The Neuropsychology Handbook

Third Edition

Arthur MacNeill Horton, Jr., EdD, ABPP, ABPN, received his EdD degree in Counselor Education from the University of Virginia in 1976. He also holds Diplomates in Clinical Psychology and Behavioral Psychology from the American Board of Professional Psychology and in Neuropsychology from the American Board of Professional Neuropsychology. Dr. Horton is the author/editor of over 15 books, more than 30 book chapters, and over 150 journal articles. He is a past-president of the American Board of Professional Neuropsychology, a doctoral-level certification board in neuropsychology, the Coalition of Clinical Practitioners in Neuropsychology (CCPN), and the National Academy of Neuropsychology (NAN). In addition, Dr. Horton was a member of the State of Maryland Board of Examiners of Psychologists for two terms. Previously, Dr. Horton was a Program Officer with the National Institute of Drug Abuse (NIDA) of the National Institutes of Health (NIH) with responsibilities for neuropsychology. He has taught at University of Virginia, The Citadel, West Virginia University, Johns Hopkins University, the University of Baltimore, Loyola College in Maryland, the Department of Psychiatry of the University of Maryland Medical School, and the Fielding Institute Graduate Program in Neuropsychology. Currently, Dr. Horton is in independent practice as Director of the Neuropsychology Clinic at Psych Associates of Maryland in Towson, Columbia, and Bethesda, Maryland and consults on neuropsychology and drug abuse research issues. He recently co-authored (with Cecil R. Reynolds, PhD, ABPN) *The Test of Verbal Conceptualization and Fluency (TVCF)*, a measure of executive functions in children, adults, and the elderly.

Danny Wedding, PhD, earned a PhD in Clinical Psychology from the University of Hawaii in 1979, after working as an Air Force medic and a VISTA volunteer. He completed a postdoctoral year of training in behavioral medicine and clinical neuropsychology at the University of Mississippi Medical Center in Jackson, Mississippi. Dr. Wedding ran the neuropsychology service for 10 years for the medical schools at East Tennessee State University and Marshall University. He subsequently completed a health policy fellowship sponsored by the Robert Wood Johnson Foundation and managed by the Institute of Medicine; during this year Dr. Wedding worked as a legislative aide for Senator Tom Daschle. He then completed a science policy fellowship in the program sponsored by the American Psychological Association; this year was spent working for Congressman John Conyers who chaired the Government Operations Committee for the House of Representatives. Since 1991, Dr. Wedding has served as a Professor of Psychiatry and Director of the Missouri Institute of Mental Health (MIMH), a health policy, research, and training center affiliated with the University of Missouri–Columbia School of Medicine. While working at MIMH, Dr. Wedding spent a sabbatical as a Fulbright Senior Scholar, teaching psychotherapy to psychiatry residents in Chiang Mai, Thailand; retired after 20 years in the Navy Reserves; and earned graduate degrees in public health and English literature. He is the author or editor of 12 books including *Current Psychotherapies, Screening for Brain Impairment, Movies and Mental Illness,* and *Behavior and Medicine.* He is also the editor of *PsycCRITIQUES: Contemporary Psychology—APA Review of Books.*

The Neuropsychology Handbook

Third Edition

Arthur MacNeill Horton, Jr., EdD, ABPP, ABPN
Danny Wedding, PhD
Editors

SPRINGER PUBLISHING COMPANY

New York

Springer Publishing Company, LLC
11 West 42nd Street
New York, NY 10036-8002
www.springerpub.com

Acquisitions Editor: Philip Laughlin
Production Editor: Carol Cain
Cover design by Joanne E. Honigman
Composition: Apex Publishing, LLC

07 08 09 10 /5 4 3 2 1

Library of Congress Cataloging-in-Publication Data

The neuropsychology handbook / Arthur M. Horton, Jr., Danny Wedding, editors. — 3rd ed.
        p. ; cm.
  Includes bibliographical references and index.
  ISBN-13: 978-0-8261-0251-5 (alk. paper)
  ISBN-10: 0-8261-0251-4 (alk. paper)
1. Clinical neuropsychology—Handbooks, manuals, etc.
2. Neuropsychological tests—Handbooks, manuals, etc. I. Horton, Arthur MacNeill, 1947- II. Wedding, Danny.
  [DNLM: 1. Neuropsychology—methods. 2. Nervous System Diseases.
3. Neuropsychological Tests. WL 103.5 N4945 2007]
  RC386.6.N48N49 2007
  616.89—dc22
                                        2007020080

Printed in the United States of America by Sheridan Books.

To my wife, Mary, with all my love.
— Arthur MacNeill Horton, Jr.

To Sara Serot, life partner.
— Danny Wedding

Contents

SECTION I

SECTION III

Practice Issues in Neuropsychology

SECTION IV

Preface

Great enthusiasm among professional psychologists in independent practice for the specialization of clinical neuropsychology can be seen in a number of events. In the last decade, a number of books dealing with clinical neuropsychology have been published for the graduate and professional markets, departments of psychology are developing courses and providing training experiences, and new journals have been established. There are also increasing numbers of requests from attorneys and judges for neuropsychologists to interact in the clinical setting by quantifying the nature and extent of cortical damage in cases of automobile or industrial accident or neurotoxin exposure.

Indeed, there is considerable evidence to support the opinion that clinical neuropsychology is rapidly expanding as a professional practice area across the nation. While managed care has reduced reimbursement for psychological services in the last decade, there has still been significant growth in the need for clinical neuropsychological services. A salient fact concerning clinical neuropsychology is that it is perhaps the prime example of an area of professional specialization that was developed by practitioners. While many clinical neuropsychologists engage in full-or part-time independent practice, there has been considerable evolution of the traditional independent practitioner role.

In order to address the urgent need for an authoritative reference work for the rapidly growing field, *The Neuropsychology Handbook*, Third Edition, has been published. The *Handbook* reviews the major areas in which clinical neuropsychologists work. Specific areas covered include the foundations of clinical neuropsychology, such as the neuropsychological basis of mental abilities, diagnostic decision making, and symptom validity testing. Specific chapters include neuroimaging, behavioral change following traumatic brain injury, and rehabilitation planning. A remaining section includes very specialized areas of practice chapters on clinical neuropsychology with children, clinical neurotoxicology, and neuropsychological assessment in sports. A concluding chapter on the future of clinical neuropsychology completes the *Handbook*.

The Neuropsychology Handbook, Third Edition, is intended for clinical neuropsychologists in practice and others who utilize neuropsychological data in their decision making. Also, other professionals who enter the clinical arena and rely on neuropsychological opinions, such as psychiatrists, neurologists, clinical psychologists, school psychologists, social workers, counselors and special educators, as well as other health care and educational professionals, will find the *Handbook* of considerable value. The hope and expectation is that the *Handbook* will make an important contribution to clinical neuropsychology and will thereby meet the challenge of alleviating human misery and promoting positive adaptation by brain-injured children and adults.

Acknowledgments

Many clinical neuropsychologists have indirectly contributed to *The Neuropsychology Handbook,* Third Edition, by their support and advice to the editors. These persons include Ralph M. Reitan, David E. Hartman, Tony Strickland, Arnold Purish, Robert J. McCaffrey, Robert W. Elliott, W. Drew Gouvier, Charles J. Long, Jim Hom, Paul Satz, Pat Pimental, Deborah Wolfson, Karen Steingarden, Sue Antell, Eric Zillmer, Joan W. Mayfield, Ralph Tarter, Gerald Goldstein, Francis J. Fishburne, J. Randall Price, Jeffrey T. Barth, Antonio E. Puente, George W. Hynd, Ira B. Gensemer, Daneen A. Milam, Randy W. Kamphaus, Robert L. Kane, Kathleen Fitzhugh-Bell, Dennis L. Reeves, James A. Moses, Jr., Jeffrey J. Webster, Alan Gessner, Bradley Sewick, Francis J. Pirozzolo, John E. Obrzut, Richard Berg, Mark Goodman, Henry Soper, Nicole McWhorter, Marvin H. Podd, Greta N. Wilkening, and Cindy K. Westergaard, among others too numerous to mention. A number of psychiatrists and neurologists have also been helpful and include Francis J. Mwaisela, Michael K. Spodak, Abdul Malik, Mahmood Jahromi, Daniel Drubach, Scott Spier, and Mohammad Haerian, among others too numerous to mention. Also, attorneys such as Tom Talbot, James Sullivan, Mitchell Blatt, Steve Van Grack, Patrick Donahue, Allison Kohler, Steven Leder, Thomas Hale, Catherine Potash, John Duud III, and Jeanie Garner, among others too numerous to mention.

Contributors

Daniel N. Allen, PhD
Department of Psychology
University of Nevada Las Vegas
Las Vegas, NV

Elizabeth Andresen, PhD
Department of Psychology
University of
    Wisconsin–Milwaukee
Milwaukee, WI

**Thomas L. Bennett, PhD, ABPN,
    ABPP-RP**
Brain Injury Recovery
    Program
and Colorado State University
Department of Psychology
Fort Collins, CO
Center for Neurorehabilitation
    Services
Fort Collins, CO

John J. Blase, PhD, ABPN
Independent Practice
Southfield, MI

Michelle Braun, PhD
Department of Psychology
University of
    Wisconsin–Milwaukee
Milwaukee, WI

Brian L. Brooks, PhD
British Columbia Mental Health
    and Addiction Services
Vancouver, British Columbia

**Shane S. Bush, PhD, ABPN,
    ABPP-RP, ABPP-CN**
Independent Practice
Long Island Neuropsychology
Lake Ronkonkoma, NY

Francis Canavan, PhD
Department of Psychology
Fielding Graduate University
Santa Barbara, CA

Christine L. Castillo, PhD
Department of Psychology
Baylor Children's Medical Center
Dallas, TX

Rik Carl D'Amato, PhD
School of Professional
  Psychology and Office of the
  Dean College of Education
  and Behavior Sciences
University of Northern
  Colorado
Greeley, CO

Andrew S. Davis, PhD
Department of Psychology
Ball State University
Muncie, IN

**Raymond S. Dean, PhD, ABPN,
  ABPP-SP**
Department of Psychology
Ball State University
Muncie, IN

John Denning, PhD
Department of Physical Medicine
  and Rehabilitation
Division of Rehabilitation
  Psychology and
  Neuropsychology
Johns Hopkins University School
  of Medicine
Baltimore, MD

Brad Donohue, PhD
Department of Psychology
University of Nevada at
  Las Vegas
Las Vegas, NV

Kevin Duff, PhD
Department of Psychology
University of Iowa
Iowa City, IA

Paul S. Ferber, JD
Vermont Law School
South Royalton, VT

Sam Goldstein, PhD
University of Utah Medical
  School
Salt Lake City, UT

William Drew Gouvier, PhD
Department of Psychology
Louisiana State University
Baton Rouge, LA

Thomas J. Grabowski, PhD
Department of Psychology
University of Iowa
Iowa City, IA

J. Josh Hall, PhD
Department of Psychology
Ball State University
Muncie, IN

**Lawrence C. Hartlage, PhD,
  ABPP-CL, ABPN**
Augusta Neuropsychology Center
Evans, GA

B. D. Hill, PhD
Department of Psychology
Louisiana State University
Baton Rouge, LA

Arthur MacNeill Horton III, BS
Eastern Virginia Medical
  School
Norfolk, VA

Grant L. Iverson, PhD
Department of Psychology
University of British Columbia
British Columbia Mental Health
  and Addiction Services
Vancouver, British Columbia

Joy Jansen, MEd
University of Utah Medical
  School
Salt Lake City, UT

Doug Johnson-Greene, PhD, MPH, ABPP-CL, ABPP-RP, ABPP-CN
Department of Physical Medicine and Rehabilitation
Division of Rehabilitation Psychology and Neuropsychology
Johns Hopkins University School of Medicine
Baltimore, MD

Katie Kendra, PhD
Department of Psychology
Louisiana State University
Baton Rouge, LA

Nancy S. Koven, PhD
Program in Neuroscience
Department of Psychology
Bates College
Lewiston, ME

Brian D. Leany, PhD
Department of Psychology
University of Nevada
    Las Vegas
Las Vegas, NV

Thomas A. Martin, PsyD, ABPP-RP
Department of Psychology
University of
    Missouri–Columbia
Columbia, MO

Tiffany J. Neal, PhD
Department of Psychology
Ball State University
Muncie, IN

David C. Osmon, PhD
Department of Psychology
University of
    Wisconsin–Milwaukee
Milwaukee, WI

Cory Patrick, PhD
Department of Psychology
University of
    Wisconsin–Milwaukee
Milwaukee, WI

Russell D. Pella, PhD
Department of Psychology
Louisiana State University
Baton Rouge, LA

Jo Cara Pendergrass, PhD
Brain Imaging Laboratory
Department of Psychiatry
Dartmouth Medical School /
    DHMC
Lebanon, NH

Dorrie L. Rapp, PhD, ABPN, ABPP-RP
Independent Practice
White River Junction, VT

Michael J. Raymond, PhD, ABPN
Neuropsychology Services
Allied Services, John Heinz
    Institute of Rehabilitation
    Medicine
Wilkes-Barre, PA

Cecil R. Reynolds, PhD, ABPN
Department of Educational
    Psychology
Texas A&M University
College Station, TX

Robert M. Roth, PhD
Brain Imaging Laboratory
Department of Psychiatry
Dartmouth Medical School /
    DHMC
Lebanon, NH

Robert J. Sbordone, PhD, ABPP-CN, ABPN
Independent Practice of
    Neuropsychology
Laguna Hills, CA

Raymond Singer, PhD, ABPN
Independent Practice
Santa Fe, NM

Henry V. Soper, PhD
Department of Psychology
Fielding Graduate University
Santa Barbara, CA

Robert A. Stern, PhD
Boston University School of
  Medicine
Department of Neurology
Boston, MA

Gregory P. Strauss, PhD
Department of Psychology
University of Nevada Las Vegas
Las Vegas, NV

Frank M. Webbe, PhD
Department of Psychology
Florida Institute of
  Technology
Melbourne, FL

Travis White, PhD
Psychological Assessment
  Resources, Inc.
Lutz, FL

Arthur D. Williams, PhD, ABPN
Independent Practice of
  Neuropsychology
Seattle, WA

Stephen Wolfson, PhD
Department of Psychology
Fielding Graduate University
Santa Barbara, CA

Section I

Foundations of Neuropsychology

1

Overview of Clinical Neuropsychology

ARTHUR MacNEILL HORTON, JR. AND
ARTHUR MacNEILL HORTON III

URING THE LAST half century, interest in human brain behavioral relationships, or *clinical neuropsychology,* has increased at a tremendous rate. There are a large number of examples of the cross-cultural validity of neuropsychological research findings as well as successful applications of neuropsychological assessment intervention methods with adults and children (Hartlage, 1975, 1986; Horton, 1994; Horton & Puente, 1986; Hynd & Willis, 1988; Reitan & Davison, 1974). These remarkable demonstrations of the power of neuropsychological methods have engendered great interest in clinical neuropsychology.

NEUROPSYCHOLOGICAL ISSUES
AND BRAIN DAMAGE

AT THIS JUNCTURE it might be helpful to provide some basic neuropsychology definitions. Neuropsychology was defined by Meier (1974) as "The scientific study of brain-behavior relationships" (p. 289).

That definition was particularly apt and is as serviceable today, more than 20 years after it was proposed, as it was at that time. It is noted by Horton and Puente (1990), that neuropsychological performance may be influenced by both organic and environmental variables.

The organic nature of neuropsychological variables has been clearly demonstrated through the work of famous neuropsychologists such as Ralph M. Reitan, Arthur L. Benton, and A. R. Luria, among others over a number of decades. Attention to the environmental determinants of neuropsychological performance, however, is of more recent origin. As an example, it should be noted that in recent years, increased attention has been focused on the practice of behavior therapy with brain-impaired adults and children (Horton, 1989, 1994; Horton & Wedding, 1984).

A brief discussion of the concepts of *brain damage* and *cerebral dysfunction* is provided to clarify the neuropsychological context in which the concepts are applied. Very briefly, *brain damage* implies clear and substantial structural injury to the brain (Horton, 1994). Contemporary neurodiagnostic imaging methods, such as Positron Emission Tomography or PET-scanning, or Magnetic Resonance Imaging (MRI) in many cases can clearly identify structural brain lesions (Kertesz, 1994). Nonetheless, in some subtle cases neuroimaging is totally inadequate to reflect changes in the physiological functioning of the brain that may result in behavioral abnormalities. It could be said that the behavioral correlates of neuroimaging are still, at this point in time, poorly understood. Although brain tumors or strokes often can be easily visualized, other neuropathological conditions such as sequela of traumatic brain injury and neurotoxic conditions may produce clear neurocognitive, sensory-perceptual, and motoric deficits without demonstrating clear structural brain changes under imaging (Horton, 1989). In situations of this sort where behavioral changes are clearly documented but structural lesions in the brain cannot be visualized, the term *cerebral dysfunction* is often used (Horton, 1994). The hope and expectation is that further research in neuroimaging and related procedures and methods will allow more precise detection of abnormalities in cerebral morphology.

ORGANICITY: LOCALIZATION VS. GENERALIZED FUNCTION

A T THIS POINT, attention might be turned to the term *organicity,* as that term is also frequently misunderstood. The classic definition by Davison (1974) is as follows:

> The concept includes the assumption that any and all kinds of brain damage lead to similar behavioral effects and that behavioral differences among the brain damaged are due primarily to severity of damage and premorbid personality characteristics. (p. 14)

The concept of *organicity* has something of an interesting history. It originated during the human potentiality/localization debates that characterized thinking regarding brain-behavior relationships approximately a century ago. The human potentiality/localization debates were concerned with how behavioral functions were organized in the human brain (Horton & Wedding, 1984). A brief review of some of the crucial scientific findings related to these debates may be helpful in understanding them. The debates began in April of 1861, when a physician named Paul Broca presented the brain of a patient at the Paris (France) Anthropological Society Meeting. Apparently, the patient had been studied, by Broca, while alive and at that time the patient had been unable to speak. Subsequently, the patient died, and his brain became available for inspection. Paul Broca found that the patient had a lesion in the posterior third portion of the inferior frontal convulsion of the left hemisphere. Simply put, the lesion was in the left frontal lobe. Broca demonstrated that the patient's language difficulty, or aphasia, was not related to either memory difficulties or motoric problems. Rather, Broca postulated the aphasia was related to the specific brain lesion. The startling hypothesis from this case study was that a specific brain area supported expressive speech; to this day that particular area is known as "Broca's area" (Horton & Wedding, 1984).

Similarly in 1874, Carl Wernicke presented a clinical case of a patient who, when he was alive, had a speech comprehension deficit. After the patient died, his brain became available for inspection and study by Wernicke. Wernicke discovered that the patient's brain had a lesion in the posterior third portion of the superior temporal lobe of the left hemisphere. This area today is known of course as "Wernicke's area" (Horton & Wedding, 1984). These scientific discoveries suggested that specific brain areas could be identified with specific behavioral functions.

Although these advances were exciting instances of the localizationist school of brain-behavior relationships, there was an opposing school of thought that proposed that all brain tissue was of equal relevance for subserving behavioral functions. That school described brain tissue as of "equal potentiality" with respect to behavioral functions. This equal potentiality school had its own series of startling scientific discoveries. For example, Marie J. P. Flourens (cited in Luria, 1966) demonstrated in animal research studies that the loss of behavioral function were related to the amount of brain tissue impaired rather than specific localization of the brain lesion. Kurt Goldstein found similar results in his work with brain-injured veterans of World War I. Goldstein's research suggested that the major difficulty with respect to brain-injured persons was concrete thinking and there was, in a rather memorable phrase, "the loss of the abstract attitude" (Goldstein, 1952). Interestingly, it appeared that the French scientists were finding evidence supporting a localization model, whereas the German scientists were finding evidence that endorsed an equal potentiality paradigm.

One somewhat questionable suggestion had been advanced that because many of these brain lesions were from the Franco-Prussian War or World War I, the different findings could be the result of the fact that the German ammunition in both conflicts was quite excellent and tended to remain intact after impact, while the French ammunition, in the same conflicts, was of lesser quality and had a tendency to fragment upon impact. Therefore, it has been suggested that brain lesions caused by German bullets produced relatively prescribed lesions, whereas lesions from French bullets tended to have widespread effects because they fragmented and therefore scattered to various portions of the brain. Whether or not this hypothesis has a basis in fact would require a certain amount of historical neuropsychological research to confirm or negate. What does seem clear now and is generally accepted is that both the localization and equal potential conceptualization of brain-behavior relationships fail to fully explain or account for the full range of human neuropsychological abilities.

MULTIPLE BRAIN LEVELS

AN INTEGRATIVE SOLUTION to the human potentiality/localization debates was proposed by Thomas Hughlings Jackson, an Englishman, who was a contemporary of Paul Broca. Jackson's concepts of brain functioning have been popularized more recently by Luria (1966, 1973). Jackson suggested that human behavioral functions were represented in multiple levels in the brain. That is to say that there was a vertical organization with brain functions subsumed at a number of levels. Luria further developed Jackson's theoretical views and described the brain as composed of distinct functional blocks with each section serving different functions. Basically, Luria saw higher mental processes as involving multiple brain areas interacting in multiple points in time (Horton, 1987). To put it another way, he suggested multicausation of behavioral functions by different brain areas. As was noted by Horton and Wedding (1984),

> Essentially, Luria thought that every complex form of behavior depended on the joint operations of several faculties located in different zones of the brain. Disturbance of any one of the number of faculties located in different areas of the brain will change behavior in a different way. But

in another way, this means no single behavior is localized in a specific brain area, and that each behavior is a result of the specific combination of separate brain areas. Also, the damage to a single brain area causes the behavior to be changed but not necessarily lost. (p. 30)

Thus, it can be seen that brain damage is a relatively difficult and complex concept to understand, and complexities go far beyond the rather simplistic conceptualizations of organicity. Although there are some similarities among brain-injured individuals, there is also a tremendous amount of heterogeneity. It might be suggested that current diagnostic frameworks only poorly capture the degree of complexity inherent in human cerebral functioning.

NEURODEVELOPMENTAL ISSUES/CONCERNS

ATTENTION NEEDS TO be paid to the theoretical ideas of A. R. Luria (1963, 1966, 1973). Luria's cultural and historical model, for example, postulates specific developmental stages that are related to phases of higher cortical developmental maturation. Luria considered the various stages of mental development encountered as children mature as a unique opportunity to study how neurocognitive processes develop (Horton, 1987). As it is particularly well known, there are great differences in child neurodevelopmental processes relative to adult neurodevelopmental processes (Rourke, Fisk, & Strang, 1986). Child brains are considerably less studied than adult brains, and there is a greater degree of variability in terms of the expression of neurocognitive abilities in a child's neuropsychological development (Horton & Puente, 1986). Children, for instance, are in a continual process of development, there are various growth spurts and developmental lags to contend with, and there may be specific learning or developmental or behavioral processes that could be related to physical illness or injury (Hynd & Obrzut, 1981; Reynolds, 1981). These complex neurodevelopmental factors make it particularly difficult to provide a clinical assessment of child neuropsychological abilities and to distinguish subtypes of learning disorders (Broder, 1973; Mattis, French, & Rapin, 1975). Among other critical problems is the difficulty of collecting appropriate normative neuropsychological data (Hartlage, 1986; Klonoff, Crockett, & Clark, 1984). Because neuropsychological abilities may vary in terms of quantity and quality depending on the various neurocognitive developmental stages, neuropsychological normative data need to be interpreted in terms of understanding the child's neurocognitive development in the various stages of neuropsychological development (Hynd & Willis, 1988;

Reynolds, 1981). The child must have had an opportunity to develop various mental skills before it can be said that the child had lost an ability due to brain injury. For example, in reading if an adult demonstrates an inability to read very simple words and phrases, that behavioral deficit might be seen as clear evidence of a brain injury if the adult had reasonably adequate education experiences as a child. It could very easily be that the child has never had the opportunity to acquire the specific academic skills, and therefore the problem is not one related to brain injury but rather inadequate educational opportunities.

It would appear straightforward that persons who intend to deliver clinical neuropsychological services will need to have a basic understanding of brain-behavior relationships. Because the primary reason that children require neuropsychological services is usually a real or presumed disorder of the brain, an appreciation of the structure and functioning of the cerebral cortex will be invaluable in determining the nature and extent of the presumed brain disorder. Indeed, the central premise upon which all of clinical neuropsychology rests is that there are direct and predictable behavioral correlates of structural lesions in the neocortex (Reitan & Davison, 1974). In child clinical neuropsychology, for example, there is an evolving research literature that has documented specific brain-behavior relationships. As will be elaborated upon later, the human brain is the "prime organ" of behavioral functioning. In a very real way, understanding of the anatomical structure and behavioral functioning of children's brains serves to provide a valuable perspective on methods of clinical neuropsychological assessment and treatment/interventions (Horton, 1994).

DEVELOPMENTAL NEUROANATOMY AND BRAIN LATERALIZATION

THIS SECTION IS intended to be a very brief and selective review of brain-behavior relationships with particular reference to developmental neuroanatomy and hemispheric lateralization of brain functioning. It should be clearly understood that this discussion is not intended to be a detailed treatment of brain-behavior relationships. Rather the reader is referred to other volumes, which more adequately address this area of developmental neuroanatomy (Hynd & Willis, 1988; Kolb & Fantie, 1989; Reitan & Wolfson, 1992; Spreen, Risser, & Edgell, 1995). It should also be mentioned that the emphasis will be upon the gross structural organization of the human brain rather than an examination of the cellular level and neurotransmitter systems. Particular areas addressed are the morphology of the central nervous system, A. R. Luria's neurodevelopmental model of brain functioning, hemispheric lateralization of functioning, specific functioning of the cerebral lobes, and a brief and selective discussion of recovery of functioning after childhood traumatic brain injury.

MORPHOLOGY OF THE CENTRAL NERVOUS SYSTEM

THE CENTRAL NERVOUS system is divided into the brain and the spinal cord. The function of the spinal cord is to transmit sensory impulses to the brain and also to send motor impulses to the brain to the muscles. Various segments (i.e., cervical, thoracic, lumbar, and sacral) make up the spinal cord and refer to various groups of nerves. Injuries to various levels of the spinal cord have serious implications with respect to motoric and sensory functioning. The division of the spinal cord into sensory and motoric areas is also reflected in the gross morphology and organization of the human brain. Understanding the extent of the sensory/motor organization of the human brain is of crucial importance in terms of understanding the structure and functioning of the central nervous system.

While the spinal cord is of great importance for the maintainability of life and mobility, its assessment is usually considered to be the domain of the pediatric neurologist, whereas child clinical neuropsychologists more commonly devote their attention to the brain. There are three major divisions to the brain: the hindbrain, the midbrain, and the forebrain. Each of these will be very briefly reviewed.

HINDBRAIN

MAJOR AREAS THAT make up the hind brain include the medulla oblongata, the pons, and the cerebellum. Locating the medulla oblongata is best done by first identifying the foramen magnum, which is the opening in the cranial cavity that allows the brain and the spinal cord to be connected. The medulla oblongata lies just above the foramen magnum. Major functions of the medulla oblongata are to control blood pressure, heart rate, and breathing. Just above the medulla oblongata is the pons, which is an enlarged section of the brain stem that has a number of functions. Of the most interest in this context, the pons allows communication to flow from the spinal cord to higher brain areas and includes particular fibers that connect the two cerebral hemispheres to hind areas of the cerebellums. The cerebellum, another hindbrain area, is located behind the pons and has the particular function of monitoring motor control and coordination and in combination with the pons coordinates motor impulses in response to movement.

MIDBRAIN

THE MIDBRAIN SITS at the point where the brain stem merges with two other brain areas, the hypothalamus and the thalamus. This area is of particular importance because brain structures in this area are thought to be in control of attention processes. For instance, the reticular activating system (RAS) lies in this area and has the function of regulating cortical tone and deciding which to focus upon of a large number of incoming stimuli. There has been some speculation that this area is of particular importance in terms of disorders such as attention-deficit/hyperactivity disorder. Often in cases of severe injury to the RAS, disorders of consciousness, such as a coma, may arise.

FOREBRAIN

THIS AREA IS often considered to be the primary focus of clinical child and experimental neuropsychology. There are a number of important areas in the forebrain, and these will each be briefly described. These include the thalamus, the hypothalamus, the limbic system, the basal ganglia, and the cerebral cortex.

Thalamus

The purpose of the thalamus is to serve as a relay center for sensory information to be transmitted to the brain. Specifically, sensory nerves come to the thalamus and are routed to appropriate cerebral sensory/perceptual areas. There is some speculation that the thalamus is the place in the brain where sensory impulses coming in are "boosted," in terms of power, so that they can be relayed to the higher level brain areas. The thalamus is also noted for controlling the brain's electrical activity, a crucial matter in terms of information processes. When the thalamus is damaged, in cases of brain injury, the most common problems associated with this site of brain injury involve short-term memory, attention, and concentration. In terms of physical location, the thalamus lies in the center of the brain above the limbic system. It is composed of two hemispheres similar to the higher level of the cerebral hemispheres.

Hypothalamus

The hypothalamus is involved in a number of important functions including the regulation of body temperature, blood pressure, sleeping, eating, drinking, and sexual activities. Clearly, brain injuries to the thalamus and the hypothalamus can have disastrous consequences in terms of life activities. The hypothalamus is generally considered to be located above the roof of the mouth.

Limbic System

The structures commonly associated with the limbic system include the amygdala, cingulate cortex, hippocampus, and septal area. There is a maze of interconnections of the limbic system to other areas of the nervous system. Perhaps the most important of these interconnections are to the frontal lobes. Of the limbic system components, the most studied are the hippocampal area and the amygdala. When the hippocampal area is damaged, the most commonly associated dysfunction is that of memory disorder particularly with respect to declarative memory of facts that were over-learned. It should be noted that this type of memory for information, as opposed to skills memory or procedural memory, is often thought to be located in this cerebellum. There also seems to be lateralization in the hippocampus. When the left hippocampus is damaged, the most common deficit is the inability to acquire new long-term verbal memories (Russell & Espir, 1961), and impairment of the right hippocampal area produces a rather dramatic difficulty with acquisition of new long-term nonverbal memories (Milner, 1971). A role in memory production has also been proposed for the amygdala (Mishkin, 1978) as well as an association with the expression of aggressive behavior. Much, however, remains to be learned about these important forebrain structures.

Basal Ganglia

The basal ganglia have been associated with the production of movement and in the unthinking coordination of movement with other components of the extrapyramidal system. The particular areas in the basal ganglia include the putamen, globus pallidus, and caudate nucleuses. The structures of the basal ganglia along with the cerebral cortex in the midbrain constitute what is often called the extrapyramidal system. The extrapyramidal system is often associated with the neurological disorder known as Parkinson's disease. Indeed, Parkinson's disease has often been cited as the classic example of an impairment of the extrapyramidal system.

Cerebral Cortex

The area that has been studied the most by clinical neuropsychologists and other brain researchers has been the cerebral cortex. Many have suggested that the functions of the cerebral cortex are unique in terms of the abilities that allow humans to be human. The most frequently used approach in the United States is to subdivide the cerebral cortex into specific functional areas. The most widely used American system proposes there are frontal, temporal, parietal, and occipital lobes and that each lobe has a unique function associated with its structure. In addition, each cerebral hemisphere is considered to have separate frontal, temporal, parietal, and occipital lobes. With respect to landmarks in the brain, it should be very clear from the earlier discussion that the frontal and parietal lobes are clearly demarcated by the central sulcus or the fissure of Rolando, and the temporal lobes are separated from the frontal and parietal lobes by the lateral cerebral fissure or the fissure of Sylvius. Although in American neuropsychology, as previously noted (Horton, 1994), four specific lobes are postulated, other brain organization systems are possible. It might be noted that the parietal and occipital lobes are not dramatically separated by a large fissure but by a relatively small fissure. The parietal and occipital fissure is used to indicate or mark where the parietal lobe ends and the occipital lobe begins. It might be noted that other non-U.S. models of brain functioning sometimes consider the parietal and occipital lobes to act together as a functional unit.

As is well known, the cerebral cortex is divided into two hemispheres, which, when looked at from above, appear similar to two footballs placed together (Horton & Wedding, 1984). The cerebral hemisphere that corresponds to the dominant hemisphere, which in the majority of human beings is the left cerebral hemisphere, often appears to be a bit larger than the nondominant hemisphere. It should be noted that the two cerebral hemispheres are interconnected by a number of brain structures. Perhaps the most important and largest of these is the corpus callosum. The corpus callosum consists of white fibers that connect areas of the cerebral hemispheres. The corpus callosum allows for direct communication between the two cerebral hemispheres. The cerebral hemispheres are separated by the longitudinal cerebral commissaries, and the surface of the cerebral hemispheres have a number of convulsions, which have been described as hills and valleys. The technical terms for these are gyris and sulcis.

The major landmarks of the brain are formed by two very deep valleys in the brain, or sulci. The most important landmark of the brain is the central valley, also called the central sulcus or fissure of Rolando, which lies in the middle of each cerebral hemisphere and divides the frontal from the parietal lobes. The unique aspects of the fissure of Rolando will be described in greater detail later. The second major landmark of the brain is a lateral valley, also called the lateral cerebral fissure or the fissure of Sylvius. This particular fissure arises from the bottom of the brain and separates the frontal and temporal lobes in the beginning, and then later, as it continues backward in the brain, it separates the temporal and parietal lobes. These major landmarks of the brain provide a means of separating the frontal and parietal lobes and the frontal and parietal lobes or temporal lobes from each other.

These functional, structural subdivisions of the brain are very important for later understanding of neuropsychology test result interpretation and, in a very real sense, form the underlying basis of the majority of treatment and management recommendations.

The particular areas of the cerebral cortex can, of course, be further classified. Although there are different ways to look at the way the surface of the cerebral cortex has been mapped out by neuroanatomical workers, the most common framework utilized is that of Brodmann (Nauta & Feintag, 1986). In Brodmann's system, particular cortical areas are identified by numbers. For example, in the parietal lobes, just behind the central sulcus or the fissure of Rolando, lie the primary tactual sensory-perceptual areas, and these have been given numbers one, two, and three to identify specific functional areas. These particular areas that are one, two, and three must be intact to enable tactile perceptions to be perceived by other portions of the cerebral cortex. In addition, in the temporal lobes lies the primary area for audition, and this is identified as area 41. Also in the occipital lobes there are a number of areas supporting primary vision, and they are identified as areas 17, 18, and 19. There are also other specific brain structures associated with various functions. If any of the particular brain areas mentioned previously are severely damaged then there is difficulty in terms of receiving tactual perceptions, hearing sounds, or seeing objects.

These primary brain areas interact with other brain areas to produce typically human behaviors, emotions, and cognitions. While there are a plethora of brain functioning theories, one particularly insightful model for understanding brain functioning is based on the work of A. R. Luria, the famous Russian neurologist and neuropsychologist. The following comments are a very oversimplified description of his theoretical paradigm but are offered for purposes of illustration.

LURIA'S MODEL OF BRAIN FUNCTIONING

A. R. LURIA (1966, 1973) was a Russian neuroscientist who developed a complex but elegant conceptual model for understanding the organization of higher mental abilities or facilities and proposed human behavioral correlates of brain functioning. In essence, Luria's model of higher cortical functioning involved dividing brain anatomy into three major brain blocks. These were: (1) lower brain stem structures, (2) the cerebral cortex posterior to the central sulcus or the fissure of Rolando, and (3) the cerebral cortex anterior to, or in front of, the central sulcus or the fissure of Rolando. The blocks of the brain are labeled one, two, and three corresponding to (1) the brain stem structures, (2) the cerebral cortex posterior to the central sulcus, and (3) the cerebral cortex anterior to the central sulcus. Those major blocks, as conceptualized by Luria, make unique contributions to human brain functioning. Each will be briefly described.

BLOCK ONE

THE LOWER BRAIN stem structures are responsible for maintaining the tone and energy supply of the cerebral cortex. In a way, a similar situation would be a personal computer and its electricity supply. For the personal computer to work in a reasonable fashion it must have a supply of electricity. In addition, the level of electricity must be constant. If the electricity supply or current voltage varies, then the arithmetic and logic section and memory banks of the personal computer will have difficulty working in an efficient manner. In a similar fashion, the lower brain stem structures provide for the tone and energy level of the cerebral cortex and must keep this stable and constant in order for the higher level areas to work in an effective manner.

BLOCK TWO

THE AREA POSTERIOR to the central sulcus or the posterior cerebral cortex is the area into which sensory impressions of a visual, auditory, and tactile nature are identified, perceived, and organized for comprehension. The processes of perceiving the incoming sensory stimuli include the function of organizing it in such a way that it can be understood by other areas of the cerebral cortex.

BLOCK THREE

BLOCK THREE is the area anterior to the central sulcus. This area is involved in the production and monitoring of motor responses. The area of the anterior cerebral cortex is the area in which the information from both the posterior sensory impressions comes and where there is a formulation of intention planning and production of motor behaviors and evaluation of the effects of motor behaviors. To carry the computer model mentioned previously a little further, in block two, the input devices to the computer, which are like the keyboard or, in the early days a card reader, are some models for the posterior cerebral cortex. Similarly, the anterior cerebral cortex is related to the arithmetic and logic unit of the personal computer, which makes decisions. The output of information by the printer or through some other output mechanism is planned by the anterior cerebral area but carried out by arms, legs, and the mouth, mostly.

PRIMARY, SECONDARY, AND TERTIARY AREAS OF BLOCKS TWO AND THREE

IT SHOULD BE noted that Luria (1966) further subdivided the second and third blocks of the cerebral cortex into smaller subareas. Luria suggested that the area posterior to the cerebral cortex and the area anterior to the cerebral cortex could be subdivided into primary, secondary, and tertiary areas. Each of these areas is arranged in some organized fashion in terms of its particular role of dealing with mental stimuli. Perhaps the simplest way to explain this concept is to use the second block or the posterior cerebral cortex to illustrate this proposed structure/function neuropsychological arrangement. Grossly oversimplified, the primary areas of the second block perform very simple functions of collecting sensory input of stimuli. More elaborate perceptions of the nature of the stimuli are performed by the secondary areas, and the tertiary areas coordinate the integration of two or more secondary areas to produce higher level mental activities.

For example, using the modalities of touch, a primary (or *the* primary) area would tell a person whether or not they had the sense of touch, but the secondary area would be necessary to determine some more complex stimuli or whether the touch was an "X" or an "O" drawn on the skin. The tertiary areas, on the other hand, would subsume more complex activities such as handwriting where the motion of the hand in a complex function and the feedback from touching various materials is important in terms of subserving complex mental activities. To put this in another way, information from different areas of the brain combines to subserve higher level mental functions.

Luria (1966) suggested that divergent areas of the brain work together in a functional matter to subsume or support behavioral or various behavioral functions. That is to say those areas of the brain in each of the three blocks were combined in order to support higher level mental activities. The postulate of this particular notion is that functional systems may use more than one set of brain areas in terms of subsuming the same behavioral functions. That is to say in rehabilitation, it may be possible to obtain the same behavioral performance but reroute or have a different organization in terms of brain areas used.

NEUROPSYCHOLOGICAL DEVELOPMENTAL STAGES

IT MIGHT BE noted that Luria (1966) postulated a number of stages by which neuropsychological functions are developed. These stages apparently interact with environmental stimuli. Luria's work to a large extent is based on Lev Vygotsky's cultural and historical theory (Horton, 1987). Vygotsky was something of a mentor or teacher to Luria and can be seen as a major influence on Luria's thinking. Vygotsky was a terribly impressive individual, as he initially worked in education but obtained his PhD based on a dissertation on his works of Shakespeare. This was quite an achievement considering that he obtained his doctorate while in Russia just after the Russian Revolution and Soviet takeover. Vygotsky developed a complex theory related to language and thought processes. He postulated that environmental/cultural influences were important in terms of interacting with neurological structures to develop higher level mental abilities such as abstraction, memory, and voluntary attention. It is indeed tragic and regrettable that Vygotsky died of tuberculosis at a young age and that he was unable to further develop his interesting neurodevelopmental theories. Nonetheless, Luria apparently used Vygotsky's thinking as his major theoretical framework throughout Luria's life (Horton, 1987).

Essentially Luria, like Vygotsky, believed that the development of higher cortical functions required both the interaction of normal neurological development and specific environmental stimuli of a cultural, historical, and social nature to flourish. The process or the result of the appropriate interaction of neurological development and the appropriate environmental stimuli would be higher cortical functioning such as language, intention memory, and abstract thought. Five stages in development were proposed by Luria (Luria, 1980). It might be expected that the specific stages of neurodevelopment are closely related to Luria's conceptualization of basic blocks of the brain.

As earlier noted, block one is related to the lower brain stem structures, block two is related to the area posterior to the central sulcus, and block three is related to the area anterior to the central sulcus. Essentially in the first stage, beginning in the first year of life, the brain stem structures are primarily developed. These brain stem structures in block one may be seen as involving the reticular activating system, which was described earlier.

The second stage is related to the activation of the primary sensory areas for vision, hearing and tactical perception, and the primary motor areas for gross motor movement. To put it in terms of neuroanatomy, these would be areas that immediately are adjacent both posterior and anterior to the central sulcus. This particular stage relies primarily upon the unfolding of "hard wired" neurological structures.

The third stage focuses on single modalities in the secondary association areas of the brain. Often, this stage is associated with movement of the child into preschool. The child at this stage recognizes and reproduces various symbolic materials and is able to model various physical movements. The different modalities of learning may be separately accessed.

The fourth stage begins about the time of first or second grade. At this time the tertiary areas of the parietal lobes become activated. The tertiary parietal lobe is the area in which the temporal, parietal, and occipital lobes come together. This enables a coordination of the three major sensory input channels. In order to help the child make sense of the sensory input coming in, environmental stimulation is particularly important. For instance, the cultural, historical, and social influences are the major factors in shaping the crucial academic skills of reading, writing, and arithmetic, which are the primary tasks a child learns in the early school years.

The fifth stage becomes activated during adolescence. In this stage the frontal area or the area anterior to the central sulcus comes on line in terms of mental functioning. As noted by Struss and Benson (1984), the area anterior to the central sulcus is important for abstract thinking, intentional memory, and the execution, monitoring, and evaluation of complex learning behavior. Luria's model (1980) suggests there are qualitative differences between children at different stages in neuropsychological development and that children could use different functional systems to perform similar tasks.

That is to say, combinations of brain areas utilized in mental functioning may vary, although the final behavior performance could be similar. In addition, Luria's thinking suggests that there must be interaction between the child's level of neuropsychological development and the sorts of environmental stimulation that are crucial in terms of developing important human adaptive and vocational skills. Luria's model (1980) should be recognized as a unique, elegant, and efficient method with which to understand neuropsychological development and environmental stimuli/stimulation.

HEMISPHERIC LATERALIZATION OF FUNCTIONS

A s is well known, the human brain is divided into two cerebral hemispheres (Dean, 1985). Each cerebral hemisphere is very similar but not identical in structure and function to the other cerebral hemisphere. The term *cerebral asymmetry* refers to the differences between the two cerebral hemispheres. As would be expected, given that human beings are dominant on one side of the body versus the other side, one cerebral hemisphere is usually larger than the other. In the vast majority of right-hand individuals, the left cerebral hemisphere is slightly larger than the right cerebral hemisphere. It is often suggested that the reason the left cerebral hemisphere is slightly larger is the fact that the left cerebral hemisphere subserves language functions in the human (Geschwind & Levitsky, 1984).

Essentially, the need to support spoken language and various symbolic methods of communication has resulted in areas of the brain that have been further developed as human beings have evolved to an information intensive society. It might be noted that there have been reports in children with dyslexia that suggest that their right cerebral hemispheres are slightly larger than their left cerebral hemispheres (Dean, 1985). Essentially, this is clear evidence for a neuroanatomical basis of reading disability. In addition to cerebral asymmetry, it is also important for the clinical child neuropsychologist to be aware of the concept of *contralateral control*. This refers to the cross-wired organization of the central nervous system at the level of the cerebral hemispheres. Essentially what this means is that while the left cerebral hemisphere controls motor and sensory functions of the right side of the body, the right cerebral hemisphere controls motor and sensory functions of the left side of the body. It might be noted that all functions of the sensory nature are not 100% lateralized; for example, visual functions do appear to be 100% lateralized, but auditory ability is 80% under contralateral control and 20% under ipsolateral, or same side, control. Similarly, tactile functions are generally thought to be 90% under contralateral control and 10% under ipsolateral control (Horton & Wedding, 1984).

HEMISPHERIC ABILITIES

AS IT IS well known by anyone who attends to popular culture or has taken a Psychology 101 course in college, the cerebral hemispheres are specialized for behavioral functions, which they subserve. Although historical understanding of the functional behavioral correlates of the cerebral hemispheres may be traced as far back as Paul Broca's 1861 clinical observations of brain-injured subjects (cited in Horton & Wedding, 1984) and the insightful theoretical formulation of Hughlings Jackson in the 1870s (cited in Horton & Wedding, 1984) , nonetheless general acceptance of hemispheric abilities by the neuroscience community only became widespread after the split brain research findings of Roger Sperry (1961) were published.

Sperry, who obtained his masters degree in psychology and his doctorate in zoology, conducted an extensive neuropsychological research program with epilepsy patients who had undergone neurosurgical procedures for patients with severe refractory epilepsy. Each patient had been through a neurosurgical procedure that involved cutting the fibers connecting the two cerebral hemispheres.

The theory underlying this surgical procedure was that refractory seizures will move from one cerebral hemisphere to another through these connecting fibers and that cutting the interconnecting fibers would reduce seizure frequency. Usually the treatment involved the corpus callosum, the largest set of interhemispheric connecting fibers. The corpus callosum, however, is not the only group of fibers connecting the cerebral hemispheres. The anterior commissure and the hippocampal commissure also connect the cerebral hemispheres but in smaller collections of fibers. As a general rule, as a result of severing these interhemispheric connecting fibers the patients were less troubled by their seizures.

Sperry carefully studied a group of patients who had operations in which the interconnecting hemispheric fibers were cut, which as a result produced disconnected cerebral hemispheres or "split brains." This "split brain" operation allows the two cerebral hemispheres to function in an independent fashion (Dean, 1985; Horton & Wedding, 1984). The split brain patients were a phenomenal and unique natural laboratory for studying cerebral lateralized brain functioning as they provided a situation where the two cerebral hemispheres were relatively intact and available for assessment, thus allowing comparison of the two reasonably well-functioning sides of the brain during particular experimental manipulation (Nebes, 1974).

In previous research, which usually involved lesion studies where patients with unilateral brain damage in one cerebral hemisphere were compared to normal subjects, there were multiple cases of confounding influences that could only be poorly controlled. By contrast, the split brain patients provided a unique situation where there was relatively exquisite control of past life experiences, demographic variables, substance abuse, psychiatric history, and many other factors (Nebes, 1974). The split brain research of Roger Sperry was so successful and produced findings of such great importance that he later received the Nobel Prize in Medicine for his contributions.

Essentially, Sperry's research team found that while split brain patients had few obvious consequences from the neurosurgical procedure there were nonetheless subtle neuropsychological changes. For example, information presented in the right visual field would go to the left cerebral hemisphere only and not be accessible to the right cerebral hemisphere (Gazzaniga, 1977). A fundamental experimental paradigm of Sperry's work was the presentation of stimuli to only one visual field of split brain patients. An example of how this could work is to present a coin to a split brain patient's right visual field. As the sensory stimuli are transmitted to the left cerebral hemisphere, the cerebral hemisphere specialized for speech and language, the split brain patient is able to identify the object by name.

On the other hand, if the coin is presented to the left visual field, then sensory information is transmitted to the right cerebral hemisphere, which is specialized for visual-spatial perception and organization (Nebes, 1974). As a result the split brain patient is unable to name the coin but can match the coin when presented with alternatives (i.e., a dime is presented and a nickel, penny, and quarter are other options). Similarly, split brain patients draw better with the left hand and right cerebral hemisphere, regardless of their pre-neurosurgical dominance pattern (Gazzaniga, Steen, & Volpe, 1979).

Research since Sperry's major contributions has focused on other aspects of hemispheric functioning. Although there is an agreement that the two cerebral hemispheres subserve different neurobehavioral functions, there is less agreement regarding at which neurodevelopment stages various behavioral abilities are mediated by particular brain structures (Dean, 1985). It has been postulated, for instance, that hemispheric lateralization of functions begins relatively early in life, and by the age of three, more than 90% of children demonstrate left hemisphere language and symbolic processing abilities (Bryden & Saxby, 1985).

Moreover, developmental preferences for hand and foot dominance follow similar age-related patterns. Preference for the right hand in most children appears by age two (Bryden & Saxby, 1985), while foot preference develops a little later, in many cases by age five (Porac & Coren, 1981).

A very basic and oversimplified overview of localization of cerebral functioning has been presented here. To a large extent, these suggestions for cerebral functioning localization are based on adult chronic lesion study data. In some cases, the relationships suggested between neurocortex and behavioral function may not generalize to child and adolescent populations. The purpose of this overview, however, is to provide a very elementary perspective on brain-behavior relationships and to demonstrate the specific neurobehavioral functions that may be developing in some children and adolescents. For a more elaborate discussion of lateralization cerebral functioning, the reader may wish to consult the excellent chapter by Dean (1985).

Left Hemispheric Functioning

As it is well known by virtually every clinical neuropsychologist and perhaps the majority of lay persons, the left cerebral hemisphere, assuming right-handedness, is specialized for language and symbolic processing. Abilities such as speech, writing, arithmetic, and reading are thought to be mediated by the left cerebral hemisphere. In short, the processes of using symbols for communication are generally thought to be subsumed by the left cerebral hemisphere. Generally, the left cerebral hemisphere is also considered to work more in a linear-sequential fashion, or step-by-step, rather than in a synthetic-simultaneous fashion. An example might be that the left hemisphere works more like someone using a cookbook recipe rather than someone cooking by intuition.

RIGHT HEMISPHERIC FUNCTIONS

AGAIN, AS IS well known thanks to contemporary popular culture, the right hemisphere is specialized for the perception and organization of visual-spatial stimuli, certain perceptual-motor skills, and emotional functioning. The various abilities subserved by the right cerebral hemisphere, assuming right-handedness, include orienting oneself in space, reproducing complex geometric and whole-part patterns, recognizing faces, and understanding different emotional tones and patterns of nonverbal behavior (Saxby & Bryden, 1984).

SPECIFIC FUNCTIONS OF THE CEREBRAL LOBES

THE KNOWLEDGE OF the specific behavioral correlates of lesions in specific cerebral lobes is based upon a considerable amount of clinical research. As alluded to earlier, the majority of these research findings were developed from the adult brain-injured population from studies of patients with chronic lesions. It should be noted that correlation of a behavioral deficit with a chronic lesion in a specific brain area does not always mean that a specific function or behavioral ability can be localized in that particular area of the brain. Rather, the chronic lesion data suggest that some important function that is involved in the production of the behavior may be absent based on some other particular impaired brain area. As was mentioned earlier, neurobehavioral functions are produced by multiple brain areas working together in a coordinated fashion.

FRONTAL LOBES

PLANNING, EXECUTION, AND evaluation of motor and cognitive behaviors are performed by the frontal lobes, working with other brain areas. The frontal lobes direct behavior toward goals, make judgments with respect to time allocation and passage, and also play a role in terms of decisions with respect to material to be remembered. In addition, there is a relationship between the frontal lobes and emotional response as many decisions with respect to emotional expression require input to the frontal lobes.

Left Frontal Lobe

As was mentioned previously, Broca's area resides in the left frontal lobe and is connected with motor speech or expressive language. With chronic lesions in the left frontal lobe, research has generally shown difficulties of modulating behavior to conform to complex internal speech and difficulties with intentional verbal memory; Luria (1966) described this syndrome as *dynamic aphasia*. An example of this problem is an inability to produce words that start with a particular letter (Benton, 1968).

Right Frontal Lobe

The right frontal lobe is particularly involved with visual-spatial integration and maze learning (Corkin, 1965; Teuber, 1963). The visuo-spatial problems, however, may be more related to integration of motor aspects than visual-perceptual components. Also, there may be difficulties in singing or the ability to tell jokes and funny stories.

TEMPORAL LOBES

THE PERCEPTION, ANALYSIS, and evaluation of auditory stimuli are the special ability of the temporal lobes (Luria, 1966). In addition, the temporal lobes subserve memory function involving both verbal and nonverbal stimuli.

Left Temporal Lobe

As would be expected, verbal stimuli such as the sounds of letters, words, and numbers are perceived by the left temporal lobe. Impairment of the left temporal lobe can make it difficult for an individual to appreciate language (Luria, 1966). Problems in the phonemic analysis can impair classic academic skills, such as reading, writing, and spelling. The decoding of language as phonics is a key component in these processes, as well as verbal short-term memory (Milner, 1958). [A distinction between episodic and declarative memory could be made here, but for the sake of ease of understanding, the somewhat dated concepts on short- and long-term memory will be used in this book.]

Right Temporal Lobe

As the left hemisphere is associated with language and verbal short-term memory, the right hemisphere is associated with perception of nonverbal stimuli, particularly auditory perception of stimuli such as rhythm and pitch (Horton & Wedding, 1984). Impairment of the right temporal lobe can cause a person to be unable to appreciate music; similarly nonverbal memory is also associated with the recall of nonverbal figures (Meier & French, 1965).

PARIETAL LOBES

TACTILE AND KINESTHETIC perception is based in the parietal lobes. Lesion studies involving the parietal lobes usually show deficits in appreciating tactile stimuli, such as an inability to recognize objects perceived through touch and problems integrating tactile and kinesthetic information (Horton & Wedding, 1984). Other deficits include the inability to consider multiple aspects of objects and problems with complex voluntary perceptual-motor skill movements (i.e., *apraxia;* Horton & Wedding, 1984).

Left Parietal Lobe

The left parietal lobe is situated in a central location between the temporal and occipital lobes, and as a result, it plays a special role in terms of verbal information processing. The left parietal lobe contains numerous connections between the temporal and occipital lobes, which are responsible for facilitating communication and integrating information from visual, auditory, and tactile sensory and modalities (Horton & Wedding, 1984). Problems in the perception and comprehension of language can be produced by impairment of this area (i.e., Wernicke's area). Lesion studies involving the area where the left parietal, occipital, and temporal lobes intersect demonstrate difficulties with reading, writing, naming, color labeling, and spelling (Horton & Wedding, 1984). Luria (1973) noted verbal memory deficits associated with the left parietal lobe usually involve difficulties in terms of organizing verbal material rather than perceiving it.

Right Parietal Lobe

Just as the left parietal lobe is important in verbal information processing so the right parietal lobe is important in the processing of nonverbal information. The parietal lobe region of the right parietal lobe is particularly important in terms of combining visual, auditory, and tactile stimuli into integrated nonverbal wholes. The perception of faces and the drawing of complex spatial figures is dependent on intact right parietal lobe functioning. In addition, arithmetic operations in which place values are important and dressing difficulties and left-sided visual neglect are related to the right parietal lobe functioning (Horton & Wedding, 1984).

OCCIPITAL LOBES

JUST AS THE temporal lobes subserve the perception of auditory stimuli, and the parietal lobes subserve the perception of tactile stimuli, the occipital lobes mediate visual functions. The occipital lobes in different cerebral hemispheres perceive the contralateral visual field. As earlier noted, the perception of the contralateral visual field is 100%.

Left Occipital Lobe

Visual discrimination and analysis of language-related visual forms such as symbolic stimuli are mediated by the left occipital lobe. This includes symbols such as letters, numbers, and words. The inability to integrate visual stimuli to comprehend multiple aspects of a visual form can be found in individuals with specific lesions in the left occipital lobe (Luria, 1966). An interesting way of testing for these types of deficits is to print a word such as "STOP" and then draw diagonal lines through the printed word. The drawing of the lines should make it more difficult for the subject to read a word he or she could read without difficulty before. The reading problem, however, comes from difficulties in visual recognition and scanning and not problems in comprehension (Horton & Wedding, 1984).

Right Occipital Lobe

Visual perception of nonverbal forms is subserved by the right occipital lobe. In chronic lesion studies of patients with impaired right occipital lobes, the patients had difficulties in visual recognition and differentiation of forms and geometric patterns (Horton & Wedding, 1984). In addition, problems with respect to differentiating color hues can be traced to right occipital lobe lesions (Scotti & Spinner, 1970).

RECOVERY OF FUNCTION AFTER BRAIN INJURY

A CONSIDERABLE DEGREE OF research on animals has demonstrated that environmental stimulation is important in terms of modifying the central nervous system. Essentially, it has been suggested that the brain may have some residual capacity to repair itself after injury and that the environment can be crucial in terms of supporting recovery functioning after brain injury. Rosenzweig (1980) performed a number of important studies in this area of research. Essentially, he demonstrated that animals raised in a rich intellectual environment (for the specific species of animal) had a larger brain and positive neurochemical changes. These physical changes were directly related to prior positive environmental experiences. This suggests that the particular environmental stimulations may be important in terms of allowing the brain to recover, at least to a degree, following some sort of brain injury. Similarly, it has been suggested that children recover from brain injury in a somewhat different fashion than adults. This is related to the fact that children are not completely developed as human beings, but are rather passing through a number of complex developmental phases.

Generally speaking, when adults have a brain injury, assuming that it is not a progressive condition such as a degenerative disease (i.e., Alzheimer's disease, Pick's disease), a degree of recovery might be expected. This is most classically seen in cases of stroke or traumatic brain injury. Often adults will recover for a period of 1 or 2 years. With children, a different picture is presented. Teuber, in a classic study (Teuber & Rudel, 1962), studied brain-injured children over a number of years to assess the residual effects of childhood brain damage. Basically three possible developmental patterns of recovery of function were postulated.

The first pattern is similar to that seen in adults. There is initial impairment of neuropsychological abilities following brain injury, but the typical progressive pattern of neuropsychological recovery would be seen over time.

The second proposed developmental pattern of neuropsychological functioning after brain injury produces constant and consistent impairment of behavioral abilities over time. This would be somewhat similar to individuals with a major stroke in the primary motor area and significant destruction of brain tissue in the area. In short, no significant recovery of functioning is expected after a brief period of time.

The third pattern is one that is only expected to be seen in children. In that pattern, there is no clear impairment of behavior abilities initially, but as the child grows and develops, behavioral impairment is demonstrated. The behavioral impairment could emerge weeks, months, or even years after the initial injury to the brain.

This last pattern relies on the fact that certain neuropsychological brain structures only become active in certain neuropsychological developmental stages. That is to say, the delayed onset of impaired brain functioning is sort of like turning on lights on a Christmas tree. The lights come on only in stages, similar to a brain injury that impairs an area that will only become active in a later neurodevelopmental stage. The initial behavioral performance will not be impaired, because the child has not found it necessary to use the particular skill that will only be needed in a later stage of neurobehavioral development. For example, the child may sustain brain injury at age 2 and only later when the child goes to school would it be apparent that functions such as reading, writing, and arithmetic were impaired to a significant degree. The crux of that matter is that only when the child is called upon to demonstrate specialized neurobehavioral functioning will some neuropsychological deficits emerge.

With respect to Teuber's study, the results were unexpected, because essentially brain-injured children displayed all three patterns depending on the particular tasks assessed. That is to say in some cases they had initial impairment followed by significant behavioral improvement overtime. In other cases, there was initial impairment of neurobehavioral functioning, which stayed current, and in the third case, there was no clear neurobehavioral impairment initially, but as the child grew up the neuropsychological deficits emerged. Due to the time lag, if the child hadn't been followed in a research project, it wouldn't have been clear that he or she was impaired due to childhood brain damage. Essentially, this research study demonstrates that the effects of brain damage to children are very complex and depend both on the characteristics of tasks under study and the normal developmental sequencing of that task, among other factors (Horton, 1994).

The third pattern is particularly problematic in cases where someone is attempting to demonstrate the extent of neuropsychological deficits from a childhood traumatic brain injury, as it essentially undermines any conclusions reached before the child has grown to maturity. It has been suggested that the lesion area is either immature or not yet utilized at the time the lesion was sustained and that only later will the degree of neurobehavioral deficit be apparent (Bolter & Long, 1985).

As might be understood after one reflects on the difficulties of longitudinal research, most studies of childhood brain injury have been of limited duration. (Teuber's study followed children for 10 years and is the clear exception to the rule.) Most research has concentrated on the first pattern, that is, the recovery of functional ability after traumatic brain injury where there is some clear evidence of progressive recovery. Researchers at the University of British Columbia (Klonoff & Low, 1974; Klonoff & Paris, 1974) have done what is considered, perhaps, the most pivotal work in this area. They initiated a number of longitudinal large studies on injuries that involved fairly comprehensive diagnostic assessments. It has been noted elsewhere that traumatic head injuries are the most common neurological problem in children and result in 15% of deaths in the 15–24 year age group (Klonoff, Crockett, & Clark, 1984).

Some of the most important findings from the British Columbia studies indicated that the most marked improvement after childhood traumatic brain injury took place in the first 2 years following head injuries, but children showed evidence of significant improvement for 5 years post injury. In addition, it may be noted that boys are more likely than girls to have head injury and that factors such as living in a congested residential area, having a lower socioeconomic status, and unstable family lives were related to the likelihood of having a childhood traumatic head injury. It might be observed that somewhat different patterns were seen for younger and older children following traumatic head injury. Younger children demonstrated irritability plus other personality changes, where older children more likely to demonstrate headaches, impaired memory function, and problems in learning (Klonoff, Crockett, & Clark, 1984).

Test data demonstrated that IQ scores for brain-injured children were lower than those for normal control subjects during the entire 5-year study and the most marked differences found at the initial assessment and at the first year follow up after injury (Klonoff & Paris, 1974). It was also noted that IQ measures appeared to recover somewhat more rapidly than did neuropsychological measures. Interestingly, the series of studies in British Columbia suggested that full scale IQ scores from the initial testing were the single best predictor of the child's recovery from traumatic brain injury. This simply underscores the importance of IQ measurements in brain-injured children. It might be noted that the IQ is of a different level of sensitivity with children than it is with adults with respect to neuropsychological functioning (Benton, 1974; Reitan, 1974). The status of the child after 5 years was best predicted by the initial full scale IQ, loss of consciousness, and memory problems immediately after injuries (Klonoff, Crockett, & Clark, 1984).

SUMMARY

THE FIELD OF clinical neuropsychology is quite new and rests on an evolving research base. Moreover, the complex nature of clinical neuropsychology makes it a very difficult but rewarding area. The hope and expectation is that this and other chapters of this book will be helpful in terms of facilitating the delivery of clinical neuropsychological services to this needy population of brain-injured adults and children.

REFERENCES

Benton, A. L. (1968). Differential effects in the minor hemisphere. *Confinia Neurologica, 6,* 53–60.

Benton, A. L. (1974). Child neuropsychology. In R. M. Reitan & L. A. Davison (Eds.), *Clinical neuropsychology: Current status and applications* (pp. 79–82). New York: Wiley.

Bolter, J. F., & Long, C. J. (1985). Methodological issues in research in developmental neuropsychology. In L. C. Hartlage & C. F. Telzrow (Eds.), *Neuropsychology of individual differences* (pp. 41–60). New York: Plenum Press.

Broder, E. (1973). Developmental dyslexia: A diagnostic approach based on three atypical reading-spelling patterns. *Developmental Medicine and Child Neurology, 15,* 663–687.

Bryden, M. P., & Saxby, L. (1985). Developmental aspects of cerebral lateraliza-
    tion. In J. E. Obrzut & G. W. Hynd (Eds.), *Clinical neuropsychology, Vol. I,
    Theory and research* (pp. 71–94). Orlando, FL: Academic Press.

Corkin, S. (1965). Tactually-guided imaging in man: Effects of unilateral exci-
    sions and bilateral hippocampus lesions. *Neuropsychologia, 3,* 339–351.

Davison, L. (1974). Introduction. In R. M. Reitan & L. A. Davison (Eds.), *Clinical
    neuropsychology: Current status and applications* (pp. 1–7). New York:
    Wiley.

Dean, R. S. (1985). Foundation and rationale for neuropsychological basis of indi-
    vidual differences. In L. C. Hartlage & C. F. Telzrow (Eds.), *Neuropsychology
    of individual differences* (pp. 7–40). New York: Plenum.

Gazzaniga, M. S. (1977). Consistency and diversity in brain organization. *Annals
    of the New York Academy of Science, 299,* 415–423.

Gazzaniga, M. S., Steen, D., & Volpe, B. T. (1979). *Functional neuroscience.* New
    York: Harper & Row.

Geschwind, N., & Levitsky, W. (1984). Human brain left-right asymmetries in
    temporal speech region. *Science, 161,* 186–187.

Goldstein, K. (1952). The effects of brain damage on personality. *Psychiatry, 1*(5),
    245–260.

Hartlage, L. C. (1975). Neuropsychological approaches to predicting outcome of
    remedial educational strategies for learning disabled children. *Pediatric
    Psychology, 3,* 23–28.

Hartlage, L. C. (1986). Pediatric neuropsychology. In D. Wedding, A. M. Horton,
    Jr., & J. S. Webster (Eds.), *The neuropsychology handbook* (pp. 441–455). New
    York: Springer.

Horton, A. M., Jr. (1987). Luria's contributions to clinical and behavioral neu-
    ropsychology. *Neuropsychology, 1*(2), 39–44.

Horton, A. M., Jr. (1989). Child behavioral neuropsychology with children. In
    C. R. Reynolds & E. Fletcher-Janzen (Eds.), *Handbook of clinical child neu-
    ropsychology* (pp. 521–534). New York: Plenum.

Horton, A. M., Jr., (1994). *Behavioral interventions with brain injured children.* New
    York: Plenum.

Horton, A. M., Jr., & Puente, A. E. (1986). Behavioral neuropsychology for chil-
    dren. In G. Hynd & J. Obrzut (Eds.), *Child neuropsychology, Vol. II, Clinical
    practice* (pp. 299–316). Orlando, FL: Academic Press.

Horton, A. M., Jr., & Puente, A. E. (1990). Lifespan neuropsychology: An over-
    view. In A. M. Horton, Jr. (Ed.), *Neuropsychology across the life span* (pp. 1–15).
    New York: Springer Publishing.

Horton, A. M., Jr., & Wedding, D. (1984). *Clinical and behavioral neuropsychology.*
    New York: Praeger.

Hynd, G. W., & Obrzut, J. E. (Eds.) (1981). *Neuropsychological assessment and the
    school-aged child: Issues and procedures.* New York: Grune & Stratton.

Hynd, G. W., & Willis, W. G. (1988). *Pediatric neuropsychology.* Orlando, FL: Grune &
    Stratton.

Kertesz, A. (Ed.) (1994). *Localization and neuroimaging in neuropsychology*. New York: Academic Press.

Klonoff, H., & Low, M. (1974). Disordered brain function in young children and early adolescents: Neuropsychological and electroencephalographic correlates. In R. M. Reitan & L. A. Davison (Eds.), *Clinical neuropsychology: Current status and applications* (pp. 121–178). New York: Wiley.

Klonoff, H., & Paris, R. (1974). Immediate, short-term and residual effects of acute head injuries in children: Neuropsychological and neurological correlates. In R. M. Reitan & L. A. Davison (Eds.), *Clinical neuropsychology: Current status and applications* (pp. 179–210). New York: Wiley.

Klonoff, A., Crockett, D. F., & Clark, G. (1984). Head trauma in children. In R. Tarter & G. Goldstein (Eds.), *Advances in clinical neuropsychology* (pp. 139–157). New York: Plenum.

Kolb, B., & Fantie, B. (1989). Development of the child's brain and behavior. In C. R. Reynolds and E. Fletcher-Janzen (Eds.), *Handbook of clinical child neuropsychology* (pp. 17–40). New York: Plenum.

Luria, A. R. (1963). *Restoration of function after brain injury*. New York: Macmillan.

Luria, A. R. (1966). *Higher cortical functioning in man*. New York: Basic Books.

Luria, A. R. (1973). *The working brain*. New York: Basic Books.

Luria, A. R. (1980). *Higher cortical functions*. New York: Basic Books.

Mattis, S., French, J. H., & Rapin, T. (1975). Dyslexia in children and adults: Three independent neuropsychological syndromes. *Developmental Medicine and Child Neurology, 17,* 150–163.

Meier, M. J. (1974). Some challenges for clinical neuropsychology. In R. M. Reitan & L. A. Davison (Eds.), *Clinical neuropsychology: Current status and applications* (pp. 289–324). New York: John Wiley.

Meier, M. J., & French, L. A. (1965). Some personality correlates of unilateral and bilateral EEG abnormalities in psychomotor epileptics. *Journal of Clinical Psychology, 21,* 3–9.

Milner, B. (1958). Psychological deficits produced by temporal lobe excision. *Association for Research in Nervous and Mental Diseases, 36,* 244–257.

Milner, B. (1971). Interhemispheric differences and psychological processes. *British Medical Journal, 27,* 272–277.

Mishkin, M. (1978). Memory in monkeys severely impaired by combined but not separate removal of amygdala and hippocampus. *Nature, 273,* 297–298.

Nauta, W. J. H., & Feintag, M. (1986). *Fundamental neuroanatomy*. New York: W. H. Freeman.

Nebes, R. W. (1974). Hemispheric specialization in commissurotomized man. *Psychological Bulletin, 81,* 1–14.

Porac, C., & Coren, S. (1981). *Lateral performances and human behavior*. New York: Springer-Verlag.

Reitan, R. M. (1974). Psychological effects of cerebral lesions in children of early school age. In R. M. Reitan & L. A. Davison (Eds.), *Clinical neuropsychology: Current status and applications* (pp. 53–90). New York: Wiley.

Reitan, R. M., & Davison, L. A. (Eds.) (1974). *Clinical neuropsychology: Current status and applications*. New York: Wiley.

Reitan, R. M., & Wolfson, D. (1992). *Neuropsychological evaluation of older children*. Tucson, AZ: Neuropsychology Press.

Reynolds, C. R. (1981). The neuropsychological basis of intelligence. In G. W. Hynd and J. E. Obrzut (Eds.), *Neuropsychological assessment and the school aged child* (pp. 87–124). New York: Grune & Stratton.

Rourke, B. P., Fisk, J. L., & Strang, J. D. (1986). *Neuropsychological assessment of children: A treatment-oriented approach*. New York: Guilford Press.

Rosenzweig, M. R. (1980). Animal models for effects of brain lesions and for rehabilitation. In D. C. Stein, J. J. Rosen, & N. Butters (Eds.), *Plasticity and recovery of function in the central nervous system*. New York: Academic Press.

Russell, E. W., & Espir, M.L.E. (1961). *Traumatic aphasia*. London: Oxford University Press.

Saxby, L., & Bryden, M. P. (1984). Left-ear superiority in children processing auditory emotional material. *Developmental Psychology, 20,* 72–80.

Scotti, G., & Spinner, H. (1970). Color imperception in unilateral hemispheric patients. *Journal of Neurology, Neurosurgery and Psychiatry, 33,* 22–41.

Sperry, R. W. (1961). Cerebral organization and behavior. *Science, 133,* 1949.

Spreen, O., Risser, A. T., & Edgell, D. (1995). *Developmental neuropsychology*. New York: Oxford University Press.

Struss, D. T., & Benson, D. F. (1984). Neuropsychological studies of the frontal lobes. *Psychological Bulletin, 95*(1), 23–38.

Teuber, H. L. (1963). Space perception and its disturbances after brain injury in man. *Neuropsychologia, 1,* 47–53.

Teuber, H. L., & Rudel, R. G. (1962). Behavior after brain lesions in children and adults. *Developmental Medicine and Child Neurology, 4,* 3–20.

2

Neurological Disorders

MICHELLE BRAUN

SINCE THE DEBUT of neuropsychological assessment in the 1970s, the demand for neuropsychological evaluations has increased exponentially. Simultaneously, neuropsychological research across a wide variety of clinical disorders has increased the scope and utility of neuropsychological assessments. Among the requisite areas of knowledge for solid practice in neuropsychology, information on neurological disorders is foundational. Individuals with neurological disorders are frequently referred not only for assessment of neurocognitive issues, but for delineation of the primary and secondary comorbid psychiatric and behavioral symptoms that are crucial to diagnosis and treatment planning. Regardless of the initial referral question, neuropsychologists who evaluate individuals with neurological disorders are often required to make fine discriminations of cognitive, behavioral, and emotional variables. Neuropsychologists provide unique contributions to several aspects of care including diagnosis, prognosis, determination of severity, tracking of cognitive and behavioral change over time, and formation of treatment recommendations.

The goal of this chapter is to provide information on the clinical features and etiology of common neurological disorders in adults and the impact of these disorders on neuropsychological, emotional, and behavioral functioning. Although the types of neurological disorders seen in practice differ as a function of several variables (clinician specialty area, age-range of patients, systemic and regional issues, type and affiliation of practice), topic areas in this chapter are ordered based on a combination of prevalence statistics and typical referral questions in general neuropsychology clinics (based upon anecdotal information from neuropsychologists across the United States). Topics include cerebrovascular disorders, dementia, mild cognitive impairment, movement disorders, epilepsy and nonepileptic attack disorder, traumatic brain injury and postconcussive syndrome, neoplasms, and finally, a note about psychiatric disorders. Although each of these disorders is presented separately, comorbidity is common, and neuropsychologists are often required to think flexibly about characterizing cognitive functioning across diagnostic categories.

CEREBROVASCULAR DISORDERS

PATIENTS WITH CEREBROVASCULAR disorders—including strokes, transient ischemic attacks, multi-infarct dementia (MID), and small vessel ischemic changes—are frequently seen in neuropsychological practice. Additionally, the role of cerebrovascular factors has emerged in two relatively more recent areas of study: vascular cognitive impairment, a developing construct that aims to characterize subtle vascular-related cognitive compromise due to issues that are more chronic and subtle than stroke, such as hypertension (Hachinksi et al., 2006); and the role of vascular risk factors in Alzheimer's disease (as reviewed in Alagiakrishnan, McCracken, & Feldman, 2006). Current coverage begins with the most common cerebrovascular disorder, stroke, or cerebrovascular accident (CVA). A stroke is characterized by a sudden interruption of blood supply to the brain. Recent U.S. statistics document that stroke is the third leading cause of death (behind heart disease and cancer), that 40,000 more women than men have a stroke at all ages, and that stroke is the leading cause of serious, long-term disability (American Heart Association, 2006). Although stroke can occur at any age, including in childhood, the risk of stroke increases with age and most people with ischemic or obstructive strokes are over the age of 60. Many people who experience a stroke have at least some vascular risk factors including high blood pressure, heart disease, a history of smoking, or diabetes. Trends are alarming: high blood pressure alone contributes to over 12.7 million strokes worldwide and, compared with whites, young African Americans have a two- to three-fold greater risk of ischemic stroke, and African American men and women are more likely to die of stroke (American Heart Association, 2006).

The brain's need for oxygen and glucose is significant. Although it comprises only about 2% of the total body weight, the brain requires approximately 20% of the body's blood and 25% of the body's oxygen to function. Compromised blood flow may lead to inefficiencies in neuronal functioning or neuronal death, depending on the size and location of the affected vessels (e.g., arteries vs. capillaries), the extent of blockage or leakage, and the compensation of surrounding blood vessels, among other variables (e.g., preexisting damage, recovery of function). Knowledge of cerebrovascular anatomy is crucial in predicting and assessing the cognitive and behavioral changes that may accompany cerebrovascular insult and in providing information on prognosis and treatment. Although a comprehensive review of cerebrovascular anatomy is beyond the scope of this chapter, the following summary by Berg, Franzen, and Wedding (1987) is offered:

> The brain is supplied bilaterally by the internal carotid arteries and by the vertebral arteries. The internal carotid divides on each side to form the anterior and middle cerebral arteries. The vertebral arteries form a single basilar artery, which divides at the top of the midbrain to form paired posterior cerebral arteries, which supply the thalamus, the occipital lobes, and the medial temporal lobes. The entire system is linked by the Circle of Willis and by the anterior and posterior communicating arteries that provide for collateral circulation (p. 6).

Strokes are classified as either ischemic or obstructive (blockages within the brain), or hemorrhagic (bleeding within the brain). About 88% of all strokes are ischemic and occur when an artery within the brain becomes blocked by the formation of a clot of blood cells, which forms due to artherosclerosis in the head and neck (in which the arteries narrow due to gradual cholesterol deposition), heart problems (usually due to atrial fibrillation or a heart attack), or various other vascular impairments. There are two types of ischemic strokes: thrombotic and embolic. If an artery becomes obstructed at the point where the clot formed, a *thrombosis* (stationary clot) results. If the clot travels to a different part of the vasculature, then an *embolis* results. Thrombotic strokes account for about 50% of all strokes.

The duration of blood vessel occlusion directly impacts later neuronal functioning. After 30 seconds of oxygen deprivation, ischemia may develop. After 1 minute of oxygen deprivation, neuronal function may cease, and after 2–5 minutes, infarcts (areas of dead or dying tissue) may develop. The hippocampus is especially sensitive to hypoperfusion, and hippocampal sclerosis may result from oxygen deprivation. Thrombotic strokes can occur in the large arteries such as the carotid or middle cerebral arteries (large-vessel thrombosis) or the smaller penetrating arteries (small vessel thrombosis or lacunar strokes). Lacunar strokes—which often form in subcortical areas such as the basal ganglia, internal capsule, white matter, and pons—are mostly thrombotic but can also be embolic. Lacunar strokes may also be referred to as lacunes, lacunar infarcts, lacunar state dementia, or subcortical ischemic vascular dementia (SIVD). Similar to MID, clinical history often involves stepwise deterioration, though lacunar strokes are often too small to be detected on neurodiagnostic tests such as CT and angiography. Lacunar states have received particular attention in regard to differential diagnosis from Alzheimer's disease (AD), because there are similarities: onset is insidious (due to the "silent" nature of lacunes), age is a risk factor for both, and AD may present with lacunes. However, neuropsychological profiles differ. Given the localization of lacunar infarcts a subcortical-frontal pattern is often observed versus the relatively poorer performance of AD patients on tests of memory and language (Kramer, Kemenoff, & Chui, 2001).

Binswanger's disease, or subcortical arteriosclerotic encephalopathy, also involves multiple infarcts, but these occur mostly in the periventricular white matter and are accompanied by myelin loss, mostly in the temporal and occipital lobes. Decline is usually insidious (versus stepwise), and deficits in executive functioning are common. Individuals with Binswanger's commonly have a history of hypertension or systemic vascular disease. When cognitive functioning becomes impaired due to repeated infarctions (often at several different brain sites, and in large versus small vessels in particular), MID may result. Decline due to MID often occurs in stepwise fashion, with neuropsychological deficits related to infarct location and often occurring in the presence of gait abnormalities or other subcortical neurological signs. Vascular dementia may also occur due to a single infarct (strategic single infarct dementia), which often occurs in the frontal white matter, basal ganglia, angular gyrus, or bilateral medial thalamic areas. Risk factors for MID include small vessel ischemic changes (often associated with artherosclerosis and diabetes) and hypertension. The Hachinski Ischemic scale is often helpful in identifying and characterizing MID in particular (Hachinski et al., 1975), but it is generally not as helpful in characterizing other vascular dementias.

The traveling clots that characterize embolic strokes originate outside of the brain in large bore vessels or the heart and travel upstream until they become lodged in smaller vessels. A common site for embolism occlusion is the middle cerebral artery on the left side of the brain. Emboli may be comprised of various materials including clotted blood cells, air bubbles, deposits of oil or fat, or pieces of tumor. Given the immediate obstruction of a traveling clot (versus the slow buildup of a thrombotic clot), immediate neurological and physical deficits often result. Secondary effects, such as hydrocephalus, can occur after any type of stroke.

Not all incidents of cerebral ischemia are caused by the sudden impairment that accompanies stroke, although cognitive functioning can be impacted nonetheless. Gradual reductions in blood flow to the brain may result from cerebral artherosclerosis (hardening and narrowing of the arteries) or from cerebral vasculitis (narrowed vessels due to inflammation or vasospasm). Episodic compromise in blood flow due to hypertension or cerebral artherosclerosis with thrombosis may result in a Transient Ischemic Attack (TIA), or cerebral vascular insufficiency. A TIA generally lasts from minutes to hours and resolves on its own (either gradually or abruptly), often without significant sequelae. It is not uncommon to observe patients with no history of significant vascular events that exhibit cognitive compromise due to chronic vascular risk factors including hypertension, diabetes, and high cholesterol (hyperlipidemia). Cognitive deficits may also be observed following cardiac surgery or other procedures in which blood and oxygen flow to the brain is compromised. Although no commonly agreed upon standards exist for identifying and describing individuals with subtle cognitive impairment due to vascular risk factors or relatively insidious and subtle vascular events, damage may present on neuroimaging as small vessel ischemic changes and may be expressed on neuropsychological tests as subcortical compromise (impairments in processing speed, motor functioning, and rapid information processing). Due to the growing awareness of the need to develop criteria for vascular-related cognitive impairment, a recent work group from the National Institute for Neurological Disorders and Stroke (NINDS) and the Canadian Stroke Network (CSN) created a consensus report on clinical and research definitions of vascular cognitive impairment (Hachinski et al., 2006).

Hemorrhagic strokes are caused by the rupture of a blood vessel in the brain that allows blood to leak inside the brain. The initial rupture may relate not only to weakness in the vessel wall itself, but to softening of the brain tissue surrounding the vessel. The vessel or tissue abnormalities leading to hemorrhage can be caused by aneurysms, angiomas (congenital collections of abnormal vessels including capillaries, veins, and arteries such as arterial venous malformations), blood diseases (such as leukemia), infections, toxic chemicals, trauma, and brain tumors. An aneurysm is a small, irregular area of swelling in an artery wall that weakens and bursts over time and is typically caused by hypertension, arterosclerosis, infection, or embolism. It is often accompanied by a headache, though there is a wide range of variability in the type and duration of headaches. For example, although 90% of headaches resulting from aneurysms are often sudden and intense ("the worst headache of my life"), and accompanied by neck stiffness ("Kernig's sign"), nausea, and pain in the occipital region, headaches may also be chronic over many years if the aneurysm is slow to develop and exerts pressure on the dura over time. Aneurysms account for 50% of all strokes in people under age 45. Hemorrhagic strokes, or intracerebral hemorrhages account for about 12% of total strokes, and 80% of these are fatal. The most common site for hemorrhage is in the basal ganglia, and the most common cause is hypertension. The onset is usually abrupt and, if accompanied by a sudden increase in brain pressure, can lead to unconsciousness or death. A subarachnoid hemorrhage occurs when a blood vessel ruptures outside the brain and pools in the subarachnoid space surrounding the brain. Most often, an aneurysm in an artery at the base of the brain is the cause. Subarachonid hemorrhages can occur at any age and are slightly more common in women than men. Angiomas are comprised of a mass of enlarged, abnormally twisted cortical vessels that are supplied by one or more large arteries and drained by one or more large veins before blood flow adequately circulates through the capillary beds. Because blood circulates predominantly from artery to vein without adequate circulation, surrounding tissue may become compromised and higher than normal blood pressure may weaken the abnormally twisted vessels over time and lead to rupture.

The location of a stroke and its possible secondary effects (e.g., swelling) is often directly linked to specific neuropsychological abnormalities. Increasingly, neurologists are emphasizing the importance of learning neuropsychological manifestations of stroke given that post-stroke presenting signs may be predominantly cognitive (Ferro, 2001). A summary of neuropsychological syndromes related to specific arterial compromise is listed in Table 2.1.

Although a review of issues related to stroke recovery is beyond the scope of this chapter, given that it is the leading cause of chronic disability in the United States, it is important to note that recent important advances have been made in this field, especially regarding the recovery of motor function. For example, landmark research has shown that Constraint-Induced Movement Therapy (in which a functional limb is immobilized and the stroke-injured limb is utilized and later strengthened by the stimulation of neural pathways) allows stroke patients to increase their use of an injured limb by about 50% as compared to patients who do not undergo physical therapy (Taub, Uswatte, & Pidikiti, 1999).

As indicated earlier, there is growing evidence that patients with Alzheimer's disease have vascular damage in addition to the beta-amyloid plaques and neurofibillary tangles that characterize Alzheimer's disease. Longitudinal studies suggest that hypertension and high cholesterol may trigger the mechanisms involved in Alzheimer's disease (Alzheimer's Association, 2006). Additional studies show that other vascular abnormalities are associated with Alzheimer's disease, including

TABLE 2.1   Arterial Blood Supply to Functional-Anatomic Divisions of the Brain Relevant to Neuropsychology

Function	Impairment	Brain structure	Blood supply
Sensorimotor	Paralysis of contralateral face, arm, and leg	Primary motor area, precentral gyrus	Middle cerebral artery, anterior cerebral artery
	Sensory impairment over face, arm, and leg	Primary sensory area postcentral gyrus	Middle cerebral artery, anterior cerebral artery
Language	Broca's aphasia	Inferior frontal gyrus in dominant hemisphere	Middle cerebral artery
	Wernicke's aphasia	Superior temporal gyrus in dominant hemisphere	Middle cerebral artery
Visual perception	Homonymous hemianopia	Optic radiation deep in temporal convolution	Middle cerebral artery, posterior cerebral artery
	Visual integration, spatial neglect, visual agnosia	Parietal-occipital lobe, nondominant hemisphere	Middle cerebral artery
	Constructional apraxia, dressing apraxia	Parietal lobe, nondominant hemisphere	Middle cerebral artery
	Gertsmann's syndrome (agraphia, acalculia, alexia, finger agnosia, right-left confusion)	Angular gyrus of the dominant hemisphere	Middle cerebral artery

(Continued)

37

TABLE 2.1 Arterial Blood Supply to Functional-Anatomic Divisions of the Brain Relevant to Neuropsychology *(Continued)*

Function	Impairment	Brain structure	Blood supply
Movement	Ideomotor and ideational apraxia	Left temporal, parietal, occipital area	Middle cerebral artery, posterior cerebral artery
Memory	Short-term and long-term memory impairment	Hippocampus, medial temporal lobes, frontal lobes, basal forebrain, medial thalamus	Medial cerebral, posterior cerebral, anterior choroidal, and posterior communicating arteries
	Working memory	Dorsolateral frontal lobes	Anterior cerebral artery
Frontal-executive	Impairment in set maintenance, problem solving, planning, self-evaluation, ability to modify behavior	Dorsolateral frontal	Anterior cerebral artery
	Impairment in inhibition, emotional regulation	Orbital frontal	Anterior cerebral artery
	Akinesia, bradykinesia	Basal ganglia, putamen, globus pallidus, caudate nucleus, amygdaloid	Anterior choroidal artery, middle cerebral artery

Source: Weinstein & Swenson (1998).

cerebral emboli (Purandare et al., 2006) and Type II diabetes (Biessels & Kappelle, 2005), and that common genetic risk factors may be present in vascular compromise and Alzheimer's pathology (Manev & Manev, 2006). It has also been demonstrated that enhanced cardiovascular functioning (and cardiovascular exercise in particular) is associated with a decreased incidence of dementia (Lautenschlager & Almeida, 2006). Given the modifiable nature of many vascular risk factors, future studies of the relationship between vascular risk factors and Alzheimer's disease may lead to additional treatment strategies that impact both conditions. These findings may prove especially important to certain subgroups of the population who suffer from disproportionately larger rates of vascular disorders, such as African Americans.

DEMENTIA

MEMORY PROBLEMS ARE a common reason for referral to a neuropsychologist, in part due to increased awareness about memory problems in the medical community and society at large, and in part due to a rapidly growing older adult demographic (the demographic most at risk for memory problems) (Budson & Price, 2005). Simultaneously, the unique role of neuropsychological assessment in differentiating between normal and abnormal memory functioning has become increasingly important as many patients present with subtle memory complaints that cannot be detected on neuroimaging or common screening tests. For example, the Mini-Mental Examination (Folstein, Folstein, & McHugh, 1975) lacks the statistical sensitivity and difficulty level to detect subtle deficits in many patients.

Although memory impairment is still required for a diagnosis of dementia according to the *Diagnostic and Statistical Manual of Mental Disorders,* 4th ed. (*DSM–IV;* American Psychiatric Association [APA], 1994), an expanded definition of dementia has recently been applied in clinical settings based on observations that intact memory functioning may present with impairment in other cognitive functions. In this case, dementia can be conceptualized as:

> The decline of cognitive functions (e.g., memory, attention, language, visual perception, reasoning) and/or comportment (e.g., insight, judgment, social appropriateness) from a prior level of functioning to the point where customary activities of daily living are negatively affected. (Weintraub, 2006, p. 142)

When declines in cognitive or daily functioning are present, it is first necessary to examine whether impairment might relate to a delirium or other reversible condition. Common reversible conditions often misdiagnosed as dementia include normal pressure hydrocephalus (NPH), which presents with the clinical triad of gait problems, incontinence, and mental decline and which often requires rapid detection for true reversibility; vitamin B12 deficiency; and infections. Importantly, reversible dementias are often caused by multiple factors, so a thorough medical history is crucial. However, it is noted that a recent meta-analysis found not only a low proportion of reversible dementias across 5,620 patients in 39 studies (9%), but that only 0.6% of reversible cases actually reversed (Clarfield, 2003). These findings, in combination with two similar meta-analytic findings in 1988, suggest both that reversible dementias may comprise a smaller proportion of total dementias than previously suggested, and that most reversible dementias may not reverse as presumed (Clarfield, 2003). Although incidence and reversibility may be relatively low, reversible conditions must still be factored in and treated. Because a number of patients assessed for dementia are adults over the age of 60, and because older adults are particularly sensitive to medication effects, it is crucial that medication regimens are clarified. Medication-related cognitive compromise can impact cognitive functioning along a continuum ranging from subtle to gross impairment and may be one or many factors impacting cognitive functioning (see Jenike, 1988, for a complete list of medications that can cause cognitive changes in older adults). A list of reversible conditions is provided in Table 2.2.

Although dementia prevalence estimates vary as a function of geographical location and sample characteristics (community dwelling individuals vs. hospital patients), consolidated findings of studies on community-dwelling elderly in North America have reported dementia in 0.8–1.6% of persons 65–74 years old, 7–8% of persons 75–84 years old, and 18–32% of persons over 85 (U.S. Preventive Services Task Force, 1996).

ALZHEIMER'S DISEASE

ESTIMATES OF ALZHEIMER'S disease (AD) vary, though all studies have found that it is the most common form of dementia, and most studies implicate Alzheimer's pathology in 50–70% of cases (Alzheimer's Association, 2006). The number of Americans with AD has more than doubled since 1980, and it is currently estimated that 4.5 million Americans have the disease (Hebert et al., 2004a). Increased age is the greatest risk factor for Alzheimer's, with some studies suggesting that it impacts about 2% of the population at age 65, with prevalence doubling for every 5 years of increasing age such that 33% or more of 85 year olds have the disease. Some studies suggest that over half of all individuals

TABLE 2.2   Causes of Reversible Dementia

Intracranial conditions
  Meningiomas
  Subdural hematomas
  Hydrocephalus
    Communicating
    Noncommunicating
  Epilepsy
  Multiple sclerosis
  Wilson's disease

Systemic illness
  Pulmonary insufficiency
  Cardiac arrhythmia
  Severe anemia
  Polycythemia vera
  Uremia
  Hyponatremia
  Portosystemic encephalopathy
  Porphyria
  Hyperlipidemia

Deficiency states
  B12 deficiency
  Pellagra
  Folate deficiency

Endocrinopathies
  Addison's disease
  Panhypopituitarism
  Myxedema

Hypoparathyroidism
  Hyperparathyroidism
  Recurrent hypoglycemia
  Cushing's disease and steroid therapy
  Hyperthyroidism

Drugs
  Methyldopa and haloperidol
  Clonidine and fluphenazine
  Disulfiram
  Lithium carbonate
  Phenothizaines
  Haloperidol and lithium carbonate
  Bromides
  Phenytoin
  Mephenytoin
  Barbituates
  Clonidine
  Methyldopa

(Continued)

TABLE 2.2   Causes of Reversible Dementia *(Continued)*

Propranolol hydrochloride
Atropine and related compounds

Heavy metals
  Mercury
  Arsenic
  Lead
  Thallium

Exogenous toxins and industrial agents
  Tricholoroethylene
  Toluene
  Carbon disulfide
  Organophosphates
  Carbon disulfide
  Alcohol

Infections
  General paresis
  Chronic meningitis
  Cerebral abscess
  Cysticercosis
  Whipple's disease
  Progressive multifocal leukoencephalopathy

Collagen-vascular and vascular disorders
  Systemic lupus erythematosus

Temporal arteritis
  Sarcoidosis
  Cogan's syndrome
  Behcet's syndrome
  Carotid artery stenosis

"Potentially recoverable dementia"
  Cerebral anoxia
  Trauma
  Excessive electroconvulsive drugs/therapy
  Encephalitis

Source: Cummings, Benson, & LoVerma (1980).

85 or older will be diagnosed with AD (Hebert et al., 2004b), especially if there is a family history of a first-degree relative with AD. A recent study on the prevalence of dementia in Sweden found that 55% of women and 37% of men aged 95 were diagnosed with dementia, but that the proportion of mild dementia and vascular dementia was lower in 95 year olds versus 85 year olds (Borjesson-Hanson, Edin, Gislason, & Skoog, 2004). A recent Delphi consensus study on the global prevalence of dementia (Ferri et al., 2005) suggests that 24.3 million people have dementia,

with 4.6 million new cases of dementia every year (one new case every 7 seconds). Additionally, the number of people affected is projected to double every 20 years to 81.1 million by 2040, with the highest increases in developing countries (60% in 2001, rising to 71% by 2040). The projected rate of increase is 100% in developed countries between 2001 and 2040, but more than 300% in India, China, and their south Asian and western Pacific neighbors.

Given that advanced age is a risk factor for dementia, an increase in the older adult population is projected to lead to a significant increase in the incidence of dementia. In the United States, the number of people age 65 and older is expected to double over the next 25 years, which may lead to a 70% increase in the prevalence of AD and an estimated 7.7 million people affected (Alzheimer's Association, 2006). United States state-specific projections of AD prevalence through 2025 suggest that specific regions of the country (e.g., the western United States) will see the greatest increase in AD due to the ratio of projected older to younger adults in the population (Hebert et al., 2004b). Recent research provides troubling new statistics about the incidence of AD in African Americans and adults younger than 65 (early-onset). First, combined findings on the incidence of AD in African Americans versus whites suggests that it occurs 14–100% more often, that there is a greater familial risk, and that genetic and environmental factors may interact differently to cause AD. For example, the combination of hypertension and high cholesterol, which is significantly higher in African Americans, creates a four-fold risk of dementia. Furthermore, African Americans have a 60% higher risk of developing Type II diabetes, which is another risk factor for AD (Alzheimer's Association, 2006).

In light of the information about the significant incidence and projected increase in AD, it is important to note recent trends suggesting that AD in its pure form may be rarer than originally thought, with autopsy findings suggesting a mixed dementia (AD and vascular disease) in 45% of cases (Alzheimer's Association, 2006) and a Lewy-body variant of AD in 20% of cases (Fields, 1998). Additionally, autopsy findings that 25% of dementias include Lewy bodies (McKeith et al., 1996) suggest the need for future advances in detecting multiple brain pathologies.

Initial symptoms of AD often relate to atrophy in the medial temporal lobe (specifically the hippocampus, amygdala, and entorhinal cortex), and include impairment in episodic memory and learning that impacts daily functioning. However, as reviewed in a recent meta-analysis of 47 studies of preclinical AD (Backman, Jones, Berger, Laukka, & Small, 2005), neuropsychological deficits were present across multiple cognitive domains in addition to memory (e.g., global cognitive functioning, executive functioning, and perceptual speed), in support of the growing hypothesis that preclinical AD is characterized by multiple areas of brain compromise in addition to medial temporal areas. In support of this hypothesis, the authors reviewed multiple research studies and found significant heterogeneity in areas of brain impairment in preclinical AD, including widespread volume reductions (anterior cingulate, temporal sulcus, posterior cingulate, neotemporoparietal regions, and frontal regions), decreased blood flow in posterior cingulate and precuneus, reduced glucose metabolism in temporoparietal regions, deposits of amyloid plaques in temporal and frontal cortices, increased white matter hyperintensities, and reduction in whole-brain glucose metabolism (see Backman et al., 2005, for a review). Other research has analyzed typical patterns of neuropsychological performance in data collected over the first 10 years of the Consortium to Establish a Registry for Alzheimer's Disease (CERAD) and identified three subgroups of neuropsychological dysfunction in patients with AD: group one exhibited severe naming impairment yet borderline normal figure copy; group two exhibited average naming ability but moderately impaired figure copy; and group three exhibited profound anomia and constructional dyspraxia (Fisher, Rourke, & Bieliasukas, 1999). The course of disease progression worsens continually over time, and the average patient usually lives from 8 to 10 years after symptom onset. Because AD cannot be confirmatively diagnosed until autopsy, the diagnosis is usually clinical. The most reliable signs are usually cognitive and behavioral manifestations of the disorders, and overreliance on or overinterpretation of laboratory findings, particularly CT and MRI results, is not recommended (Small et al., 1997). Taken together, autopsy findings of heterogeneity in dementia pathology (i.e., the finding that 45% of autopsy patients with dementia have the telltale plaques and tangles of AD, along with vascular damage), combined with clinical research on vascular contributions to AD, and also the heterogeneity of neuropsychological and physiological findings in both preclinical and established AD, suggest that AD may be more multifaceted and may co-occur with other brain pathology more than originally proposed.

The histological abnormalities of AD may occur with or without other histological and structural abnormalities that contribute to eventual dementia. At a cellular level, AD is characterized by neurofibrillary abnormalities and the presence of beta-amyloid plaques. Neurofibrillary pathology is caused by abnormal functioning of tau protein and manifests as tangles, neurophil threads (neurofibrillary pathology occurring in neuronal processes), and dystrophic neurites (neuritis surrounding plaques). Amyloid pathology generally manifests as two types of plaques—diffuse and neuritic—and is composed of beta-amyloid protein, an amino acid peptide derived from a larger transmembrane precursor protein (amyloid precursor protein, APP). Amyloid pathology may also be deposited in the walls of the cerebral vessels (amyloid angiopathy). Findings have demonstrated that neuro-pathological abnormalities precede clinical impairment. However, it has also been demonstrated that some individuals with beta-amyloid plaques and neurofibrillary tangles (even in significant amounts) do not clinically express Alzheimer's symptomology due to higher levels of resistance to pathology expression (Snowdon, 2003). Current treatment for AD includes acetylcholinesterase-inhibitor medication that increases deficient levels of acetylcholine (one neurotransmitter related to memory consolidation) and provides some level of cognitive improvement in 15–40% of patients. In addition, *N-methyl d-aspartate* (NMDA)-receptor antagonists are often used to treat moderate to severe symptoms of AD on the premise that glutamate-mediated neuro-toxicity is involved in the pathogenesis of AD and that NMDA-receptor antagonists can block that activity, resulting in slower disease progression (Wojciech & Parsons, 2003). Family education and caregiver support are of primary importance. In the case of behavioral problems that may accompany advanced dementia (e.g., wandering, verbal and physical aggression), behavioral therapy is recommended as a first-line treatment, especially given the increase in recent warnings against the off-label use of antipsychotic medication in behavioral management in light of increased mortality rates with this treatment (Schnider et al., 2006).

VASCULAR DEMENTIA

ALTHOUGH ESTIMATES VARY, vascular dementia accounts for approximately 15–25% of all dementias. As previously discussed, neuropsychological symptoms will vary as a function of lesion location and magnitude and extent of recovery. Details on various vascular conditions including MID, Binswanger's disease, lacunar states, and strategic single infarct dementia are reviewed earlier in this chapter under the "Vascular Disorders" section.

LEWY BODY DEMENTIA

A RECENT REVIEW of the prevalence of Lewy body dementia (LBD) identified wide variability in prevalence estimates across seven combined studies, with rates from 0 to 5% in the general population, and from 0 to 30.5% in patients with diagnosed dementia (Zaccai, McCracken, & Brayne, 2005). "Lewy bodies" are abnormal deposits of a protein called alpha-synuclein that forms inside neurons, and they can occur in the brains of patients with LBD, AD, and Parkinson's disease (Alzheimer's Association, 2006). Onset of LBD is often insidious, like AD, but course is relatively more rapid. Neuropsychological deficits often include memory problems, as in AD, but relatively greater deficits in attention, visuospatial and constructional abilities, psycho-motor speed, and verbal fluency (Fields, 1998). Clinical symptoms may include visual hallucinations (sometimes Lilliputian in nature), fluc-tuating mental status and attention level (e.g., a "switch-like" mental status that turns on and off), and daytime drowsiness. Rapid eye move-ment (REM) sleep disorder may also present in 50% of patients and is characterized by the acting out of dreams, sometimes vividly and vio-lently (Alzheimer's Association, 2006).

FRONTOTEMPORAL DEMENTIA

FRONTOTEMPORAL DEMENTIA (FTD) is reportedly underdiagnosed, with prevalence estimates ranging from 6–12% of all dementias (Kertesz, 2006). Onset is usually earlier than AD (50s–60s), course is usually more rapid than in AD, and incidence is generally equal among men and women, with declines after age 62. Damage occurs primarily in either the frontal areas (associated with changes in personality) or anterior temporal areas (associated with language abnormalities). Subtypes include FTD-behavioral or frontal variant/Pick's disease, Primary Progressive Aphasia (PPA)/Non-fluent Progressive Aphasia, FTD-temporal variant/Semantic Dementia (SD)/Fluent Progressive Aphasia, Corticobasal Degeneration/Progressive Supranuclear Palsy (CBD/PSP), Frontotemporal dementia with Motor Neuron Disease (FTD/MND; otherwise known as amyotrophic lateral sclerosis/Lou Gehrig's dis-ease), and Hereditary Frontotemporal Dementia with Parkinsonism-17 (FTDP-17). Abnormalities in tau protein are implicated in most forms of FTD (Kertesz, 2006). For example, Pick's bodies, which are impli-cated in frontal behavioral abnormalities such as hyperorality, impul-sivity, and stereotypied behaviors, appear as ballooned neurons with tau positive neuronal properties. While behavioral problems are the hallmark of Pick's disorder, language and movement abnormalities may or may not be present. When anterior temporal damage is pri-mary, language disorders such as SD and PPA may result. Patients with PPA present with impaired ability to produce speech, but often do not present with personality changes until much later. Patients with SD exhibit impairments in word recognition, but not speech production or personality. In FTD/MND, patients often present with behavioral and language impairments consistent with frontal-temporal pathology, but also exhibit motoric weakness and sometimes myoclonus (muscle jerks). Genetic abnormalities have been identified only in FTDP-17, a heterogenous dementia that presents with various symptoms includ-ing behavioral changes, language abnormalities, and motor impair-ment and is accompanied by genetic tests showing a mutation on chromosome 17. One study examining distinguishing neuropsychiatric features between AD and FTD showed that only altered eating behavior (e.g., hyperorality and sterotypied eating) and loss of social awareness reliably differentiated between these conditions (with FTD patients displaying more deficits). Deficits in executive functioning, poor self care, and restlessness were indistinguishable in advanced phases of both disease states (Bozeat, Gregory, Lambon, & Hodges, 2000).

PSEUDODEMENTIA

PSEUDODEMENTIA REFERS TO any condition that appears to present as a dementia but has an underlying cause that is not related to permanent brain compromise. In practice, the term *pseudodementia* is often used to refer to cognitive deficits due to depression, and neuropsychologists are commonly asked to differentiate cognitive deficits due to depression versus primary dementia. As discussed in Fields (1998), approximately 20% of older adults with depression may exhibit neuropsychological abnormalities (usually deficits in attention and short-term recall and better recognition than recall memory). Performance in domains of language, perception, and visuospatial processing may be inconsistently impaired. Behavioral features of neuropsychological compromise due to depression are also discussed, including complaints of memory problems, more "I don't know" answers, lower effort, and mood disturbance. Patients with primary depression may also have more extensive psychiatric histories than patients with primary dementia. It is noted, however, that brain compromise (e.g., lesions and organic diseases) may initially present as depression and may explain findings that patients with a diagnosis of pseudodementia due to depression are more likely to eventually convert to dementia (Gallassi, Morreale, & Pagni, 2001). It is also noted that cognitive deficits due to depression may be comorbid with cognitive deficits due to primary dementia, either as a psychological response to the dementia or a psychiatric feature of the dementia itself. There is also controversy about whether depression within pseudodementia is actually treatable.

OTHER DEMENTIAS

IN ADDITION TO the aforementioned pathologies that contribute to a majority of dementias, there are multiple less common causes of dementia, including (a) dementia due to Parkinson's disease (please see the "Movement Disorders" section for more information); (b) dementia due to Wernicke-Korsakoff syndrome, in which a thiamine deficiency (usually caused by alcoholism) can lead to significant anterograde amnesia and thus confabulation; (c) dementia due to Creutzfeldt-Jakob disease (CJD; when a prion protein that normally occurs in the brain begins to fold into a three-dimensional shape, causing a rapidly fatal disorder in one in one million people worldwide, usually over age 60); (d) dementia due to variant CJD (the human variant of "mad cow disease" that move often occurs in young adults); (e) dementia due to Huntington's disease (an inherited disorder characterized by choreic movements, emotional changes, and difficulty with memory and concentration); and (f) dementia due to multiple sclerosis (an inflammatory demyelination that can present with subcortical deficits including impaired information processing, greater difficulty with memory recall versus recognition, and impaired visuospatial and problem-solving abilities).

MILD COGNITIVE IMPAIRMENT

A S D I S C U S S E D I N Jicha and Petersen's chapter on mild cognitive impairment (MCI; in press), the concept of MCI has its roots in the nineteenth-century realization that there may be a prodromal phase to the development of dementia. They report that in 1999, Petersen and colleagues published the first study defining MCI (Petersen et al., 1999). They further note that since that time, the definition of MCI has evolved from a focus on only memory impairment (as a possible stage in eventual AD) to a focus on impairment in multiple cognitive domains with or without amnesia. Based on a 2003 International Working Group on MCI, a broader operationalization of MCI was offered as follows: (1) not normal, not demented (does not meet *DSM–IV or International Classification of Diseases-Ninth Edition* [ICD-10] criteria for dementia); (2) cognitive decline defined as self or informant report and objective impairment on cognitive tasks, or evidence of decline over time on objective cognitive tasks; and (3) preserved basic activities of daily living/minimal impairment in complex instrumental functions. It is also reported that this symposium outlined four major categories of MCI, including (1) amnestic single-domain, (2) amnestic multiple domain, (3) nonamnestic single domain, and (4) nonamnestic multiple domain. Thus, it has been proposed that MCI can be conceptualized as a transitional state to AD as well as other degenerative disease states including LBD, vascular cognitive impairment, and frontotemporal dementia. They note that there is great variability in rates of MCI conversion to dementia across studies (3–36% per year, which likely relates to the varied diagnostic criteria utilized), and that longitudinal studies show that although most cases progress to dementia over time, some cases are stable and some revert to normal functioning.

Jicha and Petersen also report that the popularized 1.5 standard deviation (SD) cutoff below the mean as an indicator of MCI has been problematic because it naturally includes the lowest 7% of the population and excludes the top 93% without necessarily factoring in individual decline. They point out that this issue may be most problematic in premorbidly high functioning individuals with cognitive reserve that have experienced relative decline but are not scoring within the 1.5 SD cutoff. Although age- and education-adjusted normative values are recommended, clinical judgment is primary in determining individual decline. It is also important to track neuropsychological functioning over time to determine intraindividual decline. They further note that common screening tests such as the Mini-Mental Status Examination (MMSE) are not sensitive to MCI, whereas the Short Test of Mental Status, which places more emphasis on learning and memory, may be more sensitive (Tang-Wai et al., 2003). They emphasize that neuropsychiatric symptoms such as apathy and aggression, but not depression, appear to influence the likelihood of progression to dementia from MCI. They further suggest that functional impairment occurs on a continuum, and that a mild degree of functional impairment is not inconsistent with, but rather may be supportive of, a diagnosis of MCI.

Recent research on conversion rates from various MCI subtypes to dementia has produced interesting results. In one study, it was found that patients with MCI amnestic multiple domain subtype were at higher risk for conversion to dementia than the MCI amnestic single domain subtype (50% versus 10% conversion; Tabert et al., 2006). It was also demonstrated that the combined predictive accuracy for two neuropsychological indices—total immediate recall on the Buschke Selective Reminding Test and the Digit Symbol Test coding—was 86% for conversion over 3 years. Another recent study identified neuropsychological indices that correctly classified 85.7% of the sample as either AD converters or MCI nonconverters, with 76.9% sensitivity and 88.9% specificity using a stepwise discriminant function analysis with Dementia Rating Scale (DRS) Initiation/Perseveration and Wechsler Memory Scale, third edition (WMS-III) Visual Reproduction Percent Retention scores (Griffithy et al., 2006). They further found that factoring in race, the presence of vascular risk factors, or cholinesterase inhibitor use to the analysis did not greatly change the classification rates obtained with neuropsychological test data.

Per Jicha and Petersen (in press), information on the pathophysiology of MCI has produced several findings. First, in regard to genetic issues, they note that although the ApoE E4 status is a strong predictor from MCI to AD, the presence or absence of an E4 allele itself lacks both the sensitivity and specificity for AD or MCI, and that the American Academy of Neurology does not recommend routine screening for ApoE status in the diagnosis of AD. Several studies are currently examining several possible MCI biomarkers and biochemical brain changes. They further note that extant studies suggest MCI amnestic subtype is accompanied by pathologic changes in the ventromedial temporal lobes and hippocampi. Jicha and Petersen provide detailed information about extant studies on MCI treatment. In summary, they note mixed evidence for treatment with cholinesterase inhibitors and report ongoing investigations into the use of nootropic agents, ampakines, anti-inflammatory agents, and subtype-specific strategies such as anti-amyloid or tau-based interventions. It is also noted that there has been promising work in the development of cognitive training, but that randomly controlled studies are needed to fully evaluate the benefit of these techniques.

MOVEMENT DISORDERS

MANY NEUROLOGICAL DISORDERS involve either hyperkinetic, involuntary movement (e.g., tremors, tics, dystonias, myoclonus), or hypokinetic movement (bradykinesia, hypokinesia). Most commonly, movement disorders involve Parkinsonian symptoms including resting tremor, bradykinesia, rigidity, and postural instability. Relatively more rare movement disorders include Huntington's disease (affecting 5 to 10 per 100,000 people), Wilson's disease, tic disorders, dystonia, myoclonus, medication-induced movement disorder, and psychogenic movement disorder (incidentally, it is noted that psychogenic movement disorders must be cautiously diagnosed given that up to 30% of such individuals are found to have a neurologic illness; Apetauerova, 2005).

PARKINSONISM AND PARKINSON'S DISEASE

FIRST DEFINED BY James Parkinson in 1817 as "the shaking palsy" (Parkinson, 1817), Parkinson's disease (PD) is the most common movement disorder, accounting for about 75% of extrapyramidal movement disorders (Troster, 1998), and is one of the most common neurological disorders overall (affecting about 98–175 per 100,000 people in the United States; Apetauerova, 2005). Parkinson's disease often initially presents with some but not all of four core Parkinsonian symptoms (resting tremor, bradykinesia, rigidity, and postural instability). Although there is no definitive test and neuroimaging results are often normal, PD—a diagnosis based mainly on clinical signs—is the most common etiological explanation for Parkinsonian symptoms (Bhat & Weiner, 2005). However, diagnosis is also incorrect 20–25% of the time (Hobson, 2003) due to complexities in ruling out both secondary causes for Parkinsonian symptoms (e.g., drugs, toxins, dementia, infections, or trauma), and degenerative causes (e.g., Huntington's disease, Wilson's disease). Furthermore, it is vital to differentiate PD from atypical Parkinsonian syndromes, or "Parkinson's plus syndromes." Atypical Parkinsonian syndromes encompass about 10% of all Parkinsonian referrals and include CBD, PSP, and multiple system atrophy (MSA). Some research has suggested that neuropsychological evaluation may help to differentiate PD from Parkinson's plus syndromes early in the diagnostic process (Soliveri et al., 2000). Parkinson's disease itself may have various underlying causes, though the idiopathic variety is most common, affecting 75% of individuals diagnosed with primary Parkinsonism. Diagnostic accuracy might be improved with the use of clinical diagnostic criteria based on autopsy studies (Gibb & Lees, 1988) or with the use of olfactory tests, given that olfactory dysfunction occurs in PD and LBD, but not PSP or CBD (Katzenschlager & Lees, 2004).

In PD, symptom onset is often mild and gradual and may begin on one side of the body (and remain stronger on that side of the body even after it generalizes to both sides). In addition to the four core Parkinsonian symptoms mentioned in the previous paragraph, "festinating gait" (walking with small, fast steps while leaning forward) may be present. Other early symptoms might include difficulty ambulating, standing, initiating movement, writing, and forming facial expressions as well as speaking loudly and mild tremor. Although the course is progressive, there are usually different rates of progression, and life expectancy is usually average. Progress in treatment and staging of the disease is often a combination of clinical judgment and response to medication, though rating scales can also be helpful. The most commonly used scale—the Unified Parkinson's Disease Rating Scale (UPDRS; Fahn & Elton, 1987)—measures multiple domains including cognitive functioning, behavior, mood, activities of daily living, and motor function. The Hoehn and Yahr scale (1967) is another commonly utilized scale.

Parkinson's disease strikes about 50% more men than women, though reasons for this discrepancy are unknown. The average age of onset is 60 years, and the incidence rises significantly with increasing age: epidemiological studies show that 1 in 100 people over the age of 65 and 1 in 10 over the age of 80 get the disease, though there are clear cross-cultural differences in prevalence (Weintraub, 2006). However, about 5–10% of people with PD have "early-onset" disease that begins before the age of 50. Early-onset forms of the disease are often inherited, and some have been linked to specific gene mutations. People with one or more close relatives who have PD have an increased risk of developing the disease themselves, but the total risk is still just 2–5% unless the family has a known gene mutation for the disease.

Parkinson's disease primarily involves the loss of dopaminergic neurons responsible for smooth, purposeful movement in a part of the brain called the nigrostriatal pathway. This pathway extends from an area of the midbrain called the *substantia nigra* to portions of the basal ganglia known as the striatum (caudate and putamen). By the time symptoms appear, Parkinson's patients have lost 60 to 80% or more of the dopamine-producing neurons in this pathway. Recent findings suggest that toxic substances released by glial cells could be involved in dopaminergic neuronal degeneration in the substantia nigra (Hirsch, Hunot, & Hartmann, 2005). Some studies have also shown that low norepinephrine/noradrenalin, a core messenger of the sympathetic nervous system, might explain several of the nonmotor features seen in PD, including fatigue and abnormalities in blood pressure regulation.

In addition to destruction of dopaminergic and noradrenergic neurons, deposits of the protein alpha-synuclein (Lewy bodies) are often, if not always, present in the brains of individuals with PD (Takahashi & Wakabayashi, 2005). Researchers do not yet know why Lewy bodies form or what role they play in development of the disease. An estimated 15–25% of people with PD have a known relative with the disease. Several studies support the role of genetic factors in early-onset PD, although most cases appear later in life and are not associated with a genetic basis (Weintraub, 2006). Although the importance of genetics in PD is increasingly recognized, most researchers believe environmental exposures increase a person's risk of developing the disease. Even in familial cases, exposure to toxins or other environmental factors may influence when symptoms of the disease appear or how the disease progresses.

At least 60% of patients with PD suffer from at least one psychiatric symptom: depression is most common, with anxiety disorders (especially obsessive-compulsive disorder) and psychotic symptoms (especially visual hallucinations) also prevalent (Weintraub, 2006). Similar to the discussion of psychiatric symptoms in dementia, the directional relationship between psychiatric symptoms and PD is unknown (it is possible that brain dysfunction leads to both, or that psychiatric symptoms are a reaction to PD symptoms). Treatment, including medication and surgery, often targets the nigrostriatal system. Three classes of medications are often used to treat PD: dopamine agonists (which may cause psychotic symptoms), anticholinergic drugs that reduce muscle stiffness, and medications that target nonmotor symptoms (such as antidepressants). When PD becomes treatment-resistant to medication therapy, deep brain stimulation (DBS) may be considered. In this procedure, electrodes are placed either unilaterally or bilaterally in the subthalamic nucleus (the most common site), the thalamus, or the globus pallidus in order to reduce tremor, bradykinesia, and rigidity. Weintraub (2006) noted mixed results about the role of DBS in later cognitive impairment. Surgical treatments include pallidotomy (destruction of the globus pallidus to improve tremor, gait, and bradykinesia) and thalamotomy (destruction of the thalamus to reduce tremor).

A recent literature review suggests that 24 to 31% of PD patients have dementia, and that 3 to 4% of the dementia in the population would be due to Parkinson's dementia disorder (PDD), with estimated prevalence of PDD in the general population aged 65 years and over at 0.2 to 0.5% (Aarsland, Zaccai, & Brayne, 2005). Dementia in PD is often characterized by primary impairment in executive function and attention and secondary memory impairment, and there is preliminary evidence that cholinesterase inhibitors may be an effective treatment for PD dementia (Emre, 2004).

EPILEPSY AND NONEPILEPTIC ATTACK DISORDER

EPILEPSY IS A condition characterized by multiple seizures, or bursts of uncontrolled electrical activity in the brain, and is best considered as a symptom of cerebral insult, rather than a disease entity. Isolated seizures—which may occur in up to 5% of the population (World Health Organization [WHO], 2006)—can have a variety of causes (e.g., syncope, hypoglycemia). When at least two seizures occur in the absence of known causes, epilepsy is often considered as a possible diagnosis (Hauser, Rich, Lee, Annegers, & Anderson, 1998).

Epilepsy is one of the most common neurological disorders, affecting about 0.5% of the population in developed countries (50 per 100,000 people) and approximately 1% of the population in developing countries (100 per 100,000 people; WHO, 2006). Epilepsy occurs across all cultures and age groups, though prevalence in men is slightly higher than in women, worldwide (e.g., in Iceland, where whole population data are available, prevalence is 53 per 100,000 for females and 57 per 100,000 for males; McManus, 2002). Contrary to previous findings that most cases of epilepsy were diagnosed within the first two decades of life, recent findings suggest that the risk is highest in adults over age 65 (McManus, 2002), and that epilepsy is the third most frequent neurologic problem in the elderly, after cerebrovascular disorders and dementia (Kramer, 2001). Although the risk of developing epilepsy is also high in the first year of life, it has dropped in this age group over the past three decades in developed countries (Duncan, Sander, Sisodiya, & Walker, 2006) and has been historically low at midlife (McManus, 2002). Epilepsy is associated with an increased risk of mortality due to underlying brain disease and seizures that occur in dangerous places, among other factors. For example, epilepsy-related deaths of young adults in the United Kingdom are three times higher than standard mortality rates (WHO, 2006).

Diagnosis of epilepsy is mostly clinical and based on patient and witness history and neurologic exam (Oster, Gutrecht, & Gross, 2005). Electroencephalographs (EEGs) are frequently used to assess possible seizure activity, given that specific wave abnormalities are highly associated with seizures (e.g., focal or generalized spikes and spike-and-wave discharges). Neuroimaging is often helpful in determining whether seizures are secondary to structural brain disease. Seizures may originate in any part of the brain, cortically or subcortically, and are classified according to where they arise in the brain (WHO, 2006). The most widely used classification system, the International Classification of Epileptic Seizures (ICES) is presented in Table 2.3. However, it is important to note that there is promising preliminary data on two other seizure classification systems compared to the ICES (Baykan et al., 2005). It is possible that improved classification of seizures may enhance our understanding of etiology (given that nearly two-thirds of causes are unknown; McManus, 2002) and treatment (given that 30% or more of patients receiving medication may have poorly controlled seizures).

Although epidemiological research suggests a cause cannot be found for about 62% of cases of epilepsy, factors such as stroke (but not TIAs), head injury (moderate trauma = 3-fold risk; severe trauma = 20-fold risk) and central nervous system infection increase the risk of developing epilepsy by 20-fold, with secondary risk factors including Alzheimer's disease (6- to 10-fold increased risk), progressive neurological disease, brain tumor, depression (6-fold risk), hypertension, migraine (4-fold risk), alcohol use (more than three drinks/day), attention-deficit disorder (3-fold risk), mental retardation (9-fold risk), cerebral palsy (12-fold risk), and mental retardation with cerebral palsy (50-fold risk). However, seizures during infancy are not related to a higher risk of developing epilepsy (McManus, 2002).

Psychiatric disorders occur in approximately 6% of people with epilepsy, though prevalence rises to 10–20% in patients with temporal lobe or treatment refractory epilepsy (Gaitatzis, Trimble, & Sander, 2004). Depression is the most frequent comorbid psychiatric disorder and can occur at about 10 times the rate compared to the general population (Kanner, 2003). Given that people with depression are at 6-fold increased risk for developing epilepsy, a possible bidirectional relationship or common pathogenic mechanisms may exist (Kanner, 2003). Other common comorbid psychiatric conditions include anxiety disorders

TABLE 2.3   The International Classification of Epileptic Seizures (ICES)

I. Partial (focal, local) seizures

    A. Simple partial seizures (no loss of consciousness)

        1. With motor signs

            a. focal motor without march

            b. focal motor with march (Jacksonian)

            c. versive

            d. postural

            e. phonatory (vocalization or arrest of speech)

        2. With somatosensory or special-sensory symptoms (simple hallucinations, e.g., tingling, light flashes, buzzing)

            a. somatosensory

            b. visual

            c. auditory

            d. olfactory

            e. gustatory

        3. With autonomic symptoms or signs (including epigastric sensation, pallor, sweating, flushing, piloerection, and pupillary dilatation)

        4. With psychic symptoms (disturbance of higher cerebral function). These symptoms rarely occur without impairment of consciousness and are much more commonly experienced as complex partial seizures.

            a. dysphasic

            b. dysmnesic (e.g., déjà vu)

            c. cognitive (e.g., dreamy states, distortions of time sense)

            d. affective (e.g., fear, anger)

            e. illusions (e.g., macropsia)

            f. structured hallucinations (e.g., music, scenes)

    B. Complex partial seizures

        1. With impairment of consciousness at onset

            a. with impairment of consciousness only

            b. with automatisms

         2. Simple partial onset followed by impairment of consciousness

            a. with simple partial features (A.1.-A.4.) followed by impaired consciousness

            b. with automatisms

    C. Partial seizures evolving to generalized tonic-clonic convulsions (GTC)

        1. Simple partial seizures (A) evolving to generalized seizures

        2. Complex partial seizures (B) evolving to generalized seizures

        3. Simple partial seizures evolving to complex partial seizures evolving to generalized seizures

II. Generalized seizures (convulsive or nonconvulsive)

    A. Absence seizures

        1. Absence (petit mal)

            a. impairment of consciousness only

            b. with mild clonic components

            c. with atonic components

            d. with tonic components

            e. with automatisms

(Continued)

TABLE 2.3   The International Classification of Epileptic Seizures (ICES)
(Continued)

      f. with autonomic components (b through f may be
         used alone or incombination)
   2. Atypical absence

B. Myoclonic seizures, myoclonic jerks (simple or multiple)
C. Clonic seizures
D. Tonic seizures
E. Tonic-clonic seizures
F. Atonic seizures (astatic)
Combinations of the above may occur (e.g., B and F, B and D)

III. Unclassified epileptic seizures (because of inadequate data)

Source: Adapted from Commission on Classification and Terminology of the International League Against Epilepsy (1981).

(in 10–25% of the epilepsy population), psychoses (2–7%), and personality disorders (1–2%; Gaitatzis et al., 2004).

While EEGs often assist in localization, reported sequential onset of behavioral manifestation of seizure activity is also important in localization, given that EEGs may not always detect abnormal wave activity (though they are more likely to do so when the patient is asleep). Forty to sixty percent of patients with epilepsy have simple-partial or complex-partial seizures of temporal lobe origin and suffer from related cognitive, emotional, personality, and behavioral alterations (Synder, 1998). Currently, genes have been detected for generalized but not partial seizures (McManus, 2002).

A 2005 survey of leading epileptologists provided the following expert opinion regarding treatment: in initial monotherapy for idiopathic generalized seizures (tonic-clonic, absence, and myoclonic), valproate was the treatment of choice. For tonic-clonic seizure, lamotrigine and topiramate were also identified as usually appropriate for initial monotherapy. For simple partial seizures and secondarily generalized tonic-clonic seizures, carbamazepine and oxcarbazepine were treatments of choice, with lamotrigine and levetiracetam usually appropriate. For complex partial seizures, carbamazepine, lamotrigine, and oxcarbazepine were treatments of choice, while levetiracetam was also usually appropriate (Martin, Bortz & Snyder, 2006). According to data obtained by WHO, after 2–5 years of successful treatment, drugs can be withdrawn in about 70% of children and 60% of adults without relapses, though some sources note that patients with chronic epilepsy may require ongoing drug treatment (Oster et al., 2005). Thirty percent or more of people with epilepsy may not have well-controlled symptoms with medication. In some cases of treatment refractor epilepsy, surgical treatment may be indicated, with the best results occurring for patients with temporal lobectomy, or with lesion resection for patients with complex partial seizures and underlying unilateral mesial temporal sclerosis (Oster et al., 2005). Sometimes neuropsychologists are called upon to assist with Wada testing in order to determine the dominant language hemisphere for patients with complex partial seizures and no obvious underlying pathology. Neuropsychological testing and psychiatric evaluations may also be helpful in such cases. Small cortical resections and palliative surgeries such as callostomy and vagal nerve stimulation may also be useful (Oster et al., 2005).

Comprehensive reviews of the neuropsychology of epilepsy are helpful in providing an overview of pertinent tests and interview questions (Lee, 2004; Rankin, Adams, & Jones, 1996; Trimble, Ring, & Schmitz, 2000), but go beyond the scope of this chapter. In brief, given the heterogeneity of epilepsy in regard to its onset and seizure localization, there does not appear to be a common neuropsychological profile associated with the disorder (Lee, 2004), though mental slowness and memory problems are not uncommon. Specific clinical interview questions are vital to thorough assessment of epilepsy (Rankin et al., 1996) and can provide information about specific tests that may be added to existing batteries, including an existing neuropsychology assessment epilepsy battery (Dodrill, 1978). Neuropsychology may have a role not only in the characterization and tracking of cognitive functioning and recommendations of compensatory strategies, but in the ability to improve classification systems by using cognitive profiles to speculate about mechanisms underlying pathology (Hommet, Sauerwein, De Toffol, & Lassonde, 2006).

Nonepileptic attack disorders (NEADs; sometimes known as "pseudoseizures") encompass behavior or reported behavior that resembles a seizure but does not present with the typical clinical or EEG characteristics. The presence of NEADs may be suspected by an abnormal clinical presentation, the presence of psychiatric factors that appear to mediate reported seizure activity, or lack of EEG evidence of seizure activity. Neuropsychologists may be consulted to assess connections between reported seizure phenomenon and psychological factors and can also help in assessing clinical differences between NEADs and epilepsy (see Rankin et al., 1996, and Lesser, 1996, for a list of differential clinical features). For example, among many other differentiating characteristics, gradual seizure onset is common in NEADs, but not in epilepsy, and movements described as quivering, flailing, or thrashing are more common to NEADs than to epilepsy (Lesser, 1996). It is important to note that an absolute diagnosis of NEADs cannot be made with clinical approaches alone, given the lack of fixed rules in making a differential diagnosis and given that a person may have epilepsy and a NEAD (Rankin et al., 1996). In addition, given the high occurrence of psychological disorders in epilepsy, as previously discussed, it can be difficult to tease apart psychological comorbidity from psychological factors that may be related to NEADs. In determining the presence of NEADs, it is often helpful to combine clinical evidence with data from simultaneous video-EEG monitoring.

TRAUMATIC BRAIN INJURY AND POSTCONCUSSIVE SYNDROME

WHEREAS STROKES AND dementia are frequently seen in neuropsychological practice with older adults, traumatic brain injury (TBI) is a frequent referral issue for young adults. Motor vehicle accidents are responsible for half of all TBIs in people under age 75, falls are responsible for the majority of TBIs in people over age 75, half of all TBIs involve alcohol use, and males are twice as likely as females to sustain a TBI (Lucas & Addeo, 2006). Every year, of the approximately 1.4 million people who experience a TBI, about 1 million are treated in hospital emergency rooms, and approximately 50,000 people die from the injury (Lucas & Addeo, 2006). Traumatic brain injuries are divided into two categories: closed head injuries and open/penetrating head injuries. Closed head injuries (CHIs) comprise the majority of TBIs, with neuropathological changes following from the physics of the injury (Lucas & Addeo, 2006). Lucas and Addeo (2006) note that in a CHI, the skull makes contact with a relatively immovable surface at a high rate of speed. Because the forces of velocity and rotation are then imparted to the brain, the brain often strikes the interior of the skull (*coup* is the point on the brain where it impacts the skull, and *contrecoup* is damage to the brain opposite the point of impact). In addition to focal contusions resulting from coup and contrecoup lesions, the strain of the brain's movement within the skull may also lead to diffuse axonal injury and hypoxia. Secondary complications can include seizures, hydrocephalus, and leaks of cerebrospinal fluid (if the skull has been fractured). Damage to blood vessels can lead to strokes or hematomas (epidural, subdural, or intercranial bleeding into or around the brain).

Head injuries can be further classified as mild, moderate, or severe based on duration of loss of consciousness, duration of posttraumatic amnesia, and Glasgow Coma Scale ratings. The majority of TBIs consist of mild CHIs such as concussions. Although concussions have historically been described by a brief loss of consciousness following a head injury, they have now become defined as any minor head injury, with or without loss of consciousness (Lucas & Addeo, 2006). In addition to impairment directly related to the site of injury, postconcussive syndrome (PCS) has been reported in approximately 40% of patients, with common symptoms including headache, dizziness, vertigo, memory and concentration problems, sleeping difficulty, restlessness, irritability, apathy, depression, and anxiety (Lucas & Addeo, 2006). A recent review of diagnostic criteria for PCS suggested further refinement of diagnostic criteria, given that the prevalence of PCS was higher using ICD-10 (64%) than *DSM–IV* criteria (11%; Boake et al., 2005).

Whether PCS arises from neuronal damage or from psychological reactions to the injury, or from a combination of both has been debated, with some researchers recommending that PCS symptoms be described as commonly co-occurring symptoms rather than as a syndromal sequela of TBI (Arciniegas, Anderson, Topkoff, & McAllister, 2005). Examination of the role of psychiatric factors in TBI is also important in light of recent findings that depression occurs in over 50% of the TBI population (Moldover, Goldberg, & Prout, 2004). Traumatic brain injury is also seen as a longitudinal risk factor for the later development of arthritis, sleep problems, and anxiety many years post injury (Colantonio, Ratcliff, Chase, & Vernich, 2004). Research on cognitive functioning following TBI has shown that cognitive functioning rapidly recovers during the first few weeks following mild TBI and returns to baseline within 1–3 months. In moderate to severe TBI, cognitive functioning also improves during the first 2 years, but continues to remain markedly impaired (Schretlen & Shapiro, 2003). It has also been shown that severe TBI is a risk factor for the development of AD, particularly in subjects lacking the ApoE 4 allele (Jellinger, 2004).

NEOPLASMS

AT TIMES, THE cognitive and behavioral changes that neuropsychologists are called upon to evaluate may relate to tumors that have grown in or around the brain (neoplasms, or new abnormal growths). More than 40,000 Americans of all ages develop brain tumors each year, though they occur most often in middle-aged and older adults. People in their 60s face the highest risk—each year 1 of every 5,000 people in this age group develops a brain tumor. However, the odds of developing a malignant brain tumor are small (5.8 per 100,000 people). The symptoms of brain tumors are often directly related to the cell type comprising the tumor, the rate of tumor growth, and the size and location of the tumor. Brain tumors may be classified as *benign* (noncancerous, slow growing, and confined to one location) or *malignant* (cancerous, quickly growing, and easily spread) and as *primary* (originating in the brain) or *secondary* (originating outside the brain). They originate from the glia and other supportive cells. Kolb and Wishaw (1996) note three categories of tumor, defined by where they originate: gliomas, meningiomas, and metastatic tumors. They summarize that gliomas include astrocytomas (about 40% of gliomas, and not usually malignant), glioblastomas (about 30% of gliomas, and highly malignant), and medulloblastomas (11% of gliomas, highly malignant, and usually found in the cerebellum of children). These tumors originate in the brain and often do not travel outside of it. Meningiomas grow in the meninges outside the brain, are usually benign, and often exert pressure effects and resultant seizures. Even though they are benign, meningiomas can be harmful in exerting pressure effects on surrounding tissue and because surgery to remove an embedded tumor may damage surrounding tissue (especially near tissue that is vital to functioning). Metastatic brain tumors are formed after tumor cells travel to the brain through blood vessel walls from another part of the body. The original site of the tumor is usually the lungs or breast, but may also be in the kidneys, immune cells, prostate, or skin.

Neuropsychological deficits may relate to deficits in the cognitive domain where the tumor is directly located (e.g., occipital tumors may relate to vision changes), or to cognitive and behavioral domains that are impacted by pressure effects due to the tumor. When increased intracranial pressure or blockage of cerebral spinal fluid occurs secondary to a brain tumor, symptoms can include headaches (in more than half of all individuals with brain tumors), seizures (sometimes a warning sign of a brain tumor if seizure onset is in adulthood), nausea, and vision problems including blurred or double vision or partial vision loss (secondary to increased intracranial pressure that decreases blood flow to the eye and swells the optic nerve). Treatment often involves tumor removal and radiation primarily, with chemotherapy sometimes indicated.

A NOTE ABOUT PSYCHIATRIC DISORDERS

OVER THE PAST decade, advances in neuroimaging and psychiatric treatment and research have led to an understanding that virtually all psychiatric symptoms have a neurophysiological basis. Furthermore, as discussed in previous sections, many patients with neurological disorders such as epilepsy, traumatic brain injury, and dementia often present with psychiatric symptoms. As with the possible bidirectional relationship between epilepsy and depression (Kanner, 2003), psychiatric symptoms and specific neurological disorders may have common neural substrates or act as risk factors for one another, or psychiatric symptoms may arise from neurological damage, depending on localization. Familiarity with the neuropsychology of emotion and the physiology of various affective and behavioral disorders is often crucial to examining the interplay of psychiatric and neurological factors and developing appropriate recommendations about treating psychiatric symptoms in the context of a neurological disorder. Although it is beyond the scope of this chapter to discuss specific features of various psychiatric disorders, there exists a wealth of data on the interplay between the physiology and clinical manifestations of psychiatric disorders including schizophrenia, major depressive disorder, bipolar disorder, panic disorder, obsessive-compulsive disorder, and other clinical disorders including drug addiction and eating disorders (Nixon, 1996; Weintraub, 2006).

CONCLUSIONS

FAMILIARITY WITH NEUROLOGICAL disorders is crucial to the practice of neuropsychology and has contributed to several advances in diagnosis and patient management. By virtue of its integrative focus on behavioral, statistical, and neurological data, neuropsychology provides a valuable lens through which to understand pathology and normal functioning. This chapter's broad focus on neurological disorders is best conceptualized as a starting point for additional inquiry into any given topic area. When possible, meta-analytic and review studies were incorporated to outline global findings. Recent developments were also highlighted, including (a) evidence on the pathophysiological and clinical heterogeneity of dementia (particularly AD), including the increasingly prominent role of vascular factors in AD, which could lead to a widespread emphasis on the importance of managing vascular risk factors over the lifespan; (b) the construct of MCI and its role in the possible prediction of eventual dementia; (c) the importance of honing diagnosis, prevention, and treatment for our rapidly growing aging population; (d) understanding the multidirectional relationship between neurological and comorbid psychiatric disorders; (e) increasing our understanding of how neuropsychological profiles differ as a function of underlying neurological and psychiatric disorders; and (f) the new construct of *vascular cognitive impairment*. As the raw numbers of neuropsychologists increase across the nation, the potential to continue advancing our understanding of diagnosis, management, and etiology of neurological disorders is at one of its highest points in history.

REFERENCES

Aarsland, D., Zaccai, J., & Brayne, C. (2005). A systematic review of prevalence studies of dementia in Parkinson's disease. *Movement Disorders, 20,* 1255–1263.

Alagiakrishnan K., McCracken P., & Feldman, H. (2006). Treating vascular risk factors and maintaining vascular health: Is this the way towards successful cognitive ageing and preventing cognitive decline? *Postgraduate Medical Journal, 82,* 101–105.

Alzheimer's Association. (2006). Fact Sheets: Alzheimer's disease and other dementias; Growth of Alzheimer's disease through 2025; African Americans and Alzheimer's disease: The silent epidemic; Mild cognitive impairment; Early onset dementia: A national challenge, a future crisis. Retrieved August 2, 2006, from http://www.alz.org

American Heart Association. (2006). Electronic references. Retrieved August 15, 2006, from http://www.strokecenter.org/pat/stats.htm

American Psychiatric Association. (1994). *Diagnostic and statistical manual of mental disorders* (4th ed.). Washington, DC: Author.

Apetauerova, D. (2005). Psychogenic movement disorders. In H. Royden Jones (Ed.), *Netter's neurology* (pp. 472–474). Teterboro, NJ: Icon Learning Systems.

Arciniegas, D. B., Anderson, C. A., Topkoff, J., & McAllister, T. W. (2005). Mild traumatic brain injury: A neuropsychiatric approach to diagnosis, evaluation, and treatment. *Neuropsychiatric Disease and Treatment, 1,* 311–327.

Backman, L., Jones, S., Berger, A., Laukka, E. J., & Small, B. J. (2005). Cognitive impairment in preclinical Alzheimer's disease: A meta-analysis. *Neuropsychology, 19,* 520–531.

Baykan, B., Ertas, N. K., Ertas, M., Aktekin, B., Saygi, S., Aysen G., et al. (2005). Comparison of classification of seizures: A preliminary study with 28 participants and 48 seizures. *Epilepsy & Behavior, 6,* 607–612.

Berg, R., Franzen, M., & Wedding, D. (1987). *Screening for brain impairment: A manual for mental health practice.* New York: Springer Publishing Co.

Bhat, V., & Weiner, W. J. (2005). Parkinson's disease: Diagnosis and the initiation of therapy. *Minerva Medica, 96,* 145–154.

Biessels, G. J., & Kappelle, L. J. (2005). Increased risk of Alzheimer's disease in Type II diabetes: Insulin resistance of the brain or insulin-induced amyloid pathology? *Biochemical Society Transactions, 33,* 1041–1044.

Boake, C., McCauley, S. R., Levin, H. S., Pedroza, C., Contant, C. F., Song, J. X., et al. (2005). Diagnostic criteria for postconcussional syndrome after mild to moderate traumatic brain injury. *Journal of Neuropsychiatry & Clinical Neurosciences, 17,* 350–356.

Borjesson-Hanson, A., Edin, E., Gislason, T., & Skoog, I. (2004). The prevalence of dementia in 95 year olds. *Neurology, 63,* 2436–2438.

Bozeat, S., Gregory, C. A., Lambon, M. A., & Hodges, J. R. (2000). Which neuropsychiatric and behavioural features distinguish frontal and temporal variants of frontotemporal dementia from Alzheimer's disease? *Journal of Neurology and Neurosurgical Psychiatry, 69,* 178–186.

Budson, A. E., & Price, B. H. (2005). Memory dysfunction. *New England Journal of Medicine, 352,* 692–699.

Clarfield, A. M. (2003). The decreasing prevalence of reversible dementias: An updated meta-analysis. *Archives of Internal Medicine, 163,* 2219–2229.

Colantonio, A., Ratcliff, G., Chase, S., & Vernich, L. (2004). Aging with traumatic brain injury: Long-term health conditions. *International Journal of Rehabilitation Research, 27,* 209–214.

Commission on Classification and Terminology of the International League Against Epilepsy. (1981). Proposal for revised clinical and electroencephalographic classification of epileptic seizures. *Epilepsia, 22,* 493–495.

Cummings, J., Benson, F., & LoVerma, S. (1980). Reversible dementia: Illustrative cases, definition and review. *Journal of the American Medical Association, 243,* 2434–2439.

Dodrill, C. B. (1978). A neuropsychological battery for epilepsy. *Epilepsia, 19,* 611–623.

Duncan, J. S., Sander, J. W., Sisodiya, S. M., & Walker, M. C. (2006). Adult epilepsy. *The Lancet, 367,* 1087–1100.

Emre, M. (2004). Dementia in Parkinson's disease: Cause and treatment. *Current Opinion in Neurology, 17,* 399–404.

Fahn, S., & Elton, R. L. (1987). Unified Parkinson's disease rating scale. In S. Fahn, C. D. Marsden, D. B. Calne, & A. Lieberman (Eds.), *Recent developments in Parkinson's disease* (pp. 153–163). Florham Park, NJ: Macmillan Health Care Information.

Ferro, J. M. (2001). Hyperacute cognitive stroke syndromes. *Journal of Neurology, 248,* 841–849.

Fields, R. B. (1998). The dementias. In P. J. Snyder and P. D. Nussbaum (Eds.), *Clinical neuropsychology: A pocket handbook for assessment* (pp. 207–214). Washington, DC: American Psychological Association.

Fisher, N. J., Rourke, B. P., & Bieliasukas, L. A. (1999). Neuropsychological subgroups of patients with Alzheimer's disease: An examination of the first 10 years of CERAD data. *Journal of Clinical and Experimental Neuropsychology, 21,* 488–518.

Folstein, M. F., Folstein, S. E., & McHugh, P. R. (1975). Mini-mental state. *Journal of Psychiatric Research, 12,* 189–198.

Gaitatzis, A., Trimble, M. R., & Sander, J. W. (2004). The psychiatric comorbidity of epilepsy. *Acta Neurologica Scandinavia, 110,* 207–220.

Gallassi, R., Morreale, A., & Pagni, P. (2001). The relationship between depression and cognition. *Archives of Gerontology and Geriatrics* (Suppl. 7), 163–171.

Gibb, W. R., & Lees, A. J. (1988). The relevance of Lewy body to the pathogenesis of idiopathic Parkinson's disease. *Journal of Neurology, Neurosurgery, and Psychiatry, 51,* 745–752.

Griffithy, H. R., Netson, K. L., Harrell, L. E., Zamrini, E. Y., Brockington, J. C., & Marson, D. C. (2006). Amnestic mild cognitive impairment: Diagnostic outcomes and clinical prediction over a two-year time period. *Journal of the International Neuropsychological Society, 12,* 166–175.

Hachinski, V., Iadecola, C., Petersen, R. C., Breteler, M. M., Nyenhuis, D. L., et al. (2006). National Institute of Neurological Disorders and Stroke-Canadian Stroke Network vascular cognitive impairment harmonization standards. *Stroke, 37,* 2220–2241.

Hachinski, V. C., Iliff, L. D., Zilhka, E., DuBoulay, G. H., McAllister, V. L., Marshall, J., et al. (1975). Cerebral blood flow in dementia. *Archives of Neurology, 32,* 632–637.

Hauser, W. A., Rich, S. S., Lee, J. R., Annegers, J. F., & Anderson, V. E. (1998). Risk of recurrent seizures after two unprovoked seizures. *New England Journal of Medicine, 338,* 429–434.

Hebert, L. E., Scherr, P. A., Bienias, J. L., Bennett, D. A., & Evans, D. A. (2004a). Alzheimer disease in the U.S. population: Prevalence estimates using the 2000 census. *Archives of Neurology, 60,* 1119–1122.

Hebert, L. E., Scherr, P. A., Bienias, J. L., Bennett, D. A., & Evans, D. A. (2004b). State-specific projections through 2025 of Alzheimer disease prevalence. *Neurology, 62,* 1645.

Hirsch, E. C., Hunot, S., & Hartmann, A. (2005). Neuroinflammatory process in Parkinson's disease. *Parkinsonism and Related Disorders, 11,* S9–S15.

Hobson, D. E. (2003). Clinical manifestations of Parkinson's disease and parkinsonism. *Canadian Journal of Neurological Sciences, 30,* S2–S9.

Hoehn, M. H., & Yahr, M. D. (1967). Parkinsonism. Onset, progression and mortality. *Neurology, 17,* 427–442.

Hommet, C., Sauerwein, H. C., De Toffol, B., & Lassonde, M. (2006). Idiopathic epileptic syndromes and cognition. *Neuroscience and Behavioral Reviews, 30,* 85–96.

Jellinger, K. A. (2004). Traumatic brain injury as a risk factor for Alzheimer's disease. *Journal of Neurology, Neurosurgery and Psychiatry, 75,* 511–512.

Jenike, M. A. (1988). Depression and other psychiatric disorders. In M. S. Albert and M. Moss (Eds.), *Geriatric neuropsychology* (p. 127). New York: Guilford Press.

Jicha, G. A., & Petersen, R. C. (in press). Mild cognitive impairment. In J. H. Growdon & M. Rossor (Eds.), *The dementias.* New York: Butterworth-Heinemann.

Kanner, A. M. (2003). Depression in epilepsy: Prevalence, clinical semiology, pathogenic mechanisms, and treatment. *Biological Psychiatry, 54,* 388–398.

Katzenschlager, R., & Lees, A. J. (2004). Olfaction and Parkinson's syndromes: Its role in differential diagnosis. *Current Opinion in Neurology, 17,* 417–423.

Kertesz, A. (2006). Progress in clinical neurosciences: Frontotemporal dementia-Pick's disease. *Canadian Journal of Neurological Sciences, 33,* 141–148.

Kolb, B., & Wishaw, I. Q. (1996). *Fundamentals of human neuropsychology* (4th ed). New York: W. H. Freeman and Company.

Kramer, G. (2001). Epilepsy in the elderly: Some clinical and pharmacotherapeutic aspects. *Epilepsia, 42,* 55–59.

Kramer, J. H., Kemenoff, L. A., & Chui, H. C. (2001). The neuropsychology of subcortical ischemic vascular dementia. In S. R. Waldstein & M. F. Elios (Eds.), *Neuropsychology of cardiovascular disease* (pp. 279–300). Mahwah, NJ: LEA.

Lautenschlager, N. T., & Almeida, O. P. (2006). Physical activity and cognition in old age. *Current Opinion in Psychiatry, 19,* 190–193.

Lee, G. P. (2004). Differential diagnosis in epilepsy. In J. H. Ricker (Ed.), *Differential diagnosis in adult neuropsychological assessment.* New York: Springer Publishing Company.

Lesser, R. P. (1996). Psychogenic seizures. *Neurology, 46,* 1499–1507.

Lucas, J. A., & Addeo, R. (2006). Traumatic brain injury. In P. J. Snyder & P. D. Nussbaum (Eds.), *Clinical neuropsychology: A pocket handbook for assessment* (2nd ed., pp. 351–380). Washington, DC: American Psychological Association.

Manev, H., & Manev, R. (2006). 5-Lipoxygenase (ALOX5) and FLAP (ALOX5AP) gene polymorphisms as factors in vascular pathology and Alzheimer's disease. *Medical Hypotheses, 66,* 501–503.

Martin, R. C., Bortz, J. J., & Snyder, P. J. (2006). Epilepsy and nonepileptic seizure disorders. In P. J. Snyder & P. D. Nussbaum (Eds.), *Clinical neuropsychology: A pocket handbook for assessment* (2nd ed., pp. 318–350). Washington, DC: American Psychological Association.

McKeith, I. G., Galsako, D., Kosaka, K., Perry, E. K., Dickson, D. W., Hansen, K. A., et al. (1996). Consensus guidelines for the clinical and pathologic diagnosis of dementia with Lewy bodies (DLB): Report of the consortium on DLB international workshop. *Neurology, 47,* 1113–1124.

McManus, R. (2002). Cause mostly unknown: Epidemiologist Hauser traces roots of epilepsy. *The NIH Record,* 8/22/02, http://www.nih.gov/news/NIH-Record/08-20-2004story/01.htm

Moldover, J. E., Goldberg, K. B., & Prout, M. F. (2004). Depression after traumatic brain injury: A review of evidence for clinical heterogeneity. *Neuropsychology Review, 14,* 143–154.

Nixon, S. J. (1996). Secondary dementias: Reversible dementia and pseudodementia. In R. Adams, O. Parsons, J. Culbertson, & S. J. Nixon (Eds.), *Neuropsychology for clinical practice* (pp. 107–130). Washington, DC: American Psychological Association.

Oster, J. M., Gutrecht, J. A., & Gross, P. T. (2005). Epilepsy and syncope. In H. R. Jones (Ed.), *Netter's neurology.* Teterboro, NJ: Icon Learning Systems.

Parkinson, J. (1817). *An essay on the shaking palsy.* London, England: Whittingham & Rowland.

Petersen, R. C., Smith, G. E., Waring, S. C., Ivnik, R. J., Tangalos, E. G., & Kokmen, E. (1999). Mild cognitive impairment: Clinical characterization and outcome. *Archives of Neurology, 56,* 303–308.

Purandare, N., Burns, A., Daly, K. J., Haricre, J., Morris, J., Macfarlane, G., et al. (2006). Cerebral emboli as a potential cause of Alzheimer's disease and vascular dementia: Case-control study. *British Medical Journal, 332,* 1104–1105.

Rankin, E. J., Adams, R. L., & Jones, H. E. (1996). Epilepsy and nonepileptic attack disorder. In R. Adams, O. Parsons, J. Culbertson, & S. J. Nixon (Eds.), *Neuropsychology for clinical practice* (pp. 131–174). Washington, DC: American Psychological Association.

Schnider, L. S., Tariot, P. N., Dagerman, K. S., Davis, S. M., Hsiao, J. K., Ismal, M. S., et al. (2006). Effectiveness of atypical antipsychotic drugs in patients with Alzheimer's disease. *New England Journal of Medicine, 355,* 1525–1538.

Schretlen, D., & Shapiro, A. M. (2003). A quantitative review of the effects of traumatic brain injury on cognitive functioning. *International Review of Psychiatry, 4,* 341–349.

Small, G. W., Rabins, P. V., Barry, P. P., Buckholtz, J. S., KeKosky, S. T., Ferris., S. H., et al. (1997). Diagnosis and treatment of Alzheimer disease and related disorders: Consensus statement of the American Association for Geriatric Psychiatry, the Alzheimer's Association, and the American Geriatrics Society. *Journal of the American Medical Association, 278,* 1363–1372.

Snowdon, D. (2003). Healthy aging and dementia: Findings from the Nun Study. *Annals of Internal Medicine, 139,* 450–454.

Snyder, P. J. (1998). Epilepsy. In P. J. Snyder & P. D. Nussbaum, *Clinical neuropsychology: A pocket handbook for assessment* (pp. 304–323). Washington, DC: American Psychological Association.

Soliveri, P., Monza, D., Paridi, D., Carella, F., Genitrini, S., Testa, D., et al. (2000). Neuropsychological follow up in patients with Parkinson's disease, striatonigral degeneration-type multisystem atrophy, and progressive supernuclear palsy. *Journal of Neurological and Neurosurgical Psychiatry, 69,* 313–318.

Tabert, M. H., Manly, J. J., Liu, X., Pelton, G. H., Rosenblum, S., Jacobs, M., et al. (2006). Neuropsychological prediction of conversion to Alzheimer disease in patients with mild cognitive impairment. *Archives of General Psychiatry, 63,* 916-924.

Takahashi, H., & Wakabayashi, K. (2005). Controversy: Is Parkinson's disease a single disease entity? Yes. *Parkinsonism and Related Disorders, 11,* S31–S37.

Tang-Wai, D. R., Knopman, D. S., Geda, Y. E., Edland, S. D., Smith, G. E., Ivnika R. J., et al. (2003). Comparison of the short test of mental status and the mini-mental state examination in mild cognitive impairment. *Archives of Neurology, 60,* 1777–1781.

Taub, E., Uswatte, G., & Pidikiti, R. (1999). Constraint-induced movement therapy: A new family of techniques with broad application to physical rehabilitation—A clinical review. *Journal of Rehabilitation Research and Development, 36,* 237–251.

Trimble, M. R., Ring, H. A., & Schmitz, B. (2000). Epilepsy. In B. S. Fogel, R. B. Schiffer, & S. M. Rao (Eds.), *Synopsis of neuropsychiatry* (pp. 469–489). Philadelphia, PA: Lippincott, Williams & Wilkins Publishers.

Troster, A. I. (1998). Assessment of movement and demyelinating disorders. In P. J. Snyder & P. D. Nussbaum (Eds.), *Clinical neuropsychology: A pocket handbook for assessment* (pp. 266–303). Washington, DC: American Psychological Association.

U.S. Preventive Services Task Force. (1996). *Guide to clinical preventive services* (2nd ed.) Washington, DC: U.S. Department of Health and Human Services.

Weinstein, A., & Swenson, R. (1998). Cerebrovascular disease. In P. J. Snyder & P. D. Nussbaum (Eds.), *Clinical neuropsychology: A pocket handbook for assessment* (pp. 381–402). Washington, DC: American Psychological Association.

Weintraub, S. (2006, May 17). Neuropsychological assessment of dementia. Presentation at Harvard Medical School course titled "Dementia: A Comprehensive Update."

Wojciech, D., & Parsons, C. G. (2003). The NMDA receptor antagonist memantine as a symptomatological and neuroprotective treatment for Alzheimer's disease: Preclinical evidence. *International Journal of Geriatric Psychiatry, 18,* S23–32.

World Health Organization. Retrieved August 15, 2006, from http://www.who.int/mediacentre/factsheets/fs165/en/

Zaccai, J., McCracken, C., & Brayne, C. (2005). A systematic review of prevalence and incidence studies of dementia with Lewy bodies. *Age & Ageing, 34,* 561–566.

3

Neuropsychology and Intelligence: An Overview

CECIL R. REYNOLDS, CHRISTINE L. CASTILLO, AND ARTHUR MacNEILL HORTON, JR.

NEUROPSYCHOLOGY AND INTELLIGENCE are abstract concepts associated in biology, overlap to a degree, and are measured through behavior. This chapter will provide a view of intelligence from a functional, clinical neuropsychology perspective to be of utility in clinical practice. The intent is to describe models of the working brain that will aid clinicians in understanding compromised brains. As is well known, intelligence as a concept was first used clinically when Binet devised an intelligence test to determine what children were appropriate for the public schools of Paris, France (Binet & Simon, 1905, 1908). In the United States, David Wechsler developed a series of intelligence scales to aid in clinical assessment (Wechsler, 1955). Wechsler adapted tests that had been devised to select officers during

Note: This chapter is based in part on a prior work of the first two authors: Reynolds, C. R., & French, C. (2003). The neuropsychological basis of intelligence: Revisited. In A. M. Horton, Jr., & L. C. Hartlage (Eds.), *Handbook of forensic neuropsychology*. New York: Springer Publishing Company. Christine L. Castillo, PhD was previously Christine L. French, PhD.

World War I (Wechsler, 1939) and standardized the administration and scoring and normed the measures in large national samples of adults (Wechsler, 1955). Neuropsychology as a field of clinical interest developed later (Horton & Wedding, 1984).

HALSTEAD'S THEORY OF BIOLOGICAL INTELLIGENCE

THE WORK OF Halstead (1947) was the basis for many of the methods of clinical neuropsychology. Halstead was interested in the study of the cerebral cortex (specifically on the role of the frontal lobes) in relation to intelligence. Halstead (1947) was interested in developing a broad theory of brain-behavior relationships. He postulated there were two types of intelligence, biological intelligence and psychometric intelligence. Psychometric intelligence was considered to be what is measured by intelligence tests (Reitan, 1994). Reitan (1994) has averred that Halstead considered biological intelligence best viewed as "the adaptive abilities represented by a healthy brain and nervous system" (p. 55). Halstead believed measures of psychometric intelligence lacked the capability to denote the true state of the nervous system (Reed, 1985). Reitan (1994) reported that in Halstead's research he found some patients with tremendous loss of brain mass continuing to score well on measures of psychometric intelligence. Halstead postulated that an examination of the biological intelligence of brain-damaged individuals would result in a greater understanding of their adaptive abilities (Shure & Halstead, 1959). Halstead clearly realized that psychometric and biological intelligence were related concepts as he routinely included a standardized test of intelligence, the Henmon-Nelson Tests of Mental Ability, in the neuropsychological test battery used in his research (Reitan, 1994). Halstead's research focused on determining the nature of biological intelligence. Halstead selected 13 measures, from a much larger number of tests, for his study of biological intelligence. The tests were selected because they "seemed likely to reflect some component of biological intelligence" (Halstead, 1947, p. 39). Based on factor analyses of this set of tests, Halstead (1947) extracted four basic factors of biological intelligence, which he labeled C, A, P, and D. Halstead defined these four factors as follows.

C, THE INTEGRATIVE FIELD FACTOR

HALSTEAD CONSIDERED THIS factor the ability to adapt to new situations and to integrate new information and stimuli that were not a part of one's previous experiences (Reitan, 1994). Halstead's factor analysis found large loadings by the Halstead Category Test, the Henmon-Nelson Tests of Mental Ability, the Speech-Sounds Perception Test, the Halstead Finger Oscillation Test, and the Halstead Time-Sense Test for the *C* factor (Halstead, 1947).

A, THE ABSTRACTION FACTOR

HALSTEAD CONSIDERED THIS factor as the ability to draw meaning away from a series of events or to hold ideas away from their concrete referents and to grasp essential similarities in the face of apparent differences and vice versa without the use or reliance upon past experience. Halstead's factor analysis found large loadings from the Carlo Hollow-Square Performance Test for Intelligence, the Halstead Category Test, the Halstead Tactual Performance Test (memory component), and the Halstead Tactual Performance Test (localization component; Halstead, 1947).

P, THE POWER FACTOR

HALSTEAD POSTULATED THIS factor to be the reserve power available to an amplifier not already functioning at peak wattage and controlled principally through the frontal lobes. Reitan (1994) stated that *P* was critical in an individual's expression of his or her biological intelligence. Halstead's factor analytic study found large loadings by the Halstead Flicker-Fusion Test, the Halstead Tactual Performance Test (recall component), the Halstead Dynamic Visual Field Test (central form), and the Halstead Dynamic Visual Field Test (central color; Halstead, 1947).

D, THE DIRECTIONAL FACTOR

HALSTEAD (1947) DESCRIBED THIS factor as the "medium of exteriorization of intelligence, either from within or from without the individual" (p. 84). Put another way, he believed the factor was an attentional factor. Halstead's factor analysis found large loadings by the Halstead Tactual Performance Test (speed component) and the Halstead Dynamic Visual Field Test (peripheral component; Halstead, 1947). The first three factors, *C*, *A*, and *P*, were considered process factors of intelligence, and *D* the factor through which expression of these processes occurred. Unfortunately, no replications of the factor analysis have been completed (Reitan, 1994), thereby limiting the validity for the concept of biological intelligence.

Halstead reasoned that individuals with known neuropathology should suffer impairment in their ability to perform tasks represented by the factors. He found that tests measuring the four factors differentiated between individuals with a definite history of head injury and with no history of head injury, but that an average of the measures performed better than any single measure (Halstead, 1947). Halstead used the 10 best discriminating tests to form an index of impairment, and this is now known as the Halstead Impairment Index (HII; Reitan, 1994). Each test was given an equal weighting. An individual scoring within the impaired range on every test was thus assigned a score of 1.0, while an individual scoring in the normal (nonimpaired) range on every test earned a score of 0. Halstead (1947) postulated that biological intelligence was principally controlled through the frontal lobes. Frontal lesions resulted in HIIs several times greater than in patients with nonfrontal lesions, and patients with nonfrontal lesions had HIIs much greater than normal subjects. The relationship between the frontal lobes and HII, however, has not been validated in subsequent research (Reitan, 1975).

Reitan (1994) recognized the need for a clinical battery of neuropsychological tests in order to make diagnoses of brain pathology and expanded Halstead's original battery of tests. Reitan completed extensive studies using test results, which were later reviewed and corroborated by others in the field of neuropsychology (Reitan, 1994), and modified the test battery based on clinical diagnostic needs (Hevern, 1980; Reed, 1985; Swiercinsky, 1979). Reitan (1975) found nonfrontal lobe lesions were most frequently associated with specific types of disorders while frontal lobe lesions resulted in more general disturbances. Reitan's work (1955, 1966, 1975; Reitan & Davison, 1974; Wheeler & Reitan, 1962) validated the Halstead-Reitan Neuropsychological Test Battery (HRNTB) as the most widely used research-based comprehensive neuropsychological assessment battery (Reitan & Wolfson, 1996).

LURIA'S BRAIN-BEHAVIOR MODEL

ALEXANDER R. LURIA, MD, PhD, was a Russian neurologist and neuropsychologist who made major contributions to the scientific discipline of neuropsychology. The major contribution Luria made to the field of clinical neuropsychology was the concept of the functional system (Horton, 1987). Luria used a variety of neuropsychological tests that were based on his prior research on the cultural-historical theory of higher cognitive functioning to obtain a qualitative evaluation of an individual's neurological status (Horton, 1987).

Luria conceptualized the working brain as organized into three major components or brain blocks. The first block of the brain consists of the brainstem, including the reticular formation, the midbrain, pons, and medulla. The second block of the brain consists of the parietal, occipital, and temporal lobes. The third block of the brain consists of the cerebral cortex anterior to the central sulcus and the sensory-motor strip. The brain blocks were considered to function in a dynamic interaction between the areas, and any deficit in one area of the brain may interact and affect the functioning of the other brain areas (Reynolds & French, 2003). While sensory and motor functions of the brain have highly specific functional localizations, complex higher level mental processes require the coordination of multiple areas of the brain. Simply put, for higher level cognitive functions, multiple areas of the brain can underlie multiple specific behaviors; for simple sensory motor functions a specific area of the brain can be localized (Reynolds & French, 2003). Specialization for higher level cognitive tasks is more process-specific and information processing requires coordination of several anatomical sections of the cortex (Ashman & Das, 1980).

Luria gives credit for developing the notion of the brain as a dynamic functional system to Hughlings Jackson, an English physician who lived in the nineteenth century (Horton, 1987). Luria (1964) noted that the higher cognitive processes were formed as a function of the process of communication and represent *"complex functional systems based on jointly working zones of the brain cortex"* (italics added) (pp. 11–12). Luria (1964) goes on to state, "It becomes completely understandable that a higher (mental) function may suffer as a result of the destruction of *any link which is a part of the structure of a complex functional system* and . . . may be disturbed even when the centres differ greatly in localization" (italics added) (pp. 11–12). In addition, Luria (1964) postulated that, "when one or another link has been lost, the whole functional system will be disturbed in a particular way, and symptoms of disturbance of one or another higher (mental) function will have a *completely different structure, depending on the location of the damage"* (italics added) (pp. 11–12).

Luria utilized his qualitative assessment methods with neurological patients by analyzing the nature of the difficulty experienced in performing a cognitive task to determine the localizing significance of the observed disturbance (Luria, 1964). These functional clinical appraisals were based on Luria's model of brain functioning that postulated three systems of functional activity or three "blocks" of the brain.

BLOCK ONE

THE FIRST BLOCK of the brain is the arousal and attention unit and has responsibility for regulating the energy level and tone of the entire cortex to provide a stable basis for the conscious organism to organize the various other functions and processes of the brain. The regulatory functions are mediated by the reticular formation, the posterior hypothalamic, and brainstem portions of the brain. The reticular formation controls the levels of activation found at any given time in the cortex. Injuries to the first block of the brain can result in lowering of the level of consciousness in the cortex, giving rise to confused behavior.

BLOCK TWO

THE SECOND BLOCK is the area posterior to the central sulcus and is composed of the parietal, occipital, and temporal lobes. The information processing of the brain, such as receiving sensory input, integrating, and storing of information, occurs in the second block. The areas in block two responsible for the analysis and synthesis of stimuli (e.g., auditory in the temporal region, visual in the occipital region, and tactile in the parietal lobe) are each organized into three hierarchical zones. The *primary zone* of block two sorts and records incoming sensory organization. The *secondary zone* receives information from the primary zone and organizes and codes the information. The *tertiary zone* merges information from multiple secondary zones and organizes complex behavior.

BLOCK THREE

LURIA (1970) HAS noted that "The third block of the brain, comprising the frontal lobes, is involved in the formation of intentions and programs for behavior" (p. 68). The third block is the executive region of the brain and takes input from the first and second blocks of the brain (Obrzut & Obrzut, 1982). The frontal lobes organize and implement conscious actions and are involved in every complex, higher order behavior of humans.

The frontal lobes are connected to the reticular formation in the first block of the brain and are involved in the activation of the remainder of the cortex. The frontal lobes regulate and focus attention in the brain. The direction of attention determines how information is processed in the brain. Higher cognitive functioning is the result of the dynamic interplay of the three blocks of the brain (Luria, 1964). A standardized version of the neurological test procedures used by Luria was developed in the United States for adults (Golden, Purisch, & Hammeke, 1979) and children (Golden, 1987).

SIMULTANEOUS AND SUCCESSIVE COGNITIVE PROCESSES

SIMULTANEOUS AND SUCCESSIVE (or sequential) cognitive processes are two complementary information-processing strategies of Luria's (1964) second block of the brain. Simultaneous and successive processes are not specific to any modality or stimulus (Ashman & Das, 1980). Stimulus information can be processed through either simultaneous or successive means, but various functions may be processed more efficiently through one process (Kaufman, 1979). The means of cognitive processing an individual uses for a task may change depending on the task demands, attention to the task, and preferred means for completing the task (Hall, Gregory, Billinger, & Fisher, 1988; Watters & English, 1995; Willis, 1985). Language is usually processed efficiently through successive methods that are linear in nature such as writing a letter. Copying a complex figure is a task that is processed efficiently through simultaneous processing strategies.

Simultaneous Processing

Das, Kirby, and Jarman (1979) note that "Simultaneous integration refers to the synthesis of separate elements into groups, these groups often taking on spatial overtones." The essential nature of this sort of processing is that "any portion of the result is at once surveyable without dependence upon its position in the whole" (p. 49). Areas of the right cerebral hemisphere occipital and parietal lobes of the brain are often associated with this mode of information processing (Naglieri, Kamphaus, & Kaufman, 1983; Willis, 1985). Traditional tests of spatial abilities have been noted to show high correlations with simultaneous processing (Kirby & Das, 1977).

Successive Processing

Das, Kirby, and Jarman (1979) describe successive (or sequential) information processing as linear processing of information. Elements of information are accessed in a serial fashion. Successive (or sequential) processing is associated with the left cerebral hemisphere frontotemporal areas (Naglieri et al., 1983; Willis, 1985).

Tasks used in research on successive processing require the maintenance of a temporal order of input of information for the generation of an appropriate response. For example, children learning to read based on a phonetic approach must identify each letter of a word in succession and pronounce the word based on the sounds each letter makes. Successful reading is best accomplished by means of successive processing (Gunnison, Kaufman, & Kaufman, 1982).

HEMISPHERIC SPECIALIZATION AND SIMULTANEOUS AND SUCCESSIVE COGNITIVE PROCESSES

THE LEFT CEREBRAL hemisphere appears to be specialized for linguistic, serial, and analytic tasks, and the right hemisphere appears to be specialized for more nonverbal, spatial, and holistic tasks (Bogen, 1969; Dean & Reynolds, 1997; Gazzaniga, 1970; Harnad, Doty,

Goldstein, Jaynes, & Krauthamer, 1977; Kinsbourne, 1997; Naglieri et al., 1983; Schwartz, Davidson, & Maer, 1975; Segalowitz & Gruber, 1977; Willis, 1985). A review of Table 3.1 indicates modes of processing are the best means of reviewing differences in hemispheric processing. Processing modes are more important to determining the efficiency of these hemispheric brain functions.

Cerebral hemispheric asymmetries of function are best seen as *process-specific* rather than *stimulus-specific*. The mode of processing for accomplishing a task may vary due to a number of factors, such as task demands, level of attention to the task, individual strengths, genetics, and sociocultural norms and traditions (Cumming & Rodda, 1985; Hall et al., 1988; McCallum & Merritt, 1983; Watters & English, 1995; Willis, 1985). Manipulation of stimuli appears to be the source of hemispheric differences (e.g., Dean, 1985; Grimshaw, 1998; Mateer, Rapport, & Kettrick, 1984; Obrzut, Obrzut, Bryden, & Bartels, 1985; Ornstein, Johnstone, Herron, & Swencionis, 1980; Piccirilli, D'Alessandro, Mazzi, Sciarma, & Testa, 1991; Tous, Fusté, & Vidal, 1995).

HEMISPHERICITY AND COGNITIVE PROCESSING

HEMISPHERICITY IS THE tendency of an individual to rely primarily upon the problem-solving or information-processing style of one hemisphere (Reynolds, 1978, 1981). Hemisphericity may be conceptualized as dominance for an information-processing style but is independent of traditional notions of cerebral dominance and the motorically determined lateral preference of the individual. Dominance is for a higher level cognitive style (Allen, 1983). The cognitive styles of the two hemispheres have also been described as modes of consciousness (Galin, 1974). Luria's model continues to serve as the foundation for current treatment and assessment processes as reviews of hemispheric specialization support Luria's model (Dean & Reynolds, 1997).

Hemispheric specialization, or preferred higher level cognitive style, has replaced cerebral dominance as a major concept in understanding human brain-behavior relationships. Assessing the dominant information-processing modality of an individual may assist in understanding intelligence (Corballis & Beale, 1976). Use of the two modes of information processing separately or in conjunction with one another and being able to shift the mode is characteristic of normal individuals (Gazzaniga, 1975). However, differences in reading ability may be due to hemisphericity disparity (Newell & Rugel, 1981; Roubinek, Bell, & Cates, 1987).

TABLE 3.1   Functions of the Right and Left Hemispheres

Right hemisphere		Left hemisphere	
Processing modes	**Representative reference**	**Processing modes**	**Representative reference**
Simultaneous	Hall, Gregory, Billinger, & Fisher, 1988	Sequential	Bell, 1990; Bloom, 2000
Holistic Visual/Nonverbal	Dimond & Beaumont, 1974 Sperry, 1974	Temporal Analytic	Mills, 1977 Morgan, McDonald, & McDonald, 1971
Imagery Spatial Reasoning	Seamon & Gazzaniga, 1973 Sperry, 1974		
Nonverbal functions	**Representative reference**	**Verbal functions**	**Representative reference**
Depth Perception	Carmon & Bechtoldt, 1969	Speech	Wada, 1949 Reitan, 1955
Melodic Perception	Shankweiler, 1966	General Language/ Verbal Abilities	Mateer, Rapport, & Kettrick, 1984
Tactile Perception (Integration)	Boll, 1974	Calculation/ Arithmetic	Mitsuda, 1991
Haptic Perception	Wittelson, 1974	Abstract Verbal Thought	Watters & English, 1995
Nonverbal Sound Recognition	Wright & Ashman, 1991	Writing (Composition)	Hecaen & Marcie, 1974
Motor Integration	Gorynia & Egenter, 2000	Complex Motor Functions	Dimond & Beaumont, 1974
Visual Constructive Performance	Capruso, Hamsher, & Benton, 1995	Body Orientation	Gerstmann, 1957
Pattern Recognition	Capruso, Hamsher, & Benton, 1995	Vigilance	Dimond & Beaumont, 1974

Note: Adapted from Kamphaus and Reynolds (1987).

Traditional concepts of cerebral dominance are being replaced with notions of hemispheric specialization. Hemisphericity is a powerful explanatory variable with many clinical implications. A great deal of recent research has focused on identifying students' preferred mode of processing (hemisphericity) in order to remediate learning problems and facilitate successful academic performance (Faust, Kravetz, & Babkoff, 1993; Gunnison et al., 1982; Paquette, Tosoni, Lassonde, & Peretz, 1996; Roubinek et al., 1987; Sonnier, 1992; Sonnier & Goldsmith, 1985).

THE ROLE OF G IN NEUROPSYCHOLOGICAL MODELS OF INTELLIGENCE

THE CONCEPT OF g is the most efficient means of describing the intellectual abilities of an individual. Rather than delineate each function, it is more efficient to ascribe all cognitive functioning to a single variable. The ancient Greek Aristotle was the first to suggest assessment of intellect could be based on a single variable, *nous* (Detterman, 1982). One wonders how Aristotle assessed the intellect of his most famous pupil, Alexander the Great. The notion of g is an average of fluctuations in an individual's cognitive abilities as measured by different tasks. In all cases, g may not be the best estimate of an individual's cognitive functioning, and an individual's scope of cognitive abilities may be best described by assessing task specific skills (Kaufman, 1994).

Researchers continue to use g as a means of denoting general intellectual ability (Aluja-Fabregat, Colom, Abad, & Juan-Espinosa, 2000; Kane, 2000). Jensen (1998), for example, avers for the presence of a general cognitive ability factor in intelligence. He postulated that "provided the number of tests in the analyzed battery is sufficiently large to yield reliable factors and the tests are sufficiently diverse in item types and information content to reflect more than a single narrow ability, a g factor always emerges" (p. 73). Jensen notes that arguments against the g factor fail to understand the need for a large assessment battery or large number of diverse item types. He surmises that because there are so many biological correlates to g there must be a general cognitive factor. Reynolds and French (2003) propose that the study of g and the study of cognitive processing styles and even more specific functions of the brain must be undertaken as complementary, not exclusionary, areas of clinical and research investigation.

Simultaneous and successive processes in the human brain can be related to a general overall cognitive ability. The verbal and performance IQ factors of the Wechsler Intelligence Scale for Children Fourth Edition (WISC-R) are examples of separate but related factors in many diverse populations (Reynolds, 1981), and the majority of individuals perform at about the same general level on the two sets of tasks. In addition, the notion of g is supported by individual differences in the level or efficiency of information processing. For example, Das, Kirby, and Jarman (1979) and Detterman (1982) have found that mentally retarded persons demonstrate the presence of simultaneous and successive cognitive processes in the same manner as normal individuals, but mentally retarded persons differ in the level and efficiency with which they perform styles of cognitive processing. On the other hand, evidence suggests that one cause of learning disorders is difficulty with specific types of information processing or an over-reliance on a single mode of cognitive information processing. However, except for brain trauma or dementia, g controls the efficiency of cognitive processing any individual is able to undertake. Travers (1977); Luborsky, Auerbach, Chandler, Cohen, and Bachrach (1971); and Lezak (1995) found in many studies of psychotherapy-outcome research, the general intellectual level (i.e., g) of the individual is the best predictor of success. Similarly, the pre-injury or pre-decline level of general intellectual functioning is the best predictor of rehabilitative success of patients with a number of neurological diseases and disorders (Golden, 1978).

The concept of g is considered to be determined by the biology (i.e., anatomy, physiology, and chemistry) of the human brain (Brand, 1996; Vernon, 1983, 1998). Arthur Jensen's (1998) research has supported a physiological determination of g. Harmony (1997) and Languis and Miller (1992) reviewed several studies utilizing EEG measures, auditory evoked responses, visual evoked responses, and event-related potentials that lended support to the notion of using physiological measures in order to determine some aspect of cognitive ability (or disability). Similarly, Jensen's research (1978, 1998) on reaction times and stimulus complexity and the study of evoked potentials leads one to define g as the general physiological efficiency of the central nervous system (Head, 1926). Contemporary conceptualizations of intelligence must take into account the method and components of information processing in the brain as well as the ability to use the available information-processing strategies to their fullest potential, such as g.

DISCUSSION: BIOLOGICAL AND PSYCHOLOGICAL INTELLIGENCE

IT APPEARS CLEAR that g represents a biological intelligence based in the physiology of the brain, while some might postulate that psychological intelligence is represented by the use of various hemispheric brain mechanisms assisted by a wealth of cultural experiences, as suggested by Luria (1966, 1973). Biological intelligence would appear to be largely genetically based, though certainly dependent on the nurturance of the environment pre- and postnatally. Psychological intelligence would appear to be largely influenced by the person's environmental history (i.e., for a discussion of Luria's cultural-historical theory, see Horton, 1987), though there is clearly a genetic influence mediating the functional development of the various anatomical structures of the brain. Biological intelligence, therefore, is the physiological efficiency of the brain, while psychological intelligence refers to the hemispheric processes through which intelligence is externalized. Biological intelligence sets an individual's level of function, while psychological intelligence mediates an individual's ability to adapt to life circumstances and challenges (Pallier, Roberts, & Stankov, 2000). The theories of intelligence referred to in this chapter are truly theories of psychological intelligence. The further development of theories of psychological intelligence will continue to elucidate how the human brain carries out higher order thinking. The further elaboration of subtle mechanisms of biological intelligence is expected to be done by noncognitive neuroscientists. The conceptualizations of biological and psychological intelligence have lead to new understanding regarding the human brain, such as hemisphericity.

The concept of level of function, or *g*, however, remains central to any contemporary theory of human intelligence. In addition, new understanding regarding the lateralization of different modes of cognitive processing in the human as noted by Das, Kirby, and Jarman (1979) are important for conceptualizing higher order thinking. New measures of psychological intelligence have been developed in the past two decades (e.g., Kamphaus, 1993; Kaufman & Kaufman, 1983; Naglieri & Das, 1988, 1990, 1996) based on new understandings of brain function. A particularly important new test of intelligence has been the Reynolds Intellectual Assessment Scales (RIAS; Reynolds & Kamphaus, 2003), which is based on the fluid and crystallized theory of intelligences of Horn and Cattell (1966). In some ways, fluid and crystallized intelligences may be other ways of conceptualizing biological intelligence and psychological intelligence. Future research with the RIAS may provide needed answers. In addition, recent research in test development has continued to explore biological intelligence as related to executive functioning (Naglieri, 1997). To assess the area of executive functioning, Reynolds and Horton (2006) recently published the Test of Verbal Conceptualization and Fluency (TVCF), which is a well-standardized measure of executive functioning. The TVCF is based on Luria's model (1970) of higher level mental processing as being subserved by multiple brain areas. In some ways the TVCF may come to be considered an appropriate measure of biological intelligence, but only future research can answer this question. Nonetheless, it is expected that the pace of new knowledge will increase rather than decrease, and new understandings of human intelligence are expected in the coming decades (Beaumont, Young, & McManus, 1984). New techniques of measurement are expected to revise past conceptualizations, and interdisciplinary research teams are expected to synthesize previously divergent views of biological and psychological intelligence and contribute to greater understanding of how the human brain processes information (Beaumont, 1997).

REFERENCES

Allen, M. (1983). Models of hemispheric specialization. *Psychological Bulletin, 93,* 73–104.

Aluja-Fabregat, A., Colom, R., Abad, F., & Juan-Espinosa, M. (2000). Sex differences in general intelligence defined as *g* among young adolescents. *Personality and Individual Differences, 28,* 813–820.

Ashman, A. F., & Das, J. P. (1980). Relation between planning and simultaneous-successive processing. *Perceptual and Motor Skills, 51,* 371–382.

Beaumont, J. G. (1997). Future research directions in laterality. *Neuropsychology Review, 7,* 107–126.

Beaumont, J. G., Young, A. W., & McManus, I. C. (1984). Hemisphericity: A critical review. *Cognitive Neuropsychology, 1,* 191–212.

Binet, A., & Simon, T. (1905). New methods for the diagnosis of the intellectual level of subnormals. *L'annee Psychologique, 11,* 191–244.

Binet, A., & Simon, T. (1908). The development of intelligence in the child. *L'annee Psychologique, 14,* 1–90.

Bogen, J. E. (1969). The other side of the brain: Parts I, II, and III. *Bulletin of the Los Angeles Neurological Society, 34,* 73–105, 135–162, 191–203.

Brand, C. (1996). Doing something about *g. Intelligence, 22,* 311–326.

Corballis, M. C., & Beale, I. L. (1976). *The psychology of left and right.* Hillsdale, NJ: Lawrence Erlbaum Associates.

Cumming, C. E., & Rodda, M. (1985). The effects of auditory deprivation on successive processing. *Canadian Journal of Behavioural Science, 17,* 232–245.

Das, J. P., Kirby, J. R., & Jarman, R. F. (1979). *Simultaneous and successive cognitive processes.* New York: Academic Press.

Dean, R. S. (1985). Foundation and rationale for neuropsychological basis of individual differences. In L. C. Hartlage & C. F. Telzrow (Eds.), *Neuropsychology of individual differences* (pp. 7–40). New York: Plenum Press.

Dean, R. S., & Reynolds, C. R. (1997). Cognitive processing and self-report of lateral preference. *Neuropsychology Review, 7,* 127–142.

Detterman, D. K. (1982). Does "g" exist? *Intelligence, 6,* 99–108.

Faust, M., Kravetz, S., & Babkoff, H. (1993). Hemisphericity and top-down processing of language. *Brain and Language, 44,* 1–18.

Galin, D. (1974). Implications for psychiatry of left and right cerebral specialization. *Archives of General Psychiatry, 31,* 78–82.

Gazzaniga, M. S. (1970). *The bisected brain.* New York: Appleton.

Gazzaniga, M. S. (1975, May). Recent research on hemispheric lateralization of the human brain: Review of the split-brain. *UCLA Educator,* 9–12.

Golden, C. J. (1978). *Diagnosis and rehabilitation in clinical neuropsychology.* Springfield, IL: Charles C. Thomas.

Golden, C. J. (1987). *Luria-Nebraska neuropsychological battery children's revision.* Los Angeles: Western Psychological Services.

Golden, C. J., Purisch, A. D., & Hammeke, T. A. (1979). *The Luria-Nebraska neuropsychological test battery: A manual for clinical and experimental uses.* Lincoln: The University of Nebraska Press.

Grimshaw, G. M. (1998). Integration and interference in the cerebral hemispheres: Relations with hemispheric specialization. *Brain and Cognition, 36,* 108–127.

Gunnison, J., Kaufman, N. L., & Kaufman, A. S. (1982). Reading remediation based on sequential and simultaneous processing. *Academic Therapy, 17,* 297–306.

Hall, C. W., Gregory, G., Billinger, E., & Fisher, T. (1988). Field independence and simultaneous processing in preschool children. *Perceptual and Motor Skills, 66,* 891–897.

Halstead, W. C. (1947). *Brain and intelligence.* Chicago: University of Chicago Press.

Harmony, T. (1997). Psychophysiological evaluation of neuropsychological disorders in children. In C. R. Reynolds & E. Fletcher-Janzen (Eds.), *Handbook of clinical child neuropsychology* (2nd ed., pp. 356–370). New York: Plenum Press.

Harnad, S., Doty, R. W., Goldstein, L., Jaynes, J., & Krauthamer, G. (Eds.) (1977). *Lateralization in the nervous system.* New York: Academic Press.

Head, H. (1926). *Aphasia and kindred disorders of speech: Vol. 1.* New York: Macmillan.

Hevern, V. W. (1980). Recent validity studies of the Halstead-Reitan approach to clinical neuropsychological assessment: A critical review. *Clinical Neuropsychology, 2,* 49–61.

Horn, J. L., & Cattell, R. B. (1966). Refinement and the test of the theory of fluid and crystallized general intelligences. *Journal of Educational Psychology, 57*(5), 253–270.

Horton, A. M., Jr. (1987). Luria's contributions to clinical and behavioral neuropsychology. *Neuropsychology, 1*(2), 39–44.

Horton, A. M., Jr., & Wedding, D. (1984). *Clinical and behavioral neuropsychology.* New York: Praeger.

Jensen, A. R. (1978, September). *"g": Outmoded concept or unconquered frontier?* Invited address at the annual meeting of the American Psychological Association, New York.

Jensen, A. R. (1998). *The g factor: The science of mental ability*. Westport, CT: Praeger.

Kamphaus, R. W. (1993). *Clinical assessment of children's intelligence*. Boston: Allyn and Bacon.

Kamphaus, R. W., & Reynolds, C. R. (1987). *Clinical and research applications of the K-ABC*. Circle Pines, MN: American Guidance Service.

Kane, H. D. (2000). A secular decline in Spearman's *g*: Evidence from the WAIS, WAIS-R and WAIS-III. *Personality and Individual Differences, 29*, 561–566.

Kaufman, A. S. (1979). Cerebral specialization and intelligence testing. *Journal of Research and Development in Education, 12*, 96–107.

Kaufman, A. S. (1994). *Intelligent testing with the WISC-III*. New York: John Wiley & Sons, Inc.

Kaufman, A. S., & Kaufman, N. L. (1983). *Administration and scoring manual for the Kaufman Assessment Battery for Children*. Circle Pines, MN: American Guidance Service.

Kinsbourne, M. (1997). Mechanisms and development of cerebral lateralization in children. In C. R. Reynolds & E. Fletcher-Janzen (Eds.), *Handbook of clinical child neuropsychology* (2nd ed., pp. 102–119). New York: Plenum Press.

Kirby, J. R., & Das, J. P. (1977). Reading achievement, IQ, and simultaneous-successive processing. *Journal of Educational Psychology, 69*, 564–570.

Languis, M. L., & Miller, D. C. (1992). Luria's theory of brain functioning: A model for research in cognitive psychophysiology. *Educational Psychologist, 27*, 493–511.

Lezak, M. D. (1995). *Neuropsychological assessment* (3rd ed.). New York: Oxford University Press.

Luborsky, L., Auerbach, A. H., Chandler, M., Cohen, J., & Bachrach, H. M. (1971). Factors influencing the outcome of psychotherapy: A review of quantitative research. *Psychological Bulletin, 75*, 145–185.

Luria, A. R. (1964). Neuropsychology in the local diagnosis of brain damage. *Cortex, 1*, 3–18.

Luria, A. R. (1966). *Higher cortical functions in man*. New York: Basic Books.

Luria, A. R. (1970). The functional organization of the brain. *Scientific American, 222*, 66–78.

Luria, A. R. (1973). *The working brain*. London: Penguin.

Mateer, C. A., Rapport, R. L., & Kettrick, C. (1984). Cerebral organization of oral and signed language responses: Case study evidence from amytal and cortical stimulation studies. *Brain and Language, 21*, 123–135.

McCallum, R. S., & Merritt, F. M. (1983). Simultaneous-successive processing among college students. *Journal of Psychoeducational Assessment, 1*, 85–93.

Naglieri, J. A. (1997). Planning, attention, simultaneous, and successive theory and the Cognitive Assessment System: A new theory-based measure of intelligence. In D. P. Flanagan, J. L. Genshaft, & P. L. Harrison (Eds.),

Contemporary intellectual assessment: Theories, tests, and issues (pp. 247–267). New York: The Guilford Press.

Naglieri, J. A., & Das, J. P. (1988). Planning-Arousal-Simultaneous-Successive (PASS): A model for assessment. *Journal of School Psychology, 26,* 35–48.

Naglieri, J. A., & Das, J. P. (1990). Planning, attention, simultaneous, and successive (PASS) cognitive processes as a model for intelligence. *Journal of Psychoeducational Assessment, 8,* 303–337.

Naglieri, J. A., & Das, J. P. (1996). *Das Naglieri cognitive assessment system.* Chicago: Riverside.

Naglieri, J. A., Kamphaus, R. W., & Kaufman, A. S. (1983). The Luria-Das simultaneous-successive model applied to the WISC-R. *Journal of Psychoeducational Assessment, 1,* 25–34.

Newell, D., & Rugel, R. P. (1981). Hemispheric specialization in normal and disabled readers. *Journal of Learning Disabilities, 14,* 296–298.

Obrzut, J. E., & Obrzut, A. (1982). Neuropsychological perspectives in pupil services: Practical application of Luria's model. *Journal of Research and Development in Education, 15,* 38–47.

Obrzut, J. E., Obrzut, A., Bryden, M. P., & Bartels, S. G. (1985). Information processing and speech lateralization in learning-disabled children. *Brain and Language, 25,* 87–101.

Ornstein, R., Johnstone, J., Herron, J., & Swencionis, C. (1980). Differential right hemisphere engagement in visuospatial tasks. *Neuropsychologia, 18,* 49–64.

Pallier, G., Roberts, R. D., & Stankov, L. (2000). Biological versus psychometric intelligence: Halstead's (1947) distinction revisted. *Archives of Clinical Neuropsychology, 15,* 205–226.

Paquette, C., Tosoni, C., Lassonde, M., & Peretz, I. (1996). Atypical hemispheric specialization in intellectual deficiency. *Brain and Language, 52,* 474–483.

Piccirilli, M., D'Alessandro, P., Mazzi, P., Sciarma, T., & Testa, A. (1991). Cerebral organization for language in Down's Syndrome patients. *Cortex, 27,* 41–47.

Reed, J. (1985). The contributions of Ward Halstead, Ralph Reitan and their associates. *International Journal of Neuroscience, 25,* 289–293.

Reitan, R. M. (1955). Certain differential effects of left and right cerebral lesions in human adults. *Journal of Comparative and Physiological Psychology, 48,* 474–477.

Reitan, R. M. (1966). A research program on the psychological effects of brain lesions in human beings. *International Review of Research in Mental Retardation, 1,* 153–218.

Reitan, R. M. (1975). Assessment of brain-behavior relationships. In P. McReynolds (Ed.), *Advances in psychological assessment: Vol. III.* San Francisco: Jossey-Bass.

Reitan, R. M. (1994). Ward Halstead's contributions to neuropsychology and the Halstead-Reitan Neuropsychological Test Battery. *Journal of Clinical Psychology, 50,* 47–69.

Reitan, R. M., & Davison, L. A. (1974). *Clinical neuropsychology: Current status and applications.* Washington, DC: V. H. Winston.

Reitan, R. M., & Wolfson, D. (1996). Theoretical, methodological, and valida-
tional bases of the Halstead-Reitan Neuropsychological Test Battery. In
I. Grant & K. M. Adams (Eds.), *Neuropsychological assessment of neuropsychiatric disorders* (2nd ed., pp. 3–42). New York: Oxford University Press.

Reynolds, C. R. (1978, April). *Current conceptualizations of hemisphericity*. Col-
loquium presented to the Department of Educational Psychology, the
University of Texas–Austin.

Reynolds, C. R., & French, C. (2003). The neuropsychological basis of intelligence: Revisited. In A. M. Horton, Jr., & L. C. Hartlage (Eds.) *Handbook of
forensic neuropsychology*. New York: Springer Publishing Company.

Reynolds, C. R., & Horton, A. M., Jr. (2006). *Test of verbal conceptualization and
fluency: Professional manual*. Austin, TX: ProEd.

Reynolds, C. R., & Kamphaus, R. W. (2003). *Reynolds Intellectual Assessment Scales
and Reynolds Intellectual Screening Test*. Professional Manual. Odessa, FL:
PAR, Inc.

Roubinek, D. L., Bell, M. L., & Cates, L. A. (1987). Brain hemispheric preference
of intellectually gifted children. *Roeper Review, 10,* 120–122.

Schwartz, G. E., Davidson, R. J., & Maer, F. (1975). Right hemisphere lateralization for emotion in the human brain: Interactions with cognition.
Science, 190, 286–288.

Segalowitz, S. J., & Gruber, F. A. (Eds.) (1977). *Language development and neurological theory*. New York: Academic Press.

Shure, G. H., & Halstead, W. C. (1959). Cerebral lateralization of individual processes. *Psychological Monographs: General and Applied, 72*(12).

Sonnier, I. L. (1992). Hemisphericity as a key to understanding individual
differences. In I. L. Sonnier (Ed.), *Hemisphericity as a key to understanding
individual differences* (pp. 6–8). Springfield, IL: Charles C. Thomas.

Sonnier, I. L., & Goldsmith, J. (1985). The nature of human brain hemispheres:
The basis for some individual differences. In I. L. Sonnier (Ed.), *Methods
and techniques of holistic education* (pp. 17–25). Springfield, IL: Charles C.
Thomas.

Swiercinsky, D. P. (1979). Factorial pattern description and comparison of functional abilities in neuropsychological assessment. *Perceptual and Motor
Skills, 48,* 231–241.

Tous, J. M., Fusté, A., & Vidal, J. (1995). Hemispheric specialization and individual differences in cognitive processing. *Personality and Individual
Differences, 19,* 463–470.

Travers, R. M. W. (1977). *Essentials of learning* (4th ed.). New York: MacMillan.

Vernon, P. A. (1983). Recent findings on the nature of *g*. *Journal of Special
Education, 17,* 389–400.

Vernon, P. A. (1998). From the cognitive to the biological: A sketch of Arthur
Jensen's contributions to the study of *g*. *Intelligence, 26,* 267–271.

Watters, J. J., & English, L. D. (1995). Children's application of simultaneous
and successive processing in inductive and deductive reasoning problems:

Implications for developing scientific reasoning skills. *Journal of Research in Science Teaching, 32,* 699–714.

Wechsler, D. (1939). *The measurement of adult intelligence.* Baltimore, MD: Williams & Wilkins.

Wechsler, D. (1955). *The manual for the Wechsler adult intelligence scale.* New York: The Psychological Corporation.

Wheeler, L., & Reitan, R. M. (1962). The presence and laterality of brain damage predicted from responses to a short aphasia screening test. *Perceptual and Motor Skills, 15,* 783–799.

Willis, W. G. (1985). Successive and simultaneous processing: A note on interpretation. *Journal of Psychoeducational Assessment, 4,* 343–346.

4

Understanding the Etiology of Psychiatric and Neurologic Disorders in Neuropsychiatry

Lawrence C. Hartlage and Rik Carl D'Amato

AGGRESSION, ANXIETY, AMNESIA, cognitive impairment, concentration problems, depression, fatigue, diminished motivation, impaired self control, headaches, personality disorders, psychosis, sexual problems, psychosocial difficulties, and sleep disorders represent but a few conditions that may have either psychiatric or neurologic etiologies (Hall, 1980; Silver, McAllister, & Yudofsky, 2005), differentiation of which can have important implications for diagnosis, treatment, prognosis, and occasionally for forensic issues.

The purpose of this chapter is to consider the etiology of both psychiatric and neurologic disorders and to examine the relationship that both types of disorders have to one another. The chapter begins with a consideration of the historical underpinnings of differential neuropsychological diagnosis, considers progress in the field, and then links current research and related thought to the basis of each disorder, focusing on implications for practice. The chapter concludes with a discussion of the impact of contemporary research on evidence-based practices and offers predictions of what the future may bring for understanding neuropsychiatric and neuropsychological practices.

UNDERSTANDING PSYCHOGENIC AND NEUROLOGIC DISORDERS AS A CONTINUUM

DIFFERENTIATION OF NEUROLOGIC (nerve function problems) verses psychogenic (psychiatric) etiologies of disordered behavior has long been a focus of applied neuropsychology in the United States. In fact, the field of neuropsychiatry emerged from attempts to unite the chasm between psychiatry and neurology, realizing that the enormous complexity of brain disorders could not be explained by research from a single field (D'Amato, Fletcher-Janzen, & Reynolds, 2005). In the years immediately following World War II, there was considerable interest in approaches to segregating postwar adjustment difficulties among veterans according to criteria classified as *functional* as opposed to *organic* (i.e., neurologic) causes, and clinical scales were devised for such purposes so they could be used to efficiently classify patients into groups. At that time, it was common practice to use a single measure for diagnosis and then to use these data to classify an individual as brain damaged or suffering from *organicity,* a unitary syndrome (Hartlage, 1966). While this practice is currently viewed as appalling, at best, it represented state-of-the-art practice at the time (D'Amato et al., 2005; Kolb & Whishaw, 2003). Indeed, when neuroimaging techniques were not sophisticated enough to detect brain abnormalities, neuropsychologists were called upon to document and clarify brain damage. Halstead's pioneering work concerning biological intelligence (Halstead, 1947), and his expanded conceptualizations of brain functioning as a multifaceted phenomenon, were compatible at that time with current approaches to neurological diagnosis. Then, neurological diagnosis addressed specific deficiencies of sensation, perception, and cognitive organization related to specific neurologic substrates of damage involving the central nervous system (Allen, Hulac, & D'Amato, 2005).

It was Halstead's student, Reitan, who refined Halstead's concepts into a comprehensive neuropsychological assessment battery with carefully validated cutting scores, which could reliably differentiate neurologic from psychiatric etiologies (Reitan, 1955a, 1955b, 1956; Reitan & Wolfson, 1985). But Reitan's work was not always well received, and he reported that the field in general was not quick to believe in, or accept a neurobiological basis of behavior (D'Amato et al., 2005;

Reitan & Wolfson, 1985). In the main, clinical neuropsychology was born, developed, and expanded by Reitan and his colleagues (Reitan & Wolfson, 1985), and his neuropsychological batteries were refined to evaluate the complexity of the human brain. For decades clinical neuropsychologists have focused on lesion detection, localization, hemispheric asymmetries, and disorder identification, with some time spent in the area of treatment planning and rehabilitation (Davis, in press). Use of Reitan's battery was remarkably accurate given the availability of instruments at the time (Davis, Johnson, & D'Amato, 2005; Reitan & Wolfson, 1985). Various researchers used the battery and demonstrated how to achieve quite remarkable group differentiation of various psychiatric groups at that time (e.g., see Gray, Dean, D'Amato, & Rattan, 1986). Nonetheless, the role of the neuropsychologist changed rapidly *with the field,* and many neuropsychologists began to practice a more ecological or systemic-based perspective to evaluating patients for behavioral understanding and rehabilitation planning (e.g., D'Amato et al., 2005).

It is quite true that our previous lack of sophistication in brain scanning technology has impeded our knowledge of brain-behavior relations. Kandel (1985) has explained "The boundary between behavior and biology is arbitrary and changing. It has been imposed not by the natural contours of the disciplines, but by lack of knowledge. As our knowledge expands, the biological and behavioral disciplines will merge..." (p. 832). Beginning about 30 years ago, neuroimaging offered a means for researchers to study, in vivo, patients with psychiatric disorders (Ron & Foong, 2003). While previous work could be done via postmortem study, or through consideration of psychogenic signs, this advance changed the face of the field, as well as our understanding of the cause of many disorders. Interestingly, Kaufman (2001) explained that deficits in the violation of the "laws of neuroanatomy" often have suggested the presence of psychogenic disorders, for example, when "temperature sensation is preserved but pain perception is 'lost'" (p. 27). But more recently such an examination has become a less significant part of the overall conceptualization of the patient. It would seem that the best approach to understanding the functioning of the brain is through direct observation of a "living brain" *processing information,* and current technology makes such an examination possible (Davis, in press; Dean, 1986). In essence, we can *watch a brain learn.* With this technological change in our understanding of the brain has come a change in the role of the neurologist, psychiatrist, and clinical neuropsychologist. Clinical neuropsychologists have continued to offer unique information about the structural functioning of the brain and its relationship to behavior (Davis, in press; Dean, 1986). This is critical information, because while two brain scans may look *alike,* the behavioral expression of these two seemingly similar patients could, in actuality, be drastically *different*. Thus, neuropsychologists are needed to understand the behavioral expression of disorders and to help plan rehabilitation services and offer treatment that match such behavioral and emotional needs. While our neuropathological sensitivity via brain scanning is impressive, limitations make the use of such techniques less than ideal for some milder brain disorders (Ron & Foong, 2003). As a result, the role of the neuropsychologist most certainly should not be in jeopardy.

Building on the luxury of some 50 years of new research, and astonishing advances in technology, some have argued that practitioners have been asking and answering the wrong neuropsychological questions (Sattler & D'Amato, 2002a, 2002b). Kolb and Whishaw (2003) have argued that:

> Psychologists are frequently asked to help determine whether patients' behavioral disturbances are 'functional' or 'organic' in nature. In other words, the psychologist is being asked for an opinion on whether the abnormal behavior in a patient can be ascribed to brain dysfunction or to some other 'mental' disorder. This question is clearly inappropriate...the question to ask is not whether or not someone's brain is functioning normally. Normal brain function is hardly a yes-or-no issue. Clinically, it may be more reasonable to ask whether a patient is experiencing neuropsychological deficits that could account for the observed behavioral symptoms, and whether the test profile is suggestive of a particular diagnosis. (p. 810)

FIGURE 4.1 Graphic portrayal of the interactive connection of psychogenic variables to neurologic variables in individual patients.

Brain reprinted by permission of BodyMind Publication from *The Human Brain: Anatomy, Functions, and Injury*, (800) 295-3346.

Recent research supports the view that many psychogenic disorders have clear organic etiology (Davis, in press; Dean, 1985, 1986; Semrud-Clikeman, Portman, & Gerrard-Morris, 2005). This has led present-day authors to advocate for a psychogenic-neurologic continuum of disorders, similar to what has been offered as the autism disorder spectrum (Dean, 1985; Semrud-Clikeman et al., 2005). The need to conceptualize disorders falling within an interactive, circular continuum seems reasonable given our current level of understanding of neuropsychiatric disorders. In fact, the very notion of a disconnected dichotomy with psychogenic at one end, unconnected to neurologic at the other end, seems static, and is not in line with the multidimensional brain-related notions of Reitan (1956) or of Luria (1966, 1980). If conceptualized as an interactive continuum, and not as an *all* or *none* occurrence, this allows neuropsychologists to answer much more than only *yes* or *no* questions regarding brain damage (Dean, 1986). In fact, this makes conceptual sense, because an organic disorder, when untreated (e.g., neurologic depression), often leads to environmental or functional changes. For instance, a child who is depressed often does not interact with friends given his or her depression. This lack of interaction leads to psychosocial changes, where friends no longer invite the child to join their social group activities. Thus, what began as an explicit neurological depression often leads to what can become a functional (psychogenic) disorder. Davis (in press) has viewed the "possible morphological alterations in children with depression" (p. 6) as a powerful finding, explaining that "if consistent organic markers can be found, early and accurate diagnosis can lead to better treatment outcomes" (p. 6). No longer are only structural markers investigated, but changes in areas such as glucose metabolism seem promising (Davis, in press). It is important to note this major shift from brain structure to neurochemical functioning. The longer a patient manifests a psychiatric disorder, the greater the chance of significant neuropsychological involvement (Dean, 1986; Semrud-Clikeman, Kamphaus, Teeter, & Vaughn, 1997).

Even when an obvious neurological insult is present, it becomes difficult to distinguish the behavior related to the physiological changes of the brain from the anxiety and distress associated with changes in functioning as recognized by the patient (Dean, 1986). Add to this mix the presence of psychotropic medication with related side effects, and the unique features of the patient and his or her disorder obviously become obscured. This leaves practitioners and researchers alike in a diagnostic quandary. Dean (1986) explains that "this in no way, of course, lessens the six times greater risk of emotional disturbance for brain-damaged children than that found with normals" (p. 85). While the specific cause of various neuropsychiatric disorders continues to be examined using our advanced technology, and progress is quite

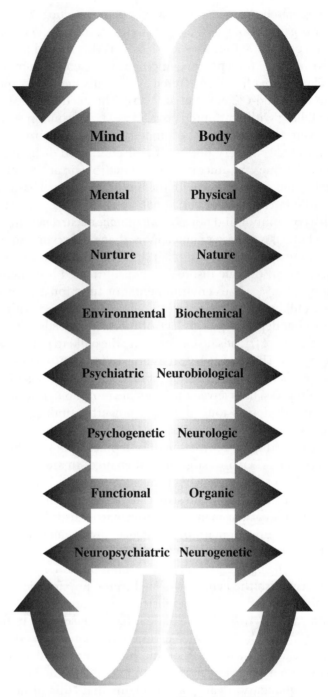

FIGURE 4.2 Visual display of the words used to describe the interactive psychogenic-neurologic continuum.

apparent, the complexity of the brain makes the study of the underlying etiology of disorders an arduous and multifarious pursuit (Luria, 1966, 1980; Shaywitz, 2003).

EXAMINING BIOCHEMICAL, ANATOMICAL, AND GENETIC MODELS OF NEUROPSYCHIATRIC DISORDERS

TEETER AND SEMRUD-CLIKEMAN (1997) argue convincingly for a variety of the mechanisms that make up the biochemical base of neuropsychiatric disorders. Specifically, they have focused on the neurochemical processes, considering their role in brain functioning, in light of the three major neurotransmitters (i.e., serotonin, dopamine, and norepinephrine). Neurotransmitters are not evenly distributed in the brain and appear in different concentrations in various regions of the brain (e.g., frontal lobes). Because "neurotransmitters are part of the electrochemical mechanisms by which neurons communicate to initiate, regulate, and inhibit simple and complex activities" (Teeter & Semrud-Clikeman, 1997, p. 107), neurotransmitters are important if one is to understand psychological behavior in general, and psychiatric disorders, specifically (Comings, 1990). Many researchers (Kolb & Whishaw, 2003; Semrud-Clikeman et al., 2005; Teeter & Semrud-Clikeman, 1997) have noted the over- or under-abundance of neurotransmitters that are present in many neuropsychiatric disorders, including patients with Tourette syndrome, attention-deficit/hyperactivity disorder, schizophrenia, depression, anxiety, and obsessive-compulsive disorders (OCD). These researchers also have discussed the effect of psychotropic medication on neurotransmitters and behavior. Such models are complicated by the fact that frontal lobe dysfunction is also found in many neuropsychiatric disorders. While they make clear that our level of understanding of much of this literature is only just beginning, the future of our practice, which should have a strong focus on evidence-based treatment, seems related to an accurate view of the etiology of each disorder (Kubiszyn, 2005; Traughber & D'Amato, 2005).

In addition, Harrison and Gittins (2003) have reported numerous cytoarchitectural abnormalities in patients with neuropsychiatric disorders. These include decreases in the number or density of glia, reduced size and density of neurons, and dendritic and synaptic alterations. Studies with children manifesting depression have implicated unique features related to specific areas of the brain including decreased cerebral activity and lower nonverbal reasoning skills (Bishop, Dalgleish, & Yule, 2004; Liotti & Mayberg, 2001; Semrud-Clikeman et al., 2005). Likewise, research focusing on children with autism and on children with seizure disorders both show neuropsychological abnormalities (Clark & Christiansen, 2005; D'Amato et al., 2005; Dawson, Webb, Carver, Panagiotides, & McPartland, 2004; Lee, Meador, Loring, & Bradley, 2002). With children falling within the autism spectrum, research has suggested a great variety of brain-related dysfunction, including hemispheric difficulties, cerebellar and brainstem problems, cortical-subcortical integration, abnormal gyri patterns, increased posterior region brain size, increased ventrical size, cerebellar abnormalities, and a smaller corpus callosum, excessive white matter, little use of the amygdala area, and genetic abnormalities (Hale & Fiorello, 2004; Kolb & Whishaw, 2003). Even though twin studies show a genetic influence, some argue for the influence of industrial toxins and viruses, however, brainstem abnormalities have also been implicated (Kolb & Whishaw, 2003). In other disorders, early coordination problems have been related to a later anxiety-withdrawal diagnosis, and linguistic deficits seem linked to child anxiety disorders (Semrud-Clikeman et al., 2005). Some have found that children with a hyperkinetic disorder suffer from general deficits of attentional orienting and response preparation problems indicating the possible involvement of a dysregulation of the central noradrenergic networks (Banaschewski et al., 2003). Again, an understanding of genetic factors may be critical to understanding the complexity of each individual patient (e.g., see Kolb & Whishaw, 2003). While environmental factors such as family support, peer pressure, and individualized help from others continue to be vital if a patient's level of psychological functioning is to be understood or predicted (D'Amato, Rothlisberg, & Leu Work, 1999), it is clear that environmental variables interact with neurobiological functioning to make each patient and the outcome of his or her recovery unique. Researchers now advocate that aberrant neurodevelopment is central to the case of disorders such as schizophrenia (Ron & Foong, 2003). Only recently has brain scanning research began to seriously investigate the cause of some of these disorders, with the hope that new information will lead to early diagnosis and treatment (Davis, in press), as well as to prevention.

Researchers have attempted to apply some of these notions to clinical practice. For instance, in the field of behavioral psychology, Davis (in press) has explained that the reason positive rewards are more effective for behavioral change than negative rewards relates to our neurological basis of behavior. It seems that positive rewards activated more areas of the brain than negative rewards. So too, impairment in frontal lobe functioning was related to planning problems, which Davis (in press) used to explain why behavior plans often do not work well with children suffering from emotional disturbance. Similar findings were offered by Bjoraker (2001), who found neuropsychologically based communication problems in children suffering from emotional disturbances. While it is difficult to derive clinical practices from many of these studies, such attempts are needed if we are to develop evidence-based neuropsychological practices (Traughber & D'Amato, 2005).

Historically, psychiatric disorders were viewed as a result of inappropriate parenting, environmental distress, or the influence of other psychosocial variables, whereas neurological disorders were viewed as medically or biologically based disorders. Of late, the biochemical foundation of both types of disorders has been developing at a rapid rate. Hale and Fiorello (2004) have argued that in neuropsychiatric disorders:

> The frontal-subcortical circuits can affect an individual's interest in the environment, with overarousal resulting in a tendency toward withdrawal (e.g., 'Everything is too over-whelming; I need to avoid others') and underarousal associated with approach behaviors (e.g., 'Everything is boring; I need to approach others'). (p. 249)

These authors also relate cortical underarousal to disorders like conduct disorders and cortical overarousal to disorders like depression. Davis (in press) advocates that violent, aggressive, and antisocial behaviors can be traced to neuroanatomical differences when patients are compared to controls—differences such as frontal lobe function problems. At the same time, Hale and Fiorello (2004) caution that comorbidity between disorders is so high that it makes clear diagnosis and treatment extremely difficult and challenging. It is apparent that contemporary ecological neuropsychiatric diagnostic procedures must cover a number of brain-based *systems* (e.g., communication, sensory, motor, cognitive, environment fit, etc.), *contexts* (e.g., family, community, peers, motivations), and *settings* (e.g., home, school), while concomitantly considering information from several *sources* (e.g., parents, teachers, adult, peers) using various *methods* (e.g., interviews, self reports, objective and projective measures, and behavioral procedures; D'Amato, Crepeau-Hobson, et al., 2005; Sattler & D'Amato, 2002a, 2002b).

As previously discussed, many researchers have studied the relationship between brain dysfunction and psychopathology (D'Amato et al., 2005; Rutter, 1977, 1983; Tramontana & Hooper, 1997). Does brain dysfunction lead to psychopathology? Do certain responses to individual's with traumatic brain injuries (TBI) cause additional brain impairment? While it is clear that many disorders have a biochemical, anatomical, or genetic base (Kolb & Whishaw, 2003), Tramontana and Hooper have explored this notion further and recapitulated, asking six questions that provide insight regarding when brain dysfunction *may* lead to psychopathology. These six questions include:

> (1) behavioral disruption that arises directly from abnormal brain activity; (2) a heightened exposure to failure, frustration, and social stigma related to associated disabilities; (3) the possible effects of brain damage on subsequent temperament and personality development; (4) adverse

family reactions ranging from overprotection to scapegoating; (5) the children's own reaction to being handicapped and its effects on his or her actual capacity to cope and compete; and (6) possible adverse effects from treatment themselves (e.g., recurrent hospitalization) that may restrict normal activities and socialization. (p. 125)

While the causes of brain damage to patients are numerous, closed head injury would seem to have the most "direct link" between structural brain lesions and emotional disorders (Gainotti, 2003, p. 371) and would require specialized intervention (D'Amato et al., 1999; Rothlisberg, D'Amato, & Palencia, 2002).

TABLE 4.1   Emotional Problems Related to TBI

Agitation
Anger
Anxiety
Behavioral control
Delusions
Depression
Emotional lability
Emotionality related to academic variability
Emotionality related to neuropsychological variability
Fatigue
Hypersensitivity
Immature behavior
Impulsiveness
Inappropriate social responses
Irritability
Loss of interest in sex
Loss of motivation
Low frustration tolerance
Low self-esteem
Mania
Over-arousal problems
Over-interest in sex
Paranoia
Poor planning
Relentlessness
Resistance to change
Social isolation
Suspiciousness
Under-arousal problems
Violence

Note: Adapted from Prigatano (1992), Semrud-Clikeman et al. (1997), and Semrud-Clikeman et al. (2005).

TRAUMATIC BRAIN INJURY OR PSYCHOGENIC DISORDER?

IN CONTEMPORARY NEUROPSYCHOLOGY, reflecting independent trends in neurology and law, there is substantial interest in identifying the etiology of adjustment problems resulting from a TBI. Advances in medical science have dramatically increased survival rates among victims of TBI, and legal attention to liability issues involving TBIs in both personal injury and workers' compensation cases has challenged neuropsychology to develop refinements in assessment procedures that can segregate and apportion behavior problems directly attributable to a given trauma from those problems representing either pre-injury conditions or adjustment difficulties of nonneurologic etiology. This has proven to be a challenge of considerable magnitude, insofar as many adjustment problems resulting from TBI share many features similar if not identical to adjustment problems referable to either innate biological disorders or to stress of social interactions and interpersonal relationships. Because mild head trauma and its sequalae represents the single most common etiology seen by neuropsychologists (Rabin, Barr, & Burton, 2005), and second only to migraine headaches in prevalence among disorders seen by neurologists (Alexander, 1995), it is appropriate to review factors that tend to obscure or obfuscate its assessment as etiologic in a marker of presenting complaints. Further, because mild TBI is the most common etiology, representing at least 80% of all TBIs, it merits special attention (Anderson & McLaurin, 1980; Miller & Jones, 1985). It is probably safe to assume that the majority of mild TBIs are neither detected nor even suspected (Hartlage, 1997; Zasler, 1993). A number of factors contribute to this problematic situation (Segalowitz & Brown, 1991). Perhaps of primary importance in the under-recognition of mild TBI is the fact that loss of consciousness is not necessary for brain injury to occur (Hartlage, 1997; Iverson, Lovell, & Smith, 2001; Zasler, 1993).

A closely associated point involves the fact that the head does not necessarily need to be struck in order for acceleration or deceleration brain injuries to occur (Hartlage & Rattan, 1992). As Varney and Varney (1995) have documented, significant brain injury can occur in, for example, motor vehicle accidents where there was no evidence of contact between the head and the vehicle. Similar to *shaken baby syndrome* (Caffey, 1974), it has been suggested that any cervical injury in an auto accident be viewed as a clue that a TBI may have occurred (Domer, Chandran & Krieger, 1979; Linn, Allen, & Willer, 1994). Another important factor involves the progressive nature of neurobehavioral problems, in that initial axonal changes resultant from mild TBI become progressively severe, with axonal injury in humans representing an evolutionary process (Christman, Grady, & Povlishock, 1992; Hartlage, 1997; Kontos, Wei, & Povlishock, 1980; Povlishock, Becker, Cheng, & Vaughn, 1983). There is a compelling body of basic science literature documenting progressive deterioration in brain function following concussion related to vascular/ischemic changes (e.g., Doberstein, Velarde, Badie, & Hovda, 1992; Hovda, Katayama, Yoshino, Kawamata, & Becker, 1992; Jenkins, Marmarou, Lewelt, & Becker, 1986; Katayama, Becker, Tamura, & Hovda, 1990; Kawamata, Katayama, Hovda, Yoshino, & Becker, 1992; Lee, Lifshitz, Hovda, & Becker, 1995; Lifshitz et al., 1995; Muizelaar, 1989; Sutton, Hovda, Adelson, Benzel, & Becker, 1994; Yamakami & McIntosh, 1989). Bigler (2001) has provided an elegant description of the neurological changes following TBI, and Hartlage and his associates have documented longitudinal neurobehavioral problems presenting at different stages following TBI (Hartlage, Durant-Wilson, & Patch, 2001; Patch & Hartlage, 2003). While Gisi and D'Amato (2000) found that individuals suffering from TBI displayed less stress in their lives if they scored higher on a forgiveness scale, and Prentiss, D'Amato, Davis, and Softas-Nall (2000) found that families were provided inadequate information and insufficient services regarding their children suffering from TBI, it is clear that many life changing problems remained chronic and severe.

Even more impediments to recognizing mild TBI resulting from accidents are the obvious physical injuries, which clearly are more noticeable and receive greater attention (Hartlage & Patch, 2003): Glasgow Coma Scale scores in the *normal* range can mask significant brain injury (Zasler, 1993); CT scan findings are often *normal* in cases of mild TBI (Tsushima & Popper, 1980; Tshusima & Wedding, 1979; Zasler, 1993); and many patients who incur mild TBIs do not seek medical attention (Zasler, 1993). Adding even further likelihood to mild TBI being overlooked is the popular recognition (enhanced by seeing NFL quarterbacks concussed and shortly thereafter returning to apparently intact playing status) that the majority of patients with mild TBI tend to make a full and quick recovery. Because of this, the approximately 15 to 20% of patients with mild or severely handicapping residua are faced with skepticism and disbelief (Alexander, 1995; Dacey, Alves, Rimel, Winn, & Jane, 1986; Gentilini, Nichelli, & Schoenhuber, 1989; Hartlage, 1997; Hatcher, Johnson, & Walker, 1996; Kurtzke & Kurland, 1993).

To be sure, the neuropsychiatric literature has documented depression as a remote sequel of even mild TBI for decades following the head injury (e.g., Busch & Alpern, 1998; Fann, Katon, Uomoto, & Esselman, 1995; Holsinger et al., 2002; Linn, Allen, & Willer, 1994; Rosenthal, Christenson, & Ross, 1998; Van Reekum, Chen, & Wong, 2000).

Current research (Killam, Cautin, & Santucci, 2005) has confirmed that even participation in sports such as hockey, lacrosse, and soccer, without history of concussion, produces subclinical cognitive impairments, presumably produced by multiple mild head trauma short of a concussion level injury. This research extends prior findings of unsuspectedly high levels of undiagnosed brain injury among both high school and collegiate athletes (e.g., Guskiewicz, Weaver, Palua, & Garrett, 2000; McKeever & Shatz, 2003; Moser & Shatz, 2002; Rutherford, Stephens, & Potter, 2003).

Accumulating evidence documenting the high incidence of undiagnosed brain injury, and the relationship of such brain injury to a range of neurocognitive and neurobehavioral disorders (Alexander, 1995; Anderson & McLaurin, 1980; Annegers, Grabow, Kurland, & Laws, 1980; Annegers & Kurland, 1979; Caveness, 1979; Centers for Disease Control, 1999; Frankowski, 1986; Gentilini, Nichelli, & Schoenhuber, 1989; Golden & Golden, 2003; Hartlage, 1990, 1991, 1999; Hatcher, Johnson, & Walker, 1996; Klonoff & Thompson, 1969; Krauss, 1980; Kurtzke & Kurland, 1993; Lishman, 1988; Montgomery, Fenton, McClelland, MacFlynn, & Rutherford, 1991; Rapoport, McCullagh, Shamin, & Feinstein, 2005; Rapoport, McCullagh, Streiner, & Feinstein, 2003; Sorenson & Krauss, 1991; Strong, 2005a, 2005b) has been paralleled by a resurgence of interest in the search for possible neurological substrates of behavior disorders and a shift away from traditional psychodynamic and psychosocial etiological explanations. Two major factors have contributed to this shift: the emergence of advanced and sensitive neuroimaging techniques allowing the study of brain metabolic substrates of disordered behavior, and the concurrent emergence of neuropsychological sophistication and involvement in sensitive and precise measurement of such disorders.

As additional evidence of such a shift, borderline personality disorder has recently been associated with damage to the brain (Driessen et al. 2000; Strong, 2005b; Van Reekum, Conway, Ganslen, White, & Bachman, 1993; Van Reekum et al., 1996), especially with damage to the frontal cortical areas, involving the orbital frontal system. Further combined neuroimaging and neuropsychological research has addressed the neuroanatomy of personality. As Rankin and colleagues (Rankin, Baldwin, Pace-Savitsky, Kramer, & Miller, 2005) observed, it is now possible to correlate abnormal personality changes with specific brain regions. With such techniques as voxel-based morphometry and neuropsychology, personality factors can now be studied in relation to specific brain areas (Balzac, 2005). This shift is noticeable both in the tendency toward classifying schizophrenia as a *brain disease* rather than resultant from *schizophrenogenic mothering* or social determinants and also in a shift toward treating depression as a symptom of impaired brain function rather than as a reaction to environmental pressures (Fisch, 2003; Leboyer & Belliver, 2003; Schmidt & Reith, 2005). For example, the *American Psychiatric Publishing Textbook* (Yudofsky & Hales, 2002) focuses on what the brain has to do with psychopathology, and books and chapters about neuroimaging are being written for psychiatrists and psychologists (e.g., Dougherty, Rauch, & Rosenbaum, 2004; Provencal & Bigler, 2005).

Each day, additional evidence is added to the corpus of research concerning neuropsychiatric disorders (Davis, in press). This chapter has argued for the consideration of neuropsychiatric disorders falling along a continuum, with neurologic causation at one end and psychogenic causation at the other. While disorders may occasionally fall at one end or the other, typically patient disorders will fall in the middle and encompass components of both ends of what we had advocated as a connected continuum. Even recently, it was improbable that we would soon be able to watch live brains learn. After advocating for a neurologic foundation for most neuropsychiatric disorders, O'Carroll (2003) posits that:

> The neuropsychological study of psychiatric disorders is still in its infancy. As C. D. Frith (1992, p. 28) stated in a commentary on a paper on a neuropsychological model of schizophrenia, 'A few years ago articles of this sort would have been unthinkable'.... Exciting novel attempts to explain abnormal behavior in terms of dysfunctional information processing are rapidly being developed. However, it is critical that such models are explicitly amenable to experimental testing and refutation. Only then will significant advances be made in our scientific understanding of abnormal experience.... Demonstrating that a particular patient or patient group has abnormal regional brain metabolism, or a specific cognitive deficit is of interest, but it does not provide a causal explanation of abnormal behavior or experience. In most instances we still await truly convincing neuropsychological explanations of psychopathological states. (pp. 628–629)

With our current rate of research, it would seem logical that, in the next decade, a clear foundation for most neuropsychiatric disorders will be demonstrated. Davis (in press) has argued that researchers may soon identify morphological markers of some disorders, which could appear before clinical symptoms, allowing practitioners to shift from providing tertiary treatments to primary prevention activities. But many challenges make such discovery difficult. In most neuropsychiatric disorders, brain lesions and localized brain damage are rare, and understanding disorders in light of abnormalities of brain systems seems to be paramount (Davis, in press; Dean, 1985, 1986; O'Carroll, 2003). Only evidence accumulated over time will be able to answer such questions.

REFERENCES

Alexander, M. D. (1995). Mild traumatic brain injury: Pathophysiology, natural history, and clinical management. *Neurology, 45,* 1253–1260.

Allen, T. R., Jr., Hulac, D., & D'Amato, R. C. (2005). The pediatric neurological examination and school neuropsychology. In R. C. D'Amato, E. Fletcher-Janzen, & C. R. Reynolds (Eds.), *The handbook of school neuropsychology* (pp. 145–171). New York: Wiley.

Anderson, D. W., & McLaurin, R. L. (1980). The national head and spinal cord injury survey. *Journal of Neurosurgery, 53,* S1–S43.

Annegers, J. F., Grabow, J. D., Kurland, L. T., & Laws, E. R. (1980). The incidence, causes, and secular trends of head trauma in Olmstead County, Minnesota. *Neurology, 30,* 912–919.

Annegers, J. F., & Kurland, L. T. (1979). The epidemiology of central nervous system trauma. In G. L. Odom (Ed.), *Central nervous system trauma research status report, 1979* (pp. 1–8). Durham, NC: Duke University Press.

Balzac, F. (2005). The neuroanatomy of personality. *Neurology Reviews, 61,* 16–22.

Banaschewski, T., Brandes, D., Heinrich, H., Allbrecht, B., Brummer, E., & Rothenberger, A. (2003). Association of ADHD and conduct disorder—brain electrical evidence for the existence of a distinct subtype. *Journal of Child Psychology and Psychiatry, 44*(3), 356–376.

Bigler, E. D. (2001). The lesion(s) in traumatic brain injury: Implications for clinical neuropsychology. *Archives of Clinical Neuropsychology, 16,* 95–131.

Bishop, S. J., Dalgleish, T., & Yule, W. (2004). Memory for emotional stories in high and low depressed children. *Memory, 12,* 214–230.

Bjoraker, K. J. (2001). *An examination of the neuropsychological basis of emotional disabilities in children.* Unpublished dissertation, University of Northern Colorado, Greeley, CO.

Busch, C. R., & Alpern, H. (1998). Depression after mild traumatic brain injury: A review of current research. *Neuropsychology Review, 8*(2), 95–99.

Caffey, J. (1974). The whiplash shaken infant syndrome. *Pediatrics, 54,* 396–403.

Caveness, W. F. (1979). Incidence of cranio-cerebral trauma in the United States. *Transactions of the American Neurological Association, 102,* 136–138.

Centers for Disease Control. (1999). *Traumatic brain injury in the United States: A report to Congress.* Washington, DC: Centers for Disease Control.

Christman, C. W., Grady, M. S., & Povlishock, J. T. (1992). Electron microscopic immunocytochemical study of diffuse axonal injury in man. *Neuroscience Abstracts, 18,* 1,088.

Clark, E., & Christiansen, E. (2005). Neurological and psychological issues for learners with seizures. In R. C. D'Amato, E. Fletcher-Janzen, & C. R. Reynolds (Eds.), *The handbook of school neuropsychology* (pp. 444–459). New York: Wiley.

Comings, D. E. (1990). *Tourette syndrome and human behavior.* Durante, CA: Hope Press.

Dacey, R. G., Alves, W. M., Rimel, R. W., Winn, H. R., & Jane, J. A. (1986). Neurosurgical complications after apparently minor head injury. *Journal of Neurosurgery, 65,* 203–210.

D'Amato, R. C., Fletcher-Janzen, E., & Reynolds, C. R. (Eds.). (2005). *The handbook of school neuropsychology.* New York: Wiley.

D'Amato, R. C., Rothlisberg, B. A., & Leu Work, P. H. (1999). Neuropsychological assessment for intervention. In T. B. Gutkin & C. R. Reynolds (Eds.), *Handbook of school psychology* (3rd ed., pp. 452–475). New York: Wiley.

Davis, A. S. (in press). The neuropsychological basis of childhood psychopathology. *Psychology in the Schools.*

Davis, A. S., Johnson, J. A., & D'Amato, R. C. (2005). Evaluating and using longstanding school neuropsychological batteries: The Halstead-Reitan and the Luria-Nebraska Neuropsychological Batteries. In R. C. D'Amato, E. Fletcher-Janzen, & C. R. Reynolds (Eds.), *The handbook of school neuropsychology* (pp. 236–263). New York: Wiley.

Dawson, G., Webb, S. J., Carver, L., Panagiotides, H., & McPartland, J. (2004). Young children with autism show atypical brain response to fearful versus neutral facial expressions of emotion. *Developmental Science, 7*(3), 340–359.

Dean, R. S. (1985). Foundation and rationale for neuropsychological basis of individual differences. In L. C. Hartlage & C. F. Telzrom (Eds.), *Neuropsychology of individual differences* (pp. 7–40). New York: Plenum Press.

Dean, R. S. (1986). Neuropsychological aspects of psychiatric disorders. In J. E. Obrzut & G. W. Hynd (Eds.), *Child neuropsychology: Clinical practice* (Vol. 2, pp. 83–112). New York: Academic Press.

Doberstein, C., Velarde, F., Badie, H., & Hovda, D. A. (1992) Changes in local cerebral blood flow following concussive brain injury. *Society for Neuroscience, 18,* 175.

Domer, F. R., Chandran, K. B., & Krieger, K. W. (1979). The effect of hyperextension-hyperflexion (whiplash) on the function of the blood-brain barrier of rhesus monkeys. *Experimental Neurology, 63,* 304–309.

Dougherty, D. D., Rauch, S. L., & Rosenbaum, J. E. (2004). *Essentials of neuroimaging for clinical practice.* Arlington, VA: American Psychiatric Publishing.

Driessen, M., Hermann, J., Stahl, K., Zwann, M., Meier, S., Hill, A., et al. (2000). Magnetic resonance imaging volumes of the hippocampus and the amygdale in women with borderline personality disorder and early traumatization. *Archives of General Psychiatry, 57,* 1115–1122.

Fann, J. R., Katon, W. J., Uomoto, J. M., & Esselman, P. C. (1995). Psychiatric disorders and functional disability in outpatients with traumatic brain injury. *American Journal of Psychiatry, 152,* 1493–1499.

Fisch, G. S. (2003). *Genetics and genomics of neurobehavioral disorders.* Towata, NJ: Humana Press.

Frankowski, R. F. (1986). Descriptive epidemiological studies of head injury in the United States 1974–1984. *Advances in Psychosomatic Medicine, 16,* 153–172.

Frith, C. D. (1992). *The cognitive neuropsychology of schizophrenia.* Hove, U.K.: Lawrence Erlbaum.

Gainotti, G. (2003). Assessment and treatment of emotional disorders. In P. W. Halligan, U. Kischka, & J. C. Marshall (Eds.), *Handbook of clinical neuropsychology* (pp. 368–386). Oxford: Oxford Press.

Gentilini, M., Nichelli, P., & Schoenhuber, R. (1989). Assessment of attention in mild head injury. In H. S. Levin, H. M. Eisenberg, & A. L. Benton (Eds.), *Mild head injury* (pp. 163–175). New York: Oxford University Press.

Gisi, T. M., & D'Amato, R. C. (2000). What factors should be considered in rehabilitation: Are anger, social desirability, and forgiveness related in adults with traumatic brain injuries? *International Journal of Neuroscience, 105,* 121–133.

Golden, Z., & Golden, C. J. (2003). Impact of brain injury severity and personality dysfunction. *International Journal of Neuroscience, 113,* 733–745.

Gray, J. W., Dean, R. S., D'Amato, R. C., & Rattan, G. (1986). Differential diagnosis of primary affective depression using the Halstead-Reitan Neuropsychological Battery. *The International Journal of Neuroscience, 35,* 43–49.

Guskiewicz, K. M., Weaver, N. L., Palua, D. A., & Garrett, W. (2000). Epidemiology of concussion in collegiate and high school football players. *American Journal of Sport Medicine, 28,* 643–650.

Hale, J. B., & Fiorello, C. A. (2004). *School neuropsychology: A practitioner's handbook.* New York: Guilford.

Hall, R. C. (Ed.). (1980). *Psychiatric presentations of medical illness.* New York: Spectrum.

Halstead, W. C. (1947). *Brain and intelligence.* Chicago: University of Chicago Press.

Harrison, P. J., & Gittins, R. (2003). The neuropathology of mood disorders. In M. A. Ron & T. W. Robbins (Eds.), *Disorders of the brain and mind 2* (pp. 291–307). New York: Cambridge University Press.

Hartlage, L. C. (1966). Common psychological tests applied to the assessment of brain damage. *Journal of Projective Techniques and Personality Assessment, 30,* 319–338.

Hartlage, L. C. (1990). *Neuropsychological evaluation of head injury.* Sarasota, FL: Professional Resource Exchange.

Hartlage, L. C. (1991). Major legal implications of minor head injuries. *The Journal of Head Injury, 2*(3), 8–11.

Hartlage, L. C. (1997). Forensic aspects of mild brain injury. *Applied Neuropsychology, 4,* 69–74.

Hartlage, L. C. (1999). Forensic aspects of mild traumatic brain injury. In M. I. Raymond, T. L. Bennet, L. C. Hartlage, & C. M. Cullum (Eds.), *Mild traumatic brain injury* (pp. 135–142). Austin, TX: Pro-Ed.

Hartlage, L. C., Durant-Wilson, D., & Patch, P. C. (2001). Persistent neurobehavioral problems following mild traumatic brain injury. *Archives of Clinical Neuropsychology, 16,* 561–570.

Hartlage, L. C., & Patch, P. C. (2003). Epidemiology of traumatic brain injury. In M. A. Horton & L. C. Hartlage (Eds.), *Handbook of forensic neuropsychology* (pp. 181–193). New York: Springer Publishing.

Hartlage, L. C., & Rattan, G. (1992). Brain injury from motor vehicle accidents. In D. Templer, L. Hartlage, & W. Cannon (Eds.), *Preventable brain damage: Brain vulnerability and brain health*. New York: Springer Publishing.

Hatcher, L., Johnson, C. C., & Walker, J. M. (1996). *More than just a bump on the head: About concussions; mild traumatic brain injuries*. Atlanta: Pritchett & Hull.

Holsinger, T., Steffins, D. C., Phillips, C., Helms, M. J., Havlik, R. J., Breitner, J. C., et al. (2002). Head injury in early adulthood and the lifetime risk of depression. *Archives of General Psychiatry, 59,* 17–23.

Hovda, D. A., Katayama, Y., Yoshino, A., Kawamata, T., & Becker, D. P. (1992). Pre or postsynaptic blocking of glutamatergic functioning prevents the increase in glucose utilization following concussive brain injury. In M. Globus & W. D. Dietrich (Eds.), *The role of neurotransmitters in brain injury* (pp. 327–332). New York: Plenum Press.

Iverson, G. L., Lovell, M. R., & Smith, S. S. (2001). Does brief loss of consciousness affect cognitive functioning after head injury? *Archives of Clinical Neuropsychology, 15,* 643–648.

Jenkins, L. W., Marmarou, A., Lewelt, W., & Becker, D. P. (1986). Increased vulnerability of the traumatized brain to early ischemia. In A. Baethmann, G. K. Go, & A. Unterberg (Eds.), *Mechanisms of secondary brain damage* (pp. 273–282). New York: Springer Publishing.

Kandel, E. R. (1985). Cellular mechanisms of learning and the biological basis of individuality. In E. R. Kandel & J. H. Schwartz (Eds.), *Principles of neural science* (2nd ed., pp. 816–833). New York: Academia Press.

Katayama, Y., Becker, D. P., Tamura, T., & Hovda, D. A. (1990). Massive increases in extra cellular potassium and the indiscriminate release of glutamate following concussive brain injury. *Journal of Neurosurgery, 73,* 889–900.

Kaufman, D. M. (2001). *Clinical neurology for psychiatrists*. New York: W. B. Saunders.

Kawamata, T., Katayama, Y., Hovda, D. A., Yoshino, A., & Becker, D. P. (1992). Administration of excitatory amino acid antagonists via microdialysis attenuates the increase in glucose utilization seen following concussive brain injury. *Journal of Cerebral Blood Flow Metabolism, 12,* 12–24.

Killam, C., Cautin, R. L., & Santucci, A. C. (2005). Assessing the enduring residual neuropsychological effects of head trauma in college athletes who participate in contact sports. *Archives of Clinical Neuropsychology, 20,* 599–611.

Klonoff, H., & Thompson, G. B. (1969). Epidemiology of head injuries in adults. *Canadian Medical Association Journal, 100,* 235–241.

Kolb, B., & Whishaw, I. Q. (2003). *Fundamentals of human neuropsychology* (5th ed.). New York: Worth.

Kontos, H. A., Wei, E. P., & Povlishock, J. T. (1980). Pathophsyiology of vascular consequences of experimental concussive brain injury. *Clinics Association Transactions, 92,* 111.

Krauss, J. F. (1980). Injury to the head and spinal cord. The epidemiological relevance of the medical literature 1960–1978. *Journal of Neurosurgery, 53,* 53–59.

Kubiszyn, T. (2005). Special issue: Findings of the Division 16 task force on psychopharmacology, learning, and behavior. *School Psychology Quarterly, 20*(2), 115–221.

Kurtzke, J. F., & Kurland, L. T. (1993). The epidemiology of neurologic disease. In R. J. Joynt (Ed.), *Clinical neurology* (pp. 66–89). Philadelphia: J. B. Lippincott.

Leboyer, M., & Belliver, F. (2003). *Psychiatric genetics.* Towata, NJ: Humana Press.

Lee, G. P., Meador, K. J., Loring, D. W., & Bradley, K. P. (2002). Lateralized changes in autonomic arousal during emotional processing in patients with unilateral temporal lobe seizures onset. *International Journal of Neuroscience, 112,* 743–752.

Lee, S. M., Lifshitz, J., Hovda, D. A., & Becker, D. P. (1995). Focal cortical-impact injury produces immediate and persistent deficits in metabolic autoregulation [Abstract]. *Journal of Cerebral Blood Flow Metabolism, 7,* 22.

Lifshitz, J., Pinanong, P., Le, H. M., Lee, S. M., Hovda, D. A., & Becker, D. P. (1995). Regional uncoupling of cerebral blood flow and metabolism in degenerating cortical areas following a lateral cortical contusion [Abstract]. *Journal of Neurotrauma, 12,* 129.

Linn, R. T., Allen, K., & Willer, B. S. (1994). Affective symptoms in the chronic stage of traumatic brain injury. *Brain Injury, 8,* 135–147.

Liotti, M., & Mayberg, H. S. (2001). The role of functional neuroimaging in the neuropsychology of depression. *Journal of Clinical and Experimental Neuropsychology, 23,* 121–136.

Lishman, W. A. (1988). Physiogenesis and psychogenesis in the "post-concussional syndrome." *British Journal of Psychiatry, 353,* 460–469.

Luria, A. R. (1966). *Human brain and psychological processes.* New York: Harper & Row.

Luria, A. R. (1980). *Higher cortical functions in man* (2nd ed.). New York: Basic Books.

McKeever, C. K., & Shatz, P. (2003). Current issues in identification, assessment, and management of concussions in sports related injuries. *Applied Neuropsychology, 10,* 4–11.

Miller, J. D., & Jones, P. A. (1985). The work of a regional head injury service. *Lancet, 1,* 1141.

Montgomery, E. A., Fenton, G. W., McClelland, R. J., MacFlynn, G., & Rutherford, W. H. (1991). The psychobiology of minor head injury. *Psychological Medicine, 21,* 375–384.

Moser, R. S., & Shatz, P. (2002). Enduring effects of concussions in youth athletes. *Archives of Clinical Neuropsychology, 17,* 91–100.

Muizelaar, J. P. (1989). Cerebral blood flow, cerebral blood volume, and cerebral metabolism after severe head injury. In D. P. Becker & S. K. Gudeman (Eds.), *Textbook of head injury* (pp. 221–240). Philadelphia: W. B. Saunders.

O'Carroll, R. (2003). The clinical presentation of neuropsychiatric disorders. In P. W. Halligan, U. Kischka, & J. C. Marshall (Eds.), *Handbook of clinical neuropsychology* (pp. 609–673). Oxford: Oxford Press.

Patch, P. C., & Hartlage, L. C. (2003). Behavioral changes following traumatic brain injury. In A. Horton & L. Hartlage (Eds.), *Handbook of forensic neuropsychology* (pp. 215–235). New York: Springer Publishing.

Povlishock, J. T., Becker, D. P., Cheng, C. L., & Vaughn, G. W. (1983). Axonal change in minor head injury. *Journal of Neuropathology and Experimental Neurology, 42,* 225.

Prentiss, D., D'Amato, R. C., Davis, A. S., & Softas-Nall, L. (2000). What can we learn from parents of brain-injured children and their families? [Research Abstract]. *Archives of Clinical Neuropsychology, 15*(8), 794–795.

Prigatano, G. P. (1992). Personality disturbances associated with traumatic brain injury. *Journal of Consulting and Clinical Psychology, 60,* 360–368.

Provencal, S. L., & Bigler, E. D. (2005). Behavioral neuroimaging: What is it and what does it tell us? In R. C. D'Amato, E. Fletcher-Janzen, & C. R. Reynolds (Eds.), *The handbook of school neuropsychology* (pp. 327–364). New York: Wiley.

Rabin, L. A., Barr, W. B., & Burton, L. A. (2005). Assessment practices of clinical neuropsychologists in the United States and Canada: A survey of INS, NAN, and APA Divide 40 workers. *Archives of Clinical Neuropsychology, 20,* 33–65.

Rankin, K. P., Baldwin, E., Pace-Savitsky, C., Kramer, J. H., & Miller, B. L. (2005). Self awareness and personality change in dementia. *Journal of Neurology, Neurosurgery and Psychiatry, 76,* 632–639.

Rapoport, M. J., McCullagh, S., Shamin, P., & Feinstein, A. (2005). Cognitive impairment associated with major depression following mild and moderate traumatic brain injury. *Journal of Neuropsychiatry and Clinical Neuroscience, 17,* 61–65.

Rapoport, M. J., McCullagh, S., Streiner, D., & Feinstein, A. (2003). The clinical significance of major depression following mild traumatic brain injury. *Psychosomatics, 44,* 31–37.

Reitan, R. M. (1955a). Certain differential effect of left and right cerebral lesions in human adults. *Journal of Comparative and Physiological Psychology, 48,* 474–477.

Reitan, R. M. (1955b). Investigation of the validity of Halstead's measures of biological intelligence. *Archives of Neurology and Psychiatry, 73*(28), 28–35.

Reitan, R. M. (1956). Investigation of relationships between "psychiatric and biological" intelligence. *Journal of Nervous and Mental Disease, 123,* 536–541.

Reitan, R. M., & Wolfson, D. (1985). *The Halstead-Reitan Neuropsychology Test Battery*. Tucson, AZ: Neuropsychology Press.

Ron, M. A., & Foong, J. (2003). The application of neuropathologically sensitive MRI techniques to the study of psychosis. In M. A. Ron & T. W. Robbins (Eds.), *Disorders of the brain and mind 2* (pp. 128–148). New York: Cambridge University Press.

Rosenthal, M., Christenson, B. K., & Ross, T. P. (1998). Depression following traumatic brain injury. *Archives of Physical Medicine & Rehabilitation, 79,* 90–103.

Rothlisberg, B. A., D'Amato, R. C., & Palencia, B. (2002). Assessment of children for intervention planning following traumatic brain injury. In C. R. Reynolds & R. W. Kamphaus (Eds.), *Handbook of psychological and educational assessment of children* (2nd ed., pp. 685–706). New York: Guilford.

Rutherford, A., Stephens, R., & Potter, D. (2003). The neuropsychology of healing and head trauma in association with football (soccer): A review. *Neuropsychology Review, 13,* 153–179.

Sattler, J. M., & D'Amato, R. C. (2002a). Brain injuries: Formal batteries and informal measures. In J. M. Sattler (Ed.), *Assessment of children: Behavioral and clinical applications* (4th ed., pp. 440–469). San Diego, CA: J. M. Sattler.

Sattler, J. M., & D'Amato, R. C. (2002b). Brain injuries: Theory and rehabilitation programs. In J. M. Sattler (Ed.), *Assessment of children: Behavioral and clinical applications* (4th ed., pp. 470–490). San Diego, CA: J. M. Sattler.

Schmidt, W. J., & Reith, M. E. (2005). *Dopamine and glutamate in psychiatric disorders*. Towata, NJ: Humana Press.

Segalowitz, S. J., & Brown, D. (1991). Mild head injury as a source of developmental disabilities. *Journal of Learning Disabilities, 24,* 551–558.

Semrud-Clikeman, M., Kamphaus, R. W., Teeter, P, & Vaughn, M. (1997). Assessment of behavior and personality in the neuropsychological diagnosis of children. In C. R. Reynolds & E. Fletcher-Janzen (Eds.), *Handbook of child clinical neuropsychology* (2nd ed., pp. 320–341). New York: Wiley.

Semrud-Clikeman, M., Portman, E., & Gerrard-Morris, A. (2005). Understanding the school neuropsychology of nosology, pediatric neuropsychology, and developmental disorders. In R. C. D'Amato, E. Fletcher-Janzen, & C. R. Reynolds (Eds.), *Handbook of school neuropsychology* (pp. 383–402). New York: Wiley.

Shaywitz, S. E. (2003). *Overcoming dyslexia: A new and complete science-based program for reading problems at any level*. New York: Knopf.

Silver, J. M., McAllister, T. W., & Yudofsky, S. C. (Eds.). (2005). *Textbook of traumatic brain injury*. Arlington, VA: American Psychiatric Publishing.

Sorenson, S., & Krauss, J. (1991). Occurrence, severity, and outcomes of brain injury. *The Journal of Head Trauma Rehabilitation, 6,* 1–10.

Strong, C. (2005a). Major depression after traumatic brain injury is associated with poor cognitive function. *Neurology Reviews, 6,* 66–68.

Strong, C. (2005b). Personality disorders following brain injury—A common problem requiring comprehensive care. *Neurology Reviews, 6,* 53–54.

Sutton, R. L., Hovda, D. A., Adelson, P. D., Benzel, E. C., & Becker, D. P. (1994). Metabolic changes following cortical contusion: Relationships to edema and morphological changes. *Acta Neurochirurgica, 60,* 446–448.

Teeter, P. A., & Semrud-Clikeman, M. (1997). *Child neuropsychology: Assessment and interventions for neurodevelopmental disorders.* Needham Heights, MA: Allyn & Bacon.

Traughber, M. C., & D'Amato, R. C. (2005). Integrating evidence-based neuropsychological services into school settings: Issues and challenges for the future. In R. C. D'Amato, E. Fletcher-Janzen, & C. R. Reynolds (Eds.), *Handbook of school neuropsychology* (pp. 383–402). New York: Wiley.

Tsushima, W. T., & Popper, J. S. (1980). Computerized tomography: A report of false negative errors. *Clinical Neuropsychology, 2*(3), 130–133.

Tsushima, W. T., & Wedding, D. (1979). Neuropsychological battery and computerized tomography in the identification of brain disorder. *Journal of Nervous and Mental Disease, 167,* 704–707.

Van Reekum, R., Chen, T., & Wong, J. (2000). Can traumatic brain injury cause psychiatric disorders (review). *Journal of Neuropsychiatry and Clinical Neuroscience, 12,* 316–327.

Van Reekum, R., Conway, C. A., Gansler, D., White, R., & Bachman, D. L. (1993). Neurobehavioral study of borderline personality disorders. *Journal of Psychiatry and Neuroscience, 18,* 121–129.

Van Reekum, R., Links, P. S., Finlayson, M. A., Boyle, M., Boiago, I., Ostrander, L. A., et al. (1996). Repeat neurobehavioral study of borderline personality disorder. *Journal of Psychiatry and Neuroscience 21,* 13–20.

Varney, N. R., & Varney, R. N. (1995). Brain injury without head injury: Some physics of automobile collisions with particular reference to brain injuries occurring without physical head trauma. *Applied Neuropsychology, 2,* 47–62.

Yamakami, I., & McIntosh, T. K. (1989). Effects of traumatic brain injury on regional cerebral blood flow in rats as measured with radiolabled microspheres. *Journal of Cerebral Blood Flow Metabolism, 9,* 117–124.

Yudofsky, S. C., & Hales, R. E. (2002). *The American Psychiatric Publishing textbook of neuropsychiatry and clinical neurosciences* (4th ed.). Arlington, VA: American Psychiatric Publishing.

Zasler, N. D. (1993). Post–concussive disorders: Facts, fallacies and fables. *The Journal of Head Injury, 3*(2), 8–13.

5

Bias and Explicit Decision Rules

ARTHUR D. WILLIAMS

BIAS

BY NATURE HUMAN beings process information selectively (Evans, 1989), therefore, we must take steps to minimize the impact of bias.

Nickerson (1998) discussed deliberate versus very spontaneous case building. He said, "There is an obvious difference between impartially evaluating evidence in order to come to an unbiased conclusion and building a case to justify a conclusion already drawn" (p. 175). In the first case, the neuropsychologist "seeks evidence on all sides of a question, evaluates it as objectively as one can, and draws the conclusion in the aggregate, that the evidence seems to dictate" (p. 175). In the second

Dr. Williams is a licensed psychologist in Washington state, California, and Alaska and a registered psychologist in British Columbia, a Diplomate of the American Board of Professional Neuropsychology, a Fellow of the American College of Professional Neuropsychology, and a Fellow of the National Academy of Neuropsychology. He was a Clinical Assistant Professor at the University of Washington and an Associate Professor at Pepperdine University. Dr. Williams received his PhD in 1977. He has written several journal articles and book chapters and co-edited *The Practice of Forensic Neuropsychology*. He has made numerous presentations in several countries. He is currently in private practice in Seattle, Washington.

case the neuropsychologist "selectively gathers or gives undue weight to evidence that supports one's position while neglecting to gather, or discounting evidence that would tell against it" (p. 175). Kahneman (2003) also delineated two generic modes of cognitive function: a controlled mode, which is deliberate and slower; and an intuitive mode, in which judgments and decisions are made automatically and rapidly. The first of these involves explicit decision rules, which can be subjected to scrutiny and scientific and logical evaluation. The second, intuition or clinical judgment, involves implicit decision rules and is more vulnerable to bias.

There are several types of bias. Confirmatory bias is the tendency to seek and value supportive evidence at the expense of contrary evidence (Wedding & Faust, 1989). Nickerson (1998) said this type of bias "connotes the seeking or interpreting of evidence in ways that are partial to existing beliefs, explanations, or a hypothesis in hand" (p. 175).

Illusory correlation involves perceiving a relationship between events or characteristics, even when there is no relationship between these characteristics.

Hindsight bias is "the tendency to believe, once the outcome of an event is known, that the outcome could have been predicted more easily than is actually the case" (Wedding & Faust, 1989, p. 237). Garb (1998) used the term labeling bias to refer to a similar concept. He wrote, "Labeling bias is said to occur when treatment recommendations are affected by being told how a person has been diagnosed by another clinician" (p. 141). He noted that diagnoses made by another clinician may be wrong. In the field of logic, one may say that the conclusion is based on a weak or false premise. Also, even if the diagnoses are correct, clinicians may make inappropriate inferences from the diagnoses, and treatment recommendations may have poor utility.

Garb (1998) also noted other biases related to race, social class, gender, sex role, age, and context (e.g., hospital setting).

DEBIASING TECHNIQUES

DEBIASING TECHNIQUES ARE "strategies designed to reduce the magnitude of judgment errors" (Williams, 2003, p. 113). Use of clinical judgment or intuition tends to be rapid but increases the likelihood of bias. A slow deliberate process, using explicit decision rules, is an effective debiasing technique. Sweet (1999) summarized several strategies: noting the limitations of judgment tasks that are not well-established, decreasing reliance on memory by documenting important case information, gathering information in a comprehensive manner, considering base rates and established diagnostic criteria, following scientific standards of assessment, and considering support for and against alternative hypotheses or premises for the conclusions in a specific case. He said, "Of course, when possible, reliance on empirically based decision rules or actuarial formulae has been recommended repeatedly in the relevant literature" (Sweet, 1999).

Regarding Sweet's (1999) suggestion to consider support for and against alternative hypotheses or premises, Galinksy and Mussweiler (2001) discussed the debiasing technique of "considering the opposite" to counter the effects of bias. For example, to consider the opposite, one would argue as vigorously as possible against the conclusions that one has made in a case, considering all alternative information. This relates to the principle of falsifiability discussed by Popper (1989) and utilized by the U.S. Supreme Court in *Daubert v. Merrell Dow Pharmaceuticals* (1993). In that case the justices relied on Hempel (1966) and Popper (1989). Hempel described the nature of the empirical sciences, which "seek to explore, to describe, to explain, and to predict the occurrences in the world we live in. The statements, therefore, must be checked against the facts of our experience, and they are acceptable only if they are properly supported by empirical evidence" (p. 1). He was describing an empirical truth claim, which must be verified or falsified. Popper discussed "the problem of *drawing a line of demarcation* between those statements…which could properly be described as belonging to empirical science, and others which might, perhaps, be described as 'pseudoscientific'" (pp. 255–256). Popper proposed "that the *refutability or falsifiability* of a theoretical system should be taken as the criterion of demarcation" (pp. 255–256).

As Nickerson (1998) has emphasized, according to the principle of falsifiability, an explanation cannot qualify as scientific unless it is falsifiable in principle. In other words, there must be a way to show an explanation is false if in fact it is false. Popper focused on the falsifiability of a theory or hypothesis (rather than verifiability) because "subscribers to…theories were likely to see confirming evidence everywhere they looked" (Nickerson, 1998, p. 206). This idea is inherent in the debiasing technique of considering the opposite.

Anchoring is a type of confirmatory bias and occurs when excessive weight is given to initial information. Neuropsychologists, particularly in the forensic arena, are likely to give excessive weight to initial information from the referral source, such as an attorney who emphasizes a particular view of the case.

Specific signs are likely to be related to a certain condition or disorder. Nonspecific signs are signs that could be attributable to a number of disorders. The clinician may be vulnerable to confirmatory bias in situations involving nonspecific signs and symptoms, such as in the case of traumatic brain injury.

Regarding nonspecific signs, Arkes (1981) and Faust and Nurcombe (1989) both described a way of determining if a sign is valid. Faust and Nurcombe described the four conditions:

1. Sign present, disorder present (S+D+)
2. Sign present, disorder absent (S+D-)
3. Sign absent, disorder present (S-D+)
4. Sign absent, disorder absent (S-D-).

If the sign contributes to a diagnosis, (S+D+)/(S+D-) must exceed (S-D+)/(S-D-). They emphasized, "A prediction should apply more often when a sign is present than when it is absent" (p. 198).

For example, Fox, Lees-Haley, Earnest, and Dolezal-Wood (1995) noted that many symptoms of postconcussive syndrome are "more frequent than normal in patients with psychiatric problems and certain medical problems" (p. 610). Iverson and McCracken (1997) wrote that many "postconcussive" symptoms were reported by a majority of chronic pain patients. Alves, Macciocchi, and Barth (1993) found that memory problems were present at discharge in 4.3% of patients with mild brain injury. Iverson and McCracken (1997) found that 29% of chronic pain patients had forgetfulness. Fox et al. (1995) found that 27% of health maintenance organization (HMO) patients (with no loss of consciousness in the last 2 years) had memory problems. Using the aforementioned formula, there would be serious concerns about using memory problems as a specific sign of traumatic brain injury.

Consideration of base rates is also important in another debiasing technique, using probability theory, which is discussed in Williams (1997).

USE OF EXPLICIT DECISION RULES

As NICKERSON (1998) stated, a slow deliberate process is necessary to reach an unbiased conclusion and be able to justify an empirical truth claim. First, it would be helpful if practitioners used the Structured Clinical Interview for the American Pyschiatric Association's (APA) *Diagnostic and Statistical Manual of Mental Disorders,* 4th ed. (*DSM–IV;* 1994) to make their diagnoses. There are forms for Axis I and Axis II disorders and for dissociative disorders. For children, there is the Children's Interview for Psychiatric Syndromes. These allow for a systematic way to review the criteria for many of the diagnostic categories.

Garb (1998) has presented the LEAD procedure. This is an acronym for Longitudinal, Expert, All Data. This involves administering a structured interview and making diagnoses, following the patient for a period of time and making LEAD diagnoses. Longitudinal data are used to validate diagnoses. For example, in one case a neuropsychologist diagnosed a 20-year-old man with amnestic disorder due to a traumatic brain injury. Two years later the man was on the dean's list at a major university without any accommodations and had traveled alone to several foreign countries. The longitudinal data did not support the diagnosis.

In conjunction with this concept, it would be helpful if there were a universal definition of the severity of traumatic brain injuries. The World Health Organization (WHO; 2004) states, "There is no universally accepted definition of MTBI [mild traumatic brain injury], and the studies are so heterogeneous that it is difficult to compare incidence rates and risk factors. Different authors use different criteria to define and ascertain cases of MTBI, and these criteria are all susceptible to information bias and misclassification of cases.... There is an urgent need for workable clinical and surveillance definitions of MTBI and subsequent studies to validate various methods of capturing cases" (p. 47).

It would also be helpful if practitioners were to agree on certain meta-analytic reviews of the literature as a basis for decision making. For example, WHO (2004) published "Best Evidence Synthesis on Mild Traumatic Brain Injury."

Another recommendation is that neuropsychologists follow the Standards for Educational and Psychological Testing (APA, 1999). The Standards for Educational and Psychological Testing (APA, 1985, 1999) are the standards of care for testing in psychology. The authors of the 1999 book stated, "Unless otherwise specified in the standards or commentary, and with the caveats outlined below, standards should be met before operational use" (p. 2).

The 1999 Standard 5.1 states, "Test administrators should follow carefully the standardized procedures for administering and scoring specified by the test developer, unless the situation or a test taker's disability dictates that an exception should be made" (APA, 1999, p. 63). The 1999 Standard 11.19 states, "When a test user contemplates an approved change in test format, mode of administration, instructions, or the language used in administering the test, the user should have a sound rationale for concluding that validity, reliability, and appropriateness of norms will not be compromised" (p. 117). For example, the manual for the Wechsler Memory Scale-III (WMS-III) (Wechsler, 1997c) states, "To maintain the validity and reliability of the WMS-III, the uniformity of the administration and scoring procedures, as well as testing conditions, must be adhered to. To obtain results that can be interpreted according to national norms, you should carefully follow all directions in the Stimulus Booklets. Deviations from the standard subtest administration…could reduce the validity of the test results" (p. 28). Omitting mandatory subtests in a clinical or forensic setting would not be consistent with the manual.

The Wechsler Adult Intelligence Scale-III (WAIS-III) administration manual (Wechsler, 1997a) states, "The norms on the WAIS-III were established on the basis of standard administration and scoring procedures under uniform testing conditions. So that an individual's test results are interpretable according to national norms, the WAIS-III should be administered according to the administration and scoring procedures as well as the recommended testing conditions.…Deviation from the standard procedures, such as changes in phrasing or presentation of a test item or modifications of time limits, could reduce the validity and reliability of test results (American Psychological Association, 1985)" (p. 28).

There are serious issues that need to be considered when testing people of other linguistic, cultural, and ethnic backgrounds. It is important to follow the guidelines from the International Test Commission, which are available online. The WAIS-III manual states, "You may be…challenged when testing individuals who are not fluent in English or individuals for whom English is a second language.…The WAIS-III normative data were collected on individuals who speak fluent English. Attempts to translate the test on an individual basis do not constitute a standardized administration; therefore, the normative information may be invalid…" (p. 41).

The WMS-III manual states, "When testing individuals who are not fluent in English or individuals for whom English is their second language, several approaches have been suggested, including administering the test with the assistance of a translator, translating the test prior to administration and administering it in the examinee's native language, or administering the test bilingually. All of these methods have their strengths and weaknesses, but all are problematic because the normative information was collected on individuals who spoke fluent English. Any attempt to translate the test on an individual basis will not constitute a standard administration; therefore, the normative information will be invalid" (p. 28).

The 1999 Standards include one chapter each on validity and reliability with relevant standards. A desirable minimal level of reliability is .80. Many tests have no available reliability data or the reliability coefficients fall below this level. The 1999 Standard 2.1 states, "For each total score, subscore, or combination of scores that is to be interpreted, estimates of relevant reliabilities and standard errors of measurement or test information functions should be reported" (APA, 1999, p. 31).

The 1999 Standard 1.4 states, "If a test is used in a way that has not been validated, it is incumbent on the user to justify the new use, collecting new evidence if necessary" (APA, 1999, p. 18). Many tests have not been empirically validated.

The 1999 Standard 12.5 states, "The selection of a combination of tests to address a complex diagnosis should be appropriate for the purposes of the assessment as determined by available evidence of validity" (APA, 1999, p. 132). The neuropsychologist needs to be ready to provide "available evidence of validity" (APA, 1999, p. 132) for each test used or the battery as a whole.

The 1999 Standard 12.16 states, "Test interpretations should not imply that empirical evidence exists for a relationship among particular test results...unless empirical evidence is available for populations similar to those representative of the examinee" (APA, 1999, p. 134).

Most psychological tests rely on an assumption that the scores are distributed on a normal curve. While some issues that are tested are normally distributed, such as intelligence, many are not. Dodrill (1997) stated, "Unlike intelligence, the normal versus abnormal continuum of brain function is not normally distributed. Most people have normal brain functions, and distributions of overall indices of brain functions...are highly skewed" (p. 10).

Mitrushina, Boone, and D'Elia (2005) wrote, "The interpretation of individual test scores respective to the normative distribution is based on an assumption of the normality of this distribution. To avoid interpretive errors the basis for test score interpretation should be different, if distribution is asymmetrical" (p. 38). They noted the distribution of scores on the Boston Naming Test and the Rey-Osterrieth Complex Figure Test were negatively skewed and the distribution on the Raven's Advanced Progressive Matrices was positively skewed. They concluded, "In both of the above cases resulting in skewed score distributions, the use of z score conversions is inappropriate, since such conversions are based on the assumption of normality (particularly symmetry) of the distribution" (p. 39).

It is incumbent upon test publishers to provide data regarding the distribution of scores in the test manuals and for researchers to provide these data in published studies. Otherwise, the clinician may use inappropriate score conversions and present misleading interpretations.

In any case percentiles are likely to be misleading, because they are not equally distributed. Anastasi (1988) stated, "The chief drawback of percentile scores arises from the marked inequality of their units, especially at the extremes of the distribution. If the distribution of raw scores approximates the normal curve,...then raw score differences near the median or center of the distribution are exaggerated in the percentile transformation, whereas raw score differences near the ends of the distribution are greatly shrunk" (p. 82). Merely comparing a score on a test to a normative group, usually a small sample, and using a percentile to describe this score relative to the normative group, is likely to be misleading.

In addition to assessing the level of performance of scores, it is very helpful to evaluate a pattern of scores in a battery. Scores from tests that have been normed on different samples cannot be compared to one another, because the relationship of the scores to one another is unknown. This has been pointed out by Lezak, Howieson, Loring, Hannay, and Fisher (2004, p. 142) and Spreen and Strauss (1998, p. 26) on a chart these authors have reproduced with the following text: "This chart cannot be used to equate scores on one test to scores on another test....[Scores from different tests] do not represent 'equal' standings because the scores were obtained from different groups." Lezak et al. (2004) elaborated on this issue: "In evaluating a patient's performance, the examiner can only compare scores from different tests when the standardization populations of each of the tests are identical or at least reasonably similar, with respect to both demographic characteristics and score distribution...Otherwise, even though their scales and units are statistically identical, the operational meaning of the different values are as different as the populations from which they are drawn" (pp. 143–144). They continue, "Different norms, derived on different samples in different places, and sometimes for different reasons, can produce quite different evaluations for some subjects resulting in false positives or false negatives, depending on the subject's score, condition, and the norm against which the score is compared...Thus, finding appropriate norms for each patient is still a challenge for clinicians...This problem with norms is very important in forensic cases...when the choice of norms can introduce interpretation bias" (p. 147). This raises questions about the use of pattern analysis with tests that have not been researched together.

The 1999 Standard 6.1 states, "Test documents (e.g., test manuals, technical manuals, user's guides, and supplemental material) should be made available to prospective test users and other qualified persons at the time a test is published or released for use" (APA, 1999, p. 68). Standard 11.1 states, "Prior to adoption and use of a published test, the test user should study and evaluate the materials provided by the test publisher...*Comment:* A prerequisite to sound test use is knowledge of the materials accompanying the instrument. As a minimum, these include manuals provided by the test developer" (p. 445).

For many tests with no manuals neuropsychologists rely on short descriptions in Lezak et al. (2004) and Spreen and Strauss (1998). Spreen and Strauss stated about the Consonant Trigrams Test and the Buschke Selective Reminding Test, "that no commercial source exists for these tests." Designing one's own material makes standardized administration difficult.

The 1985 Standard 6.12 indicates, "In school, clinical, and counseling applications, tests developed for screening should be used only for identifying test takers who may need further evaluation. The results of such tests should not be used to characterize a person or to make any decision about a person, other than the decision for referral for further evaluation, unless adequate reliability and validity for these other uses can be demonstrated" (APA, 1985, p. 43). Many of the tests used by neuropsychologists are only screening tests, including the Stroop Color and Word Test (Golden, 1978) and the Hooper Visual Organization Test (Hooper, 1983). Regarding the Wechsler Abbreviated Scale of Intelligence (WASI), the WASI manual (Wechsler, 1999) states, "Like all brief tests, the WASI sacrifices some degree of clinical accuracy for the conservation of time. The WASI cannot provide a comprehensive evaluation of an individual's intellectual functioning because it includes only four subtests of the Wechsler full batteries, samples only limited areas of the domains of cognitive functioning, and does not include subtests from the third and fourth factors of the full batteries. Consequently the main uses of the WASI are retesting and screening for a quick estimate of cognitive functioning.... The WASI does not substitute for more comprehensive measures of intelligence ... and should not be used in isolation for diagnosis or classification. In general, it should not be used for legal, judicial, or quasi-legal purposes (e.g., a statutorily mandated diagnosis or determination of disability)" (p. 8). Therefore, it is not appropriate for a forensic evaluation.

The 1999 Standard 3.27 states, "If a test or part of a test is intended for research use only and is not distributed for operational use [for decision-making], statements to this effect should be displayed prominently on all relevant test administration and interpretations materials that are provided to the test user" (APA, 1999, p. 48). For example, the computerized version of the Wisconsin Card Sorting Test is published as a research edition.

The 1999 Standard 12.6 states, "When differential diagnosis is needed, the professional should choose, if possible, a test for which there is evidence of the test's ability to distinguish between the two or more diagnostic groups of concern rather than merely to distinguish abnormal cases from the general population. *Comment:* Professionals will find it particularly helpful if evidence of validity is in a form that enables them to determine how much confidence can be placed in inferences regarding an individual" (APA, 1999, p. 132). This is an important standard because many neuropsychological tests are based on an assumption of a normal distribution, and impairment is inferred based on a score on this normal distribution. If the distribution is skewed, as is the case with many tests, derived scores such as z scores, T-scores and percentiles are likely to be misleading. Lezak et al. (2004) emphasized this point: "A number of…tests…have been devised for studies of particular neuropsychological problems in which the standardization groups are relatively small (often under 20).… Standard score conversions are inappropriate if not impossible in such cases" (p. 144).

There are also implications in terms of criterion validity. If no studies have been conducted with the test involving samples similar to the examined (APA, 1999), the test or battery may not meet the requirements of this Standard.

Related to this concern, it would be helpful if neuropsychologists could agree on a definition of impairment. Mitrushina et al. (2005) noted ranges for performance levels that were consistent with the traditional Wechsler ranges, for which scores were considered to be impaired if they were below the second percentile. Lezak et al. (2004) stated, "In general, differences of two standard deviations or more may be considered significant, whereas differences of one or two standard deviations suggest a trend" (p. 143).

Related to this standard is the 1999 Standard 12.4, which states, "If a publisher suggests that tests are to be used in combination with one another, the professional should review the evidence on which the procedures for combining tests is based and determine the rationale for the specific combinations of tests and the justification of the interpretation based on the combined scores. *Comment:* For example, if…a neuropsychological battery is being applied, then supporting validity data for such combinations of scores should be available" (APA, 1999, p. 131). The Halstead-Reitan Battery and the Luria-Nebraska Neuropsychological Battery provide research about the known relationships between the various tests. Regarding psychoeducational assessment, the Woodcock-Johnson Tests would also meet the requirements of this standard. Choosing a battery that has been developed "to distinguish between the two or more diagnostic groups of concern rather than merely to distinguish abnormal cases from the general population" (APA, 1999, p. 131) is strongly recommended. It would be helpful if commonly used tests, such as the WAIS-III and the WMS-III, indicated evidence of their ability to distinguish abnormal cases from the general population at the time they are published.

With high-functioning individuals, neuropsychological scores are likely to be overpathologized, because they are based on a questionable assumption that the scores are all expected to be similar to high average or superior intelligence scores. Hawkins and Tulsky (2003) stated that in intellectual-memory discrepancy analysis on the WAIS-III and WMS-III, "the employment of a simple difference approach using a single set of base rates will cause high rates of *false positives* among subjects with higher IQs. Clinicians expecting high IQ scores to be accompanied by equally high memory scores will be vulnerable to false positive error with regard to memory decline. The corrective is simple: use either the predicted difference method of the Technical Manual, or reference to the IQ stratified base rates provided in the chapter, and in Hawkins and Tulsky (2001)" (p. 252). However, these authors noted caution should be used with the discrepancy analyses: "[T]he presentation within this chapter of unidirectional discrepancy data is predicated on the assumption that clinicians will be selective in their examination of differences between scores.... In that regard they are disadvantaged by the limited clinical data yet available. The validation of [discrepancy analysis] with these instruments calls for the generation of data across a broad range of clinical circumstances and conditions, and there remains much work to be done" (Hawkins & Tulsky, 2003, p. 258). This limits the amount of weight to be given to discrepancy analysis, and it remains a weak premise on which to base a strong conclusion, such as a diagnosis.

Many neuropsychologists use the WAIS-III and the WMS-III for evaluation of traumatic brain injury. There are a number of limitations to these tests that must be kept in mind related to debiasing and the use of explicit decision rules, because any decision rules that do exist must be used with caution. It is instructive to examine the studies related to these tests and traumatic brain injury (TBI), because of the popularity of the use of these tests for diagnostic purposes. According to the WAIS-III Technical Manual (Wechsler, 1997b), the WAIS-III and WMS-III have only been studied on "22 adults who had experienced a moderate to severe single closed head injury who were administered the WAIS-III and the WMS-III" (p. 155). This is too small a sample to generalize from, and this sample did not include any subjects with mild brain injury.

Taylor and Heaton (2001) explored the sensitivity and specificity of WAIS-III/WMS-III demographically-corrected factor scores. The sample sizes for the various clinical groups (n = 9 to 39), including only 21 with TBI, limit the generalizability of the findings. Zhu, Tulsky, Price, and Chen (2001) examined the reliability for clinical groups, but again the sample sizes for the groups, with the exception of mental retardation, were small and limit generalizability. There were 22 subjects with TBI. Tulsky and Haaland (2001) wrote, "Given the extent of the revisions within the tests, a much more detailed exploration of their reliability, construct validity, and clinical utility is clearly warranted.... [M]uch more work is needed in these areas to convince neuropsychologists that these tests should be incorporated in their evaluations" (p. 861).

Langeluddecke and Lucas (2003) used the Australian version of the WAIS-III. They said the Processing Speed Index of the WAIS-III had been found to be the index most sensitive to brain injury. They suggested using six subtests to screen for intellectual impairment in relation to traumatic brain injury: Digit Symbol, Symbol Search, Comprehension, Similarities, Picture Completion, and Picture Arrangement. Their study had 50 controls, 35 people with moderate brain injury, 74 with severe brain injury, and 41 with extremely severe brain injury. Again there is a problem of using small samples. The moderate TBI group had similar scores to those in the control group who had no brain damage. In both groups all subtest and index scores were average. They concluded, "Persons with a history of severe to extremely severe brain injury generally show significant, and indeed fairly global, impairment in intellectual functioning on the WAIS-III. The clinical utility of the WAIS-III in assessing long term outcome in persons with mild to moderate brain injury receives less support" (p. 195).

Langeluddecke and Lucas (2003) also studied WMS-III findings with 25 mild brain injury litigants who met the criteria for probable malingered neurocognitive dysfunction compared with 50 nonmalingering subjects. They found the auditory recognition-delayed score to be "highly effective in detecting malingering" (p. 181). There were small samples in this study limiting generalizability.

Langeluddecke and Lucas (2005) examined WMS-III findings in litigants with moderate to extremely severe brain trauma patients. There were 50 controls, 44 people with moderate brain injury, 86 with severe brain injury, and 50 with extremely severe brain injury. They concluded, "The WMS-III appears to be useful in documenting long-term impairment in immediate memory functioning following severe to extremely severe brain injury, but has limited sensitivity in relation to less severe TBI" (pp. 587–588).

Strong, Donders, and Van Dyke (2005) examined the diagnostic validity of the new demographically corrected WAIS-III norms using a sample of 100 patients with traumatic brain injury and a matched control group from the standardization sample. They found that the demographically corrected norms do not offer a clear advantage or disadvantage compared to traditional age-corrected norms in the assessment of patients with TBI who are Caucasian and have at least a middle-school education.

The updated Technical Manual (Wechsler, 2002) also noted two other studies. Fisher, Ledbetter, Cohen, Marmor, and Tulsky (2000) compared score profiles of 23 patients with mild brain injury (12 men and 11 women with a mean age of 35.73), only 11 of whom reported a loss of consciousness; 22 patients with moderate to severe brain injury (14 men and 8 women with a mean age of 26.9); and a matched control group of 45 people. The authors found significant differences on the WAIS-III between the moderate to severe group and the control group, but no significant differences between the mild brain injury group and controls. On the WMS-III the mild brain-injured subjects performed significantly lower than the controls, though all scores were low average to average. The small samples in this study limit generalizability.

Donders, Tulsky, and Zhu (2001) evaluated 41 mild brain injury patients, defined as having no intracranial lesions and no prolonged delays until they followed commands. This was a somewhat vague definition of mild brain injury, and it was unclear how this definition related to other studies of mild TBI. This group was compared to 59 patients with documented CT or MRI evidence of intracranial lesion, patients with a duration of coma of at least 24 hours or both. The idiosyncratic definitions of the mild and moderate-to-severe TBI make generalization of the findings of this study difficult. The WAIS-III Index scores for all groups was average except for the moderate-severe group for which Processing Speed was low average. They concluded, "Digit-Symbol-Coding and Symbol Search both demonstrated medium effect sizes in distinguishing patients with moderate-severe injuries from both demographically matched standardization controls and patients with mild TBI" (p. 896).

In 1999, Millis, Malina, Bowers, and Ricker published an article stating that only separate constructs of Working Memory, Visual Memory, and Auditory Memory had the strongest support. They particularly found problems with the subtests including the Faces subtest in the Visual Memory factor. David Tulsky, one of the Project Directors of the WMS-III, and others (Tulsky, Chiaravalloti, Palmer, & Chelune, 2003) stated, "[R]eplication studies confirm that the distinction between immediate and delayed memory cannot be supported, and the construct validity for this model of memory in this test battery has not yet been supported" (p. 131). They proposed a six-factor WAIS-III/WMS-III factor structure. Auditory Composite and Visual Composite scales were developed. Since the factor structure of the WAIS-III and WMS-III has been changed, neuropsychologists need to be aware of these changes and rescore the Indexes. It is recommended that this factor structure be considered for more accurate interpretation of these tests.

CONCLUSION

IT IS RECOMMENDED that neuropsychologists use the deliberate reasoning process noted by Nickerson (1998) rather than intuition or "clinical judgment." In the deliberation process the explicit decision rules and other debiasing techniques outlined in this chapter can be considered. While the Wechsler tests are widely used, caution is necessary when forming conclusions based on these tests, because further research is needed with diagnostic groups.

ACKNOWLEDGMENTS

SPECIAL THANKS TO Silvie Opatrna and Amy Miyako for their assistance.

REFERENCES

Alves, W., Macciocchi, S., & Barth, J. (1993). Postconcussive symptoms after uncomplicated mild brain injury. *Journal of Head Trauma Rehabilitation, 8*(3), 48–59.

American Psychiatric Association. (1994). *Diagnostic and statistical manual of mental disorders* (4th ed.). Washington, DC: Author.

American Psychological Association. (1985). *Standards for educational and psychological testing*. Washington, DC: Author.

American Psychological Association. (1999). *Standards for educational and psychological testing*. Washington, DC: Author, American Educational Research Association, National Council on Measurement in Education.

Anastasi, A. (1988). *Psychological testing* (6th ed.). New York: Macmillan Publishing Company.

Arkes, H. (1981). Impediments to accurate clinical judgment and possible ways to minimize their impact. *Journal of Consulting and Clinical Psychology, 49*(3), 323.

Daubert v. Merrell Dow Pharmaceuticals, 113 S. Ct. 2786 (1993). Ohio.

Dodrill, C. (1997). Myths of neuropsychology. *The Clinical Neuropsychologist, 11*(1), 1–17.

Donders, J., Tulsky, D., & Zhu, J. (2001). Criterion validity of new WAIS-III subtest scores after brain injury. *Journal of the International Neuropsychological Society, 7*, 892–898.

Evans, J. (1989). *Bias in human reasoning*. Hillsdale, NJ: Lawrence Ehrlbaum.

Faust, D., & Nurcombe, B. (1989). Improving the accuracy of clinical judgment. *Psychiatry, 52*, 197–208.

Fisher, D., Ledbetter, M., Cohen, N., Marmor, D., & Tulsky, D. (2000). WAIS-III and WMS-III profiles of mildly to severely brain-injured patients. *Applied Neuropsychology, 7*(3), 126–132.

Fox, D., Lees-Haley, P., Earnest, K., & Dolezal-Wood, S. (1995). Base rates of postconcussive symptoms in health maintenance organization patients and controls. *Neuropsychology, 9*(4), 606–611.

Galinsky, A., & Mussweiler, T. (2001). First offers as anchors: The role of perspective-taking and negotiator focus. *Journal of Personality and Social Psychology, 81*(4), 657–669.

Garb, H. (1998). *Studying the clinician*. Washington, DC: American Psychological Association.

Golden, C. J. (1978). *Stroop Color and Word Test: Manual for clinical and experimental uses*. Chicago, IL: Stroelting Company.

Hawkins, K., & Tulsky, D. (2001). The influence of IQ stratification on WAIS-III/WMS-III FSIQ-general memory index discrepancy base-rates in the standardization sample. *Journal of the International Neuropsychological Society, 7*(7), 875–880.

Hawkins, K., & Tulsky, D. (2003). WAIS-III WMS-III discrepancy analysis. In D. Tulsky et al. (Eds.), *Clinical interpretation of the WAIS-III and WMS-III.* New York: Academic Press.

Hempel, C. (1966). *Philosophy of natural science.* New York: Prentice-Hall.

Hooper, H. E. (1983). *The Hooper Visual Organization Test Manual.* Los Angeles, CA: Western Psychological Services.

Iverson, G., & McCracken, L. (1997). "Postconcussive" symptoms in persons with chronic pain. *Brain Injury, 11*(11), 783–790.

Kahneman, D. (2003). A perspective on judgment and choice: Mapping bounded rationality. *American Psychologist, 58*(9), 697–720.

Langeluddecke, P., & Lucas, S. (2003). Quantitative measures of memory malingering on the Wechsler Memory Scale-Third Edition in mild head injury litigants. *Archives of Clinical Neuropsychology, 18,* 181–197.

Langeluddecke, P., & and Lucas, S. (2005). Wechsler Adult Intelligence Scale-Third Edition findings in relation to severity of brain injury litigants. *The Clinical Neuropsychologist, 17*(2), 273–284.

Lezak, M., Howieson, D., Loring, D., Hannay, H., & Fisher, J. (2004). *Neuropsychological assessment* (4th ed.). New York: Oxford University Press.

Millis, S., Malina, A., Bowers, D., & Ricker, J. (1999). Confirmatory factor analysis of the Wechsler Memory Scale-III. *Journal of Clinical and Experimental Neuropsychology, 21*(1), 87–93.

Mitrushina, M., Boone, K., & D'Elia, L. (2005). *Handbook of normative data for neuropsychological assessment.* New York: Oxford University Press.

Nickerson, R. (1998). Confirmation bias: A ubiquitous phenomenon in many guises. *Review of General Psychology, 2*(2), 175–220.

Popper, K. (1989). *Conjectures and refutations.* London: Routledge.

Spreen, O., & Strauss, E. (1998). *A compendium of neuropsychological tests.* New York: Oxford University Press.

Strong, C., Donders, J., & Van Dyke, S. (2005). Validity of demographically corrected norms for the WAIS-III. *Journal of Clinical and Experimental Neuropsychology, 27,* 746–758.

Sweet, J. (1999). Conclusion: Toward objective decision-making in adversarial assessments. In J. Sweet (Ed.), *Forensic neuropsychology: Fundamentals and practice* (pp. 255–285). Exton, PA: Swets & Zeitlinger.

Taylor, M., & Heaton, R. (2001). Sensitivity and specificity of WAIS-III/WMS-III demographically corrected factor scores in neuropsychological assessment. *Journal of the International Neuropsychological Society, 7,* 867–874.

Tulsky, D., Chiaravalloti, N., Palmer, B., & Chelune, G. (2003). The Wechsler Memory Scale, Third Edition: A new perspective. In D. Tulsky et al. (Eds.),

Clinical interpretation of the WAIS-III and WMS-III (pp. 93–139). New York: Academic Press.

Tulsky, D., & Haaland, K. (2001). Exploring the clinical utility of WAIS-III and WMS-III. *Journal of the International Neuropsychological Society, 7,* 860–862.

Wechsler, D. (1997a). *WAIS-III Administration and Scoring Manual.* San Antonio, TX: Psychological Corp.

Wechsler, D. (1997b). *WAIS-III – WMS-III Technical Manual.* San Antonio, TX: Psychological Corp.

Wechsler, D. (1997c). *WMS-III Administration and Scoring Manual.* San Antonio, TX: Psychological Corp.

Wechsler, D. (1999). *WASI Administration and Scoring Manual.* San Antonio, TX: Psychological Corp.

Wechsler, D. (2002). *WAIS-III – WMS-III Technical Manual.* San Antonio, TX: Psychological Corp.

Wedding, D., & Faust, D. (1989). Clinical judgment and decision making in neuropsychology. *Archives of Clinical Neuropsychology, 4,* 233–265.

Williams, A. (1997). The forensic evaluation of adult traumatic brain injury. In R. McCaffrey, A. Williams, J. Fisher, & L. Laing (Eds.), *The practice of forensic neuropsychology* (pp. 37–56). New York: Plenum Press.

Williams, A. (2003). Diagnostic decision making in neuropsychology. In A. M. Horton & L. C. Hartlage (Eds.), *Handbook of forensic neuropsychology* (pp. 113–136). New York: Springer Publishing Company.

World Health Organization. (2004). Best evidence synthesis on mild traumatic brain injury. *Journal of Rehabilitation Medicine,* February Supplement No. 43 (pp. 1–52).

Zhu, J., Tulsky, D., Price, L., & Chen, H. (2001). WAIS-III reliability data for clinical groups. *Journal of the International Neuropsychological Society, 7,* 862–866.

6

Assessing for Exaggeration, Poor Effort, and Malingering in Neuropsychological Assessment

GRANT L. IVERSON

THE PURPOSE OF this chapter is to provide a critical review and discussion of poor effort, exaggeration, and malingering within the context of neuropsychological assessment. The explicit goal is to assist the practitioner with developing a best practice approach for assessing effort in clinical and forensic practice. The chapter is divided into the following sections: (a) conceptual issues and terminology,

Author Notes: This chapter was adapted, revised, and updated from two previous works (Iverson, 2003; Iverson, in press). The author thanks Jennifer Bernardo for help with manuscript preparation.

(b) diagnostic criteria for malingering in neuropsychology, (c) assessing for exaggerated symptom reporting, (d) conceptualizing and assessing poor effort in neuropsychology, (e) ethical issues, (f) sample text for reports, and (g) conclusions and recommendations for clinical practice.

CONCEPTUAL ISSUES AND TERMINOLOGY

MALINGERING IS THE intentional production of false or greatly exaggerated symptoms for the purpose of attaining some identifiable external reward (American Psychiatric Association [APA], 1994). Within the context of a psychological or neuropsychological evaluation, an individual who is malingering typically exaggerates symptoms. The person might exaggerate memory problems, concentration difficulty, depression, anxiety, pain, dizziness, sleep disturbance, or personality change, for example. During neuropsychological testing, a person who is malingering deliberately underperforms. People might malinger to (a) influence the outcome of a personal injury lawsuit, (b) receive worker's compensation or disability benefits, (c) obtain prescription medications, (d) avoid prosecution for criminal activities (vis-à-vis a determination of incompetency to stand trial), or (e) avoid criminal responsibility (i.e., not guilty by reason of insanity).

Resnick (1997) described three types of malingering, labeled *pure malingering, partial malingering,* and *false imputation.* Pure malingering is characterized by a complete fabrication of symptoms. Partial malingering is defined by exaggerating actual symptoms or by reporting past symptoms as if they are continuing. False imputation refers to the deliberate misattribution of actual symptoms to the compensable event. Appreciating these types is important, because mental health and legal professionals might have a simplistic view of malingering (i.e., only *pure malingering* is considered malingering).

Many lawyers and health care professionals adopt a rather extreme position regarding malingering. They assume that malingering represents total fabrication (i.e., fraud). An example would be the person who pretends to not be able to walk who is videotaped walking. Less blatant malingering is conceptualized differently, such as exaggeration. Exaggeration is seen as common in personal injury litigation, and part of the function of the adversarial system is to illustrate to the trier of fact that exaggeration is present. Some professionals are tempted to believe that if a person has a well-documented psychiatric condition or visible brain damage on MRI that the person could not be malingering or exaggerating. However, it would be naïve to assume that a person with a psychiatric problem or the lingering effects of a traumatic brain injury could not malinger. That would be tantamount to concluding that people with these conditions are not capable of engaging in goal-directed behavior (e.g., exaggeration of symptoms to influence their litigation).

Resnick's (1997) conceptualization deals with malingering in the context of a medical, psychiatric, or psychological evaluation and primarily relates to the self-report of symptoms and problems. Neuropsychologists must, of course, estimate the extent to which a person appears to be putting forth his or her best effort during testing. The clinician must then make an inference regarding underlying motivation to perform. Effort is not a binary phenomenon. It falls on a continuum from very poor to outstanding.

To conclude that a person might be malingering, the clinician must make an inference regarding the person's underlying motivation or reasons for presumed poor effort, exaggeration, or fabrication of symptoms and problems. There are many possible underlying motivations for exaggeration (singly or in combination). These include (a) a "cry for help"; (b) anger, frustration, self-justification, a sense of entitlement, and greed; (c) a deep-rooted psychological need to be seen as sick or disabled (i.e., a factitious disorder); (d) attention or avoidance as reinforcers, such as attention from others, avoidance of unpleasant activities, and other reinforcers or so-called secondary gains; (e) concerns about not being taken seriously; (f) personality style or disorder; (g) depressive, negativistic thinking; and (h) deliberate exaggeration to influence litigation.

First, the "cry for help" euphemism implies that the person has serious psychological or psychiatric problems and is desperately seeking recognition of, and attention for, these problems. There is a long history of conceptualizing exaggeration as a cry for help in psychology and neuropsychology, whereas in psychiatry and general medicine clinicians are inclined to attribute exaggeration to psychological factors, psychiatric problems, nonorganic factors, or secondary gains. Some physicians even use vague and obfuscating terms, such as supratentorial, to communicate that the patient's problems are "in his head" (technically, the location of the problems would be above the tentorium cerebri). Second, in personal injury litigation, a person often feels angry about being injured and by perceived mistreatment from an insurance company. Some people feel justified in aggressively pursuing their litigation and feel entitled to generous compensation. Through a series of independent evaluations they might feel the need to exaggerate their symptoms or problems in order to be taken seriously, or to communicate how bad off they were in the past. There might be a number of reinforcing benefits relating to exaggerating one's problems, such as attention from family and friends, or avoidance of unpleasant activities.

Third, some people with depression have an extremely negative view of themselves, the world, and their future. This negativistic thinking can manifest in exaggeration of symptoms and problems. Some people have a personality style that is prone to dramatizing and exaggerating their problems. Fourth, a person might deliberately exaggerate because he has a deep-seated psychological need to be perceived as sick and disabled. The motivation is not the litigation, per se, but to be seen and treated as a sick and disabled person. Under these circumstances, the person would be diagnosed with a factitious disorder. Finally, a person might deliberately exaggerate or underperform during testing because he is trying to influence the outcome of his evaluations in order to influence the outcome of his litigation. This latter behavior is what we consider malingering. The reporting of symptoms and problems falls on a continuum, from underreporting, to accurate reporting, to exaggeration, as illustrated in Figure 6.1. A person's reporting of symptoms and problems can move along this continuum during an evaluation and over time, from evaluation to evaluation.

Over the past 15 years, many terms have been used to describe reduced effort during neuropsychological testing, including but not limited to nonoptimal effort, suboptimal effort, incomplete effort, poor effort, biased responding, and negative response bias. Faking, feigning, simulating, dissimulating, magnifying, amplifying, and exaggerating are some of the terms used to describe interview behavior, responses on psychological tests, and performance on neuropsychological tests. Those familiar with the literature will appreciate that nearly all of these terms have been used to describe *both* test performance and symptom endorsement.

It is important conceptually to separate test performance and symptom endorsement. My preferred terms are *poor effort,* for describing underperforming on neuropsychological tests, and *exaggeration,* for describing self-reported symptoms and problems during interview or on psychological tests, such as the MMPI-2. Sometimes the terms

| Under-
Endorsement | Accurate
Reporting | Possible
Exaggeration | Probable
Exaggeration | Definite
Exaggeration |

FIGURE 6.1 Continuum of symptom reporting.

Note: Most people provide reasonably accurate portrayals of their symptoms and problems. Some people downplay or minimize their problems (underendorsement). Information is provided in this chapter regarding how to estimate probable or definite exaggeration using Bayesian methods.

poor effort or *exaggeration* seem too strong for the clinical situation, such as when there is somewhat equivocal evidence for their presence. There are also occasions when I might describe a person's effort on testing as suboptimal, or variable. I try to use the word *variable* on rare occasion. I occasionally use the expressions *amplifying* or *magnifying* in relation to symptom reporting.

In general, the terms *poor effort* and *exaggeration* are simple, descriptive, and communicative. Many other researchers and clinicians will adopt the expression *symptom validity assessment,* used in the National Academy of Neuropsychology (NAN) position paper (Bush et al., 2005), to refer to *all methods and procedures* that the practitioner can draw upon to make inferences regarding poor effort during testing and exaggeration of symptoms or problems during interview or on psychological tests. There is nothing wrong with this terminology provided that the conceptual issues conveyed by the terminology are understood. I think there has been longstanding conceptual confusion amongst clinicians and researchers regarding the similarities and differences between exaggeration and poor effort. Exaggeration and poor effort are related but not synonymous behavioral constructs. Unfortunately, the distinction between them has often been blurred. For example, clinicians frequently refer to poor performance on an effort test as exaggeration, such as *symptom exaggeration* or *cognitive exaggeration.* The term *exaggeration* is less ambiguous conceptually if it is used to describe symptom reporting during interview, symptom endorsement on psychological tests, or behavioral observations (e.g., facial expressions or pain behaviors). *Poor effort,* on the other hand, refers to *clearly suboptimal effort during testing.* This simply means the person underperformed during testing. The clinician might wish to *infer* that this underperformance constitutes *exaggeration* of problems, such as memory problems, but it is important to appreciate that this is a *secondary clinical inference;* the primary clinical inference is *poor effort, underperformance,* or *submaximal effort.*

The conceptual overlap among exaggeration, poor effort, and malingering is illustrated in Figure 6.2. The shaded circle represents malingering, the dotted circle exaggeration, and the solid circle poor effort. Malingering in a neuropsychological evaluation typically involves both exaggeration and poor effort (most of the shaded circle). However, it can occur with only one of these constructs being present (or accurately detected). Notice the small shaded area at the top, within malingering, which does not involve exaggeration or poor effort. This could be a situation involving false imputation, in that a person reports legitimate symptoms and problems, reasonably accurately, but deliberately attributes them to a false cause (such as a motor vehicle accident). False imputation, without question, occurs in forensic evaluations. It can be difficult, even impossible at times, to determine if a person is deliberately

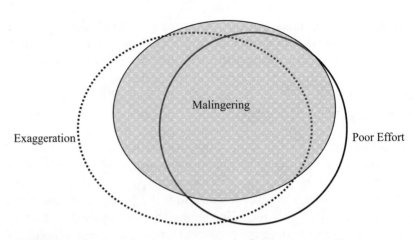

FIGURE 6.2 Conceptual and assessment overlap between exaggeration, poor effort, and malingering.

FIGURE 6.3 Continuum of accuracy of causal attributions.

falsely attributing symptoms or problems to a compensable cause (i.e., *false imputation* to a person injury tort). Attribution of cause also falls on a continuum of accuracy, as illustrated in Figure 6.3.

As seen in Figure 6.2, exaggeration and poor effort, singly or in combination, can occur without the person malingering. Some degree of exaggeration is likely ubiquitous in civil and criminal forensic evaluations, and it is believed to be relatively common in clinical settings especially among people with somatoform disorders, fibromyalgia, chronic pain, and certain personality disorders. In inpatient adult or geriatric psychiatric settings, or outpatient adolescent psychiatric settings, poor effort during testing might occur simply because the person does not want to undergo the assessment. In some psychiatric settings, the patient is simply too disturbed and disorganized to meaningfully participate in the assessment process. Under these circumstances, the person might be deemed to be providing poor effort, but the clinical inference for the behavior would *not* be malingering.

DIAGNOSTIC CRITERIA FOR MALINGERING IN NEUROPSYCHOLOGY

SLICK, SHERMAN, AND Iverson (1999) proposed diagnostic criteria for definite, probable, and possible malingering (see Table 6.1 for a partial reproduction of the criteria). These criteria have been used in numerous studies (e.g., Bianchini, Greve, & Love, 2003; Bianchini, Love, Greve, & Adams, 2005; Bianchini, Houston, et al., 2003; Curtis, Greve, Bianchini, & Brennan, 2006; Etherton, Bianchini, Greve, & Heinly, 2005; Greve et al., 2006a, 2006b; Greve, Bianchini, & Doane, 2006; Greve, Bianchini, Love, Brennan, & Heinly, 2006; Greve, Bianchini, Mathias, Houston, & Crouch, 2002, 2003; Heinly, Greve, Bianchini, Love, & Brennan, 2005; Larrabee, 2003c; Mathias, Greve, Bianchini, Houston, & Crouch, 2002). For a diagnosis of *definite malingering,* there must be clear and compelling evidence of poor effort on testing (i.e., below chance performance). To be considered malingering, the person's behavior should be conceptualized as volitional and rational. In addition, there must not be plausible alternative explanations for this behavior (e.g., factitious disorder or somatoform disorder). Moreover, it should be determined that the exaggeration or fabrication of impairment is not the result of diminished capacity to appreciate laws or mores against malingering or an inability to conform behavior to such standards, as may be the case in persons with certain psychiatric (e.g., a schizophrenia spectrum disorder), developmental (e.g., mental retardation), or neurological disorders (e.g., dementia).

The foundation of an opinion regarding malingered cognitive impairment is deliberately poor performance on testing. Evidence of poor effort on neuropsychological testing can be demonstrated by one of the following: (a) *below chance* performance ($p < .05$) on one or more forced-choice measures of cognitive function, (b) poor effort on one or more well-validated tests or indices designed to measure this behavior, (c) compelling inconsistency between test results and known patterns of brain functioning (e.g., biological severity indexing), (d) compelling inconsistency between test results and observed behavior, (e) compelling inconsistency between test results and reliable collateral reports, and (f) compelling inconsistency between test results and documented background history.

According to Slick et al. (1999), evidence from the patient's self-report can be used to *support* a diagnosis of malingering. The following factors may be considered suspicious and should be examined carefully: (a) self-reported history that is inconsistent with documented history, (b) self-reported symptoms that are inconsistent with known patterns of brain functioning, (c) self-reported symptoms that are inconsistent with behavioral observations, (d) self-reported symptoms that

TABLE 6.1   Criteria for Definite, Probable, and Possible Malingering of Cognitive Impairment

Definite Malingering is indicated by the presence of clear and compelling evidence of volitional exaggeration or fabrication of cognitive impairment and the absence of plausible alternative explanations. The specific diagnostic criteria necessary for Definite Malingering are:

1. Presence of a substantial external incentive [Criterion A]
2. Definite poor effort on testing characterized by *below chance* performance [Criterion B1]
3. Behaviors meeting necessary criteria from group B are not fully accounted for by psychiatric, neurological, or developmental factors [Criterion D]

Probable Malingering is indicated by the presence of evidence strongly suggesting volitional exaggeration or fabrication of cognitive impairment and the absence of plausible alternative explanations. The specific diagnostic criteria necessary for Probable Malingering are:

1. Presence of a substantial external incentive [Criterion A]
2. Two or more types of evidence from neuropsychological testing, excluding definite (i.e., below chance) poor effort [two or more of Criteria B2–B6]
   Or
   One type of evidence from neuropsychological testing, excluding definite poor effort, and one or more types of evidence from Self-Report [one of Criteria B2–B6 and one or more of Criteria C1–C5]
3. Behaviors meeting necessary criteria from groups B or C are not fully accounted for by psychiatric, neurological, or developmental factors [Criterion D]

Possible Malingering is indicated by the presence of evidence suggesting volitional exaggeration or fabrication of cognitive impairment and the absence of plausible alternative explanations. Alternatively, Possible Malingering is indicated by the presence of criteria necessary for Definite or Probable Malingering except that other possible causes cannot reasonably be ruled out. The specific diagnostic criteria for Possible Malingering are:

1. Presence of a substantial external incentive [Criterion A]
2. Evidence from Self-Report [one or more of Criteria C1–C5]
3. Behaviors meeting necessary criteria from groups B or C are not fully accounted for by psychiatric, neurological, or developmental factors [Criterion D]
   Or
   Criteria for Definite or Probable Malingering are met except for Criterion D (i.e., primary psychiatric, neurological, or developmental etiologies cannot reasonably be ruled out). In such cases, the alternate etiologies that cannot be ruled out should be specified.

Source: Adapted with minor terminology modifications from Slick, Sherman, & Iverson (1999). Reprinted with permission.

are inconsistent with information obtained from reliable collateral informants, or (e) evidence of exaggerated or fabricated self-reported problems on psychological tests (e.g., MMPI-2). A checklist for using the diagnostic criteria is provided in Table 6.2.

TABLE 6.2   Malingering Criteria Checklist

☐	A.	Clear and substantial external incentive
☐	B1.	Definite poor effort (below chance)
☐	B2.	Probable poor effort
☐	B3.	Discrepancy between known patterns of brain function/dysfunction and test data
☐	B4.	Discrepancy between observed behavior and test data
☐	B5.	Discrepancy between reliable collateral reports and test data
☐	B6.	Discrepancy between history and test data
☐	C1.	Self-reported history is discrepant with documented history
☐	C2.	Self-reported symptoms are discrepant with known patterns of brain functioning
☐	C3.	Self-reported symptoms are discrepant with behavioral observations
☐	C4.	Self-reported symptoms are discrepant with information obtained from collateral informants
☐	C5.	Evidence of exaggerated or fabricated psychological dysfunction on standardized measures
☐	D.	Behaviors satisfying Criteria B and/or C were volitional and directed at least in part towards acquiring or achieving external incentives as defined in Criterion A
☐	E.	The patient adequately understood the purpose of the examination and the possible negative consequences of exaggerating or fabricating cognitive impairments
☐	F.	Test results contributing to Criterion B are sufficiently reliable and valid

Note: See Slick et al., 1999.

ASSESSING FOR EXAGGERATED SYMPTOM REPORTING

SEVERAL MULTISCALE PSYCHOLOGICAL tests have validity scales. These validity scales have varying degrees of accuracy for detecting exaggeration. Examples of tests with validity scales include the Minnesota Multiphasic Personality Inventory—Second Edition (MMPI-2; Butcher et al., 2001), Personality Assessment Inventory (PAI; Morey, 1991), Ruff Neurobehavioral Inventory (Ruff & Hibbard, 2003), and the Behavior Rating Inventory of Executive Function—Adult Version (BRIEF-A; Roth, Isquith, & Gioia, 2005).

MINNESOTA MULTIPHASIC PERSONALITY INVENTORY—SECOND EDITION (MMPI-2)

THERE IS AN enormous amount of literature relating to detecting exaggeration on the Minnesota Multiphasic Personality Inventory—Second Edition (MMPI-2; e.g., see reviews by Greene, 2000; Guriel & Fremouw, 2003; Iverson & Lange, 2005; Lees-Haley, Iverson, Lange, Fox, & Allen, 2002; Meyers, Millis, & Volkert, 2002; Nelson, Sweet, &

Demakis, 2006; Rogers, Sewell, Martin, & Vitacco, 2003). Researchers frequently have reported that the traditional and supplemental infrequency validity scales, such as F, F_B, and F(p) are effective for identifying exaggeration. There is no doubt that some personal injury litigants will substantially elevate these scales. When this occurs, it often represents frank and somewhat unsophisticated exaggeration. It is important to note, however, that these scales are more useful for identifying exaggeration of severe mental illness, such as in criminal forensic evaluations involving competency to stand trial. Validity scales and indices that might be more useful for identifying exaggeration in civil forensic evaluations include the Fake Bad Scale, Obvious-Subtle scales, and the Dissimulation Scale—Revised. Iverson and Lange (2005) provided numerous tables summarizing the literature on these various validity scales. A recent meta-analysis is essential reading for practitioners using the MMPI-2 validity scales (Nelson et al., 2006). Nelson and colleagues concluded that the Fake Bad Scale performed as well or better than the other MMPI-2 validity scales for identifying exaggeration. Based on a large amount of literature (e.g., Bagby, Nicholson, Buis, & Bacchiochi, 2000; Dearth et al., 2005; Greiffenstein, Baker, Axelrod, Peck, & Gervais, 2004; Greiffenstein, Baker, Gola, Donders, & Miller, 2002; Guez, Brannstrom, Nyberg, Toolanen, & Hildingsson, 2005; Larrabee, 1997, 1998, 2003b, 2003c; Lees-Haley, 1992; Lees-Haley, English, & Glenn, 1991; Nelson et al., 2006; Ross, Millis, Krukowski, Putnam, & Adams, 2004; Tsushima & Tsushima, 2001), this scale seems particularly useful in civil forensic evaluations.

Meyers and colleagues (2002) developed the MMPI-2 Validity Index. The Validity Index combines seven validity scales from the MMPI-2 (i.e., F-K, F, FBS, F(p), Ds-r, Es, and O-S). Each validity index is assigned a weighting of 1 or 2 points based on an arbitrarily defined score range on each validity scale. Scores on the Validity Index can range from 0 to 14. A cutoff score of 5 or higher was recommended as a preliminary criterion for exaggeration based on the Validity Index scores of 100 nonlitigant chronic pain patients, 100 litigating chronic pain patients, and 30 sophisticated simulators instructed to feign the emotional and cognitive difficulties demonstrated by chronic pain patients. Using a cutoff score of 5 or above, 100% of nonlitigant chronic pain patients were successfully classified as honest responders, and 86% of the simulators were correctly identified as exaggerating symptomatology. In the litigating chronic pain patients sample, 33% scored 5 points or higher on this index. Meyers and colleagues concluded that the MMPI-2 Validity Index appears to be superior to any single validity scale, however, replication of these findings was recommended.

Greve and colleagues (Greve, Bianchini, Love, et al., 2006) recently published the most sophisticated, elaborate, and clinically useful study ever conducted on interpreting the MMPI-2 validity scales in brain-injury litigation. They examined the MMPI-2 validity scales in 259 patients with traumatic brain injuries in comparison to 133 patients not involved in litigation who were referred for neuropsychological evaluations for a variety of neurological, medical, or psychiatric reasons. Fb, DS-r, and Ego Strength appeared to be the most effective scales. The Fake Bad Scale and Meyers Validity Index also were useful. The authors provided sensitivity, specificity, and predictive value statistics for various cutoffs on the validity scales. This article is essential reading for anyone using the MMPI-2 in civil forensic neuropsychological evaluations.

The MMPI-2 is the most well-researched and well-validated psychological test for identifying exaggerated symptom reporting. Over decades, the research has evolved from identifying "fake bad" to malingered insanity to exaggerated physical and psychological problems in forensic psychological and neuropsychological evaluations.

PERSONALITY ASSESSMENT INVENTORY (PAI)

THE PERSONALITY ASSESSMENT Inventory (PAI; Morey, 1991) is an objective personality inventory designed to measure psychological functioning across multiple domains. Unlike the MMPI-2, there is no item overlap on the scales. In addition, items are answered on a 4-point Likert scale as opposed to a true-false format. In addition to the clinical scales, the PAI has four validity scales. The Inconsistency scale is comprised of 10 highly correlated items. The Infrequency scale contains 8 items that are rarely endorsed by healthy adults, and these items are believed to be minimally related to psychopathology. The Positive Impression Management scale (PIM) is designed to evaluate fake good responding; and the Negative Impression Management scale (NIM) contains 9 items that are rarely endorsed by persons in the general population and are considered to reflect exaggerated psychological problems. Morey (1996) described eight score patterns that comprise a "Malingering Index" on the PAI. If the patient demonstrates three or more of these score patterns, malingering is suspected; five or more score patterns represent likely malingering. Rogers and colleagues conducted a large-scale study of the PAI validity scales, using undergraduates and psychology graduate students as simulators. A discriminant function analysis provided better classification accuracy than the single validity scales (Rogers, Sewell, Morey, & Ustad, 1996). This discriminant function is now included in the computerized scoring program for the PAI.

In general, the PAI is a well-designed and validated measure for identifying psychological, behavioral, and personality problems. Unfortunately, there has been relatively little research directed toward identifying exaggeration and malingering on the PAI, and most has been directed toward identifying severe psychopathology (Bagby, Nicholson, Bacchiochi, Ryder, & Bury, 2002; Calhoun, Earnst, Tucker, Kirby, & Beckham, 2000; Liljequist, Kinder, & Schinka, 1998; Morey & Lanier, 1998; Rogers et al., 1996; Rogers, Ornduff, & Sewell, 1993; Rogers, Sewell, Cruise, Wang, & Ustad, 1998; Veazey, Wagner, Hays, & Miller, 2005; Wang et al., 1997). From a clinical perspective, one method for screening for exaggeration is to determine whether the person's symptom reporting seems extreme relative to the clinical sample. If so, do the assessment results converge to suggest that this extreme symptom reporting is reflective of the person's true condition? That is, when considering interview findings, behavioral observation, medical records, and other collateral information, does it make sense that the person could be experiencing the extreme symptoms and problems reported on this test (such as depression and anxiety in excess of 99% of the clinical sample)? Psychologists should be cautious about over-relying on the NIM or the Malingering Index. These measures are more likely to detect extreme and bizarre symptom reporting, such as that seen in a criminal forensic evaluation of someone who is faking insanity. These measures are considerably less sensitive to exaggeration in civil forensic evaluations.

RUFF NEUROBEHAVIORAL INVENTORY (RNBI)

THE RUFF NEUROBEHAVIORAL Inventory (RNBI; Ruff & Hibbard, 2003) is a 243-item self-report questionnaire that assesses a person's perception of the important dimensions of their daily life activities following a traumatic brain injury. The RNBI uses two different types of questions to assess both pre-injury and post-injury functioning. The test yields 4 validity scales, 4 composite scores (Cognitive, Emotional, Physical, and Quality of Life), and 18 basic scales (e.g., Learning & Memory, Executive Functions, Anger & Aggression, Depression, Pain, Activities of Daily Living, and Vocation & Finance). Premorbid and postmorbid normative scores are derived for nearly every scale.

The Inconsistency Scale contains 12 pairs of items with similar content that are scattered throughout the test. Respondents are expected to answer the items consistently. The Infrequency Scale contains items that were endorsed in an extreme manner by the normative sample and the clinical validation sample. Six items from the premorbid scales and six items from the postmorbid scales were selected based on low levels of endorsement. There are two Negative Impression Scales. These scales contain six items from the premorbid scales and six from the postmorbid scales. These scales are designed to identify frank exaggeration. The items describe unusually negative and exaggerated problems. Most of the items are emotional or psychological in content. There are two Positive Impression Scales that contain six items each (premorbid and postmorbid). These scales are designed to measure a person's denial of flaws or difficulties.

By design, the validity scales seem promising for identifying random or highly inconsistent responding; fairly extreme exaggeration, primarily in the psychological/emotional domain; and positive response bias, such as denying common and presenting oneself in an overly favorable light. To my knowledge, however, there has been no published research as of mid-2006 relating to detecting exaggeration or malingering using the RNBI validity scales.

The self-report of symptoms and problems, especially in cases involving personal injury litigation or disability-related evaluations, has obvious inherent limitations. Getting the person's perspective, nonetheless, is critical. The RNBI is an excellent instrument for gathering comprehensive and diverse information from the patient's perspective. We use the RNBI on a regular basis because of its large normative sample, unique design, and obvious clinical relevance. However, I have concerns about the ability of the validity scales to identify exaggerated symptoms and problems, when present, in forensic neuropsychological evaluations. To date, we have rarely seen any elevated validity scales in patients seen for forensic evaluations. On several occasions I have evaluated patients with extreme symptom reporting and frank effort test failures who have not elevated the validity scales. I anticipate that a new RNBI validity scale will need to be developed and validated to more reliably identify exaggeration in civil forensic neuropsychological evaluations. After which, we can have increased confidence in the reliability and accuracy of the symptom reporting on this inventory.

BEHAVIOR RATING INVENTORY OF EXECUTIVE FUNCTION—ADULT VERSION (BRIEF-A)

THE BEHAVIOR RATING Inventory of Executive Function—Adult Version (BRIEF-A; Roth et al., 2005) contains 75 items that yield 9 non-overlapping theoretically and clinically derived scales that measure different aspects of executive functioning. The clinical scales are combined to form two broad index scores, the Behavioral Regulation Index and the Metacognition Index, and an overall composite score, the Global Executive Composite. The clinical scales comprising the Behavioral Regulation Index are labeled Inhibit, Shift, Emotional Control, and Self-Monitor. The clinical scales comprising the Metacognition Index are labeled Initiate, Working Memory, Plan/Organize, Task Monitor, and Organization of Materials. The BRIEF-A can be completed rapidly (approximately 15 minutes), it has broad coverage of executive functioning, and it is normed based on self-report and informant-report. Norming the test for use with a collateral informant (e.g., a spouse or family member) makes it inherently useful in mainstream clinical practice.

The BRIEF-A contains three validity scales labeled Negativity, Infrequency, and Inconsistency. Each validity scale is on the self-report and informant versions of the test. The Negativity scale contains 10 items. They are scored only if the respondent rates them in the most extreme direction (i.e., Never, Sometimes, Often; to get a point they must be rated as Often). Thus, there is a maximum score of 10 points for the scale. Obtaining a raw score of 6 or greater on this scale occurs in less than 1% of the normative sample and the clinical sample. The Infrequency scale is designed to measure the extent to which individuals respond to the test in an atypical manner. The scale contains five items that people would customarily respond to in a single direction. These items, if responded to in the extreme directions, might represent an overly favorable or overly negative point of view. Elevations on this scale might also reflect a haphazard approach to completing the test. A cutoff score is provided above which 1% or fewer of the normative sample or clinical sample scored. The Inconsistency scale contains 10 pairs of items with similar content. Thus, it is expected that a person who is carefully and thoughtfully responding to the items will rate these pairs similarly. Extreme cutoff scores for the Inconsistency scale are provided (i.e., a person must score above 99.7% of the combined normative and clinical samples to be considered to have responded inconsistently). To my knowledge, as of mid-2006, there has been no published research evaluating the BRIEF-A validity scales. Similar to the RNBI, it might be necessary, over time, for clinical researchers to develop modified or alternative validity scales and indices that can reliably and accurately identify exaggeration. In the meantime, of course, research is needed on the current validity scales.

CONCEPTUALIZING AND ASSESSING POOR EFFORT IN NEUROPSYCHOLOGY

NEUROPSYCHOLOGICAL TESTING IS exquisitely dependent upon effort. Effort is a state, not a trait. Effort is variable, not constant. Effort is behavior that falls on a continuum. On occasion, in clinical practice, we assess people who are extremely motivated to perform well. Most of the time, however, our patients' effort is likely *good* or *adequate* for the purposes of the evaluation. It is likely that the normative data upon which we compare our patients' test results are comprised of subjects who gave adequate, good, or excellent effort (with the possibility of a subset of subjects who gave relatively poor effort due to lack of interest or other reasons). Most subjects in normative studies likely gave *good* or *adequate* effort, although this assumption is ultimately unknowable.

A continuum for conceptualizing effort is illustrated in Figure 6.4. This figure reminds us to approach effort as a spectrum of behavior, not simply a dichotomous construct. It would be a mistake to conclude, for example, that a person provided *exceptional* effort, or even *good* effort, on the basis of performing normally on a single effort test. Conclusions about level of effort should be based on several sources of converging evidence, not a single test score. As a general rule, passing one or more effort tests suggests *adequate* effort, or possibly *good* effort, provided that there are not other indicators in the battery or the behavioral observations of possible poor effort.

There are two types of tests that are used to identify poor effort in neuropsychology: traditional and specialized. Traditional tests simply are tests that have been developed to measure a specific skill or ability that have been used by researchers to identify poor effort. Examples of traditional tests that have been used to identify poor effort are provided in Table 6.3. These are simply examples. Many tests have been used in this manner. Specialized tests, in contrast, have been designed and validated specifically for the detection of poor effort. Examples of specialized tests are provided in Table 6.4.

As seen in Figure 6.5, poor effort can have a dramatic adverse impact on neuropsychological test performance. Clinicians know that poor effort can result in a global suppression of neuropsychological test performance or scattered low scores across a battery of tests. Researchers have reported that poor effort results in suppressed test scores on a variety of neuropsychological tests (e.g., Backhaus, Fichtenberg, &

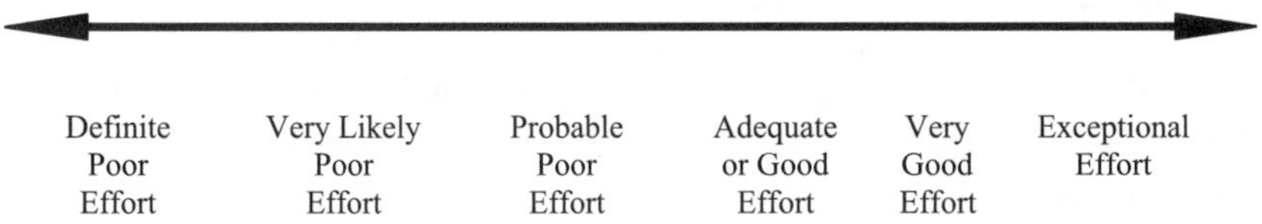

| Definite Poor Effort | Very Likely Poor Effort | Probable Poor Effort | Adequate or Good Effort | Very Good Effort | Exceptional Effort |

FIGURE 6.4 Continuum of effort.

Note: Some people provide exceptional effort. They are extremely motivated to perform well on testing. Most people provide adequate effort during testing. Information is provided in this chapter regarding how to estimate probable or very likely poor effort. The difference between them can be differentiated based on Positive and Negative Predictive Value statistics. *Definite poor effort* can be used when a person performs below the probable range of random responding (i.e., below the 90% confidence interval for chance), or there is converging and compelling evidence of poor effort. The definitional categories in Figures 6.2 and 6.4 are similar to the categories for malingering presented in Slick, Sherman, & Iverson (1999).

TABLE 6.3   Examples of Traditional Tests That Have Been Used
to Identify Poor Effort

Digit Span, Reliable Digit Span, & Vocabulary-Digit Span Difference Scores

DiCarlo, Gfeller, & Oliveri (2000); Forrest, Allen, & Goldstein (2004); Sweet & King (2002); Tenhula & Sweet (1996); Binder & Willis (1991); Greiffenstein, Baker, & Gola (1994); Meyers & Volbrecht (1998); Iverson & Franzen (1994, 1996); Iverson & Tulsky (2003); Suhr, Tranel, Wefel, & Barrash (1997); Trueblood & Schmidt (1993); Merten, Green, Henry, Blaskewitz, & Brockhaus (2005); Heinly et al. (2005); Etherton, Bianchini, Greve, & Heinly (2005); Etherton, Bianchini, Ciota, & Greve (2005); Fisher & Rose (2005); Axelrod & Rawlings (1999); Mittenberg, Theroux-Fichera, Zielinski, & Heilbronner (1995); Millis, Ross, & Ricker (1998); Miller, Ryan, Carruthers, & Cluff (2004); Vagnini et al. (2006); Babikian, Boone, Lu, & Arnold (2006); Shum, O'Gorman, & Alpar (2004); Larrabee (2003b); Nelson et al. (2003); Greve et al. (2003); Mittenberg, Aguila-Puentes, Patton, Canyock, & Heilbronner (2002)

Wechsler Memory Scale–Third Edition (WMS-III)

Killgore & DellaPietra (2000a, 2000b); Langeluddecke & Lucas (2003); Glassmire et al. (2003); Hilsabeck et al. (2003); Miller et al. (2004); Lange, Sullivan, & Anderson (2005); Mittenberg, Aguila-Puentes, Patton, Canyock, & Heilbronner (2002); Langeluddecke & Lucas (2004)

Category Test

DiCarlo, Gfeller, & Oliveri (2000); Forrest et al. (2004); Sweet & King (2002); Tenhula & Sweet (1996); Williamson, Green, Allen, & Rohling (2003)

Halstead-Reitan Neuropsychological Battery

Goebel (1983); Heaton, Smith, Lehman, & Vogt (1978); McKinzey & Russell (1997); Mittenberg, Rotholc, Russell, & Heilbronner (1996); Arnold et al. (2005); Reitan & Wolfson (1996a, 1996b, 2002)

California Verbal Learning Test

Ashendorf, O'Bryant, & McCaffrey (2003); Demakis (1999); Moore & Donders (2004); Baker, Donders, & Thompson (2000); Coleman, Rapport, Millis, Ricker, & Farchione (1998); Trueblood (1994); Trueblood & Schmidt (1993); Millis, Putnam, Adams, & Ricker (1995); Slick, Iverson, & Green (2000); Sweet et al. (2000); Moore & Donders (2004); Demakis (2004); Bauer, Yantz, Ryan, Warden, & McCaffrey (2005)

Rey Auditory Verbal Learning Test

Barrash, Suhr, & Manzel (2004); Suhr, Gunstad, Greub, & Barrash (2004); Powell, Gfeller, Hendricks, & Sharland (2004); Sherman, Boone, Lu, & Razani (2002); Bernard, Houston, & Natoli (1993); Silverberg & Barrash (2005); Boone, Lu, & Wen (2005)

Rey Complex Figure

Lu, Boone, Cozolino, & Mitchell (2003); Sherman et al. (2002); Bernard et al. (1993)

Recognition Memory Test

Iverson & Franzen (1994, 1998); Iverson & Binder (2000); Millis (1992, 1994, 2002); Millis & Dijkers (1993); Barrash et al. (2004); Silverberg & Barrash (2005); Nelson et al. (2003); Tardif, Barry, Fox, & Johnstone (2000); Ross, Putnam, & Adams (2006); Nelson et al. (2006)

TABLE 6.4 Examples of Specialized Tests That Have Been Used to Identify Poor Effort

Portland Digit Recognition Test

Binder (1993); Binder & Kelly (1996); Binder & Willis (1991); Ju & Varney (2000); Rose, Hall, Szalda-Petree, & Bach (1998); Doane, Greve, & Bianchini (2005); Temple, McBride, David Horner, & Taylor (2003); Larrabee (2003a); Bianchini, Mathias, Greve, Houston, & Crouch (2001); Gunstad & Suhr (2001); Binder, Salinsky, & Smith (1994); Vickery, Berry, Inman, Harris, & Orey (2001); Binder, Kelly, Villanueva, & Winslow (2003); Rosen & Powel (2003); Binder (2002); Gunstad & Suhr (2004)

Computerized Assessment of Response Bias (CARB)

Allen, Conder, Green, & Cox (1997); Green & Iverson (2001a, 2001b); Allen, Iverson, & Green (2002); Lynch (2004); Gervais, Rohling, Green, & Ford (2004); Dunn, Shear, Howe, & Ris (2003); Iverson (2001); Slick, Iverson, & Green (2000)

Victoria Symptom Validity Test

Doss, Chelune, & Naugle (1999); Grote et al. (2000); Slick, Hopp, Strauss, Hunter, & Pinch (1994); Slick, Hopp, Strauss, & Spellacy (1996); Slick, Hopp, Strauss, & Thompson (1997); Loring, Lee, & Meador (2005); Macciocchi, Seel, Alderson, & Godsall (2006); Vagnini et al. (2006); Thompson (2002)

Amsterdam Short-Term Memory Test

Merten et al. (2005); van Hout, Schmand, Wekking, Hageman, & Deelman (2003); Bolan, Foster, Schmand, & Bolan (2002); van der Werf, Prins, Jongen, van der Meer, & Bleijenberg (2000); Schmand et al. (1998); Schagen, Schmand, de Sterke, & Lindeboom (1997)

Word Memory Test

Green, Allen, & Astner (1996); Green, Iverson, & Allen (1999); Iverson, Green, & Gervais (1999); Dunn et al. (2003); Gervais et al. (2001); Gorissen, Sanz, & Schmand (2005); Green & Flaro (2003); Green, Lees-Haley, & Allen (2002); Green, Rohling, Iverson, & Gervais (2003); Green, Rohling, Lees-Haley, & Allen (2001); Rohling, Allen, & Green (2002); Rohling, Green, Allen, & Iverson (2002); Tan, Slick, Strauss, & Hultsch (2002); Green & Iverson (2001a); Williamson et al. (2003); O'Bryant & Lucas (2006)

Medical Symptom Validity Test

Green (2004); Merten et al. (2005); Richman et al. (2006)

21 Item Test

Arnett & Franzen (1997); Gontkovsky & Souheaver (2000); Iverson, Franzen, & McCracken (1991, 1994); Iverson (1998); Rose et al. (1998); Vickery et al. (2001)

(Continued)

141

TABLE 6.4   Examples of Specialized Tests That Have Been Used to Identify Poor Effort *(Continued)*

Validity Indicator Profile

Frederick (1997, 2000); Frederick & Crosby (2000); Frederick, Crosby, & Wynkoop (2000); Frederick & Foster (1991); Frederick, Sarfaty, Johnston, & Powel (1994); Rose et al. (1998); Vallabhajosula & van Gorp (2001); Frederick (2002b)

Test of Memory Malingering

Tombaugh (1996, 1997); Rees, Tombaugh, Gansler, & Moczynski (1998); Ashendorf, Constantinou, & McCaffrey (2004); Constantinou & McCaffrey (2003); Hill, Ryan, Kennedy, & Malamut (2003); Rees, Tombaugh, & Boulay (2001); Teichner & Wagner (2004); Weinborn, Orr, Woods, Conover, & Feix (2003); Powell et al. (2004); Yanez, Fremouw, Tennant, Strung, & Coker (2005); Greve & Bianchini (2006); Donders (2005); Duncan (2005); Gierok, Dickson, & Cole (2005); Etherton, Bianchini, Ciota, & Greve (2005); Gavett, O'Bryant, Fisher, & McCaffrey (2005); Moore & Donders (2004); van Hout et al. (2003); Vagnini et al. (2006); Horner, Bedwell, & Duong (2006); O'Bryant & Lucas (2006); Haber & Fichtenberg (2006); Greve et al. (2006a); Vallabhajosula & van Gorp (2001); McCaffrey, O'Bryant, Ashendorf, & Fisher (2003); Tombaugh (2002); Bolan et al. (2002); Brennan & Gouvier (2006)

Dot Counting Test

Erdal (2004); Nelson et al. (2003); Strauss et al. (2002); Vickery et al. (2001); Lee et al. (2000); Rose et al. (1998); Hayes, Hale, & Gouvier (1998); Arnett & Franzen (1997); Binks, Gouvier, & Waters (1997); Boone et al. (1995); Beetar & Williams (1995); Frederick (2002a); Brennan & Gouvier (2006)

Rey 15 Items Test

Arnett, Hammeke, & Schwartz (1995); Bernard & Fowler (1990); Goldberg & Miller (1986); Greiffenstein, Baker, & Gola (1996); Guilmette, Hart, Giuliano, & Leininger (1994); Hays, Emmons, & Stallings (2000); Lee, Loring, & Martin (1992); Millis & Kler (1995); Iverson & Binder (2000); Kelly, Baker, van den Broek, Jackson, & Humphries (2005); Reznek (2005); Fisher & Rose (2005); McCaffrey et al. (2003); Frederick (2002a); Brennan & Gouvier (2006)

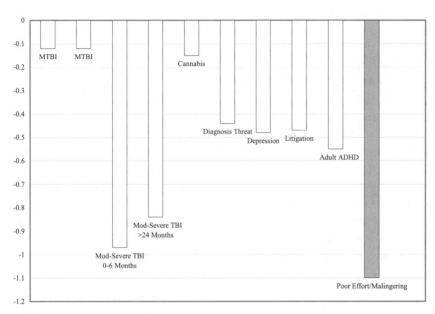

FIGURE 6.5 Effect sizes on overall neuropsychological functioning.

Note: Effect sizes typically are expressed in pooled, weighted standard deviation units. However, across studies, there are some minor variations in the methods of calculation. By convention, effect sizes of .2 are considered small, .5 medium, and .8 large. This is from a statistical, not necessarily clinical, perspective. For this figure, the overall effect on cognitive or neuropsychological functioning is reported. The effect sizes are displayed in a negative direction to visually illustrate the negative, or adverse effect on cognitive functioning. Effect sizes less than .3 should be considered very small and difficult to detect in individual patients, because the patient and control groups largely overlap. First mild traumatic brain injury (MTBI), moderate-severe traumatic brain injury (TBI) 0–6 months, > 24 months, all in Schretlen & Shapiro (2003), 39 studies, N = 1,716 TBI, N = 1,164 controls; second MTBI (Binder, Rohling, & Larrabee, 1997), 11 studies, N = 314 MTBI, N = 308 controls; cannabis (Grant, Gonzalez, Carey, Natarajan, & Wolfson, 2003), long-term regular use, 11 studies, N = 623 users, N = 409 non or minimal users; depression (Christensen, Griffiths, Mackinnon, & Jacomb, 1997), 97 comparisons for depression; Diagnosis Threat (Suhr & Gunstad, 2002, 2005), 2 studies, 23 comparisons; litigation/financial incentives (Binder & Rohling, 1996), 17 studies, N = 2,353 total; attention deficit hyperactivity disorder (ADHD; Schoechlin & Engel, 2005) based on "Focused Attention," 22 studies, 1,493 subjects; exaggeration/malingering (Vickery et al., 2001), 32 studies published between 1985 and 1998, 41 independent comparisons.

Diagnosis Threat: Suhr and Gunstad (2002, 2005), through innovative research designs, reported that *simply calling attention* to the fact that people with past MTBIs might have cognitive difficulties actually results in substantially worse test performance than not calling attention to this belief. This is a remarkable finding illustrating the *adverse effects of suggestion and expectations* on neuropsychological test performance.

Hanks, 2004; Constantinou, Bauer, Ashendorf, Fisher, & McCaffrey, 2005; Henry, 2005).

The impact of *varying degrees* of poor effort on neuropsychological test performance is illustrated in Figures 6.6–6.8. These figures were derived from a sample of 531 patients seen for neuropsychological evaluations long after sustaining a mild traumatic brain injury (MTBI). All patients met the following inclusion criteria: (a) loss of consciousness less than 30 minutes, (b) Glasgow Coma Scale between 13 and 15, and (c) post-traumatic amnesia less than 24 hours. All patients were administered the Word Memory Test (WMT) and a battery of neuropsychological tests. The patients were sorted by level of performance on the Delayed Recognition subtest of the WMT. As seen in Figure 6.6, there is a linear decrease in performance on the Short Delay Free Recall task of the California Verbal Learning Test associated with decreasing performance on an effort test. Keep in mind that all patients were being evaluated in the context of having a previous MTBI. What is varying in this figure is not injury severity, it is level of effort. Similar findings are

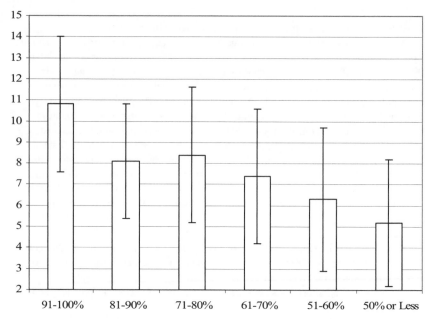

FIGURE 6.6 California Verbal Learning Test (CVLT; 15 words) Short Delay Free Recall performance by level of effort (Word Memory Test; Delayed Recognition % correct).

Note: The total sample (N = 531) was comprised of patients seen for neuropsychological evaluations in the post-acute period following a mild traumatic brain injury (MTBI). The average WMT Delayed Recognition scores by group were as follows: 97.0 (n = 288), 85.5 (n = 87), 76.1 (n = 58), 66.0 (n = 47), 56.0 (n = 34), 45.0 (n = 17). The bars represent the mean scores, and the error lines represent one standard deviation. Data provided by Paul Green, PhD, Green's Publishing, Edmonton.

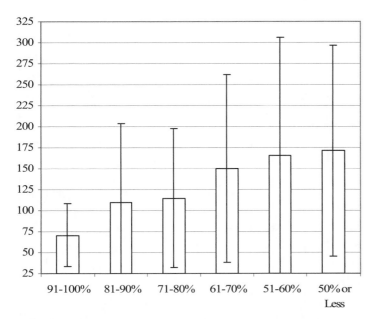

FIGURE 6.7 Trails B (seconds) performance by level of effort (Word Memory Test; Delayed Recognition % correct).

Note: The total sample (N = 531) was comprised of patients seen for neuropsychological evaluations in the post-acute period following a mild traumatic brain injury (MTBI). The average WMT Delayed Recognition scores by group were as follows: 97.0 (n = 288), 85.5 (n = 87), 76.1 (n = 58), 66.0 (n = 47), 56.0 (n = 34), 45.0 (n = 17). The bars represent the mean scores and the error lines represent one standard deviation. Data provided by Paul Green, PhD, Green's Publishing, Edmonton.

illustrated for the Trail Making Test Part B (Figure 6.7) and Warrington's Recognition Memory Test for Faces (Figure 6.8). The bars represent the linear trends (mean scores) for worse performance relating to level of effort, and the error lines illustrate the substantial within-group variability in performance (standard deviations).

BAYESIAN METHODS/DIAGNOSTIC ACCURACY STATISTICS/ODDS RATIOS

HOW DO WE draw accurate inferences regarding possible, probable, very likely, or definite poor effort? Over the past several years, researchers have been encouraging the use of Bayesian methods (e.g., Mossman, 2000, 2003) for effort testing (e.g., Barrash et al., 2004; Bianchini, Mathias, Greve, Houston, & Crouch, 2001; Etherton, Bianchini, Greve, & Heinly, 2005; Glassmire et al., 2003; Greve et al., 2003; Lange et al., 2005; Millis & Volinsky, 2001; Slick et al., 1997). This encouragement is similar to other areas of professional neuropsychological research and

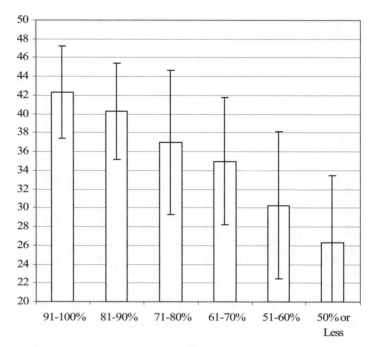

FIGURE 6.8 Warrington's Recognition Memory Test for Faces (50 faces) performance by level of effort (Word Memory Test; Delayed Recognition % correct).

Note: The total sample (N = 531) was comprised of patients seen for neuropsychological evaluations in the post-acute period following a mild traumatic brain injury (MTBI). The average WMT Delayed Recognition scores by group were as follows: 97.0 (n = 288), 85.5 (n = 87), 76.1 (n = 58), 66.0 (n = 47), 56.0 (n = 34), 45.0 (n = 17). The bars represent the mean scores and the error lines represent one standard deviation. Data provided by Paul Green, PhD, Green's Publishing, Edmonton.

practice (e.g., Barr & McCrea, 2001; Benedict et al., 2004; Benedict et al., 2003; Iverson, Mendrek, & Adams, 2004; Ivnik et al., 2001; Labarge, McCaffrey, & Brown, 2003; Rasquin, Lodder, Visser, Lousberg, & Verhey, 2005; Sawrie et al., 1998; Shapiro, Benedict, Schretlen, & Brandt, 1999; Tierney, Szalai, Dunn, Geslani, & McDowell, 2000; Woods, Weinborn, & Lovejoy, 2003). Unfortunately, Bayesian methods, and other interesting statistical methodologies (e.g., Crawford, Garthwaite, Howell, & Venneri, 2003; Godber, Anderson, & Bell, 2000), including odds and likelihood ratios (e.g., Bieliauskas, Fastenau, Lacy, & Roper, 1997; Dori & Chelune, 2004; Ivnik et al., 2001; Ivnik et al., 2000), are rarely used in mainstream clinical practice.

O'Bryant and Lucas (2006) recently calculated predictive value statistics for the Test of Memory and Malingering (TOMM) based on data published by Gervais, Rohling, Green, and Ford (2004). The sample was 519 non–head-injured disability evaluation cases. The predictive value statistics for the TOMM were based on two assumptions: (a) claimants failing the Word Memory Test provided poor effort (i.e., the WMT was the "gold standard"), and (b) the base rate of poor effort in disability claimants is 30%. With these assumptions, predictive value statistics for the TOMM were computed. The positive predictive value was .98 and the negative predictive value was .78. This means that the clinician can be 98% sure that a person who fails the TOMM is providing poor effort. Moreover, a clinician can be 78% sure that a person who passes the TOMM is not providing obviously poor effort. Note that the TOMM is much more specific than sensitive, meaning it will fail to identify poor effort in a subset of cases. Thus, using predictive value statistics, a clinician can have much more confidence conceptualizing a patient's *poor* effort along the continuum (Figure 6.4).

Two-group contingency analyses also can be used to provide meaningful information regarding effort test scores. Two-group analyses can be conducted by collecting or combining large groups of subjects with similar characteristics. Using the TOMM as an example, performances from highly specific groups reported in the literature were selected (see Table 6.5). These groups can be combined to create specific two-group comparisons. Odds ratios can be calculated to represent the likelihood of belonging to one group versus another based on poor effort on Trial 2 of the TOMM. A number of straightforward, easy-to-use statistical calculators are readily available on the Internet for calculating this information. The results of these two-group comparisons are listed here.

1. People who score below the cutoff on Trial 2 of the TOMM are 1,069 times more likely to be in the laboratory malingering group than the traumatic brain injury group (95% confidence interval = 165.4 to 6,600.5; see Table 6.5).
2. People who score below the cutoff on Trial 2 of the TOMM are 1,144 times more likely to be in the laboratory malingering group than in the combined group of adults with depression, severe mental illness, or chronic pain (95% confidence interval = 266.4 to 4,767.6; see Table 6.5).
3. People who score below the cutoff on Trial 2 of the TOMM are 1,828 times more likely to be in the laboratory malingering group than in the combined group of children and elderly subjects (95% confidence interval = 426.7 to 7,602.9; see Table 6.5).
4. People who score below the cutoff on Trial 2 of the TOMM are 1,115 times more likely to be in the laboratory malingering group than in a group of children with psychiatric or neurological problems (95% confidence interval = 172.6 to 6,882.3; see Table 6.5).

TABLE 6.5 TOMM Trial 2 Performances in Known Clinical Groups

Group	Source	N	Trial 1	Trial 2	Retention	% Passing
Children & the Elderly						
Elderly Community Subjects	Ashendorf et al. (2004)	197	48.9 (1.6)	49.9 (0.3)	n/a	100
Greek Children—Ages 5–12	Constantinou & McCaffrey (2003)	61	46.8 (3.4)	49.5 (1.7)	n/a	96.7
American Children—Age 5–12	Constantinou & McCaffrey (2003)	67	45.9 (3.7)	49.9 (0.3)	n/a	100
Children/Adolescents: Neurological or Psychiatric Problems	Donders (2005)	97[1]	46.5 (4.2)	49.7 (0.7)	n/a	99 97/98
Traumatic Brain Injury Samples						
Patients with Traumatic Brain Injuries	Tombaugh (1997)	45	45.9 (4.7)	49.4 (1.3)	49.6 (1.1)	98
Patients with Traumatic Brain Injuries	Rees et al. (1998)	13	45.3 (5.0)	49.5 (1.0)	50.0 (0.0)	100
Traumatic Brain Injury	Greve et al. (2006a)	14	47.4 (2.9)	49.4 (1.0)	49.6 (0.8)	100
Traumatic Brain Injury	Haber & Fichtenberg (2006)	22	n/a	n/a	n/a	100
Depression, Psychiatric Problems, & Pain Samples						
Psychiatric Inpatients with Major Depression	Rees et al. (2001)	26	47.8 (2.9)	49.9 (0.2)	49.9 (0.3)	100
Elderly Community Subjects with Mild Depression	Ashendorf et al. (2004)	31	48.9 (1.3)	49.9 (0.3)	n/a	100

		N	Trial 1	Trial 2	Retention	% Failing
Healthy Young Adults in Acute Pain	Etherton, Bianchini, Greve, & Ciota (2005)	20	44.8 (4.1)	49.7 (0.9)	49.9 (0.4)	100
Psychiatric Inpatients	Gierok et al. (2005)	19	45.1 (3.9)	49.3 (2.7)	49.3 (1.8)	95
Psychiatric Inpatients with Psychotic Disorders	Duncan (2005)	50	44.2 (5.1)	49.0 (1.7)	48.9 (2.4)	96
Fibromyalgia–Chronic Pain & Psych. Distress	Iverson, LePage, Koehler, Shojania, & Badii (in press)	54	48.8 (1.9)	49.8 (0.5)	49.6 (0.9)	100
Psychiatric Inpatients						
Psychiatric Inpatients	Gierok et al. (2005)	20	45.1 (3.9)	49.3 (2.7)	49.3 (1.8)	95
Psychiatric Inpatients with Psychotic Disorders	Duncan (2005)	50	44.2 (5.1)	49.0 (1.7)	48.9 (2.4)	96
Experimental Subjects Instructed to Malinger		N	Trial 1	Trial 2	Retention	% Failing
University Students Instructed to Malinger[2]	Tombaugh (1997)	20	27.2 (6.8)	27.9 (7.2)	26.4 (7.5)	100
University Students—Symptom Coached[3]	Powell et al. (2004)	27	26.6 (8.5)	26.7 (10.4)	26.7 (9.9)	93
University Students—Test Coached[3]	Powell et al. (2004)	25	32.3 (4.8)	34.6 (6.1)	34.5 (6.6)	96
University Students Instructed to Malinger	Rees et al. (1998)	25	32.6 (7.8)	35.7 (8.9)	34.3 (8.2)	84

(Continued)

149

TABLE 6.5 TOMM Trial 2 Performances in Known Clinical Groups *(Continued)*

Experimental Subjects Instructed to Malinger		N	Trial 1	Trial 2	Retention	% Failing
Subjects with TBIs Instructed to Malinger	Rees et al. (1998)	8	28.1 (7.8)	32.1 (7.3)	31.6 (8.0)	100
Students Faking Cognitive Impairment from Pain	Etherton, Bianchini, Greve, & Ciota (2005)	20	19.7 (11.4)	21.7 (14.9)	18.7 (13.0)	85

[1]There were 100 participants; two were deemed to have provided poor effort during testing and one was considered a false positive.

[2]The university students were given a week to prepare, using any materials they wanted, to malinger believable problems relating to a head injury sustained in a motor vehicle accident.

[3]Symptom coached students were told to fake cognitive impairment, and they were given information describing typical symptoms and problems in people with traumatic brain injuries. Test coached students were given instructions describing effective test-taking strategies that would help them avoid detection.

Based on a large amount of literature to date, when a person fails the TOMM, clinicians can be confident that this performance reflects probable poor effort. However, clinicians should be very cautious about overinterpreting the results of patients who *pass* the TOMM. The TOMM is highly specific to poor effort, but its sensitivity might be lower than some other tests. Gervais and colleagues have suggested that the TOMM is less sensitive to poor effort than the Word Memory Test (Gervais et al., 2004). Tan and colleagues also reported that the TOMM is less sensitive than the Word Memory Test (Tan et al., 2002)., and the TOMM appears to be less sensitive to poor effort than the Amsterdam Short-Term Memory Test (van Hout et al., 2003).

The two-group contingency analysis reported previously for the TOMM can also be applied to the Medical Symptom Validity Test (MSVT; Green, 2004). This Windows-based program is patterned after the Word Memory Test, but it is briefer and easier. The examiner reads aloud the instructions while the patient sits at the computer. The patient is asked to watch the screen while a list of 10 word pairs is presented twice at a rate of 6 seconds per pair. Then, the computer successively presents one word from each pair that was shown previously (i.e., the target) and one that was not shown (i.e., a foil), and the person is required to select the word shown previously in the original list. This produces a total of 20 test items on the immediate recognition (IR) trial. After a 10-minute filled delay (for example, with nonverbal testing), the same recognition testing is performed again using different foil words in the delayed recognition (DR) trial. A consistency score (CNS) between the two trials is calculated by the computer. After the DR trial, testing proceeds to the paired associates (PA) trial, in which the person is asked to sit where the computer screen cannot be seen. The tester reads the first word of each pair from the screen and the person is asked to say the word that went with it in the original list. Finally, the person is asked to recall as many words as possible from the original list in the free recall (FR) trial. The tester records the person's responses using the computer.

In the MSVT manual, data from 228 Brazilians (tested in Portuguese), between the ages of 6 and 68, who were instructed to try their best can be compared to data from 70 additional subjects instructed to simulate memory impairment. Of those instructed to try their best, 96% scored above the cutoffs on Immediate Recognition, Delayed Recognition, and Consistency. In contrast, 97% of those instructed to simulate memory impairment scored below the cutoff on at least one of these measures. Therefore, a person who scores below the cutoff on any one of the three scales is 827 times more likely to be in the group simulating memory impairment than in the normal effort group (95% confidence interval = 188.4 to 3,515.3).

To further illustrate the ease of the MSVT effort scales, healthy children were compared to adults seen for civil forensic evaluations who were very likely to be providing poor effort. The children were in grades 2–5 (N = 75[1]). The adults were seen for disability-related evaluations involving chronic pain, psychological problems, or both (N = 37[2]). All of these adults failed the TOMM relatively early in the evaluation process. The children performed nearly perfectly on the MSVT's Immediate Recognition (M = 98.9, SD = 3.6), Delayed Recognition (M = 98.6, SD = 3.9), and Consistency scales (M = 98.1, SD = 5.5). Only one child scored below 85 on any of these scales. In contrast, adults known to be providing poor effort performed very poorly on the Immediate Recognition (M = 74.3, SD = 21.9), Delayed Recognition (Mean = 68.0, SD = 24.8), and Consistency (Mean = 69.6, SD = 20.6) scales, and 70% frankly failed the MSVT. Based on these data, a person who failed the MSVT is 174.9 times more likely to fall in the poor effort adult group than in the healthy child group (95% confidence interval = 26.6 to 1,096.3).

Without question, there is a major gap between research and practice regarding the use of innovative statistical and psychometric approaches to identifying exaggerated symptoms and poor effort. As a profession, we are very close to being able to provide clinical inferences regarding where a person falls on the continuum of symptom reporting (Figure 6.1) and effort (Figure 6.4) using predictive accuracy statistics with known confidence intervals. Clinicians should be encouraged to conceptualize poor effort, exaggeration, and malingering not in simple dichotomous terms, but through probabilistic estimations. The use of Bayesian methods provide strong statistical evidence to underpin a clinical inference regarding where a person falls along the spectrum of symptom reporting accuracy (Figure 6.1) and effort (Figure 6.4).

ETHICAL ISSUES

THE CENTRAL ISSUES regarding symptom validity assessment, from an ethical perspective, relate to competence, objectivity, clarity in communication, and the proper use of tests (Slick & Iverson, 2003). Common sense dictates that effort testing is essential. However, it is, by its very nature, controversial. Ten ethical concerns, issues, and considerations are summarized in the following list. These ethical concerns and issues are discussed in detail elsewhere (Iverson, in press).

1. Failing to use well-researched effort tests.
2. Using effort tests only for defense cases.

3. Using *more or fewer* effort tests, systematically, depending on whether you were retained by the defendant or the plaintiff.

4. Using *different* effort tests, or using effort tests *differently* depending on which side retains you. For example, using the Rey 15 Items Test for plaintiff cases and the Word Memory Test for defense cases. The former test has lower sensitivity (e.g., Arnett et al., 1995; Guilmette et al., 1994; Iverson & Binder, 2000; Millis & Kler, 1995); therefore, the clinician would be systematically, with forethought, reducing the likelihood of detecting poor effort. An obvious example of using the same test differently would be to give simple effort tests at the end of the evaluation, or after much more difficult tests, such as a battery of memory tests. Researchers have cautioned that from a common sense perspective this practice might reduce the sensitivity of the effort test (e.g., Bernard, 1990; Iverson, 2003), and there is some empirical support for this concern (e.g., Guilmette, Whelihan, Hart, Sparadeo, & Buongiorno, 1996).

5. Warning or prompting patients immediately before taking an effort test.

6. Interpreting effort test results differently, systematically, depending on which side retains you. The most extreme examples would be to *systematically* interpret effort test failure as a "cry for help" or "distraction due to psychological factors or pain" for plaintiff cases and due to "malingering" for defense cases. Of course, these examples are extreme. The point is to be careful and self-reflective of one's clinical approach to interpreting effort test results. It might be useful for clinicians to write out, for personal reflection, their decision rules or clinical criteria for inferring a patient's probable underlying motivation for exaggeration or poor effort.

7. Assuming that someone who passes a single effort test gave his full, complete, or best effort during the evaluation. Passing an effort test simply means the person passed the effort test. It cannot be used, especially in isolation, to infer that the client gave his best effort throughout the evaluation. It can be one piece of converging evidence to suggest adequate or good effort throughout the evaluation.

8. Interpreting effort test failure or exaggerated symptoms, in isolation, as malingering. The research literature is filled with inappropriate use of the term *malingering*. In many studies, the term is used synonymously with *poor effort*. Clinicians should be careful to not assume, automatically, the probable poor effort is diagnostic of malingering. Concluding that someone is malingering

requires multiple sources of converging evidence and the systematic ruling out of probable alternative explanations.

9. Inappropriately interpreting exaggeration or poor effort as a cry for help. A clinician should provide the foundations for an opinion of a "cry for help" as the probable underlying cause of exaggeration or poor effort just as a clinician needs to provide the foundations for an opinion regarding malingering. Unfortunately, most clinicians who rely regularly on the euphemistic "cry for help" do not provide the foundations for this clinical inference.

10. Competent, responsible, informed use of tests. Practitioners cannot simply rely on test manuals. The literature on specific tests is constantly evolving. Thus, clinicians should actively keep up with the literature for the specific tests used. The citations in Tables 6.3 and 6.4 are provided to assist the clinician with this.

Clinicians can avoid most ethical problems by following four recommendations. First, neuropsychologists should routinely assess for poor effort and exaggerated symptoms and problems. Second, neuropsychologists should explain to examinees that it is important to provide their best effort and to report their symptoms and problems accurately. Neuropsychologists should notify them that failure to do so can often be detected. Third, neuropsychologists should be familiar with the literature on poor effort, exaggeration, and malingering and be very familiar with the literature regarding the specific tests and measures used. Finally, neuropsychologists should state conclusions about poor effort, exaggeration, and malingering carefully, explicitly, and clearly.

SAMPLE TEXT FOR REPORTS

CLINICIANS SHOULD AVOID using vague or misleading terminology to describe exaggerated symptoms or deliberately poor test performances. Some psychologists use expressions such as, "psychological factors interfered with the test performance," when there is obvious evidence of poor effort. Some psychologists also overstate the results of effort testing, such as: "The patient passed the TOMM, a well-validated effort test. Therefore, there was absolutely no evidence that poor effort or symptom exaggeration contributed to these test findings." In general, psychologists should avoid overstating effort test results, in either direction (excellent effort or poor effort). Psychologists should avoid terminology that obfuscates rather than informs. Instead, the clinician should consider phraseology that is clear and unambiguous. Some examples of how to report effort test results in a clinical report are provided here.

GOOD EFFORT: SAMPLE REPORT TEXT

THE CAREFUL ASSESSMENT of effort underlies proper test interpretation. In neuropsychology we have numerous well-validated tests and measures that are designed to detect deliberately poor effort. He was administered two well-validated effort tests, and he passed both of them. Moreover, other tests and measures that can indicate poor effort were examined carefully (e.g., Digit Span, Category Test, and Recognition Memory Test), and there was no indication of poor effort during testing. In addition, he was administered psychological tests that have built-in validity scales designed to detect exaggerated symptom reporting. His symptom reporting on all of these validity scales was broadly normal. In summary, Mr. Smith was pleasant and cooperative during the testing, he appeared to work hard on the challenging tasks, and he responded well to encouragement. He did not appear to have motor, sensory, or language problems that would interfere with testing. He passed effort testing. Therefore, the results of this evaluation will be interpreted as a reasonably reliable, valid, and accurate reflection of his current neuropsychological functioning.

POOR EFFORT: SAMPLE REPORT TEXT

Example A
There is evidence of poor effort during this evaluation. Ms. Johnson performed poorly on a well-validated effort test (TOMM: 34/42/36). Her performance on the Recognition Memory Test for Words, a simple forced-choice memory test, was extremely low (30/50). In addition, her performance across many cognitive measures was extremely low and inconsistent with her injury or her estimated preinjury level of functioning. The research literature indicates that performance on these measures of effort is not negatively impacted by a mild concussion, depression, or pain. Therefore, it is likely that the results of this evaluation are not reliable and accurate; they likely *underrepresent* her true abilities in certain areas of cognitive functioning.

Example B
It is not possible to determine if the plaintiff has significant decrements in his cognitive functioning, because it is very likely that he did not put forth his best effort during testing.

Example C
Mr. Frank's test results are grossly inconsistent with his history of sustaining a remote mild concussion. On some relatively simple tests (i.e.,

TOMM, Recognition Memory Test for Words), his performance was so poor that it is not likely to be accurate. For example, on the TOMM he performed far worse than small children (for example 5-year-olds), psychiatric inpatients with schizophrenia, psychiatric inpatients with depression, or patients with traumatic brain injuries. His performance on the Recognition Memory Test for Words was in the probable range of random responding. This performance was far worse than expected from patients with moderate or severe traumatic brain injuries. Overall, there was compelling evidence of poor effort during some of the testing. The cause of this poor effort cannot be determined, but it is unlikely to be explained simply by his symptoms of depression. Therefore, the test results cannot be considered a reliable or valid estimate of his neuropsychological abilities at the time of this evaluation

Example D

The patient scored below chance on a two-alternative forced choice procedures indicating that she knew some of the correct answers and deliberately chose the incorrect answers. This is compelling evidence of poor effort. Therefore, the neuropsychological test results cannot be interpreted as reliable or accurate. They very likely underestimate her true abilities.

Example E

There is compelling evidence that the patient exaggerated his symptoms and provided poor effort during testing. The patient's performances on neuropsychological tests, as well as specialized tests designed to detect poor effort, are very similar to the performances of research participants who are given instructions to malinger. Based on a careful review of the contemporaneous medical record, behavioral observations, and the neuropsychological test results, in my opinion the patient meets criteria for probable malingering. The presence of malingering during the current evaluation does not preclude the possibility that the patient has some residual problems from the accident in question, but it does preclude a meaningful opinion regarding the nature and severity of these problems.

Example F

Mr. Doe has undergone two evaluations. In both evaluations, there was considerable evidence of exaggerated symptoms and problems. In both evaluations, there was also evidence of poor effort during testing. In any case involving frank exaggeration, there are several potential underlying explanations, causes, or motives, including frank psychosis, severe depression, a conversion disorder, a "cry for help," a deep-rooted psychological need to be seen as sick and disabled (i.e., a factitious disorder), an extremely negative self-perception, a personality disorder, a desire to look worse than is actually the case to influence the outcome of litigation, or malingering. Regardless of the underlying motivation, the presence of major exaggeration and poor effort makes it impossible to determine the true nature and extent of his psychiatric, psychological, or neurocognitive problems, and resultant disability (if any), through this evaluation.

Example G

Dr. Jones attributed this exaggeration and poor effort to a "cry for help." During my evaluation, he did not appear to be acutely psychologically distressed. Moreover, he did not appear to be seeking psychological help. When asked specifically about counseling or psychotherapy, he was ambivalent. He did not seem interested. Therefore, I cannot agree that a cry for help is the most likely explanation for his exaggeration and poor effort. In my opinion, his exaggeration of symptoms and problems and his poor performance during testing was not due to severe mental illness or brain damage. In my opinion the primary reason that he behaved this way was to influence the outcome of this independent evaluation in relation to his personal injury litigation. Secondarily, it is possible that he has a very negative perception of himself and his functioning. Moreover, he might derive direct and indirect benefits from being perceived by others as being very disabled. Either one or both of these factors could have contributed to this behavior.

DEFINITE POOR EFFORT: ELABORATE REPORT WRITE-UP

MR. LEE SUSTAINED a mild concussion approximately 2.5 years ago. He sustained a blow to the head, and he felt dazed immediately thereafter. He did not lose consciousness. He did not experience retrograde amnesia or frank post-traumatic amnesia. However, he felt dazed and generally unwell for at least 1 hour following this injury. His recovery from this injury has been unusual and highly atypical. He reported that his symptoms and problems have not improved at all since the first week post injury.

Proper interpretation of neuropsychological test results requires careful and systematic consideration of a wide range of factors that can influence performance on any given test. Before assuming that a test score reflects compromised brain functioning secondary to an injury or disease, the psychologist must determine that the patient understood the requirements of the test and put forth his or her best effort.

Mr. Lee was administered several effort tests over the course of the 2-day assessment. His performance on all the measures was grossly atypical and indicative of poor effort. He performed extremely poorly on standard neuropsychological tests, too. However, these test results are not a reliable, valid, or an accurate reflection of his true abilities.

Mr. Lee grossly failed all effort tests. His performance on these tests was either within or *below* the probable range of chance (i.e., random) responding. His performance on these measures was far worse than the performance of small children, children with mental retardation, children with brain injuries, adults with severe mental illness, adults with severe traumatic brain injuries, or adults with dementia who require institutional care.

Mr. Lee was administered the TOMM, a well-validated effort test. He grossly failed this test (Trial 1 = 15, Trial 2 = 17, Retention = 22). His performance was much worse than would be expected from young children (for example 5–8-year-olds), elderly adults, psychiatric inpatients with depression, psychiatric inpatients with schizophrenia spectrum disorders, or people with traumatic brain injuries (who all tend to score above 45 on Trial 2 and Retention). His performances on two of the three trials of this test were actually below chance. That is, *he scored statistically worse than random guessing* on this simple effort test. If Mr. Lee had a blindfold on while taking the test, and thus did not see any of the items, and then he randomly guessed the answers, he would obtain a score greater than 17 out of 50 98% of the time (i.e., 98 times out of 100 administrations of the test). When a person scores statistically lower than random responding, this is compelling evidence that the person knows the correct answer and is choosing the incorrect answer.

Mr. Lee was also administered the Recognition Memory Test. This test has been used in many studies for identifying poor effort (e.g., Iverson & Franzen, 1994, 1996, 1998; Millis, 1992, 1994, 2002; Millis & Dijkers, 1993). On Recognition Memory for Words, he obtained a score of 16/50. On Recognition Memory for Faces he obtained a score of 10/50. As seen in Figures 6.9 and 6.10, his performance on this test is far below expectations for patients with severe traumatic brain injuries tested during their inpatient rehabilitation. Moreover, his score was worse than the average score for patients with moderate Alzheimer's disease (Diesfeldt, 1990) who cannot live independently.

Again, his performance on this test was actually far worse than random guessing. In fact, his performance was so poor it would be virtually impossible to obtain a score that low by random guessing. For example, if he randomly guessed while blindfolded he would obtain a score greater than 16/50 or 10/50 99% of the time. In fact, he would have less than a 1 in 10,000 chance of obtaining a score of 10 or less by random guessing. Therefore, the only reasonable and probable explanation for this extraordinarily low performance was that he must have known the correct responses and deliberately chose incorrect responses.

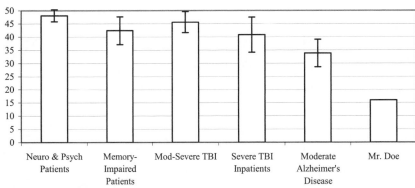

FIGURE 6.9   Mr. Lee's performance on the Recognition Memory Test (Words) compared to known groups.

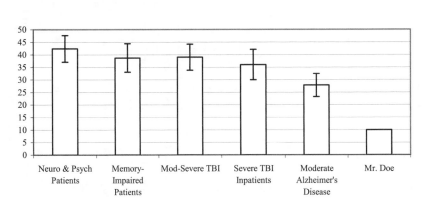

FIGURE 6.10   Mr. Lee's performance on the Recognition Memory Test (Faces) compared to known groups.

CONCLUSIONS AND RECOMMENDATIONS FOR CLINICAL PRACTICE

N EUROPSYCHOLOGICAL TEST PERFORMANCE is exquisitely dependent upon effort. Effort is variable, not constant, and when conceptualized globally it falls on a continuum. This has not been articulated well in the literature over the past 20 years. Passing one or more effort tests does not mean that the patient provided excellent, good, or adequate effort throughout the entire evaluation. Passing one or more effort tests does not ensure that the patient was not exaggerating symptoms and problems. Failing one or more effort tests does not necessarily mean that the patient is malingering. Failing one or more effort tests does not necessarily mean that the patient was exaggerating his symptoms or problems. A flowchart for the assessment of malingering is presented in Figure 6.11.

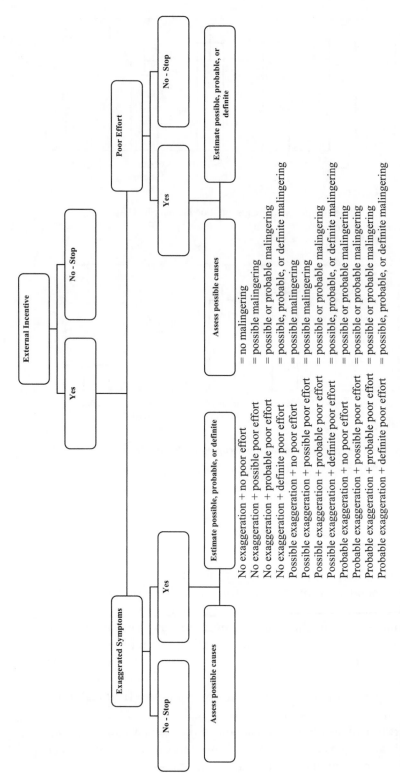

FIGURE 6.11 Assessment of malingering.

Note: A person might exaggerate symptoms or perform poorly on effort testing yet not be malingering. There is always the possibility of a false positive diagnosis (except if the person admits to malingering, of course). See Slick et al. (1999) for a complete discussion of criteria for possible, probable, and definite malingering. The practitioner must consider carefully the possible underlying cause, or causes, for exaggeration or poor effort. If exaggeration or poor effort are present, practitioners should be just as cautious ruling out possible malingering as they are concluding probable or definite malingering.

Hundreds of studies and reviews relating to the detection of exaggerated symptoms, poor effort during neuropsychological testing, and malingering have been published in the past 15 years. It is virtually impossible for practitioners to keep up with the research in this area. Fortunately, there are many good reviews of this literature (e.g., Bianchini, Mathias, & Greve, 2001; Hayes, Hilsabeck, & Gouvier, 1999; Hom & Denney, 2003; Iverson, 2003; Iverson & Binder, 2000; Larrabee, 2005; Millis & Volinsky, 2001; Reynolds, 1998; Rogers, 1997; Sweet, 1999; Vickery et al., 2001). Specific guidelines and recommendations for identifying malingering in a neuropsychological evaluation have been available for several years (Slick et al., 1999), and have recently been published for pain-related disability evaluations (Bianchini, Greve, & Glynn, 2005). The key for practitioners is to (a) have a solid plan for how to conduct and interpret this aspect of the evaluation, and (b) stay abreast of the literature relating to the specific tests used.

The National Academy of Neuropsychology recently published a position paper on *symptom validity assessment* (Bush et al., 2005). In that paper, symptom validity assessment refers to *all methods and procedures* that the practitioner can draw upon to make inferences regarding poor effort during testing and exaggeration of symptoms or problems during interview or on psychological tests. The NAN position paper clearly states that symptom validity assessment is not optional. This position paper solidifies the recommendation for routine effort and validity testing made by clinical researchers for many years (e.g., Doss et al., 1999, p. 17; Green et al., 2001, p. 1059; Greve et al., 2003, p. 179; Iverson & Binder, 2000, p. 853; Iverson & Franzen, 1996, p. 38; Lu et al., 2003, p. 426; Mateer, 2000, p. 54; Millis et al., 1998, p. 172; Slick et al., 1996, p. 920; Suchy & Sweet, 2000, p. 56; Suhr & Boyer, 1999, p. 701; Sweet, 1999, p. 278; Tombaugh, 2002, p. 68).

In forensic practice, clinicians who fail to properly administer and interpret effort testing are not conducting a thorough or competent independent neuropsychological evaluation. This is because: (a) poor effort during testing is, unfortunately, common (Larrabee, 2003b; Mittenberg, Patton, Canyock, & Condit, 2002); (b) the effect of poor effort on neuropsychological test results is major (Vickery et al., 2001), and, in fact, dwarfs the effect of mild traumatic brain injuries (see Figure 6.5) or other conditions that have modest effects on cognitive functioning; (c) there are well-validated tests for detecting poor effort that have low false positive rates; (d) in forensic practice special effort must be made to address causation and to rule out factors that might lead to incorrect inferences or interpretations; and (e) it is considered standard practice in forensic psychology and neuropsychology to do so. A thorough review of ethical issues associated with the assessment of exaggeration, poor effort, and malingering is available elsewhere

(Iverson, in press). Effort testing should not, however, be limited to forensic practice. Screening for poor effort should be part of routine clinical assessments, too.

Clinicians should be encouraged to conceptualize poor effort, exaggeration, and malingering not in simple dichotomous terms, but through probabilistic considerations. Without doubt, we are faced with clinical, statistical, and ethical challenges, issues, and considerations associated with the assessment of poor effort. Commercially available tests, well-written manuals, and dozens of research studies facilitate, but do not ensure, proper and responsible test use. Individual practitioners, clinical researchers, professional organizations, and regulatory bodies are all stakeholders in responsible test use, but the ultimate responsibility lies with the practitioner. I recommend that the clinician keep abreast of the literature and follow the multi-step procedure listed here. Approach the evaluation proactively, not reactively. Planning for the evaluation of poor effort and exaggerated symptoms should be done just as you would plan to evaluate any specific area of functioning. Don't wait for obvious evidence of poor effort or exaggeration before giving specialized tests. Evaluate for poor effort or exaggerated symptoms with the same or greater effort as you evaluate other things, like concentration, memory, or depression.

1. Use a combination of approaches, including specialized tests and examination of performance patterns on traditional tests.
2. Use well-validated specialized tests (e.g., Word Memory Test, Medical Symptom Validity Test, Victoria Symptom Validity Test, CARB, or TOMM). Give "simple" specialized tests (e.g., TOMM, Rey 15 Item Test, or 21 Item Test) at the beginning of the evaluation, not the middle or end.
3. Intersperse validity indicators throughout the evaluation. These can be specific tests or general ability tests for which certain "abnormal performance patterns" may be associated with poor effort.

It is the responsibility of the neuropsychologist to identify and explain test scores that do not make biological or psychometric sense. If the patient demonstrates clear evidence of poor effort on any test within the evaluation, the entire set of test results is questionable. Practitioners should avoid trying to use clinical judgment (i.e., making an educated guess) to determine which test performances are valid, questionable, or biased. Some patients who give poor effort might have demonstrable evidence of structural brain damage documented on neuroimaging (Bianchini, Greve, & Love, 2003; Boone & Lu, 2003; Iverson, 2003). Obviously, it would be inappropriate to conclude that they have no neuropsychological decrements or subjective symptoms. Rather, the clinician must conclude that because the patient did not put forth his or her best performance, it is not possible to determine relative strengths or weaknesses in the neuropsychological profile.

Some neuropsychologists are very reluctant to infer the underlying motivation for exaggerated symptoms or deliberately poor test performance. Without inferring the underlying motivation (i.e., the antecedents), it is impossible to differentiate malingering from a factitious disorder, somatoform disorder, or uncooperativeness. Those psychologists who refuse to infer motivation in regards to exaggerated symptoms should be equally cautious in regards to inferring motives for less contentious behaviors. The neuropsychologist might simply wish to state that: "There is considerable evidence that the patient exaggerated his level of disability and gave poor effort during neuropsychological testing. I am not comfortable, based on the evidence available to me, providing an opinion as to whether this behavior was motivated by general uncooperativeness, a desire for monetary gain (i.e., malingering), or a psychological need to assume the sick or disabled role (i.e., factitious disorder)."

A competent forensic neuropsychological assessment should in most cases be comprised of (a) review of records (e.g., medical and educational), (b) interviews with the plaintiff and other informants such as spouse or employer if possible, (c) behavioral observations, (d) neuropsychological measures covering all major domains of cognitive function, (e) measures of psychological adjustment and psychiatric symptoms, and (f) measures for detecting poor effort (Slick & Iverson, 2003). An evaluation that does not include these elements might lead to incorrect conclusions about the nature and cause of any observed deficits and may thus be considered incompetently conducted. A thorough assessment provides the best, and in many cases, only acceptable basis for an expert opinion.

NOTES

1. Data provided by Lloyd Flaro, PhD.
2. Data provided by Roger Gervais, PhD.

REFERENCES

Allen, L. M., Conder, R. L., Green, P., & Cox, D. R. (1997). *CARB 97 manual for the Computerized Assessment of Response Bias*. Durham, NC: CogniSyst.

Allen, L. M., Iverson, G. L., & Green, P. (2002). Computerized Assessment of Response Bias in forensic neuropsychology. *Journal of Forensic Neuropsychology, 3*, 205–225.

American Psychiatric Association. (1994). *Diagnostic and statistical manual of mental disorders* (4th ed.). Washington, DC: Author.

Arnett, P. A., & Franzen, M. D. (1997). Performance of substance abusers with memory deficits on measures of malingering. *Archives of Clinical Neuropsychology, 12*(5), 513–518.

Arnett, P. A., Hammeke, T. A., & Schwartz, L. (1995). Quantitative and qualitative performance on Rey's 15-Item Test in neurological patients and dissimulators. *The Clinical Neuropsychologist, 9*(1), 17–26.

Arnold, G., Boone, K. B., Lu, P., Dean, A., Wen, J., Nitch, S., et al. (2005). Sensitivity and specificity of finger tapping test scores for the detection of suspect effort. *The Clinical Neuropsychologist, 19*(1), 105–120.

Ashendorf, L., Constantinou, M., & McCaffrey, R. J. (2004). The effect of depression and anxiety on the TOMM in community-dwelling older adults. *Archives of Clinical Neuropsychology, 19*(1), 125–130.

Ashendorf, L., O'Bryant, S. E., & McCaffrey, R. J. (2003). Specificity of malingering detection strategies in older adults using the CVLT and WCST. *The Clinical Neuropsychologist, 17*(2), 255–262.

Axelrod, B. N., & Rawlings, D. B. (1999). Clinical utility of incomplete effort WAIS-R formulas: A longitudinal examination of individuals with traumatic brain injuries. *Journal of Forensic Neuropsychology, 1*, 15–27.

Babikian, T., Boone, K. B., Lu, P., & Arnold, G. (2006). Sensitivity and specificity of various digit span scores in the detection of suspect effort. *The Clinical Neuropsychologist, 20*(1), 145–159.

Backhaus, S. L., Fichtenberg, N. L., & Hanks, R. A. (2004). Detection of suboptimal performance using a floor effect strategy in patients with traumatic brain injury. *The Clinical Neuropsychologist, 18*(4), 591–603.

Bagby, R. M., Nicholson, R. A., Bacchiochi, J. R., Ryder, A. G., & Bury, A. S. (2002). The predictive capacity of the MMPI-2 and PAI validity scales and indexes to detect coached and uncoached feigning. *Journal of Personality Assessment, 78*(1), 69–86.

Bagby, R. M., Nicholson, R. A., Buis, T., & Bacchiochi, J. R. (2000). Can the MMPI-2 validity scales detect depression feigned by experts? *Assessment, 7*(1), 55–62.

Baker, R., Donders, J., & Thompson, E. (2000). Assessment of incomplete effort with the California Verbal Learning Test. *Applied Neuropsychology, 7*(2), 111–114.

Barr, W. B., & McCrea, M. (2001). Sensitivity and specificity of standardized neurocognitive testing immediately following sports concussion. *Journal of the International Neuropsychological Society, 7*, 693–702.

Barrash, J., Suhr, J., & Manzel, K. (2004). Detecting poor effort and malingering with an expanded version of the Auditory Verbal Learning Test

(AVLTX): Validation with clinical samples. *Journal of Clinical and Experimental Neuropsychology, 26*(1), 125–140.

Bauer, L., Yantz, C. L., Ryan, L. M., Warden, D. L., & McCaffrey, R. J. (2005). An examination of the California Verbal Learning Test II to detect incomplete effort in a traumatic brain-injury sample. *Applied Neuropsychology, 12*(4), 202–207.

Beetar, J. T., & Williams, J. M. (1995). Malingering response styles on the memory assessment scales and symptom validity tests. *Archives of Clinical Neuropsychology, 10*(1), 57–72.

Benedict, R. H., Cox, D., Thompson, L. L., Foley, F., Weinstock-Guttman, B., & Munschauer, F. (2004). Reliable screening for neuropsychological impairment in multiple sclerosis. *Multiple Sclerosis, 10*(6), 675–678.

Benedict, R. H., Munschauer, F., Linn, R., Miller, C., Murphy, E., Foley, F., et al. (2003). Screening for multiple sclerosis cognitive impairment using a self-administered 15-item questionnaire. *Multiple Sclerosis, 9*(1), 95–101.

Bernard, L. C. (1990). Prospects for faking believable memory deficits on neuropsychological tests and the use of incentives in simulation research. *Journal of Clinical and Experimental Neuropsychology, 12*(5), 715–728.

Bernard, L. C., & Fowler, W. (1990). Assessing the validity of memory complaints: Performance of brain-damaged and normal individuals on Rey's task to detect malingering. *Journal of Clinical Psychology, 46*(4), 432–436.

Bernard, L. C., Houston, W., & Natoli, L. (1993). Malingering on neuropsychological memory tests: Potential objective indicators. *Journal of Clinical Psychology, 49*(1), 45–53.

Bianchini, K. J., Greve, K. W., & Glynn, G. (2005). On the diagnosis of malingered pain-related disability: Lessons from cognitive malingering research. *Spine Journal, 5*(4), 404–417.

Bianchini, K. J., Greve, K. W., & Love, J. M. (2003). Definite malingered neurocognitive dysfunction in moderate/severe traumatic brain injury. *The Clinical Neuropsychologist, 17*(4), 574–580.

Bianchini, K. J., Houston, R. J., Greve, K. W., Irvin, T. R., Black, F. W., Swift, D. A., et al. (2003). Malingered neurocognitive dysfunction in neurotoxic exposure: An application of the Slick criteria. *Journal of Occupational and Environmental Medicine, 45*(10), 1087–1099.

Bianchini, K., Love, J. M., Greve, K. W., & Adams, D. (2005). Detection and diagnosis of malingering in electrical injury. *Archives of Clinical Neuropsychology, 20*(3), 365–373.

Bianchini, K. J., Mathias, C. W., & Greve, K. W. (2001). Symptom validity testing: A critical review. *The Clinical Neuropsychologist, 15*(1), 19–45.

Bianchini, K. J., Mathias, C. W., Greve, K. W., Houston, R. J., & Crouch, J. A. (2001). Classification accuracy of the portland digit recognition test in traumatic brain injury. *The Clinical Neuropsychologist, 15*(4), 461–470.

Bieliauskas, L. A., Fastenau, P. S., Lacy, M. A., & Roper, B. L. (1997). Use of the odds ratio to translate neuropsychological test scores into real-world outcomes: From statistical significance to clinical significance. *Journal of Clinical and Experimental Neuropsychology, 19*(6), 889–896.

Binder, L. M. (1993). An abbreviated form of the Portland Digit Recognition Test. *The Clinical Neuropsychologist, 7,* 104–107.

Binder, L. M. (2002). The Portland Digit Recognition Test: A review of validation data and clinical use. *Journal of Forensic Neuropsychology, 2*(3/4), 27–42.

Binder, L. M., & Kelly, M. P. (1996). Portland Digit Recognition Test performance by brain dysfunction patients without financial incentives. *Assessment, 3,* 403–409.

Binder, L. M., Kelly, M. P., Villanueva, M. R., & Winslow, M. M. (2003). Motivation and neuropsychological test performance following mild head injury. *Journal of Clinical and Experimental Neuropsychology, 25*(3), 420–430.

Binder, L. M., & Rohling, M. L. (1996). Money matters: A meta-analytic review of the effects of financial incentives on recovery after closed-head injury. *American Journal of Psychiatry, 153*(1), 7–10.

Binder, L. M., Rohling, M. L., & Larrabee, J. (1997). A review of mild head trauma. Part I: Meta-analytic review of neuropsychological studies. *Journal of Clinical and Experimental Neuropsychology, 19*(3), 421–431.

Binder, L. M., Salinsky, M. C., & Smith, S. P. (1994). Psychological correlates of psychogenic seizures. *Journal of Clinical and Experimental Neuropsychology, 16*(4), 524–530.

Binder, L. M., & Willis, S. C. (1991). Assessment of motivation after financially compensable minor head trauma. *Psychological Assessment, 3,* 175–181.

Binks, P. G., Gouvier, W. D., & Waters, W. F. (1997). Malingering detection with the dot counting test. *Archives of Clinical Neuropsychology, 12*(1), 41–46.

Bolan, B., Foster, J. K., Schmand, B., & Bolan, S. (2002). A comparison of three tests to detect feigned amnesia: The effects of feedback and the measurement of response latency. *Journal of Clinical and Experimental Neuropsychology, 24*(2), 154–167.

Boone, K. B., & Lu, P. (2003). Noncredible cognitive performance in the context of severe brain injury. *The Clinical Neuropsychologist, 17*(2), 244–254.

Boone, K. B., Lu, P., & Wen, J. (2005). Comparison of various RAVLT scores in the detection of noncredible memory performance. *Archives of Clinical Neuropsychology, 20*(3), 301–319.

Boone, K. B., Savodnik, I., Ghaffarian, S., Lee, A., Freeman, D., & Berman, N. G. (1995). Rey 15-Item memorization and Dot counting scores in a "stress" claim worker's compensation population: Relationship to personality (MCMI) scores. *Journal of Clinical Psychology, 51*(3), 457–463.

Brennan, A. M., & Gouvier, W. D. (2006). Are we honestly studying malingering? A profile and comparison of simulated and suspected malingerers. *Applied Neuropsychology, 13*(1), 1–11.

Bush, S. S., Ruff, R. M., Troster, A. I., Barth, J. T., Koffler, S. P., Pliskin, N. H., et al. (2005). Symptom validity assessment: Practice issues and medical necessity

NAN policy & planning committee. *Archives of Clinical Neuropsychology, 20*(4), 419–426.

Butcher, J. N., Graham, J. R., Ben-Porath, Y. S., Tellegen, A., Dahlstrom, W. G., & Kaemmer, B. (2001). Minnesota multiphasic personality inventory 2—manual for adminstration and scoring. Minneapolis, MN: University of Minnesota Press.

Calhoun, P. S., Earnst, K. S., Tucker, D. D., Kirby, A. C., & Beckham, J. C. (2000). Feigning combat-related posttraumatic stress disorder on the personality assessment inventory. *Journal of Personality Assessment, 75*(2), 338–350.

Coleman, R. D., Rapport, L. J., Millis, S. R., Ricker, J. H., & Farchione, T. J. (1998). Effects of coaching on detection of malingering on the California Verbal Learning Test. *Journal of Clinical and Experimental Neuropsychology, 20*(2), 201–210.

Constantinou, M., Bauer, L., Ashendorf, L., Fisher, J. M., & McCaffrey, R. J. (2005). Is poor performance on recognition memory effort measures indicative of generalized poor performance on neuropsychological tests? *Archives of Clinical Neuropsychology, 20*(2), 191–198.

Constantinou, M., & McCaffrey, R. J. (2003). Using the TOMM for evaluating children's effort to perform optimally on neuropsychological measures. *Neuropsychology Development and Cognition. Section C, Child Neuropsychology, 9*(2), 81–90.

Crawford, J. R., Garthwaite, P. H., Howell, D. C., & Venneri, A. (2003). Intra-individual measures of association in neuropsychology: Inferential methods for comparing a single case with a control or normative sample. *Journal of the International Neuropsychological Society, 9*(7), 989–1000.

Curtis, K. L., Greve, K. W., Bianchini, K. J., & Brennan, A. (2006). California Verbal Learning Test indicators of malingered neurocognitive dysfunction: Sensitivity and specificity in traumatic brain injury. *Assessment, 13*(1), 46–61.

Dearth, C. S., Berry, D. T., Vickery, C. D., Vagnini, V. L., Baser, R. E., Orey, S. A., et al. (2005). Detection of feigned head injury symptoms on the MMPI-2 in head injured patients and community controls. *Archives of Clinical Neuropsychology, 20*(1), 95–110.

Demakis, G. J. (1999). Serial malingering on verbal and nonverbal fluency and memory measures: An analog investigation. *Archives of Clinical Neuropsychology, 14*(4), 401–410.

Demakis, G. J. (2004). Application of clinically-derived malingering cutoffs on the California Verbal Learning Test and the Wechsler Adult Intelligence Test-Revised to an analog malingering study. *Applied Neuropsychology, 11*(4), 222–228.

DiCarlo, M. A., Gfeller, J. D., & Oliveri, M. V. (2000). Effects of coaching on detecting feigned cognitive impairment with the Category test. *Archives of Clinical Neuropsychology, 15*(5), 399–413.

Diesfeldt, H. F. (1990). Recognition Memory for Words and Faces in primary degenerative dementia of the Alzheimer type and normal old age. *Journal of Clinical and Experimental Neuropsychology, 12*(6), 931–945.

Doane, B. M., Greve, K. W., & Bianchini, K. J. (2005). Agreement between the abbreviated and standard Portland Digit Recognition Test. *The Clinical Neuropsychologist, 19*(1), 99–104.

Donders, J. (2005). Performance on the test of memory malingering in a mixed pediatric sample. *Neuropsychology, Development, and Cognition. Section C, Child Neuropsychology, 11*(2), 221–227.

Dori, G. A., & Chelune, G. J. (2004). Education-stratified base-rate information on discrepancy scores within and between the Wechsler Adult Intelligence Scale—Third Edition and the Wechsler Memory Scale—Third Edition. *Psychological Assessment, 16*(2), 146–154.

Doss, R. C., Chelune, G. J., & Naugle, R. I. (1999). Victoria Symptom Validity Test: Compensation-seeking vs. non-compensation-seeking patients in a general clinical setting. *Journal of Forensic Neuropsychology, 1*(4), 5–20.

Duncan, A. (2005). The impact of cognitive and psychiatric impairment of psychotic disorders on the Test of Memory Malingering (TOMM). *Assessment, 12*(2), 123–129.

Dunn, T. M., Shear, P. K., Howe, S., & Ris, M. D. (2003). Detecting neuropsychological malingering: Effects of coaching and information. *Archives of Clinical Neuropsychology, 18*(2), 121–134.

Erdal, K. (2004). The effects of motivation, coaching, and knowledge of neuropsychology on the simulated malingering of head injury. *Archives of Clinical Neuropsychology, 19*(1), 73–88.

Etherton, J. L., Bianchini, K. J., Ciota, M. A., & Greve, K. W. (2005). Reliable digit span is unaffected by laboratory-induced pain: Implications for clinical use. *Assessment, 12*(1), 101–106.

Etherton, J. L., Bianchini, K. J., Greve, K. W., & Ciota, M. A. (2005). Test of Memory Malingering performance is unaffected by laboratory-induced pain: Implications for clinical use. *Archives of Clinical Neuropsychology, 20*(3), 375–384.

Etherton, J. L., Bianchini, K. J., Greve, K. W., & Heinly, M. T. (2005). Sensitivity and specificity of reliable digit span in malingered pain-related disability. *Assessment, 12*(2), 130–136.

Fisher, H. L., & Rose, D. (2005). Comparison of the effectiveness of two versions of the Rey memory test in discriminating between actual and simulated memory impairment, with and without the addition of a standard memory test. *Journal of Clinical and Experimental Neuropsychology, 27*(7), 840–858.

Forrest, T. J., Allen, D. N., & Goldstein, G. (2004). Malingering indexes for the Halstead Category Test. *The Clinical Neuropsychologist, 18*(2), 334–347.

Frederick, R. I. (1997). *Validity Indicator Profile manual.* Minneapolis, MN: NCS Assessments.

Frederick, R. I. (2000). A personal floor effect strategy to evaluate the validity of performance on memory tests. *Journal of Clinical and Experimental Neuropsychology, 22*(6), 720–730.

Frederick, R. I. (2002a). A review of Rey's strategies for detecting malingered neuropsychological impairment. *Journal of Forensic Neuropsychology, 2*(3/4), 1–26.

Frederick, R. I. (2002b). Review of the Validity Indicator Profile. *Journal of Forensic Neuropsychology, 2*(3/4), 125–146.

Frederick, R. I., & Crosby, R. D. (2000). Development and validation of the Validity Indicator Profile. *Law and Human Behavior, 24*(1), 59–82.

Frederick, R. I., Crosby, R. D., & Wynkoop, T. F. (2000). Performance curve classification of invalid responding on the Validity Indicator Profile. *Archives of Clinical Neuropsychology, 15*(4), 281–300.

Frederick, R. I., & Foster, H. G. (1991). Multiple measures of malingering on a forced-choice test of cognitive ability. *Psychological Assessment, 3*(4), 596–602.

Frederick, R. I., Sarfaty, S. D., Johnston, J. D., & Powel, J. (1994). Validation of a detector of responses bias on a forced-choice test of nonverbal ability. *Neuropsychology, 8*, 118–125.

Gavett, B. E., O'Bryant, S. E., Fisher, J. M., & McCaffrey, R. J. (2005). Hit rates of adequate performance based on the Test of Memory Malingering (TOMM) Trial 1. *Applied Neuropsychology, 12*(1), 1–4.

Gervais, R. O., Rohling, M. L., Green, P., & Ford, W. (2004). A comparison of WMT, CARB, and TOMM failure rates in non-head injury disability claimants. *Archives of Clinical Neuropsychology, 19*(4), 475–487.

Gervais, R. O., Russell, A. S., Green, P., Allen, L. M., 3rd, Ferrari, R., & Pieschl, S. D. (2001). Effort testing in patients with fibromyalgia and disability incentives. *Journal of Rheumatology, 28*(8), 1892–1899.

Gierok, S. D., Dickson, A. L., & Cole, J. A. (2005). Performance of forensic and non-forensic adult psychiatric inpatients on the Test of Memory Malingering. *Archives of Clinical Neuropsychology, 20*(6), 755–760.

Glassmire, D. M., Bierley, R. A., Wisniewski, A. M., Greene, R. L., Kennedy, J. E., & Date, E. (2003). Using the WMS-III Faces subtest to detect malingered memory impairment. *Journal of Clinical and Experimental Neuropsychology, 25*(4), 465–481.

Godber, T., Anderson, V., & Bell, R. (2000). The measurement and diagnostic utility of intrasubtest scatter in pediatric neuropsychology. *Journal of Clinical Psychology, 56*(1), 101–112.

Goebel, R. A. (1983). Detection of faking on the Halstead-Reitan Neuropsychological Test Battery. *Journal of Clinical Psychology, 39*(5), 731–742.

Goldberg, J. O., & Miller, H. R. (1986). Performance of psychiatric inpatients and intellectually deficient individuals on a test that assesses the validity of memory complaints. *Journal of Clinical Psychology, 42*, 792–795.

Gontkovsky, S. T., & Souheaver, G. T. (2000). Are brain-damaged patients inappropriately labeled as malingering using the 21-Item Test and the WMS-R

Logical Memory Forced Choice Recognition Test. *Psychological Reports, 87*(2), 512–514.

Gorissen, M., Sanz, J. C., & Schmand, B. (2005). Effort and cognition in schizophrenia patients. *Schizophrenia Research, 78*(2–3), 199–208.

Green, P. (2004). *Green's Medical Symptom Validity Test for Windows user's manual.* Edmonton, AB: Green's Publishing, Inc.

Green, P., Allen, L. M., & Astner, K. (1996). *The Word Memory Test: A user's guide to the oral and computer-administered forms, US Version 1.1.* Durham, NC: CogniSyst, Inc.

Green, P., & Flaro, L. (2003). Word Memory Test performance in children. *Neuropsychology, Development, and Cognition. Section C, Child Neuropsychology, 9*(3), 189–207.

Green, P., & Iverson, G. L. (2001a). Effects of injury severity and cognitive exaggeration on olfactory deficits in head injury compensation claims. *NeuroRehabilitation, 16*(4), 237–243.

Green, P., & Iverson, G. L. (2001b). Validation of the Computerized Assessment of Response Bias in litigating patients with head injuries. *The Clinical Neuropsychologist, 15*, 492–497.

Green, P., Iverson, G. L., & Allen, L. (1999). Detecting malingering in head injury litigation with the Word Memory Test. *Brain Injury, 13*(10), 813–819.

Green, P., Lees-Haley, P. R., & Allen, L. M. (2002). The Word Memory Test and the validity of neuropsychological test scores. *Journal of Forensic Neuropsychology, 2*(3/4), 97–124.

Green, P., Rohling, M. L., Iverson, G. L., & Gervais, R. O. (2003). Relationships between olfactory discrimination and head injury severity. *Brain Injury, 17*(6), 479–496.

Green, P., Rohling, M. L., Lees-Haley, P. R., & Allen, L. M., 3rd. (2001). Effort has a greater effect on test scores than severe brain injury in compensation claimants. *Brain Injury, 15*(12), 1045–1060.

Greene, R. L. (2000). *The MMPI-2: An interpretive manual* (2nd ed.). Boston: Allyn and Bacon.

Greiffenstein, M. F., Baker, W. J., Axelrod, B., Peck, E. A., & Gervais, R. (2004). The Fake Bad Scale and MMPI-2 F-family in detection of implausible psychological trauma claims. *The Clinical Neuropsychologist, 18*(4), 573–590.

Greiffenstein, M. F., Baker, W. J., & Gola, T. (1994). Validation of malingered amnesia measures with a large clinical sample. *Psychological Assessment, 6*, 218–224.

Greiffenstein, M. F., Baker, W. J., & Gola, T. (1996). Comparison of multiple scoring methods for Rey's malingered amnesia measures. *Archives of Clinical Neuropsychology, 11*, 283–293.

Greiffenstein, M. F., Baker, W. J., Gola, T., Donders, J., & Miller, L. (2002). The Fake Bad Scale in atypical and severe closed head injury litigants. *Journal of Clinical Psychology, 58*(12), 1591–1600.

Greve, K. W., & Bianchini, K. J. (2006). Should the retention trial of the Test of Memory Malingering be optional? *Archives of Clinical Neuropsychology, 21*(1), 117–119.

Greve, K. W., Bianchini, K. J., Black, F. W., Heinly, M. T., Love, J. M., Swift, D. A., et al. (2006a). Classification accuracy of the Test of Memory Malingering in persons reporting exposure to environmental and industrial toxins: Results of a known-groups analysis. *Archives of Clinical Neuropsychology, 21*(5), 439–448.

Greve, K. W., Bianchini, K. J., Black, F. W., Heinly, M. T., Love, J. M., Swift, D. A., et al. (2006b). The prevalence of cognitive malingering in persons reporting exposure to occupational and environmental substances. *Neurotoxicology*. (In press.)

Greve, K. W., Bianchini, K. J., & Doane, B. M. (2006). Classification accuracy of the Test of Memory Malingering in traumatic brain injury: Results of a known-groups analysis. *Journal of Clinical and Experimental Neuropsychology, 28*(7), 1176–1190.

Greve, K. W., Bianchini, K. J., Love, J. M., Brennan, A., & Heinly, M. T. (2006). Sensitivity and specificity of MMPI-2 validity scales and indicators to malingered neurocognitive dysfunction in traumatic brain injury. *The Clinical Neuropsychologist, 20*(3), 491–512.

Greve, K. W., Bianchini, K. J., Mathias, C. W., Houston, R. J., & Crouch, J. A. (2002). Detecting malingered performance with the Wisconsin Card Sorting Test: A preliminary investigation in traumatic brain injury. *The Clinical Neuropsychologist, 16*(2), 179–191.

Greve, K. W., Bianchini, K. J., Mathias, C. W., Houston, R. J., & Crouch, J. A. (2003). Detecting malingered performance on the Wechsler Adult Intelligence Scale. Validation of Mittenberg's approach in traumatic brain injury. *Archives of Clinical Neuropsychology, 18*(3), 245–260.

Grote, C. L., Kooker, E. K., Garron, D.C., Nyenhuis, D. L., Smith, C. A., & Mattingly, M. L. (2000). Performance of compensation seeking and non-compensation seeking samples on the Victoria Symptom Validity test: Cross-validation and extension of a standardization study. *Journal of Clinical and Experimental Neuropsychology, 22*(6), 709–719.

Guez, M., Brannstrom, R., Nyberg, L., Toolanen, G., & Hildingsson, C. (2005). Neuropsychological functioning and MMPI-2 profiles in chronic neck pain: A comparison of whiplash and non-traumatic groups. *Journal of Clinical and Experimental Neuropsychology, 27*(2), 151–163.

Guilmette, T. J., Hart, K. J., Guiliano, A. J., & Leininger, B. E. (1994). Detecting simulated memory impairment: Comparison of the Rey Fifteen-Item Test and the Hiscock forced-choice procedure. *The Clinical Neuropsychologist, 8,* 283–294.

Guilmette, T. J., Whelihan, W. M., Hart, K. J., Sparadeo, F. R., & Buongiorno, G. (1996). Order effects in the administration of a forced-choice procedure for detection of malingering in disability claimants' evaluations. *Perceptual and Motor Skills, 83*(3 Pt 1), 1007–1016.

Gunstad, J., & Suhr, J. A. (2001). Efficacy of the full and abbreviated forms of the Portland Digit Recognition Test: Vulnerability to coaching. *The Clinical Neuropsychologist, 15*(3), 397–404.

Gunstad, J., & Suhr, J. A. (2004). Use of the Abbreviated Portland Digit Recognition Test in simulated malingering and neurological groups. *Journal of Forensic Neuropsychology, 4*(1), 33–48.

Guriel, J., & Fremouw, W. (2003). Assessing malingered posttraumatic stress disorder: A critical review. *Clinical Psychology Review, 23*(7), 881–904.

Haber, A. H., & Fichtenberg, N. L. (2006). Replication of the Test of Memory Malingering (TOMM) in a traumatic brain injury and head trauma sample. *The Clinical Neuropsychologist, 20*(3), 524–532.

Hayes, J. S., Hale, D. B., & Gouvier, W. D. (1998). Malingering detection in a mentally retarded forensic population. *Applied Neuropsychology, 5*(1), 33–36.

Hayes, J. S., Hilsabeck, R. C., & Gouvier, W. D. (1999). Malingering in traumatic brain injury: Current issues and caveats in assessment and classification. In N. R. Varney & R. J. Roberts (Eds.), *The evaluation and treatment of mild traumatic brain injury* (pp. 249–290). Mahwah, NJ: Lawrence Erlbaum Associates.

Hays, J. R., Emmons, J., & Stallings, G. (2000). Dementia and mental retardation markers on the Rey 15-Item Visual Memory Test. *Psychological Reports, 86*(1), 179–182.

Heaton, R. K., Smith, H. H., Jr., Lehman, R. A., & Vogt, A. T. (1978). Prospects for faking believable deficits on neuropsychological testing. *Journal of Consulting and Clinical Psychology, 46*(5), 892–900.

Heinly, M. T., Greve, K. W., Bianchini, K. J., Love, J. M., & Brennan, A. (2005). WAIS digit span-based indicators of malingered neurocognitive dysfunction: Classification accuracy in traumatic brain injury. *Assessment, 12*(4), 429–444.

Henry, G. K. (2005). Probable malingering and performance on the test of variables of attention. *The Clinical Neuropsychologist, 19*(1), 121–129.

Hill, S. K., Ryan, L. M., Kennedy, C. H., & Malamut, B. L. (2003). The relationship between measures of declarative memory and the Test of Memory Malingering in patients with and without temporal lobe dysfunction. *Journal of Forensic Neuropsychology, 3*(3), 1–18.

Hilsabeck, R. C., Thompson, M. D., Irby, J. W., Adams, R. L., Scott, J. G., & Gouvier, W. D. (2003). Partial cross-validation of the Wechsler Memory Scale-Revised (WMS-R) General Memory-Attention/Concentration Malingering Index in a nonlitigating sample. *Archives of Clinical Neuropsychology, 18*(1), 71–79.

Hom, J., & Denney, R. L. (2003). *Detection of response bias in forensic neuropsychology*. New York: Haworth Medical Press.

Horner, M. D., Bedwell, J. S., & Duong, A. (2006). Abbreviated form of the test of memory malingering. *International Journal of Neuroscience, 116*(10), 1181–1186.

Iverson, G. L. (1998). *21 Item Test research manual:* unpublished.

Iverson, G. L. (2001). Can malingering be identified with the judgment of the line orientation test? *Applied Neuropsychology, 8*(3), 167–173.

Iverson, G. L. (2003). Detecting malingering in civil forensic evaluations. In A. M. Horton & L. C. Hartlage (Eds.), *Handbook of forensic neuropsychology* (pp. 137–180). New York: Springer Publishing.

Iverson, G. L. (in press). Ethical issues associated with the assessment of exaggeration, poor effort, and malingering. *Applied Neuropsychology*.

Iverson, G. L., & Binder, L. M. (2000). Detecting exaggeration and malingering in neuropsychological assessment. *Journal of Head Trauma Rehabilitation, 15*(2), 829–858.

Iverson, G. L., & Franzen, M. D. (1994). The Recognition Memory Test, Digit Span, and Knox Cube Test as markers of malingered memory impairment. *Assessment, 1,* 323–334.

Iverson, G. L., & Franzen, M. D. (1996). Using multiple objective memory procedures to detect simulated malingering. *Journal of Clinical and Experimental Neuropsychology, 18*(1), 38–51.

Iverson, G. L., & Franzen, M. D. (1998). Detecting malingered memory deficits with the Recognition Memory Test. *Brain Injury, 12*(4), 275–282.

Iverson, G. L., Franzen, M. D., & McCracken, L. M. (1991). Evaluation of a standardized instrument for the detection of malingered memory deficits. *Law and Human Behavior, 15,* 667–676.

Iverson, G. L., Franzen, M. D., & McCracken, L. M. (1994). Application of a forced-choice memory procedure designed to detect experimental malingering. *Archives of Clinical Neuropsychology, 9*(5), 437–450.

Iverson, G. L., Green, P., & Gervais, R. (1999). Using the Word Memory Test to detect biased responding in head injury litigation. *Journal of Cognitive Rehabilitation, 2,* 4–8.

Iverson, G. L., & Lange, R. T. (2005). Detecting exaggeration and malingering in psychological injury claims. In W. J. Koch, K. S. Douglas, T. L. Nicholls, & M. O'Neill (Eds.), *Psychological injuries: Forensic assessment, treatment and law* (pp. 76–112). New York: Oxford University Press.

Iverson, G. L., LePage, J., Koehler, B. E., Shojania, K., & Badii, M. (in press). TOMM scores are not affected by chronic pain or depression in patients with fibromyalgia. *The Clinical Neuropsychologist*.

Iverson, G. L., Mendrek, A., & Adams, R. L. (2004). The persistent belief that VIQ-PIQ splits suggest lateralized brain damage. *Applied Neuropsychology, 11*(2), 85–90.

Iverson, G. L., & Tulsky, D. S. (2003). Detecting malingering on the WAIS-III. Unusual Digit Span performance patterns in the normal population and in clinical groups. *Archives of Clinical Neuropsychology, 18*(1), 1–9.

Ivnik, R. J., Smith, G. E., Cerhan, J. H., Boeve, B. F., Tangalos, E. G., & Petersen, R. C. (2001). Understanding the diagnostic capabilities of cognitive tests. *The Clinical Neuropsychologist, 15*(1), 114–124.

Ivnik, R. J., Smith, G. E., Petersen, R. C., Boeve, B. F., Kokmen, E., & Tangalos, E. G. (2000). Diagnostic accuracy of four approaches to interpreting neuropsychological test data. *Neuropsychology, 14*(2), 163–177.

Ju, D., & Varney, N. R. (2000). Can head injury patients simulate malingering? *Applied Neuropsychology, 7*(4), 201–207.

Kelly, P. J., Baker, G. A., van den Broek, M. D., Jackson, H., & Humphries, G. (2005). The detection of malingering in memory performance: The sensitivity and specificity of four measures in a UK population. *British Journal of Clinical Psychology, 44*(Pt. 3), 333–341.

Killgore, W. D., & DellaPietra, L. (2000a). Item response biases on the Logical Memory Delayed Recognition subtest of the Wechsler Memory Scale-III. *Psychological Reports, 86*(3 Pt. 1), 851–857.

Killgore, W. D., & DellaPietra, L. (2000b). Using the WMS-III to detect malingering: Empirical validation of the Rarely Missed Index (RMI). *Journal of Clinical and Experimental Neuropsychology, 22*(6), 761–771.

Labarge, A. S., McCaffrey, R. J., & Brown, T. A. (2003). Neuropsychologists' abilities to determine the predictive value of diagnostic tests. *Archives of Clinical Neuropsychology, 18*(2), 165–175.

Lange, R. T., Sullivan, K., & Anderson, D. (2005). Ecological validity of the WMS-III Rarely Missed Index in personal injury litigation. *Journal of Clinical and Experimental Neuropsychology, 27*(4), 412–424.

Langeluddecke, P. M., & Lucas, S. K. (2003). Quantitative measures of memory malingering on the Wechsler Memory Scale—Third edition in mild head injury litigants. *Archives of Clinical Neuropsychology, 18*(2), 181–197.

Langeluddecke, P. M., & Lucas, S. K. (2004). Validation of the Rarely Missed Index (RMI) in detecting memory malingering in mild head injury litigants. *Journal of Forensic Neuropsychology, 4*(1), 49–64.

Larrabee, G. J. (1997). Neuropsychological outcome, post concussion symptoms, and forensic considerations in mild closed head trauma. *Seminars in Clinical Neuropsychiatry, 2*(3), 196–206.

Larrabee, G. (1998). Somatic malingering on the MMPI and MMPI-2 in litigating subjects. *The Clinical Neuropsychologist, 12*, 179–188.

Larrabee, G. (2003a). Detection of symptom exaggeration with the MMPI-2 in litigants with malingered neurocognitive dysfunction. *The Clinical Neuropsychologist, 17*(1), 54–68.

Larrabee, G. J. (2003b). Detection of malingering using atypical performance patterns on standard neuropsychological tests. *The Clinical Neuropsychologist, 17*(3), 410–425.

Larrabee, G. J. (2003c). Exaggerated MMPI-2 symptom report in personal injury litigants with malingered neurocognitive deficit. *Archives of Clinical Neuropsychology, 18*(6), 673–686.

Larrabee, G. J. (2005). Assessment of malingering. In G. J. Larrabee (Ed.), *Forensic neuropsychology: A scientific approach* (pp. 115–158). New York: Oxford University Press.

Lee, A., Boone, K. B., Lesser, I., Wohl, M., Wilkins, S., & Parks, C. (2000). Performance of older depressed patients on two cognitive malingering tests: False positive rates for the Rey 15-Item memorization and Dot Counting tests. *The Clinical Neuropsychologist, 14*(3), 303–308.

Lee, G. P., Loring, D. W., & Martin, R. C. (1992). Rey's 15-Item Visual Memory Test for the detection of malingering: Normative observations on patients with neurological disorders. *Psychological Assessment, 4*, 43–46.

Lees-Haley, P. R. (1992). Efficacy of MMPI-2 validity scales and MCMI-II modifier scales for detecting spurious PTSD claims: F, F-K, Fake Bad Scale, ego strength, subtle-obvious subscales, DIS, and DEB. *Journal of Clinical Psychology, 48*(5), 681–689.

Lees-Haley, P. R., English, L. T., & Glenn, W. J. (1991). A Fake Bad Scale on the MMPI-2 for personal injury claimants. *Psychological Reports, 68*(1), 203–210.

Lees-Haley, P. R., Iverson, G. L., Lange, R. T., Fox, D. D., & Allen, L. M. (2002). Malingering in forensic neuropsychology: *Daubert* and the MMPI-2. *Journal of Forensic Neuropsychology, 3*, 167–203.

Liljequist, L., Kinder, B. N., & Schinka, J. A. (1998). An investigation of malingering posttraumatic stress disorder on the Personality Assessment Inventory. *Journal of Personality Assessment, 71*(3), 322–336.

Loring, D. W., Lee, G. P., & Meador, K. J. (2005). Victoria Symptom Validity Test performance in non-litigating epilepsy surgery candidates. *Journal of Clinical and Experimental Neuropsychology, 27*(5), 610–617.

Lu, P. H., Boone, K. B., Cozolino, L., & Mitchell, C. (2003). Effectiveness of the Rey-Osterrieth Complex Figure Test and the Meyers and Meyers recognition trial in the detection of suspect effort. *The Clinical Neuropsychologist, 17*(3), 426–440.

Lynch, W. J. (2004). Determination of effort level, exaggeration, and malingering in neurocognitive assessment. *Journal of Head Trauma Rehabilitation, 19*(3), 277–283.

Macciocchi, S. N., Seel, R. T., Alderson, A., & Godsall, R. (2006). Victoria Symptom Validity Test performance in acute severe traumatic brain injury: Implications for test interpretation. *Archives of Clinical Neuropsychology, 21*(5), 395–404.

Mateer, C. A. (2000). Assessment issues. In S. A. Raskin & C. A. Mateer (Eds.), *Neuropsychological management of mild traumatic brain injury* (pp. 39–72). New York: Oxford University Press.

Mathias, C. W., Greve, K. W., Bianchini, K. J., Houston, R. J., & Crouch, J. A. (2002). Detecting malingered neurocognitive dysfunction using the reliable digit span in traumatic brain injury. *Assessment, 9*(3), 301–308.

McCaffrey, R. J., O'Bryant, S. E., Ashendorf, L., & Fisher, J. M. (2003). Correlations among the TOMM, Rey-15, and MMPI-2 validity scales in a sample of TBI litigants. *Journal of Forensic Neuropsychology, 3*(3), 45–54.

McKinzey, R. K., & Russell, E. W. (1997). A partial cross-validation of a Halstead-Reitan Battery malingering formula. *Journal of Clinical and Experimental Neuropsychology, 19*(4), 484–488.

Merten, T., Green, P., Henry, M., Blaskewitz, N., & Brockhaus, R. (2005). Analog validation of German-language symptom validity tests and the influence of coaching. *Archives of Clinical Neuropsychology, 20*(6), 719–726.

Meyers, J. E., Millis, S. R., & Volkert, K. (2002). A validity index for the MMPI-2. *Archives of Clinical Neuropsychology, 17*(2), 157–169.

Meyers, J. E., & Volbrecht, M. (1998). Validation of reliable digits for detection of malingering. *Assessment, 5*(3), 303–307.

Miller, L. J., Ryan, J. J., Carruthers, C. A., & Cluff, R. B. (2004). Brief screening indexes for malingering: A confirmation of Vocabulary minus Digit Span from the WAIS-III and the Rarely Missed Index from the WMS-III. *The Clinical Neuropsychologist, 18*(2), 327–333.

Millis, S. R. (1992). The Recognition Memory Test in the detection of malingered and exaggerated memory deficits. *The Clinical Neuropsychologist, 6*, 406–414.

Millis, S. R. (1994). Assessment of motivation and memory with the Recognition Memory Test after financially compensable mild head injury. *Journal of Clinical Psychology, 50*(4), 601–605.

Millis, S. R. (2002). Warrington's Recognition Memory Test in the detection of response bias. *Journal of Forensic Neuropsychology, 2*, 147–166.

Millis, S. R., & Dijkers, M. (1993). Use of the Recognition Memory Test in traumatic brain injury: Preliminary findings. *Brain Injury, 7*(1), 53–58.

Millis, S. R., & Kler, S. (1995). Limitations of the Rey Fifteen-Item Test in the detection of malingering. *The Clinical Neuropsychologist, 9*(3), 241–244.

Millis, S. R., Putnam, S. H., Adams, K. H., & Ricker, J. H. (1995). The California Verbal Learning Test in the detection of incomplete effort in neuropsychological testing. *Psychological Assessment, 7*, 463–471.

Millis, S. R., Ross, S. R., & Ricker, J. H. (1998). Detection of incomplete effort on the Wechsler Adult Intelligence Scale-Revised: A cross-validation. *Journal of Clinical and Experimental Neuropsychology, 20*(2), 167–173.

Millis, S. R., & Volinsky, C. T. (2001). Assessment of response bias in mild head injury: Beyond malingering tests. *Journal of Clinical and Experimental Neuropsychology, 23*(6), 809–828.

Mittenberg, W., Aguila-Puentes, G., Patton, C., Canyock, E. M., & Heilbronner, R. L. (2002). Neuropsychological profiling of symptom exaggeration and malingering. *Journal of Forensic Neuropsychology, 3*(1/2), 227–240.

Mittenberg, W., Patton, C., Canyock, E. M., & Condit, D. C. (2002). Base rates of malingering and symptom exaggeration. *Journal of Clinical and Experimental Neuropsychology, 24*(8), 1094–1102.

Mittenberg, W., Rotholc, A., Russell, E., & Heilbronner, R. (1996). Identification of malingered head injury on the Halstead-Reitan battery. *Archives of Clinical Neuropsychology, 11*(4), 271–281.

Mittenberg, W., Theroux-Fichera, S. T., Zielinski, R. E., & Heilbronner, R. L. (1995). Identification of malingered head injury on the Wechsler Adult Intelligence Scale-Revised. *Professional Psychology: Research and Practice, 26*, 491–498.

Moore, B. A., & Donders, J. (2004). Predictors of invalid neuropsychological test performance after traumatic brain injury. *Brain Injury, 18*(10), 975–984.

Morey, L. C. (1991). *Personality Assessment Inventory professional manual*. Odessa, FL: Psychological Assessment Resources.

Morey, L. C. (1996). *An interpretive guide to the Personality Assessment Inventory (PAI)*. Odessa, FL: Psychological Assessment Resources.

Morey, L. C., & Lanier, V. W. (1998). Operating characteristics of six response distortion indicators for the Personality Assessment Inventory. *Assessment, 5*(3), 203–214.

Mossman, D. (2000). The meaning of malingering data: Further applications of Bayes' theorem. *Behavioral Sciences and the Law, 18*(6), 761–779.

Mossman, D. (2003). Daubert, cognitive malingering, and test accuracy. *Law and Human Behavior, 27*(3), 229–249.

Nelson, N. W., Boone, K., Dueck, A., Wagener, L., Lu, P., & Grills, C. (2003). Relationships between eight measures of suspect effort. *The Clinical Neuropsychologist, 17*(2), 263–272.

Nelson, N. W., Sweet, J. J., & Demakis, G. J. (2006). Meta-analysis of the MMPI-2 Fake Bad Scale: Utility in forensic practice. *The Clinical Neuropsychologist, 20*(1), 39–58.

O'Bryant, S. E., & Lucas, J. A. (2006). Estimating the predictive value of the Test of Memory Malingering: An illustrative example for clinicians. *The Clinical Neuropsychologist, 20*(3), 533–540.

Powell, M. R., Gfeller, J. D., Hendricks, B. L., & Sharland, M. (2004). Detecting symptom- and test-coached simulators with the Test of Memory Malingering. *Archives of Clinical Neuropsychology, 19*(5), 693–702.

Rasquin, S. M., Lodder, J., Visser, P. J., Lousberg, R., & Verhey, F. R. (2005). Predictive accuracy of MCI subtypes for Alzheimer's disease and vascular dementia in subjects with mild cognitive impairment: A 2-year follow-up study. *Dementia and Geriatric Cognitive Disorders, 19*(2–3), 113–119.

Rees, L. M., Tombaugh, T. N., & Boulay, L. (2001). Depression and the Test of Memory Malingering. *Archives of Clinical Neuropsychology, 16*(5), 501–506.

Rees, L. M., Tombaugh, T. N., Gansler, D. A., & Moczynski, N. P. (1998). Five validation experiments of the Test of Memory Malingering (TOMM). *Psychological Assessment, 10*, 10–20.

Reitan, R. M., & Wolfson, D. (1996a). Consistency of responses on retesting among head-injured subjects in litigation versus head-injured subjects not in litigation. *Applied Neuropsychology, 2*, 67–71.

Reitan, R. M., & Wolfson, D. (1996b). The question of validity of neuropsychological test scores among head-injured litigants: Development of a dissimulation index. *Archives of Clinical Neuropsychology, 11*(7), 573–580.

Reitan, R. M., & Wolfson, D. (2002). Detection of malingering and invalid test results using the Halstead-Reitan battery. *Journal of Forensic Neuropsychology, 3*(1/2), 275–314.

Resnick, P. J. (1997). Malingering of posttraumatic disorders. In R. Rogers (Ed.), *Clinical assessment of malingering and deception* (2nd ed., pp. 130–152). New York: Guilford.

Reynolds, C. R. (Ed.). (1998). *Detection of malingering during head injury litigation.* New York: Plenum Press.

Reznek, L. (2005). The Rey 15-Item Memory test for malingering: A meta-analysis. *Brain Injury, 19*(7), 539–543.

Richman, J., Green, P., Gervais, R., Flaro, L., Merten, T., Brockhaus, R., et al. (2006). Objective tests of symptom exaggeration in independent medical examinations. *Journal of Occupational and Environmental Medicine, 48*(3), 303–311.

Rogers, R. (1997). *Clinical assessment of malingering and deception* (2nd ed.). New York: Guilford Press.

Rogers, R., Ornduff, S. R., & Sewell, K. W. (1993). Feigning specific disorders: A study of the Personality Assessment Inventory (PAI). *Journal of Personality Assessment, 60*(3), 554–560.

Rogers, R., Sewell, K. W., Cruise, K. R., Wang, E. W., & Ustad, K. L. (1998). The PAI and feigning: A cautionary note on its use in forensic-correctional settings. *Assessment, 5*(4), 399–405.

Rogers, R., Sewell, K. W., Martin, M. A., & Vitacco, M. J. (2003). Detection of feigned mental disorders: A meta-analysis of the MMPI-2 and malingering. *Assessment, 10*(2), 160–177.

Rogers, R., Sewell, K. W., Morey, L. C., & Ustad, K. L. (1996). Detection of feigned mental disorders on the Personality Assessment Inventory: A discriminant analysis. *Journal of Personality Assessment, 67*(3), 629–640.

Rohling, M. L., Allen, L. M., & Green, P. (2002). Who is exaggerating cognitive impairment and who is not? *CNS Spectrums, 7*(5), 387–395.

Rohling, M. L., Green, P., Allen, L. M., & Iverson, G. L. (2002). Depressive symptoms and neurocognitive test scores in patients passing symptom validity tests. *Archives of Clinical Neuropsychology, 17*(3), 205–222.

Rose, F. E., Hall, S., Szalda-Petree, A. D., & Bach, P. J. (1998). A comparison of four tests of malingering and the effects of coaching. *Archives of Clinical Neuropsychology, 13*(4), 349–363.

Rosen, G. M., & Powel, J. E. (2003). Use of a symptom validity test in the forensic assessment of posttraumatic stress disorder. *Journal of Anxiety Disorders, 17*(3), 361–367.

Ross, S. R., Millis, S. R., Krukowski, R. A., Putnam, S. H., & Adams, K. M. (2004). Detecting incomplete effort on the MMPI-2: An examination of the

Fake-Bad Scale in mild head injury. *Journal of Clinical and Experimental Neuropsychology, 26*(1), 115–124.

Ross, S. R., Putnam, S. H., & Adams, K. M. (2006). Psychological disturbance, incomplete effort, and compensation-seeking status as predictors of neuropsychological test performance in head injury. *Journal of Clinical and Experimental Neuropsychology, 28*(1), 111–125.

Roth, R. S., Isquith, P. K., & Gioia, G. A. (2005). *BRIEF-A: Behavior Rating Inventory of Executive Function—Adult Version.* Lutz, FL: Psychological Assessment Resources.

Ruff, R. M., & Hibbard, K. M. (2003). *Ruff Neurobehavioral Inventory.* Lutz, FL: Psychological Assessment Resources, Inc.

Sawrie, S. M., Martin, R. C., Gilliam, F. G., Roth, D. L., Faught, E., & Kuzniecky, R. (1998). Contribution of neuropsychological data to the prediction of temporal lobe epilepsy surgery outcome. *Epilepsia, 39*(3), 319–325.

Schagen, S., Schmand, B., de Sterke, S., & Lindeboom, J. (1997). Amsterdam Short-Term Memory test: A new procedure for the detection of feigned memory deficits. *Journal of Clinical and Experimental Neuropsychology, 19*(1), 43–51.

Schmand, B., Lindeboom, J., Schagen, S., Heijt, R., Koene, T., & Hamburger, H. L. (1998). Cognitive complaints in patients after whiplash injury: The impact of malingering. *Journal of Neurology, Neurosurgery and Psychiatry, 64*(3), 339–343.

Shapiro, A. M., Benedict, R. H., Schretlen, D., & Brandt, J. (1999). Construct and concurrent validity of the Hopkins Verbal Learning Test-revised. *The Clinical Neuropsychologist, 13*(3), 348–358.

Sherman, D. S., Boone, K. B., Lu, P., & Razani, J. (2002). Re-examination of a Rey auditory verbal learning test/Rey complex figure discriminant function to detect suspect effort. *The Clinical Neuropsychologist, 16*(3), 242–250.

Shum, D. H., O'Gorman, J. G., & Alpar, A. (2004). Effects of incentive and preparation time on performance and classification accuracy of standard and malingering-specific memory tests. *Archives of Clinical Neuropsychology, 19*(6), 817–823.

Silverberg, N., & Barrash, J. (2005). Further validation of the expanded auditory verbal learning test for detecting poor effort and response bias: Data from temporal lobectomy candidates. *Journal of Clinical and Experimental Neuropsychology, 27*(7), 907–914.

Slick, D., Hopp, G., Strauss, E., Hunter, M., & Pinch, D. (1994). Detecting dissimulation: Profiles of simulated malingerers, traumatic brain-injury patients, and normal controls on a revised version of Hiscock and Hiscock's Forced-Choice Memory Test. *Journal of Clinical and Experimental Neuropsychology, 16*(3), 472–481.

Slick, D. J., Hopp, G., Strauss, E., & Spellacy, F. J. (1996). Victoria Symptom Validity Test: Efficiency for detecting feigned memory impairment and relationship to neuropsychological tests and MMPI-2 validity scales. *Journal of Clinical and Experimental Neuropsychology, 18*(6), 911–922.

Slick, D. J., Hopp, G., Strauss, E., & Thompson, G. (1997). *The Victoria Symptom Validity Test*. Odessa, FL: PAR.

Slick, D. J., & Iverson, G. L. (2003). Ethical issues arising in forensic neuropsychological assessment. In I. Z. Schultz & D. O. Brady (Eds.), *Handbook of psychological injuries* (pp. 2014–2034). Chicago: American Bar Association.

Slick, D. J., Iverson, G. L., & Green, P. (2000). California Verbal Learning Test indicators of suboptimal performance in a sample of head-injury litigants. *Journal of Clinical and Experimental Neuropsychology, 22*(5), 569–579.

Slick, D. J., Sherman, E. M., & Iverson, G. L. (1999). Diagnostic criteria for malingered neurocognitive dysfunction: Proposed standards for clinical practice and research. *The Clinical Neuropsychologist, 13*(4), 545–561.

Strauss, E., Slick, D. J., Levy-Bencheton, J., Hunter, M., MacDonald, S. W., & Hultsch, D. F. (2002). Intraindividual variability as an indicator of malingering in head injury. *Archives of Clinical Neuropsychology, 17*(5), 423–444.

Suchy, Y. J., & Sweet, J. J. (2000). Information/Orientation subtest of the Wechsler Memory Scale-Revised as an indicator of suspicion of insufficient effort. *The Clinical Neuropsychologist, 14*(1), 56–66.

Suhr, J. A., & Boyer, D. (1999). Use of the Wisconsin Card Sorting Test in the detection of malingering in student simulator and patient samples. *Journal of Clinical and Experimental Neuropsychology, 21*(5), 701–708.

Suhr, J., Gunstad, J., Greub, B., & Barrash, J. (2004). Exaggeration index for an expanded version of the auditory verbal learning test: Robustness to coaching. *Journal of Clinical and Experimental Neuropsychology, 26*(3), 416–427.

Suhr, J., Tranel, D., Wefel, J., & Barrash, J. (1997). Memory performance after head injury: Contributions of malingering, litigation status, psychological factors, and medication use. *Journal of Clinical and Experimental Neuropsychology, 19*(4), 500–514.

Sweet, J. J. (1999). Malingering: Differential diagnosis. In J. J. Sweet (Ed.), *Forensic neuropsychology: Fundamentals and practice* (pp. 255–285). Lisse, The Netherlands: Swets & Zeitlinger.

Sweet, J. J., & King, J. H. (2002). Category Test validity indicators: Overview and practice recommendations. *Journal of Forensic Neuropsychology, 3*(1/2), 241–274.

Sweet, J. J., Wolfe, P., Sattlberger, E., Numan, B., Rosenfeld, J. P., Clingerman, S., et al. (2000). Further investigation of traumatic brain injury versus insufficient effort with the California Verbal Learning Test. *Archives of Clinical Neuropsychology, 15*(2), 105–113.

Tan, J. E., Slick, D. J., Strauss, E., & Hultsch, D. F. (2002). How'd they do it? Malingering strategies on symptom validity tests. *The Clinical Neuropsychologist, 16*(4), 495–505.

Tardif, H. P., Barry, R. J., Fox, A. M., & Johnstone, S. J. (2000). Detection of feigned recognition memory impairment using the old/new effect of the event-related potential. *International Journal of Psychophysiology, 36*(1), 1–9.

Teichner, G., & Wagner, M. T. (2004). The Test of Memory Malingering (TOMM): Normative data from cognitively intact, cognitively impaired, and elderly patients with dementia. *Archives of Clinical Neuropsychology, 19*(3), 455–464.

Temple, R. O., McBride, A. M., David Horner, M. D., & Taylor, R. M. (2003). Personality characteristics of patients showing suboptimal cognitive effort. *The Clinical Neuropsychologist, 17*(3), 402–409.

Tenhula, W. N., & Sweet, J. J. (1996). Double cross-validation of the booklet category test in detecting malingered traumatic brain injury. *The Clinical Neuropsychologist, 10*, 104–116.

Thompson, G. B. (2002). The Victoria Symptom Validity Test: An enhanced test of symptom validity. *Journal of Forensic Neuropsychology, 2*(3/4), 43–68.

Tierney, M. C., Szalai, J. P., Dunn, E., Geslani, D., & McDowell, I. (2000). Prediction of probable Alzheimer disease in patients with symptoms suggestive of memory impairment. Value of the Mini-Mental State Examination. *Archives of Family Medicine, 9*(6), 527–532.

Tombaugh, T. N. (1996). *Test of Memory Malingering.* North Tonawanda, NY: Multi-Health Systems.

Tombaugh, T. N. (1997). The Test of Memory Malingering (TOMM): Normative data from cognitively intact and cognitively impaired individuals. *Psychological Assessment, 9*(3), 260–268.

Tombaugh, T. N. (2002). The Test of Memory Malingering (TOMM) in forensic psychology. *Journal of Forensic Neuropsychology, 2*(3/4), 68–96.

Trueblood, W. (1994). Qualitative and quantitative characteristics of malingered and other invalid WAIS-R and clinical memory data. *Journal of Clinical and Experimental Neuropsychology, 16*(4), 597–607.

Trueblood, W., & Schmidt, M. (1993). Malingering and other validity considerations in the neuropsychological evaluation of mild head injury. *Journal of Clinical and Experimental Neuropsychology, 15*(4), 578–590.

Tsushima, W. T., & Tsushima, V. G. (2001). Comparison of the Fake Bad Scale and other MMPI-2 validity scales with personal injury litigants. *Assessment, 8*(2), 205–212.

Vagnini, V. L., Sollman, M. J., Berry, D. T., Granacher, R. P., Clark, J. A., Burton, R., et al. (2006). Known-groups cross-validation of the letter memory test in a compensation-seeking mixed neurologic sample. *The Clinical Neuropsychologist, 20*(2), 289–304.

Vallabhajosula, B., & van Gorp, W. G. (2001). Post-Daubert admissibility of scientific evidence on malingering of cognitive deficits. *Journal of the American Academy of Psychiatry and the Law, 29*(2), 207–215.

Van der Werf, S. P., Prins, J. B., Jongen, P. J., van der Meer, J. W., & Bleijenberg, G. (2000). Abnormal neuropsychological findings are not necessarily a sign of cerebral impairment: A matched comparison between chronic fatigue syndrome and multiple sclerosis. *Neuropsychiatry, Neuropsychology, and Behavioral Neurology, 13*(3), 199–203.

Van Hout, M. S., Schmand, B., Wekking, E. M., Hageman, G., & Deelman, B. G. (2003). Suboptimal performance on neuropsychological tests in patients with suspected chronic toxic encephalopathy. *Neurotoxicology, 24*(4–5), 547–551.

Veazey, C. H., Wagner, A. L., Hays, J. R., & Miller, H. A. (2005). Validity of the Miller forensic assessment of symptoms test in psychiatric inpatients. *Psychological Reports, 96*(3 Pt. 1), 771–774.

Vickery, C. D., Berry, D. T., Inman, T. H., Harris, M. J., & Orey, S. A. (2001). Detection of inadequate effort on neuropsychological testing: A meta-analytic review of selected procedures. *Archives of Clinical Neuropsychology, 16*(1), 45–73.

Wang, E. W., Rogers, R., Giles, C. L., Diamond, P. M., Herrington-Wang, L. E., & Taylor, E. R. (1997). A pilot study of the Personality Assessment Inventory (PAI) in corrections: Assessment of malingering, suicide risk, and aggression in male inmates. *Behavioral Sciences and the Law, 15*(4), 469–482.

Weinborn, M., Orr, T., Woods, S. P., Conover, E., & Feix, J. (2003). A validation of the Test of Memory Malingering in a forensic psychiatric setting. *Journal of Clinical and Experimental Neuropsychology, 25*(7), 979–990.

Williamson, D. J. G., Green, P., Allen, L., & Rohling, M. L. (2003). Evaluating effort with the Word Memory Test and Category Test—or not: Inconsistencies in a compensation-seeking sample. *Journal of Forensic Neuropsychology, 3*(3), 19–44.

Woods, S. P., Weinborn, M., & Lovejoy, D. W. (2003). Are classification accuracy statistics underused in neuropsychological research? *Journal of Clinical and Experimental Neuropsychology, 25*(3), 431–439.

Yanez, Y. T., Fremouw, W., Tennant, J., Strunk, J., & Coker, K. (2006). Effects of severe depression on TOMM performance among disability-seeking outpatients. *Archives of Clinical Neuropsychology, 21*, 161–166.

7

Lateralization of Cerebral Functions

J. JOSH HALL, TIFFANY J. NEAL, AND RAYMOND S. DEAN

THE HUMAN BRAIN is clearly divided into hemispheres by a deep longitudinal fissure. Although these hemispheres are similar from a gross anatomical point of view, research over the past century suggests that they have specialized functions. Anatomically, right-handed individuals display asymmetries between the hemispheres of the primary motor cortex (M1), whereas individuals who are left-handed do not show these same asymmetries (Solodkin, Hlustik, Noll, & Small, 2001). The anatomical difference of M1 between left- and right-handed individuals suggests that motor physiology (i.e., sequential movements) may differ between right- and left-handed individuals (Solodkin et al., 2001). Asymmetries are also found in the frontal, temporal, and parietal lobes (Hugdahl, 1996).

Microanatomical and psychophysiological differences in hemispheres of the brain have been observed as early as the 30th week of gestation (Molfese, Freeman, & Palermo, 1975; Wada, Clarke, & Hamm, 1975). Others have argued that lateralization begins as early as 12 weeks gestation (McCartney & Hopper, 1999). While elementary lateralization is measurable in perinatal stages, more complex patterns of hemispheric specialization continue to develop during childhood and into adulthood (Dean & Anderson, 1997; Satz, Bakker, Teunissen, Goebel, & van der Blugt, 1975). Research incorporating functional magnetic resonance imaging (fMRI) and positron emission topography (PET) affirms early evidence that structural differences between hemispheres may lead to functional differences and thus specialization for tasks and activities within each hemisphere (Robichon, Levrier, Farnarier, & Habib, 2000; Xu et al., 2001).This chapter examines aspects of hemispheric lateralization of functions that may hold clinical insights. Following a review of a number of critical issues in the assessment and understanding of hemispheric differences, the clinical significance of a lack of secure hemispheric lateralization will be examined for language disorders.

HISTORICAL ANTECEDENTS

EARLY IN THE nineteenth century a number of papers were published that began to link complex psychological functions to specific areas of the brain. Although efforts in the specific localization of functions to microstructures of the brain have not fared well, broad organizational principles of the relationship between anatomical features of the brain and behavior remain the focus of neuropsychology (Dean, 1985a). It is now well recognized that an individual's developmental history and normal differences in both the structure and the chemistry of the brain interact in such a way that highly specific structural localization of functions is a tenuous pursuit. Thus, although hemispheric differences are acknowledged, highly specific localization of function does not appear as robust as once portrayed. Parallel increases in neuropsychological instruments and neuroimaging have shifted the foci of neuropsychology toward examination of the relationship between behaviors and the structural functioning of the brain (Dean & Anderson, 1997).

Serious consideration of functional asymmetry of hemispheres may be traced to Broca's (1861) and Dax's (1865) clinical observations of brain-damaged subjects. Moreover, patients with damage to the left hemisphere were reported to have compromised linguistic processes. Specifically, Broca (1861) concluded that with damage to the third convolution of the left cerebral cortex, many aspects of the patient's speech were impaired. Jackson's seminal work in the late nineteenth century began to articulate more fully the idea of two different yet coexisting modes of cognitive processing that followed hemispheric lines of the brain (1932). Summarizing his clinical observations, Jackson argued that "in most people, the left side of the brain is the leading side—the side of the so-called will, and the right is the automatic side" (1932, p. 141). Although Jackson also described the left hemisphere as serving functions of sensation and perception.

These conclusions extended Dax's (1865) and Broca's (1861) observations and provided the underpinnings of what has been referred to as the bimodal theory of hemispheric processing. The evolving notion of hemispheric dominance was originally articulated to distinguish the hemisphere that most clearly served language functions and has only recently taken on more global connotations associated with control functions. The luxury of retrospect allows criticisms of reports that offered conclusions on normal function based on the study of diseased brains. However, these early papers are the antecedents of continued research efforts.

Congruent with increased experimental sophistication of recent investigations has come debate as to the nature of the lateralization process. Thus, although consistent hemispheric differences are acknowledged by more neuroscientists, debate continues as to whether hemispheric differences in processing (e.g., Geschwind & Levitsky, 1968; Petersen, Fox, Posner, Mintun, & Raichle, 1989), attention (e.g., Kinsbourne, 1975), or storage (e.g., Hardyck, Tzeng, & Wang, 1978) are responsible. Although most investigators have found the arguments favoring processing differences to be more heuristic, Hardyck and colleagues' (1978) data concerning hemispheric lateralization in memory storage and Kinsbourne's (1970) reports regarding the direction of attention between hemispheres need to be seriously addressed when attempting conclusions concerning the underlying neurological mechanism.

LATERALIZATION OF FUNCTIONS

THE NOTION THAT hemispheres of the brain selectively serve rather different psychological functions has gained scientific credence (Dean, 1985b). Although acknowledging interhemispheric communication, laboratory and clinical researchers portray distinct hemispheric differences for more complex cognitive functions. As may be gathered from Table 7.1, investigations of patients who have undergone surgical section of the corpus callosum and those with localized brain damage to one hemisphere indicate rather clear differences in the functional efficiency between hemispheres. As suggested early on by Dax, Broca, Wernicke, and Jackson, the left hemisphere has been more closely linked to processing involving speech, language, and calculation (Reitan, 1955; Sperry, 1969) than has the right. Poizner, Bellugi, and Klima (1990) have offered similar data with deaf individuals who have had either a right or a left hemispheric lesion. Furthermore, Jackson implicated that lateralization of speech to the left hemisphere and thus localization of speech ability to this area of the brain does not imply that all damage that impacts speech is inherently within such areas. Brain injury resulting in speech impairments could occur in processes

TABLE 7.1   Lateralized Functions of the Right and Left Hemispheres

Function	Reference
Right hemisphere	
Processing modes	
Simultaneous	Sperry (1974)
Holistic	Sperry (1969); Dimond & Beaumont (1974)
Visual/nonverbal	Sperry (1974); Savage & Thomas (1993)
Imagery	Seamon & Gazzaniga (1973)
Spatial Reasoning	Sperry (1974); Poizner, Bellugi, & Klima (1990)
Nonverbal functions	
Depth perception	Carmon & Bechtoldt (1969)
Melodic perception	Shankweiler (1966)
Tactile perception (integration)	Boll (1974b)
Haptic perception	Witelson (1974)
Nonverbal sound recognition	Milner (1962)
Motor integration	Kimura (1967)
Visual constructive performance	Parsons, Vega, & Burn (1969)
Pattern recognition	Eccles (1973)
Memory/learning	
Nonverbal memory	Stark (1961)
Face recognition	Milner (1967); Hecaen & Angelergues (1962)
Left hemisphere	
Processing modes	
Sequential	Sperry, Gazzaniga, & Bogen (1969)
Temporal	Mills (1977); Efron (1963)
Analytic	Morgan, McDonald, & McDonald (1971); Eccles (1973)
Verbal functions	
Speech	Wada (1949); Reitan (1955); Posner, Petersen, Fox, & Raichle (1988)
General language/verbal abilities	Gazzaniga (1970); Smith (1974)
Calculation/arithmetic	Reitan (1955); Eccles (1973); Gerstmann (1957)
Abstract verbal thought	Gazzaniga & Sperry (1962)
Writing (composition)	Sperry (1974); Hecaen & Marcie (1974)
Complex motor functions	Dimond & Beaumont (1974)
Body orientation	Gerstmann (1957)
Vigilance	Dimond & Beaumont (1974)
Learning/memory	
Verbal paired-associates	Dimond & Beaumont (1974)
Short-term verbal recall	Kimura (1961)
Abstract and concrete words	McFarland, McFarland, Bain, & Ashton (1978); Seamon & Gazzaniga (1973)
Verbal mediation/rehearsal	Dean (1983); Seamon & Gazzaniga (1973)
Learning complex motor functions	Dimond & Beaumont (1974)

necessary to create speech within either hemisphere. Thus, localizing function or damage is independent of the localization of speech (Zillmer & Spiers, 2001).

The study of sign language with brain-damaged individuals allows another perspective of hemispheric specialization, as it is a combination of visual-spatial elements and language. These differences seem more heuristically attributed to the mode in which information is processed than to the specific stimuli or modality of presentation (Brown & Hecaen, 1976). That is to say, the left hemisphere has been shown to be better prepared to process information in a more analytical, logical, or sequential fashion; as such, language is an excellent tool for such processing (Kimura, 1961). Research that has examined the electrical activity of the brain (electroencephalographic studies) and relies on perceptual asymmetries reinforces the duality of cerebral processing (Gordon, 1978; Kimura, 1967; Morgan, McDonald, & McDonald, 1971).

Studies of autism also demonstrate the effects of lateralization upon language. Recent evidence concerning autism has implicated abnormal lateralization as a cause of language deficits (Escalante-Mead, Minshew, & Sweeney, 2003). The authors suggested that language disturbances in autism may be associated with the left hemisphere not developing as a specialized area for language skills. For example, patients diagnosed with autism, characterized by delayed language development, exhibited reduced rates of established lateral hand preference (Escalante-Mead et al., 2003). Alternatively, patients with high-functioning autism with normal language development were more likely to demonstrate an established lateral hand preference.

Generally, the linguistic dependence of the left hemisphere is not seen in tasks shown to be typically served by the right hemisphere. As shown in Table 7.1, the right hemisphere is more closely linked to a direct representation of visual-spatial reality. Indeed, the right hemisphere is shown to be prepotent (Sperry, 1969) in the presence of nonverbal-spatial task requirements. The frequent inference that this verbal–nonverbal distinction follows hemispheric lines seems something of an overstatement (Dean, 1985b). Moreover, research indicates that one must closely examine the requirements of and cognitive processes involved in the individual task before assuming hemispheric differences. Examination of the requirements associated with the task rather than the stimuli involved in the task provides greater insight into hemispheric specialization as confirmed through fMRI studies (Stephan et al., 2003). Such research supports assessment of the hemispheres through the information-processing model rather than discrete localization or task approaches and gives way to assessment implications (Springer & Deutsch, 1998).

Research findings with patients who have suffered right hemispheric damage contrasts, in many ways, with the research findings for patients with damage to the left hemisphere. In general, it seems that the right hemisphere more efficiently serves tasks that require the holistic, or simultaneous, processing of nonverbal gestalts and the complex transformations of complex visual patterns (e.g., Milner, 1962). As such, incoming information of a parallel or spatial nature that requires cognitive manipulation has been shown to be closely linked to processing in the right hemisphere (e.g., Gordon, 1970). It also seems that information that does not lend itself to verbal mediation, such as diffuse representation of the environment, is most efficiently served by the right cortical hemisphere (Levy, Trevarthen, & Sperry, 1972). Recent research has expanded the commonly assumed nonverbal functions of the right hemisphere to include aspects of memory, depth perception, and motor integration (see Table 7.1). More recently, visual-half field techniques demonstrate a right-field preference for word recognition in regards to laterality while visuo-spatial tasks and face processing demonstrate a left-field preference, which supports the notion that the right hemisphere more efficiently processes simultaneous processing of nonverbal gestalts and complex visual patterns (Hugdahl, 1996). However, some cross-over in functions may exist. Indeed, hearing-impaired subjects with right hemispheric lesions have been found to have visual-spatial deficits, although they possessed the ability to sign and comprehend sign language. Conversely, left-hemispheric signers showed signing or interpreting deprivation but retained nonlanguage spatial functions (Poizner et al., 1990).

Apparently, individuals have some control over the mode of processing that will be utilized and thus the specific hemisphere. Dean and Hua (1982) have offered data portraying hemispheric specialization as an active constructive process, with the specific form of encoding dependent on constraints of attention and individual differences in the lateralization of functions. Hemispheric specialization is also often used to denote differences between hemispheres when processing sensory information (Hugdahl, 1996). Evidence for this position also comes from investigations showing that visual-spatial stimuli may be encoded semantically (Conrad, 1964) and that verbal material can be represented as visual traces (Paivio, 1971). Apparently, individuals can process and encode information in at least two qualitatively distinct but interconnected systems (see Bower, 1970; Paivio, Clark, Digdon, & Bons, 1989). These processing modes have been shown to follow in part the left–right functional distinction. In essence, learners can readily generate nonverbal or verbal processing strategies regardless of the form of the original stimulus. These rather different modes of processing correspond to function ordinarily seen as hemisphere-specific (Bower, 1970; Dean, 1985a; Paivio et al., 1989).

A corollary view, in concert with Luria's (1966) theory, has been articulated by Das (1973). These researchers have characterized differences in hemispheric processes as complementary and coexisting modes. Research seems consistent with cortical functions of the right and left cerebral hemispheres (e.g., Luria, 1966), spoken of as simultaneous and successive modes of information processing. While Luria acknowledged discrete cortical zones, equipotentiality theory proposes that all parts of the cortex contribute to cortical processing of complex functions. Thus, research relevant to hemispheric specialization and cerebral dominance remains conflicted as to the functional roles of each hemisphere in cortical processing (Dronkers, 2001; Rains, 2002).

HEMISPHERIC FUNCTIONAL SIMILARITIES

DESPITE COMPELLING EVIDENCE favoring hemispheric lateralization of functions, a good deal of symmetrical processing occurs. Research with normal individuals and patients who have suffered unilateral lesions indicates equal proficiency of hemispheres in registering and storing sensory information (Milner, 1962). The magnitude of functional lateralization would seem to increase in direct proportion to the amount of conceptual reformulation or, if you will, cognitive processing necessary for interpretation and encoding (Gordon, 1974).

Patients with unilateral lesions to either hemisphere generally show deficit performance in the extraction of stimulus features (e.g., brightness, color, pitch, and elements of somatosensory perception) compared with normal controls (e.g., Gordon, 1974; Milner, 1962; Scotti & Spinnler, 1970). In contrast to higher-order differences in function between groups of patients with unilateral left and right hemispheric lesions, lower-level sensory discrimination differences between patients with localized lesions lack robustness (e.g., Gordon, 1974; McKeever & Gill, 1972). Apparently, specific performance deficits that correspond to the hemisphere in which the patient has suffered damage occur only when patients are required to reorder, categorize, integrate, or abstract stimulus elements. It would seem that as the degree of cognitive processing necessary for a task increases, so too does the extent to which that function is asymmetrically lateralized.

Using split visual field (e.g., McKeever & Gill, 1972), auditory evoked potentials (Gordon, 1974), and dichotic listening (Darwin, 1974, 1975) techniques with normal subjects, a number of investigators have shown hemispheric symmetry in the extraction of low-order visual, auditory, and tactile elements with normal adults. Such findings seem robust and have been found even in cases in which the target stimuli are embedded in a verbal or nonverbal context (e.g., Rabinowicz, 1976; Wood, 1975). Apparently, then, when normal subjects must discriminate simple sensory elements such as brightness, pitch, color, pressure, sensitivity, sharpness, or contour, few hemispheric differences in processing are evident. However, when the task requires higher-order cognitive processing beyond that found in such simple discrimination, rather clear hemispheric differences become evident.

Evidence indicates that hemispheric asymmetries are also related to the amount of previously encoded information that must be used to interpret incoming sensory information (e.g. Goodglass & Peck, 1972; Moscovitch, 1976). Moscovitch (1979) argues elegantly that accentuated hemispheric asymmetries occur after a delay in the recognition or recall of incoming stimuli (e.g., Goodglass & Peck, 1972; Milner, 1968). Functional lateralization varies in proportion to the degree of transformation that has occurred prior to encoding. In sum, then, it appears that hemispheric asymmetries in function are more clearly evidenced in tasks requiring higher-order processing or when incoming information must be interpreted in light of prior knowledge.

Subcortical structures also show a left–right asymmetry. Hugdahl, Wester, and Asbjornsen (1990) studied patients with Parkinson's disease who were undergoing stereotactic thalamotomy surgery in an attempt to reduce tremors and rigidity. Using a dichotic listening technique, the authors compared patients operated either in the left or right thalamus. The results demonstrated that patients with operations in the left thalamus demonstrated cognitive dysfunction, while those patients with right side thalamus surgery did not demonstrate the same cognitive dysfunction (Hugdahl, 1996). The authors determined that a subcortical activating gating mechanism in the left ventrolateral thalamic nucleus controlled the flow of auditory language information to the corresponding cortical area. More importantly, the study revealed the importance of the subcortical structures for functional asymmetry in cognition (Hugdahl, 1996). Wittling (1995) also supported the notion that brain asymmetry involves the entire nervous system, not just the cortical hemispheres.

DEVELOPMENTAL ASPECTS

STRUCTURAL DIFFERENCES IN the hemispheres of the brain exist prior to birth (Geschwind & Levitsky, 1968). Left hemispheric structures (left temporale planum), most often considered to serve speech, language, and reading functions, are significantly larger than temporal structures of the right hemisphere early in gestation (Geschwind & Levitsky, 1968; Robichon et al., 2000; Witelson & Pallie, 1973). Rather clear structural differences have also been noted in the rate at which the pyramidal tract develops projections to hemispheres of the brain. Yakovlev and Rakic (1966) have shown consistently earlier crossing of projections from the left hemisphere than seen for the right hemisphere. Such research has begun to outline early structural differences between hemispheres that may be the precursors of functional differences in cerebral hemispheres.

Equipotentiality, most clearly attributed to Lenneberg (1967), portrays the cerebral hemispheres of the brain as having equal potential in the development of functional specialization for language. Although this is an appealing notion, neurophysiological differences between hemispheres (Molfese et al., 1975; Wada et al., 1975) and early neuroanatomical differences limit its explanatory power. Of course, rejection of the notion of early equal potential of hemispheres does not rule out the possibility that functional lateralization is a progressive, developmental process.

The extent to which functions are progressively lateralized to cerebral hemispheres is still a matter of controversy (Kinsbourne, 1975; Satz, 1976). Cerebral lateralization has been portrayed to follow patterns similar to that for the development of numerous psychological functions (Bruner, 1974; Piaget, 1952). From this point of view, the functional lateralization of hemispheres is seen to follow a progressive pattern of consolidation of functions corresponding to the child's neurological development (e.g., Dean, 1985a; Satz et al., 1975). Although arguments favoring early specific specialization continue (Kinsbourne, 1975), a large corpus of data exists supporting developmental progression in the lateralization of functions (see Dean, 1985a). While left hemispheric asymmetries related to language are present at birth, further research has demonstrated that language may still develop normally in children who sustain a unilateral lesion in the left hemisphere (Dean & Anderson, 1997). Neuroimaging studies have postulated two sides to the development or presence of functional lateralization such that language is either bilaterally organized at birth and becomes specialized to the left hemisphere or language is localized to the left hemisphere at birth (Balsamo et al., 2002; Booth et al., 2001).

The lateralization of language of the left hemisphere has been argued to correspond to the continuing maturation of secondary association areas, which begins some time after the 5th year of life (Peiper, 1963). Indeed, we find a decrease in the role played by the right hemisphere in language, which covaries with the child's neurological development (see Krashen, 1973). Sperry (1968, 1969) has suggested that this progressive lateralization of function may well relate to the rather slow maturation of the commissure-associative cortex. In this regard, numerous reports suggest that the rate of lateralization varies with the specific function being examined (Molfese, 1977; Waber, 1977). Clearly, it would seem that although hemispheric asymmetries for certain functions are observable in the neonate, patterns of functional lateralization continue to develop in an orderly fashion throughout the early childhood years (see Satz et al., 1975).

Related to developmental aspects of hemispheric specialization is the notion of functional plasticity. Plasticity here refers to the degree to which functions of a damaged hemisphere are preempted by the other. As early as the nineteenth century, clinical reports suggested that the effects of damage to the left hemisphere before adolescence were less severe and language disturbances more transient than those from similar lesions occurring in adults (Dax, 1865). Since these early reports, numerous investigators have presented data favoring what amounts to a "critical period" occurring between 5 and 7 years of age. Prior to this critical period, functions normally served by the left hemisphere may more completely be subserved by the right cerebral hemisphere following damage to the language center (Chelune & Edwards, 1981; Dikman, Matthews, & Harley, 1975; Pirozzolo, Campanella, Christensen, & Lawson-Kerr, 1981). In contrast, damage to similar areas occurring after this critical period is more severe and less transient (e.g., Dikman et al., 1975). These conclusions are consistent with Krashen's (1973) data suggesting a decreasing role of the right hemisphere for language with age. Neuroimaging studies have demonstrated that by 8 years of age language is no longer bilaterally evident (Balsamo et al., 2002).

The completeness of the transfer of functions between hemispheres is also positively related to the severity with which the brain is damaged (e.g., Pirozzolo et al., 1981). This conclusion is evidenced in patients who have undergone a left hemispherectomy before this critical period. In such cases, the behavioral effects are less devastating in terms of later language function than disabilities that occur with relatively minor damage to the left hemisphere (Dikman et al., 1975; Pirozzolo et al., 1981; Springer & Deutsch, 1998). Smith and Sugar (1975) have hypothesized that, with the removal of the left hemisphere, "competition for language" functions is less likely to occur than is true when more localized damage has occured. The heuristic value of plasticity as an explanatory term has begun to be questioned. Research suggests the process of plasticity and ability of the right hemisphere to subsume language functions occurs over time and is most evident in children under 5 years of age (Springer & Deutsch, 1998; Zillmer & Spiers, 2001). The interested reader is directed to Fletcher and Satz (1983) for the subtleties of the counterargument.

SEX DIFFERENCES IN LATERALIZATION

SUBTLE STRUCTURAL NEUROLOGICAL differences have been observed between males and females (see MacLusky & Naftolin, 1981). However, neuropsychological dissimilarity between adult males and females is more heuristically attributed to functional-organizational factors than to an obvious central nervous system disparity (Dean, 1985a; Kolata, 1979). Although genetic and morphological differences exist between males and females from conception, sex hormones have been shown to have more striking effects on the structure and function of the central nervous system (Baum, 1979; MacLusky & Naftolin, 1981; Weintraub, 1981). These sex steroids have a dramatic effect on the function and development of the nervous system because they are permeable to the blood-brain barrier. Hence, rapid changes in some sex-related brain functions may be due in part to the structure of androgens, which enable rapid access to the brain (Schmeck, 1980). Importantly, these sex hormones have privileged access to the brain early in gestation, when rates of development heighten their sensitivity (Baum, 1979; Gur, Gunning-Dixon, Bilker, & Gur, 2002).

The extent to which genetic-hormonal sex differences are responsible for hemispheric lateralization remains in dispute (see Maccoby, 1966). Of course, one must be careful not to attribute differences in neuropsychological functioning to gender when behavior could heuristically be attributed to social-cultural variables. With this caveat in mind, numerous neuropsychological differences between normal males and females have been reported that relate directly to an appreciation of the lateralization of brain functions. For example, the superior spatial ability of males and relatively greater verbal facility of females have been attributed to sex differences in hemispheric specialization arising from sex-specific steroids (Dean, 1985a; Levy & Levy, 1978). Several studies suggest that certain sex hormones (e.g., testosterone) stimulate growth in right hemispheric regions or delay development in left hemispheric regions (de Lacoste, Horvath, & Woodward, 1991; Tan, 1991). Indeed Reinisch and Sanders (1992) concluded that prenatal exposure to diethylstilbestrol (DES), a synthetic estrogen, reduced hemispheric laterality and lowered spatial ability.

Conversely, several studies argue that females with high androgen levels possess spatial abilities comparable to males (Kolb & Whishaw, 1990; Shute, Pelligrino, Hubert, & Reynolds, 1983). In this regard, Witelson (1976) offers data favoring earlier right hemispheric specialization for spatial processing in males than is found for females, who more often exhibit bilateral representation of these functions until early adolescent years. Hemispheric specialization for language has also been observed earlier in males than in females, who show less consistent lateralization throughout the life span (Levy, 1973). MacLusky and Naftolin (1981) argue convincingly that such findings may more heuristically be attributed to genetic-hormonal differences than to developmental rates in general. Goy and McEwen (1980) have presented data suggesting that sex hormonal differences also result in a proclivity to rely on specific cues (e.g., verbal, spatial) in learning and differences in the rate of acquisition for verbal and spatial stimuli.

Findings of less secure hemispheric specialization for females stand in contrast to the consistent report of more coherent lateral preference (handedness, eye preference, etc.) for females (Annett, 1976; Dean, 1986; Levy, 1973). In fact, a study by Cappa et al. (1988) suggested that the role of gonadal hormones and lateralization have little significance on the establishment of asymmetries. With the frequently drawn association between lateral preference and the functional lateralization of hemispheres, such findings seem rather paradoxical. Although lateral preference will be examined in greater depth later in this chapter, it suffices to say at this point that the one-to-one relationship between hand preference and hemispheric specialization for language may be rather naïve.

Although males evidence more consistent hemispheric lateralization of verbal and nonverbal functions, this consistency does not seem to occur without a consequence (Dean, 1985a; Nottebohm, 1979). The consequence here seems to be exhibited in a higher risk of specific expressive and receptive language disorders for males (Benton, 1975; Brain, 1965; Dean, 1981). Benton (1975) has reported a risk of language disorders for males 10 times greater than that for female cohorts. Assessment of demographic data reflects a greater percentage of males referred for assessment and special education services as well as a higher percentage of males with reading problems (D'Amato, Dean, Rattan, & Nickell, 1988; Share & Silva, 2003).

INFERRING FUNCTIONAL LATERALIZATION

UNDOUBTEDLY, THE MOST predominant difficulty in the measurement and study of functional lateralization is the inaccessibility of the human brain. Indeed, the vast majority of our knowledge of human neuropsychology and the study of functional lateralization has come about as the result of inferential methods. Neuropsychological assessment grew out of a need to objectively describe the behavioral effects of known brain damage. Thus, until quite recently, functions of specific areas of the brain were inferred from behavioral deficits that correspond to localized lesions. Correlational in nature, these data have been the basis of the quantitative-actuarial approach that has dominated neuropsychology in North America. Clearly, attempts to link structure and function from this database often become a tautological pursuit.

With this limitation in mind, one can state that damage to the left hemisphere of the brain in most right-handed individuals corresponds to deficits in speech, language, and calculation (Boll, 1974a, 1974b; Reed & Reitan, 1963; Reitan, 1955), whereas damage to the right hemisphere correlates with functional deficits of a more nonverbal nature (Reitan, 1955). Although handedness will be examined in greater detail later in this chapter, it suffices to say that language disturbances for left-handed individuals after left hemispheric damage are less severe and more transient than those for right-handers (Hecaen, 1962). These results are often cited as the basis for inferring less secure left hemispheric lateralization of language for most left-handed individuals. Such data have been cited as the basis for making inferences from scores on neuropsychological test batteries (Reitan, 1969).

Sperry and his associates (Gazzaniga & Sperry, 1962; Sperry, 1968; Sperry, Gazzaniga, & Bogen, 1969) have confirmed and extended the neuropsychological findings for patients with localized lesions in research involving surgical section of the corpus callosum as a treatment for intractable seizures. The amount of communication between hemispheres is drastically reduced with this procedure, and functions of individual hemispheres can be more completely examined. Although difficulties exist in drawing conclusions about normal hemispheric functioning from such patients, the contribution of Sperry and his associates to our understanding of hemispheric function has been seminal. In general, research with split-brain subjects has refined our understanding of functional lateralization and confirmed that, in most right-handed and many left-handed individuals, complex linguistic functions are served by the left hemisphere (Dean & Hua, 1982; Kimura, 1961; Sperry, 1968; Springer & Deutsch, 1998) and visual-spatial reality is more closely linked to the right hemisphere (Milner, 1962).

In addition to the research concerning functions that are compromised with lateralized lesions, most neuropsychological batteries utilize tasks that allow comparison of right side performance with left side performance. This is possible, of course, because simple unimanual performance and sensory perception to one side of the body are served by the contralateral hemisphere. Thus, left versus right differences in strength of grip, finger tapping, and finger localization are compared against normal values. With larger than expected differences, inferences can be made concerning lateralized impairment. In turn, these results are interpreted in conjunction with functions (e.g., language) most often associated with either left or right hemisphere impairment. Although less useful in making diagnostic statements, most neuropsychology batteries include a measure of lateral preference for motor tasks (e.g., Halstead-Reitan Lateral Dominance examination, Dean-Woodcock Sensory Motor Battery Lateral Preference subtest) as an indicator of the degree to which functions ordinarily ascribed to one hemisphere or the other can be applied to a given patient. Lateral preference percentages match distributions for planum temporale asymmetries in the general population and thus provide additional evidence for assessment of language processing (Richardson, 1995).

NORMAL PERCEPTUAL ASYMMETRY

THE WADA TEST (Wada, 1949), which involves the intracarotid injection of amytal to one hemisphere or the other, has been considered to be the most emphatic measure of hemispheric functional specialization. Obviously, the use of this method with basically normal subjects is questionable. However, recent advances in neural imaging technology employing positron emission tomography (PET) and magnetic resonance imaging (MRI) have allowed more precise anatomical-functional correlations in the primary and secondary sensory and motor areas of the human brain (Damasio & Damasio, 1992; Petersen et al., 1989). Nevertheless, because these are rather new techniques, expense and accessibility can be somewhat problematic. Short of these techniques, the use of perceptual asymmetry techniques to infer functional lateralization based on a left–right difference in performance remains the most extensively used procedure with normal subjects (Dean, 1983).

In the dichotic listening technique, which was first introduced by Broadbent (1954) and refined by Kimura (1961), auditory asymmetries for various verbal and nonverbal stimuli are assessed. Specifically, the ear advantage is measured when different stimuli are presented simultaneously to each ear. In this way, hemispheric differences are inferred because there are a greater number of contralateral than ipsilateral ear-to-hemisphere "nerve connections"; and ipsilateral input from one ear is "blocked" by simultaneous stimuli presented to the contralateral ear. Thus, the dominant hemisphere for a particular stimuli (e.g., consonant-vowel letter groups) is inferred from more consistent recall or recognition of specific stimuli presented to the ear opposite that hemisphere. Therefore, if a given subject reports more correctly or reacts more quickly for a specific signal to one ear than the other (ear advantage), the contralateral hemisphere to the ear is considered to be specialized for that function (Kimura, 1961).

Although any simple comparison of individual studies is difficult due to differences in specific stimuli and subtleties in procedures, it may safely be concluded that for normal adults (Dean & Hua, 1982; Kimura, 1961) and children (Dean, 1983; Hynd & Obrzut, 1977; Summers & Taylor, 1972) a right-ear advantage exists for linguistic stimuli when presented in a dichotic fashion. Thus, data with normals support a left hemisphere specialization for language often inferred from clinical studies of brain-damaged patients (e.g., Reitan, 1955). In contrast, dichotic presentation of nonverbal tones most often has been shown to produce a left-ear advantage for most normal right-handed subjects (Kimura, 1967). While results obtained from dichotic listening tests tend to align with Wada Test findings, other results may prove contradictory especially for non–right-handed subjects (Bryden, 1988; Hugdahl, Carlsson, Uvebrant, & Lundervold, 1997; Segalowitz, 1986). Although distinct methodological difficulties exist (Berlin & Cullen, 1977; Birkett, 1977; Bryden, 1978; Satz, 1976), the dichotic listening technique is considered by many to be the most valid noninvasive indicator for inferring functional hemispheric lateralization for language.

The split visual field technique is similar to the dichotic listening paradigm in terms of neurological assumptions. Because the visual half fields in humans are contralaterally served by the hemispheres of the brain, stimuli presented to one visual field (e.g., right) have privileged access to the opposite hemisphere (e.g., left). The presentation of stimuli is most often accomplished with a tachistoscope, which allows exposure to different stimuli by both visual fields simultaneously. Very brief exposure periods reduce the methodological difficulties that would be attributed to the possibility of eye movements during presentation. Early on, research utilizing the visual half field technique employed unilateral presentations (e.g., Heron, 1957). Recent research has been more sensitive to the methodological difficulties associated with unilateral presentations and has focused on simultaneous bilateral exposures. In this research, we would expect and indeed we find an advantage to the right visual half (left hemispheric) for linguistically related material (Kershner, 1977; Marcel & Rajan, 1975).

Because of the possibility of post-exposure attentional scanning (Witelson, 1977) and other difficulties related to the visual mode of presentation (Dean, 1981), methodological difficulties continue in the use of this technique with linguistic stimuli. A left-field advantage has consistently been reported when tasks involve more nonverbal spatial stimuli (Kimura & Durnford, 1974). Indeed, McLaren and Bryson (1987) demonstrated similar findings when nonverbal emotional stimuli (pairs of expressive and neutral faces) presented in the left visual field (i.e., right hemisphere) enhanced subjects' emotional responses. However, a recent study by Gainotti, Caltagirone, and Zoccolotti (1993) argued that there may be some interconnection between the left/right and cortical/subcortical structures, because the right hemisphere is dominant for basic levels of emotional arousal and response, whereas the left hemisphere may be more involved in the cortical aspects of inhibition and may dominate the subcortical emotional functions.

Kinsbourne and Cook (1971) have reported data favoring hemispheric lateralization when subjects are required to perform different tasks, both of which are lateralized in a single hemisphere simultaneously. The consistent finding using this paradigm has been significantly greater interference for verbal tasks in the right-hand performance of motor tasks than that found for the left hand. Comparing left- and right-hand performance on dowel-balancing and finger-tapping tasks, researchers have inferred greater lateralization of language functions in the left hemisphere because of greater interference in the performance of the right hand (e.g., Hiscock, Antoniuk, & Prisciak, 1985; Kinsbourne & Cook, 1971).

Research that has examined the electrical activity of the brain also reinforces the hemispheric lateralization of functions. When utilizing electroencephalographic (EEG) leads, decreased activity is inferred from the presence of alpha waves. The majority of studies that employ this technique have shown increased alpha activity in the right hemisphere (post-central area) when normal right-handed subjects are involved in verbal analytic tasks (Morgan et al., 1971). Conversely, greater alpha activity has been noted in the left hemisphere of normal individuals when they have been required to perform spatial or musical tasks (Davidson & Schwartz, 1977; Morgan et al., 1971). Thus, in concert with research involving other research paradigms, EEG studies indicate a verbal-analytical versus spatial-holistic processing difference that corresponds to the left and right hemispheres of the brain.

Recently, Savage and Thomas's (1993) data of visual evoked potentials (VEP; i.e., subjects pressed a button when a stimulus appeared), measured by EEG, showed that reaction time was faster and right hemisphere activity was more prevalent for right-handers, whereas hemispheric asymmetries were less consistent for left-handers. Moreover, PET studies of normal right-handed subjects have indicated that specific processing differences do indeed exist (e.g., Petersen et al., 1989; Posner et al., 1988). These studies identified specific brain areas related to lexical (i.e., single word) processing. However, it is the underlying process requirements of the task that are localized rather than the actual task itself (Posner et al., 1988).

LATERAL PREFERENCE

THE PERFORMANCE OF unimanual activities on one side of the body is served by the contralateral hemisphere of the brain. Consistent with the rather antiquated notion of cerebral dominance, it has long been inferred that lateral preference may be a behavioral expression of the degree of functional specialization of the left hemisphere for language and other control functions. Indeed, most clinical examinations and neuropsychological batteries have incorporated some measure of lateral preference (handedness, eye preference, etc.) as an indicator of the underlying functional organization of cortical hemispheres. A corollary to the notion of hemispheric dominance is the long-held hypothesis that anomalous preference patterns may underlie many functional disorders (e.g., Orton, 1937). The relationship between atypical patterns of lateral preference and cortical functioning remains one of the most studied and controversial issues in neuropsychology (Dean, 1985a).

The implicit assumption has been that observable patterns of preference would reflect functional lateralization of cortical hemispheres (Harris, 1947). Although measures have varied from direction of eye gaze (Reynolds, 1978) to left or right turning of the individual's hair whorl (Tjossen, Hansen, & Ripley, 1961), research has concentrated on hand preference (Dean, 1983). This concentration probably relates to the deceptive ease in assessment and various reports of a higher incidence rate of mixed-hand preference for individuals with a number of expressive and receptive language disorders (e.g., Orton, 1937).

Population estimates based on large samples suggest that some 90% of normal individuals may be considered as right-handed. The remaining 10% consists of individuals who are either consistently left-handed or without a clear hand preference (Annett, 1976; Oldfield, 1971). Although a number of clinical reports have stressed the importance of assessing hand preference, it has become obvious that simple handedness does not relate directly to functional lateralization for language (Dean, 1982; Kinsbourne & Hiscock, 1977).

Inconsistent findings in the study of lateral preference seem understandable when in many cases simple hand preference for writing is the only measure of laterality. Dean (1982) has argued that confusion in past research that has used lateral preference as a measure of hemispheric lateralization may well be related to the specific index of preference used. Indeed, it seems that the relationship between simple hand preference and cerebral lateralization is less than robust (Dean, 1978, 1982). In fact, conclusions concerning hemispheric specialization based on hand preference are more likely to be in error than if the assumption is made that language is served by the left hemisphere in all subjects regardless of handedness (Dean, 1986). This conclusion is reflected in research showing that for most right- and left-handed individuals, complex linguistic functions are served by the left hemisphere (Lake & Bryden, 1976). Milner (1974) reported that some 95% of right-handed and 70% of left-handed individuals have secure left hemispheric specialization for language. For some 30% of left-handed individuals, language has been shown to be served by the right hemisphere, or symmetrically organized.

These data stand in contrast to early speculations of right hemispheric language dominance for all left-handed individuals. Other than the social learning that occurs, differences between left-handers in language lateralization may be attributed to differences in the etiology of left-hand preference (Satz, 1976). Moreover, although there has been shown to be a distinct genetic factor in left-handedness (Levy & Nagylaki, 1972), a number of researchers have argued in favor of a form of left-handedness that arises out of pathological factors relating to early brain damage or a developmental anomaly in the left hemisphere. Specifically, Lucas, Rosenstein, and Bigler (1989) suggested that mentally retarded left-handed subjects had a higher incidence of impairment. Furthermore, there was a greater degree of expressive and receptive language impairment for females than for males.

Satz (1976) has argued convincingly against measures of lateral preference based on simple handedness as an index of cerebral dominance for language. This seems reasonable when the degree of social learning and environmental constraints are considered in the establishment of hand preference. Clearly, early theoretical notions that offered handedness as a definitive indicator of cortical specialization appear naïve in light of our present research base (Dean, 1981). It seems then, that although preference for peripheral activities may reflect cortical organization, the relationship is not a simple one.

Measures of lateral preference have often been used to classify respondents in a rather arbitrary, nominal fashion (left, right, mixed) (e.g., Annett, 1976; Harris, 1947; Jasper & Raney, 1937; Oldfield, 1971). Like other individual difference variables, lateral preference seems more heuristically considered as a continuous variable, and one would expect individuals to show various degrees of preference (see Dean, 1978; Shankweiler & Studdert-Kennedy, 1975; Whitaker & Ojemann, 1977). From this point of view, it is not surprising to find confusion between studies that have relied on methodologies that portray lateral preference as an all-or-nothing variable.

Dunlop, Dunlop, and Fenelon (1973) presented data showing little reliable variance associated with simple hand preference as a predictor of language. However, these authors showed a clear association between inconsistent eye/hand use and confused hemispheric lateralization for language. This finding seems consistent with other research showing discrepancies in ear/hand preference (e.g., Bryden, 1967) and more confused hand preference for fine motor activities requiring visual guidance (Dean, Schwartz, & Smith, 1981; Kaufman, Zalma, & Kaufman, 1978), which may be more sensitive indicators of language confusion. Examining preference for a large number of items in a continuous fashion, Dean (1982) offered data favoring lateral preference as a factorial complex variable that is best represented on a continuum from entirely right to entirely left. Given that hand preference falls along such a continuum, lateral preference is most appropriately assessed through this fashion (Dean, 1982). Dean (1982) argued that the neurological significance of lateral preference may well have been masked in methodologies that summed across subjects' preferences for individual activities with little more than intuitive support.

Dean et al. (1981) hypothesized that much of the inconsistency in results of studies on lateral preference may well vary as a function of the specific tasks chosen to infer lateral dominance. Using factor analysis, Dean (1982) isolated six distinct dimensions that accounted for some 90% of the variability in subjects' preferences for activities involving the hands, arms, eyes, ears, and feet. Research comparing individual factors with sophisticated measures of hemispheric language lateralization indicates a more robust relationship with that factor, which involves preference for visually guided motor tasks (Dean, 1985b). These data suggest that the choice of preference items (writing, etc.) in past research may have played an interactive role with other neuropsychological variables (Dean & Hua, 1982). Thus, lateral preference patterns would seem not only to vary from individual to individual but, more important to the present discussion, for each individual as a function of the cerebral system under study. For example, assessment of lateral preference data indicates that the percentage breakdown of handedness in the general population reflects the distribution of planum temporale asymmetry and thus contributes to the assessment of language processing disorders (Richardson, 1995).

Using a multifactor measure of lateral preference, Dean (1981) has offered data favoring a greater mixed tendency for males than for females. Although these results are consistent with Oldfield's (1971) data, sex differences in lateral preference are not as simplistic as once proposed (Oldfield, 1971). Moreover, Dean (1979, 1982) showed males to present a significantly more mixed pattern in lateralization for factors involving strength and those requiring visual guidance in their performance. Although genetic factors that would predict such differences have been proposed (Levy & Levy, 1978), sex steroids and specific social learning cannot be dismissed (see McGlone, 1980).

ATYPICAL LATERALIZATION AND LANGUAGE DISORDERS

INCOMPLETE HEMISPHERIC LATERALIZATION of language has long been hypothesized as a predisposing factor for a number of disorders. The most often articulated view speculates that language-related disorders may result from the bilateral representation of language functions in the brain and thus some form of competition between hemispheres (e.g., Arnett, 1976; Orton, 1937). Orton's (1937) early hypothesis of confused lateralization for severe reading disorders was based on his clinical observations of a higher incidence of confused lateral preference (hand and/or hand/eye preference) for children referred for reading problems. As outlined previously because purposeful unimanual activities are served by the contralateral hemisphere of the brain, observed confusion for such behaviors was seen to reflect confused lateralization of cortical functions (Annett, 1976; Orton, 1937; Zangwill, 1962). In support of this notion, Zangwill (1960) offers data showing that some 88% of "congenital dyslexics" present with some form of confused lateral preference. Although over a half century has passed since Orton's (1937) hypothesis, cerebral dominance as an etiological factor in reading disorders remains one of the most controversial issues in neuropsychology.

As mentioned previously, measures of hemispheric specialization based on simple handedness do not relate to language lateralization in a one-to-one fashion. In the Dunlop et al. (1973) study, little relationship between handedness in isolation and language-related disorders was found. However, when crossed eye-hand preference was examined, this index was shown to be clearly associated with such disorders. Similarly, Dean et al. (1981) have offered data favoring less coherently lateralized systems of lateral preference for children diagnosed as learning-disabled. Interestingly, when summed across systems of lateral preference, learning-disabled children differed little from normal controls.

Inconsistencies in this area exist not only in how lateral preference is measured but also in a lack of a consistent rationale for inclusion of individuals in nosological categories. Moreover, classifications such as reading disabilities, dyslexia, and the like are both overlapping and confounded. Using a more descriptive approach to reading disorders, Dean (1978, 1979) has reported significantly greater mixed systems of lateralization for children with adequate decoding skills who experience problems in reading comprehension. However, in the same investigation, poor readers deficient in decoding also were similar to good readers in their lateral preference patterns. Thus, refined diagnostic specificity in considering language disorders is as important as the measure of lateralization used. A good deal of research indicates a consistent right-ear advantage for language-disabled patients when verbal stimuli are presented in a dichotic fashion (Dean & Hua, 1982; Hynd, Obrzut, Weed, & Hynd, 1979; Satz et al., 1975), a pattern similar to that found for normals. Thus, these data would suggest that language lateralization for language-disabled patients, when measured in an auditory fashion, is similar to that reported for normals (Dean & Hua, 1982). However, when language lateralization is inferred from a visual presentation (split visual field), the majority of studies show a smaller right visual field superiority as well as differential neuronal size of the visual pathway for linguistic material in language-disabled patients than that found for normal controls (Kershner, 1977; Marcel, Katz, & Smith, 1974; Marcel & Rajan, 1975).

Interestingly then, it appears that although evidence of normal language lateralization exists when measured in an auditory fashion, many language-disabled individuals show less secure visual language lateralization. The etiology of such deficits has been attributed to developmental aberrations (Satz, 1976), early insult (Geschwind, 1974), genetic factors (Levy & Reid, 1976), and the interaction of these factors. Evidence of left-right symmetry or reversed right asymmetry on measures of temporal lobe size has been demonstrated in individuals with dyslexia (Dalby, Elbro, & Stodkilde-Jorgensen, 1998; Duara et al., 1991; Leonard et al., 1993). Indeed, professional controversy persists concerning neuropsychological aspects of reading disorders in general and the heuristic value of Orton's (1937) original hypothesis of inconsistent cerebral dominance for many linguistically disabled patients. In one study, dysphasic and autistic subjects demonstrated reversed direction of hemispheric asymmetry (Dawson, Finley, Phillips, & Lewy, 1989). However, when language ability was analyzed, the autistic subjects demonstrated more right hemispheric activity, whereas the dysphasic subjects appeared to have more left hemispheric activity (Dawson et al., 1989).

Beaumont and Rugg (1978) have offered an interesting hypothesis that attempts to reconcile findings of normal auditory (right-ear advantage) and less secure visual (split visual field) language asymmetries for patients who present with severe reading disorders. In concert with Pizzamiglio's (1976) and Geschwind's (1974) conceptualizations, Beaumont and Rugg (1978) have hypothesized a functional disassociation in the lateralization of auditory and visual language systems. The deficit here is seen as integration of visual-verbal systems in the presence of normal auditory-verbal functioning. From this point of view, functional lateralization for language may vary for an individual as a function of the specific system (i.e., visual-verbal) examined (Beaumont & Rugg, 1978; Dean & Rothlisberg, 1983; Luria, 1966).

Although empirical attempts to subtype linguistic disorders in the selection of subjects is encouraging (Boder, 1970; Pirozzolo, 1979), the lack of relevant diagnostic criteria represents a major difficulty in drawing conclusions in this area of research (Dean, 1986). The reader should be particularly alert to the myriad of practical assessment and complex theoretical issues when drawing clinical inferences of functional lateralization as part of a comprehensive neuropsychological evaluation. Moreover, although inconsistent patterns of functional lateralization may be viewed as having potential clinical implications, there is little robust evidence that atypical lateralization should be considered pathogenic in isolation.

REFERENCES

Annett, M. (1976). Hand preference and the laterality of cerebral speech. *Cortex, 11*, 305–329.

Balsamo, L. M., Xu, B., Grandin, C. B., Petrella, J. R., Braniecki, S. H., Elliot, T. K., et al. (2002). A functional magnetic resonance imaging study of left hemispheric language dominance in children. *Archives of Neurology, 59*, 1168–1174.

Baum, M. J. (1979). Differentiation of coital behavior in mammals. A comparative analysis. *Neuroscience and Biobehavioral Reviews, 3*, 265–284.

Beaumont, J. G., & Rugg, M. D. (1978). Neuropsychological laterality of function and dyslexia: A new hypothesis. *Dyslexia Review, 1*, 18–21.

Benton, A. L. (1975). Development dyslexia: Neurological aspects. In W. J. Friedlander (Ed.), *Advances in neurology* (Vol. 7; pp. 1–47). New York: Raven Press.

Berlin, C. I., & Cullen, J. K. (1977). Acoustic problems in dichotic listening tasks. In S. J. Segalowitz & F. A. Gruber (Eds.), *Language development and neurological theory* (pp. 77–88). New York: Academic Press.

Birkett, P. (1977). Measures of laterality and theories of hemispheric process. *Neuropsychologia, 15*, 693–696.

Boder, E. (1970). Developmental dyslexia: A new diagnostic approach based on the identification of three subtypes. *Journal of School Health, 40*, 289–290.

Boll, T. J. (1974a). Behavioral correlates of cerebral damage in children aged 9 through 14. In R. M. Reitan & L. A. Davison (Eds.), *Clinical neuropsychology: Current status and applications* (pp. 91–120). New York: Wiley.

Boll, T. J. (1974b). Right and left cerebral hemisphere damage and tactile perception: Performance of the ipsilateral and contralateral sides of the body. *Neuropsychologia, 12*, 235–238.

Booth, J. R., MacWhinney, B., Thulborn, K. R., Sacco, K., Voyvodic, J. T., & Feldman, H. M. (2001). Developmental and lesion effects in brain activation during sentence comprehension and mental rotation. *Developmental Neuropsychology, 18*, 139–169.

Bower, G. H. (1970). Analysis of a mnemonic device. *American Scientist, 58*, 496–510.

Brain, L. (1965). *Speech disorders*. London: Butterworths.

Broadbent, P. E. (1954). The role of auditory localization in attention and memory span. *Journal of Experimental Psychology, 47*, 191–196.

Broca, P. (1861). Nouvelle observation d'aphemie produite par une lesion de la moite posterieure des deuxieme et troiseme circonvolutions frontales. *Bulletin de la Societe Anatomique de Paris, 36*, 398–407.

Brown, J. W., & Hecaen, H. (1976). Lateralization and language representation. *Neurology, 26*, 183–189.

Bruner, J. S. (1974). *Beyond the information given*. London: George Allen & Unwin.

Bryden, M. P. (1967). An evaluation of some models of laterality effects in dichotic listening. *Acta Otolaryngol (Stockh), 63*, 595–604.

Bryden, M. P. (1978). Strategy effects in the assessment of hemispheric asymmetry. In G. Underwood (Ed.), *Strategies of information processing* (pp. 392–404). London: Academic Press.

Bryden, M. P. (1988). Cerebral specialization: Clinical and experimental assessment. In F. Boller & J. Grafman (Eds.), *Handbook of neuropsychology* (Vol. 1; pp. 143–159). Amsterdam: Elsevier.

Cappa, S. F., Guariglia, C., Papagno, C., Pizzamiglio, L., Vallar, G., Zoccolotti, P., et al. (1988). Patterns of lateralization and performance levels for verbal and spatial tasks in congenital androgen deficiency. *Behavioral Brain Research, 31*(2), 177–183.

Carmon, A., & Bechtoldt, H. (1969). Dominance of the right cerebral hemisphere for stereopsis. *Neuropsychologia 7*, 29–39.

Chelune, G. J., & Edwards, P. (1981). Early brain lesions: Ontogenic-environmental considerations. *Journal of Consulting and Clinical Psychology, 39*, 777–790.

Conrad, R. (1964). Acoustic confusions in immediate memory. *British Journal of Psychology, 55*, 75–83.

Dalby, M. A., Elbro, C., & Stodkilde-Jorgensen, H. (1998). Temporal lobe asymmetry and dyslexia: An in vivo study using MRI. *Brain and Language, 62*, 51–69.

Damasio, A. R., & Damasio, H. (1992). Brain and language. *Scientific American, 267*(3), 88–95.

D'Amato, R. C., Dean, R. S., Rattan, G., & Nickell, K. (1988). A study of psychological referrals for learning disabled children. *Journal of Psychoeducational Assessment, 6*, 118–124.

Darwin, C. J. (1974). Ear differences and hemispheric specialization. In F. O. Schmitt & F. G. Worden (Eds.), *The neurosciences: Third study program* (pp. 57–63). Cambridge, MA: MIT Press.

Darwin, C. J. (1975). Speech perception. In E. C. Carterette & M. P. Freedman (Eds.), *Handbook of perception* (Vol. 7; pp. 175–226). New York: Academic Press.

Das, J. P. (1973). Structure of cognitive abilities: Evidence for simultaneous and successive processing. *Journal of Educational Psychology, 65*, 103–108.

Davidson, R. J., & Schwartz, G. (1977). The influence of musical training on patterns of EEG asymmetry during musical and nonmusical self-generation tasks. *Psychophysiology, 14*, 58–63.

Dawson, G, Finley, C., Phillips, S., & Lewy, A. (1989). A comparison of hemispheric asymmetries in speech-related brain potentials of autistic and dysphasic children. *Brain and Language, 37*(1), 26–41.

Dax, G. (1865). Lesions de la moitie gauche de l'encephale coincident avec l'oubli des signes de la pensee. *Gazette Hebdomadaire de Medicine et de Chirurgie, 2*, 250–262.

de Lacoste, M. C., Horvath, D. S., & Woodward, D. J. (1991). Possible sex differences in the developing human fetal brain. *Journal of Clinical and Experimental Neuropsychology, 13*, 831–846.

Dean, R. S. (1978). Cerebral laterality and reading comprehension. *Neuropsychologia, 16, 633–636.*

Dean, R. S. (1979, September). *Lateral preference and reading comprehension.* Paper presented at the annual meeting of the American Psychological Association, New York.

Dean, R. S. (1981). Cerebral dominance and childhood learning disorders: Theoretical perspectives. *School Psychology Review, 10, 373–380.*

Dean, R. S. (1982). Assessing patterns of lateral preference. *Journal of Clinical Neuropsychology, 4, 124–128.*

Dean, R. S. (1983, February). *Dual processing of prose and cerebral laterality.* Paper presented at the annual meeting of the International Neuropsychological Society, Mexico City.

Dean, R. S. (1985a). Foundation and rationale for neuropsychological bases of individual differences. In L. C. Hartlage & C. F. Telzrow (Eds.), *The neuropsychology of individual differences: A developmental perspective* (pp. 8–39). New York: Plenum.

Dean, R. S. (1985b). Neuropsychological assessment. In J. D. Cavenar, R. Michels, H. K. H. Brodie, A. M. Cooper, S. B. Guze, L.L. Judd, et al. (Eds.), *Psychiatry* (pp. 7–40). Philadelphia: J. B. Lippincott.

Dean, R. S. (1986). Perspectives on the future of neuropsychological assessment. In B. S. Plake & J. C. Witt (Eds.), *Buros-Nebraska series on measurement and Testing* (pp. 203–244). New York: Lawrence Erlbaum.

Dean, R. S., & Anderson, J. L. (1997). Lateralization of cerebral functions. In A. M. Horton, Jr., D. Wedding, & J. Webster (Eds.), *The neuropsychology handbook foundations and assessment* (Vol. 1; pp. 139–198). New York: Springer Publishing Company.

Dean, R. S., & Hua, M. S. (1982). Laterality effects in cued auditory asymmetries. *Neuropsychologia, 20, 685–690.*

Dean, R. S., & Rothlisberg, B. A. (1983). Lateral preference patterns and cross-modal sensory integration. *Journal of Pediatric Psychology, 8, 285–292.*

Dean, R. S., Schwartz, M. H., & Smith, L. S. (1981). Lateral preference patterns as a discriminator of learning difficulties. *Journal of Consulting and Clinical Psychology, 49, 227–235.*

Dikman, S., Matthews, C. G., & Harley, I. P. (1975). The effect of early versus late onset of major motor epilepsy upon cognitive intellectual performance. *Epilepsia, 16, 73–77.*

Dimond, S., & Beaumont, J. (1974). *Hemisphere function in the human brain.* London: Elek Scientific Books.

Dronkers, N. F. (2001). The pursuit of brain-language relationships. *Brain and Language, 71, 59–61.*

Duara, R., Kushch, A., Gross-Glenn, K., Barker, W. W., Jallad, B., Pascal, S., et al. (1991). Neuroanatomic differences between dyslexic and normal readers on magnetic resonance imaging scans. *Archives of Neurology, 48, 410–416.*

Dunlop, D. B., Dunlop, P., & Fenelon, B. (1973). Vision laterality analysis in children with reading disability: The results of new techniques of examination. *Cortex, 9,* 227–236.

Eccles, J. C. (1973). *The understanding of the brain.* New York: McGraw-Hill.

Efron, R. (1963). The effect of handedness on the perception of simultaneity and temporal order. *Brain, 86,* 261–284.

Escalante-Mead, P. R., Minshew, N. J., & Sweeney, J. A. (2003). Abnormal brain lateralization in high-functioning autism. *Journal of Autism and Developmental Disorders, 33,* 539–543.

Fletcher, J. M., & Satz, P. (1983). Age, plasticity, and equipotentiality: A reply to Smith. *Journal of Consulting and Clinical Psychology, 31,* 763–767.

Gainotti, G., Caltagirone, C., & Zoccolotti, P. (1993). Left/right and cortical/subcortical dichotomies in the neuropsychological study of human emotions. *Cognition and Emotion, 7*(1), 71–93.

Gazzaniga, M. S. (1970). *The bisected brain.* New York: Appleton-Century-Crofts.

Gazzaniga, M. S., & Sperry, R. W. (1962). Language after section of the cerebral commissures. *Brain, 90,* 131–148.

Gerstmann, J. (1957). Some notes on the Gerstmann syndrome. *Neurology, 7,* 866–869.

Geschwind, N. (1974). *Selected papers on language and the brain.* The Netherlands: D. Reidel.

Geschwind, N., & Levitsky, W. (1968). Human brain: Left-right asymmetries in temporal speech region. *Science, 161,* 186–187.

Goodglass, H., & Peck, E. A. (1972). Dichotic ear order effects in Korsakoff and normal subjects. *Neuropsychologia, 10,* 211–217.

Gordon, H. W. (1970). Hemispheric asymmetries in the perception of musical chords. *Cortex, 6,* 387–398.

Gordon, H. W. (1974). Auditory specialization of the right and left hemispheres. In M. Kinsbourne & W. L. Smith (Eds.), *Hemispheric disconnection and cerebral function* (pp. 126–136). Springfield, IL: Charles C. Thomas.

Gordon, H. W. (1978). Left hemisphere dominance for rhythmic elements in dichotically-presented melodies. *Cortex, 14,* 58–70.

Goy, R. W., & McEwen, B. S. (1980). *Sexual differentiation of the brain.* Cambridge, MA: MIT Press.

Gur, R., Gunning-Dixon, F., Bilker, W., & Gur, R. (2002). Sex differences in temporo-limbic and frontal brain volumes of healthy adults. *Cerebral Cortex, 12,* 998–1003.

Hardyck, C., Tzeng, O. J. L., & Wang, W. S-Y. (1978). Lateralization of function and bilingual judgements: 1. Thinking lateralized. *Brain and Language, 5,* 56–71.

Harris, A. J. (1947). *Harris tests of lateral dominance.* New York: Psychological Corporation.

Hecaen, H. (1962). Clinical symptomatology in right and left hemisphere lesions. In V. G. Mountcastle (Ed.), *Interhemispheric relations and cerebral dominance* (pp. 215–243). Baltimore: Johns Hopkins University Press.

Hecaen, H., & Angelergues, R. (1962). Agnosia for faces (prosopagnosia). *Archives of Neurology, 24*–32.

Hecaen, H., & Marcie, P. (1974). Disorders of written language following right hemisphere lesions: Spatial dysgraphia. In S. J. Dimond & J. G. Beaumont (Eds.), *Hemisphere function in the human brain* (pp. 345–366). New York: Wiley.

Heron, W. (1957). Perception as a function of retinal locus and attention. *American Journal of Psychology, 70*, 38–48.

Hiscock, M., Antoniuk, D., & Prisciak, K. (1985). Generalized and lateralized interference between concurrent tasks performed by children: Effects of age, sex, and skill. *Devekionebtak Beyriostcgikigtm 1*(1), 29–48.

Hugdahl, K. (1996). Brain laterality—beyond the basics. *European Psychologist, 1*, 206–220.

Hugdahl, K., Carlsson, G., Uvebrant, P., & Lundervold, A. J. (1997). Dichotic-listening performance and intracarotid injections of amobarbital in children and adolescents. Preoperative and postoperative comparisons. *Archives of Neurology, 54*, 1494–1500.

Hugdahl, K. Wester, K., & Asbjornsen, A. (1990). The role of the left and right thalamus in language asymmetry: dichotic listening in Parkinsonian-patients undergoing stereotactic thalamotomy. *Brain and Language, 39*, 1–13.

Hynd, G. W., & Obrzut, J. E. (1977). Effects of grade level and sex on the magnitude of the dichotic ear advantage. *Neuropsychologia, 15*, 689–692.

Hynd, G. W., Obrzut, J. E., Weed, W., & Hynd, C. R. (1979). Development of cerebral dominance: Dichotic listening asymmetry in normal and learning disabled children. *Journal of Experimental Child Psychology, 28*, 445–454.

Jackson, J. H. (1932). On the duality of the brain. In J. Taylor (Ed.), *Selected writings of John Hughlings Jackson* (Vol. 2; pp. 146–252). London: Hodder and Stoughton. (Original work published 1874.)

Jasper, H. H., & Raney, E. T. (1937). The phi-test of lateral dominance. *American Journal of Psychology, 49*, 450–457.

Kaufman, A. S., Zalma, R., & Kaufman, N. L. (1978). The relationship of right hand dominance to motor coordination, mental ability, and right-left advantages of young normal children. *Child Development, 49*, 885–888.

Kershner, J. B. (1977). Cerebral dominance in disabled readers, good readers, and gifted children: Search for a valid model. *Child Development, 48*, 61–67.

Kimura, D. (1961). Cerebral dominance and the perception of verbal stimuli. *Canadian Journal of Psychology, 15*, 166–171.

Kimura, D. (1967). Functional asymmetry of the brain in dichotic listening. *Cortex, 3*, 163–178.

Kimura, D., & Durnford, M. (1974). Normal studies on the function of the right hemisphere in vision. In S. J. Dimond & J. G. Beaumont (Eds.), *Hemisphere function in the human brain* (pp. 25–47). London: Elek Scientific Books.

Kinsbourne, M. (1970). The cerebral basis of lateral asymmetries in attention. *Acta Psychologia, 33,* 193–201.

Kinsbourne, M. (1975). Cerebral dominance, learning, and cognition. In H. R. Myklebust (Ed.), *Progress in learning disabilities* (pp. 201–218). New York: Grune & Stratton.

Kinsbourne, M., & Cook, J. (1971). Generalized and lateralized effects of concurrent verbalization on a unimanual skill. *Quarterly Journal of Experimental Psychology, 23,* 341–345.

Kinsbourne, M., & Hiscock, M. (1977). Does cerebral dominance develop? In S. J. Segalowitz & F. A. Gruber (Eds.), *Language development and neurological theory* (pp. 255–334). New York: Academic Press.

Kolata, G. B. (1979). Sex hormones and brain development. *Science, 205,* 985–987.

Kolb, B., & Whishaw, I. Q. (1990). *Fundamentals of human neuropsychology.* New York: W. H. Freeman.

Krashen, S. D. (1973). Lateralization, language learning, and the critical period: Some new evidence. *Language Learning, 23,* 63–74.

Lake, D., & Bryden, M. (1976). Handedness and sex differences in hemispheric asymmetry. *Brain and Language, 3,* 266–282.

Lenneberg, E. H. (1967). *Biological foundations of language.* New York: Wiley.

Leonard, C. M., Voeller, K.K.S., Lombardino, L. J., Morris, M. J., Hynd, G. W., Alexander, A. W., et al. (1993). Anomalus cerebral structure in dyslexia revealed with magnetic resonance imaging. *Archives of Neurology, 50,* 461–469.

Levy, J. (1973). Lateral specialization of the human brain: Behavioral manifestations and possible evolutionary basis. In J. Kriger (Ed.), *The biology of behavior* (pp. 159–180). Corvallis, OR: Oregon State University Press.

Levy, J., & Levy, J. M. (1978). Human lateralization from head to foot: Sex-related factors. *Science, 200,* 1291–1292.

Levy, J., & Nagylaki, T. (1972). A model for the genetics of handedness. *Genetics, 72,* 117–128.

Levy, J., & Reid, M. (1976). Variations in writing posture and cerebral organization. *Science, 194,* 337–339.

Levy, J., Trevarthen, C., & Sperry, R. W. (1972). Perception of bilateral chimeric figures following hemispheric deconnection. *Brain, 95,* 61–78.

Lucas, J. A., Rosenstein, L. D., & Bigler, E. D. (1989). Handedness and language among the mentally retarded: Implications for the model of pathological left-handedness and gender differences in hemispheric specialization. *Neuropsychologia, 27,* 713–723.

Luria, A. R. (1966). *Human brain and psychological processes.* New York: Harper & Row.

Maccoby, E. E. (1966). *The development of sex differences.* Stanford, CA: Stanford University Press.

MacLusky, M. J., & Naftolin, F. (1981). Sexual differentiation of central nervous system. *Science, 211,* 1294–1302.

Marcel, T., Katz, L., & Smith, M. (1974). Laterality and reading proficiency. *Neuropsychologia, 12,* 133–139.

Marcel, T., & Rajan, P. (1975). Lateral specialization for recognition of words and faces in good and poor readers. *Neuropsychologia, 13,* 489–497.

McCartney, G., & Hopper, P. (1999). Development of lateralized behavior in the human fetus from 12 to 27 weeks' gestation. *Developmental Medicine and Child Neurology, 41,* 83–86.

McFarland, K., McFarland, M. L., Bain, J. D., & Ashton, R. (1978). Ear differences of abstract and concrete word recognition. *Neuropsychologia, 13,* 555–561.

McGlone, J. (1980). Sex differences in human brain asymmetry: A critical review. *Behavioral and Brain Sciences, 3,* 215–263.

McKeever, W. F., & Gill, K. M. (1972). Interhemispheric transfer time for visual stimulus information varies as a function of the retinal locus of stimulation. *Psychonomic Science, 26,* 308–310.

McLaren, J., & Bryson, S. E. (1987). Hemispheric asymmetries in the perception of emotional and neutral faces. *Cortex, 23,* 645–654.

Mills, L. (1977). *Left-hemispheric specialization in normal subjects for judgements of successive order and duration of nonverbal stimuli.* Unpublished doctoral dissertation, University of Western Ontario, London, Ontario, Canada.

Milner, B. (1962). Laterality effects in audition. In V. B. Mountcastle (Ed.), *Interhemispheric relations and cerebral dominance.* Baltimore: Johns Hopkins University Press.

Milner, B. (1967). Brain mechanisms suggested by studies of temporal lobes. In C. H. Millikan and F. L. Darley (Eds.), *Brain mechanisms underlying speech and Language* (pp. 381–414). New York: Grune & Stratton.

Milner, B. (1968). Visual recognition and recall after right temporal-lobe excision in man. *Neuropsychologia, 6,* 191–209.

Milner, B. (1974). Hemispheric specialization: Scope and limits. In F. O. Schmitt & F. G. Warden (Eds.), *The neurosciences: Third study programme* (pp. 75–89). Cambridge, MA: MIT Press.

Molfese, D. L. (1977). Infant cerebral asymmetry. In S. J. Segalowitz & F. A. Gruber (Eds.), *Language development and neurological theory.* New York: Academic Press.

Molfese, D. L., Freeman, R. B., & Palermo, D. S. (1975). The ontogeny of brain lateralization for speech and non-speech stimuli. *Brain and Language, 2,* 356–368.

Morgan, A., McDonald, P. J., & McDonald, H. (1971). Differences in bilateral alpha activity as a function of experimental tasks, with a note on lateral eye movements and hypnotizability. *Neuropsychologia, 9,* 459–469.

Moscovitch, M. (1976, September). *Verbal and spatial clustering in free recall of drawings following left or right temporal lobectomy; Evidence for dual encoding.* Paper presented at the Canadian Psychological Association meeting, Toronto.

Moscovitch, M. (1979). Information processing and the cerebral hemispheres. In M. S. Gazzaniga (Ed.), *Handbook of behavioral neurobiology: Vol 2, Neuropsychology* (pp. 379–446). New York: Plenum Press.

Nottebohm, F. (1979). Origins and mechanisms in the establishment of cerebral dominance. In M. S. Gazzaniga (Ed.), *Handbook of behavioral neurobiology: Vol. 2, Neuropsychology* (pp. 295–344). New York: Plenum Press.

Oldfield, R. C. (1971). The assessment and analysis of handedness: The Edinburgh Inventory. *Neuropsychologia, 9,* 97–113.

Orton, S. T. (1937). Specific reading disability—strephosymobolia. *Journal of the American Medical Association, 90,* 1095–1099.

Paivio, A. (1971). *Imagery and verbal processes.* New York: Holt, Rinehart and Winston.

Paivio, A., Clark, J. M., Digdon, N., & Bons, T. (1989). Referential processing: Reciprocity and correlates of naming and imaging. *Memory and Cognition, 17*(2), 163–174.

Parsons, O. A., Vega, A., Jr., & Burn, J. (1969). Different psychological effects of lateralized brain damage. *Journal of Consulting and Clinical Psychology, 33,* 551–557.

Peiper, A. (1963). *Cerebral function in infancy and childhood* (3rd rev. ed., B. Nagler & M. Nagler, Trans.). New York: Consultants Bureau.

Petersen, S. E., Fox, P. T., Posner, M. I., Mintun, M., & Raichle, M. E. (1989). Positron emission tomographic studies of the processing of single words. *Journal of Cognitive Neuroscience, 1*(2), 153–170.

Piaget, J. (1952). *The origins of intelligence in children.* New York: International Universities Press.

Pirozzolo, F. J. (1979). *The neuropsychology of developmental reading disorders.* New York: Praeger.

Pirozzolo, F. J., Campanella, D. J., Christensen, K., & Lawson-Kerr, K. (1981). Effects of cerebral dysfunction on neurolinguistic performance in children. *Journal of Consulting and Clinical Psychology, 49,* 791–806.

Pizzamiglio, L. (1976). Cognitive approach to hemispheric dominance. In R. M. Knights & D. Bakker (Eds.), *The neuropsychology of learning disorders* (pp. 265–272). Baltimore: University Park Press.

Poizner, H., Bellugi, U., & Klima, E. S. (1990). Biological foundations of language: Clues from sign language. *Annual Review of Neuroscience, 13,* 283–307.

Posner, M. I., Petersen, S. E., Fox, P. T., & Raichle, M. E. (1988). Localization of cognitive operation in the human brain. *Science, 240,* 1627–1631.

Rabinowicz, B. H. (1976). *A non-lateralized auditory process in speech perception.* Unpublished master's thesis, University of Toronto.

Rains, G. D. (2002). *Principles of human neuropsychology.* Boston: McGraw-Hill.

Reed, H., & Reitan, R. (1963). Intelligence test performances in brain damaged subjects with lateralized motor deficits. *Journal of Consulting Psychology, 17*(2), 101–106.

Reinisch, J. M., & Sanders, S. A. (1992). Effects of prenatal exposure to diethylstilbestrol (DES) on hemispheric laterality and spatial ability in human males. *Hormones and Behavior, 26*(1), 62–75.

Reitan, R. M. (1955). Certain differential effects of left and right cerebral lesions in human adults. *Journal of Comparative and Physiological Psychology, 48,* 474–477.

Reitan, R. M. (1969). *Manual for administration of neuropsychological test batteries for adults and children.* Indianapolis: Author.

Reynolds, C. R. (1978). Latency to respond and conjugate lateral eye movements: A methodological and theoretical note. *Perceptual and Motor Skills, 47,* 843–847.

Richardson, A. J. (1995). Handedness and visual motion sensitivity in adult dyslexics. *The Irish Journal of Psychology, 16,* 229–247.

Robichon, F., Levrier, O., Farnarier, P., & Habib, M. (2000). Developmental dyslexia: Atypical cortical asymmetries and functional significance. *European Journal of Neurology, 7,* 35–46.

Satz, P. (1976). Cerebral dominance and reading disability: An old problem revisited. In R. M. Knights & D. Bakker (Eds.), *The neuropsychology of learning disorders* (pp. 273–294). Baltimore: University Park Press.

Satz, P., Bakker, D. J., Teunissen, J., Goebel, R., & van der Blugt, H. (1975). Developmental parameters of the ear asymmetry: A multivariate approach. *Brain and Language, 2,* 71–85.

Savage, C. R., & Thomas, D. G. (1993). Information processing and interhemispheric transfer in left- and right-handed adults. *International Journal of Neuroscience, 71*(1–4), 201–219.

Schmeck, H. H., Jr. (1980). His brain, her brain. *Science and Living Tomorrow, 15,* 23–24.

Scotti, G., & Spinnler, H. (1970). Colour imperception in unilateral hemisphere-damaged patients. *Journal of Neurology, Neurosurgery, and Psychiatry, 33,* 22–28.

Seamon, J. G., & Gazzaniga, M. D. (1973). Coding strategies and cerebral laterality effects. *Cognitive Psychology, 5,* 240–256.

Segalowitz, S. J. (1986). Validity and reliability of noninvasive lateralization measures. In J. E. Obrzut & G. W. Hynd (Eds.), *Child neuropsychology* (Vol. 1; pp. 191–208). New York: Academic Press.

Shankweiler, D. (1966). Effects of temporal-lobe damage on perception of dichotically presented melodies. *Journal of Comparative Psychology, 62,* 115–119.

Shankweiler, D., & Studdert-Kennedy, M. (1975). A continuum of lateralization for speech perception. *Brain and Language, 2,* 212–225.

Share, D., & Silva, P. (2003). Gender bias in IQ-discrepancy and post-discrepancy definitions of reading disability. *Journal of Learning Disabilities, 36,* 4–14.

Shute, V. J., Pelligrino, J. W., Hubert, L., & Reynolds, R. W. (1983). The relationship between androgen levels and human spatial abilities. *Bulletin of the Psychonomic Society, 21,* 465–468.

Smith, A. (1974). Dominant and nondominant hemispherectory. In M. Kinsbourne & W. L. Smith (Eds.), *Hemispheric deconnection and cerebral function* (pp. 5–33). Springfield, IL: Charles C. Thomas.

Smith, A., & Sugar, O. (1975), Development of above normal language and intelligence 21 years after left hemispherectomy. *Neurology, 25,* 813–818.

Solodkin, A., Hlustik, P., Noll, D. C., & Small, S. L. (2001). Lateralization of motor circuits and handedness during finger movements. *European Journal of Neurology, 8,* 425–434.

Sperry, R. W. (1968). Hemispheric deconnection and unity in conscious awareness. *American Psychologist, 23,* 723–733.

Sperry, R. W. (1969). A modified concept of consciousness. *Psychological Review, 76,* 532–536.

Sperry, R. W. (1974). Lateral specialization in the surgically separated hemispheres. In F. O. Schmitt & F. G. Worden (Eds.), *The neurosciences: Third study program* (pp. 163–185). New York: Wiley.

Sperry, R. W., Gazzaniga, M. S., & Bogen, J. H. (1969). Interhemispheric relationship: The neocortical commissures: Syndromes of hemisphere disconnection. In P. Vinken & G. W. Bruyn (Eds.), *Handbook of clinical neurology* (Vol. 4; pp. 273–290). New York: Wiley.

Springer, S. P., & Deutsch, G. (1998). *Left brain, right brain: Perspectives from cognitive neuroscience.* New York: Freeman.

Stark, R. (1961). An investigation of unilateral cerebral pathology with equated verbal and visual-spatial tasks. *Journal of Abnormal and Social Psychology, 62,* 282–287.

Stephan, K. C., Marshall, J. C., Friston, K. J., Rowe, J. B., Ritzl, A., Zilles, K., et al. (2003). Lateralized cognitive processes and lateralized task control in the human brain. *Science, 301,* 384–386.

Summers, R. K., & Taylor, M. L. (1972). Cerebral speech dominance in language-disordered and normal children. *Cortex, 8,* 224–232.

Tan, U. (1991). Serum testosterone levels in male and female subjects with standard and anomalous dominance. *International Journal of Neuroscience, 58*(3–4), 211–214.

Tjossen, R. D., Hansen, T. J., & Ripley, H. S. (1961, August). *An investigation of reading difficulty in young children.* Paper presented at the 117th Annual Meeting of the American Psychological Association, Chicago.

Waber, D. P. (1977). Sex differences in mental abilities, hemispheric lateralization, and rate of physical growth at adolescence. *Developmental Psychology, 13,* 29–38.

Wada, J. (1949). A new method for the determination of the side of cerebral speech dominance: A preliminary report on the intra-carotid injection of sodium amytal in man. *Medical Biology, 14,* 221.

Wada, J. A., Clarke, R., & Hamm, A. (1975). Cerebral hemispheric asymmetry in humans. *Archives of Neurology, 32,* 239–246.

Weintraub, P. (1981). The brain: His and hers. *Discover, 2,* 14–20.

Whitaker, H. A., & Ojemann, G. A. (1977). Lateralization of higher cortical functions: A critique. In S. J. Dimond & D. A. Blizard (Eds.), *Evaluation and lateralization of the brain* (pp. 459–473). New York: New York Academy of Sciences.

Witelson, S. F. (1974). Hemispheric specialization for linguistic and nonlinguistic tactual perception using a dichotomous stimulation technique. *Cortex, 10,* 1–17.

Witelson, S. F. (1976). Early hemisphere specialization and interhemisphere plasticity: An empirical and theoretical review. In S. Segalowitz & F. Gruber (Eds.), *Language and development and neurological theory* (pp. 213–287). New York: Academic Press.

Witelson, S. F. (1977). Developmental dyslexia: Two right hemispheres and none left. *Science, 195,* 309–311.

Witelson, S. F., & Pallie, W. (1973). Left hemispheric specialization for language in the newborn: Neuroanatomical evidence of asymmetry. *Brain, 96,* 641–646.

Wittling, W. (1995). Brain asymmetry in the control of autonomic-physiologic activity. In R. J. Davidson and K. Hugdahl (Eds.), *Brain asymmetry* (pp. 305–358). Cambridge, MA: MIT Press.

Wood, C. C. (1975). Auditory and phonetic levels of processing in speech perception: Neurophysiological and information processing analyses. *Journal of Experimental Psychology: Human Perception and Performance, 104,* 3–20.

Xu, B., Grafman, J., Gaillard, W. D., Ishii, K., Vega-Bermudez, F., Pietrini, P., et al. (2001). Conjoint and extended neural networks for the computation of speech codes: The neural basis of selective impairment in reading words and pseudowords. *Cerebral Cortex, 11,* 267–277.

Yakovlev, P. I., & Rakic, P. (1966). Patterns of decussation of bulbar pyramids and distribution of pyramidal tracts on two sides of the spinal cord. *Transactions of the American Neurology Association, 91,* 366–367.

Zangwill, O. L. (1960). *Cerebral dominance and its relationship to psychological function.* London: Oliver & Boyd.

Zangwill, O. L. (1962). Dyslexia in relation to cerebral dominance. In J. Money (Ed.), *Reading disability* (pp. 103–113). Baltimore: Johns Hopkins University Press.

Zillmer, E., & Spiers, M. (2001). *Principles of neuropsychology.* Belmont, CA; Wadsworth.

Section II

Assessment in Neuropsychology

8

An Introduction to Structural and Functional Neuroimaging

ROBERT M. ROTH, NANCY S. KOVEN, AND
JO CARA PENDERGRASS

INTRODUCTION

A CURSORY GLANCE AT any number of health-related scientific journals, or a walk though many modern medical facilities, would bear witness to the explosion of novel neuroimaging technologies and their research and clinical applications, since the inception of x-ray computed tomography over 30 years ago (Hounsfield, 1973). Take as a case in point functional magnetic resonance imaging (fMRI), commonly employed to study the neural substrates of cognitive and other processes. We conducted a simple (and by no means exhaustive) literature search using the search terms "fMRI and working memory," starting from the first publications on the topic in 1995 (Casey et al., 1995; D'Esposito et al., 1995; Mellers et al., 1995) and then for every other year until 2005. As can be seen from Figure 8.1, the volume of publications on the topic of fMRI and working memory has burgeoned over the years.

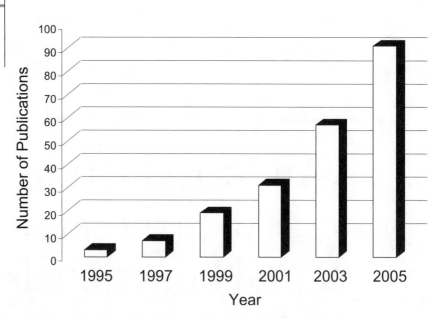

FIGURE 8.1 Estimated number of publications on the topic of "fMRI and working memory" from 1995 to 2005.

The panoply of methods for investigating brain structure and function, in both animals and humans, has played an increasingly important role in augmenting our understanding of the healthy and abnormal brain. And while state-of-the art research in neuroimaging tends to be slowly translated into valuable and widely available clinical tools, some of the advances have already resulted in significant benefits for the understanding of the etiology and treatment of patients with illnesses commonly seen in the offices of neuropsychologists and other clinicians.

In the present chapter, we provide the reader with an introduction to several modern structural and functional neuroimaging technologies, including some basics regarding how they work, and what they can tell us about the brain. We supplement the description of the methods with examples illustrating applications to healthy and clinical populations.

IMAGING BRAIN STRUCTURE

COMPUTED TOMOGRAPHY

COMPUTED TOMOGRAPHY (CT) imaging, also known as CAT scanning (computed axial tomography), produces topographic images of the living human body (McRobbie, Moore, Graves, & Prince, 2003). A rotating x-ray device creates detailed cross-sectional images of the brain and bodily structures, including organs, bone, and blood vessels, based on the attenuation of the x-rays by the tissues. In using x-rays, a type of ionizing radiation, CT has an excellent ability to generate high resolution images of dense tissue such as bone and bony structures, in addition to soft tissue and blood vessels. CT imaging is commonly conducted to evaluate complicated bone fractures; bone mineral density; anatomy of the spine; chest and abdominal tumors; cysts or infections; brain tumors; traumatic injuries to the head, such as skull fractures or blood clots; and when magnetic resonance (MR) imaging is contraindicated due to an implanted metal device. Due to shorter scan times, CT imaging can be used for all anatomic regions and is often used for immediate assessment of trauma patients. Contrast agents also may be used in CT imaging to enhance delineation of normal from abnormal anatomical structures. CT imaging is comparable in exposure to radiation as that associated with other x-ray examinations.

MAGNETIC RESONANCE IMAGING

MAGNETIC RESONANCE IMAGING (MRI) is a noninvasive, in-vivo imaging technique that uses magnetic fields and the natural magnet properties of the human body to image biological tissue, including detection of different tissue properties and types. The technique is based principally upon sensitivity to the presence and properties of water, which makes up 70 to 90% of most tissues (McRobbie et al., 2003). MR signals are produced within a person's tissue in response to pulse sequences generated by the MR scanner. These sequences consist of radio frequency (RF) and gradient pulses that are produced through a series of changing magnetic gradients and oscillating electromagnetic fields. MRI scanners generally produce frequencies consistent with that of hydrogen nuclei, which are most common given the presence of water molecules in the human body (Huettel, Song, & McCarthy, 2004). Different types of human tissue (e.g., gray matter, white matter, cerebrospinal fluid) produce different signal intensities or brightness on MR images due to the varying amounts of electromagnetic energy absorbed and later emitted by the tissue, which is dependent on the number and type of nuclei present in the tissue (McRobbie et al., 2003). Contrast agents, such as a gadolinium compound, may be used to enhance detection of anatomy or pathology in specific areas of interest. Because MR imaging relies on the natural magnetization of the human body, it is harmless to an individual unless the individual has metal in their body. Therefore, MR imaging is usually contraindicated if an individual has an implanted metal device, including but not limited to a cardiac pacemaker, implanted defibrillator, or brain aneurysm clip, or otherwise has ferromagnetic metal (i.e., exhibits spontaneous magnetization) in their body (e.g., shrapnel; McRobbie et al., 2003).

MANUAL SEGMENTATION

SEVERAL PROCEDURES HAVE been developed to investigate aspects of brain morphology quantitatively. The vast majority of studies have applied these procedures to images acquired using MRI rather than CT, given the former's greater spatial resolution.

Researchers have commonly employed manual segmentation to obtain the volume of brain regions of interest (ROI). Segmentations are carried out following standardized instruction manuals that detail the boundaries defining a given brain region. For example, the lateral border of the caudate nucleus is defined by the internal capsule, while its medial border is defined by the lateral ventricle. Most studies have traced ROIs on high resolution T1-weighted images, thus facilitating the identification of boundaries between gray matter, white matter, and cerebrospinal fluid. Furthermore, while the majority of studies have focused on cortical and subcortical gray matter, one can also segment the ventricles and ROIs within white matter (e.g., Jernigan et al., 2001), though the latter is somewhat tenuous given the lack of obvious boundaries between different white matter pathways, at least as seen on T1-weighted images.

Manually segmented ROI measurements generally show good reliability between different tracers following the same guidelines, but several limitations must be taken into consideration. The procedure is very time intensive, and the reason for volume loss in a given patient or patient population cannot be addressed. Volume loss may be due to such factors as decreased neuron size, loss of neurons, reduced dendritic arborization, or even factors related to hydration (Zipursky, Lim, & Pfefferbaum, 1989). Direct comparison of results between laboratories is difficult given variations in the resolution of images obtained (e.g., 1 mm versus 3 mm slice thickness), ROI boundary definitions, and other parameters such as tracing the ROI on contiguous slices in which it appears versus every other slice and then extrapolating to obtain overall volume. Such variations contribute to the difficulty in establishing a normative database of ROI volumes for use in clinical studies. While automated segmentation software is also available and can provide reliable ROI volume measurements, several methodological limitations have been noted (Carmichael et al., 2005; Walhovd et al., 2005).

Despite the limitations of ROI volumetry, this procedure has been used to study the neuroanatomy of a wide variety of clinical populations. This has included psychiatric populations such as schizophrenia (Nelson, Saykin, Flashman, & Riordan, 1998; Roth, Flashman, Saykin, McAllister, & Vidaver, 2004; Shenton, Dickey, Frumin, & McCarley, 2001) and posttraumatic stress disorder (Gilbertson et al., 2002; Vythilingam et al., 2005); neurological illnesses such as epilepsy (Lawson et al., 2000; Seeck et al., 2005), Alzheimer's disease, and mild cognitive impairment (Callen, Black, Gao, Caldwell, & Szalai, 2001; Copenhaver et al., 2006; Xu et al., 2000); as well as neurodevelopmental disorders (Carper & Courchesne, 2005; Kates et al., 2002). Others have investigated the relationship between volume loss and cognitive deficits. What is evident from this latter type of study is that the relationship between brain function and brain structure is not always consistent with what one may expect. For example, while the hippocampus is known to play an important role in episodic memory (Small, 2002), volume of the structure has been reported to be associated with performance on neuropsychological tests of episodic memory in some studies (e.g., Martin et al., 1999; Tate & Bigler, 2000) but not others (e.g., Serra-Grabulosa et al., 2005; Torres, Flashman, O'Leary, Swayze, & Andreasen, 1997).

SHAPE ANALYSIS

SEVERAL INVESTIGATORS HAVE sought to gain further information about the morphology of the brain by employing computational methods, such as deformation-based morphometry and tensor-based morphology (Ashburner et al., 1998; Chung et al., 2001; Golland, Grimson, Shenton, & Kikinis, 2005), which allow for the quantification of the shape of brain regions. Most of these methods require that a ROI first be segmented from the rest of the brain. Although there is no single accepted method for evaluating the shape of a brain region, there are several processing steps that are typically applied to the neuroanatomical images (Golland et al., 2005). The brains employed in a study are commonly warped into a standard three-dimensional stereotactic space, such as that provided by the Montreal Neurological Institute or Talairach (Talairach & Tournoux, 1988) atlases, a procedure also referred to as spatial normalization. This step allows one to remove the effects of size, orientation, and position of the ROI, thus focusing on shape alone. The shape features of the ROI are then extracted through the use of one of several techniques such as dense surface meshes (Figure 8.2; Shen, Makedon, & Saykin, 2004; Shenton, Gerig, McCarley, Szekely, & Kikinis, 2002). Such meshes allow one to calculate distance measures to each point on the surface from, for example, the central point of the structure. Once the features of the surface have been extracted, statistical models can be constructed that evaluate differences between the features of two or more groups, such as comparing healthy adults to patients with schizophrenia. The results of the statistical model (which are purely mathematical, not anatomical) are then mapped back onto the neuroanatomy in order to permit visualization and interpretation of local shape differences between groups or time points such as in treatment or longitudinal studies. It should be noted that the majority of work thus far has focused on the shape of gray matter. Recently, tools have been developed for analyzing the shape of white matter fiber tracts (Batchelor et al., 2006).

The majority of clinical studies of shape have focused on determining whether there are areas of abnormal shape along the surface of discrete brain structures such as the hippocampus, or along the entire cortical surface (Chung et al., 2003). Results of these analyses allow one to identify areas of local surface expansion and contraction in one group relative to another. A limitation of the surface-based approach, however, is that it cannot determine whether changes seen along the surface of a ROI are actually due to changes in that specific location or are secondary to changes located more internal to the structure. More recent studies have begun to explore ways to gain information about the shape of medial surfaces of brain structures (Bouix, Pruessner, Louis Collins, & Siddiqi, 2005; Styner, Gerig, Lieberman, Jones, & Weinberger, 2003; Styner, Lieberman, Pantazis, & Gerig, 2004).

Shape analysis has been applied to the study of normal aging (McHugh et al., 2007) and several illnesses such as schizophrenia (Csernansky et al., 1998), depression (Posener et al., 2003), epilepsy (Hogan, Bucholz, & Joshi, 2003; Hogan et al., 2004), and Alzheimer's disease (AD; Csernansky et al.,

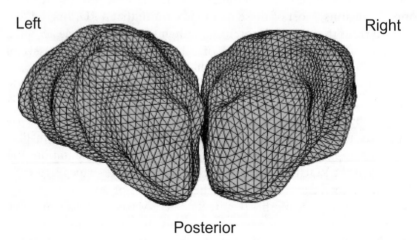

Left   **Right**

Posterior

FIGURE 8.2 Example of shape analysis using meshes over the surface of the left and right thalamus.
Morphometry provided by Franklin Brown, PhD, Eastern Connecticut State University; surface mesh illustration provided by Li Shen, PhD, Image and Pattern Analysis Lab, University of Massachusetts–Dartmouth.

2000). Patients with very mild AD, for example, have been shown to not only have reduced overall volume of the hippocampus, but also inward deformation of the lateral surface of the hippocampus (Csernansky, Wang, Miller, Galvin, & Morris, 2005). Furthermore, degree of abnormality of hippocampus surface shape is reported to be predictive of conversion to very mild dementia (Csernansky, Wang, Swank, et al., 2005), as well as predicting response to donepezil in patients with very mild or mild AD (Csernansky, Wang, Miller, et al., 2005). Further support for the potential clinical utility of shape analysis is seen in a study of two patients with occlusive hydrocephalus (Preul, Hubsch, Lindner, & Tittgemeyer, 2006). Analyses showed regional differences between the patients in their pattern of pre- to post-surgical change as revealed by shape analysis of the third and lateral ventricles, despite equivalent change in overall ventricular volume.

Voxel-Based Morphometry

Voxel-based morphometry (VBM) is a computational neuroanatomic technique that allows one to quantify the density or concentration of gray matter (or white matter) on a voxel-by-voxel basis relative to other tissue types (white matter, cerebrospinal fluid) in a brain region (Ashburner & Friston, 2000, 2001). VBM is most commonly applied to T1-weighted MRI images. There are several image processing steps typically employed in VBM. The acquired images are spatially normalized to the same stereotactic space, using a template brain or a locally developed normative template. The spatial normalization removes shape and location differences between individual brains. It should be noted, however, that this is a global rather than exact matching of the individual brains to the template brain. The gray matter is then extracted from the normalized images using automated procedures based on voxel intensities. The resulting images are spatially smoothed, resulting in each voxel having the average concentration of its surrounding voxels, the number and extent of which depends upon the size of the smoothing kernel. Smoothing helps compensate for inexact normalization and renders the data more normally distributed, thus increasing the power of parametric statistical tests to detect significant effects.

The output of VBM statistical analyses is a color-coded map overlaid on the brain template showing where significant effects are located. More recently, an *optimized* VBM procedure was introduced that involves normalizing the segmented tissue compartments rather than the whole brain, which helps to avoid confounds in global normalization that may be introduced when one group has significant structural changes unrelated to gray and white matter volumes, such as enlarged ventricles (Good et al., 2001b). A further processing step may also be included that would allow one to measure the volume (i.e., absolute amount) of gray or white matter within a region (Good et al., 2001b).

VBM has an advantage over manual segmentation in being able to provide a quantitative measure of structural integrity throughout the brain simultaneously, rather than having to trace individual ROIs one by one. VBM has been employed to study the relationship between sex and handedness (Good et al., 2001a) as well as normal aging (Good et al., 2001b) on brain structure. VBM is also being employed in an increasing number of studies of patient populations. For example, Saykin and colleagues recently used VBM to demonstrate abnormalities of gray matter concentration in elderly with mild cognitive impairment, as well as in healthy elderly with significant cognitive complaints but intact cognitive functioning (Saykin et al., 2006). Others have reported correlations between neuropsychological test performance and gray matter concentration in patient groups such as those with Huntington's disease (Kassubek, Juengling, Ecker, & Landwehrmeyer, 2005) and traumatic brain injury (Gale, Baxter, Roundy, & Johnson, 2005). Furthermore, recent evidence has implicated a genetic contribution to gray matter concentration in healthy adults (Wishart et al., 2006), raising the possibility that gray matter changes in clinical populations may also have at least partly a genetic basis.

DIFFUSION TENSOR IMAGING

DIFFUSION TENSOR IMAGING (DTI) involves the acquisition of MRI data using scan parameters that permit determination of the magnitude and direction in which water molecules diffuse along white matter fibers (Le Bihan et al., 2001; Mori & Zhang, 2006; Sundgren et al., 2004). The more directions (i.e., angles) from which the scanner acquires diffusion information, the less direction sampling bias is introduced, generally resulting in greater ability to accurately resolve diffusion direction in any given voxel in the brain (Wozniak & Lim, 2006). DTI provides information about the brain that cannot be obtained from conventional MRI in which white matter appears homogeneous and pathways connecting different brain regions, such as the arcuate fasciculus, cannot be readily separated from adjacent or overlapping white matter pathways.

One of the most common measures obtained from DTI data is fractional anisotropy, which reflects the degree to which water molecules are diffusing (i.e., moving) in the same direction within a given voxel or area of the brain. This is based on the principle that water molecules should diffuse more easily along axon bundles than perpendicular to bundles because there are fewer membranous barriers to motion (Figure 8.3). Areas of the brain where diffusion is largely unidirectional, such as the corpus callosum, have high fractional anisotropy (i.e., anisotropic).

Fractional anisotropy is lower in gray matter where axons generally project in multiple directions. It is close to zero in cerebrospinal fluid where the diffusion of water molecules has little specific directionality (i.e., isotropic). Researchers have obtained fractional anisotropy maps in the whole brain and then either calculated the measure for the whole brain using voxel-based techniques (such as in VBM) or in manually or automatically defined ROIs, such as the cingulum bundle or uncinate fasciculus. Others have obtained maps of fractional anisotropy values for the whole brain using voxel-based techniques. Reduced fractional anisotropy in white matter is typically interpreted as reflecting white matter abnormality, although the specific nature of the abnormality remains unclear, potentially reflecting any number of mechanisms (e.g., demyelination). Other measures that can be obtained include axial diffusivity, which reflects the diffusion of water parallel to axon fibers; radial diffusivity, which reflects diffusion orthogonal in panes orthogonal to the long axis of axons; relative anisotropy, which is a ratio of anisotropic

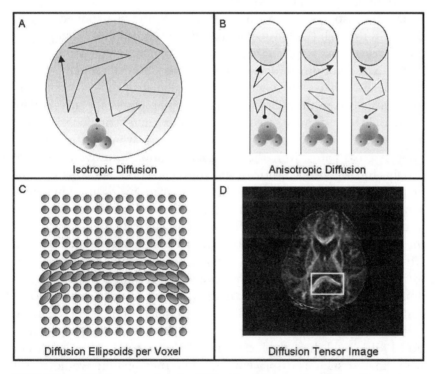

FIGURE 8.3 Diffusion tensor imaging (DTI) with graphic representation of isotropic (a) and anisotropic (b) diffusion. The matrix of mathematical values that represents the average molecular mobility of water in multiple directions for each voxel or tensor is often represented geometrically by an ellipsoid (c). The summation of this information across all voxels results in a 3-D map of the relative anisotropy across the entire brain, the diffusion tensor image (d).

to isotropic diffusion; and mean diffusivity, which is a combination of axial and radial diffusivity.

Several illnesses in which white matter changes have been identified using conventional MRI have also demonstrated abnormal fractional anisotropy using DTI, including multiple sclerosis (Ge, Law, & Grossman, 2005), brain tumor (Stieltjes et al., 2006), and schizophrenia (Kubicki, Westin, McCarley, & Shenton, 2005; Szeszko et al., 2005). DTI may also be useful for detecting subtle white matter abnormalities when other neuroimaging modalities may fail to do so, such as in traumatic brain injury (Nakayama et al., 2006), epilepsy (Gross, Concha, & Beaulieu, 2006), and in normal appearing white matter in patients with multiple sclerosis (Filippi, Cercignani, Inglese, Horsfield, & Comi, 2001; Vrenken et al., 2006). Furthermore, recent research has shown that DTI can provide novel information on the neural correlates of cognitive deficits. For example, reduced fractional anisotropy in the uncinate fasciculus and cingulate bundle have been reported to correlate with deficits in verbal episodic memory and executive function, respectively, in patients with schizophrenia (Nestor et al., 2004).

DTI has also opened up a new avenue for studying connectivity in the brain through three-dimensional fiber tractography. Tractography is based on the assumption that the orientation of a given white matter fiber can be determined for each voxel of the DTI image and the degree of association between adjacent voxels calculated, thus allowing one to track its course through the brain. Tractography is a relatively new methodology with many assumptions and analytic complexities such as difficulty resolving specific pathways in areas where different fiber bundles cross paths. Nonetheless, tractography can provide valuable insights into the contribution of specific connections and broader neural networks underlying regional neural activations in functional neuroimaging studies of healthy and clinical populations. Tractography is also likely to prove highly informative in clinical populations given the information it can provide with respect to the integrity of specific white matter tracts including deformation, deviation, infiltration, and interruption. Recent studies have shown its usefulness in the longitudinal tracking of patients with traumatic brain injury (Le et al., 2005) and in neurosurgical settings (Lazar, Alexander, Thottakara, Badie, & Field, 2006). In the case of brain tumor patients, for example, conventional MRI could show the location of the tumor and gross changes to white matter such as displacement, while tractography would reveal the effects of the tumor on specific white matter pathways.

Magnetic Resonance Spectroscopy

Magnetic resonance spectroscopy (MRS) is a noninvasive tool for the evaluation of tissue biochemistry. The majority of studies investigating in-vivo metabolism in the human brain have focused on nuclei such as hydrogen (^{1}H) and phosphorus (^{31}P) because of their high sensitivity and abundance in the brain. Proton (^{1}H) MRS has become particularly prominent because of the abundance of protons, its good spatial resolution, sensitivity to magnetic manipulation, and simplicity relative to imaging of other nuclei (Gujar, Maheshwari, Bjorkman-Burtscher, & Sundgren, 2005; Vigneron, 2006).

MRS uses essentially the same procedures as high field MRI. An important difference, however, is that, in MRS, external pulses are sent into the brain in order to suppress the signal generated by water (Rubaek Danielsen & Ross, 1999). This is necessary because the concentration of water is 10,000 or more times greater than metabolites of interest. Thus, the most dominant peak (resonance) in the ^{1}H spectrum is water, which would otherwise overwhelm the other peaks, which are on the order of millimolars in concentration.

The concentration of metabolites within the MR spectra may be quantified in a small volume of tissue (a ROI) at a time (single voxel spectroscopy) with a spatial resolution of between 1 and 8 cubic centimeters (note that voxel in MRS refers to the entire area in which signal is acquired, in contrast to the typical meaning of voxel in MRI). Simultaneous signal acquisition in a large volume of tissue within a two- or three-dimensional section of the brain, allowing for interrogation of multiple smaller voxels (1 cubic centimeter or larger) within the larger volume, is also possible (multivoxel spectroscopy or chemical shift imaging), though it is less commonly used and takes longer to complete than single voxel studies (Gujar et al., 2005; Nelson, 2003).

The output of an MRS scan is displayed as a series of peaks typically reflecting the concentration of various metabolites in parts per million. Concentrations are expressed as absolute values, relative to one another (e.g., ratios), or even relative tissue water or cerebrospinal fluid. Some peaks are difficult to quantify accurately and reliably, however, because of their proximity to the water peak, thus being affected by the water suppression pulse (e.g., myo-inositol). Other metabolites are hard to measure because of their close proximity to one another in the spectra (e.g., gamma amino butyric acid, glutamate, and glutamine). It is also difficulty to acquire reliable data in brain regions adjacent to bone, fat, or air pockets (e.g., sinuses) because of the distortion of the magnetic field in these areas. Metabolites investigated most commonly to date in clinical populations are choline (Cho), creatine (Cre), glutamate and glutamine (Glx), lactate (Lac), myo-inositol (mI), and N-acetyl aspartate (NAA); their putative functions are described in Table 8.1 (Gujar et al., 2005).

MRS has been applied to numerous clinical populations. For example, NAA concentration has been reported to be reduced and predictive of cognitive outcome in patients with traumatic brain injury (Brooks, Friedman, & Gasparovic, 2001). MRS has been used extensively

TABLE 8.1 Metabolites Commonly Investigated in Proton Magnetic Resonance Spectroscopy (MRS) Studies of the Brain

Metabolite	Acronym	Function
Choline	Cho	Believed to reflect cell membrane turnover in neurons and glia. Abnormal choline concentration may signal changes in cell synthesis or cellular membrane breakdown.
Creatine	Cre	Believed to reflect cellular energy metabolism in neurons and glia.
Glutamate and Glutamine	Glx	MRI scanners of high magnet field (3T or more) can be used to investigate the levels of the neurotransmitter glutamate/glutamine in the brain.
Lactate	Lac	Believed to reflect anaerobic metabolism. The presence of lactate in the brain is thought to indicate a failure of oxidative phosphorylation and anaerobic glycolysis.
Myo-inositol	mI	An organic osmolyte believed to be present mainly in glial cells and thought to be a marker of glial integrity.
N-acetyl aspartate	NAA	Believed to reflect neuronal or axonal integrity, reduced NAA concentration is commonly interpreted as indicating neuronal loss or damage.

to investigate neuropathological changes in the brains of patients with multiple sclerosis (Caramanos, Narayanan, & Arnold, 2005; Gonzalez-Toledo, Kelley, & Minagar, 2006; Tartaglia & Arnold, 2006). Changes in the concentrations of various metabolites have been reported in relation to brain ischemia (Demougeot, Marie, Giroud, & Beley, 2004), brain tumors (Nelson, 2003), substance abuse (Haselhorst et al., 2002), as well as in relation to brain activation during working memory task performance in patients infected with the human immunodeficiency virus (Ernst, Chang, & Arnold, 2003). Others have employed MRS to predict or monitor the effects of treatment on the brain in patients such as those with epilepsy (Kuzniecky, 2004), bipolar disorder (Delbello & Strakowski, 2004), and obsessive-compulsive disorder (Jang et al., 2006).

IMAGING BRAIN FUNCTION

FUNCTIONAL MAGNETIC RESONANCE IMAGING

FUNCTIONAL MAGNETIC RESONANCE imaging (fMRI) refers to a series of in-vivo MRI techniques employed most frequently to provide a link between brain anatomy and neural processes such as cognition, perception, and sensation. The blood oxygenation level dependent (BOLD) response is the basis of the most commonly used fMRI technique employed to image neural processes. BOLD fMRI is based on the assumption that there is a disproportionate increase in the supply of oxygenated blood to the site of increased neuronal activity (Huettel et al., 2004). Hemoglobin is diamagnetic when bound to oxygen, but deoxygenated hemoglobin is paramagnetic. Thus, alterations in hemoglobin oxygenation result in local distortions to the magnetic field that the MR system has applied to the brain (Jezzard, Matthews, & Smith, 2001). Essentially, BOLD fMRI produces image contrasts based on the ratio of oxyhemoglobin to deoxyhemoglobin that accompanies neuronal responses (Ogawa, Menon, Kim, & Ugurbil, 1998). Ogawa and colleagues (Ogawa, Lee, Kay, & Tank, 1990) were able to demonstrate that in-vivo changes in blood oxygenation could be detected with MRI, and several demonstrations of BOLD signal changes in normal humans during stimulus presentations and task performance quickly followed (Bandettini, Wong, Hinks, Tikofsky, & Hyde, 1992; Kwong et al., 1992; Ogawa et al., 1992). It should be noted, however, that researchers continue to debate scientifically with regards to what BOLD fMRI truly measures (Logothetis, 2002).

Because the BOLD response is based on the oxygen content of brain vasculature, the peak of the hemodynamic response (increased oxygenated blood flow to the site of neuronal response) typically occurs within 6 to 9 seconds after the actual firing of the neurons. Similarly, this lag results in the BOLD effect lasting longer than neural activity within a brain region (McRobbie et al., 2003). Delay of the hemodynamic response results in the BOLD signal typically rising and falling within 12 to 20 seconds of the assumed neuronal firing in response to the presentation of a stimulus or event, which must be taken into consideration when analyzing fMRI data.

A fundamental limitation to experimental design with fMRI is that the measured signal changes are small (Jezzard et al., 2001). The *blocked design* has been the primary type of experimental design utilized in fMRI experiments and is statistically powerful. Blocked designs consist of multiple, discrete epochs (time periods) that alternate the presentation of two or more experimental conditions. Each epoch is many seconds in duration, and epochs of like conditions are averaged together to obtain neural responses that are contrasted with responses for other conditions. For example, in a study of response inhibition, one may have condition A where both a respond cue and an inhibit cue are presented on multiple occasions in a random manner. The control condition may involve only presentation of the respond cues, with the contrast between conditions A and B interpreted as reflecting neural processes related to inhibitory control. Such blocked designs are disadvantageous in part because of the limited information regarding the time course of neural response to a given stimulus type that may be obtained, as well as the increased risk of confounding influences from fluctuations of attention or arousal over time that may differentially affect the experimental conditions given their extended durations.

In contrast to blocked designs, event-related fMRI designs allow one to investigate brain activation in response to individual event types, because these are interspersed among each other. Using our example from the blocked design described previously, an event-related design would involve random or pseudo-random presentation of the respond and inhibit cues within the same epochs, with subsequent off-line averaging of brain activation for all stimuli of a given type presented in the experiment. Event-related designs thus have several advantages such as reducing the potential confound of having separate conditions of interest in different epochs, allowing for increased flexibility in the use of stimuli, exploring changes in neural response over time, and facilitating post-hoc binning of stimuli or responses based on experimenter interest (e.g., correct versus incorrect responses to a stimulus). A significant disadvantage of event-related designs is a reduced signal-to-noise ratio (SNR) and loss of statistical power, which may be addressed in part by increasing the number of stimulus trials.

The resulting functional MR images of the brain are typically presented as colored blobs superimposed on a grey-scale two-dimensional anatomical background image, or as a color overlay on a 3D-surface rendered image of the cortical surface (Jezzard et al., 2001). It is important to consider that BOLD fMRI does not measure neuronal activity directly, but is believed to be an indirect measure of changes in synaptic activity in gray matter (Jezzard et al., 2001). Therefore, the colored blobs may not represent neuronal activity per se, but areas of statistically different MR signal, with the intensity of the color usually representing the degree of statistical confidence in the results of the contrast of interest.

As noted in the introduction, fMRI has been employed increasingly since its inception to investigate the neural correlates of various functions of the brain in healthy and ill individuals. For example, fMRI studies have demonstrated brain abnormality during performance of a variety of cognitive tasks in patients with schizophrenia (Ford et al., 2004; Tan, Choo, Fones, & Chee, 2005), bipolar disorder (Altshuler et al., 2005; Roth et al., 2006), multiple sclerosis (Wishart et al., 2004), and traumatic brain injury (McAllister et al., 2001). fMRI has also been employed to study neural correlates of developmental changes in cognitive processes (Booth et al., 2003; Konrad et al., 2005), and recently to investigate the effects of medications on brain activation in various clinical populations (e.g., Saykin et al., 2004).

Positron Emission Tomography

Positron emission tomography (PET) is a diagnostic and research tool in which an individual is injected with a small dose of a radioactively labeled substance that is nearly identical in structure to naturally occurring molecules in the brain, such as neurotransmitters, glucose, or water. As part of the natural decay process of the radioisotope, positrons (i.e., antimatter counterparts of electrons) are emitted, which collide with nearby electrons. The result of this annihilation reaction is the production of two equally opposed gamma rays or photons (Figure 8.4), which travel through the brain unimpeded by surrounding brain tissue, leave the skull, and are detected by a gamma ray camera that surrounds the individual's head. The gamma ray camera, which typically consists of photodiodes arranged in a ring, is designed to detect photons that arrive simultaneously in pairs. This "coincidence detection" permits localization of the source of the original annihilation reaction. With the collection of tens of thousands of photon pairs during the scanning process, a whole brain "map" can be obtained that displays the relative concentration of the radioactive probe on a

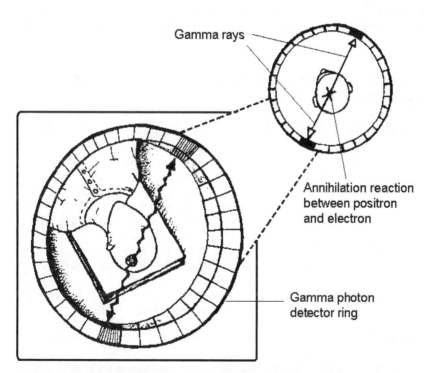

Gamma rays

Annihilation reaction
between positron
and electron

Gamma photon
detector ring

FIGURE 8.4 In positron emission tomography, gamma rays are created by an annihilation reaction and subsequently detected outside the head by a circular gamma ray camera (illustration by Madelyn Rubin, Bates College).

voxel-by-voxel basis throughout the brain. This map can also be co-registered to a structural MRI scan to achieve greater spatial resolution than possible with the PET scanner itself, thus facilitating anatomical localization.

The choice of radioisotope to use depends upon the biochemical process in the brain that the clinician or researcher desires to study. For example, fluorodeoxyglucose (FDG) is glucose with the addition of a radioactive fluorine atom. The resulting gamma radiation from FDG decomposition permits spatial resolution of brain regions actively metabolizing glucose at the time of scanning, either while the individual under study is at rest or is responding to experimental stimuli. Table 8.2 presents several such radioisotopes and their common uses. The half-life of these substances (i.e., the time it takes for half of the atoms to disintegrate) is an unavoidable limiting factor for research applications of PET, as the half-life dictates the window of time available to present experimental stimuli to research participants. If the half-life of a desired radiopharmaceutical is particularly short, as is the case of radioactive oxygen and nitrogen, the researcher must also consider the time between production of the isotope and delivery of the isotope to the research site (which may take several hours) and the time of distribution of the isotope from injection site to the brain (which may take up to an hour). The use of PET is also limited by the need to have

TABLE 8.2 Common Radioactive Isotopes Used in PET, Their Half-Lives, and Some of Their Research Applications

Radioisotope	Half-life	Applications in PET
Fluorine-18	~110 min	• glucose metabolism via F^{18} labeled glucose • dopaminergic function via F^{18} labeled haloperidol and L-dopa
Bromine-75	~98 min	• GABAergic function via Br^{75} labeled benzodiazepine
Carbon-11	~20 min	• opiate function via C^{11} labeled carfentanil • biochemical effects of cocaine via C^{11} labeled cocaine • MAO inhibition via C^{11} labeled deprenyl • dopaminergic function via C^{11} labeled N-methylspiperone and raclopride
Nitrogen-13	~10 min	• glutamate function via N^{13} labeled ammonia
Oxygen-15	~2 min	• oxygen metabolism via O^{15} directly • blood flow via O^{15} labeled water and carbon dioxide

ready access to a cyclotron and radiochemistry laboratories to produce the expensive radioisotopes; otherwise one must rely on third-party suppliers where the transportation time for the decaying radioisotopes may be too long.

The application of PET to questions of relevance to neuropsychology continues to grow, despite the limitations and expense associated with the manufacture of radioisotopes. Numerous studies have demonstrated good concordance between PET and fMRI in the localization of brain regions active during sensory, motor, and cognitive processes such as mental imagery, attention and working memory, language processing, semantic memory retrieval, and episodic memory encoding and retrieval (for a review, see Cabeza & Nyberg, 2000). PET has been shown to improve prediction of the conversion from mild cognitive impairment to Alzheimer's disease, especially in combination with the APOE genotype (Mosconi et al., 2004). PET has also been used to demonstrate that persistent post-concussive symptoms in patients with mild traumatic brain injury may be associated with cerebral changes during cognitive challenges despite normal resting state metabolism (Chen, Kareken, Fastenau, Trexler, & Hutchins, 2003). Other recent clinical applications include using PET to study the role of opioids in the pathophysiology of cluster headaches (Sprenger et al., 2006); refine source localization of seizure activity in epileptic surgical candidates (Knowlton, 2006); assess and monitor disease severity using dopaminergic ligands in Parkinson's disease and essential tremor (Breit, Reimold, Reischl, Klockgether, & Wüllner, 2006); and track pathological changes in cortical gray matter as associated with aspects of cognitive decline in multiple sclerosis (Herholz, 2006).

OPTICAL IMAGING

OPTICAL IMAGING FIRST appeared in 1949 when a relationship between neuronal activity and light diffusion was observed in the crab (Hill & Keynes, 1949). It was not until nearly 50 years later, however, that optical signal detection began to be employed with greater frequency in clinical and research contexts with humans. Optical imaging is a noninvasive technique that measures cortical activity through the intact cranium either during a resting state or in response to external stimuli. The technique capitalizes on the intrinsic optical properties of living tissue known to be affected by changes in neuronal activity, including absorption, reflection, and scattering of light (Hochman, 2000; Pouratian, Sheth, Martin, & Toga, 2003). Brain tissue is illuminated by a near infrared light source placed directly over the scalp, with the optical characteristics of the tissue captured by an optical detector (Gratton & Fabiani, 2001).

Optical imaging devices are designed to measure one of two properties of light-tissue interaction, the scattering and absorption of light, using light in the near-infrared (690–1,000 nm) window (Gratton, Fabiani, Elbert, & Rockstroh, 2003). Degree of scattering varies significantly across types of brain tissue: blood and cerebrospinal fluid scatter very little light; skin, bone, and gray matter scatter moderate degrees of light; and white matter scatters almost all light (Pouratian, Cannestra, Martin, & Toga, 2002; Pouratian et al., 2003; Taddeucci, Martelli, Barilli, Ferrari, & Zaccanti, 1996). Degree of scattering in gray matter is directly associated with action potential summation, with changes in light scattering occurring as a consequence of the reorientation of molecules in neuronal membranes and passage of ions and water across membranes (Gratton et al., 2003). In general, neurons become more transparent, scattering less light, during periods of inhibition. In contrast, during periods of activation, neurons become less transparent, scattering more light, with these changes in light scattering following the same time course as the action potential (Frostig, Lieke, Ts'o, & Grinvald, 1990). Changes in light absorption by brain tissue are larger than changes in light scattering and are therefore easier to measure (Gratton et al., 2003). Light absorption by gray matter is related to hemodynamic changes, given that oxygenated and deoxygenated hemoglobin have distinct absorption abilities, such that the resulting measure indexes oxy- and deoxyhemoglobin concentration as a function of neural activity (Gratton et al., 2003; Malonek & Grinvald, 1996). This parallels the approach used in BOLD fMRI.

Although additional hardware to amplify, filter, and analyze the resulting data is needed, optical imaging remains one of the least expensive modalities by which to quantify cortical activity (Hochman, 2000). Even with amplification, however, the physics of light diffusivity in human brain tissue is such that accurate mapping of brain activity is possible only for a maximum depth of 3 to 5 centimeters below the cortical surface (Gratton et al., 2003). Thus it is not well suited to examine activity in deeper brain structures such as the basal ganglia or relationships between cortical and subcortical structures. Nevertheless, optical imaging techniques have been useful for mapping cortical language (Watanabe et al., 1998), motor (Gratton et al., 1995), somatosensory (Tommerdahl, Favorov, & Whitsel, 2002), visual (Gratton & Fabiani, 2003), and auditory (Rinne et al., 1999) areas. It has also been successfully applied to study cross-hemispheric interaction in cognitive processes that rely on more superficial gray matter (Rykhlevskaia, Fabiani, & Gratton, 2006).

Optical imaging can be performed at bedside and across a number of outpatient or nonhospital research and school settings, given the noninvasive approach and high degree of equipment portability (Zabel

& Chute, 2002). Furthermore, as optical imaging permits participant movement, it is a particularly useful imaging modality for populations in which holding still for extended periods of time is difficult, such as infants (Hebden, 2003) and patients with schizophrenia (Fallgatter & Strik, 2000). Applications of optical imaging to improve our understanding of the healthy brain and clinical populations are growing. For example, studies in healthy adults have identified frontal cortex activity during performance of the Wisconsin Card Sorting Test (Fallgatter & Strik, 1998; Sumitani et al., 2006), activation of left inferior frontal cortex (Ehlis, Herrmann, Wagener, & Fallgatter, 2005) and bilateral motor cortices (DeSoto, Fabiani, Geary, & Gratton, 2001) during the Stroop interference trial, and bilateral inferior frontal activation during response inhibition in a go/no-go task (Herrmann, Plichta, Ehlis, & Fallgatter, 2005). Additional research suggests a promising role for optical imaging in the search for early cognitive biomarkers of Alzheimer's disease (Hock et al., 1996) as well as cortical functional mapping (Nariai et al., 2005; Schwartz, 2005) and localization of cortical epileptiform activity (Haglund & Hochman, 2004) during neurosurgery. As a low-cost and portable technology, optical imaging has been envisioned as a promising addition to the neuropsychologist's toolbox to supplement existing paper-and-pencil brain-based approaches to assess cognition (Zabel & Chute, 2002). With advances in wireless extended-duration optical imaging, it may soon be possible to collect data outside the laboratory, such as examining brain processes in children in their schools and homes (Zabel & Chute, 2002).

QUANTITATIVE ELECTROENCEPHALOGRAPHY AND MAGNETOENCEPHALOGRAPHY

CURRENT METHODS FOR measuring intracranial currents noninvasively in humans originally developed from more invasive procedures such as single unit recording, in which microelectrodes record electrical activity of neurons in vivo (e.g., during neurosurgery) or in vitro in cell preparations of animal tissue. The quest to capture small changes in electrical potentials at the surface of the scalp as a direct function of manipulation of cognitive and emotional processes in many ways fostered the growth of clinical neuropsychology (Shenal, Rhodes, Moore, Higgins, & Harrison, 2001). Electroencephalography (EEG) is a noninvasive means by which to study the timing of neural activity associated with cognitive and emotional processes with precision in the millisecond range (Kahana, 2006). Quantitative EEG (QEEG) offers the additional advantage of statistical comparison of patient-recorded electrical activity to data from healthy comparison subjects or normative databases. Employment of statistical techniques in QEEG rests on the theoretical assumption that clinically significant cognitive disturbance is associated with statistically significant EEG disturbance (Coburn et al., 2006).

EEG data may be conceptualized as a time series of local voltage changes detected by electrodes placed systematically over the scalp. The electrodes record the frequency and amplitude of electrical potentials that correspond to intracranial currents whether they occur spontaneously or in direct response to stimulation. EEG rhythms are typically classified as belonging to a particular bandwidth based on frequency (oscillations per second), with slower frequency waves associated with relaxation and sleep and higher frequency waves associated with focused mental work (Table 8.3). QEEG has been used to corroborate interview and neuropsychological sources of information concerning diagnosis, as well as to further subdivide individuals within a single diagnostic category for whom different electrophysiological processes may manifest in similar cognitive symptoms (Coburn et al., 2006). QEEG has been applied to numerous clinical conditions including mild cognitive impairment and Alzheimer's disease (Huang et al., 2000), Creutzfeldt-Jakob disease (Adams, Sahu, & Treloar, 2005), learning disabilities (Chabot, di Michele, & Prichep, 2005), attention-deficit/hyperactivity disorder (White, Hutchens, & Lubar, 2005), and mild traumatic brain injury (Thornton, 2003).

While EEG has historically been known to have poor spatial resolution, its ability to identify anatomical sources of electric potentials has improved tremendously with increases in channel capacity. Caps with 256-electrodes are widely available and 512-electrode caps are expected soon. As a relatively inexpensive unit that is portable, noninvasive, and capable of detecting excitatory and inhibitory cortical responses with excellent temporal resolution and continued improvements in spatial resolution, QEEG stands in good stead for continued contribution to differential diagnosis and treatment planning across numerous patient populations.

Magnetoencephalography (MEG), often conceptualized as the progeny of EEG, capitalizes on the fact that all electrical currents,

TABLE 8.3 Level of Consciousness and Their Associated EEG Frequencies

Rhythm	Correlate of awareness	Typical frequencies (Hz)
Delta	Deep sleep	0.5–4
Theta	Drowsy; light sleep	4–8
Alpha	Awake; relaxed	8–13
Beta	Awake; alert	13–30
Gamma	Awake; focused concentration	30–80

regardless of the generator, produce orthogonally oriented magnetic fields. Changes in local magnetic fields at the surface of the scalp serve as a proxy for voltage changes associated with ion movement during action potentials (Papanicolaou, 1995). MEG signals have an advantage over electrical fields in that they are minimally distorted despite passage through the brain, meninges, cerebrospinal fluid, blood, and bone. Furthermore, biomagnetic signals are less affected than bioelectric signals by variations in tissue and skull thickness over different regions of the cortex, facilitating source localization in the brain. Magnetic field signals are recorded as temporally dependent waveforms, similar in appearance to EEG data, which are used to generate a functional visuospatial map that can be coregistered with structural MRI data. Taken together, MEG possesses superb temporal resolution and reasonable spatial resolution (Hari, Levänen, & Raij, 2000), greatly facilitating the study of the anatomical origins of evoked responses to experimental stimuli.

The surface magnetic fields in MEG are usually measured in the femtotesla (10^{-15}) range, which is quite small relative to the earth's own magnetic field. In lieu of electrodes applied directly to the scalp, MEG uses extremely sensitive superconducting coil sensors called SQUIDs (superconducting quantum interference devices) to record the magnetic potentials. Because SQUIDs must be kept at a very low temperature to maintain their superconducting properties, they are encased in a large liquid helium-filled device called a *dewar*, which is helmet shaped to follow the natural curvature of the head without directly touching the scalp (Figure 8.5). Current models can support a dense array of more than 300 SQUIDs for full-head coverage, typically achieving source localization within millimeters (Ioannides, 2006). The entire contraption is designed to minimize contributions from peripheral biomagnetic sources such as the heart and eyes and, furthermore, is housed in a shielded room to obstruct external artifacts from moving metallic objects (Hari et al., 2000).

MEG has been used clinically for noninvasive localization of seizure foci in epileptic patients who are candidates for surgical resection (Otsubo & Snead, 2001), as well as for presurgical mapping of eloquent cortex to supplement data normally derived from sodium amobarbitol tests (Breier et al., 1999). MEG has also been used to localize abnormal low frequency magnetic activity in symptomatic mild traumatic brain injury despite normal EEG and structural MRI (Lewine, Davis, Sloan, Kodituwakku, & Orrison, 1999). Other MEG studies have identified abnormal delta and theta activity in bilateral temporoparietal areas that is predictive of impaired cognitive performance and functional status in patients with Alzheimer's disease (Fernandez et al., 2002), activation in the fusiform face area in response to facial stimuli (Halgren, Raij,

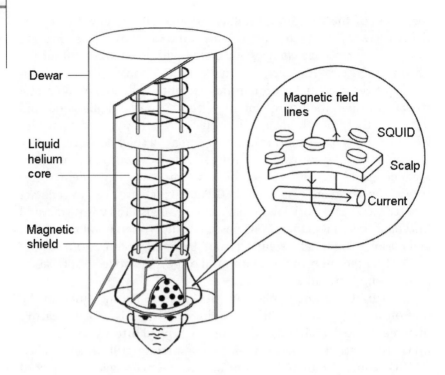

FIGURE 8.5 In magnetoencephalography, changes in local magnetic fields at the surface of the scalp are detected by superconducting coil sensors called SQUIDs (superconducting quantum interference devices). To maintain their superconducting properties, SQUIDs are encased in a large liquid helium-filled dewar, which is helmet-shaped to follow the natural curvature of the head without directly touching the scalp (illustration by Jessica C. Ricker, Bates College).

Marinkovic, Jousmäki, & Hari, 2000), and delayed activation in the left superior temporal cortex during semantic analysis in individuals with dyslexia (Helenius, Salmelin, Service, & Connolly, 1999).

SUMMARY

STATE-OF-THE-ART STRUCTURAL AND functional neuro-imaging is playing a key role in the growth of our scientific understanding of the brain in health and illness. Each of the techniques described herein have their strengths and weaknesses (for a summary, see Table 8.4), and their applicability to specific empirical and clinical questions vary. Nonetheless, many of the techniques are already making significant contributions to clinical practice, while others are poised to make contributions in the not too distant future.

TABLE 8.4   A Summary of Some of the Advantages and Disadvantages of
Various Neuroimaging Techniques

Technique	Advantages	Disadvantages
DTI	• noninvasive • good spatial resolution • ideal for examining white matter pathways • can be coupled with MRI as it uses the same equipment	• equipment is not mobile; scan must be conducted in a shielded room • cannot use in human with ferromagnetic implants • patient must hold very still for several minutes
fMRI	• noninvasive • excellent spatial resolution • good temporal resolution	• equipment is not mobile; scan must be conducted in a shielded room • cannot use in human with ferromagnetic implants • patient must hold very still for several minutes
PET	• excellent spatial resolution • permits examination of brain's use of various molecules and distribution of neurotransmitters	• invasive; radioactive tracer is injected • limited temporal resolution • radioactive isotopes are costly to produce and require a cyclotron • radiation involved limits the number of scans a participant can receive per year • equipment is not mobile • patient must hold very still for several minutes
Optical imaging	• noninvasive • excellent temporal resolution • good spatial resolution just below cortical surface • relatively inexpensive and mobile machinery • body movement is acceptable	• spatial resolution below cortical surface is very limited
qEEG	• noninvasive • excellent temporal resolution • relatively inexpensive and mobile machinery	• spatial resolution can be poor if few electrodes are used • application of electrodes to scalp can be time intensive
MEG	• noninvasive • excellent temporal and good spatial resolution	• equipment is not mobile; scan must be conducted in a shielded room • patient must hold very still for several minutes

REFERENCES

Adams, D., Sahu, S., & Treloar, A. (2005). The utility of EEG in dementia: A clinical perspective. *International Journal of Geriatric Psychiatry, 20*, 1038–1045.

Altshuler, L. L., Bookheimer, S. Y., Townsend, J., Proenza, M. A., Eisenberger, N., Sabb, F., et al. (2005). Blunted activation in orbitofrontal cortex during mania: A functional magnetic resonance imaging study. *Biological Psychiatry, 58*(10), 763–769.

Ashburner, J., & Friston, K. J. (2000). Voxel-based morphometry—The methods. *Neuroimage, 11*(6 Pt 1), 805–821.

Ashburner, J., & Friston, K. J. (2001). Why voxel-based morphometry should be used. *Neuroimage, 14*(6), 1238–1243.

Ashburner, J., Hutton, C., Frackowiak, R., Johnsrude, I., Price, C., & Friston, K. (1998). Identifying global anatomical differences: Deformation-based morphometry. *Human Brain Mapping, 6*(5–6), 348–357.

Bandettini, P. A., Wong, E. C., Hinks, R. S., Tikofsky, R. S., & Hyde, J. S. (1992). Time course EPI of human brain function during task activation. *Magnetic Resonance in Medicine, 25*, 390–397.

Batchelor, P. G., Calamante, F., Tournier, J. D., Atkinson, D., Hill, D. L., & Connelly, A. (2006). Quantification of the shape of fiber tracts. *Magnetic Resonance in Medicine, 55*(4), 894–903.

Booth, J. R., Burman, D. D., Meyer, J. R., Lei, Z., Trommer, B. L., Davenport, N. D., et al. (2003). Neural development of selective attention and response inhibition. *Neuroimage, 20*(2), 737–751.

Bouix, S., Pruessner, J. C., Louis Collins, D., & Siddiqi, K. (2005). Hippocampal shape analysis using medial surfaces. *Neuroimage, 25*(4), 1077–1089.

Breier, J. I., Simos, P. G., Zouridakis, G., Wheless, J. W., Willmore, L. J., Constantinou, J. E. C., et al. (1999). Language dominance determined by magnetic source imaging: A comparison with the Wada procedure. *Neurology, 53,* 938–945.

Breit, S., Reimold, M., Reischl, G., Klockgether, T., & Wüllner, U. (2006). [(11)C]d-threo-methylphenidate PET in patients with Parkinson's disease and essential tremor. *Journal of Neural Transmission, 113,* 187–193.

Brooks, W. M., Friedman, S. D., & Gasparovic, C. (2001). Magnetic resonance spectroscopy in traumatic brain injury. *Journal of Head Trauma Rehabilitation, 16*(2), 149–164.

Cabeza, R., & Nyberg, L. (2000). Imaging cognition II: An empirical review of 275 PET and fMRI studies. *Journal of Cognitive Neuroscience, 12*(1), 1–47.

Callen, D. J., Black, S. E., Gao, F., Caldwell, C. B., & Szalai, J. P. (2001). Beyond the hippocampus: MRI volumetry confirms widespread limbic atrophy in AD. *Neurology, 57*(9), 1669–1674.

Caramanos, Z., Narayanan, S., & Arnold, D. L. (2005). ¹H-MRS quantification of tNA and tCr in patients with multiple sclerosis: A meta-analytic review. *Brain, 128*(Pt 11), 2483–2506.

Carmichael, O. T., Aizenstein, H. A., Davis, S. W., Becker, J. T., Thompson, P. M., Meltzer, C. C., et al. (2005). Atlas-based hippocampus segmentation in Alzheimer's disease and mild cognitive impairment. *Neuroimage, 27*(4), 979–990.

Carper, R. A., & Courchesne, E. (2005). Localized enlargement of the frontal cortex in early autism. *Biological Psychiatry, 57*(2), 126–133.

Casey, B. J., Cohen, J. D., Jezzard, P., Turner, R., Noll, D. C., Trainor, R. J., et al. (1995). Activation of prefrontal cortex in children during a nonspatial working memory task with functional MRI. *Neuroimage, 2*(3), 221–229.

Chabot, R. J., di Michele, F., & Prichep, L. S. (2005). The role of quantitative electroencephalography in child and adolescent psychiatric disorders. *Child and Adolescent Psychiatric Clinics of North America, 14*, 21–53.

Chen, S.H.A., Kareken, D. A., Fastenau, P. S., Trexler, L. E., & Hutchins, G. D. (2003). A study of persistent post-concussion symptoms in mild head trauma using positron emission tomography. *Journal of Neurology, Neurosurgery, and Psychiatry, 74*, 326–332.

Chung, M. K., Worsley, K. J., Paus, T., Cherif, C., Collins, D. L., Giedd, J. N., et al. (2001). A unified statistical approach to deformation-based morphometry. *Neuroimage, 14*(3), 595–606.

Chung, M. K., Worsley, K. J., Robbins, S., Paus, T., Taylor, J., Giedd, J. N., et al. (2003). Deformation-based surface morphometry applied to gray matter deformation. *Neuroimage, 18*(2), 198–213.

Coburn, K. L., Lauterbach, E. C., Boutros, N. N., Black, K. J., Arciniegas, D. B., & Coffey, C. E. (2006). The value of quantitative electroencephalography in clinical psychiatry: A report by the Committee on Research of the American Neuropsychiatric Association. *Journal of Neuropsychiatry and Clinical Neurosciences, 18*, 460–500.

Copenhaver, B., Rabin, L. A., Saykin, A. J., Roth, R. M., Wishart, H. A., Flashman, L. A., et al. (2006). Reduced fornix and mammilary body volume in Alzheimer's disease but not MCI or elderly with cognitive complaints. *Psychiatry Research: Neuroimaging, 147*, 93–103.

Csernansky, J. G., Joshi, S., Wang, L., Haller, J. W., Gado, M., Miller, J. P., et al. (1998). Hippocampal morphometry in schizophrenia by high dimensional brain mapping. *Proceedings of the National Academy of Sciences of the United States of America, 95*(19), 11406–11411.

Csernansky, J. G., Wang, L., Joshi, S., Miller, J. P., Gado, M., Kido, D., et al. (2000). Early DAT is distinguished from aging by high-dimensional mapping of the hippocampus. *Neurology, 55*(11), 1636–1643.

Csernansky, J. G., Wang, L., Miller, J. P., Galvin, J. E., & Morris, J. C. (2005). Neuroanatomical predictors of response to donepezil therapy in patients with dementia. *Archives of Neurology, 62*(11), 1718–1722.

Csernansky, J. G., Wang, L., Swank, J., Miller, J. P., Gado, M., McKeel, D., et al. (2005). Preclinical detection of Alzheimer's disease: Hippocampal shape and volume predict dementia onset in the elderly. *Neuroimage, 25*(3), 783–792.

Delbello, M. P., & Strakowski, S. M. (2004). Neurochemical predictors of response to pharmacologic treatments for bipolar disorder. *Current Psychiatry Reports, 6*(6), 466–472.

Demougeot, C., Marie, C., Giroud, M., & Beley, A. (2004). N-acetylaspartate: A literature review of animal research on brain ischaemia. *Journal of Neurochemistry, 90*(4), 776–783.

DeSoto, M. C., Fabiani, M., Geary, D. C., & Gratton, G. (2001). When in doubt, do it both ways: Brain evidence of the simultaneous activation of conflicting motor responses in a spatial stroop task. *Journal of Cognitive Neuroscience, 13*(4), 523–536.

D'Esposito, M., Detre, J. A., Alsop, D. C., Shin, R. K., Atlas, S., & Grossman, M. (1995). The neural basis of the central executive system of working memory. *Nature, 378*(6554), 279–281.

Ehlis, A. C., Herrmann, M. J., Wagener, A., & Fallgatter, A. J. (2005). Multi-channel near-infrared spectroscopy detects specific inferior-frontal activation during incongruent Stroop trials. *Biological Psychology, 69*(3), 315–331.

Ernst, T., Chang, L., & Arnold, S. (2003). Increased glial metabolites predict increased working memory network activation in HIV brain injury. *Neuroimage, 19*(4), 1686–1693.

Fallgatter, A. J., & Strik, W. K. (1998). Frontal brain activation during the Wisconsin Card Sorting Test assessed with two-channel near-infrared spectroscopy. *European Archives of Psychiatry & Clinical Neuroscience, 248*(5), 245–249.

Fallgatter, A. J., & Strik, W. K. (2000). Reduced frontal functional asymmetry in schizophrenia during a cued continuous performance test assessed with near-infrared spectroscopy. *Schizophrenia Bulletin, 26*(4), 913–919.

Fernandez, A., Maestu, F., Amo, C., Gil, P., Fehr, T., Wienbruch, C., et al. (2002). Focal temporoparietal slow activity in Alzheimer's disease revealed by magnetoencephalography. *Biological Psychiatry, 52,* 764–770.

Filippi, M., Cercignani, M., Inglese, M., Horsfield, M. A., & Comi, G. (2001). Diffusion tensor magnetic resonance imaging in multiple sclerosis. *Neurology, 56*(3), 304–311.

Ford, J. M., Gray, M., Whitfield, S. L., Turken, A. U., Glover, G., Faustman, W. O., et al. (2004). Acquiring and inhibiting prepotent responses in schizophrenia: Event-related brain potentials and functional magnetic resonance imaging. *Archives of General Psychiatry, 61*(2), 119–129.

Frostig, R. D., Lieke, E. E., Ts'o, D. Y., & Grinvald, A. (1990). Cortical functional architecture and local coupling between neuronal activity and the microcirculation revealed by in vivo high-resolution optical imaging of intrinsic signals. *Proceedings of the National Academy of Sciences of the United States of America, 87*(16), 6082–6086.

Gale, S. D., Baxter, L., Roundy, N., & Johnson, S. C. (2005). Traumatic brain injury and grey matter concentration: A preliminary voxel based morphometry study. *Journal of Neurology, Neurosurgery & Psychiatry, 76*(7), 984–988.

Ge, Y., Law, M., & Grossman, R. I. (2005). Applications of diffusion tensor MR imaging in multiple sclerosis. *Annals of the New York Academy of Sciences, 1064*, 202–219.

Gilbertson, M. W., Shenton, M. E., Ciszewski, A., Kasai, K., Lasko, N. B., Orr, S. P., et al. (2002). Smaller hippocampal volume predicts pathologic vulnerability to psychological trauma. *Nature Neuroscience, 5*(11), 1242–1247.

Golland, P., Grimson, W. E., Shenton, M. E., & Kikinis, R. (2005). Detection and analysis of statistical differences in anatomical shape. *Medical Image Analysis, 9*(1), 69–86.

Gonzalez-Toledo, E., Kelley, R. E., & Minagar, A. (2006). Role of magnetic resonance spectroscopy in diagnosis and management of multiple sclerosis. *Neurological Research, 28*(3), 280–283.

Good, C. D., Johnsrude, I., Ashburner, J., Henson, R. N., Friston, K. J., & Frackowiak, R. S. (2001a). Cerebral asymmetry and the effects of sex and handedness on brain structure: A voxel-based morphometric analysis of 465 normal adult human brains. *Neuroimage, 14*(3), 685–700.

Good, C. D., Johnsrude, I. S., Ashburner, J., Henson, R. N., Friston, K. J., & Frackowiak, R. S. (2001b). A voxel-based morphometric study of ageing in 465 normal adult human brains. *Neuroimage, 14*(1 Pt 1), 21–36.

Gratton, G., & Fabiani, M. (2001). The event-related optical signal: A new tool for studying brain function. *International Journal of Psychophysiology, 42*(2), 109–121.

Gratton, G., & Fabiani, M. (2003). The event-related optical signal (EROS) in visual cortex: Replicability, consistency, localization, and resolution. *Psychophysiology, 40*(4), 561–571.

Gratton, G., Fabiani, M., Elbert, T., & Rockstroh, B. (2003). Seeing right through you: Applications of optical imaging to the study of the human brain. *Psychophysiology, 40*(4), 487–491.

Gratton, G., Fabiani, M., Friedman, D., Franceschini, M. A., Fantini, S., Corballis, P., et al. (1995). Rapid changes of optical parameters in the human brain during a tapping task. *Journal of Cognitive Neuroscience, 7*, 446–456.

Gross, D. W., Concha, L., & Beaulieu, C. (2006). Extratemporal white matter abnormalities in mesial temporal lobe epilepsy demonstrated with diffusion tensor imaging. *Epilepsia, 47*(8), 1360–1363.

Gujar, S. K., Maheshwari, S., Bjorkman-Burtscher, I., & Sundgren, P. C. (2005). Magnetic resonance spectroscopy. *Journal of Neuro-Ophthalmology, 25*(3), 217–226.

Haglund, M. M., & Hochman, D. W. (2004). Optical imaging of epileptiform activity in human neocortex. *Epilepsia, 45*(Suppl 4), 43–47.

Halgren, E., Raij, T., Marinkovic, K., Jousmäki, V., & Hari, R. (2000). Cognitive response profile of the human fusiform face area detected by MEG. *Cerebral Cortex, 10,* 69–81.

Hari, R., Levänen, S., & Raij, T. (2000). Timing of human cortical functions during cognition: Role of MEG. *Trends in Cognitive Sciences, 4,* 455–462.

Haselhorst, R., Dursteler-MacFarland, K. M., Scheffler, K., Ladewig, D., Muller-Spahn, F., Stohler, R., et al. (2002). Frontocortical N-acetylaspartate reduction associated with long-term i.v. heroin use. *Neurology, 58*(2), 305–307.

Hebden, J. C. (2003). Advances in optical imaging of the newborn infant brain. *Psychophysiology, 40*(4), 501–510.

Helenius, P., Salmelin, R., Service, E., & Connolly, J. F. (1999). Semantic cortical activation in dyslexic readers. *Journal of Cognitive Neuroscience, 11,* 535–550.

Herholz, K. (2006). Cognitive dysfunction and emotional-behavioural changes in MS: The potential of positron emission tomography. *Journal of the Neurological Sciences, 245,* 9–13.

Herrmann, M. J., Plichta, M. M., Ehlis, A. C., & Fallgatter, A. J. (2005). Optical topography during a Go-NoGo task assessed with multi-channel near-infrared spectroscopy. *Behavioural Brain Research, 160*(1), 135–140.

Hill, D. K., & Keynes, R. D. (1949). Opacity changes in stimulated nerve. *Journal of Physiology, 108,* 278–281.

Hochman, D. W. (2000). Optical monitoring of neuronal activity: Brain-mapping on a shoestring. *Brain and Cognition, 42,* 56–59.

Hock, C., Villringer, K., Muller-Spahn, F., Hofmann, M., Schuh-Hofer, S., Heekeren, H., et al. (1996). Near infrared spectroscopy in the diagnosis of Alzheimer's disease. *Annals of the New York Academy of Sciences, 777,* 22–29.

Hogan, R. E., Bucholz, R. D., & Joshi, S. (2003). Hippocampal deformation-based shape analysis in epilepsy and unilateral mesial temporal sclerosis. *Epilepsia, 44*(6), 800–806.

Hogan, R. E., Wang, L., Bertrand, M. E., Willmore, L. J., Bucholz, R. D., Nassif, A. S., et al. (2004). MRI-based high-dimensional hippocampal mapping in mesial temporal lobe epilepsy. *Brain, 127*(Pt 8), 1731–1740.

Hounsfield, G. N. (1973). Computerized transverse axiel scanning (tomography). *British Journal of Radiology, 46,* 1016–1022.

Huang, C., Wahlund, L. O., Dierks, T., Julin, P., Winblad, B., & Jelic, V. (2000). Discrimination of Alzheimer's disease and mild cognitive impairment by equivalent EEG sources: A cross-sectional and longitudinal study. *Clinical Neurophysiology, 111,* 1961–1967.

Huettel, S. A., Song, A. W., & McCarthy, G. (2004). *Functional magnetic resonance imaging.* Sunderland, MA: Sinauer Associates, Inc.

Ioannides, A. A. (2006). Magnetoencephalography as a research tool in neuroscience: State of the art. *Neuroscientist, 12,* 524–544.

Jang, J. H., Kwon, J. S., Jang, D. P., Moon, W. J., Lee, J. M., Ha, T. H., et al. (2006). A proton MRSI study of brain N-acetylaspartate level after 12 weeks of citalopram treatment in drug-naive patients with obsessive-compulsive disorder. *American Journal of Psychiatry, 163*(7), 1202–1207.

Jernigan, T. L., Archibald, S. L., Fennema-Notestine, C., Gamst, A. C., Stout, J. C., Bonner, J., et al. (2001). Effects of age on tissues and regions of the cerebrum and cerebellum. *Neurobiology of Aging, 22*(4), 581–594.

Jezzard, P., Matthews, P. M., & Smith, S. M. (2001). *Functional MRI: An introduction to methods.* New York: Oxford University Press.

Kahana, M. J. (2006). The cognitive correlates of human brain oscillations. *The Journal of Neuroscience, 26,* 1669–1672.

Kassubek, J., Juengling, F. D., Ecker, D., & Landwehrmeyer, G. B. (2005). Thalamic atrophy in Huntington's disease co-varies with cognitive performance: A morphometric MRI analysis. *Cerebral Cortex, 15*(6), 846–853.

Kates, W. R., Frederikse, M., Mostofsky, S. H., Folley, B. S., Cooper, K., Mazur-Hopkins, P., et al. (2002). MRI parcellation of the frontal lobe in boys with attention deficit hyperactivity disorder or Tourette syndrome. *Psychiatry Research: Neuroimaging, 116*(1–2), 63–81.

Knowlton, R. C. (2006). The role of FDG-PET, ictal SPECT, and MEG in the epilepsy surgery evaluation. *Epilepsy and Behavior, 8,* 91–101.

Konrad, K., Neufang, S., Thiel, C. M., Specht, K., Hanisch, C., Fan, J., et al. (2005). Development of attentional networks: An fMRI study with children and adults. *Neuroimage, 28*(2), 429–439.

Kubicki, M., Westin, C. F., McCarley, R. W., & Shenton, M. E. (2005). The application of DTI to investigate white matter abnormalities in schizophrenia. *Annals of the New York Academy of Sciences, 1064,* 134–148.

Kuzniecky, R. (2004). Clinical applications of MR spectroscopy in epilepsy. *Neuroimaging Clinics of North America, 14*(3), 507–516.

Kwong, K. K., Belliveau, J. W., Chesler, D. A., Goldberg, I. E., Weiskoff, R. M., Poncelet, B. P., et al. (1992). Dynamic magnetic resonance imaging of human brain activity during primary sensory stimulation. *Proceedings of the National Academy of Sciences of the United States of America, 89,* 5675–5679.

Lawson, J. A., Vogrin, S., Bleasel, A. F., Cook, M. J., Burns, L., McAnally, L., et al. (2000). Predictors of hippocampal, cerebral, and cerebellar volume reduction in childhood epilepsy. *Epilepsia, 41*(12), 1540–1545.

Lazar, M., Alexander, A. L., Thottakara, P. J., Badie, B., & Field, A. S. (2006). White matter reorganization after surgical resection of brain tumors and vascular malformations. *American Journal of Neuroradiology, 27*(6), 1258–1271.

Le, T. H., Mukherjee, P., Henry, R. G., Berman, J. I., Ware, M., & Manley, G. T. (2005). Diffusion tensor imaging with three-dimensional fiber tractography of traumatic axonal shearing injury: An imaging correlate for the posterior callosal "disconnection" syndrome: Case report. *Neurosurgery, 56*(1), 189.

Le Bihan, D., Mangin, J. F., Poupon, C., Clark, C. A., Pappata, S., Molko, N., et al. (2001). Diffusion tensor imaging: Concepts and applications. *Journal of Magnetic Resonance Imaging, 13*(4), 534–546.

Lewine, J. D., Davis, J. T., Sloan, J. H., Kodituwakku, P. W., & Orrison, W. W. (1999). Neuromagnetic assessment of pathophysiological brain activity induced by minor head trauma. *American Journal of Neuroradiology, 20,* 857–866.

Logothetis, N. K. (2002). The neural basis of the blood-oxygen-level-dependent functional magnetic resonance imaging signal. *Philosophical Transactions of the Royal Society of London—Series B: Biological Sciences, 357*(1424), 1003–1037.

Malonek, D., & Grinvald, A. (1996). Interactions between electrical activity and cortical microcirculation revealed by imaging spectroscopy: Implications for functional brain mapping. *Science, 272,* 551–554.

Martin, R. C., Hugg, J. W., Roth, D. L., Bilir, E., Gilliam, F. G., Faught, E., et al. (1999). MRI extrahippocampal volumes and visual memory: Correlations independent of MRI hippocampal volumes in temporal lobe epilepsy patients. *Journal of the International Neuropsychological Society, 5*(6), 540–548.

McAllister, T. W., Sparling, M. B., Flashman, L. A., Guerin, S. J., Mamourian, A. C., & Saykin, A. J. (2001). Differential working memory load effects after mild traumatic brain injury. *Neuroimage, 14*(5), 1004–1012.

McHugh, T. L., Saykin, A. J., Wishart, H. A., Flashman, L. A., Cleavinger, H. B., Rabin, L. A., et al. (2007). Hippocampal volume and shape analysis in an older adult population. *The Clinical Neuropsychologist, 21,* 131–146.

McRobbie, D. W., Moore, E. A., Graves, M. J., & Prince, M. R. (2003). *MRI: From picture to proton.* New York: Cambridge University Press.

Mellers, J. D., Bullmore, E., Brammer, M., Williams, S. C., Andrew, C., Sachs, N., et al. (1995). Neural correlates of working memory in a visual letter monitoring task: An fMRI study. *Neuroreport, 7*(1), 109–112.

Mori, S., & Zhang, J. (2006). Principles of diffusion tensor imaging and its applications to basic neuroscience research. *Neuron, 51*(5), 527–539.

Mosconi, L., Perani, D., Sorbi, S., Herholz, K., Nacmias, B., Holthoff, V., et al. (2004). MCI conversion to dementia and the APOE genotype: A prediction study with FDG-PET. *Neurology, 63,* 2332–2340.

Nakayama, N., Okumura, A., Shinoda, J., Yasokawa, Y. T., Miwa, K., Yoshimura, S. I., et al. (2006). Evidence for white matter disruption in traumatic brain injury without macroscopic lesions. *Journal of Neurology, Neurosurgery & Psychiatry, 77*(7), 850–855.

Nariai, T., Sato, K., Hirakawa, K., Ohta, Y., Tanaka, Y., Ishiwata, K., et al. (2005). Imaging of somatotopic representation of sensory cortex with intrinsic optical signals as guides for brain tumor surgery. *Journal of Neurosurgery, 103*(3), 414–423.

Nelson, M. D., Saykin, A. J., Flashman, L. A., & Riordan, H. J. (1998). Hippocampal volume reduction in schizophrenia as assessed by magnetic resonance imaging: A meta-analytic study. *Archives of General Psychiatry, 55*(5), 433–440.

Nelson, S. J. (2003). Multivoxel magnetic resonance spectroscopy of brain tumors. *Molecular Cancer Therapeutics, 2*(5), 497–507.

Nestor, P. G., Kubicki, M., Gurrera, R. J., Niznikiewicz, M., Frumin, M., McCarley, R. W., et al. (2004). Neuropsychological correlates of diffusion tensor imaging in schizophrenia. *Neuropsychology, 18*(4), 629–637.

Ogawa, S., Lee, T. M., Kay, A. R., & Tank, D. W. (1990). Brain magnetic resonance imaging with contrast dependent on blood oxygenation. *Proceedings of the National Academy of Sciences of the United States of America, 87*, 9868–9872.

Ogawa, S., Menon, R. S., Kim, S. G., & Ugurbil, K. (1998). On the characteristics of functional magnetic resonance imaging of the brain. *Annual Review of Biophysics & Biomolecular Structure, 27*, 447–474.

Ogawa, S., Tank, D. W., Menon, R., Ellermann, J. M., Kim, S. G., Merkle, H., et al. (1992). Intrinsic signal changes accompanying sensory stimulation: Functional brain mapping with magnetic resonance imaging. *Proceedings of the National Academy of Sciences of the United States of America, 89*, 5951–5955.

Otsubo, H., & Snead, O. C. (2001). Magnetoencephalography and magnetic source imaging in children. *Journal of Child Neurology, 16*, 227–235.

Papanicolaou, A. C. (1995). An introduction to magnetoencephalography with some applications. *Brain and Cognition, 27*, 331–352.

Posener, J. A., Wang, L., Price, J. L., Gado, M. H., Province, M. A., Miller, M. I., et al. (2003). High-dimensional mapping of the hippocampus in depression. *American Journal of Psychiatry, 160*(1), 83–89.

Pouratian, N., Cannestra, A. F., Martin, N. A., & Toga, A. W. (2002). Intraoperative optical intrinsic signal imaging: A clinical tool for functional brain mapping. *Neurosurgical Focus, 13*(4), e4.

Pouratian, N., Sheth, S. A., Martin, N. A., & Toga, A. W. (2003). Shedding light on brain mapping: Advances in human optical imaging. *Trends in Neurosciences, 26*(5), 277–282.

Preul, C., Hubsch, T., Lindner, D., & Tittgemeyer, M. (2006). Assessment of ventricular reconfiguration after third ventriculostomy: What does shape analysis provide in addition to volumetry? *American Journal of Neuroradiology, 27*(3), 689–693.

Rinne, T., Gratton, G., Fabiani, M., Cowan, N., Maclin, E., Stinard, A., et al. (1999). Scalp-recorded optical signals make sound processing in the auditory cortex visible? *Neuroimage, 10*(5), 620–624.

Roth, R. M., Flashman, L. A., Saykin, A. J., McAllister, T. W., & Vidaver, R. (2004). Apathy in schizophrenia: Reduced frontal lobe volume and neuropsychological deficits. *American Journal of Psychiatry, 161*(1), 157–159.

Roth, R. M., Koven, N. S., Randolph, J. J., Flashman, L. A., Pixley, H. S., Ricketts, S. M., et al. (2006). Functional magnetic resonance imaging of executive control in bipolar disorder. *Neuroreport, 17*(11), 1085–1089.

Rubaek Danielsen, E., & Ross, B. (Eds.). (1999). *Magnetic resonance spectroscopy diagnosis of neurological disease*. New York: Marcel Dekker, Inc.

Rykhlevskaia, E., Fabiani, M., & Gratton, G. (2006). Lagged covariance structure models for studying functional connectivity in the brain. *Neuroimage, 30*(4), 1203–1218.

Saykin, A. J., Wishart, H. A., Rabin, L. A., Flashman, L. A., McHugh, T. L., Mamourian, A. C., et al. (2004). Cholinergic enhancement of frontal lobe activity in mild cognitive impairment. *Brain, 127*, 1574–1583.

Saykin, A. J., Wishart, H. A., Rabin, L. A., Santulli, R. B., Flashman, L. A., West, J. D., et al. (2006). Older adults with cognitive complaints show brain atrophy similar to that of amnestic MCI. *Neurology, 67*(5), 834–842.

Schwartz, T. H. (2005). The application of optical recording of intrinsic signals to simultaneously acquire functional, pathological and localizing information and its potential role in neurosurgery. *Stereotactic & Functional Neurosurgery, 83*(1), 36–44.

Seeck, M., Dreifuss, S., Lantz, G., Jallon, P., Foletti, G., Despland, P. A., et al. (2005). Subcortical nuclei volumetry in idiopathic generalized epilepsy. *Epilepsia, 46*(10), 1642–1645.

Serra-Grabulosa, J. M., Junque, C., Verger, K., Salgado-Pineda, P., Maneru, C., & Mercader, J. M. (2005). Cerebral correlates of declarative memory dysfunctions in early traumatic brain injury. *Journal of Neurology, Neurosurgery & Psychiatry, 76*(1), 129–131.

Shen, L., Makedon, F., & Saykin, A. J. (2004). Shape-based discriminative analysis of combined bilateral hippocampi using multiple object alignment. *Medical Imaging, 5370*, 274–282.

Shenal, B. V., Rhodes, R. D., Moore, T. M., Higgins, D. A., & Harrison, D. W. (2001). Quantitative electroencephalography (qEEG) and neuropsychological syndrome analysis. *Neuropsychology Review, 11*, 31–43.

Shenton, M. E., Dickey, C. C., Frumin, M., & McCarley, R. W. (2001). A review of MRI findings in schizophrenia. *Schizophrenia Research, 49*(1–2), 1–52.

Shenton, M. E., Gerig, G., McCarley, R. W., Szekely, G., & Kikinis, R. (2002). Amygdala-hippocampal shape differences in schizophrenia: The application of 3D shape models to volumetric MR data. *Psychiatry Research, 115*(1–2), 15–35.

Small, S. A. (2002). The longitudinal axis of the hippocampal formation: Its anatomy, circuitry, and role in cognitive function. *Reviews in the Neurosciences, 13*(2), 183–194.

Sprenger, T., Willoch, F., Miederer, M., Schindler, F., Valet, M., Berthele, A., et al. (2006). Opioidergic changes in the pineal gland and hypothalamus in cluster headache: A ligand PET study. *Neurology, 66*, 1108–1110.

Stieltjes, B., Schluter, M., Didinger, B., Weber, M. A., Hahn, H. K., Parzer, P., et al. (2006). Diffusion tensor imaging in primary brain tumors: Reproducible quantitative analysis of corpus callosum infiltration and contralateral involvement using a probabilistic mixture model. *Neuroimage, 31*(2), 531–542.

Styner, M., Gerig, G., Lieberman, J., Jones, D., & Weinberger, D. (2003). Statistical shape analysis of neuroanatomical structures based on medial models. *Medical Image Analysis, 7*(3), 207–220.

Styner, M., Lieberman, J. A., Pantazis, D., & Gerig, G. (2004). Boundary and medial shape analysis of the hippocampus in schizophrenia. *Medical Image Analysis, 8,* 197–203.

Sumitani, S., Tanaka, T., Tayoshi, S., Ota, K., Kameoka, N., Ueno, S., et al. (2006). Activation of the prefrontal cortex during the Wisconsin Card Sorting Test as measured by multichannel near-infrared spectroscopy. *Neuropsychobiology, 53*(2), 70–76.

Sundgren, P. C., Dong, Q., Gomez-Hassan, D., Mukherji, S. K., Maly, P., & Welsh, R. (2004). Diffusion tensor imaging of the brain: Review of clinical applications. *Neuroradiology, 46*(5), 339–350.

Szeszko, P. R., Ardekani, B. A., Ashtari, M., Kumra, S., Robinson, D. G., Sevy, S., et al. (2005). White matter abnormalities in first-episode schizophrenia or schizoaffective disorder: A diffusion tensor imaging study. *American Journal of Psychiatry, 162*(3), 602–605.

Taddeucci, A., Martelli, F., Barilli, M., Ferrari, M., & Zaccanti, G. (1996). Optical properties of brain tissue. *Biomedical Optics, 1,* 117–123.

Talairach, J., & Tournoux, P. (1988). *Co-planar stereotaxic atlas of the human brain.* Stuttgart: Thieme.

Tan, H. Y., Choo, W. C., Fones, C. S., & Chee, M. W. (2005). fMRI study of maintenance and manipulation processes within working memory in first-episode schizophrenia. *American Journal of Psychiatry, 162*(10), 1849–1858.

Tartaglia, M. C., & Arnold, D. L. (2006). The role of MRS and fMRI in multiple sclerosis. *Advances in Neurology, 98,* 185–202.

Tate, D. F., & Bigler, E. D. (2000). Fornix and hippocampal atrophy in traumatic brain injury. *Learning & Memory, 7*(6), 442–446.

Thornton, K. (2003). The electrophysiological effects of a brain injury on auditory memory functioning: The QEEG correlates of impaired memory. *Archives of Clinical Neuropsychology, 18,* 363–378.

Tommerdahl, M., Favorov, O., & Whitsel, B. L. (2002). Optical imaging of intrinsic signals in somatosensory cortex. *Behavioural Brain Research, 135*(1–2), 83–91.

Torres, I. J., Flashman, L. A., O'Leary, D. S., Swayze, V., 2nd, & Andreasen, N. C. (1997). Lack of an association between delayed memory and hippocampal and temporal lobe size in patients with schizophrenia and healthy controls. *Biological Psychiatry, 42*(12), 1087–1096.

Vigneron, D. B. (2006). Magnetic resonance spectroscopic imaging of human brain development. *Neuroimaging Clinics of North America, 16*(1), 75–85.

Vrenken, H., Pouwels, P. J., Geurts, J. J., Knol, D. L., Polman, C. H., Barkhof, F., et al. (2006). Altered diffusion tensor in multiple sclerosis normal-appearing brain tissue: Cortical diffusion changes seem related to clinical deterioration. *Journal of Magnetic Resonance Imaging, 23*(5), 628–636.

Vythilingam, M., Luckenbaugh, D. A., Lam, T., Morgan, C. A., 3rd, Lipschitz, D., Charney, D. S., et al. (2005). Smaller head of the hippocampus in Gulf War-related posttraumatic stress disorder. *Psychiatry Research, 139*(2), 89–99.

Walhovd, K. B., Fjell, A. M., Reinvang, I., Lundervold, A., Dale, A. M., Eilertsen, D. E., et al. (2005). Effects of age on volumes of cortex, white matter and subcortical structures. *Neurobiology of Aging, 26*(9), 1261–1270.

Watanabe, E., Maki, A., Kawagucki, F., Takashiro, K., Yamashita, Y., Koizumi, H., et al. (1998). Non-invasive assessment of language dominance with near-infrared spectroscopic mapping. *Neuroscience Letters, 256*, 49–52.

White, J. N., Hutchens, T. A., & Lubar, J. F. (2005). Quantitative EEG assessment during neuropsychological task performance in adults with attention deficit hyperactivity disorder. *Journal of Adult Development, 12*, 113–121.

Wishart, H. A., Saykin, A. J., McAllister, T. W., Rabin, L. A., McDonald, B. C., Flashman, L. A., et al. (2006). Regional brain atrophy in cognitively intact adults with a single APOE €4 allele. *Neurology, 67*, 1221–1224.

Wishart, H. A., Saykin, A. J., McDonald, B. C., Mamourian, A. C., Flashman, L. A., Schuschu, K. R., et al. (2004). Brain activation patterns associated with working memory in relapsing-remitting MS. *Neurology, 62*(2), 234–238.

Wozniak, J. R., & Lim, K. O. (2006). Advances in white matter imaging: A review of in vivo magnetic resonance methodologies and their applicability to the study of development and aging. *Neuroscience & Biobehavioral Reviews, 30*(6), 762–774.

Xu, Y., Jack, C. R., Jr., O'Brien, P. C., Kokmen, E., Smith, G. E., Ivnik, R. J., et al. (2000). Usefulness of MRI measures of entorhinal cortex versus hippocampus in AD. *Neurology, 54*(9), 1760–1767.

Zabel, T. A., & Chute, D. L. (2002). Educational neuroimaging: A proposed neuropsychological application of near-infrared spectroscopy (nIRS). *Journal of Head Trauma Rehabilitation, 17*, 477–488.

Zipursky, R. B., Lim, K. C., & Pfefferbaum, A. (1989). MRI study of brain changes with short-term abstinence from alcohol. *Alcoholism: Clinical & Experimental Research, 13*(5), 664–666.

9

The Halstead-Reitan Neuropsychological Test Battery: Past, Present, and Future

ARTHUR MacNEILL HORTON, JR.

PAST

A SIGNIFICANT NUMBER OF clinical neuropsychologists have used a standardized *fixed* battery approach, in which the same set of neuropsychological tests has been given to patients as a general rule for many years. This approach has the advantage of providing the clinical neuropsychologist with similar clinical information for each patient and allows for comprehensive assessment of a wide variety of brain-related behaviors (Horton & Wedding, 1984). Also, the use of similar measures facilitates the development of clinical skills and provides a consistent information base for research purposes from which validated data interpretations may emerge. At the same time, there is

Portions of this chapter were drawn from chapter 7 in Horton and Wedding's (1984) *Clinical and Behavioral Neuropsychology* and the Halstead-Reitan chapters in the first and second editions of *The Neuropsychology Handbook*.

the potential disadvantage that a particular set of tests may be inappropriate for a particular patient.

The fixed battery approach has been widely accepted in clinical neuropsychology. The premier battery of neuropsychological tests, The Halstead-Reitan Neuropsychological Test Battery, was developed from research studies by Ward Halstead and his doctoral student Ralph M. Reitan (Halstead, 1947; Reitan & Davison, 1974; Horton & Wedding, 1984; Reitan, 1994). The battery was based on experimental psychology procedures first used by Halstead to investigate the human abilities that were compromised by brain injury. Halstead was interested in the concept of *biological intelligence,* which he defined as the adaptive capacity of the brain dependent upon its organic integrity and assumed to be related to frontal lobe functioning (Halstead, 1947). Halstead tested many neurosurgical patients who had documented brain injuries with his battery of tests. Halstead factor analyzed the test results from his battery and proposed a four factor model of neuropsychological abilities. The factors were a central integrative field factor, an abstraction factor, a power factor, and a directional factor (Halstead, 1947). In some ways, these factors appear to mirror the factors found on the Wechsler Intelligence Scales for adults and children (Wechsler, 1991). Ralph M. Reitan modified and augmented the Halstead-Reitan Neuropsychology Test Battery to make it clinical brain damage assessment battery (Reitan & Davison, 1974; Horton & Wedding, 1984: Reitan & Wolfson, 1993). Reitan added the Wechsler Intelligence scale, measures of aphasia, constructional dyspraxia, sensory-perceptual functioning, and grip strength, the Trail Making Test and the Minnesota Multiphasic Personality Inventory (MMPI; Horton & Wedding, 1984).

The Halstead-Reitan Neuropsychology Test Battery is the most frequently used fixed neuropsychological test battery in neurological, neurosurgical, rehabilitation, and psychiatric settings (Guilmette, Faust, Hart & Arkes, 1990; Hartlage & Telzrow, 1980; Seretny, Dean, Gray, & Hartlage, 1986). This popularity is due to the extensive body of research conducted by Ralph M. Reitan, PhD, and a variety of investigators demonstrating the validity of this battery for assessing brain-damaged patients (Reitan & Wolfson, 1986; Reitan, 1994). In a national survey of neuropsychologists that assessed preference for either the Halstead-Reitan or Luria-Nebraska Neuropsychological Test Batteries (Guilmette & Faust, 1991), the majority preferred the Halstead-Reitan. The Halstead-Reitan Neuropsychological Test Battery was seen as more comprehensive, with superior validity data and greater sensitivity for more complex and subtle deficits, among other advantages (Guilmette & Faust, 1991). As was stated by Drs. Reitan and Wolfson (1986):

> The Halstead-Reitan Battery has probably been researched in more detail than any other set of neuropsychological tests. Through the

close cooperation between neuropsychologists, neurologists, neurological surgeons, and neuropathologists it has been possible to compose groups of subjects with definite, unequivocal evidence of cerebral damage and compare these persons with subjects who have no history or present evidence of cerebral damage or disease. This approach has a tremendous advantage over research oriented toward development of constructs such as intelligence, affective disorders, emotional maturity, and so forth. In attempting to validate psychological measures against such constructs, there has been the continual criterion problem of not having an unequivocal definition of the condition being evaluated. In neuropsychology, however, it has been possible not only to identify the presence or absence of cerebral damage but also to provide more detailed information regarding localization type, duration, and acuteness or chronicity of lesion.

The research approach used was to compare control subjects to persons known to have heterogeneous types of lesions in various locations and to identify the procedures that were sensitive to the general condition of the brain. The research of the validity of the Halstead Reitan Battery is extensive (Boll, Heaton, & Reitan, 1974; Doehring & Reitan, 1961; Fitzhugh, Fitzhugh, & Reitan, 1960, 1961, 1962a; Reed & Reitan, 1962, 1963a, 1963b, Reitan, 1955a, 1955b, 1958, 1959a, 1959b, 1960, 1964, 1970a; Wheeler, Burke, & Reitan, 1963; Wheeler & Reitan, 1962, 1963).

The validation approach to the Halstead-Reitan Neuropsychology Test Battery that has been most impressive has been with the use of sophisticated multivariate statistical techniques, such as discriminant functions analysis. This is a statistical technique for predicting group classification. Reitan, Wheeler and their colleagues (Wheeler, 1964; Wheeler et al., 1963; Wheeler & Reitan, 1963) used Halstead-Reitan Neuropsychological Test Battery subtest scores as predictor variables in discriminant functions to predict classification groups composed on the basis of independent neurological findings. The Halstead-Reitan Neuropsychological Test Battery subtest scores accurately predicted patients into lateralized brain-damaged groups. On cross-validation to control for shrinkage still about 8 out of 10 subjects were correctly classified.

The Halstead-Reitan Neuropsychological Test Battery was developed to be sensitive to neurological as opposed to behavioral variables (Reitan & Wolfson, 1986). Age, education, personality, socioeconomic status, vocational skills, and medical history can influence psychological test performance, but the crucial concern for clinical neuropsychologists is the biological condition of the human brain. Reitan used an empirical method to determine if psychological tests were "brain-related" rather than "behavior-related." As noted by Reitan and Wolfson (1986):

> We have found that the best way to answer this question has been to examine carefully an individual's neuropsychological test data and,

from that information, predict the neurological status. To implement this procedure data were collected on thousands of patients using a three-step process: (1) administering a comprehensive battery of neuropsychological tests to the patient without knowing any of the patient's neurological findings; (2) making a written prediction of the patient's neurological status based solely on his or her neuropsychological test results; and (3) comparing the neurological diagnosis with the neuropsychological test results.

Using this procedure, we have learned that certain variables contribute little to neurological conclusions (even though they may serve as comparison variables in certain respects), whereas other combinations of test results are of unequivocal significance. This procedure has permitted us to gradually refine clinical interpretation of results on individual subjects to a high degree of accuracy, as will be illustrated later.

Certain neuropsychological test data are particularly helpful in determining whether brain damage is present; other test results are especially useful for lateralizing and localizing cerebral damage; certain patterns of results relate to generalized or diffuse cerebral damage; other test results, particularly as they reflect the entire configuration of data, are used to differentiate the chronic, static lesion from the recent acutely destructive or rapidly progressive lesion; and still different findings aid the interpreter in deciding whether the cerebral damage was sustained during the developmental years or adulthood.

One can readily see that in addition to formal, controlled research studies (the type usually published in the literature) there are challenging tasks that involve development of valid clinical interpretation of results for individual subjects. Achieving this aim required the development of a test battery that represented at least a reasonable approximation of the behavioral correlates of brain function. (p. 136)

The Halstead-Reitan Neuropsychological Test Battery research has allowed a theoretical-conceptual model of brain-behavior relationships to be developed (Reitan & Wolfson, 1986). As noted by Reitan and Wolfson (1986):

The battery consists of tests in five categories: (1) input measures; (2) tests of verbal abilities; (3) measures of spatial, sequential, and manipulatory abilities; (tests of abstraction, reasoning, logical analysis, and concept formation; and (5) output measures. The tests cover a broad range of difficulty: both very simple and quite complex tasks are included. Attention, concentration, and memory are distributed throughout the tests in the battery, just as they appear to occur in the tasks that people face in everyday living. Many of the tests require immediate problem-solving capabilities, others depend on stored information, and some require simple perceptual skills that focus principally upon the sensory modalities of vision, hearing, and touch. (pp. 136–137)

A large number of tests make up the Halstead-Reitan Neuropsychology Test Battery. The core tests were developed in Ward Halstead's laboratory at the University of Chicago (Halstead, 1947; Reitan, 1994). As mentioned earlier, others were added by Reitan (e.g., Trail Making Test, parts A and B, etc.). Reitan deleted tests that were theoretically interesting but that failed to statistically discriminate between brain-damaged and normal subjects (e.g., Critical Flicker Frequency and the Time Sense Test). The tests remaining include the Category Test, Tactual Performance Test, Speech Sounds Perception Test, Rhythm Test, Trail Making Test, a Finger Oscillation Test (Finger Tapping), the Reitan-Klove Sensory Perceptual Examination, the Reitan-Indiana Aphasia Examination, and the Lateral Dominance Examination. In addition, the age-appropriate Wechsler Intelligence Scale is included in the Halstead-Reitan Neuropsychology Test Battery to assess general intellectual functions, and many users include an objective personality inventory, such as the Minnesota Multiphasic Personality Inventory-2 (MMPI-2) or the Millon Clinical Multiphasic Inventory-III (MCMI-III), to assess mood state and personality variables. Also tests of academic achievement and memory may be added to assess particular problems. Information from these tests is integrated with sociodemographic variables (age, sex, education, etc.) and the patient's complaints. The Halstead-Reitan Neuropsychology Test Battery forms a matrix of data that can provide considerable information about the patient (Reitan & Wolfson, 1993).

Ralph M. Reitan's most important methodological contribution has been the recognition of the need to use multiple methods of inference (Horton & Wedding, 1984). Reitan postulated that multiple levels of inference, level of performance, patterns of performance, pathognomonic signs, and right–left comparisons needed to be considered when evaluating neuropsychological test data. As described by Reitan and Wolfson (1986):

> First, it is necessary to determine how well the subject performs on each of the measures included in the battery. This approach essentially refers to level of performance and, on most of the measures, is represented by a normal distribution for non-brain-damaged subjects. Since some persons perform quite well and others perform more poorly, it clearly would not be possible to accept a level-of-performance strategy alone as a basis for diagnosing cerebral damage. In other words, there are some persons who demonstrate above-average ability levels in spite of having sustained cerebral damage and some persons with below-average ability levels who do not have cerebral damage. A level-of-performance approach represents an interindividual inferential model. It is useful for comparing subjects, but offers relatively little direct information regarding the brain functions of the individual

subject. (As the reader has probably noted, this is the model used in most research studies.)

A second approach, introduced by Babcock (1930), postulated that differences in levels of performance on various tests might denote impaired brain functions, or at least a loss of efficiency in psychological performances. This approach has also been used to compute the Deterioration Quotient, based on comparison of scores from different subtests of the Wechsler Scale (Wechsler, 1955). This method represents an intraindividual comparison procedure (a comparison of the subject's own performances on various tests) and helps identify the uniqueness of an individual's ability structure. Research with the tests included in the Halstead-Reitan Battery has produced a number of intraindividual patterns that are quite useful for assessing differential functions of the brain and identifying impaired areas within the brain.

A third approach incorporated into the Halstead-Reitan Battery is the identification of specific deficits on simple tasks of the type that occur almost exclusively among brain-damaged persons. Deficits on these simple tasks may not only identify the presence of cerebral damage but also indicate areas of maximal involvement (Wheeler & Reitan, 1962). The reader should be aware, however, that this inferential strategy fails to identify a significant proportion of brain-damaged persons who do not show the specific deficit in question (false negatives).

The fourth measurement strategy used in the Halstead-Reitan Battery to identify cerebral damage is one which compares motor and sensory-perceptual performances of the same type on the two sides of the body, thus permitting inferences regarding the functional status of homologous areas of the two cerebral hemispheres. This method is also based on intraindividual comparisons, using the subject as his or her control. When positive findings occur they may have unequivocal significance for cerebral damage. (pp. 138–139, citations may be found in the original source)

PRESENT

THE MAJOR TESTS most commonly used in the Halstead-Reitan Neuropsychological Test Battery are described here.

THE CATEGORY TEST

THE CATEGORY TEST is a visual abstraction concept formation test that measures the patient's ability to learn general abstract principles from sets of stimulus items. The traditional administration utilized a slide projector to display slides. A recently developed modification has been to use a booklet form of the same stimuli as the slides. The adult version of the Category Test includes 7 subtests made up from 208 stimulus slides. The patient responds to each stimulus by selecting a number from one to four to represent the principle that is used in a particular subtest. If a correct response was made, feedback is given that the choice was correct; if an incorrect choice was made, feedback is given that the choice was wrong. Only one response is permitted for each stimulus presentation. The patient is required to deduce abstract principles and to use immediate feedback to modulate response patterns.

The first six subtests involve single principles, and in the last subtest, the patient is to use memories of past responses to provide correct responses for stimulus items that have already been presented. There isn't a time limit for the test, but most patients take an hour to complete the test. The Category Test is believed by many to be the Halstead-Reitan Neuropsychology Test Battery subtest most sensitive to brain damage (Reitan & Wolfson, 1993).

TACTUAL PERFORMANCE TEST

THE TACTUAL PERFORMANCE Test (TPT) is administered using a form board that has 10 geometric spaces. The adult version of this test requires a blindfolded patient to place 10 geometric blocks into 10 matching geometric spaces on the form board where the blocks fit. The board is slanted on a stand at a 45° angle. The test is performed multiple times: first with the dominant hand, next with the nondominant hand, and, finally, with both hands. The time for each trial is recorded and summed along with the number of blocks correctly placed.

After the last trial on the TPT, the form board is removed and the patient's blindfold removed. The patient is requested to draw the geometric shapes that were on the form board and to place as many blocks as can be remembered (Memory score) in their correct location (Location score), relative to the other blocks. The patient was not told that there would be a requirement to draw the blocks. Memory and Localization scores of this test are conceptualized to be measures of incidental spatial learning.

The TPT assesses a number of neuropsychological abilities. These include integration of tactile and kinesthetic feedback, psychomotor skills, and spatial memory. In addition, disparities between the performance of the left and right hands is evidence for lateralization of cerebral damage. The expectation is that the nondominant hand should be about one-third faster than the dominant hand, and both hands are one-third faster than the nondominant hand because of practice effects. To the extent that either hand or both hands are slower than expected, the integrity of the contralateral hemisphere can be questioned. Alternative explanations for unilateral difficulties, such as peripheral damage (e.g., broken wrist, carpel tunnel syndrome), can complicate interpretation at the level of the cerebral hemispheres. There are different time limits used for the three trials of the TPT. Reitan and Wolfson (1993) suggested that a maximum of 15 minutes be allowed per trial. Russell, Neuringer, and Goldstein (1970) recommend that each trial be terminated at 10 minutes.

SPEECH SOUNDS PERCEPTION TEST

THE SPEECH SOUNDS Perception Test requires that the patient attend to 60 tape-recorded stimulus words that are variations of an "ee" sound formed by using different first and last consonants. The auditory stimuli items are matched with the correct word made up by the sound. The patient is to circle or underline the correct alternative for each spoken syllable from four alternatives of which one is correct. The test requires the ability to sustain attention, perceive speech sounds, and read words.

RHYTHM TEST

THE RHYTHM TEST is from the Seashore Tests of Musical Talent (Reitan & Wolfson, 1993). Thirty rhythmic pairs are presented via a tape recording. The patient must identify each pair as either the same or different and write a response ("S" for same or "D" for different) on a test form. The test measures auditory memory, rhythmic discrimination, and attention ability.

TRAIL MAKING TEST

THE TRAIL MAKING Test consists of two parts labeled "A" and "B." Trails A consists of 25 numbered circles (1–25), which the patient connects by drawing a line to each circle of a higher number. Trails B consists of circles with series of numbers (1–13) and letters (A–L) printed within the circles on the same page. The patient is required to draw a line that alternately connects numbers and letters (i.e., 1-A-2-B-3-C...). The patient is instructed to complete the task as rapidly as possible. Errors are included in the timing and pointed out by the examiner. The patient is redirected and continues the test from the point at which the error was first initiated. The major scores for Parts A and B are the amounts of time required to complete each page.

This test requires visual tracking, set-shifting, and sequencing ability. Trails Part B, along with the Categories Test, TPT-Localization, and the Halstead Impairment Index, has been considered one of the four best general indicators of cerebral dysfunction (Russell et al., 1970).

Similarly, Mezzich and Moses (1980) have demonstrated that Trails B is highly correlated (r = .78) with the Average Impairment Rating, a summary index of performance on the Halstead-Reitan Battery similar to the Halstead Impairment Index.

FINGER TAPPING TEST

THE FINGER TAPPING Test is a measure of motor speed. The patient is required to quickly tap a key counter that is mounted on a board for multiple trials. Finger tapping speed is assessed for each hand. The score for each hand is the mean of five consecutive trials. The most common practice is to give five trials with a range of no more than five taps.

The Finger Tapping Test provides valuable lateralizing information. Performance with the dominant hand is expected to be 10% better than the performance with the nondominant hand. The general relationship works best for right-handed subjects. For left-handed subjects the proposed relationship did not always hold, and indeed, in some cases reversals of the expected relationship were found in normal left-handed subjects (Jarvis & Barth, 1994). Interpretations regarding lateralization of brain damage require that there are no significant peripheral injuries that could account for poor unilateral performance (e.g., hand or arm injury, arthritis). Comparison of performances on the Finger Tapping Test and the Tactual Performance Test is helpful for localization of brain injuries (Horton & Wedding, 1984).

REITAN-INDIANA APHASIA SCREENING TEST

THE REITAN-INDIANA APHASIA Screening Test is a modification of the earlier Halstead-Wepman Aphasia Screening Test (Reitan & Wolfson, 1993). It assesses symbolic language-related deficits such as difficulty reading, writing, naming, spelling, performing arithmetic, and repeating words and phrases. The patient also performs nonlanguage tasks such as to draw quasi-geometric figures and left–right confusion. The test is a screening measure of language skills (Russell et al., 1970). The test has proved to be sensitive to lateralized brain damage (Wheeler & Reitan, 1962).

REITAN-KLOVE SENSORY-PERCEPTUAL EXAMINATION

THE REITAN-KLOVE SENSORY-PERCEPTUAL Examination is an adaptation and standardization of a behavioral neurologist examination (Reitan & Wolfson, 1993). The examination assesses visual, auditory, and tactual sensory abilities, as well as examination of tactual perceptual functioning. The functioning of the two cerebral hemispheres can be assessed by comparisons of sensory-perceptual function for visual, auditory, and tactual stimuli on either side of the body.

REITAN-KLOVE LATERAL DOMINANCE EXAMINATION

THE LATERAL DOMINANCE Examination assesses dominance, an important variable in clinical neuropsychology. Patient preferences for use of hand, foot, and eye are determined by brief requests. Lateral dominance is important in interpreting tests that compare the two sides of the body such as the Finger Tapping, Strength of Grip, and Tactual Performance Test.

STRENGTH OF GRIP

GRIP STRENGTH IS assessed by using a piece of mechanical apparatus, a Smedly hand dynometer. The patient squeezes the dynometer with each hand. Two alternating trials are given for each hand and the mean of the two trials for each hand used as the test score.

ADDITIONAL TESTS FOR THE HALSTEAD-REITAN NEUROPSYCHOLOGY TEST BATTERY

THE HALSTEAD-REITAN NEUROPSYCHOLOGICAL Test Battery also includes a measure of intelligence, and most recently the Wechsler Intelligence Scales have been used, but other intelligence tests have been used such as the Henmon-Nelson Test of Mental Ability. Also, it is common to use a measure of academic achievement such as the Wide Range Achievement Test. In addition, an objective personality inventory such as the original MMPI has been used, but many clinical neuropsychologists now use the MMPI-2, the MCMI-III, or the PAI. In addition, other tests of memory or executive functioning may be used to supplement the Halstead-Reitan Neuropsychological Test Battery.

CHILDREN'S VERSIONS OF THE HALSTEAD-REITAN NEUROPSYCHOLOGICAL TEST BATTERY

IN ADDITION TO testing adults, Reitan wished to assess brain damage in children, also. In order to do this, Reitan further modified the Halstead-Reitan Neuropsychological Test Battery for testing children (Reitan & Wolfson, 1992a, 1992b). In Reitan's research, the adult version of the Halstead-Reitan Neuropsychological Test Battery was found to be adequate for assessing brain behavior relationships in adolescents down to age 15 (Reitan & Wolfson, 1993). Below age 15, however, further modifications of test materials and procedures were necessary.

Older children, defined by Reitan as between the ages of 9 and 14, were able to be assessed with a test battery that was similar to the adult battery except that the Category Test, the Trail Making Test, and the Tactual Performance Test were shortened, and the number of choices for responding on the Speech Sounds Perception Test was reduced from four to three (Reitan & Wolfson, 1992b). For the neuropsychological assessment of younger children, defined by Reitan as between the ages of 5 and 8, a larger number of changes to test material and procedures were required. Because young children have smaller hands, an electric finger tapper is used. Also, a number of new tests were developed for younger children. For example, the Progressive Figures Test is a visual modification of the Trail Making Test that uses figures within figures rather than numbers and letters to guide the patient in set-shifting. Similarly the Category Test and Tactual Performance Test stimuli and the Reitan-Klove Sensory-Perceptual Examination were all simplified (Reitan, 1974a; Reitan & Wolfson, 1992a).

HALSTEAD-REITAN NEUROPSYCHOLOGY TEST BATTERY: SUMMARY MEASURES

RESEARCHERS HAVE PROPOSED a number of actuarial and statistical approaches to interpretation of the Halstead-Reitan Neuropsychological Test Battery. There are a number of summary indices that can be computed from scores on the Halstead-Reitan Neuropsychological Test Battery in order to answer the question of neuropsychological impairment (Horton, 1995a; Horton & Wedding, 1984). These include the Halstead Impairment Index (HII), a linear composite of 7 neuropsychological test scores (Halstead, 1947); the Average Impairment Rating (AIR), a weighted average of 12 selected subtest scores; the General Neuropsychological Deficit Scale (GNDS), a total of weighted scores from 42 measures (Reitan & Wolfson, 1988); the Short-Form Impairment Index, a total of 3 neuropsychological test scores (Horton, Anilane, Slone, & Shapiro, 1986); the Alternate Impairment Index, a total of 7 neuropsychological test scores (Horton, 1995a, 1995b, 1996, 1997); and the Global Deficit Score (GDS), a mean of 21 demographically corrected test scores (Heaton, Miller, Taylor, & Grant, 2004).

HALSTEAD IMPAIRMENT INDEX

THE FIRST SUMMARY index is Halstead's Impairment Index (HII), which was devised by Ward Halstead. Halstead noted that a linear composite of neuropsychological test scores was more sensitive to brain damage than any single neuropsychological test. The HII is a linear composite measure currently derived from seven neuropsychological tests. The HII ranges from .0 (no evidence for brain damage) to 1.0 (evidence for severe brain damage). The HII is the percentage of selected tests that fall in the brain-damaged range using preset cutoff points. Halstead uses 10 test scores, and each test score that falls in the brain damaged range contributes .1 to the impairment index (Halstead, 1947). Reitan deleted two test scores that were less sensitive to brain damage (the Time Sense Test and Critical Flicker Fusion Test). The Halstead-Reitan Neuropsychology Test Battery's HII is calculated from seven test scores from the Category Test, the Rhythm Test, the Speech Sounds Perception Test, the Finger Tapping Test (only the score for the dominant hand), and the Tactual Performance Test (scores for Total Time, Memory, and Localization). The HII score is prorated from 7 to 10 tests to maintain the .0 to 1.0 score distribution.

The cutoff score for the HII initially used by Reitan was .5, with .4 considered a borderline score. Research by Reitan (1985) lead to a modification of the procedure as a significant relationship between intelligence and the HII was noted. The modification was to use a cutting score of .4 with patients with an IQ of 100 or better and a cutting score of .5 with patients when the IQ is below 100. With different patient groups, additional adjustments may be required. In elderly populations, some patients with no evidence of cerebral damage can earn mildly impaired HII scores without clinical evidence of brain damage.

AVERAGE IMPAIRMENT RATING

THE HII HAS been criticized for the use of dichotomous cutoff scores. Simply put, a patient with a score that is just over a cutting score is different from a patient with a score that is significantly over the cutting score. The HII described both groups of patients as impaired with no further differentiation. Philip Rennick (a later Ward Halstead doctoral student) developed an alternative to the HII that he termed the Average Impairment Index (AIR) (Horton & Wedding, 1984). The AIR uses weighted scores to calculate an average summary measure of brain impairment. While working at the Menninger Foundation in Topeka, Kansas, Rennick assembled data from the Halstead-Reitan Battery. He found that the best cutting score for brain damage was about a standard deviation below the mean and that each standard deviation further below the mean represented increasing levels of impairment. Rennick proposed a weighted numerical scale where a score of 0 was better than average (above the mean value), 1 was normal (between the mean and one standard deviation below the mean), and 2 (below one standard deviation from the mean), 3, and 4 (increasingly below the mean) represented mild, moderate, and severe levels of brain impairment, respectively (Russell et al., 1970). This standardization of scores allowed comparison of Halstead-Reitan Battery subtests using a common metric.

The AIR averages the weighted scores of 12 of the Halstead-Reitan Neuropsychology Test Battery test scores: the Category Test, Tactual Performance Test, Total Time, Memory, Localization, Rhythm, Speech Sounds, Finger Tapping Test (dominant hand), Trails B, Digit Symbol from WAIS, and weighted rated scores for Aphasia and Spatial Relations. On the AIR, an average score of 1.55 can be used in a manner similar to the .5 on the HII to evaluate which patients are brain damaged.

The AIR has the advantage of providing a measure of the severity of brain damage. Subtests given a 3 or 4 can be averaged with subtests given a 0 or 1, to arrive at a better assessment of the severity of brain damage. Goldstein and Shelly (1972) validated the AIR as a measure of brain damage similar to the HII.

GENERAL NEUROPSYCHOLOGICAL DEFICIT SCORE (GNDS)

REITAN AND WOLFSON (1988) devised a new summary index of brain damage, the General Neuropsychological Deficit Scale (GNDS), in order to provide a measure that would be a valid indication of an individual subject's overall neuropsychological competence. The GNDS utilizes 42 separate test variables from the Halstead-Reitan Neuropsychological Test Battery. The test variables are arranged according to Reitan's methodological methods of inferences (Horton & Wedding, 1984; Reitan, 1974a). The groupings include test scores that demonstrate the patient's level of performance, specific deficits/pathognomonic signs, patterns of performance, and comparisons of the two sides of the patient's body on motor and sensory-perceptual measures. Similar to the AIR, each test score is put on a weighted rating scale. Ratings of test scores are on a 4-point scale. Ratings of 0 indicate above average performance, ratings of 1 indicate average performance, ratings of 2 indicate mild brain damage, and ratings of 3 indicate moderate to severe brain damage. Research findings with medical, psychiatric, and normal controls (Reitan & Wolfson, 1988), a cross-validation study with pseudoneurologic controls (Sherer & Adams, 1993), and subsequent cross-validation by Reitan and Wolfson (1995a) have demonstrated fairly impressive hit rates.

Similarly, Horton and Sobelman (1994) examined how the severity of brain damage is evaluated by the GNDS relative to the HII.

In the Horton and Sobelman (1994) study, the hit rate for agreement on severity of brain damage was 60% (i.e., 15/25), with the greatest number of false negatives in the classification of severe by the HII and moderate on the GNDS. Pearson product-moment correlations for age on the GNDS and the HII were on the edge of statistical significance for the GNDS .382 (p < .06) and not statistically significant for the HII, .177 (p = .40), respectively. Pearson correlations for education on both scales were nonsignificant, GNDS -.186 (p = .374), and HII -.191 (p = .362), respectively. The Pearson correlation between the two scales was statistically significant, .43 (p < .02) confirming a strong relationship between the two summary indexes.

This finding suggests that the GNDS appears to have an advantage over the HII in assessing the severity of brain injury. The above almost significant correlation between age and the GNDS agrees with earlier work (Sherer & Adams, 1993). On the other hand, the lack of significant education effects is in contrast to earlier work (Sherer & Adams, 1993). Possibilities for the different finding may be either sample size, or the composition of the types of brain injury in the samples influenced whether education effects were found. The significant but less robust correlation between the GNDS and HII found by Horton and Sobelman (1994) could also be due to sample size or subject composition issues.

Reitan and Wolfson (1992b) have also extended the thinking behind the GNDS and developed a Neuropsychological Deficit Scale for Older Children (GNDS-OC). As might be expected, The GNDS-OC measure has a similar format to the adult GNDS. The GNDS-OC includes 45 test scores from the Halstead-Reitan Neuropsychological Test Battery for Older Children (Reed, Reitan, & Klove, 1965).

SHORT-FORM IMPAIRMENT INDEX

HORTON ET AL. (1986) developed a Short Form Impairment Index (SFII) from measures Reitan had included in the Brain Age Quotient (BAQ). The SFII was composed of scores from the Trail Making Test Part B and the Block Design and Coding subtests from the Wechsler Adult Intelligence Scale and used normative tables that Reitan had developed for the BAQ. The SFII was validated and twice cross-validated with a Pearson r = .90 for the initial study and both cross-validations (Horton et al., 1986).

ALTERNATIVE IMPAIRMENT INDEX (AII)

THE ALTERNATIVE IMPAIRMENT Index (AII; Horton, 1995a) is a recently developed measure of neuropsychological impairment that is composed of selected scores from a number of tests of the Halstead-Reitan Neuropsychological Test Battery (Halstead, 1947; Reitan & Wolfson, 1993). The AII scores are from the Category Test, the Rhythm Test, the Speech Sounds Perception Test, the Finger Tapping Test for both dominant and nondominant hands, and the Trail Making Test, both Parts A and B. The reason for developing a new index is to indicate the existence of brain damage when time and resource constraints prevent the entire Halstead-Reitan Neuropsychological Test Battery from being given. Horton (1995a) examined how the severity of brain damage is evaluated by the AII relative to the GNDS and the HII. Horton (1995a) found that the AII hit rates for severity of brain damage of 60% with the HII and 64% with the GNDS. Cross-validation of the initial results (Horton, 1995b) found a hit rate for severity of brain damage between the AII and the HII of 66%. In order to improved the AII hit rates it was decided to use a weighted set of the test scores that form the AII. The notion of using weighted scores follows from the AIR (Russell et al., 1970). Horton (1997) evaluated a modified AII, which used a set of weighted scores, the Alternative Impairment Index-Revised (AII-R). The AII-R was compared to the HII and GNDS. Agreement hit rates for level of severity for the HII and AII-R were 60% (i.e., 15/25), and for the GNDS and AII-R were 72% (i.e., 18/25). The findings suggested the AII-R better reflects severity of brain damage on the GNDS than on the HII. The AII-R grades the severity of brain injury with a better degree of accuracy than the AII relative to the GNDS. An attempt to develop subscales for the AII, however, produced very poor results (Horton, 2000a).

In summary, comparisons with the AII and AII-R (Horton, 1995a) found similar results for the AII-R/HII (60%) versus AII/HII comparison (60%) but better results for the AII-R/GNDS (72%) versus AII/GNDS (64%) comparison. AII-R appears able to reflect severity of brain damage to a modest degree with the GNDS and to a much lesser degree with the HII. Additional research with the AII-R appears warranted.

CHILDREN'S VERSION OF THE ALTERNATIVE IMPAIRMENT INDEX

GIVEN PROMISING RESULTS with the AII and AII-R, a children's version of the AII was developed. The first study on the Alternative Impairment Index—Children's Version (AII-CV; Horton, 1995c) found prediction of the level of severity of brain damage (56% correct prediction) was at a chance level. Development of the Revised Children's Version of the Alternative Impairment Index (AII-CV-R; Horton, 1996) modified the AII-CV. The new AII-CV-R utilized the sum of selected weighted scores divided by the number of test measures contributing to the sum of weighted scores as a summary measure. The study compared the hit rate for severity of the AII-CV-R with the GNDS-OC (Reitan & Wolfson, 1992). Poor agreement (i.e., 50%, or 8/16 correct agreement) for severity of brain damage was found for the AII-CV-R and GNDS-OC.

It might be noted that the sensitivity of subtests from the Wechsler Scales to brain damage has been shown to be superior to those from subtests of the Halstead-Reitan Neuropsychology Test Battery (Reed, Reitan, & Klove, 1965; Reitan, 1974b) for older children and children of early school age. Horton (1998) demonstrated that a short form screening index based on performance subtests from the Wechsler Intelligence

Scale for Children—Revised (WISC-R) was able to significantly predict severity of brain damage on the GNDS-OC (hit rate 75%, or 15/20 correct agreement). Further evaluation of WISC-R subtests found that a subtest measuring processing speed was best (70%) able to predict severity of brain damage on the GNDS-OC (Horton, 1999b). The future development of a short screening index composed on age-appropriate Wechsler subtests might be a productive research project.

GLOBAL DEFICIT SCALE

THIS MEASURE IS composed of 21 test scores from the expanded Halstead-Reitan Neuropsychological Test Battery, which are demographically corrected for age, education, gender, and ethnicity using published norms and assigned deficit scores based on T-score values and averaged to create the GDS (0-T score 40 and above, 1-T score 35–39, 2-T score 30–34, etc.; Heaton et al., 2004). These norms are an updated version of earlier published demographically corrected norms (Heaton, Grant, & Matthews, 1991). The 21 measures include the Category Test, Trail Making Test (both Parts A and B), Tactual Performance Test (Total Time, Memory, and Location scores), Rhythm Test, Speech Sounds Perception Test, Digit Vigilance Test (Time and Error components), Story Memory Test (Learning and Delayed Recall components), Figure Memory Test (Learning and Delayed Recall components), Aphasia Screening Test, Boston Naming Test, Thurston Word Fluency Test, Spatial Relations, Sensory-Perceptual-Total, Finger Tapping-worse hand, and Grooved Pegboard-worse hand. Heaton et al. (2004) reported sensitivity of 91.4% and specificity of 87.66% for differentiating brain damage from control adults for an over all hit rate of 89% for a GDS of .5; it is interesting to note that .5 is the cut-off value first used for the HII. Also, it is noteworthy that the GDS was noted to be relatively unaffected by missing data or modifications in the GDS test battery as deleting three randomly selected test scores and prorating the remaining 18 scores resulted in a correlation of .98 between the full GDS and prorated GDS (Heaton et al., 2004), or put another way, the correlation between the full and prorated GDS was about the same as might be expected between the test-retest of the full GDS. This result is similar to the results of Horton (2000b), which noted that removing IQ values from the GNDS didn't significantly change the overall GNDS scores. It appears that comprehensive fixed neuropsychological batteries such as the HRNTB are like the "F" statistic and relatively "robust" to minor variations, as long as the fixed battery is reasonably comprehensive in including adequate coverage of cognitive, motor, and sensory-perceptual abilities. Heaton et al. (2004) also compared the GDS to the AIR and the WAIS Full Scale IQ scores and found that while the AIR was more sensitive to brain injury than the

WAIS IQ (74.6% vs. 52.2), the GDS was more sensitive than the AIR (91.4% vs. 74.6%). Heaton et al. (2004) make an important point that for the GDS to be valid for neuropsychological assessment the GDS test scores must not be impaired due to peripheral problems such as hearing or vision loss or a broken arm. The GDS is an interesting new summary measure, but there have been few studies of the GDS from research groups other than at the University of California at San Diego Department of Psychiatry where the method was developed. It would be helpful to see studies that cross-validate the results of the study of the GDS and AIR presented previously (Heaton et al., 2004).

The Heaton et al. (1991) norms for demographic correction were evaluated relative to the GNDS procedure by Reitan and Wolfson (1993), and they found that the 1991 Heaton et al. norms had the effect of producing a normal score 1.74 times more often than the Reitan and Wolfson method in 52 individuals who had neurologically verified brain damage. They concluded the effect of using the 1991 norms was to identify impairment in brain-damaged persons less often than the Reitan and Wolfson (1986) method.

Sweeney (1999) compared the 1991 Heaton et al. norms and normative data from Reitan and Wolfson (1993) for 33 adults with nonimpact acceleration force injuries in motor vehicle accidents. Results for the GNDS found neuropsychological impairment, but the Heaton et al. (1991) results suggested normal cognitive skills. Moses, Pritchard, and Adams (1999) examined the ability of the Heaton et al. (1991) norms in correcting for age and education and found 10% in HRNTB test score variance could be predicted by patient age and education; after conversion to age and education were corrected, T-scores less than 1% of the variance could be predicted by age and education. Golden and van den Broek (1998) assessed 64 patients with localized injuries to four quadrants of the brain with both HRNTB raw scores and the Heaton et al. (1991) norms. They found the HRNTB raw scores were more sensitive in detecting brain damage, but both the raw scores and T-scores were statistically equal in their abilities to separate localized groups. Yantz, Gavett, Lynch, and McCaffrey (2006) evaluated the performance of the Heaton et al. (2004) revised demographically corrected norms versus the GNDS (Reitan & Wolfson, 1993) and found the Heaton et al. (2004) system was statistically more likely to identify litigants as unimpaired than the Reitan and Wolfson (1993) GNDS procedure.

CLINICAL INTERPRETATION OF THE HALSTEAD-REITAN NEUROPSYCHOLOGICAL BATTERY

REITAN HAS DEVISED a method of interpreting the test data from the Halstead-Reitan Neuropsychological Test Battery (Reitan

& Wolfson, 1986). The first step requires consideration of the Wechsler Intelligence Scale subtest results to attempt an estimation of the patient's premorbid level of functioning. The particular subtests scale scores that Reitan finds most useful are Information, Comprehension, Similarities, and Vocabulary (Reitan & Wolfson, 1986). As noted by Reitan and Wolfson (1986):

> If these subtest scores are low, one cannot use them as a contrast for poor scores on neuropsychological (brain-sensitive) tests. If these scores are relatively good, one can presume that circumstances in the past have been adequate to permit development of these abilities; poorer scores on tests that are more specifically sensitive to the biological condition of the brain may be subject to interpretation as evidence of impairment. The Wechsler subtests may be used for more specific aspects of interpretation as well but only after reviewing the results obtained with the remaining tests of the Halstead-Reitan Battery. (p. 142)

The next step in interpretation is to consider the results on the most sensitive measures of the Halstead-Reitan Neuropsychological Test Battery. With the development of the General Neuropsychological Deficit Scale, Reitan has added that measure as a general indicator of brain integrity and considers it along with other particularly sensitive single measures of brain damage, the Halstead Impairment Index, Category Test, Part B of the Trail-Making Test, and the Localization score of the Tactual Performance Test. As noted by Reitan and Wolfson (1986):

> If these tests were performed poorly and the Wechsler scores suggest that the person had developed relatively normal abilities in the past, a presumption may be made that the person has suffered some neuropsychological deficit resulting from brain damage; inferences of severity may also be drawn. However, each of these four measures is a general indicator and does not have significance for localization of cerebral damage, even though focal lesion (regardless of localization) and generalized or diffuse damage may have pronounced effects on general indicators. (p. 142)

The next step in interpretation of the Halstead-Reitan Neuropsychological Test Battery is to consider indicators of lateralization and localization of functions. This step utilizes the measures of inference other than level of performance such as patterns of performance, pathognomic deficits, and comparison of the two sides of the body on motor and sensory-perceptual measures. The most useful indicators are the Wechsler Verbal and Performance scales and subtests, motor and sensory perceptual findings on the finger tapping test, Tactual Performance Test, the Strength of Grip Test, and the Reitan-Klove Sensory-Perceptual Examination, evidence for language and/or constructional dyspraxia on the Reitan Indiana Aphasia Screening Test, and visual field losses (Reitan & Wolfson, 1986). Clinical neuropsychologists often add measures of verbal and nonverbal short-term memory to supplement the Halstead-Reitan Neuropsychological Test Battery and these measures in the interpretation (Horton & Wedding, 1984).

The fourth step in interpretation involves making a prediction of brain injury progression. The three progression possibilities are either progressive, chronic, or recovery from a brain lesion. Focal lesions are most commonly associated with a static or chronic course. A progressive course shows severe generalized effects. Test measures that are particularly helpful in predicting degree of recovery (Reitan & Wolfson, 1986) include the Speech-Sounds Perception Test and the Rhythm Test. The Trail Making Test, Part B is often a very good measure of recovery from a brain injury (Reitan & Wolfson, 1986). Another option for prediction course of brain damage is to conduct repeated evaluations over time and thereby demonstrate if there is progressive improvement or continued deterioration.

The fifth and last step in interpretation is to identify the type of neurological condition present such as brain tumor, stroke, head trauma, Alzheimer's disease, Parkinson's disease, or some other neurotoxic condition. As noted by Reitan and Wolfson (1986):

> Skill in this area obviously requires knowledge of neurology and neuropathology, and the neuropsychologist should be familiar with the major categories of neurological disease and damage. (p. 143)

Drawing neurological inferences from neuropsychological test data is the traditional task of the clinical neuropsychologist. More recently clinical neuropsychologists have been requested to make psychological inferences from neuropsychological test data (Heaton & Pendleton, 1981). Drawing psychological inferences from neuropsychological test data is a complex task and involves knowledge bases in personality assessment, treatment of psychiatric disorders, and vocational rehabilitation, among other areas of expertise.

Supplementation of the HRNTB with additional tests as well as collateral information and school and work records is often wise when faced with this complex task. Clinical neuropsychologists must draw on their clinical experience, and a discussion of ecological validity of neuropsychological assessment is available in an edited book (Sbordone & Long, 1996).

ISSUES WITH THE HALSTEAD-REITAN NEUROPSYCHOLOGICAL TEST BATTERY

A SIGNIFICANT CONCERN is that the HRNTB may require 10 or more hours to be administered, scored, and interpreted by a clinical neuropsychologist. In addition, the HRNTB apparatus is difficult to transport, and it is difficult to test patients at bedside. Also, memory and language measures may need to be added to supplement the HRNTB. In addition, ecological validity studies of the HRNTB are few. Also, adequate clinical interpretation of the complex HRNTB test results requires great expertise and many years of clinical experience with varied neurological and psychiatric patient populations.

Moreover, questions have been raised concerning the need to use demographic normative corrections with the test scores (Heaton, Grant, & Matthews, 1986; Heaton et al., 2004). Data demonstrate that many of the tests included in the HRNTB are sensitive to the effects of age, education, and gender. For example, in terms of test variance accounted for by age, the Category Test, Trails B, and Tactual Performance Test are influenced by age (Heaton et al., 1986; Heaton et al., 2004). Similarly, Trails B, Speech Sounds Perception, Aphasia Screening, and the Category Test are influenced by education effects (Heaton et al., 1986; Heaton et al., 2004). The measures that are least age- and education-related are Finger Tapping, Sensory Perceptual Functioning, and Strength of Grip (Heaton et al., 1986; Heaton et al., 2004).

In order to address this issue of demographic effects on the various subtests of the HRNTB, Heaton et al. (1991) developed age, education, and gender correction norms, and Heaton et al. (2004) revised the demographic norms and added ethnic norms for Caucasians and African Americans. The use of demographic corrections for age, education, gender (Heaton et al., 1991), and ethnicity (Heaton et al., 2004) has been an important advance in clinical neuropsychology, but there is a degree of controversy regarding the demographic norms.

Reitan and Wolfson (1995b, 2005a) have averred that the effects of age and education in brain-damaged samples must be further studied before raw scores are corrected for brain-damaged patients. Reitan and Wolfson (1995b) argue that the Heaton et al. (1991) norms were developed on a normal population, and while normative corrections are important in normal samples, the effects of brain damage may obliterate age and education effects in a brain-damaged population. They argue that adding a demographic correction developed in a normal sample to a brain-damaged sample has the effect of removing a portion of the effects of brain damage. Brain-damaged and normal samples manifest different degrees of correlation with demographic variables (Finlayson, Johnson, & Reitan, 1977). The problem is application of demographic corrections as developed could result in patients not being appropriately diagnosed as brain damaged (Horton, 1999a). At this point, additional research is clearly in order to clarify the worth and value of demographic normative corrections of neuropsychological test data from the expanded Halstead-Reitan Neuropsychology Test Battery.

In addition, prediction of every day functioning from the HRNTB scores (Heaton & Pendleton, 1981) is a work in progress, and additional work is needed (Sbordone & Long, 1996).

THE FUTURE OF THE HALSTEAD-REITAN NEUROPSYCHOLOGICAL TEST BATTERY

THERE IS A continued need to learn more regarding various uses and developments and possible new uses of the HRNTB. Some possible areas for future research are presented here.

SCREENING FOR BRAIN DAMAGE

SUGGESTIONS FOR JUDGING the need for comprehensive neuropsychological evaluations with the HRNTB might be predicated upon the referral question. For example, it would appear clear that the differentiation of brain-based disease states (i.e., Alzheimer's' disease dementia, vascular dementia, adult attention-deficit/hyperactivity disorder, dementia due to HIV disease, etc.) with contrasting treatment implications, as well as prognosis and course, would require comprehensive neuropsychological evaluations with the HRNTB.

In addition, assessments of the patient's behavior in demanding work settings (Heaton & Pendleton, 1981) or for complex forensic proceedings with significant liability issues are situations that would seem to require the full HRNTB, and at times multiple assessments over time would be needed.

On the other hand, when screening of a great number of patients is needed and the base rate estimate of organic conditions is very low, then brief screening procedures would be indicated. For the HRNTB, Reitan and Wolfson (2004a, 2004b, 2006) have developed methods to screen for brain damage in samples with predominantly normal brain function. These screening procedures are able to correctly identify brain-damaged children and adults at impressive rates (young children, 88%; older children, 91%; adults, 90%), and further research appears warranted.

INTERPRETATION OF NEUROPSYCHOLOGICAL TESTING

HORTON, VAETH, AND Anilane (1990) and Russell et al. (1970) demonstrated that objective rules for interpreting neuropsychological test data could yield reasonably adequate results. An important consideration, however, is the adequacy of the neuropsychological data set for drawing conclusions. Heaton et al. (2004) found that the GDS was not sensitive to missing data, and the Horton (2000b) study showed that not including IQ values didn't significantly reduce the ability of the GNDS to assess severity of brain damage. Briefly put, the GNDS, GDS, and likely other neuropsychological summary indices are "robust" to minor changes in neuropsychological tests that are combined to make up the indices.

CONATION

REITAN AND WOLFSON (2004c) define conation as the ability to apply effective effort in comparing a task over time. Another way of describing conation would be stamina. Reitan and Wolfson (2004c) have demonstrated that brain-damaged subjects are more sensitive to the effects of conation then normal subjects over performance on three intelligence tests that varied in the degree of which the intelligence tests required conation. In a subsequent study Reitan and Wolfson (2005b) found a significant relationship between neuropsychological test scores relationship to conation and their sensitivity to determining differences between a brain-damaged and control group.

FACTOR STRUCTURE OF THE HRNTB

AS NOTED EARLIER, Halstead (1947) conducted a factor analysis of the measures included in the HII. A later study of adult neuropsychiatric patients (Fowler, Zillmer, & Newman, 1988) found five factors (Verbal Comprehension, Perceptual Organization, Sensory-Attention, Primary-Motor, and Tactual-Spatial abilities). A study of the young children's version of the HRNTB with children aged 5 to 7 years (Foxcroft, 1989) found six factors (Analytic-Synthetic Visual Motor ability, Perceptual Organization, Cross-Modality Motoric Efficiency, directed Motor Speed Patterned Critical Discrimination, and Strength). A study with older children (Brooks, Dean, & Gray, 1989) found four factors (Simple Motor, Tactile Kinesthesis, Memory/Attention, and Nonverbal Visual-Spatial Memory). Another study with children ages 9 to 12 (Francis, Fletcher, Rourke, & York, 1992) found a five factor model (Simple Motor Skill, Complex Visual-Spatial Relations, Simple Spatial Motor Operations, Motor Steadiness, and Speeded Motor Sequencing). Clearly, there is great need for confirmation of the factors that underlie the HRNTB at all three age ranges of the battery.

CHANGE SCORES

DIKMEN, HEATON, GRANT, and Temkin (1999) have presented test–retest data for the expanded HRNTB and also have presented data regarding change scores. Being able to reliably predict change over time for the HRNTB is important as serial testing is often needed as brain diseases progress or a patient recovers from a brain injury. Much additional work is needed to develop methods for reliable estimation of change over time on the HRNTB.

CONCLUSION

T HE HRNTB PROVIDES the best and most complete comprehensive assessment available in clinical neuropsychology. A large research database supports use of the HRNTB in clinical settings, from neurological and neurosurgical departments to psychiatry wards and rehabilitation centers. It is the "gold standard" in clinical neuropsychology.

REFERENCES

Boll, T. J., Heaton, R. K., & Reitan, R. M. (1974). Neuropsychological and emotional correlates of Huntington's chorea. *Journal of Nervous and Mental Disease, 158,* 61–69.

Brooks, D. A., Dean, R. S. & Gray, J. W. (1989). HRNB factors with simultaneous-successive marker variables. *International Journal of Neuroscience, 46*(3–4), 157–160.

Dikmen, S. S., Heaton, R. K., Grant, I., & Temkin, N. R. (1999). Test-retest reliability and practice effects of expanded Halstead-Reitan Neuropsychological Test Battery. *Journal of the International Neuropsychological Society, 5*(4), 346–356.

Doehring, D. G., & Reitan, R. M. (1961a). Behavioral consequences of brain damage associated with homonymous field visual defects. *Journal of Comparative and Physiological Psychology, 54,* 489–492.

Finlayson, M. A., Johnson, K. A., & Reitan, R. (1977). Relationship of the level of education to neuropsychological measures in brain-damaged and non-brain-damaged adults. *Journal of Consulting and Clinical Psychology, 45,* 534–540.

Fitzhugh, K. B., Fitzhugh, L. C., & Reitan, R. M. (1962a). Psychological deficits in relation to acuteness of brain dysfunction. *Journal of Consulting Psychology, 25,* 61–66.

Fitzhugh, K.B., Fitzhugh, L. C., & Reitan, R. M. (1962a). The relationship of acuteness of organic brain dysfunction to Trail Making test performances. *Perceptual and Motor Skills, 15,* 399–403.

Fitzhugh, L. C., Fitzhugh, K. B., & Reitan, R. M. (1960). Adaptive abilities and intellectual functioning in hospitalized alcoholics. *Quarterly Journal of Studies on Alcohol, 21,* 414–423.

Fowler, P. C., Zillmer, E., & Newman, A. C. (1988). A multifactor model of the Halstead-Reitan Neuropsychological Test Battery and its relationship to cognitive status and psychiatric diagnosis. *Journal of Clinical Psychology, 44*(6), 898–906.

Foxcroft, C. D. (1989). Factor analysis of the Reitan-Indiana Neuropsychological Test Battery. *Perceptual and Motor Skills, 69*(3 pt. 2), 1303–1313.

Francis, D. J., Fletcher, J. M., Rourke, B. P., & York, M. J. (1992). A five-factor model for the motor, psychomotor and visual-spatial tests used in the neuropsychological assessment of children. *Journal of Clinical and Experimental Neuropsychology, 14*(4), 625–637.

Golden, C. J., & van den Broek, A. (1998). Potential impact of age and education scores on HRNB score patterns in participants with local brain injury. *Archives of Clinical Neuropsychology, 13*(8), 683–694.

Goldstein, G., & Shelly, C. H. (1972). Statistical and normative studies of the Halstead-Reitan Neuropsychological Test Battery relevant to a neuropsychiatric hospital setting. *Perceptual and Motor Skills, 34,* 603–620.

Guilmette, T. J., & Faust, D. (1991). Characteristics of neuropsychologists who prefer the Halstead-Reitan or the Luria-Nebraska Neuropsychology Battery. *Professional Psychology: Research and Practice, 22*(1), 80–83.

Guilmette, T. J., Faust, D., Hart, K., & Arkes, H. R. (1990). A national survey of psychologists who offer neuropsychological services. *Archives of Clinical Neuropsychology, 5,* 371–392.

Halstead, W. C. (1947). *Brain and intelligence: A quantitative study of the frontal lobes.* Chicago: University of Chicago Press.

Hartlage, L. C., & Telzrow, C. F. (1980). The practice of clinical neuropsychology in the U.S. *International Journal of Clinical Neuropsychology, 2,* 200–202.

Heaton, R. K., Grant, I., & Matthews, C. G. (1986). Differences in neuropsychological test performance associated with age, education and sex. In I. Grant & K. Adams (Eds.), *Neuropsychological assessment of neuropsychiatric disorders* (pp. 100–120). New York: Oxford.

Heaton, R. K., Grant, I., & Matthews, C. G. (1991). *Comprehensive norms for an expanded Halstead-Reitan Battery.* Odessa, FL: Psychological Assessment Resources.

Heaton, R. K., Miller, S. W., Taylor, M. J., & Grant, I. (2004). *Revised comprehensive norms for an expanded Halstead-Reitan Battery.* Odessa, FL: Psychological Assessment Resources.

Heaton, R. K., & Pendleton, M. G. (1981). Use of neuropsychological tests to predict adult patients every day functioning. *Journal of Consulting and Clinical Psychology, 49,* 807–821.

Horton, A. M., Jr. (1995a). The Alternative Impairment Index: A measure of neuropsychological deficit. *Perceptual and Motor Skills, 80,* 336–338.

Horton, A. M., Jr. (1995b). Cross-validation of the Alternative Impairment Index. *Perceptual and Motor Skills, 81,* 1153–1154.

Horton, A. M., Jr. (1995c) Children's version of the Alternative Impairment Index. *Perceptual and Motor Skills, 81*, 217–218.

Horton, A. M., Jr. (1996). Revised children's version of the Alternative Impairment Index. *Applied Neuropsychology, 3*, 178–180.

Horton, A. M., Jr. (1997). Alternative Impairment Index-Revised: A neuropsychological pilot study. *Applied Neuropsychology, 4*, 176–179.

Horton, A. M., Jr. (1998). Development of a short-form screening index for severity of brain damage in older children. *Applied Neuropsychology, 5*, 48–50.

Horton, A. M., Jr. (1999a). Prediction of brain damage severity: Demographic corrections. *International Journal of Neuroscience, 97*, 179–183.

Horton, A. M., Jr. (1999b). Prediction of severity of brain damage by a processing speed variable in older children: A brief report. *International Journal of Neuroscience, 99*, 233–238.

Horton, A. M., Jr. (1999c). Above-average intelligence and neuropsychological test score performance. *International Journal of Neuroscience, 99*, 221–231.

Horton, A. M., Jr. (2000a). Prediction of brain injury severity by subscales of the Alternative Impairment Index. *International Journal of Neuroscience, 105*, 97–100.

Horton, A. M., Jr. (2000b). General Neuropsychological Deficit Scale sans IQ. *International Journal of Neuroscience, 103*, 127–130.

Horton, A. M., Jr., Anilane, J., Slone, D. G., & Shapiro, S. (1986). Development and cross-validation of a short-form impairment index. *Archives of Clinical Neuropsychology, 1*, 243–246.

Horton, A. M., Jr., & Sobelman, S. A., (1994). The General Neuropsychological Deficit Scale and the Halstead Impairment Index: Comparison of severity. *Perceptual and Motor Skills, 78*, 888–890.

Horton, A. M., Jr., Vaeth, J., & Anilane, J. (1990). Computerized interpretation of the Luria-Nebraska Neuropsychological Test Battery. *Perceptual and Motor Skills, 71*, 83–86.

Horton, A. M., Jr., & Wedding, D. (1984). *Clinical and behavioral neuropsychology.* New York: Praeger.

Jarvis, P. E., & Barth, J. T. (1994). *Halstead-Reitan Test Battery: An interpretive guide* (2nd ed.). Odessa, FL: Psychological Assessment Resources.

Mezzich, J. E., & Moses, J. A. (1980). Efficient screening for brain dysfunction. *Biological Psychiatry, 15*, 333–337.

Moses, J. A., Jr., Pritchard, D. A., & Adams, R. L. (1999). Normative corrections for the Halstead Reitan neuropsychological battery. *Archives of Clinical Neuropsychology, 14*(5), 445–454.

Reed, H. B. C., & Reitan, R. M. (1962). The significance of age in the performance of a complex psychomotor task by brain-damaged and non-brain-damaged subjects. *Journal of Gerontology, 17*, 193–196.

Reed, H. B. C., & Reitan, R. M. (1963a). Changes in psychological test performances associated with the normal aging process. *Journal of Gerontology,*
18, 271–274.

Reed, H. B. C., & Reitan, R. M. (1963b). A comparison of the effects of the normal aging process with the effects of organic brain damage on adaptive
abilities. *Journal of Gerontology, 18,* 177–179.

Reed, H. B. C., Reitan, R. M., & Klove, H. (1965). The influence of cerebral lesions
on psychological test performance of older children. *Journal of Consulting Psychology, 29,* 247–251.

Reitan, R. M. (1955a). Certain differential effects of left and right cerebral lesions
in human adults. *Journal of Comparative and Physiological Psychology, 48,*
474–477.

Reitan, R. M. (1955b). Discussion: Symposium on the temporal lobe. *Archives of
Neurology and Psychiatry, 74,* 569–570.

Reitan, R. M. (1958). The validity of the Trail Making test as an indicator of
organic brain damage. *Perceptual and Motor Skills, 8,* 271–276.

Reitan, R. M. (1959a). The comparative effects of brain damage on the Halstead
Impairment Index and the Wechsler–Bellevue Scale. *Journal of Clinical
Psychology, 15,* 281–285.

Reitan, R. M. (1959b). *The effects of brain lesions on adaptive abilities in human
beings.* Tucson, AZ: Reitan Neuropsychology Laboratories, Inc.

Reitan, R. M. (1960). The significance of dysphasia for intelligence and adaptive
abilities. *Journal of Psychology, 50,* 355–376.

Reitan, R. M. (1962). The comparative psychological significance of aging in
groups with and without organic brain damage. In C. Tibbitts & W.
Donahue (Eds.), *Social and psychological aspects of aging* (pp. 880–887).
New York: Columbia University Press.

Reitan, R. M. (1964). Psychological deficits resulting from cerebral lesions in
man. In J. M. Warren & K. A. Akart (Eds.), *The frontal granular cortex and
behavior* (pp. 295–312). New York: McGraw-Hill.

Reitan, R. M. (1970a). Measurement of psychological changes in aging. *Duke
University Council on Aging and Human Development,* Proceedings of
Seminars. Durham, NC: Duke University Press.

Reitan, R. M. (1974a). Methodological problems in clinical neuropsychology.
In R. M. Reitan & L. A. Davison (Eds.), *Clinical neuropsychology: Current
status and applications* (pp. 19–46). New York: Wiley.

Reitan, R. M. (1974b). Psychological effects of cerebral lesions in children of
early school age. In R. M. Reitan & L. A. Davison (Eds.), *Clinical neuropsychology: Current status and applications* (pp. 53–90). New York: Wiley.

Reitan, R. M. (1985). Relationships between measures of brain functions and
general intelligence. *Journal of Clinical Psychology, 41,* 245–253.

Reitan, R. M. (1994). Ward Halstead's contributions to neuropsychology and
the Halstead-Reitan Neuropsychological Test Battery. *Journal of Clinical
Psychology, 50*(1), 47–70.

Reitan, R. M., & Wolfson, D. (1986). The Halstead-Reitan Neuropsychology Test Battery. In D. Wedding, A. M. Horton, Jr., and J. S. Webster (Eds.). *The neuropsychology handbook* (pp. 134–160). New York: Springer Publishing Company.

Reitan, R. M., & Wolfson, D. (1988). *Traumatic brain injury: Vol. 2. Recovery and rehabilitation*. Tucson, AZ: Neuropsychology Press.

Reitan, R. M., & Wolfson, D. (1992a). *Neuropsychological evaluation of younger children*. Tucson, AZ: Neuropsychology Press.

Reitan, R. M., & Wolfson, D. (1992b). *Neuropsychological evaluation of older children*. Tucson, AZ: Neuropsychology Press.

Reitan, R. M., & Wolfson, D. (1993). *The Halstead-Reitan Neuropsychological Test Battery: Theory and clinical interpretation* (2nd ed.). Tucson, AZ: Neuropsychology Press.

Reitan, R. M., & Wolfson, D. (1995a). Cross-validation of the General Neuropsychological Deficit Scale (GNDS). *Archives of Clinical Neuropsychology, 10*, 125–131.

Reitan, R. M., & Wolfson, D. (1995b). Influence of age and education on neuropsychological test results. *The Clinical Neuropsychologist, 9*, 151–158.

Reitan, R. M., & Wolfson, D. (2004a). The Trail Making Test as an initial screening procedure for neuropsychological impairment in older children. *Archives of Clinical Neuropsychology, 19*, 281–288.

Reitan, R. M., & Wolfson, D. (2004b). Use of the Progressive Figures Test in evaluating brain damaged children, children with academic problems, and normal controls. *Archives of Clinical Neuropsychology, 19*, 305–312.

Reitan, R. M., & Wolfson, D. (2004c). The differential effect of conation on intelligence test scores among brain-damaged and control subjects. *Archives of Clinical Neuropsychology, 19*, 29–35.

Reitan, R. M., & Wolfson, D. (2005a). The effect of age and education transformations on neuropsychological test scores of persons with diffuse or bilateral brain damage. *Applied Neuropsychology, 12*(4), 181–189.

Reitan, R. M., & Wolfson, D. (2005b). The effect of conation in determining differential variance among brain-damaged and nonbrain-damaged persons across a broad range of neuropsychological tests. *Archives of Clinical Neuropsychology, 20*, 957–966.

Reitan, R. M., & Wolfson, D. (2006, January). *Screening for neuropsychological impairment using subtests from the Halstead-Reitan Battery*. Workshop Presented at the Third Annual Meeting of the Coalition of Clinical Practitioners in Neuropsychology, Las Vegas, Nevada.

Russell, E. W., Neuringer, C., & Goldstein, G. (1970). *Assessment of brain damage: A neuropsychological key approach*. New York: John Wiley.

Sbordone, R. J., & Long, C. J. (Eds.). (1996). *Ecological validity of neuropsychological testing*. Delray Beach, FL: St. Lucie Press.

Seretny, M. L., Dean, R. S., Gray, J. W., & Hartlage, L. C. (1986). The practice of clinical neuropsychology in the United States. *Archives of Clinical Neuropsychology, 1*, 5–12.

Sherer, M., & Adams, R. L. (1993). Cross-validation of Reitan and Wolfson's neuropsychological deficit scales. *Archives of Clinical Neuropsychology, 8,* 429–435.

Sweeney, J. E. (1999). Raw, demographically altered and composite Halstead-Reitan Battery data in the evaluation of adult victims of nonimpact acceleration forces in motor vehicle accidents. *Applied Neuropsychology, 6*(2), 79–87.

Wechsler, D. (1991). *Wechsler Intelligence Scale for Children* (3rd ed.). San Antonio, TX: Psychological Corporation.

Wheeler, L. (1964). Complex behavioral indices weighted by linear discriminant functions for the prediction of cerebral damage. *Perceptual and Motor Skills, 19,* 907–923.

Wheeler, L., Burke, C. J., & Reitan, R. M. (1963). An application of discriminant functions to the problem of predicting brain damage using behavioral variables. *Perceptual and Motor Skills, 16,* 417–440.

Wheeler, L., & Reitan, R. M. (1962). The presence and laterality of brain damage predicted from responses to a short Aphasia Screening test. *Perceptual and Motor Skills, 15,* 789–799.

Wheeler, L., & Reitan, R. M. (1963). Discriminant functions applied to the problem of predicting cerebral damage from behavior tests: A cross validation study. *Perceptual and Motor Skills, 16,* 681–701.

Yantz, C. L., Gavett, B. E., Lynch, J. K., & McCaffrey, R. J. (2006). Potential for litigation disparities of Halstead-Reitan Neuropsychological Battery performance in a litigating sample. *Archives of Clinical Neuropsychology, 21*(8), 809–817.

10

Neuropsychological Assessment Battery: Introduction and Advanced Interpretation

GRANT L. IVERSON, BRIAN L. BROOKS,
TRAVIS WHITE, AND ROBERT A. STERN

OVERVIEW

THE NEUROPSYCHOLOGICAL ASSESSMENT Battery (NAB; Stern & White, 2003a) is comprehensive, conormed, and it can be used in a fixed or flexible manner. The normative sample is large, and the coverage of neuropsychological abilities assessed is broad.

The NAB has six optional modules: Screening, Attention, Language, Memory, Spatial, and Executive Functions. The Screening Module is a self-contained battery of tests that can be administered in less than 1 hour. It yields individual test scores and index scores in the same areas as the full NAB (i.e., Attention, Language, Memory, Spatial, and Executive Functions). If the Screening Module is administered, the clinician can choose to administer specific NAB modules to assess more thoroughly areas of interest or concern that were identified using the Screening Module.

The full NAB can be administered in its entirety, as a fixed battery, in approximately 3 hours (without the Screening Module). Alternatively, selected modules and tests can be administered in a flexible battery approach. An overview of the tests comprising the NAB modules is provided in Table 10.1; more specific descriptions of each module and the tests are provided later in this chapter.

The NAB was carefully designed based on feedback from an Advisory Council of distinguished neuropsychologists, as well as from surveys from members of the International Neuropsychological Society, the National Academy of Neuropsychology, and Division 40 of the American Psychological Association. Based on the survey responses, several features that were given high ratings of importance were incorporated into the development of the NAB. These features are listed here.

TABLE 10.1 Overview of the NAB Modules

Attention Module: Orientation (person, place, time), digit span (Digits Forward and Digits Backward), Dots (visual-spatial attention), four graphomotor tests measuring attention, processing speed, and working memory (Numbers & Letters tests), and Driving Scenes (visual-spatial attention; images of driving scenes are presented, followed by other scenes with aspects missing, added, or changed).

Language Module: Oral Production (expressive language), Auditory Comprehension (language comprehension), Naming (confrontation naming), Writing (narrative writing), and Bill Payment (a test measuring one's ability to pay bills).

Memory Module: Word list learning (12 words, 3 trials, distracter list, short delay free recall, long delay free recall, recognition), Shape Learning (9 shapes, 3 learning trials with immediate recognition after each trial, delayed recognition memory, delayed forced-choice recognition), Story Learning (one story presented twice with immediate free recall following each presentation and delayed free recall), and Daily Living Memory (medication instructions presented over 3 trials with immediate free recall following each presentation, delayed free recall, delayed recognition memory; name, address, and phone number presented three times with free recall after each trial, delayed free recall, and delayed recognition memory).

Spatial Module: Visual Discrimination (visual perception and discrimination), Design Construction (visual-spatial and constructional skills, assembling pieces into a design), Figure Drawing (visual-constructional skills, copying a complex figure followed by immediate free recall of the figure), and Map Reading (ability to read and understand increasingly complex maps).

Executive Functions Module: Mazes (seven increasingly difficult mazes), Judgment (questions regarding everyday judgment), Categories (conceptual reasoning, flexible thinking), and Word Generation (verbal fluency).

---

1. The battery has screening capability to rapidly identify those patients who require in-depth assessment.
2. The battery provides comprehensive assessment of neuropsychological functioning that is suitable for most clinical applications.
3. The battery combines the strengths of both fixed and flexible batteries.
4. The battery, in general, avoids ceiling and floor effects, thus providing a wide enough range for most clinical settings.
5. The battery is comprehensive, yet still brief enough to allow inclusion of other tests as desired.
6. The battery provides coordinated norming with intelligence (Reynolds Intellectual Screening Test [RIST]; Reynolds & Kamphaus, 2003).
7. The battery has demographically corrected normative data (i.e., age, education, and sex).
8. The battery has equivalent/alternate forms.
9. Several new tests were specifically developed to increase the ecological validity of the comprehensive battery.

The purpose of this chapter is to provide a comprehensive overview of the NAB, as well as to provide new analyses that facilitate more sophisticated interpretation of test performance. The chapter is divided into the following sections: (a) Screening Module, (b) NAB main modules, (c) standardization sample, (d) types of normative scores, (e) norming method, (f) intelligence–NAB index discrepancy scores, (g) neuropsychological profile analysis, (h) reliability and validity, and (i) conclusions.

SCREENING MODULE

THE NAB SCREENING Module was designed to be a relatively brief assessment of cognitive abilities, more in depth and informative than rapid screening tests (e.g., MMSE), though less time-consuming than a comprehensive battery. The Screening Module can be used in isolation or to facilitate and guide further neuropsychological assessment. It requires approximately 45 minutes to administer and consists of 12 brief tests, producing 16 T-scores, of which 14 T-scores contribute to the five Screening Domain scores (i.e., Attention, Language, Memory, Spatial, and Executive Functions) and the Total Screening Index score. In addition, the tests provide several secondary and descriptive scores.

The *Screening Attention Domain* score is a composite score of an individual's attentional capacity, working memory, psychomotor speed, selective attention, divided attention, and sustained attention. The *Screening Language Domain* score briefly examines both comprehension and naming. The *Screening Memory Domain* score is a composite of immediate and delayed verbal (story) and visual (shapes) nonmotor memory. The *Screening Spatial Domain* is a composite measure of the examinee's visual-perceptual skills, attention to visual detail, and visual-constructional ability. The *Screening Executive Functions Domain* is a composite measure of planning, mental flexibility, verbal fluency, and generativity. The *Total Screening Index* is based on the sum of the five screening module domain scores. It is meant to be an omnibus screening measure of neuropsychological functioning in the domains of attention, language, memory, spatial, and executive functions.

As seen in Table 10.2, the Screening Module consists of tests measuring orientation; digit span; attention, working memory, and processing speed (numbers and letters); language comprehension; confrontation naming; immediate and delayed recognition memory for shapes; immediate and delayed memory for stories; visual perception and discrimination; visual-motor construction; speeded visual-motor planning and problem solving (mazes); and verbal fluency.

Clinicians can choose to use the Screening Module as a freestanding neuropsychological screening battery. The obvious advantage of this screening battery is that all the tests are conormed with each other (i.e., across the Screening Module), with the full NAB battery, as well as with a measure of intellectual abilities (i.e., RIST; Reynolds & Kamphaus, 2003). The Screening Module was designed to be used in a sequential manner with the main modules of the NAB. The Screening Domain scores fairly accurately predict full NAB index scores that fall in the extremely low range. Thus, a clinician might choose to not administer certain main modules if the respective Screening Domain score is extremely low. We believe, however, that in most clinical situations involving thorough neuropsychological assessment, the full NAB should be administered. From a practical perspective, when using the Screening Module as a sequential screening tool, most patients will be administered at least three of the five main modules. Thus, if the clinician simply chose, a priori, to administer all five modules (and omit the Screening Module), then the total administration time might be comparable to administering the Screening Module followed by most of the modules.

The Screening Module can also be used as part of a battery of tests designed for a specific population. For example, one author (RS) uses the Screening Module in combination with the Memory Module for the assessment of older adults in a memory disorders clinic. Using the Screening Module in this manner can be illustrated by examining the dementia sample reported in the *Psychometric and Technical Manual* (White &

TABLE 10.2   Screening Module Tests

Test	Acronym	Description	Possible interpretation of impairment
Screening Orientation	S-ORN	Questions about orientation to self, time, place, and situation	Compromised awareness of one's self in relation to one's environment
Screening Digits Forward	S-DGF	Repetition of orally presented digits	Reduced auditory attentional capacity
Screening Digits Backward	S-DGB	Reversal of orally presented digits	Reduced working memory for orally presented information
Screening Numbers & Letters	S-N&L	Two timed tasks (Parts A and B) involving letter cancellation and letter cancellation plus serial addition, respectively	Reduced focused or selective attention, distractibility or reduced concentration, diminished sustained attention, and reduced divided attention and information processing speed
Screening Auditory Comprehension	S-AUD	Three-part test that requires the examinee to demonstrate comprehension of orally presented commands	Compromised auditory comprehension
Screening Naming	S-NAM	Visual confrontation naming task in which the examinee states the name of an object depicted in a photograph; semantic and phonemic cues are provided if necessary	Compromised word-finding ability or possible dysnomia or anomia
Screening Shape Learning	S-SHL	Single-trial visual learning task involving multiple-choice immediate recognition recall of five visual stimuli, followed by a delayed recognition task	Poor initial learning, storage, and 5–10 minute delayed recall of visually presented information
Screening Story Learning	S-STL	Verbal learning task involving immediate and delayed free recall of a two-sentence story	Compromised initial learning, storage, and 5–10 minute delayed recall of orally presented verbal information

(Continued)

TABLE 10.2   Screening Module Tests *(Continued)*

Test	Acronym	Description	Possible interpretation of impairment
Screening Visual Discrimination	S-VIS	Visual match-to-target paradigm, in which the examinee matches a target visual design from an array of four similar designs presented beneath the target	Difficulties with visuo-perception and visuospatial skills, as well as attention to detail
Screening Design Construction	S-DES	Visuoconstruction assembly task using plastic manipulatives (tans) to copy two-dimensional target designs (tangrams)	Compromised visuo-construction or the inability to manipulate materials to copy of visual stimulus
Screening Mazes	S-MAZ	Three timed paper-and-pencil mazes of increasing difficulty	Difficulties with planning and foresight but may also be associated with reduced impulse control and decreased psychomotor speed
Screening Word Generation	S-WGN	Timed task in which the examinee creates three-letter words from a group of six letters (two vowels, four consonants) that are presented visually	Reduced generativity or verbal fluency

Note: Adapted from Table 1.2 (page 6) and Table 6.11 (page 130) of the *NAB Administration, Scoring, and Interpretation Manual* (Stern & White, 2003b). Reprinted with permission. Further reproduction is prohibited without permission from PAR, Inc.

Stern, 2003b). Participants in this sample were community-dwelling older adults who had clinical dementia ratings between 0.5 (questionable dementia) and 1.5 (mild-to-moderate dementia), with the majority having a 1.0 rating (mild dementia). Their average age was 78.0 years (SD = 4.9), and their average education was 13.0 years (SD = 3.0). Their Screening Module and Memory Module test scores are presented in Table 10.3.

The most sensitive Screening Module tests for measuring cognitive problems associated with dementia appeared to be Numbers and Letters

TABLE 10.3 NAB Screening Module and Memory Module in Patients With Dementia (N = 20)

	Mean	SD	% < 1 SD	% ≤ 5th percentile	% < 2 SD
Screening Attention Domain	82.2	15.7	50	35	20
Screening Language Domain	81.2	15.1	60	30	15
Screening Memory Domain	80.3	11.1	65	40	20
Screening Spatial Domain	89.5	16.9	45	20	15
Screening Executive Functions Domain	84.9	15.2	55	35	20
Total Screening Index	75.7	13.2	65	50	35
Individual Screening Tests					
Screening Digits Forward	45.9	10.1	20	10	10
Screening Digits Backward	43.8	7.9	30	20	5
Screening Numbers and Letters Part A Speed	37.8	12.1	55	55	25
Screening Numbers and Letters Part A Errors	48.7	9.9	20	20	10
Screening Numbers and Letters Part A Efficiency	38.1	11.9	60	50	25
Screening Numbers and Letters Part B Efficiency	39.3	11.0	60	35	15
Screening Auditory Comprehension	43.3	14.6	40	40	20
Screening Naming	34.4	12.4	70	50	45
Screening Shape Learning Immediate Recognition	45.3	9.1	25	20	5
Screening Shape Learning Delayed Recognition	49.0	9.6	15	10	0
Screening Story Learning Immediate Recall	39.1	8.4	50	30	5
Screening Story Learning Delayed Recall	29.9	7.7	90	70	55
Screening Visual Discrimination	41.7	14.1	55	30	20
Screening Design Construction	46.6	10.7	30	15	5
Screening Mazes	41.4	7.7	40	25	5
Screening Word Generation	42.4	11.8	50	25	10
Full Module Memory Index	67.6	14.5	89.3	84.3	79.0
List Learning List A Immediate Recall	33.8	9.4	80	55	30
List Learning List B Immediate Recall	38.3	7.9	55	25	15
List Learning List A Short Delayed Recall	27.5	11.0	85	85	85

(Continued)

TABLE 10.3 NAB Screening Module and Memory Module in Patients With Dementia (N = 20) *(Continued)*

	Mean	SD	% < 1 SD	% ≤ 5th percentile	% < 2 SD
List Learning List A Long Delayed Recall	32.0	8.4	90	65	45
Shape Learning Immediate Recognition	37.4	10.3	60	35	20
Shape Learning Delayed Recognition	38.2	11.2	50	40	20
Story Learning Phrase Unit Immediate Recall	32.1	10.7	85	75	45
Story Learning Phrase Unit Delayed Recall	35.0	9.6	90	70	30
Daily Living Memory Immediate Recall	32.3	9.5	85	60	35
Daily Living Memory Delayed Recall	25.8	12.1	84.2	84.2	84.2
Other Test Scores					
MMSE total raw score	23.1	3.1			
DRS-2 total raw score	117.1	14.4			
DRS-2 total age-corrected scaled score	4.9	2.7			
DRS-2 total age- and education-corrected scaled score	4.1	3.3			

Note: Adapted from Tables 6.36 (page 202), 6.37 (page 203), 6.38 (page 204), and 6.39 (page 205) of the *NAB Psychometric and Technical Manual* (White & Stern, 2003b). Reprinted with permission. Further reproduction is prohibited without permission from PAR, Inc. The Full Module percentages falling below the three cutoff scores are reported as 89.3%, 84.3%, and 79.0% in the *Psychometric and Technical Manual,* due to missing data.

Part A Speed and Efficiency, Naming, and Story Learning Delayed Recall; 50–70% of the sample scored at or below the 5th percentile on these tests. The Module Memory tests were more sensitive than the screening tests. The average Memory Index score for the dementia sample was more than two standard deviations (SDs) below the mean (67.6, SD = 14.5). The average List Learning, Story Learning, and Daily Living Memory test scores ranged from approximately 1.5 to 2 SDs below the mean and 55–85% of the sample scored at or below the 5th percentile on these tests.

NAB MAIN MODULES

THE FULL NAB (i.e., the five main modules) consists of 24 individual tests across the five cognitive domains. From these 24 tests, 36 T-scores are derived, 30 of which contribute toward five separate index scores and one total battery index score. Tests on the NAB also provide several secondary and qualitative scores. Total administration time for the NAB is estimated to be 3–3.5 hours. Individual modules range in administration time from 25 (Spatial) to 45 (Attention and Memory) minutes (White & Stern, 2003b). Clinicians can administer the entire NAB, selected modules, or selected tests. Similar to the Screening Module, the full NAB tests are conormed with each other, with the Screening NAB, as well as with a brief measure of intellectual abilities (i.e., the RIST). A description of the individual tests within each module is provided in this section.

ATTENTION MODULE TESTS

THE SYSTEMATIC ASSESSMENT of attention, concentration, and processing speed is routinely included in a comprehensive neuropsychological assessment. Problems with attention, working memory, and processing speed are common in patients with diverse diseases, disorders, and conditions, including Alzheimer's, Parkinson's, and Huntington's disease; ADHD; traumatic brain injury; multiple sclerosis; depression; and schizophrenia.

The Attention Module consists of six tests: (a) Orientation, (b) Digits Forward, (c) Digits Backward, (d) Dots, (e) Numbers and Letters, and (f) Driving Scenes. These tests measure different aspects of attention and processing speed in the verbal and visual domain. The *Attention Index* is a composite score representing diverse neurocognitive abilities such as attentional capacity, working memory, selective attention, divided attention, distractibility, sustained attention, attention to detail, and information processing speed. The entire module can be administered in approximately 45 minutes. Descriptions of the tests comprising this module and possible interpretations for low scores are provided in Table 10.4.

LANGUAGE MODULE TESTS

LANGUAGE CAN BE compromised by many different conditions affecting the brain. The Language Module tests can be interpreted from a classic syndromal perspective, descriptive perspective, or psycholinguistic perspective. A reasonably thorough assessment of language includes spontaneous speech, auditory and reading comprehension, naming, and writing. The Language Module tests can be used to examine for some of the classic aphasic syndromes, such as the following:

- Broca's Aphasia: Major disturbance in expressive speech
- Wernicke's Aphasia: Major disturbance in auditory comprehension
- Pure Word Deafness: Inability to recognize spoken words with broadly normal spontaneous speech

TABLE 10.4 Individual Tests

Test	Acronym	Description	Possible interpretation of impairment[1]
Attention Module			
Orientation	ORN	Questions about orientation to self, time, place, and situation	Compromised awareness of one's self in relation to one's environment
Digits Forward	DGF	Repetition of orally presented digits	Reduced auditory attentional capacity
Digits Backward	DGB	Reversal of orally presented digits	Reduced working memory for orally presented information
Dots	DOT	Delayed recognition span paradigm, in which an array of dots is exposed for a brief period, followed by a blank interference page, followed by a new array with one additional dot; examinee points to "new" dot	Compromised visuospatial working memory, as well as visual scanning
Numbers and Letters	N&L	Four timed tasks (Parts A, B, C, and D) involving letter cancellation, letter counting, serial addition, and letter cancellation plus serial addition, respectively	Difficulties in psychomotor speed, concentration, sustained attention, focused or selective attention, divided attention, and information processing speed
Driving Scenes	DRV	Daily Living task in which the examinee is first presented with a drawing of a driving scene as viewed from behind a steering wheel, and then shown another scene and asked to say and point to everything that is new, different, or missing relative to the previous scene; this is continued for four additional scenes	Compromised visuospatial working memory, as well as visual scanning, attention to detail, and selective attention

(Continued)

TABLE 10.4 Individual Tests *(Continued)*

Test	Acronym	Description	Possible interpretation of impairment[1]
Language			
Oral Production	OPD	Speech output task in which the examinee orally describes a picture of a Family scene	Diminished speech output or fluency
Auditory Comprehension	AUD	Six-part test that requires examinee to demonstrate comprehension of orally presented instructions; tasks include performing one- to four-step commands, the concepts of before/after, above/below and right/left, body-part identification, yes/no questions, and paper folding	Compromised auditory comprehension
Naming	NAM	Visual confrontation naming task in which the examinee states the name of a pictured object; semantic and honemic cues are provided if necessary	Compromised word-finding ability or possibly dysnomia or anomia
Reading Comprehension	RCN	Two-part test that requires the examinee to demonstrate reading comprehension of single words and of sentences by pointing to multiple choice written words and sentences that match visual stimuli	Reduced reading comprehension of words and sentences
Writing	WRT	Narrative writing task in which the examinee is shown the same drawing of a family scene used in the Oral Production test and asked to write about it; the writing sample is scored with regard to legibility, syntax, spelling, and conveyance	Poor narrative writing and possibly dysgraphia or agraphia

(Continued)

TABLE 10.4 Individual Tests *(Continued)*

Test	Acronym	Description	Possible Interpretation of Impairment[1]
Bill Payment	BIL	Daily Living task in which the examinee is given a utility bill statement, check ledger, check, and envelope, and asked to follow a series of eight commands requiring oral and written responses of increasing complexity	Difficulties with auditory comprehension, reading comprehension, writing skills, simple calculations, and speech output
Memory			
List Learning	LL	Verbal list learning task involving three learning trials of a 12-word list, followed by an interference list, and then short delay free recall, long delay free recall, and long delay forced-choice recognition tasks; the word list includes three embedded semantic categories with four words in each category	Difficulties with the learning, storage, and 10- to 15-minute delayed free recall and recognition of discrete pieces of verbal information
Shape Learning	SHL	Visual learning task involving three learning trials and multiple-choice immediate recognition of nine visual stimuli, followed by delayed recognition and forced-choice recall	Poor initial learning, storage, and 10- to 15-minute delayed recognition of visually-presented nonverbal information
Story Learning	STL	Verbal learning task involving immediate and delayed free recall of a five-sentence story; two learning trials are provided, and recall is scored for both verbatim and gist elements	Compromised initial learning and 10- to 15-minute delayed free recall of logically organized, orally-presented verbal information

(Continued)

TABLE 10.4   Individual Tests *(Continued)*

Test	Acronym	Description	Possible interpretation of impairment[1]
Daily Living Memory	DLM	Verbal learning task involving three-trial learning with immediate recall, delayed recall, and delayed multiple-choice recognition of information encountered in daily living, including medication instructions, and a name, address, and phone number	Difficulties with the learning, storage, and 5- to 10-minute delayed free recall and recognition of information frequently encountered in daily living
Spatial			
Visual Discrimination	VIS	Visual match-to-target paradigm, in which the examinee matches a target visual design from an array of four similar designs presented beneath the target	Difficulties with visuoperception and visuospatial skills, as well as attention to detail
Design Construction	DES	Visuoconstruction assembly task using plastic manipulatives (tans) to copy two-dimensional target designs (tangrams)	Compromised visuoconstruction or the inability to manipulate materials to copy a visual stimulus
Figure Drawing	FGD	Visuoconstruction drawing task involving a copy and immediate recall of a geometric figure of moderate complexity; the production is scored for the presence, accuracy, and placement of the elements, as well as overall organizational skill	Compromised visuoconstruction or the inability to accurately draw a geometric design from a two-dimensional stimulus, as well as poor visual-organizational skills and poor encoding and immediate processing of visuospatial material
Map Reading	MAP	Daily Living task in which the examinee answers questions (presented both orally and in writing) about a city map that has a compass rose and mileage legend	Compromised visuospatial skills, with possible spatial/directional disorientation, right-left disorientation, and visual scanning difficulties

(Continued)

TABLE 10.4   Individual Tests *(Continued)*

Test	Acronym	Description	Possible interpretation of impairment[1]
Executive Functions			
Mazes	MAZ	Seven timed paper-and-pencil mazes of increasing difficulty	Difficulties with planning and foresight, but may also be associated with reduced impulse control and decreased psychomotor speed
Judgment	JDG	Daily Living test in which the examinee answers 10 judgment questions pertaining to home safety, health, and medical issues	Poor problem solving, poor knowledge of important aspects of home safety and health/medical issues, and possibly reduced decisional capacity in these areas
Categories	CAT	Classification and categorization task in which the examinee generates different two-group categories based on photographs and verbal information (e.g., name, occupation, place of birth, date of birth, marital status) about six people	Poor concept formation, cognitive response set, mental flexibility, and generativity
Word Generation	WGN	Timed task in which the examinee creates three-letter words from a group of eight letters (two vowels, six consonants) that are presented visually	Reduced generativity or verbal fluency, poor self-monitoring, and perseverative tendencies

Note: [1] There are several possible explanations for poor performance on a measure, which must be carefully considered when interpreting any neuropsychological test. Adapted from Tables 1.3 (page 7), 1.4 (page 8), 1.5 (page 9), 1.6 (page 9), 1.7 (page 10), 6.12 (page 135), 6.13 (page 138), 6.14 (page 141), 6.19 (page 146), and 6.20 (page 148) of the *NAB: Administration, Scoring, & Interpretation Manual* (Stern & White, 2003b). Reprinted with permission. Further reproduction is prohibited without permission from PAR, Inc.

- Anomic Aphasia: Difficulty producing single words, such as common nouns; globally intact repetition and comprehension
- Global Aphasia: Major disturbance in all language functions

It should be noted that the formal assessment of repetition is not included in the NAB and, therefore, results based *solely* on the NAB Language Module cannot be used to diagnose aphasic conditions marked by the presence or absence of intact repetition (e.g., transcortical aphasias, conduction aphasia).

The Language Module tests also can be used to screen for several of the acquired dyslexias, most notably pure alexia (alexia without agraphia). Some disorders of writing, the agraphias, also can be identified. Pure agraphia, for example, is an isolated disturbance in writing, without co-occurring language disturbance. Of course, writing problems typically co-occur with language problems.

The Language Module consists of six individual tests: (a) Oral Production, (b) Auditory Comprehension, (c) Naming, (d) Reading Comprehension, (e) Writing, and (f) Bill Payment. When administering the Language Module tests, the examiner is encouraged to take notes regarding qualitative aspects of the person's expressive and receptive language, including articulation problems, dysprosody, halting or telegraphic speech, phonemic and semantic paraphasias, neologisms, and perseverations. The *Language Index* is a composite score of overall language functioning. This module can be administered in approximately 35 minutes.

The Language Module is comprised of sophisticated language tests designed for people with language disorders. Most healthy adults, and patients with mild brain-related problems, perform normally on these tests. Therefore, unlike the other four NAB Main Modules, performance on the Language Module is not meant to have a normal distribution. Descriptions of the tests comprising this module and possible interpretations for low scores are provided in Table 10.4.

MEMORY MODULE TESTS

THE THOROUGH ASSESSMENT of memory typically involves measuring encoding, storage/retention, retrieval, and recognition. Encoding refers to the acquisition of new information. New information might be processed and analyzed superficially by some people. Thus, the initial acquisition of the information is faulty. With storage/retention problems, a person might fail to consolidate the information in memory, or the person might have an abnormal rate of forgetting. A person might have encoded and stored the information, yet have problems retrieving this information from memory. A person with retrieval problems often performs dramatically better on recognition memory tasks.

The NAB Memory tests measure explicit learning and memory in verbal (auditory) and visual modalities. These tests incorporate immediate and delayed free recall tasks, and delayed recognition tasks. The Memory Module consists of four tests: (a) List Learning, (b) Shape Learning, (c) Story Learning, and (d) Daily Living Memory. These tests measure verbal learning and memory for a word list, immediate and delayed recognition memory for shapes, immediate and delayed memory for stories, and memory for everyday information (e.g., medication instructions, name, address, phone number). The *Memory Index* is a composite score for the four learning and memory tests. The Memory Module can be administered in approximately 45 minutes. Descriptions of the tests comprising this module and possible interpretations for low scores are provided in Table 10.4.

SPATIAL MODULE TESTS

PERCEPTUAL AND SPATIAL functioning can be influenced by injuries, diseases, or conditions affecting diverse brain regions, particularly the occipital lobe and the right parietal lobe. The tests in the Spatial Module measure basic and complex integrative abilities in this domain. Several visual-perceptual and spatial neurobehavioral disorders can be assessed using Spatial Module and Language Module tests. Examples of neurobehavioral disorders that might be identified using the NAB are:

- Achromotopsia: Acquired color blindness (Auditory Comprehension test)
- Hemi-Spatial Neglect: This could manifest on numerous tests across several modules
- Visual Agnosia: Impairment in the recognition of objects (object agnosia)
- Constructional Apraxia: Impairment in drawing or assembling

The Spatial Module consists of four tests: (a) Visual Discrimination, (b) Design Construction, (c) Figure Drawing, and (d) Map Reading. The *Spatial Index* score is a composite score for these tests. This module can be administered in approximately 25 minutes. Descriptions of the tests comprising this module and possible interpretations for low scores are provided in Table 10.4.

EXECUTIVE FUNCTIONS MODULE TESTS

THE EXECUTIVE FUNCTIONS are a set of neurocognitive abilities and behaviors that become important in situations involving non-routine thinking and behavior. From a neurocognitive perspective, examples include situations involving flexible problem solving, thinking abstractly, planning, conceptualization, organizing, sequencing, or shifting mental set. There is no consensus on the definition of the executive functions, and there is no consensus on which tests are believed to measure these functions.

The Executive Functions Module consists of four tests: (a) Mazes, (b) Judgment, (c) Categories, and (d) Word Generation. Several neurocognitive abilities, including planning, judgment, conceptualization, cognitive response set, mental flexibility, verbal fluency, and generativity, are measured by these tests. The *Executive Functions Index* is a composite score based on these four tests. This module can be administered in approximately 30 minutes. Descriptions of the tests comprising this module and possible interpretations for low scores are provided in Table 10.4.

STANDARDIZATION SAMPLE

THE NAB STANDARDIZATION sample consists of 1,448 healthy, community-dwelling adults from the United States (men = 775 and women = 673). Rigorous exclusion criteria were used to ensure the sample did not include people with a neurological disease, acquired brain injury, psychiatric illness, treatment/medication, or physical impairment that would negatively impact test performance. Participants for the standardization sample were recruited and tested at five sites across the country, including Rhode Island Hospital, University of Florida Health Sciences Center, Indiana University, University of California at Los Angeles School of Medicine, and the Psychological Assessment Resources (PAR) offices in Lutz, Florida. These sites were chosen to provide representation of the four geographical regions of the country (Northeast, Midwest, West, and South). The normative sample was collected in 2001 and 2002. The entire sample (N = 1,448) was used to create demographically corrected norms, based on age (18–97), sex, and education (≤11, 12, 13–15, and ≥16 years).

A portion of the entire sample (N = 950) was matched to the 2001 U.S. Census statistics with respect to age, sex, education, race/ethnicity (Caucasian, African American, Hispanic, and others), and geographical region. Norms were created for the census-matched group. However, it is recommended that the demographically corrected normative data set be used for routine clinical interpretation (Stern & White, 2003b).

TYPES OF NORMATIVE SCORES

ALL NORMATIVE SCORES can be obtained by using either (a) the NAB Scoring Program (NAB-SP), or (b) the calculations on the record forms and the accompanying normative manuals (White & Stern, 2003a). For ease and accuracy, we strongly recommend the scoring program, which results in detailed and graphic screen-based and printed reports.

An overview of the types of normative scores and interpretive classification ranges is presented in Tables 10.5 to 10.7. Note that all NAB scores are scaled such that higher normative scores indicate better performance. The *Domain and Index scores* are scaled with a mean of 100 and a standard deviation of 15 (M = 100, SD = 15). The *primary test scores* are T-scores (M = 50, SD = 10). In general, only scores with acceptable-to-high reliability or adequate distributional characteristics were selected as primary scores; those with weaker reliability or highly skewed distributions were relegated to secondary or descriptive status. The primary scores are demographically corrected normative scores. They are corrected for age, education, and sex. The age ranges used for the presentation of these normative scores are as follows: 18–29, 30–39, 40–49, 50–59, 60–64, 65–69, 70–74, 75–79, 80–97, and 18–97. The education ranges used for these scores are as follows: ≤11, 12, 13–15, and ≥16 years. Examples of index and primary test scores include the Memory Index = 72 (3rd percentile) and the List Learning List A Immediate Recall, T-Score = 38 (12th percentile), respectively.

The *secondary test scores* are age-corrected percentile ranks. Most secondary scores have skewed score distributions or limited score ranges. These scores do *not* correct for education or sex. An example of a secondary test score is List Learning List A Percent Retention = 50th percentile. The *descriptive scores* represent very basic abilities that are highly skewed in healthy adults at all levels of age and education (e.g., orientation to time and place). Therefore, they are presented as cumulative percentages for the *entire* standardization sample. That is, these scores are not corrected for age, education, or sex. They represent normative scores for all healthy adults.

The NAB classification ranges (Table 10.6) are consistent with those used by Heaton and colleagues for the Expanded Halstead-Reitan

TABLE 10.5 Overview of Normative Scores

Type of score	Normative metric	Demographic correction
Domain and Index (Standard scores)	M = 100; SD = 15	Age, education, & sex
Primary Test Score (T scores)	M = 50; SD = 10	Age, education, & sex
Secondary Test Score	Percentile rank	Age only
Descriptive Score	Cumulative percentage	None. All healthy adults.

TABLE 10.6 NAB Classification Ranges

Clinical interpretation / classification range	Index score range M = 100, SD = 15	T-score range M = 50, SD = 10	Percentile ranks
Very superior	130–155	70–81	98+
Superior	115–129	60–69	84–97
Above average	107–114	55–59	68–82
Average	92–106	45–54	30–66
Below average	85–91	40–44	16–27
Mildly impaired	77–84	35–39	6–14
Mildly-to-moderately impaired	70–76	30–34	2–5
Moderately impaired	62–69	25–29	0.6–1.9
Moderately-to-severely impaired	55–61	20–24	0.13–0.5
Severely impaired	45–54	19	< .12

Note: The NAB scoring program combines above average, superior, and very superior into a single "above average" classification for the individual tests listed on the printout. Clinicians can modify that terminology, as desired, in their clinical reports.

TABLE 10.7 Wechsler Normative Scores and Classification Ranges

Clinical interpretation/ classification range	Scaled scores M = 10, SD = 3	IQs/Index score range M = 100, SD = 15	T-score range M = 50, SD = 10	Percentile ranks
Very superior	16–19	130+	70+	98+
Superior	14–15	120–129	64–69	91–97
High average	13	110–119	57–63	76–90
Average	8–12	90–109	44–56	25–75
Low average	7	80–89	37–43	10–24
Borderline/unusually low	5–6	70–79	30–36	2–9
Extremely low	≤ 4	≤ 69	≤ 29	≤ 1.9

Note: Clinicians might choose to use this classification system out of personal preference or to maintain consistent terminology for all tests in a clinical report.

Neuropsychological Battery (Heaton, Grant, & Matthews, 1991; Heaton, Miller, Taylor, & Grant, 2004). They differ from the traditional Wechsler classification ranges (Table 10.7). The NAB Scoring Program utilizes the classifications presented in Table 10.6. Of course, the choice of classification descriptors is one of personal preference for individual clinicians. To avoid confusion, we find it helpful to use the same classification descriptors for all tests presented in a report. Thus, a clinician might choose one set of descriptors or the other (i.e., Table 10.6 or 10.7, but not both).

NORMING METHOD

Approximately half of the normative sample received each form of the NAB (Form 1, N = 711; Form 2, N = 737). An equipercentile equating method was used to equate the primary scores for the two forms. It is important to note that secondary and descriptive scores are not equated by form. Normative data for these scores are provided separately for each form.

The first step was to compute the cumulative frequency distribution of each primary raw score for each form separately. With these distributions, the percentile rank that corresponds to each possible raw score was determined. The cumulative percentile distributions of raw scores were plotted and inspected visually. The second step was to assign a z score to each derived percentile rank (done separately for each form). The raw score to z score conversion preserved the shape of the distribution of raw scores. The cumulative percentile rank distributions for the z scores were then plotted and inspected visually.

The normative method used to derive the demographically corrected normative data was continuous norming (see Gorsuch, 1983; Zachary & Gorsuch, 1985 for an overview). This method has been used for a number of tests, such as the Wisconsin Card Sorting Test (Heaton, Chelune, Talley, Kay, & Curtiss, 1993), Wisconsin Card Sorting Test—64 Card Version (Kongs, Thompson, Iverson, & Heaton, 2000), and the Canadian Standardization of the Wechsler Adult Intelligence Scale—3rd Edition (The Psychological Corporation, 2001).

Continuous norming was originally used with psychological and neuropsychological measures to correct for ongoing problems in normative samples. For example, Zachary and Gorsuch (1985) discussed problems with the normative sample of the Wechsler Adult Intelligence Scale-Revised (WAIS-R; Wechsler, 1981) that were acknowledged by the test publisher, particularly 'jumps' in intelligence between adjacent age groups and the necessity for post hoc smoothing of the normative data. In contrast, continuous norming uses polynomial regression analyses to estimate the entire sample's means and standard deviations, given an individual's exact placement on one or more demographic variables used to stratify the sample (e.g., age, education, and sex). The calculations are based on the entire normative sample, not subgroups of the normative sample, such as an age cohort. The norms are *presented* for subgroups (e.g., 30–39-year-old men with 12 years of education), but they are *derived* from regression analyses conducted on the entire normative sample.

INTELLIGENCE–NAB INDEX DISCREPANCY SCORES

CLINICIANS AND RESEARCHERS are interested in the psychometric relation between intelligence and neuropsychological test performance, especially intelligence-memory discrepancy scores (e.g., Atkinson, 1991; Bornstein, Chelune, & Prifitera, 1989; Dori & Chelune, 2004; Franzen & Iverson, 2000; Hall & Bornstein, 1991; Hawkins & Tulsky, 2001, 2003, 2004; Nadolne, Adams, Scott, Hoffman, & Tremont, 1997; Oresick & Broder, 1988). With the conorming of the WAIS-III and WMS-III it is now standard practice to interpret intelligence-memory discrepancy scores (The Psychological Corporation, 1997).

The Reynolds Intellectual Screening Test (RIST; Reynolds & Kamphaus, 2003) was administered during the NAB standardization. This allowed us to create RIST-NAB discrepancy scores (Iverson, Brooks, & White, 2006a). These discrepancy scores are conceptually similar to the WAIS-III and WMS-III discrepancy scores.

The RIST is an abbreviated administration of the Reynolds Intellectual Assessment Scales (RIAS; Reynolds & Kamphaus, 2003). It is normed across the life span (i.e., ages 3 through 94). The RIST normative sample (N = 2,438) was recruited from 41 states and stratified to represent the U.S. population based on age, sex, ethnicity, education, and region. The RIST was designed as a brief intellectual screening test. The T-scores for the tests Guess What (which assesses verbal reasoning, vocabulary, language development, and one's general fund of knowledge) and Odd Item Out (which measures nonverbal reasoning, spatial ability, and visual imagery) are summed to produce a composite index score (mean 100, standard deviation of 15).

Uncommon RIST-NAB discrepancy scores are presented in Table 10.8. These results are presented for the entire standardization sample and the sample stratified by level of intelligence. The discrepancy score required for a RIST-Attention Index difference to be considered *unusual* (i.e., occurring in less than 15% of healthy adults) is 21 points for the entire standardization sample. When stratified by level of intelligence, the unusual RIST-Attention discrepancy scores are as follows: low average intelligence = 13, average intelligence = 16, high average intelligence = 24, and superior or very superior intelligence = 33. Unusual discrepancy scores are not presented for those with a RIST IQ score ≤ 79 because of the small sample size (N < 30).

As seen in Table 10.8, healthy adults with high average or superior intelligence are not expected to have comparably high scores across an entire battery of neuropsychological tests. On average, people with high average or superior intellectual abilities have greater discrepancy scores than people with average or low average intellectual abilities.

Similar findings have been reported for the relation between WAIS-III and WMS-III scores. For example, the regression-predicted WMS-III Index scores for a person with a Full Scale IQ of 120 are as follows: Auditory Immediate Index = 112, Visual Immediate Index = 107, Auditory Delayed Index = 111, Visual Delayed Index = 108, and Working Memory Index = 114 (The Psychological Corporation, 2002). Thus, people with superior intelligence are expected to have average to high average memory abilities.

There remains a common belief in the profession that people with high average or superior intelligence should have high average or superior scores across a battery of neuropsychological tests. Dodrill (1997, 1999)

TABLE 10.8 Uncommon RIST-NAB Discrepancy Scores by Level of Intelligence

	Uncommon (<20%)	Unusual (<15%)	Very unusual (<10%)	Rare (<5%)	Very rare (<1%)
Total Sample					
RIST—Attention Index	18–20	21–23	24–29	30–40	41+
RIST—Language Index	17–18	19–21	22–26	27–37	38+
RIST—Memory Index	17–18	19–22	23–26	27–35	36+
RIST—Spatial Index	17–19	20–22	23–27	28–34	35+
RIST—Executive Functions Index	17–19	20–22	23–27	28–36	37+
RIST—Total NAB Index	16–17	18–20	21–24	25–32	33+
RIST 80–89					
RIST—Attention Index	9–12	13–14	15–18	19–22	23+
RIST—Language Index	11	12–13	14–18	19–33	34+
RIST—Memory Index	11–13	14	15–17	18–27	28+
RIST—Spatial Index	11–12	13–15	16–18	19–23	24+
RIST—Executive Functions Index	11–13	14	15–16	17–28	29+
RIST—Total NAB Index	12–12	14–16	17–20	21–25	26+
RIST 90–109					
RIST—Attention Index	13–15	16–18	19–24	25–35	36+
RIST—Language Index	13–14	15–17	18–21	22–29	30+
RIST—Memory Index	12–14	15–17	18–20	21–30	31+
RIST—Spatial Index	13–14	15–17	18–22	23–31	32+
RIST—Executive Functions Index	13–15	16–18	19–22	23–29	30+
RIST—Total NAB Index	13–14	15–16	17–20	21–26	27+

(Continued)

TABLE 10.8   Uncommon RIST-NAB Discrepancy Scores by Level of Intelligence *(Continued)*

	Uncommon (<20%)	Unusual (<15%)	Very unusual (<10%)	Rare (<5%)	Very rare (<1%)
RIST 110–119					
RIST—Attention Index	22–23	24–26	27–31	32–41	42+
RIST—Language Index	19–20	21–23	24–26	27–34	35+
RIST—Memory Index	21–23	24–25	26–29	30–34	35+
RIST—Spatial Index	21–22	23–26	27–30	31–34	35+
RIST—Executive Functions Index	20–21	22–24	25–29	30–36	37+
RIST—Total NAB Index	19–21	22	23–25	26–33	34+
RIST 120+					
RIST—Attention Index	32	33–36	37–44	45–49	50+
RIST—Language Index	33–34	35–36	37–41	42–61	62+
RIST—Memory Index	28–30	31–33	34–37	38–48	49+
RIST—Spatial Index	27–29	30–33	34–36	37–46	47+
RIST—Executive Functions Index	27–29	30–32	33–36	37–48	49+
RIST—Total NAB Index	26–29	–	30–35	36–48	49+

Note: This information was not presented in the *Psychometric and Technical Manual*. Produced by special permission of the Publisher, Psychological Assessment Resources, Inc., 16204 North Florida Avenue, Lutz, Florida 33549, from the standardization data presented in the *Neuropsychological Assessment Battery Psychometric and Technical Manual* by Travis White, PhD and Robert A. Stern, PhD. Copyright 2001, 2003 by PAR, Inc. (White & Stern, 2003b). Further reproduction is prohibited without permission from PAR, Inc. The difference scores were created by subtracting the NAB index score from the RIST score. Uncommon difference scores occur in less than 20% of healthy adults and rare difference scores occur in less than 5% of healthy adults. Sample sizes, presented as ranges due to missing values, are as follows: Total Sample = 1254–1267; 80–89 = 134–135; 90–109 = 670–676; 110–119 = 287–290; ≥ 120 = 137–138. Discrepancy scores for adults with RIST scores less than 80 are not presented due to small sample sizes (RIST ≤ 79 = 26–28).

referred to this belief as a "myth" in clinical neuropsychology. Although it is true that people with high average or superior intelligence score higher on many (but not all) neuropsychological tests (Horton, 1999), as intelligence increases there appears to be a leveling off (asymptote) in the relation between intelligence and many neuropsychological abilities (e.g., Dodrill, 1999). This leveling off creates a greater spread of test scores in people with superior intelligence, for example, than in people with low average intelligence (as illustrated in Table 10.8).

Clinicians are encouraged to administer the RIST with the NAB. The RIST provides a quick estimate of intellectual abilities. If the clinician believes that the person's RIST score has not been significantly influenced by their presenting problem (i.e., it is believed to represent an estimate of premorbid intellectual functioning), then RIST-NAB discrepancy scores can be interpreted. This assumption requires clinical judgment; there is very little direct empirical data to use to inform this judgment.

For example, the RIST has been administered to only a few clinical groups with small sample sizes. According to the test manual, in a sample of 44 patients with traumatic brain injuries, their average RIST score was 94.05 (SD = 10.85). In a sample of 19 patients with strokes/CVAs, their average RIST score was 95.05 (SD = 14.57). In contrast, in a sample of 27 patients with dementia, their average RIST score was 75.48 (SD = 19.98). Thus, one could infer from these limited data that TBI and stroke have modest adverse effects on RIST performance whereas dementia has a pronounced adverse effect. Similar findings have been reported for the WAIS-III. The Processing Speed Index is most affected by acquired brain damage (e.g., Donders, Tulsky, & Zhu, 2001; Fisher, Ledbetter, Cohen, Marmor, & Tulsky, 2000; Hawkins, 1998; Martin, Donders, & Thompson, 2000; The Psychological Corporation, 1997), and the Verbal Comprehension Index appears to be the least affected. The RIST tests are not timed, and there is not a significant processing speed or working memory component to them. Thus, by inference, they are likely less affected by acquired brain damage than tests requiring speed or working memory.

The RIST-NAB discrepancy data presented in Table 10.8 are ready for clinical use. However, these data are best used *descriptively,* not *diagnostically.* Research is needed to determine if RIST-NAB discrepancies differ between specific clinical groups and the healthy adult population. Moreover, additional research is needed to determine the diagnostic validity of specific RIST-NAB discrepancy scores and the incremental validity of these discrepancy scores over interpreting the index scores alone. A sample write-up using the RIST-NAB discrepancy data is illustrated here.

Mr. Smith is a 47-year-old man who suffered a moderate traumatic brain injury when he fell approximately 20–30 feet to the ground (lowest GCS = 11, post-traumatic amnesia for approximately 1 day, depressed skull fracture, and CT scan results revealing subarachnoid hemorrhage, cortical effacement, and midline displacement). On assessment 2 years after the accident, Mr. Smith performed in the high average range (Index = 118, 88th percentile) on an intellectual screening test (RIST). His Total NAB Index, an omnibus measure of neuropsychological functioning, was in the below average range (Index = 85, 16th percentile). His Attention Index was in the moderately impaired range (Index = 69, 2nd percentile), Language Index was in the below average range (Index = 86, 18th percentile), Memory Index was in the average range (Index = 100, 50th percentile), Spatial Index was in the average range (Index = 103, 58th percentile), and his Executive Functions Index was in the below average range (Index = 86, 18th percentile).

Based on Mr. Smith's estimated high average intellectual abilities, the discrepancies between his RIST Index and Memory (-18 points) and Spatial (-15 points) Indexes are *not uncommon* and found in more than 20%

of healthy adults. The difference between his RIST and Language Index scores (-32 points) is *rare* and found in less than 5% of healthy adults. The differences between his RIST Index and his Attention (-49 points), Executive Functions (-32 points), and Total (-33 points) Indexes are *very rare* and found in less than 1% of healthy adults.

NEUROPSYCHOLOGICAL PROFILE ANALYSIS

NEUROPSYCHOLOGISTS DO NOT interpret test scores in isolation. In routine clinical assessment, the practitioner considers individual test results, patterns of test results, and the entire profile as it relates to the patient's history and presenting problem. As a general rule, however, it is not possible for the clinician to know the base rate of low (i.e., impaired) scores in healthy adults across an entire battery of tests. This is because neuropsychologists use flexible neuropsychological test batteries (Rabin, Barr, & Burton, 2005; Sweet & Moberg, 1990; Sweet, Moberg, & Suchy, 2000; Sweet, Moberg, & Westergaard, 1996); the base rates of low scores across these batteries are unknowable unless the same battery is given to a normative sample or a large control sample (e.g., de Rotrou et al., 2005; Palmer, Boone, Lesser, & Wohl, 1998). Unfortunately, it is not possible to calculate mathematically the estimated number of low scores to expect in healthy adults given any particular flexible battery, because there are too many variables to take into account (e.g., diverse normative samples, normal versus nonnormal test distributions, varying degrees of correlation among tests, varying degrees of measurement error among tests, and varying numbers of tests and test scores considered). Even with conormed batteries of tests, such as the Wechsler Adult Intelligence Scale—Third Edition (WAIS-III; Wechsler, 1997a) and the Wechsler Memory Scale—Third Edition (WMS-III; Wechsler, 1997b), or the Delis-Kaplan Executive Function System (DKEFS; Delis, Kaplan, & Kramer, 2001), this information has not been provided in the test manuals or by researchers examining the standardization data.

Therefore, unfortunately, very little is known about how healthy adults perform across an entire battery of tests. If we set our criterion for a deficit at one standard deviation below the mean, we accept a priori that 15% of healthy adults will score in this range on any given test, without actually having an acquired deficit. We accept a priori that the more tests we give the more likely we are to obtain low scores. Although common sense and clinical experience support the psychometric fact that giving more tests increases the probability of obtaining low scores, this issue has been infrequently and inadequately studied. The reason for this is simple: most neuropsychologists, and neuropsychology researchers, use flexible batteries of tests, and these batteries are not co-normed. Therefore, the research is very difficult to accomplish.

Clinicians using the Halstead-Reitan Neuropsychological Battery (HRNB; Reitan & Wolfson, 1985, 1993) have known for many years that healthy adults routinely obtain low scores when given a battery of tests. Traditionally, a Halstead Impairment Index score of 0.3 was considered normal (i.e., 30% of the 7 tests comprising the index could fall in the impaired range; Reitan & Wolfson, 1993). If the General Neuropsychological Deficit Scale (GNDS) norms are used then Halstead Impairment Indexes from 0–0.4 are considered broadly normal (Reitan & Wolfson, 1993).

The manual of normative data for the Expanded Halstead-Reitan Neuropsychological Battery (Heaton et al., 1991) provides more specific information on the base rate of low scores in healthy adults when a fixed battery of tests is administered. Similar to the NAB, these authors defined impairment as a T-score of 39 or less on the Expanded Halstead-Reitan Neuropsychological Battery. Using this definition, 15% of healthy normal subjects would be classified as impaired on any single test. However, when multiple tests are given, the probability of obtaining impaired scores goes up dramatically. For example, in a healthy sample of 455 adults, 90% had one or more impaired scores (the median number of impaired scores was 4). Approximately one-third of the normative subjects (i.e., 32.5%) had 7 or more scores in the impaired classification range, and over half (i.e., 53.3%) had 4 or more impaired scores (see Figure 6, page 37, in Heaton et al., 1991). Heaton and colleagues noted that the "important point to recognize is that some poor test results are to be expected in most normal persons, especially when a large battery of tests is administered" (p. 36). The same analyses, with very similar results, were completed for the Revised Comprehensive Norms for an Expanded Halstead-Reitan Battery based on 25 scores and yielded similar results (see Figure 9, page 73, in Heaton et al., 2004).

Clinicians using flexible batteries with age-based normative data should expect the number of low scores to vary by both education and intelligence. It has been reported repeatedly in the literature that neuropsychological test performance is correlated with education (e.g., Heaton et al., 1991) and with intelligence (e.g., Boone, Lesser, Hill-Gutierrez, Berman, & D'Elia, 1993; Brittain, La Marche, Reeder, Roth, & Boll, 1991; Dodrill, 1999; Kane, Parsons, & Goldstein, 1985; The Psychological Corporation, 2002). People with below average intelligence tend to perform worse on many neuropsychological tests than people with average intelligence (e.g., Dodrill, 1999; Horton, 1999; Reitan, 1985).

Iverson, White, and Brooks (2006b) introduced neuropsychological profile analysis for the NAB. In this section, we illustrate (a) base rates of the number of scores below specific cutoff scores when the five index scores are considered simultaneously, and (b) base rates of the number of scores below specific cutoff scores when the 36 individual test scores are considered simultaneously. These analyses are conducted for the standardization sample between the ages of 18 and 79 years (N = 1,269) and by level of RIST performance.

The base rates of low index scores on the NAB in the standardization sample are presented in Table 10.9. These base rates are presented for the entire sample and then by level of estimated intellectual abilities (i.e., RIST). The categories for estimated intellectual abilities are based on the Wechsler classification system (see Table 10.7), which include low average (RIST = 80–89), average (RIST = 90–109), high average (RIST = 110–119), and superior/very superior (RIST = 120+). Base rates are not presented for persons with intellectual abilities below low average (RIST < 80) because of small sample size.

When the five index scores are considered simultaneously, 37% of healthy adults had one or more scores below 1 SD, 25% had one or more index scores below the 10th percentile, 14% had one or more scores at or below the 5th percentile, and 6% had one or more scores below 2 SDs. Notice that 11% of the sample had three or more index scores that fell below 1 SD from the mean. Analyses based on education-level subgroups (≤11, 12, 13–15, and ≥16 years) revealed results very similar to Table 10.9.

If the total sample is divided into subgroups based on level of intelligence, differential base rates emerge. The base rates of low index scores on the NAB by level of RIST are also presented in Table 10.9. The base rates of low scores decrease systematically as level of intelligence increases. Notice that 82% of adults with RIST scores in the low average range (i.e., 80–89) have at least one low score compared to 12% of adults with RIST in the superior or very superior range (i.e., 120+). Using a cutoff score of 1 SD, 63% of adults with low average RIST scores (i.e., 80–89) have two or more low scores, whereas 3.7% of adults with superior/very superior RIST scores (i.e., 120+) have two or more low index scores.

The base rates of low scores for the Primary Test scores on the NAB for the standardization sample are presented in Table 10.10. These base rates are presented for the entire sample and then by level of estimated intellectual abilities (i.e., RIST). When considering the 36 primary test scores simultaneously, nearly half of the sample (i.e., 44%) had five or more scores below one standard deviation from the mean, and 24% had five or more scores below the 10th percentile. One or more extremely low scores (below 2 SDs) occur in 44% of healthy adults.

Again, if the total sample is divided into subgroups based on level of intelligence (i.e., low average, RIST = 80–89; average, RIST = 90–109;

TABLE 10.9 Base Rates of Low NAB Index Scores by Level of RIST and for the Total Sample

<1 SD	80–89		90–109		110–119		120+		Total sample	
	p	cp	p	cp	p	cp	p	cp	p	cp
5	10.4	10.4	0.7	0.7	–	–	–	–	2.5	2.5
4	17.2	27.6	2.2	3.0	–	–	–	–	3.4	6.0
3	14.2	41.8	4.6	7.6	0.7	0.7	1.5	1.5	4.6	10.6
2	20.9	62.7	9.0	16.6	4.5	5.2	2.2	3.7	8.7	19.3
1	19.4	82.1	22.5	39.1	11.5	16.7	8.0	11.7	17.7	36.9
0	17.9	100	60.9	100	83.3	100	88.3	100	63.1	100
<10th percentile										<10th percentile
5	7.5	7.5	–	–	–	–	–	–	1.3	1.3
4	7.5	14.9	0.9	0.9	–	–	–	–	1.9	3.2
3	15.7	30.6	1.5	2.4	–	–	0.7	0.7	2.9	6.1
2	14.2	44.8	5.8	8.2	1.0	1.0	1.5	2.2	5.5	11.5
1	18.7	63.4	16.7	24.9	8.0	9.1	2.9	5.1	13.3	24.8
0	36.6	100	75.1	100	90.9	100	94.9	100	75.2	100

≤5th percentile											≤5th percentile
5	4.5	4.5	–	–	–	–	–	–	0.6	0.6	5
4	5.2	9.7	0.1	0.1	–	–	–	–	1.1	1.8	4
3	9.0	18.7	0.4	0.6	–	–	–	–	1.8	3.6	3
2	11.9	30.6	3.0	3.6	–	–	0.7	0.7	3.3	6.8	2
1	13.4	44.0	9.9	13.4	1.7	1.7	1.5	2.2	7.6	14.4	1
0	56.0	100	86.6	100	98.3	100	97.8	100	85.6	100	0
<2 SDs											<2 SDs
5	0.7	0.7	–	–	–	–	–	–	0.2	0.2	5
4	2.2	3.0	0.1	0.1	–	–	–	–	0.5	0.6	4
3	0.7	3.7	0.0	0.1	–	–	–	–	0.2	0.9	3
2	5.2	9.0	0.0	0.1	–	–	–	–	1.2	2.1	2
1	10.4	19.4	4.5	4.6	0.3	0.3	0.7	0.7	4.2	6.3	1
0	80.6	100	95.4	100	99.7	100	99.3	100	93.7	100	0

Note: Analyses based on subjects between 18 and 79 years of age (N = 1,269). These results are presented in Iverson, White, and Brooks (2006b). Produced by special permission of the publisher, Psychological Assessment Resources, Inc., 16204 North Florida Avenue, Lutz, Florida 33549, from the standardization data presented in the *Neuropsychological Assessment Battery Psychometric and Technical Manual* by Travis White, PhD and Robert A. Stern, PhD. Copyright 2001, 2003 by PAR, Inc. Further reproduction is prohibited without permission from PAR, Inc. There are slight variations due to rounding.

high average, RIST = 110–119; and superior/very superior, RIST = 120+), differential base rates of low primary test scores emerge. The base rates of low primary test scores on the NAB by level of RIST are presented in Tables 10.11–10.14. The base rates of low scores decrease systematically as level of intelligence increases. Approximately half of the sample

TABLE 10.10 Test Scores in the NAB Standardization Sample: Percentages and Cumulative Percentages of Scores At or Below the Cutoffs

	Cutoff scores								
	< 1 SD		< 10th%		≤ 5th%		< 2 SD		
Number of scores	%	cp	%	cp	%	cp	%	cp	Number of scores
25+	0.6	0.6	0.1	0.1	–	–	–	–	25+
25	0.4	1.0	0.1	0.2	–	–	–	–	25
24	0.2	1.1	0.1	0.2	0.1	0.1	–	–	24
23	0.3	1.4	0.1	0.3	0.1	0.2	–	–	23
22	0.2	1.6	0.4	0.7	0.0	0.2	–	–	22
21	0.3	1.9	0.2	1.0	0.1	0.2	–	–	21
20	0.3	2.2	0.0	1.0	0.2	0.5	–	–	20
19	0.6	2.9	0.2	1.1	0.2	0.6	0.1	0.1	19
18	0.8	3.7	0.4	1.5	0.2	0.8	0.0	0.1	18
17	0.9	4.6	0.3	1.8	0.2	1.0	0.0	0.1	17
16	0.6	5.1	0.4	2.2	0.2	1.2	0.0	0.1	16
15	1.1	6.3	0.3	2.6	0.1	1.3	0.1	0.2	15
14	1.0	7.3	0.7	3.3	0.6	1.8	0.2	0.3	14
13	2.0	9.3	0.6	3.9	0.5	2.3	0.2	0.5	13
12	1.4	10.7	1.1	5.1	0.6	2.9	0.1	0.6	12
11	2.8	13.6	1.5	6.6	0.6	3.5	0.2	0.7	11
10	1.9	15.5	1.3	7.9	1.0	4.6	0.4	1.1	10
9	3.2	18.7	1.6	9.5	1.3	5.9	0.5	1.6	9
8	3.2	21.9	1.9	11.4	1.4	7.2	0.2	1.8	8
7	5.6	27.5	3.2	14.6	1.8	9.0	1.0	2.7	7
6	6.9	34.3	4.1	18.7	3.0	12.0	1.0	3.7	6
5	9.2	43.6	4.9	23.6	3.5	15.6	1.5	5.2	5
4	11.0	54.6	9.0	32.6	5.9	21.4	2.6	7.8	4
3	11.2	65.8	11.3	43.9	9.9	31.3	4.4	12.2	3
2	12.6	78.4	16.4	60.3	17.2	48.5	9.6	21.8	2
1	13.1	91.5	19.9	80.2	21.7	70.2	22.5	44.3	1
0	8.5	100	19.8	100	29.8	100	55.7	100	0

Note: Analyses based on adults between 18 and 79 years of age (N = 1,269). These are original analyses for this chapter. Produced by special permission of the publisher, Psychological Assessment Resources, Inc., 16204 North Florida Avenue, Lutz, Florida 33549, from the standardization data presented in the *Neuropsychological Assessment Battery Psychometric and Technical Manual* by Travis White, PhD and Robert A. Stern, PhD. Copyright 2001, 2003 by PAR, Inc. Further reproduction is prohibited without permission from PAR, Inc. There are 36 primary test scores that yield T-scores that were considered for these analyses. There are slight variations due to rounding.

(i.e., 52%) with RIST scores in the *low average* range (i.e., 80–89) had 10 or more scores below one standard deviation from the mean, whereas only 2.5% of adults with *high average* RIST scores (i.e., 110–119) had 10 or more low scores (see Table 10.11). Using a cutoff score below the 10th percentile (see Table 10.12), 51% of adults with low average RIST scores (i.e., 80–89) had seven or more low scores, 46.5% of adults with average RIST scores (i.e., 90–109) had three or more low scores, and 33–45% of adults with high average or superior RIST scores had two or more low scores. As seen in Table 10.14, most adults (i.e., 71%) with low average RIST scores (i.e., 80–89) have one or more test scores below two standard deviations from the mean (< 30T). Having two or more extremely low scores is relatively uncommon in adults with average or greater RIST scores.

Tables 10.11–10.14 illustrate psychometrically what practitioners should already know clinically, that (a) the more tests that are administered the more likely a person is to obtain low scores, (b) setting a cutoff score for *impairment* at one standard deviation below the mean across a battery of tests will result in many low scores in healthy adults, and (c) the number of low scores across a battery of neuropsychological tests varies with level of intelligence.

From a clinical perspective, the base rate tables presented in this chapter (Tables 10.9–10.14) are ready for routine use. They can be added as one step in the sequential interpretation of the NAB. A sample write-up using the neuropsychological profile analysis is provided here.

> Mr. Smith is a 47-year-old man who suffered a moderate traumatic brain injury when he fell approximately 20–30 feet to the ground (lowest GCS = 11, post-traumatic amnesia for approximately 1 day, depressed skull fracture, and CT scan results revealing subarachnoid hemorrhage, cortical effacement, and midline displacement). On assessment 2 years after the accident, Mr. Smith performed in the high average range (88th percentile; SS = 118) on an intellectual screening test (RIST). His Total NAB Index, an omnibus measure of neuropsychological functioning, was in the below average range (16th percentile). His Attention Index was in the moderately impaired range (2nd percentile), Language Index was in the below average range (18th percentile), Memory Index was in the average range (50th percentile), Spatial Index was in the average range (58th percentile), and his Executive Functions Index was in the below average range (18th percentile). His Attention Index score was more than two standard deviations below average.
>
> Having one or more index scores more than two standard deviations below the mean occurs in less than 1% of healthy adults with high average intellectual abilities. When considering the 36 primary test scores from the NAB simultaneously, Mr. Smith obtained 9 scores below the 16th percentile. This many low scores occurs in less than 5% of healthy

TABLE 10.11 Base Rate of Low NAB Test Scores (< 1 SD) by Level of RIST

Number of scores	80–89 %	80–89 cp	90–109 %	90–109 cp	110–119 %	110–119 cp	120+ %	120+ cp	Number of scores
26+	3.0	3.0	–	–	–	–	–	–	26+
25	2.2	5.2	0.2	0.2	–	–	–	–	25
24	0.7	6.0	0.0	0.2	–	–	–	–	24
23	0.0	6.0	0.2	0.3	–	–	–	–	23
22	0.7	6.7	0.0	0.3	–	–	–	–	22
21	1.5	8.2	0.0	0.3	–	–	–	–	21
20	2.2	10.4	0.0	0.3	–	–	–	–	20
19	3.0	13.4	0.2	0.5	–	–	–	–	19
18	3.0	16.4	0.8	1.2	–	–	–	–	18
17	3.7	20.1	0.9	2.1	–	–	–	–	17
16	3.0	23.1	0.5	2.6	–	–	–	–	16
15	3.7	26.9	0.9	3.5	0.4	0.4	–	–	15
14	4.5	31.3	0.8	4.2	0.0	0.0	0.7	0.7	14
13	6.7	38.1	1.7	5.9	0.4	0.7	0.0	0.0	13
12	3.7	41.8	1.7	7.5	0.7	1.4	0.0	0.0	12
11	6.7	48.5	3.0	10.5	0.7	2.1	0.7	1.5	11
10	3.7	52.2	2.3	12.8	0.4	2.5	2.2	3.6	10
9	5.2	57.5	3.8	16.5	2.1	4.6	1.5	5.1	9
8	6.0	63.4	3.0	19.5	2.8	7.4	2.2	7.3	8
7	6.7	70.1	7.4	26.9	3.5	11.0	1.5	8.8	7
6	1.5	71.6	9.5	36.3	5.7	16.7	3.6	12.4	6
5	6.7	78.4	11.0	47.3	8.2	24.8	7.3	19.7	5
4	10.4	88.8	11.1	58.4	14.2	39.0	5.8	25.5	4
3	4.5	93.3	11.6	70.0	13.5	52.5	13.9	39.4	3
2	3.0	96.3	13.1	83.0	13.5	66.0	20.4	59.9	2
1	3.0	99.3	11.0	94.0	19.5	85.5	22.6	82.5	1
0	0.7	100	6.0	100	14.5	100	17.5	100	0

Note: Analyses based on adults between 18 and 79 years of age (N =1,269). These are original analyses for this chapter. Produced by special permission of the publisher, Psychological Assessment Resources, Inc., 16204 North Florida Avenue, Lutz, Florida 33549, from the standardization data presented in the *Neuropsychological Assessment Battery Psychometric and Technical Manual* by Travis White, PhD and Robert A. Stern, PhD. Copyright 2001, 2003 by PAR, Inc. Further reproduction is prohibited without permission from PAR, Inc. There are slight variations due to rounding.

adults with high average intelligence. He had 4 scores below two standard deviations from the mean, which occurs in less than 1% of healthy adults with high average intelligence.

RELIABILITY AND VALIDITY

THE RELIABILITY AND validity of the NAB is summarized, in detail, in the *Psychometric and Technical Manual* (White & Stern, 2003b). Dozens of tables and hundreds of correlations are provided.

TABLE 10.12 Base Rate of Low NAB Test Scores (<10th Percentile) by Level of RIST

Number of scores	80–89		90–109		110–119		120+		Number of scores
	%	cp	%	cp	%	cp	%	cp	
21+	3.7	3.7	0.2	0.2	–	–	–	–	21+
20	0.0	3.7	0.0	0.2	–	–	–	–	20
19	0.7	4.5	0.2	0.3	–	–	–	–	19
18	2.2	6.7	0.0	0.3	–	–	–	–	18
17	1.5	8.2	0.2	0.5	–	–	–	–	17
16	0.7	9.0	0.3	0.8	–	–	–	–	16
15	2.2	11.2	0.0	0.8	–	–	–	–	15
14	2.2	13.4	0.3	1.1	–	–	–	–	14
13	2.2	15.7	0.6	1.7	–	–	–	–	13
12	5.2	20.9	0.8	2.4	–	–	0.7	0.7	12
11	6.0	26.9	1.4	3.8	–	–	0.0	0.7	11
10	3.7	30.6	1.2	5.0	–	–	0.0	0.7	10
9	6.7	37.3	1.4	6.3	0.4	0.4	0.0	0.7	9
8	6.0	43.3	1.8	8.1	0.4	0.7	1.5	2.2	8
7	7.5	50.7	3.6	11.7	1.8	2.5	0.7	2.9	7
6	6.0	56.7	5.1	16.8	2.1	4.6	2.2	5.1	6
5	4.5	61.2	6.2	23.0	4.3	8.9	0.7	5.8	5
4	11.9	73.1	10.8	33.8	6.7	15.6	2.9	8.8	4
3	8.2	81.3	12.8	46.5	13.1	28.7	5.1	13.9	3
2	7.5	88.8	18.3	64.9	16.7	45.4	19.0	32.8	2
1	5.2	94.0	18.3	83.2	25.5	70.9	34.3	67.2	1
0	6.0	100	16.8	100	29.1	100	32.8	100	0

Note: Analyses based on adults between 18 and 79 years of age (N = 1,269). These are original analyses for this chapter. Produced by special permission of the Publisher, Psychological Assessment Resources, Inc., 16204 North Florida Avenue, Lutz, Florida 33549, from the standardization data presented in the *Neuropsychological Assessment Battery Psychometric and Technical Manual* by Travis White, PhD and Robert A. Stern, PhD. Copyright 2001, 2003 by PAR, Inc. Further reproduction is prohibited without permission from PAR, Inc. There are slight variations due to rounding.

TABLE 10.13 Base Rate of Low NAB Test Scores (≤ 5th Percentile) by Level of RIST

Number of scores	80–89		90–109		110–119		120+		Number of scores
	%	cp	%	cp	%	cp	%	cp	
21+	1.5	1.5	—	—	—	—	—	—	21+
20	0.7	2.2	—	—	—	—	—	—	20
19	0.0	2.2	—	—	—	—	—	—	19
18	0.7	3.0	—	—	—	—	—	—	18
17	1.5	4.5	—	—	—	—	—	—	17
16	0.7	5.2	0.2	0.2	—	—	—	—	16
15	0.0	5.2	0.2	0.3	—	—	—	—	15
14	1.5	6.7	0.3	0.6	—	—	—	—	14
13	1.5	8.2	0.2	0.8	—	—	—	—	13
12	3.0	11.2	0.5	1.2	—	—	—	—	12
11	4.5	15.7	0.0	1.2	—	—	—	—	11
10	3.0	18.7	1.1	2.3	—	—	—	—	10
9	5.2	23.9	0.8	3.0	—	—	0.7	0.7	9
8	4.5	28.4	1.5	4.5	—	—	0.0	0.7	8
7	6.7	35.1	1.5	6.0	0.7	0.7	0.0	0.7	7
6	6.0	41.0	3.2	9.2	1.4	2.1	2.2	2.9	6
5	8.2	49.3	4.2	13.4	1.4	3.5	0.7	3.6	5
4	8.2	57.5	7.4	20.7	4.3	7.8	0.0	3.6	4
3	14.2	71.6	10.2	30.9	10.3	18.1	5.1	8.8	3
2	11.2	82.8	20.4	51.4	16.7	34.8	10.2	19.0	2
1	6.7	89.6	21.9	73.3	23.4	58.2	36.5	55.5	1
0	10.4	100	26.7	100	41.8	100	44.5	100	0

Note: Analyses based on adults between 18 and 79 years of age (N =1,269). These are original analyses for this chapter. Produced by special permission of the Publisher, Psychological Assessment Resources, Inc., 16204 North Florida Avenue, Lutz, Florida 33549, from the standardization data presented in the *Neuropsychological Assessment Battery Psychometric and Technical Manual* by Travis White, PhD and Robert A. Stern, PhD. Copyright 2001, 2003 by PAR, Inc. Further reproduction is prohibited without permission from PAR, Inc. There are slight variations due to rounding.

TABLE 10.14 Base Rate of Low NAB Test Scores (< 2 SDs) by Level of RIST

Number of scores	80–89		90–109		110–119		120+		Number of scores
	%	cp	%	cp	%	cp	%	cp	
13+	1.5	1.5	–	–	–	–	–	–	13+
12	0.7	2.2	–	–	–	–	–	–	12
11	0.7	3.0	–	–	–	–	–	–	11
10	1.5	4.5	0.2	0.2	–	–	–	–	10
9	0.7	5.2	0.3	0.5	–	–	–	–	9
8	0.0	5.2	0.0	0.0	–	–	–	–	8
7	5.2	10.4	0.6	1.1	–	–	–	–	7
6	3.7	14.2	0.8	1.8	–	–	–	–	6
5	6.0	20.1	1.1	2.9	–	–	0.7	0.7	5
4	5.2	25.4	3.0	5.9	0.4	0.4	0.7	1.5	4
3	10.4	35.8	4.8	10.7	1.4	1.8	2.2	3.6	3
2	14.9	50.7	10.4	21.0	9.6	11.3	2.9	6.6	2
1	20.1	70.9	25.4	46.4	19.1	30.5	19.7	26.3	1
0	29.1	100	53.6	100	69.5	100	73.7	100	0

Note: Analyses based on adults between 18 and 79 years of age (N = 1,269). These are original analyses for this chapter. Produced by special permission of the Publisher, Psychological Assessment Resources, Inc., 16204 North Florida Avenue, Lutz, Florida 33549, from the standardization data presented in the *Neuropsychological Assessment Battery Psychometric and Technical Manual* by Travis White, PhD and Robert A. Stern, PhD. Copyright 2001, 2003 by PAR, Inc. Further reproduction is prohibited without permission from PAR, Inc. There are slight variations due to rounding.

The purpose of this section is to summarize some of that information and to present new information.

INTERNAL CONSISTENCY RELIABILITY

INTERNAL CONSISTENCY RELIABILITY refers to the consistency of results across items within a test. For some of the primary Screening Module tests, internal consistency was examined using Cronbach's alpha. However, internal consistency reliability cannot be determined for certain types of neuropsychological tests. For the NAB, this is because of (a) use of unique item format presentations, (b) interitem dependency issues that would artificially inflate the reliability estimate, and (c) the use of speed of performance formats for several measures.

Alpha coefficients were calculated for 9 tests on the screening module and 15 tests on the entire battery. In addition, the alpha coefficients were averaged for all age groups. White and Stern (2003b) provide further breakdown of the alpha coefficients across four age groups (18–34, 35–49, 50–69, and 70–97).

For the Screening Module, the average alpha coefficients, for Form 1 and 2 combined, for the entire standardization sample were as follows: Screening Digits Forward ($r = .78$), Screening Digits Backward ($r = .79$), Screening Auditory Comprehension ($r = .48$), Screening Naming ($r = .36$), Screening Story Learning Immediate Recall ($r = .69$), Screening Story Learning Delayed Recall ($r = .72$), Screening Visual Discrimination ($r = .24$), Screening Design Construction ($r = .31$), and Screening Mazes ($r = .55$).

For the Full NAB tests, the average alpha coefficients, for Form 1 and 2 combined, for the entire standardization sample were as follows: Digits Forward ($r = .78$), Digits Backwards ($r = .79$), Oral Production ($r = .84$), Auditory Comprehension ($r = .48$), Naming ($r = .76$), Bill Payment ($r = .69$), Shape Learning Immediate Recognition ($r = .69$), Shape Learning Delayed Recognition ($r = .47$), Story Learning Phrase Unit Immediate Recall ($r = .86$), Story Learning Phrase Unit Delayed Recall ($r = .86$), Visual Discrimination ($r = .67$), Design Construction ($r = .67$), Map Reading ($r = .65$), Mazes ($r = .77$), and Judgment ($r = .45$).

TEST–RETEST RELIABILITY

TEST–RETEST RELIABILITY REFERS to the consistency of scores on a measure from one time to another. Typically, examination of the retest reliability for measures consists of a series of correlations between scores at time 1 and at time 2 (see White & Stern, 2003b). However, it is often difficult for clinicians to use correlations in everyday practice when determining how performance during a second evaluation compares to the initial evaluation. Several other analyses can assist clinicians with understanding neuropsychological performance over time. It is important to understand whether there are practice effects on retest, which can be examined through paired sample T-tests and effect sizes. Another type of retest analysis, designed to assist clinicians when making decisions regarding consistency of performance on retest, involves examining how many people obtain scores at retest that remain within a specified score range or within the same classification (i.e., clinical retest reliability). To examine clinical retest reliability, a sample of healthy adults (N = 95) between 18 and 85 years of age (mean age = 50.5, SD = 17.6) was administered the NAB on two separate occasions (mean time = 193.1 days, SD = 20.3 days). This 6-month test–retest interval is uncommon for neuropsychological tests; most test authors and developers use a test–retest interval ranging from 2 to 12 weeks.

Test–retest reliability for the Screening Domain scores is presented in Table 10.15. On the six Screening Module Domain and Index scores, the 6-month uncorrected retest correlations for the sample were: Screening Attention Domain (r = .73), Screening Language Domain (r = .69), Screening Memory Domain (r = .50), Screening Spatial Domain (r = .56), Screening Executive Functions Domain (r = .67), and Total Screening Index (r = .75). When examining the mean Screening Domain scores over the two administrations, only the Screening Memory Domain (t (94) = 4.37, p < .001, Effect size, d = .45) and Total Screening Index (t (94) = 3.09, p = .003, d = .22) had significant practice effects. When considering the number of Screening Domain scores at retest that remained within 1/2 SD or within the same classification as the initial performance, the percentages ranged from 58.9% for Screening Memory Domain to 83.2% for Screening Language Domain. The percentage of people who remained within 1 SD or within the same classification ranged from 74.7% on the Screening Memory Domain to 89.5% on the Screening Attention Domain.

Test–retest reliabilities for the 16 Screening Module primary scores are presented in Table 10.16. The 6-month uncorrected retest correlations for the sample were significant at the p = .001 for all Screening Module test scores, with the exception of Screening Shape Learning Immediate Recognition and Screening Visual Discrimination. When examining the mean Screening Module primary scores over the two administrations, several tests had significant practice effects based on the paired samples T-tests. The effect sizes for these practice effects ranged from small (d = .17) to medium (d = .45). When considering the number of scores at retest that remained within 1/2 SD or within the same classification as the initial performance, the percentages ranged from 40.0% for Screening Shape Learning Immediate Recognition to 92.6% for Screening Auditory Comprehension. The percentage of people

TABLE 10.15 Test-Retest Reliability of the NAB Screening Module Scores (Form 1 and Form 2 Combined)

Score	Mean (SD) time 1	Mean (SD) time 2	Correlation (p)[1]	t test (p)[2]	Effect size	±7 points OR same class[3]	±15 points OR same class[3]	% ≤ -1 SD	% ≥ 1 SD
Screening Attention Domain	103.1 (16.1)	102.2 (15.7)	.73 (<.001)	0.76 (.45)	0.06	76.8	89.5	7.4	7.4
Screening Language Domain	96.6 (15.5)	96.9 (15.2)	.69 (<.001)	0.24 (.81)	0.02	83.2	85.3	5.3	9.5
Screening Memory Domain	97.3 (14.2)	103.6 (13.8)	.50 (<.001)	4.37 (<.001)	0.45	58.9	74.7	6.3	23.2
Screening Spatial Domain	99.7 (15.5)	102.4 (14.8)	.56 (<.001)	1.90 (.061)	0.18	61.1	82.1	6.3	17.9
Screening Executive Domain	97.8 (17.2)	100.3 (15.7)	.67 (<.001)	1.82 (.072)	0.15	66.3	82.1	7.4	11.6
Total Screening Index	98.4 (15.2)	101.8 (15.5)	.75 (<.001)	3.09 (.003)	0.22	69.5	85.3	2.1	13.7

Note: N = 95. Participants ranged in age from 20 to 87 years, with the mean age = 50.5 (SD = 17.6).
[1] Uncorrected Pearson correlation (p value). [2] Values represent a paired-samples t test with df = 94 (p value). [3] Classification ranges were set at "Moderate–Severe Impairment" (Index <70); "Mild Impairment" (Index = 70–84); "Below Average–Average" (Index = 85–106); and "Above Average–Superior" (Index = 107+).

who remained within 1 SD or within the same classification ranged from 65.3% for Screening Shape Learning Immediate Recognition to 92.6% for Screening Auditory Comprehension.

Test–retest reliabilities for the NAB Index scores are presented in Table 10.17. On the six NAB Index scores, the 6-month uncorrected retest correlations for the sample were: Attention Index (r = .85), Language Index (r = .55), Memory Index (r = .50), Spatial Index (r = .70), Executive Functions Index (r = .67), and Total NAB Index (r = .81). When examining the mean Index scores over the two administrations, the Attention (t (94) = 5.71, p < .001), Language (t (94) = 2.69, p = .008), Memory (t (94) = 4.81, p < .001), and Total NAB Index (t (94) = 3.10, p = .003) had significant practice effects. However, the effect sizes were very small (d = .14) to medium (d = .40) for these practice effects. Performance on the Spatial Index decreased significantly over the 6-month interval (t (94) = 3.42, p < .001), although the effect size was small (d = .28). When considering the number of index scores at retest that remained within 1/2 SD or within the same classification as the initial performance, the percentages ranged from 66.3% for the Language Index to 79.3% for the Total NAB Index. The percentage of people who remained within 1 SD or within the same classification ranged from 77.7% on the Spatial Index to 94.7% on the Attention Index.

Test–retest reliabilities for the 36 NAB primary scores are presented in Table 10.18. The 6-month uncorrected retest correlations for the sample were significant at the p < .01 for all NAB scores, with the exception of Oral Production and Figure Drawing Copy. Several tests had significant practice effects based on the paired samples t tests, with practice effects ranging from small (d = .17) to medium (d = .50). Performance on the Figure Drawing Copy Test decreased significantly over time (t (94) = 6.39, p < .001, d = .88). When considering the number of scores at retest that remained within 1/2 SD or within the same classification as the initial performance, the percentages ranged from 36.2% for Figure Drawing Copy to 82.1% for Numbers and Letters Part A Efficiency. The percentage of people who remained within 1 SD or within the same classification ranged from 53.2% for Figure Drawing Copy to 98.9% for Numbers and Letters Part A Efficiency.

The clinical retest reliability information provided in Tables 10.15–10.18 allows clinicians to easily determine (1) which indexes and tests have significant practice effects on retest and (2) how often scores remain within a specific range (i.e., 1/2 or 1 SD) or within the same classification. Obviously, this information goes beyond the retest correlations supplied in most test manuals. The goal of presenting the clinical retest reliability is to supplement the *NAB Psychometric and Technical Manual* (White & Stern, 2003b) and make this information easier to understand and use in everyday clinical practice. For example,

TABLE 10.16   Test–Retest Reliability of the 16 NAB Screening Module Primary T-Scores (Form 1 and Form 2 Combined)

Screening module test	Mean (SD) time 1	Mean (SD) time 2	Correlation (p)[1]	t test (p)[2]	Effect size	±5 points OR same class[3]	±10 points OR same class[3]	% ≤ -1 SD	% ≥ 1 SD
Screening Attention Domain									
Screening Digits Forward	50.0 (11.1)	50.2 (10.5)	.71 (<.001)	0.16 (.87)	0.02	76.8	82.1	12.6	10.5
Screening Digits Backward	49.7 (10.5)	51.4 (10.1)	.69 (<.001)	2.06 (.04)	0.17	66.3	82.1	10.5	15.8
Screening Numbers & Letters Part A Speed	52.8 (11.6)	49.7 (11.8)	.71 (<.001)	3.33 (.001)	0.26	78.9	89.5	7.4	1.1
Screening Numbers & Letters Part A Errors	49.3 (10.6)	53.2 (6.7)	.34 (.001)	3.70 (<.001)	0.45	81.1	81.1	2.1	12.6
Screening Numbers & Letters Part A Efficiency	52.7 (11.8)	50.4 (11.7)	.74 (<.001)	2.64 (.01)	0.20	82.1	89.5	3.2	1.1
Screening Numbers & Letters Part B Efficiency	53.2 (11.8)	52.0 (11.2)	.59 (<.001)	1.10 (.27)	0.10	74.7	81.1	8.4	5.3
Screening Language Domain									
Screening Auditory Comprehension	48.6 (10.8)	48.4 (11.4)	.71 (<.001)	0.31 (.75)	0.02	92.6	92.6	4.2	3.2

Screening Naming	49.3 (10.0)	49.9 (9.1)	.47 (<.001)	0.65 (.52)	0.06	85.3	86.3	4.2	7.4
Screening Memory Domain									
Screening Shape Learning Immediate Recognition	48.7 (10.8)	52.1 (9.9)	.12 (.26)	2.41 (.02)	0.33	40.0	65.3	11.6	21.1
Screening Shape Learning Delayed Recognition	50.3 (9.5)	51.6 (9.5)	.33 (.001)	1.13 (.26)	0.14	54.7	75.8	7.4	11.6
Screening Story Learning Immediate Recall	48.2 (10.1)	51.6 (8.8)	.45 (<.001)	3.27 (.002)	0.36	53.7	73.7	3.2	11.6
Screening Story Learning Delayed Recall	48.1 (9.8)	51.9 (9.9)	.43 (<.001)	3.54 (.001)	0.39	56.8	74.7	4.2	10.5
Screening Spatial Domain									
Screening Visual Discrimination	50.3 (10.3)	50.8 (9.1)	.15 (.14)	0.40 (.69)	0.05	56.8	57.9	10.5	8.4
Screening Design Construction	49.3 (10.3)	51.8 (10.2)	.61 (<.001)	2.65 (.009)	0.24	65.3	81.1	1.1	9.5

(Continued)

TABLE 10.16 Test–Retest Reliability of the 16 NAB Screening Module Primary T-Scores (Form 1 and Form 2 Combined) *(Continued)*

Screening module test	Mean (SD) time 1	Mean (SD) time 2	Correlation (p)[1]	t test (p)[2]	Effect size	±5 points OR same class[3]	±10 points OR same class[3]	% ≤ -1 SD	% ≥ 1 SD
Screening Executive Functions Domain									
Screening Mazes	49.5 (11.7)	50.1 (10.4)	.69 (<.001)	0.60 (.55)	0.05	63.2	82.1	3.2	6.3
Screening Word Generation	48.0 (10.5)	50.1 (10.7)	.66 (<.001)	2.37 (.02)	0.20	68.4	80.0	2.1	4.2

Note: N = 95. Participants ranged in age from 20 to 87 years, with the mean age = 50.5 (SD = 17.6).
[1]Uncorrected Pearson correlation (p value). [2]Values represent a paired-samples T-test with df = 94 (p value). [3]Classification ranges were set at "Moderate–Severe Impairment" (T < 30); "Mild Impairment" (T = 30–39); "Below Average–Average" (T = 40–54); and "Above Average–Superior" (T = 55+).

320

TABLE 10.17 Test–Retest Reliability of the NAB Index Scores (Form 1 and Form 2 Combined)

NAB Index	Mean (SD) time 1	Mean (SD) time 2	Correlation (p)[1]	t test (p)[2]	Effect Size	± 7 points OR same class[3]	± 15 points OR same class[3]	% ≤ -1 SD	% ≥ 1 SD
Attention	98.1 (15.5)	102.8 (14.2)	.85 (<.001)	5.71 (<.001)	0.32	78.9	94.7	1.1	6.3
Language	94.3 (13.6)	98.0 (13.9)	.55 (<.001)	2.69 (.008)	0.27	66.3	83.2	4.2	13.7
Memory	98.8 (13.8)	104.4 (14.2)	.67 (<.001)	4.81 (<.001)	0.40	69.5	85.3	2.1	14.7
Spatial	99.0 (15.8)	94.6 (16.1)	.70 (<.001)	3.42 (<.001)	0.28	66.0	77.7	21.3	4.3
Executive Functions	97.1 (15.0)	99.2 (16.1)	.67 (<.001)	1.60 (.112)	0.14	67.7	82.8	6.5	15.1
Total	96.8 (14.4)	99.7 (15.0)	.81 (<.001)	3.10 (.003)	0.20	79.3	90.2	2.2	7.6

Note: N = 95. Participants ranged in age from 20 to 87 years, with the mean age = 50.5 (SD = 17.6).
[1]Uncorrected Pearson correlation (p value). [2]Values represent a paired-samples T-test with df = 94 (p value). [3]Classification ranges were set at "Moderate–Severe Impairment" (Index <70); "Mild Impairment" (Index =70–84); "Below Average–Average" (Index = 85–106); and "Above Average–Superior" (Index =107+).

clinicians can quickly look at Table 10.17 and know that approximately 80% of Attention Index scores remain within 1/2 SD or within the same classification at retest. As seen in Table 10.18, there is a very small practice effect for Digits Backward, and 66% of retest scores fall within 1/2 SD or in the same classification as initial scores.

The final column of Table 10.18 illustrates the tests that are most likely to have a pronounced practice effect in healthy adults retested at 6 months. Twenty percent or more improved by at least one SD on the following tests: Dots, Numbers and Letters Part A Errors, Driving Scenes, Oral Production, List Learning List A Immediate Recall, Shape Learning Immediate Recognition and Delayed Recognition, Story Learning Delayed Recall, Daily Living Memory Immediate Recall, and Design Construction. As seen in the second to last column in Table 10.18, large declines in performance across a 6-month retest interval are uncommon for most tests. This information facilitates interpretation of deterioration in test scores.

CONTENT VALIDITY

THE INITIAL THEORETICAL rationale for selection of the NAB tests came from existing knowledge about the various cognitive domains that are generally assessed in a neuropsychological evaluation. Further guidance for the content of the NAB tests came from the survey results (N = 888) from members of the International Neuropsychological Society (INS), the National Academy of Neuropsychology (NAN), and Division 40 of the American Psychological Association (APA), which indicated that respondents preferred that a new battery include measures of attention/working memory, language, learning/memory, perceptual/spatial, and executive functions/problem solving. Respondents preferred to maintain using already established measures of sensori-motor abilities and personality, emotional, and adaptive functioning, as well as measures of effort. After the authors created the initial tests and item pools, the Advisory Council, which consisted of distinguished neuropsychologists from around North America, used the theoretical rationale and respondent information contained in the surveys to rate the tests and items to determine whether they assessed the desired functions.

CONSTRUCT VALIDITY

CONSTRUCT VALIDITY REFERS to the examination of how well a test is measuring what we believe it should be measuring. Construct validity of the NAB was examined using (a) intercorrelations, (b) factor analyses, and (c) the relationship between the Screening Module

TABLE 10.18 Test–Retest Reliability of the 36 NAB Primary T-Scores (Form 1 and Form 2 Combined)

NAB test	Mean (SD) time 1	Mean (SD) time 2	Correlation (p)[1]	t test (p)[2]	Effect size	± 5 points OR same class[3]	± 10 points OR same class[3]	% ≤ -1 SD	% ≥ 1 SD
Attention Module									
Digits Forward	50.0 (11.1)	50.2 (10.5)	.71 (<.001)	0.16 (.87)	0.02	76.8	82.1	12.6	10.5
Digits Backward	49.7 (10.5)	51.4 (10.1)	.69 (<.001)	2.06 (.04)	0.17	66.3	82.1	10.5	15.8
Dots	48.3 (10.7)	51.2 (9.9)	.47 (<.001)	2.62 (.01)	0.28	52.6	72.6	11.6	24.2
Numbers & Letters Part A Speed	51.1 (11.2)	51.2 (11.4)	.89 (<.001)	0.23 (.82)	0.01	81.1	97.9	2.1	2.1
Numbers & Letters Part A Errors	50.7 (10.7)	52.1 (9.7)	.59 (<.001)	1.44 (.15)	0.14	56.8	71.6	14.7	21.1
Numbers & Letters Part A Efficiency	51.1 (10.8)	51.2 (11.5)	.88 (<.001)	0.22 (.83)	0.01	82.1	98.9	3.2	2.1
Numbers & Letters Part B Efficiency	49.6 (9.8)	51.7 (10.0)	.54 (<.001)	2.16 (.03)	0.21	63.2	78.9	10.5	14.7
Numbers & Letters Part C Efficiency	49.1 (11.1)	52.9 (10.3)	.60 (<.001)	3.82 (<.001)	0.36	70.5	83.2	5.3	16.8
Numbers & Letters Part D Efficiency	50.3 (11.1)	52.1 (10.3)	.73 (<.001)	2.25 (.03)	0.17	72.6	89.5	7.4	17.9
Numbers & Letters Part D Disruption	50.9 (10.2)	52.5 (9.7)	.45 (<.001)	1.49 (.14)	0.16	67.4	76.8	12.6	17.9
Driving Scenes	45.9 (10.1)	49.1 (8.9)	.65 (<.001)	3.84 (<.001)	0.34	58.9	82.1	5.3	22.1

(Continued)

TABLE 10.18 Test–Retest Reliability of the 36 NAB Primary T-Scores (Form 1 and Form 2 Combined) (*Continued*)

NAB test	Mean (SD) time 1	Mean (SD) time 2	Correlation (p)[1]	t test (p)[2]	Effect size	±5 points OR same class[3]	±10 points OR same class[3]	% ≤ -1 SD	% ≥ 1 SD
Language Module									
Oral Production	43.1 (9.2)	47.1 (8.5)	.19 (.06)	3.46 (.001)	0.45	53.7	64.2	8.4	32.6
Auditory Comprehension	49.1 (9.6)	51.1 (8.9)	.28 (.006)	1.77 (.08)	0.22	75.8	76.8	5.3	17.9
Naming	49.1 (11.2)	48.7 (10.8)	.75 (<.001)	0.42 (.68)	0.04	75.8	84.2	9.5	10.5
Writing	49.3 (10.8)	50.1 (10.6)	.29 (.004)	0.63 (.53)	0.07	66.3	68.4	13.7	17.9
Bill Payment	49.7 (10.0)	50.1 (10.3)	.46 (<.001)	0.40 (.69)	0.04	77.9	77.9	9.5	12.6
Memory Module									
List Learning List A Immediate Recall	48.6 (9.0)	50.5 (9.4)	.34 (.001)	1.79 (.08)	0.21	57.9	73.7	10.5	22.1
List Learning List B Immediate Recall	49.3 (10.1)	47.8 (10.1)	.40 (<.001)	1.37 (.17)	0.15	50.5	65.3	21.1	13.7
List Learning List A Short Delayed Recall	49.1 (9.3)	50.4 (9.8)	.41 (<.001)	1.22 (.23)	0.14	64.2	77.9	10.5	17.9
List Learning List A Long Delayed Recall	48.9 (9.5)	51.7 (8.7)	.39 (<.001)	2.70 (.008)	0.31	68.4	82.1	6.3	18.9
Shape Learning Immediate Recognition	51.1 (10.2)	54.8 (11.4)	.43 (<.001)	3.11 (.002)	0.34	62.1	67.4	9.5	31.6
Shape Learning Delayed Recognition	50.2 (10.1)	52.2 (11.2)	.40 (<.001)	1.70 (.09)	0.19	45.3	64.2	15.8	26.3
Story Learning Phrase Unit Immediate Recall	49.0 (9.8)	51.3 (8.5)	.58 (<.001)	2.72 (.008)	0.25	64.2	82.1	6.3	17.9

Story Learning Phrase Unit Delayed Recall	50.4 (9.0)	52.7 (8.9)	.57 (<.001)	2.67 (.009)	0.26	65.3	81.1	4.2	20.0
Daily Living Memory Immediate Recall	50.2 (10.0)	55.0 (9.2)	.49 (<.001)	4.83 (<.001)	0.50	53.7	64.2	10.5	34.7
Daily Living Memory Delayed Recall	49.6 (10.8)	51.0 (10.0)	.53 (<.001)	1.37 (.17)	0.13	66.3	75.8	10.5	18.9
Spatial Module									
Visual Discrimination	50.5 (10.4)	49.8 (10.6)	.38 (<.001)	0.61 (.54)	0.07	51.6	68.4	18.9	14.7
Design Construction	48.0 (11.7)	50.5 (11.1)	.72 (<.001)	2.81 (.006)	0.22	67.4	78.9	8.4	21.1
Figure Drawing Copy	51.5 (9.8)	42.2 (11.4)	.14 (.19)	6.39 (<.001)	0.88	36.2	53.2	47.9	9.6
Figure Drawing Copy Organization	49.6 (9.7)	49.8 (9.1)	.37 (<.001)	0.20 (.85)	0.02	51.1	75.5	13.8	16.0
Figure Drawing Immediate Recall	49.3 (9.9)	46.7 (10.9)	.49 (<.001)	2.38 (.02)	0.25	59.6	75.5	19.1	12.8
Map Reading	48.5 (11.1)	47.3 (10.4)	.56 (<.001)	1.13 (.26)	0.11	61.1	72.6	25.3	14.7
Executive Functions Module									
Mazes	49.8 (12.5)	51.4 (11.5)	.67 (<.001)	1.59 (.12)	0.13	64.5	79.6	7.5	21.5
Judgment	47.6 (9.5)	44.5 (10.1)	.42 (<.001)	2.83 (.006)	0.32	50.5	64.2	30.5	15.8
Categories	47.7 (9.8)	51.8 (10.9)	.51 (<.001)	3.89 (<.001)	0.40	58.9	71.6	9.5	26.3
Word Generation	49.7 (10.5)	50.9 (9.7)	.64 (<.001)	1.36 (.18)	0.12	72.6	83.2	7.4	13.7

Note: N = 95. Participants ranged in age from 20 to 87 years, with the mean age = 50.5 (SD = 17.6).

[1] Uncorrected Pearson correlation (p value). [2] Values represent a paired-samples T-test with df = 94 (p value). [3] Classification ranges were set at "Moderate–Severe Impairment" (T < 30); "Mild Impairment" (T = 30–39); "Below Average–Average" (T = 40–54); and "Above Average–Superior" (T = 55+).

Domains and full Module Indexes. The intercorrelations are presented in numerous tables in the *Psychometric and Technical Manual* (White & Stern, 2003b). The correlations between individual NAB tests and their respective index scores (e.g., List Learning Test and Memory Index) are higher than the correlations between these tests and the other index scores (e.g., List Learning Test and Attention Index). Most of the correlations between individual tests and their respective indexes ranged from .50 to .76.

The normative data for the Screening Module and the five main NAB modules initially were subjected to exploratory factor analyses. Principal axis factoring with Promax rotation was used. Factors were interpreted through traditional methods, such as visually examining screen plots and considering eigenvalues. This was not a purely statistical approach, however. The theoretical underpinnings of the NAB and the clinical meaningfulness of the constructs also were considered. The next step was to use confirmatory factor analysis to derive the final module structure of the NAB. Using structural equation modeling, several factor models were tested for both the Screening Module and the full NAB. The confirmatory factor analyses yielded the modules described earlier in this chapter.

Exploratory and confirmatory factor analyses, as is often the case, can be difficult to interpret in isolation. These analyses, combined with the bivariate intercorrelations, support the multifactorial nature of many neuropsychological tests. A test of verbal memory, for example, also requires adequate attention and intact receptive and expressive language. A test of spatial working memory also requires basic visual-perceptual skills and memory. Thus, not surprisingly, individual tests do not always cleanly load on factors. Without question, success on many neurocognitive tests requires multiple specific abilities. Clinicians need to consider carefully which specific abilities contribute to success or failure on any given test (cf., Table 10.4).

CRITERION VALIDITY

CRITERION VALIDITY REFERS to whether a test is accurately measuring the construct it was intended to measure, and in particular, how the test compares to other measures that are believed to measure a similar ability. The correlations between the NAB and numerous other tests for 50 healthy adults (mean age = 59.5, SD = 17.5 years) were reported in numerous tables in the *Psychometric and Technical Manual* (White & Stern, 2003b). Correlations between tests for small clinical samples also are reported. Both the Screening Module and Total NAB Index scores, which are indicators of global cognitive performance, correlated reasonably well with other measures of global cognitive abilities.

The Screening Module Total Screening Index had medium-sized correlations with the Modified Mini Mental Status Exam (3MS; $r = .46$), Mini Mental Status Exam (MMSE; $r = .55$), and Repeatable Battery of the Assessment of Neuropsychological Status (RBANS; $r = .65$). Similar results were found for correlations between the Total NAB Index score and the 3MS ($r = .40$), MMSE ($r = .45$), and RBANS ($r = .65$).

Correlations between the Screening Module and full NAB Modules and several other neuropsychological measures were examined. The Screening Attention Domain and Attention Module Attention Index had low to medium correlations with attention/working memory tests from the Wechsler Memory Scale-III (WMS-III), Trail Making Test A and B, RBANS Digit Span and Coding tests, and indices from the Ruff 2&7 Test. The NAB Language Index had low to medium correlations with the Boston Naming Test, Verbal Fluency (FAS and Animal Naming), and RBANS Picture Naming and Semantic Fluency. The Screening Language Domain correlated well with the Boston Naming Test and RBANS Picture Naming.

Both the Screening Memory Domain and Memory Module Memory Index scores had low to medium correlations with many of the memory scores from the WMS-III, the California Verbal Learning Test-II (CVLT-II), and the RBANS memory tests. The Spatial Module Spatial Index and Screening Spatial Domain scores had low to medium correlations with many visual-spatial measures, including WMS-III Visual Reproduction Copy, WAIS-III Block Design, most scores from the Boston Qualitative Scoring System for the Rey-Osterrieth Complex Figure, RBANS Figure Copy and Line Orientation, and the Judgment of Line Orientation Test.

The Screening Module Executive Functions Domain and the Executive Functions Module Executive Functions Index scores both had medium correlations with the WAIS-III Comprehension test. The Executive Functions Index also had medium correlations with Wisconsin Card Sorting Test Perseverative Responses ($r = .47$), Trails B ($r = .50$), and Verbal Fluency (FAS; $r = .48$).

The intercorrelations amongst individual NAB tests and the correlations with external tests can be difficult to interpret. Clinicians know, from reading test manuals, that academic, intellectual, memory, and neuropsychological tests are intercorrelated. Low to medium intercorrelations across tests are very common. When examining intercorrelations, one typically looks for a general pattern or specific relations. General patterns typically should reveal that tests measuring similar constructs should correlate more highly than tests measuring dissimilar constructs. Sometimes clinicians are interested in specific tests and how those tests correlate with other tests. These specific relations can be examined in the *Psychometric and Technical Manual* (White & Stern,

2003b). An obvious limitation of the study comparing the NAB to external tests is (a) the relatively small sample size of participants who received the NAB and selected other measures (N = 50); (b) the fact that the healthy adults produced a limited range of scores, which served to attenuate the magnitude of the validity coefficients; and (c) the small sample sizes for clinical groups. Additional criterion-related validity research in clinical samples is needed.

Grohman and Fals-Stewart (2004) examined the validity of the Screening Module compared with the Neuropsychological Screening Battery (NSB; Heaton, Thompson, Nelson, Filly, & Franklin, 1990; O'Malley, Adams, Heaton, & Gawin, 1992) for detecting general cognitive impairment in a group of substance-abusing patients. Both instruments were administered to 84 detoxified substance-abusing patients upon entering a residential treatment program. NSB performance was used as the criterion measure with which to compare NAB Screening Module performance. Thirty patients (36%) were identified as cognitively impaired based on the NSB (i.e., 6 or more scores more than 1 SD below the mean), whereas the NAB Screening Module classified 32 patients (38%) as cognitively impaired (i.e., S-NAB Total Index more than 1 SD below the mean). Overall agreement between the two instruments was excellent (i.e., classification accuracy, based on true positives plus true negatives divided by sample size, was .88).

CLINICAL GROUP VALIDATION

CLINICAL GROUP VALIDATION is important for examining whether a neuropsychological test can identify cognitive deficits in various clinical samples and differentiate the samples from a control group. Performance on the Screening Module and full NAB was examined across several clinical groups, including multiple sclerosis (MS), traumatic brain injury (TBI), human immunodeficiency virus/acquired immunodeficiency syndrome (HIV/AIDS), adult attention-deficit/hyperactivity disorder (ADHD), aphasia, rehabilitation inpatients, and dementia. Unlike individual tests, administration of the NAB to various clinical groups allows for a better understanding of how those groups perform across a full neuropsychological battery. A description of the clinical groups is provided here.

- Multiple sclerosis (N = 31): Participants ranged in age from 24 to 59 years (M = 43.4 years, SD = 9.9 years) and averaged 14.1 years of education (SD = 3.1 years). Of the 31 participants, 23 had relapsing/remitting form of MS, 1 had primary progressive, 6 had secondary progressive, and 1 had an unclear subtype.

- Traumatic brain injury (N = 31): This group consisted of patients with varying severity of TBIs. Their average age was 42.0 years (SD = 11.2 years) and their average level of education was 14.4 years (SD = 2.9 years). Positive CT or MRI results were found in 39% of the sample. Their loss of consciousness (LOC) status was as follows: 27% had none, 49% had brief LOC (<10 minutes), 4% had 10–30 minutes, and 20% had more than 30 minutes (range = 30 minutes to 5 days). Nearly 75% of the patients had less than 1 day of post-traumatic amnesia. Time between injury and assessment varied across the group, with 15% examined within 3 months, more than 1/3 examined within the first year, 1/3 examined within the second year, and 12% examined after more than 2 years. Although 85% of the TBI sample was involved in litigation at the time of testing, all patients performed adequately on a measure of effort.
- HIV/AIDS (N = 19): This group ranged in age from 35 to 55 years (M = 45.1, SD = 6.2 years) and had an average of 12.0 years of education (SD = 2.2 years). HIV/AIDS participants were recruited from infectious disease/HIV clinics, and none of the participants had HIV-associated dementia.
- Adults with ADHD (N = 30): This group had an average age of 30.7 years (SD = 13.3 years), ranged between 18 and 59 years, and averaged 13.3 years (SD = 1.7 years) of education. The majority of the ADHD participants (63%) were taking stimulant medication at the time of testing with the NAB.
- Aphasia (N = 27): This group ranged in age from 26 to 79 years (M = 58.9, SD = 12.4 years) and had 14.5 years of education (SD = 3.4 years). Breakdown for the types of aphasia included nonfluent (n = 19), fluent (n = 2), global (n = 1), and unspecified (n = 5).
- Rehabilitation inpatients (n = 39): This group had an average age of 65.5 years (range = 21 to 92, SD = 16.0 years), 12.5 years of education (SD = 2.2 years), and a wide variety of diagnoses (e.g., TBI, stroke).
- Dementia group (N = 20): This group ranged in age from 69 to 88 years (M = 78.0 years, SD = 4.9 years) and averaged 13.0 years of education (SD = 3.0 years). Participants in this sample were community-dwelling older adults who had Clinical Dementia Ratings between 0.5 (questionable dementia) and 1.5 (mild-to-moderate dementia), with the majority having a 1.0 rating (mild dementia). They were tested either in their homes or in an outpatient clinic.

The percentages of patients in each of the clinical groups that obtained scores more than one standard deviation below the mean (<16th percentile) and less than or equal to the 5th percentile on the

Screening Module and full NAB were examined. These results are presented in Tables 10.19 and 10.20. These tables are intended to be descriptive, not diagnostic, of performance on the Screening Module and the full NAB.

In general, for the Screening Module, the Attention Domain, Executive Functions Domain, and Total Screening Index seemed to have the highest proportions of low scores across the groups. The individual tests that seemed to have the highest proportions of low scores were Screening Numbers and Letters (Parts A and B) and Screening Mazes. Of course, the percentage of subjects in each group that obtained low index and individual test scores varied considerably. In general, for the full NAB, all the indexes had a fairly high proportion of low scores across groups (with the exception of the Language Index). The proportions of low scores across individual tests varied considerably by group, with no particular set of tests emerging as clearly more sensitive.

ECOLOGICAL VALIDITY

IT IS A longstanding goal in neuropsychology to (a) study the ecological validity of tests, and (b) develop tests that have greater ecological validity (Sbordone, 1996; Williams, 1996). A unique feature of the NAB is the inclusion of five Daily Living tests. These tests were developed with the goal of being more representative of real world behavior and functioning than typical neuropsychological tests.

There are five Daily Living tests on the NAB, one in each module. For Driving Scenes, in the Attention Module, the examinee is first presented with a drawing of a driving scene as viewed from behind a steering wheel, and then shown another scene and asked to say and point to everything that is new, different, or missing relative to the previous scene. For Bill Payment, in the Language Module, the examinee is given a utility bill statement, check ledger, check, and envelope, and asked to follow a series of eight commands requiring oral and written responses of increasing complexity. For Daily Living Memory, in the Memory Module, the examinee is asked to learn and remember medication instructions and a name, address, and phone number. For Map Reading, in the Spatial Module, the examinee answers questions (presented both orally and in writing) about a city map that has a compass rose and mileage legend. For Judgment, in the Executive Functions Module, the examinee answers 10 judgment questions pertaining to home safety, health, and medical issues. These standardized tests examine everyday, real-world skills in a laboratory environment.

The premises of the five NAB Daily Living tests are common in other stand-alone objective measures of functional or real world abilities. For example, the Independent Living Scale (ILS; Loeb, 1996)

TABLE 10.19 Low Scores on the Screening NAB Module in the Clinical Groups

Domain, index or test	Multiple sclerosis[1]		Traumatic brain injury[2]		HIV/AIDS[3]		Adult ADHD[4]		Aphasia[5]		Rehabilitation[6]		Dementia[7]	
	<1SD	≤5%&8	<1SD	≤5%	<1SD	≤5%	<1SD	≤5%	<1SD	≤5%	<1SD	≤5%	<1SD	≤5%
Screening Attention Domain	58.1	32.3	28.1	12.5	31.6	21.1	33.2	9.9	90.0	80.0	91.7	75.0	50.0	35.0
Screening Language Domain	9.7	0.0	12.9	0.0	21.1	0.0	16.7	0.0	82.6	65.2	35.9	15.4	60.0	30.0
Screening Memory Domain	29.0	12.9	21.8	6.2	26.4	10.6	13.7	3.4	60.8	47.8	30.7	12.8	65.0	40.0
Screening Spatial Domain	32.3	19.4	12.5	3.1	26.4	15.9	6.6	3.3	39.1	13.0	55.4	31.7	45.0	20.0
Screening Executive Functions Domain	51.6	41.9	21.8	18.7	42.1	31.6	36.6	16.6	90.8	77.2	73.6	55.2	55.0	35.0
Total Screening Index	45.2	35.5	22.5	6.4	36.8	26.3	13.7	3.4	94.8	89.5	85.3	64.7	65.0	50.0
Screening Digits Forward	38.7	16.1	25.0	12.5	26.4	10.6	33.4	6.7	85.1	66.6	30.9	15.5	20.0	10.0
Screening Digits Backward	25.8	16.1	15.7	6.3	26.3	15.8	16.7	13.4	77.7	74.0	48.7	23.1	30.0	20.0
Screening Numbers & Letters Part A Speed	45.2	38.7	34.4	25.0	21.1	5.3	33.3	20.0	79.2	66.7	84.5	66.6	55.0	55.0
Screening Numbers & Letters Part A Errors	29.1	29.1	12.5	9.4	15.8	5.3	10.0	10.0	26.8	23.0	41.1	36.0	20.0	20.0
Screening Numbers & Letters Part A Efficiency	48.4	35.5	37.6	25.1	15.8	5.3	30.0	20.0	80.0	68.0	94.8	76.9	60.0	50.0
Numbers & Letters Part B Efficiency	54.9	35.5	31.3	18.8	31.6	15.8	30.1	30.1	84.6	80.8	77.8	63.9	60.0	35.0
Auditory Comprehension	3.2	3.2	9.7	9.7	21.1	21.1	13.3	13.3	77.8	77.8	25.7	20.6	40.0	40.0
Naming	13.0	6.5	6.3	6.3	0.0	0.0	3.3	3.3	66.7	66.7	33.3	25.6	70.0	50.0
Shape Learning Immediate Recognition	16.1	12.9	6.2	3.1	15.8	5.3	23.3	10.0	18.5	3.7	23.0	17.9	25.0	20.0

(Continued)

TABLE 10.19 Low Scores on the Screening NAB Module in the Clinical Groups (Continued)

Domain, index or test	Multiple sclerosis[1]		Traumatic brain injury[2]		HIV/AIDS[3]		Adult ADHD[4]		Aphasia[5]		Rehabilitation[6]		Dementia[7]	
	<1 SD	≤5%[8]	<1 SD	≤5%	<1 SD	≤5%	<1 SD	≤5%	<1 SD	≤5%	<1 SD	≤5%	<1 SD	≤5%
Shape Learning Delayed Recognition	38.7	16.1	12.5	3.1	26.3	10.5	10.3	0.0	18.5	7.4	20.5	12.8	15.0	10.0
Story Learning Immediate Recall	22.7	16.2	18.7	15.6	31.7	15.9	16.7	6.7	66.6	62.9	25.6	17.9	50.0	30.0
Story Learning Delayed Recall	29.1	25.9	31.2	15.6	26.3	15.8	16.7	10.0	70.3	59.2	43.7	28.3	90.0	70.0
Visual Discrimination	29.1	25.9	9.4	3.1	26.4	26.4	9.9	9.9	18.5	11.1	35.8	23.0	55.0	30.0
Design Construction	35.5	12.9	15.7	9.4	31.6	15.8	10.0	10.0	51.8	22.2	63.2	39.5	30.0	15.0
Mazes	51.6	35.5	25.1	22.0	26.4	26.4	30.0	23.3	73.1	57.7	81.7	60.6	40.0	25.0
Word Generation	54.9	29.1	25.0	9.4	36.9	15.8	33.3	23.3	77.7	40.7	33.4	23.1	50.0	25.0

Note: [1]N = 31; [2]N = 31; [3]N = 19; [4]N = 30; [5]N = 27; [6]N = 39; [7]N = 20; [8] ≤5% = Index scores less than or equal to 76 and test scores less than or equal to 34. Adapted from Tables 6.37 (page 203), 6.38 (page 204), 6.40 (page 207), 6.41 (page 208), 6.43 (page 211), 6.44 (page 212), 6.50 (page 218), 6.51 (page 219), 6.57 (page 225), 6.58 (page 227), 6.64 (page 233), 6.65 (page 234), 6.72 (page 241), and 6.73 (page 242) of the *NAB Psychometric and Technical Manual* (White & Stern, 2003b). Reprinted with permission. Further reproduction is prohibited without permission from PAR, Inc.

TABLE 10.20 Low Scores on the Full NAB in Various Clinical Groups

Index or test	Multiple sclerosis[1]		Traumatic brain injury[2]		HIV/AIDS[3]		Adult ADHD[4]		Aphasia[5]		Dementia[6]	
	<1 SD	≤5%[7]	<1 SD	≤5%	<1 SD	≤5%	<1 SD	≤5%	<1 SD	≤5%	<1 SD	≤5%
Attention Index	58.1	38.7	34.4	21.9	47.4	31.6	40.1	13.4	–	–	–	–
Language Index	19.4	9.7	13.8	0.0	36.8	26.3	19.9	6.6	86.2	81.7	–	–
Memory Index	58.0	29.0	25.1	6.3	52.7	26.4	26.6	3.3	–	–	89.3	84.3
Spatial Index	48.5	25.9	12.5	9.4	57.9	21.1	16.6	6.6	–	–	–	–
Executive Functions Index	41.9	25.8	40.6	15.6	42.2	21.1	34.4	13.7	–	–	–	–
Total NAB Index	54.9	35.5	27.6	20.7	52.7	31.6	24.0	6.8	–	–	–	–
Digits Forward	38.7	16.1	25.0	12.5	26.4	10.6	33.4	6.7	–	–	–	–
Digits Backward	25.8	16.1	15.7	6.3	26.3	15.8	16.7	13.4	–	–	–	–
Dots	38.7	32.2	25.0	15.6	31.6	15.8	13.3	0.0	–	–	–	–
Numbers & Letters Part A Speed	51.6	38.7	40.8	25.2	21.1	5.3	29.9	16.6	–	–	–	–
Numbers & Letters Part A Errors	38.7	29.0	31.3	12.5	26.4	10.6	20.0	13.3	–	–	–	–
Numbers & Letters Part A Efficiency	55.0	48.5	40.7	31.3	26.3	15.8	30.0	13.3	–	–	–	–
Numbers & Letters Part B Efficiency	48.5	29.1	31.3	21.9	31.6	10.5	36.7	20.0	–	–	–	–
Numbers & Letters Part C Efficiency	42.0	22.6	25.0	12.5	21.1	5.3	20.0	10.0	–	–	–	–
Numbers & Letters Part D Efficiency	67.8	42.0	28.1	25.0	26.4	10.6	53.4	30.1	–	–	–	–
Numbers & Letters Part D Disruption	29.0	16.1	21.9	18.8	26.4	5.3	43.4	26.7	–	–	–	–
Driving Scenes	51.7	29.1	34.4	9.4	63.2	52.7	26.6	6.6	–	–	–	–
Oral Production	41.9	19.3	9.7	9.7	36.8	26.3	36.7	13.4	65.1	60.8	–	–
Auditory Comprehension	19.4	16.2	3.4	3.4	26.3	26.3	16.7	10.0	88.9	81.5	–	–
Naming	9.7	3.2	6.5	0.0	21.1	10.6	6.6	3.3	76.9	73.1	–	–

(Continued)

333

TABLE 10.20 Low Scores on the Full NAB in Various Clinical Groups *(Continued)*

Index or test	Multiple sclerosis[1]		Traumatic brain injury[2]		HIV/AIDS[3]		Adult ADHD[4]		Aphasia[5]		Dementia[6]	
	<1 SD	≤5%[7]	<1 SD	≤5%	<1 SD	≤5%	<1 SD	≤5%	<1 SD	≤5%	<1 SD	≤5%
Writing	16.1	9.6	12.8	9.6	31.6	15.8	9.9	6.6	66.7	66.7	–	–
Bill Payment	16.1	12.9	16.0	12.8	31.7	26.4	26.6	23.3	88.8	81.4	–	–
List Learning List A Immediate Recall	38.8	32.3	34.5	12.6	26.4	15.9	33.3	13.3	–	–	80.0	55.0
List Learning List B Immediate Recall	35.4	22.5	25.0	3.1	63.1	36.8	13.3	6.6	–	–	55.0	25.0
List Learning List A Short Delayed Recall	35.5	25.8	28.1	28.1	21.1	10.6	20.0	10.0	–	–	85.0	85.0
List Learning List A Long Delayed Recall	42.1	22.7	25.0	15.6	42.2	26.4	16.6	6.6	–	–	90.0	65.0
Shape Learning Immediate Recognition	58.1	32.3	18.8	9.4	52.6	26.3	13.4	6.7	–	–	60.0	35.0
Shape Learning Delayed Recognition	42.0	22.6	25.0	12.5	42.2	10.6	20.1	13.4	–	–	50.0	40.0
Story Learning Phrase Unit Immediate Recall	22.5	6.4	15.6	3.1	42.2	21.1	6.7	0.0	–	–	85.0	75.0
Story Learning Phrase Unit Delayed Recall	38.7	22.6	15.6	6.2	52.7	31.6	6.6	3.3	–	–	90.0	70.0
Daily Living Memory Immediate Recall	29.0	16.1	18.7	9.3	26.3	10.5	13.3	3.3	–	–	85.0	60.0
Daily Living Memory Delayed Recall	51.6	35.5	28.2	25.1	42.2	26.4	23.3	13.3	–	–	84.2	84.2
Visual Discrimination	45.2	19.4	9.3	6.2	36.8	21.0	16.7	13.4	–	–	–	–

Design Construction	38.7	25.8	9.4	3.1	31.6	15.8	20.1	13.4	–	–	–	–
Figure Drawing Copy	32.2	16.1	31.3	18.8	47.5	26.4	26.6	13.3	–	–	–	–
Figure Drawing Copy Organization	26.7	13.4	29.1	9.7	15.8	10.5	13.7	3.4	–	–	–	–
Figure Drawing Immediate Recall	32.2	29.0	28.1	12.5	47.4	15.8	23.4	16.7	–	–	–	–
Map Reading	38.8	16.2	18.7	15.6	36.9	31.6	16.6	6.6	–	–	–	–
Mazes	35.5	25.8	18.7	15.6	21.0	10.5	27.5	17.2	–	–	–	–
Judgment	22.6	3.2	40.6	18.7	31.6	10.6	37.9	20.7	–	–	–	–
Categories	35.5	12.9	40.7	18.8	31.6	26.4	6.8	3.4	–	–	–	–
Word Generation	35.5	22.6	28.2	9.4	26.3	21.1	30.9	20.6	–	–	–	–

Note: [1]N = 31; [2]N = 31; [3]N = 19; [4]N = 30; [5]N = 27; [6]N = 20; [7]≤ 5% = Index scores less than or equal to 76 and test scores less than or equal to 34.

Adapted from Tables 6.39 (page 205), 6.40 (page 207), 6.42 (page 209), 6.43 (page 211), 6.45 (page 213), 6.46 (page 214), 6.47 (page 215), 6.48 (page 216), 6.49 (page 216), 6.50 (page 218), 6.52 (page 220), 6.53 (page 221), 6.54 (page 222), 6.55 (page 223), 6.56 (page 224), 6.57 (page 225), 6.59 (page 228), 6.60 (page 229), 6.61 (page 230), 6.62 (page 231), 6.63 (page 232), 6.64 (page 233), 6.66 (page 235), 6.67 (page 236), 6.68 (page 237), 6.69 (page 238), and 6.70 (page 239) of the *NAB Psychometric and Technical Manual* (White & Stern, 2003b). Reprinted with permission. Further reproduction is prohibited without permission from PAR, Inc.

is a 68-item measure of functional abilities, composed of five scales: Memory/Orientation (i.e., immediate recall of a shopping list; recall of items presented at the beginning of the test, including a pen, credit card, driver's license, key, $10 bill, a quarter, and a check; and recall of a doctor's appointment), Managing Money (i.e., questions pertaining to financial knowledge, counting money, and bill payment), Managing Home and Transportation (i.e., knowledge of home safety, knowledge of transportation safety and issues, brief map reading, addressing an envelope, proper use of a telephone book, and operation of a telephone), Health and Safety (i.e., knowledge of personal medical issues, medication safety, home and personal safety, and knowledge of self-care), and Social Adjustment.

As an initial assessment of the ecological validity of the Driving Scenes test, Brown and colleagues (2005) examined its relationship with an on-road driving evaluation in 24 healthy elderly controls (EC; CDR = 0) and 31 individuals with very mild dementia (MD; CDR = 0.5), who were all currently driving. Participants were administered a modified Washington University Road Test (WURT; Hunt et al., 1997) that resulted in both a continuous WURT score and a categorical global rating of driving ability (safe, marginal, or unsafe). Participants were also administered the Driving Scenes test as part of an office-based assessment. The control group performed significantly better than the mild dementia group on both the WURT and Driving Scenes. The correlation between Driving Scenes and WURT was strong ($r (55) = -.55$, $p < .01$), and there were significant group differences [$F (2,52) = 7.75$, $p < .01$)] between Driving Scenes scores and global ratings of driving ability. Post-hoc analyses revealed that *safe* drivers scored better on Driving Scenes than those rated *marginal* or *unsafe*. A discriminant function analysis was significant (Wilks' lambda = .77, $p < .01$), with a 66% correct classification rate. These findings support the ecological validity of the NAB Driving Scenes in healthy elderly and those with mild dementia. Additional studies of the ecological validity of the NAB Daily Living tests are needed.

CONCLUSIONS

THE NAB IS a comprehensive, modular battery of tests, focusing on multiple areas of cognitive functioning (i.e., attention, language, memory, spatial, and executive functions). The tests in the battery are all new, but most are based on tests commonly used in neuropsychology (see Tables 10.2 and 10.4). The entire battery has an equivalent form. All tests were administered to the standardization sample; thus, the normative data apply to every test singly and in combination.

The NAB consists of a Screening Module and five main battery modules (Attention, Language, Memory, Spatial, and Executive Functions). The Screening Module is self-contained and can be administered in less than 1 hour. The Screening Module yields individual test scores and Domain scores in the same areas as the full NAB. The Screening Module can be used as a stand-alone screening measure or to determine further testing with the main modules. Alternatively, a clinician can simply choose to administer the five main modules in a fixed battery approach. This can be typically accomplished in 3 to 3.5 hours.

The main modules of the NAB can be administered in their entirety (fixed battery) or selected modules or tests can be administered (flexible battery). The full NAB consists of 24 individual tests. These tests yield 36 demographically corrected (age, education, and sex) T-scores, five index scores, and a Total NAB Index score, all based on continuous norming of scores from a sample of 1,448 healthy adults between the ages of 18 and 97.

Each of the main modules of the NAB includes one test designed to be more ecologically valid than traditional neuropsychological tests. These tests are Driving Scenes (Attention Module), Bill Payment (Language Module), Daily Living Memory (Memory Module), Map Reading (Spatial Module), and Judgment (Executive Functions Module). Brown and colleagues (2005) reported that the Driving Scenes test correlated .55 with a 108-point on-road driving test. Moreover, performance on the test differed in relation to the driving instructor's global ratings (safe, marginal, and unsafe). This study provides preliminary evidence of ecological validity for this NAB test. Additional research on the ecological validity of the other tests is needed.

The Reynolds Intellectual Screening Test (RIST) was administered to the NAB standardization sample. The RIST is comprised of one verbal and one nonverbal test. RIST-NAB discrepancy scores were not presented in the *Psychometric and Technical Manual* (White & Stern, 2003). These discrepancy scores are presented in user-friendly manner in Table 10.8. The discrepancies are presented for the entire standardization sample and subgroups stratified by level of intelligence. As seen in Table 10.8, the magnitude of discrepancy between intelligence and NAB index scores increases with level of intelligence. For example, it is uncommon for a person with low average intelligence to have an Attention Index that is 9 points lower than their RIST score. In contrast, it is uncommon for a person with high average intelligence to have an Attention Index that is 22 points lower than their RIST score.

Neuropsychological profile analysis for the NAB has recently been introduced (Iverson, White, & Brooks, 2006b). This is a new method for interpreting a battery of neuropsychological test results. The method is conceptually similar, but goes well beyond, the Halstead Impairment Index. The base rates of the number of low index scores and individual test scores are provided, in detail, in Tables 10.9–10.14. Different cutoff scores are applied, and the results are presented for the entire standardization sample and subgroups stratified by level of intelligence. At present, no test battery has such sophisticated base rate analyses allowing the clinician to determine how an individual patient performs across an entire battery of tests *simultaneously*. For example, 36 T-scores are derived from the 24 NAB tests. Considering these 36 T-scores simultaneously, the percentage of healthy adults who obtain *six or more* scores below specific cutoffs are as follows: (a) < 1 SD = 34.4%, (b) < 10th percentile = 18.7%, (c) ≤ 5th percentile = 12.0%, and (d) < 2 SDs = 3.7% (Table 10.10). It is essential to note that the base rates of low scores vary considerably based on level of intelligence. Considering these 36 T-scores simultaneously, the percentage of healthy adults stratified by level of intelligence who obtain *six or more* scores below the 10th percentile (Table 10.12) are as follows: (a) low average (RIST = 80–89) = 56.7%, (b) average (RIST = 90–109) = 16.8%, (c) high average = 4.6%, and (d) superior = 5.1%.

Individual test scores that remain the most consistent from over a 6-month test–retest interval for the main modules of the NAB include all five index scores, the Total NAB Index score, and the following individual test scores: Digits Forward, Digits Backward, Numbers and Letters Part A Speed, Numbers and Letters Part A Efficiency, Numbers and Letters Part C Efficiency, Numbers and Letters Part D Efficiency, Numbers and Letters Part D Disruption, Auditory Comprehension, Naming, Bill Payment, List Learning List A Long Delayed Recall, Daily Living Memory Delayed Recall, Design Construction, and Word Generation. For all of these scores, at least 66% of the sample scored within 1/2 SD or in the same classification range at 6-month retest as they did at initial testing (Tables 10.17–10.18).

Some NAB tests are more likely to be affected by practice than others. As seen in the final column of Table 10.18, 20% or more of healthy adults retested at 6 months improved by at least one SD on the following tests: Dots, Numbers and Letters Part A Errors, Driving Scenes, Oral Production, List Learning List A Immediate Recall, Shape Learning Immediate Recognition and Delayed Recognition, Story Learning Phrase Unit Delayed Recall, Daily Living Memory Immediate Recall, and Design Construction. In regards to evaluating a decline in functioning, large declines in performance across a 6-month retest interval are uncommon for most tests (second to last column of Table 10.18).

There is tremendous opportunity for future research with this relatively new test battery. Research on the psychometric properties in clinical groups is needed. Short forms of "flexible batteries" could be developed for specific clinical groups. Once developed and applied, neuropsychological profile analyses could be undertaken to refine the interpretation of the new flexible battery. Research is needed to examine RIST-NAB discrepancy scores in clinical groups to determine if they improve the identification of cognitive problems incrementally over the interpretation of the index scores alone. Future researchers might wish to determine if cutoff scores, based on neuropsychological profile analyses, can be used to identify widespread cognitive impairment in specific clinical groups.

The purpose of this chapter was to provide an introduction to the Neuropsychological Assessment Battery and to present new information to facilitate advanced interpretation. The goal of this chapter is to supplement the *Administration, Scoring, and Interpretation Manual* (Stern & White, 2003b) and the *Psychometric and Technical Manual* (White & Stern, 2003b). A substantial amount of new information is presented. Uncommon RIST-NAB discrepancy scores are presented in Table 10.8, and Tables 10.9–10.14 allow the clinician to do sophisticated profile analyses. It is our hope that this chapter facilitates the routine clinical use of the battery.

REFERENCES

Atkinson, L. (1991). Concurrent use of the Wechsler Memory Scale-Revised and the WAIS-R. *British Journal of Clinical Psychology, 30*(1), 87–90.

Boone, K., Lesser, I., Hill-Gutierrez, E., Berman, N., & D'Elia, L. (1993). Rey-Osterrieth Complex Figure performance in healthy, older adults: Relationship to age, education, sex, and IQ. *The Clinical Neuropsychologist, 7*, 22–28.

Bornstein, R. A., Chelune, G. J., & Prifitera, A. (1989). IQ-memory discrepancies in normal and clinical samples. *Psychological Assessment, 1*(3), 203–206.

Brittain, J., La Marche, J., Reeder, K., Roth, D., & Boll, T. (1991). Effects of age and IQ on Paced Auditory Serial Addition Task (PASAT) performance. *The Clinical Neuropsychologist, 5*, 163–175.

Brown, L. B., Stern, R. A., Cahn-Weiner, D. A., Rogers, B., Messer, M. A., Lannon, M. C., et al. (2005). Driving Scenes test of the Neuropsychological Assessment Battery (NAB) and on-road driving performance in aging and very mild dementia. *Archives of Clinical Neuropsychology, 20*(2), 209–215.

Delis, D. C., Kaplan, E., & Kramer, J. H. (2001). *Delis-Kaplan Executive Function System technical manual.* San Antonio, TX: The Psychological Corporation.

de Rotrou, J., Wenisch, E., Chausson, C., Dray, F., Faucounau, V., & Rigaud, A. S. (2005). Accidental MCI in healthy subjects: A prospective longitudinal study. *European Journal of Neurology, 12*(11), 879–885.

Dodrill, C. B. (1997). Myths of neuropsychology. *The Clinical Neuropsychologist, 11*, 1–17.

Dodrill, C. B. (1999). Myths of neuropsychology: Further considerations. *The Clinical Neuropsychologist, 13*(4), 562–572.

Donders, J., Tulsky, D. S., & Zhu, J. (2001). Criterion validity of new WAIS-II subtest scores after traumatic brain injury. *Journal of the International Neuropsychological Society, 7*(7), 892–898.

Dori, G. A., & Chelune, G. J. (2004). Education-stratified base-rate information on discrepancy scores within and between the Wechsler Adult Intelligence Scale—Third Edition and the Wechsler Memory Scale—Third Edition. *Psychological Assessment, 16*(2), 146–154.

Fisher, D. C., Ledbetter, M. F., Cohen, N. J., Marmor, D., & Tulsky, D. S. (2000). WAIS-III and WMS-III profiles of mildly to severely brain-injured patients. *Applied Neuropsychology, 7*(3), 126–132.

Franzen, M. D., & Iverson, G. L. (2000). The Wechsler Memory Scales. In G. Groth-Marnat (Ed.), *Neuropsychological assessment in clinical practice* (pp. 195–222). New York: John Wiley & Sons.

Gorsuch, R. L. (1983). *The theory of continuous norming.* Paper presented at the Annual meeting of the American Psychiatric Association (June), Anaheim, CA.

Grohman, K., & Fals-Stewart, W. (2004). The detection of cognitive impairment among substance-abusing patients: The accuracy of the neuropsychological assessment battery-screening module. *Experimental and Clinical Psychopharmacology, 12*(3), 200–207.

Hall, S., & Bornstein, R. A. (1991). The relationship between intelligence and memory following minor or mild closed head injury: Greater impairment in memory than intelligence. *Journal of Neurosurgery, 75*(3), 378–381.

Hawkins, K. (1998). Indicators of brain dysfunction derived from graphic representations of WAIS-III/WMS-III technical manual clinical samples data. *The Clinical Neuropsychologist, 12*, 535–551.

Hawkins, K. A., & Tulsky, D. S. (2001). The influence of IQ stratification on WAIS-III/WMS-III FSIQ-general memory index discrepancy base-rates in the standardization sample. *Journal of the International Neuropsychological Society, 7*(7), 875–880.

Hawkins, K. A., & Tulsky, D. S. (2003). WAIS-III WMS-III discrepancy analysis: Six-factor model index discrepancy base rates, implication, and preliminary consideration of utility. In D. S. Tulsky, D. H. Saklofske, G. J. Chelune, R. K. Heaton, R. J. Ivnik, R. Bornstein, et al. (Eds.), *Clinical interpretation of the WAIS-III and WMS-III* (pp. 211–272). Amsterdam: Academic Press.

Hawkins, K. A., & Tulsky, D. S. (2004). Replacement of the Faces subtest by Visual Reproductions within Wechsler Memory Scale—Third Edition (WMS-III) visual memory indexes: Implications for discrepancy analysis. *Journal of Clinical and Experimental Neuropsychology, 26*(4), 498–510.

Heaton, R. K., Chelune, G. J., Talley, J. L., Kay, G. G., & Curtiss, G. (1993). *Wisconsin Card Sorting Test (WCST) manual, revised and expanded.* Odessa, FL: Psychological Assessment Resources.

Heaton, R. K., Grant, I., & Matthews, C. G. (1991). *Comprehensive norms for an extended Halstead-Reitan Battery: Demographic corrections, research findings, and clinical applications.* Odessa, FL: Psychological Assessment Resources.

Heaton, R. K., Miller, S. W., Taylor, M. J., & Grant, I. (2004). *Revised comprehensive norms for an expanded Halstead-Reitan Battery: Demographically adjusted neuropsychological norms for African American and Caucasian adults–professional manual.* Lutz, FL: Psychological Assessment Resources.

Heaton, R. K., Thompson, L. L., Nelson, L. M., Filly, C. M., & Franklin, G. M. (1990). Brief and intermediate length screening of neuropsychological impairment in multiple sclerosis. In S. M. Rao (Ed.), *Multiple sclerosis: A psychological perspective* (pp. 149–160). New York: Oxford University Press.

Horton, A. M., Jr. (1999). Above-average intelligence and neuropsychological test score performance. *International Journal of Neuroscience, 99*(1–4), 221–231.

Hunt, L. A., Murphy, C. F., Carr, D., Duchek, J. M., Buckles, V., & Morris, J. C. (1997). Reliability of the Washington University Road Test. A performance-based assessment for drivers with dementia of the Alzheimer type. *Archives of Neurology, 54*(6), 707–712.

Iverson, G. L., Brooks, B. L., & White, T. (2006a). New discrepancy scores for the Neuropsychological Assessment Battery. *Canadian Psychology, 47*(2a), 110.

Iverson, G. L., White, T., & Brooks, B. L. (2006b). Base rates of low scores on the Neuropsychological Assessment Battery (NAB). *Canadian Psychology, 47*(2a), 110.

Kane, R. L., Parsons, O. A., & Goldstein, G. (1985). Statistical relationships and discriminative accuracy of the Halstead-Reitan, Luria-Nebraska, and Wechsler IQ scores in the identification of brain damage. *Journal of Clinical and Experimental Neuropsychology, 7*(3), 211–223.

Kongs, S. K., Thompson, L. L., Iverson, G. L., & Heaton, R. K. (2000). *Wisconsin Card Sorting Test—64 Card Version, professional manual.* Odessa, FL: Psychological Assessment Resources.

Loeb, P. A. (1996). *Independent Living Scales.* San Antonio, TX: Psychological Corporation.

Martin, T. A., Donders, J., & Thompson, E. (2000). Potential of and problems with new measures of psychometric intelligence after traumatic brain injury. *Rehabilitation Psychology, 45*, 402–408.

Nadolne, M. J., Adams, R. L., Scott, J. G., Hoffman, R. G., & Tremont, G. (1997). Clinical utility of Wechsler Memory Scale-Revised and predicted IQ discrepancies in closed head injury. *Archives of Clinical Neuropsychology, 12*(8), 757–762.

O'Malley, S., Adams, K. M., Heaton, R. K., & Gawin, F. H. (1992). Neuropsychological impairment in chronic cocaine abusers. *American Journal of Drug and Alcohol Abuse, 18*, 131–144.

Oresick, R. J., & Broder, S. N. (1988). The psychometric structure of the Wechsler Memory Scale in comparison to the WAIS-R in a low-IQ clinical population. *Journal of Clinical Psychology, 44*(4), 549–557.

Palmer, B. W., Boone, K. B., Lesser, I. M., & Wohl, M. A. (1998). Base rates of "impaired" neuropsychological test performance among healthy older adults. *Archives of Clinical Neuropsychology, 13*(6), 503–511.

The Psychological Corporation. (1997). *WAIS-III/WMS-III technical manual*. San Antonio, TX: Author.

The Psychological Corporation. (2001). *Wechsler Adult Intelligence Scale—Third Edition. Canadian technical manual*. Toronto, ON: Harcourt Canada.

The Psychological Corporation. (2002). *Updated WAIS-III/WMS-III technical manual*. San Antonio, TX: Author.

Rabin, L. A., Barr, W. B., & Burton, L. A. (2005). Assessment practices of clinical neuropsychologists in the United States and Canada: A survey of INS, NAN, and APA Division 40 members. *Archives of Clinical Neuropsychology, 20*(1), 33–65.

Reitan, R. M. (1985). Relationships between measures of brain functions and general intelligence. *Journal of Clinical Psychology, 41*(2), 245–253.

Reitan, R. M., & Wolfson, D. (1985). *The Halstead-Reitan Neuropsychological Test Battery: Theory and clinical interpretation*. Tucson, AZ: Neuropsychology Press.

Reitan, R. M., & Wolfson, D. (1993). *The Halstead-Reitan Neuropsychological Test Battery: Theory and clinical interpretation* (2nd ed.). Tucson, AZ: Neuropsychology Press.

Reynolds, C. R., & Kamphaus, R. W. (2003). *Reynolds Intellectual Assessment Scales and Reynolds Intellectual Screening Test professional manual*. Lutz, FL: Psychological Assessment Resources.

Sbordone, R. J. (1996). Ecological validity: Some critical issues for the neuropsychologist. In R. J. Sbordone & C. J. Long (Eds.), *Ecological validity of neuropsychological testing* (pp. 15–41). Delray Beach, FL: GR Press/St. Lucie Press.

Stern, R. A., & White, T. (2003a). *Neuropsychological Assessment Battery*. Lutz, FL: Psychological Assessment Resources.

Stern, R. A., & White, T. (2003b). *Neuropsychological Assessment Battery: Administration, scoring, and interpretation manual*. Lutz, FL: Psychological Assessment Resources.

Sweet, J. J., & Moberg, P. J. (1990). A survey of practices and beliefs among ABPP and non-ABPP clinical neuropsychologists. *The Clinical Neuropsychologist, 4*, 101–120.

Sweet, J. J., Moberg, P. J., & Suchy, Y. (2000). Ten-year follow-up survey of clinical neuropsychologists: Part I. Practices and beliefs. *The Clinical Neuropsychologist, 14*(1), 18–37.

Sweet, J. J., Moberg, P. J., & Westergaard, C. K. (1996). Five-year follow-up survey of practices and beliefs of clinical neuropsychologists. *The Clinical Neuropsychologist, 10,* 202–221.

Wechsler, D. (1981). *Wechsler Adult Intelligence Scale-3rd.* San Antonio, TX: The Psychological Corporation.

Wechsler, D. (1997a). *Wechsler Adult Intelligence Scale—Third Edition.* San Antonio, TX: Psychological Corporation.

Wechsler, D. (1997b). *Wechsler Memory Scale—3rd Edition.* San Antonio, TX: The Psychological Corporation.

White, T., & Stern, R. A. (2003a). *NAB demographically corrected norms manual.* Lutz, FL: Psychological Assessment resources.

White, T., & Stern, R. A. (2003b). *Neuropsychological Assessment Battery: Psychometric and technical manual.* Lutz, FL: Psychological Assessment Resources.

Williams, J. M. (1996). A practical model of everyday memory assessment. In R. J. Sbordone & C. Long (Eds.), *Ecological validity of neuropsychological testing.* Delray Beach, FL: GR Press/St. Lucie Press.

Zachary, R. A., & Gorsuch, R. L. (1985). Continuous norming: Implications for the WAIS-R. *Journal of Clinical Psychology, 41*(1), 86–94.

11

Multicultural Neuropsychological Assessment: The Future of Neuropsychology

ARTHUR MACNEILL HORTON, JR.

INTRODUCTION

THE U.S. POPULATION increased in terms of cultural diversity in recent years (U.S. Census Bureau, 2002) and there are questions regarding the application of clinical neuropsychological assessment to culturally diverse populations (Wong, Strickland, Fletcher-Janzen, Ardilla, & Reynolds, 2000). While neuropsychological research findings have been successfully cross-validated in different cultures and foreign countries (Fletcher-Janzen, Strickland, & Reynolds, 2000; Klove, 1974; Reitan, 1986; Reitan & Wolfson, 1993) it would be premature to suggest that clinical neuropsychological assessment has escaped cultural biases (Adams, Boake, & Crain, 1982; Amante, VanHouten, Grieve, Bader, & Margules, 1977). Understanding the cultural sensitivity of neuropsychological assessment procedures is necessary because of an increasingly culturally diverse U.S. population. Neuropsychology as a field has been called to task for not addressing cultural biases in neuropsychological assessment (Fletcher-Janzen et al., 2000). This chapter will discuss the issue of cultural factors in neuropsychological assessment, consider current limitations in neuropsychological assessment, and propose best practices in clinical neuropsychology across diverse cultural domains.

SUGGESTED NEUROPSYCHOLOGY ASSESSMENT APPROACHES

THE MULTIFACETED NATURE of clinical neuropsychological assessment is best addressed by the use of standardized neuropsychological test measures and batteries (Horton & Wedding, 1984). When neuropsychologically assessing individuals from diverse cultural and ethnic groups, a standardized neuropsychological battery is usually recommended. A standardized battery allows for the use of multiple levels of inference (Reitan & Wolfson, 1993) rather than simply relying on a level of performance model. The use of multiple levels of inference provides some control over false-positive and false-negative errors in diagnosis. A battery of carefully selected neuropsychological tests is most helpful for comprehensively describing strengths and weaknesses exhibited by brain-impaired patients and for limiting the degree of cultural bias that is induced by assessing patients from diverse cultural groups (Evans, Miller, Byrd, & Heaton, 2000).

At the same time, single neuropsychological test measures can be helpful in screening assessments and when the question is of a specific area of brain functioning. It is acknowledged that in some cases circumstances such as time and money dictate that single measures or collections of single measures will be used when assessing individuals from diverse cultural and ethnic groups. Still, given the limited space available for discussion of this area, the most profitable use would be to mention only a limited number of procedures. These will include the most widely used fixed standardized clinical neuropsychological batteries and a new measure of executive functioning. The neuropsychological test battery identified is the *Halstead-Reitan Neuropsychological Test Battery* (HRNTB; Reitan & Wolfson, 1993), and the measure of executive functioning will be the *Test of Verbal Conceptualization and Fluency* (Reynolds & Horton, 2006). It should be noted that fixed neuropsychological test batteries are often supplemented by additional tests based on specific needs of the assessment situation, such as the patient's reported problem/chief complaint and particular educational, medical, neurological, and social characteristics as well as special circumstances when assessing individuals from diverse cultural and ethnic groups. There are too many neuropsychological test batteries and measures to cover all of them, so the treatment in this chapter must be selective.

The term *standard* may not be entirely applicable with diverse cultural and ethnic groups. *Standard* indicates that the fixed neuropsychological test battery has been administered in a standard fashion to a sample of persons that includes a representative number of persons in the sample from which the results of this group can be generalized to the population group in question. All neuropsychological batteries and most single measures have included far too few members of diverse cultural and ethnic groups in their standardization. The majority of neuropsychological test batteries and measures can be assumed to be likely skewed to the values and beliefs of the dominant cultural and ethnic group in the country in which the test was developed (Fletcher-Janzen et al., 2000). Additional research is necessary to identify appropriate strategies for correcting inherent problems of standardization and correcting for cultural biases.

CRITICAL ISSUES IN NEUROPSYCHOLOGICAL TESTING BIASES AND LIMITATIONS CROSS-CULTURALLY

CULTURE IS AN important variable in clinical neuropsychological assessment (Campbell et al., 1996; Manly et al., 1998). Wong et al. (2000) define culture as:

> a broad and overarching concept that refers to a body of customary beliefs and social norms that are shared by a particular group of people. It includes behaviors, beliefs, values, and other shared elements. (p. 4)

Exactly how and to what degree culture determines and influences performance on clinical neuropsychological tests is controversial (Artiola i Fortuny & Mullaney, 1998; Campbell et al., 1996; Ford-Booker et al., 1993; Roberts & Hamsher, 1984). For example, there is the previously mentioned lack of representativeness of widely used clinical neuropsychological instruments due to failure to include diverse groups in the normative samples when the instruments were standardized (Betancourt & Lopez, 1993, 1995; Ford-Booker et al., 1993; Lichtenberg, Ross, & Christensen, 1994; Wong et al., 2000).

CULTURE AS A CONCEPT

ETHNOCENTRISM

ETHNOCENTRISM IS THE concept that individuals identify with their own native culture and have difficulties understanding and appreciating differences between their own and other cultures and that this identification is outside of the individuals' awareness (Campbell et al., 1996; Helms, 1992; Raminez & Price-Williams, 1974). Membership in the dominant U.S. cultural group is frequently an underlying assumption in psychological assessment in the United States. Neuropsychology has devoted little study to biases in assessment instruments. Ignorance and unawareness of clinical neuropsychological assessment biases directed attitudes, perceptions, and beliefs in test construction, validation, and interpretations (Campbell et al., 1996; Helms, 1992). The dominant Euro-American culture has been the de facto standard to the detriment of other non-Euro-American cultural groups (Padilla & Marsella, 1996). The unique cultural identities of non-Euro-American cultural groups have differences from the dominant Euro-American culture, which may contribute to clinical neuropsychological test error, and these differences should be appreciated (Campbell et al., 1996). American society is increasingly more multicultural in the twenty-first century, and clinical neuropsychologists will be expected to provide clinical neuropsychological assessment services to non-Euro-American cultural groups (O'Bryant, 2007). In order to serve these clinical needs it will be important to separate the error variance of cultural biases from the true scores of brain-related variables (Reynolds, 2000).

ACCULTURATION

ACCULTURATION IS THE process by which individuals from a non-dominant culture inculcate the new beliefs, values, and practices of a dominant culture (Westermeyer, 1993); for example, persons from Mexico moving to the United States, learning to speak English, and adopting the speech patterns, dress, physical mannerisms, and values of the dominant U.S. Euro-American culture (i.e., wearing jeans, listening to rap music, eating at McDonalds, etc.). Acculturation has recently emerged as an important issue in the general psychological assessment literature. Standard psychological assessment measures are not sensitive to acculturation factors and behaviors (Campbell et al., 1996). Variables related to acculturation include the following:

1. The person's age when they enter the new culture
2. The person's educational and occupational status
3. The person's gender
4. The person's degree of interactions and involvement with the dominant culture
5. The person's relationships with their extended family
6. The person's access to cultural support systems, such as their native language (Berry, Trimble, & Olmedo, 1986; Culler, Harris, & Jasso,

1980; Landrine & Klonoff, 1995; Rogler, Malgady, & Rodriguez, 1989; Suinn, Richard-Figueroa, Lew, & Vigil, 1985)

Acculturation is a complex concept, and the process can take many forms. These forms can include the following:

1. Bicultural, the person maintains both a native and new cultural identity
2. Blended, the person combines elements of both cultures together
3. Assimilated, the person adopts the new cultural identity completely
4. Marginal, the person avoids adopting the new cultural identity

As is apparent from the previous discussion, acculturation can't be determined by simply counting the number of years a person has lived in a dominant culture. Frequently, cultural groups remain immersed in their culture of origin while living in a country that sponsors a different culture (Berry, 1980; Berry et al., 1986). A particularly telling example is Ralph M. Reitan, PhD, ABPP, ABPN, and the father of American neuropsychology was not a native English speaker (1986). His first language was Norwegian; he grew up in Norwegian-speaking Lutheran communities in the upper Midwest and only learned the English language after he went to public school. Similarly, the German language was used for teaching in the public schools of Wisconsin for many years, because the state was largely settled by German-speaking immigrants. In addition, in the city of Chicago, there were Polish-language newspapers in wide circulation serving the Polish-speaking population of the city. Moreover, celebrating Saint Patrick's Day is a major event in the cities of New York, Boston, and Savannah, Georgia due to large Irish immigrant populations. Examples for other cultural groups could be easily generated.

In addition to the variety of combinations of native and new cultures there is also *transculturation*. Briefly, *transculturation* is a new hybrid culture that can develop from interactions between a nondominant and a dominant culture (DeGranda, 1968). Modern American trends in music and food may be seen as hybrids of Euro-American, Hispanic American, Asian American, and African American cultural influences. For example, it would not be unusual for an American to listen to rap music, drink margaritas, and eat Asian fusion cooking all at the same time. Acculturation is important to consider in clinical neuropsychological assessment. If a person to be assessed is from a nondominant culture and not acculturated to the Euro-American culture within which the clinical neuropsychological assessment procedures were developed, then there is great potential for test bias error due to lack of acculturation. Manly et al. (1998) studied acculturation and neuropsychological test performance among African Americans and Euro-Americans. African Americans who self-reported less acculturation to the dominant Euro-American culture scored lower on neuropsychological tests such as the Wechsler Adult Intelligence Scale Revised (WAIS-R) Information subtest, the Boston Naming Test, and on the Trail Making Test-Part B. In addition, HIV-infected African Americans obtained lower scores than HIV-infected Euro-Americans on the Halstead Category Test, Trails B, WAIS Block Design and Vocabulary subtests, and the learning components of the Story and Figure Memory Tests. Demonstrations of cultural differences related to neuropsychological test performance suggest that controlling for acculturation influences will improve the diagnosing accuracy of neuropsychological assessment.

ETHNO-CULTURAL VARIABLES CRITICAL TO CLINICAL NEUROPSYCHOLOGICAL ASSESSMENT

LANGUAGE

VALID NEUROPSYCHOLOGICAL ASSESSMENT requires that the person being assessed be able to understand the instruction of the person conducting the assessment, and the person conducting the assessment must be able to understand the answers of the person being assessed (Artiola i Fortuny & Mullaney, 1998). The expressive language ability of the clinical neuropsychologist administering tests is crucial to appropriate neuropsychological assessment, as mistakes could be made in multiple aspects of language such as wording, form and content, modulations of phrasing, and accent (Artiola i Fortuny & Mullaney, 1997; Sandoval & Duran, 1998). In short, a two-way street of understandable communication is essential for a valid clinical neuropsychological assessment. However, in some cases it is not possible to have a clinical neuropsychologist who speaks a patient's language. In those cases, a professional interpreter should be used to interpret the clinical neuropsychologist's questions and instructions and the patient's answers, but the best situation is to have a clinical neuropsychologist who speaks the patient's language.

Another issue is the cultural appropriateness of the neuropsychological tests to be administered. In some cases, clinical neuropsychological test measures have been translated into another language, but concerns remain, because the clinical neuropsychological tests may or may not have been appropriately translated (Artiola i Fortuny et al., 2005; Figueroa, 1990).

Culture Specific Knowledge

A CRUCIAL DEFICIENCY in clinical neuropsychological assessment is the dearth of information regarding cultural differences, because graduate programs in clinical psychology have not introduced graduate courses in ethnic and cultural diversity topics. Understanding cultural diversity issues must be integrated into the graduate clinical psychology curriculum in order to teach psychology graduate students essential practice information (Wong et al., 2000).

Socioeconomic Status

SOCIOECONOMIC STATUS (SES) is related to social class and economic standing and is often seen as the same as occupational status (Dohrenwend & Dohrenwend, 1969, 1974; Gray-Little, 1995). Disparities between the occupational status of the diagnostician and patient may influence diagnostic biases (Bernard, 1989; Betancourt & Lopez, 1993, 1995; O'Bryant, 2007; Strickland, Jenkins, Myers, & Adams, 1988).

Subpopulation Cultural Differences

CULTURAL DIFFERENCES MAY exist on many levels. In the United States, recognized minority groups include African Americans, Hispanic Americans, Asian Americans, Pacific Islanders, and Native Americans, but not all members within these minority groups self-identify as having exactly the same cultural influences. Rather there are significant subpopulation cultural differences, which are a major difficulty in addressing the problem of minimizing cultural influences in neuropsychological assessment (O'Bryant, 2007; Wong et al., 2000). In the United States, for example, three large Hispanic American subpopulation groups are Puerto Ricans (in the New York Metropolitan area), Cubans (Florida), and Mexican Americans (southwestern United States). These subpopulations of Hispanic Americans describe themselves as having significant cultural differences and consider their groups as distinct from the other groups. Indeed, multiple culturally distinct subgroups of Hispanic Americans have been proposed, so it is an oversimplification to mention but three subgroups of Hispanic Americans. To mention but a few it would be important to consider other Hispanic subgroups such as Santo Dominicans, Colombians, Salvadorians, Peruvians, Argentineans, Ecuadorians, Brazilians, and so on. Thinking that all of these culturally distinct groups have intracultural homogeneity of neuropsychological abilities is not currently supported by research data. Similarly, an important question is the level of cultural subpopulation; which is the appropriate basis of analyses? The multiple numbers of cultural subpopulations in Hispanic Americans are also mirrored in other cultural groups such as Asian Americans, African Americans, and Native Americans. For example, Asian American subpopulations would include Japanese Americans, Korean Americans, Chinese Americans (i.e., Northern Chinese Americans, Southern Chinese Americans, etc.), and Vietnamese Americans, to cite a very few and not considering the very many culturally distinct subgroups on the Indian subcontinent or Pacific Islanders, who would also be considered Asian Americans. Indeed, the usual categories of cultures employed in the United States ignore the many forms of Middle-Eastern cultures.

MULTICULTURAL RESEARCH AND NEUROPSYCHOLOGICAL ASSESSMENT

CLINICAL NEUROPSYCHOLOGY RESEARCHERS have postulated that culture and ethnicity have significant influences on brain processes (Adams et al., 1982; Parsons & Prigatano, 1978; Penk et al., 1981; Raminez & Price-Williams, 1974; Seidenberg et al., 1984; Stodolsky & Lesser, 1967). While international in scope, clinical neuropsychology has seen the largest extent of test development in the United States. Therefore, the largest number of clinical neuropsychological test instruments was developed by Euro-Americans, standardized on Euro-Americans, and are constructed using assumptions based on Euro-American traditions, values, and culture (Wong et al., 2000). A major problem with clinical neuropsychological tests is that members of culturally diverse groups have not been included in normative samples used in clinical neuropsychological test standardization studies in the past. Due to the lack of representation from members of diverse cultural groups, many clinical neuropsychological tests may lack the proper normative data to assess non-Euro-American cultural groups. It is important to obtain data on the performances of culturally diverse groups, because brain-behavior relationships may be influenced by the cultural social context in which the behavior develops (Cole & Bruner, 1971; Cole & Scribner, 1974; Helms, 1992; Miller-Jones, 1989). Boykin (1991) and Miller-Jones (1989) have noted that psychological test items may be culturally related. To cite an example, the Wechsler Intelligence Scales have included a number of psychological test items that were related to the identification and use of umbrellas. The developer of the Wechsler Intelligence Scales, David Wechsler, first developed his intelligence scales while he worked in Manhattan, in New York City. Manhattan is an island next to the Atlantic Ocean. Living on an island next to an ocean it might be expected that it would rain from time to time. Dr. Wechsler, when developing the scales that bear his name, may have often used an umbrella. Because it rained frequently in New York City, carrying and using an umbrella was a common cultural event. Another intelligence test, developed by authors who lived in the south and southwest, included test items related to sundials as it is sunny much of the time in the south and southwest. The selections of these intelligence test items that reflect geographical weather conditions are cogent examples of how cultural influences may influence the assessment of neuropsychological processes in specific test situations (Miller-Jones, 1989). It would be a serious mistake, however, to think that David Wechsler was not aware of cultural difference on intelligence testing, because Dr. Wechsler was born in Budapest, Hungary, and came to the United States as an immigrant. The major point, however, is that neuropsychological assessment occurs in the context of culture, and these potential cultural test biases must be considered or misinterpretations of neuropsychological test data will occur (Reynolds, 2000).

AFRICAN AMERICANS

Children

There are significant concerns when using a race-comparative paradigm with African American children in clinical neuropsychology. Knuckle and Campbell (1984) assessed normal African American middle-school aged children on the Purdue Pegboard test and the Benton Visual Retention test. They found that published Euro-American norms misclassified almost half of the children as neuropsychologically impaired. Heverly, Isaac, and Hynd (1986) found low scores on tactile-visual discrimination for elementary-school aged African American children and considered a possible neurodevelopmental delay of the left tertiary region in the parietal lobe. Vincent (1991) found that the degree of differences between African American and Euro-American children on a number of intelligence tests seemed to be time linked as smaller differences were noted after 1980, suggesting poorer education and SES prior to 1980 could be the reason for discrepancies. Studies showing neuropsychological impairments in normal African American children may be attributable to the race-comparison model's inability to control for the effects of education and SES.

Adults

Campbell et al. (1996) administered normal African Americans a number of neuropsychological tests that included the Symbol Digit Modalities Test (SDMT; Smith, 1982), the Benton Visual Retention

Test (BVRT), Administration A and C (Sivan, 1992), the Visual Form Discrimination Test (VFD) of the BVRT (Benton, Hamsher, Varney, & Spreen, 1983), the Purdue Pegboard Test (Costa, Vaughn, Levita, & Farber, 1963), and the Hooper Visual Organization Test (VOT; Boyd, 1981; Hooper, 1983). They found a high percentage of diagnostic errors (i.e., SDMT, BVRT and Purdue Pegboard Test). In addition, Lewis-Jack et al. (1997) found misclassifications with the Russell's Revision of the Wechsler Memory Scale (Russell, 1975, 1988) Logical Memory subtest but not with the Visual Reproduction subtest. Campbell et al. (2002) tested normal African American adults with six clinical neuropsychological tests and found a high percentage of diagnostic errors for a non–brain-damaged sample on five of the tests. Roberts and Hamsher (1984) found that normal African Americans did worse than normal Euro-Americans on a measure of visual naming ability. In addition, Bernard (1989) reported that African American males scored lower on the Halstead Category test and higher on the Seashore Rhythm Test than did Euro-Americans and Hispanic Americans. These studies have reported some differences between African Americans and Euro-Americans on neuro-psychological tests, but the actual significance of the reported differences from a brain organization point of view is unclear.

In studies of African Americans with strokes, the Verbal Intelligence Quotient (VIQ) and Performance Intelligence Quotient (PIQ) scores of African Americans with left hemisphere strokes are similar, but African American patients with right hemisphere strokes have lower mean PIQ scores than VIQ scores (Ford-Booker et al., 1993). The significance of the patterns of IQ scores observed in different groups of ethnic patients with lateralized brain damage will require additional study and research (Campbell et al., 1996).

One possible alternative would be the development of normal normative data for African Americans so that proper comparisons could be made and overdiagnosis of neuropathology could be avoided. In response to this need researchers have developed demographic corrections for neuropsychological tests scores (Heaton, Grant, & Mathews, 1991), and these demographic corrections were expanded to include a culturally different sample of African Americans (Heaton, Miller, Taylor, & Grant, 2004). Unfortunately, the African American sample was drawn primarily from a single geographical region (San Diego, California; Heaton et al., 2004). Similarly, Strickland, D'Elia, James, and Stern (1997) developed Stroop Color Word Test Norms for African Americans, but again a geographically restricted sample was drawn (Los Angeles, California). Despite these important efforts to equate Euro-American and African American groups on demographic variables such as age, education, sex, and socio-economic status, cultural discrepancies have remained, underscoring the difficulties of a race comparative strategy to cultural differences.

In assessing African American adults, clinical neuropsychologists need to be aware of possible biases found in neuropsychological tests score norms developed for Euro-Americans and not diagnose neuropsychological impairment when none exists (Adams et al., 1982).

New research has demonstrated the viability of a different strategy however. The new research demonstrated that an educational variable could explain differences in neuropsychological test scores between African Americans and Euro-Americans (Manly, Jacobs, Touradji, Small, & Stern, 2002). The researchers used a standard test of academic achievement, the Wide Range Achievement Test third edition (WRAT-3) Reading Recognition test, to adjust neuropsychological test scores and found that cultural diversity differences were removed. The researchers postulated that adjustments for self-reported or obtained years of education were ineffective. Rather, the researchers demonstrated that assessing actual reading skills was more effective to determine educational level. When disparities in educational skills were removed and controlled for, neuropsychological test score differences were removed. The data suggested that the primary reasons for previous research findings of discrepancies between ethnic groups were simply discrepancies in educational attainment in terms of actual word reading skills. New research data suggest that development of actual clinical assessment of word reading level corrections for clinical neuropsychological tests to prevent misclassification errors is a critical issue for clinical neuropsychology (Manly, Byrd, Touradji, & Stern, 2004). Interestingly, there have been views questioning the need for establishing separate neuropsychological test norms for African Americans (Manly, 2005), and others have reaffirmed the need for separate neuropsychological test norms for African Americans (Byrd et al., 2006).

HISPANIC AMERICANS

NEUROPSYCHOLOGICAL ASSESSMENT OF Hispanic Americans confronts different issues than assessment of African Americans. With the neuropsychological assessment of Hispanic Americans the most crucial issue is language. Often clinical neuropsychological tests have been translated into the Spanish language to be used with Hispanic Americans, but there may be problems due to language inadequacy in test translations and adaptations (Artiola i Fortuny & Mullaney, 1997; Artiola i Fortuny & Mullaney, 1998; Artiola i Fortuny et al., 2005). In addition, there are questions regarding possible cultural differences on specific clinical neuropsychological tests. For example, on Trail Making Test-parts A and B and the Fuld Object Memory Test, Euro-Americans had higher scores than Hispanic Americans (Lowenstein, Rubert, Arguelles, & Duara, 1995). In contrast, Bernard's (1989) study that used the entire Halstead-Reitan Neuropsychological Test Battery found no cultural differences in overall rates of impairment in samples that included African Americans, Euro-Americans, and Hispanic Americans, but there were some cultural group differences on selected neuropsychological tests such as the Halstead Category test, Seashore Rhythm test, and Finger Tapping test. Interestingly, the Wisconsin Card Sorting Test (Grant & Berg, 1948), which was thought to be relatively culture free, was shown to be related to degree of acculturation in a Mexican American sample (Coffey, Marmol, Schock, & Adams, 2005).

Lowenstein, Duara, Arguelles, and Arguelles (1995) found different patterns of functional abilities in Euro-American and Hispanic American patients on clinical neuropsychological tests. Cultural biases can possibly influence neuropsychological tests even when linguistic factors are taken into consideration. Hispanic Americans may be able to speak English and yet not be acculturated to the dominant Euro-American culture in the United States for a number of reasons. Lack of acculturation other than for language could still influence clinical neuropsychological test performance of Hispanic Americans. As previously mentioned, the best clinical neuropsychological assessment situation would have a Spanish-speaking clinical neuropsychologist assessing a Spanish-speaking Hispanic American with clinical neuropsychological tests that were developed for Spanish speaking populations. Professional translators are a less desirable alternative when clinical neuropsychological testing is necessary but a Spanish speaking clinical neuropsychologist is not available.

Hispanic Americans may also be bilingual, and that may have implications for clinical neuropsychological assessment. When bilinguals, who were unbalanced in proficiency in the two languages, were assessed on verbal learning they did worse in learning and memory. However, bilinguals, who were balanced in their proficiency in the two languages, were assessed in their dominant language, and the results were not different from monolingual English-speaking non-Hispanic subjects (Harris, Cullum, & Puente, 1995).

Another study found that Hispanic American bilinguals did better on clinical neuropsychological testing based on how long they had lived in the United States (Artiola i Fortuny, Heaton, & Hermosillo, 1997). The clear implication is longer residence in the United States resulted in a greater degree of acculturation, and that may result in better clinical neuropsychological test performance.

ASIAN AMERICANS

IN COMPARISON TO other culturally diverse groups, relatively few studies of cultural difficulties on neuropsychological testing could be identified for Asian Americans (Wong, 2000; Wong & Fujii, 2004). In one of the few studies found, Boyer and Tsuhima (1975) cross-validated the HRNTB with an Asian American sample in Hawaii and found good identification of brain-damaged Asian Americans but a high level of misclassification of normal Asian Americans. Application of revisions of the HRNTB in China for adults (Gong, 1986) and children (Xie & Gong, 1993) found the adapted batteries very useful for identification of neuropsychological impairment. Additional research on cultural issues regarding neuropsychological testing of Asian Americans is warranted to investigate possible cultural differences that could bias clinical neuropsychological test results against Asian Americans (Sue & Sue, 1987). Investigation of acculturation issues is particularly important (Suinn, Richard-Figueroa, Lew, & Vigil, 1987).

NATIVE AMERICANS

NATIVE AMERICANS, SIMILAR to Asian Americans, have not frequently been the focus of clinical neuropsychological test studies (King & Fletcher-Janzen, 2000). Indeed, there is a relative dearth of research on cultural influences on neuropsychological test performance of Native Americans. In one study that could be identified, Ferraro (2002) found that elderly Native American adults had negatively correlated results for neuropsychological test scores and depression test scores. Interestingly, on a neuropsychological screening battery, no differences were found between Native Americans and Euro-Americans (Whyte et al., 2005). Research on the cultural influences of Native American status on clinical neuropsychological test performance appears to be urgently needed.

NEUROPSYCHOLOGICAL TEST INTERPRETATION

RESEARCH STUDIES OF cultural factors identified, except for Bernard (1989), have interpreted tests scores by means of a level of performance model. On the other hand, clinical neuropsychological test interpretation of a standardized battery, such as the HRNTB uses multiple levels of inference (Reitan & Wolfson, 1993). Briefly put, a level of performance model is how high or low a specific test score is. A level of performance simply means the level of the score; an IQ test score would be an example. The use of the multiple levels of inference paradigm includes the additional factors of pathognomonic signs, patterns of performance, and right-left comparisons, as well as the level of performance model (see Horton, 1994; Reitan & Wolfson, 1993). A pathognomonic sign is a test performance that is impossible in a normal developing person, such as the inability to read simple letters or words or doing simple arithmetic problems. Patterns of performance refer to discrepancies among test score such as differences between IQ scores that should be similar. Right-left differences refer to differences that are beyond the norm between the right and left sides of the body on motor and tactual-perceptual tasks. A standardized comprehensive neuropsychological test battery, such as the HRNTB, has a significant advantage because it is designed to utilize the multiple methods of inference. Also, there is a wealth of accumulated clinical experience in using the multiple levels of inference methodological approach. The level of performance method is more subject to cultural bias than other methods of inference. The other measures of inference are more associated with biological variables that are common for all humans. These are invariable as the number of eyes, arms, and legs and not expected to be as subject to cultural bias as level of performance. Use of multiple levels of inference would be expected to reduce the influence of cultural bias in the clinical neuropsychological assessment. The methods of inference other than level of performance are based on biological rather than behavioral variables.

The use of a standardized comprehensive neuropsychological test battery, such as the HRNTB, is the preferred strategy for the comprehensive neuropsychological assessment of non-Euro-American ethnic group members. Also it might be noted that the HRNTB has the most developed demographic correction norms available (Heaton et al., 2004). At the same time it is noted that, as previously mentioned, the geographically restricted sample of African Americans (from the San Diego, California area) may not be reflective of African Americans from other geographical areas. Alternatively, new test measures for specific domains of neuropsychological abilities, such as the TVCF (Reynolds & Horton, 2006), that have been demonstrated to not be biased relative to cultural differences may be useful in assessment of culturally diverse groups.

SUMMARY AND CONCLUSIONS

RESEARCH ON CLINICAL neuropsychological assessment suggests that specific cross-cultural assessment competencies need to be developed for the practice of clinical neuropsychology with members of culturally diverse groups. While there is agreement that clinical neuropsychological assessment should be sensitive to discrepancies between and among members of culturally diverse groups, the available research literature is quite limited. Few studies of cultural differences on clinical neuropsychological test performance have compared African Americans and Hispanic Americans with Euro-Americans, fewer have investigated Asian Americans, and almost none have been completed for Native Americans. The studies addressing cultural assessment issues are also problematic with respect to methodological flaws, such as inappropriate statistical controls for educational differences and Type I error rates (Gasquoine, 2001). Future research with culturally diverse groups will need to be better controlled for educational differences, which may require testing for word reading recognition levels (Manly et al., 2002; Manly, Byrd, Touradji, Sanchez, & Stern, 2004), adequacy of English/Spanish translations (Artiola i Fortuny & Mullaney, 1997), and acculturation/bilingualism (Artiola i Fortuny, Heaton, & Hermosillo, 1997; Artiola i Fortuny & Mullaney, 1998; Manly et al., 1998), among other issues.

Another important concern that involves all of the culturally diverse groups considered in this chapter is the appropriate characterization of cultural subpopulations. While there has been some progress in developing normative neuropsychological test score databases that include African American samples (Brown et al., 1991; Heaton et al., 2004) the largest sample is not nationally representative and may not be generalized to African American samples from other geographical locations. Characterization of subpopulations is crucial to investigation of cultural diversity. For example the situation of Asian Americans and Pacific Islanders may be considered. A question might be raised if separate subpopulation normative databases should be constructed for Japanese Americans, Korean Americans, Chinese Americans, and Vietnamese Americans, to cite a very few of the possible Asian American subpopulations and not even beginning to consider the many cultural diverse subgroups on the Indian subcontinent or Pacific Islands, who would also be considered Asian Americans. The situations for Hispanic Americans (Mexican Americans, Cuban Americans, Puerto Rican Americans, etc.), African Americans, and Native Americans are likely to have similar subdivisions.

Adequate separate normative databases for cultural diverse subpopulations are not currently available, and not everyone agrees that they are the best option (Manly, 2005). Given that situation, what can be done when the clinical neuropsychologist is assessing someone from a different culture? It would appear clear that clinical neuropsychologists need to be sensitive to the cultural aspects of the clinical neuropsychological assessment process. In addition, clinical neuropsychologists need to be knowledgeable regarding various non-Euro-American cultures. Also, it is recommended that clinical neuropsychologists administer a standardized clinical neuropsychological test battery, such as the HRNTB, that was designed to allow for the use of multiple levels of inference. The HRNTB also has the advantage of having existing normative data sets on cultural differences. As earlier mentioned it is suggested that the use of multiple levels of inference may minimize the influence of cultural factors (Bernard, 1989). In addition, clinical neuropsychologists should have strong evidence from more than one level of inference before making any conclusions regarding brain damage in non-Euro-Americans when using tests standardized on Euro-American populations. Moreover, an important component of any clinical neuropsychological assessment is assessment of acculturation issues or degree of bilingualism for any non-Euro-American patient. The hope, expectation, and sincere desire are that this chapter will assist in improving clinical neuropsychological assessments conducted in a multicultural context.

REFERENCES

Adams, R., Boake, C., & Crain, C. (1982). Bias in a neuropsychological test classification related to education, age, and ethnicity. *Journal of Consulting and Clinical Psychology, 50,* 143–145.

Amante, D., VanHouten, V., Grieve, J., Bader, C., & Margules, P. (1977). Neuropsychological deficit, ethnicity, and socioeconomic status. *Journal of Consulting and Clinical Psychology, 45*(4), 524–535.

Artiola i Fortuny, L., Garolera, M., Hermosillo Romo, D., Feldman, E., Fernandez Barillas, H., Keefe, R., et al. (2005). Research with Spanish-speaking populations in the United States: Lost in translation. A commentary and a plea. *Journal of Clinical and Experimental Neuropsychology, 27*(5), 555–564.

Artiola i Fortuny, L., Heaton, R. K., & Hermosillo, D. (1997). Neuropsychological comparisons of Spanish-speaking participants from the U.S.-Mexico border region versus Spain. *Journal of the International Neuropsychological Society, 4*(4), 363–379.

Artiola i Fortuny, L., & Mullaney, H. A. (1997). Neuropsychology with Spanish-speakers: Language proficiency issues for test development. *Journal of Clinical and Experimental Neuropsychology, 19,* 615–622.

Artiola i Fortuny, L., & Mullaney, H. A. (1998). Assessing patients whose language you do not know or, can the absurd be ethical. *The Clinical Neuropsychologist, 12,* 113–126.

Benton, A., Hamsher, K., Varney, N., & Spreen, O. (1983). *Contributions to neuropsychological assessment.* New York: Oxford University Press.

Bernard, L. C. (1989). Halstead-Reitan Neuropsychological Test performance of black, Hispanic, and white young adult males from poor academic backgrounds. *Archives of Clinical Neuropsychology, 4,* 267–274.

Berry, J. W. (1980) Acculturation as varieties of adaptation, In A. M. Padillo (Ed.), *Acculturation: Theory, models and some new findings* (pp. 9–26). Boulder, CO: Westview Press.

Berry, J. W., Trimble, J. E., & Olmedo, E. L. (1986). Assessment of acculturation. In W. J. Lonner & J. W. Berry (Eds.), *Field methods in cross-cultural research* (pp. 291–324). Beverly Hills, CA: Sage.

Betancourt, H., & Lopez, S. R. (1993). The study of culture, ethnicity, and race in American psychology. *American Psychologist, 48,* 629–637.

Betancourt, H., & Lopez, S. R. (1995). The study of culture, ethnicity, and race in American psychology. In N. R. Goldberger & J. B. Veroff (Eds.), *The culture and psychology reader* (pp. 87–107). New York: New York University Press.

Boyd, J. (1981). A validity study of the Hooper Visual Organization Test. *Journal of Consulting and Clinical Psychology, 49,* 15–19.

Boyer, J. I., & Tsuhima, W. T. (1975). Cross-validation of the Halstead-Reitan Neuropsychology Battery: Application in Hawaii. *Hawaii Medical Journal, 34*(3), 94–96.

Boykin, A. (1991). Black psychology and experimental psychology: A functional confluence. In R. Jones (Ed.), *Black psychology* (3rd ed.; pp. 22–38). Berkeley: Cobb and Henry Publishers.

Brown, A., Campbell, A., Wood, D., Hastings, A., Lewis-Jack, O., Dennis, G., et al. (1991). Neuropsychological studies of blacks with cerebrovascular disorders: A preliminary investigation. *Journal of the National Medical Association, 83*(3), 217–229.

Byrd, D. A., Walden Miller, S., Reilly, J., Weber, S., Wall, T., & Heaton, R. K. (2006). Early environmental factors, ethnicity, and adult cognitive test performance. *The Clinical Neuropsychologist, 20*(2), 243–260.

Campbell, A. L., Ocampo, C., Deshawn Rorie, K., Lewis, S., Combs, P., Ford-Booker, P., et al. (2002). Caveats in the neuropsychological assessment of African-Americans. *Journal of the National Medical Association, 94*(7), 591–601.

Campbell, A. L., Rorie, K. D., Dennis, G., Wood, D., Combs, S., Hearn, L., et al. (1996). Neuropsychological assessment of African Americans: Conceptual and methodological considerations. In R. Jones (Ed.), *Handbook of tests and measurements for black populations* (pp. 197–209). Berkeley: Cobb & Henry.

Coffey, D. M., Marmol, L., Schock, L., & Adams, W. (2005). The influence of acculturation on the Wisconsin Card Sorting Test by Mexican Americans. *Archives of Clinical Neuropsychology, 20*(6), 795–803.

Cole, M., & Bruner, J. (1971). Cultural differences and inferences about psychological processes. *American Psychologist, 26,* 867–876.

Cole, M., & Scribner, S. (1974). *Culture and thought: A psychological introduction.* New York: John Wiley & Sons, Inc.

Costa, L., Vaughn, H., Levita, E., & Farber, N. (1963). Purdue Pegboard as a predictor of presence and laterality of cerebral lesions. *Journal of Consulting Psychology, 27,* 133–137.

Cullar, I., Harris, L. C., & Jasso, R. (1980). An acculturation scale for Mexican-Americans normal and clinical population. *Hispanic Journal of Behavioral Sciences, 2,* 199–217.

DeGranda, G. (1968). *Transculturation & linguistic interference in contemporary Puerto Rico*. Bogata, Colombia: Ediciones Bogata.

Dohrenwend, B. P., & Dohrenwend, B. S. (1969). *Social status and psychological disorder*. New York: John Wiley & Sons.

Dohrenwend, B. P., & Dohrenwend, B. S. (1974). Social and cultural influences on psychotherapy. *Annual Review of Psychology, 25,* 417–452.

Evans, J. D., Miller, S. W., Byrd, D. A., & Heaton, R. K. (2000). Cross-cultural applications of the Halstead-Reitan Batteries. In E. Fletcher-Janzen, T. L. Strickland, & C. R. Reynolds (Eds.), *Handbook of cross-cultural neuropsychology* (pp. 287–303). New York: Plenum Publishers.

Ferraro, F. R. (Ed.). (2002). *Minority and cross-cultural aspects of neuropsychological assessment*. Lisse, The Netherlands: Swets & Zeitlinger.

Figueroa, R. (1990). Best practices in the assessment of bilingual children. In A. Thomas & J. Grimes (Eds.), *Best practices in school psychology* (Vol. 2, pp. 93–106). Washington, DC: National Association of School Psychologists.

Fletcher-Janzen, E., Strickland, T. L., & Reynolds, C. R. (2000). *Handbook of cross-cultural neuropsychology*. New York: Plenum Publishers.

Ford-Booker, P., Campbell, A., Combs, S., Lewis, S., Ocampo, C., Brown, A., et al. (1993). The predictive accuracy of neuropsychological tests in a normal population of African Americans. *Journal of Clinical and Experimental Neuropsychology, 15,* 64.

Gasquoine, P. G. (2001). Research in clinical neuropsychology with Hispanic American participants: A review. *The Clinical Neuropsychologist, 15*(1), 2–12.

Gong, Y. (1986). The Chinese revision of the Halstead-Reitan Neuropsychological Test Battery for adults. *Acta Psychologica Sinica, 18,* 433–442.

Grant, D. A., & Berg, E. A. (1948). A behavioral analysis of the degree of reinforcement and ease of shifting to new responses in a Weigl-type card sorting problem. *Journal of Experimental Psychology, 38,* 404–411.

Gray-Little, B. (1995). The assessment of psychopathology in racial and ethnic minorities. In J. N. Butcher (Ed.), *Clinical personality assessment* (pp. 140–157). New York: Oxford University Press.

Harris, J. G., Cullum, C. M., & Puente, A. E. (1995). Effects of bilingualism on verbal learning and memory in Hispanic adults. *Journal of the International Neuropsychological Society, 1*(1), 10–16.

Heaton, R., Grant, I., & Mathews, C. (1991). *Comprehensive norms for an expanded Halstead-Reitan Battery*. Odessa, FL: Psychological Assessment Resources.

Heaton, R., Miller, S. W., Taylor, M. J., & Grant, I. (2004). *Revised comprehensive norms for an expanded Halstead-Reitan Battery: Demographically adjusted neuropsychological norms for African American and Caucasian adults*. Odessa, FL: Psychological Assessment Resources.

Helms, J. (1992). Why is there no study of cultural equivalence in standardized cognitive ability testing? *American Psychologist, 47,* 1083–1101.

Heverly, L., Isaac, W., & Hynd, G. (1986). Neurodevelopmental and racial differences in tactile-visual (cross-modal) discrimination in normal black and white children. *Archives of Clinical Neuropsychology, 1,* 139–145.

Hooper, H. (1983). *The Hooper Visual Organization Test manual.* Los Angeles: Western Psychological Services.

Horton, A. M., Jr. (1994). *Behavioral interventions with brain injured children.* New York: Plenum.

Horton, A. M., Jr., & Wedding, D. (1984). *Clinical and behavioral neuropsychology.* New York: Praeger.

King, J., & Fletcher-Janzen, E. (2000). Neuropsychological assessment and intervention with Native Americans. In E. Fletcher-Janzen, T. L. Strickland, & C. R. Reynolds (Eds.), *Handbook of cross-cultural neuropsychology* (pp. 105–122). New York: Plenum Publishers.

Klove, H. (1974). Validation studies in clinical neuropsychology. In R. M. Reitan & L. A. Davison (Eds.), *Clinical neuropsychology: Current status and applications* (pp. 211–235). Washington, DC: V. H. Winton.

Knuckle, E., & Campbell, A. (1984). *Suitability of neuropsychological tests norms with black adolescents.* Paper presented at the International Neuropsychological Society Meeting, Houston, Texas.

Landrine, H., & Klonoff, E. A. (1995). The African-American Acculturation Scale II: Cross-validation and short form. *Journal of Black Psychology, 21,* 124–152.

Lewis-Jack, O., Campbell, A., Ridley, S., Ocampo, C., Brown, A., Dennis, G., et al. (1997). Unilateral brain lesions and performance on Russell's version of the Wechsler Memory Scale in an African American population. *International Journal of Neuroscience, 91*(3–4), 229–240.

Lichtenberg, P. A., Ross, T., & Christensen, B. (1994). Preliminary normative data on the Boston Naming Test for an older urban population. *The Clinical Neuropsychologist, 8,* 109–111.

Lowenstein, D. A., Duara, R., Arguelles, T., & Arguelles, S. (1995). Use of the Fuld Object-Memory Evaluation in the detection of mild dementia among Spanish and English-speaking groups. *American Journal of Geriatric Psychiatry, 3,* 300–307.

Lowenstein, D. A., Rubert, M. P., Arguelles, T., & Duara, R. (1995). Neuropsychological test performances and prediction of functional capacities among Spanish speaking and English speaking patients with dementia. *Archives of Clinical Neuropsychology, 10,* 75–88.

Manly, J. J. (2005). Advantages and disadvantages of separate norms for African Americans. *The Clinical Neuropsychologist, 19*(2), 270–275.

Manly, J. J., Byrd, D., Touradji, P., Sanchez, D., & Stern, Y. (2004). Literacy and cognitive change among ethnically diverse elders. *International Journal of Psychology, 39,* 47–60.

Manly, J. J., Byrd, D. A., Touradji, P., & Stern, Y. (2004). Acculturation, reading level, and neuropsychological test performance among African American elders. *Applied Neuropsychology, 11*(1), 37–46.

Manly, J., Jacobs, D. M., Touradji, P., Small, S. A., & Stern, Y. (2002). Reading level attenuates differences in neuropsychological test performance between African American and White elders. *Journal of the International Neuropsychological Society, 8,* 341–348.

Manly, J., Miller, S. W., Heaton, R. K., Byrd, D., Reilly, J., Velasquez, R. J., et al. (1998). The effect of African American acculturation on neuropsychological test performance in normal and HIV-positive individuals. *Journal of the International Neuropsychology Society, 4,* 291–302.

Miller-Jones, D. (1989). Culture and testing. *American Psychologist, 44,* 360–366.

O'Bryant, S. E. (2007, January). *Conducting neuropsychological assessments with culturally diverse patient populations.* Workshop presented at the Coalition of Clinical Practitioners of Neuropsychology (CCPN) Convention, Orlando, Florida.

Padilla, A. M., & Marcella, A. (1996). Cross-cultural sensitivity in assessment: Using tests in culturally appropriate ways. In L. A. Suzuki, F. J. Meller, & J. G. Ponterotto (Eds.), *Handbook of multicultural assessment: Clinical psychological and educational applications* (pp. 3–28). San Francisco: Jossey-Bass.

Parsons, O., & Prigatano, G. (1978). Methodological considerations in clinical neuropsychological research. *Journal of Consulting and Clinical Psychology, 46,* 608–619.

Penk, W. E., Brown, A., Roberts, W. R., Dolan, M., Atkins, H., & Robinowitz, R. (1981). Visual memory of male Hispanic-American heroin users. *Journal of Consulting and Clinical Psychology, 49,* 771–772.

Raminez, M., & Price-Williams, D. (1974). Cognitive styles of children of three ethnic groups in the United States. *Journal of Cross-Cultural Psychology, 5,* 212–219.

Reitan, R. (1986). Theoretical and methodological basis of the Halstead-Reitan Neuropsychological Test Battery. In I. Grant & K. Adams (Eds.), *Neuropsychological assessment of neuropsychiatric disorders* (pp. 3–42). New York: Oxford University Press.

Reitan, R. M., & Wolfson, D. (1993). *The Halstead-Reitan Neuropsychological Test Battery: Theory and clinical interpretation* (2nd ed.). Tucson, AZ: Neuropsychology Press.

Reynolds, C. R. (2000). Methods for detecting and evaluating cultural bias in neuropsychological assessment tests. In E. Fletcher-Janzen, T. L. Strickland, & C. R. Reynolds (Eds.), *Handbook of cross-cultural neuropsychology* (pp. 249–286). New York: Plenum Publishers.

Reynolds, C. R., & Horton, A. M., Jr. (2006). *Test of Verbal Conceptualization and Fluency, Examiner's Manual.* Austin, TX: Pro-ED.

Roberts, R. J., & Hamsher, K. (1984). Effects of minority status on facial recognition and naming performance. *Journal of Clinical Psychology, 40,* 539–540.

Rogler, L. H., Malgady, R. G., & Rodriguez, O. (1989). *Hispanics and mental health: A framework for research*. Malabar, FL: Krieger Publishing Company.

Russell, E. W. (1975). A multiple scoring method for the assessment of complex memory functions. *Journal of Clinical and Experimental Neuropsychology, 43*, 800–809.

Russell, E. W. (1988). Renorming Russell's version of the Wechsler Memory Scale. *Journal of Clinical and Experimental Neuropsychology, 10*, 235–249.

Sandoval, J., & Duran, R. (1998). Language. In J. Sandoval, C. Frisby, K. Gelsinger, J. Scheuneman, & J. Grenick (Eds.), *Test interpretation and diversity: Achieving equity in assessment* (pp. 181–203). Washington, DC: American Psychological Association.

Seidenberg, M., Gamache, M., Beck, N., Smith, M., Giordani, B., Serent, S., et al. (1984). Subject variables and performances on the Halstead Neuropsychological Test Battery: A multivariate analysis. *Journal of Consulting and Clinical Psychology, 52*, 658–662.

Sivan, A. (1992). *Benton Visual Retention Test Manual* (5th ed.). San Antonio, TX: The Psychological Corporation.

Smith, A. (1982). *Symbol Digit Modalities Test (SDMT) Manual* (Revised). Los Angeles: Western Psychological Services.

Stodolsky, S., & Lesser, G. (1967). Learning patterns in the disadvantaged. *Harvard Educational Review, 37*, 546–593.

Strickland, T. L., D'Elia, L. F., James, R., & Stern, R. (1997). Stroop color word performance of African-Americans. *The Clinical Neuropsychologist, 11*(1), 87–90.

Strickland, T. L., Jenkins, J. O., Myers, H. F., & Adams, H. E. (1988). Diagnostic judgments as a function of client and therapist race. *Journal of Psychopathology and Behavioral Assessment, 10*, 141–151.

Sue, D., & Sue, S. (1987). Cultural factors in the clinical assessment of Asian Americans. *Journal of Consulting and Clinical Psychology, 55*, 479–487.

Suinn, R. M., Richard-Figueroa, K., Lew, S., & Vigil, P. (1985). Career decisions and an Asian acculturation scale. *Journal of the Asian American Psychological Association, 10*, 20–28.

Suinn, R. M., Richard-Figueroa, K., Lew, S., & Vigil, P. (1987). The Suinn-Lew Asian Self-Identity Acculturation Scale: An initial report. *Educational and Psychological Measurement, 47*, 401–407.

U.S. Census Bureau. (2002). *Statistical abstract of the United States*. Washington, DC: Author.

Vincent, K. R. (1991). Black-white IQ differences: Does age make a difference? *Journal of Clinical Psychology, 47*, 266–270.

Westermeyer, J. J. (1993). Cross-cultural psychiatric assessment. In A. Gaw (Ed.), *Culture, ethnicity and mental illness* (pp. 125–144). Washington, DC: American Psychiatric Press.

Whyte, S. R., Cullum, C. M., Hynan, L. S., Lacritz, L. H., Rosenberg, R. N., & Weiner, M. F. (2005). Performance of elderly Native Americans and

Caucasians on the CERAD Neuropsychology Battery. *Alzheimer's Disease and Associated Disorders, 19*(2), 74–78.

Wong, T. M. (2000). Neuropsychological assessment and intervention with Asian Americans. In E. Fletcher-Janzen, T. L. Strickland, & C. R. Reynolds (Eds.), *Handbook of cross-cultural neuropsychology* (pp. 43–53). New York: Plenum Publishers.

Wong, T. M., & Fujii, D. E. (2004). Neuropsychological assessment of Asian Americans: Demographic factors, cultural diversity, and practical guidelines. *Applied Neuropsychology, 11*(1), 23–36.

Wong, T. M., Strickland, T. L., Fletcher-Janzen, E., Ardilla, A., & Reynolds, C. R. (2000). Theoretical and practical issues in neuropsychological assessment and treatment of cultural dissimilar patients. In E. Fletcher-Janzen, T. L. Strickland, & C. R. Reynolds (Eds.), *Handbook of cross-cultural neuropsychology* (pp. 3–18). New York: Plenum Publishers.

Xie, Y., & Gong, Y. (1993). The revision of the Halstead-Reitan Neuropsychological Test Battery for children in China. *Chinese Mental Health Journal, 7*(2), 49–53.

12

Ecological Validity of Neuropsychological Testing: Critical Issues

ROBERT J. SBORDONE

INTRODUCTION

THE FOCUS OF neuropsychological testing has gradually evolved from the time that psychologists initially began utilizing existing and familiar psychological tests, such as the Wechsler Scales and the Rorschach or Bender-Gestalt Test, to identify the patients who had "organic brain damage." Halstead put together a battery or collection of tests based on his observations of brain-damaged patients (Halstead, 1947, 1950). Reitan (1955) developed the Halstead-Reitan battery based on a modification of Halstead's neuropsychological battery. He and his associates utilized this battery to identify the patients who had focal or diffuse brain damage. Teuber and his associates (Teuber, 1972; Teuber, Battersby, & Bender, 1960) developed psychological tests that were sensitive to the patients who had lesions in the frontal and parietal lobes.

A group of prominent psychologists associated with the Boston Veterans Administration Medical Center in the Boston University School of Medicine, under the leadership of Herald Goodglass, Edith

Kaplan, and Nelson Butters, were instrumental in developing what they termed *qualitative* methods of analyzing the psychological and behavioral manifestations of damage to specific parts of the brain, rather than relying on the patient's quantitative test data. In the late 1970s, work by Charles Golden, Thomas Hammeke, and Arnold Purisch (1978) resulted in the development of a comprehensive neuropsychological test battery based on the qualitative bedside testing procedures that had been developed by the late professor Alexander Romanovich Luria in the Soviet Union. They found that their battery could discriminate brain-damaged patients from normal controls with a very statically reliable level of significance. Although these tests and batteries developed by these investigators were effective in identifying the presence of brain damaged and neuropsychological impairments resulting from specific cortical lesions, they were never designed to address the issue of how the test data could predict how patients would function in real-world settings.

With the occurrence of acquired brain damage (e.g., traumatic brain injuries, carbon monoxide poisoning, toxic exposure, etc.) caused by the fault of another party, neuropsychologists were often called upon to evaluate these patients and determine on the basis of their neuropsychological test data whether a patient could live independently, return to work or school, or maintain competitive employment, even though the tests that they relied upon were never designed to be used for this purpose (Sbordone, 1996; Sbordone & Guilmette, 1999). Neuropsychologists found that whenever they were asked to testify about such issues in the courtroom based on their test data, their opinions often had little empirical support and were often based on their faulty assumptions about neuropsychological testing (Bach, 1993; Long & Kibby, 1995; Sbordone, 1996, 1997; Wilson, 1993).

Stemming largely from the involvement of neuropsychologists in the courtroom, considerable pressure was placed on neuropsychologists to broaden the traditional concepts of test reliability and validity to include the issue of whether the neuropsychological tests they utilized possessed ecological validity. Thus, although many neuropsychologists could claim that the test or batteries they utilized possessed high test reliability and validity, they were often forced to admit that a particular test score or set of test scores might not accurately predict how a patient would function in his or her environment, particularly when the test scores were normal or mild to moderately impaired.

This chapter will examine critical issues that deal with the ecological validity of standardized neuropsychological tests, their ability to predict a patient's behavioral and cognitive functioning in real-world settings, the validity of some of our widely held assumptions about testing, and the shortcomings of our tests to assess a patient's frontal lobes and executive functions, and predict everyday and vocational functioning.

ECOLOGICAL VALIDITY

D EFINITION ECOLOGICAL VALIDITY in the area of neuro-psychological testing refers to the functional and predictive relationship between a patient's performance on a particular test or battery and their behavior at home, work, school, or in the community (Sbordone, 1996; Sbordone & Guilmette, 1999).

Neuropsychologists have utilized two major approaches to enhance the ecological validity of their neuropsychological test data. The first approach involves utilizing tests that mimic the demands of the patient's everyday functioning. The second approach involves using neuropsychological tests that have been empirically shown to be correlated or can be used to predict the patient's everyday or work functioning.

The first approach is known as *verisimilitude* and refers to the degree to which the tests and measures utilized mimic the cognitive demands of the patient's environment (Franzen & Wilhelm, 1996). This definition assumes that the neuropsychologists' choice of tests should be determined by the cognitive demands of the settings the patient currently functions within, or will function within in the future. Several tests have been developed for this purpose. For example, the Rivermead Behavioural Memory Test (Wilson, Cockburn, & Baddeley, 1985) tries to mimic the demands that are made on a patient's memory in everyday life.

The primary focus of this approach is to avoid using tests that were primarily designed to diagnose brain damage, but rather to utilize tests that simulate the cognitive demands of the patient's everyday environment. This approach, however, often overlooks whether the data obtained from such tests, often under highly artificial conditions (e.g., the testing laboratory), irrespective of their apparent verisimilitude, accurately reflect the demands of the patient's environment. Neuropsychologists frequently ignore this issue and use tests that were primarily designed to detect brain damage rather than mimic the demands of the patient's environment. They often do not interview significant others who are familiar with the demands of these environments and routinely observe how the patient functions in these environments. They rarely leave their laboratories or offices to determine whether the tests and the environment in which the tests were administered accurately represent the demands of the patient's environment, and whether the test data obtained under such conditions corroborate the observations of significant others.

The second approach is the degree to which the administered tests are empirically related to measures of everyday functioning (Franzen & Wilhelm, 1996). This approach has been labeled *veridicality* and typically involves the use of statistical techniques to relate a patient's performance on traditional neuropsychological tests to measures of real-world functioning such as work performance evaluations, questionnaires completed by significant others, or clinician ratings (Chaytor & Schmitter-Edgecombe, 2003). One issue that confounds the validity of this approach is whether the chosen outcome measure accurately reflects the patient's real-world functioning, because the use of inappropriate outcome measures could lead to inaccurate predictions of the ecological validity of a particular neuropsychological test or battery.

Chaytor and Schmitter-Edgecombe (2003) found, in a careful review of 17 empirical studies of the ecological validity of neuropsychological tests and outcome measures of everyday functioning, that there was considerable variability in the choices of neuropsychogical tests and outcome measures that were utilized, even within the same cognitive domain. They found that these studies frequently ignored the issue of specificity between the tests and the outcome measures that were utilized. For example, many of these studies did not specify a priori which neuropsychological tests should be expected to be related to specific measures of everyday functioning and which should not. Irrespective of these methodological issues, tests of memory had the best ecological validity, while tests of executive functions had the poorest. They noted that in these studies many clinicians seemed perplexed that patients whose test scores on neuropsychological tests were within normal limits had impaired executive functions.

THE DEMAND CHARACTERISTICS OF THE ENVIRONMENT

THE DEMAND CHARACTERISTICS of a patient's environments (e.g., work, school, home, etc.) can vary considerably. For example, the demand characteristics within a particular patient's workplace may fluctuate considerably as a result of factors such as economic pressures, absenteeism, sickness, organizational or administrative changes, competition from other companies, changes in the market place, changes in equipment, marketing goals, and so on. Depending on the interface between the patients' cognitive strengths and deficits, and the demand characteristics of the particular work setting that a patient finds herself or himself within, the setting may either compensate or exacerbate the patient's cognitive and behavioral impairments. When the former occurs, persons in this setting often serve as the patient's ancillary frontal lobes by structuring the environment to compensate for the patient's cognitive impairments. When the latter occurs, the patient's functioning often declines and the decline is hypothesized to be based on the principle of a conditional neurological lesion (Sbordone, 1996, 1997; Sbordone & Guilmette, 1999). This principle argues that factors such as stress, fatigue, lack of sleep, and so on can have a deleterious effect on the patient's behavioral, cognitive, and emotional functioning. When this occurs, patients can develop secondary psychiatric disorders (e.g., generalized anxiety disorder, adjustment reaction with a depressed or anxious mood, or major depression), which frequently exacerbate their behavioral and cognitive impairments.

Obtaining Information About the Demand Characteristics of the Patient's Environment

Because the demand characteristics of each setting are unique, it is essential that neuropsychologists obtain as much information as possible about the behavioral and cognitive demands that a particular environment places on a patient. This information should be obtained not only from the patient, but also from the patient's family, friends, coworkers, and supervisors, not to mention specialists in the fields of vocational and occupational rehabilitation. This information helps us understand how these environments interact with the patient's behavioral problems (e.g., disinhibition, mood swings, irritability, etc.), cognitive strengths and impairments, goals and objectives, premorbid skills and abilities, attitudes, awareness of their impairments, and biological systems (e.g., medical conditions, general health, etc.). Unfortunately, such information is rarely obtained by neuropsychologists.

In the absence of a clear understanding of the demand characteristics of the patient's environments, predictions about the patient's ability to function at work, school, in the community, or live independently, based solely on neuropsychological test data, are likely to be inaccurate or misleading. Such predictions may also be viewed as "sheer speculation" when they are presented in the courtroom, where such issues are of major importance in determining the extent of the patient's damages and needs.

Although the vast majority of our widely used neuropsychological tests were never specifically designed to assess the patient's functioning in real-world settings, within the past decade, some effort has been made to determine whether many of our widely used neuropsychological tests and measures possessed ecological validity in predicting real-world functions such as job performance, activities of daily living, academic performance, work behavior, shopping, everyday life problems, executive functions, adaptive decision making, functional status, and driving and work-related skills (Chaytor & Schmitter-Edgecombe, 2003).

The major problem inherent in such studies is that the environments in which these patients were tested typically had little or no resemblance to real-world settings. For example, individuals who undergo neuropsychological testing are usually tested in quiet and highly structured settings that are relatively free of extraneous or distracting stimuli to optimize their test performance. This type of environment has been a standard in the field for the expressed purpose of reducing extraneous negative influences during the evaluation process and allows different psychologists to compare the patient's test data (Cronbach, 1984). Unfortunately, while these particular conditions may optimize the patient's performance, particularly on tests that require a high level of attention and concentration, the real issue is whether the test results obtained under such artificial conditions can generalize to the patient's environment, which is often unstructured, chaotic, noisy, contains numerous extraneous and distracting stimuli, and is highly dissimilar to the conditions under which the test data were obtained.

Testing brain-injured patients in such quiet, structured, and artificial settings, combined with the gentle and calm manner of the examiner, not to mention the examiner's patience and concerted efforts to prevent the patient from becoming fatigued or emotionally upset, frequently mask many of the patient's behavioral and cognitive symptoms that may only appear when the patient is placed in unstructured, complex, noisy, stressful, and cognitively demanding situations, particularly when they are fatigued. Under such conditions, a patient's cognitive and behavioral functioning is often highly discrepant from any predictions of how they will function in real-world situations based on their quantitative test data.

Case Example

A 27-year-old female was referred for neuropsychological testing after she had sustained a severe closed head injury during a bicycle versus motor vehicle accident. She was rendered comatose for 2 weeks. CT and MRI studies revealed bilateral contusions to her frontal and temporal lobes. Prior to the accident, she worked as a TV news broadcaster, spoke several languages, and had earned a Master's Degree in Economics. During testing, she appeared articulate, demure, and cooperative. Testing revealed a Wechsler full scale IQ of 138 that was consistent with her academic and vocational achievements. She was found to have relatively mild cognitive impairments on tests that assessed her divided attention skills. Testing revealed no evidence of impairment on neuropsychological tests that assessed her intellectual functioning, memory, language, perceptual, judgment, executive functions, motor, problem solving, and cognitive processing skills.

To assess how this patient functioned in a highly unstructured, complex, and noisy environment with numerous distracting stimuli, she was taken to a large crowded nearby mall on a Saturday afternoon. Prior to being taken to the mall, she was given a total of $100 by her husband, who instructed her to purchase five specific items. Her behavior in this setting was videotaped using a concealed camera that was hidden in the jacket of a male professional investigator. Another investigator (a strikingly attractive woman in her late 20s) covertly recorded whatever she said. Both investigators were never introduced to her, but remained at her side throughout the entire time (4 hours) that she spent at the mall. At no time was either investigator more than 3 feet away from her. Despite the fact that these individuals were constantly at her side the entire time she spent at the mall, she never recognized their presence, or questioned why they were following her so closely. Their presence, however, was often noted by other shoppers and a security guard who came over and asked what was going on.

As soon as she entered into the mall, she walked up to a large directory trying to locate the kitchen utensils that her husband had asked her to purchase. Although the directory listed where the household items were located, she indicated that she could not find where the kitchen utensils were located. She walked aimlessly throughout the mall without any apparent goal or plan even though her husband had written down on a sheet of paper the items he had wished her to purchase. At no time did she ever pull out this list from her purse to examine its contents or check to see if any of the items she had purchased were on the list. She walked throughout the mall with little or no regard to other shoppers, which resulted in her walking into three shoppers. At no time did she apologize or seem to be the least bit concerned about what had occurred. On several occasions, she walked to the front of a long line of shoppers and demanded the immediate attention of the salesperson. When she was told by the salesperson that she was waiting on another shopper and to please stand in line, she began cursing at the salesperson very loudly. She also appeared to have no regard for the rights of other shoppers.

When she went into a department store, she walked around one of the floors several times without realizing that she had done this. She would often pick up items and walk away with them rather than take them to the checkout line. She was taken to a restaurant at the mall where she was seated only a few feet away from several young children. When the waitress would not immediately wait on her, she began uttering expletives in a very loud manner, which created a scene in the restaurant that resulted in her being asked to leave by the manager. Although she had spent the $100 that had been given to her by her husband, she did not purchase any of the items he had requested, and instead had only purchased items that she had wanted.

This case example demonstrates the discrepancies that can occur between the patient's neuropsychological test results when they are tested in a very quiet and highly structured artificial setting and their behavior in a highly unstructured, complex, novel, noisy, and crowded setting. This patient's behavior in this latter setting would have not been predicted by observing her behavior in the quiet and highly structured artificial test setting or by a review of her neuropsychological test data. In fact, the neuropsychologist who examined her had recommended that she could return to work.

CONDITIONALITY

IF MOST PEOPLE were asked if they could fly a 747 passenger jet, they would probably emphatically state that they could not do this. The truth is that most people are capable of flying a 747 even without ever going to flight school if the pilot were sitting next to them in the cockpit, instructing them what to do in a gentle and reassuring manner, and providing them with considerable praise for doing such a good job. If the pilot suddenly passed out or died, the individual, who had been following the instructions of the pilot, would no longer be able to continue flying the aircraft. In other words, under the right set of conditions many individuals would be capable of piloting an aircraft without ever attending flight school. If these conditions changed, then the person would be unable to fly the aircraft.

This principle was initially described by the philosopher Plato in one of his dialogues, Meno, when he demonstrated how Socrates was able to convince Meno that a simple slave boy knew all the principles of geometry by asking him leading questions to prove to Meno that all knowledge was innate (Plato, 1952). This phenomenon, with respect to the ecological validity of our test data, has been termed *conditionality* (Sbordone, 1987, 1988, 1996, 1997; Sbordone & Guilmette, 1999). It refers to specific modifications of the test protocol or instructions during testing and the use of compensatory techniques provided by the examiner during testing that allow the patient to ignore extraneous or distracting stimuli, attend to the examiner and the task, comprehend and recall the test instructions, perform according to the test requirements, utilize cues and prompts to minimize their problems of initiation and organization, and foster a positive emotional and psychological state and attitude during the examination to compensate for the patient's cognitive deficits, thus allowing them to perform at an optimal level of cognitive efficiency throughout the entire test or battery.

Do Neuropsychologists Ever Utilize Conditionality?

Many neuropsychologists consciously or unconsciously modify standard test instructions or procedures when they are evaluating patients with cognitive impairments. For example, the examiner may repeat the test instructions several times or permit the patient to spend more time warming up prior to administering a test to them. The examiner may also provide frequent cues and prompts throughout testing to minimize the patient's problems of initiation and the effects of fatigue, frequently redirect the patient back to the task, and keep the patient as motivated as possible to facilitate their performance (e.g., using praise or rewards). Unfortunately, these modifications are often not recorded, because the traditional focus in testing has been placed on the patient's quantitative test performance rather than on their behavior during testing. If the examiner follows strict test guidelines and does not provide any cues, prompts, or any more rehearsal or practice time than is specified by the test manual, the patient's test scores will most likely be significantly impaired, which will often cause the neuropsychologist to report that the patient has significant cognitive deficits that render them unable to return to the job they held prior to their brain injury. However, if such patients are placed in a highly structured and familiar work setting that provides them with frequent cues, prompts, and contains caring and patient individuals who compensate for the patient's deficits, brain-injured patients can often function reasonably well at their job even though their neuropsychological test scores are impaired.

Case Example

A 40-year-old attorney who had sustained a traumatic brain injury in a motor vehicle accident was referred for neuropsychological testing. Review of his medical records revealed that he had sustained bilateral contusions to the anterior frontal and temporal lobes, a subdural hematoma, and an arachnoid hemorrhage. The damage to his right temporal lobe was so severe that 6 cm had to be removed surgically. The neuropsychologist who tested him at 1 year post injury strongly felt that this patient was incapable of ever practicing law based on his poor neuropsychological test scores. When he was later seen by another neuropsychologist after he had gone back to work, he indicated that he was doing well at his job, and as a husband and father at home.

When the staff at his law firm was interviewed they admitted they liked him and felt sorry for him when he returned to work. They admitted that they had been providing him organization, structure, cues, and frequent prompts and reminders to help him function effectively at work. For example, although the other attorneys in the firm had shared a secretary with one or two other attorneys, this patient needed three full-time secretaries and two legal assistants to help him perform his job even though he was billing considerable less than any of the other attorneys in the firm. He compensated for his cognitive impairments by putting in long hours (usually 11–12 hours a day) and working weekends in comparison to working 6 or 7 hours a day only 4 days a week, as he had prior to his accident.

At home, his wife, who had once practiced law with her husband, was no longer practicing law, because she had decided to become a full-time homemaker to care for their two young children. She had taken over their finances and was making virtually all of the decisions at home, which her husband had made prior to his accident. She had also taken over the household duties and responsibilities that had previously been held by her husband and would often assist her husband in performing his legal work.

This case illustrates that when a brain-injured patient is placed in a highly structured work environment in the presence of individuals who serve as their "ancillary frontal lobes," who provide frequent reminders, cues, prompts, guidance, structure, feedback, and take over many of their responsibilities to compensate for their cognitive impairments, they can often return to work and create the superficial appearance that they have made an excellent recovery.

Neuropsychologists should recognize the issue of conditionality when they are asked to predict whether a patient can return to work and maintain their job. Unfortunately, neuropsychologists often fail to interview the patient's family, coworkers, employers, friends, or spouses to determine how the patient is performing at work and under what conditions the patient actually performs his job duties and responsibilities.

THE ECOLOGICAL VALIDITY OF THE BRAIN-INJURED PATIENT'S COMPLAINTS

NEUROPSYCHOLOGISTS OFTEN RELY on questionnaires that are completed by the patient while seated in the waiting room to determine their behavioral and cognitive symptoms rather than directly interview the patient. This is typically done to save time and reduce the costs of the examination, particularly when it is being paid for by an insurance company. This policy, unfortunately, ignores the fact that the vast majority of brain-injured patients have a limited or poor awareness of their symptoms and typically fail to recognize their behavioral and cognitive symptoms that are readily observed by their significant others, even when their symptoms are pointed out to them (Sbordone, Seyranian, & Ruff, 1998).

When patients are interviewed, they will often only exhibit cognitive deficits when they are asked broad, open-ended questions. In such circumstances, these patients may exhibit circumstantial and tangential thinking, confusion, memory difficulties (e.g., being unable to recall the question), a loss of their train of thought, or confabulation, even though they did not identify such symptoms on the questionnaires they completed.

Although some neuropsychologists have assumed that the patient's test performances should be consistent with their subjective complaints, nothing could be further from the truth, because the neuropsychological test results are usually consistent with the observations of the significant others and are typically inconsistent with the patient's reported subjective complaints. When the patient's subjective complaints are consistent with the patient's neuropsychological test data, malingering should be suspected (Sbordone, Seyranian, & Ruff, 2000).

The presence of family members or significant others during such interviews can shed considerable light on the patient's symptoms and improve the ecological validity of the psychologist's opinions about the patient's ability to return to school or work, live independently, or function in the community. When neuropsychologists rely on the brain-injured reported assessment of their ability to function at work, they are apt to make predictions about the patient's ability to return to work or school that are often inaccurate and potentially harmful to the patient's economic welfare.

Case Example

A 37-year-old male laborer had fallen 12 feet off a ladder at work. He was rendered unconscious for less than a minute. A CT scan did not identify any evidence of intracranial abnormalities. He was placed on medical leave and was referred by his physician for neuropsychological testing to determine if he could return to work. This patient denied any behavioral or cognitive deficits when he was interviewed. He tested in the normal range on all of the cognitive tests that were administered to him. When the psychologist asked him if he felt that he was ready to return to work, he said he did not see any reason why he could not return to work. Based on this, the psychologist recommended that this patient return to work. After this patient had returned to work, his coworkers and supervisor observed that he frequently cursed, became easily fatigued, yelled at them, and made serious mistakes that jeopardized his and their safety. Eventually, he was terminated and had considerable difficulty finding a similar job.

COMMON ASSUMPTIONS HELD BY NEUROPSYCHOLOGISTS

MANY NEUROPSYCHOLOGISTS, THROUGH their particular training or theoretical orientation, hold assumptions about the practice of neuropsychological testing that may handicap them in dealing with the issue of ecological validity as a construct. For example, many neuropsychologists often take workshops where they are told that it is not necessary to take a detailed clinical history or interview collateral sources, because such information may bias test interpretation. What are often emphasized in such workshops are the primary importance of the patient's neuropsychological test data and the unbiased interpretation of the test data to arrive at accurate opinions about the patient's cognitive impairments and localization of brain dysfunction. They are taught that it is essential that standardized tests and batteries should be utilized to arrive at any meaningful opinions about the presence or absence of cognitive dysfunction and brain damage. They are told in such workshops that any changes in the patient's cognitive functioning can best be determined by a careful examination of the patient's serial test data. They are taught that a neuropsychologist's primary responsibility is to record the patient's quantitative responses to specific test stimuli during testing. Neuropsychologists who hold such assumptions often feel that it is not important to record the amount and type of practice or the various cues, prompts, or various strategies that are given to the patient or are utilized by the patient during testing, because they believe that a review of the patient's raw test data is sufficient to determine the patient's cognitive impairments.

Many neuropsychologists assume that neuropsychological test data can be best interpreted in the absence of information from other sources (e.g., historical information, medical records, academic records, interviews with significant others, etc.). Observation of the patient's behavior outside of the testing environment is also seen as irrelevant, because it is assumed that careful interpretation of the test data will provide a sufficient basis to predict how the patient is likely to respond in real world settings.

Many neuropsychologists assume that intact performance on standardized neuropsychological tests or batteries will determine whether the patient has cognitive deficits or has sustained a brain injury. Some neuropsychologists have assumed that it is not necessary to review the patient's medical chart if they are trying to determine whether the patient has sustained a brain injury, because this can best be determined by examination of the test data. Many often assume that it is not necessary to review the patient's educational or vocational records to determine whether the patient is able to return to school or work if the neuropsychological test data show no evidence of cognitive impairment.

Irrespective of whether such assumptions are faulty or have any merit, psychologists who hold such assumptions are likely to find it difficult to determine the ecological validity of their neuropsychological test data. For example, if you fail to observe the patient's ability to function outside of the test environment, and do not interview significant others to obtain information about the patient functioning at home and in the community, both prior and following their brain injury, it is difficult to determine whether the patient's test data have any ecological validity.

Many neuropsychologists assume that using standardized neuropsychological tests and careful interpretation of the test data are more scientific than observing the patient function in real-world settings, because they often assume that any information obtained from significant others is biased and unscientific. In other words, they assume that any digression from standard test protocols would not yield valid or reliable data. While this assumption may have held some merit prior to the advent of brain imaging, it is outdated with respect to the issue of whether the patient's test data are ecologically valid. For example, how can this approach be assumed to be "scientific" if it produces inaccurate and misleading information about the patient's ability to function in real-world settings?

CURRENT USES OF NEUROPSYCHOLOGICAL TESTING

MOST NEUROPSYCHOLOGISTS WHO are practicing today use neuropsychological tests to identify the patient's cognitive strengths and deficits, rather than determine whether the patient has brain damage, because this is typically determined by the patient's medical history and neuroimaging studies. Neuropsychological testing is primarily used today to determine whether a patient has sustained brain damage when the neurological examination is normal, and the neuroimaging studies are negative. However, with the advent of increasing sophistication in neuroimaging, it is unlikely that neuropsychological testing will be utilized in the future to determine whether a patient is brain damaged if the presence of the damage can be accurately identified, localized, and quantified. On the positive side, this is likely to place more emphasis on the development of innovative methods of assessing how the brain injury or dysfunction affects the patient's functioning in real-world situations.

LIMITATIONS OF NEUROPSYCHOLOGICAL TESTING

NEUROPSYCHOLOGISTS FREQUENTLY ASSUME that whatever cognitive deficits the patient has, such deficits can be detected by neuropsychological tests. In other words, the patient's test performance should provide us with reliable information about their cognitive functioning. Unfortunately, in many cases, neuropsychological testing often fails to detect the patient's behavioral and cognitive deficits. The following story illustrates this point:

A man, upon arriving home at approximately 2 a.m., sees a man in the middle of the street on his hands and knees apparently searching for something on the street. Out of curiosity, he walks over and asks the other man if he needs assistance. The man replies that he has lost his car keys. The passerby asks where he had lost them. The man kneeling on the asphalt responds "about two blocks away." Puzzled by this response, he asks "why are you looking here if your keys are two blocks away?" The man states, "the light here is better."

This amusing story illustrates how we are often bound by the insensitivity of the many of the tests we use to detect a patient's behavioral and cognitive deficits. As a consequence, many of the patient's behavioral and cognitive deficits go undetected, particularly when neuropsychologists rely heavily on the patient's scores on standardized neuropsychological tests, which often show no cognitive deficits and give us little information about a patient's behavioral problems (e.g., irritability, rapid mood swings, poor safety judgment, and difficulty regulating their emotions and behavior, etc.).

Although standardized neuropsychological tests are commonly used to assess patients with frontal lobe injuries, Damasio (1985) reported that patients, who had most of their prefrontal lobes surgically removed often tested in the normal range on IQ and other standardized neuropsychological tests. He found, however, that in real-world settings these patients exhibited a loss of initiative, curiosity, exploratory behavior, motivation, creativity, and libido. They were unable to regulate their behavior and emotions. They were unable to organize their thoughts, plan, remain on tasks, monitor their actions, problem solve, recognize their mistakes, or rectify them when they were made aware of them. They exhibited impaired social behavior, inflexible thinking, poor judgment, impulsivity, egocentricity, an inability to show affection or feel compassion toward others, and crude or coarse language. They had no plans or concern for future events, were unable to profit from experience, and often confabulated when they were asked to recall remote information.

USE OF IQ TESTS TO ASSESS BRAIN-DAMAGED PATIENTS

MANY PSYCHOLOGISTS COMMONLY administer the Wechsler Adult Intelligence Scale to patients who have sustained brain damage to determine whether there has been any change in the patient's intellectual functioning, even though IQ tests were never designed to assess brain-damaged patients and are typically insensitive to their behavioral and cognitive deficits. As a consequence, the results from such tests often provide inaccurate and misleading information about the patient's ability to function in real-world settings. The following case example illustrates this.

Case Example

An 18-year-old male had sustained a severe closed head injury as a result of a serious motor vehicle accident on the night of his high school graduation. He was referred by his treating neurologist for neuropsychological testing approximately 6 months post injury to determine if he was able to attend college. Prior to his accident he had been given an academic scholarship to attend a prestigious Ivy League university based on his excellent high school grades and SAT scores. He had planned on becoming a physician or attorney. He was administered the Wechsler Adult Intelligence Scale and was found to have a full scale IQ of 140, which placed him in the very superior range (99th percentile). As soon as he had completed this test, the examiner went to the restroom.

Upon his return a few minutes later, the patient did not recognize the examiner and denied that he had ever previously seen him or had undergone any testing that day. Interviews with his family corroborated this patient's severe cognitive deficits.

Based on his IQ score, one would be tempted to say that he was capable of going to college and becoming either an attorney or physician. Had the neuropsychologist recommended that this patient attend college based on his high IQ score, he would have most likely flunked out of school.

THE POTENTIAL HAZARDS OF USING INAPPROPRIATE TESTS AND NORMS

NEUROPSYCHOLOGISTS OFTEN ADMINISTER inappropriate tests to individuals of different ethnic backgrounds whose understanding and competence in English is marginal, or who are raised in a different culture. Ignoring a patient's cultural and linguistic background may make it difficult for neuropsychologists to predict how that patient will function if they return to school or work, or their particular community.

Case Example

A 53-year-old male accountant had sustained a mild closed head injury. He was referred for neuropsychological testing by his physician. He was born and raised in the Philippines. He completed his education in the Philippines, and relocated to Hawaii 5 years ago. Although he spoke with a heavy accent, his command of English seemed adequate. He was administered a variety of standardized neuropsychogical tests in English rather than his native language (Tagalog) to assess his cognitive and intellectual functioning. He tested with a full-scale IQ of 88 on the Wechsler and performed poorly on tests of confrontational naming, language, verbal memory, and on a test that was used to assess his "executive functioning" (e.g., Controlled Oral Word Association Test). These results convinced the psychologist who examined him that he sustained an injury to his left hemisphere. The psychologist concluded that this patient was severely impaired and was unable to work as an accountant.

When he was retested by another psychologist in his native language 2 months later, he was found to have an IQ of 133 on the Test of Non-Verbal Intelligence. When the stories on the Logical Memories subtest of the Wechsler were administered to him in his native language, he tested in the 98th percentile. When he was asked to name the pictures on the Boston Naming Test in his native language rather than English, he made a score of 59 out of 60 rather than 42 when he had been earlier tested in English. When he was asked to generate words in his native language on the Controlled Oral Word Association Test, he tested in the 95th percentile rather than the 12th percentile when he earlier had been asked to respond in English. Based on these findings the psychologist recommended that this patient could return to work as an accountant. A 6-month follow-up revealed that he had successfully returned to work duties and responsibilities.

Psychologists often fail to use appropriate norms when scoring neuropsychological tests. Neuropsychologists often fallaciously assume that the test norms they utilize should apply to all individuals irrespective of their age, education, or cultural or ethnic background as if they were fixed in stone, even though research has shown that there is considerable variability in many of the norms that have been published for the same neuropsychological test (Mitrushina, Boone, & D'Elia, 1999). Such variability most often reflects variables such as the patient's age, prior level of intellectual functioning, educational background, geographic location, and the patient's ethnic or cultural background. For example, how appropriate is it to utilize norms obtained from college graduates born in the United States ranging in age 25 though 39 to a foreign-born 64-year-old individual who has only completed 6 years of formal education? Such invidious comparisons are likely to result in this individual's test scores falling in the impaired range and the psychologist concluding that this individual would have significant difficulty functioning in their community even though this individual's functioning in his or her environment is seen as normal by the vast majority of people who reside in his or her environment. The real issue is what should we rely upon, our test data or the observations of significant others?

IS POOR PERFORMANCE ON TESTING INDICATIVE OF BRAIN DAMAGE?

ALTHOUGH IT IS often widely assumed that poor performance on neuropsychological testing is indicative of brain damage or cognitive dysfunction, Sbordone and Purisch (1996) identified a number of confounding factors that can produce poor performance during testing, regardless of whether or not the patient is brain damaged. The factors they identified were: prior brain injury or insult, congenital or preexisting neurological conditions, absences (seizures), acute pain, symptoms and impairments secondary to physical injuries, peripheral sensory impairment, peripheral motor impairment, current and chronic medical illness, sleep deprivation, excessive fatigue, history of alcohol/drug abuse, medications, psychiatric illness, recent psychosocial stressors, suboptimal motivation or malingering, negative patient/examiner interactions, cultural/linguistic discrepancies, the patient's vocational and avocational background, test sophistication, and practice effects. Thus, psychologists who arrive at the opinion that a particular patient has sustained brain damage solely based on their relatively poor test performance without carefully considering these factors is likely to make inaccurate and misleading predictions of the patient's ability to function in real-world settings, particularly when the factors that accounted for the patients poor performance have resolved or are no longer present.

Case Example

A 49-year-old male was referred for neuropsychological testing after he began to complain of headaches, dizziness, concentration and memory difficulties, irritability, fatigue, and sleep difficulties after being involved in a motor vehicle accident 7 months ago. His medical records revealed that he had a questionable loss of consciousness, but did not appear confused or disoriented at the scene of the accident or when he was later seen in the ER. He was recently placed on medical leave by his physician as a result of his complaints. Neuropsychological testing indicated that his attention and recent memory were mild to moderately impaired. The psychologist, who relied on the patient's complaints and test results, decided that this patient had sustained a closed head injury and should not return to work at this time. He did not obtain a history of the patient's injury or background, review the patient's medical records, or interview any significant others.

This patient was evaluated by another psychologist who took a careful clinical history, reviewed the patient's medical records, and interviewed the patient's 24-year-old daughter. Based on this information, this psychologist learned that at the time of the last examination the patient had been going through a nasty divorce; had been taking a variety of anxiety, antidepressant, and pain medications; and had been in a great deal of pain and discomfort as a result of injuring his lower back after he had fallen down a flight of stairs while he was heavily intoxicated.

Since his last examination, he had met an attractive woman who he was now dating. He had been sleeping much better, and he was considerably less anxious and depressed than he had been at the time of his prior examination. He was no longer drinking or taking any medications, and he was no longer experiencing back pain and discomfort. His neuropsychological test scores fell into the normal range. This psychologist recommended that this patient should return to work.

This case demonstrates that this patient's test results when he was initially tested were most likely due to several factors that had a deleterious effect on his cognitive functioning at the time he was examined. These factors were not present at the time of the second examination.

NEUROPSYCHOLOGICAL TESTS ARE POOR AT ASSESSING THE FRONTAL LOBES OF THE BRAIN

STUSS AND BENSON (1986) have stressed that neuropsychological tests were not specifically designed to evaluate the frontal lobes of the brain. They emphasized that identification of the behavioral and cognitive symptoms of frontal lobe pathology depended to a large degree on the competence and experience of the neuropsychologist. They stressed that the patient's neuropsychological test data needed to be supplemented by interviews with significant others, observations of the patient's behavior in real-world settings, and the patient's medical records to determine how the patient was functioning while they were hospitalized or receiving treatment in a brain-injury rehabilitation program.

A number of prominent neuropsychologists and behavioral neurologists have also pointed out how inadequate neuropsychological testing is to assess damage to the frontal lobes and the regions connected to the frontal lobes. For example, Bigler (1988) stressed that traditional neuropsychological tests and measures are generally insensitive to alterations in the patient's behavior caused by frontal lobe damage. He stressed that the patients themselves lacked awareness that such alterations had occurred. As a consequence, he strongly emphasized the importance of careful observations of the patient's behavior and detailed interviews of family members and significant others who have observed the patient to assess any alterations in the patient's executive functions. Mesulam (1986) felt that the behavioral changes associated with frontal lobe damage were almost impossible to quantify through traditional neuropsychological tests and batteries. He felt that our traditional methods of testing the frontal lobes were often overly simplistic. For example, this writer has seen numerous reports in which neuropsychologists have stated that they assessed the patient's frontal lobes by administering the Trail Making Test. Thus, if the patient's test scores fall in the average or expected range, they will often conclude that the patient's frontal lobes are intact. Other psychologists may administer the Wisconsin Card Sorting Test to assess the functional integrity of the patient's frontal lobes, even though individuals who sustain significant damage to their orbital frontal lobes typically perform well on this test (Stuss & Benson, 1986).

Luria (1996) observed that while many patients with frontal lobe lesions did fairly well on neuropsychological tests, they approached problem-solving tasks quite differently in that they were generally unable to formulate a plan that was needed to solve the problem when the task required a preliminary analysis of the problem itself. Zangwill (1966) had earlier pointed out that those patients who had sustained frontal lobe injuries would often perform in the normal range on standardized neuropsychological tests. He strongly felt that these tests were inadequate to assess the cognitive deficits caused by these injuries.

Many neuropsychologists do not understand the effects of damage to the medial or lateral orbital frontal lobes. Injuries to these regions of the brain are common when patients have struck their head on the ground as a result of falling from ladders or been struck by a motor vehicle while walking across the street.

Although individuals who sustain damage to the medial orbital frontal lobes typically perform in the normal range on standardized neuropsychological tests, they frequently exhibit a loss of motivation, loss of energy and drive, loss of pleasure from the environment, depression (pseudodepression), psychomotor retardation, a change in their eating habits, loss of sex drive, loss of curiosity, and increase in obsessive-compulsive behavior.

Although these patients with lateral orbital frontal lobe will deny any behavioral or cognitive symptoms and test in the normal range on standardized neuropsychological tests, they will typically exhibit a dramatic change in their personality, which is observed by their family and significant others, but not by the patient. They are unable to control their behavior and regulate their emotions, exhibit a loss of social tact, are unable to empathize with others, exhibit marked egocentricity, frequently use crude and coarse language at home, exhibit poor frustration tolerance, exhibit frequent mood swings, and are unaware of how their symptoms effect others.

Why aren't patients with these injuries identified by neuropsychologists? This typically occurs when neuropsychologists spend little time with their patients; fail to interview their significant others; base their opinions on the patient's performance on standardized tests, which are usually administered by a technician or someone in training often without the neuropsychologist being present; have a poor or limited understanding of the behavioral symptoms of orbital frontal lobe pathology; take inadequate histories; and assume that poor performance on neuropsychological tests indicates brain damage and relatively normal performance indicates no brain damage. It also occurs when they do not observe the patient's function outside the test environment, particularly in unstructured, noisy, complex, and novel settings.

Although some neuropsychologists (i.e., Reitan & Wolfson, 1993) have stressed the importance of not biasing the interpretation of the patient's test data by reviewing the patient's clinical history and medical records, this practice often can result in the neuropsychologist forming opinions based solely on tests that are insensitive to the behavioral consequences of orbital frontal lobe damage. This increases the likelihood that the neuropsychologist's predictions about the patient's ability to function in real-world settings will be inaccurate and misleading. This practice also has the potential of arriving at opinions that are potentially harmful to the patient and the patient's significant others.

Case Example

A 27-year-old male sustained a blunt head trauma as a result of falling from a ladder and striking his head on the ground. He sustained a brief loss of consciousness and was observed to be combative at the scene of the accident. He was taken to the ER and released later that day after his CT head scan was normal. Within a few weeks his wife observed a dramatic change in her husband's personality in that he now had a great deal of difficulty controlling his emotions and temper and would often hit her and throw things with little or no provocation. She denied that he had ever acted this way prior to his accident. He was referred by his family physician for neuropsychological testing. He denied any cognitive symptoms or problems controlling his emotions. All of his test scores fell into the normal range. The psychologist contacted the referring physician and indicated that this patient showed no evidence of brain damage or cognitive deficits. Three weeks later this patient struck his wife with a heavy metal crowbar during an argument and killed her. The psychologist had not interviewed the patient's wife, or had ever observed this patient's behavior outside of his office, or in a stressful situation.

NEUROPSYCHOLOGICAL TESTS ARE POOR AT ASSESSING THE EXECUTIVE FUNCTIONS OF THE BRAIN

THE EXECUTIVE FUNCTIONS are a complex process of integrated cognitive activities. For example, Sbordone (2000) has proposed that the executive functions of the brain be defined as the complex process by which an individual goes about performing a novel problem-solving task from its inception to its completion. This process includes the awareness that a particular problem or need exists, an evaluation of the particular problem or need, an analysis of the conditions of the problem, the formulation of specific goals necessary to solve this problem, the development of a set of plans that determine which actions are needed to solve this problem, evaluation of the potential effectiveness of these plans, the selection and initiation of a particular plan to solve the problem, evaluation of any progress made toward solving the problem or need, modification of the plan if it was not effective, disregarding ineffective plans and replacing them with more effective plans, comparing the results achieved by the new plan with the conditions of the problem, terminating the plan when the conditions of the problem have been satisfied, storing the plan, and retrieving it later if the same or similar problem appears.

Neuropsychological tests were primarily designed to assess whether a patient had brain damage. They were not designed to assess the executive functions of the brain. Much like the man on the street trying to find his keys that are located two blocks away, psychologists frequently rely on neuropsychological tests that are believed to be sensitive to frontal lobe damage to assess the executive functions of the brain, because they apparently assume that the executive functions are located in the frontal lobes. This assumption is faulty, because injuries to subcortical and other nonfrontal brain structures that have connections to the frontal lobes can produce executive dysfunction even though the patient's frontal lobes are intact (Cummings, 1995). For example, subcortical disorders such as Parkinson's disease, progressive supranuclear palsy, Huntington's disease, Korsakoff's syndrome, and dementia caused by carbon monoxide exposure and inhalation of organic solvents produce executive dysfunction (Sbordone, 2000).

Many neuropsychologists seem to believe that the best way to assess the executive functions of the brain is to administer the following tests: The Wisconsin Card Sorting Test, the Halstead Category Test, the Verbal Concept Attainment Test, Controlled Oral Word Association Test, the Verbal Fluency Test, Designed Fluency, Ruff Figural Fluency Test, Porteus Maze Test, Tinker Toy Test, Stroop Test, Trail Making Test, Purdue Pegboard Test, Finger Tapping Test, Rey Complex Figure Test, and more recently the Delis-Kaplan Executive Function System. The patient's performance on these tests may not provide accurate information about their executive functions, because they may only assess some, but not all of the complex steps that are involved in the executive functions of the brain (Cripe, 1996; Sbordone, 2000). By analogy, using these tests to assess a patient's executive functions is comparable to being asked to write a review of the movie Titanic after watching only 10 minutes of the film. This would not provide sufficient time to comprehend the complexity, richness, and drama of this movie. The only way to fully appreciate the movie and write a meaningful review would be to watch the entire movie from start to finish. Unfortunately, the manner in which neuropsychologists currently practice (e.g., administering tests rather than observing a patient function in real-world settings) is the primary reason why we do not understand the executive functions of the brain, or how to adequately assess them.

A VECTOR ANALYSIS APPROACH TO DETERMINE THE ECOLOGICAL VALIDITY OF OUR TEST DATA

SBORDONE, 1997; SBORDONE and Guilmette, 1999; and Sbordone and Purisch (1996) have recommended that neuropsychologists utilize a "vector analysis approach" to evaluate the ecological validity of a patient's neuropsychological test data. They have argued that if the information about the patient's behavior obtained from different sources (e.g., significant others, medical, academic, vocational records, etc.) is consistent or forms a vector with the patient's neuropsychological test data, there is a high probability that the test data is ecologically valid. On the other hand, if the test data is inconsistent with this information (e.g., the test data indicate that the patient is severely impaired 3 years post motor vehicle accident in the face of medical records indicating no loss of consciousness, amnesia, disorientation or brain or head trauma combined with academic and vocational records that document appreciable educational and vocational attainments subsequent to the accident), there is a high probability that the ecological validity of the test data is poor. When the latter occurs, these authors recommend that neuropsychologists explore alternative explanations of the test data and avoid at arriving at premature diagnoses, opinions, or predictions about the patient's functioning in real-world situations.

PREDICTION OF EVERYDAY FUNCTIONING FROM NEUROPSYCHOLOGICAL TESTS

PREDICTION OF EVERYDAY functioning based on the patient's neuropsychological test data to a large degree depends on the type of neurobehavioral disorder that the brain injury has generated. For example, the nature of the aphasia examination itself lends itself to greater ecological validity than many laboratory measures of cognitive functioning. In this case, the examiner is directly assessing the skills that the patient will need to demonstrate outside of the testing environment (e.g., comprehension, fluency, naming, etc.) to allow them to communicate effectively. Thus, the better a clinician can test skills that approximate specific real-world ability, the greater the likelihood of accurate prediction of real-world functioning. When neuropsychological tests are utilized to predict the patient's ability to perform everyday skills, more often than not patients who perform very poorly and who are not malingering would most often have considerable difficulty at home and functioning at any job. The ecological validity of neuropsychological test is poorest when evaluating traumatic brain injury cases that test in the normal to mildly impaired range. For example, Williams (1996) stressed that such predictions of these patients are often no better than guesses. Individuals who test with severely impaired test scores who are not malingering and putting forth good effort frequently have impaired functional skills. Their test performance is more likely to have better ecological validity than patents that test in the normal or mildly impaired range. Consequently, it is important to supplement standardized test procedures with observations and descriptions of the patient during testing and from others who observe the patient under more varied and frequent circumstances. It is also important to obtain a careful history of the patient's planning and organizational skills and initiative prior to his or her injury to accurately gauge the effects, if any, the injury has had on these abilities.

Most studies have shown that the overall relationship between neuropsychological measures and everyday skills ranges from low-to-moderate, with Pearson correlations ranging from 0.2 to as high as 0.5 (Chaytor & Schmitter-Edgecombe, 2003). The modest ability of neuropsychological tests to predict everyday functioning suggests that although some test measures may provide some beneficial information under some circumstances, they should not be used in isolation. Clinicians should acknowledge the limitations of their measures in this domain. More importantly, neuropsychologists need to determine whether a test is being used as a diagnostic measure of some clinical syndrome or cognitive deficit versus the test being used to predict everyday skills.

While neuropsychological tests and measures are used routinely and usually quite helpful in identifying differences between clinical groups and normal subjects, predicting a patient's performance outside of an office or laboratory setting is an entirely different matter. Thus, while a neuropsychological test or measure may be diagnostically useful, it may not be useful in predicting a patient's everyday functioning (Chaytor & Schmitter-Edgecombe, 2003; Sbordone & Guilmette, 1999), because the behavioral domains are too complex and our understanding of our everyday skill too elementary. As a consequence, neuropsychologists need to seek convergent and consistent sources of information to increase our ability to predict an individual's everyday functioning. This is particularly true in a forensic context where all of the neuropsychologists' assumptions and the information upon which they based their opinions can be challenged in the courtroom (Sbordone & Guilmette, 1999).

Research has shown that no one specific neuropsychological test or measure can accurately predict the patient's everyday functioning or skills for all persons. Thus, neuropsychologists should combine information gathered from neuropsychological tests with information gathered from behavioral observations, interviews, rating scales, self-report measures, and other assessment procedures. In short, it is not enough to rely solely on the patient's neuropsychological test performance when predicting everyday competence (Wilson, 1993), because it is important that psychologists seek convergent and consistent sources of information to increase our understanding and ability to predict the individual patient's everyday competencies. Research has suggested that neuropsychological assessment may be more predictive if the tests used closely match or simulate everyday abilities (Sbordone & Guilmette, 1999).

PREDICTING VOCATIONAL FUNCTIONING FROM NEUROPSYCHOLOGICAL TESTS

THE USE OF neuropsychological test data to predict the patient's vocational functioning is difficult. Although research studies have shown that neuropsychological tests and measures can be helpful in identifying brain-injured patients who may or may not be successful in the workplace, the predicted relationship between the test data and the patient's vocational skills and functioning is far from perfect (e.g., Sbordone & Guilmette, 1999). Unfortunately many neuropsychologists in forensic settings are often pressured to utilize their neuropsychologic test data to predict a patient's work potential even though the empirical relationship between the test data that were utilized in the patient's work potential has not been empirically demonstrated.

Neuropsychologists should be aware of such variables as specific jobs skills, skills necessary for success in the patient's workplace, routine versus unpredictability of the patient's work day, availability of supervision, the amount of interaction with coworkers and the public, degree to which the job matches the patient's behavioral and cognitive strengths, degree to which demands of the job and workplace will have on the patient's behavioral and cognitive weaknesses, level of distraction in the job environment, whether the job duties require multitasking, the patient's ability to recall novel information, the degree to which the workplace contains coworkers or supervisors who are tolerant or intolerant of the patient's behavioral and cognitive problems, the availability of part-time or less cognitively demanding work, the likelihood of integrating the patient slowly back into the work environment, and job coaching. A formal work site evaluation by a vocational specialist or occupational therapist may be helpful in some cases.

Interviewing family members to assess their observations of the patient's organizational skills, initiation, motivation, behavioral controls, emotional lability, social skills and functioning, concentration, persistence, fatigability, and executive functions can also provide useful information about a patient's ability to function in real-world settings. This information can help us determine whether there has been a change in the patient's functioning and whether they feel that the patient can and is willing to work. While obtaining this information is quite labor intensive, it is crucial in helping us determine the patient's vocational potential.

While research has shown that no single variable or test can predict all vocational outcomes, Dikmen and Machamer (1995) found that patients who had sustained mild traumatic brain injuries based on their Glasgow Coma Scale (GCS) scores had an 80% chance of returning to work at 1 year post injury, which was identical with a trauma control group. These investigators found, however, that if the individual had a pre-existing history of an unstable work history, low educational background, was over the age of 50, and had sustained severe injuries to other parts of his or her body, the likelihood of returning to work dropped to 15%. They also found that individuals over the age of 60 were less likely to return to work than younger persons. Individuals who failed to graduate from high school were less likely to return to work at 1 year post injury than those who had completed high school (Greenspan, Wrigley, Kresnow, Branche-Dorsey, & Fine, 1996). Sbordone and Guilmette (1999) found in their review of the research literature that an individual patient's pre-existing history of dependability on the job, absenteeism, ability to manage frustration at work, and length of employment were important factors in predicting future job success, particularly following a mild traumatic brain injury.

SUMMARY

NEUROPSYCHOLOGICAL TESTS ARE developed to identify individuals with brain damage. They were never designed to predict how these individuals would behave in real-world situations. Over the past decade more attention has been directed to this problem. Psychologists have tried to increase the ecological validity of standardized tests by selecting tests that have some resemblance to real-world settings. Psychologists have also used statistical techniques to correlate the patient's neuropsychological test scores to measures of real-world functioning. While both approaches have their merits, they also have serious shortcomings.

Psychologists need to assess the demand characteristics of a patient's environment by interviewing persons who are familiar with the patient and have observed the patient function in these settings (Sbordone, 1987). Psychologists should observe the patient function in settings that are highly dissimilar to the environment in which they were tested. These settings will permit the patient to exhibit pathological behaviors and cognitive deficits that were masked by the highly structured and artificial testing environment and were not predicted by the patient's test data.

Psychologists hold a number of assumptions as a result of their education and training that prevents them from understanding the concept of ecological validity. These assumptions have allowed psychologists to routinely utilize insensitive tests to patients to assess their cognitive and executive functions and arrive at inaccurate and misleading opinions about the patient's ability to function in real-world settings. For example, IQ tests were never designed to assess brain-injured patients and frequently produce misleading and inaccurate predictions about the patient's ability to function in real-world settings.

Standardized neuropsychological tests are generally poor at assessing patients with frontal lobe injuries, particularly when the damage involves the orbital frontal lobes. Many neuropsychologists do not understand the executive functions of the brain or how to assess them. They typically administer tests that are believed to be sensitive to frontal lobe damage even though damage to a number of subcortical structures can produce executive dysfunction when the frontal lobes are intact.

Neuropsychological tests have been utilized to predict a patient's ability to work and maintain employment even though the empirical data supporting their use and effectiveness is quite limited. Psychologists should seek out information from significant others, vocational specialists, and occupational rehabilitation professionals to assess the patient's work potential (Sbordone, 1988).

REFERENCES

Bach, P. J. (1993). Demonstrating relationships between natural history, assessment results and functional loss in civil proceedings. In H. V. Hall and R. J. Sbordone (Eds.), *Disorders of executive functions: Civil and criminal law applications* (pp. 135–159). Delray Beach, FL: St. Lucie Press.

Bigler, E. D. (1988). Frontal lobe damage and neuropsychological assessment. *Archives of Clinical Neuropsychology, 3,* 279–297.

Chaytor, N., & Schmitter-Edgecombe, M. (2003). The ecological validity of neuropsychological tests: A review of the literature on everyday cognitive skills. *Neuropsychological Review, 13*(4), 181–197.

Cripe, L. I. (1996). The ecological validity of executive function testing. In R. J. Sbordone & C. Long (Eds.), *Ecological validity of neuropsychogical testing* (pp. 129–146). Delray Beach, FL: GR Press/St. Lucie Press.

Cronbach, L. J. (1984). *Essentials of psychological testing* (4th ed.). New York: Harper & Row.

Cummings, J. L. (1995). Anatomic and behavioral aspects of frontal-subcortical circuits. In J. Grafman, K. J. Holyoak, & F. Boller (Eds.), Structure and function of the human pre-frontal cortex. *Annals of the New York Academy of Sciences, 769,* 1–13.

Damasio, A. R. (1985). The frontal lobes. In K. M. Heilman & E. Valenstein (Eds.), *Clinical neuropsychology* (2nd ed., pp 409–460). New York: Oxford University Press.

Dikmen, S., & Machamer, J. E. (1995). Neurobehavioral outcomes and their determinants. *Journal of Head Trauma Rehabilitation, 10,* 48–67.

Franzen, M. D., & Wilhelm, K. L. (1996). Conceptual foundations of ecological validity in neuropsychology. In R. J. Sbordone & C. J. Long (Eds.), *The ecological validity of neuropsychological testing* (pp. 51–69). Orlando: GR Press/St. Lucie Press.

Golden, C. J., Hammeke, T. A., & Purisch, A. D. (1978). Diagnostic validity of a standardized neuropsychological battery derived from Luria's neuropsychological tests. *Journal of Consulting and Clinical Psychology, 5,* 221–238.

Greenspan, A. I., Wrigley, J. M., Kresnow, M., Branche-Dorsey, C. M., & Fine, P. R. (1996). Factors influencing failure to return to work due traumatic brain injury. *Brain Injury, 10,* 207–218.

Halstead, W. C. (1947). *Brain and intelligence: A quantitative study of the frontal lobes.* Chicago: University of Chicago Press.

Halstead, W. C. (1950). Frontal lobe functions and intelligence. *Bulletin of the Los Angeles Neurological Society, 15,* 205–212.

Long, C. J., & Kibby, M. Y. (1995). Ecological validity of neuropsychological tests: A look at neuropsychology's past and the impact that ecological issues may have on its future. *Advances in Medical Psychotherapy, 8,* 59–78.

Luria, A. R. (1996). *Human brain and psychological processes.* New York: Harper and Row.

Mesulam, M. M. (1986). Frontal cortex and behavior: Editorial. *Annals of Neurology, 19,* 320–325.

Mitrushina, M. N., Boone, K. B., & D'Elia, L. F. (1999). *Handbook of normative data for neuropsychological assessment.* New York: Oxford University Press.

Plato. (1952). The dialogues of Plato, translated by B. Jowett. In R. M. Hutchins (Eds.), *Great books of the Western World, Volume 7.* Chicago: Encyclopedia Britannica.

Reitan, R. M. (1955). The distribution according to age of a psychologic measure dependent upon organic brain functions. *Journal of Gerontology, 10,* 338.

Reitan, R. M., & Wolfson, D. (1993). Validity of the Trail Making Test as an indicator of organic brain damage. *Perceptual and Motor Skills, 8,* 271–276.

Sbordone, R. J. (1987). A neuropsychological approach to cognitive rehabilitation within a private practice setting. In B. Caplan (Ed.), *Handbook of contemporary rehabilitation* (pp. 323–342). New York: Charles Thomas.

Sbordone, R. J. (1988). Assessment and treatment of cognitive communicative impairments in the closed head injury patient: A neurobehavioral systems approach. *Journal of Head Trauma Rehabilitation, 3*(2), 55–62.

Sbordone, R. J. (1996). Ecological validity: Some critical issues for the neuropsychologist. In R. J. Sbordone & C. J. Long (Eds.), *The ecological validity of neuropsychological testing* (pp. 15–41). Orlando, FL: GR Press/St. Lucie Press.

Sbordone, R. J. (1997). The ecological validity of neuropsychological testing. In A. M. Horton, D. Wedding, & J. Webster (Eds.), *The neuropsychology handbook, Vol. 1: Foundations and assessment* (2nd ed., pp. 365–392). New York: Springer Publishing.

Sbordone, R. J. (2000). The executive functions of the brain. In G. Groth-Marnat (Ed.), *Neuropsychological assessment in clinical practice: A guide to test interpretation and integration* (pp. 437–456). New York: Wiley.

Sbordone, R. J., & Guilmette, T. J. (1999). Ecological validity: Prediction of everyday and vocational functioning from neuropsychological test data. In J. J. Sweet (Ed.), *Forensic neuropsychology* (pp. 227–254). Lisse, The Netherlands: Swets and Zeitlinger.

Sbordone, R. J., & Purisch, A. D. (1996). Hazards of blind analysis of neuropsychological data in assessing cognitive disability. *Neurorehabilitation, 7,* 15–26.

Sbordone, R. J., Seyranian, G. D., & Ruff, R. M. (1998). Are the subjective complaints of brain-injured patients reliable? *Brain-Injury, 12*(6), 505–515.

Sbordone, R. J., Seyranian, G. D., & Ruff, R. M. (2000). The use of significant others to enhance the detection of malingers from traumatic brain-injured patients. *Archives of Clinical Neuropsychology, 15,* 465–477.

Stuss, D. T., & Benson, D. F. (1986). *The frontal lobes.* New York: Raven Press.

Teuber, H. L. (1972). Unity and diversity of frontal lobe function. *Acta Neurobiologica Experimentalis, 32,* 615–656.

Teuber, H. L., Battersby, W. S., & Bender, M. B. (1960). *Visual field defects after penetrating missible wounds of the brain.* Cambridge, MA: Harvard University Press.

Williams, J. M. (1996). A practical model of everyday memory assessment. In R. J. Sbordone & C. Long (Eds.), *Ecological validity of neuropsychogical testing* (pp. 129–146). Delray Beach, FL: GR Press/St. Lucie Press.

Wilson, B. A. (1993). Ecological validity of neuropsychological assessment: Do neuropsychological indexes predict performance in everyday activities? *Applied and Preventive Psychology, 2,* 209–215.

Wilson, B. A., Cockburn, J., & Baddeley, A. D. (1985). *The Rivermead Behavioural Test manual.* Bury St. Edmunds, U.K.: Thames Valley Test Company.

Zangwill, O. L. (1966). Psychological deficits associated with frontal lobe lesions. *International Journal of Neurology, 5,* 395–402.

13

The Dean-Woodcock Neuropsychological Assessment System

RAYMOND S. DEAN AND ANDREW S. DAVIS

THE DEAN-WOODCOCK NEUROPSYCHOLOGICAL Assessment System (DWNAS) (Dean & Woodcock, 2003a, 2003b, 2003c, 2003d) was designed to be interpreted on at least two levels, depending on the training of the examiner and the intended use of the test results. As Dean (1989) and others have argued, a neuropsychological assessment offers the most complete psychological picture of a subject possible. Indeed the neuropsychological battery includes measures of cognitive, sensory-motor, and emotional status. From this point of view, interpretation of the DWNAS may be accomplished at an information processing or functional level consistent with the CHC (Gf-Gc) model (see Schrank, Flanagan, Woodcock, & Mascolo, 2001 for a review). A second level of interpretation includes a consideration of the neurological implications of a patient's performance.

This chapter provides an introduction to the Dean-Woodcock Neuropsychological Assessment System. The Woodcock-Johnson III Tests of Cognitive Ability and the Woodcock-Johnson III Tests of Achievement are the core of the cognitive neuropsychological model offered by (Dean & Woodcock, 1999). The Dean-Woodcock Sensory Motor Battery (DWSMB) and the Dean-Woodcock Structured Interview and Emotional Status Exam round out the assessment of the neuropsychological functions. The Structured Interview and Mental Status Examination assess the "Facilitator-Inhibitors," which may influence neuropsychological functioning.

Although the Dean-Woodcock Neuropsychological Battery (DWNB) is extensive, including measures of simple and complex sensory and motor behavior, family and medical history, and emotional functioning, it, too, is not complete without a measure of cognitive ability. Despite a number of excellent measures of cognitive functioning, the Woodcock-Johnson III Tests of Cognitive Ability (WJ-III COG) and Achievement (WJ-III ACH) were selected as the best cognitive measure to round out the DWNAS, because of its construction around a single theory, which has a longstanding reputation in the history of cognitive assessment, theoretical foundation, technical properties, and ability to provide practical, functional, and predictive information regarding cognitive profiles. The Woodcock-Johnson-III (WJ-III) is a wide range, comprehensive battery of individually administered tests measuring cognitive abilities and achievement. It is composed of two major parts: the WJ-III COG and the WJ-III ACH, as mentioned previously. Both parts may be further subdivided into a Standard Battery and a Supplemental Battery. Depending on the purpose and extent of the assessment, the Standard Batteries of the WJ-III COG and WJ-III ACH may be used alone or in conjunction with tests from the Supplemental Batteries.

The DWSMB was designed to offer a comprehensive group of tests that complement measured cognitive functioning. As the name would imply, the battery is comprised of two major sections: sensory and motor. The sensory section consists of eight tests that evaluate simple and complex visual, auditory, and tactile perception. Motor functions are assessed with nine individual tests. Three of these measures are standardized adaptations of neurological tests of subcortical functioning. The assessment of subcortical motor functions is important, because impairment at this level may often mimic cortical dysfunction (Dean, 1988). The six remaining motor tests are meant to measure motor functioning predominantly at the cortical level. This chapter provides an overview of the history and development of each test as well as detailed administration and scoring procedures, which are offered in both English and Spanish.

Regardless of whether a *flexible* or *fixed* battery approach is utilized, the combination or melding of different tests to form a battery can be problematic. This is because the different measures were likely normed on different samples. This can negatively impact intraindividual interpretations, especially when the normative samples were collected over a period of years. This is especially problematic for measures of cognitive processing due to the "Flynn Effect" (Flynn, 1984, 1987).

This has led test companies and test developers to link, conorm, and concurrently develop tests that assess different functions. This can be seen in the commonly used Wechsler scales. A deficit in short-term auditory working memory uncovered on the Letter-Word Identification or Digit Span subtests on the Wechsler Adult Intelligence Scale—Third Edition (WAIS-III; Wechsler, 1997) could be substantiated by the Wechsler Memory Scale—Third Edition (WMS-III; The Psychological Corporation, 1997).

This idea of creating a comprehensive neuropsychological battery that relies upon a singular theoretical orientation and connected normative data is realized with the introduction of the DWNAS (Dean & Woodcock, 2003a). The DWSMB can be used as a stand-alone measure or in conjunction with the WJ-III COG (Woodcock, McGrew, & Mather, 2001a) and the WJ-III ACH (Woodcock, McGrew, & Mather, 2001b). The combination of the DWNB, WJ-III COG, and the WJ-III ACH allows for a complete assessment of neurofunctional status. This includes measures of cortical and subcortical sensory-motor functioning, a full range of higher order cognitive processing abilities, and current academic achievement skills.

The raw scores obtained on the subtest from both the DWSMB and WJ-III are transformed to yield W-scores and W-difference scores with normative samples of individuals ranging from 4 to over 90 years of age. Most traditional measures of sensory–motor functioning use cutoff scores that indicate the presence or lack of impairment. The W-scores on the DWSMB and WJ-III allow for increased ipsative comparison and are especially useful for tracking longitudinal changes as may be seen in degenerative disorders. W-scores also contain a greater range than cutoff scores, which increases the sensitivity to subtle impairment. The DWSMB instructional manual contains instructions in both Spanish and English. The following section will briefly describe each subtest of the DWSMB and the functions of the WJ-III; for more details on the administration and interpretation the reader is directed to the *Examiner's Manual* (Dean & Woodcock, 2003b).

DEAN-WOODCOCK SENSORY MOTOR BATTERY

REGARDING THE NEED for a comprehensive measure of sensory-motor functions, Reitan and Wolfson (2003) indicated that, "the close dependence of sensory-motor functions on the biological status of the nervous system permits measured deficits to be related to brain impairment, as contrasted with the much greater dependence of higher-level brain functions on environmental opportunities, educational advantage, and so forth" (p. 13). It is also essential to recognize that the nervous system deficits revealed on measures of sensory-motor tests can profoundly impact higher-order cognitive processing. This was recently demonstrated in a study by Davis, Finch, Dean, & Woodcock (under review). The authors conducted a canonical correlation of 265 children with mixed neurological and psychiatric disorders. It was demonstrated that sensory motor skills shared 92% of the variance with a measure of cognitive processing, while sensory-motor skills shared 90% of the variability with a measure of academic achievement. The potential impact of sensory-motor deficits is quite profoundly related to higher order functional ability. This relationship has been further expanded by recent research, which is increasingly implicating the cerebellum, formerly primarily associated with motor functioning, in the role of executive functioning, language, memory, and reading (Gottwald, Wilde, Mihajlovic, & Mehdorn, 2004; Nicolson, Fawcett, & Dean, 2001).

The development of the DWSMB was guided by a need for a comprehensive neuropsychological battery that would not only yield measurement of current neurofunctional status, but would be psychometrically sound. The paucity of psychometric rigor is especially evident for traditional modalities of assessing sensory-motor skills. The assessment of sensory and motor skills is not unique to neuropsychology; indeed, the measurement of sensory and motor skills is a standard part of a neurological exam. However, neurologists tend to rely upon qualitative measurement of functions, while traditional neuropsychological sensory-motor measures are troubled by a lack of standardization and inadequate reliability and validity (Woodward, Ridenour, Dean, & Woodcock, 2002). Even the most widely used neuropsychological battery has been criticized for difficulties with standardization and the normative samples. Regarding the Halstead-Reitan Neuropsychological Battery (HRNB; Reitan & Wolfson, 1993), Lezak, Howieson, and Loring (2004) wrote, "However, the battery was never standardized on a representative, stratified sample of healthy subjects. As with other procedures lacking appropriate standardization and a set of widely accepted norms, there is much variability both in how HRB data are obtained as well as in their interpretation. With so many available norms, it is possible to choose ones based on desired outcomes" (p. 673).

Another psychometric concern of traditional sensory-motor batteries is their lack of sensitivity to age-related developmental differences. Until recently, developmental differences in sensory and motor skills may have been overlooked based upon the hypothesis that sensory and motor skills can be similarly assessed and interpreted throughout the life span (i.e., Dean & Woodcock, 1994, 1999). However, recent research indicates that not only do developmental differences exist for sensory-motor skills, but developmental differences in sensory-motor skills can predict cognitive achievement, academic performance, and special education placement. Arceneaux, Hill, Chamberlin, and Dean (1997) used the *Dean-Woodcock Sensory Motor Battery* to consider if differences in sensory-motor skills exist for younger and older children. The results supported the connection between maturation, motor abilities, and sensory skills (i.e., Huttenlocher, Levine, Huttenlocher, & Gates, 1990; Statham & Murray, 1971). Some developmental sensory-motor differences are obvious, such as an infant or toddler lacking the subcortical development to walk, run, or balance; while other sensory-motor skills may not be as salient age markers, but may be indicative of future learning problems. Huttenlocher et al. (1990) investigated normal and at-risk children for learning disabilities with a series of simple sensory-motor tasks. These data showed that differential performance on sensory-motor tasks was not only able to distinguish between normal and at-risk children, but sensory-motor tasks were found to be linked to intelligence and special education placement. The differential sensory-motor abilities exhibited by normal and at-risk children throughout the lifespan indicate that sensory-motor assessment measures should provide age-specific normative data.

The importance of using reliable and valid neuropsychological measures is magnified for sensory-motor tests, because even one error may be pathognomic of dysfunction. This is in direct contrast to most measures of higher order processing in which a patient may miss several items and still be in the average or above range. The DWNB is easy to administer, and a computer scoring system is available. Even with impaired patients, the DWSMB is typically administered in about 30 to 45 minutes. The Structured Neuropsychological Interview and the Emotional Status Examination take about 30 minutes each to administer.

The DWNAS contains 18 subtests, 8 of which were designed to measure *sensory* functions and 10 of which were designed to measure *motor* functioning. The subtests of the DWNAS, along with a brief description of each, are displayed in Table 13.1.

The sensory section consists of eight tests that evaluate simple and complex visual, auditory, and tactile perception. Motor functions are assessed with nine individual tests. Three of these measures are standardized adaptations of neurological tests of subcortical functioning. The assessment of subcortical motor functions is important, because impairment at this level may often mimic cortical dysfunction (Dean, 1988). The six remaining motor tests are meant to measure motor functioning predominantly at the cortical level.

TABLE 13.1 Dean-Woodcock Neuropsychological Assessment System

Subtest	Ability or symptom assessed
Sensory Subtests	
Lateral Preference Scale	Laterality and handedness
Near-Point Visual Acuity	Visual acuity, Visual perception
Visual Confrontation	Peripheral visual fields
Naming Pictures of Objects	Dysnomia, anomia, visual dysgnosia, visual agnosia, confrontation naming
Auditory Acuity	Auditory acuity
Palm Writing	Graphesthesia, tactile discrimination
Object Identification	Astereognosis
Finger Identification	Asomatognosia, finger agnosia
Simultaneous Localization (hands only, hand and cheek)	Asomatognosia, broad sensory and tactile reception left-right confusion
Motor Tests	
Gait and Station	Ataxia, coordination, lower extremity gross motor functioning, presence of subcortical lesions, spasticity
Romberg	Cerebellar dysfunction, vestibular dysfunction
Construction	Construction dyspraxia, visual motor integration, visuospatial awareness and memory
Coordination (finger to nose, hand to thigh)	Coordinated motor movement at the cerebral and cerebellar levels, myoclonic jerks, upper extremity motor functioning
Mime Movements	Ideomotor dyspraxia, receptive language, verbal agnosia
Left-Right Movements	Left-right confusion, perseveration
Finger Tapping	Fine motor speed, manual dexterity, overall functioning of the motor strip and precentral gyrus
Expressive Speech	Dysarthria, dysnomia, peripheral speech mechanisms
Grip Strength	Deficits in the contralateral motor strip, overall integrity of the cerebral hemispheres, upper extremity motor strength

Adapted from Dean-Woodcock Neuropsychological Assessment System

Broad abilities	Subtests
Comprehension Knowledge	Verbal Comprehension
	Picture Vocabulary
	Synonyms
	Antonyms
	Verbal Analogies
	Expressive Speech (D-WNB)

(Continued)

TABLE 13.1 Dean-Woodcock Neuropsychological Assessment System
(Continued)

Long-Term Retrieval	Visual Auditory Learning
	Visual Auditory Learning-Delayed
Visual-Spatial Thinking	Spatial Relations
	Picture Recognition
Auditory Processing	Sound Blending
	Incomplete Words
Fluid Reasoning	Concept Formation
	Analysis-Synthesis
	Planning
Processing Speed	Visual Matching
	Decision Speed
Short-Term Memory	Memory for Words
	Numbers Reversed
	Auditory Working Memory
	Picture Recognition
Quantitative Knowledge	Calculation Test
	Applied Problems
Reading/Writing	Letter-Word Identification
	Spelling Test
	Passage Comprehension
	Writing Samples
Sensory Assessment	Visual Acuity
	Visual Confrontation Test
	Object Naming
	Auditory Perception
	Tactile Perception
Motor Assessment	Gait and Station
	Romberg
	Traditional
	One Foot
	Heel to Toe
	Coordination/Gross Cerebellar Assessment
	Construction
	Mime Movements
	Left–Right Movements
	Finger Tapping
	Grip Strength
History/Emotional Status	Structured Interview
	History
	Medical
	Psychiatric
	Social
	Family
	Mental Status

Adapted from Davis, Finch, Dean, and Woodcock (2006).

SENSORY MOTOR TESTS

LATERAL PREFERENCE SCALE

MOST MEASURES OF sensory and motor functioning vary with the subject's dominant and nondominant preference (Dean, 1988), therefore, this measure may not necessarily determine hemispheric laterality for functions. However, Reitan and Davison (1974) showed that close to 100% of unimpaired subjects maintain the same dominant hand after a 5-year span. The test is scored with a 5-point Likert Scale.

NEAR-POINT VISUAL ACUITY

NEUROPSYCHOLOGISTS OFTEN RELY upon patient report or a review of records regarding visual acuity. This may be an oversight, because even slight visual impairment may have a salient effect on test performance. A recent study with a large sample of 2,946 participants found that impairments in visual acuity were related to cognitive decline (Clemons, Rankin, & McBee, 2006). These authors hypothesized that age-related macular degeneration and cognitive impairment have the same pathogenesis, namely, the loss of neurons in the central nervous system. For the Near Point Visual Acuity Test, using one eye at a time, the patient reads series of numbers on an eye chart about 14 inches away (using Snellen notations; e.g., 20/20 vision).

VISUAL CONFRONTATION

THE ASSESSMENT OF peripheral visual fields is useful for assessing the contralateral visual field as this tends to be sensitive to sudden onset. The examinee keeps his or her eyes forward and attempts to identify finger movements in the peripheral visual fields. The measure is useful also in localization of the lesion in the prechiasmal, chiasmal, or postchiasmal area (Dean & Woodcock, 2003b).

NAMING PICTURES OF OBJECTS

ALTHOUGH DESIGNED AS a sensory measure to detect visual agnosia, the Naming Pictures of Objects Test is also a qualitative measure of dysnomia and dysarthria. Difficulty with confrontation naming can result from a variety of neurological conditions. On this task the examinee is required to name 21 objects, which are presented in a stimulus booklet. Although visual agnosia or dysgnosia may exist independent of other language problems, it is more likely that difficulty with confrontational naming will indicate more broad receptive or expressive language impairment (Dean & Woodcock, 2003b).

AUDITORY ACUITY

AUDITORY DEFICITS CAN have profound impact on the patient's test taking skills. This is especially true when the problem is undiagnosed. For example, a prominent theory postulates sensory-motor deficits are present in the etiology of dyslexia, including auditory processing (e.g., Ramus et al., 2003). As in clinical neurology, the examinee gently rubs his or her fingers together about 3 inches away from the examinee's ears one at a time as well as bilaterally. Thus determination of lateral impairment is in keeping with difference in between the left and right auditory channels (Dean & Woodcock, 2003b).

TACTILE IDENTIFICATION

Palm Writing
Measures of graphesthesia are classic measures of tactile perception and appear on other batteries (Halstead-Reitan Neuropsychological Test Battery; Reitan & Wolfson, 1993). On this task the examinee must first determine if an X or an O was written on his or her palm, while the second part of the test requires the identification numbers. Due to the simple nature of the tasks, this measure is extremely sensitive to impairment, and even one error may be pathognomic of dysfunction. This subtest also can aid in lateralization of brain dysfunction. Agraphesthesia may initially present as clumsiness or maladroitness (Dean & Woodcock, 2003b).

Object Identification
Difficulty in identifying common objects by tactile manipulation without the aid of vision is indicative of astereognosis, and similar to agraphesthesia. Errors are not expected and may be viewed as pathognomic signs of cerebral dysfunction. Because the examinee attempts these tasks with both hands, difficulty on this measure can also contribute to information regarding lateralization of impairment.

Finger Identification
Finger agnosia (inability to recognize tactile stimulation of one's own specific fingers) is also generally pathognomic of dysfunction and contributes information regarding lateralization. Finger agnosia is also

important in the recognition of Gerstmann's syndrome, a disorder that will greatly contribute to academic problems. Indeed, recent research demonstrated that finger agnosia was able to significantly predict number skill difficulty in a group of children between the first and second grade (Noel, 2005). The patient is required to determine which finger is being touched without aid of vision. Like many of the other tactile sensory tasks, difficulty on this task is generally associated with contralateral parietal lobe lesions (Reitan & Wolfson, 1993).

Simultaneous Localization

This is the fourth of the tactile subtests, all of which contribute lateralization information concerning cortical impairment. Double sensory and unilateral stimulation are used, because double sensory stimulation has been shown to often be a more sensitive measure of tactile perception (e.g., Kahn, Goldfarb, Pollack, & Peck, 1960). On this subtest the patient's hands and cheeks are lightly touched in a series and combination of right only, left only, and right and left together, and the patient is required to identify the source of the tactile stimulation.

GAIT AND STATION

MANY VOLITIONAL MOTOR functions assessed by traditional measures are associated with the motor strip anterior to the central gyrus. However, the DWSMB attempts to assess both cortical and subcortical motor functioning. One of the problems with traditional measures of sensory and motor functioning is an emphasis on upper extremity. Motor deficits in the lower extremity can aid in the localization of neuropsychological impairment. Although lower extremity motor skills are often assessed qualitatively, this test provides empirically derived standard scores, which offer baseline measures of neurologic functioning. The DWSMB assesses gait through three tasks thought to be sensitive to subcortical functioning (Dean & Woodcock, 2003b) requiring lower extremity gross motor movement, coordination, balance, and speed with three subtests (gait free-walking; steadiness and balance; station).

ROMBERG

THE ROMBERG TEST is commonly found on most neurological exams, although there is a dearth of standardized measures. Tell, Lefkowitz, Diehr, and Elster (1998) linked cerebral changes, including white matter disease and ventricular size, with balance. Patients undergo the Romberg test by standing erect with their eyes closed. They are observed for signs of swaying and impaired balance for three progressively more difficult tasks (Dean & Woodcock, 2003b).

CONSTRUCTION

ALTHOUGH CONSTRUCTION TASKS are typically associated with right parietal involvement, construction tasks are extremely sensitive to gross neurological impairment. The task on the DWSMB primarily assesses visual-motor integration, visuo-spatial, and other signs of construction dyspraxia. The Construction subtest on the DWSMB is composed of two tasks. The examinee is required to copy a cross from a stimulus book and to draw a clock with the hands indicating a directed time. Clock drawing tests have been shown to predict impairment with several patient populations, including being able to differentially diagnose Alzheimer's disease (Dean & Woodcock, 2003b).

COORDINATION

THE MOTOR COORDINATION test assesses upper extremity motor capacity with two tasks. The first task requires the subject to move his or her finger to his or her nose and then to touch the examiner's finger as the examiner moves his or her finger across the examinee's field of vision. The second task requires the examinee to alternatively tap his or her thigh with the front and back of his or her hand. Both tasks are completed with both of the examinee's hands, which allows laterality and assessment of motor movement at the cerebral and cerebellar levels (Dean & Woodcock, 2003b).

MIME MOVEMENTS

MIME MOVEMENTS IS a derivation of classic measures of ideomotor dyspraxia in which difficulty is revealed in motor execution. Difficulty with miming motor movements may occur in initiation, execution, control, motor planning, or kinesthetic praxis. The patient is required to execute simple motor acts that involve the hands, mouth, and head. This test is particularly useful when a patient is presenting with motor problems that may be secondary to receptive language deficits, because dyspraxia can be assessed without language-based commands.

LEFT-RIGHT MOVEMENTS

CONFUSION DETERMINING THE left and right side of the body is rare in children over the age of nine and thus should be considered a pathognomic indicator when it occurs (Dean & Woodcock, 2003b). Left-right confusion is also another hallmark of Gerstmann's syndrome (Dean, 1988).

FINGER TAPPING

FINGER TAPPING TASKS are one of the most commonly used measures of manual dexterity (Sattler & D'Amato, 2002). As with several other well-known measures in the Battery, this version on the DWSMB offers standardization and normative samples. Like earlier versions of this task, the Finger Tapping Test on the DWSMB assesses fine motor speed and dexterity and can serve as a measure of the overall integrity of the motor strip and precentral gyrus (Dean & Woodcock, 2003b).

EXPRESSIVE SPEECH

DIFFICULTIES WITH PRODUCING speech and language may have many causes, including deficits in the typical language centers of the brain such as Broca's area, Wernicke's area, or the arcuate fasciculus. Difficulty may also arise from dysarthria (difficulty or weakness with the motor muscles of speech system). The Expressive Speech subtest requires examinees to repeat a series of simple words and phrases (Dean & Woodcock, 2003b).

GRIP STRENGTH

MEASURING A PATIENT'S grip for symmetry weakness is a standard part of a neurological and neuropsychological examination using a hand dynometer. Grip strength is a sensitive measure of overall cortical integrity, and deficits with either hand may be linked to contralateral dysfunction in the motor strip (Dean & Woodcock, 2003b).

COGNITIVE FUNCTIONING

THE IDEA OF creating a comprehensive neuropsychological battery that relies upon a singular theoretical orientation and connected normative data was recently realized with the introduction of the DWNB (Dean & Woodcock, 2003a). The DWNB can be used as a stand-alone measure or in conjunction with the WJ-III COG (Woodcock et al., 2001a) and the WJ-III ACH (Woodcock et al., 2001b). When the DWNB is combined with the measures of cognitive processing and academic achievement, the comprehensive battery is referred to as the

DWNAS. Table 13.1 also provides an overview of the functions and individual tests that comprise each.

SHORT-TERM / WORKING MEMORY

SHORT-TERM MEMORY IS a critical component of most cognitive activities and is an aspect of cognitive efficiency. It is defined as the ability to hold information in conscious awareness and then use it within a few seconds. Short-term memory's goal is limited: hold the information briefly until it is used, then disregard it. A classic example of this ability is remembering a telephone number long enough to dial it. Among the consequences of a short-term memory deficit is difficulty in remembering just imparted instructions or information. Evaluation of short-term memory in the DWNAS is provided by four subtests. The stimuli presented in these subtests are arbitrary and meaningless, so as to emphasize the role of memory as opposed to stored knowledge.

COMPREHENSION KNOWLEDGE (CRYSTALLIZED INTELLIGENCE)

ORIGINALLY IDENTIFIED AS crystallized intelligence, comprehension knowledge represents the breadth and depth of knowledge, including the ability for verbal communication and reasoning based on previously learned experiences. This form of crystallized intelligence is primarily language-based and highly environmentally sensitive, relying on degree of personal investment, education, and general life experiences. A patient with a deficit in this general ability may present with limited knowledge of word meanings, poor ability to interchange words of the same or opposite meaning, and an overall poor grasp of language skills.

LONG-TERM RETRIEVAL

LONG-TERM RETRIEVAL IS the ability to store information and fluently retrieve it later. This ability incorporates a number of narrow abilities including associative memory, ideational fluency, meaningful memory, associative fluency, naming facility, expressional fluency, and word fluency. Long-term retrieval should not be confused with long-term memory. Whereas long-term memory is the actual storage of information, long-term retrieval is procedural in nature, emphasizing the actual transfer of knowledge from short-term memory. The tests of the DWNAS that measure this look at both storage and retrieval of information. They further emphasize the ability to associate meaningful information (old and new), which, in turn, provides for more organized thought and improved long-term memory. Of note, although long-term memory and long-term retrieval are distinct abilities, the processes used to measure them are the same.

VISUAL-SPATIAL THINKING

VISUAL-SPATIAL THINKING IS the ability to perceive, analyze, synthesize, and think with visual patterns. Storage and recall of visual stimuli is also a component of visual-spatial thinking. A number of specific subabilities contribute to this, including the abilities to manipulate objects or patterns mentally and identify visual representations that are abstract or obscure. A patient with difficulties in this area may demonstrate poor spatial orientation, misperceive object-space relationships (e.g., the distance between the patient's car and the one in front of them), and have difficulty orienting on a map.

AUDITORY PROCESSING

AUDITORY PROCESSING IS the ability to analyze, synthesize, and discriminate auditory stimuli, even when distorted. Narrow abilities that contribute to it include phonological awareness and processing, tonal discrimination, and ability to track/sequence auditory temporal events. Deficits in this area likely present as an inability to discriminate or recognize sounds of speech (e.g., unable to hear the difference between "free" and "three") or to detect subtle changes in tone, which might provide significant social clues (e.g., detect sarcasm).

FLUID REASONING

FLUID OR NOVEL reasoning is defined as an ability to form concepts, reason, and problem solve in unfamiliar situations. Key to this ability are the contributions of both inductive and deductive reasoning. Fluid reasoning is manifested in the reorganization, transformation, and extrapolation of information. Deficits in this area may present as difficulty in generalizing rules, forming concepts, and seeing the implications of behavior. Deficits in fluid reasoning often underlie social and emotional problems.

PROCESSING SPEED

PROCESSING SPEED IS the ability to perform automatic or simple cognitive tasks rapidly. This ability is generally assessed utilizing a timed component, thereby requiring the ability to maintain focused attention. It is this element of time restriction that makes the task difficult and demands cognitive efficiency. Although the tasks included for measurement in the DWNAS are simple, it should be noted that impaired processing speed clearly also affects the completion of complex tasks.

QUANTITATIVE KNOWLEDGE AND READING-WRITING ABILITY

THE LAST TWO broad ability classifications are quantitative knowledge and reading-writing ability. These are largely reflected in academic achievement and, as such, will be discussed together. Quantitative knowledge is the ability to comprehend quantitative concepts and relationships and to manipulate numerical symbols. It involves skills of addition, subtraction, multiplication, and division. The ability to solve word problems, determine rate calculations, and use percentages and statistics are also subsumed in the quantitative knowledge component. In simple, quantitative knowledge measures mathematical skills drawn from stored mathematical knowledge.

THE DEAN-WOODCOCK STRUCTURED INTERVIEW AND EMOTIONAL STATUS EXAMINATION

THE EMOTIONAL STATUS Examination provides the clinician with information regarding the patient's emotional functioning in a structured format. Constructed in a similar fashion to the Structured Interview, information can be collected from either the patient or a reliable informant. There are three sections of the Emotional Status Examination. The first section is for the patient to enter their information. The second section is structured with a series of questions that are designed to explore the symptomology of psychiatric disorders. The final section, Clinical Observations and Impressions, allows for the qualitative observation of orientation, physical appearance, behavioral observations, emotional status, and cognitive status. The Emotional Status Examination will provide a format for report writing, because much of the information that is typically in a behavioral observation section of a report will be collected on the Emotional Status Examination.

RESEARCH OF THE DEAN-WOODCOCK NEUROPSYCHOLOGICAL BATTERY

AT THIS TIME, a review of the literature reveals that the vast majority of the research with the DWNB has been conducted by the authors of the measure and their colleagues. An early version of the DWSMB was administered to 95 participants to assess the reliability, which was gauged to be adequate to excellent (Woodward et al., 2002). Even though many of the measures of the DWSMB were adapted from classic neurological and neuropsychological measures, the size of the standardization sample and the extensive standardization warrant investigations regarding construct validity. The test manual reports a construct validity study, which examined the underlying factor structure of the DWSMB. Hill, Lewis, Dean, and Woodcock (2001) investigated the scores of 617 participants between the ages of 2 and 88 and used exploratory factor analysis, which showed that a three factor solution best fit the data, with the following three factors emerging: (1) sensory functions, (2) cortical motor functions, and (3) subcortical motor functions.

The largest study to date involving the DWSMB was conducted by Davis et al. (2006) and examined the factor structure of 701 neurologically impaired participants and 950 normal individuals. Three factors emerged which accounted for 58.2% of the total test variation and were labeled simple sensory skills, motor and complex sensory skills, and subcortical motor skills and auditory/visual acuity. The results of that exploratory factor analysis are presented in Table 13.2.

There were several cross loadings present. This was expected, because there seems to be a hierarchical ranking in regard to the complexity of the cortical sensory-motor tasks. As tasks became more complex there were more cross loadings between the two factors. The combination of subcortical motor tasks and auditory/visual acuity tasks, which loaded on the third factor, likely reflects the primitive, or more basic, components of these DWSMB tasks. Davis et al. (2006) wrote "Although normal functioning would be impaired if an individual demonstrated extreme deficits on any task of the DWSMB, it is likely that severely impaired performance on any task of Factor Three would indicate critical neurological problems, such as deafness, blindness, inability to walk or stand upright" (p. 1168). It seems as if a simple approach to differentiating between sensory and motor factors on the DWSMB would not yield accurate results. This is primarily due to the overlap between sensory and motor functions due to their morphological neurological proximity, as well as to the investigation of both cortical and subcortical sensory-motor skills on the DWSMB. Thus, practitioners should exercise caution when interpreting the DWSMB unless they possess a thorough understanding of the relationship and function of the sensory strip, motor strip, subcortical functions, as well as the equipotential nature of sensory-motor processing.

Volpe, Davis, and Dean (2006) compared performance on the DWSMB for 250 normal and 250 neurologically impaired individuals and demonstrated the DWSMB was able to correctly identify 92.8% of

TABLE 13.2 Promax Factor Loading Matrix For Three Factor Solution

DWSMB Subtest	Factor		
	1	2	3
Simultaneous Localization—hand/left	**.973**	−1.60	−0.52
Simultaneous Localization—hand/right	**.968**	−1.58	−0.56
Simultaneous Localization—hand/both	**.935**	−1.60	−0.20
Simultaneous Localization—hands & cheeks/left	**.802**	.066	.020
Simultaneous Localization—hands & cheeks/right	**.798**	.076	.009
Simultaneous Localization—hand and cheek/simultaneous	**.756**	.095	.033
Visual Confrontation—total/right	**.688**	.027	.048
Visual Confrontation—total/both	**.664**	.000	.130
Visual Confrontation—total/left	**.657**	.052	.093
Finger Identification—right	**.462**	.375	−.036
Finger Identification—left	**.450**	.403	−.042
Grip Strength—dominant	−.043	**.884**	−.137
Grip Strength—nondominant	−.049	**.859**	−.113
Finger Tapping—nondominant	−.129	**.815**	.025
Finger Tapping—dominant	−.098	**.742**	.050
Coordination—hand–thigh/right	−.252	**.721**	.235
Coordination—hand–thigh/left	−.253	**.719**	.231
Construction—Part B	.161	**.688**	−.082
Object Identification—right	.270	**.549**	−.088
Construction—Part A	.144	**.548**	.145
Palm Writing—total/nondominant	.380	**.538**	−.104
Object Identification—left	.196	**.537**	−.009
Palm Writing—total/dominant	.395	**.509**	−.095
Left–Right Movements—total	.332	**.422**	−.141
Expressive Speech	.158	**.402**	.042
Mime Movements	.252	**.370**	.103
Auditory Acuity—both	.078	−.099	**.836**
Auditory Acuity—left	.108	−.109	**.800**
Auditory Acuity—right	.150	−.111	**.768**
Gait and Station	.103	.168	**.622**
Romberg	.077	.131	**.583**
Near Point Visual Acuity—right eye	−.180	.020	**.611**
Near Point Visual Acuity—left eye	−.197	.018	**.588**
Coordination—finger-to-nose/right	−.146	.171	**.384**
Coordination—finger-to-nose/left	.163	.175	**.351**

Adapted from Davis et al. (2006).

the participants. This figure included 94.4% of the normal controls and
91.2% of the neurologically impaired sample. This was an impressive
finding when it is considered that only sensory-motor measures were
used (no measures of higher order cognitive processing were included).

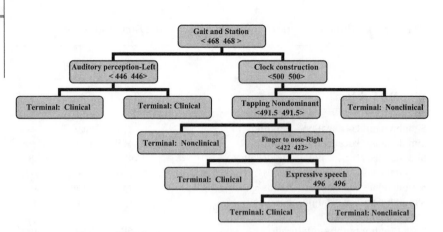

FIGURE 13.1 Classification and regression tree for the DWSMB from the Davis, Finch, Trinkle, Dean, and Woodcock (2006) study.

To further explore the validity of the DWSMB, Davis, Finch, Trinkle, Dean, and Woodcock (in press) investigated the ability of the DWSMB to differentiate between neurologically impaired and normal individuals. Classification and Regression Tree Analysis (CART) was able to identify several clinically useful nodes, which provided a hierarchical decision tree in determining impairment. The results from this study are displayed in Figure 13.1.

A cross validation revealed the model correctly predicted 84.5% of the normal group and 71.4% of the neurologically impaired sample. The primary separation variable was the Gait and Station subtest, while Auditory Acuity and Clock Construction also provided important pathognomic information. This figure demonstrates the clinical utility of the tasks of the DWSMB. Davis et al. (in press) wrote

> Gait and Station can be considered a subtest with a high predictive pathognomic value. Individuals who exhibit errors on Gait and Station are demonstrating problems with lower extremity movement and lower motor coordination and balance, which is pathognomic for ataxia or other gait and balance problems. Individuals with subcortical motor lesions are also likely to demonstrate other obvious behavioral cognitive skills as well. Similarly, the finding that Auditory Acuity demonstrated high differential power along with the Gait and Station subtest can also be hypothesized to be linked to its pathognomic value. On the Davis, Finch, Dean, & Woodcock (2005) exploratory factor analysis study, Auditory Acuity had the highest loading (.836) on the Subcortical Motor tasks and Auditory/Visual Acuity Skills factor. Again, it is likely that even a small error on Auditory Acuity is indicative of neurological impairment. Difficulty with the underlying constructs measured by Gait and Station and Auditory Acuity

will serve to impair other test taking skills. If an individual can not hear the stimulus accurately, or is unable to maintain balance, motor coordination, and posture, it is likely that other neuropsychological test results will be affected. (p. 12 of the manuscript)

In general, the early studies of the clinical utility and validity of the DWSMB are promising. However, the DWSMB, along with the other components of the DWNB, will need to continue to undergo independent validity and reliability studies before the psychometrics of this promising instrument can be fully understood.

REFERENCES

Arceneaux, J. M., Hill, S. K., Chamberlin, C. M., & Dean, R. S. (1997). Developmental and sex differences in sensory and motor functioning. *International Journal of Neuroscience, 89,* 253–263.

Clemons, T. E., Rankin, M. W., & McBee, W. L. (2006). Cognitive impairment in the age-related eye disease study: AERDS report no. 16. *Archives of Ophthalmology, 124,* 537–543.

Davis, A. S., Finch, W. H., Dean, R. S., & Woodcock, R. W. (2006). Cortical and constructs of the Dean-Woodcock Sensory Motor Battery: A construct validity study. *International Journal of Neuroscience, 116,* 1157–1171.

Davis, A. S., Finch, W. H., Dean, R. S., & Woodcock, R. W. (under review). The relationship between sensory-motor skills, cognitive processing, and academic achievement in children with neurological and psychiatric impairment. *School Psychology Quarterly.*

Davis, A. S., Finch, W. H., Trinkle, J., & Dean, R. S. (in press). Classification and regression tree analysis of a neurologically impaired and normal sample using sensory-motor tasks. *International Journal of Neuroscience.*

Dean, R. S. (1988). *Lateral Preference Schedule: Professional manual.* Odessa, FL: Psychological Assessment Resources.

Dean, R. S. (1989). Foundations of rationale for neuropsychological bases of individual differences. In L. C. Hartlage & C. F. Telzrow (Eds.), *The neuropsychology of individual differences: A developmental perspective* (pp. 8–46). New York: Plenum Press.

Dean, R. S., & Woodcock, R. W. (1994). *Dean-Woodcock Neuropsychological Assessment System: Sensory and Motor Assessment Battery.* Itasca, IL: Riverside.

Dean, R. S., & Woodcock, R. W. (1999). *The WJ-R and Bateria-R in neuropsychological assessment—Research report number 3.* Itasca, IL: Riverside Publishing.

Dean, R. S., & Woodcock, R. W. (2003a). *Dean-Woodcock Neuropsychological Battery.* Itasca, IL: Riverside Publishing.

Dean, R. S., & Woodcock, R. W. (2003b). Examiners manual. *Dean-Woodcock Neuropsychological Battery.* Itasca, IL: Riverside Publishing.

Dean, R. S., & Woodcock, R. W. (2003c). Emotional Status Examination. *Dean-Woodcock Neuropsychological Battery*. Itasca, IL: Riverside Publishing.

Dean, R. S., & Woodcock, R. W. (2003d). Structured Neuropsychological Interview. *Dean-Woodcock Neuropsychological Battery*. Itasca, IL: Riverside Publishing.

Flynn, J. R. (1984). The mean IQ of Americans: Massive gains 1932 to 1978. *Psychological Bulletin, 95*, 29–51.

Flynn, J. R. (1987). Massive IQ gains in 14 nations: What IQ tests really measure. *Psychological Bulletin, 101*, 171–191.

Gottwald, B., Wilde, B., Mihajlovic, Z., & Mehdorn, H. M. (2004). Evidence for cognitive deficits after focal cerebellar lesions. *Journal of Neurology, Neurosurgery, and Psychiatry, 75*, 1524–1531.

Hill, S. K., Lewis, M. N., Dean, R. S., & Woodcock, R. S. (2001). Constructs underlying measures of sensory-motor functioning. *Archives of Clinical Neuropsychology, 15*, 631–641.

Huttenlocher, P. R., Levine, S. C., Huttenlocher, J., & Gates, J. (1990). Discrimination of normal and at-risk preschool children on the basis of neurological tests. *Developmental Medicine and Child Neurology, 32*, 394–402.

Kahn, R. L., Goldfarb, A. I., Pollack, M., & Peck, A. (1960). Brief objective measures for the determination of mental status in the aged. *American Journal of Psychiatry, 117*, 326–328.

Lezak, M. D., Howieson, D. B., & Loring, D. W. (2004). *Neuropsychological assessment*. New York: Oxford University Press.

Nicolson, R. I., Fawcett, A. J., & Dean, P. (2001). Developmental dyslexia: The cerebellar deficit hypothesis. *Trends in Neuroscience, 24*, 508–511.

Noel, M. P. (2005). Finger agnosia: A predictor of numerical abilities in children? *Child Neuropsychology, 11*, 413–430.

The Psychological Corporation. (1997). *Wechsler Memory Scale—Third Edition*. San Antonio, TX: Author.

Ramus, F., Rosen, S., Dakin, S. C., Day, B. L., Castellote, J. M., White, S., et al. (2003). Theories of developmental dyslexia: Insights from a multiple case study of dyslexic adults. *Brain, 126*, 841–865.

Reitan, R. M., & Davison, L. A. (1974). *Clinical neuropsychology: Current status and applications*. Washington, DC: Hemisphere Publishing.

Reitan, R. M., & Wolfson, D. (1993). *The Halstead-Reitan Neuropsychological Test Battery*. Tucson, AZ: Neuropsychology Press.

Reitan, R. M., & Wolfson, D. (2003). The significance of sensory-motor functions as indicators of brain dysfunction in children. *Archives of Clinical Neuropsychology, 18*, 11–18.

Sattler, J. M., & D'Amato, R. C. (2002). Brain injuries: Formal batteries and informal measures. In J. M. Sattler (Ed.), *Assessment of children: Behavioral and clinical application* (4th ed., pp. 440–469). San Diego: Jerome M. Sattler.

Schrank, F. A., Flanagan, D. P., Woodcock, R. W., & Mascolo, J. T. (2001). *The essentials of WJ III Cognitive Abilities Assessment.* New York: Wiley and Sons.

Statham, L., & Murray, M. (1971). Early walking patterns of normal children. *Clinical Orthopedics, 79,* 8–24.

Tell, G. S., Lefkowitz, D. S., Diehr, P., & Elster, A. D. (1998). Relationship between balance and abnormalities in cerebral magnetic imaging in older adults. *Archives of Neurology, 55,* 73–79.

Volpe, A. G., Davis, A. S., & Dean, R. S. (2006). Predicting global and specific neurological impairment with sensory-motor functioning. *Archives of Clinical Neuropsychology, 21,* 203–210.

Wechsler, D. (1997). *Wechsler Adult Intelligence Scale—Third Edition.* San Antonio, TX: The Psychological Corporation.

Woodcock, R. S., McGrew, K. S., & Mather, N. (2001a). *Woodcock-Johnson III Tests of Cognitive Ability.* Itasca, IL: Riverside Publishing.

Woodcock, R. S., McGrew, K. S., & Mather, N. (2001b). *Woodcock-Johnson III Tests of Achievement.* Itasca, IL: Riverside Publishing.

Woodward, H. R., Ridenour, T., Dean, R. S., & Woodcock, R. S. (2002). Generalizability of sensory and motor tests. *International Journal of Neuroscience, 112,* 1115–1137.

Section III

Practice Issues in Neuropsychology

14

Cognitive Rehabilitation With Brain-Damaged Patients

Russell D. Pella, Katie Kendra, B. D. Hill, and William Drew Gouvier

WITH ADVANCES IN medical technology, the number of individuals surviving initial life-threatening incidents and medical conditions has increased over the past two decades. Two of the most common causes of cognitive dysfunction secondary to physical problems are stroke-related complications and traumatic brain injury (TBI). A survey of 122 rehabilitation programs within the American Hospital Association Section for Rehabilitation Hospitals and Programs reported strokes were by far the most commonly treated condition with TBI second (Springer, 2003). The effects of brain damage on individuals and society are complex, multifaceted, and challenging to address therapeutically. Individuals with brain damage and those within their social fabric often experience dramatic acute and lingering post-acute changes, altering many areas of daily functioning. Substantial residual cognitive problems often go unnoticed once overt physical problems have been resolved.

Based on statistics from the American Heart Association (AHA), nearly 700,000 people have a new or recurrent stroke each year, with 163,000 persons dying from the incident (AHA, 2005). In 2003, 5.1 million noninstitutionalized adults had a stroke at some time in their life (Lethbride-Cejku & Vickerie, 2005). The AHA projected the United States spent $57 billion for stroke-related medical costs and disability in 2005. Thus, strokes are the leading cause of severe long-term disability in the United States.

Langlois, Rutland-Brown, and Thomas (2004) estimated 1.4 million people incur a TBI each year, with 50,000 dying, 235,000 hospitalized, and 1.1 million treated and released from emergency departments. In 1995, the estimated medical and indirect costs of TBI were approximately $56.3 billion in the United States (Thurman, 2001). According to other figures from the Centers for Disease Control and Prevention (CDC, 1999), at least 5.3 million individuals in the United States are disabled presently from the risidual squelae of TBI (Thurman, Alverson, Dunn, Guerro, & Sniezek, 1999). The CDC also indicated an additional 80,000 people will acquire long-term disabilities resulting from TBI each year.

In addition to strokes and TBI, several other medical conditions have been associated with cognitive problems (e.g., multiple sclerosis, HIV/AIDS, etc.). Although each of those disorders may share certain neuropsychological symptomatology (i.e., memory problems, etc.) with various other disorders, they are the result of unique physiological and environmental pathogens. Despite cognitive problems in those disorders, few programs specifically offer cognitive rehabilitation services for dementia, demyelinating diseases, or central nervous system infection. Likewise, cognitive rehabilitation for brain tumors and anoxia lag far behind most conditions treated by rehabilitation programs (Springer, 2003).

Because addressing each disorder in turn is beyond the scope of this chapter, we will present rehabilitation approaches that may prove beneficial for a number of disorders and deficits. However, the combination of course, prognosis, and outcome of specific conditions, along with their psychosocial and environmental factors, determine the relative applicability of any approach. For instance, clinicians cannot simply assume procedures used for attentional deficits accompanying TBI will be equally applicable to attentional problems associated with a subcortical infarct.

Only through the systematic incorporation of theory, research, and application across multiple fields of study can clinicians meet the needs of individual patients. Also, valid models of psychosocial functioning, behavior, learning, emotion, physiology, and cognition add a useful dimension to treatment planning (Wilson, 2002). No matter what types

421

*Cognitive
Rehabilitation
With Brain-
Damaged
Patients*

of approach or techniques are selected for rehabilitation, the explicit goal includes promoting the highest possible level of functional independence for the patient while attending to cognitive limitations, extreme physical challenges, disrupted social functioning, emotional alteration, and a pervading sense of personal loss, which often accompany brain injury (Mateer, Sira, & O'Connell, 2005; McGrath, in press).

This chapter presents specific techniques, approaches, and methods to compensate for or remediate cognitive deficits associated with nonprogressive brain dysfunction. An overview of Luria's formulation of higher cortical functions and neuropathology of acquired injuries describes some concerns facing rehabilitation patients. Moreover, we illustrate relevant contemporary trends of rehabilitation service delivery that are firmly rooted in long-standing principles, along with methods of measuring rehabilitation progress. Because people with brain injuries cannot be reduced to a simple, fragmented collection of cognitive deficits, accompanying complications in the rehabilitation setting are addressed as well.

HIGHER CORTICAL FUNCTIONS

LURIA **(1966, 1980)** proposed a theory of functional cortical sys - tems that has utility for conceptualizing the impact of brain injury and rehabilitation efficacy. His method of discerning the connection between brain structure and function views cognitive retraining as more than just a clinical service. He viewed cognitive retraining as a means of furthering knowledge of brain-behavioral relationships through examining "the dynamics of the disturbed function in the course of retraining" through a theory driven approach (Luria, 1980, p. 396). Through such a process, clinicians explore the true nature of the impairment and distinguish between primary deficits and impairments of functional systems.

Luria's view of the organizational structure of the brain indicates that higher cortical functions have a plexiform nature, arising from coordinated output of several brain areas instead of a cortical discrete area. While he strongly rejected a strict localizationist approach, he also abandoned the theory of cortical equipotentiality. Instead, Luria stated that the brain has broad, specialized regions suited for discrete functional activities. Thus, no single brain area or structure is responsible for a specific function. Rather, behavior is the byproduct of multiple cortical areas forming a series of functional systems with individual brain areas participating in more than one functional system.

Luria (1966) and other Russian contemporaries contended regions of specificity are hierarchically organized, but change with experience and development. Thus, executive impairment varies as a function of ontogenetic state. For example, damage to auditory analyzers for phonemic analysis have greater functional consequences in children than adults, because children are in the process of forming a lexicon and highly depend on learning surface properties of language, whereas adults have mastered phonetics and are primarily concerned with processing semantics and syntax.

The core of Lurian theory is that three units account for normal functional activity and guide mental operations (Luria, 1966). The first unit (Unit 1), composed of the reticular formation, limbic system, and mesial basal frontal lobes, is hypothesized to regulate activation and vigilance. It provides the required level of arousal and emotional "drive" to regulate higher cortical functions. Injuries to those structures can result in lethargy and flatness of affect resulting in compromised higher functional activity.

The second functional unit (Unit 2) accounts for the registration, analysis, and storage of environmental information and includes occipital, parietal, and temporal lobes. Luria's third hypothesized functional unit (Unit 3) initiates behavioral programs and regulates mental activity producing "on-line" adjustments necessary for complex, flexible human activity and are predominately comprised of the frontal lobes. Luria advocated testing functional systems to determine which systems are responsible for cognitive deficits.

By taking a Lurian approach, the rehabilitation neuropsychologist must go beyond simply identifying areas of weakness and generate clinical hypotheses about why complex tasks failed, and then test those hypotheses. Hypotheses generation requires both an understanding of the nervous system's functional organization and knowledge of the extent of damage secondary to a given neurological insult.

NEUROPATHOLOGY

DAMAGE TO BRAIN tissue produced by cerebrovascular events or head trauma results in both primary and secondary effects. Primary injuries involve neuronal death at the time of the injury, which can be caused by a number of events, such as: direct trauma, indirect trauma (e.g., whiplash), diffuse axonal injury (DAI; stretching and/or shearing of axonal fibers due to torque), and hypoxia. Secondary effects occur post-injury and involve either a global loss of neuronal efficiency resulting from the brain's general response to the injury, or a specific time-limited decrease in neuronal function associated with the primary injury.

423

*Cognitive
Rehabilitation
With Brain-
Damaged
Patients*

PRIMARY INJURY

AFTER AN INJURY to the brain, neurons die, which is associated with a rapid biochemical cascade leading to a series of destructive cellular events. Some of these negative events are: the release of massive amounts of excitatory neurotransmitters, dysregulated modulation of inhibitory neurotransmitters, increased free radical production, lipid membrane peroxidation (Sutkovoĭ et al., 1999), and the degradation of the blood-brain barrier (Chen, Constantini, Trembovier, Weinstock, & Shohami, 1996). The particular pattern of dysfunction in such cases is largely determined by the type of injury incurred. Focal lesions are often produced by cerebrovascular accidents and nonmetastic tumors, while TBI typically causes both diffuse and focal neuronal death. Because tissue lost to primary injury does not regenerate, knowing the etiology of injury is helpful in predicting which brain functions will recover.

In closed head injury, focal injuries result in contusions, hematomas, and lacerations, usually affecting anterior temporal and orbitofrontal cortices. Cortical penetration may also occur and involve subcortical white matter (Richardson, 1990). In closed head injury, contusional damage, hemorrhagic lesions in gray matter or at the gray-white matter junctions, is widely considered the hallmark of clinical significance (Büki, Okonkwo, Wang, & Povlishock, 2000). Neuronal necrosis (cell death due to acute cellular injury) and apoptosis (genetically programmed cell death) frequently accompany contusional damage (Raghupathi, 2004) often leading to inflammatory responses. It is also important to consider that patients may be asymptomatic immediately after a hemorrhagic injury, but experience bleeding hours or days post-injury.

In contrast, nonhemorrhagic contusions are confined to the subcortical matter and are associated with diffuse damage. Diffuse lesioning, such as that observed in DAI, also results in neuronal death. A rotational component is usually required for consciousness to be impaired and DAI to occur in head trauma (Richardson, 1990), but symptoms may not become apparent until 12 to 24 hours post-injury. Typical DAI damage is thought to result from mechanical forces changing the axonal membrane in such a way that hinders axonal transport, leading to focal swelling and eventual axonal detachment (Büki, Okonkwo, Wang, & Povlishock, 2000). The corpus callosum, rich with axonal fibers, is often associated with DAI leading to impaired interhemispheric transfer (Wilson, Hadley, Wiedmann, & Teasdale, 1995).

Spreading neuronal degeneration is also commonly observed following TBI. Retrograde or primary degeneration refers to cell death that occurs proximal to the axonal lesion. This pattern of deterioration is distinguished by movement and disfigurement of the nucleus, loss of Nissl bodies, and cellular edema. Axonal degeneration is usually limited to the first few internodes surrounding the injury site, but may progress back toward the cell body, resulting in cell death remote from the initial injury. Necrosis is believed to occur due to loss of tropic support from the postsynaptic neuron (Büki, Okonkwo, Wang, & Povlishock, 2000). However, if the axotomized neuron is supplied with the critical substance produced by the postsynaptic neuron, retrograde degeneration can be prevented. Additionally, if the neuron is given an alternative target, as in a transplant, degeneration is stymied.

Anterograde degeneration (i.e., Wallerian, orthograde, or secondary degeneration) occurs when the axon becomes necrotic distal to the point of injury (Nicholls, Martin, Wallace, & Fuchs, 2001). This occurs as distal Schwann cells dedifferentiate and, with the aid of macrophages, phagotize the remains of the axon and myelin that fragmented after the injury. While new axons will sprout from the injury area, they typically die or atrophy. Further, neurons that are innervated by an injured neuron may die due to transneuronal degeneration.

SECONDARY INJURY—GENERAL RESPONSE TO INJURY

LIKE OTHER ORGAN tissue, brain matter displays an inflammatory response when damaged by trauma or ischemia. Microvascular injury results in swelling due to excess neuronal fluid but can also occur in TBI due to decreased blood plasma during vasodilation (Richardson, 1990). Cerebral edema results in neuronal death due to prolonged increases in intracranial pressure, which may result in herniation (displacement of tissue, fluid, or blood vessels) and pressure necrosis. Intracranial pressure also increases the risk of ischemic damage by reducing cerebral blood flow.

A number of other harmful events may occur after the primary injury. These include delayed neuronal injury and hypometabolism. After TBI, both hypoxia and decreased systemic blood pressure increase mortality and morbidity risk (Greenwald, Burnett, & Miller, 2003). While the hypoxic environment is harmful to neural cells, reperfusion can actually increase the magnitude of initial hypoxic damage. This is predominantly due to increased hydrogen peroxide and free radicals (Cernak, Wang, Jiang, Bian, & Savic, 2001) that accompany the influx of oxygenated blood into previously hypoxic brain tissue (Morimoto, Globus, Busto, Martinez, & Ginsburg, 1996). These products disrupt neuronal DNA, resulting in an energy consumption effect that increases the neural damage associated with TBI (Yamamoto, Uchigata, & Okamoto, 1981). Pharmacological agents that prevent secondary neural damage related to reperfusion are particularly important as there is an increased use of clot dissolving agents in acute treatment for cerebrovascular incidents.

425

*Cognitive
Rehabilitation
With Brain-
Damaged
Patients*

RECOVERY OF FUNCTIONING
IN ACQUIRED INJURIES

THE TYPICAL CLINICAL strategy is to minimize initial damage and, thereby, reduce the amount of functional recovery that is necessary. However, after the infliction of the injury, recovery and rehabilitation becomes the primary clinical focus. There is hope for recovery even long past the period of spontaneous recovery and acute rehabilitation. In fact, improvement in neuropsychological functioning is generally observed for at least 2 years after TBI (Lannoo, Colardyn, Jannes, & DeSoete, 2001). Still, many patients will not return to previous levels of functioning and must cope with at least some serious residual impairment (Hochstenbach, den Otter, & Mulder, 2003). Typically, these patients will partially recover some damaged functions and learn to substitute intact functions for post-injury deficits. However, Robertson and Murre (1999) indicated there are generally three groups of patients in terms of likelihood of recovery: (1) spontaneous recovery, (2) assisted recovery, and (3) no recovery.

Even with ever-improving understanding of neural mechanisms, the exact process of recovery of cognitive function is still a mystery in many respects (Stein, 2000). What is known is that injury and recovery follow a general pattern. Coma often accompanies TBI and is followed by an emergence from unconsciousness. Next, a state of confusion and dense anterograde amnesia is commonly observed. Finally, a slow recovery of impaired cognitive functions occurs, which is marked by improvements in autoregulation and social competence. Usually, resolution time for each phase is progressively longer than the one that preceded it.

Kolb and Whishaw (2000) outlined three ways in which recovery is possible following brain injury. First, endogenous recovery may occur. Intact neural circuits may reorganize to accommodate functions that previously resided in damaged neural areas by dendritic proliferation. However, because functions are more densely localized in the adult brain, younger developing brains tend to show more neuroplasticity than mature brains. Second, recovery may have an exogenous origin in that cerebral reorganization may be prompted or accelerated by therapeutic interventions such as pharmacological agents or behavioral therapy. The neurophysiological goal of such treatments is to prevent dendritic atrophy. Third, recovery may not involve reorganization at all, but instead involve the replacement of injured neurons. This can theoretically take place either by neurogenesis or through transplantation of healthy neurons. However, research in neuronal transplantation is still in its infancy and is presently not a therapeutic option.

APPROACHES TO REHABILITATION

THE MOST PROMINENT deficits treated by rehabilitation programs are attentional and memory impairments, followed by visuoperceptual and executive disturbances (Springer, 2003). However,
each patient has a unique combination of cognitive problems with
varying degrees of impairment. Additionally, no specific treatment
protocol or theoretical framework addresses how to treat problems at
a complex individual level. Further, there are controversies regarding
recovery of cognitive functioning and cognitive models of normal
and disrupted brain functioning. As a result, particular neuroscientific models of brain function and recovery may differentially apply
across individuals, which could influence what strategies are effective
in particular cases. Therefore, it is important to avoid single therapeutic packages for specific neuropsychological disorders, because underlying physiology and psychosocial context may not be shared across
patients (Robertson, 1994).

Despite the lack of a recognized "gold standard" approach for cognitive rehabilitation, there are essential methodologies. Furthermore,
within the past decade significant effort has been made to draft appropriate standards of care and paradigm changes for cognitive rehabilitation based on recent reviews of empirical studies (Cappa et al., 2003;
Carney et al., 1999; Chestnut et al., 1999; Cicerone et al., 2000, 2005; Ma &
Trombly, 2002; Malia & Duckett, 2001; Nadeau, 2002; Sohlberg et al.,
2003; Trombly & Ma, 2002; Ylvisaker, Hanks, & Johnson-Greene, 2003).
A cross-disciplinary panel of professionals developed the National
Institutes of Health (NIH) Consensus Statement on Rehabilitation of
Persons with Traumatic Brain Injury (TBI). This panel recommended
that "rehabilitation services should be matched to the needs, strengths,
and capacities of each person with TBI and modified as those needs
change over time; and rehabilitation of persons with TBI should
include cognitive and behavioral assessment and intervention" (NIH
Consensus Statement, 1999, p. 23). Such efforts have provided a structure for post-injury rehabilitation based in science.

There are two basic, but not mutually exclusive, distinctions in rehabilitation techniques that appear consistently throughout the literature:
(1) remediation, and (2) compensation. These are typically implemented
through an interdisciplinary team-oriented approach with the use of
goal-setting strategies. Such treatment can be delivered at any point
during recovery, and the treatment settings can range from intensive
inpatient to periodic outpatient.

The remediation, or restorative, model assumes underlying weaknesses in basic cognitive functioning or that processing subcom-
ponents can be recovered through repeated practice (Ben-Yishay,

427

Cognitive
Rehabilitation
With Brain-
Damaged
Patients

Piasetsky, & Rattok, 1987; Meier, Benton, & Diller, 1987; Perna, Bekanich, Williams, & Boozer, 2000; Sohlberg & Mateer, 1989). Remediation techniques include tabletop activities and repetitive drills that are assumed to correct, reduce, or eliminate underlying pathology or deficient cognitive mechanisms and are accomplished through a series of highly structured psychometric exercises chosen to address specific impairments. The tasks are completed in a hierarchical fashion in which the level of complexity, quality, speed of presentation, and amount of cuing are tapered (Blundon & Smits, 2000). Once basic skills have been mastered, it is postulated that they will generalize, enabling the person to perform real-life applications (Lee, Powell, & Esdaile, 2001). Thus, remediation proponents assert that fundamental cognitive processes are developed in order to accomplish higher order processes.

However, there is an assumption that those with brain dysfunction struggle to generalize learning associated with discrete trials (as with strict remediation) to new contexts. Learning in a limited, sterile clinic atmosphere does not appear to generalize spontaneously to novel situations (Boman, Lindstedt, Hemmignsson, & Bartfai, 2004). This has prompted some to suggest learning in rehabilitation should be held in patients' well-known, natural settings (Fisher, 1998).

On the other hand, adaptive or compensatory approaches use learning and psychological processes and consider environmental influences and interventions (Ben-Yishay & Diller, 1993). Compensation focuses on using strengths of intact processes to carry out previous functioning through alternative means. These methods attempt to bypass affected areas through novel strategies for functional deficits. Repetitive practice of specific functional activities directed toward daily living is generally performed. When treating via compensation, it is important to consider the patient's deficit awareness and level of cognitive functioning (Prigatano, 1987).

Rehabilitation professionals, through integrative approaches, should shift beyond the simple remediation/compensation dichotomy to view rehabilitation in terms of skill transfer and generalization. Rehabilitation should teach useful mental sets that can be applied to a range of situations by teaching specific skills, being concerned with germane tasks, using a mix of training examples, and establishing a pattern of over-learning and verifying learning processes (Parente & Hermann, 1996). Cicerone et al. (2000) further indicated interventions are likely to be aided through a combination of the following:

1) reinforcing, strengthening, or establishing previously learned patterns of behavior,
2) establishing new patterns of cognitive activity through compensatory cognitive mechanisms for impaired neurologic systems,

3) establishing new patterns of activity through external compensatory mechanisms such as personal orthoses or environmental
   structuring and supports, and
4) enabling persons to adapt to their cognitive disability. (p. 1597)

One commonality across rehabilitation models is that each usually
includes explicitly teaching coping strategies (Lee et al., 2001).

Remediation and compensation are critical components of rehabilitation, but their relative prominence in a patient's treatment is
a matter of controversy. Ylvisaker et al. (2003) have explained that
the "Traditional Paradigm" has utilized cognitive remediation as first line
treatment followed by attempts at compensatory behaviors or assistive
devices if remediation techniques prove inadequate. Robertson and
Murre (1999) suggested that compensatory strategies should be used for
those showing little capacity for recovery, remedial techniques can be
applied to those needing assisted recovery, while spontaneously recov-
ering patients require little intervention. Thus, cognitive restoration
approaches should comprise the majority of rehabilitation at the beginning of treatment (Gianutsos, 1991; Pépin, Laranger, & Benoit, 1995),
which was adapted empirically by Boman et al. (2004).

Similarly, Lee et al. (2001) proposed a Functional Model of Cognitive Rehabilitation, which attempts to bridge gaps in current service
provision. They offered a brief overview of 10 cognitive rehabilitation
models from an occupational therapy perspective and indicated that
no model universally applies to individuals throughout all levels of
recovery. Some apply more readily to early stages of disruption rather
than to recovery in advanced post-acute stages (see also Turner-Stokes,
2002). Lee et al. (2001) ranked techniques on a remedial-functional
continuum where simulated tasks are gradually supplanted by functional, real-world tasks. Thus, their proposed model provides a framework for rehabilitation that corresponds with stages of recovery,
beginning in coma care and continuing for an indefinite time period
until adequate recovery goals are met.

Their approach is similar to Ylvisaker et al.'s (2003) "Contextualized
Paradigm" wherein the broad goal is to aid individuals to achieve functional objectives and engage personally relevant activities blocked
by present impairment. This has also been adapted to include body
structure/function-oriented interventions within a meaningful real-
life context extending beyond simple remediation/compensatory tasks
(Wilson, 2002). This type of rehabilitation may capitalize on neuroplasticity, because it is thought neurogenesis occurs in enriched environments (Ogden, 2000). However, Lee et al. (2001) provided a caveat that
those in acute stages may gain little from complex, functional activity training, because they become overwhelmed and confused when

429

*Cognitive
Rehabilitation
With Brain-
Damaged
Patients*

multistage, multimodal tasks are involved. Even self-care in the early stages can prove challenging and overtaxing. In such cases remediation appears to be of value.

Therefore, in contrast to traditional methods of rehabilitation, a contextual model is not composed exclusively of either remedial or adaptive methods, but is an incorporation of various techniques through an integrative fashion with a metacognitive emphasis (see also Wilson, 2002; Ylvisaker et al., 2003). Rehabilitation requires a particular combination of activity/participation interventions (i.e., compensation) and context-oriented interventions (e.g., reducing the impact of disability, modifying expectations, and eliciting social support; Perna et al., 2000). Using adaptation, remediation, and compensation strategies in concert appears to be the clinical and research zeitgeist influencing the rehabilitation field. Ylvisaker et al. have provided expanded delineation between traditional and context oriented approaches (p. 62).

Current service delivery patterns suggest rehabilitation centers use compensation-based interventions at a rate comparable to rehearsal strategies (Mazmanian, Kreutzer, Devany, & Martin; 1993; Springer, 2003). Virtually every rehearsal program in the Springer study used daily tasks and paper or pencil methods with work-related tasks, board games, computer cognitive rehabilitation, and computer games following in turn. The most frequently used compensation strategies were written aids with few programs using electronic aids. Blundon and Smits' (2000) survey of occupational therapists in Canada also revealed popular use of paper and pencil tasks, tabletop games, computer software, and graded occupations for addressing orientation, attention, and memory deficits. They provided a list of specific tasks used for each domain.

A "client-centered goal planning" strategy is an important part of rehabilitation (McGrath, Marks, & Davis, 1995). This approach is based on concepts promoted by Davis et al. (1992) and continues to be systematically applied at the Rivermead Rehabilitation Centre. McGrath, Davis, and colleagues have created a comprehensive goal-planning program with techniques and protocol including participation from professionals in various disciplines working as a team to establish meaningful goals (McGrath, in press). McGrath suggested that goal planning is arguably more essential than any specific techniques used in rehabilitation. She also noted that rather than working in parallel, professionals should approach rehabilitation in an explicitly interdisciplinary manner. This overall concept has also been supported elsewhere (Stichbury, Davenport, & Middleton, 1980). The interdisciplinary approach requires the team to comprehend the patients' motivation, premorbid goals, and values and see the patient as a whole, unfragmented person within the context of his own environment, while addressing subjective feelings as well as performance on specific tasks (McGrath, in press).

Two relevant features to this approach are: (1) realizing the extent and complexity of difficulties arising from injury, including the overwhelming feelings shared by patients and family members; and (2) understanding dramatic alterations in patients' sense of self. Their multilayered approach includes administering the Life Goals Questionnaire, a brief structured interview, and goal formulation by the team in conjunction with the patient and family (Davis et al., 1992). This enables treatment to include goals that are specific, measurable, achievable, relevant, and timed (SMART). Goals addressing psychological functioning should also be given equal weight as goals for physical and cognitive functioning.

Another issue within the cognitive rehabilitation literature concerns whether inpatient treatment is more advantageous than outpatient/ home intervention (Cicerone, Mott, Azulay, & Friel, 2004; Salazar et al., 2000; Warden et al., 2000). While there is a debate as to the comparative cost-effectiveness and treatment efficacy of outpatient programs versus inpatient modalities, few empirical investigations have been reported (Salazar et al., 2000). In terms of the traditional rehabilitation models, intensive inpatient treatment is preferred, especially for acute cases. However, treatment in the community well after the acute phase has shown promise to long-term recovery (Cicerone et al., 2005; Powell, Heslin, & Greenwood, 2002). In his review of rehabilitation treatment centers, Springer (2003) reported that while services offered more inpatient programs (48%) than outpatient (19%), a substantial number provided both inpatient and outpatient services equally (33%). One concerning observation about treatment delivery is that the overwhelming majority of programs only treat patients between 1 and 6 months. Only a small percentage of programs continue treatment beyond 6 months, despite the fact that recovery of functioning occurs throughout the year following injury (Harrison-Felix, Newton, Hall, & Kreutzer, 1996).

POTENTIAL COMPLICATIONS AND FACTORS TO CONSIDER IN THE REHABILITATION SETTING

SOMATIC

NO MATTER WHAT treatment approach is chosen, providers have to attend to potential somatic problems that may have an indirect influence on rehabilitation progress. Sensory and motor complications, including pain and paralysis, provide challenges. In particular, dysautonomia, neuropathic pain, spasticity, headaches, heterotopic ossification, deep venous thrombosis, orthopedic trauma, genitourinary and

431

*Cognitive
Rehabilitation
With Brain-
Damaged
Patients*

gastrointestinal problems, and shoulder pain commonly cause pain in rehabilitation patients (Ivanhoe & Hartman, 2004). Furthermore, dizziness and posttraumatic seizure disorders, hearing impairments, and motoric tremor are sources of physical dysfunction in brain injury as well. Finally, cardiovascular concerns, particularly with stroke patients, are potential contributors to additional cognitive deterioration and general health decline.

PSYCHOSOCIAL

BRAIN INJURIES ALSO interact with a patient's psychosocial characteristics. While early outcome measures based on physiological and neurological functioning have consistently predicted functional outcome (Watanabe, 2003), other factors include psychological functioning, family factors, motivation and impaired deficit awareness, premorbid intellectual functioning, age, and cerebral organization. Thus, patients are not simply a manifestation of underlying cognitive problems, but are complex organisms within social and psychic environments (Wilson, 1997).

Emotional problems occur in patients with and without premorbid histories of psychological problems. It has been noted that individuals often have problematic premorbid character traits that impact their ability to perform effective behavior and rehabilitation tasks, which could extend recovery (Golden & Golden, 2003). Patients with TBI often display marked liability, reactivity to difficulties, psychotic symptoms, dissociation, and sexually inappropriate behavior (Fujii & Ahmend, 2002). These are often long-term problems (Koponen et al., 2002; Novack, Alderson, Bush, Meythaler, & Canupp, 2000). Thus, it is not surprising that social and family adjustment problems last for years after initial brain injury (Lezak & O'Brien, 1988; Oddy, Coughlan, Tyerman, & Jenkins, 1985). Because of their often enduring nature, researchers have urged clinicians to not treat cognitive functioning, personality, and emotional reactions as separate entities within the individual (Mateer et al., 2005; Prigatano, 1987).

Motivation and awareness of deficits has also been shown to negatively affect rehabilitation. This is a profound problem, because while they may acknowledge deficits, a large proportion of patients tend to overestimate their behavioral competencies (Ownsworth, McFarland, & Young, 2000). Some have referred to awareness as a prerequisite for successful rehabilitation, because if the patient does not realize or understand cognitive deficits are present, motivation for treatment suffers (for recent treatment models for awareness, see Lucas & Flemming, 2005). There are conflicting data in regards to the association of awareness to employment outcome (Coetzer &

du Toit, 2002; Trudel, Tryon, & Purdum, 1998). A recently validated model of factors influencing brain-injury outcome indicated that being either younger or older, being unemployed, and being poorly educated significantly factor into rehabilitation outcome (Bush et al., 2003). Handedness research has also suggested that left-handers tend to recover more favorably than right-handers.

OUTCOME IN REHABILITATION

MEASURING OUTCOME IN cognitive rehabilitation has evolved along with conceptualizations on how to implement certain procedures. While no comprehensive taxonomy in rehabilitation outcome measurement exists (Mermis, 2005), the World Health Organization (WHO; 1999, 2001) has provided significant direction in that area with the publication of the *International Classifications of Functioning and Disability* (ICIDH–2) and the *International Classification of Functioning, Disability, and Health* (ICF). The ICF is a conceptual framework for measuring functional outcome that includes: (1) body structure/function, (2) activity, (3) participation, and (4) environmental factors. Within that system, body/structure/function limitations refer to the amount of damage and impairment to underlying psychological, physiological, and other bodily functioning. Activity dysfunctions are the degree to which persons' can independently perform daily tasks. Participation, which is the ultimate goal of rehabilitation by going beyond activity, pertains to level of productivity along with integration into family and community. Environmental factors include physical, social, age, education, coping skills, and attitudinal environments influencing persons' functioning (Gray & Hendershot, 2000). The ICF attempts to address how treatment targets deficits by dividing affected areas of functioning into a common nomenclature.

Within that framework, clinicians should be aware of how treatments address which level of patients' functioning. Additionally, the outcome should monitor the interventions to assess effects of specific treatments. For instance, if participation is the aim of treatment, the level of participation should be the focus of outcome assessment (Perna et al., 2000). This allows clinicians to make more inferences regarding how treatment influences particular aspects of patients' lives. This also puts rehabilitation components into relation to all other interventions the person may be engaged in.

However, measuring outcome in cognitive rehabilitation is challenging. Beaumont, Connolly, and Rogers (1999) indicated that difficulties assessing outcomes include a lack of standardized measures for particular domains (i.e., ICF levels of dysfunction), decreased generalization across individuals, the fact that follow-up studies often require

433

*Cognitive
Rehabilitation
With Brain-
Damaged
Patients*

a funding separate from treatment, and that most outcome measures are limited in breadth of assessment. Rehabilitation measures must meet minimum standards for reliability and validity, be sensitive to change, have consistent scoring criteria and normative data, and be translatable to clinical practice.

Neuropsychological testing is an important factor in the outcome process, which addresses body function and structure. Controversies surrounding the ecological validity of neuropsychological testing (i.e., the degree of relationship of testing and gains in day-to-day functioning) call into question the utility of using cognitive measures as outcome data (Perna et al., 2000). But, neuropsychological testing has, in fact, been shown to be associated with reported functional ratings in rehabilitation patients (Hajek, Gagnon, & Ruderman, 1997; Larson et al., 2003). In addition to traditional neuropsychological measures, improvement in cognitive functioning and neuroplasticity may be substantiated with neuroimaging techniques such as functional magnetic resonance imaging (fMRI), and electroencephalographic (EEG) imaging (Laatsch et al., 1997; Laatsch, Pavel, Jobe, Qing, & Quintana, 1999; Laatsch, Thulborn, Krisky, Shobat, & Sweeney, 2004; Sathopoulou & Lubar, 2004). New developments in diffuse-weighted imaging and perfusion MRI will be beneficial for tracking cerebral blood flow in stroke patients (Ashwal & Holshouser, 1997).

In real-world practice, a large majority of rehabilitation centers use goal attainment or performance on simulated tasks as the measure for treatment success (Springer, 2003). These are related to measuring areas most germane in the lives of individuals. Thus, neuropsychological testing as an outcome measure appears to be the least used method for evaluating treatment outcome, which is used with similar frequency as patient observations, therapist rating scales, or other measures (Springer, 2003). For instance, treatment of "attention" is not necessarily for "attention's" sake. However, outcome measures of most functional abilities lack the standardization and psychometric stability neuropsychological tests provide. Thus, neuropsychological tests are limited to primarily measuring cognitive impairment (i.e., body structure/function) and cannot sufficiently pinpoint the nature of daily problems encountered by a person in an expanded context (Wilson, 2002).

Nevertheless, testing is needed early on in the process to provide feedback to the patient and family regarding cognitive status and capacity for performing daily tasks (Sherer et al., 2002). Results can be used as a tool to improve patients' deficit awareness and to assess baseline functioning, initial problem identification, problem analysis, and progress/outcome tracking (Oddy, Alcott, Francis, Jenkins, & Fowlie, 1999). Post-acute cognitive testing may aid in predicting employment outcome beyond post-traumatic amnesia duration, as post-acute testing likely reveals focal strengths and weaknesses not elucidated by testing in the acute phase.

It is also necessary to survey patients' perceptions of how neuropsychological techniques help them in daily life in context of the community and personal functioning (Cicerone et al., 2004; Pioth, 1992; Prigatano, 2003). Patient satisfaction surveys with brain-injured patients who participated in compensatory cognitive retraining have perceived the activities as useful for functional life (Dirette, 2002). Nearly 74% reported using cognitive strategies to complete job tasks in that particular study. While traditional models of cognitive rehabilitation have employed neuropsychological testing as a central outcome, meaningful outcomes depend upon more than neuropsychological variables.

In addition to structure and functional aspects of body structure and functioning, outcomes have also focused on measuring activities of daily living (ADL) and participation. Traditional measures, such as the Galveston Orientation and Amnesia Test (GOAT), Glasgow Coma Scale (GCS), Comprehensive Level of Consciousness Scale (CLCS), Disability Rating Scale (DRS), and Levels of Cognitive Function Scale (LCFS), largely fail in this endeavor. Thus, there has been an effort to standardize outcome measurement and provide reviews of existing measures of functional abilities spanning various domains (Turner-Stokes, 2002).

However, there is a lingering problem within the functional measurement modality, because most measure heterogeneous content, are not appropriately conceptualized, and lack psychometric integrity (Heinemann, 2005). For instance, even one of the most popular measures for rehabilitation outcome, the Functional Independence Measure (FIM), predominately assesses change during medical rehabilitation, and few items address cognitive, emotional, and social difficulties. The addition of the Functional Assessments Measure (FAM) helps to bridge this gap. Yet, participation and independent living approaches that focus on environmental factors within the persons' functional sphere need to be represented within clinical practice (Minnes, Harrick, Carlson, & Johnston, 1998).

In addition to the aforementioned problems in outcome measurement, other factors cloud the issue of whether particular rehabilitation strategies are effective and actually affect the areas to which they purport. In terms of examining rehabilitation effectiveness, research is confounded by those who recover spontaneously, by providers' pressure to justify long-term outcomes, and by patients' premorbid functioning (Turner-Stokes, 2002). Given that there is no preferred outcome measure among over 42 available scales for cognitive rehabilitation measurement, comparing outcomes across studies is daunting.

435

*Cognitive
Rehabilitation
With Brain-
Damaged
Patients*

Fortunately, several extensive reviews of cognitive rehabilitation outcomes have been systematically undertaken within the past few years (Cappa et al., 2003; Carney et al., 1999; Chestnut et al., 1999; Cicerone et al., 2000; Cicerone et al., 2005, Ma & Trombly, 2002; Malia & Duckett, 2001; Nadeau, 2002; Sohlberg et al., 2003; Trombly & Ma, 2002; Ylvisaker et al., 2003). Together, they have provided guidance regarding what rehabilitation techniques have substantial support from dividing studies according to the level of scientific rigor. Such studies included single subject and group designs, although few randomized control designs are found in the rehabilitation literature.

Though practice guidelines and years of professional commentary have urged outcome measurement and treatment to target individuals' problems at the level of participation, few well-designed studies explore such interventions. In order to promote evidence-based practices, in the next section of this chapter we elaborate on retraining techniques suggested as efficacious, probably efficacious, practice options, and others that may prove clinically useful.

SPECIFIC AREAS FOR REHABILITATION

ATTENTION AND VIGILANCE

ONE OF THE most common disruptions secondary to TBI is dysfunctional attentional regulation. Brain injury affects multiple aspects of attention including shorter attention span, distractibility, and increased effort for harnessing attentional resources (Bennett, Malia, Linton, Raymond, & Brewick, 1998; Palmese & Raskin, 2000; Wood, 1988). Functionally, these deficits may cause problems with information processing, communication, social awareness, memory, task completion, and the ability to self-monitor behavior (Bennett et al., 1998). Furthermore, impaired orientation may translate into misinterpreting the environment in terms of person, place, time, and circumstance, which may lead to confusion, aggression, and inappropriate social responses (Watanabe, Black, Zafonte, Millis, & Mann, 1998).

Although attentional rehabilitation has received increased research emphasis in recent years, few techniques exist for isolating attention in rehabilitation (Wood, 1988). Existing interventions often target specific dimensions of attention (i.e., focused, sustained, selective, alternating/shifting, divided, and orientation). While many patients with severe head injury are able to recover the fundamental components of attention (e.g., sleep/wake cycle and arousal), problems often persist at higher levels (e.g., sustained and divided attention; Mateer, Kerns,

& Eso, 1996). Currently, the most commonly used treatment for brain-injured patients is the retraining of cognitive function.

Retraining

Engelberts et al. (2002) compared compensation versus retraining. In the retraining group, patients had to rehearse responses on a divided attention task, wherein task difficulty automatically increased. Patients in the compensation group were made aware of their functional attention and memory failures and were taught rules to compensate for those failures. Daily homework assignments were used to help patients apply these strategies. While both methods were found to be effective, compensation showed slightly more benefits, and the authors suggested that the methods be applied together.

Training aimed either specifically at a particular area of attention, or at a level subordinate to targets has produced positive results in patients with localized vascular lesions (Sturm, Willmes, Orgass, & Hartje, 1997). Although significant results were found for training sustained and divided attention, these findings were even more favorable for deficits in alertness and vigilance.

The Attention Process Training-II (APT-II) program is also hierarchical and allows fundamental skills to be stimulated while increasingly complex skills are added. Repetition of the exercises serves to establish new neural organization, which is reinforced by intensifying exercises. Eventually, skills are trained to generalize to daily activities and should improve quality of life through application of skills to real situations (Palmese & Raskin, 2000).

Compensation and Environmental Restructuring

Behavioral approaches may involve rewarding behaviors that resemble appropriate attention and can include punishment for failure to attend to designated information (Robinson & Winner, 1998). Although it has low generalizability, response-cost contingencies have been employed in treatment for attentional problems, along with direct retraining, which includes repeated exposures and practice (Mateer et al., 1996). Shaping strategies have also been implemented to improve functioning of processing speed (Park & Ingles, 2001).

External interventions require the individual and caregivers to structure the environment to optimize preserved abilities and minimize reliance on areas of impaired functioning. Examples include: reducing distractions, providing prompts such as checklists and cuing systems, altering expectations for performance, and didactic training (Robinson & Winner, 1998). Special seating in crowded rooms and the use of earplugs are also useful for managing the environment (Mateer et al., 1996). Computers and task lists that clearly outline the steps

437

*Cognitive
Rehabilitation
With Brain-
Damaged
Patients*

required to perform a task can be motivating and facilitate appropriate responses (Robinson & Winner, 1998).

Having patients slow down or perform tasks at their own pace, when appropriate, may enhance functioning (Madigan, DeLuca, Diamond, Tramontano, & Averill, 2000). Other strategies have been able to improve functioning by helping patients better manage their time. Time Pressure Management (TPM) is a compensatory therapy to assist with completing activities of daily living (Fasotti, Kovacs, Eling, & Brouwer, 2000). The aims of TPM are prevention and management of problems due to processing speed. TPM teaches patients to rely on decision making at a high level, as this is often an area that has been preserved from impairment. By performing subtasks at a high level, the individual is afforded more time to process at the operational level. Thus, the patient plans for the task prior to presentation and, during the initial presentation, attempts to clarify anything that may be unclear, as well as review and rehearse information. Therefore, when a time pressure is applied, the individual can focus on executing the task at hand.

The GOAT is a 10-item measure to assess for disorientation following head trauma that has been adapted to create a technique for assessing and treating disorientation (Zencius, Wesolowski, & Rodriguez, 1998). Treatment gains in orientation to person, place, and time have been shown to have lasting effects. Clocks, calendars, and other relevant cuing devices (Watanabe et al., 1998) can be used in conjunction with orientation groups and individual interactions (Zencius et al., 1998) to promote reorientation. Patients that are able to become reoriented prior to discharge are more likely to regain cognitive and motor functioning and preserve activities of daily living than those who do not become reoriented (Alderson & Novack, 2002).

UNILATERAL NEGLECT AND RELATED DISORDERS

UNILATERAL NEGLECT OCCURS when patients do not report, respond, or orient to stimuli presented to the contralesional hemisphere, given that the deficit cannot be attributed to sensory or motor impairments (Heilman, 1979). Neglect deficits can be personal or spatial (body, environment, object centered). Several behaviors are associated with neglect and differ across patients including inattention/sensory neglect, extinction/suppression to simultaneous stimulation, motor neglect, spatial neglect, allesthesia and allokinesia, and anosognosia (Heilman, Watson, & Valenstein, 2003).

Overall, there are few rigorous studies examining the effects of treatment for visuospatial deficits in those without neglect. Moreover, studies that have investigated this have shown that patients have nominal improvement compared with treatment for those with severe neglect (Cicerone et al., 2000). For example, Kasten, Müller-Oehring, and Sabel (2001) indicated significant visual field improvements with computer restitution training. But, these changes are likely due to compensatory effects rather than remediation of damaged neurological tissue (i.e., regeneration of the optic tract), and the effects may only apply to specific subpopulations.

Most rehabilitation research has focused on those with sensory, motor, and spatial neglect syndromes. Because those problems are associated with right cerebral damage, a number of other cognitive challenges often co-occur (e.g., visual agnosias, dyscalculia, body schema dysfunction, etc.). Accordingly, the majority of evidence within the rehabilitation literature consists of interventions for those with right hemisphere strokes. Generally, the greatest rehabilitation effects are demonstrated for those with substantial rather than mild deficits.

Review of the literature for intervening in right hemisphere strokes suggests visuospatial rehabilitation and scanning training have the most empirical support followed by training in visuospatial and organizational skills in acute rehabilitation (not for those with left hemisphere strokes or TBI without neglect), limb activation, use of electric technology for visual scanning, and computers for visual field deficits in TBI and stroke (Cicerone et al., 2000, 2005). Effective strategies combine techniques to maximize generalizability and intervention outcome (i.e., scanning, sensory awareness, spatial organization, etc.) and are likely more beneficial than conventional rehabilitation. Less support has been offered for prism lenses, eye patches, optokinetic stimulation, caloric vestibular stimulation, and neck muscle vibration (Manly, 2002).

Simply cuing individuals to the neglected zones is not enough to instill habitual left-sided attention direction. Visual scanning was among the first interventions for neglect (Weinberg et al., 1977) and is an empirically supported approach to neglect rehabilitation. Conceptually, this technique serves to automatize the patient's focus to the neglected area. Current recommended practice standards suggest that intensive visual scanning (20 1-hour sessions over 4 weeks) that tasks the visual periphery is superior to standard occupational therapy and conventional rehabilitation and is probably critical in neglect rehabilitation (Cicerone et al., 2005). Scanning paradigms have also been shown effective for those who are anosognosic (Zoccolotti et al., 1992).

One popular scanning training exercise is to present repeated trials of tracking a light that moves from right to left. However, generalizing this type of training has proven problematic (Gouvier, Bua, Blanton, & Urey, 1987). One way to counter decreased generalization is to create training exercises that resemble real-world activities. For instance,

439

*Cognitive
Rehabilitation
With Brain-
Damaged
Patients*

Webster et al. (2001) demonstrated improved wheelchair navigation in complex situations with task-specific scanning exercises. Their particular approach employed a hierarchical module-based program utilizing computer training.

Covert, self-cued scanning has also been applied to both functional and training tasks (Niemeier, 1998). For instance, Bailey, Riddoch, and Crome (2002) trained patients to imagine their eyes as the beam of a lighthouse sweeping the horizon from right to left, emphasizing the left field. As a part of that program, patients were presented a series of graded tasks (copying, drawing, locating objects) composed of real-life materials; left-sided visual, tactile, and verbal cuing (e.g., a red ribbon placed on the left of the patient when reading) for tasks; left-limb activation; and were given performance feedback and praise for each task. Furthermore, integration of visual scanning, somatosensory awareness, size estimation training, and complex visual perceptual organization has been shown to increase effectiveness (Gordon et al., 1985). Forced activation of the neglected limb combined with scanning appears beneficial for visual and sensory neglect (Cicerone et al., 2005). It is also likely that generalization would increase if paired with monocular patching and lateralized visual stimulation (Butter & Kirsch, 1992).

However, when scanning techniques fail, visuo-spatio-motor cuing may offer an effective alternative that generalizes to ADLs (Samuel et al., 2000). With this approach, Samuel et al. (2000) trained patients to move and look at their left arm. In a given activity, patients were prompted to move their left arm when failing to spontaneously explore the left side of a stimulus. Implementing this approach is obviously not an option in those with dense left hemiparesis. Voluntary trunk rotation has also shown to improve ADL functioning in neglect when combined with spatial reconditioning (Wiart et al., 1997).

Because important attentional networks are generally lateralized in the right hemisphere, neglected patients often show problems engaging tasks (i.e., poor vigilance, arousal, and alertness). In fact, Robertson et al. (1997) reported that the attentional performance on nonspatial tasks was correlated with degree of left neglect. To address such problems, Wilson, Manly, Coyle, and Robertson (2000) used sustained attention training in conjunction with errorless learning on self-care tasks and indicated improvement on neuropsychological measures and independent everyday activities. Benefits were shown to last beyond the training period.

MEMORY

MEMORY TRAINING INTERVENTIONS have been shown to be effective in older adults with subjective and objective memory decline (De Vreese, Belloi, Iacono, Finelli, & Neri, 1998) and in those with severe brain injury. However, there appears to be a deficit in the literature investigating the ecological generalizability of such techniques. The literature also lacks comparisons of memory rehabilitation strategies across types of brain damage in varied ages and levels of recovery (Cappa et al., 2003).

Current strategies for remediation include external aids such as checklists, notebooks, cuing cards, tape recorders, computers, and personal storage devices. Comprehensive treatment also includes individualized strategies incorporating feedback, family involvement, and environmental restructuring. Didactic training and homework assignments are also an important aspect of therapy. Other rehabilitative strategies include: rehearsal, visual imagery, verbal strategies, implicit memory tasks, and employment of mnemonic devices (Cicerone et al., 2000).

Repetitive Recall Drills

Despite insufficient empirical support for this practice, repetitive recall drills have been identified as the most commonly utilized technique in memory rehabilitation (Cuesta, 2003). This method attempts to enhance memory by providing multiple exposures to information as well as repeated recall. If utilized, it is important to note that "depth of encoding" is a significant predictor of accurate recall (Chiaravalloti, Demaree, & Gaudino, 2003). Their findings suggested that initial thorough learning may be more important than repeated exposures to information.

Mnemonic Techniques

Designed for use with normal populations, mnemonic techniques are widely used in rehabilitation. This strategy requires the patient to structure and package information for enhanced retrieval and recall. Critics of mnemonic techniques argue the gains do not generalize from artificial settings to real experiences (Cuesta, 2003). Because mnemonic strategies often require increased skill, they may be more appropriate for those with mild, rather than severe, neurocognitive deficits (Kaschel et al., 2002). There is also evidence that younger individuals benefit significantly more from mnemonic strategies to recall word lists than older adults (Richardson & Rossan, 1994).

Visual Imagery

This strategy requires individuals to produce images of nonvisual information to facilitate storage and to cue retrieval. Storage should occur even with distraction and should hold over time (Kaschel et al., 2002). One commonly used technique is the rhyming peg method (one-bun, two-shoe, etc.) where the first item to be remembered is visually paired

441

*Cognitive
Rehabilitation
With Brain-
Damaged
Patients*

with a bun, the second item paired with a shoe, and so forth. Another method, the face–name association, involves pairing a feature of the to-be-remembered person's name with a visual cue to their name. For example, to recall Barry Locke, the patient could visualize a blueberry with a padlock around it. For both of these techniques, learning is enhanced by breaking down material into simple components (Tate, 1997).

Biofeedback

Biofeedback involves positioning devices on a participant's body, which promotes awareness of physiological activity. Thus, a patient is presented with information regarding their brain activity. According to Thornton (2000), 59 patients receiving Quantitative EEG (QEEG) biofeedback achieved normal levels of functioning, with dramatic improvement for some patients. Improvements ranged from 68% to 181% and were experienced in participants with brain injury as well as normal participants.

External Memory Aids

External memory aids are commonly used and consist of storage devices, cuing devices, and restructured environments. These devices, when taught to be used properly, can be inexpensive, enhance daily functioning, and increase patient autonomy.

Storage Devices

Notebooks are inexpensive and easy to use. According to one review, notebooks were particularly beneficial for persons with severe memory impairment, whereas other memory strategies for individuals with mild impairments were deemed more useful (Cicerone et al., 2005). Schmitter-Edgecombe, Fahy, Whelan, and Long (1995) reported that notebook training initially serves to reduce everyday memory failures more than supportive therapy, but these results were not maintained over time. A group setting was found to be beneficial in that it allowed for social contact, encouragement, and sharing between participants. However, patients in groups progressed more slowly and did not achieve the same level of mastery as those in individual therapy.

Squires, Hunkin, and Parkin (1996) were able to train a severely amnesic stroke survivor to look up answers in a memory notebook before asking his wife for the answers. His questions about recent events were reduced to zero, questions about current events were reduced by 42%, and questions about future events declined 47%. The authors indicated the patient generalized training and continued to use it following the study.

Two problems with memory notebooks have been identified. First, people may want to simply rely on their own memories, because they believe recall will only be strengthened by training their endogenous memory systems. Secondly, individuals may hesitate to use the notebooks because of perceived social embarrassment or stigmatization (Tate, 1997). Instead of a notebook, patients may more readily accept an electronic organizer (Tate, 1997).

Cuing Devices

Cuing devices serve as reminders or prompts for events or actions and can be mechanical or electrical. Van den Broek, Downes, Johnson, Dayus, and Hilton (2000) used a handheld electronic device for cuing to reduce prospective memory errors in daily routines. Patients showed significant improvements on message-passing and domestic tasks. There is some evidence that computerized cued recall is more successful for face–naming than word recall tasks (Goldstein, Beers, Longmore, & McCue, 1996).

Restructuring Environments

This primarily works by rearranging objects so patients will be prompted to remember information. Examples include placing medications where they will be seen at the same time everyday, which prompts the patient to take them; and labeling everyday items (keys, glasses, personal care items). Signs (e.g., sticky notes) may also be helpful and can be used to label cabinets and drawers, as well as to cue instructions (e.g., medication schedules). Language functioning must be considered before implementing these strategies (Hutchinson & Marquardt, 1997).

Domain Specific Learning

The principle with this type of learning is that it should be highly practical by teaching tasks and providing exposure to useful information to increase generalization. Vanishing cues, based on shaping and backward chaining, addresses the problem that information may be cued, but it is not readily accessible. This technique requires the therapist to begin with complete stimulus cuing with progressive cues fading across trials. Training is individualized and specific and emphasizes priming and procedural learning.

Use of external aids and time management are some techniques successfully aided by vanishing cues (Hutchinson & Marquardt, 1997). Glisky and Schacter (1988) found learning this way to be superior to standard repetition and to have little decay over a 6-week period. One identified problem with this method is that errors tend to be difficult to extinguish, because they have been strengthened by repeated occurrence (Tate, 1997).

443

*Cognitive
Rehabilitation
With Brain-
Damaged
Patients*

Errorless Learning

The errorless learning method was developed in response to observed learning difficulties in amnesic patients in the 1950s. While implicit memory is still relatively intact in most amnestic patients, explicit memory is usually deficient. Although common trial-and-error methods address explicit memory deficits, errors may be implicitly primed and create stores of "error" memories (Bier, Vanier, & Meulemans, 2002). Thus, errorless learning may be better for severely impaired individuals, but may only work for short periods of time (Evans et al., 2000). However, errorless learning has been found to reduce forgetting better than errorful training (Wilson, Baddeley, Evans, & Shiel, 1994).

Squires, Hunkin, and Parkin (1997) found that errorless learning produced more accurate recall than errorful conditions for immediate memory conditions. However, under delayed conditions, there was no difference between the two groups. The problem identified with the errorful learning method is that patients often recall the error answer as opposed to the correct answer.

LANGUAGE

THOUGH CLASSICAL NOMENCLATURE of aphasia and language syndromes is not without its problems (e.g., lack of treatment validity, overlapped symptoms, heterogeneous categorization, etc.), most studies of language rehabilitation continue to utilize those traditional descriptions (Caplan, 2003). Moreover, any given patient may present with various deficits affecting lexical, phonological, semantic, pragmatics, and syntactic language processes. Keeping this in mind, we review rehabilitation techniques as they apply to commonly referenced conditions and deficits.

Despite questionable effectiveness of language interventions with brain-injured clients in early research, there is current optimism that some methods are helpful for increasing functioning. Converging evidence from randomized control studies, semi-experimental designs, and rigorous single subject work has led to more confidence when recommending some approaches. For a more detailed review of intervention strategies for language deficits see Chapey (2002).

Aphasia

Cicerone et al. (2005) suggested that a series of group interventions promoting social and pragmatic communication are beneficial. Within those approaches, feedback, self-monitoring communication behavior, and behavioral techniques such as correction contingency (e.g., actively correcting inappropriate remarks) appear to be worthy components

(Lewis, Nelson, Nelson, & Reusink, 1988). For instance, Ehrlich and Sipes (1985) reported a positive outcome for a model of pragmatic-based interventions that focused on improving nonverbal communication, communication in context, and message repair (becoming aware of communication breakdown, etc.). Those authors indicated that group members actively evaluated each others' videotaped role plays.

Four-month group communication treatment has shown promise as an approach to chronic aphasia (Elman & Bernstein-Ellis, 1999). This consisted of two sessions per week (5 hours) for a total of 32 sessions. Strategies included methods for conveying messages in any manner, encouraging conversation initiation, education about communication disorders, promoting insight to establish and measure personal goals, and trying to increase efficacy in communication attempts. While in groups, participants were encouraged to discuss daily activities and participated in a host of activities including communicative drawing, role playing, natural gestures, maps, notebooks, prompting, graphic choices, and scripting. Participants were also asked to lead group discussions, prompt others to participate, and encourage feedback. A family social interaction component was also added in the form of a coffee break to elicit conversation. Other group interventions for aphasic patients have been described by Kearns and Elman (2001).

Individual approaches, such as Worrall and Yiu's (2000) module-based Speaking Out intervention have also shown promise. They utilized a 10-module program implemented by volunteers visiting stroke patients in the home. Modules included: what is aphasia?, communication breakdown, communication repair, starting a conversation, managing finances, using the telephone, leisure going out, leisure at home, daily planning, along with surprises and gift giving. The tasks chosen in this program were relevant to daily activities.

Additional well-supported therapies include intensive functional stimulation communication therapy and cognitive linguistic therapies. Research has also supported the use of cognitive interventions for specific language impairments in reading comprehension and language formation in left hemisphere stroke patients. Moreover, cuing techniques for dysnomic and agrammatic conditions have proven useful. In general, the interventions should be intense, target specific functional communication, and be tailored to patients' needs.

Alexia/Agraphia

Another language-based complication of brain injury relates to reading and writing functions. While multiple disorders can arise, many do not occur in strict isolation of one another (Coslett, 2003; Roeltgen, 2003). Alexia is a disturbance of reading with relatively preserved writing skills. A number of techniques have been used to address such problems, including tactile-kinesthetic letter identification approach, motor cross-cuing strategy, speeded stimulus presentation, rapid whole word recognition, along with rapid whole word reading and multiple oral re-reading (Cherney, 2004). Moreover, computer-based programs with hierarchical language stimuli have been shown to improve comprehension (Cicerone et al., 2000).

Lott and Friedmen (1999) used letter naming or letter-by-letter reading in a two-stage process. The first stage stressed improving accuracy with a tactile-kinesthetic strategy, and the second stage encouraged speed of reading. Seki, Yajima, and Sugishita (1995) also reported favorable results using kinesthetic reading (reading by tracing or copying the outline of each letter with the patient's finger). Viswanathan and Kiran (2005) reported improvement with a case implementing several stages in word reading. The patient first read target words orally, then graphically spelled targets, selected target words from phonological and orthographic foils, identified letters of target words presented randomly, read letters in target words aloud, analyzed semantic attributes of targets, and read aloud the words again.

Agraphia refers to the lack of ability to express thoughts into written words (Roeltgen, 2003). Interventions for agraphia are dependent upon the type of agraphic deficits (e.g., pure agraphic versus apraxic agraphia). Some effectiveness has been shown for cuing hierarchies to correct spelling of nouns and verbs (Beeson, 1999). For instance, arranging scrambled letters of target words and repeated copying of the word (Anagram and Copy Treatment) with intensive copying and recall homework trials (Copy and Recall Treatment) has shown promise (Beeson, Hirsch, & Rewega, 2002). Such rehabilitation has been shown valuable in post-acute stages, particularly with aphasic agraphia.

EXECUTIVE FUNCTIONS AND PROBLEM SOLVING

GOAL-SETTING, PLANNING, MONITORING/ORGANIZING behaviors, and making adjustments toward a goal are all considered executive functions. These abilities are commonly impaired after TBI and typically associated with damage to the frontal and prefrontal cortex. They are frequently barriers to community reentry and prevent patients from resuming normal premorbid activities (Sohlberg, Mateer, & Stuss, 1993; Stuss, 1987).

Sohlberg and Mateer (1989) developed one of the first interventions that specifically targeted remediation of executive functions. Their program emphasized organization and structure. Generally, the patient is trained in time management, self-regulation, and how to appropriately select cognitive plans and then execute them. Specific treatment components are planning, initiation, speed of response, time scheduling, awareness, and impulse control. The focus is on real-world application. For example, training for impaired time-scheduling may involve having the patient inform the therapist when a set number of minutes have passed. To remediate awareness, the patient may be asked to keep a record of how many times they engage in a specific behavior. In this exercise, the therapist would also record target behaviors in order to gauge the accuracy of the patient's awareness. This intervention has only been supported by case studies to this point.

Problem interventions frequently target isolated components of problem solving instead of rehabilitating general reasoning abilities. One approach gaining popularity within rehabilitation settings is Goal Management Training (GMT), which is based on goal neglect theory (Duncan, Emslie, Williams, Johnson, & Freer, 1996). Goal neglect is the failure to adhere to task requirements and is postulated to be a core executive deficit. In GMT, paper and pencil training exercises are employed to teach the patient to utilize five stages of goal management. The patient is taught to stop, define the main task, list the necessary steps required for the task, learn the steps and complete the task, and check that they are engaging in the planned activity.

Levine et al. (2000) employed a randomized control GMT trial resulting in improvement on typically problematic tasks for patients with TBI. However, the treatment only entailed an hour of instruction, and generalization has not been demonstrated. However, the efficacy of behavioral interventions for impaired problem solving in TBI was clearly shown in their study.

Several less stringently designed studies have reported benefits from cognitive-behavioral approaches emphasizing self-awareness and self-instructional procedures (Medd & Tate, 2000; Ownsworth et al., 2000; Tham, Ginsburg, Fisher, & Tegner, 2001). The typical strategy in these studies was to enhance the patient's awareness of their executive deficits. However, others have suggested that increased self-awareness of deficits is not a necessary component of behavioral change (Cicerone et al., 2005).

Another common therapeutic practice is to increase strategies for dealing with everyday events. Integrating effective strategies into the patient's skill set can be accomplished via feedback and self-monitoring. Generally, in group therapy situations, the therapist presents problems to the group before guiding members through problem-solving processes. Problem-solving deficits may be addressed by introducing problematic situations that resemble problems of members of the group, viewing problem-solving vignettes, using flow sheets with the steps necessary to solve a problem, and scheduling to work through problematic situations in a controlled fashion (Wesolowski & Zencius, 1994). To ameliorate impaired planning ability,

447

*Cognitive
Rehabilitation
With Brain-
Damaged
Patients*

therapy may also involve recreational and menu planning groups, use of planning forms and checklists, and situational exposure. The object is to have the group member self-generate effective solutions.

Others have examined whether training in specific executive tasks generalizes to other executive functions. Stablum, Umilta, Mogentale, Carlan, and Geurrini (2000) utilized the dual-task paradigm wherein the primary instruction is to respond whether two stimuli are presented to the left or right of a fixation point while the secondary instruction is to respond whether the stimuli are the same or different. The primary response is speeded while the secondary response is not. Stablum et al. (2000) found that training resulted in response time improvement, which extended to other measures of executive functioning.

COMPUTERS AND OTHER TECHNOLOGIES IN COGNITIVE REHABILITATION

SINCE THE LATE 1970s computers have shown potential in cognitive rehabilitation. Continuing in the twenty-first century, advances in computers, increased Internet access, and various electronic devices are quickly shaping the role assistive technologies play in the lives of those with disabilities. Devices have become smaller, personalizable, flexible, content-laden, and multifunctioning. Although there are few systematic studies supporting efficacy of such devices in cognitive rehabilitation, there are some areas in which progress has been achieved (Lynch, 2002). On the other hand, little support has been endorsed for playing video games and other discrete, repetitive "learning" tasks aimed at restoring acquired deficits. Contemporary use of technologies in rehabilitation focuses on ways to improve individuals' functional independence through targeting specific ADLs (i.e., driving, daily math skills, memory for faces and names, remembering appointments, etc.). Some of the task-specific technologies have advantages in that they allow the client to complete tasks without a therapist and are often self-paced. Rehabilitation can also be accessed by obtaining existing technologies for the general population and devices specifically designed for those with special needs. Also, telerehabilitation and virtual reality modalities are becoming more prominent in the field.

Electronic prosthetics include tone, text, and voice alarms; alarm enabled text watches; timers; Personal Digital Assistants; mobile phones; text pagers;, and digital dictation/memo takers. For instance, Neuropage is a personal paging system that auditorily alerts the patient and provides text content for reminders to take medication or attend appointments. Also available are prompts and organizers that instruct individuals with procedural information (i.e., task-oriented instructions; Bergman, 2003). Some handheld and desktop programs aid with scheduling, organizing, and information retrieval. Such devices can both send and receive information and transfer data to personal computers and central data centers for therapist review (Kapur, Glisky, & Wilson, 2004). One of the most comprehensive tailored programs, Essential Steps, is based on learning, cognitive, and neuropsychological theory, to include journals, personal directory, conversation telephone center, appointments scheduler, to do lists, money manager, text writer, information section, and activity sequencing (Bergman, 2003).

Driving ability can both be assessed and trained through the computer medium (e.g., Cognitive Behavioral Driver's Inventory, Driving School). Math skill software includes virtual shopping malls and shops as well as tasks to engage the user in purchasing and tracking inventory (e.g., Math Shop Deluxe). Through other educational software patients can learn vocabulary, grammatical, and spelling skills. Some of those areas include word-finding problems, sentence construction, comprehension, and simple word recognition. Another advance in communication-related concerns is personal computer dictation software that can be integrated with popular software including word-processing programs and operating systems. Through most of the programs, patients can self-pace through hierarchical modules while receiving immediate feedback.

Virtual rehabilitation and telerehabilitation provide even further options. Some programs are presented as 3-D atmospheres mimicking potential life challenges faced in an individuals' environment (e.g., kitchen, stores, etc.) or offer rehabilitation resources online (e.g., social support, educational modules, etc.; Diamond et al., 2003). Both types of technologies can allow therapists to interact with patients by video link and review data to track patient progress. LoPresti, Mihailidis, and Kirsch (2004) have provided a more comprehensive review of assistive technology.

BEHAVIORAL AND PSYCHOLOGICAL DISORDERS

BEHAVIORAL AND PSYCHOLOGICAL problems are prominent aspects in the clinical picture of those with acquired brain injury. While there is no one syndrome or cluster of psychiatric symptoms unique to brain damage, there are a number of symptoms commonly encountered. Of particular concern to caregivers is disruptive aggressiveness coupled with liability, decreased frustration tolerance, increased lability, and disinhibition. Symptom severity and patterns of psychological distress in such patients have multiple co-occurring causes (i.e., focal brain injury, familiar/spouse relationships, employment problems, etc.). Irrespective of the etiological mechanism, behavioral disturbances often lead to staff and caregiver burnout, social isolation, and perhaps

449

*Cognitive
Rehabilitation
With Brain-
Damaged
Patients*

adversely affect more life domains than cognitive deficits. While such problems can be addressed pharmacologically, we briefly review behaviorally and cognitively oriented approaches.

One factor that can exacerbate symptoms is stress. Because of decreased cerebral efficiency, brain-injured patients often have problems coping with routine activities that would have been performed with ease and mastery premorbidly. Those caring for patients should be acutely aware of this decreased coping capacity and ensure difficult tasks are not presented too early in the rehabilitation process as failure could lead to feelings of being overwhelmed, hopelessness, and decreased treatment motivation. Another salient source of stress is a hostile, overinvolved familial environment (i.e., expressed emotion). Researchers have indicated expressed emotion has a causal role in exacerbating psychiatric and behavioral symptoms in those with various mental illnesses and has a role in relapse of mood symptoms and decompensation (Johnson, Winett, Meyer, Greenhouse, & Miller, 1999). Therefore, it is likely counterproductive for a range of brain-damage conditions.

Behavioral interventions (e.g., relaxation training, stress inoculation, etc.) are popular for treating stress, anxiety, and depression. The nature of those interventions is largely dependent upon the setting (e.g., inpatient versus outpatient) and extent of injury. For instance, token economies employing response cost, and so forth are more effective in a circumscribed, well-controlled inpatient environment (Glynn, 1990) and are most relevant in acute institutional rehabilitation. On the other hand, behavioral contracts, reinforcing differential behaviors, offering alternative reinforcers, and contingency management can be utilized in treatment plans regardless of setting.

Beyond behavioral methods, empirically validated psychotherapy for symptoms and behavioral medicine techniques for pain and treatment adherence should be explored (Chambless et al., 1998). However, the effectiveness of any particular intervention will be limited by accompanying cognitive dysfunction. For instance, session-to-session progress may be hindered by memory and executive problems that disrupt integrity of treatment continuity. Therefore, any treatment technique must account for patients' cognitive limitations. In more severe cases of brain injury, intervention strategies will likely resemble methods traditionally enlisted for those with intellectual disabilities, developmental disabilities, or dementia conditions (Allen-Burge, Stevens, & Burgio, 1999).

AGING, DEMENTIA, AND OTHER NEUROLOGICAL DISORDERS

AFTER MANY YEARS of consideration, the "use it or lose it" motto has been challenged (Neri, Iacono, Renzetti, & De Vreese, 2001) within the dementia literature. Early identification of deficits may allow for improvement of cognitive functioning via multiple therapies: behavioral strategies, environmental modifications, and emotional therapies (Piccoloni, Amandio, Spazzafumo, Moroni, & Freddi, 1992). The treatment of dementia is multifaceted and includes intervening with both cognitive and affective functioning (Koltai, Welsh-Bohmer, & Schmechel, 2001). Studer (2004) has identified five areas that should be considered in the treatment of cognitive impairment in dementia: (1) understand pathophysiology of presenting problem; (2) assign level of awareness; (3) assign level of learning; (4) assess personality, premorbid interests, and current goals; and (5) identify/objectify any potential barriers to learning (e.g., attention and memory).

Some research has targeted improving semantic deficits with demented patients successfully; however, results also have indicated that performance may decline once learning is no longer practiced, and gains may not generalize (Graham, Patterson, Pratt, & Hodges, 2001). Interventions concentrating on encoding and emphasizing learning have been shown to facilitate long-term gains and most likely semantic learning (Clare, Wilson, Carter, Hodges, & Adams, 2001). Bucks et al. (2003) recommended inclusion of psychoeducation to enhance coping skills and problem solving and for greater improvement of behavioral, emotional, and cognitive functioning.

Other approaches have focused on enhancing procedural skills in dementia patients (Farina et al., 2002; Zanetti et al., 2001). Clare et al. (2003) reported that interventions should attempt to build upon preserved areas of functioning and impairment through compensation that targets functioning and alleviates stress.

Combining pharmacological and nonpharmacological treatments may be the most efficacious (Bucks et al., 2002). Acetylcholinesterase inhibitors are the most widely used pharmacological treatment (Moore, Sandman, McGrady, & Kesslak, 2001) and should be considered for use in conjunction with behavioral therapies.

Reality orientation was one of the first treatments used for dementia rehabilitation. This therapy repetitiously exposes patients to orientation-related information to help better understand their environment. However, critics of this method have commented that the technique is rigid and insensitive (Spector, Orrell, Davies, & Woods, 2001).

Reminiscence therapy, which involves individual or group sessions that promote the discussion of past events with external aids (e.g., photographs), serves to preserve temporal and spatial orientation. Validation therapy aims to provide validation for the feelings by focusing on the meaning of behavior, as opposed to attempting to correct it (Spector et al., 2001). Recreational (e.g., games, time with pets) and art (e.g., dance and crafts) therapies (Farina et al., 2002) have been

451

*Cognitive
Rehabilitation
With Brain-
Damaged
Patients*

identified as nonpharmacological treatments, although initial studies lack methodological rigor. Aerobic training has also been explored and found to significantly improve the cognitive functions in demented patients (Palleschi et al., 1996). Errorless learning (Komatsu, Mimura, Kato, Wakamatsu, & Kashima, 2000) spaced-retrieval (Hawley & Cherry, 2004), domain-specific learning, mnemonic methods (Clare, Wilson, Carter, & Hodges, 2003), and sensorimotor skill stimulation (De Vreese, Neri, Fioravanti, Belloi, & Zanetti, 2001) have all been employed and are discussed elsewhere in this chapter.

The use of external memory aids, both electric and nonelectric, have become more popular in the treatment of dementia. The NeuroPage service has been found to be useful for reminders (Wilson, Scott, Evans, & Emslie, 2003). Examples of nonelectric memory aids include: diaries, calendars, large clocks (Spector et al., 2001), memory boards (De Vreese et al., 2001) post-it pads, beepers, alarm clocks, tape recorders (Moore et al., 2001), memory boxes, memory books, memory posters (McPherson et al., 2001), and memory wallets (Bourgeois, 1992). These devices tend to be easy to use, are inexpensive, and enhance both daily and social functioning. Bourgeois et al. (2003) highlighted the obvious problem with external memory aids—the patient often forgets their existence or location, or fails to use them at appropriate times.

CASE CONCEPTUALIZATION

THUS FAR, THE chapter has centered on specific interventions. However, the rehabilitation clinician needs a methodology to integrate data on recovery of functioning and cognitive retraining. To this end, a useful approach to case conceptualization is presented. Efficacious case conceptualization rests on the assumption that cognitive training is a continuously evolving process dependent upon multidisciplinary integration of diverse data. This emphasizes the necessity of being well-versed in neuropathology and experimental neuropsychology, as well as other interrelated disciplines. Conceptual flexibility and an open approach to new information, even if it contradicts long-held assumptions, is essential to advancing the field and ensuring patients receive the highest level of care.

While no empirically validated case conceptualization model has been demonstrated, good case conceptualization of head injury should involve the following components: (1) patient/collateral interview, (2) neuropsychological evaluation, (3) functional inspection of test performance, and (4) initiation of training and progressive modifications.

STEP 1: PATIENT/COLLATERAL INTERVIEW

THE PATIENT'S CURRENT neuropsychological status is the culmination of a number of variables such as premorbid functioning, current situational stressors, time elapsed since the injury, and severity of injury. In order to gain a complete and accurate clinical picture, it is necessary to gather pertinent information from diverse sources. Relevant information includes demographics, medical history (particularly pre-existing sensory impairments), behavioral observations, and the psychologist's analysis of the patient's and caregivers' observations of functional impairments. The patient's academic and occupational record is also extremely important as this may be the most accurate indicator of the individual's premorbid functioning (Lezak, Howieson, & Loring, 2004). Additional information regarding level of functioning can be gathered using rating forms completed by the patient or their family. Such rating forms can also provide an objective way to gauge the progress of the patient's recovery over time.

STEP 2: NEUROPSYCHOLOGICAL EVALUATION

AN INITIAL COMPREHENSIVE neurocognitive evaluation assessing a wide array of cognitive abilities is an important component of case conceptualization. This allows the clinician to quantify the degree of deficits and extent of residual strengths from the outset. From that point, the therapist can form a plan of interventions that best compliments the assessment results. A thorough evaluation of neuropsychological functioning should encompass the following domains: intelligence (current and premorbid estimations), memory, attention and concentration, sensory/perceptual and motor, visuoperceptual, language, executive, problem solving, academic, and personality/emotional.

STEP 3: FUNCTIONAL INSPECTION OF TEST PERFORMANCE

WHILE IDENTIFICATION OF functional impairment is an important and valid goal, the overriding purpose of this step is to determine why specific mental functions are impaired. Discovering what is responsible for deficient neuropsychological status is a necessary foundational step that must be completed before treatment interventions can be designed. Luria's concept of hypothesis testing of functional deficits plays an important clinical role at this stage of case conceptualization. First, areas of brain dysfunction should be identified through the neuropsychological evaluation. Next, the clinician should apply knowledge of cognitive functions and architecture and identify the

453

*Cognitive
Rehabilitation
With Brain-
Damaged
Patients*

underlying functional impairment that produces patterns of strengths and weaknesses. Finally, this information is used to gauge potential for treatment and, if appropriate, develop intervention strategies. Moreover, the patient's neuropsychological status should be conceptualized as it relates to the patient's current and predicted functional status.

STEP 4: INITIATION OF TRAINING AND PROGRESSIVE MODIFICATION

AT THIS LAST stage, therapeutic interventions are implemented and data is gathered concerning patient performance. Treatment decisions are then made based on analysis of this data. If analysis of daily performance data indicates the patient is mastering the rehabilitation task, the therapist may decide to progress to the next task level. Conversely, if data analysis reveals that the patient is not making appreciable gains, then the task may need to be restructured or a different intervention strategy considered. Such structured performance analysis is especially important in the context of a large therapeutic team, because it allows team members to have a similar level of understanding progress and functional ability. It also provides data to justify current and future service delivery. Working through these four levels of assessment and rehabilitation is the basis of good case conceptualization in head injury. Periodic reevaluation at each level, particularly steps two and three, is recommended to confirm training efficacy.

REFERENCES

Alderson, A. I., & Novack, T. A. (2002). Measuring recovery of orientation during acute rehabilitation for traumatic brain injury: Value and expectations of recovery. *Journal of Head Trauma and Rehabilitation, 17*(3), 210–219.

Allen-Burge, R., Stevens, A. B., & Burgio, L. D. (1999). Effective behavioral interventions for decreasing dementia-related challenging behavior in nursing homes. *International Journal of Geriatric Psychiatry, 14,* 213–232.

American Heart Association. (2005). *Heart Disease and Stroke Statistics—2005 Update*. Dallas, TX: American Heart Association.

Ashwal, S., & Holshouser, B. A. (1997). New neuroimaging techniques and their potential role in patients with acute brain injury. *Journal of Head Trauma Rehabilitation, 12*(4), 13–35.

Bailey, M. J., Riddoch, M. J., & Crome, P. (2002). Treatment of visual neglect in elderly patients with stroke: A single-subject series using either a scanning and cuing strategy or a left-limb activation strategy. *Physical Therapy, 82*(8), 782–797.

Beaumont, J. G., Connolly, S.A.V., & Rogers, M.J.C. (1999). Inpatient cognitive and behavioral rehabilitation: Assessing the outcomes. *Neuropsychological Rehabilitation, 9*(3/4), 401–411.

Beeson, P. M. (1999). Treating acquired writing impairment: Strengthening graphemic representations. *Aphasiology, 13*(9–11), 767–785.

Beeson, P. M., Hirsch, F. M., & Rewega, M. A. (2002). Successful single-word writing treatment: Experimental analyses of four cases. *Aphasiology, 16*(4–6), 473–491.

Bennett, T., Malia, K., Linton, B., Raymond, M., & Brewick, K. (1998). Rehabilitation of attention and concentration deficits following brain injury. *The Journal of Cognitive Rehabilitation, March/April,* 8–13.

Ben-Yishay, Y., & Diller, L (1993). Cognitive remediation in traumatic brain injury: Update and issues. *Archives of Physical Medicine and Rehabilitation, 74*(2), 204–213.

Ben-Yishay, Y., Piasetsky, E. B., & Rattok, J. (1987). A systematic model for ameliorating disorders in basic attention. In M. J., Meier, A. Benton, & L. Diller (Eds.), *Neuropsychological rehabilitation* (pp. 165–181). London: Churchill Livingstone.

Bergman, M. M. (2003). The Essential Steps cognitive orthotic. *Neuro-Rehabilitation, 18,* 31–46.

Bier, N., Vanier, M., & Meulemans, T. (2002). Errorless learning: A method to help amnesic patients learn new information. *The Journal of Cognitive Rehabilitation, 20*(3), 12–18.

Blundon, G., & Smits, E. (2000). Cognitive rehabilitation: A pilot survey of therapeutic modalities used by Canadian occupational therapists with survivors of traumatic brain injury. *Canadian Journal of Occupational Therapy, 67*(3), 184–196.

Bourgeois, M. S., Camp, C., Rose, M., White, B., Malone, M., Carr, J., et al. (2003). A comparison of training strategies to enhance use of external aids by persons with dementia. *Journal of Communication Disorders, 36,* 361–378.

Bourgeois, M. S. (1992). Evaluating memory wallets in conversations with persons with dementia. *Journal of Speech and Hearing Research, 35*(6), 1344–1358.

Boman, I. L., Lindstedt, M., Hemmignsson, H., & Bartfai, A. (2004). Cognitive training in home environment. *Brain Injury, 18*(10), 985–995.

Bucks, R. S., Byrne, L., Haworth, J., Wilcock, G., Hyde, J., Emmerson, C., et al. (2002). Interventions in Alzheimer's disease. *International Journal of Geriatric Psychiatry, 17*(5), 492–493.

Büki, A., Okonkwo, D. O., Wang, K. K., & Povlishock, J. T. (2000). Cytochrome *c* release and caspase activation in traumatic axonal injury. *Journal of Neuroscience, 20*(8), 2825–2834.

Bush, B. A., Novack, T. A., Malec, J. F., Stringer, A. Y., Millis, S. R., & Madan, A. (2003). Validation of a model for evaluating outcome after traumatic brain injury. *Archives of Physical Medicine and Rehabilitation, 84,* 1803–1807.

455

*Cognitive
Rehabilitation
With Brain-
Damaged
Patients*

Butter, C. M., & Kirsch, N. (1992). Combined and separate effects of eye patching and visual stimulation on unilateral neglect following stroke. *Archives of Physical Medicine and Rehabilitation, 73*(12), 1133–1139.

Caplan, D. (2003). Aphasic syndromes. In K. M. Heilman & E. Valenstein (Eds.), *Clinical neuropsychology* (pp. 14–34). New York: Oxford University Press.

Cappa, S. F., Benke, T., Clarke, S., Rossi, B., Stemmer, B., & van Heugten, C. M. (2003). EFNS guidelines on cognitive rehabilitation: Report of an EFNS task force. *European Journal of Neurology, 10,* 11–23.

Carney, N., Chesnut, R. M., Maynard, H., Mann, N. C., Patterson, P., & Helfand, M. (1999). Effect of cognitive rehabilitation on outcomes for persons with traumatic brain injury: A systematic review. *Journal of Head Trauma Rehabilitation, 14*(3), 277–307.

Centers for Disease Control. (1999). *Traumatic brain injury in the United States: A Report to Congress.* Retrieved from http://www.cdc.gov/doc.do/id/0900f3ec8001011c.

Cernak, I., Wang, Z., Jiang, J., Bian, X., & Savic, J. (2001). Cognitive deficits involved in blast injury-induced neurotrauma: Possible involvement of nitric oxide. *Brain Injury, 15*(7), 593–612.

Chambless, D. L., Baker, M. J., Baucon, D. H., Beutler, L. E., Calhoun, K. S., Crits-Christoph, P., et al. (1998). Update on empirically validated therapies II. *The Clinical Psychologist, 51*(1), 3–21.

Chapey, R. (2002). *Language intervention strategies in aphasia and related neurogenic communication disorders* (4th ed.). Baltimore, MD: Lippincott Williams & Wilkins.

Chen, Y., Constantini, S., Trembovier, V., Weinstock, M., & Shohami, E. (1996). An experimental model of closed head injury in mice: Pathophysiology, histopathology, and cognitive deficits. *Journal of Neurotrauma, 13*(10), 557–568.

Cherney, L. R. (2004). Aphasia, alexia, and oral reading. *Topics in Stroke Rehabilitation, 11*(1), 22–36.

Chestnut, R. M., Carney, N., Maynard, H., Mann, N. C., Patterson, P., & Helfand, M. (1999). Summary report: Evidence for the effectiveness of rehabilitation for persons with traumatic brain injury. *Journal of Head Trauma Rehabilitation, 14*(2), 176–188.

Chiaravalloti, N. D., Demaree, H., & Gaudino, E. A. (2003). Can the repetition effect maximize learning in multiple sclerosis? *Clinical Rehabilitation, 17,* 58–68.

Cicerone, K. D., Dahleberg, C., Kalmar, K., Langenbahn, D. M., Malec, J. F., Berquist, T. F., et al. (2000). Evidence-based cognitive rehabilitation: Recommendations for clinical practice. *Archives of Physical Medicine and Rehabilitation, 81*(12), 1596–1615.

Cicerone, K. D., Dahleberg, C., Malec, J. F., Langenbahn, D. M., Felicetti, T., Kneipp, S., et al. (2005). Evidence-based cognitive rehabilitation: Updated review of the literature from 1998 through 2002. *Archives of Physical Medicine and Rehabilitation, 86,* 1681–1692.

Cicerone, K. D., Mott, T., Azulay, J., & Friel, J. C. (2004). Community integration and satisfaction with functioning after intensive cognitive rehabilitation for traumatic brain injury. *Archives of Physical Medicine and Rehabilitation, 85,* 943–950.

Clare, L., Wilson, B. A., Carter, G., & Hodges, J. R. (2003). Cognitive rehabilitation as a component of early intervention in Alzheimer's disease: A single case study. *Aging and Mental Health, 7*(1), 15–21.

Clare, L., Wilson, B. A., Carter, G., Hodges, J. R., & Adams, M. (2001). Long-term maintenance of treatment gains following a cognitive rehabilitation intervention in early dementia of Alzheimer type: A single case study. *Neuropsychological Rehabilitation, 11*(314), 477–494.

Coetzer, B. R., & du Toit, R. L. (2002). Impaired awareness following brain injury and its relationship to placement and employment outcome. *The Journal of Cogntive Rehabilitation, 20*(2), 20–24.

Coslett, H. B. (2003). Acquired dyslexia. In K. M. Heilman & E. Valenstein (Eds.), *Clinical neuropsychology* (pp. 108–125). New York: Oxford University Press.

Cuesta, G. M. (2003). Cognitive rehabilitation of memory following stroke: Theory, practice, and outcome. *Ischemic Stroke: Advances in Neurology, 92,* 415–421,

Davis, A. M., Davis, S., Moss, N., Marks, J., McGrath, J., Hovard, L., et al. (1992). First steps towards an interdisciplinary approach to rehabilitation. *Clinical Rehabilitation, 6,* 237–244.

De Vreese, L. P., Belloi, L., Iacono, S., Finelli, C., & Neri, M. (1998). Memory training programs in memory complainers: Efficacy on objective and subjective memory functioning. *Archives of Gerontology and Geriatrics, 6S*(Suppl), 141–154.

De Vreese, L. P., Neri, M., Fioravanti, M., Belloi, L., & Zanetti, O. (2001). Memory rehabilitation in Alzheimer's disease: A review of progress. *International Journal of Geriatric Pyschiatry, 16,* 794–809.

Diamond, B. J., Shreve, G. M., Bonilla, J. M., Johnston, M. V., Morodan, J., & Branneck, R. (2003). Telerehabilitation, cognition, and user-accessibility. *NeuroRehabilitation, 18,* 171–177.

Dirette, D. (2002). The use of cognitive strategies by adults with acquired brain injuries: Results of a two-year post-treatment survey. *The Journal of Cognitive Rehabilitation, 20*(4), 6–11.

Duncan, J., Emslie, H., Williams, P., Johnson, R., & Freer, C. (1996). Intelligence and the frontal lobe: The organization of goal-directed behavior. *Cognitive Psychology, 30,* 257–303.

Ehrlich, J. S., & Sipes, A. L. (1985). Group treatment of communication skills for head trauma patients. *Cognitive Rehabilitation, 3*(1), 32–37.

Elman, R. J., & Bernstein-Ellis, E. (1999). The efficacy of group communication treatment in adults with chronic aphasia. *Journal of Speech, Language & Hearing Research, 42*(2), 411–419.

457

*Cognitive
Rehabilitation
With Brain-
Damaged
Patients*

Engelberts, N., Klein, M., Ader, H., Heimans, J., Trenite, D., & van der Ploeg, H. (2002). The effectiveness of cognitive rehabilitation for attention deficits in focal seizures: A randomized controlled study. *Epilepsia, 43*(6), 587–595.

Evans, J. J., Wilson, B. A., Schuri, E., Andrade, J., Baddeley, A., Bruna, O., et al. (2000). A comparison of "errorless" and "trial-and-error" learning methods for teaching individuals with acquired memory deficits. *Neuropsychological Rehabilitation, 10*(1), 67–101.

Farina, E., Fioravanti, R., Chiavari, L., Imbornone, E., Alberoni, M., Pomati, S., et al. (2002). Comparing two programs of cognitive training in Alzheimer's disease: A pilot study. *Acta Neurologica Scandinavica, 105*, 365–371.

Fasotti, L., Kovacs, F., Eling, P., & Brouwer, W. H. (2000). Time pressure management as a compensatory strategy training after closed head injury. *Neuropsychological Rehabilitation, 10*(1), 47–65.

Fisher, A. (1998). Uniting practice in an occupational framework. *The American Journal of Occupational Therapy, 52*(7), 509–521.

Fujii, D., & Ahmend, I. (2002). Psychotic disorder following traumatic brain injury: A conceptual framework. *Cognitive Neuropsychiatry, 7*(1), 41–62.

Gianutsos, R. (1991). Cognitive rehabilitation: A neuropsychological specialty comes of age. *Brain Injury, 5*(4), 353–368.

Glisky, E. L., & Schacter, D. L. (1988). Acquisition of domain-specific knowledge in patients with organic memory disorders. *Journal of Learning Disabilities, 21*(6), 333–351.

Glynn, S. M. (1990). Token economy approaches for psychiatric patients. *Behavior Modification, 14*(4), 383–407.

Golden, Z., & Golden, C. J. (2003). The differential impacts of Alzheimer's dementia, head injury, and stroke on personality dysfunction. *International Journal of Neuroscience, 113*, 869–878.

Goldstein, G., Beers, S. R., Longmore, S., & McCue, M. (1996). Efficacy of memory training: A technological extension and replication. *The Clinical Neuropsychologist, 10*(1), 66–72.

Gordon, W. A., Hibbard, M. R., Egelko, S., Diller, L., Shaver, M. S., Lieberman, A., et al. (1985). Perceptual remediation in patients with right brain damage: A comprehensive program. *Archives of Physical Medicine and Rehabilitation, 66*(6), 353–359.

Gouvier, W., Bua, B., Blanton, P., & Urey, J. (1987). Behavioral changes following visual scanning training: Observation of five cases. *International Journal of Clinical Neuropsychology, 9*, 74–80.

Graham, K. S., Patterson, K., Pratt, K. H., & Hodges, J. R. (2001). Can repeated exposure to "forgotten" vocabulary help alleviate word-finding difficulties in semantic dementia? An illustrative case study. *Neuropsychological Rehabilitation, 11*(314), 429–454.

Gray, D. B., & Hendershot, G. E. (2000). The ICIDH-2: Developments for a new era of outcomes research. *Archives of Physical Medicine and Rehabilitation, 81*(Suppl 2), S10–S14.

Greenwald, B. D., Burnett, D. M., & Miller, M. A. (2003). Congenital and acquired brain injury. 1. Brain injury: Epidemiology and pathophysiology. *Archives of Physical Medicine and Rehabilitation, 84*(Suppl1), s3–s7.

Hajek, V. E., Gagnon, S., & Ruderman, J. E. (1997). Cognitive and functional assessments of stroke patients: An analysis of their relation. *Archives of Physical Medicine and Rehabilitation, 78*, 1331–1337.

Harrison-Felix, C., Newton, C. N., Hall, K. M., & Kreutzer, J. S. (1996). Descriptive findings from the traumatic brain injury model systems national database. *Journal of Head Trauma Rehabilitation, 11*(5), 1–14.

Hawley, K. S., & Cherry, K. E. (2004). Spaced-retrieval effects on name-face recognition in older adults with probable Alzheimer's disease. *Behavior Modification, 28*(2), 276–296.

Heilman, K. M. (1979). Neglect and related disorders. In K. M. Heilman & E. Valenstein (Eds.), *Clinical neuropsychology* (pp. 268–307). New York: Oxford University Press.

Heilman, K. M., Watson, R. T., & Valenstein, E. (2003). Neglect and related disorders. In K. M. Heilman & E. Valenstein (Eds.), *Clinical neuropsychology* (pp. 296–346). New York: Oxford University Press.

Heinemann, A. W. (2005). Putting outcome measurement in context: A rehabilitation psychology perspective. *Rehabilitation Psychology, 50*(1), 6–14.

Hochstenbach, J. B., den Otter, R., & Mulder, T. W. (2003). Cognitive recovery after stroke: A 2-year follow-up. *Archives of Physical Medicine and Rehabilitation, 84*, 1499–1504.

Hutchinson, J., & Marquardt, T. P. (1997). Functional treatment approaches to memory impairment following brain injury. *Topics in Language Disorders, 18*(1), 45–57.

Ivanhoe, C. B., & Hartman, E. T. (2004). Clinical caveats on medical assessment and treatment of pain after TBI. *Journal of Head Trauma Rehabilitation, 19*(1), 29–39.

Johnson, S., Winett, C., Meyer, D., Greenhouse, W., & Miller, I. (1999). Social support and the course of bipolar disorder. *Journal of Abnormal Psychology, 108*, 558–566.

Kapur, N., Glisky, E. L., & Wilson, B. A. (2004). Technological aids for people with memory deficits. *Neuropsychological Rehabilitation, 14*(1/2), 41–60.

Kaschel, R., Sala, S. D., Cantagallo, A., Fahlbock, A., Laaksonen, R., & Kazen, M. (2002). Imagery mnemonics for the rehabilitation of memory: A randomized group controlled trial. *Neuropsychological Rehabilitation, 12*(2), 127–153.

Kasten, E., Müller-Oehring, E., & Sabel, B. A. (2001). Stability of visual field enlargements following computer-based restitution training—Results of a follow-up. *Journal of Clinical and Experimental Neuropsychology, 23*(3), 297–305.

Kearns, K., & Elman, R. (2001). Group therapy for aphasia: Theoretical and practical considerations. In R. Chapey (Ed.), *Language intervention strategies in adult aphasia* (4th ed., pp. 316–337). Baltimore, MD: Lippincott Williams & Wilkins.

Kolb, B., & Whishaw, I. Q. (2000). Reorganization of function after cortical lesions in rodents. In H. Levin & J. Grafman (Eds.), *Cerebral reorganization of function after brain damage,* (pp. 109–129). New York: Oxford University Press.

Koltai, D. C., Welsh-Bohmer, K. A., & Schmechel, D. E. (2001). Influence of anosognosia on treatment outcome among dementia patients. *Neuropsychological Rehabilitation, 11*(314), 455–475.

Komatsu, S., Mimura, M., Kato, M., Wakamatsu, N., & Kashima, H. (2000). Errorless and effortful processes involved in the learning of face-name associations by patients with alcoholic Korsakoff's syndrome. *Neuropsychological Rehabilitation, 10*(2), 113–132.

Koponen, S., Taiminen, T., Portin, R., Himanen, L., Isoniemi, H., Heinonen, H., et al. (2002). Axis I and II psychiatric disorders after traumatic brain injury: A 30-year follow-up study. *American Journal of Psychiatry, 159*(8), 1315–1321.

Laatsch, L. K., Thulborn, K. R., Krisky, C. M., Shobat, D. M., & Sweeney, J. A. (2004). Investigating the neurobiological basis of cognitive rehabilitation therapy with fMRI. *Brain Injury, 18*(10), 957–974.

Laatsch, L., Pavel, D., Jobe, T., Qing, L., & Quintana, J. C. (1999). Incorporation of SPECT imaging in a longitudinal cognitive rehabilitation therapy programme. *Brain Injury, 13*(8), 555–570.

Laatsch, L., Pavel, D., Jobe, T., Sychra, J., Lin, Q., & Blend, M. (1997). Impact of cognitive rehabilitation therapy on neuropsychological impairments as measured by brain perfusion SPECT: A longitudinal study. *Brain Injury, 11*(12), 851–863.

Langlois J. A., Rutland-Brown, W., & Thomas, K. E. (2004). *Traumatic brain injury in the United States: Emergency department visits, hospitalizations, and deaths.* Atlanta, GA: Centers for Disease Control and Prevention, National Center for Injury Prevention and Control.

Lannoo, E., Colardyn, F., Jannes, C., & DeSoete, G. (2001). Course of neuropsychological recovery from moderate-to-severe head injury: A 2-year follow-up. *Brain Injury, 15*(1), 1–13.

Larson, E. B., Kirschner, K., Bode, R. K., Heinemann, A. W., Clorfene, J., & Goodman, R. (2003). Brief cognitive assessment and prediction of functional outcome in stroke. *Topics in Stroke Rehabilitation, 9*(4), 10–21.

Lee, S. S., Powell, N. J., & Esdaile, S. (2001). A functional model of cognitive rehabilitation in occupational therapy. *Occupational Therapy, 68*(1), 41–50.

Lethbride-Cejku, M., & Vickerie, J. (2005). Summary health statistics for U.S. adults: National Health Interview Survey, 2003. *National Center for Health Statistics. Vital Health Statistics, 10*(225).

Levine, B., Robertson, I. H., Clare, L., Carter, G., Hong, J., Wilson, B. A., et al. (2000). Rehabilitation of executive functioning: An experimental-clinical validation of goal management training. *Journal of the International Neuropsychology Society, 6*(3), 299–312.

Lewis, F. D., Nelson, J., Nelson, C., & Reusink, P. (1988). Effects of three feedback contingencies on the socially inappropriate talk of a brain-injured adult. *Behavior Therapy, 19*(2), 203–211.

Lezak, M. D., Howieson, D. B., & Loring, D. W. (2004). *Neuropsychological assessment*. New York: Oxford University Press.

Lezak, M. D., & O'Brien, K. P. (1988). Longitudinal study of emotional, social, and physical changes after traumatic brain injury. *Journal of Learning Disabilities, 21*(8), 456–463.

LoPresti, E. F., Mihailidis, A., & Kirsch, N. (2004). Assistive technology for cognitive rehabilitation: State of the art. *Neuropsychological Rehabilitation, 14*(1/2), 5–39.

Lott, S. N., & Friedmen, R. B. (1999). Can treatment for pure alexia improve letter-by-letter reading speed without sacrificing accuracy? *Brain and Language, 67*(3), 188–201.

Lucas, S. E., & Flemming, J. M. (2005). Interventions for improving self-awareness following acquired brain injury. *Australian Occupational Therapy Journal, 52,* 160–170.

Luria, A. R. (1966). *Higher cortical functions in man*. Andover: Tavistock Publications.

Luria, A. R. (1980). *Higher cortical functions in man* (2nd Ed.). New York: Basic Books.

Lynch, B. (2002). Historical review of computer-assisted cognitive retraining. *Journal of Head Trauma Rehabilitation, 17*(5), 446–457.

Ma, H., & Trombly, C. A. (2002). A synthesis of the effects of occupational therapy for persons with stroke, part II: Remediation of impairments. *The American Journal of Occupational Therapy, 56*(3), 260–274.

Madigan, N. K., DeLuca, J., Diamond, B. J., Tramontano, G., & Averill, A. (2000). Speed of information processing in traumatic brain injury: Modality-specific factors. *Journal of Head Trauma Rehabilitation, 15*(3), 943–956.

Malia, K., & Duckett, S. (2001). Establishing minimum recommended standards for post-acute brain injury rehabilitation. *Brain Injury, 15*(4), 357–362.

Manly, T. (2002). Cognitive rehabilitation for unilateral neglect: Review. *Neuropsychological Rehabilitation, 12*(4), 289–310.

Mateer, C. A., Kerns, K. A., & Eso, K. L. (1996). Management of attention and memory disorders following traumatic brain injury. *Journal of Learning Disabilities, 29*(6), 618–632.

Mateer, C. A., Sira, C. S., & O'Connell, M. E. (2005). Putting Humpty Dumpty together again: The importance of integrating cognitive and emotional interventions. *Journal of Head Trauma Rehabilitation, 20*(1), 62–75.

Mazmanian, P. E., Kreutzer, J. S., Devany, C. W., & Martin, K. O. (1993). A survey of accredited and other rehabilitation facilities: Education, training, and cognitive rehabilitation in brain-injury programmes. *Brain Injury, 7*(4), 319–331.

McPherson, A., Furniss, F. G., Sdogati, C., Cesaroni, F., Tartaglini, B., & Lindesay, J. (2001). Effects of individualized memory aids on the conversation of persons with severe dementia: A pilot study. *Aging and Mental Health, 5*(3), 289–294.

McGrath, J. R. (in press). Interdisciplinary goal planning in neurological rehabilitation. In P. Frommelt & H. Groezbach (Eds.), *NeuroRehabilitation*. Berlin: ABW-Wissenschaftsverlag.

McGrath, J. R., Marks, J. A., & Davis, A.M. (1995). Towards interdisciplinary rehabilitation: Further developments at Rivermead Rehabilitation Centre. *Clinical Rehabilitation, 9*, 320–326.

Medd, J., & Tate, R. L. (2000). Evaluation of an anger management therapy programme following ABI: A preliminary study. *Neuropsychological Rehabilitation, 10*, 185–201.

Meier, M. J., Benton, A., & Diller L. (1987). *Neuropsychological rehabilitation*. New York: The Guilford Press.

Mermis, B. J. (2005). Developing a taxonomy for rehabilitation outcome measurement. *Rehabilitation Psychology, 50*(1), 15–23.

Minnes, P., Harrick, L., Carlson, P., & Johnston, J. (1998). A transitional living environment for persons with brain injuries: Staff and client perceptions. *Brain Injury, 12*(11), 987–992.

Moore, S., Sandman, C. A., McGrady, K., & Kesslak, J. P. (2001). Memory training improves cognitive ability in patients with dementia. *Neuropsychological Rehabilitation, 11*(314), 245–261.

Morimoto, T., Globus, M. Y. T., Busto, R., Martinez, E., & Ginsburg, M. D. (1996). Simultaneous measurement of salicylate hydroxylation and glutamate release in the penumbral cortex following transient middle cerebral artery occlusion in rats. *Journal of Cerebral Blood Flow and Metabolism, 16*, 92–99.

Nadeau, S. E. (2002). A paradigm shift in neurorehabilitation. *The Lancet— Neurology, 1*, 126–129.

Neri, M., Iacono, S., Renzetti, C., & De Vreese, L. P. (2001). Cognitive training in aging and disease (COTRAD): Does it really work in Italy? *Archives of Gerontology and Geriatrics, 7*(Suppl), 285–293.

Nicholls, J. G., Martin, A. R., Wallace, B. G., & Fuchs, P. A. (2001). *From neuron to brain*. Sunderland, MA: Sinauer Associates, Inc.

Niemeier, J. P. (1998). The Lighthouse Strategy: Use of a visual imagery technique to treat visual inattention in stroke patients. *Brain Injury, 12*(5), 399–406.

NIH Consensus Statement. (1999). NIH Consensus Development Panel on Rehabilitation of Persons with Traumatic Brain Injury Rehabilitation of persons with traumatic brain injury. *JAMA: Journal of the American Medical Association, 282*(10), 974–983.

Novack, T. A., Alderson, A. L., Bush, B. A., Meythaler, J. M., & Canupp, K. (2000). Cognitive and functional recovery at 6 and 12 months post-TBI. *Brain Injury, 14*(11), 987–996.

Oddy, M., Alcott, D., Francis, E., Jenkins, K., & Fowlie, C. (1999). Methods of evaluation in a cognitive-behavioural rehabilitation programme for brain injury: The experiences of Ticehurst House and Unsted Park Hospitals. *Neuropsychological Rehabilitation, 9*(3/4), 373–384.

Oddy, M., Coughlan, T., Tyerman, A., & Jenkins, D. (1985). Social adjustment after closed head injury: A further follow-up seven years after injury. *Journal of Neurology, Neurosurgery, and Psychiatry, 48*, 564–568.

Ogden, J. A. (2000). Neurorehablitation in the third millennium: New roles for our environment, behaviors, and mind in brain damage and recovery? *Brain and Cognition, 42*, 110–112.

Ownsworth, T. L., McFarland, K., & Young, R. (2000). Self-awareness and psychosocial functioning following acquired brain injury: An evaluation of a group support programme. *Neuropsychological Rehabilitation, 10*(5), 465–484.

Palleschi, L., Vetta, F., De Gennaro, E., Idone, G., Sottosanti, G., Gianni, W., et al. (1996). Effect of aerobic training on the cognitive performance of elderly patients with senile dementia of Alzheimer type. *Archives of Gerontology and Geriatrics, 5*(Suppl), 47–50.

Palmese, C. A., & Raskin, S. A. (2000). The rehabilitation of attention in individuals with mild traumatic brain injury, using the APT-II Programme. *Brain Injury, 14*(6), 535–548.

Parente, R., & Hermann, D. (1996). *Retraining cognition: Techniques and applications*. Gaithersburg, MD: Aspen Publishers.

Park, N. W., & Ingles, J. L. (2001). Effectiveness of attention rehabilitation after an acquired brain injury: A meta-analysis. *Neuropsychology, 15*(2), 199–210.

Pépin, M., Laranger, M., & Benoit, G. (1995). Efficiency of cognitive training: Review and prospects. *The Journal of Cognitive Rehabilitation, 13*(4), 8–14.

Perna, R. B., Bekanich, M., Williams, K. R., & Boozer, R. H. (2000). Cognitive rehabilitation: What's the problem? *The Journal of Cognitive Rehabilitation, 18*(4), 16–21.

Piccoloni, C., Amandio, L., Spazzafumo, L., Moroni, S., & Freddi, A. (1992). The effects of a rehabilitation program with mnemotechniques on the institutionalized elderly subject. *Archives of Gerontology and Geriatrics, 15*, 141–149.

Pioth, P. (1992). Perceptions of interventions post mild head injury. *The Journal of Cognitive Rehabilitation, 10*(2), 34–38.

Powell, J., Heslin, J., & Greenwood, R. (2002). Community based rehabilitation after severe traumatic brain injury: A randomised controlled trial. *Journal of Neurology, Neurosurgery, and Psychiatry, 72*, 193–202.

Prigatano, G. P. (1987). Recovery and cognitive retraining after craniocerebral trauma. *Journal of Learning Disabilities, 20*(10), 603–613.

463

*Cognitive
Rehabilitation
With Brain-
Damaged
Patients*

Prigatano, G. P. (2003). What do brain dysfunctional patients report following memory compensation training? *NeuroRehabilitation, 18*, 47–55.

Raghupathi, R. (2004). Cell death mechanisms following traumatic brain injury. *Brain Pathology, 14*, 215–222.

Richardson, J. T. (1990). *Clinical and neuropsychological aspects of closed head injury*. Hillsdale, NJ: Lawrence Erlbaum.

Richardson, J. T. E., & Rossan, S. (1994). Age limitations on the efficacy of imagery mnemonic instructions. *Journal of Mental Imagery, 18*, 151–163.

Robertson, I. H. (1994). Editorial: Methodology in neuropsychological rehabilitation research. *Neuropsychological Rehabilitation, 4*(1), 1–6.

Robertson, I. H., Manly, T., Beschin, N., Daini, R., Haeske-Dewick, H., Homberg, V., et al. (1997). Auditory sustained attention is a marker of unilateral spatial neglect. *Neuropsychologia, 35*(12), 1527–1532.

Robertson, I. H., & Murre, J. M. J. (1999). Rehabilitation after brain damage: Brain plasticity and principles of guided recovery. *Psychological Bulletin, 125*(5), 544–575.

Robinson, K., & Winner, D. (1998). Rehabilitation of attentional deficits following brain injury. *The Journal of Cognitive Rehabilitation, January/February*, 8–15.

Roeltgen, D. P. (2003). Agraphia. In K. M. Heilman & E. Valenstein (Eds.), *Clinical neuropsychology* (pp. 126–145). New York: Oxford University Press.

Salazar, A.M., Warden, D. L., Schwab, K., Spector, J., Braverman, S., Wlater, J., et al. (2000). Cognitive rehabilitation for traumatic brain injury. A randomized trial. *JAMA: The Journal of the American Medical Association, 283*(23), 3075–3081.

Samuel, C., Louis-Dreyfus, A., Kaschell, R., Makiela, E., Troubat, M., Anselmi, N., et al. (2000). Rehabilitation of very severe unilateral neglect by visuo-spatio-motor cuing: Two single case studies. *Neuropsychological Rehabilitation, 10*(4), 385–399.

Sathopoulou, S., & Lubar, J. F. (2004). EEF changes in traumatic brain injured patients after cognitive rehabilitation. *Journal of Neurotherapy, 8*(2), 21–51.

Schmitter-Edgecombe, M., Fahy, J. F., Whelan, J. P., & Long, C. J. (1995). Memory remediation after severe closed head injury: Notebook training versus supportive therapy. *Journal of Consulting and Clinical Psychology, 63*(3), 484–489.

Seki, K., Yajima, M., & Sugishita, M. (1995). The efficacy of kinesthetic reading treatment for pure alexia. *Neuropsychologia, 33*(5), 595–609.

Sherer, M., Sander, A. M., Nick, T. G., High, W. M., Malec, J. F., & Rosenthal, M. (2002). Early cognitive status and productivity outcome after traumatic brain injury: Findings from the TBI model systems. *Archives of Physical Medicine and Rehabilitation, 83*, 183–192.

Sohlberg, M., & Mateer, C. (1989). *Introduction to cognitive rehabilitation: Theory and practice*. New York: The Guilford Press.

Sohlberg, M. M., Avery, J., Kennedy, M., Ylvisaker, M., Coelho, C., Turkstra, L., et al. (2003). Practice guidelines for direct attention training. *Journal of Medical Speech-Language Pathology, 11*(3), 19–39.

Sohlberg, M. M., Mateer, C., & Stuss, D. T. (1993). Contemporary approaches to the management of executive control dysfunction. *Journal of Head Trauma Rehabilitation, 8*(1), 45–58.

Spector, A., Orrell, M., Davies, S., & Woods, B. (2001). Can reality orientation be rehabilitated? Development and piloting of an evidence-based programme of cognition-based therapies for people with dementia. *Neuropsychological Rehabilitation, 11*(314), 377–397.

Springer, A. Y. (2003). Cognitive rehabilitation practive patterns: A survey of American Hospital Association rehabilitation programs. *The Clinical Neuropsychologist, 17*(1), 34–44.

Squires, E. J., Hunkin, N. M., & Parkin, A. J. (1997). Errorless learning of novel associations in amnesia. *Neuropsychologia, 35*(8), 1103–1111.

Squires, E. J., Hunkin, N., & Parkin, A. J. (1996). Memory notebook training in a case of severe amnesia: Generalizing from paired associate learning to real life. *Neuropsychological Rehabilitation, 6*(1), 55–65.

Stablum, F., Umilta, C., Mogentale, C., Carlan, M., & Geurrini, C. (2000). Rehabilitation of executive deficits in closed head injury and anterior communicating artery aneurysm patients. *Psychological Research, 63*, 265–278.

Stein, D. G. (2000). Brain injury and theories of recovery. In A. L. Christensen and B. P. Uzzell (Eds.), *International handbook of neuropsychological rehabilitation* (pp. 9–15). New York: Kluwer Academic/Plenum Publishers.

Stichbury, J. C., Davenport, M. J., & Middleton, F. R. I. (1980). Head-injured patients—A combined therapeutic approach. *Physiotherapy, 66*(9), 288–292.

Studer, M. (2004). Cognitive rehabilitation in the frail elderly patient: Never too old to learn? *Topics in Geriatric Rehabilitation, 20*(1), 21–33.

Sturm, W., Willmes, K., Orgass, B., & Hartje, W. (1997). Do specific attention deficits need specific training? *Neuropsychological Rehabilitation, 7*(2), 81–103.

Stuss, D. T. (1987). Contributions of frontal lobe injury to cognitive impairment after closed head injury: Methods of assessment and recent findings. In H. S. Levin, J. Grafman, & D. M. Eisenberg (Eds.), *Neurobehavioral recovery from head injury* (pp. 166–177). New York: Oxford University Press.

Sutkovoǐ, D. A., Pedachenko, E. G., Malyshev, O. B., Guk, A. P., Troian, A. I., Morozov, A. N., et al. (1999). The activity of free-radical lipid-peroxidative reactions in the acute and late periods of severe craniocerebral trauma. *Likars'ka Sprava/Ministerstvo Okhorony Zdorov'ia Ukrainy, Mar, 2*, 57–59.

Tate, R. L. (1997). Beyond one-bun, two-shoe: Recent advances in the psychological rehabilitation of memory disorders after acquired brain injury. *Brain Injury, 11*(12), 907–918.

Tham, K., Ginsburg, E., Fisher, A., & Tegner, R. (2001). Training to improve awareness of disabilities in clients with unilateral neglect. *American Journal of Occupational Therapy, 55*, 46–54.

Thornton, K. (2000). Improvement/Rehabilitation of memory functioning with neuropathy/QEEG biofeedback. *The Journal of Head Trauma Rehabilitation, 15*(6), 1285–1296.

Thurman, D. (2001). The epidemiology and economics of head trauma. In L. Miller, R. Hayes, & J. K. Newcomb (Eds.), *Head trauma: Basic, preclinical, and clinical directions* (pp. 327–347). New York: Wiley & Sons.

Thurman, D., Alverson, C., Dunn, K., Guerro, J., & Sniezek, J. (1999). Traumatic brain injury in the United States: A public health perspective. *Journal of Head Trauma Rehabilitation, 14*(6), 602–615.

Trombly, C. A., & Ma, H. (2002). A synthesis of the effects of occupational therapy for persons with stroke, part I: Restoration of roles, tasks, and activities. *The American Journal of Occupational Therapy, 56*(3), 250–259.

Trudel, T. M., Tryon, W. W., & Purdum, C. M. (1998). Awareness of disability and long-term outcome after brain injury. *Rehabilitation Psychology, 43*(4), 267–281.

Turner-Stokes, L. (2002). Standardized outcome assessment in brain injury rehabilitation for younger adults. *Disability and Rehabilitation, 24*(7), 383–389.

van den Broek, M. D., Downes, J., Johnson, Z., Dayus, B., & Hilton, N. (2000). Evaluation of an electronic memory aid in the neuropsychological rehabilitation of prospective memory deficits. *Brain Injury, 14*(5), 455–462.

Viswanathan, M., & Kiran, S. (2005). Treatment for pure alexia using a model based approach: Evidence from one acute aphasic individual. *Brain and Language, 95*(1), 204–206.

Warden, D. L., Salazar, A. M., Martin, E. M., Schwab, K. A., Coyle, M., Walter, J., et al. (2000). A home program of rehabilitation for moderately severe traumatic brain injury patients. *Journal of Head Trauma Rehabilitation, 15*(5), 1092–1102.

Watanabe, T. K. (2003). Congenital and acquired brain injury. 5. Outcomes after acquired brain injury. *Archives of Physical Medicine and Rehabilitation, 84*(Suppl 1), S23–S26.

Watanabe, T. K., Black, K. L., Zafonte, R. D., Millis, S. R., & Mann, N. R. (1998). Do calendars enhance posttraumatic temporal orientation?: A pilot study. *Brain Injury, 12*(1), 81–85.

Webster, J. S., McFarland, P. T., Rapport, L. J., Morrill, B., Roades, L. A., & Abadee, P. S. (2001). Computer-assisted training for improving wheelchair mobility in unilateral neglect patients. *Archives of Physical Medicine and Rehabilitation, 82*(6), 769–775.

Weinberg, J., Diller, L., Gordon, W., Gerstman, L., Lieberman, A., Lakin, P., et al. (1977). Visual scanning training effect on reading-related tasks in acquired right brain damage. *Archives of Physical Medicine and Rehabilitation, 58*, 479–486.

Wesolowski, M. D., & Zencius, A. H. (1994). *A practical guide to head injury rehabilitation: A focus on postacute residential treatment.* New York: Plenum.

Wiart, L., Bon Saint Come, A., Debelleix, X., Petit, H., Joseph, P. A., Mazaux, J. M., et al. (1997). Unilateral neglect syndrome rehabilitation by trunk rotation and scanning training. *Archives of Physical Medicine and Rehabilitation, 78*(4), 424–429.

Wilson, B. (1997). Cognitive rehabilitation: How it is and how it might be. *Journal of International Neuropsychological Society, 3*(5), 487–496.

Wilson, B. A. (2002). Cognitive rehabilitation in the 21st century. *Neurorehabilitaton & Neuronal Repair, 16*(2), 207–210.

Wilson, B. A., Baddeley, A., Evans, J., & Shiel, A. (1994). Errorless learning in the rehabilitation of memory impaired people. *Neuropsychological Rehabilitation, 4*(3), 307-326.

Wilson, B. A., Scott, H., Evans, J., & Emslie, H. (2003). Preliminary report of a NeuroPage service within a health care system. *NeuroRehabilitation, 18*, 3–8.

Wilson, F. C., Manly, T., Coyle, D., & Robertson, I. H. (2000). The effect of contralesional limb activation training and sustained attention training for self-care programmes in unilateral spatial neglect. *Restorative Neurology and Neuroscience 16*, 1–4.

Wilson, J. T., Hadley, D. M., Wiedmann, K. D., & Teasdale, G. M. (1995). Neuropsychological consequences of two patterns of brain damage shown by MRI in survivors of severe head injury. *Journal of Neurology, Neurosurgery, and Psychiatry, 59*(3), 328–331.

Wood, R. L. (1988). Attention disorders in brain injury rehabilitation. *Journal of Learning Disabilities, 21*(6), 327–351.

World Health Organization. (1999). *ICIHD–2: International classification of functioning and disability.* Geneva, Switzerland: Author.

World Health Organization. (2001). *International classification of functioning, disability, and health.* Geneva, Switzerland: Author.

Worrall, L., & Yiu, E. (2000). Effectiveness of functional communication therapy by volunteers for people with aphasia following stroke. *Aphasiology, 14*(9), 911–924.

Yamamoto, H., Uchigata, Y., & Okamoto, H. (1981). Streptozocin and alloxan induce DNA strand breaks and poly (ADP-ribose) synthetase in pancreatic islets. *Nature, 294*, 284–286.

Ylvisaker, M., Hanks, R., & Johnson-Greene, D. (2003). Rehabilitation of children and adults with cognitive-communication disorders after brain injury. *ASHA Supplement, 23*, 59–72.

Zanetti, O., Zanieri, G., Di Giovanni, G., De Vreese, L. P., Pezzini, A., Metitieri, T., et al. (2001). Effectiveness of procedural memory stimulation in mild Alzheimer's disease patients: A controlled study. *Neuropsychological Rehabilitation, 11*(314), 263–272.

467

*Cognitive
Rehabilitation
With Brain-
Damaged
Patients*

Zencius, A. H., Wesolowski, M. D., & Rodriguez, I. M. (1998). Improving orientation in head injured adults by repeated practice, multi-sensory input and peer participation. *Brain Injury, 12*(1), 53–61.

Zoccolotti, P., Guariglia, C., Pizzamiglio, L., Judica, A., Razzano, C., & Pantano, P. (1992). Good recovery in visual scanning in a patient with persistent anosognosia. *The International Journal of Neuroscience, 63*(1–2), 93–104.

15

Unresolved Issues About Release of Raw Test Data and Test Materials

DORRIE L. RAPP, PAUL S. FERBER, AND SHANE S. BUSH

INTRODUCTION

FORENSIC NEUROPSYCHOLOGISTS OFTEN spend professional time responding to lawyers' requests, subpoenas, and court orders to produce raw test data from evaluations and trying to explain to attorneys and judges the ethical and contractual dilemmas these requests present for the neuropsychologist. From the lawyers' perspective there is no problem. Legal procedure is designed to reach

Disclaimer: This chapter gives the opinions of the authors and does not provide legal advice, nor is it intended to be a substitute for the advice of an attorney in your jurisdiction, as relevant law varies substantially from state to state and context to context. The information contained here does not supersede the APA Ethical Code nor any other rules or regulations that may apply to practitioners in their home states and provinces.

appropriate trial decisions by ensuring that all parties have full access to all relevant material and information. To lawyers, test materials and raw test data are no different than an X-ray. The lawyer "wants it all," and the procedural rules that govern civil litigation generally say "give it all."

Beyond the practicalities of negotiating such requirements of daily practice, we believe that there are much larger issues to be considered, including the integrity and future of the profession of neuropsychology and the perceived value of the profession's usefulness to the judicial system. In Rapp and Ferber (1994), an attempt was made to resolve these conflicts and improve communication between the legal and neuropsychological professions. That article was intentionally published in a journal that *attorneys* would read when not in the heat of an adversarial battle. It appeared to be well-received and was subsequently abstracted in the American Trial Lawyers' Association *Professional Negligence Reporter*. The first edition of this chapter (Rapp & Ferber, 2003) expanded on the relevant issues and offered pragmatic solutions for use by forensic neuropsychologists. Personal experience and feedback from other practitioners indicated that some headway had been made with regard to negotiating appropriate handling of test materials and raw test data when copies of these publications were appended to response letters to attorneys and courts dealing with these issues.

At the time of publication of Rapp and Ferber (2003), it was hoped there would not be a future need for articles and chapters on the topic of release of raw test data. It was hoped that the definitions of test data and materials and guidelines for handling requests for raw test data materials would be sufficiently clarified with the implementation of the 2002 revision of the American Psychological Association's (APA's) Ethical Principles of Psychologists and Code of Conduct (hereinafter referred to as the Ethics Code)[1]. Unfortunately, as has also been stated elsewhere (Bush, 2005; Bush, Connell, & Denny, 2006; Bush & Lees-Haley, 2005; Bush & Macciocchi, 2003), the implementation of the 2002 Ethics Code appears to have resulted in contradictory requirements, and much confusion remains for the practitioner regarding the issue of release of raw test data, as well as wider ethical issues impacting the integrity of the profession. Although we are unlikely to resolve all of these issues in this chapter, we hope to provide current information to enable practitioners to make informed decisions regarding handling requests for raw test data.

This chapter will attempt to facilitate effective interprofessional communication by addressing the release of raw test data within the contexts of legal and ethical resources, including the following: Federal Rules of Civil Procedure, Federal and State Rules of Evidence, case law, the APA Ethics Code (2002), the Association of State and Provincial

Psychology Boards (ASPPB) Code of Conduct (2005), the Speciality Guidelines for Forensic Psychologists (SGFP; Committee on Ethical Guidelines for Forensic Psychologists, 1991),[2] and position papers of professional organizations. We also examine the issue of release of test data within the broader scope of scientific and professional integrity and the future of the practice of neuropsychology. Finally, we will provide practical proactive and reactive strategies for coping with the inevitable requests, subpoenas, and court orders that are commonplace in the practice of forensic neuropsychology.

In order to provide a context for the discussion of those resources we present the following scenario.[3]

Scenario

In between reading records, interviewing patients, administering and scoring tests, and writing reports, you receive a telephone call from a plaintiff's attorney who wishes to retain your services as a forensic neuropsychologist to assess his client who he states was injured in an auto accident and sustained a brain injury. You reach an agreement regarding the terms and logistics of the evaluation. You then conduct a comprehensive neuropsychological evaluation and produce a report containing the basis for your opinions. All is going well until you are served with a *subpoena duces tecum* that states the following:

> BY THE AUTHORITY OF THE STATE OF [your state], you are hereby summoned to appear and produce the following documents at the law offices of [defendant's counsel], With respect to your evaluation of [Plaintiff], produce all documents in your possession or control, *including,* but not limited to: *all test materials including tests and test forms used, normative tables and test manuals, all test data generated, interview notes,* documents, and narratives or drawings made by [Plaintiff]. This you may not omit, or you will answer for the default under the pains and penalties of the law in such case made and provided.

You call the attorney who retained you. You explain that you can only turn over test materials or raw test data to someone qualified and bound to maintain test security under the same ethical requirements (e.g., Ethical Standards 9.11 and 9.04) and test manufacturer contractual requirements. You hope this will convey that you must ethically "refrain from releasing test data…from substantial harm or misuse or misinterpretation of the data or test" (Ethical Standard 9.04). Therefore, your plan is to express a willingness to release the raw test data to a designated qualified psychologist or neuropsychologist retained by the defense, who by virtue of his or her training and experience should be in the position to both appropriately interpret the meaning of the test scores and understand the necessity of protecting the information from misuse or misrepresentation. However, the actual conversation with the attorney goes something like this:

Neuropsychologist: I just received this subpoena, and although I want to comply with the order, I cannot release some of the

Attorney:

materials requested directly to attorneys due to ethical and contractual constraints.

I have a copy of the subpoena. The language in the subpoena is standard. The rules of civil procedure generally entitle parties to all documents related to the case. We are making a claim for a brain injury based on your evaluation. The rules of civil procedure require us to turn over everything you used relating to your evaluation and any other material you used to form your opinions. We call it "discovery." We have no basis to deny the defense all relevant information. We have to turn those documents over or the court might not let you testify and might bar us from asserting a claim of brain injury.

Neuropsychologist: I agree that they have a right to review the materials that form the basis of my opinions, to determine whether I have administered, scored, and interpreted the tests correctly, and to see if I have a valid foundation for my opinions. I will be glad to turn over all of those documents directly to the defense's expert if the neuropsychologist will sign a letter of agreement to not further distribute the materials, but I have contractual and ethical requirements preventing me from just turning it all over to the opposing attorney. I won't divulge the raw test data or test materials without taking reasonable steps to maintain the integrity of the tests.

Attorney: The psychologist working with the defense will just turn all the test data over to the opposing attorney anyway. I have been told by other neuropsychologists that under HIPAA and your current Ethics Code you are required pursuant to a client release, to provide test data to the client or anyone else identified in the release. You have a signed release by my client directing you to release the test data to me and the defense attorneys. But that's not really relevant. I am the one who retained you, so *I am your client*. Because I am your client, your Ethics Code and the law require you to release the test data to me and to anyone that I specify. You're covered ethically and legally, so I don't understand why you feel you have a problem.

Neuropsychologist: First, the neuropsychologist retained by the defense is bound by the same contractual and ethical requirements pertaining to test security that I am, so a failure by that person to safeguard test materials would also be inappropriate. Second, the right to review medical records that HIPAA established for clinical cases does not apply to forensic cases (Bush & Lees-Haley, 2005;

Connell & Koocher, 2003). Third, the APA Ethics Code is not the only authoritative reference on this matter. There are additional guidelines and rules of conduct that must be considered. Fourth, if I release the requested raw test data to a nonpsychologist, I run a serious risk of invalidating the test instruments for future use with this or any other client, which would undermine the basis of my opinions and hence my usefulness as an expert in this or any other case, as well as the integrity of the field of neuropsychology itself. Therefore, I propose that we obtain a protective order that clearly defines handling and limited use of the raw test data. I'd be happy to provide you with the necessary information and references that you can use in constructing the order.

Attorney: Well, I'll talk to the opposing attorney and see what we can agree to short of needing the hassle of making motions to the court for a protective order. I still don't understand your ethical objections, and I don't think you understand the rules of evidence. This will really slow things down with this case, cause me additional unnecessary work and expenses that the client won't want to pay for, and will create conflicts with opposing counsel.

Result

The attorney eventually calls back saying that the opposing attorney verbally agrees that you should send all the requested materials including raw test data, directly to a designated neuropsychologist expert. This course of action is appropriate. You made known the perceived conflicts between professional ethics and the requirements of the law and rules of evidence, and you took steps to resolve the conflict. It appears that you received a commitment that will maintain the integrity of the raw test data and the security of the tests. You comply with the original subpoena by sending a package of all of the requested information to the neuropsychologist designated by the defense attorney.

Several months later you find out that the "expert" designated by the defense turned out to be an unlicensed self-proclaimed neuropsychologist without training or experience in test administration or interpretation, and who is without commitment or obligation to maintain test security (Shapiro, 1991; Tranel, 1994; *Watts v. United States,* 1977). The defense expert promptly made a copy of everything and sent it to the opposing attorney. During your cross examination at trial, you are presented with enlarged exhibits of actual sections of the copyrighted test protocols, displaying the questions and your clients' answers, which are entered as exhibits into the public record. You are later served notice that you are to appear before your state board for psychology to respond to a complaint that you violated multiple regulations in your state, which are based on the Ethics Code and ASPPB Code of Conduct. You have no written documents indicating your efforts to resolve the conflict in an ethical manner. You desperately try to remember if you purchased the optional liability insurance coverage for expenses incurred in responding to such complaints.

End of Scenario

For most forensic neuropsychologists, this scenario would likely only be a bad dream and not a situation that is actually encountered. Diligence, forethought, and the exercise of informed judgment would likely help prevent such a scenario. However, determining the realistic and appropriate choices for neuropsychologists may be challenging. Our experience suggests a wide spectrum of opinions and practice. At one end of the spectrum, some give all materials to whomever is specified in the release signed by the client. This view is supported by APA Ethical Standard 9.04 (Release of Test Data). Other practitioners write letters of explanation to the retaining attorney, including providing attachments of supporting citations and documents, and request that the attorney obtain a protective order ensuring the maintenance of the integrity of the tests and data, followed by compliance with whatever order the court issues. Such an approach is consistent with the position statement of the National Academy of Neuropsychology Policy and Planning Committee (2003). The neuropsychologist may also wish to seek independent legal counsel (SGFP, Second draft 1.1.06, section 10.02, Release of Information), as the neuropsychologist's interests may diverge from the attorney–client's interests through the course of legal proceedings (APA, 2006). Independent counsel may be necessary to craft a protective order to submit to the court that covers all aspects of exposure and handling of the test data. This may be necessary to ensure that the integrity of the test data and materials are maintained throughout the case, including sealing those sections of the court record that involve discussion or presentation of test data and returning or destroying all test data after the conclusion of the case.

THE PROBLEM IDENTIFIED

T HE UNLIMITED DISCLOSURE of raw test data presents a unique problem: how to balance the law's interest in providing full disclosure of everything a party will rely on at trial, against the scientific, ethical, and contractual obligations of the neuropsychologist and against the test publisher's proprietary interests in the testing instruments. The problem arises because of a clash of values and interests of two professions.

In the ordinary course of litigation, an attorney will request "all data" used by the neuropsychologist in evaluating the plaintiff in a civil case or the defendant in a criminal case and in arriving at his or her conclusions. In legal proceedings such requests are common and proper (Committee on Legal Issues, 1996, 2006). Federal courts, and most state courts, follow the basic rule that anything relating to the subject matter of the action or that is likely to lead to admissible evidence is fair game in preparing for trial. The fundamental principle underlying the rules of discovery is that our legal system will function more fairly if both parties are aware of the strengths and weaknesses of both sides. Full disclosure by both sides is more likely to result in appropriate decisions in cases than a result based on one party's ability to hide evidence until trial and catch the other side by surprise. Such disclosure also allows both parties to accurately assess their position and thereby encourages settlement at an appropriate level without the need for a trial.

On the other hand, full disclosure may well ignore the function, values, and ethical and contractual obligations of the neuropsychologist. For the neuropsychologist, the basic goal of the evaluation is to determine the current levels of cognitive brain-behavior functioning of the patient and offer professional opinions responding to the referral or legal questions. For that to happen, the neuropsychologist requires valid tests. If the tests and manuals become widely available to the public, they will lose their validity. The consequence is not just that the neuropsychologist will not have valid tests to use in treating patients. Unlimited disclosure will destroy the economic value to the test publishers and have potentially serious negative impact on the research and development of new tests.

Rarely will the attorneys or the courts fully understand the unique and highly sensitive aspects of this discovery issue from the neuropsychologist's perspective. Therefore, it is important for the neuropsychologist to be able to explain the problem and propose resolutions in the *attorney's language*.

THE NEUROPSYCHOLOGIST'S OBLIGATIONS

THE NEUROPSYCHOLOGIST HAS ethical and contractual obligations to protect test data and test materials.

ETHICAL REQUIREMENTS

The Ethics Code

The Code's Ethical Standards set forth enforceable rules for conduct as psychologists. The Ethical Standards are intentionally written broadly to apply to psychologists in varied roles, and they are not exhaustive. Because they were not written specifically to address the issues and situations encountered by neuropsychologists acting as forensic experts, they must at times be supplemented with more specific guidelines.

Although it is necessary to abide by the specific enforceable ethical standards, following only the enforceable letter of the Code is not always sufficient. The Preamble and General Principles of the Ethics Code provide *aspirational* goals to guide psychologists toward the highest ideals of psychology. The issues of test integrity and security clearly involve all of the General Principles and may also directly affect the validity and hence future existence of the practice of neuropsychology.

The 2002 Ethics Code substantially changed the standard on release of test data. Standard (9.04) states:

> Pursuant to a client/patient release, psychologists provide test data to the client/patient or other persons identified in the release. Psychologists may refrain from releasing test data to protect a client/patient or others from substantial harm or misuse or misrepresentation of the data or the test, recognizing that in many instances release of confidential information under these circumstances is regulated by law. (See Standard 9.11, Maintaining Test Security.) (b) In the absence of a client/patient release, psychologists provide test data only as required by law or court order.

Compared to the 1992 version of the Code, this change appears to substantially relieve the enforceable ethical burden on neuropsychologists and does not indicate that neuropsychologists need to obtain protective orders when raw test data is subpoenaed.

Even if the 2002 APA Ethics Code appears to allow release of raw test data to attorneys based on a client's release, this does not mean that neuropsychologists should automatically release such raw test data into the public domain. In addition to the Ethics Code, there are other rules and regulations regarding evaluations and test security that may also apply to the individual neuropsychologist in his or her state.

Association of State and Provincial Psychology Boards (ASPPB) Code of Conduct

Many states have incorporated the ASPPB Code of Conduct (2005) as part of their rules and regulations for psychologist licensure. The ASPPB Code of Conduct is a distillation of regulatory codes representing geographic and professional diversity from a wide range of U.S. and Canadian jurisdictions, which were scrutinized and debated by the Model Licensure Committee. Rules of conduct differ in function in critical ways from professional association ethics codes, with which they are sometimes confused. The ASPPB requirements primarily protect the public interest and pertain to the process or "mechanics" of the professional relationship, not to the content of the professional judgment itself. They are essentially unambiguous concerning what behavior is acceptable and what is not. They are sufficient unto themselves, without dependence for interpretation on additional explanatory materials, because they will be applied in a judicial/legal context interpreting the regulatory code of which they are a part. They are coercive, not advisory or aspirational. They are nontrivial, to the extent that any violation is basis for formal disciplinary action, including loss of licensure.

The ASPPB code (2005) specifically states (III. F.7) "**Release of confidential information.** The psychologist may release confidential information upon court order, as defined in Section II of this Code, or to conform with state, federal or provincial law, rule, or regulation." The following section (III. I) on Assessment Procedures is clear, specific, and unchanged from the 1991 version.

1. *Confidential information.* The psychologist shall treat an assessment result or interpretation regarding an individual as confidential information.
2. *Communication of results.* The psychologist shall accompany communication of results of assessment procedures to the client, parents, legal guardians or other agents of the client by adequate interpretive aids or explanations.
3. *Reservations concerning results.* The psychologist shall include in his/her report of the results of a formal assessment procedure for which norms are available, any deficiencies of the assessment norms for the individual assessed and any relevant reservations or qualification which affect the validity, reliability, or other interpretation of results.
4. Protection of integrity of assessment procedures. The psychologist shall not reproduce or describe in popular publications, lectures, or public presentations psychological tests or other assessment devices in ways that might invalidate them." [Italics added for emphasis]

Specialty Guidelines for Forensic Psychologists

In addition to the enforceable Ethics Code and ASPPB Code of Conduct, there are other rules and regulations regarding evaluations and test security that may also apply to the individual neuropsychologist in each state. Whereas the APA Ethics Code describes the enforceable standards for *competent and adequate professional conduct,* the SGFP (Committee on Ethical Guidelines for Forensic Psychologists, 1991) are intended to describe (but not mandate) the *most desirable and highest level professional conduct* for psychologists when engaged in the practice of forensic psychology. The SGFP are educative and designed to provide more specific and thorough guidance to psychologists engaging in forensic conduct. The SGFP were developed by the American

Psychology-Law Society and Division 41 of APA, and the guidelines were endorsed by the American Board of Forensic Psychology. The SGFP are currently undergoing revision due to advancements in the field and the need to address the wide variety of professional forensic practice areas that have developed and expanded since 1991. (See www. ap-ls.org for the status of the current draft revision, Second Official Draft was released online January 1, 2006).

For example, the SGFP contain very specific guidance regarding release of client information. The guidelines advise that when a forensic psychologist receives a properly served subpoena or court order to release records, the forensic psychologist should comply by making available all records specified in the order *unless there is a compelling reason not to do so*. The SGFP suggest that compelling reasons to offer an objection to complying could include contractual obligations, federal or state privacy, confidentiality or privilege regulations, or notice of a counsel's intent to quash or otherwise petition the court to amend or void the subpoena or order for the records. When in doubt about an appropriate response or course of action, the guidelines advise that forensic psychologists may formally notify the drafter of the subpoena of their uncertainty, seek assistance from the counsel that has retained him or her in the matter, seek his or her own independent counsel, or defer to and request direction from the court or other tribunal.

HIPAA

The Health Insurance Portability and Accountability Act (HIPAA) states that information compiled in anticipation of use in civil, criminal, and administrative proceedings is *not* subject to the same right of review and amendment as is health care information in general [§164.524(a)(1)(ii)] (U.S. Department of Health and Human Services, 2003). Therefore, in forensic contexts HIPAA does not prohibit neuropsychologists from withholding raw test data, and minimizing the possibility of misuse or misinterpretation of the data may require practitioners to withhold data or take other steps (described previously in the chapter) to safeguard the data (Bush et al., 2006).

Test Data Regulations in Specific States and Provincial Provinces

Rapp and Ferber (2003) surveyed all 58 of the State and Provincial Psychological Association Executive Directors regarding any written statutes, rules, and regulations or the ethical standards each used to safeguard release of test data. Of the 20 responses received (34% response rate), 6 responses indicated that they had written statutes that addressed release of test data, and 6 stated they had rules and regulations 3 of these indicated that handling of test data was subsumed under general confidentiality rules, and 1 indicated test data was subsumed under release of medical records). Utah's response stated it has a 6-page position statement regarding handling of test data, compiled by members of the Professional Standard's Committee of the Utah Psychological Association. However, Utah has no restriction on the release of raw test data to nonpsychologists. Seven States cited reliance on APA's Ethical Code in their rules and regulations. Vermont for example, has a statute incorporating the APA Ethical Code and the ASPPB Code of Conduct.

Some states and provinces have much more specific enforceable standards. Texas's State Board of Examiners of Psychologists Rules and Regulations (1999) states under the Psychological Records, Test Data and Test Protocols "Test data are not part of a patient's or client's record. Test data are not subject to subpoena. Test data shall be made available only to another qualified mental health professional and only upon receipt of a written release from the patient or client for purposes of continuity of care or pursuant to a court order."

Illinois' *Mental Health and Developmental Disabilities Confidentiality Act*, paragraph 803 (c) states:

> Psychological test material whose disclosure would compromise the objectivity or fairness of the testing process may not be disclosed to anyone including the subject of the test and is not subject to disclosure in any administrative, judicial or legislative proceeding. However, any recipient who has been the subject of the psychological test shall have the right to have all records relating to that test disclosed to any psychologist designated by the recipient. Requests for such disclosure shall be in writing.

Maryland's *Confidentiality of Medical Records Act* (1994) includes section III (E) (1) stating:

> Except as otherwise provided in paragraphs (3), (4), and (5) of this subsection, if the disclosure of a portion of a medical record relating to a psychological test would compromise the objectivity or fairness of the test or the testing process, a mental health care provider may not disclose that portion of the medical record to any person including the subject of the test. (2) The raw test data relating to a psychological test is only discoverable or admissible as evidence in a criminal, civil, or administrative action on the determination by the court or administrative hearing officer that the expert witness for the party seeking the raw test data is qualified by the appropriate training, education, or experience to interpret the results of that portion of the raw test data relating to the psychological test.

In addition to Texas, Maryland, and Illinois, an informal survey conducted by Grote (2005) revealed that Florida and Iowa have also adopted legislation that prohibits the release of raw test data to nonpsychologists. Quebec's Code of Ethics of Psychologists (1998) also states under Standards for Psychological Tests Use "A Psychologist shall not entrust the raw, uninterpreted data from a Psychological consultation to anyone but another Psychologist" (p. 4).

Neuropsychologist practitioners should confirm the specific currently applicable regulations in their state. It may also be beneficial to work with each state psychological association and legislators to introduce specific bills to legally resolve the issue of how and when to release test data while preserving test security.

Integrity of the Profession of Neuropsychology

In addition to the array of statutes and rules, there are other reasons to protect test data. The profession of neuropsychology depends heavily on the scientific validity, reliability, and integrity of the tests they use in evaluating a patient. Therefore, ethics issues aside, preventing the unlimited release of raw test data and test security is critical to the neuropsychologist. As Adams and Putnam (1994) stated, "Psychologists called to court are best advised to act as psychologists first and best, allowing the legal arena to evolve as it must and will. Psychologists and lawyers are professionals with different goals, cultures, and rules who operate in epistemologically diverse ways" (p. 6).

The proposition that forensic neuropsychologists should take an active role in promoting high standards is not new. An observation made more than 25 years ago remains equally true today:

> There is a commensurate responsibility for psychologists to adequately prepare themselves to meet the special ethical demands of the expert witness role, not only because they represent the profession in the public's eye but also for the welfare of the clients who are served…[They] urge psychologists to be assertive concerning the establishment of a truly collaborative relationship with the attorney and client…Careful joint preparation will reduce the number of 'surprises' encountered by psychologists in the courtroom and allow the psychologists to avoid various ethical pitfalls. It is also through active involvement with the attorney that the psychologist can best educate the attorney regarding ethical problems as they arise. (Anderten, Staulcup, & Grisso, 1980, p. 274)

One should never forget that:

> The psychologist who conducts forensic assessments holds a sometimes overwhelming power over the lives of others…Our responsibility as forensic practitioners includes not only upholding these standards in

our own work of conducting assessments but also constantly rethinking the nature of these standards, their presence in our education and training, the degree to which the profession ensures accountability or, alternatively, passively tolerates and tacitly accepts or encourages violations, and the care with which we spell out responsibilities that fit the current and constantly evolving demands of forensic assessment. (Butcher & Pope, 1993, p. 285)

Therefore, part of the solution to the current problem involves the neuropsychologist's ability and willingness to facilitate communication between two professions (psychology and law) having very different procedures, ethical codes, codes of conduct, and rules of practice.

WHAT THE NEUROPSYCHOLOGIST NEEDS TO KNOW ABOUT THE LAW AND ATTORNEYS

The Law of Discovery

The Federal Rules of Civil Procedure, Rule 26, which has been adopted as the rule in most states as well as all Federal District Courts, broadly defines the scope of discovery. Litigants are entitled to have access to "any matter, not privileged, which is relevant to the subject matter involved in the pending action" (Federal Rules of Civil Procedure, Rule 26(b)(1)). Rule 26 further allows discovery of the identity of the other side's expert, the subject matter of his or her expected testimony, the substance of the expert's substantive facts and opinions, and the bases for the opinion.

The consequence of these rules is that all information dealing with the evaluation of the plaintiff's psychological and cognitive brain-behavior functioning is within the scope of discovery in cases in which the plaintiff seeks damages for brain injury or raises a brain injury as a factor in a criminal prosecution. The other side is entitled to the plaintiff's expert's written opinion and to take the expert's deposition. The other side is also *entitled to obtain all data underlying the expert's opinion* in order to determine the accuracy of testing procedures and scoring and to evaluate, challenge, or attempt to discredit the expert's opinions.

Attorneys' "requests" for this information may be in the form of an informal telephone call or letter, which can be responded to equally informally in an attempt to negotiate a satisfactory resolution for all parties. The request also may be in the form of a *subpoena* (an order to appear to provide testimony) or *subpoena duces tecum* (an order to appear and bring specific documents) automatically issued by a court officer on request of an attorney; both require a timely response. Finally, a *court order* signed by the judge may be issued for testimony or documents, and it must be responded to in a timely manner or the neuropsychologist can be held in contempt of court for failing to comply.

The Ethics Code, ASPPB Code of Conduct, and the SGFP all recognize that the practitioner should take steps to attempt to resolve the conflict between the legal rules of discovery and the ethical and professional obligations of the neuropsychologist. If the conflict cannot be resolved informally, court orders and rules supersede ethical rules of conduct and guidelines.

In a case in which one of the authors was the expert, because the plaintiff's attorney had not informed the defense attorney that a re-evaluation had occurred, the judge stated during trial testimony that he would leave it up to the neuropsychologist to decide whether to give all of the raw test data to the opposing attorney to review over the lunch break. If the neuropsychologist chose not do so, all of her testimony would be stricken from the record. Faced with this dilemma, the neuropsychologist asked to speak with the judge, succinctly explained the contractual and ethical conflict this "choice" placed on the neuropsychologist, and asked that the judge issue a court order requiring the production of the raw test data. In this case, the judge understood the dilemma of the neuropsychologist's conflict between the law and ethics and issued a court order for release of the raw test data and its immediate return to the neuropsychologist after the lunch break. This case suggests that some courts may be willing to listen and respond appropriately if the problem is properly presented to them.

Under Rule 26, the matter is not resolved by determining that the raw test data is within the broad rule of discovery. Rule 26 recognizes that there may be circumstances that justify limiting discovery and specifically allows the court to enter an order limiting the use or access to sensitive information. The neuropsychologist is entitled to protection under Rule 26 ©) as a *"person from whom discovery is sought."*

It is incumbent on the attorney to request, through a motion to the court, that the subpoena or court order be modified or "quashed" (made void or invalid). In support of this motion, the attorney must explain the reasons justifying the relief. Rule 26 provides some of that explanation. The rule allows the court to "make any order which justice requires to protect a party or person." Specifically, it empowers the court to enter an order that a *trade secret or other confidential research, development, or commercial information* **not be disclosed or be disclosed only in a designated way***"* Rule 26 (c)(7) [emphasis added]. Substantially the same protection is provided specifically for subpoenas under Federal Rule 45 (c)(3).

Relying on Rule 26(c)(7), courts have entered protective orders limiting *who has access* to such information and *how that information can be used.* For example, in *Quotron Systems, Inc. v. Automatic Data Processing, Inc.* (1992), the court entered a protective order limiting the category of people who could have access to the confidential commercial information. Indeed, where justified, courts have even kept information out of the hands of attorneys. In *Digital Equipment Corp v. Micro Technology, Inc.* (1992) the District Court entered a protective order limiting access to the confidential information to only "independent experts, consultants, or translators for a part...whose advice and consultation are being or will be used by such party in connection with preparation for trial."

Attorneys may mistakenly believe that the completed test response forms belong to the examinee. Although in some contexts examinees or their guardians may be entitled to inspect and have the data explained to them by the neuropsychologist, the test protocols are the property of the neuropsychologist. The neuropsychologist's opinions, and the basis for those opinions, are typically included in the report. Depending on the context, the report may be released to the examinee if it is explained by the neuropsychologist. The report is freely given to parties in litigation, pending appropriate patient release, or waiver of doctor–patient privilege.

The Lawyers

In civil litigation, the test security problem varies slightly depending on whether the neuropsychologist is retained by the plaintiff or the defense attorney. While generalizations are dangerous, most plaintiffs' attorneys are focused on showing that their client is seriously injured and that it is the defendant's fault. The plaintiff's attorney has no interest in slowing down the case by arguing with the defense attorney over "little things," such as the neuropsychologist's ethical and contractual obligations, or a testing company's commercial interests.

Conversely, most defendants' attorneys are focused on showing that the plaintiff is not injured, or at least not severely, and that it is not the defendant's fault in any event. A defendant's attorney will immediately be skeptical of any attempt by the plaintiff's neuropsychologist to withhold anything.

The starting point for the neuropsychologist is to recognize that the average attorney is unaware of the need for test security, the effects of test disclosure on future public welfare, or the effects on the field of neuropsychology itself. Indeed, some continuing legal education programs provide advice to attorneys on how to prepare their clients for independent psychological evaluations, including seeking advanced disclosure of what tests will be administered (Lees-Haley, 1997). Attorneys who have test data, including the test questions and answers from prior cases, have been encouraged to use the information to prepare their client to attempt to achieve a specific result on a specific test.

A survey of 70 practicing attorneys conducted by Wetter and Corrigan (1995) found that 79–87% of two groups of attorneys surveyed believed they should discuss with the client what psychological testing is involved before an evaluation, and 48% of the attorneys believed they should usually or always inform a client about validity measures in psychological tests. The authors noted that the term "discuss" used in the questions was open to wide interpretation; the attorneys were not directly asked if they "coached" their clients before testing. However, Youngjohn (1995) described an attorney who argued that *not counseling* the client how to answer questions prior to undergoing a psychological evaluation may be considered legal malpractice. Rosen (1995) confirmed the existence of coaching by plaintiffs' attorneys in personal injury litigation regarding psychological sequelae of traumatic events. As reported by Lees-Haley (1997), even some other experts, for example, the psychiatrist involved in the mass tort case *Lailhengue v. Mobil* (1990), do not see a problem with providing copies of the criteria from the *Diagnostic and Statistical Manual of Mental Disorders,* 4th ed. (*DSM–IV*; APA, 1994) to clients to review prior to holding further interviews with the clients. The availability of test information on the Internet and effects of coaching on test performance continue to be threats, as recently discussed by Bauer and McCaffrey (2006).

The results of the Wetter and Corrigan (1995) and Youngjohn (1995) surveys are surprising in view of the fact that the improper use of test information, such as coaching a client to achieve a particular result, probably is unethical for attorneys and could result in a sanction, which could be as severe as losing the license to practice law. The Model Rules of Professional Conduct (2006), which are the ethical rules governing lawyers in all but a few states, have several provisions that would seem to be violated by an attorney's use of protected testing information to coach a client to achieve a specific result. This situation may stem partly from attorneys not thinking through the full ramifications of their conduct. By understanding the following, the neuropsychologist should be able to put the problem in language that will bring home to attorneys their own liability for improper use of test materials.

Rule 1.2(d) provides that:

> A lawyer shall not counsel a client to engage, or *assist a client, in conduct that the lawyer knows is* criminal or *fraudulent,* but a lawyer may discuss the legal consequences of any proposed course of conduct with a client and may counsel or assist a client to make a good faith effort to determine the validity, scope, meaning or application of the law. [italics added]

The essence of fraud is misrepresenting a fact or facts. Lawyers can understand that using a doctored X-ray is fraud. The neuropsychologist needs to make the lawyer understand that preparing a client to achieve a result on a psychological test that does not reflect accurately the examinee's abilities is no different than doctoring an X-ray. It is no different than swearing that a fact is true when the witness knows it is not.

In addition, Rule 3.3(a)(4) provides that an attorney shall not "offer evidence that the lawyer knows to be false." A lawyer would recognize that Rule 3.3 is violated if he or she offers as evidence test scores she knows were improperly changed after testing. The neuropsychologist needs to help the lawyer understand that preparing a client to achieve a result on a test that does not reflect accurately the examinee's abilities is no less false than altered test scores. When an attorney knows that psychological test results have been manipulated by the client's reviewing the test questions and preparing answers in advance, the attorney knows that the results are "false." Therefore, offering those results at trial violates Rule 3.3.

Such conduct also violates Model Rule 3.4 (a) and (b), which provide that an attorney shall not:

> (a) …unlawfully alter, destroy or conceal a document or other material having potential evidentiary value. *A lawyer shall not counsel or assist another person to do any such act;*
> (b) *falsify evidence,* counsel or assist a witness to testify falsely, or offer an inducement to a witness that is prohibited by law.…

Lawyers know that it is unethical to change an original document or the condition of a piece of evidence to change its meaning or significance. The neuropsychologist needs to help the lawyer understand that preparing a client to achieve a result on a test that does not reflect accurately the examinee's abilities is altering the "potential evidentiary value" of neuropsychological testing and its results and is falsifying evidence.

THE NEUROPSYCHOLOGIST'S ROLE IN OBTAINING A PROTECTIVE ORDER

THE INITIAL STEP for the neuropsychologist in obtaining a protective order is to disabuse the attorney of a mistaken belief that the issue is one of confidentiality of the test materials. The protective order is necessary to maintain the integrity and security of the test materials. The next step is to provide the retaining attorney with a standard prepared motion and documents supporting the legal, contractual, and ethical obligations justifying the request for a protective order. The materials provided to the attorney should address the three categories of information that courts look to in deciding whether to enter a protective order and what the terms of the order should be:

1. Significant harm will result from unrestricted disclosure of the test materials;
2. The significant harm from disclosure can be avoided while still accommodating the opposing side's legitimate need for information to prepare its case; and
3. The exact proposed restrictions the protective order should contain.

The starting point in obtaining a protective order is to establish the need to protect the test questions and answers from unrestricted disclosure. There are at least three reasons supporting the need for limiting access to raw test data. First, the test instruments have commercial and scientific value that will be impaired without the protective order. Second, the neuropsychologist agreed to contractual obligations imposed as part of the purchase of the tests and test forms. Third, the forensic neuropsychologist is required by ethical rules to protect the tests from improper disclosure.

Harm to the Scientific and Commercial Value of the Test Instruments

Unlimited disclosure will destroy the scientific value of the tests. Neuropsychological tests are unlike most tests used by other medical and scientific experts where there is no equivalent discovery problem, because the test results are not manipulatable. For example, the technology used to create an X-ray is not divulged by disclosure of the patient's X-ray. Further, a patient's X-ray film cannot be manipulated by explaining to the patient the underlying science of X-rays.

Neuropsychological test interpretation, the test materials, and the test data are only valid and reliable if the answers are not artificially manipulated. A person with access to the questions and manual for the examiner of a neuropsychological test can prepare in advance to answer the questions in a way that produces a desired result. The main control for preventing "faking" or exaggerating deficits is maintaining the security of the test protocol. Failure to keep the questions, answers, and evaluation purposes of each test out of the public domain will allow the opportunity for widespread "coaching" and "faking" of test performances, which ultimately could destroy the validity of the tests. Thus, without maintaining their security, the tests will lose their usefulness to the medical and psychological communities, as well as their value for forensic purposes. For attorneys having difficulty grasping these concepts, it can be helpful to ask them to consider what would happen to the validity of the Law School Admission Test or the Multi-state Bar Examination if the questions and correct answers were freely available.

Second, undercutting test validity also destroys the commercial value of the psychological tests, which have been developed at an enormous cost by private parties. Indeed, the owners of the tests go to great lengths to preserve the security of the tests by including nondisclosure provisions in every sale contract and selling the tests only to individuals meeting specific levels of qualifications (e.g., doctorate, licensed psychologist, member of APA), and even those qualified buyers must agree to accept terms and conditions, which include releasing any of the material only to other qualified psychologists. The attorneys should understand that the end result of unprotected neuropsychological tests could be to make the test results inadmissible, because the tests would no longer have the validity and reliability required under the *Daubert* (1993) standard.

Although most practitioners probably have not recently read the terms and conditions at the back of their test catalogs, a great deal of useful (and legally enforceable) information is available there. For example, the PsychCorp Psychological Assessment Products Annual Catalog (2006) specifically states that by placing a test order, the purchaser agrees to accept all terms including the following:

> **Protective Orders.** *Purchaser agrees to seek a protective order safeguarding the confidentiality of test materials classified by Harcourt Assessment as C-level assessments[4] if Purchaser is required to produce such materials in court or administrative proceedings.*
>
> **Governing Law and Venue.** *This Agreement, each transaction entered into in connection with this Agreement, and all matters arising from or related to this Agreement (including validity and interpretation), are governed by, construed, and enforced in accordance with the laws of the* State of Texas, *without reference to any conflict of law principles. Purchaser submits to the exclusive jurisdiction of the federal and state courts located in Bexar County, in the State of Texas[5].*
>
> **Maintenance of Test Security and Test Use....** *Access to test materials must be limited to qualified persons with a responsible, professional interest who agree to safe-guard their use. Test materials and scores may be released only to persons qualified to interpret and use them properly.* If a test taker or the parent of a child who has taken a test wishes to examine test responses or results, the parent or test taker may be permitted to review the test and the test answers in the presence of a representative of the school, college or institution that administered the test. Such review should not be permitted in those jurisdictions where applicable laws require the institution to provide a photocopy of the test subsequent to review.

Compliance with HIPAA. *Harcourt Assessment would like to advise its customers that they are* **not** *obligated to disseminate copies of test record forms or protocols to persons who erroneously claim that they are entitled to copies under HIPAA's Privacy Rule.* This position is consistent with a guidance letter Harcourt received from the Department of Health and Human Services which states that so long as test items (which may be disclosed in record forms) are trade secrets, such information is not required to be disclosed under HIPAA. Harcourt Assessment has claimed trade secret status for its test record forms and protocols for many years in order to preserve the validity of these tools used by the professional community for the benefit of the general public. Please go to **PsychCorp.com** for a more detailed explanation of our position regarding HIPAA. Questions should be directed to the Legal Department of Harcourt Assessment at 800–228–0752. [italics added].

The position statement of The Psychological Corporation regarding releasing test materials under HIPAA was also discussed in detail in the National Academy of Neuropsychology *Bulletin* (2004).

Unlimited Disclosure Forces Neuropsychologists to Breach Contractual Obligations

Neuropsychologists accept legal obligations by purchasing and using the tests. Failure to abide by those obligations constitutes a breach of the contract under which the tests were purchased. Thus, by forcing unlimited disclosure of test materials, a court is in effect ordering the neuropsychologist to commit a breach of the contract with the test publishers. The courts have recognized that such a result would be improper. For example, in *Snowden v. Connaught Labs., Inc.* (1991), the court affirmed a magistrate's protective order, which was based on the fact that the "defendants should not be required to produce documents or records which will require them to violate their contract with [a non-party]." That is the exact situation we are addressing.

Interpretation of Test Results

The typical approach to using evidence does not apply to neuropsychological test data. Typically, only a licensed psychologist or neuropsychologist has the qualifications, training, and competence to evaluate and interpret the test results (Frumkin, 1995; Shapiro, 1991; Tranel, 1994, 1999). Many questions on psychological and neuropsychological tests do not call for "yes" or "no" answers. The neuropsychologist often must consider gender, age, race and ethnicity, national origin, primary language, culture and religion, formal education level, socioeconomic status, premorbid functioning, and past evaluation experience, as well as all other test results in their entirety, in order to meaningfully interpret the test results (per APA Ethical Standards 2.01b and 9.06; ASPPB Code of Conduct sections III.D.3, III.I.3; and SGFP 2006 Second Official Draft sections 4.08, 12.02, 12.03). For example, if three people, who differ in age, education levels, and other social and cultural factors give exactly the same answers to a set of test questions, they will obtain different scores on the test, and those scores must be interpreted differently. The examinees' test answers, without the psychologist's analysis, are meaningless to, and likely to be misinterpreted by, anyone other than a specifically trained psychologist or neuropsychologist.

Courts have recognized that neuropsychological testing is unique and such tests can only be understood by specially trained professionals. For example, in *Watts v. the United States* (1977), the appellate court rejected the claim that a psychiatrist was a "qualified person" to receive psychological test data, because there was no evidence that the psychiatrist had the specialized training necessary to interpret that data. With rare exceptions, attorneys are not qualified to interpret psychological or neuropsychological test data.

An example of the dangers of misuse and misinterpretation of released raw test data by an attorney was illustrated in a scenario in Tranel (1994). In that scenario, an attorney selected test items from the memory test and presented them to the jury in an attempt to point out that the items the plaintiff failed were so difficult that it would be unreasonable to expect any normal person to pass them. Individual items taken out of context can be quite misleading, yet this tactic may be quite compelling to laypersons.

Therefore, the opposing expert psychologist or neuropsychologist is the appropriate person to receive raw test data in discovery. The opposing expert can review the data along with the original neuropsychologist's report and supporting information and then advise the attorney of any scoring errors, omissions, or misinterpretations of the data. To the extent that there is an alleged error in scoring or interpreting any particular question or test result, the neuropsychologist being questioned has all of the raw test data in his or her position at the time of deposition or trial testimony. There is no need for the attorney to have a copy of the raw test data in order to pursue this line of questioning.

The neuropsychologist should determine that the requesting party's designated recipient of the raw test data is actually a psychologist who is qualified to interpret the test data (i.e., do they meet the specific requirements for C level tests as defined by the test manufacturer with whom you have contracted?). One suggested strategy is to request and review the recipient's curriculum vitae (Tranel, 1994). The neuropsychologist may wish to obtain a written agreement from the expert designated to receive the raw test data indicating that he or she agrees to maintain test security, or at least document expectations of the standard of conduct in a cover letter included with the raw test data being released. The cover letter can be used as evidence of an attempt to resolve the conflicts between law pertaining to discovery and ethical and legal obligations to maintain test security.

Proactive Strategies for the Neuropsychologist

Forensic neuropsychologists should prepare in advance for demands for records, including raw test data. Practitioners are advised to create and have available for use the following documents.

1. A standard letter to send to each referring attorney at the outset, before conducting the evaluation of the client, which contains not only the fee agreement and other arrangements, but also a clear statement of how you will handle release of raw test data (e.g., only to another qualified expert, through a protective order, motion to seal the portion of the transcript dealing with specifics of test materials). Some attorneys may object, but at least you will know this up front and can attempt to resolve the conflict *before* becoming involved. Some attorneys expect a written contract from the neuropsychologist and view this as evidence that the expert is straightforward, organized, and professional.

2. A standard cover letter to send to the "other qualified expert" stating that by accepting the packet of raw test data he or she agrees to maintain test integrity and security and adhere to the test manufacturer contracts.

3. Multiple pre-prepared packets containing a sample protective order and supporting documents, ready to forward to attorneys upon receipt of an informal request, subpoena, or court order.

In addition, forensic neuropsychologists may be well served by working with state psychological associations and legislators to introduce bills that will explicitly define how raw test data and test materials are to be handled and define who is qualified to receive these materials. Rapp and Ferber (2003) and Grote (2005) provided examples of states and provinces that prohibit the release of raw test data to nonpsychologists (e.g., Illinois, Florida, Iowa, Texas, Maryland, Alberta, and Quebec). Where such laws exist, the citation should be included with the other materials provided to attorneys and the courts.

ACCOMMODATING THE OPPOSING SIDE'S LEGITIMATE DISCOVERY NEEDS WHILE AVOIDING UNNECESSARY HARM

THE NEXT STEP in demonstrating the appropriateness of a protective order is to establish that legitimate discovery interests will not be compromised by the protective order. Issuing a protective order limiting access to the test materials and raw test data to qualified psychologists or neuropsychologists retained by the side seeking discovery protects the security and maintains the integrity of the tests and still allows adequate discovery.

Even with the protective order covering all test materials and raw test data, the attorney will obtain the neuropsychological evaluation report and other written notes and records reviewed, as part of normal discovery. The neuropsychologist's report is analogous to the hospital "medical record" for a physical injury. The report should contain all of the information on which the neuropsychologist based his or her opinions, including sources of the patient's history, the details of any interviews with third parties, identification of all of the records reviewed and tests used, the demographic and other variables that were considered, the interpretation of the raw data results, and the opinions themselves. Thus, disclosure of the evaluation report should provide the attorney with adequate discovery.

Importance of Appropriate Attitude and Demeanor

Throughout the process of explaining ethical and contractual issues to the attorneys and the court, it is critical that the neuropsychologist demonstrate an appreciation of the importance of the goals of the discovery process. It is also critical that the neuropsychologist make clear that he or she is not seeking to withhold rightful discovery and that the issue has nothing to do with doctor–patient confidentiality, which was waived when the examinee placed his or her mental status at issue in the legal claim. Rather, the neuropsychologist must make clear the ways in which neuropsychological tests and their results differ from other medical and scientific tests as discussed earlier in this chapter, and why the protective order is necessary for test integrity and security. And as Tranel (1994) stated:

> [T]he attitude or demeanor of the psychologist can influence substantially the degree of cooperation from members of the legal profession (lawyers, judges, etc.). When an attorney senses that the psychologist is trying to conceal something, or to resist cooperation, the attorney is likely to mount an all-out effort to get everything possible out of the psychologist. By contrast, if the attorney senses that the psychologist is attempting to cooperate fully with the spirit of the proceedings, within the bounds of his or her ethical principles, the attorney is far more likely to go along with the psychologist's recommended course of action. The Ethical Principles do not, in fact, have the force of law; thus, it is very much in the best interest of psychologists to solicit cooperation and collegiality from attorneys. (p. 33)

PROVISIONS OF A PROPOSED PROTECTIVE ORDER

THE TRIAL JUDGE has broad discretion in fashioning a protective order. The specific provisions of a protective order that would accommodate the party's legitimate discovery while protecting test security are simple. First, the protective order should cover "all test materials and raw test data generated in the case of [patient's name] by [neuropsychologist's name]."

Second, the order should limit the disclosure of such information "to [name of expert] who is a licensed psychologist or neuropsychologist qualified to administer and interpret such tests, who certifies that he or she will maintain test integrity and security and not further copy or distribute the materials." If the party seeking disclosure of the test data has not disclosed the identity of their expert, the protective order should state that the "Raw test data shall be placed in a sealed envelope and delivered to the clerk of the court where the action is proceeding. The clerk shall release the sealed envelope only to the designated licensed psychologist or neuropsychologist who has been determined to be qualified to receive and interpret the test materials." Enclosing a copy of the user qualifications pages from a well-known test catalog with the protective order can facilitate this determination.

If the matter reaches the trial stage, the court should also be requested to seal all parts of the record containing any of the test materials and any exhibits or testimony that make specific reference to any of the test materials. The court order should also prohibit copying of test materials that are not destroyed or returned to the expert at the conclusion of the trial.

Example Letters

Example response letters to informal requests for raw test data that can be adapted for use by individual neuropsychologists are provided in Frumkin (1995), Rapp and Ferber (1994), and Shapiro (1991, 1999).

CONCLUSION

FORENSIC NEUROPSYCHOLOGISTS ARE frequently called upon to release records, including raw test data. If the need for maintenance of test security is properly understood by the attorneys on both sides, the matter of handling raw test data can be easily stipulated to in a protective order. If the attorney seeking discovery refuses to stipulate to an appropriate protective order, the attorney resisting discovery should be prepared, through the neuropsychologist, to provide the court with sufficient acceptable documentation to allow the court to determine that a protective order is appropriate, can provide effective

TABLE 15.1 Resources That Address Test Security

Resource	Distinguishes between test data and materials	Release to psychologists with client release	Release to nonpsychologists with client release (not including court order)*
APA Ethics Code	X	X	X
NAN		X	
SEPT		X	
SGFP		X	

Note: APA Ethics Code refers to the 2002 version. NAN= National Academy of Neuropsychology position paper on test security. SEPT= Standards for Educational and Psychological Testing.
SGFP= Specialty Guidelines for Forensic Psychologists.
*All resources support compliance with court orders, although steps can be taken to maximize the security of test data even when compelled by a court order to release the data.

discovery, and at the same time protect the legitimate need for test integrity and security. Mutual professionalism, cooperation, and civility will go a long way toward achieving the objectives of all parties.

OTHER SOURCES OF SUPPORTING INFORMATION

THE FOLLOWING PUBLICATIONS provide additional sources of information and guidance: *Test Security, Protecting the Integrity of Tests* (APA, 1999b); *Standards for Educational and Psychological Testing* (APA, 1999a); *Statement on the Disclosure of Test Data* (APA, 1996); *Test Security* position statements (NAN, 2000, 2003); and *Strategies for Coping With Subpoenas or Compelled Testimony for Test Data* (Committee on Legal Issues, 1996, 2006) Committee on the Revision of the Specialty Guidelines for Forensic Psychology (2006). *Specialty Guidelines for Forensic Psychology.* The APA (2006) article includes a useful subpoena decision flow chart to help the neuropsychologist decide exactly how to proceed when a specific subpoena is received.

Table 15.1 graphically presents which of these resources distinguish between release of test data and materials and release to psychologists versus nonpsychologists with client releases (other than by court order).

NOTES

1. The Ethics Code Standard 9.11 provides clear definitions, that is, "*test materials* refers to manuals, instruments, protocols, and test questions or stimuli and does not include *test data*." Standard 9.04 "*test data* refers to raw and scaled

scores, client/patient responses to test questions or stimuli, and psychologists' notes and recordings concerning client/patient statements and behavior during an examination. Those portions of test materials that include client/patient responses are included in the definition of *test data*." Therefore, *test materials* apparently convert to *test data* once the patient's responses are recorded on the test protocol forms (Behnke, 2003).

2. The Committee on Ethical Guidelines for Forensic Psychologists is currently undertaking a multiyear revision process of the SGFP. The status of the latest draft of the revised guidelines is available at www.ap-ls.org. (Second Official Draft—released 1.11.06—will be referred to in this chapter when discussing the current revision status.)

3. This scenario is fictional and does not represent real events of any known practitioner. It does, however, represent a compilation of situations and near-miss experiences encountered by many different forensic neuropsychologists.

4. "C-level tests require verification of a doctorate in psychology, education, or a related field or licensure" (The Psychological Corporation, 2006, p. 178). The following examples of tests commonly used by neuropsychologists are all C-level tests: Wechsler Adult and Children's Intelligence Scales (WAIS-III, WCIS-IV); Wechsler Memory Scale (WMS-III); Wechsler Abbreviated Scale of Intelligence (WASI); Wechsler Adult Reading Test (WART) Test of Memory Malingering (TOMM); Wide Range Assessment of Memory and Learning (WRAML-2), Children's Memory Scale (CMS), California Verbal Learning Test (CVLT-2), NEPSY, MicroCog, Dementia Rating Scale-2 (DMR-2), Children's Category Test (CCT; Boll, 1993), Delis-Kaplan Executive Function System (D-KEFS) and Wisconsin Card Sorting Test (WCST).

5. This is important because the Texas law *prohibits the release of raw data to nonpsychologists* (Title 22 Texas Statutes Part 21, Rule 465.22).

REFERENCES

Adams, K. M., & Putnam, S. H. (1994). Coping with professional skeptics: Reply to Faust. *Psychological Assessment, 6,* 5–7.

American Psychiatric Association. (1994). *Diagnostic and statistical manual of mental disorders* (4th ed.). Washington DC: Author.

American Psychological Association. (1992). Ethical principles of psychologists and code of conduct. *American Psychologist, 47,* 1597–1611.

American Psychological Association. (1996). Statement on the disclosure of test data. *American Psychologist, 51,* 644–648.

American Psychological Association. (1999a). *Standards for educational and psychological testing.* Washington, DC: American Educational Research Association.

American Psychological Association. (1999b). Test security: Protecting the integrity of tests. *American Psychologist, 54,* 1078.

American Psychological Association. (2002). Ethical principles of psychologists and code of conduct. *American Psychologist, 57*(12), 1060–1073.

American Psychological Association. (2006). Strategies for private practitioners coping with subpoenas or compelled testimony for client records or test data. *Professional Psychology: Research and practice, 37*(2), 215–222.

Anderten, P., Staulcup, V., & Grisso, T. (1980). On being ethical in legal places. *Professional Psychology, 11,* 764–773.

Anderten, P., Staulcup, V., & Grisso, T. (1999). On being ethical in legal places. In D. N. Bersoff (Ed.), *Ethical conflicts in psychology* (2nd ed., pp. 541–542). Washington, DC: American Psychological Association.

Association of State and Provincial Psychology Boards Code of Conduct. (2005). Montgomery: Author. (www.asppb.org/publications).

Bauer, L., & McCaffrey, R. J. (2006). Coverage of the Test of Memory Malingering, Victoria Symptom Validity Test, and Word Memory Test on the Internet: Is test security threatened? *Archives of Clinical Neuropsychology, 21,* 121–126.

Bush, S. S. (Ed.). (2005). *A casebook of ethical challenges in neuropsychology.* New York: Psychology Press.

Bush, S. S., & Lees-Haley, P. R. (2005). Threats to the validity of forensic neuropsychological data: Ethical considerations. *Journal of Forensic Neuropsychology, 4*(3), 45–66.

Bush, S., & Macciocchi, S. (2003). The 2002 APA Ethics Code: Select changes relevant to neuropsychology. *Bulletin of the National Academy of Neuropsychology, 18*(2), 1–2, 7–8.

Bush, S. S., Connell, M. A., & Denny, R. L. (2006). Ethical issues in forensic psychology: A systemic model for decision making. Washington, DC: American Psychological Association.

Butcher, J. N., & Pope, K. S. (1993). Seven Issues in conducting forensic assessments: Ethical responsibility in light of new standards and new tests. *Ethics and Behavior, 3,* 267–288.

Committee on Ethical Guidelines for Forensic Psychologists. (1991). Specialty guidelines for forensic psychologists. *Law and Human Behavior, 15,* 655–665.

Committee on the Revision of the Specialty Guidelines for Forensic Psychology. (2006). *Specialty guidelines for forensic psychology.* Second Official Draft, released on January 1, 2006, at www.ap-ls.org.

Committee on Legal Issues. (1996). Strategies for coping with subpoenas or compelled testimony for test data. *Professional Psychology: Research and Practice, 27*(3), 245–251.

Committee on Legal Issues. (2006). Strategies for coping with subpoenas or compelled testimony for test data. *Professional Psychology: Research and practice, 37*(2), 215–222.

Confidentiality of Medical Records Act. Section 4–307 of the Health General Article, Annotated Code of Maryland. 1994 replacement, vol. 2000 supplement.

Connell, M., & Koocher, G. (2003). HIPAA & forensic practice. *American Psychology Law Society News, 23*(2), 16–19.

Daubert v. Merrell Dow Pharmaceuticals, 113 S. Ct. 2786 (1993).

Digital Equipment Corp v. Micro Technology, Inc. 142 F.R.D. 488 1992.

Frumkin, I. B. (1995). How to handle attorney requests for psychological test data. *Innovations in Clinical Practice: A Source Book, 14,* 275–292.

Grote, C. (2005). Ethical practice of forensic neuropsychology. In G. L. Larrabee (Ed.), *Forensic neuropsychology: A scientific approach* (pp. 92–114). New York: Oxford University Press.

Illinois *Mental Health and Developmental Disabilities Confidentiality Act* (740 ILCS 110/3 (c), formerly Ill. Rev. Statutes. 1991 ch. 91 1/2, 803.

Lailhengue v. Mobil (1990). Civil Action No. 90–4425, U.S. Dist. Ct. For E. Dist. of LA.

Law School Admission Test. Princeton: Law School Admission Services.

Lees-Haley, P. R. (1997). Attorneys influence expert evidence in forensic psychological and neuropsychological cases. *Assessment, 4,* 321–324.

Model Rules of Professional Conduct. (2006). *American Bar Association.* Chicago: Author.

Multi-State Bar Examination. *National Conference of Bar Examiners.* Iowa City: Author.

National Academy of Neuropsychology. (2000). Test Security. Official Position Statement of the National Academy of Neuropsychology. *Archives of Clinical Neuropsychology, 15*(5), 383–386.

National Academy of Neuropsychology Policy and Planning Committee. (2003). Test Security: An Update. Official statement of the National Academy of Neuropsychology. Retrieved February 17, 2004, from http://nanonline. org/paio/security_update.shtm

National Academy of Neuropsychology. (2004). Releasing test materials: Position of the Psychological Corporation. *Bulletin, 19*(1), 1–2, 7–8.

Quebec Code of Ethics of Psychologists. (1998). *Editeur officiel du Quebec.*

Quotron Systems, Inc. v. Automatic Data Processing, Inc. 141 F.R.D. 37 (S.D.N.Y. 1992).

Rapp, D. L., & Ferber, P. S. (1994). Discovery and protective orders relating to raw data in psychological or neuro-psychological testing. *The Vermont Bar Journal & Law Digest,* December, 22–34.

Rapp, D. L., & Ferber, P. S. (2003). To release, or not to release raw test data, that is the question. In A. M Horton, Jr., & L. C. Hartlage (Eds.), *Handbook of forensic neuropsychology* (pp. 337–368). New York: Springer Publishing.

Rosen, G. M. (1995). The Aleutian Enterprise sinking and posttraumatic stress disorder: Misdiagnosis in clinical and forensic settings. *Professional Psychology, 26,* 82–87.

Rule 26 and 45. *Federal Rules of Civil Procedure.*

Shapiro, D. L. (1991). *Forensic psychological assessment: An integrative approach.* Needham Heights, MA: Allyn and Bacon.

Shapiro, D. L. (1999). *Criminal responsibility evaluations: A manual for practice.* Sarasota: Professional Resource Press.

Snowden v. Connaught Labs., Inc. 137 F.R.D. 325, 332 (D. Kan. 1991).

Texas State Board of Examiners of Psychologists. (1999). *Rules and regulations.* Austin: Author (22 Texas Statutes, Part 21, Rule 465.22).

The Psychological Corporation. (2006). *Psychological Assessment Products Catalog.* San Antonio, TX: Harcourt Brace.

Tranel, D. (1994). The release of psychological data to nonexperts: Ethical and legal considerations. *Professional Psychology, 25,* 33–38.

Tranel, D. (1999). The release of psychological data to nonexperts: Ethical and legal considerations. In D. N. Bersoff (Ed.), *Ethical conflicts in psychology* (2nd ed., pp. 303–307). Washington, DC: American Psychological Association.

Watts v. the United States, 77–1428, U.S. Ct. Of App., DC., 1977.

Wetter, M. W., & Corrigan, S. K. (1995). Providing information to clients about psychological tests: A survey of attorneys' and law students' attitudes. *Professional Psychology, 26,* 474–477.

U.S. Department of Health and Human Services. (2003). *Public Law 104–191: Health Insurance Portability and Accountability Act of 1996.* Retrieved November 24, 2003, from www.hhs.gov/ocr/hipaa/

Youngjohn, J. R. (1995). Confirmed attorney coaching prior to neuropsychological evaluation. *Assessment, 2,* 279–283.

16

Trained Third-Party Presence During Forensic Neuropsychological Evaluations

JOHN J. BLASE

THE PRESENCE OF an observer during forensic neuropsychological evaluations is an issue that has created much controversy and discussion in the field of neuropsychology. The interest has been spearheaded by the decision in many, if not most, jurisdictions that an outside observer is permissible as part of the discovery process in litigated matters. Some courts have ruled that attorneys may be present at the evaluation of their clients, and others have advised that the evaluee has a right to have a doctor of their choice present during such an evaluation. The opinions of neuropsychologists as to the appropriateness of this type of observation are mixed, but the strength with which each side presents their opinion speaks to the depth of feeling in this matter. McCaffrey, Fisher, Gold, and Lynch (1996) present several reasons to oppose the presence of observers during neuropsychological examinations. The main position McCaffrey espouses is based on the theory of social facilitation, and an extensive bibliography on the subject is offered. Other objections cited include: (a) the compromise of test security and misuse of tests, (b) potential ethical violations because tests were not standardized with a third party present, and (c) the impact of ethical and professional standards on a request to a neuropsychologist to be a third-party observer. Since the appearance of McCaffrey et al.'s article in 1996, there has been a published opinion by McSweeny et al. (in press) and a policy statement made by the National Academy of Neuropsychology (1999). Neither appears to rely on an independent review of the literature but, rather, on McCaffrey et al.'s analysis and a reiteration of the Ethical Principles of Psychologists and Code of Conduct (APA, 1992).

A policy statement for the American Academy of Clinical Neuropsychology authored by Hamsher, Baron, and Lee (1999) makes the important distinction between an involved third party such as an attorney, parent, relative, and so forth and an uninvolved third party such as a health care professional, student professional, or technical personnel. Of note is Hamsher's opinion that the purpose of the presence of uninvolved parties is to learn about test procedure and to focus on observation of the examiner. In 2005, the *Journal of Forensic Neuropsychology* devoted an entire issue (volume 4, issue 2) to the research pertaining to third-party observers with several articles presented primarily by authors from the Albany Psychological Associates, P.C. These articles ostensibly present new research and new findings that support the exclusion of third-party observers from neuropsychological evaluations.

This chapter proposes to look at and clarify the issues being addressed concerning the presence of a trained third-party observer during a forensic neuropsychological evaluation. The focus of this chapter is purposely narrowed to consider only trained third-party observers who are defined as neuropsychologists or technicians trained in the use and administration of neuropsychological tests. This definition is akin to Hamsher's uninvolved third party. This restriction to using only trained third-party observers should obviate the concern about test security or the misuse of tests. The current author would not suggest or condone as appropriate the presence of any untrained observer such as a parent, spouse, attorney, or the like during a neuropsychological assessment. He also would have concerns about audio or videotaping that could allow future viewing by untrained individuals unless assurances by the court could be provided that such a recording would not be released into the public domain. Use of trained observers would help to insure that the observer acts professionally and does not engage in distraction or any other behavior that would interfere with the test administration. This chapter will present a review of the literature on social facilitation that has been proposed as relevant research impacting on the issue of third-party observers. Known research findings will be presented as well as suggestions concerning trained third-party observers and future research topics.

Finally, there will be a discussion of the relevance of observing the examiner rather than the examinee during forensic assessments. To date, the focus has been on the observation of the individual being evaluated and how that observation will affect the validity of neuropsychological testing. It would seem that this should not be the sole focus of attention in such evaluations, because it is the examiner's methods that are to be observed and not necessarily the examinee's behavior. McCaffrey et al. (1996) point out that "attorneys, especially those who fear that the examiner would elicit incriminating information concerning how the injury occurred, or who felt that the exam would otherwise be conducted in a biased manner, were usually permitted to attend" (p. 435). Clearly, the emphasis in this statement is on the observation of the examiner, not the examinee. The request for a trained third party at an evaluation should be to address concerns about what questions will be asked, how these questions will be phrased, and what questions are omitted. Questions about what tests are employed, whether the tests are administered in a standardized fashion, if appropriate time is allowed for examinee response, and similar methodological inquiries are appropriate. These are behaviors that cannot be observed by merely reviewing the raw test data. The concern is clearly focused on how the examinee is evaluated by the examiner; not on how the examinee performs. The importance on this focus will become evident in the discussion that follows.

The request for a trained third-party observer is almost always confined to the forensic examination. Forensic neuropsychological assessments are substantially different from clinical assessments. For instance, in a forensic assessment there is no doctor–patient relationship established. The person being evaluated is not a "patient" in the clinical sense and is usually referred to as an examinee or a plaintiff. There is limited confidentiality for the information gathered and no promise or attempt to provide treatment. The evaluating neuropsychologist has a relationship with a third party—usually an insurance company, municipality, or a defense attorney—and no therapeutic relationship with the examinee. The examinee is not evaluated voluntarily, and not infrequently there is an adversarial aspect to the evaluation.

The forensic examinee or plaintiff is quite different from clinical patients in that they have made their injury complaints public and should be aware of the fact that their behavior is open to scrutiny. This scrutiny can take the form of interrogations, depositions, or sworn testimony in a court of law before a jury of peers. The examinees or plaintiffs in forensic evaluations are generally aware that their actions may be observed, recorded, or videotaped for public scrutiny. Insurance companies routinely assign case managers who accompany examinees into medical exams—a practice rarely, if ever, tolerated in a clinical examination. In other words, plaintiff examinees are accustomed to and expect a different set of rules to apply during litigation. Clearly, a forensic assessment is vastly different from a clinical assessment.

The ethical codes for psychologists that are liberally invoked as a reason to prevent a trained third-party observer at a neuropsychological examination were never intended to apply to the forensic assessment. The current author would agree that a third-party observer is not appropriate during a clinical assessment with the two notable exceptions being to provide clinical supervision and the need for an interpreter. In the clinical supervision setting it is also obvious that the person being assessed is the examiner and not the patient. Supervised test results are generally considered reliable and valid. Both clinical supervision and observation of a forensic examination are designed to answer the same question—Is the test administration being conducted properly and according to established practices? If distraction presents a problem, it exists equally in a supervisory session and a forensic examination. If controlled properly, there is no reason to believe that distractions would be significant factors influencing the outcome of either a supervised clinical assessment or a forensic evaluation. Sanders and Baron (1975) concluded: "To the question 'Does distraction *necessarily* impair task performance?' the present research provides a firm 'No.' Even though distraction does take time and/or attention away from the task at hand, additional factors are apparently involved" (p. 962). Both simple and complex tasks were studied, and the authors concluded that a compensatory process most likely in the form of an increase in general drive level of the performer accompanies the process of distraction. Trained third-party observers would be aware of appropriate testing procedures and would also understand the importance of maintaining a nonpresence by not interfering with the examination in any way. Reports of inappropriate interference by a trained observer are rare if they exist at all. However, inappropriate behavior by a relative or attorney that interrupts the testing process is an all too commonly reported phenomenon.

SOCIAL FACILITATION

SOCIAL FACILITATION IS a concept that has been part of the social psychology literature for nearly a century. Zajonc (1965, 1980) championed an instinct theory of social facilitation by proposing that the mere presence of others was the sufficient condition to bring about a change in another person's behavior. He proposed further that the presence of another produced an increased drive state resulting in social facilitation on simple tasks and socially mediated impairment on complex tasks. Thus, Zajonc suggests that an audience will impair the acquisition of new responses and facilitate the emission of responses that are well learned or instinctive. Key to Zajonc's theory is that the mere presence of a third party is sufficient to produce these changes in behavior. Cottrell (1972) proposed a revision to Zajonc's theory by suggesting that the presence of others is a learned source of drive, rather than a source of drive that is innate or "wired-into" the organism. He designed experiments that allowed for the presence of another during an experiment but had the third party blindfolded. Because the mere presence of the blindfolded third party did not have the predicted influence proposed by Zajonc, Cottrell concluded that the presence of others will enhance the emission of dominant responses only when the spectators can evaluate the individual's performance. Various researchers (Henchy & Glass, 1968; Paulus & Murdock, 1971) conducted experiments that demonstrated that the mere presence of others is not a sufficient condition to enhance emission of dominant responses, but that these effects do occur when there is the anticipation of later praise or criticism. Guerin and Innes (1982) presented a summary of the research up to then that demonstrated that approximately 50% of the research studying social facilitation appeared to lend support to the drive theory proposed by Zajonc, and 50% favored the learning theory of Cottrell. Schmitt, Gilovich, Goore, and Joseph (1986) conducted a study that strongly supported Zajonc's contention that mere presence of another person is sufficient to increase people's generalized arousal and to produce the standard social facilitation effects. However, he goes on to state "no advocate of the mere presence hypothesis, for example, would deny that evaluation apprehension is an important variable that can indeed increase people's general arousal level and thus further facilitate their dominant response tendencies" (Schmitt et al., 1986, p. 246). Whether one accepts the instinct theory or the learning theory being proposed, there is no dispute that the presence of another does influence the behavior of a person being examined. This would seem to lend support to the conclusions of McCaffrey et al. (1996) that the phenomenon called social facilitation may pose an important threat to the validity of a neuropsychological evaluation in the presence of a third-party observer.

McCaffrey et al. (1996) state further that "the literature on social facilitation provides empirical evidence to suggest that the presence of an observer(s) alters cognitive/motor performance" and "the social facilitation literature provides a theoretical framework to support arguments that the presence of a third party observer during neuropsychological evaluation may alter the results of the evaluation" (p. 441). The question that needs to be addressed is just how the presence of a third party during neuropsychological evaluation alters the result of the evaluation.

WHO IS THE OBSERVER?

A REVIEW OF THE extensive bibliography provided by McCaffrey et al. (1996) will reveal that the vast majority of the research refers to studies in which the experimental design provided for a comparison of an individual working alone with an individual working with an examiner/experimenter. The process of social facilitation in either the drive theory proposed by Zajonc or the learning theory proposed by Cottrell refers to the influence upon the examinee by the mere presence of the examiner (Zajonc) and the evaluative characteristic of the examiner (Cottrell). Manstead and Semin (1980) note "While it might be argued that an experimenter does not constitute an audience, it is difficult to see how, from the perspective of a mere presence theorist, our experimenter did not satisfy the conditions of being 'merely present,' because to suggest that there is some phenomenological difference between the mere presence of an experimenter and that of a third party is to invoke the very cognitive processes which mere presence must by definition not involve" (p. 131). In some studies (Guerin, 1983; Knowles, 1983;) the examiner was blindfolded, sometimes placed behind the examinee, sometimes in front of the examinee, and sometimes at a distance simulating indifference or nonattention. In each, the comparison was between the "alone condition" and one in which an examiner was present. In other words, social facilitation occurred by virtue of the presence of an examiner; not the presence of a third party. Thus, because social facilitation already exists by virtue of the fact that neuropsychological examinations involve the presence of both an examinee and an examiner, what is the possible effect on the examinee by introducing another person into the testing situation? This question has relevance for the presence of a third-party observer, a clinical supervisor, or an interpreter for non-English speaking evaluees. It has relevance for the presence of a third-party observer such as a parent, an attorney, or any other untrained observer as opposed to a trained third-party observer. A trained third-party observer is defined as a neuropsychologist or a neuropsychological technician who is familiar with the tests being used, is not related to the examinee, and is present during the neuropsychological testing solely for the purpose of observing the examiner in order to assure that testing is administered in a standardized fashion.

Knowles (1983) measured the effects of audience size and distance on social judgments and behavior. The audience size varied from 2 to 4 to 8 members and distances varied from 3 to 10 to 24 feet. The distance of the audience had no reliable effects on the drive-related measures, even though subjects accurately recalled the distance of the audience and were influenced by it in judging their crowdedness. There was a tendency for the alone condition to take somewhat less time per trial than the audience conditions, but within audience conditions, the size and distance of the audience did not significantly effect times. Laughlin and Wong-McCarthy (1975) designed an experiment requiring the solving of three concept-attainment problems in an orthogonal design. The variables to be manipulated were the number of observers comparing the examiner alone with an additional observer. Videotaping, audiotaping, and task complexity did not differ in the ability to effect poorer performance when compared to the control condition of no observer. The presence of an additional observer had no effect on performance. They point out that previous findings in which the presence of an observer degrades performance may be due to the observer as a recorder of information about performance, rather than to his physical presence per se. Laughlin and Jaccard (1975) compared individuals and cooperative pairs varying the size of the audience between zero, one, or two persons as they solved three successive concept attainment problems. Their findings indicated that an audience of either one or two persons hindered the performance of individuals relative to unobserved controls, but had no effect upon the performance of cooperative pairs. Cohen and Davis (1973) emphasize that the presence of others is a vague psychological dimension. While the most parsimonious conclusion from research is that presence of others generally implies evaluation and the saliency of evaluation can clearly be increased by instruction. Evaluation of performance may or may not imply a relationship to the needs and purposes of the person being evaluated.

THE IMPACT OF BEING OBSERVED

TOLMAN (1965) COMMENTED on animal behavior and noted that the running of chicks in a 4-foot runway for food was facilitated by the mere presence of conspecific companions. It should be noted that this effect was a disinhibitory one. A similar interpretation was given to data obtained on rhesus monkeys by Stamm (1961) and by Ross and Ross (1949) in discussing their results on feeding behavior in dogs. Cottrell (1972) opined that humans are trained by their past experience in that other persons who watch them as spectators often praise or criticize them. He cites several authors who produce research findings akin to his demonstrating that when anticipations of praise or criticism are eliminated, the presence of others does not increase the individual's drive level. When a nonrivalrous coaction arrangement is encountered, the presence of coactors does not serve to increase the individual's drive level. Sasfy and Okun (1974) concluded that audience characteristics and the form of evaluation could be considered interactive determinants of evaluation potential. Their findings supported Cottrell's notion that the potential for evaluation characterized a social situation that is the chief source of audience and coaction effects in humans. Green (1983) conducted an experiment comparing subjects evaluated with the promise of future help with those evaluated with no such promise. His conclusion was that evaluation apprehension was reduced when subjects were told that an otherwise evaluative observer would be a source of future help. He concluded further that such a finding suggests that evaluation apprehension during observation is a function of the anticipation of negative outcomes. Evaluation resulting from being observed facilitates performance on an easy task even though it inhibits performance on a more difficult one. Green (1985) noted that fear of failure engendered by test anxiety and experimenter evaluation caused subjects to become overly cautious and withhold responding. Shaver and Liebling (1976) state "there is probably no such thing as the 'mere presence' of an observer *in a task situation;* a task observer will always be perceived as somewhat evaluative or will at least arouse some uncertainty concerning evaluation and hence will tend to increase task-relevant drive" (p. 270).

Evaluative audiences are frequently noted in social facilitation research with the conclusions emphasizing the importance of audience expectation on the test performance (Bond, 1982; Criddle, 1971; Ganzer, 1968; Green, 1979; Guerin, 1983, 1986; Haas & Roberts, 1975; Innes & Gordon, 1985; Innes & Young, 1975; Lombardo & Catalano, 1975; Robinson-Staveley & Cooper, 1988; Sanna & Shotland, 1990; Seta, Donaldson, & Wang, 1988; Zajonc, 1980). As recent as 1990, Sanna and Shotland conclude that whether the presence of an evaluative audience improves or impairs performance depends upon whether a positive or a negative evaluation is anticipated. Robinson-Staveley and Cooper (1988) studied the effects of mere presence, expectations for success, gender, and level of computer experience on reactions to computers. They conclude "It is not inconsistent with models of social facilitation that performance could be impaired because of low expectations for success...low expectations could result in the energization of irrelevant response tendencies, in embarrassment, or in withdrawal, all of which would be expected to impair performance. When expectations for success are high, however, the result could be increases in task-relevant drive, self-presentational strategies, and matching to standards that would lead to facilitation of performance" (p. 181). Lombardo and Catalano (1975) note that their findings indicate that anticipation of performance evaluation is the mediating mechanism for drive arousal. Zajonc (1980) reports the effects of stress on performance. He concludes that stress often elicits fixed response patterns, and different stress conditions elicit different responses in different species. Furthermore, to the extent that stress responses conflict with the behavior under observation, the presence of others will interact with the performance of this observed behavior accordingly. The level of stress in companions promoting efficient behavior is unimportant; and implied evaluative threats may increase stress. Additionally, the possibility exists that others may prevent the occurrence of avoidance responses and thus reduce emotional reactions to stress. Green and Gange (1977) note that the presence of others leads to increased arousal only when the others are stimuli for anticipation of negative outcomes. Reassuring subjects viewing a stressful film in the presence of a familiar and trusted figure inhibited the anxiety normally elicited by the film.

FOCUSING THE ISSUE

THE PRESENCE OF a trained third-party observer is distinctively different than the presence of a third party during a forensic neuropsychological evaluation. The role of the observer as understood by the evaluee is of critical importance. This author believes that following certain criteria pertaining to trained third-party observers will eliminate any undo influence on neuropsychological assessments.

The issue of trained third-party observers during forensic neuropsychological assessments requires the following:

1. The evaluation is a forensic rather than clinical assessment.
2. The trained observer is a third party in addition to the examiner who is clearly performing some evaluative process.
3. The trained observer is a professional who is knowledgeable about the testing to be administered and is not a family member, attorney, or any other individual without specific knowledge about test procedures.
4. The evaluee is advised prior to the evaluation that the observer is an ally who is present only to evaluate the examiner to make sure that testing is administered in a standardized manner.
5. The evaluee understands that his/her performance on testing is not being evaluated.

RECENT STUDIES AND OPINIONS

MᴄCᴀꜰꜰʀᴇʏ, Lʏɴᴄʜ, Yᴀɴᴛᴢ, Constantinou, Ashendorf, Gavett, Duff, and Fisher recently authored a series of articles presented in the *Journal of Forensic Neuropsychology,* Vol. 4(2) 2005. In the first article, McCaffrey et al. reference some of the literature pertaining to social facilitation but fail to point out that this research is largely based on a comparison of an individual being tested in isolation compared to being tested by an examiner. In fact, the social facilitation research says very little about the presence of a third party and in the few studies where this issue is addressed, the majority found no significant influence on the examinee even when the observer was not a trained observer. McCaffrey et al. refer to a study by Binder and Johnson-Greene (1995) pertaining to a mother observing her child that clearly has nothing to do with a trained third-party examiner.

A study by Constantinou, Ashendorf, and McCaffrey (2005) involved examining the impact of audio recording on neuropsychological test performance of 40 undergraduate university students. This was not a forensic evaluation, and there is no evidence that the 40 undergraduate students were advised as to who was being evaluated. These same authors conducted a similar examination with the use of a video camera as observer. Sixty-five students were recruited for this study and were randomly assigned to either a visual recording group or a no visual recording group. Participants in the visual recording group were advised that their performance was being recorded. No instruction as to why the recording was being done or for what purpose was offered. As with the previous study, this was not a forensic evaluation, and there was no evidence to suggest that the recorded subjects were advised as to who was being evaluated.

Lynch (2005) offered an article on the effects of a third-party observer on neuropsychological testing following a closed head injury. Participants were randomly assigned to one of two groups. The unobserved group received a standard administration while the observed group was administered tests in the presence of a male graduate student who was introduced as a colleague of the examiner who was assuming the role that a legal representative would assume in cases in which legal parties wanted to be present. The observer held a pen and legal pad. The evaluee was not advised that the observer was a trained professional there to assess the examiner rather than the examinee.

Yantz and McCaffrey (2005) reported the findings of a study designed to examine the effects of a supervisor's observation on memory test performance. The performance of observed group members was attended by the examiner's supervisor during test administration. The subjects were informed before the start of testing that the observer was the examiner's supervisor, present solely to monitor the consistency of the examiner's test administration, and that she would not be evaluating the subject's performance in any way. On memory testing, two of the four summary scores were found to have significant relationship with supervisory observation. Both verbal memory and global memory scores were significantly higher for the unobserved group while there was no difference in scores for visual memory or short-term memory. Seventeen additional variables were examined, and there was no significant difference between the observed and unobserved groups. Because the two effected memory summary scores were in the normal range of performance for both the observed and the unobserved group, the authors could only conclude that "the supervisor's evaluative presence could have effected the examiner's concentration and/or anxiety level which impacted test administration procedures" (p. 36). The supervisor in this study was a colleague of the examiner and not an ally of the examinee involved in a forensic assessment. Even with this departure from recommended criteria for a trained third-party examination, the significant findings appear to be not that two summary scores (both falling in the normal range) were statistically different but that the vast majority of analyzed scores demonstrated no significant difference, and the vast majority of scores demonstrated none or very small effect size.

Gavett, Lynch, and McCaffrey (2005) took the results of three of the previously referenced studies in order to evaluate effect size and included the findings of 42 additional published reports, including 36 from the social facilitation literature. Many of these studies do not meet the necessary criteria for the evaluation of trained third-party observation during forensic neuropsychological evaluations and included data from studies that compared evaluees being assessed in isolation compared to those being evaluated by an examiner with no third party present. The conclusion that "Effect size estimates associated with findings from third-party observer research were, on average, medium for memory measures and small for motor and attention/executive measures. These findings indicate that the presence of an observer during neuropsychological evaluation should be expected to have a clinically meaningful impact on an examinee's test performance, with memory measures particularly vulnerable" (pp. 49–50) appears to have little or no relevance for forensic evaluations involving trained third-party observers who meet the criteria defined in this article.

Finally, Duff and Fisher (2005) present an opinion based on all of the previously cited research by McCaffrey et al. titled "Ethical Dilemmas with Third Party Observers." Contained within this article are unlikely examples of inappropriate third-party presence during an examination with subsequent disruption of the exam process that could have been avoided with the use of a trained third-party observer.

CONCLUSIONS

T HE CURRENT REVIEW of the literature suggests that the use
of social facilitation research to support the objections to third-
party observation is questionable. Social facilitation research does
not provide convincing evidence to suggest that the presence of an
observer in addition to the examiner alters cognitive/motor performance. Social facilitation research does suggest that there is no appreciable effect on the examinee by the introduction of an observer in
addition to the examiner. Social facilitation research raises some concerns about the conclusions in the August 1999 published opinions of
the executive board of National Academy of Neuropsychology (NAN)
concerning third-party observers in forensic evaluations. Social facilitation research would support the presence of a trained third-party
observer during both forensic evaluations and training sessions requiring supervision of the examiner.

Social facilitation research does posit some interesting questions
concerning the instructions given to an examinee regarding the presence of a trained third-party observer and how this perception could
actually enhance test performance. Advising evaluees that an observer,
either a person or a recording device, will be present to observe the
examiner may have a beneficial effect on those evaluees anticipating
a negative outcome. It is reasonable to conclude that the presence
of a trained third-party observer who is perceived as a monitor of
the examination process could raise the examinee's drive level and
thereby improve test performance. Also, the presence of a perceived
neutral party observing the process in a forensic Independent Medical
Examination (IME) evaluation could help to reduce the anticipated
negative evaluation in this sometimes adversarial situation. While
it is not reasonable to conclude that all IME evaluations are biased
or will generate negative expectations from evaluees, this is a common enough perception that it may warrant the recommendation
for a trained third-party observer in many situations. Social facilitation research would suggest that other IME evaluations in addition to
neuropsychological assessments are likely candidates for some type
of observation. What forensic neuropsychologist has not heard of
the 10-minute complete and comprehensive neurology or orthopedic
examination? Because we have little or no scientific research that supports an objection to trained third-party observation during forensic
evaluations, it is recommended that neuropsychologists utilize trained
third-party observers in order to adhere to the principles of freedom
of information and full disclosure. At the same time, neuropsychologists would be preventing distribution of the tests in the public
domain that would jeopardize the validity of our instruments. Future

research pertaining to the effects of trained third-party observers on the evaluation process could investigate: (1) the effect of advising that the focus of attention is on the evaluator versus the evaluee, and (2) the effect of advising the evaluee that the evaluator is a biased versus an impartial IME evaluator.

REFERENCES

American Psychological Association. (1992). Ethical principles of psychologists and code of conduct. *American Psychologist, 47,* 1597–1611.

Binder, L. M., & Johnson-Greene, D. (1995). Observer effects on neuropsychological performance: A case report. *The Clinical Neuropsychologist, 9,* 74–78.

Bond, C. F. (1982). Social facilitation: A self-presentational view. *Journal of Personality and Social Psychology, 42,* 1042–1050.

Cohen, J. L., & Davis, J. H. (1973). Effects of audience status, evaluation, and time of action on performance with hidden-word problems. *Journal of Personality and Social Psychology, 27,* 74–85.

Constantinou, M., Ashendorf, L., & McCaffrey, R. (2005). Effects of a third party observer during neuropsychological assessment: When the observer is a video camera. *Journal of Forensic Neuropsychology, 4*(2), 39–63.

Cottrell, N. B. (1972). Social facilitation. In C. G. McClintock (Ed.), *Experimental social psychology* (pp. 185–236). New York: Holt.

Criddle, W. D. (1971). The physical presence of other individuals as a factor in social facilitation. *Psychonomic Science, 22,* 229–230.

Duff, K., & Fisher, J. M. (2005). Ethical dilemmas with third party observers. *Journal of Forensic Neuropsychology, 4*(2), 65–81.

Ganzer, D. (1968). Effects of audience presence and test anxiety on learning and retention in a serial learning situation. *Journal of Personality and Social Psychology, 8,* 194–199.

Gavett, B. E., Lynch, J. K., & McCaffrey, R. L. (2005) Third party observers: The effect size is greater than you might think. *Journal of Forensic Neuropsychology, 4*(2), 49–63.

Green, R. G. (1979). Effects of being observed on learning following success and failure experiences. *Motivation and Emotion, 3,* 355–371.

Green, R. G. (1983). Evaluation apprehension and the social facilitation/inhibition of learning. *Motivation and Emotion, 7,* 203–211.

Green, R. G. (1985). Evaluation apprehension and response withholding in solution of anagrams. *Personality and Individual Differences, 6,* 293–298.

Green, R. G., & Gange, J. J. (1977). Drive theory of social facilitation: Twelve years of theory and research. *Psychological Bulletin, 84,* 1267–1288.

Guerin, B. (1983). Social facilitation and social monitoring: A test of three models. *British Journal of Social Psychology, 22,* 203–214.

Guerin, B. (1986). The effects of mere presence on a motor task. *The Journal of Social Psychology, 126,* 99–401.

Guerin, B., & Innes, J. M. (1982). Social facilitation and social monitoring: A new look at Zajonc's mere presence hypothesis. *British Journal of Social Psychology, 21,* 7–18.

Haas, J., & Roberts, G. C. (1975). Effect of evaluative others upon learning and performance of a complex motor task. *Journal of Motor Behavior, 7,* 81–90.

Hamsher, K., Baron, I. S., & Lee, G. P. (1999). Third party observers. *Policy Statement for the American Academy of Clinical Neuropsychology.*

Henchy, T., & Glass, D. C. (1968) Evaluation apprehension and the social facilitation of dominant and subordinate responses. *Journal of Personality and Social Psychology, 4,* 446–454.

Innes, J. M., & Gordon, M. I. (1985). The effects of mere presence and a mirror on performance. *The Journal of Social Psychology, 125,* 479–484.

Innes, J. M., & Young, R. F. (1975). The effect of an audience, evaluation apprehension, and objective self awareness on learning. *Journal of Experimental Social Psychology, 11,* 35–42.

Knowles, E. S. (1983). Social physics and the effects of others: Tests of audience size and distance on social judgment and behavior. *Journal of Personality and Social Psychology, 45,* 1263–1279.

Laughlin, P. R., & Jaccard, J. J. (1975). Social facilitation and observational learning of individuals and cooperative pairs. *Journal of Personality and Social Psychology, 32,* 873–879.

Laughlin, P. R., & Wong-McCarthy, W. J. (1975). Social inhibition as a function of observation and recording of performance. *Journal of Experimental Social Psychology, 11,* 560–571.

Lombardo, J. P., & Catalano, J. F. (1975). The effect of failure and the nature of the audience on performance of a complex motor task. *Journal of Motor Behavior, 7,* 29–35.

Lynch, J. K. (2005) Effect of a third party observer on neuropsychological test performance following closed head injury. *Journal of Forensic Neuropsychology, 4*(2), 17–25.

Manstead, A. S. R., & Semin, G. R. (1980). Social facilitation effects: Mere enhancement of dominant responses? *British Journal of Social and Clinical Psychology, 19,* 119–136.

McCaffrey, R. J., Fisher, J. M., Gold, B. A., & Lynch, J. K. (1996). The presence of third parties during neuropsychological evaluations: Who is evaluating whom? *The Clinical Neuropsychologist, 10*(4), 435–449.

McCaffrey, R. J., Lynch, J. K., & Yantz, C. L. (2005). Third party observers: Why all the fuss? *Journal of Forensic Neuropsychology, 4*(2), 1–15.

McSweeny, A. J., Becker, B. C., Naugle, R. I., Snow, W. G., Binder, L. M., & Thompson, L. L. (in press). Ethical issues related to third party observers in clinical neuropsychological evaluations. *The Clinical Neuropsychologist.*

Miller, F. G., Hurkman, M. F., Robinson, J. B., & Feinberg, R. A. (1979). Status and evaluation potential in the social facilitation and impairment of task performance. *Personality and Social Psychology Bulletin, 5,* 381–385.

National Academy of Neuropsychology. (Summer, 1999). Official statement.

Paulus, P., & Murdock, R. (1971). Anticipated evaluation and audience presence in the enhancement of dominant responses. *Journal of Experimental Social Psychology, 7,* 280–291.

Robinson-Staveley, K., & Cooper, J. (1990). Mere presence, gender, and reactions to computers: Studying human-computer interaction in the social context. *Journal of Experimental Social Psychology, 26,* 168–183.

Ross, R., & Ross, S. (1949). Social facilitation of feeding behavior in dogs: I. Group and solitary feeding. *Journal of Genetic Psychology, 74,* 97–108.

Sanders, G. S., & Baron, R. S. (1975). The motivating effects of distraction on task performance. *Journal of Personality and Social Psychology, 32,* 956–963.

Sanna, L. J., & Shotland, R. L. (1990). Valence of anticipated evaluation and social facilitation. *Journal of Experimental Social Psychology, 26,* 82–92.

Sasfy, J., & Okun, M. (1974). Form of evaluation and audience expertness as joint determinants of audience effects. *Journal of Experimental Social Psychology, 10,* 461–467.

Schmitt, B. H., Gilovich, T., Goore, N., & Joseph, L. (1986). Mere presence and social facilitation: One more time. *Journal Of Experimental Social Psychology, 22,* 242–248.

Seta, J. J., Donaldson, S., & Wang, M. A. (1988). The effects of evaluation on organizational processing. *Personality and Social Psychology Bulletin, 14,* 604–609.

Shaver, P., & Liebling, B. A. (1976). Explorations in the drive theory of social facilitation. *The Journal of Social Psychology, 99,* 259–271.

Stamm, S. (1961). Social facilitation in monkeys. *Psychological Reports, 8,* 470–484.

Tolman, C. W. (1965). The role of the companion in social facilitation of animal behavior. In E. Simmel, R. Hoppe, & G. Milton (Eds.), *Social facilitation and initiative behavior* (pp. 33–54). Boston, MA: Allyn & Bacon.

Yantz, C. L., & McCaffrey, R. L. (2005). Effects of a supervisor's observation on memory test performance of the examinee: Third party observer effect confirmed. *Journal of Forensic Neuropsychology, 4*(2), 27–37.

Zajonc, R. B. (1965). Social facilitation. *Science, 149,* 269–274.

Zajonc, R. B. (1980). Compresence. In P. Paulus (Ed.), *Psychology of group influence* (pp. 35–60). Hillsdale, NJ: Lawrence Erlbaum.

17

Confidentiality in Neuropsychological Practice

SHANE S. BUSH AND THOMAS A. MARTIN

What I may see or hear in the course of the treatment or even outside
of the treatment in regard to the life of men, which on no account one
must spread abroad, I will keep to myself, holding such things shameful
to be spoken about.

—Hippocrates[1]

THE ABILITY OF patients to communicate openly and honestly
with psychologists has traditionally served as the foundation of
medical and mental health treatment. Patients[2] must feel confident that their innermost thoughts and sensitive aspects of their past
can be safely divulged. Trust that the therapist will maintain the privacy of this sensitive information is central in promoting the sincere
communication between parties that is the cornerstone of the therapeutic process. Discussion of the patient's private information outside of the therapeutic context, without the consent of the patient or
a designated representative, may destroy the patient's trust, possibly
harm the patient in significant ways, and end the patient's willingness
to engage in further treatment with any therapist. Patients expect that
the information conveyed to mental health professionls will be kept
within the therapeutic dyad (Appelbaum, 2002). With few exceptions,
protecting privacy protects patients. Thus, the importance of protecting

patient information in most psychological treatment contexts cannot be overstated, and this importance is reflected in the jurisdictional laws and codes of ethics that govern psychological practice.

The willingness of patients to convey information that may render them vulnerable to embarrassment or other harmful consequences is as essential for neuropsychological evaluations as it is for psychological treatment. Diagnostic accuracy and the usefulness of recommendations depend upon the accuracy and completeness of relevant patient information. However, neuropsychologists and patients face multiple threats to confidentiality (see Table 17.1).

Consistent with intuitive expectations, research indicates that individuals have a reduced willingness to disclose personal information when they are informed that there are limits to confidentiality (Haut & Muehleman, 1986; Nowell & Spruill, 1993; Woods & McNamara, 1980), particularly for patients with more severe problems (Taube & Elwork, 1990). In addition, fear of confidentiality infringement reduces the willingness of patients to disclose relevant and necessary information regardless of their personality traits or demographic background (Kremer & Gesten, 1998). As the result of either wishing to facilitate patient openness or an insufficient appreciation of the importance of educating patients about these matters, many mental health professionals fail to provide full disclosure of the limits of confidentiality (Appelbaum, 2002), resulting in inaccurate patient expectations and increased likelihood of an adverse outcome.

The goals of this chapter are to examine the legal, ethical, and practical considerations pertaining to confidentiality in the context of neuropsychological practice and to offer suggestions for anticipating and negotiating threats to confidentiality. Because confidentiality requirements

TABLE 17.1   Examples of Threats to Confidentiality in Neuropsychological Practice

---

- Practical limitations associated with inpatient settings, such as roommates
- Team approach to evaluation and treatment
- Third-party observers, such as interpreters and parents
- Mandated reporting requirements, such as harm to self or others
- Government monitoring of services funded by public payers such as Medicare
- Managed care oversight, including utilization review
- Practitioner disclosure to resolve unpaid debts
- Electronic storage and transfer of patient information
- Litigation
- Requests for services by third parties, such as employers and disability insurance carriers

---

Note: The examples listed do not include a client's request for the practitioner to disclose information or a patient's waiver of privilege in litigated matters.

and threats to confidentiality may vary in different professional contexts and settings, a case vignette and utilization of an ethical decision-making model will be employed to illustrate relevant issues.

DEFINITIONS

PRIVACY, CONFIDENTIALITY, AND privilege are related terms pertaining to the protection of communications from a patient to his or her neuropsychologist in a professional context. In *Webster's 9th New Collegiate Dictionary* (Merriam-Webster, 1988), *privacy* is defined as "freedom from unauthorized intrusion" (p. 936). Privacy pertains to individuals (Smith-Bell & Winslade, 1999)—their thoughts, feelings, beliefs, and experiences. Privacy stems from a core societal value—autonomy, the right of individuals to self-determination (Behnke, Perlin, & Bernstein, 2003).

Confidentiality is defined as "intimacy or willingness to confide" (Merriam-Webster, 1988, p. 275). It is based on the disclosure of private information to the neuropsychologist; as such, it is a subset of privacy. Confidentiality requires a professional relationship between patient and neuropsychologist, and it represents the responsibility of the neuropsychologist to not disclose information shared by the patient in the professional relationship.

Privilege is defined as "a right or immunity granted as a peculiar benefit, advantage, or favor" (Merriam-Webster, 1988, p. 936). Privilege relieves the neuropsychologist from having to testify in court about a patient's communications; thus, it is a narrower concept than confidentiality. By "invoking privilege," the patient can prevent the neuropsychologist from testifying or releasing records about intimate personal details shared with the neuropsychologist (Behnke et al., 2003). By "waiving privilege," the patient allows the neuropsychologist to testify or release records in a legal proceeding. Accordingly, privilege belongs to the patient and is invoked or waived at the patient's discretion. Without a privilege statute or a common-law rule, the neuropsychologist can be charged with contempt of court for refusing to testify about information shared by a patient in a professional context (Smith-Bell & Winslade, 1999).

LEGAL CONSIDERATIONS

A CONSTITUTIONAL RIGHT

THE SPECIFIC RIGHTS and restrictions regarding privacy have been established at both the federal and state levels. Despite the absence of the word *privacy* in the U.S. Constitution, the U.S. Supreme Court has recognized privacy as a constitutional right (*Eisenstadt v. Baird,* 1972; *Griswold v. Connecticut,* 1965; *Hawaii Psychiatric Society v. Ariyoshi,* 1979), reflecting the importance that society has long placed on privacy as a primary value and fundamental right (Bersoff, 1999; Smith-Bell & Winslade, 1999). Nevertheless, the protection of sensitive disclosures by patients is not absolute. Courts have placed limitations on the right to privacy (*Bowers v. Hardwick,* 1985; *Roe v. Wade,* 1973; *Tarasoff v. Regents of the University of California,* 1976; *Whalen v. Roe,* 1976), indicating that under certain circumstances, the value of human safety, especially for vulnerable individuals such as children and the elderly, outweighs the importance placed on a patient's right to privacy.

HIPAA

THE HEALTH INSURANCE Portability and Accountability Act (HIPAA) is a federal statute that regulates the manner in which patient information is maintained, used, and disclosed (U.S. Department of Health and Human Services, 2003). The aspect of HIPAA that addresses the privacy of health care information is known as the *privacy rule.* Section 160.102(3) states that the privacy rule applies to practitioners who transmit health information in electronic form (including fax) in connection with a transaction; the rule applies to all of a covered practitioner's health-related information, not just that transmitted electronically (Behnke et al., 2003).

The health information that is regulated is referred to as *protected health information.* HIPAA grants patients access to their protected health information with the exception of psychotherapy notes; however, the definition of psychotherapy notes excludes the results of clinical tests and any summary of the patient's symptoms, diagnosis, functional status, treatment plan, and prognosis. Thus, HIPAA does not prevent patients from having access to much of the information contained in a neuropsychological report. In addition, raw test data are not considered psychotherapy notes; therefore, HIPAA does not allow for neuropsychologists to withhold raw test data from patients (Behnke et al., 2003; Fisher, 2003).

The Ethics Code of the American Psychological Association (2002) offers circumstances under which raw test data should not be released. Ethical Standard 9.04a states, "Psychologists may refrain from releasing test data to protect a client/patient or others from substantial harm or misuse or misinterpretation of the data or the test, recognizing that in many instances release of confidential information under these circumstances is regulated by law." "Substantial harm" has been defined as "reasonably likely to endanger the life or physical safety of the individual or another person or cause equally substantial harm" (Fisher, 2003, p. 12). Rapp and Ferber (2003) stated, "The client's test answers, with the psychologist's analysis, are meaningless to, and likely to be misinterpreted by, anyone other than a specifically trained psychologist" (p. 353). Thus, it is difficult to imagine how such information would not be misinterpreted or misused when in the hands of individuals not trained to understand them.

Regarding raw test data, Fisher (2003) also stated, "The extent to which HIPAA, state privacy rules, and Standard 9.04 of the Ethics Code will conflict with test copyright laws will be determined over time" (p. 12). Such clarification has been provided by Richard Campanelli, Director of the Office for Civil Rights at the U.S. Department of Health and Human Services, which is responsible for the administration of HIPAA. Campanelli stated, "[A]ny requirement for disclosure of protected health information pursuant to the Privacy Rule is subject to Section 1172(e) of HIPAA, 'Protection of Trade Secrets.' As such, we confirm that it would not be a violation of the Privacy Rule for a covered entity to refrain from providing access to an individual's protected health information, to the extent that doing so would result in a disclosure of trade secrets" (Harcourt Assessment, 2003, p. 1). Thus, HIPAA does not prohibit neuropsychologists from withholding test data when such a release would violate copyright law or when the potential for misinterpretation or misuse exists; in such situations withholding test data would seem to be the preferred action (Bush, 2005a; Bush, Connell, & Denney, 2006).

"At times HIPAA will preempt state law and at other times state law will preempt HIPAA" (Behnke et al., 2003, p. 164). The neuropsychologist must comply with the law that affords the patient greatest access to health information and greatest privacy from third parties.

Forensic Considerations

When an individual places his or her mental state at issue in a legal matter, certain rights are waived in the interest of justice, including the right to privacy of relevant information. Discovery requirements allow the defense (in civil litigation) access to all relevant information, including neuropsychological records. In forensic evaluation contexts, HIPAA constraints are limited (Connell & Koocher, 2003; Fisher, 2003). HIPAA states that information compiled in anticipation of use in *civil, criminal, and administrative* proceedings is not subject to the same right of review and amendment as is health care information in general [§164.524(a)(1)(ii)] (U.S. Department of Health and Human Services, 2003). In addition, HIPAA's privacy rule allows covered practitioners to disclose protected health information in response to a court order (§164.524), but such disclosure should be limited to the information explicitly covered by the order.

In many forensic contexts the person being evaluated is not "the client." That is, the neuropsychologist is retained by a third party, such as an attorney. In such contexts, the doctor–patient relationship differs in important ways from that of clinical contexts (Bush et al., 2005), including control over the release of confidential information. The neuropsychologist must clarify with all parties from the outset the nature of confidentiality and the manner in which information and data obtained during the evaluation will be protected and released.

ETHICAL CONSIDERATIONS

THE CODE OF ETHICS of a profession is based on the collective values of the professionals, which typically parallel the values of the larger society. The Code of Ethics of the National Association of Social Workers (1999), for example, explicitly ties each ethical principle to an underlying value. U.S. citizens place maximum value on their right to decide how much access others should have to their thoughts, feelings, and other personal information. Beauchamp and Childress (2001) stated, "rules of informed consent and medical confidentiality are rooted in the more general moral requirements of respecting the autonomy of persons and protecting them from harm" (p. 5). Necessary to ensure dignity and freedom of self-determination (Koocher & Keith-Spiegel, 1998), privacy is a core value protected by mental health ethics codes.

The Ethical Principles of Psychologists and Code of Conduct (herein after referred to as the Ethics Code) of the APA (2002) addresses privacy and confidentiality requirements in Ethical Standard 4. Standard 4.01 (Maintaining Confidentiality) states that psychologists have a *primary* obligation to protect confidential information. In addition, psychologists must discuss with persons with whom they have a professional relationship, including competent patients and retaining parties, the relevant limits of confidentiality and the foreseeable uses of the information generated through the services provided (Ethical Standard 4.02, Discussing the Limits of Confidentiality). Ethical Standard 4.05 (Disclosures) states,

> (a) Psychologists may disclose confidential information with the appropriate consent of the organizational client, the individual client/patient, or another legally authorized person on behalf of the client/patient unless prohibited by law.
>
> (b) Psychologists disclose confidential information without the consent of the individual only as mandated by law, or where permitted by law for a valid purpose such as to (1) provided needed professional services; (2) obtain appropriate professional consultations; (3) protect the client/patient, psychologist, or others from

harm; or (4) obtain payment for services from a client/patient, in which instance disclosure is limited to the minimum that is necessary to achieve the purpose.

These sections of the APA Ethics Code underscore the importance that is placed on maximizing patient privacy and allowing patients to exercise as much control as possible over when and to whom information about them is released.

In addition to the Ethics Code, the Standards for Educational and Psychological Testing (American Educational Research Association, 1999) provide guidelines specific to confidentiality in the use of tests. Standard 8.2 states, "Where appropriate, test takers should be provided, in advance, as much information about the test, the testing process, the intended test use, test scoring criteria, testing policy, and confidentiality protection as is consistent with obtaining valid responses" (p. 86). Standard 8.6 states, "Test data maintained in data files should be adequately protected from improper disclosure. Use of facsimile transmission, computer networks, data banks, and other electronic data processing should be restricted to situations in which confidentiality can be reasonably assured" (p. 88). Also, Standard 12.11 states, "Professionals and others who have access to test materials and test results should ensure the confidentiality of the test results and test materials consistent with legal and professional ethics requirements" (pp. 132–133).

An additional resource for neuropsychologists practicing in forensic contexts is the most recent draft of the revised Specialty Guidelines for Forensic Psychologists (Committee on Specialty Guidelines, 2005). Guideline 10 (Privacy, Confidentiality, and Privilege) states, "A forensic psychologist keeps private and in confidence information relating to a client or a party except so far as disclosure is consented to by the client or required or allowed by law." In the following eight subsections of Guideline 10, additional clarification is provided regarding confidentiality in forensic contexts.

PRACTICAL CONSIDERATIONS

NEUROPSYCHOLOGISTS WORK IN a variety of evaluation and treatment contexts, with each context having both shared and unique confidentiality requirements. For example, a neuropsychologist may work in an inpatient or outpatient setting in which multiple health care professionals provide services to the patient. In such settings, patient information is typically shared in a collaborative team process to enhance the patient's treatment experience and ability to benefit from services. However, the patients may not be aware, or because of cognitive deficits may not understand or remember, that the information discussed with the neuropsychologist is shared with the other members of the treatment team. Similarly, with bedside evaluations, the unavoidable presence of roommates and the intrusion of other care providers or custodial personnel may intrude on the patient's privacy.

In some settings, electronic medical records, including neuropsychological records, may be accessible to a variety of employees, including those who do not have direct involvement with the patient. In other instances, such as neuropsychological evaluations of children, or of older adults suspected of having dementia, family members or caregivers may be closely involved in the evaluation and feedback process. In forensic contexts, the potential exists for neuropsychological records to become available to the public. Also, neuropsychological testing performed by a technician or with the use of a translator immediately inserts a third party into the doctor–patient relationship. As these examples illustrate, neuropsychologists frequently provide services in contexts with inherent limitations to patient privacy and confidentiality. As Beauchamp and Childress (2001) stated, "We necessarily surrender some of our privacy when we grant others access to our personal histories and bodies, but we also retain some control over information generated about us, at least in diagnostic and therapeutic contexts and in research" (p. 303).

Despite the traditionally fundamental emphasis on confidentiality in psychology, and in medicine more broadly, most neuropsychological evaluations are performed with the advanced knowledge and expectation of all parties that the results will be shared with others, whether it is a referring doctor, an attorney, a family member, a school district, or another interested party. Except in cases of severe cognitive impairment, the person being evaluated typically understands before they enter the neuropsychologist's office that the information provided by the patient and the test results obtained will be disclosed to other identified parties. Nevertheless, patients generally do not fully appreciate all of the potential threats to confidentiality, and they may expect more rigorous safeguarding of personal information than actually exists (Weiss, 1982). Some have argued that the traditional notion of confidentiality in medicine is outdated and no longer exists, given that so many unidentified parties (e.g., clinical and support staff in medical settings and employees of managed care companies) often have access to patient information (Friedland, 1994; Siegler, 1982). Patient expectations and the multitude of possible threats to confidentiality not withstanding, neuropsychologists have a fundamental responsibility to describe to all relevant parties the foreseeable limits to confidentiality and the anticipated uses of the information obtained.

Patients, with few exceptions, have the right to rescind their prior consent to have information about them released to third parties.

However, rescinding such consent is paramount to breaking a promise and puts the neuropsychologist in a difficult position with regard to the referral source, payor, and other involved parties after having performed an evaluation in good faith. When a patient revokes consent to release evaluation results, it is likely because the results are not favorable (e.g., a diagnosis of malingering) or the recommendations run counter to their wishes (e.g., recommending supervised living for an older adult diagnosed with dementia).

VIGNETTE

DR. A. CONDUCTED A neuropsychological evaluation of Mrs. M. who tripped and fell at work, reportedly striking her head on a cabinet. Her payment source is worker's compensation, and she is involved in personal injury litigation. However, she was referred to Dr. A. by her neurologist for clinical services, not from an attorney for forensic purposes.

During the informed consent process, it was clearly established that worker's compensation would be the payor and would require a copy of the neuropsychological report before providing payment for services. Mrs. M. understood all information conveyed during the informed consent process, and she provided her written consent to the evaluation. Dr. A. conducted a clinical interview and then submitted to the worker's compensation carrier a bill, a copy of the brief interview report, and a request for authorization of testing. Dr. A. received written authorization from the worker's compensation carrier for 11 hours of neuropsychological testing.

Dr. A. subsequently performed the testing, which revealed that the patient had put forth poor effort (i.e., she failed symptom validity tests and had numerous other indicators that she was exaggerating or fabricating symptomatology), wrote the report, and had a feedback session with Mrs. M. and her husband. As expected, Mrs. M. was not pleased to hear that the test results were consistent with invalid responding. She became very angry and voiced her concern about the possible implications the evaluation could have for her worker's compensation benefits and her lawsuit. She also took issue with a number of Dr. A.'s recommendations; for example, based on her report that she had left a shirt on a stove while cooking and started a fire and that her driving had become unsafe, Dr. A. recommended that she not cook unless supervised and not drive until she passed a driving evaluation performed by a qualified driving instructor.

By the end of the feedback session Mrs. M. was extremely angry and, while yelling, stated that she did not want Dr. A. to release the report to anyone. In effect, she rescinded her original consent to have the evaluation results sent to her referring neurologist and to her worker's compensation carrier. Dr. A.'s reminder that he needed to release the report for clinical and billing purposes was met with no reply. Dr. A. then offered to discuss the issue further with Mrs. M. at a later time or to refer her to another clinician, but she stated that she never wanted to speak to Dr. A. again.

Following the feedback session, Dr. A. was confronted with two questions related to confidentiality: (1) Is it ethical to release the report to the worker's compensation carrier in order to get paid?, and (2) What kind of feedback, if any, should be given to the referring neurologist? He turned to an ethical decision-making model (Bush, 2005b; Bush et al., 2006) to help clarify his options. He first pursued direction related to billing.

Identify the Problem

Dr. a. wanted to be paid for his services and felt an obligation to inform the referring neurologist of the outcome of the evaluation.

Consider the Significance of the Context and Setting

Although the patient was seen for a clinical evaluation, she was involved in litigation and initially elected to have her worker's compensation carrier pay for the neuropsychological evaluation, thereby bringing into the evaluation context the limitations to confidentiality inherent in forensic contexts.

Identify and Utilize Ethical and Legal Resources

Dr. a. reviewed the laws of his jurisdiction and found that they were silent on this specific matter. He then reviewed the APA Ethics Code, which states, in Ethical Standard 4.05 (Disclosures), subsection b, "Psychologists disclose confidential information without the consent of the individual only as mandated by law, or where permitted by law for a valid purpose such as to...obtain payment for services from a client/payment, in which instance disclosure is limited to the minimum that is necessary to achieve the purpose." To be thorough, Dr. A. also consulted trusted and experienced colleagues, an ethics committee, and his liability insurance carrier.

Consider Personal Beliefs and Values

Dr. A. believed that he provided services in good faith, based upon the agreement with the patient established in the initial session, and he was confident that he should be paid for the evaluation. He also valued the relationship with the referring neurologist and believed that he had a responsibility to inform the neurologist of the outcome of the neuropsychological evaluation. In addition, although angry at the patient, Dr. A. respected both her desire to control her personal information and her right to do so.

DEVELOP POSSIBLE SOLUTIONS TO THE PROBLEM

A. Submit the report with the bill as instructed by the worker's compensation carrier. Dr. A. had already been informed that the neuropsychological report was the minimum information necessary to obtain payment.

B. Give the patient the option of paying for the evaluation herself.

C. Employ the services of a collection agency, which would require the release of minimal identifying and personal information rather than a copy of a potentially damaging report.

D. Consider the situation a learning experience and not pursue payment.

E. Submit the bill to the worker's compensation carrier with the hope that payment would follow without a request for further documentation.

During this process, Dr. A. began to question the manner in which consent was rescinded. He considered that because consent was provided in writing, consent would also have to be rescinded in writing, which Mrs. M. had not done. However, he determined that such a requirement was not established by law and, as a result, reliance on this assumption was too risky.

CONSIDER THE POTENTIAL CONSEQUENCES OF VARIOUS SOLUTIONS

A. Dr. A. realized that, from the perspective of professional ethics, he may be able to defend releasing his report in order to obtain payment; however, he also understood that he risked facing a complaint to the state psychology board from the patient for doing so. Even if it were determined that his actions were appropriate, such a determination would be quite costly in terms of time, finances, and emotional duress.

B. The worker's compensation carrier was already aware that the evaluation had been performed and could subpoena the report, even if the carrier were no longer being billed for the evaluation. In this scenario, the patient risked losing both the money for the evaluation and containment of the findings.

C. Dr. A. considered that a collection agency may be able to obtain the fees due; however, he also worried that use of a collection may provide the impetus needed for Mrs. A. to file a complaint with the state psychology board, the defense of which was not worth his effort.

D. Dr. A. considered forgiving the debt to be a reasonable, albeit personally painful, option. While there was no benefit from this option, there was no risk either.

E. Dr. A. saw in this option the remote possibility of receiving payment without going against the wishes of the patient and risking an adverse reaction from the patient.

CHOOSE AND IMPLEMENT A COURSE OF ACTION

DR. A. ELECTED to pursue option E. He submitted only the bill to the worker's compensation carrier, with the hope that it would be paid without the usual supporting documentation.

With regard to discussing the results of the evaluation with the referring neurologist, Dr. A. found no guidelines describing the nature or extent of the information that should be conveyed to the referral source in such situations. He determined that consistent with Ethical Principle B (Fidelity and Responsibility), he had an obligation to convey some information about the evaluation to the referring neurologist. He decided to inform the neurologist that the evaluation had been performed as requested but that, following the evaluation, the patient rescinded her consent to have the results conveyed to anyone, including the neurologist.

ASSESS THE OUTCOME AND IMPLEMENT CHANGES AS NEEDED

DR. A. NEVER received payment for the neuropsychological evaluation. However, he was determined to avoid this dilemma in the future by, in cases of third-party payors, adopting a policy of not providing feedback to patients until the bills and supporting documentation were already submitted. This policy would be fully explained to patients, and their consent would be obtained prior to conducting the evaluation.

The neurologist was sympathetic to the neuropsychologist's dilema. Being experienced with medicolegal work, the neurologist made what were ultimately correct assumptions about the results of the neuropsychological evaluation.

RECOMMENDATIONS

O NCE A DETERMINATION has been made that patient communications must be disclosed, it is important to determine
which information will be shared and the manner in which the information will be disclosed. In making these determinations, two principles should be considered, the *Parsimony Principle* and the *Law of No
Surprises* (Behnke et al., 2003).

The Parsimony Principles indicates that only the information necessary to achieve the purpose of the disclosure should be released. The
Law of No Surprises indicates that all reasonable steps should be taken
to inform patients at the outset of the relationship of the circumstances
under which disclosure of information to a third party will occur. This
principle "is founded upon a clinical truism: You never want your client
to be surprised when you disclose confidential information...disclo-
sure of information should be done together with the client whenever
possible" (Behnke et al., 2003, p. 30).

Informing patients of the extent and limits of confidentiality should
occur at the beginning of the professional relationship during the informed consent process and thereafter as needed to ensure the
patient's continued understanding of their privacy rights and the
exceptions to such rights. When dilemmas arise, the use of an ethical
decision-making model can help facilitate an acceptable resolution.
However, an attempt should be made to anticipate dilemmas that
may be encountered in the context(s) in which one practices, using
the decision-making model to derive solutions to avoid or quickly and
appropriately resolve ethical challenges. Although it is impossible to
anticipate all of the potential threats to confidentiality, a personal
commitment to ethical practice and a proactive approach to identifying and resolving ethical challenges will maximize the likelihood
that the values deemed important by the patient, the neuropsychologist, and the profession will find a point of mutual acceptance and
satisfaction.

CONCLUSIONS

N EUROPSYCHOLOGISTS OFTEN PRACTICE in contexts that
have the potential to limit patient privacy and confidentiality. In
addition, working with patients who possess impaired mental status
poses unique challenges to practitioners. As a result, neuropsychologists must be proactive in anticipating potential ethical challenges and
in identifying appropriate courses of action to meet the challenges
confronted while performing professional activities. The freedom of

competent adults to allow or restrict access to their bodies, thoughts, and feelings has long been a fundamental value of medicine and the cornerstone of clinical psychology, and neuropsychologists are obligated to defend that value. With solid training and a personal commitment to patient welfare, neuropsychologists are well positioned to do so.

NOTES

1. From the Hippocratic Oath; translated from Greek by Ludwig Edelstein. Retrieved June 23, 2006, from HYPERLINK "http://www.pbs.org/wgbh/nova/doctors/oath_classical.html" www.pbs.org/wgbh/nova/doctors/oath_classical.html.

2. The term "patient" is used throughout the chapter to refer to individuals seen for evaluation or treatment. Other terms such as "examinee," "client," or "consumer" may be used to describe more specific types of relationships between the practitioner and other individuals.

REFERENCES

American Educational Research Association. (1999). *Standards for educational and psychological testing.* Washington, DC: American Educational Research Association, American Psychological Association, National Council on Measurement in Education.

American Psychological Association. (2002). Ethical principles of psychologists and code of conduct. *American Psychologist, 57*(12), 1060–1073.

Appelbaum, P. S. (2002). Privacy in psychiatric treatment: Threats and responses. *American Journal of Psychiatry, 159,* 1809–1818.

Beauchamp, T. L., & Childress, J. F. (2001). *Principles of biomedical ethics* (5th ed.). New York: Oxford University Press.

Behnke, S. H., Perlin, M. L., & Bernstein, M. (2003). *The essentials of New York mental health law: A straightforward guide for clinicians of all disciplines.* New York: W. W. Norton & Company.

Bersoff, D. N. (1999). Confidentiality, privilege, and privacy. In D. N. Bersoff (Ed.), *Ethical conflicts in psychology* (2nd ed., pp. 149–150). Washington, DC: American Psychological Association.

Bowers v. Hardwick, 478 U.S. 186. (1985).

Bush, S. S. (2005a). Differences between the 1992 and 2002 Ethics Codes: A brief overview. In S. S. Bush (Ed.), *A casebook of ethical challenges in neuropsychology* (pp. 1–8). New York: Psychology Press.

Bush, S. S. (2005b). Ethical issues in forensic neuropsychology: Introduction. *Journal of Forensic Neuropsychology, 4*(3), 1–9.

Bush, S. S., Barth, J. T., Pliskin, N. H., Arffa, S., Axelrod, B. N., Blackburn, L. A., et al. (2005). Independent and court-ordered forensic neuropsychological examinations: Official statement of the National Academy of Neuropsychology. *Archives of Clinical Neuropsychology, 20*(8), 997–1007.

Bush, S. S., Connell, M. A., & Denney, R. L. (2006). *Ethical issues in forensic psychology: A systematic model for decision making.* Washington, DC: American Psychological Association.

Committee on Specialty Guidelines. (2005). *Specialty guidelines for forensic psychologists,* revision draft. Retrieved July 5, 2006, from www.ap-ls.org/links/SGFP%20version%202.0%20of%2002–14–05%20for%20posting%20to%20the%20discussion%20list.pdf

Connell, M., & Koocher, G. (2003). HIPAA & forensic practice. *American Psychology Law Society News, 23,* 16–19.

Eisenstadt v. Baird, 405 U.S. 438. (1972).

Fisher, C. B. (2003). Test data standard most notable change in new APA ethics code. *The National Psychologist,* Jan/Feb, 12–13.

Friedland, B. (1994). Physician-patient confidentiality: Time to re-examine a venerable concept in light of contemporary society and advances in medicine. *Journal of Legal Medicine, 15,* 249–277.

Griswold v. Connecticut, 381 U.S. 479. (1965).

Harcourt Assessment. (2003). *HIPAA position statement.* Retrieved April 5, 2004, from http://marketplace.psychcorp.com

Haut, M. W., & Muehleman, T. (1986). Informed consent: The effects of clarity and specificity on disclosure in a clinical interview. *Psychotherapy, 23,* 93–101.

Hawaii Psychiatric Society v. Ariyoshi, 481 F. Supp. 1028. (D. Hawaii, 1979).

Koocher, G. P., & Keith-Spiegel, P. (1998). *Ethics in psychology: Professional standards and cases* (2nd ed.). New York: Oxford University Press.

Kremer, T. G., & Gesten, E. L. (1998). Confidentiality limits of managed care and clients' willingness to self-disclose. *Professional Psychology: Research and Practice, 29,* 553–558.

Merriam-Webster. (1988). *Webster's 9th new collegiate dictionary.* Springfield, MA: Merriam-Webster, Inc.

National Association of Social Workers. (1999). *Code of Ethics of the National Association of Social Workers.* Retrieved July 5, 2006, from www.socialworkers.org/pubs/codenew/code.asp

Nowell, D., & Spruill, J. (1993). If it's not absolutely confidential, will information be disclosed? *Professional Psychology: Research and Practice, 24,* 367–369.

Rapp, D. L., & Ferber, P. S. (2003). To release, or not to release raw test data, that is the question. In A. M. Horton, Jr., & L. C. Hartlage (Eds.), *Handbook of forensic neuropsychology* (pp. 337–368). New York: Springer Publishing Company.

Roe v. Wade, 410 U.S. 113. (1973).

Siegler, M. (1982). Confidentiality in medicine—A decrepit concept. *New England Journal of Medicine, 307*, 1518–1521.

Smith-Bell, M., & Winslade, W. J. (1999). Privacy, confidentiality, and privilege in psychotherapeutic relationships. In D. N. Bersoff (Ed.), *Ethical conflicts in psychology* (2nd ed., pp. 151–155). Washington, DC: American Psychological Association.

Tarasoff v. Regents of the University of California, 551 P.2d 334 (Cal. 1976).

Taube, D. O., & Elwork, A. (1990). Researching the effects of confidentiality law on patients' self-disclosures. *Professional Psychology: Research and Practice, 2*, 72–75.

U.S. Department of Health and Human Services. (2003). *Public Law 104–191: Health Insurance Portability and Accountability Act of 1996.* Retrieved November 24, 2003, from www.hhs.gov/ocr/hipaa/

Weiss, B. D. (1982). Confidentiality expectations of patients, physicians, and medical students. *Journal of the American Medical Association, 247*, 2695–2697.

Whalen v. Roe, 429 U.S. 589. (1976).

Woods, K. M., & McNamara, J. R. (1980). Confidentiality: Its effect on interviewee behavior. *Professional Psychology, 11*, 714–721.

Section IV

Special Populations in Neuropsychology

18

The Neuropsychology of Traumatic Brain Injury

Thomas L. Bennett and Michael J. Raymond

THE ANNUAL INCIDENCE of traumatic brain injury (TBI) in the United States varies among leading experts and published articles. However, it is clear that well over 1 million TBIs occur at varying degrees (e.g., mild–severe). According to Langlois, Marr, Mitchko, and Johnson (2005), approximately 1–4 million TBIs were estimated to have occurred. However, they prefaced this estimate by suggesting that "this number most likely underestimates this problem" as the result of many individuals having never sought treatment or subsequently never being diagnosed, hence, the term or reference, the "silent epidemic" was established. Approximately one-quarter to one-third of those who received only emergency room evaluation and care will still experience persisting sequelae secondary to their brain injuries (e.g., Rimel, Giordani, Barth, Boll, & Jane, 1981). Of the millions of annual TBI cases, about 500,000 require acute hospitalization (Caveness, 1977; Frankowski, 1986), and these latter individuals are at even greater risk for persisting difficulties including sensory and motor deficits, cognitive impairments, personality change, and noncognitive sequelae that can lead to prolonged or permanent disability. Indeed, it is estimated that each year 70,000 to 90,000 TBI survivors are left with serious physical and cognitive impairments that preclude their reintegration into the community (Finlayson & Garner, 1994). Approximately 300,000 fatalities are reported each year (Rimel et al., 1981). These observations underscore the fact that TBI is a major medical and socioeconomic concern.

After Congress passed the TBI Act of 1996 (Public Law 104–166), an effort by the Center for Disease Control and Prevention (CDC) was made to systematically gather data and track the incidence of TBI. Data, as described in Table 18.1 is part of the "surveillance" that is conducted by the CDC to assist in designing, evaluating, and implementing programs for public health (Langlois et al., 2005).

EPIDEMIOLOGY AND ETIOLOGY OF TBI

THE IMPACT OF TBI on our society is underscored by the fact that 70% of injured individuals are 30 years old or younger; the peak incidence of TBI is in the age range of 15–24 (Rimel, Jane, & Bond, 1990).

TABLE 18.1 TBI Surveillance Data

Abbreviated Injury Score-Head*
Age
Blood Alcohol Concentration*
County of Injury
County of Residence
Date of Admission
Date of Birth
Date of Death
Date of Discharge
Date of Injury
Diagnosis Codes (ICD-9-CM or ICD-10)
Ethnicity (Hispanic versus non-Hispanic)
External Cause of Injury Codes (E Codes)
Glasgow Coma Scale Score*
Glasgow Outcome Scale Score (modified, abstractor assigned)*
Intracranial Lesion*
Level of Consciousness
Motor Vehicle Position (e.g., driver, passenger)*
Payment Source
Personal Protective Equipment*
Race
Sex
Skull Fracture*
Sports and Recreation-related*
State of Injury
State of Residence
Work-related

*Abstracted from medical records.

TBI is the leading cause of death in adults under the age of 35. Survivors of severe TBI may have disabling persisting deficits that will require life-long care, and even among those whose problems are relatively mild to moderate, career goals and achievement may be significantly adversely impacted. While the causes of TBI are varied, motor vehicle accidents continue to be the primary source of such injuries.

In an epidemiological study of approximately 3,400 mild TBI victims conducted in San Diego County by Kraus and Nourjah (1989), almost 42% of brain injuries involved a motor vehicle crash in which the injured person was an occupant of the vehicle (64%), a motorcyclist (20%), a pedestrian (10%), or riding a bicycle (6%). Falls were the second most frequent cause of brain injuries (23%), and assaults, including bullet wounds, were the third leading cause of brain injury. Sports, recreational activities, as well as bicycle accidents not involving a motor vehicle, each accounted for 6% of the total. Unfortunately, these statistics (e.g., percentages) have not drastically changed over the years despite research and implementation of preventable measures (e.g., airbags, helmets). Guidelines regarding management strategies for sports concussion have been published by Kelly (1990) and updated by Collins et al. (2003).

Gender differences were noted by Kraus and Nourjah (1989), an observation that has been confirmed by other investigators. In the San Diego County study, it was found that the rate for males was about twice the rate as for females. Thus, the person at greatest risk for TBI is a male in the age range of 15–24. This is related to a number of factors including inexperience in operating a motor vehicle and knowing its limits, risk-taking behavior, a sense of invincibility, and experimentation with drugs and alcohol (and many times not being aware that they are under its influence). Alcohol has been implicated in at least one-third of all brain injuries (Rimel et al., 1990). Approximately 70% of automobile related deaths result from brain injury. As previously noted, automobile safety devices will certainly lower the risk, but it is clear that severe TBI will continue to occur in individuals who are restrained and whose airbag deploys; statistics have not drastically changed!

NEUROPATHOLOGY OF TRAUMATIC BRAIN INJURY

PRIMARY AND SECONDARY BRAIN INJURY

TRAUMATIC BRAIN INJURY results in two categories of brain injury: primary and secondary. As discussed by Pang (1989), primary brain injury occurs at the instant of impact, and it produces direct damage to brain tissue. Secondary brain injury, on the other hand, occurs as a result of epiphenomena causally related to the primary injury, and these events in turn can produce damage to the brain. Among the latter, for example, are such events as epidural, subdural, or intracerebral hematomas and cerebral edema; these may, in turn, raise intracerebral pressure (ICP) and cause brain shift, herniation, or ischemia, which may produce brain infarction and necrosis. Unlike brain damage produced by primary impact injury, secondary brain injury may be preventable if the antecedent epiphenomena (i.e., hematomas and/or cerebral edema) are promptly treated. Modern acute medical management of TBI affects outcome through minimization of the occurrence of secondary brain injuries.

Focal Brain Injury

For an excellent discussion of the physics and pathophysiology of TBI, the reader is referred to Pang (1989). Mechanisms that produce primary brain damage result in two categories of brain injury: focal brain injury and diffuse axonal injury (DAI). When focal brain injury is present, it is typically superimposed on a background of more generalized brain damage (Bigler, 1990, 1996). Focal injury results from the collision of the brain with the rough interior surface of the skull at the instant of impact. The greatest brain-bone interfaces occur in the orbitofrontal region of the frontal lobes and in the anterior two-thirds of the temporal lobes, and these are the most common sites for cerebral contusions to occur. Such contusions result regardless of the site or the direction of the initial impact (Bigler, 1990, 1996). A coup (site of impact) or contrecoup (opposite site) injury is likely and will produce focal or multifocal brain damage.

Diffuse Axonal Injury (Generalized Brain Damage)

As indicated, focal injury, when present, is observed against a background of generalized brain damage, and neuropsychological deficits observed in TBI patients are predominantly the consequence of generalized brain injury. We refer to generalized brain damage as diffuse axonal injury (DAI) to emphasize that the physiological basis of such brain damage is direct damage to the axons or their interfaces with adjacent neurons at the synapse. The forces that produce such injury are referred to as the shear-strain effect. This shear-strain effect, as originally observed by Holbourn (1943) and later by Strich (1961) and Gennarelli (1990), was the result of rapid brain movement within the cranial vault causing stretching of white matter fibers and eventual degeneration. These "microscopic" injuries were attributed to even mild brain trauma and eventually verified by Nevin (1967) and Oppenheimer (1968) through their histological (cell) staining techniques. Damage at the cellular level was often diffused, involving both cortical and subcortical regions. Loss of consciousness often occurs following alterations of the brainstem and subsequent interference of the ascending reticular activating pathways. In addition to the upper and lower brainstem, the frontotemporal regions are especially prone to damage due to bony contours of the skull.

Acceleration and deceleration forces at the instant of brain injury produce rotational or twisting effects on brain tissue. This action stretches neuronal fibers that interconnect different brain regions. This frequently results in the tearing of axons or the shearing of synaptic connections. Damage to supportive oligodendroglia cells can disrupt brain myelin. While superficial contusions are undoubtedly the basis for focal sensorimotor deficits and post-traumatic seizures, DAI is the basis for irreversible disturbance of consciousness and most of the generalized cognitive dysfunction seen in TBI victims (e.g., decreased processing speed, distractibility, forgetfulness, etc.). While DAI effects are widely distributed, they are understandably most notable in regions that have high white matter concentrations. DAI is most frequently observed in the gray–white matter junctional regions around the basal ganglia, the periventricular zone of the hypothalamus, the superior cerebellar peduncles, the fornices, the corpus callosum, and fiber tracts of the brainstem (Pang, 1989).

The clinical significance of DAI is obvious when one considers the fact that in severe TBI countless microscopic shearing injuries occur simultaneously and can virtually isolate different cortical regions from one another and disconnect the cortex from subcortical structures. This phenomenon is most vividly demonstrated by individuals in a persistent vegetative state. Such individuals may cough, chew, and swallow, and they appear to visually follow or track a noise or bright light, but there is no content to their apparent consciousness, because they do not show any signs of either interpreting or responding to the external world in any meaningful way. These individuals appear as if cortical regions are isolated from all external and internal input, have no way of interacting with one another, and have no means of projecting responses outward through the subcortical motor pathways (Pang, 1989).

METABOLIC CHANGES

METABOLIC CHANGES FOLLOWING TBI are common and likely more readily identified or suspected in mild (e.g., concussion) versus more significant injuries. This is due to a dearth of structural brain changes following concussions; neuroradiological studies (e.g., CT Scan, MRI) typically yield negative results.

In animal research (rodent model), Hovda, Prins, Becker, et al. (1999) reported metabolic alterations and intra/extra cellular changes following TBI. While it is often difficult to extrapolate any type of pathological change from animal to human studies, it is clear that individuals, following even mild TBI, are prone for hyperglycolysis (Bergschneider, Hovda & Shalmon, 2003). This reaction occurs following the release of excitatory amino acids and activation of increased sodium and potassium. The end result may be neurovascular constriction and subsequent reduced cerebral blood flow. It is surmised that this reaction is the result of initial increased "cerebral energy" and possible storage of endothelial calcium following cerebral trauma. The duration of such changes remains unclear, however, they may persist for weeks post trauma.

NEUROIMAGING IN TBI EVALUATION

BECAUSE OF TECHNOLOGICAL advances in brain imaging since the 1970s, the structural integrity of the brain can be studied in TBI patients via computerized tomography (CT) or magnetic resonance imaging (MRI). Neuroimaging has revolutionized neurosurgical management of TBI in the acute treatment stages. While the details and clarity of the images obtained via MRI are typically superior to those obtained via CT scans, the time and sustained compliance required to obtain MRI images may prove problematic in neurologically compromised individuals. As reviewed by Ruff, Cullum, and Luerrsen (1989), CT scanning appears to be of sufficient sensitivity to detect those mass lesions that would necessitate immediate surgical intervention. Focal cerebral contusions can also be demonstrated using either imaging methodology.

Once the patient is medically stable, they enter into the chronic treatment stages. Brain imaging is beneficial at this point for tracking the size of hematomas; expansion of a hematoma may require its evacuation. While both CT and MRI studies can detect the location and size of surgically significant hematomas, MRI is clearly better for detecting smaller hematomas, particularly in areas not well visualized by CT such as the anterior temporal lobes (Ruff et al., 1989). Brain swelling and cerebral edema can likewise be detected or serially investigated by both neuroimaging techniques, but MRI is more sensitive to these phenomena. Common signs of acute brain swelling include midline shift and compression of the ventricles.

One of the most common delayed changes in gross brain morphology following severe TBI is ventricular enlargement, and this is an obvious sign that can be detected via neuroimaging techniques. In some cases, this reflects an obvious hydrocephalus secondary to the cerebrospinal fluid (CSF) pathways being obstructed in some way following TBI. Symptomatically, we observe a cessation in recovery followed by a slow deterioration in cognitive skills, increased ataxia, and decreased bladder control. This is a relatively rare occurrence, but it can be treated by ventricular peritoneal (VP) shunting, and subsequently further recovery will be observed (Miller, Pentland, & Berrol, 1990).

Unfortunately, the most common cause of a delayed increase in the size of the ventricles in TBI patients is related to DAI. In this case, the enlarged ventricles are simply a consequence of a reduction in the bulk of cerebral white matter allowing the ventricles to expand to replace the volume within the skull; this expansion process typically stabilizes at around 9–12 weeks post injury (Bigler, Kurth, Blatter, & Abildskov, 1992). This type of ventricular enlargement is called *hydrocephalus ex-vacuo,* and CSF shunting is of no benefit in these cases. As would be expected, *ex-vacuo* ventricular enlargement is strongly correlated with the presence of severe neuropsychological impairment of TBI survivors, and it seems to be correlated in a relatively linear way (e.g., Cullum & Bigler, 1986; Johnson, Bigler, Burr, & Blatter, 1994).

CT and MRI studies are anatomical studies that seek to clarify brain injury by depicting structural lesions resulting in the brain following trauma. This contrasts with neuropsychological testing, as will be discussed later in this chapter, which seeks to determine the integrity of brain cognitive functions regardless of the gross structural status of the brain. Neuroimaging studies that evaluate functions of the brain indirectly by evaluating changes in the brain region's metabolism or blood flow (under the assumption that abnormalities reflect disruption of brain function) include PET, SPECT, and fMRI. A review of these methods is beyond the scope of this chapter. A recent review of the efficacy of SPECT as a diagnostic tool in mild TBI is provided by Davalos and Bennett (2002). All of these methods, from a forensic perspective, are still considered investigational, and it has generally been concluded that these methodologies do not meet the Daubert rule for admissibility in the court room. On the other hand, many would conclude that such data can be confirmatory of neuropsychological testing data, and certainly more research is needed on this topic. Recent published studies have concluded that SPECT, for example, is valuable in detecting neurophysiologic abnormalities in mild TBI patients that are not detectable with conventional CT and MRI imaging techniques (Audenaert et al., 2003; Bonne et al., 2003; Umile, Sandel, Alavi, Terry, & Plotkin, 2002).

CONCEPTUALIZING THE SEVERITY OF TRAUMATIC BRAIN INJURY

THE SEVERITY OF traumatic brain injury is typically conceptualized by resorting to medical descriptors such as duration of loss of consciousness, duration of post-traumatic amnesia, the occurrence of a skull fracture, the presence of extracerebral or intracerebral hematomas, and so forth. This has led to erroneous conclusions in research investigating the effects of TBI on behavior, because much research on this topic assumes that people with a common attribute, for example, duration of loss of consciousness, are similar on other dimensions as well (e.g., preinjury characteristics, type and/or amount of physical brain damage, late complication producing brain injury or lack thereof). Some of the most common medical descriptors that are used to classify the severity of brain injury include the following (Bennett, 1992a).

SKULL AND BRAIN TRAUMAS AS DESCRIPTORS

USING THE *International Classification of Diseases, 9th Revision, Clinical Modification* (ICD-9-CM) diagnostic classification manual, one can describe traumatic brain injury as being a closed head injury (diagnostic codes 850–854), one that is accompanied by a skull fracture (diagnostic categories 800–801 and 803–804), or one that is accompanied by an open wound of the head (diagnostic codes 851–854). Each of these categories can additionally be described, using appropriate modifiers, as being accompanied by cerebral contusion or laceration and by extradural, subdural, subarachnoid, or intracerebral hemorrhage or hematomas (Hart, Hopkins, & Ford, 2005). These diagnostic categories describe the observable events that the trauma produces (via the use of X-ray, CT scan, or MRI methods). Needless to say, the more pronounced the physical damage to the skull and brain, the worse the outcome will be when group data are summarized (e.g., Cullum & Bigler, 1986).

However, these descriptors do not take into account behavioral measures of the acute trauma stage that could prove to be better predictors of eventual outcome than the physical measures often are. For example, a person with an open prefrontal gunshot wound might never experience a loss of consciousness and might appear to function normally according to many behavioral indices, while a person without skull fracture, brain contusion, brain laceration, or intracranial hemorrhage might be rendered permanently comatose. Two relatively simple behavioral measures that have had some success in predicting outcome for groups of TBI victims at the acute stage following injury include duration of loss of consciousness and duration of post-traumatic amnesia. These measures can be considered together as levels of awareness measures.

LEVELS OF AWARENESS MEASURES:
LOSS OF CONSCIOUSNESS

DURATION OF LOSS of consciousness and duration of post-traumatic amnesia are the most common measures used to assess severity of injury and outcome from traumatic brain injury. The ICD-9-CM describes 5 levels of increasing severity according to duration of loss of consciousness. A concussion or brain injury can be accompanied by mental confusion or disorientation, without loss of consciousness (850.0), by loss of consciousness for less than one hour (850.1), by loss of consciousness for 1–24 hours, by loss of consciousness for greater than 24 hours with complete recovery, and by loss of consciousness for greater than 24 hours without return to pre-existing consciousness level. In general, people who experience longer durations of unconsciousness have more brain injury and more enduring impairment (e.g., Jennett & Teasdale, 1981).

However, coma or loss of consciousness is not an all-or-none phenomenon. As a result, it is difficult to use the simple ICD-9-CM categories, and a better approach is to assess the level of consciousness of the acute TBI victim. Teasdale and Jennett's (1974) Glasgow Coma Scale (GCS) allows one to make such an assessment. This simply administered procedure consists of evaluating the person on three continua: eyes opening, motor responses, and verbal responses to standard stimuli. The highest score obtained on each factor is added together, and the highest possible score is 15. Ninety percent of patients with a score of 8 or less are in coma and regarded as having a severe injury. Patients who score 9 or greater are not in coma. While as indicated, duration of loss of consciousness correlates with severity of eventual impairment (e.g., Brooks, 1990), the correlation is far from perfect, as can be illustrated by cases of so-called "mild brain injury" or mild TBI (e.g., postconcussion). This will be further discussed in this chapter.

The Mild Traumatic Brain Injury Committee of the Head Injury Interdisciplinary Special Interest Group of the American Congress of Rehabilitation Medicine provided a revised definition of mild TBI (1993). According to these criteria, a person with mild TBI is a person who has traumatically induced physiological disruption of brain function as manifested by *at least one* (not necessarily all) of the following:

1. Any period of loss of consciousness up to approximately 30 minutes duration. After 30 minutes, the person must obtain an initial Glasgow Coma Scale of 13–15 (of a possible 15);
2. Any loss of memory for events immediately before or after the accident (retrograde or anterograde amnesia);
3. Any alteration of mental state at the time of the accident (e.g., feeling dazed, disoriented, or confused);
4. Focal neurological deficit, which may or may not be transient (in the past, mild head trauma was ruled out if focal signs persisted);
5. Post-traumatic amnesia not greater than 24 hours.

This definition includes instances in which TBI is produced by hitting the head, the head being struck, or instances in which TBI is produced by a whiplash injury in which the head is not hit. In essence, an individual *does not* need to hit their head to sustain a TBI and, conversely, if an individual does hit their head, it does not necessarily result in a TBI. Thus, the reason why the term "head injury" is considered obsolete and replaced by the term TBI. CT or MRI scans may be read as normal. However, it is important to note that CT and MRI will, at times, albeit rarely, detect intracranial lesions following mild TBI (Jenkins, Teasdale, Hadley, MacPhearson, & Rowan, 1986; Levin, Amparo et al., 1987), even in individuals with no documented loss of consciousness (Levi, Guildburd, Lemberger, Soustiel, & Feinsod, 1990). While we continue to use the term, such findings would question the validity of the concept of "mild or minor" brain injury.

While a single uncomplicated mild TBI typically produces no significant permanent neurocognitive or behavioral impairment in the majority of individuals (Levin, Mattis et al., 1987), it is also the case that mild brain injuries are capable of producing persisting neuropsychological deficits (e.g., Barth et al., 1983; Carlson, Svardsudd, & Welin, 1987; Leinenger, Gramling, Fanell, Kreutzer, & Peck, 1990; Rimel et al., 1981; Yarnell & Rossi, 1988).

Thus, duration of loss of consciousness, while a good predictor of group outcomes, does not adequately predict outcome on a case by case basis. A second level of awareness measure used to index severity of TBI and to predict outcome is duration of post-traumatic amnesia. It may improve prediction of outcome over duration of loss of consciousness, because it likely reflects the health of the brain after the acute insult.

LEVELS OF AWARENESS MEASURES: DURATION OF POST-TRAUMATIC AMNESIA

FOR MOST TBI victims, duration of loss of consciousness if experienced, is short, but cognitive processes may be significantly disrupted for a prolonged period of time. Post-traumatic amnesia (PTA) has been used as an alternative assessment procedure, because it reflects neuropsychological functioning, to some extent, after the acute injury. PTA is the period of time from the injury (including coma time) until the point at which on-going memory for events becomes fairly stable. Russell (1932) was the first to propose the use of this measure, and he viewed the duration of PTA as an index of the extent of brain damage. In a recent study by Collins and associates (2003) regarding outcomes of sports-related concussion (e.g., group of 78 college and high school athletes), they determined that PTA, rather than LOC, was a better marker and more predictive of post-concussive problems at 3 days post trauma.

Although beneficial, this measure does not possess the specificity we would hope for as a predictor of eventual outcome. As with duration of loss of consciousness, there is a statistically significant relationship between PTA duration and cognitive performance, with an increasing duration of PTA being positively correlated with increasing cognitive impairment (Brooks, 1990). However, these correlations, while statistically significant, are far from linear, leaving much variance unexplained, and in fact, relatively brief PTA (less than an hour) has been associated with significant brain injury (Brooks, 1990; Jennett, 1986). With this limitation in mind, in his original paper, Russell related duration of PTA to severity of injury in the following way:

1. Less than 5 minutes = very mild injury
2. 5 minutes to less than 1 hour = mild injury
3. 1 hour to less than 24 hours = moderate injury
4. 1 to 7 days = severe injury
5. Longer than 7 days = very severe injury

Length of PTA can often be established by asking the patient questions about the accident and later events or by asking such questions as "What is the first thing you remember after the accident?" One needs to be careful in this regard because often, particularly if days or weeks have passed since the accident, the patient may report information that has been provided to them by friends or family. This is an inherent difficulty in querying a patient retrospectively.

Determining the end of PTA is also complicated by the fact that patients may communicate and visit with others while still experiencing PTA. In addition, many patients will also have "islands" of memory prior to the onset of continuous memory (e.g., remembering a visit from a friend), but these can usually be identified by the patient as such. Questioning relatives can be helpful in establishing the end of PTA. They will often describe it as a time when the patient became lucid and began remembering recent conversations and events.

Sometimes the end stage of PTA and the return of continuous memory will coincide with a specific event, such as seeing a particular visitor in the hospital, being moved from one unit of the hospital to another, or being discharged home. Indeed, Bond (1990) indicated that full consciousness may be reestablished in children, for whom PTA is prolonged, by sending them home to a familiar environment. Jennet and Teasdale (1981) report that an approximate guide to the relationship between the return of speech and the end of PTA is to multiply the return of speech interval by a factor of four (assuming that the patient does not have a specific factor delaying the return of speech).

Recently, tests have been devised to move us from retrospectively assessing the end of PTA to prospectively doing so. Such bedside brief mental status evaluation tools assess the patient's ability to recall recent events and the extent of his or her orientation with respect to person, place, and time. The Galveston Orientation and Amnesia Test (GOAT) has been used widely in the United States for this purpose (Levin, O'Donnell, & Grossman, 1979).

Duration of PTA appears to be a better predictor of eventual outcome than duration of loss of consciousness, but Jennett and Teasdale (1981) point out that severe long-term disability typically only results from PTA of greater than 14 days. Even in individuals who have suffered PTA of greater than 14 days, a majority of these individuals were found to make a favorable recovery. As stated earlier, this lack of predictive validity in early measures likely results because of the heterogeneity of the population for which one is attempting to make predictions. Heterogeneity is present because of preinjury differences among the total TBI population (e.g., gender, age, educational level, preinjury I.Q., communication skills, career achievement, personality and psychological adjustment, family support system, etc.) and because of differences in characteristics of the neural insult (in addition to such global characterizations as coma duration, length of PTA, etc.).

MILD TRAUMATIC BRAIN INJURY (MTBI)

AS PREVIOUSLY DISCUSSED, the vast majority of all TBIs are considered "mild" (MTBI). The term or reference to MTBI is often considered analogous to other terms such as concussion or post-concussive syndrome (Raymond, 1989). Most individuals with MTBI have uneventful recoveries, but, depending on the specific research study, it has been estimated that as many as 25–35% of these individuals might experience persistent neurocognitive and behavioral problems at 3–6 months post trauma (Raymond & Bennett, 1999; Raymond, Bennett, Hartlage, & Cullum, 1999). Kibby and Long (1999) opined that many of these individuals with persisting problems who were diagnosed or classified as having a MTBI may have actually sustained a more significant (e.g. moderate) brain injury, and they may have been misclassified because the duration of LOC was the only criterion utilized to evaluate or determine the severity of injury.

Recently, an influx of research studies involving MTBI has come from those individuals gathering data on sports-related concussion. As noted previously, Collins and colleagues (2003), as well as others (e.g., Erlanger et al., 2003), indicated that the best predictor for outcomes and subsequent "return to play" decisions was based on PTA, rather than LOC. Over the years, post-concussion management was based on a set of guidelines and concussion grading system (AAN, 1997; Cantu, 1992, 2001; Kelly, Nichols, & Filley, 1991). As the result of individual variables (e.g., age, LOC, PTA, reported symptoms, prior concussion), these guidelines were revisited and deemed in need of change. Specifically, it was determined that management strategies should be individually developed and not based on a generic grading system.

While formal neuropsychological assessment is the standard in evaluating documented or suspected cognitive or behavioral changes following brain injury, this evaluation system is often prolonged and cumbersome. This is especially true when return-to-play decisions are required shortly after the injury. To address this concern, a number of computerized evaluations were developed including Headminders, Cog State, ANAM (Automated Neuropsychological Assessment Metric), and ImPACT (Immediate Post-Concussion Assessment and Cognitive Testing). Please review the current literature regarding the development and clinical utility of each.

The authors are most familiar with the latter computerized assessment, ImPACT. ImPACT was developed by Lovell, Collins, Podell, Powell, and Maroon (2000) and is utilized throughout the country. It assesses various neurocognitive and behavioral abilities that are often compromised following any degree of TBI. Six composite scores are generated including: verbal memory; visual memory; visual motor speed; reaction time; and impulse control. A symptom score based on a subjective report of symptoms (e.g., checklist) is also included. Baseline and follow-up scores are instrumental in making clinical decisions regarding an individual's ability to resume premorbid activities and to reduce the risk for premature re-entry into sporting activities. This is particularly true in an individual who has sustained a prior concussion, thus, rendering them prone for a second or third concussion, commonly referred to as Second Impact Syndrome (Cantu & Voy, 1995).

ASSESSMENT OF INJURY SEVERITY BASED ON OUTCOME

THE BEST INDICATOR of the severity of a person's TBI is their degree of impairment post-discharge from the hospital. This is reflected by the TBI victim's ability to re-engage in normal activities of daily living (ADL), such as home-making, career, school, and social relationships. In our clinical practices, we have found that one's ability to actually re-engage is best assessed through evaluation by an occupational therapist. Neuropsychological evaluation can investigate one's potential to re-engage in normal activities. An evaluation by a speech and language pathologist can determine the effect that communication difficulties, even if these are not immediately apparent, might have on one's attempts to resume normal daily activities and challenges. The point to be made here is that long-term TBI outcome is best clarified by assessing the post-acute consequences of the injury. The person's level of impairment and persisting brain-injury produced deficits as they are discharged from the hospital and then attempt to resume normal activities at home, work, or school are better predictors of eventual outcome than is a person's condition at the time of the TBI or shortly thereafter.

CLINICAL FEATURES OF TBI SURVIVORS

IN OUR DISCUSSION, we will focus on survivors of TBI who have resultant mild–moderate deficits in cognitive functioning. From a neuropsychological perspective, these individuals are considered the most interesting, and they present with the most challenging assessment and long term rehabilitation issues. Typically, these individuals do not present with significant signs of sensory and motor dysfunction, although, as will be discussed later in this section, they certainly may present with subtle deficits in those areas, which thereby compromise their ability to function at their pre-injury level. In making our observations regarding the characteristics of TBI survivors, we will draw on our clinical experience based on thousands and thousands of evaluations of survivors of brain injury as well as on relevant experimental literature. However, as we have indicated earlier in this chapter, much of the research on brain-injured individuals has lacked proper experimental controls or has been compounded by selection errors; thus, conclusions from these studies must always be viewed cautiously.

The survivor of TBI presents with a constellation of cognitive, affective/personality, and noncognitive symptoms that interact to produce the post-concussive or post-TBI syndrome we observe in these individuals. From a neuropathological perspective, these symptoms primarily reflect the interactions of focal and diffuse brain injury, although diffuse injury appears to be the primary causative factor underlying the symptoms in most individuals. The primary effect of diffuse injury is to cause a slowing or disruption of signal conduction, transmission, or processing. This results in decreased processing speed and efficiency of thinking, difficulty ignoring nonrelevant environmental information, and increased difficulty in retrieval processes. These factors, in turn, result in a disruption of dependent cognitive processes such as attention, learning and memory, perception, communication, problem-solving skills, and general intelligence. Other TBI related problems such as sensory deficits (blurred vision, dizziness, tinnitus), post-traumatic headaches, post-traumatic epilepsy, and psychological factors, such as anxiety and depression may certainly compound any impairments produced by the brain injury itself. Assessment of the TBI survivor requires that all of these factors be considered; this will be further discussed.

MAJOR COGNITIVE SEQUELAE OF TBI

THE MAJOR COGNITIVE sequelae that are present following TBI may include decreased speed and efficiency of information processing, disrupted attention and concentration, problems with learning and memory, mild perceptual disturbances, disorders of communication, difficulties with executive functions, and decreased general intelligence. Clarification of the presence, severity, and contributions of each to the TBI survivor's presenting symptoms is dependent, of course, on clinical interview, behavior observations, and neuropsychological assessment. In our practices, we use an expanded Halstead-Reitan Neuropsychological Test Battery (HRNTB) to neuropsychologically assess our patients (Bennett, 1988b). We will indicate neuropsychological assessment procedures that we have found helpful to clarify each of the following cognitive domains.

DECREASED SPEED AND EFFICIENCY OF INFORMATION PROCESSING

DECREASED SPEED AND efficiency of information is a universal complaint from individuals suffering from the after-effects of TBI, regardless of whether their presenting symptoms are judged to be mild, moderate, or severe. Patients complain of slower thinking, difficulty attending to information being presented quickly, slower problem solving, and a perception that things seem to be going on at a faster speed than normal. As indicated, this constellation of symptoms appears to be related to diffuse brain injury. It also is reflective of an overall decreased level of arousal secondary to TBI. Decreased speed of processing will be reflected in timed tests such as the performance subtests of the Wechsler Adult Intelligence Scale-III (WAIS-III; Wechsler, 1997), particularly in those cases when the person can do the task but not in the required time. Other indicators include relatively impaired performance on the Seashore Rhythm Test as compared to the Speech Sounds Perception Test from the HRNTB. Slow performance on a visual scanning task, such as Digit Vigilance or the Stroop Test (Trennery, Crosson, DeBoe, & Leber, 1989), or an increased difficulty in task performance as the interstimulus interval decreases on the Paced Auditory Serial Addition Task (PASAT; Gronwall, 1986) are further indicators. Gronwall (1989) refers to these cognitive processes as information processing capacity. She has presented a great deal of data that indicates that recovery from post-concussive symptoms is reflected by a return to normal performance on the PASAT, but she also stresses the finding that "the return of test scores to the normal range does not necessarily imply full recovery from the trauma" (p. 153).

ATTENTION AND CONCENTRATION

DEFICITS IN ATTENTION and concentration are closely related to such complaints as decreased speed and efficiency of information processing or decreased information processing capacity. All patients with post-TBI symptoms report that it takes more cognitive effort to attend, that their attention span is shorter, and that they are more distractible. Most of them will complain of being unable to do more than one thing at a time (e.g., multitask) since the injury, or being unable to juggle more than one idea or task at the same time. When distractions become significantly more than they can handle, many such individuals will complain of "overload," "going blank," or "shutting down." The tests we indicated for evaluating speed and efficiency of information processing or information processing capacity are obviously appropriate for evaluating basic and higher-level attention and concentration skills. A continuous performance task, such as that found in Gordon's Diagnostic System (e.g., Gordon & Mettelman, 1988), is an excellent way to evaluate sustained attention. A relatively greater impairment in Trails B as compared to Trails A is often indicative of alternating or divided attention deficits.

CONTINUOUS PERFORMANCE

CONTINUOUS PERFORMANCE TESTS (CPTs) have been developed and utilized over the years as an adjunct to the assessment of attention/concentration and learning efficiency. While administered to individuals with TBI and other neurological etiologies, the origin for such testing arose from individuals (children–adults) with attention deficit disorder (ADD) or attention deficit hyperactivity disorder (ADHD). CPTs are also considered "screening tests" and are often incorporated into more comprehensive neuropsychological assessment batteries (e.g., HRNTB). The scope of this chapter precludes an in-depth description or analysis of many of these tests. However, we recommend to the readers that they review the text by Riccio, Reynolds, & Lowe (2004), which describes the clinical applications of CPTs. Those noted tests are the Conner's Continuous Performance Test, Test of Variables of Attention (TOVA), Gordon Diagnostic System, and Integrated Visual and Auditory Continuous Performance Test (IVA). These tests are thoroughly discussed and address such issues as clinical application, test administration, diagnostic usage, potential problems or limitations, and efficacy for treatment planning. Undoubtedly, CPTs are, and should be, used during formal assessment of those individuals with TBI (mild–severe). As previously noted, attentional deficits are pronounced and are a common subjective concern in this patient population.

LEARNING AND MEMORY

AFTER A BRAIN injury of any kind, forgetfulness is the most common area of cognitive concern. Memory difficulties occur across a wide range of daily activities, and difficulty in remembering things that happened before the accident may also be reported. However, for most individuals with TBI, pre-injury memories are retained and are accessible, although possibly less efficiently, while new memories are difficult to establish, are poorly consolidated, and subsequently difficult to retrieve. For most individuals with TBI, forgetfulness is a problem secondary to cognitive fatigue, reduced speed and efficiency of information processing, or deficits in attention and concentration. An experience or event cannot be consolidated unless it is appropriately attended to, processed, and encoded. For such individuals, forgetfulness improves as these underlying difficulties resolve. However, primary consolidation deficits, secondary to medial temporal lobe (hippocampal) damage, do not improve significantly with improvements in such basic processes as attention and concentration. Such individuals are left with permanent amnestic disorders whose impact can only be reduced by utilizing structured compensatory strategies (Bennett, 1990; Malia, Bewick, Raymond, & Bennett, 1997).

There are many choices available to investigate learning and memory skills in the TBI patient. The Tactual Performance Test (TPT) from the HRNTB provides a good measure of nonverbal learning and memory skills. The TPT Memory and Localization scores are indices of incidental learning. Percent correct of Subtest 7 of the adult Category Test is another nonverbal memory test within the HRNTB. Benton's Visual Retention Test provides information regarding visual-perceptual, constructional, and nonverbal learning and memory skills in brain-injured people. The Rivermead Behavioral Memory Test is a test of everyday verbal and nonverbal learning and memory skills and appears to have sound ecological validity in predicting memory problems in unstructured activities of daily living (Wilson, Cockburn, Baddeley, & Hiorns, 1989). The California Verbal Learning Test (CVLT) is a word list learning task like its predecessor the Rey Auditory Verbal Learning Test (Delis, Kramer, Kaplan, & Ober, 1987). The computer analyses and comparative norms available for the CVLT allow the examiner to make a detailed assessment of the patient's strengths, weaknesses, and factors contributing to difficulties in verbal learning abilities. Reitan's Story Memory and Figure Memory Tests continue to be widely used, and demographically adjusted norms are available to evaluate a patient's verbal and nonverbal memory skills (Heaton, Grant, & Matthews, 1991). For those who would rather use a battery approach to assessing learning and memory skills, there are the Wechsler Memory Scales or Williams' (1991) Memory Assessment Scales.

PERCEPTION

AS A COGNITIVE process, perception requires information processing and integration. It is highly dependent on attention, and it can involve information processing capacity within a sensory modality or across sensory modalities. Neuropsychological assessment of perception in TBI patients is typically fairly primitive, and in our own practices, we often incorporate the results of our occupational therapy evaluation. Spatial skills are often assessed by neuropsychologists through administration of tests such as Trails A and B, the Category Test, and the TPT. Difficulty in mastering the TPT can result from a number of problems other than spatial difficulties. However, poor performance on the TPT Localization Score in the face of good performance on the TPT Memory Score may indicate a lack of spatial awareness, as may poor performance on subtests four, five, and six of the Category Test. Difficulties with perceptual (and constructional) skills may also be apparent in one's copies of the patterns from the HRNTB Aphasia Screening Test or Benton's Visual Retention Test. Higher-level perceptual processing deficits appear to contribute to unawareness syndromes (e.g., McGlynn & Schacter, 1989), such as unilateral neglect and anosognosia (unawareness of deficits), which are observed in more severely brain-injured individuals.

LANGUAGE AND COMMUNICATIONS

LANGUAGE DISABILITIES THAT are of a severity level that they would be classified as aphasias (such as those observed in those with cerebrovascular accidents) are relatively rare. In an early survey, Heilman, Safran, and Geschwind (1971) screened all patients who presented with TBI at a Boston hospital during 1 year. Of 750 cases, only 2% were judged to have residual aphasia. Groher (1990) made the important point that TBI victims who present with aphasia exhibit this acquired language disorder along with other significant cognitive problems such as deficits in information processing capacity, perception, attention, memory, and executive functions. Thus, individuals who exhibit language deficits after TBI are probably best described as having problems with language and communication.

Common language and communication problems seen in our program can be summarized as follows. Dysarthria (difficulty in pronouncing words) is often seen in individuals who suffered severe TBI that resulted in brain stem injuries that produced enduring motor and movement disabilities. Injuries that resulted in residual mild–moderate cognitive difficulties overall often result in subtle communication problems such as problems in fluency, word-recall, sentence organization, listening and comprehension, reading comprehension, and verbal reasoning which, as suggested previously, are really symptomatic of general problems in cognitive processes. The Aphasia Screening Test from the HRNTB, which requires the patient to perform a series of simple language tasks, is a useful way to screen for gross disturbances of language and communication skills (e.g., pathognomonic signs). Items from this test require the patient to name common objects, spell simple words, identify individual numbers and letters, read, write, enunciate, understand spoken language, identify body parts, calculate simple math problems, and distinguish between right and left. The extent to which mild communication difficulties will interfere with one's normal activities depends on just how language-based his or her daily activities typically are. Deficits in word-recall would have a greater effect on a trial lawyer than on a construction worker, and indeed, what appears superficially to be mild word-recall deficits would be major if they made it impossible for a trial lawyer to resume their previously high level of verbal communication.

EXECUTIVE FUNCTIONS

EXECUTIVE FUNCTIONS INCLUDE problem solving, sequencing, thought flexibility, planning, starting an activity, and completing a task. These activities require that a person be organized, and of course, that the person have good information processing capacity, attention and concentration, memory, perceptual skills, and communication abilities. However, a shortcoming of neuropsychological assessment of executive functions is that we typically use structured tests such as the Trail Making Test and the Category Test from the HRNTB and the Wisconsin Card Sorting Test. The use of such highly structured tasks may make it difficult, if not impossible, to adequately investigate the integrity of the executive control system, because the very process of formally testing executive functions may mask an existing impairment (Ylvisaker & Szekeres, 1989). This occurs because the structure provided by the testing environment can be a prosthetic for deficits that potentially impaired individuals may have with respect to task initiation, maintenance, and completion. The examiner gives the patient instructions on what to do and when to begin, and the examiner keeps the client on task until the task is completed. Formal testing can thus reduce or eliminate our ability to evaluate the demands the patient might meet in their activities of daily living with respect to planning, initiation, or organizational skills. Because of this, some researchers have argued that executive functions should be evaluated through naturalistic observation of the patient (e.g., Kay & Silver, 1989) or by the use of less structured assessment protocols (Ben-Yishay & Diller, 1993; Lezak, 1995).

Individuals who report cognitive difficulties after TBI always experience some degree of disruption of executive functions. This occurs, quite simply, because the brain acts as an integrated whole in regulating executive functions, and any disruption or cerebral cortical processes following TBI will result in a disruption of these skills. While the frontal lobes appear to be critical for the planning, initiation, and completion of activities and for self-monitoring and self-correcting, they cannot do these functions if information received by them from posterior regions of the brain is impaired because of posterior cerebral damage. Thus, the frontal lobes can only modulate executive functions if information sent to them by other regions of the brain is accurate. This is why individuals with damage to virtually any specific region of the brain, or individuals who experience diffuse brain injury, will often show deficits on formal tests of executive functions. Such tests require the highest level of cognitive processing available. However, it is also clear that certain deficits in executive functions are dramatic examples of the critical role the frontal lobes perform in this cognitive process. These are specific to different regions of the frontal lobes, and they can be summarized as follows.

According to Lezak (1995), the medial aspects of the frontal lobes appear to be necessary for maintenance of drive, motivation, and capacity for emotional expression. Damage to this region will result in a person who appears to be apathetic and who seems to be uninterested in or incapable of initiating and completing activities. With significant damage to this region, the person will be incapable of initiating even primitive or mundane behaviors such as getting out of bed and eating, and they will become virtually devoid of affect or emotional responsivity. Even with mild damage to this region, we often observe a loss of spontaneity and creativity, accompanied by flattened affect. This may be misinterpreted as depression by well-meaning but uninformed psychotherapists who may institute a nonproductive course of psychotherapy to deal with a problem that is organically and not psychologically induced.

The orbitofrontal region of the frontal lobes, lying just above the rough boney orbital ridge, primarily houses behaviors. According to Lezak (1995), TBI patients who sustain orbitofrontal injury tend to exhibit behavioral dyscontrol manifested by impulsivity, disinhibition, and social unawareness. Judgment and insight may be significantly disrupted. These changes are quite apparent to family members and friends. They can result in a significant impairment in one's behavioral interactions with others and can quickly alienate a person from their social support network. In such individuals, we may see well-preserved attention, memory, and even problem-solving skills—at least in structured testing settings. However, the person's self-awareness and altered behavior may be so significant as to prevent them from functioning independently.

Problems with self-awareness and other executive functions are a common consequence of TBI. Metacognitive processes, in close alliance with executive functions, are viewed as integral components of new learning and awareness. According to Bewick, Raymond, Malia, and Bennett (1995), combining these areas may be necessary to achieve a beneficial treatment plan for improving or enhancing executive functions. Metacognitive processes, which foster knowledge about an individual's own cognitive capabilities and the ability to monitor one's own performance, represent the core of executive functioning.

General Intelligence

Neuropsychological evaluation of general intelligence is typically based on performance on the Wechsler Adult Intelligence Test-III (WAIS-III) and occasionally achievement testing, although some investigators use overall performance on their test battery as an indication of general intelligence. Individuals who experience a good recovery from the effects of TBI experience a return to normal with respect to IQ scores as well. This was demonstrated in an early study by Levin and coworkers (Levin, Grossman, Rose, & Teasdale, 1979). They found that patients who had made a good recovery, as assessed by the Glasgow Outcome Scale, usually functioned within the normal range of intelligence, while those with severe disabilities exhibited significant intellectual impairments.

While the WAIS-III is commonly used to evaluate brain injury, it is inappropriate to do so unless it is a component of a comprehensive neuropsychological battery. The WAIS-III, as well as other Wechsler scales (e.g., WAIS-R), was not designed as an instrument to evaluate brain injury, and performance on this instrument may be perfectly normal after mild brain injury, even though performance on tests that are brain-injury sensitive may be concomitantly significantly disrupted. Indeed, IQ testing in mild brain-injured individuals can often provide an accurate estimate of a person's range of premorbid intellectual functioning.

In contrast, it is certainly true that IQ scores are likely to be significantly compromised after moderate to severe brain injury. However, when this occurs, the finding does not necessarily reflect a concomitant of the brain injury itself. Lowered IQ may be the product of or reflect a lowered arousal level; decreased speed and efficiency of information processing, retrieval, and responding; impaired attention and concentration; memory deficits; or underlying impairments in perceptual or language skills.

MAJOR AFFECTIVE/PERSONALITY SEQUELAE OF TBI

CHANGES IN EMOTIONAL reactivity and personality are common consequences of TBI. These individuals often experience a number of emotional difficulties including increased lability and irritability, decreased tolerance to frustration, difficulty with temper control, and mild to moderate depression. Brain injury itself may produce such changes in emotionality, but certainly, the compromise of one's ability to function as well as they did before the injury, due to difficulties in cognitive skills, is an important contributor to the development of emotional problems after brain injury. The loss of self-esteem that occurs because of difficulties performing at preinjury levels would also be expected to cause an emotional reaction (Bornstein, Miller, & vanSchoor, 1989).

Another factor that influences emotional adjustment is the person's preinjury personality and level of psychological adjustment. Individuals who were well-adjusted emotionally and were well-entrenched in their occupation prior to their injury are likely to experience less emotional difficulty secondary to TBI than are those who were more poorly adjusted or who had less stability in their lives. Individuals performing higher-level occupations will often times show less emotionality, because they can defer work challenges to coworkers whom they supervise, while individuals in less skilled occupations typically have to deal with all the demands that they experienced at work prior to their injury. The degree of family support and support from significant others can also affect a person's level of adjustment post trauma.

As noted previously, a number of factors can contribute to difficulty in emotional adjustment after TBI. The basis for the changes is not always clear, but what is evident is the fact that patients will need emotional support to help them deal with the challenges they will face secondary to their cognitive problems. Indeed, some individuals with TBI may need more help dealing with the emotional consequences related to their cognitive losses and diminished self-esteem than they will need dealing with their cognitive difficulties. Certainly, we also see patients who have very little emotional disturbance following brain injury, but even these individuals will benefit greatly from education regarding the effects of brain injury and from learning techniques to cope with their altered level of functioning.

NATURE AND BASIS FOR EMOTIONAL CHANGES FOLLOWING TBI

As PREVIOUSLY INDICATED, changes that occur in personality and emotionality in individuals who have sustained TBI depend (in addition to brain injury itself) upon a variety of factors that include preinjury adjustment, cognitive loss, and reactions to the loss of cognitive competence that the brain injury produces. Certainly, negative personality traits that existed before the accident may be accentuated by the injury. Interestingly, in contrast, some rare individuals have experienced a loss of objectionable personality traits secondary to brain trauma. It is often difficult to separate changes in personality and emotionality that are due to the brain injury versus those that are a reaction to the brain injury (Bennett & Raymond, 1999).

ORGANIC PERSONALITY CHANGES

SIGNIFICANT PERSONALITY CHANGE can result from the brain injury itself, although this is more commonly seen in individuals who have sustained moderate to severe brain injuries than in persons who have suffered mild brain injuries. When an individual sustains a TBI, particularly if it is a "closed head injury," injury to the frontal and temporal lobes normally occurs. The frontal and temporal lobes are involved in emotional behavior, and thus, one would expect significant changes to occur in personality. Injury to the frontal lobes (e.g., frontal lobe syndrome) often manifests with flattened affect, indifference, apathy, and difficulty initiating and completing activities (e.g., Damasio & Anderson, 1993; Jorge & Starkstein, 2005, Levin, Eisenberg, & Benton, 1991). Such individuals, while appearing flat in their affect will, at times, show emotionality. Unfortunately, when they do, it is often poorly regulated and poorly directed, and the person may show episodes of what appears to be "explosive" behavior. Many times, calm individuals with significant frontal lobe injury will show aggressive behavior because it is an attempt to direct attention to the difficulties that they are experiencing or needs that they are attempting to meet.

Individuals with frontal lobe injury may also show evidence of socially inappropriate behavior. They may be more impulsive in their actions and less aware of the impact that their actions and behaviors are having on others. This is part of the brain injury, and it is not purposely motivated. Many times, it is important to allow individuals to have the freedom to express themselves, understanding that this is a means for them to achieve goals in their environment. The strategy in dealing with objectionable behaviors after frontal lobe injury needs to be one of determining the goal of the patient's behavior and then teaching them other ways (acceptable behaviors) to achieve that same goal.

Temporal lobe injury may also affect behavior and emotionality. Individuals with temporal lobe injury may report heightened emotionality ranging from "feeling things more deeply than I did before" to irritability and reduced control of aggressive impulses. The latter, as with frontal lobe injury, partly reflects loss of inhibitory control. Temporal lobe injury may also produce flattened affect, and finally, such injury may also result in hypersexuality, as seen in the Kluver-Bucy Syndrome (Kluver & Bucy, 1939). A combination of impulsivity, lack of impulse control, and hypersexuality following frontal-temporal injury can result in a significant degree of behavior dyscontrol.

Reactive Personality Changes

Depression, guilt, anxiety about the future, and feelings of helplessness and hopelessness are often seen in people with TBI, particularly those with mild to moderate impairment. Many individuals with more severe injury are not at a level of awareness where they can actually appreciate the severity of their impairments and the impact that it will have on their day to day functioning. Unfortunately, when many mental health therapists see individuals with brain injury who are showing behavior such as depression and anxiety, they interpret these behaviors as being related to adjustment problems independent of the head injury. The point to be made here is that emotional reactions to brain injury, such as depression and anxiety, are perfectly appropriate. Indeed, if they are not present, the person may not have the potential to benefit from formal rehabilitation because of their unawareness of the difficulties that they are experiencing.

As suggested earlier in this chapter, compromise of adaptive cognitive skills represents an important factor in the development of emotional disturbance following brain injury because of a loss of self-esteem related to reduced ability to perform at preinjury levels. The following is a typical scenario shown by a person who suffers even a MTBI.

An individual may or may not have been hospitalized, and after a week or so, they return to work. The injured person has been assured by their physician, family, and friends that they "look great." The person, however, feels like "something is missing" but proceeds with plans to return to school or work. The person "looks good" because there are not obvious fractures, cuts, or scars to remind one of the injury.

The TBI survivor then returns to work or school with the assurance that no problems should occur, and everyone has said that they "look great." They then go about interacting with the world as they had done in the past. However, the feedback now received from teachers, fellow workers, supervisors, and others is not the same. Where challenges were easily met in the past, the feedback now received is often negative. The person discovers that they have lost or forgotten a message, missed an appointment, done poorly on exams, made errors at work, and if things occur too rapidly around them, they have a tendency to feel overloaded or overwhelmed.

Because of these experiences, the individual may feel unsure as to their capabilities, actions, and judgment. Because they have been told everything is OK, the feeling may be one that "I am losing my mind." As you would expect, this will produce a great blow to both self-confidence and self-esteem. Some of these patients were perfectionists in the past, and they achieved a great deal of their self-esteem, self-confidence, and self-image from performing at a high level. Now, because of their cognitive difficulties, these patients may develop anxiety and depression, become socially withdrawn, and become angry or resentful. Suspiciousness and paranoia may result. Some may cling excessively to family or friends, seeking reassurance that they are still "normal." When one considers the effects of the brain trauma itself and a person's reaction to it, it is quite understandable that an individual with even mild cognitive loss may experience significant emotional difficulties secondary to the impact that the cognitive difficulties are having on their daily activities. The process of addressing these issues in individual psychotherapy with individuals who have sustained mild to moderate TBI is noted (Bennett, 1987a; 1987b; Bennett & Raymond, 1999).

NONCOGNITIVE SEQUELAE OF TBI

NONCOGNITIVE SEQUELAE ARE commonly reported by individuals with TBI. These symptoms include blurred vision, dizziness and imbalance, headaches, post-traumatic seizures, and sleep disorders (McIntosh, 1999). It is thus surprising that many of the major texts that have been written about brain injury, with the exception of the comprehensive book by Rosenthal, Griffith, Bond, and Miller (1990), do not address many of these symptoms. Their contribution to the whole neuropsychological presentation of the TBI survivor, as well as neuropsychological consequences of medications used to manage these symptoms, must be considered in any comprehensive evaluation.

Sensory Complaints

Diplopia and blurred vision are present in about one-third of patients who experience brain injury. When evaluated, acuity is typically normal, however, this is because the basis for these complaints lies in difficulties with such processes as visual accommodation, convergence, and coordinated bilateral eye tracking movements. These difficulties may sometimes be alleviated by prism lenses; vision therapy to retrain these skills may be indicated (Raymond, Bennett, Malia, & Bewick, 1996). These possible difficulties are evaluated and treated by various professionals including ophthalmologists, optometrists, cognitive therapists, or occupational therapists.

Tinnitus (buzzing/ringing in the ears), hearing impairment, and even hypersensitivity to noise (e.g., sonophobia) are also common complaints following TBI. These symptoms may represent problems with central auditory processing, and, in this regard, it is interesting to note a high incidence of abnormality in brainstem auditory evoked potentials in TBI patients, even in individuals with mild TBI (Rowe & Carlson, 1980).

Tinnitus often is reflective of inner ear concussion, and consequently, it is typically associated with complaints of dizziness and balance problems. As a noncognitive symptom, dizziness ranks second to headache in the frequency of reported symptoms in TBI patients (Rutherford, Merrett, & McDonald, 1977). Dizziness complaints can be severe, and, unfortunately medical management can be problematic. Medications such as meclizine, which is typically used for motion sickness, tend to be sedating and often provide minimal benefit. Benzodiazepines have similar side effects and similar low efficacy. Vestibular exercises, which involve periodic changes in body posture or head turning to stimulate the vestibular system, can be effective in relieving the symptoms and produce positive results by raising the threshold to dizziness onset.

Complaints of anosmia (loss of sense of smell) are less common than symptoms involving either the visual or auditory/vestibular systems after TBI. Post-traumatic anosmia usually results from shearing of the olfactory fibers that pass through the cribiform plate (Jafek, Eller, Esses, & Moran, 1989). Scar tissue typically prevents regeneration. The degree of anosmia is generally correlated with the severity of TBI. Complete anosmia is often correlated with significant orbitofrontal damage, and consequently, is seen in individuals who have a poor prognosis for successful return to work (Varney, 1988). Disorders of taste often accompany anosmia (Schechter & Henken, 1974), which is understandable when one considers the interactions between the senses of olfaction and taste in determining how a food "tastes" to us (Bennett, 1978).

Post-Traumatic Headaches

Post-traumatic headaches are the most common noncognitive complaint of TBI victims. However, this symptom is more common in mild TBI patients than in individuals who have survived moderate to severe TBIs for reasons that are not entirely clear (Haas, 1993). Many of the headaches reported by these individuals fall into the pattern typical for migraine, with or without aura. Another large group of post-traumatic headaches are more of the tension type. A third group seems to be associated with disorders of the cervical spine occurring at the same time as the TBI (cervicogenic headaches). Symptoms may include combinations of any of these three factors, to varying degrees, but the most common presentation is that of the migraine type (Weiss, Stern, & Goldberg, 1991).

Medical management of post-traumatic headaches can be problematic as they can be very refractory to medications. A variety of medication approaches are used, and it is always important to consider effects of medications on cognitive processes, as well as distracting effects and fatigue produced by the headache pain, in evaluating the possible effects of TBI on cognition. Whenever possible, behavioral treatments such as stress management, pain management, and biofeedback should be utilized (Medina, 1992), and we have found these strategies very helpful in our own patients (Bennett, 1988a).

Post-Traumatic Epilepsy

Post-traumatic epilepsy is a complication that can develop months or years after TBI. It may limit the ability or career opportunities of a person who has otherwise recovered, or it may further compromise the abilities of a TBI survivor who is still experiencing significant cognitive sequelae (Bennett, 1987a). The incidence of post-traumatic epilepsy in TBI survivors as a group is 5%, and the incidence increases with the severity of the physical injury to the brain (Jennett & Teasdale, 1981). It is generally believed that the development of epilepsy after TBI is due to the formation of scar tissue in the brain, but the extent of overall damage to the brain and a family history of seizures are significant interactional factors (Caveness et al., 1979).

Seizures associated with TBI are usually simple or complex with or without secondary generalization. Therefore, post-traumatic seizures arise as focal events, and most typically as complex partial seizures, rather than as generalized seizures. This is related to the mechanics of TBI and the typical frontotemporal focal injuries that TBI produces. The hallmark of complex partial seizures is altered consciousness, although a variety of symptoms may precede or accompany this state (Bennett, 1987a, 1992b). It can often be difficult to ascertain whether or not episodes of dissociation or altered consciousness are actually caused by electrocerebral discharges and are, therefore, seizure events. They may instead simply reflect fluctuations in attentiveness in the TBI survivor. However, it is also true that the EEG studies of individuals who actually have complex partial seizures are often normal. A higher likelihood of obtaining EEG confirmation of complex partial seizures results from repeated studies, use of nasopharyngeal leads, or 24-hour ambulatory recording.

Individuals who have post-traumatic seizures may suffer additional cognitive compromise. Side effects from antiepileptic drugs may interfere with processing speed, attention, and memory. The seizure event may impair the person's ability to maintain continuity of consciousness and may lead to deficits (or exacerbate existing ones) in cognitive processes. If the individual's seizures secondarily generalize, they may experience a post-ictal neurological depression which, in turn, would compromise cognitive processes. However, while post-traumatic epilepsy may further compromise the cognitive abilities of TBI survivors, it is also clear that the major factor that produces cognitive compromise in such individuals is the brain injury itself which, among other symptoms, is reflected by the seizure disorder (Dikmen & Reitan, 1978; Haynes & Bennett, 1990).

Disturbance of Sleep After TBI

Because the neural mechanisms that regulate arousal and sleep cycles are widely distributed throughout the brain, one would expect that TBI, among its various consequences, would result in disorders of the sleep–wake schedule. This is clearly the case, although relatively few experimental studies have addressed this issue. Some early studies attempted to relate sleep disturbances to both the cognitive and behavioral problems that were also the result of TBI (Prigatano, Stahl, Orr, & Zeimer, 1982; Ron, Algom, Harry, & Cohen, 1980). These studies seemed to demonstrate a correlation between the recovery of normal sleep patterns and cognitive improvement, although it is certainly important to note that this finding does not indicate a causal relationship but rather a parallel process of recovery.

More recently, in a population of severely brain-injured individuals, Cohen, Oksenberg, Snir, Stern, and Groswasser (1992) indicated that sleep complaints were common in patients with recent brain injury (median = 3–5 months) as well as those who sustained brain injury 2 to 3 years previously. The incidence of such complaints in both groups was far greater than in the general population. The nature of the predominant sleep complaints differed in the two groups. Patients with recent injuries had more complaints of difficulties in initiating and maintaining sleep (DIMS), while patients with older injuries suffered mostly from disorders of excessive somnolence (DOES).

A relationship between mild to moderate TBI and sleep disturbance was reported by O'Hara and Lankford (1993). TBI victims averaged 18 months post injury at the time of evaluation; all of them were studied neuropsychologically and via overnight polysomnography. About half of the patients studied complained of excessive daytime somnolence (DOES) and all complained of sleep disturbance sufficient to warrant referral for overnight polysomnography. A variety of sleep disorders were identified including disorders in initiating and maintaining sleep (DIMS), sleep apnea, periodic limb movement disorder (e.g., restless leg syndrome), and narcolepsy. The authors concluded that all of these individuals warranted dual diagnoses in describing the sequelae of their TBI. That is, the patients suffered from cognitive impairment as well as sleep disturbance secondary to their brain injuries.

Are sleep disturbances and cognitive impairments causally related? Probably they are not. Despite some highly publicized, dramatic outcomes of prolonged abstinence from sleep in humans (described between 1955 and 1967), systematic studies of total sleep deprivation in humans revealed no permanent cognitive effects and few significant temporary deficits (Anch, Browman, Mitler, & Walsh, 1988). Studies that have deprived people of sleep for up to 264 hours (11 days) corroborate this general statement (Dement, 1972).

As one would predict, studies of partial sleep deprivation have produced even less evidence that sleep deprivation or disruption directly influences cognitive skills. Webb and Agnew (1974) limited 15 males to 5.5 hours of sleep per night for 60 days; mood and performance were assessed once each week. A deficit in performance was observed only on a 30-minute vigilance task over the 8-week study. It was felt that this was reflective more of decreased motivation rather than inability to perform. Shorter tasks and measures of affect showed no changes. In a similar study, Friedman et al. (1977) studied 8 young adults for 6–8 months following a gradual (over 2–3 months) reduction in total night sleep from 7–8 hours. Mood and performance measures, even on a 45-minute vigilance task, showed no effect during and after 6–8 months of sleep reduction.

In combination, the aforementioned studies on partial and complete sleep deprivation demonstrate remarkably minimal detrimental effects on performance and affect. Such procedures produce fatigue, but fatigue alone does not seem to produce adverse effects. These findings can be used to convincingly argue that while sleep disturbance may exist concomitantly with or contribute to the cognitive dysfunction and the fatigue/inertia seen in TBI patients, sleep disturbance itself is not the cause of these latter difficulties. One exception might be obstructive sleep apnea, which over time could result in some degree of hypoxia (Gale & Hopkins, 2004). Undoubtedly, this could have a deleterious effect on both cognitive functions and "healing" of the brain following injury.

SUMMARY AND CONCLUSIONS

TRAUMATIC BRAIN INJURY (TBI) is a major health problem in the United States, as well as throughout the world. The statistics are staggering while the consequences are often tragic. With the advent of improved medical treatment and growth of designated trauma centers, our ability to manage the primary and secondary effects of TBI has improved dramatically. While this is admirable, it has also proven problematic due to the increase of survivors with permanent and debilitating residual effects. As discussed in this chapter, however, even seemingly mild to moderate TBI can produce long-lasting changes in a survivor's capabilities, which in turn have significant consequences for career potential and social interactions. While we tend to predict outcome based on the physical characteristics of the brain injury or such nebulous concepts as duration of loss of consciousness and duration of post-traumatic amnesia, it appears that an accurate prediction of the consequences of TBI can only be established through evaluation of residual deficits after the post-acute stage of recovery has begun. A major flaw of TBI research is the common attempt to equate subjects on this basis of TBI descriptors rather than on post-injury sequelae.

The epidemiology and pathophysiology of TBI were discussed. Neuroimaging techniques, particularly the MRI and assessment procedures that evaluate regional brain metabolism, hold great promise for defining the physical parameters of neural damage following TBI. However, conclusions from those studies will be of greatest benefit as researchers combine this methodology with neuropsychological testing results. While EEG analysis has not yet proven reliable in assessment of TBI, it is expected that brain mapping and ERP analyses, which should currently be viewed as research in progress rather than validated clinical tools, will likely prove beneficial in the future. As with neuroimaging, these types of studies must be combined with neuropsychological assessment measures if they are to provide significant answers regarding the functional consequences of TBI on a given person's ability to fully integrate into their previous activities.

Clinical features of the TBI survivor were discussed. It is important to note that a person's outcome from TBI reflects the cumulative effects of alterations in cognitive abilities, affective/personality interactions, and noncognitive symptoms, such as headaches, sensory/motor skills, and post-traumatic seizures. Medications given to the person to manage these symptoms may exacerbate cognitive or personality sequelae from the TBI.

In conclusion, medical science has made significant advances in the survival rate of seriously injured TBI patients in recent years. A disproportionate percentage of them are older children or young adults, and this will pose serious social and economic problems. It is essential that long-term rehabilitation needs of these survivors be addressed through comprehensive rehabilitation programs that can demonstrate their efficacy via outcome studies. Research aimed at improving rehabilitation methods for these survivors should be encouraged and funded.

REFERENCES

American Academy of Neurology. (1997). Practice parameter: The management of concussion in sports. Report of the Quality Standards Subcommittee. *Neurology, 4,* 581–585.

Anch, A. M., Browman, C. P., Mitler, M. M., & Walsh, J. K. (1988). *Sleep: A scientific perspective.* Englewood Cliffs, NJ: Prentice-Hall.

Audenaert, K., Jansen, H. M. L., Otte, A., Peremans, K., Vervaet, M., Crombez, R., et al. (2003). Imaging of mild traumatic brain injury using 57Co and 99mTc HMPAO SPECT as compared to other diagnostic procedures. *Medical Science Monitor, 9*(10), 112–117.

Barth, J. T., Macchocchi, S. N., Giordani, B., Rimel, R., Jane, J. A., & Boll, T. J. (1983). Neuropsychological sequelae of minor head injury. *Neurosurgery, 13,* 529–533.

Bennett, T. L. (1978). *The sensory world: An introduction to sensation and perception.* Monterey, CA: Brooks/Cole.

Bennett, T. L. (1987a). Neuropsychological aspects of complex partial seizures: Diagnostic and treatment issues. *International Journal of Clinical Neuropsychology, 9,* 37–45.

Bennett, T. L. (1987b). Post-traumatic epilepsy: Its nature and implications for head injury recovery. *Journal of Cognitive Rehabilitation, 5*(5), 14–18.

Bennett, T. L. (1988a). Post-traumatic headaches: Subtypes and behavioral treatments. *Journal of Cognitive Rehabilitation, 6*(2), 34–39.

Bennett, T. L. (1988b). Use of the Halstead-Reitan Neuropsychological Test Battery in the assessment of head injury. *Cognitive Rehabilitation, 6*(3), 18–24.

Bennett, T. L. (1990). The persistence of memory deficits. *Bulletin of the National Academy of Neuropsychology, 8*(2), 6–8.

Bennett, T. L. (1992a). Conceptualizing traumatic brain injuries. *Journal of Head Injury, 3*(1), 21–28.

Bennett, T. L. (1992b). *The neuropsychology of epilepsy*. New York: Plenum.

Bennett, T. L., & Raymond, M. J. (1999). Psychotherapeutic intervention for individuals with mild traumatic brain injury. In M. J. Raymond, T. L. Bennett, L. C. Hartlage, & C. M. Cullum (Eds.), *Mild traumatic brain injury: A clinician's guide* (pp. 219–229). Austin, TX: Pro-Ed.

Ben-Yishay, Y., & Diller, L. (1993). Cognitive remediation in traumatic brain injury: Update and issues. *Archives of Physical Medicine and Rehabilitation, 74*, 204–213.

Bergschneider, M., Hovda, D. A., & Shalmon, E. (2003). Cerebral hyperglycolysis following severe human traumatic brain injury: A positron emission tomography study. *Journal of Neurosurgery, 86*, 241–251.

Bewick, K. C., Raymond, M. J., Malia, K. B., & Bennett, T. L. (1995). Metacognition as the ultimate executive: Techniques and tasks to facilitate executive functions. *NeuroRehabilitation, 5*, 367–375.

Bigler, E. D. (1990). Neuropathology of traumatic brain injury. In E. D. Bigler (Ed.), *Traumatic brain injury* (pp. 13–49). Austin, TX: Pro-Ed.

Bigler, E. D. (1996). Neuroimaging in traumatic brain injury. In E. D. Bigler (Ed.), *Neuroimaging II: Clinical applications* (pp. 261–278). New York: Plenum Press.

Bigler, E. D., Kurth, S. M., Blatter, D., & Abildskov, T. J. (1992). Degenerative changes in traumatic brain injury: Post-injury magnetic resonance identified ventricular expansion compared to pre-injury levels. *Brain Research Bulletin, 28*, 651–653.

Bond, M. R. (1990). Standardized methods of assessing and predicting outcome. In M. Rosenthal, E. R. Griffith, M. R. Bond, & J. D. Miller (Eds.), *Rehabilitation of the adult and child with traumatic brain injury* (2nd ed., pp. 59–74). Philadelphia: F.A. Davis.

Bonne, O., Gilboa, A., Louzuon, Y., Kempf-Sherf, O., Katz, M., Fishman, Y., et al. (2003). Cerebral blood flow in chronic symptomatic mild traumatic brain injury. *Psychiatry Research: Neuroimaging, 124*, 141–152.

Bornstein, R. A., Miller, H. B., & vanSchoor, J. T. (1989). Neuropsychological deficits and emotional disturbance in head injured patients. *Journal of Neurosurgery, 70*, 509–513.

Brooks, D. N. (1990). Cognitive deficits. In M. Rosenthal, E. R. Griffith, M. R. Bond, & J. D. Miller (Eds.), *Rehabilitation of the adult and child with traumatic brain injury* (2nd ed., pp. 163–178). Philadelphia: F.A. Davis.

Cantu, R. C. (1992). Cerebral concussion in sport: Management and prevention. *Physician and Sportsmedicine, 14*, 64–74.

Cantu, R. C. (2001). Posttraumatic retrograde and anterograde amnesia: Pathophysiology and implications in grading and safe return to play. *Journal of Athletic Training, 36*, 244–248.

Cantu, R. C., & Voy, R. (1995). Second impact syndrome: A risk in any sport. *Physician and Sportsmedicine, 23*, 27–36.

Carlson, G. S., Svardsudd, K., & Welin, L. (1987). Long-term effects of head injuries sustained during life in three male populations. *Journal of Neurosurgery, 67,* 197–205.

Caveness, W. E. (1977). Incidence of craniocerebral trauma in the United States. *Transitions of the American Neurological Association, 102,* 136–138.

Caveness, W. E., Meirwoski, A. M., Rish, B. L., Mohr, J. P., Kistler, J. P., Dillon, J. D., et al. (1979). The nature of post-traumatic epilepsy. *Journal of Neurosurgery, 50,* 545–553.

Centers for Disease Control and Prevention, National Center for Health Statistics. Surveys and data collection systems. Retrieved October 19, 2004, from//www.cdc.gov/nchs/express.htm

Cohen, M., Oksenberg, A., Snir, D., Stern, M. J., & Groswasser, Z. (1992). Temporally related changes of sleep complaints in traumatic brain injured patients. *Journal of Neurology, Neurosurgery and Psychiatry, 55,* 313–315.

Collins, M. W., Iverson, G. L., Lovell, M. R., McKeag, D. B., Norwig, J., & Maroon, J. (2003). On-field predictors of neuropsychological and symptom deficit following sports-related concussion. *Clinical Journal of Sport Medicine, 13,* 222–229.

Cullum, C. M., & Bigler, E. D. (1986). Ventricle size, cortical atrophy, and the relationship with neuropsychological status in closed head injury. *Journal of Clinical and Experimental Neuropsychology, 8,* 437–452.

Damasio, A. R., & Anderson, S. W. (1993). The frontal lobes. In K. M. Heilman & E. Valenstein (Eds.), *Clinical neuropsychology* (3rd ed., pp. 409–460). New York: Oxford University Press.

Davalos, D. B., & Bennett, T. L. (2002). A review of the use of SPECT as a diagnostic tool in mild traumatic brain injury. *Applied Neuropsychology, 9,* 92–105.

Delis, D. C., Kramer, J. H., Kaplan, E., & Ober, B. A. (1987). *The California Verbal Learning Test.* San Antonio, TX: Psychological Corporation.

Dement, W. C. (1972). *Some must watch while some must sleep.* New York: Norton.

Dikman, S., & Reitan, R. M. (1978). Neuropsychological performance in post-traumatic epilepsy. *Epilepsia, 19,* 177–183.

Erlanger, D., Kausik, T., Cantu, R., Barth, J., Broshek, D., & Freeman, J. (2003). Symptom-based assessment of the severity of concussion. *Journal of Neurosurgery, 98,* 34–39.

Finlayson, M. A. J., & Garner, S. H. (1994). Challenges in rehabilitation of individuals with acquired brain injury. In M. A. J. Finlayson and S. H. Garner (Eds.), *Brain injury rehabilitation: Clinical considerations* (pp. 3–10). Maryland: Williams & Wilkins.

Frankowski, R. F. (1986). Descriptive and epidemiological studies of head injury in the United States: 1974–1984. *Advances in Psychosomatic Medicine, 16,* 153–172.

Friedman, J. K., Globus, G., Huntley, A., Mullaney, D., Naitoh, P., & Johnson, L. (1977). Performance and mood during and after gradual sleep reduction. *Psychophysiology, 14*, 245–250.

Gale, S. D., & Hopkins, R. O. (2004). Effects of hypoxia on the brain: Neuro-imaging and neuropsychological findings following carbon monoxide poisoning and obstructive sleep apnea. *Journal of International Neuropsychological Society, 10*, 60–71.

Gennarelli, T. A., (1990). Mechanisms of cerebral concussion, contusion, and other effects of head injury. In J. R. Youmans (Ed.), *Neurological surgery* (pp. 163–175). Philadelphia: Saunders.

Gordon, M., & Mettelman, B. B. (1988). The assessment of attention: 1. Standardization and reliability of a behavior based measure. *Journal of Clinical Psychology, 44*, 682–690.

Groher, M. (1990). Communication disorders in adults. In M. Rosenthal, E. R. Griffith, M. R. Bond, & J. D. Milles (Eds.), *Rehabilitation of the adult and child with traumatic brain injury* (2nd ed., pp. 148–162). Philadelphia: F.A. Davis.

Gronwall, D. (1986). Rehabilitation programs for patients with mild head injury: Components, problems, and evaluation. *Journal of Head Trauma Rehabilitation, 1*, 53–62.

Gronwall, D. (1989). Cumulative and persisting effects of concussion on attention and cognition. In H. S. Levin, H. M. Eisenberg, & A. L. Benton (Eds.), *Mild head injury* (pp. 153–162). New York: Oxford University Press.

Haas, D. C. (1993). Chronic post-traumatic headache. In J. Olesen, P. T. Felt-Hansen, & K. M. A. Welch (Eds.), *The headaches* (pp. 629–637). New York: Raven Press.

Hart, A. C., Hopkins, C. A., & Ford, B. (2005). *ICD-9-CM Professional*. Salt Lake City, UT: Ingenix.

Haynes, S. D., & Bennett, T. L. (1990). Cognitive impairments in adults with complex partial seizures. *International Journal of Clinical Neuropsychology, 12*, 74–81.

Heaton, R. K., Grant, I., & Matthews, C. G. (1991). *Comprehensive norms for an expanded Halstead-Reitan Battery: Demographic corrections, research findings, and clinical applications*. Odessa, FL: Psychological Assessment Resources.

Heilman, K. M., Safran, A., & Geschwind, N. (1971). Closed head injury and aphasia. *Journal of Neurology, Neurosurgery, and Psychiatry, 34*, 265–271.

Holbourn, A. (1943). Mechanism of head injuries. *Lancet, 2*, 438–441.

Hovda, D. A., Prins, M., Becker, D. P., et al. (1999). Neurobiology of concussion. In J. E. Bailes, M. Lovell, & J. C. Maroon (Eds.), *Sports related concussion* (pp. 12–51). St. Louis, MO: Quality Medical Publishing.

Jafek, B. W., Eller, P. M., Esses, B. A., & Moran, D. T. (1989). Posttraumatic anosmia: Ultrastructural correlate. *Archives of Neurology, 46*, 300–304.

Jenkins, A., Teasdale, G., Hadley, M., MacPhearson, P., & Rowan, J. (1986). Brain lesions detected by brain magnetic imaging in mild and severe head injuries. *Lancet, 2,* 445–446.

Jennet, B., & Teasdale, G. (1981). *Management of head injuries.* Philadelphia: F.A. Davis.

Jennet, B. (1986). Head trauma. In A. K. Asbury, G. M. McKann, & W. I. McDonald (Eds.), *Diseases of the nervous system* (pp. 1282–1291). Philadelphia: W.B. Saunders.

Johnson, S. C., Bigler, E. D., Burr, R. B., & Blatter, D. B. (1994). White matter atrophy, ventricular dilation, and intellectual functioning following traumatic brain injury. *Neuropsychology, 8,* 307–315.

Jorge, R. E., & Starkstein, S. E. (2005). Pathophysiologic aspects of major depression following traumatic brain injury. *Journal of Head Trauma Rehabilitation, 20*(6), 475–487.

Kay, T., & Silver, S. M. (1989). Closed head trauma: Assessment for rehabilitation. In M. D. Lezak (Ed.), *Assessment of the behavioral consequences of head trauma* (pp. 145–170). New York: Alan R. Liss.

Kelly, J. P. (1990). Report of the Sports Medicine Committee: Guidelines for the management of concussion in sports. *Colorado Medical Society, August* (Revised, May, 1991).

Kelly, J. P., Nichols, J. S., & Filley, C. M. (1991). Concussion in sports: Guidelines for the prevention of catastrophic outcome. *Journal of the American Medical Association, 266,* 2867–2869.

Kibby, M., & Long, C. J. (1999). Effective treatment of mild traumatic brain injury and understanding of its neurological consequences. In M. J. Raymond, T. L. Bennett, L. C. Hartlage, & C. M. Cullum (Eds.), *Mild traumatic brain injury: A clinician's guide* (pp. 203–217). Austin, TX: Pro-Ed.

Kluver, H., & Bucy, P. C. (1939). Preliminary analysis of the functions of the temporal lobe in monkeys. *Archives of Neurology and Psychiatry, 42,* 979–1000.

Kraus, J. F., & Nourjah, P. (1989). The epidemiology of mild head injury. In H. S. Levin, H. M. Eisenberg, & A. L. Benton (Eds.), *Mild head injury* (pp. 8–22). New York: Oxford University Press.

Langlois, J. A., Marr, A., Mitchko, J., & Johnson, R. L. (2005). Tracking the silent epidemic and educating the public. *Journal of Head Trauma Rehabilitation, 20,* 196–204.

Leinenger, B. E., Gramling, S. E., Fanell, H. D., Kreutzer, J. S., & Peck, E. A. (1990). Neuropsychological deficits in symptomatic minor head injury patients after concussion and mild concussion. *Journal of Neurology, Neurosurgery, and Psychiatry, 53,* 293–296.

Levi, L., Guilburd, J. M., Lemberger, A., Soustiel, J. F., & Feinsod, M. (1990). Diffuse axonal injury: Analysis of 100 patients with radiological signs. *Neurosurgery, 27,* 429–432.

Levin, H. S., Amparo, E. G., Eisenberg, H. M., Williams, D. H., High, W. M., McArdle, C. B., et al. (1987). Magnetic resonance imaging and computerized tomography in relation to the neurobehavioral sequelae of mild and moderate head injuries, *Journal of Neurosurgery, 66,* 706–713.

Levin, H. S., Eisenberg, H. M., & Benton, A. L. (1991). *Frontal lobe function and dysfunction.* New York: Oxford University Press.

Levin, H. S., Grossman, H. G., Rose, J. E., & Teasdale, G. (1979). Long-term neuropsychological outcome of closed head injury. *Journal of Neurosurgery, 50,* 412–422.

Levin, H. S., Mattis, S., Ruff, R. M., Eisenberg, H. M., Marshall, M. F., Tabaddor, K., et al. (1987). Neurobehavioral outcome following minor head injury: A three center study. *Journal of Neurosurgery, 66,* 234–243.

Levin, H. S., O'Donnell, V. M., & Grossman, R. G. (1979). The Galveston Orientation and Amnesia Test: A practical test to assess cognition after head injury. *Journal of Nervous and Mental Disease, 167,* 675–684.

Lezak, M. D. (1995). *Neuropsychological assessment* (3rd ed.) New York: Oxford University Press.

Lovell, M., Collins, M., Podell, K., Powell, J. W., & Maroon, J. (2000). *The comparison of computerized versus traditional neuropsychological testing in developing objective criteria for return to play following concussion in high school athletes.* 27th Annual Meeting of the National Academy of Neuropsychology, Orlando, FL.

Malia, K. B., Bewick, K. C., Raymond, M. J., & Bennett, T. L. (1997). *Brainwave-R: Cognitive strategies and techniques for brain injury rehabilitation.* Austin, TX: Pro-Ed.

McGlynn, S., & Schacter, D. L. (1989). Unawareness of deficits in neuropsychological syndromes. *Journal of Clinical and Experimental Neuropsychology, 11,* 143–205.

McIntosh, G. C. (1999). The medical management of noncognitive sequelae of mild traumatic brain injury. In M. J. Raymond, T. L. Bennett, L. C. Hartlage, & C. M. Cullum (Eds.), *Mild traumatic brain injury; A clinician's guide* (pp. 255–265). Austin, TX: Pro-Ed.

Medina, J. L. (1992). Efficacy of an individualized outpatient program in the treatment of post-traumatic headache. *Headache, 32,* 180–182.

Mild Traumatic Brain Injury Committee of the Head Injury Interdisciplinary Special Interest Group of the American Congress of Rehabilitation Medicine. (1993). Definition of mild traumatic brain injury. *Journal of Head Trauma Rehabilitation, 8,* 86–87.

Miller, J. D., Pentland, B., & Berrol, S. (1990). Early evaluation and management. In M. Rosenthal, E. R. Griffith, M. R. Bond, & J. P. Miller (Eds.), *Rehabilitation of the adult and child with brain injury* (pp. 21–51). Philadelphia: F.A. Davis.

Nevin, N. (1967). Neuropathological changes in the white matter following head injury. *Journal of Neuropathology and Experimental Neurology, 26,* 77–84.

O'Hara, C., & Lankford, D. A. (1993). *Sleep disorders in patients with mild to moderate closed head injury.* Workshop presented at the Thirteenth Annual

Conference of the National Academy of Neuropsychology, Dallas, Texas.

Oppenheimer, D. (1968). Microscopic lesions in the brain following head injury. *Journal of Neurology, Neurosurgery, & Psychiatry, 31,* 299–306.

Pang, D. (1989). Physics and pathophysiology of closed head injury. In M. D. Lezak (Ed.), *Assessment of the behavioral consequences of head trauma* (pp. 1–17). New York: Alan R. Liss.

Prigatano, G. P., Stahl, M. L., Orr, W. C., & Zeimer, H. K. (1982). Sleep and dreaming disturbances in closed head injury patients. *Journal of Neurology, Neurosurgery, and Psychiatry, 45,* 78–80.

Raymond, M. J. (1989). Major consequences of minor head injury. *JMA Bulletin, 2,* 4–7.

Raymond, M. J., & Bennett, T. L. (1999). Introduction and overview. In M. J. Raymond, T. L. Bennett, L. C. Hartlage, & C. M. Cullum (Eds.). *Mild traumatic brain injury: A clinician's guide* (pp. 1–8). Austin, TX: Pro-Ed.

Raymond, M. J., Bennett, T. L., Hartlage, L. C., & Cullum, C. M. (1999). *Mild traumatic brain injury: A clinician's guide.* Austin, TX: Pro-Ed.

Raymond, M. J., Bennett, T. L., Malia, K. B., & Bewick, K. C. (1996). Rehabilitation of visual processing deficits following brain injury. *Neuro Rehabilitation, 6*(3) 229–240.

Riccio, C. A., Reynolds, C. R., & Lowe, P. A. (2004). *Clinical applications of continuous performance tests: Measuring attention and impulsive responding in children and adults.* Hoboken, NJ: Wiley Publishers.

Rimel, R. W., Giordani, B., Barth, J. T., Boll, T. J., & Jane, J. A. (1981). Disability caused by minor head injury. *Neurosurgery, 9,* 221–228.

Rimel, R. W., Jane, J. H., & Bond, M. R. (1990). Characteristics of the head injured patient. In M. Rosenthal, E. R. Griffith, M. R. Bond, & J. D. Miller (Eds.), *Rehabilitation of the adult and child with brain injury* (2nd ed., pp. 8–16). Philadelphia: Davis.

Ron, S., Algom, D., Harry, D., & Cohen, M. (1980). Time related changes in the distributions of sleep stages in brain injured patients. *Electroencephalography and Clinical Neuropsychology, 48,* 432–441.

Rosenthal, M., Griffith, E. R., Bond, M. R., & Miller, J. D. (1990). *Rehabilitation of the adult and child with traumatic brain injury* (2nd ed.). Philadelphia: F.A. Davis.

Rowe, M. J., & Carlson, L. (1980). Brainstem auditory evoked potentials in post-traumatic dizziness. *Archives of Neurology, 37,* 679–683.

Ruff, R. N., Cullum, C. M., & Luerrsen, T. G. (1989). Brain imaging and neuropsychological outcome in traumatic brain injury. In E. D. Bigler, R. A. Yeo, & E. Turkheimer (Eds.), *Neuropsychological function and brain imaging* (pp. 161–183). New York: Plenum Publishing.

Russell, W. R. (1932). Cerebral involvement in head injury. *Brain, 55,* 549–603.

Rutherford, W. H., Merrett, J. D., & McDonald, J. R. (1977). Sequelae of concussion caused by minor head injuries. *Lancet, 1,* 1–4.

Schechter, P. J., & Henken, R. Z. (1974). Abnormalities of taste and smell after head injury. *Journal of Neurology, Neurosurgery and Psychiatry, 37,* 802–810.

Strich, S. (1961). Shearing of nerve fibers as a cause of brain damage due to head injury: A pathological study of twenty cases. *Lancet, 1,* 1–5.

Teasdale, G., & Jennett, B. (1974). Assessment of coma and impaired consciousness: A practical scale. *Lancet, 2,* 81–84.

Trennery, M. R., Crosson, B., DeBoe, J., & Leber, W. R. (1989). *Stroop Neuropsychological Test manual.* Odessa, FL: Psychological Assessment Resources.

Umile, E. M., Sandel, E., Alavi, A., Terry, C. M. & Plotkin, R. C. (2002) Dynamic imaging in mild traumatic brain injury: Support for the theory of medial temporal vulnerability. *Archives of Physical Medicine and Rehabilitation, 83,* 1506–1513.

Varney, N. A. (1988). Prognostic significance of anosmia in patients with closed head injury trauma. *Journal of Clinical and Experimental Neuropsychology, 10,* 250–254.

Webb, W. B., & Agnew, H. W., Jr. (1974). The effects of chronic limitation of sleep length. *Psychophysiology, 11,* 265–274.

Wechsler, D. (1997). *Wechsler Adult Intelligence Test—3rd Edition.* San Antonio, TX: The Psychological Corporation.

Weiss, H. D., Stern, B. J., & Goldberg, J. (1991). Post-traumatic magazine: Chronic migraine precipitated by minor head or neck trauma. *Headache, 31,* 451–456.

Williams, J. M. (1991). *The Memory Assessment Scales.* Odessa, FL: Psychological Assessment Resources.

Wilson, B., Cockburn, J., Baddeley, A., & Hiorns, R. (1989). The development and validation of a test battery for detecting and monitoring everyday problems. *Journal of Clinical and Experimental Neuropsychology, 11,* 855–870.

Yarnell, P. R., & Rossi, G. V. (1988). Minor whiplash head injury with major debilitation. *Brain Injury, 2,* 255–258.

Ylvisaker, M., & Szekeres, S. F. (1989). Metacognition and executive impairments in head injured children and adults. *Topics in Language Disorders, 9,* 34–49.

19

Normal Aging, Mild Cognitive Impairment, and Dementia

KEVIN DUFF AND THOMAS J. GRABOWSKI

SINCE THE LAST edition of *The Neuropsychology Handbook,* three events have occurred that will lead to an increased need for geriatric neuropsychological services:

1. As Baby Boomers turn 65, later adulthood is poised to become one of the largest segments of the U.S. population. For example, the U.S. Census Bureau projects that the 65 and older population will increase by 147% by 2050, whereas the population as a whole will only increase by 49%. These older adults will be concerned about their normal and abnormal aging changes.
2. Refinement in the definition of subsyndromal cognitive disorders (e.g., mild cognitive impairment [MCI], cognitive impairment no dementia [CIND]) has sparked clinical interest and research endeavors. For example, whereas only 15 Medline citations referenced MCI in 1996, 322 referenced this condition in 2005.
3. Interventions and services for patients with dementia are skyrocketing. For example, Tacrine was the only FDA-approved medication

for Alzheimer's disease (AD) in 1995. Currently, however, there are multiple classes of medications (e.g., cholinesterase inhibitors, glutamate regulators, lipid-lowering drugs) that are being utilized for this and other types of dementias.

Clearly, cognitive functioning, both normal and abnormal, will be a focus of clinical and research work in the beginning of the twenty-first century, and neuropsychology is well-positioned to address many of these upcoming concerns. Therefore, the current chapter will briefly review cognition in normal aging, subsyndromal cognitive disorders such as MCI, and several of the most commonly occurring dementias.

NORMAL CHANGING WITH AGING

IN ADDITION TO physical and sensory declines, changes in cognitive abilities across the life span have been widely documented in the literature. Several large scale longitudinal studies, including the Seattle Longitudinal Study (Schaie, 1996), Victoria Longitudinal Study (Hertzog, Dixon, Hultsch, & MacDonald, 2003), and Berlin Aging Study (Baltes & Mayer, 1999), have tracked the cognitive abilities of adults from their 20s to their 100s. These studies have consistently demonstrated that certain cognitive abilities decline during the 6th, 7th, and 8th decades of life, whereas other cognitive abilities remain quite stable across time. For example, in a review of the findings from his Seattle Longitudinal Study, Schaie (Schaie, 1994) noted that the cognitive constructs of perceptual speed and numerical ability steadily decline from 25 to 88 years old (see Figure 19.1). Other cognitive abilities, such as verbal ability, inductive reasoning, and verbal memory, start their decline at a much later point, around age 53. Modest declines, however, are observed on these abilities into the 70s and 80s. Similarly, Baltes and colleagues (Singer, Verhaeghen, Ghisletta, Lindenberger, & Baltes, 2003) observed that perceptual speed, episodic memory, and verbal fluency decline with age in 70–100 year olds, whereas word knowledge was stable into a person's 90s.

Oftentimes, many of these latent cognitive constructs vary together. For example, declines in episodic memory are strongly related to declines in working memory and perceptual speed (Hertzog et al., 2003), which has prompted some to theorize about an overarching cognitive domain such as "processing speed" (Salthouse, 1996). As perceptual/processing speed declines, an individual's ability to perform other cognitive tasks, whether learning and memory, verbal fluency, or solving arithmetic problems, also declines. Many of these *perceived* declines are largely moderated by the *true* decline in processing speed

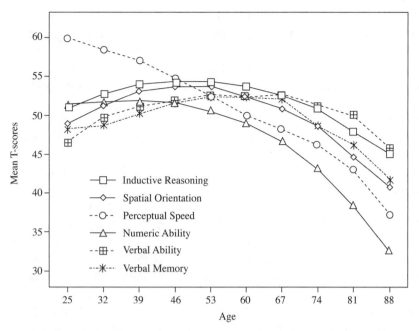

FIGURE 19.1 Longitudinal changes in latent cognitive variables across adulthood.
Note. Reprinted with permission from Schaie (1994).

(Verhaeghen & Salthouse, 1997). If the processing speed deficit could be remediated, then the other declines would be less pronounced.

Although these large longitudinal studies have provided neuropsychology with a great deal of insight into normal and abnormal cognitive aging, their applicability to clinical practice and research is somewhat limited (e.g., group data tells us little about the individual patient, latent variables are commonly reported, cognitive measures are different from clinical practice). Recently, several newer longitudinal aging studies have employed commonly used clinical measures across clinically relevant time frames and analyzed the data in a way that is both applicable to groups and the individual patient/participant.

MOANS

PERHAPS BEST KNOWN of these newer longitudinal studies in neuropsychology is the Mayo's Older American Normative Studies (MOANS), which has been run by the Mayo Clinic in Rochester, MN, for the past 20 years (Ivnik et al., 1992). Originally designed to compliment their local Alzheimer's Disease Research Center, participants were recruited from their primary care physicians if they were age 55 or older, community-dwelling and independently functioning, and free from active neurological or psychiatric disorder that could negatively affect cognition. Nearly 400 "normals" participated in the baseline assessment, and the MOANS group has continued to recruit both normal and impaired participants, which now number close to 1,900 participants. The original cognitive battery included the Wechlser Adult Intelligence Scale—Revised, Wechsler Memory Scale—Revised, and the Rey Auditory Verbal Learning Test, and has been supplemented across time with other standardized neuropsychological measures (e.g., Trail Making Test, Controlled Oral Word Association Test, Dementia Rating Scale).

Consistent with its name, the MOANS baseline assessment provides extensive normative data for individuals from age 55–98 (Harris, Ivnik, & Smith, 2002; Ivnik et al., 1992; Lucas et al., 1998a; Lucas et al., 1998b; Malec et al., 1992; Smith, Ivnik, Malec, Kokmen, et al., 1994; Tangalos et al., 1996), as well as additional corrections for African Americans (Lucas et al., 2005) and different IQ levels (Steinberg, Bieliauskas, Smith, & Ivnik, 2005a, 2005b; Steinberg, Bieliauskas, Smith, Ivnik, & Malec, 2005; Steinberg, Bieliauskas, Smith, Langellotti, & Ivnik, 2005). Factor analytic studies have also identified five cognitive factors from these various tests (Mayo Cognitive Factor Scores; Smith, Ivnik, Malec, Petersen et al., 1994): Verbal Comprehension, Perceptual Organization, Attention-Concentration, Learning, and Retention. Both the individual normative data and the factor scores can be applied to the individual patient or research participant.

Many of these MOANS participants have also been followed across time with yearly retest intervals that are much more consistent with clinical practice. Across 3–4 years, participants tend to show significant improvements on the Mayo Cognitive Factor Scores from the baseline assessment to the first follow-up, but they do not tend to show additional improvements across subsequent follow-up evaluations (Ivnik et al., 1999). Not only do these findings globally define normal variance in cognitive testing in late life, but these authors provide data to calculate Reliable Change Indexes (Chelune, Naugle, Luders, Sedlak, & Awad, 1993), which are useful for defining significant changes for the individual patient/research participant.

OKLAHOMA

ANOTHER RECENT LONGITUDINAL study that examined cognitive functioning in older adults with clinically relevant applications is the Oklahoma Longitudinal Assessment of Health Outcomes in Mature Adults (OKLAHOMA) study. This study recruited individuals who were 65–94, living in the community, and regularly attending primary care appointments. In addition to completing a number of questionnaires that asked about medical conditions, physical symptoms, and perceptions of primary care, all participants were administered the Repeatable Battery for the Assessment of Neuropsychological Status (RBANS; Randolph, 1998). Over 800 participants were involved in the baseline assessment, which provided age-, education-, and gender-corrected normative data (Duff et al., 2003; Duff, Schoenberg, Mold, Scott, & Adams, in press), as well as corrections for African American participants (Patton et al., 2003). Over 500 participants were reassessed after 1 year and over 300 were reassessed after 2 years, and these data were used to develop base rates of change scores (Patton et al., 2005), Reliable Change Indexes (Duff, Beglinger et al., 2005), and regression-based change formulas (Duff et al., 2004; Duff, Schoenberg, Patton et al., 2005).

CHAP AND SALSA

NOT ONLY IS the U.S. population aging, but it is also becoming more diverse. Therefore, there is a need for longitudinal studies that examine different racial and ethnic groups as they age. The Chicago Health and Aging Project (CHAP) is a longitudinal study of risk factors for chronic disease among black and white older adults in the south side of Chicago (Bienias, Beckett, Bennett, Wilson, & Evans, 2003). Over 4,000 participants are enrolled in this study, with over 60% being non-Hispanic African Americans. Participants were examined at baseline with four cognitive tests (East Boston Tests of Immediate and Delayed Recall, Mini Mental Status Examination, Symbol Digit Modalities Test), as well as other indicators of physical and daily functioning. Follow-up visits occurred every 2–3 years. Although the cognitive battery was relatively limited, this study has provided a good deal of information about cognitive health and decline in these urban-dwelling seniors (Barnes et al., 2003, 2005; Barnes, Mendes de Leon, Wilson, Bienias, & Evans, 2004; Barnes, Wilson, Bienias et al., 2005; Barnes, Wilson, Li et al., 2005; Sturman et al., 2005).

Another longitudinal study that will add to our knowledge of cognitive changes in diverse elders is the Sacramento Area Latino Study on Aging (SALSA). Nearly 1,800 self-designated older Latinos in the Sacramento area enrolled in this study, which was designed to track the incidence of physical and cognitive impairment, dementia, and cardiovascular diseases in this sample. Baseline and yearly follow-up visits included assessment of lifestyle factors, depressive symptoms, acculturation, medical history, physical functioning tests, and cognitive screening (Modified Mini Mental Status Examination and Spanish and English Verbal Learning Test). If cognitive screening scores fell below the 20th percentile, then participants were referred for a more comprehensive neuropsychological evaluation (Spanish English Neuropsychological

Assessment Scales). As with the CHAP study, SALSA has already begun providing new findings on the relationships between medical disease and neuropsychiatric conditions in Latinos (Farias, Mungas, Reed, Haan, & Jagust, 2004; Haan et al., 2003; Miller et al., 2003; Petkov et al., 2004; Ramos et al., 2005; Wu et al., 2003), as well as normative data and new measures to assess this expanding population (Gonzalez, Mungas, & Haan, 2002, 2005; Gonzalez, Mungas, Reed, Marshall, & Haan, 2001; Mungas, Reed, Haan, & Gonzalez, 2005).

Despite the valuable information gathered from these and other longitudinal studies, they are not without their problems. One of the main criticisms of them is sampling bias, in that their samples do not adequately represent the population of community-dwelling older adults. Overall, participants in these studies tend to be highly educated, largely Caucasian (e.g., MOANS and OKLAHOMA), and generally healthy. There is concern that older adults with low education, diverse racial/ethnic backgrounds, and multiple medical comorbidities are not well-represented. A second, but related, concern involves possible retention biases in these longitudinal studies. Individuals who are doing well (physically, emotionally, and cognitively) tend to return for follow-up appointments, whereas individuals who are doing poorly are less likely to stay in the study. For example, those who returned in the OKLAHOMA study were more intact at baseline than those who didn't return (RBANS Total Time 1 for returners = 100.2 [15.4] vs. nonreturners = 89.8 [15.8]; Duff, Beglinger et al., 2005). These two types of biases can cloud our perceptions of "true" cognitive aging. Despite their limitations, these types of longitudinal studies have provided neuropsychological practitioners and researchers with a wealth of relevant information about cognitive changes in older adults on widely used assessment measures, and this information has been particularly useful in diagnosing dementia and other types of cognitive disorders in the elderly.

SUBSYNDROMAL COGNITIVE DISORDERS

WITHIN MEDICINE, PSYCHOLOGY, and neuropsychology, there has been a recent emphasis on identifying disorders in their prodromal phases. For example, within psychiatry, subsyndromal depression is being studied as a harbinger of major depressive disorder (Lyness et al., 2006). Prediagnostic stages of cognitive disorders also have been identified. Although there is considerable disagreement as to whether these prodromal stages represent truly distinct diagnostic entities or merely very early or mild forms of the eventual diagnostic condition, these prodromal stages have been receiving considerable attention. The most widely investigated prodromal disorder is MCI.

Mild Cognitive Impairment

FROM A HISTORICAL perspective, MCI might not be an entirely new concept, as similar constructs have been previously identified (e.g., benign senescent forgetfulness [Kral, 1962], age-associated memory impairment [Crook et al., 1986], aging-associated cognitive decline [Levy, 1994]). Nonetheless, clinical research efforts at the Mayo Clinic and Washington University throughout the 1990s led to two similar, but distinct, views of this transitional stage between normal aging and dementia.

Petersen and his colleagues (Petersen et al., 1999) followed a large cohort of older clinical patients in the Rochester, MN, area. Whereas many of these individuals remained cognitively stable (see MOANS section), some have declined. Within this group that declined, some developed dementia, and some declined but not to the point of dementia. This latter group was categorized as MCI (see Figure 19.2). The initial criteria by the Mayo group for MCI were:

- Subjective memory complaint
- Objective memory deficit compared to age-matched peers
- Otherwise cognitively intact
- Otherwise intact daily functioning
- Not demented

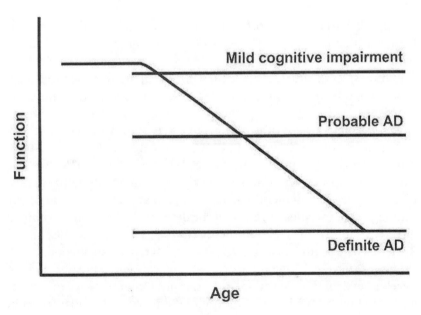

FIGURE 19.2 Theoretical progression from MCI to AD.
Note. Reprinted with permission from Petersen (2003).

Subsequently, these criteria have been modified based on new findings (e.g., collateral information on subjective memory complaint is useful [Petersen & Morris, 2003], memory deficit should be relative to age- and education-corrected normative data [Smith & Ivnik, 2003], some slight declines in other cognitive abilities are expected [Guarch, Marcos, Salamero, & Blesa, 2004], mild deficits in activities of daily living might be present [Griffith et al., 2003; Perneczky et al., 2006; Tabert et al., 2002]), but the concept has endured (Petersen, 2003).

MCI has also evolved from its initial conception as a purely amnestic condition to several different subtypes of MCI, including single domain impairment (either memory or nonmemory) and multiple domain impairments (with or without memory impairment; Petersen et al., 2001). It has been theorized that each subtype of MCI could progress to its own dementia outcome. For example, the single, memory domain subtype of MCI is likely to progress to AD, whereas the single, nonmemory domain subtype (e.g., executive dysfunction) might reflect a prodromal stage of frontotemporal dementia. Multiple domain MCI (e.g., deficits in memory and processing speed) might be indicative of eventual vascular dementia. Although this theoretical framework has drawn some criticism and has not yet been empirically tested, it provides countless avenues for exploration, both clinically and in research.

Although the Mayo definition of MCI has been most widely referenced, a second view of MCI comes from groups such as those at Washington University. There are many similarities with the Mayo concept of MCI (i.e., not normal but not demented), but the major difference is that the Washington University group notes that individuals with MCI are in a very early or mild, but definite, stage of AD (Morris & Cummings, 2005; Morris et al., 2001). This is supported by eventual diagnostic outcome in that most progress to AD (Storandt, Grant, Miller, & Morris, 2002) and by neuropathological findings in that most already have the hallmark signs of AD (Morris & Price, 2001; Morris et al., 2001).

Regardless of the definition of MCI, it has attracted so much attention because of its prognostic value. Whereas community-dwelling elders develop dementia at 1–2% per year, individuals with amnestic MCI developed dementia at 12–15% per year (Petersen et al., 1999). Although other studies have varied the definition of MCI and obtained different rates of progression (Bennett et al., 2002; Busse, Bischkopf, Riedel-Heller, & Angermeyer, 2003; Fisk, Merry, & Rockwood, 2003; Ritchie, Artero, & Touchon, 2001), all indicate an increased risk of developing dementia in this "at-risk" sample. Other negative outcomes associated with MCI include: mortality (Bennett et al., 2002; Storandt et al., 2002), institutionalization (Fisk et al., 2003; Storandt et al., 2002), disability (Boyle et al., 2005; Tabert et al., 2002), and psychiatric symptoms (Feldman et al., 2004; Lyketsos et al., 2002).

Although MCI progresses to dementia at a higher-than-normal rate, not everyone with MCI will progress. Even over 6 years, 20–30% of the original Mayo sample of MCI participants did not develop dementia (Petersen et al., 1999). Other longitudinal studies have also found that not all MCI cases progress. This has caused many to search for predictors of progression from MCI to dementia. Demographically, increasing age and lower education have been most consistently linked to progression to dementia. Clinically, collateral reports of memory problems were more suggestive of dementia conversion (Isella et al., 2006; Li, Ng, Kua, & Ko, 2006). Neuropsychologically, more severe memory deficits have been associated with transition from MCI to dementia (Arnaiz et al., 2004; Collie et al., 2001; DeCarli et al., 2004; Fowler, Saling, Conway, Semple, & Louis, 2002; Griffith et al., 2006; Guarch et al., 2004), as has mild executive dysfunction (DeCarli et al., 2004; Griffith et al., 2006; Guarch et al., 2004). An absence of expected practice effects has also been linked to continued cognitive decline (Duff, Beglinger et al., in press). Structural imaging has focused on medial temporal lobe volumes as indicators of potential progression. For example, Jack and colleagues (Jack et al., 1999) found that baseline hippocampal volumes on MRI were related to rates of progression from MCI to dementia. This group has also demonstrated the predictive value of sequential imaging by determining rates of hippocampal volume change in patients with stable MCI vs. progressive MCI (Jack et al., 2000). Structures outside the medial temporal lobe have also demonstrated significant changes in MCI patients, but fewer of these structures have been linked with predicting conversion to dementia. Functional imaging (e.g., PET, fMRI) has also been utilized in longitudinal studies of MCI. For example, patients who cognitively declined across 3 years had 18% lower resting metabolism in the entorhinal cortex compared to nondecliners (de Leon et al., 2001). Lastly, several biomarkers have been identified as potentially useful in the detection of disease progression, including APOE e4 (Aggarwal et al., 2005; Caselli et al., 2004; Mosconi et al., 2004), increased cerebrospinal fluid levels of total tau protein and phosphorylated tau protein (Blennow & Hampel, 2003; Buerger et al., 2002; Hampel et al., 2004; Maruyama et al., 2004), and decreased cerebrospinal fluid and blood levels of amyloid beta (Aβ) 40 and 42 (Andreasen, Vanmechelen, Vanderstichele, Davidsson, & Blennow, 2003; de Leon et al., 2006; Hampel et al., 2004; Herukka, Hallikainen, Soininen, & Pirttila, 2005; Ivanoiu & Sindic, 2005; Pesaresi et al., 2006). Despite extensive investigation and many promising leads, no one demographic, clinical, neuropsychological, imaging, or biomarker has become the "gold standard" for identifying which participants will progress to dementia and which will not. It is likely that future efforts will identify combinations of markers (e.g., baseline hippocampal volume, executive dysfunction, and APOE e4) that best predict conversion.

Cognitive Impairment No Dementia (CIND)

The Canadian Study of Health and Aging sought to determine prevalence rates of dementia across Canada, which it reports at 8%. It also identified a condition that was not dementia, but had "the presence of various categories of [cognitive] impairment identified in the clinical examination and in a battery of neuropsychological tests" (Graham et al., 1997). This condition, CIND, was subtyped by likely cause of the cognitive impairments: delirium, substance abuse, depression, other psychiatric illness, circumscribed memory impairment, and mental retardation. The prevalence of CIND was reported as 16.8% of Canadian seniors, with the circumscribed memory subtype representing 5.3% of the sample. It is this latter group that most closely matched the definition of MCI. When followed across 5 years, individuals with CIND had two times the risk of death, two times the risk of being admitted to an institution, and five times the risk of being diagnosed with dementia (Tuokko et al., 2003). Although MCI and CIND do not completely overlap, the concept of CIND broadens the view of subsyndromal cognitive disorders and attempts to identify the underlying cause of the disorder. Additionally, both disorders appear to be gateways to dementia.

DEMENTIA

Most globally, dementia can be defined as a loss of mental functions that is both acquired and persistent and affects multiple cognitive and behavioral domains (Mendez & Cummings, 2003). By this definition, some decline from a formerly higher level has occurred (i.e., "loss"). This loss is primarily due to mental abilities, rather than physical disabilities (e.g., hemiparalysis). This loss is acquired, rather than lifelong (e.g., mental retardation). This loss is persistent, rather than transitory (e.g., delirium). And this loss affects multiple spheres, rather than one circumscribed domain (e.g., aphasia, amnestic disorder). Despite the specifics of this definition, dementia remains a vague concept that varies greatly in its presentation and causes.

Alzheimer's Disease (AD)

Diagnostic Criteria and Prevalence

AD is the most common type of dementia, with prevalence rates as high as 10% in community-based samples (Fitzpatrick et al., 2004) and 68% in memory disorder clinics (Paulino Ramirez Diaz et al., 2005). Although a definite diagnosis still requires a post-mortem neuropathological

TABLE 19.1   NINCDS-ADRDA Criteria for Alzheimer's Disease

Probable AD

Dementia established by clinical examination, documented by mental status scales, and confirmed by neuropsychological tests.

Deficits in two or more cognitive domains.

Progressive deterioration of memory and other cognitive domains.

No disturbance of consciousness.

Onset between 40 and 90 years of age.

Absence of systemic or other brain diseases that could cause dementia.

Note. Modified from McKhann et al. (1984).

examination of brain tissue for the hallmark signs of neuritic plaques and neurofibrillary tangles, two pre-mortem sets of diagnostic criteria are widely employed in clinical and research settings. Clinically, the diagnosis can be made with evidence of memory impairment plus at least one other cognitive disturbance (aphasia, apraxia, agnosia, or executive dysfunction), a significant decline from a premorbid level, and a gradual onset with progressive course (American Psychiatric Association [APA], 2000). The National Institute of Neurological and Communicative Disorders and Stroke and Alzheimer's Disease and Related Disorders Association (NINCDS-ADRDA) criteria for probable AD (McKhann et al., 1984), however, are more commonly used in research studies (see Table 19.1).

Neuropsychological Evaluation Findings

The cognitive complaint that often leads to a clinical evaluation of possible AD is memory problems (Godbolt et al., 2005; Lehrner et al., 2005). Subjective reports of difficulties with learning and recall may come from the patient or family members. Specific examples of these memory problems could include: forgetting conversations, misplacing items, difficulties recalling names, missing appointments, and repeating him/herself. It is likely that these memory problems have been gradually worsening over the course of several years. Other cognitive deficits (e.g., language, problem solving) could be present, but are of less concern to the patient/family. As the disease progresses, some lack of awareness of deficits by the patient is common (Barrett, Eslinger, Ballentine, & Heilman, 2005; Kalbe et al., 2005). Some mild disturbances of mood or anxiety might be noted. It is likely that the patient has cut back on certain responsibilities (e.g., managing finances, managing medications, arranging appointments) or that other family members have taken over those responsibilities. Additionally, a recent significant change in life circumstances (e.g., death of spouse, move to new home) can highlight previously mild deficits in functional capabilities.

Behavioral observations during the clinical interview and formal testing are likely to support the reported changes in daily behavior. For example, the patient might have difficulty learning the name of the examiner, even after several repetitions of the information. He might demonstrate mild word finding difficulties when trying to describe his symptoms. He could get "lost" when returning from a break in the testing. He might struggle to understand some of the instructions for more complicated tests. All of this evidence is just as valuable as the scores on the formal neuropsychological measures when making the diagnosis of AD.

Consistent with the patient report and behavioral observations, performance across a comprehensive battery of neuropsychological assessment measures is likely to primarily identify learning and memory deficits (Harciarek & Jodzio, 2005), especially in an early or mild stage of AD. Both on verbal (e.g., lists, stories, or paired associates) and visual (e.g., concrete or abstract figures) tests, learning is likely to be well below expectations. Learning curves across successive trials tend to be flat. Delayed recall, however, is usually relatively more impaired (Moulin, James, Freeman, & Jones, 2004), and intrusion errors are expected. Because AD is often characterized by a rapid forgetting of information, >50% recall of information initially learned is not unusual (Au, Chan, & Chiu, 2003). Performance on recognition trials is equally impaired (Delis et al., 2005), with few correct "hits" and relatively high numbers of false positive errors. Even in the early or mild stages of AD, other cognitive difficulties are likely to be present (although they might not yet reach the point of impairment). Relative weaknesses in executive functioning, confrontational naming, semantic fluency, complex construction, and orientation to time or place are all possible (Harciarek & Jodzio, 2005). Simple attention (e.g., forward digit span) is surprisingly intact. As the dementia progresses to moderate stages, learning and memory performances are likely to reach floor effects for many standardized neuropsychological measures. More profound deficits are apparent across other cognitive domains, including complex attention, language, visuospatial perception and construction, and executive functioning. Deficits in praxis are apparent. As multiple cognitive deficits become impaired, AD often becomes difficult to distinguish from other types of dementia. Formal neuropsychological testing is not usually needed or possible in the later stages of AD.

Psychiatric dysfunction can be present throughout the natural history of AD (Cummings & McPherson, 2001). Similar to the cognitive profile, less severe symptoms appear first, and are followed by more pronounced symptoms later in the course. Depression and other changes in mood, social withdrawal, and even suicidal ideation have been reported in the majority of patients up to 2 years before diagnosis of AD (Jost & Grossberg, 1996). Within the first year after diagnosis, irritability, agitation, and aggression become common. In the later stages, hallucinations, paranoia, and accusatory behavior were present in nearly half of these patients. Given this course, formal assessment of neuropsychiatric symptoms can be useful in identifying disease progression during later stages of the illness.

Imaging and Other Laboratory Findings

Although structural imaging (e.g., CT or MRI) might be used to rule out other potential causes of the cognitive deficits in suspected AD (e.g., tumor, stroke), it can also be useful in identifying the characteristic pattern of brain degeneration. Atrophy of the hippocampal and mesial temporal regions is most pronounced in AD, especially as the disease progresses. Early in the course of the illness, radiological findings might appear "unremarkable for age" on visual inspection of the scans, but formal volumetric studies suggest that pathology has occurred (Jack et al., 1999, 2004). Functional neuroimaging (e.g., PET, fMRI) also tends to display indicators of AD: bilateral hypometabolism/hypoperfusion of the temporoparietal regions (De Santi et al., 2001; Machulda et al., 2003; Mosconi et al., 2005, 2006). Additionally, current studies are examining the benefits of specific radiotracers that bind to sites of AD pathology (Klunk et al., 2004).

Much of what we know about the biomarkers of MCI was developed out of findings related to AD. APOE e4, for example, is a risk factor for developing AD (Aggarwal et al., 2005; Baxter, Caselli, Johnson, Reiman, & Osborne, 2003; Levy et al., 2004; Qiu, Kivipelto, Aguero-Torres, Winblad, & Fratiglioni, 2004; Tierney et al., 1996). Similarly, amyloid beta and tau are related to disease onset and progression (Andreasen et al., 2003; Blennow & Hampel, 2003; de Leon et al., 2004, 2006; Ghoshal et al., 2002; Hampel et al., 2004; Ivanoiu & Sindic, 2005; Maruyama et al., 2001; Mitchell et al., 2002).

Vascular Dementia

Diagnostic Criteria and Prevalence

Occurring less frequently than AD, the prevalence of vascular dementia (VaD) is approximately 2–4% in community elders (Fitzpatrick et al., 2004) and 10% in patients seen in specialty clinics (Paulino Ramirez Diaz et al., 2005). Despite its relatively smaller numbers, it is considerably more heterogeneous in its presentation and definition than AD. VaD has also been called multi-infarct dementia, and could be due to either hemorrhagic or ischemic events affecting large or small blood vessels. Because the clinical diagnosis of VaD in the

TABLE 19.2   NINDS-AIREN Criteria for Vascular Dementia

Probable VaD

Evidence of dementia (i.e., impairments of memory and other cognitive domains).

Evidence of cerebrovascular disease (e.g., focal neurological signs, brain imaging).

Relationship between dementia and cerebrovascular disease (e.g., dementia within 3 months post-stroke, fluctuating or stepwise course of cognitive deficits).

Other features that support the diagnosis: gait disturbance, falls, incontinence, pseudobulbar palsy, mood changes.

Note. Modified from Roman et al. (1993).

APA (2000) *Diagnostic and Statistical Manual of Mental Disorders,* 4th ed., text revision *(DSM–IV—TR)* is quite similar to that of AD, other diagnostic criteria have developed to further separate these two common types of dementia. Perhaps most widely used in research settings is the National Institute of Neurological Disorders and Stroke—Association Internationale pour la Recherche et l'Enseignement en Neurosciences (NINDS-AIREN) criteria (Roman et al., 1993), which provides criteria for possible and probable VaD (see Table 19.2).

Neuropsychological Evaluation Findings

The clinical presentation of VaD is also likely to be varied, but we will describe a relatively common one. As with AD, one of the initial complaints by the patient or family is "memory problems." Upon further questioning, some examples of these difficulties will appear, but others will be different than those typically seen in AD. For example, although problems with remembering names, appointments, and medications might be reported, so will problems with other complex activities of daily living (e.g., managing finances, difficulties following directions and "figuring things out"). Apathy, depression, and emotional lability could be reported. The onset of these symptoms is likely to be more recent than AD (i.e., these deficits might lead to more immediate clinical attention than the slowly progressive symptoms in AD). The course might appear stepwise or gradually progressive, depending on the frequency and severity of additional vascular accidents.

Behavioral observations and formal testing are likely to reveal a pattern of deficits that is quite different from AD. Although initial learning and delayed recall might look quite similar to the memory deficits in AD (e.g., relatively impaired learning, flat learning curve, poor recall), performance on recognition trials are relatively intact (Tierney et al., 2001). Unlike patients with AD, patients with VaD are much more likely to demonstrate adequate encoding and storage of information across time by identifying near-normal numbers of "hits" and few (if any) false positive errors. This retrieval deficit appears to be quite common in subcortical dementias, with which VaD appears to have several components in common. Speeded processing, complex attention, and executive functioning tasks (e.g., mental arithmetic, Digit Symbol, Trail Making Test Part B) are also likely to be below expectations for patients with this type of dementia (Boyle, Paul, Moser, & Cohen, 2004; Paul, Garrett, & Cohen, 2003; Paul, Cohen et al., 2003). In contrast to patients with AD, patients with VaD tend to perform more poorly on phonemic fluency tasks compared to semantic fluency tasks. Depression, irritability, and anxiety can occur, as can hallucinations (Srikanth, Nagaraja, & Ratnavalli, 2005). Insight is usually more preserved than AD (Starkstein et al., 1996). Again, as additional small strokes occur, the nature and severity of these deficits will progress, but not necessarily in a well-defined pattern.

Imaging and Other Laboratory Findings
Neurological examination will often reveal focal abnormalities in patients with VaD. Structural imaging, especially MRI, can identify the vascular events that are purportedly responsible for the behavioral and cognitive deficits. These events might be relatively normal (e.g., diffuse white matter lesions or unidentified bright objects) or quite significant (e.g., basal ganglia strokes). Functional imaging patterns in VaD have been reported to include patchy or global hypometabolism. Cerebral angiography might also be used to identify major perfusion limitations.

MIXED DEMENTIA

IN ADDITION TO AD and VaD in their pure forms, the combination of these two conditions, often referred to as mixed dementia, also appears to be quite common. Across several studies, from 25–50% of patients with AD also have sufficient vascular pathology to be deemed VaD (Langa, Foster, & Larson, 2004; Zekry, Hauw, & Gold, 2002). Neuropsychological and neuroimaging comparisons between AD, VaD, and mixed dementia tend to show that the latter two conditions are most similar (Zekry et al., 2002). Whether these conditions are truly separate and warrant distinct diagnostic criteria is unclear. It is clear, however, that multiple types of dementia pathology can co-occur, with each leading to its own type of deficits and impairments.

FRONTOTEMPORAL DEMENTIA (FTD)

Diagnostic Criteria and Prevalence
Perhaps the third most common type of dementia, FTD is one of several dementias that falls under the spectrum of Frontotemporal

TABLE 19.3 Consensus Criteria for Frontotemporal Dementia

Presence of all core diagnostic features (i.e., insidious onset and gradual progression, early decline in social interpersonal functioning, early impairment in regulating personal conduct, early emotional blunting, early loss of insight).

Other features that support the diagnosis: behavioral disorder (e.g., decline in hygiene, mental rigidity, hyperorality, utilization behavior), speech/language disorder (e.g., altered output, echolalia, mutism), physical signs (e.g., primitive reflexes, incontinence, rigidity), diagnostic procedures (e.g., executive dysfunction on neuropsychological testing, anterior abnormalities on brain imaging).

Note. Modified from Neary et al. (1998).

Lobar Degeneration (e.g., Pick's disease, primary progressive aphasia, corticobasal degeneration, motor neuron disease). About 2–5% of memory disorder patients will be diagnosed with FTD (Lund & Manchester, 1994), and it is frequently misdiagnosed as AD. Consensus clinical criteria for FTD are presented in Table 19.3 (Neary et al., 1998), although additional criteria are also available (Lund & Manchester, 1994).

Neuropsychological Evaluation Findings

Although cognitive deficits are clearly evident on formal testing, the most common and initial complaint in cases of FTD is behavioral/personality changes (Neary, Snowden, & Mann, 2005). As the diagnostic criteria imply, these changes often reflect a significant decline in social/interpersonal functioning. For example, the formerly mild-mannered and conscientious patient might now present as overly frank, crass, and lacking empathy. There may be a decline in personal hygiene. Spouses and adult children are usually embarrassed by the patient's behavior, but the patient is indifferent. The indifference to others likely reflects an inability of the patient to recognize emotions or perspectives in others (Gregory et al., 2002). The symptoms are usually viewed as progressive, but some "straw that broke the camel's back" often leads to the clinical evaluation.

Formal neuropsychological testing will likely reveal deficits in executive functioning, especially if the FTD is primarily affecting the frontal lobes (and less so if primarily affecting the temporal lobes; Harciarek & Jodzio, 2005; Thompson, Stopford, Snowden, & Neary, 2005). Impairments have been reported across a wide range of these tests, including Wisconsin Card Sorting Test, Trail Making Test Part B, and Stroop Color Word Test. Phonemic fluency is often more impaired than semantic fluency (which is contrary to the characteristic pattern in AD). As the disease progresses, even simple go–no go tasks are beyond the patient with FTD. Language deficits can also be prominent

(Elderkin-Thompson, Boone, Hwang, & Kumar, 2004), especially if the temporal lobes are primarily affected. Decreased output of speech can be common, and eventual mutism is possible. Learning and memory is relatively intact compared to patients with AD (Harciarek & Jodzio, 2005), but might still fall below normative data due to the relationship between memory and executive functioning (Duff, Schoenberg, Scott, & Adams, 2005). Recognition memory will also tend to be relatively normal, although advancing executive dysfunction might eventually lead to high false positive error rates. Despite these significant and relative deficits, visuospatial functioning tends to be well-preserved in FTD patients, and some suggest that this domain might be useful in the differential diagnosis of AD versus FTD (Harciarek & Jodzio, 2005).

Imaging and Other Laboratory Findings

Primitive reflexes (e.g., grasp, snout, sucking) could be present on neurological examination, even in the early stages (Sjogren, Wallin, & Edman, 1997). Later in the disease, extrapyramidal signs could occur (Forman et al., 2006). As its name implies, structural and functional imaging often reveal atrophy and hypoperfusion/hypometabolism in the frontotemporal regions (Jeong et al., 2005; Short, Broderick, Patton, Arvanitakis, & Graff-Radford, 2005), which tends to be more anterior abnormalities than in AD. Although some cerebrospinal fluid and plasma biomarkers (e.g., APOE e4, amyloid beta) have been linked to FTD (Pijnenburg et al., 2006), these findings are less robust than in AD.

DEMENTIA WITH LEWY BODIES

Diagnostic Criteria and Prevalence

Although the prevalence of Lewy body inclusions in dementia cases is relatively common, the actual prevalence of dementia with Lewy bodies (DLB) remains unclear (Zaccai, McCracken, & Brayne, 2005). The application of the formal diagnostic criteria (McKeith et al., 1996; see Table 19.4), however, might begin to clarify this picture. Nonetheless, this disorder has several striking features that make DLB a "high profile" dementia.

Neuropsychological Evaluation Findings

The clinical evaluation will yield evidence of fluctuating attention and alertness (Bradshaw, Saling, Hopwood, Anderson, & Brodtmann, 2004), which may be reported as a history of delirium episodes. Recurrent, well-formed visual hallucinations might also be reported. Although parkinsonism is not typically reported by the family, other evidence, such

TABLE 19.4   Diagnostic Criteria for Dementia With Lewy Bodies

Probable DLB
Cognitive deficits sufficient to interfere with normal functioning. Deficits of attention, frontal-subcortical, and visuospatial abilities are prominent. Memory deficits might not be prominent, especially early in the course.
Two of the following: fluctuating cognition/consciousness, recurrent visual hallucinations, parkinsonisms.
Other features that support the diagnosis: repeated falls, syncope, neuroleptic sensitivity, systematized delusions, hallucinations in other modalities.

Note. Modified from McKeith et al. (1996).

as repeated falls, stiffness, and trouble initiating movements, might be. Sensitivity to neuroleptic medications, especially following attempted treatment of the hallucinations, has also been identified (Baskys, 2004).

The most prominent cognitive deficits involve attention, executive functioning, and visuospatial skills. Attention impairments include difficulties on Digit Span, Arithmetic, and Trail Making Test Part A (Ballard et al., 2001). Poor performances on verbal fluency, Similarities, and Trail Making Test Part B can characterize the executive dysfunction (Kraybill et al., 2005). Visuospatial deficits can occur on relatively simple constructional tasks (e.g., clock drawing) or more complex ones (e.g., Block Design; Johnson, Morris, & Galvin, 2005). Learning and memory profiles are more consistent with the "retrieval deficit" seen in VaD, than the amnestic syndrome of AD (Kraybill et al., 2005).

Imaging and Other Laboratory Findings

Neurological examination often reveals parkinsonism and other motor abnormalities. Neuroimaging results, both structural and functional, are similar to those seen in AD (Small, 2004), although there may be greater primary visual cortex hypometabolism in DLB patients with visual hallucinations (Minoshima et al., 2002). Functional imaging tasks that utilize complex visual stimuli (e.g., faces, motion) might be useful in differentiating DLB from AD (Sauer, Ffytche, Ballard, Brown, & Howard, 2006), although there are many clinical features that distinguish these two conditions. Evidence of the clinical utility of functional neuroimaging is still lacking. Lewy body inclusions can be diffuse (brainstem and cortex) or more focused, and greater numbers of these inclusions in the frontal and temporal regions of the cortex have been linked to greater cognitive impairment.

REVERSIBLE "DEMENTIAS"

Diagnostic Criteria and Prevalence

There are many medical conditions that can lead to the cognitive and behavioral disturbances of dementia (e.g., vitamin deficiencies, substance abuse, endocrine pathologies, normal pressure hydrocephalus), and many of these dementias can be reversed with proper medical care (Mendez & Cummings, 2003). One of the more prevalent reversible dementias that falls within this category is depression-associated dementia. Separate diagnostic criteria have not yet been developed for depression-associated dementia, but the symptoms of major depressive disorder include: depressed mood, anhedonia, changes in weight/appetite, changes in sleep, feelings of worthlessness/guilt, poor concentration, and thoughts of death/dying (APA, 2000).

Neuropsychological Evaluation Findings

Depression will likely be one of the primary rule-out conditions in these cases, and the patient will likely admit to a long history or recent onset of depression. Despite the relatively obvious psychiatric symptoms, cognitive complaints will also usually be reported, including poor attention/concentration/short-term memory. The patient might be hypervigilant of his cognitive problems and have excellent recall of each episode of his memory impairment. There might also be a dissociation between the patient's complaints (e.g., "I can't remember anything") and his actual functioning (e.g., making it to the appointment despite a short-notice room change). Unlike the progressive nature of other dementias, depression-associated dementia is more likely to have a variable and mood-dependent course.

Behavioral observations should suggest some depressed mood/affect (e.g., sad expression, tearfulness, slumped posture, head in hands). Variable or suboptimal effort is possible, especially on tasks that require considerable effort. This variable performance should not be interpreted as symptom exaggeration, but as symptom manifestation (i.e., this is how the patient functions in daily life—sometimes things go well and sometimes they don't). "I don't know" might be a relatively common response to clinical interview questions and testing items.

Formal testing will also likely yield an inconsistent/variable pattern. Attention deficits, which are part of the diagnostic criteria for major depressive disorder, can appear as impairments on Digit Span, cancellation tasks, and mental arithmetic. Slowed processing speed, which can also be related to the depressive symptoms, might lead to lowered performance on Digit Symbol, Trail Making Test, and other timed tasks (Lockwood, Alexopoulos, & van Gorp, 2002). Learning and memory may have a "retrieval deficit" pattern, with below-expectation performances on initial learning and delayed recall (Bierman, Comijs, Jonker, & Beekman, 2005). Recognition trials, however, should be relatively better, although a conservative response bias could lead to many false negative errors, but few false positive errors. As many executive functioning tasks are timed, relative weaknesses/deficits could also appear within this domain (Lockwood et al., 2002).

Imaging and Other Laboratory Findings

Although not necessarily hallmark signs of the condition, depression-associated dementia can present with various neuroimaging features (Kumar & Miller, 1997). For example, small vessel disease/white matter changes can be present on MRI. Similarly, hypometabolism of certain brain regions is more common during depressive episodes. Treatment of depression leads to cognitive improvements in some patients, yet another subset do not return to normal (Butters et al., 2000).

CONCLUSIONS

As noted at the beginning of this chapter, normal and abnormal cognitive functioning will continue to provide many opportunities for clinical and research work throughout the next 50 years. Neuropsychology is well-positioned to address many of these upcoming concerns, and should strive to be at the forefront of assessment, diagnosis, and intervention for the elderly.

REFERENCES

Aggarwal, N. T., Wilson, R. S., Beck, T. L., Bienias, J. L., Berry-Kravis, E., & Bennett, D. A. (2005). The apolipoprotein E epsilon4 allele and incident Alzheimer's disease in persons with mild cognitive impairment. *Neurocase, 11*(1), 3–7.

American Psychiatric Association. (2000). *Diagnostic and statistical manual of mental disorders* (4th ed., text revision ed.). Washington, DC: author.

Andreasen, N., Vanmechelen, E., Vanderstichele, H., Davidsson, P., & Blennow, K. (2003). Cerebrospinal fluid levels of total-tau, phospho-tau and A beta 42 predicts development of Alzheimer's disease in patients with mild cognitive impairment. *Neurologica Scandinavica Supplement, 179*, 47–51.

Arnaiz, E., Almkvist, O., Ivnik, R. J., Tangalos, E. G., Wahlund, L. O., Winblad, B., et al. (2004). Mild cognitive impairment: A cross-national comparison. *Journal of Neurology, Neurosurgery, and Psychiatry, 75*(9), 1275–1280.

Au, A., Chan, A. S., & Chiu, H. (2003). Verbal learning in Alzheimer's dementia. *Journal of the International Neuropsychological Society, 9*(3), 363–375.

Ballard, C., O'Brien, J., Gray, A., Cormack, F., Ayre, G., Rowan, E., et al. (2001). Attention and fluctuating attention in patients with dementia with Lewy bodies and Alzheimer disease. *Archives of Neurology, 58*(6), 977–982.

Baltes, P. B., & Mayer, K. U. (1999). *The Berlin Aging Study: Aging from 70 to 100.* Cambridge, England: Cambridge University Press.

Barnes, L. L., Mendes de Leon, C. F., Wilson, R. S., Bienias, J. L., & Evans, D. A. (2004). Social resources and cognitive decline in a population of older African Americans and whites. *Neurology, 63*(12), 2322–2326.

Barnes, L. L., Wilson, R. S., Bienias, J. L., Schneider, J. A., Evans, D. A., & Bennett, D. A. (2005). Sex differences in the clinical manifestations of Alzheimer disease pathology. *Archives of General Psychiatry, 62*(6), 685–691.

Barnes, L. L., Wilson, R. S., Li, Y., Aggarwal, N. T., Gilley, D. W., McCann, J. J., et al. (2005). Racial differences in the progression of cognitive decline in Alzheimer disease. *American Journal of Geriatric Psychiatry, 13*(11), 959–967.

Barnes, L. L., Wilson, R. S., Li, Y., Gilley, D. W., Bennett, D. A., & Evans, D. A. (2006). Change in cognitive function in Alzheimer's disease in African-American and white persons. *Neuroepidemiology, 26*(1), 16–22.

Barnes, L. L., Wilson, R. S., Schneider, J. A., Bienias, J. L., Evans, D. A., & Bennett, D. A. (2003). Gender, cognitive decline, and risk of AD in older persons. *Neurology, 60*(11), 1777–1781.

Barrett, A. M., Eslinger, P. J., Ballentine, N. H., & Heilman, K. M. (2005). Unawareness of cognitive deficit (cognitive anosognosia) in probable AD and control subjects. *Neurology, 64*(4), 693–699.

Baskys, A. (2004). Lewy body dementia: The litmus test for neuroleptic sensitivity and extrapyramidal symptoms. *Journal of Clinical Psychiatry, 65 Suppl 11,* 16–22.

Baxter, L. C., Caselli, R. J., Johnson, S. C., Reiman, E., & Osborne, D. (2003). Apolipoprotein E epsilon 4 affects new learning in cognitively normal individuals at risk for Alzheimer's disease. *Neurobiology of Aging, 24*(7), 947–952.

Bennett, D. A., Wilson, R. S., Schneider, J. A., Evans, D. A., Beckett, L. A., Aggarwal, N. T., et al. (2002). Natural history of mild cognitive impairment in older persons. *Neurology, 59*(2), 198–205.

Bienias, J. L., Beckett, L. A., Bennett, D. A., Wilson, R. S., & Evans, D. A. (2003). Design of the Chicago Health and Aging Project (CHAP). *Journal of Alzheimer's Disease, 5*(5), 349–355.

Bierman, E. J., Comijs, H. C., Jonker, C., & Beekman, A. T. (2005). Effects of anxiety versus depression on cognition in later life. *American Journal of Geriatric Psychiatry, 13*(8), 686–693.

Blennow, K., & Hampel, H. (2003). CSF markers for incipient Alzheimer's disease. *Lancet Neurology, 2*(10), 605–613.

Boyle, P. A., Paul, R. H., Moser, D. J., & Cohen, R. A. (2004). Executive impairments predict functional declines in vascular dementia. *Clinical Neuropsychology, 18*(1), 75–82.

Boyle, P. A., Wilson, R. S., Aggarwal, N. T., Arvanitakis, Z., Kelly, J., Bienias, J. L., et al. (2005). Parkinsonian signs in subjects with mild cognitive impairment. *Neurology, 65*(12), 1901–1906.

Bradshaw, J., Saling, M., Hopwood, M., Anderson, V., & Brodtmann, A. (2004). Fluctuating cognition in dementia with Lewy bodies and Alzheimer's disease is qualitatively distinct. *J Neurol Neurosurg Psychiatry, 75*(3), 382–387.

Buerger, K., Teipel, S. J., Zinkowski, R., Blennow, K., Arai, H., Engel, R., et al. (2002). CSF tau protein phosphorylated at threonine 231 correlates with cognitive decline in MCI subjects. *Neurology, 59*(4), 627–629.

Busse, A., Bischkopf, J., Riedel-Heller, S. G., & Angermeyer, M. C. (2003). Mild cognitive impairment: Prevalence and predictive validity according to current approaches. *Acta Neurol Scand, 108*(2), 71–81.

Butters, M. A., Becker, J. T., Nebes, R. D., Zmuda, M. D., Mulsant, B. H., Pollock, B. G., et al. (2000). Changes in cognitive functioning following treatment of late-life depression. *Am J Psychiatry, 157*(12), 1949–1954.

Caselli, R. J., Reiman, E. M., Osborne, D., Hentz, J. G., Baxter, L. C., Hernandez, J. L., et al. (2004). Longitudinal changes in cognition and behavior in asymptomatic carriers of the APOE e4 allele. *Neurology, 62*(11), 1990–1995.

Chelune, G. J., Naugle, R. I., Luders, H., Sedlak, J., & Awad, I. A. (1993). Individual change after epilepsy surgery: Practice effects and base-rate information. *Neuropsychology, 7*(1), 41—52.

Collie, A., Maruff, P., Shafiq-Antonacci, R., Smith, M., Hallup, M., Schofield, P. R., et al. (2001). Memory decline in healthy older people: Implications for identifying mild cognitive impairment. *Neurology, 56*(11), 1533–1538.

Crook, T., Bartus, R. T., Ferris, S. H., Whitehouse, P., Cohen, G. D., & Gershon, S. (1986). Age-associated memory impairment: Proposed diagnostic criteria and measures of clinical change. Report of a National Institute of Mental Health Work Group. *Dev Neuropsychol, 2,* 261–276.

Cummings, J. L., & McPherson, S. (2001). Neuropsychiatric assessment of Alzheimer's disease and related dementias. *Aging (Milano), 13*(3), 240–246.

de Leon, M. J., Convit, A., Wolf, O. T., Tarshish, C. Y., DeSanti, S., Rusinek, H., et al. (2001). Prediction of cognitive decline in normal elderly subjects with 2-[(18)F]fluoro-2-deoxy-D-glucose/poitron-emission tomography (FDG/PET). *Proc Natl Acad Sci U S A, 98*(19), 10966–10971.

de Leon, M. J., DeSanti, S., Zinkowski, R., Mehta, P. D., Pratico, D., Segal, S., et al. (2004). MRI and CSF studies in the early diagnosis of Alzheimer's disease. *J Intern Med, 256*(3), 205–223.

de Leon, M. J., DeSanti, S., Zinkowski, R., Mehta, P. D., Pratico, D., Segal, S., et al. (2006). Longitudinal CSF and MRI biomarkers improve the diagnosis of mild cognitive impairment. *Neurobiol Aging, 27*(3), 394–401.

De Santi, S., de Leon, M. J., Rusinek, H., Convit, A., Tarshish, C. Y., Roche, A., et al. (2001). Hippocampal formation glucose metabolism and volume losses in MCI and AD. *Neurobiology of Aging, 22*(4), 529–539.

DeCarli, C., Mungas, D., Harvey, D., Reed, B., Weiner, M., Chui, H., et al. (2004). Memory impairment, but not cerebrovascular disease, predicts progression of MCI to dementia. *Neurology, 63*(2), 220–227.

Delis, D.C., Wetter, S. R., Jacobson, M. W., Peavy, G., Hamilton, J., Gongvatana, A., et al. (2005). Recall discriminability: Utility of a new CVLT-II measure in the differential diagnosis of dementia. *Journal of the International Neuropsychological Society, 11*(6), 708–715.

Duff, K., Beglinger, L. J., Schoenberg, M. R., Patton, D. E., Mold, J., Scott, J. G., et al. (2005). Test-retest stability and practice effects of the RBANS in a community dwelling elderly sample. *Journal of Clinical and Experimental Neuropsychology, 27*(5), 565–575.

Duff, K., Beglinger, L. J., Schultz, S. K., Moser, D. J., McCaffrey, R. J., Haase, R. F., et al. (in press). Practice effects in the prediction of long-term cognitive outcome in three patient samples: A novel prognostic index. *Archives of Clinical Neuropsychology*.

Duff, K., Patton, D., Schoenberg, M. R., Mold, J., Scott, J. G., & Adams, R. L. (2003). Age- and education-corrected independent normative data for the RBANS in a community dwelling elderly sample. *Clinical Neuropsychology, 17*(3), 351–366.

Duff, K., Schoenberg, M. R., Mold, J. W., Scott, J. G., & Adams, R. L. (in press). Gender differences on the RBANS subtests in older adults: Baseline and retest data. *Journal of Clinical and Experimental Neuropsychology*.

Duff, K., Schoenberg, M. R., Patton, D., Mold, J., Scott, J. G., & Adams, R. L. (2004). Predicting change with the RBANS in a community dwelling elderly sample. *Journal of the International Neuropsychological Society, 10*(6), 828–834.

Duff, K., Schoenberg, M. R., Patton, D., Paulsen, J. S., Bayless, J. D., Mold, J., et al. (2005). Regression-based formulas for predicting change in RBANS subtests with older adults. *Archives of Clinical Neuropsychology, 20*(3), 281–290.

Duff, K., Schoenberg, M. R., Scott, J. G., & Adams, R. L. (2005). The relationship between executive functioning and verbal and visual learning and memory. *Archives of Clinical Neuropsychology, 20*(1), 111–122.

Elderkin-Thompson, V., Boone, K. B., Hwang, S., & Kumar, A. (2004). Neurocognitive profiles in elderly patients with frontotemporal degeneration or major depressive disorder. *Journal of the International Neuropsychological Society, 10*(5), 753–771.

Farias, S. T., Mungas, D., Reed, B., Haan, M. N., & Jagust, W. J. (2004). Everyday functioning in relation to cognitive functioning and neuroimaging in community-dwelling Hispanic and non-Hispanic older adults. *Journal of the International Neuropsychological Society, 10*(3), 342–354.

Feldman, H., Scheltens, P., Scarpini, E., Hermann, N., Mesenbrink, P., Mancione, L., et al. (2004). Behavioral symptoms in mild cognitive impairment. *Neurology, 62*(7), 1199–1201.

Fisk, J. D., Merry, H. R., & Rockwood, K. (2003). Variations in case definition affect prevalence but not outcomes of mild cognitive impairment. *Neurology, 61*(9), 1179–1184.

Fitzpatrick, A. L., Kuller, L. H., Ives, D. G., Lopez, O. L., Jagust, W., Breitner, J. C., et al. (2004). Incidence and prevalence of dementia in the Cardiovascular Health Study. *J Am Geriatr Soc, 52*(2), 195–204.

Forman, M. S., Farmer, J., Johnson, J. K., Clark, C. M., Arnold, S. E., Coslett, H. B., et al. (2006). Frontotemporal dementia: Clinicopathological correlations. *Ann Neurol, 59*(6), 952–962.

Fowler, K. S., Saling, M. M., Conway, E. L., Semple, J. M., & Louis, W. J. (2002). Paired associate performance in the early detection of DAT. *J Int Neuropsychol Soc, 8*(1), 58–71.

Ghoshal, N., Garcia-Sierra, F., Wuu, J., Leurgans, S., Bennett, D. A., Berry, R. W., et al. (2002). Tau conformational changes correspond to impairments of episodic memory in mild cognitive impairment and Alzheimer's disease. *Exp Neurol, 177*(2), 475–493.

Godbolt, A. K., Cipolotti, L., Anderson, V. M., Archer, H., Janssen, J. C., Price, S., et al. (2005). A decade of pre-diagnostic assessment in a case of familial Alzheimer's disease: Tracking progression from asymptomatic to MCI and dementia. *Neurocase, 11*(1), 56–64.

Gonzalez, H. M., Mungas, D., & Haan, M. N. (2002). A verbal learning and memory test for English- and Spanish-speaking older Mexican-American adults. *Clin Neuropsychol, 16*(4), 439–451.

Gonzalez, H. M., Mungas, D., & Haan, M. N. (2005). A semantic verbal fluency test for English- and Spanish-speaking older Mexican-Americans. *Arch Clin Neuropsychol, 20*(2), 199–208.

Gonzalez, H. M., Mungas, D., Reed, B. R., Marshall, S., & Haan, M. N. (2001). A new verbal learning and memory test for English- and Spanish-speaking older people. *J Int Neuropsychol Soc, 7*(5), 544–555.

Graham, J. E., Rockwood, K., Beattie, B. L., Eastwood, R., Gauthier, S., Tuokko, H., et al. (1997). Prevalence and severity of cognitive impairment with and without dementia in an elderly population. *Lancet, 349*(9068), 1793–1796.

Gregory, C., Lough, S., Stone, V., Erzinclioglu, S., Martin, L., Baron-Cohen, S., et al. (2002). Theory of mind in patients with frontal variant frontotemporal dementia and Alzheimer's disease: Theoretical and practical implications. *Brain, 125*(Pt 4), 752–764.

Griffith, H. R., Belue, K., Sicola, A., Krzywanski, S., Zamrini, E., Harrell, L., et al. (2003). Impaired financial abilities in mild cognitive impairment: A direct assessment approach. *Neurology, 60*(3), 449–457.

Griffith, H. R., Netson, K. L., Harrell, L. E., Zamrini, E. Y., Brockington, J. C., & Marson, D. C. (2006). Amnestic mild cognitive impairment: Diagnostic outcomes and clinical prediction over a two-year time period. *J Int Neuropsychol Soc, 12*(2), 166–175.

Guarch, J., Marcos, T., Salamero, M., & Blesa, R. (2004). Neuropsychological markers of dementia in patients with memory complaints. *Int J Geriatr Psychiatry, 19*(4), 352–358.

Haan, M. N., Mungas, D. M., Gonzalez, H. M., Ortiz, T. A., Acharya, A., & Jagust, W. J. (2003). Prevalence of dementia in older latinos: The influence of type 2 diabetes mellitus, stroke and genetic factors. *J Am Geriatr Soc, 51*(2), 169–177.

Hampel, H., Teipel, S. J., Fuchsberger, T., Andreasen, N., Wiltfang, J., Otto, M., et al. (2004). Value of CSF beta-amyloid1–42 and tau as predictors of Alzheimer's disease in patients with mild cognitive impairment. *Mol Psychiatry, 9*(7), 705–710.

Harciarek, M., & Jodzio, K. (2005). Neuropsychological differences between frontotemporal dementia and Alzheimer's disease: A review. *Neuropsychol Rev, 15*(3), 131–145.

Harris, M. E., Ivnik, R. J., & Smith, G. E. (2002). Mayo's Older Americans Normative Studies: Expanded AVLT Recognition Trial norms for ages 57 to 98. *J Clin Exp Neuropsychol, 24*(2), 214–220.

Hertzog, C., Dixon, R. A., Hultsch, D. F., & MacDonald, S. W. (2003). Latent change models of adult cognition: Are changes in processing speed and working memory associated with changes in episodic memory? *Psychol Aging, 18*(4), 755–769.

Herukka, S. K., Hallikainen, M., Soininen, H., & Pirttila, T. (2005). CSF Abeta42 and tau or phosphorylated tau and prediction of progressive mild cognitive impairment. *Neurology, 64*(7), 1294–1297.

Isella, V., Villa, L., Russo, A., Regazzoni, R., Ferrarese, C., & Appollonio, I. M. (2006). Discriminative and predictive power of an informant report in mild cognitive impairment. *J Neurol Neurosurg Psychiatry, 77*(2), 166–171.

Ivanoiu, A., & Sindic, C. J. (2005). Cerebrospinal fluid TAU protein and amyloid beta42 in mild cognitive impairment: Prediction of progression to Alzheimer's disease and correlation with the neuropsychological examination. *Neurocase, 11*(1), 32–39.

Ivnik, R. J., Malec, J. F., Smith, G. E., Tangalos, E. G., Petersen, R. C., Kokmen, E., et al. (1992). Mayo's Older Americans Normative Studies: WAIS-R norms for ages 56 to 97. *The Clinical Neuropsychologist, 6*, 1–30.

Ivnik, R. J., Smith, G. E., Lucas, J. A., Petersen, R. C., Boeve, B. F., Kokmen, E., et al. (1999). Testing normal older people three or four times at 1- to 2-year intervals: Defining normal variance. *Neuropsychology, 13*(1), 121–127.

Jack, C. R., Jr., Petersen, R. C., Xu, Y., O'Brien, P. C., Smith, G. E., Ivnik, R. J., et al. (2000). Rates of hippocampal atrophy correlate with change in clinical status in aging and AD. *Neurology, 55*(4), 484–489.

Jack, C. R., Jr., Petersen, R. C., Xu, Y. C., O'Brien, P. C., Smith, G. E., Ivnik, R. J., et al. (1999). Prediction of AD with MRI-based hippocampal volume in mild cognitive impairment. *Neurology, 52*(7), 1397–1403.

Jack, C. R., Jr., Shiung, M. M., Gunter, J. L., O'Brien, P. C., Weigand, S. D., Knopman, D. S., et al. (2004). Comparison of different MRI brain atrophy rate measures with clinical disease progression in AD. *Neurology, 62*(4), 591–600.

Jeong, Y., Cho, S. S., Park, J. M., Kang, S. J., Lee, J. S., Kang, E., et al. (2005). 18F-FDG PET findings in frontotemporal dementia: An SPM analysis of 29 patients. *J Nucl Med, 46*(2), 233–239.

Johnson, D. K., Morris, J. C., & Galvin, J. E. (2005). Verbal and visuospatial deficits in dementia with Lewy bodies. *Neurology, 65*(8), 1232–1238.

Jost, B. C., & Grossberg, G. T. (1996). The evolution of psychiatric symptoms in Alzheimer's disease: A natural history study. *J Am Geriatr Soc, 44*(9), 1078–1081.

Kalbe, E., Salmon, E., Perani, D., Holthoff, V., Sorbi, S., Elsner, A., et al. (2005). Anosognosia in very mild Alzheimer's disease but not in mild cognitive impairment. *Dement Geriatr Cogn Disord, 19*(5–6), 349–356.

Klunk, W. E., Engler, H., Nordberg, A., Wang, Y., Blomqvist, G., Holt, D. P., et al. (2004). Imaging brain amyloid in Alzheimer's disease with Pittsburgh Compound-B. *Ann Neurol, 55*(3), 306–319.

Kral, V. A. (1962). Senescent forgetfulness: Benign and malignant. *Canadian Medical Association Journal, 86,* 257–260.

Kraybill, M. L., Larson, E. B., Tsuang, D. W., Teri, L., McCormick, W. C., Bowen, J. D., et al. (2005). Cognitive differences in dementia patients with autopsy-verified AD, Lewy body pathology, or both. *Neurology, 64*(12), 2069–2073.

Kumar, A., & Miller, D. (1997). Neuroimaging in late-life mood disorders. *Clin Neurosci, 4*(1), 8–15.

Langa, K. M., Foster, N. L., & Larson, E. B. (2004). Mixed dementia: Emerging concepts and therapeutic implications. *Jama, 292*(23), 2901–2908.

Lehrner, J., Gufler, R., Guttmann, G., Maly, J., Gleiss, A., Auff, E., et al. (2005). Annual conversion to Alzheimer disease among patients with memory complaints attending an outpatient memory clinic: The influence of amnestic mild cognitive impairment and the predictive value of neuropsychological testing. *Wien Klin Wochenschr, 117*(18), 629–635.

Levy, J. A., Bergeson, J., Putnam, K., Rosen, V., Cohen, R., Lalonde, F., et al. (2004). Context-specific memory and apolipoprotein E (ApoE) epsilon 4: Cognitive evidence from the NIMH prospective study of risk for Alzheimer's disease. *J Int Neuropsychol Soc, 10*(3), 362–370.

Levy, R. (1994). Aging-associated cognitive decline. *International Psychogeriatrics,* *6, 63–68.*

Li, M., Ng, T. P., Kua, E. H., & Ko, S. M. (2006). Brief informant screening test for mild cognitive impairment and early Alzheimer's disease. *Dement Geriatr Cogn Disord, 21*(5–6), 392–402.

Lockwood, K. A., Alexopoulos, G. S., & van Gorp, W. G. (2002). Executive dysfunction in geriatric depression. *Am J Psychiatry, 159*(7), 1119–1126.

Lucas, J. A., Ivnik, R. J., Smith, G. E., Bohac, D. L., Tangalos, E. G., Graff-Radford, N. R., et al. (1998a). Mayo's older Americans normative studies: Category fluency norms. *J Clin Exp Neuropsychol, 20*(2), 194–200.

Lucas, J. A., Ivnik, R. J., Smith, G. E., Bohac, D. L., Tangalos, E. G., Kokmen, E., et al. (1998b). Normative data for the Mattis Dementia Rating Scale. *J Clin Exp Neuropsychol, 20*(4), 536–547.

Lucas, J. A., Ivnik, R. J., Willis, F. B., Ferman, T. J., Smith, G. E., Parfitt, F. C., et al. (2005). Mayo's Older African Americans Normative Studies: Normative data for commonly used clinical neuropsychological measures. *Clin Neuropsychol, 19*(2), 162–183.

Lund, T. S, & Manchester, B. J. (1994). Clinical and neuropathological criteria for frontotemporal dementia. The Lund and Manchester Groups. *J Neurol Neurosurg Psychiatry, 57*(4), 416–418.

Lyketsos, C. G., Lopez, O., Jones, B., Fitzpatrick, A. L., Breitner, J., & DeKosky, S. (2002). Prevalence of neuropsychiatric symptoms in dementia and mild cognitive impairment: Results from the cardiovascular health study. *JAMA, 288*(12), 1475–1483.

Lyness, J. M., Heo, M., Datto, C. J., Ten Have, T. R., Katz, I. R., Drayer, R., et al. (2006). Outcomes of minor and subsyndromal depression among elderly patients in primary care settings. *Ann Intern Med, 144*(7), 496–504.

Machulda, M. M., Ward, H. A., Borowski, B., Gunter, J. L., Cha, R. H., O'Brien, P. C., et al. (2003). Comparison of memory fMRI response among normal, MCI, and Alzheimer's patients. *Neurology, 61*(4), 500–506.

Malec, J. F., Ivnik, R. J., Smith, G. E., Tangalos, E. G., Petersen, R. C., Kokmen, E., et al. (1992). Mayo's Older Americans Normative Studies: Utility of corrections for age and education for the WAIS-R. *The Clinical Neuropsychologist, 6,* 31–47.

Maruyama, M., Arai, H., Sugita, M., Tanji, H., Higuchi, M., Okamura, N., et al. (2001). Cerebrospinal fluid amyloid beta(1–42) levels in the mild cognitive impairment stage of Alzheimer's disease. *Exp Neurol, 172*(2), 433–436.

Maruyama, M., Matsui, T., Tanji, H., Nemoto, M., Tomita, N., Ootsuki, M., et al. (2004). Cerebrospinal fluid tau protein and periventricular white matter lesions in patients with mild cognitive impairment: Implications for 2 major pathways. *Arch Neurol, 61*(5), 716–720.

McKeith, I. G., Galasko, D., Kosaka, K., Perry, E. K., Dickson, D. W., Hansen, L. A., et al. (1996). Consensus guidelines for the clinical and pathologic diagnosis of dementia with Lewy bodies (DLB): Report of the consortium on DLB international workshop. *Neurology, 47*(5), 1113–1124.

McKhann, G., Drachman, D., Folstein, M., Katzman, R., Price, D., & Stadlan, E. M. (1984). Clinical diagnosis of Alzheimer's disease: Report of the NINCDS-ADRDA Work Group under the auspices of Department of Health and Human Services Task Force on Alzheimer's Disease. *Neurology, 34*(7), 939–944.

Mendez, M. F., & Cummings, J. L. (2003). *Dementia: A clinical approach* (3rd ed.). Philadelphia: Butterworth Heinemann.

Miller, J. W., Green, R., Ramos, M. I., Allen, L. H., Mungas, D. M., Jagust, W. J., et al. (2003). Homocysteine and cognitive function in the Sacramento Area Latino Study on Aging. *Am J Clin Nutr, 78*(3), 441–447.

Minoshima, S., Foster, N. L., Petrie, E. C., Albin, R. L., Frey, K. A., & Kuhl, D. E. (2002). Neuroimaging in dementia with Lewy bodies: Metabolism, neurochemistry, and morphology. *J Geriatr Psychiatry Neurol, 15*(4), 200–209.

Mitchell, T. W., Mufson, E. J., Schneider, J. A., Cochran, E. J., Nissanov, J., Han, L. Y., et al. (2002). Parahippocampal tau pathology in healthy aging, mild cognitive impairment, and early Alzheimer's disease. *Ann Neurol, 51*(2), 182–189.

Morris, J. C., & Cummings, J. (2005). Mild cognitive impairment (MCI) represents early-stage Alzheimer's disease. *J Alzheimers Dis, 7*(3), 235–239; discussion 255–262.

Morris, J. C., & Price, A. L. (2001). Pathologic correlates of nondemented aging, mild cognitive impairment, and early-stage Alzheimer's disease. *J Mol Neurosci, 17*(2), 101–118.

Morris, J. C., Storandt, M., Miller, J. P., McKeel, D. W., Price, J. L., Rubin, E. H., et al. (2001). Mild cognitive impairment represents early-stage Alzheimer disease. *Arch Neurol, 58*(3), 397–405.

Mosconi, L., De Santi, S., Li, Y., Li, J., Zhan, J., Tsui, W. H., et al. (2006). Visual rating of medial temporal lobe metabolism in mild cognitive impairment and Alzheimer's disease using FDG-PET. *Eur J Nucl Med Mol Imaging, 33*(2), 210–221.

Mosconi, L., Perani, D., Sorbi, S., Herholz, K., Nacmias, B., Holthoff, V., et al. (2004). MCI conversion to dementia and the APOE genotype: A prediction study with FDG-PET. *Neurology, 63*(12), 2332–2340.

Mosconi, L., Tsui, W. H., De Santi, S., Li, J., Rusinek, H., Convit, A., et al. (2005). Reduced hippocampal metabolism in MCI and AD: Automated FDG-PET image analysis. *Neurology, 64*(11), 1860–1867.

Moulin, C. J., James, N., Freeman, J. E., & Jones, R. W. (2004). Deficient acquisition and consolidation: Intertrial free recall performance in Alzheimer's disease and mild cognitive impairment. *J Clin Exp Neuropsychol, 26*(1), 1–10.

Mungas, D., Reed, B. R., Haan, M. N., & Gonzalez, H. (2005). Spanish and English neuropsychological assessment scales: Relationship to demographics, language, cognition, and independent function. *Neuropsychology, 19*(4), 466–475.

Neary, D., Snowden, J. S., Gustafson, L., Passant, U., Stuss, D., Black, S., et al. (1998). Frontotemporal lobar degeneration: A consensus on clinical diagnostic criteria. *Neurology, 51*(6), 1546–1554.

Neary, D., Snowden, J., & Mann, D. (2005). Frontotemporal dementia. *Lancet Neurol, 4*(11), 771–780.

Patton, D. E., Duff, K., Schoenberg, M. R., Mold, J., Scott, J. G., & Adams, R. L. (2003). Performance of cognitively normal African Americans on the RBANS in community dwelling older adults. *Clin Neuropsychol, 17*(4), 515–530.

Patton, D. E., Duff, K., Schoenberg, M. R., Mold, J., Scott, J. G., & Adams, R. L. (2005). Base rates of longitudinal RBANS discrepancies at one- and two-year intervals in community-dwelling older adults. *Clin Neuropsychol, 19*(1), 27–44.

Paul, R., Garrett, K., & Cohen, R. (2003). Vascular dementia: A diagnostic conundrum for the clinical neuropsychologist. *Appl Neuropsychol, 10*(3), 129–136.

Paul, R. H., Cohen, R. A., Moser, D. J., Ott, B. R., Sethi, M., Sweet, L., et al. (2003). Clinical correlates of cognitive decline in vascular dementia. *Cogn Behav Neurol, 16*(1), 40–46.

Paulino Ramirez Diaz, S., Gil Gregorio, P., Manuel Ribera Casado, J., Reynish, E., Jean Ousset, P., Vellas, B., et al. (2005). The need for a consensus in the use of assessment tools for Alzheimer's disease: The Feasibility Study (assessment tools for dementia in Alzheimer Centres across Europe), a European Alzheimer's Disease Consortium's (EADC) survey. *Int J Geriatr Psychiatry, 20*(8), 744–748.

Perneczky, R., Pohl, C., Sorg, C., Hartmann, J., Komossa, K., Alexopoulos, P., et al. (2006). Complex activities of daily living in mild cognitive impairment: Conceptual and diagnostic issues. *Age Ageing, 35*(3), 240–245.

Pesaresi, M., Lovati, C., Bertora, P., Mailland, E., Galimberti, D., Scarpini, E., et al. (2006). Plasma levels of beta-amyloid (1–42) in Alzheimer's disease and mild cognitive impairment. *Neurobiol Aging, 27*(6), 904–905.

Petersen, R. C. (2003). *Mild cognitive impairment.* New York: Oxford Press.

Petersen, R. C., Doody, R., Kurz, A., Mohs, R. C., Morris, J. C., Rabins, P. V., et al. (2001). Current concepts in mild cognitive impairment. *Arch Neurol, 58*(12), 1985–1992.

Petersen, R. C., & Morris, J. C. (2003). Clinical features. In R. C. Petersen (Ed.), *Mild cognitive impairment* (pp. 15–40). New York: Oxford University Press.

Petersen, R. C., Smith, G. E., Waring, S. C., Ivnik, R. J., Tangalos, E. G., & Kokmen, E. (1999). Mild cognitive impairment: Clinical characterization and outcome. *Arch Neurol, 56*(3), 303–308.

Petkov, C. I., Wu, C. C., Eberling, J. L., Mungas, D., Zrelak, P. A., Yonelinas, A. P., et al. (2004). Correlates of memory function in community-dwelling elderly: The importance of white matter hyperintensities. *J Int Neuropsychol Soc, 10*(3), 371–381.

Pijnenburg, Y. A., Schoonenboom, S. N., Barkhof, F., Knol, D. L., Mulder, C., Van Kamp, G. J., et al. (2006). CSF biomarkers in frontotemporal lobar degeneration: Relations with clinical characteristics, apolipoprotein E genotype, and neuroimaging. *J Neurol Neurosurg Psychiatry, 77*(2), 246–248.

Qiu, C., Kivipelto, M., Aguero-Torres, H., Winblad, B., & Fratiglioni, L. (2004). Risk and protective effects of the APOE gene towards Alzheimer's disease in the Kungsholmen project: Variation by age and sex. *J Neurol Neurosurg Psychiatry, 75*(6), 828–833.

Ramos, M. I., Allen, L. H., Mungas, D. M., Jagust, W. J., Haan, M. N., Green, R., et al. (2005). Low folate status is associated with impaired cognitive function and dementia in the Sacramento Area Latino Study on Aging. *Am J Clin Nutr, 82*(6), 1346–1352.

Randolph, C. (1998). *Repeatable Battery for the Assessment of Neuropsychological Status.* San Antonio, TX: The Psychological Corporation.

Ritchie, K., Artero, S., & Touchon, J. (2001). Classification criteria for mild cognitive impairment: A population-based validation study. *Neurology, 56*(1), 37–42.

Roman, G. C., Tatemichi, T. K., Erkinjuntti, T., Cummings, J. L., Masdeu, J. C., Garcia, J. H., et al. (1993). Vascular dementia: Diagnostic criteria for research studies. Report of the NINDS-AIREN International Workshop. *Neurology, 43*(2), 250–260.

Salthouse, T. A. (1996). The processing-speed theory of adult age differences in cognition. *Psychol Rev, 103*(3), 403–428.

Sauer, J., Ffytche, D. H., Ballard, C., Brown, R. G., & Howard, R. (2006). Differences between Alzheimer's disease and dementia with Lewy bodies: An fMRI study of task-related brain activity. *Brain, 129*(7), 1780–1788.

Schaie, K. W. (1994). The course of adult intellectual development. *Am Psychol, 49*(4), 304–313.

Schaie, K. W. (1996). *Intellectual development in adulthood: The Seattle Longitudinal Study.* Cambridge, England: Cambridge University Press.

Short, R. A., Broderick, D. F., Patton, A., Arvanitakis, Z., & Graff-Radford, N. R. (2005). Different patterns of magnetic resonance imaging atrophy for frontotemporal lobar degeneration syndromes. *Arch Neurol, 62*(7), 1106–1110.

Singer, T., Verhaeghen, P., Ghisletta, P., Lindenberger, U., & Baltes, P. B. (2003). The fate of cognition in very old age: Six-year longitudinal findings in the Berlin Aging Study (BASE). *Psychol Aging, 18*(2), 318–331.

Sjogren, M., Wallin, A., & Edman, A. (1997). Symptomatological characteristics distinguish between frontotemporal dementia and vascular dementia with a dominant frontal lobe syndrome. *Int J Geriatr Psychiatry, 12*(6), 656–661.

Small, G. W. (2004). Neuroimaging as a diagnostic tool in dementia with Lewy bodies. *Dement Geriatr Cogn Disord, 17*(Suppl 1), 25–31.

Smith, G. E., & Ivnik, R. J. (2003). Normative neuropsychology. In R. C. Petersen (Ed.), *Mild cognitive impairment* (pp. 63–88). New York: Oxford Press.

Smith, G. E., Ivnik, R. J., Malec, J. F., Kokmen, E., Tangalos, E., & Petersen, R. C. (1994). Psychometric Properties of the Mattis Dementia Rating Scale. *Assessment, 1*(2), 123–132.

Smith, G. E., Ivnik, R. J., Malec, J. F., Petersen, R. C., Kokmen, E., Tangalos, E., et al. (1994). The Mayo Cognitive Factor Scales (MCFS): Derivation of a short battery and norms for factor scores. *Neuropsychology, 8,* 194–202.

Srikanth, S., Nagaraja, A. V., & Ratnavalli, E. (2005). Neuropsychiatric symptoms in dementia-frequency, relationship to dementia severity and comparison in Alzheimer's disease, vascular dementia and frontotemporal dementia. *J Neurol Sci, 236*(1–2), 43–48.

Starkstein, S. E., Sabe, L., Vazquez, S., Teson, A., Petracca, G., Chemerinski, E., et al. (1996). Neuropsychological, psychiatric, and cerebral blood flow findings in vascular dementia and Alzheimer's disease. *Stroke, 27*(3), 408–414.

Steinberg, B. A., Bieliauskas, L. A., Smith, G. E., & Ivnik, R. J. (2005a). Mayo's Older Americans Normative Studies: Age- and IQ-adjusted norms for the Trail-Making Test, the Stroop Test, and MAE Controlled Oral Word Association Test. *Clin Neuropsychol, 19*(3–4), 329–377.

Steinberg, B. A., Bieliauskas, L. A., Smith, G. E., & Ivnik, R. J. (2005b). Mayo's Older Americans Normative Studies: Age- and IQ-adjusted norms for the Wechsler Memory Scale—Revised. *Clin Neuropsychol, 19*(3–4), 378–463.

Steinberg, B. A., Bieliauskas, L. A., Smith, G. E., Ivnik, R. J., & Malec, J. F. (2005). Mayo's Older Americans Normative Studies: Age- and IQ-adjusted norms for the Auditory Verbal Learning Test and the Visual Spatial Learning Test. *Clin Neuropsychol, 19*(3–4), 464–523.

Steinberg, B. A., Bieliauskas, L. A., Smith, G. E., Langellotti, C., & Ivnik, R. J. (2005). Mayo's Older Americans Normative Studies: Age- and IQ-adjusted norms for the Boston Naming Test, the MAE Token Test, and the Judgment of Line Orientation Test. *Clin Neuropsychol, 19*(3–4), 280–328.

Storandt, M., Grant, E. A., Miller, J. P., & Morris, J. C. (2002). Rates of progression in mild cognitive impairment and early Alzheimer's disease. *Neurology, 59*(7), 1034–1041.

Sturman, M. T., Morris, M. C., Mendes de Leon, C. F., Bienias, J. L., Wilson, R. S., & Evans, D. A. (2005). Physical activity, cognitive activity, and cognitive decline in a biracial community population. *Arch Neurol, 62*(11), 1750–1754.

Tabert, M. H., Albert, S. M., Borukhova-Milov, L., Camacho, Y., Pelton, G., Liu, X., et al. (2002). Functional deficits in patients with mild cognitive impairment: Prediction of AD. *Neurology, 58*(5), 758–764.

Tangalos, E. G., Smith, G. E., Ivnik, R. J., Petersen, R. C., Kokmen, E., Kurland, L. T., et al. (1996). The Mini-Mental State Examination in general medical practice: Clinical utility and acceptance. *Mayo Clin Proc, 71*(9), 829–837.

Thompson, J. C., Stopford, C. L., Snowden, J. S., & Neary, D. (2005). Qualitative neuropsychological performance characteristics in frontotemporal dementia and Alzheimer's disease. *J Neurol Neurosurg Psychiatry, 76*(7), 920–927.

Tierney, M. C., Black, S. E., Szalai, J. P., Snow, W. G., Fisher, R. H., Nadon, G., et al. (2001). Recognition memory and verbal fluency differentiate probable Alzheimer disease from subcortical ischemic vascular dementia. *Arch Neurol, 58*(10), 1654–1659.

Tierney, M. C., Szalai, J. P., Snow, W. G., Fisher, R. H., Tsuda, T., Chi, H., et al. (1996). A prospective study of the clinical utility of ApoE genotype in the prediction of outcome in patients with memory impairment. *Neurology, 46*(1), 149–154.

Tuokko, H., Frerichs, R., Graham, J., Rockwood, K., Kristjansson, B., Fisk, J., et al. (2003). Five-year follow-up of cognitive impairment with no dementia. *Arch Neurol, 60*(4), 577–582.

Verhaeghen, P., & Salthouse, T. A. (1997). Meta-analyses of age-cognition relations in adulthood: Estimates of linear and nonlinear age effects and structural models. *Psychol Bull, 122*(3), 231–249.

Wu, J. H., Haan, M. N., Liang, J., Ghosh, D., Gonzalez, H. M., & Herman, W. H. (2003). Impact of diabetes on cognitive function among older Latinos: A population-based cohort study. *J Clin Epidemiol, 56*(7), 686–693.

Zaccai, J., McCracken, C., & Brayne, C. (2005). A systematic review of prevalence and incidence studies of dementia with Lewy bodies. *Age Ageing, 34*(6), 561–566.

Zekry, D., Hauw, J. J., & Gold, G. (2002). Mixed dementia: Epidemiology, diagnosis, and treatment. *J Am Geriatr Soc, 50*(8), 1431–1438.

20

Learning Disorders

DAVID C. OSMON, CORY PATRICK,
AND ELIZABETH ANDRESEN

PROBLEMS IN LEARNING have been associated with disability (impediments in living) since Samuel A. Kirk coined the term learning disability in a talk to the Association for Children with Learning Disabilities. However, the term disability carries a sociopolitical connotation associated with high rates of impairment. The Centers for Disease Control and Prevention found that of the 3.8 million persons under age 18 who qualified as disabled (7.9% of this segment of the population) the most frequent category was learning disability, accounting for 29.5% of the diagnoses. Compare this rate to mental retardation and asthma (each around 6–7%), speech problems (13.1%), and emotional disorders (6.3%) as other significant contributors to the ranks of disability among children.

While this trend is alarming, further estimates suggest an increase in the ranks of the disabled (U.S. Department of Education, 2002). As part of this increase, those with a learning disability seem to be the fastest-growing segment of disabled. For example, individuals self-reporting learning disability grew from 25% of the total disability population in 1991 to 41% in 1998, according to the Department of Education report. Perhaps part of the increase in self-reporting of learning disability is a tendency to confound terminology. For example, using the term *disability* encourages confusion of sociopolitical discussions and definitions of *being disabled* in the educational activities of life with *having a disorder* that adversely impacts learning. For this reason, the current chapter uses the psychiatric label learning disorder (LD) instead of the more common term, learning disability. The term *disorder* invokes, as intended in most definitions of LD, a neurological dysfunction that instills an inherent cognitive processing deficit that underlies the learning problem and makes that individual learn differently.

Disability in general and learning disability in particular represents a substantial problem for the education of our populace. However, our understanding of learning disability and disorder must precede any hope of providing an educational environment sufficient to bring our populace to reading competence. The current chapter takes another look at the definition of LD in light of recent neuroscientific advances in hopes of reinvigorating past attempts to place LD on an etiological foundation rooted in neurobiology. In doing so, a taxonomy might be constructed that takes advantage of known neurocognitive characteristics of LD and that will ultimately be more informative for treatment decisions.

LD DEFINITION

THE NEUROLOGICAL BASIS of learning disorder can be traced to the late 1800s in studies of psychic blindness, congenital word blindness, word alexia, and letter-by-letter reading (see Lange, 1988). Recent definitions of LD include one by the National Joint Committee on Learning Disabilities (Hammill, Leigh, McNutt, & Larsen, 1981; NJCLD, 1988) and a more recent one from 2002 by the International Dyslexia Association. The NJCLD definition is as follows:

> Learning disabilities is a generic term that refers to a heterogeneous group of disorders manifested by significant difficulties in the acquisition and use of listening, speaking, reading, writing, reasoning or mathematical abilities. These disorders are intrinsic to the individual and presumed to be due to central nervous system dysfunction. Even though a learning disability may occur concomitantly with other handicapping conditions (e.g., sensory impairment, mental retardation, social and emotional disturbance) or environmental influences (e.g., cultural differences, insufficient-inappropriate instruction, psychogenic factors), it is not the direct result of those conditions or influences. (p. 1)

While this definition was revised to include the life-long nature of the disorder and to refute a movement to include social skills as the basis for a subtype of LD, this revision includes only minor wording changes and is not included here because of exclusionary statements about social skills and self-regulatory deficits.

LD definitions include several key components: (a) the organic and congenital nature of the disorder, (b) the presence of specific cognitive deficits apart from general intellectual disturbance, (c) the existence of cognitive processing disorders underlying the academic deficiencies, and (d) the heterogeneous nature of the disorder's clinical manifestations. It is these key aspects of the disorder that give it a neurological etiology and a neuropsychological flavor in the clinic.

LD ETIOLOGY

THE NEUROBIOLOGICAL BASIS of LD seems indisputable but cannot be done justice in the current format. Likewise, it is not yet well understood, so will be reviewed in general outline only. There are several findings consonant with the type of cause that might be expected according to the definition of the disorder described previously. These findings are suggestive of a focal dysplasia that could impair specific cognitive abilities (e.g., phonologic) without disrupting general intelligence. Additionally, the damaged site can be anatomically variable such that different specific cognitive impairments are possible in the various subtypes of LD (e.g., various perceptual, decoding, and semantic/syntactic deficits in subtypes of dyslexia or visuospatial, executive, and socioemotional deficits in subtypes of nonverbal LD). Furthermore, the damage is congenital, or at least perinatal, static, and chronic to satisfy the life-long and nonprogressive natural history of LD.

The earliest clear evidence for the cause of LD satisfying the aforementioned conditions was the finding of ectopias (also known as microdysgenesis), which are the result of migration errors of cells during the first trimester of fetal development (Galaburda, 1989). The migration errors lead to "wiring problems" in the layering of the cortex, causing congenital and life-long focal disruptions in cortical functioning. In concert with such focal dysplasia accounts, LD individuals have been found to lack the normal asymmetry of the planum temporale (Miller, Sanchez, & Hynd, 2003), which can be several times larger on the left in normals and is particularly prominent in language areas (Steinmetz, 1996). Additionally, dyslexics have been found to have reduced gyrification and smaller brain volumes (Casanova, Araque, Giedd, & Rumsey, 2004), a finding consistent with focal, early damage of the sort that might occur with ectopias. Variations in gyral morphology of the perisylvian region and callosal size have also been found to relate to both diagnosis and reading test performance (also reviewed in Miller et al., 2003).

While these findings have been routinely criticized, they are suggestive and warrant further study as the neurobiologic basis of LD. Future work needs to correlate neuroanatomy with functional imaging and neuropsychological strengths and weaknesses utilizing current knowledge of LD subtypes. As an example of the kind of integrative work that will help elucidate the etiology of LD, Leonard, Lombardino, Giess, and King (2005) cluster analytically defined groups based upon phonologic, orthographic, and semantic indices. Four groups lined up according to severity of language deficits in a manner consistent with current thought, including: the most impaired group labeled Language Impaired; the next impaired group called Double Deficit, because of both phonological and orthographic deficits; the third group with only orthographic deficits called Rate Deficit; and a final dyslexic group labeled Gifted/Discrepant, because of above average verbal intelligence but only average reading scores. Anatomical asymmetry varied according to the severity associated with these four groups with the most severe groups having abnormal symmetry and smaller cerebral volume of the left planum.

In addition to neuroanatomic dysfunction in LD, there is considerable evidence for genetic transmission of brain morphology underlying language ability and for the transmission of LD. For example, identical twins show almost no variation (within-pair r = .9) in total gray matter according to MRI defined three-dimensional maps (Thompson et al., 2001). Likewise, similar lack of variation was seen in language and tertiary cortex with indications of greater genetic determination of left language-related areas than homologous right hemisphere regions. Such results argue that the neurobiologic substrate for specific cognitive ability is largely heritable.

In concert with heritability of the cognitive substrate, several groups have found strong heritability of LD. Dale et al. (1998) found that among 3,000 twin pairs studied subjects in the lower fifth percentile of ability had heritability coefficients of 73% compared to only 25% in the entire sample, and the shared environment effect was only 18% compared to 69% for the entire sample. These figures are generally consistent with extensive twin studies by the Colorado School-Age Twin Study (summarized by Olson & Byrne, 2005). The Colorado study answered many criticisms of LD genetic research by using continuous measures of general and specific deficits of dyslexia. Measures of phoneme awareness, short-term memory, rapid naming skills, auditory perceptual processing, and homophone selection found genetic contributions to both phonologic and orthographic deficits in dyslexia. In general, estimates for heritability were large (h^2 for phonology = .71 and for orthography = .67) while shared environment (c^2 phonology = .18 and for orthography = .17), and nonshared environment (e^2 phonology = .12 and for orthography = .16) were small. Results of the Colorado study series also showed that genetic differences in word reading were partly independent of Full Scale IQ, as demonstrated by the genetic correlation between word reading and WAIS-R FSIQ (r_g = .53). Such a finding is consistent with previous research demonstrating that specific factors of intelligence predict reading problems independent of and beyond predictions from general intelligence (Floyd, Evans, & McGrew, 2003).

Like all cognitive abilities, the genetic basis of reading (and LD in general) is too complex to be Mendelian (trait is due to a single gene). Therefore, nonparametric methods (e.g., Quantitative Trait Locus mapping) have been important in identifying multiple gene sites associated with disorders of reading in general and core deficits of reading in particular (see Fisher & DeFries, 2002 for a review). Extant studies point tentatively in the direction that at least phonologic and orthographic deficits have distinct genetic origins.

TAXONOMY

CERTAINLY, THERE ARE many instantiations of a taxonomy for LD that can be concocted, and none yet holds wide acceptance. The present one is meant only to be representative of the current literature. Figure 20.1 identifies three broad types of LD (verbal, nonverbal, dysexecutive), each having subtypes based upon clinically identifiable

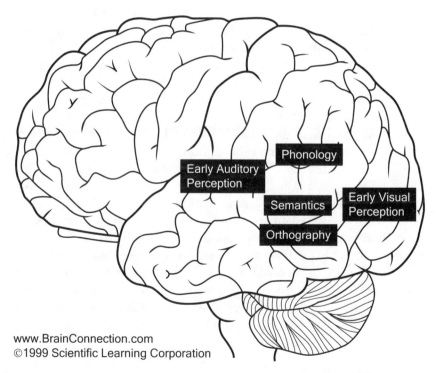

www.BrainConnection.com
©1999 Scientific Learning Corporation

FIGURE 20.1 Dorsal reading route relating to auditory perceptual and phonologic processes and ventral reading route relating to visual perceptual and orthographic processes.

processing disorders. The neuropsychological features of the verbal and nonverbal subtypes are reviewed in the following paragraphs. The dysexecutive type is not reviewed, because Chapter 21 of this book is devoted to attention-deficit/hyperactivity disorder (ADHD), and neither it nor motor incoordination disorder has been traditionally associated with LD. They are added to be theoretically consistent with the definition of LD as a neurobiologically based disorder affecting a specific neuropsychological function.

A general model of LD is assumed in presenting the various subtypes in the following paragraphs. Specifically, the model assumes that specific processing disorders (i.e., cognitive deficits) underlie low achievement and that the subtype of LD is determined by the nature of the cognitive deficits. Furthermore, the cognitive deficit is a manifestation of an anatomically circumscribed neurological pathology (e.g., microdysgenesis, abnormal gyral morphology, etc.). Thus, an attempt is made to link the cognitive profile of strengths and weaknesses to what is known about the neuroanatomy of the achievement process.

VERBAL TYPE LD

THREE RECOGNIZABLE CLINICAL subtypes of verbal LD (phonologic, orthographic, phonologic-orthographic) are consistently found to have differentiated neuroanatomy, assessment profiles of strengths and weaknesses, and response to treatment. Another less recognized subtype (semantic/syntactic) has been consistently identified though variously labeled. Additionally, two other potential subtypes are considered: auditory and visual perceptual dyslexia.

Consistent with the apt quote: "Every child is like all other children, some other children, and no other children" (Fletcher, Morris, & Lyon, 2003), it is estimated that 60% of children with verbal LD have an admixture of deficits in phonology, orthography, reading comprehension, and probably auditory or visual perception (Ellis, 1993). However, cases exist with selective deficits that demonstrate both the separateness of these sundry verbal and perceptual abilities and the viability of identifying subtypes of verbal LD around deficits in these abilities. A similar subtyping approach is considered by those who ascribe to a cognitive neuropsychology (intensive single case study methodology) approach. However, this approach is not reviewed here, although it is important to note the similarities of subtypes from this approach (phonologic, surface, and deep dyslexia) with those covered here (Ellis, 1993).

Phonological Dyslexia

There are two contrasting models of dyslexia. First, the phonological core model of dyslexia (Morris et al., 1998; Vukovic & Siegel, 2006) specifies deficits in phonological processing as the core feature of all dyslexia, giving rise to ancillary problems in orthographic processing that arise out of the phonological problems and are not separate cognitive deficits. Second, the double deficit model specifies that the phonologic and orthographic deficits are independent aspects of reading difficulty that have unique contributions to the reading process and are differentially important at different developmental stages of reading maturity (Wolf, 1999). Despite their differences, both models agree that phonological skills are crucial components of reading and are primary at least in the early stages of learning to read (Wolf & Bower, 1999).

Various aspects of phonology exist on which readers' competence can vary. An important distinction is between phonetic ability (discerning speech sounds), grapheme-phoneme correspondence rules (matching speech sounds or phonemes to printed symbols or graphemes), phonological memory (holding phonemes in mind to gain appreciation of entire words, especially when manipulating phonemes) and phonological awareness (the broader skill of manipulating individual phonemes within words and word segments, such as recognizing what word is made of *lake* by substituting *b* for *l*). All of these skills depend heavily upon the dorsal reading route according to functional neuroimaging studies. For example, Pugh et al. (2001) found the dorsal route activates during auditory discrimination and word attack type tasks and is generally considered to mediate phonological and phoneme-to-grapheme conversion processes.

Further relationships were noted between three aspects of phonology. Specifically, phonological awareness (Lindamood Auditory Conceptualization task) related to left temporal and left inferior frontal areas, phonetic retrieval (Rapid Automatized Naming) related to bilateral frontal and temporal areas, and phonological working memory (Digit Span) related only to left inferior parietal lobule areas. Such results suggest that early school experience is important in integrating multiple brain areas in support of reading and that better development of reading skill was associated with moving from bilateral to left hemisphere processing and that right temporo-occipital hemisphere (presumably whole word reading) strategies become less important in favor of left temporal (dorsal route) phonological strategies. Additionally, only adult subjects in this study were associated with strong left frontal activation, suggesting that linguistic development moves from a decoding (temporal lobe) to a complex semantic level of analysis (left frontal areas: Pugh et al., 2001).

Some aspects of the natural history of dyslexia have also been suggested by neuroimaging studies comparing dyslexics and normal readers. Primary findings suggest that dyslexics tend to underactivate dorsal and ventral routes (see Figure 20.1 and following discussion) and overactivate frontal and homogenous right temporal areas (Corina et al., 2001; Shaywitz et al., 2003). Thus, reading may be seen as a network consisting of connected areas, including the posterior and anterior language systems (e.g., Paulesu, Frith, & Snowling, 1996), and that phonology is centrally situated in this reading network.

Given these results, it is not surprising that specific processing disorders are associated with dyslexia, including crystallized intelligence (Gc), auditory processes (Ga), and short-term memory (Gsm). Specific cognitive abilities have been found to be more related to dyslexia than general intelligence (Floyd et al., 2003), consistent with the definition of LD as a disorder that does not impact general intelligence. While these processing disorders have been found associated with dyslexia in general, there has been no attempt to look at processing disorders associated with subtypes of dyslexia.

Given these imaging and neuropsychological results, a specific cognitive profile of phonological dyslexia becomes evident. First, this subtype captures those with early reading problems who tend to have difficulty analyzing words into their component speech sounds. Such individuals often tend to over-rely upon whole-word recognition and semantic (Nation & Snowling, 1998) strategies that emphasize long-term visual memory and language comprehension while having difficulty spelling phonetically regular words. In fact, word attack ability, often measured as ability to spell (e.g., Spelling of Sounds on WJ-III) or pronounce (e.g., Word Attack on the Woodcock-Johnson-III: WJ-III) phonetically regular nonsense words (to minimize orthographic ability relating to familiarity of real words), is a common method of assessing for phonological difficulty. Phonological dyslexics have difficulty early in school with reading tasks and respond well to phonologic treatment methods (Lyon & Cutting, 1998), but once they get behind they tend to stay behind normal readers throughout their educational career without specific and intense phonics and phonological awareness training (Byrne & Fielding-Barnsley, 1993).

Orthographic Dyslexia

English is an "orthographically deep" language as exemplified by the differences in majority opinion on how to pronounce a phonologically regular word sugh as *jat* versus an ambiguous word like *jough* (Fiez, 2000). As Fiez notes, most English speakers would agree that *jat* should rhyme with *bat*; however, opinions for *jough* might range from rhyming with *cough, tough, dough,* or *bough*. These complexities make it clear that orthographic knowledge contributes to reading fluency. Otherwise, phonology would not lead to such ambiguity. It was the awareness of orthography's importance that led to the development of the double deficit hypothesis (Badian, 2005).

This hypothesis has been developing a great deal of support in demonstrating that phonologic and orthographic abilities are separate processes, and both are important toward the ultimate goal of reading, namely comprehension. The support arises from multiple methodologies, including case study methods of cognitive neuropsychology, functional neuroimaging methods of neuroscience, test performance methods of psychometry, intervention research from educational psychology, and characteristics of hyperlexia, among others. As an example of the psychometric research, kindergarten performance in orthographic tasks predicts better seventh-grade reading skills than does phonologic task performance (Badian, 2001). Likewise, Van der Leij and van Daal (1999) furthered the double deficit hypothesis notion that orthographic (and to some extent phonologic) problems arise from processing speed deficits by showing the importance of automaticity in reading. In this study dyslexics' response latencies were slower in identifying familiar words, letter clusters, and nonwords with larger word frequency, word length, and subword frequency effects, indicating that dyslexics' reading had not attained automaticity. Such processing speed deficits have been identified for quite a while (e.g., Badian, 2005; Elrod & Ryckman, 1984; and Kranzler, 1994).

These results suggest that subword processes are at play in word recognition that allow skilled readers to read more quickly, especially irregular words for which phonological ability is of little help. Such a result was supported by Butler, Jared, and Hains (1984) who found that high vocabulary college students were much less affected by word length in word recognition performance than low vocabulary subjects. It was also found that a difference between high and low vocabulary subjects was evident, with high vocabulary subjects being more sensitive to syllable (sublexical) structure.

The distinctness of sublexical, orthographic processes apart from phonology gives rise to the disorder of hyperlexia. Hyperlexia is a disorder characterized by early reading (often before age 5) with better than expected word recognition skills but poor reading comprehension in the context of impaired phonologic skills and better than expected orthographic skills (Sparks, 2004). Such a profile of reading skills demonstrates that whole word recognition can occur from orthographic skills, resulting in fluent reading.

Consistent with the notion that orthography is distinct from phonology, neuroimaging results demonstrate the importance of visual perceptual regions of the brain for orthographic aspects of reading. Specifically, early striate (bilaterally) and left extrastriate visual cortex is activated by the visual perceptual requirements of reading (McCrory, Mechelli, Frith, & Price, 2005). From here two perceptual routes of reading diverge (see Figure 20.1). The auditory–phonologic route takes a dorsal course in the temporal lobe, including primary auditory cortices (Heschl's gyri bilaterally), superior temporal gyrus, and posterior portions of the inferior parietal lobule, as reviewed previously in the phonological dyslexia section. A more ventral left temporo-occipital route including portions of the fusiform gyrus and known as the Visual Word Form Area (VWFA) activates during word recognition and orthographic tasks (Temple et al., 2001).

Such results suggest that formal reading develops initially, consistent with Frith (1985), by mastering the alphabetic principle. Normal readers attain the alphabetic principle and develop auditory analytic facility, proceeding beyond the level of individual speech sounds (phonemes) to the level of meaningful units (morphemes). Decoding larger units speeds up reading ability by allowing visual recognition of sublexical units. However, deficits in orthographic ability at this stage would impair the visual perceptual basis of moving from single phoneme to syllable and morphemic level chunking of these sublexical units. Dysfunction of the VWFA corresponds with failure at this level of competence, giving rise to the other core deficit of dyslexia, namely orthographic deficits such as poor rapid naming skills. In addition to rapid automatic naming, there is evidence that a host of orthographic abilities exist and hang together as different factors of visual word recognition skills. Thus, Mano (unpublished) factor analyzed several experimental orthographic tasks culled from the literature and found confirmatory evidence for three orthographic factors: lexical/sublexical processing speed, early visual perceptual letter/word identification accuracy, and lexico-semantic word identification accuracy.

Based on such evidence the orthographic dyslexic subtype has a unique set of cognitive strengths and weaknesses. Such individuals, by definition, are relatively better in phonologic abilities. In contrast, this subtype is more impaired in orthographic processes such as whole word recognition, spelling phonetically irregular words, grasping sublexical regularities, and reading fluently and automatically (Badian, 1996). Such an individual tends to perform relatively well in early reading instruction, because phonological awareness is emphasized. Thus, reading problems of this type of dyslexic are often not recognized until reading speed and comprehension is emphasized later in elementary school when orthographic ability is more in play (Badian, 2001). As word recognition by phonological analysis becomes firmly developed by third grade, automatic word recognition via visual memory becomes the favored mode of reading. Vocabulary should now begin to develop quickly, and comprehension should leap forward as reading becomes more automatic and executive processes are freed to begin focusing on meaning.

Double Deficit Dyslexia

In addition to the predominately phonologic and orthographic sub-types, a third subtype is the mixed phonologic–orthographic dyslexic, the so-called double deficit dyslexic. Such individuals tend to have more severe reading problems that are less amenable to remediation because of their deficits in both elements of reading (Wolf & Bowers, 1999). However, they are otherwise an amalgam of the previous two subtypes and are not further reviewed here.

Semantic–Syntactic Dyslexia

Traditionally, dyslexia has been characterized solely as a disorder of decoding (phonologic and/or orthographic problems) and not language (i.e., verbal conceptual) facility. However, many poor decoders attain normal levels of comprehension. Additionally, a significant minority have greater problems with language then with decoding skills (5% in a sample of 1,285 older elementary school children [Cornold, De Beni, & Pazzaglia, 1996]; 3–10% in kindergarteners [Tomblin et al., 1997]). Therefore, it is untenable to assume that reading and listening comprehension difficulties occur only as secondary effects of decoding problems.

Based upon the aforementioned findings, comprehension must be considered a deficit in dyslexia that is at least semi-independent of decoding problems (Stothard, 1994) but not entirely unrelated to phonologic and orthographic processes (Torgesen, Wagner, & Rashotte, 1999a). In fact, poor comprehenders have much in common with various types of poor readers known by terms such as specific language disorder (Catts & Kamhi, 2005), oral language disorder, hyperlexia (Seymour & Evans, 1994), and language impaired (Montgomery, Windsor, & Stark, 1991). While characterizations of the language deficits of these types are varied, they tend to share a general impairment in crystallized intelligence (Gc or verbal-conceptual ability; Mather & Jaffe, 2002).

Ullman (2001) espouses a model of language processes that relates the semantic and syntactic processes of this subtype of dyslexia. This model, reminiscent of many language models, argues that a posterior system memorizes entries in the mental lexicon while an anterior system stores the procedures of mental grammar for the purpose of deriving meaning by storing syntactic rules for combining lexical entries in a novel fashion.

The semantic–syntactic subtype is distinct from decoding subtypes for deficits in verbal understanding in both reading and listening comprehension tasks. That is, because reading and listening comprehension scores correlate, and one includes decoding (reading) and the other does not (listening), then individuals without phonologic and orthographic deficits on other tasks but impairment in both reading and listening comprehension must be a general semantic deficit. In contrast, those with a selective problem in reading comprehension and intact listening comprehension must have decoding problems in the absence of comprehension problems. Such results have been found by Hoover and Gough (1990). Likewise, a factor analysis showed reading comprehension measures load equally on a decoding factor and a listening comprehension factor, supporting this dissociation (Nation & Snowling, 1998).

Oakhill, Cain, and Bryant (2003) identify several difficulties in poor comprehenders, including: syntactic difficulties involving sentence and phrase structure, problems inferring and integrating across ideas, awareness of text structure in the sense of following the plot by identifying main characters and tracking events to provide an organizing coherence that facilitates memory, monitoring understanding (what some call metacognitive skills; Stothard, 1994), and working memory.

Based upon the etiologic perspective of this chapter, it would seem likely that poor reading could occur solely on the basis of focal neuropathology (e.g., microdysgenesis) confined to semantic processing regions (Wible et al., 2006) without affecting decoding skills. If such were the case then the poor readers characterized as having comprehension problems in the absence of decoding difficulties would fit this variety of dyslexia. Only future studies will bear out this assumption. In the meantime, the empirical existence of poor comprehenders needs to be better characterized.

Auditory Perceptual Dyslexia

From a neuropsychological perspective, LD needs to be viewed as a disorder that can affect both early perceptual as well as linguistic level decoding processes and semantic–syntactic levels of processing. While some have questioned whether deficits in such low-level perceptual processes play an etiologic role in LD (Mody, Studdert-Kennedy, & Brady, 1997), deficits at both the auditory and visual perceptual level have been found in dyslexia.

While some researchers argue that the perceptual deficits are incidental to the disorder and not causative, there is reason to believe otherwise. For example, Stefanatos, Gershkoff, and Madigan (2005) have shown in a case of pure auditory word deafness from a left superior temporal infarct that the disorder is related to disruption of transitioning low level auditory information into lexical representations of words. This case was deficient in perceiving isolated formant transitions of less than 200 ms and in perceiving both speech and nonspeech sounds that required analysis of rapid spectrotemporal variations in frequency.

Beyond individual cases, damage to the left superior temporal region is known to cause early perceptual deficits (Temple et al., 2003), although other evidence is required to demonstrate these kinds of difficulties in developmental dyslexia. In this regard, early phonetic/phonologic deficits, rather than later phonologic/lexical difficulty, are suggested by abnormal latencies in evoked response N100 and N200 waveforms rather than N400 waveforms in dyslexics (Milene, Bonte, & Blomert, 2004). Furthermore, auditory perceptual deficits are not limited to linguistic material, as tonal memory tasks requiring rapid auditory perceptual processing and detection and discrimination of temporal envelopes in nonspeech sounds (Rocheron, Lorenzi, Fullgrabe, & Dumont, 2002) are also impaired in dyslexics compared to normal readers and are associated with reduced right temporal cortical activation (Rumsey, Andreason, Zametkin, & King, 1994).

An impressive body of work supports the impairment of rapid perception of dynamic sound changes in dyslexia, and such deficits are thought to underlie the problems of phonological discriminations in speech in dyslexia (Tallal & Gaab, in press). Such discriminations must occur on durations of tens of milliseconds in both speech and nonspeech perception. In fact, Zaehle, Wustenberg, Meyer, and Jancke (2004) have demonstrated that these rapid auditory perceptions in both speech and nonspeech sounds activate overlapping regions in primary and secondary auditory cortex in the superior temporal gyrus, and separate studies have demonstrated disruption of rapid auditory processing in dyslexics and increased left temporo-parietal activation after FastForWord remediation (e.g., Temple et al., 2000; Temple et al., 2003). Furthermore, Benasich and Tallal (2002) have shown that the auditory temporal processing deficits are more prevalent in infants with a positive family history for LD-type problems compared to infants without such risk. Such group differences suggest that temporal deficits represent a biological marker for language problems and may be predictive of later developing learning problems, although longitudinal follow-up through early to middle elementary school years is required.

While evidence for the auditory temporal processing disorder in dyslexia seems currently overwhelming, lingering concerns revolve around whether these deficits are causative of reading problems or just associated with dyslexia (Mody et al., 1997). Also, many other questions need further study. For example, the basis of the psychophysical tasks used in this research requires significant attention skills that may be the cause for poor performance rather than temporal discrimination ability. Likewise, some find only a small subset of individuals with reading disability to have the auditory discrimination deficits (Olson & Byrne, 2005).

Such criticisms notwithstanding, these lower level auditory perceptual deficits mirror lower level perceptual deficits found in the visual modality and suggest that prelexical, perceptual processes, in addition to linguistic level difficulties, are impaired in dyslexia. Therefore, appropriate clinical assessment instruments need to be developed in both visual and auditory rapid perceptual processing. Such instruments will facilitate appropriate diagnosis of specific core deficits in dyslexia that involve auditory and visual temporal processing that may underlie the phonologic and orthographic deficits. Such research will further our understanding of appropriate treatment methods for these core deficits, although much work has already been done on the auditory temporal processing deficit and appropriate treatment approaches (Tallal & Gaab, in press).

Visual Perceptual Dyslexia

Just as low-level auditory perceptual deficits are associated with dyslexia, so are low-level visual perceptual deficits. Such deficits have given rise to a number of theories, including the magnocellular theory and simultaneous dysgnosia theory in which basic visual deficits in motion and contrast sensitivity or apprehension of a single digit in a multidigit array (Hawelka & Wimmer, 2005) are thought to lead to linguistic level deficits that impair reading. Both conceptions of dyslexia have received some support (Cornelissen & Hansen, 1998; Demb, Boynton, & Heeger, 1998; Solan, Hansen, Shelley-Tremblay, & Ficarra, 2003; Talcott, Hansen, Assoku, & Stein, 2000). Also, the two deficits in visual perception have been dissociated from one another. However, clinical validation of these conceptualizations has been difficult to come by at present. For example, Birch and Chase (2004) failed to find deficits in magnocellular tasks in either compensated or uncompensated adult dyslexic samples that nevertheless had word recognition problems compared to controls. Nevertheless, in concert with subtypes of dyslexia reviewed previously, a case is being made for a visual perceptual subtype of dyslexia.

In addition to the magnocellular and simultaneous dysgnosia conceptualizations, neuroimaging results consistently identify ventral temporal reading route problems in dyslexia (Cohen, Dehaene, Naccache, et al., 2000). Problems in this brain region correspond to orthographic deficits (Temple et al., 2001) and align better with current neuropsychological findings of the second core deficit in dyslexia. Therefore, ventral reading route dysfunction and orthographic deficits suggest what might be labeled a parvocellular theory of dyslexia.

In summary, the perceptual subtypes of dyslexia proposed in this chapter have not gained acceptance as true disorders causing reading impairments. However, the existence of deficits in these abilities in association with reading problems seems indisputable. Furthermore, the etiology of dyslexia as focal dysfunction capable of causing life-long specific cognitive impairment in the absence of disruption of general intelligence is consistent with the expectation of perceptual subtypes of LD. However, the existence of these subtypes must be considered highly tentative at present.

Optometric Abnormalities in Dyslexia

Given the aforementioned low-level visual perceptual difficulties in dyslexia, it is natural to be concerned about optometric issues. Even if visual sensory difficulty does not directly cause dyslexia, vision problems may decrease the amount, quality, and speed of reading leading to eye strain and fatigue such that reading is less enjoyable and learning is hampered. As a result, many optometrists prescribe vision therapy when reading difficulties are present (47% referral rate in dyslexic students compared to 35% in nonreading impaired students [Kiely, Crewther, & Crewther, 2001]), although the research support for such therapies is scant and not clearly supportive.

Because of space limitations, this literature will not be completely reviewed here (see Cohen, 1988 and Borsting & Rouse, 1994 for supportive review). As a representative sample of this literature, Kiely et al. (2001) found no statistically reliable relationships between typical optometric test results (stereopsis, near point convergence, accommodation, and various measures of heterophoria) and reading ability. Likewise, in a controlled, randomized trial, Christenson, Griffin, and Taylor (2001) found no difference in reading comprehension or reading speed after 2–5 weeks of using blue filter glasses and concluded that diagnosed dyslexics obtained no advantage with such therapy.

It should be noted that these results do not bear upon the binocular stability issue in dyslexic reading. Some dyslexic individuals report problems reading because the text appears to move, wave, or jump on the page (an aspect of the disputed Irlen Syndrome). This subjective report can be associated with difficulty establishing a stable binocular image while reading and is exacerbated because of the visual motion required during reading (Stein & Fowler, 1993).

Again, however, binocular instability has not been etiologically linked to dyslexia. At the present time, optometric deficits in dyslexia must be considered unsupported as a cause of reading problems and even as an associated deficit of dyslexia. However, peripheral visual difficulties need to be ruled out in individuals with academic problems, because they certainly may interfere with learning, making reading less engaging and more effortful. Given the import of print exposure (Cunningham, Perry, & Stanovich, 2001) in developing reading skills, any vision difficulty must be taken seriously.

Dysgraphia

A single model of written expression LD (dysgraphia) has not been widely accepted. In fact, the distinction between developmental dyslexia and dysgraphia has not always been clearly and universally drawn out. However, a distinction between reading and writing ability finds support in a canonical correlation analysis (Shanahan, 1984) where reading measures shared no more than 45% of their variance with writing measures.

Thus, it appears that reading and writing represent different but overlapping processes and that distinguishing between reading and written expression LD is plausible. Early writing-related skills that predict response to intervention focus on penmanship and spelling, while later skill development focuses on the composition and executive aspects of the writing process (Graham & Harris, 2003). Thus, Berninger and Amtmann (2003) identify handwriting, spelling, and composition as separable components to assess in writing problems and propose the "simple view of writing" that includes three processes: (1) transcription, such as handwriting, keyboarding, spelling; (2) text generation, such as composition and discourse; and (3) executive functions, such as attention, planning, reviewing, and revising. These three processes are thought to be coordinated via working memory.

Another complementary yet more theoretically guided approach to writing comes from cognitive neuropsychology and is instructive given the inchoate nature of thought on writing LD. Four types of dysgraphia are identified. Surface dysgraphia has deficits in lexical (whole word) processing, but sublexical (phoneme) processing is intact analogous to the deficit profile of orthographic dyslexia. The opposite pattern occurs in phonologic dysgraphia. Deep dysgraphia, similar to deep dyslexia, is apparently a rare developmental disorder (Ellis, 1993) and shows an analogous pattern in which the hallmark symptom is semantic paragraphic errors (e.g., writing *table* when intending to write *chair*). These subtypes can shed light on any given LD individual's unique clinical picture. Thus, for example, finding a predominance of semantic paragraphias may point to reasons why typical phonics/phonological awareness training or some other writing-intensive training may be failing a child.

Given these issues, it may be efficacious to consider two broad levels of writing disorder, keeping in mind the four types of dysgraphia identified by cognitive neuropsychology. The first level involves the basic writing skills of penmanship and spelling. This level needs to be evaluated early in school in order to identify children at-risk for writing LD and in need of intervention for transcription skills. Berninger and Amtmann (2003) provide diagnostic and intervention strategies at this level of writing disorder that are organized around phonologic, orthographic, and morphologic errors. As an example, children showing phonemic errors (e.g., deleting a sound, such as writing pinsiss for princess) benefit from early phonologic awareness training. Despite the fact that most children manifest a mixed typology, if a selective dysgraphia occurs with these kinds of writing problems it will fit the phonologic dysgraphic pattern best. Alternately, orthographic–phonologic errors (e.g., making orthographically implausible spelling errors, writing *sithed* for *sight*), when selective, often manifests as the surface dysgraphic subtype and responds to training in the alphabet principle (i.e., phonics). Likewise, morphological awareness training is available for writing errors involving prefixes (e.g., inpolite for impolite) and inflectional and derivational suffixes (e.g., writing bumpd for bumped; see Berninger and Amtmann, 2003, for more detail).

The second level of writing disorder involves compositional skills and the attendant cognitive abilities of verbal comprehension and executive/self-regulation functions. As noted by Berninger and Amtmann (2003), adequate basic writing skills are important preparation for developing the later high level composition skills. However, composition skills are separate from basic writing skills, calling on much different cognitive abilities, and the two types of skills can be independently impaired. For example, executive functions such as self-regulation, insight about areas for improvement, and even personality characteristics such as perseverance and conscientiousness are important in the second aspect of dysgraphia. Executive ability figures prominently in the planning, revision, and self-critical steps to composing that differentiate normally achieving writers from those with a writing LD (Graham & Harris, 2003). As Graham and Harris note, the writing of LD students is mostly characterized by brevity, reflecting the reduced and unproductive efforts at content generation and the lack of sustained effort in composing. They further identified impaired executive retrieval of overlearned knowledge as a composition problem, because poor compared to good writers benefited from repeated prompts to elaborate content.

In summary, dyslexia and dysgraphia are overlapping disorders, much like aphasia and apraxia. However, the executive aspects of writing often make the distinction between the two disorders a clinically meaningful process.

Nonverbal LD

Much as with the controversy of subtyping in verbal LD, nonverbal LD subtypes are in perhaps even greater dispute. Perhaps this dispute arises from a tension between the long-standing tendency to consider right hemisphere functions as less localized than left hemisphere functions (Semmes, 1968) and the current neuroimaging zeitgeist favoring fractionation of subtypes. The "levelers" argue for one general type of nonverbal LD (NLD) while the "sharpeners" distinguish differing presentations among visuospatial, math, socioemotional, and perhaps even attentional subtypes. For purposes of this chapter two broad subtypes will be reviewed (general NLD and math LD).

General NLD

The diagnostic criteria of NLD have been well characterized by Rourke (1995) as consisting of both deficits and strengths. Deficits in nonverbal LD are listed in Table 20.1 and account for both the cognitive/academic and social characteristics of the disorder. It is important to recognize that both hallmark visuospatial and neighborhood (e.g., tactile perceptual and socioemotional) deficits are included in Rourke's criteria. Notable in the characterization is the inclusion of not just visuospatial cognitive/academic deficits but also the other nonverbal deficiencies (e.g., tactile perception, time sense, nonlinguistic aspects of math, pragmatic and complex semantic aspects of language, among others). Interesting in this discussion of NLD, difficulties in dealing with novelty are described that are associated with reasoning, problem solving, and immediate adaptive deficits.

Additionally, there are good descriptions of the socioemotional deficits of this disability and how those aspects relate to the cognitive/academic deficits (Rourke, 1995, pp. 1–26). Specifically, Rourke describes how the right hemisphere aspects of language control understanding of high-level meaning and pragmatics. These nonpropositional aspects of language, such as gesture and prosody, convey emotional meaning and contribute to intimacy and social relationships. Beyond the connection between visuospatial deficits and nonverbal communication skills, Rourke notes that novelty deficits become central to the individual, leading to difficulty with the spontaneous and unpredictable nature of interpersonal interaction.

TABLE 20.1 Taxonomy of Learning Disorders

Verbal LD	Nonverbal LD	Dysexecutive LD
Phonologic	General nonverbal	Hyperactive/impulsive ADHD
Orthographic	Dyscalculia	Inattentive ADHD
Double Deficit	(Socioemotional)	(Motor incoordination)
Semantic–syntactic		
Auditory perceptual		
Visual perceptual		

TABLE 20.2 Nonverbal LD Strengths and Weaknesses

Neuropsychological assets:
  Auditory processes
  Verbal abilities

Academic assets:
  Graphomotor ability
  Word decoding
  Spelling
  Verbatim memory

Neuropsychological deficits:
  Tactile and visual processes
  Complex psychomotor
  Novel material
  Exploratory behavior
  Concept formation
  Problem solving
  Nonpropositional aspects of language

Academic deficits:
  Graphomotor
  Reading comprehension
  Mechanical arithmetic and mathematics
  Science

Socioemotional/adaptive deficits:
  Adaptation to novelty
  Social competence
  Emotional stability
  Activity level

TABLE 20.3 Rourke's Nonverbal LD Treatment Considerations

1. Observe behavior closely, especially in novel or complex situations.
2. Adopt a realistic attitude about expectations for ability.
3. Teach in a systematic, "step-by-step" fashion.
4. Encourage description in detail of important events that are transpiring in the patient's life.
5. Teach appropriate strategies for dealing with particularly troublesome situations that occur on a frequent, everyday basis.
6. Encourage the generalization of learning strategies and concepts.
7. Teach the patient to refine and use appropriately their verbal (expressive) skills.
8. Teach better use of visual-spatial-organizational skills.
9. Teach to interpret visual information when there is "competing" auditory information.
10. Teach appropriate nonverbal behavior.

(Continued)

TABLE 20.3   Rourke's Nonverbal LD Treatment Considerations *(Continued)*

11. Facilitate structured peer interactions.
12. Promote, encourage, and monitor "systematic" explorative activities.
13. Teach how to use age-appropriate aids to reach a specific goal.
14. Help to gain insight into situations that are easy for the patient and those that are potentially troublesome.
15. Work with all caregivers to help the person with insight and direction regarding the most salient development needs.
16. Various educational recommendations (see Rourke, 1995, Appendix).
17. Be cognizant of the therapist's/remedial specialist's role in preparing the person with NLD for adult life.

Thus, deficits in these abilities and others (tactile and psychomotor deficits) lead to dysfunctional interpersonal transactions. Of note is the description of a proclivity toward externalized disorders in early childhood that evolves into more internalizing disorders in late childhood and adolescence as a result of accumulated years of ill effects of socioemotional and communication problems (e.g., impaired prosody leading to poor communication of emotion, humor, and complex semantic meaning; poor reception of nonverbal communication leading to difficulties understanding pragmatic language; "cocktail party" communication style with wordy, low meaning issuances and attendant interpersonal difficulty). The confluence of NLD, Asperger's disorder, and high functioning autism has been well recognized (Goldstein, Beers, Siegel, & Minshew, 2001; Howlin, 2003; Klin, Volkmar, Sparrow, Cicchetti, & Rourke, B. P., 1995).

This characterization of NLD also delineates the distinction of this disorder from the verbal LD varieties by noting the relative preservation of auditory perception, rote verbal abilities such as single word reading and oral language in the context of more poorly developed reading, and listening comprehension skills. However, like verbal subtypes of LD, NLD results in poor vocational outcomes with an increased probability of being underemployed or unemployed (Telzrow & Koch, 2003).

Rourke (1995) identifies poor arithmetic skills as a fundamental academic deficit of NLD that issues from primary cognitive deficits of the disorder. The question naturally arises as to whether math LD is distinguishable from NLD. In this regard, estimates are that 40–65% of children with nonverbal LD also have a specific math LD. While this number is high, it is remarkable that cases can be identified in which fractionations of the main symptoms of NLD are seen. Additionally, math problems can arise in association with nonverbal and verbal deficits and have an unusually central educational role apart from either reading or nonverbal problems. Thus, many believe that math and general NLD are important to distinguish and may even be different entities (Drummond, Ahmad, & Rourke, 2005; Pelletier, Ahmad, & Rourke, 2001).

Math LD

The neuropsychological explanation and intervention of math LD has received much less attention than verbal types of LD.

Nevertheless, it has been shown that children at risk for developing this disability can be identified early with math achievement measures (e.g., reading numerals, number constancy, magnitude judgments of one-digit numbers; Mazzocco & Thompson, 2005). Furthermore, those who start behind tend to stay behind and have difficulty catching up (Ding & Davison, 2005), indicating the importance of applying greater educational resources toward recognizing math problems in young children. As greater understanding develops, math delay and disability may differentiate much like at-risk readers and dyslexics, as discussed previously. That is, there may be a significant percentage of children requiring extra instruction in early grade school but who do not have a true LD. In fact, there are initial indications pointing in this direction.

Evidence pointing toward the efficacy of distinguishing early at-risk math performers from individuals with math LD includes a study by Geary (1993). He notes that using only a math achievement score criterion typical in the field (20–25th percentile or below) identifies many children who have no underlying cognitive processing disorder and show normal achievement in subsequent years. Consequently, he recommends an achievement criterion over two consecutive years and an underlying cognitive processing disorder in order to identify a true math LD. Much as it is important to treat preschoolers with poor pre-reading skills, it is also important to provide early and extra instruction for children low in pre-math skills. However, care is necessary in diagnosing a math LD.

Work on acquired acalculia from cognitive neuropsychology provides some guidance about processing disorders underlying math LD that help in the diagnostic process. Generally, three main cognitive components are acknowledged, including verbal semantic, verbally based math operations, and spatial ability representing left and right inferior parietal lobule contributions. However, a dissociation between left and right hemisphere aspects of the network has eluded complete explication. Psychometric group studies from neuropsychology offer greater detail.

Geary (1993) finds evidence for three types of math LD, including procedural, visuospatial, and semantic math LD. These types fit well with the processing disorders associated with math LD according to Cattell-Horn-Carroll intelligence test studies. Thus, Floyd et al. (2003)

found crystallized intelligence, fluid reasoning, processing speed, and long-term retrieval processing disorders to be associated with math LD. Although no difficulty in visual processing (Gv) was found in this study, spatial ability deficits are a consistent feature of other studies (e.g., Geary, 1993; Osmon, Smerz, Braun, & Plambeck, 2006). A likely reason for the lack of Gv deficits in this study has to do with the nature of the visual processing factor on the WJ-III. It combines two types of visual processing, namely object recognition and spatial types of visual processing, making it less sensitive to the spatial specific disorder associated with math LD.

These processing disorders are consistent with initial imaging studies. For example, studies show activation during math challenge in parietal cortex (spatial ability; Cohen, Dehaene, Chochon, Lehericy, & Naccache, 2000) and prefrontal areas (fluid intelligence; Burbaud et al., 1999). Additionally, the occurrence of both spatial and semantic reasoning ability in conjunction with math achievement is consistent with an imaging study showing bilateral temporal activation with math reasoning challenge and with greater overall glucose metabolism in high compared to low SAT math scores (at least in men; Haier & Benbow, 1995).

While group studies indicate multiple processing disorders, each math LD subtype (procedural, visuospatial, and semantic) is likely to be associated with unique deficit combinations. The procedural subtype is characterized by use of immature calculation tactics in problem solving (e.g., adding 2+3 by counting both two and three instead of "counting on" from three), poor conceptual grasp of math procedures (not recognizing that counting does not have to start at one), and difficulties organizing multiple step procedures. This subtype is associated with an executive function processing disorder especially in working memory and would likely be associated with difficulties in long-term retrieval and fluid reasoning factors of intelligence. For example, Keeler and Swanson (2001) identified both verbal and visuospatial working memory to be predictive of math difficulty and suggested that the working memory deficit related more to retrieval of long-term memory information than to processing issues, consistent with a procedural disability.

In contrast to the procedural subtype, the visuospatial subtype has spatial deficits causing impairment in representing the categorical nature of number (ones, tens, hundreds) and in early learning of spatial arrays to represent number that are the basis of later arithmetic concepts. The spatial basis of number has been demonstrated in numerous ways, yielding the Spatial-Numerical Association of Response Codes effect (SNARC; see review by Hubbard, Piazza, Pinel, & Dehaene, 2005). The fundamental finding in the SNARC effect is that larger numbers are responded to more quickly when presented on the right side of space while smaller numbers lead to quicker responses in left space. This lateralized effect probably holds clues to the spatial versus semantic basis of number. For example, the subitizing process (automatic apprehension of one to three events or things without counting; Dehaene & Cohen, 1994) appears to relate to the right hemisphere preference for small numbers found in the SNARC effect. Contrariwise, representing larger numbers requires counting, a process that lends itself more to linguistic than spatial forms of representation.

The final math LD, the semantic subtype, is associated with language-related LD and a verbal–semantic processing disorder that leads to difficulty retrieving math facts and a problem maturing from a procedural approach to a memory approach to math. The visuospatial and executive function processing disorders have been replicated in a college sample, although the semantic deficits were not, perhaps because of the selective nature of the sample and the exclusion of comorbid reading LD (Osmon, Smerz et al. 2006).

In addition to cognitive processing disorders underlying math achievement, a growing awareness that person and situation variables, such as self-efficacy and the adverse effect of social stereotypes (females and African Americans are poorer in math), can adversely affect achievement (Ryan & Ryan, 2005). Because of the difficulty of the subject matter, it is likely that these issues are especially prominent in learning math. Several approaches in this vein have been recently introduced. A broad perspective is offered by Buxton (2005) in which student self-efficacy in math and science is defined, transformed, and effected institution wide.

LD ASSESSMENT

T HE FIELD HAS been undergoing tumult over the proper way of diagnosing and establishing eligibility for treatment of LD. The traditional method of using an IQ and achievement battery and looking for a discrepancy in scores that signals an unexpected lack of academic progress seems to have been discredited (Vukovic & Siegel, 2006), perhaps prematurely.

There is little dispute about the three problems with the discrepancy approach noted in the following paragraphs. First, such an approach overidentifies many children as LD who have higher IQ scores. When such individuals' academics lag behind their IQ score but they have no processing disorder associated with LD, their discrepancy is more likely to arise from environmental disadvantage or motivational/behavioral issues, and LD is an inappropriate diagnosis. Second, a discrepancy approach misses children with lower IQ scores who do not have enough room in the numbers to allow a discrepancy between IQ and achievement and yet have clear processing problems associated with LD, such as the phonological awareness deficits of dyslexia. Finally, the discrepancy approach also tends to promote the detrimental practice of "waiting to fail" in which a child with LD falls irreparably behind in achievement.

While the aforementioned diagnostic and treatment issues are very real dilemmas, their blame may not reside in the tools used for diagnosis or even the discrepancy approach per se. Instead, the practices of those using the tools and procedures seem at fault. For example, relying exclusively on discrepancy scores to make a diagnosis is a bad practice, as is any practice in which only one indicator is used to make a diagnosis. Discrepancy scores are only one actuarial in a proper diagnostic assessment, and use of them without knowledge of their limitations and in the absence of absolutely low achievement and clear processing disorders that underlie the LD in question are to be avoided. Furthermore, state-of-the-art literature clearly shows that preschool performance can identify children at-risk for LD in many cases (especially reading and math problems), and those children are too numerous to all be learning disordered. As an example, one study identified at-risk preschool children, and 69% were good readers by 3rd grade (Felton, 1992). These results reinforce the notion that reading problems arise from numerous causes, and a thorough neuropsychological evaluation is helpful in identifying processing disorders that signal enduring and serious disorders of learning.

Therefore, the true LD population is likely to be among the nonresponders to extra instruction applied to the at-risk children. At the time of nonresponse a thorough-going cognitive evaluation is needed that examines for processing disorders associated with the various LD subtypes in an attempt to determine the reason for nonresponse. Thus, IQ tests, achievement tests, and discrepancy scores should not be eliminated from the clinician's armamentarium in the assessment of LD. Instead, they should be used in at-risk children who have not responded to intensive training, along with a thorough history, school-based assessments, medical history, and other clinical information, in the challenge to provide a diagnosis that informs treatment decisions according to the current state of the empirical literature.

While this approach seems sound, it ignores a very powerful socio-political force in the field of LD. The hotly contested issue of eligibility for treatment looms over the diagnostic process, as does the seeming remoteness of nationally normed standardized testing. Curriculum-based measurement is a process complementary to traditional testing techniques.

Based on an impressive body of work coming out of the Minnesota Institute for Research on Learning Disabilities (Kavale, Fuchs, & Scruggs, 1994), the field of LD has been increasingly advocating curriculum-based measurement in the eligibility/treatment decision-making process. The idea to base eligibility and treatment decisions on performance in classroom-based measures that are closer to the student's problem than nationally normed measures is a sound one. This approach may be important to track student progress in the classroom and function in concert with independent consultation when students do not respond to traditional instruction and add-on intensive training.

Consistent with the etiologic and taxonomic issues covered in earlier sections of this chapter and the assessment model previous, a thorough-going assessment battery will need to cover the processing disorders and achievement areas in a fine-grained fashion. Thus, a wide-range of cognitive abilities will need to be examined from the auditory processing, crystallized, short-term memory, and other abilities associated with verbal LD to the visual processing, fluid IQ/executive, and other abilities in nonverbal LD. Additionally, factors associated with disorders comorbid with LD, such as attention and personality factors, must also be covered in the battery. Such an extensive battery necessarily requires a great deal of testing time if it is to be widely applicable to LD in general. Thus, it is often necessary to triage clients ahead of time in order to trim a test battery to the limited time available in many settings.

Because of space limitations all relevant tests cannot be reviewed here. Thus, a generally applicable assessment battery is reviewed and supplemental tests that address specific assessment issues are covered, as well.

WOODCOCK-JOHNSON-III BATTERIES

WHILE THE WECHSLER series of tests are undoubtedly the most widely used intelligence and achievement measures in clinical psychology, they are no longer the best instruments for use in learning disability (and many other situations). Despite the vast research backing of the Wechsler series, the tests in this series are simply out of date, possessing no theoretical backing and taking no advantage of about 100 years of factor analytic work demonstrating a seven-factor model of intelligence that can no longer be ignored (Flanagan & Harrison, 2005). The Woodcock-Johnson-III (WJ-III) is the only current intelligence battery that evaluates all seven factors of intelligence specified by the Cattell-Horn-Carroll model of intelligence (Flanagan & Harrison, 2005). Additionally, it has been verified by confirmatory factor analysis as fitting the seven-factor structure (Floyd et al., 2003).

For this reason alone, it is the best all around intelligence battery in the diagnostic assessment of LD. In addition, the WJ-III is a single, comprehensively age normed battery and includes specific phonemic awareness subtests and composite scores. Also, the conormed WJ-III achievement battery provides multiple regression-corrected discrepancy scores that compare predicted to actual achievement performance using various comparisons, unlike the Wechsler series that uses only intellectual score comparisons (Floyd et al., 2003). And, while the battery is not without growing pains and lacks the Wechsler's vast empirical foundation, it represents a marked theoretical improvement in measuring intelligence and achievement, because it better represents the abilities and skills associated with both intelligence and learning disorders as they are currently understood.

Another point of departure for the WJ-III from traditional IQ tests also arises from its CHC theoretical orientation. Specifically, rather than choosing subtests and items that all have a high g loading, the construction of the WJ-III was based on Rasch model item selection procedures, which chooses items measuring a narrow, factor facet ability (McGrew & Woodcock, 2001). In this way, the test measures multiple specific factors of intelligence rather than predominately global intelligence like many other major IQ tests. This feature is especially important in LD because it has been repeatedly shown that deficits in LD are domain-specific, especially in the phonological and orthographic domains (Share & Stanovich, 1995), so global g measures of intelligence are not as relevant as factor facet measures.

Because of these characteristics the WJ-III represents a new generation battery. Some of its advantages are listed here:

1. Unlike most batteries, the WJ-III takes advantage of recent psychometric developments in providing both norm-referenced and criterion-referenced scores that provide information about level of development, proficiency, and relative standing within either an age or grade normative group. Thus, the W score, as a Rasch scale transformation, centers ability on average 10-year-old performance level and provides a measurement of cognitive growth. Additionally, the Relative Proficiency Index (RPI, also Rasch based) represents a person's proficiency relative to age or grade peers by expressing performance as a function of both item difficulty and ability level. For example, an RPI of 45/90 says that this individual will perform at 45% proficiency what age or grade peers perform at 90% proficiency. Such an index provides a direct measure of an individual's mastery of a task, unlike typical standard scores of intelligence tests that provide only a relative, rank ordering of performance compared to peers. As such, both Rasch and standard

score measures are necessary, because they may lead to differing conclusions. For example, it is possible to have a standard score in the average range and yet have limited proficiency because of wide variability in the normal population (Mather & Jaffe, 2002). Other psychometric advances include regression to the mean corrected multiple discrepancy measures based on all cognitive, achievement, or both cognitive and achievement performance and principal component analysis weighted derivation of the overall IQ scores (unlike equal weighting schemes for most batteries; McGrew & Woodcock, 2001).

2. Factor scores have been specifically constructed to tap at least two (three in most cases if supplement tests are administered) different facets of a factor, making the factor scores more representative of the construct and lending greater fidelity to the measurement process. Additionally, Rasch model criteria were used to insure fidelity in the item selection of the facet of each subtest (McGrew & Woodcock, 2001).

3. All seven factors of intelligence from the Cattell-Horn-Carroll model (Flanagan & McGrew, 1998) are measured, including Long-term Retrieval (Glr), Short-term Memory (Gsm), Auditory Processes (Ga), Visual Processes (Gv), Processing Speed (Gs), Crystallized (Gc), and Fluid Reasoning (Gf). Other intelligence tests measure only some of these abilities, and yet growth curves demonstrate that each factor is unique and varies across the age range. Therefore, any general intelligence quotient needs representation from each factor in order to be an adequate estimate of general ability (McGrew & Woodcock, 2001). Thus, other batteries lacking representation from all seven factors necessarily give inaccurate estimates of intelligence.

4. The dual nature of crystallized and fluid reasoning abilities are distinguished by separate subtests (Gc and Gf), rather than comingled within subtest scores. Crystallized and fluid reasoning are very different processes, having different development trajectories (Horn, 1968) and different neuroanatomical bases (Duncan, Burgess, & Emslie, 1995) and, therefore, need to be separately measured. However, tests developed without benefit of a theoretical backing typically fail to make this important distinction. For example, subtests on the Wechsler test (e.g., Comprehension, Similarities, and Block Design, among others) mix crystallized and fluid abilities, contaminating the measurement process.

5. The Visual Processes factor includes different subtests that separately measure dorsal-spatial visual stream (Spatial Relations) and ventral, object recognition stream abilities (Picture Recognition). Furthermore, as demonstrated by cross-battery factor analysis

(Flanagan & McGrew, 1998), the Gv measurement is not contaminated by mental speed and fluid reasoning abilities as occurs on many batteries (e.g., PIQ and PO factor on the WAIS-III).

6. Processing disorders underlying LD are specifically addressed in the Cognitive battery (e.g., Phonemic Analysis and Rapid Picture Naming subtests), unlike most other intelligence tests.

7. Differentiation of academic skills is greater than other global achievement measures. For example, in addition to the typical reading, writing, and math scores, an oral language composite is provided. This composite is useful for measuring the important skills of oral expression and listening comprehension and for use in a discrepancy comparison against the typical LD deficits in reading, writing, and math. Additionally, composites and subject-specific subtest scores are available for evaluating important ancillary aspects of academic performance, including automaticity of academic ability (Academic Fluency), general fund of academic knowledge (Academic Knowledge), and the ability to apply academic knowledge in problem situations (Academic Applications). Another important score comparison is between broad and basic academic skills or reading, writing, and math areas. This comparison is important because of developmental trajectories in skill development and the need to distinguish between difficulties in early (e.g., phonology) and later (e.g., orthography) childhood learning ability. Further advantages along these lines are discussed in greater detail in McGrew and Woodcock (2001).

COMPREHENSIVE TEST OF PHONOLOGICAL PROCESSING

THE COMPREHENSIVE TEST of Phonological Processing (CTOPP) is a recently developed test including two versions, one for readers between the ages of 5 and 6, and another for ages 7 to 24 (Manual; Wagner, Torgesen, & Rashotte, 1999). It was based upon the phonological core model and measures: phonological awareness, phonological memory, and rapid naming. Strong relationships were identified between phonological awareness and phonological memory and a moderate relationship of both these factors and rapid naming, which decreases as children age. The composite scores each include two subtests (three subtests for phonological awareness for 5–6 year olds) for fidelity of measurement. Subtests are specifically designed to measure reading skills (e.g., memory includes a faster presentation rate to tax short-term memory and minimize executive aspects of working memory). Administration time is reported in the manual to be about 30 minutes for the core six subtests.

GRAY ORAL READING TEST-3

THE GRAY ORAL Reading Test-3 (GORT-3) is a measure of reading fluency that is short to administer and score. The test has been reviewed favorably as a measure of reading fluency (Marlow & Edwards, 1998), correlating moderately with the Gates-MacGinitie, having incremental validity with the WISC-R, improving as a result of various reading intervention programs (Ryckman, 1982; Solan et al., 2003). Additionally, various studies have shown that GORT-3 scores are affected by minority dialect but less than other reading measures and that dyslexics benefited less than normal readers, suggesting the test focuses on disability related issues well (e.g., Craig, Thompson, Washington, & Potter, 2004).

NELSON-DENNY TEST

THIS TEST PROVIDES measures of comprehension, reading rate, and vocabulary. However, factor analysis suggested the test to measure efficiency, accuracy, and rate factors, and one study suggested that only the accuracy factor was measured well (Carver, 1992). Furthermore, the test appears to be best calibrated for above average readers, as revealed by a review (Perkins, 1984), correlating well with SAT (.79) and ACT scores (.71) but less well with grade point averages (.39 for high school and .33 for college freshman GPAs), and identifying learning problems in medical students and physicians referred for evaluation (Banks, Guyer, & Guyer, 1995). Thus, limited to use in higher level populations, the test performs well as a general reading screening device.

TEST OF WORD READING EFFICIENCY

THE TEST OF Word Reading Efficiency (TOWRE) was designed to measure two basic reading abilities (sight word reading and phonemic decoding efficiency) by examining both accuracy and fluency in individuals from 6–24 years of age. Additionally, the test can be administered in about 5 minutes (the manual recommends giving both forms for diagnostic purposes to improve fidelity of measurement) and is ideal for tracking reading development. The scores are suited to therapy recommendations with low scorers on both Phonemic Decoding Efficiency and Sight Word Efficiency responding best to explicit and intensive multimodal phonological training. Reliability values of both subtests are strong and all range from .90 to .95, and numerous validity studies attest to the construct measurement fidelity of the instrument and its subtest scores.

Effort and Malingering Testing

Empirical literature on symptom validity in LD is virtually non-existent, but clinical experience suggests that the incentives for attention, classroom accommodations, and better grades makes cognizance of effort issues mandatory. Traditional symptom validity measures are the only options for objective indicators of effort at this time. Use of multiple domains of abilities is advisable, including memory (e.g., the Word Memory Test: Green, 1995), personality validity scales, and visuospatial (e.g., Dot Counting Test; Boone, Lu, & Herzberg, 2002a). Boone, Lu, and Herzberg's (2002b) b Test may prove to be a useful approach given that many people associate letter reversal with LD and do not distinguish between dyslexia and other types of LD. In fact, one experimental measure (Word Reading Test; Osmon, Plambeck, Klein, & Mano, 2006) has been shown to distinguish simulators from nonsimulators in an analogue study. Furthermore, different types of simulators ("dyslexic" vs. "slow mental speed") could be distinguished, suggesting the need for specific types of symptom validity tests that fit people's preconceived notions of the deficits associated with the population in question. Unfortunately, no symptom validity test has yet been specifically normed for an LD population. So, clinician's are left with qualitative methods (e.g., inconsistent test performance and the like) and traditional effort measures that are as yet unproven (Manual; Torgesen, Wagner, & Rashotte, 1999b).

Personality Testing

Personality and psychopathology factors are important in LD with both internalizing and externalizing factors playing a role in dyslexia (Willcutt & Pennington, 2000). In one study, dyslexic individuals had been found to use social interaction information less well than normal readers, impeding communication and interpersonal relationships (Fine, 1985). Additionally, academic self-concept has been found to be an important predictor in academic outcome. For example, Stevenson and Newman (1986) found that reading and math are viewed differently by males and females and that expectancies for success, perceived difficulty level, and self-concept of ability are important variables to consider in academic success. Global self-concept generally does not relate to reading ability, although popularity is inversely related to reading ability (Hettinger, 1982). In addition to self-concept, personality traits have been found to influence reading level. For example, relationships have been found between the NEO ("Big Five") factors of openness and conscientiousness (Costa & McCrae, 1992) and academic performance. High openness is associated with an intellective attitude that facilitates tolerance of new ideas and an interest in academic pursuits. Likewise, the sense of industriousness, organization, task-oriented deliberateness, and responsibility associated with high conscientious also bodes well for academic performance.

LD TREATMENT

AS IN ETIOLOGY and diagnosis, most research in LD intervention has been done with reading problems, and this research guides understanding of treatment in LD in general. It appears that 90–95% of poor readers can be brought to average reading levels by focusing on basic reading skills (phonemic awareness, phonics, fluency, comprehension; Lyon & Cutting, 1998), and similar success is reported in math LD. However, as noted earlier, those with true LD may require different and more extensive instruction because of processing disorders that preclude learning by typical training methods.

PHONOLOGIC DEFICITS

THE U.S. DEPARTMENT of Education commissioned the National Reading Panel to examine research literature for the most effective methods of reading instruction, and in 2000 the Panel reported their findings. Components of reading that require systematic instruction included phonemic awareness, phonics, fluency, vocabulary, and comprehension. And yet, despite this knowledge, the National Center for Education Statistics estimates that greater than one-third of America's students (about twice that figure in disadvantaged populations) cannot read fluently and with adequate comprehension. However, starting with the Reading Excellence Act signed into law in President Clinton's term in 1998, Congress defined an approach to reading intervention based on solid empirical evidence that was continued in President G. W. Bush's administration with Reading First, which led to the No Child Left Behind Act.

Lyon and Cutting (1998) have set out the elemental components of reading that form the basis for any multipronged reading instruction program. First, phonics and phonological awareness (awareness of and ability to segment words: what word would be made if the *r* was taken out of *drill;* what word would be made by changing *l* to *m* in *lake,* etc.) training is necessary to develop basic word recognition and to set the stage for learning orthographic regularities in the language. Furthermore, "systematic, explicit" instruction in phonics is now recognized as crucial (Foorman, Francis, Fletcher, Schatschneider, & Mehta, 1998). Beyond simple exposure to phonics as occurs in regular classroom instruction, further extensive systematic and explicit phonics instruction beyond the typical 20 minutes/day is needed for those with phonological deficits (Torgesen, Wagner, Rashotte, Rose et al., 1999). Second, fluency must be developed by training orthography until sight–word reading skills are attained, not unlike Orton's (1937) original suggestion to go beyond training in individual letter–sound correspondences to sublexical components. Third, sufficient print exposure is necessary to develop reading vocabulary and comprehension skills.

While these components go together to develop normal reading, brain-related deficits in any one or more of these components lead to problems with normal reading training. For example, Forell and Hood (1985) found the most severe third-grade disabled readers (scoring at the preprimer level) continued to need LD instruction in high school despite continued reading instruction. Perhaps individuals with underlying processing disorders are unable to make the leap from the alphabetic principle to phonological awareness, as suggested by some studies conducted with LD, as opposed to typically developing, readers.

Using 2nd graders more likely to be reading disordered, Torgesen, Wagner, Rashotte, Rose, et al. (1999c) found that spending time predominately in explicit instruction at the word level increased decoding and word identification compared to embedded instruction that had roughly equal parts word and text level instruction. Thus, this study demonstrated the importance of training in both phonological awareness and phonics instruction in individuals selected for marked difficulties in phonological ability. Likewise, this study also demonstrated that children with frank impairment can benefit from training, but the training must be intensive (88 hours from late kindergarten through 2nd grade) and wide-ranging (explicit multiple phonologic abilities at both the word and text level of instruction).

The Torgesen et al. (1999c) study is also an important demonstration of the influence of nonacademic training factors and that components of reading ability are distinct and require separate, specific types of remedial instruction. Both issues are consistent with the notion that individual differences influence success in learning. So, home background and behavior in class contribute uniquely to explaining remedial training benefits independent from type of instruction. Likewise, type of instruction was shown to benefit the targeted ability. For example, the type of instruction that included training in multiple phonologic areas predominately at the word level led to significantly greater improvement in word level skills such as word attack, word identification, and reading phonologically regular nonwords. However, this type of instruction led to no greater improvements in text level skills, such as passage and reading comprehension, than instruction that focused mainly on text level instruction with less word level phonologic training.

One important component of successful treatment appears to be simple repetition and, by extension, print exposure. For example, Gray (2003) found that preschoolers with specific language impairment needed at least twice the number of repetitions as nonimpaired students to comprehend and produce new words. Such findings point toward the importance of orthographic interventions.

ORTHOGRAPHIC DEFICITS

LATE DEVELOPING POOR readers seem to respond less well to phonologic approaches with evidence that orthographically based interventions help in these cases. For example, Small, Flores, and Noll (1998) showed a progression from an angular gyrus to an inferior temporal activation from before to after intervention, suggesting that readers move from a phonologic to orthographic reading strategy as skills improve. In line with this interpretation, Hayes, Masterson, and Roberts (2004) demonstrated a procedure for addressing reading rate problems in adult developmental dyslexics. Improvement in reading rate was obtained by repeated presentation of a word set with gradual reduction in exposure time to encourage quicker reading. Repeated readings of the same text and simply amount of reading have been shown to improve reading fluency in young readers (Vaugh et al., 2000). In essence, print exposure is crucial to develop reading fluency and likely contributes greatly to the relationship between orthography and reading comprehension.

Thus, making reading easier and facilitating motivation to read is important to help readers with adequate phonologic skills increase print exposure. The most well-known orthographically oriented treatment program is the RAVE-O (Retrieval skills, Automaticity in sublexical processes, Vocabulary elaboration, Engagement with language, Orthographic pattern recognition). While this program is commonly associated with orthographic remediation alone, it in fact addresses phonologic and semantic, as well as fluency and word-retrieval skills and is meant to co-occur with phonological awareness and phonics instruction. It is based upon developing automaticity of word retrieval through practice over 70 sessions of training. Training sessions include experience with orthographic regularities to speed decoding and word identification skills (Wolf, Miller, & Donnelly, 2000).

RAPID TEMPORAL PROCESSING DEFICITS

IN ADDITION TO traditional phonologic and orthographic based approaches, Tallal and Gaab (in press) advocate a different approach based upon findings of auditory perceptual temporal processing deficits in dyslexia. The Fast ForWord program is based upon the idea that the window of dyslexics rate of processing auditory perceptual information is beyond what is required to make the speech sound discriminations. In order to sequence the sounds contained in a single word at tens of milliseconds, it is contended that dyslexics need to have the words slowed in order to perceive the words.

Numerous studies demonstrate the effectiveness of the Language and Reading Training versions of Fast ForWord with reading and language impaired children. The task has been used with over 650,000 children, and random clinical trials have been run in the field, demonstrating the efficacy of this approach for improving phonological processing. Additionally, Temple et al. (2003) have demonstrated both behavioral changes (improved Woodcock Reading Mastery and Comprehensive Evaluation of Language Fundamentals scores pre- to post- compared to nonreading impaired controls) and increased activation in left inferior frontal and left temporo-parietal regions associated with the Fast ForWord Language intervention compared to no training.

While these results are impressive, the hypothesis is not without criticism. One study oft cited in critique of the auditory temporal processing difficulty in dyslexia is Mody et al. (1997). These authors have argued that the fundamental deficit is subsequent to early auditory perceptual discrimination and is located in the phonological representation. Furthermore, these authors maintain that improvements associated with Fast ForWord are due to nonspecific effects on phonologic awareness. However, the Mody et al. (1997) study used an experimental group that is suspect for dyslexic level deficits, because their reading scores were in the average range and low only relative to a superior reading control sample, and the balance of evidence seems to favor low level auditory temporal processing deficits in dyslexics (Tallal & Gaab, in press). Additionally, some studies suggest that Fast ForWord is no more effective in this regard than traditional treatments and challenge the assumption that improving rapid auditory processing leads to better reading (Hook, 2001; Studdert-Kennedy & Mody, 1995).

In response to some of these criticisms, some evidence already suggests that rapid auditory training is an important ingredient, given that musical training that includes rapid auditory processing training is also associated with improved language ability as well as quicker auditory evoked responses and greater activation in language specific areas of the brain (Tallal & Gaab, in press). Additionally, it is logical to assume that a subtype of true dyslexia has dorsal reading route impairment in auditory perceptual processing, and that this subtype should be most responsive to the treatment method. A crucial test of Tallal's thesis will be to use the Fast ForWord methods on a group of poor readers who were nonresponders to traditional multipronged reading instruction in phonological awareness, phonics, fluency, and comprehension.

DYSGRAPHIC DEFICITS

INTERVENTIONS FOR DYSGRAPHIA have been found to be effective. Graham and Harris (2003) reported on a meta-analysis on 26 Self-Regulated Strategy Development studies that promote effective writing by prompting development of strategic knowledge, subject matter knowledge, and motivation. The meta-analysis demonstrated large effect sizes for improving quality, structure, and length of written products of a wide-range of 4th–8th grade students, including writing and other LDs, low achieving, and gifted students. Likewise, effect sizes were generally large (>.8) demonstrating improvements in LD students' ability to make substantive revisions of their written products and for maintaining and generalizing writing improvements at follow-up. The meta-analysis also evaluated teaching effectiveness at implementing the intervention technique and found strong effect sizes (most >1.0).

This meta-analysis demonstrates that writing instruction is effective. However, the literature remains small both in absolute number of studies and independent replications. Graham and Harris (2003) also admit that the active components of the intervention have not been definitively identified. As a result, other intervention techniques are needed to arm the clinician to address sundry individual differences in writing ability encountered in practice. Fortunately, many writing instruction techniques exist, including NWREL (Six Trials of Writing+One), the SRA Expressive Writing, Mulipulative Visual Language and Sentence Writing Strategy for grammar skills, semantic maps and graphic organizers to organize ideas for writing, STORE the story, and WWW, What = 2, How = 2 for thematic structure in writing, among others (see Mather & Jaffe, 2002 for a review of recommendations and intervention strategies in LD).

NLD DEFICITS

ROURKE (1995) PROVIDES an excellent summary of 17 points to consider in providing treatment for NLD (see appendix). He notes that it is easy for caregivers and helpers to overestimate the NLD child's ability because of the unique character of nonverbal cognitive abilities and the somewhat invisible role they play in daily life. Rourke further emphasizes the importance of recognizing how these deficits play out in the academic arena in order to develop appropriate expectations for the child and balance rehabilitative attempts with adaptation of the environment to the child's abilities. An important aspect of treating the NLD individual is utilizing the verbal strengths to better advantage. As Rourke notes, the NLD individual is unlike many in a preference for the not fast, very repetitive teaching. So, that strategy can be used to have the individual talk through difficulties in a "reteaching" strategy that has them rehearse the pat, rote routines. Using such a detail-oriented strategy can also help the NLD individual exercise a weakness in generating problem-solving strategies.

Finally, Rourke (1995) emphasizes the importance in advocating for the NLD child both because of their limited insight into their deficits and because of the general lack of awareness of the NLD syndrome and the invisible deficits associated with the disorder. The more people in the child's life aware of the child's difficulty the better, and parent training is a major part of Rourke's strategy. Tanguay (2001) provides a parent's guide to the disorder. Additionally, Cermak and Murray (1992) provide guidelines for the NLD adult and the manifestation of the disorder in a job situation. Also, see Foss (1991) for further ideas on intervention strategies in NLD.

MATH DEFICITS

VARIOUS TECHNIQUES EXIST for teaching introductory arithmetic skills, such as counting (e.g., Touch method; Simon & Hanrahan, 2004), and other beginning skills (see Mather & Jaffe, 2002 for a review). However, little empirical research has been completed in support of such techniques, and even less research has looked at diagnosis and intervention for higher level algebraic and geometry skills.

Tutoring has been shown to provide gains not only in math skills for the tutee but also for the student tutor and for skills other than math, such as academic self-efficacy (Robinson, Schofield, & Steers-Wenzel, 2005). Robinson et al. also demonstrated that longer intervention programs may not always be better than shorter ones and that same-sex tutoring pairs frequently work better than opposite-sex pairs.

Communal contexts in which students work together have been found to improve math performance, at least in minority students (Hurley, Boykin, & Allen, 2005). One example of this kind of communal environment is the Math Talk Community in which learners assist each other in building a math-based dialogue (Hufferd-Ackles, Fusion, & Sherin, 2004). Also, learning environments that facilitate math self-efficacy are associated with better grades, especially for girls (Crombie et al., 2005), and fluency training may result in more lasting learning (Singer-Dudek & Greer, 2005).

Math self-efficacy is facilitated by students' appraisals of adults' beliefs of the importance of math and of their own competence in math (Bleeker & Jacobs, 2004; Bouchey & Harter, 2005). Additionally, performance pressure adversely affects math performance but only when working under high working memory demands (Beilock & Carr, 2005), although this may vary depending upon the difficulty of the material. For example, Lannie and Martens (2004) found that accuracy-based contingencies worked best when the math problems were difficult, but a time-based contingency was best for most students when doing easy math problems. Math anxiety predicts math performance and is related primarily to visual, rather than verbal, working memory, arguing that math anxiety is unlike other types of anxiety (Miller & Bichsel, 2004).

ACCOMMODATIONS

IN ADDITION TO remedial intervention, compensatory interventions have been found helpful and often preferable, especially later in the educational career. For example, Lesaux, Pearson, and Siegel (2006) found that extra time on reading comprehension tests benefited dyslexic but not normally reading controls. Similarly, Ofiesh, Mather, and Russell (2005) found group differences on all speeded tasks between college LD versus nondisabled students. They found that WJ-III Reading Fluency and Academic Fluency measures were the best predictors of who needed extra-time accommodations.

Further research is needed to determine who benefits from which accommodation. Thus, at what level of reading impairment are taped books or computer readers beneficial, and what determines when other accommodations are needed, such as tutoring, a quiet environment to take exams, spell and grammar checker, among others?

SUMMARY

LEARNING IS A fundamental life task important enough to be remediated in the face of brain disorder and to be accommodated in the case of disability. Unfortunately, there has been a tendency to confound disorder and disability, resulting in overidentification of LD and misallocation of resources. Much research remains to develop a taxonomy of LD that is etiologically informed and will promote effective intervention and accommodation to remediate learning disorders and to moderate the malaise of disability. Surely, there are few pursuits with wider ranging implications than the education of the world's populace.

REFERENCES

Badian, N. A. (1996). Dyslexia: A validation of the concept at two age levels. *Journal of Learning Disabilities, 29,* 102–112.

Badian, N. A. (2001). Phonological and orthographic processing: Their roles in reading prediction. *Annals of Dyslexia, 51,* 179–202.

Badian, N. A. (2005). Does a visual-orthographic deficit contribute to reading disability? *Annals of Dyslexia, 55,* 28–52.

Banks, S. R., Guyer, B. P., & Guyer, K. E. (1995). A study of medical students and physicians referred for learning disabilities. *Annals of Dyslexia, 45,* 233–245.

Beilock, S. L., & Carr, T. H. (2005). When high-powered people fail: Working memory and "choking under pressure" in math. *Psychological Science, 16,* 101–105.

Benasich, A. A., & Tallal, P. (2002). Infant discrimination of rapid auditory cues predicts later language impairment. *Behavioral and Brain Research, 136,* 31–49.

Berninger, V. W., & Amtmann, D. (2003). Preventing written expression disabilities through early and continuing assessment and intervention for handwriting and/or spelling problems: Research into practice. In H. L. Swanson, K. R. Harris, & S. Graham (Eds.), *Handbook of learning disabilities* (pp. 345–363). New York: Guilford Press.

Birch, S., & Chase, C. (2004). Visual and language processing deficits in compensated and uncompensated college students with dyslexia. *Journal of Learning Disabilities, 37,* 389–410.

Bleeker, M. M., & Jacobs, J. E. (2004). Achievement in math and science: Do mothers' beliefs matter 12 years later? *Journal of Educational Psychology, 96,* 97–109.

Boone, K., Lu, P., & Herzberg, D. S. (2002a). *The Dot Counting Test Manual.* Los Angeles: Western Psychological Services.

Boone, K., Lu, P., & Herzberg, D. S. (2002b). *The b Test Manual.* Los Angeles: Western Psychological Services.

Borsting, E., & Rouse, M. W. (1994). Detecting learning-related visual problems in the primary care setting. *Journal of the American Optometric Association, 65*(9), 642–650.

Bouchey, H. A., & Harter, S. (2005). Reflected appraisals, academic self-perceptions, and math/science performance during early adolescence. *Journal of Educational Psychology, 97,* 673–686.

Burbaud, P., Camus, O., Guehl, D., Bioulac, B., Caillé, J. M., & Allard, M. (1999). A functional magnetic resonance imaging study of mental subtraction in human subjects. *Neuroscience Letters, 273*(3), 195–9.

Butler, B. E., Jared, D., & Hains, S. (1984). Reading skill and the use of orthographic knowledge by mature readers. *Psychological Research, 46,* 337–353.

Buxton, C. A. (2005). Creating a culture of academic success in an urban science and math magnet high school. *Science Education, 89,* 392–417.

Byrne, B., & Fielding-Barnsley, R. (1993). Evaluation of a program to teach phonemic awareness to young children: A 2- and 3-year follow-up, and a new preschool trial. *Journal of Educational Psychology, 87,* 488–503.

Carver, R. P. (1992). What do standardized tests of reading comprehension measure in terms of efficiency, accuracy, and rate? *Reading Research Quarterly, 27*, 346–359.

Casanova, M. F., Araque, J., Giedd, J., & Rumsey, J. M. (2004). Reduced brain size and gyrification in the brains of dyslexic patients. *Journal of Child Neurology, 19*, 275–281.

Catts, H. W., & Kamhi A. G. (2005), *The connections between language and reading disabilities*. Mahwah, NJ: Lawrence Erlbaum Associates, Publishers.

Centers for Disease Control and Prevention. Retrieved from http://www.cdc. gov/mmwr/preview/mmwrhtml/00038522.htm

Cermak, S. A., & Murray, E. (1992). Noverbal learning disabilities in the adult framed in the model of human occupation. In N. Katz (Ed.), *Cognitive rehabilitation models for intervention in occupational therapy* (pp. 258–291). Boston: Andover Medical.

Christenson, G. N., Griffin, J. R., & Taylor, M. (2001). Failure of blue-tinted lenses to change reading scores of dyslexic individuals. *Optometry: Journal of the American Optometric Association, 72*, 627–633.

Cohen, A. H. (1988). The efficacy of optometric vision therapy. *Journal of the American Optometric Association, 59*, 95–105.

Cohen, L., Dehaene, S., Chochon, F., Lehericy, S., & Naccache, L. (2000). Language and calculation within the parietal lobe: A combined cognitive, anatomical and fMRI study. *Neuropsychologia, 38*(10), 1426–1440.

Cohen, L., Dehaene, S., Naccache, L., Lehericy, S., Dehaene-Lambertz, G., Henaff, M. A., et al. (2000). The visual word form areas: Spatial and temporal characterization of an initial stage of reading in normal subjects and posterior split-brain patients. *Brain, 123*(Pt 2), 291–307.

Corina, D. P., Richards, T. L., Serafini, S., Richards, A. L., Steury, K., Abbott, R. D., et al. (2001). fMRI auditory language differences between dyslexic and able reading children. *Neuroreport: For Rapid Communication of Neuroscience Research, 12*(6), 1195–1201.

Cornelissen, P. L., & Hansen, P. C. (1998). Motion detection, letter position encoding, and single word reading. *Annals of Dyslexia, 48*, 155–188.

Cornold, C., De Beni, R., & Pazzaglia, F. (1996). Profiles of reading comprehension difficulties: An analysis of single cases. In C. Cornoldi, & J. Oakhill (Eds.), *Reading comprehension difficulties: Processes and intervention* (pp. 113–136). Mahwah, NJ: Lawrence Erlbaum Associates, Publishers.

Costa, P. T., & McCrae, R. R. (1992). *NEO PI-R: Professional manual, revised NEO personality inventory (NEO PI-R) and NEO five-factor inventory (NEO-FFI)*. Lutz, FL: Psychological Assessment Resources, INC.

Craig, H. K., Thompson, C. A., Washington, J. A., & Potter, S. L. (2004). Performance of elementary-Grade African American students on the gray oral reading tests. *Language, Speech, and Hearing Services in Schools, 35*, 141–154.

Crombie, G., Sinclair, N., Silverthorn, N., Byrne, B. M., DuBois, D. L., & Trinneer, A. (2005). Predictors of young adolescents' math grades and course enrollment intentions: Gender similarities and differences. *Sex Roles, 52,* 351–367.

Cunningham, A. E., Perry, K. E., & Stanovich, K. E. (2001). Converging evidence for the concept of orthographic processing. *Reading and Writing, 14,* 549–568.

Dale, P. S., Simonoff, E., Bishop, D.V.M., Eley, T. C., Oliver, B., Price, T. S., et al. (1998). Genetic influence on language delay in two-year-old children. *Nature Neuroscience, 1*(4), 324–328.

Dehaene, S., & Cohen, L. (1994). Dissociable mechanisms of subitizing and counting: Neuropsychological evidence from simultanagnosis patients. *Journal of Experimental Psychology: Human Perception and Performance, 20,* 958–975.

Demb, J. B., Boynton, G. M., & Heeger, D. J. (1998). Functional magnetic resonance imaging of early visual pathways in dyslexia. *Journal of Neuroscience, 18*(17), 6939–6951.

Ding, C. S., & Davison, M. L. (2005). A longitudinal study of math achievement gains for initially low achieving students. *Contemporary Educational Psychology, 30,* 81–95.

Drummond, C. R., Ahmad, S. A., & Rourke, B. P. (2005). Rules for the classification of younger children with nonverbal learning disabilities and basic phonological processing disabilities. *Archives of Clinical Neuropsychology, 20,* 171–182.

Duncan, J., Burgess, P., & Emslie, H. (1995). Fluid intelligence after frontal lobe lesions. *Neuropsychologia, 33,* 261–268.

Ellis, A. W. (1993). *Reading, writing and dyslexia: A cognitive analysis.* Hove, UK: Lawrence Erlbaum Associates, LTD.

Elrod, G. F., & Ryckman, D. B. (1984). An examination of WISC-R profiles of learning disabled children. *Educational & Psychological Research, 4,* 185–193.

Felton, R. H. (1992). Early identification of children at risk for reading disabilities. *Topics in Early Childhood Special Education, 12,* 212–229.

Fiez, J. A. (2000). Sound and meaning: How native language affects reading strategies. *Nature Neuroscience, 3,* 3–5.

Fine, J. (1985). Cohesion as an index of social-cognitive factors: Oral language of the reading disabled. *Discourse Processes, 8,* 91–112.

Fisher, S. E., & DeFries, J. C. (2002). Developmental dyslexia: Genetic dissection of a complex cognitive trait. *Nature Reviews: Neuroscience, 3,* 767–780.

Flanagan, D. P., & Harrison, P. L.. (2005). *Contemporary intellectual assessment: Theories, tests, and issues.* New York: Guilford Press.

Flanagan, D., & McGrew, K. (1998). *The intelligence test desk reference (ITDR): Gf-Gc cross-battery assessment.* Needham Heights, MA: Allyn & Bacon.

Fletcher, J. M., Morris, R. D., & Lyon, G. R. (2003). Classification and definition of learning disabilities: An integrative perspective. In H. L. Swanson,

K. R. Harris, & S. Graham (Eds.), *Handbook of learning disabilities* (pp. 30–57). New York: The Guildford Press.

Floyd, R. G., Evans, J. J., & McGrew, K. S. (2003). Relations between measures of Cattell-Horn-Carroll (CHC) cognitive abilities and mathematics achievement across the school age years. *Psychology in the Schools, 40,* 155–171.

Foorman, B. R., Francis, D. J., Fletcher, J. M., Schatschneider, C., & Mehta, P. (1998). The role of instruction in learning to read: Preventing reading failure in at-risk children. *Journal of Educational Psychology, 90,* 37–55.

Forell, E. R., & Hood, J. (1985). A longitudinal study of two groups of children with early reading problems. *Annals of Dyslexia, 35,* 97–116.

Frith, U. (1985). Beneath the surface of developmental dyslexia. In K. E. Patterson, J. C. Marshall, & M. Coltheart (Eds.), *Surface dyslexia* (pp. 301–330). London: Lawrence Erlbaum Associates.

Galaburda, A. M. (1989). Ordinary and extraordinary brain development: Anatomical variation in developmental dyslexia. *Annals of Dyslexia, 39,* 67–79.

Geary, D. C. (1993). Mathematical disabilities: Cognitive, neuropsychological, and genetic components. *Psychological Bulletin, 114,* 345–362.

Goldstein, G., Beers, S. R., Siegel, D. J., & Minshew, N. J. (2001). A comparison of WAIS-R profiles in adults with high-functioning autism or differing subtypes of learning disability. *Applied Neuropsychology, 8,* 148–154.

Graham, S., & Harris, K. P. (2003). Students with learning disabilities and the process of writing: A meta-analysis of SRSD studies. In H. L. Swanson, K. R. Harris, & S. Graham (Eds.), *Handbook of learning disabilities* (pp. 323–344). New York: The Guildford Press.

Gray, S. (2003). Word-learning by preschoolers with specific language impairment: What predicts success? *Journal of Speech, Language, and Hearing Research, 46,* 56–67.

Green, P. (1995). *Green's Word Memory Test for Microsoft Windows: User's manual.* Edmonton, WA: Green's Publishing Inc.

Haier, R. J., & Benbow, C. P. (1995). Sex differences and lateralization in temporal lobe glucose metabolism during mathematical reasoning. *Developmental Neuropsychology, 11,* 405–414.

Hammill, D. D., Leigh, J. E., McNutt, G., & Larsen, S. C. (1981). A new definition of learning disabilities. *Learning Disability Quarterly, 4,* 336–342.

Hawelka, S., & Wimmer, H. (2005). Impaired visual processing of multi-element arrays is associated with increased number of eye movements in dyslexic reading. *Vision Research, 45,* 855–863.

Hayes, M., Masterson, J., & Roberts, M. J. (2004). Improvement in reading speed in an adult with developmental dyslexia of the "mixed" type. *Neuropsychological Rehabilitation, 14,* 365–382.

Hettinger, C. C. (1982). The impact of reading deficiency on the global self-concept of the adolescent. *Journal of Early Adolescence, 2,* 293–300.

Hook, P. E. (2001). Efficacy of Fast ForWord training on facilitating acquisition of reading difficulties—A longitudinal study. *Annuals of Dyslexia, 51,* 75–96.

Hoover, W. A., & Gough, P. B. (1990). The simple view of reading. *Reading and Writing, 2*(2), 127–160.

Horn, J. L. (1968). Organization of abilities and the development of intelligence. *Psychological Review, 75,* 242–259.

Howlin, P. (2003). Outcome in high-functioning adults with autism with and without early language delays: Implications for the differentiation between autism and Asperger syndrome. *Journal of Autism and Developmental Disorders, 33,* 3–13.

Hubbard, E. M., Piazza, M., Pinel, P., & Dehaene, S. (2005). Interactions between number and space in parietal cortex. *Nature Reviews Neuroscience, 6,* 435–448.

Hufferd-Ackles, K., Fusion, K. C., & Sherin, M. G. (2004). Describing levels and components of a math-talk learning community. *Journal for Research in Mathematics Education, 35,* 81–116.

Hurley, E. A., Boykin, A. W., & Allen, B. A. (2005). Communal versus individual learning of a math-estimation task: African American children and the culture of learning contexts. *Journal of Psychology: Interdisciplinary and Applied, 139,* 513–527.

International Dyslexia Association. (2002). *What is dyslexia?* Retrieved July 1, 2007, from http://www.interdys.org/servlet/compose?section_id=5& page_id=95.

Kavale, K. A., Fuchs, D., & Scruggs, T. E. (1994). Setting the record straight on learning disability and low achievement: Implications for policymaking. *Learning Disabilities Research & Practice, 9,* 70–77.

Keeler, M. L., & Swanson, H. L. (2001). Does strategy knowledge influence working memory in children with mathematical disabilities? *Journal of Learning Disabilities, 34,* 418–434.

Kiely, P. M., Crewther, S. G., & Crewther, D. P. (2001). Is there an association between functional vision and learning to read? *Clinical and Experimental Optometry, 84,* 346–353.

Klin, A., Volkmar, F. R., Sparrow, S. S., Cicchetti, D. V., & Rourke, B. P. (1995). Validity and neuropsychological characterization of Asperger syndrome: Convergence with nonverbal learning disabilities syndrome. *Journal of Child Psychology and Psychiatry, 36,* 1127–1140.

Kranzler, J. (1994). Application of the techniques of mental chronometry to the study of learning disabilities. *Personality & Individual Differences, 16*(6), 853–859.

Lange, J. (1988). Agnosia and apraxia. In J. S. Brown (Ed.), *Agnosia and apraxia: Selected papers of Liepmann, Lange, and Poetzl* (pp. 43–228). Hillsdale, NJ: LEA.

Lannie, A. L., & Martens, B. K. (2004). Effects of task difficulty and type of contingency on students' allocation of responding to math worksheets. *Journal of Applied Behavior Analysis, 37,* 53–65.

Leonard, C. M., Lombardino, L. J., Giess, S. A., & King, W. M. (2005). Behavioral and anatomical distinctions between dyslexia and SLI. In H. W. Catts & A. G. Kamhi (Eds.), *The connections between language and reading disabilities* (pp. 155–172). Mahwah, NJ: Lawrence Erlbaum Associates, Publishers.

Lesaux, N. K., Pearson, M. R., & Siegel, L. S. (2006). The effects of timed and untimed testing conditions on the reading comprehension performance of adults with reading disabilities. *Reading and Writing, 19,* 21–48.

Lyon, G. R., & Cutting, L. E. (1998). Learning disabilities. In E. J. Mash & R. A. Barkley (Eds.), *Treatment of childhood disorders* (2nd ed., pp. 468–498). New York: Guilford Press.

Mano, Q. R. (unpublished master's thesis). Visuoperceptual-orthographic aspects of reading: Validating an achievement-construct.

Marlow, A., & Edwards, R. P. (1998). Test review: Gray Oral Reading Test, Third Edition (GORT-3). *Journal of Psychoeducational Assessment, 16,* 90–94.

Mather, N., & Jaffe, L. E. (2002). *Woodcock-Johnson-III: Reports, recommendations, and strategies.* New York: John Wiley & Sons, Inc.

Mazzocco, M. M., & Thompson, R. E. (2005). Kindergarten predictors of math learning disability. *Learning Disabilities Research & Practice, 20,* 142–155.

McCrory, E. J., Mechelli, A., Frith, U., & Price, C. J. (2005). More than words: A common neural basis for reading and naming deficits in developmental dyslexia? *Brain: A Journal of Neurology, 128,* 261–267.

McGrew, K. S., & Woodcock, R. W. (2001). *Woodcock-Johnson-III technical manual.* Itasca, IL: Riverside Publishing.

Milene, L., Bonte, M., & Blomert, L. (2004). Developmental dyslexia: ERP correlates of anomalous phonological processing during spoken word recognition. *Cognitive Brain Research, 21,* 360–376.

Miller, C. J., Sanchez, J., & Hynd, G. W. (2003). Neurological correlates of reading disabilities. In H. L. Swanson, K. R. Harris, & S. Graham (Eds.), *Handbook of learning disabilities* (pp. 242–255). New York: The Guildford Press.

Miller, H., & Bichsel, J. (2004). Anxiety, working memory, gender, and math performance. *Personality and Individual Differences, 37,* 591–606.

Mody, M., Studdert-Kennedy, M., & Brady, S. (1997). Speech perception deficits in poor readers: Auditory processing or phonological coding? *Journal of Experimental Child Psychology, 64*(2), 199–231.

Montgomery, J. W., Windsor, J., & Stark, R. E. (1991). Specific speech and language disorders. In J. E. Obrzut, & G. W. Hynd (Eds.), *Neuropsychological foundations of learning disabilities: A handbook of issues, methods, and practice* (pp. 573–601). San Diego: Academic Press, Inc.

Morris, R. D., Stuebing, K. K., Fletcher, J. M., Shaywitz, S. E., Lyon, G. R., Shankweiler, D. P., et al. (1998). Subtypes of reading disability: Variability around a phonological core. *Journal of Educational Psychology, 90,* 347–373.

Nation, K., & Snowling, M. J. (1998). Individual differences in contextual facilitation: Evidence from dyslexia and poor reading comprehension. *Child Development, 69,* 996–1011.

National Center for Education Statistics (1999). *Disabilities among children aged less than or equal to 17 years—United States, 1991–1992.* Retrieved from www.nces.ed.gov/pubsearch/pubintro.asp/pubid=199950o

National Joint Committee on Learning Disabilities. (1988). Letter to NJCLD Member Organizations.

Oakhill, J. V., Cain, K., & Bryant, P. E. (2003). The dissociation of word reading and text comprehension: Evidence from component skills. *Language and Cognitive Processes, 18,* 443–468.

Ofiesh, N., Mather, N., & Russell, A. (2005). Using speeded cognitive, reading, and academic measures to determine the need for extended test time among university students with learning disabilities. *Journal of Psychoeducational Assessment, 23,* 35–52.

Olson, R., & Byrne, B. (2005). Genetic and environmental influences on reading and language ability and disability. In H. W. Catts & A. G. Kamhi (Eds.), *The connections between language and reading disabilities* (pp. 173–200). Mahwah, NJ: Lawrence Erlbaum Associates, Publishers.

Orton, S. T. (1937). *Reading, writing, and speech problem in children.* New York: W. W. Norton & Company, Inc.

Osmon, D. C., Plambeck, E. A., Klein, L., & Mano, Q. (2006). The Word Reading Test of effort in adult learning disability: A simulation study. *The Clinical Neuropsychologist, 20,* 315–324.

Osmon, D. C., Smerz, J. M., Braun, M. M., & Plambeck, E. (2006). Processing abilities associated with math skills in adult learning disability. *Journal of Clinical and Experimental Neuropsychology, 28,* 84–95.

Paulesu, E., Frith, U., & Snowling, M. (1996). Is developmental dyslexia a disconnection syndrome—evidence from PET scanning. *Brain, 119,* 143–157.

Pelletier, P. M., Ahmad, S. A., & Rourke, B. P. (2001). Classification rules for basic phonological processing disabilities and nonverbal learning disabilities: Formulation and external validity. *Child Neuropsychology, 7,* 84–98.

Perkins, D. (1984). Assessment of the use of the Nelson Denny Reading Test. *Forum for Reading, 15,* 64–69.

Pugh, K. R., Mencl, W. E., Jenner, A. R., Katz, L., Frost, S. J., Lee, J. R., et al. (2001). Neurobiological studies of reading and reading disability. *Journal of Communication Disorders, 34,* 479–492.

Robinson, D. R., Schofield, J. W., & Steers-Wentzell, K. L. (2005). Peer and cross-age tutoring in math: Outcomes and their design implications. *Educational Psychology Review, 17,* 327–362.

Rocheron, I., Lorenzi, C., Fullgrabe, C., & Dumont, A. (2002). Temporal envelope perception in dyslexic children. *Neuroreport, 13*(13), 1683–1687.

Rourke, B. P. (1995). *Syndrome of nonverbal learning disabilities: Neurodevelopmental manifestations.* New York: Guilford Press.

Rumsey, J. M., Andreason, P., Zametkin, A. J., & King, A. C. (1994). Right fronto-temporal activation by tonal memory in dyslexia, an O-1-5 PET study. *Biological Psychiatry, 36*(3), 171–180.

Ryan, K. E., & Ryan, A. M. (2005). Psychological processes underlying stereotype threat and standardized math test performance. *Educational Psychologist, 40,* 53–63.

Ryckman, D. B. (1982). Gray Oral Reading Tests: Some reliability and validity data with learning-disabled children. *Psychological Reports, 50*(2), 673–674.

Semmes, J. (1968). Hemispheric specialization: A possible clue to mechanism. *Neuropsychologia, 6,* 11–26.

Seymour, P. H. K., & Evans, H. M. (1994). Levels of phonological awareness and learning to read. *Reading and Writing, 6*(3), 221–250.

Shanahan, T. (1984). Nature of the reading-writing relation: An exploratory multivariate analysis. *Journal of Educational Psychology, 76,* 466–477.

Share, D., & Stanovich, K. E. (1995). Cognitive processes in early reading development: A model of acquisition and individual differences. *Issues in Education: Contributions from Educational Psychology, 1,* 1–57.

Shaywitz, S. E., Shaywitz, B. A., Fulbright, R. K., Skudlarski, P., Mencl, W. E., Constable, R. T., et al. (2003). Neural systems for compensation and persistence: Young adult outcome of childhood reading disability. *Biological Psychiatry, 54*(1), 25–33.

Simon, R., & Hanrahan, J. (2004). An evaluation of the Touch Math method for teaching addition to students with learning disabilities in mathematics. *European Journal of Special Needs Education, 19,* 191–209.

Singer-Dudek, J., & Greer, R. D. (2005). A long-term analysis of the relationship between fluency and the training and maintenance of complex math skills. *Psychological Record, 55,* 361–376.

Small, S. L., Flores, D. K., & Noll, D. C. (1998). Different neural circuits subserve reading before and after therapy for acquired dyslexia. *Brain & Language, 62*(2), 298–308.

Solan, H. A., Hansen, P. C., Shelley-Tremblay, J., & Ficarra, A. (2003). Coherent motion threshold measurements for M-cell deficit differ for above- and below-average readers. *Optometry: Journal of the American Optometric Association, 74,* 727–734.

Sparks, R. L. (2004). Orthographic awareness, phonemic awareness, syntactic processing, and working memory skill in hyperlexic children. *Reading and Writing, 17,* 359–386.

Stefanatos, G. A., Gershkoff, A., & Madigan, S. (2005). On pure word deafness, temporal processing, and the left hemisphere. *Journal of the International Neuropsychological Society, 11,* 456–470.

Stein, J. F., & Fowler, M. S. (1993). Unstable binocular control in dyslexic children. *Journal of Research in Reading, 16,* 30–45.

Steinmetz, H. (1996). Structure, functional and cerebral asymmetry: *In vivo* morphometry of the planum temporals. *Neuroscience and Biobehavioral Reviews, 20,* 587–591.

Stevenson, H. W., & Newman, R. S. (1986). Long-term prediction of achievement and attitudes in mathematics and reading. *Child Development, 57,* 646–659.

Stothard, S. E. (1994). The nature and treatment of reading comprehension difficulties in children. In C. Hulme & M. Snowling (Eds.), *Reading development and dyslexia* (pp. 200–238). Philadelphia: Whurr Publishers, Ltd.

Studdert-Kennedy, M., & Mody, M. (1995). Auditory temporal perception deficits in reading-impaired: A critical review of the evidence. *Psychonomic Bulletin Review, 2,* 508–514.

Talcott, J. B., Hansen, P. C., Assoku, E. L., & Stein, J. F. (2000). Visual motion sensitivity in dyslexia: Evidence for temporal and energy integration deficits. *Neuropsychologia, 38,* 935–943.

Tallal, P., & Gaab, N. (in press). Dynamic auditory processing and musical training in language development and disorders. *Trends in Neuroscience.*

Tanguay, P. B. (2001). *Nonverbal learning disabilities at home: A parent's guide.* London: Jessica Kingsley Publishers.

Telzrow, C. F., & Koch, L. C. (2003). Nonverbal learning disability: Vocational implications and rehabilitation treatment approaches. *Journal of Applied Rehabilitation Counseling, 34,* 9–16.

Temple, E., Deutsch, G. K., Poldrack, R. A., Miller, S. L., Tallal, P., Merzenich, M. M., et al. (2003). Neural deficits in children with dyslexia ameliorated by behavioral remediation: Evidence from functional MRI. *Proceedings of the National Academy of Sciences, 100*(5), 2860–2865.

Temple, E., Poldrack, R. A., Protopapas, A., Nagarajan, S., Salz, T., Tallal, P., et al. (2000). Disruption of the neural response to rapid acoustic stimuli in dyslexia: Evidence from fMRI. *Proceedings of the National Academy of Science, 97,* 13907–13912.

Temple, E., Poldrach, R. A., Salidis, J., Deutsch, G. K., Tallal, P., Merzenich, M. M., et al. (2001). Disrupted neural responses to phonological and orthographic processing in dyslexic children: An fMRI study. *Neuroreport: For Rapid Communication of Neuroscience Research, 12*(2), 299–307.

Thompson, P. M., Cannon, T. D., Narr, K. I., Huttunen, M., et al. (2001). Genetic influences on brain structure. *Nature Neuroscience, 4,* 1253–1258.

Tomblin, J. B., Records, N. L., Buckwalter, P., Zhang, X., Smith, E., & O'Brien, M. (1997). Prevalence of specific language impairment in kindergarten children. *Journal of Speech & Hearing Research, 40*(6), 1245–1260.

Torgesen, J. K., Wagner, R. K., & Rashotte, C. A. (1999a). Preventing reading failure in young children with phonological processing disabilities : Group and individual responses to instruction. *Journal of Educational Psychology, 91*(4), 579–593.

Torgesen, J. K., Wagner, R. K., & Rashotte, C. A. (1999b). *Test of word reading efficiency (TOWRE).* Austin, TX: Pro-Ed.

Torgesen, J. K., Wagner, R. K., Rashotte, C. A., Rose, E., Lindamood, P., Conway, T., et al. (1999c). Preventing reading failure in young children with phonological processing disabilities: Group and individual responses to instruction. *Journal of Educational Psychology, 91, 579–593.*

Ullman, M. T. (2001). The declarative/procedural model of lexicon and grammar. *Journal of Psycholinguistic Research, 30*(1), 37–69.

U.S. Department of Education. (2002). Students with disabilities in postsecondary education: A profile of prepara tion, participation, and outcomes. Available free, 1-877-4ED-Pubs.

Van der Leij, A., & van Daal, H. P. (1999). Automatization aspects of dyslexia: Speed limitations in word identification, sensitivity to increasing task demands, and orthographic compensation. *Journal of Learning Disabilities, 32*(5), 417–428.

Vaugh, S., Chard, D. J., Pedrotty-Brynant, D., Coleman, M., Tyler, B., Livan-Thompson, S., et al. (2000). Fluency and comprehension interventions for third-grade students. *Remedial and Special Education, 21,* 325–335.

Vukovic, R. K., & Siegel, L. S. (2006). The double-deficit hypothesis: A comprehensive analysis of the evidence. *Journal of Learning Disabilities, 39,* 25–47.

Wagner, R. K., Torgesen, J. K., & Rashotte, C. A. (1999). *Examiner's manual: The Comprehension Test of Phonological Processing.* Austin, TX: Pro-Ed.

Wible, C. G., Han, S. D., Spencer, M. H., Kubicki, M., Niznikiewicz, M. H., Jolesz, F. A., et al. (2006). Connectivity among semantic associates: An fMRI study of semantic priming. *Brain and Language, 97,* 294–305.

Willcutt, E. G., & Pennington, B. F. (2000). Psychiatric comorbidity in children and adolescents with reading disability. *Journal of Child Psychology and Psychiatry, 41,* 1039–1048.

Wolf, M. (1999). What time may tell: Towards a new conceptualization of developmental dyslexia. *Annals of Dyslexia, 49,* 3–28.

Wolf, M., & Bower, P. G. (1999). The double-deficit hypothesis for the developmental dyslexias. *Journal of Educational Psychology, 91,* 415–438.

Wolf, M., Miller, L., & Donnelly, K. (2000). Retrieval, automaticity, vocabulary elaboration, orthography (RAVE-O): A comprehensive, fluency-based reading intervention program. *Journal of Learning Disabilities, 33*(4), 375.

Zaehle, T., Wustenberg, T., Meyer M., & Jancke, L. (2004). Evidence for rapid auditory perception as the foundation of speech processing: A sparse temporal sampling fMRI study. *European Journal of Neuroscience, 20,* 2447–2456.

21

The Neuropsychology of ADHD

SAM GOLDSTEIN AND JOY JANSEN

INTRODUCTION

THROUGH THE MID-1980S and into the 1990s, many children, adolescents, and adults affected with attention-deficit/hyperactivity disorder (ADHD) went unreferred, undiagnosed, and untreated. In the child and adolescent years their problems were suggested as reflecting poor motivation, ineffective parenting, or simple disobedience. In adulthood, affective illness and personality disturbance were often the explanations offered for characteristic symptoms of ADHD in adults. Rarely were neuropsychological deficits proposed as explanatory factors of the condition or related impairments. The rate of referral for ADHD and neuropsychological research on the condition has steadily increased in the past 10 years as has treatment with medication, the primary intervention (Medco Health Solutions, 2005; Safer, Zito, & Fine, 1996). Concurrently questions and criticisms have increased concerning not just the prevalence of the condition, treatment as well is debated (Diller, 2006; Diller & Goldstein, 2006). Despite these criticisms and questions, the rates of diagnosis and treatment continue to rise with greatest increases noted during the adult years (Medco Health Solutions, 2005). Converging lines of evidence reflect the significant adverse outcome of adults with ADHD (Kessler et al., 2006; Biederman et al., 2006) and estimated incidence rates of 4–5% of the adult population (Kessler et al., 2006). Yet it is still the case that by the time an appropriate referral is made, the neuropsychologist is presented with a complex set of problems often affected by a variety of social and non-social factors. Evaluation is complicated by the fact that there continues to be no critical diagnostic test for ADHD. This phenomena is not the result of a lack of effort on the part of researchers but reflects the complex interaction of ADHD symptoms with the environment.

It continues to be the case that there are few exclusionary developmental criteria and no unequivocal, positive, developmental or neuropsychological markers for the diagnosis of ADHD. ADHD appears to be distinct from other psychiatric and developmental conditions due to its intensity and persistence as well as the clustering of symptoms rather than the simple presence or absence of symptoms that drives impairment and ultimately confirms the diagnosis. This phenomena was first observed by Ross and Ross in 1982 and continues to be the case today (Goldstein & Naglieri, 2006). In many ways, ADHD reflects an exaggeration of what is normal behavior, either too much or not enough of what is expected in certain settings. The high rate of comorbid conditions makes differential diagnosis and treatment a complex process.

Symptoms considered characteristic of ADHD confront all neuropsychologists. Opinions about ADHD as a diagnostic entity distinct from other neuropsychological conditions often reflect a broad diversity of beliefs among neuropsychologists. Most, if not all, agree that on a biological basis, there are individuals who struggle from a young age to manage impulses, control movement, sustain attention, and engage in self-disciplined behavior. Yet controversy continues to fuel around the biological cause and neuropsychological impairments of this symptom profile and not surprisingly the solution. The increasing rate of diagnosis and treatment for ADHD, particularly in the adult years, is most likely a reflection of the greater community, professional, and parental awareness of the symptoms of the condition as well as a broadening of the diagnostic criteria to include additional subgroups. Thus, more individuals are referred, diagnosed, and treated.

Not surprisingly in our market economy, as a particular problem becomes popular, controversy and opinion concerning that problem as well as a recommended diversity of solutions comes to the forefront (Goldstein, 2006). Many more lay than clinical texts are published on this subject. The field continues to be over-represented by opinion. Fifteen years ago in 1992, Goodman and Poillion, in a review of articles and books about ADHD, identified 69 characteristics and 38 causes. At the time there was no clear cut pattern for identifying the condition and little agreement upon its cause.

Though it is true that many symptoms of ADHD share common ground with other psychiatric and developmental conditions (Jiron,

Sherrill, & Chiodo, 1995), a solid body of scientific evidence demonstrates that the cluster of symptomatic problems currently used to define ADHD clinically represents a disorder distinct from other conditions (Biederman et al., 1996). Multiple physical and biological differences have been identified (Dickstein et al., 2005; Pliszka, 2005; Unnever & Cornell, 2003) as well as genetic differences (Fisher et al., 2005). Since the 1970s, however, research has increasingly suggested that the core problem for ADHD is not excessive activity but deficits in executive functions (Douglas & Peters, 1979; for review, see Barkley, 1997, 2006). Though the current *Diagnostic and Statistical Manual of Mental Disorders* of the American Psychiatric Association (4th ed., text revision; *DSM–IV–TR*) diagnostic criteria continue to weigh heavily upon symptoms of inattention, the emerging literature across the life span provides strong contrary evidence that deficits in self-regulation and executive functioning offer a better explanation of this condition and its impairments (Barkley & Murphy, 2006). Yet the change in focus to problems of poor self-regulation and executive dysfunction, both likely driven by impulsivity as the core symptom of ADHD causing the most serious impairments, has not come easily. Just as the lay public begins to accept that inattentiveness is a problem for some, the preponderance of the research literature in the past 10 years suggests that in laboratory settings the problem is not that these individuals cannot pay attention but that they do not pay attention efficiently or effectively. Their inconsistent attention occurs in repetitive, effortful situations in which inhibition, planning, and working memory are required. Converging lines of evidence including measures of physiological functioning, laboratory tests, and neuroimaging studies increasingly support disinhibition as a core deficit in ADHD (for review see Barkley, 2006; Harrier & DeOrnellas, 2005; Wellington, Semrud-Clikeman, Gregory, Murphy, & Lancaster, 2006).

Barkley (1994) suggests that "ADHD represents a profound disturbance in self-regulation and organization behavior across time" (p. vii). These functions are subserved by prefrontal, mid-brain, and cerebellar regions in the human brain (Fuster, 1989). ADHD appears to be a condition that affects the organism's ability to organize behavior over time and meet demands for present and future performance. To understand the condition one has to go where it lives, at the point of performance (Ingersoll & Goldstein, 1993). ADHD is a condition best captured and understood by the observation and measurement of real life behavior. As Barkley (1997) notes, pervasive impairments caused by ADHD are driven by:

- difficulty fixing on and sustaining mental images or messages that relate to external events so that you can act or not act upon them;

- problems referencing the past in relation to those events;
- difficulty imagining hypothetical futures that might result from those events;
- problems establishing goals and plans of actions to implement them;
- difficulty avoiding reacting to stimuli likely to interfere with goal-directed behaviors;
- poor utilization of internal speech in the service of self-regulation and goal-directed behaviors;
- inefficient regulation of affect and motivation or response to situational demands;
- problems separating affect from information or feelings from facts; and
- difficulty analyzing and synthesizing information.

Thus, ADHD, a problem occurring at the point of performance, well defines a disorder of executive functioning. It is a problem that results from being capable of learning from experiences but incapable of acting efficiently on that learning at the point of performance (Ingersoll & Goldstein, 1993). It is thus a disorder of inadequate response inhibition; a problem of performance not skills; of inconsistency rather than inability.

DEFINITION AND DIAGNOSIS

THOUGH ABNORMAL EEG patterns, smaller brain structures, physiological correlates, and neuropsychological performance measures have been proposed in making the diagnosis of ADHD (for review see Loo & Barkley, 2005; Goldstein & Naglieri, 2006; Kaiser & Othmer, 2000), this is a diagnosis formulated and defined currently by the text revision of the 4th Edition of the *Diagnostic and Statistical Manual* of the American Psychiatric Association (APA, 2000). Despite advocacy by some proponents that these measures, particularly SPECT and QEEG, facilitate the diagnosis and identification of theoretical subtypes (Amen, 2002), clinical subtypes (El-Sayed, Larsson, Persson, & Rydelius, 2002), and avoidance of false positive diagnoses, in the current clinical climate they are technically unnecessary in making the diagnosis of ADHD (for review see Barkley, 2006). Until such time as these measures are incorporated into the diagnostic criteria, their utilization may best lie as sources of adjunctive information that facilitate an appreciation of the nature of the condition and possibly treatment choice.

For practicing neuropsychologists, the *DSM–IV–TR* is a standard desk reference. As such, due to chapter space only a brief review of these criteria are provided. The criteria require that the child meet five basic guidelines. These are summarized here:

A. The child must present with either 6 of 9 inattentive symptoms (e.g., often fails to give close attention to details or makes careless mistakes in school work, work, or other activities), 6 of 6 hyperactive symptoms (e.g., often fidgets with hands or feet or squirms in seat) and 3 impulsive symptoms (e.g., has difficulty awaiting turn), or both.
B. Some of these symptoms cause impairment and were present before 7 years of age.
C. Some impairment is present in two or more settings (e.g., school and home).
D. There is clear evidence of clinically significant impairment in social, academic, or occupational functioning.
E. The symptoms do not occur exclusively as the result of other psychiatric conditions.

The diagnosis of ADHD, based on *DSM–IV–TR* criteria, does not require neuropsychological tests or for that matter measures such as EEG, MRI, or SPECT. The value of neuropsychological measures may lie in their potential to define patterns of strengths and weaknesses that can be then utilized to guide treatment planning and expectations for treatment response. Although a number of studies have suggested differences between those with subtypes of ADHD as well as between ADHD and psychiatric as well as normal controls, the preponderance of the literature does not provide a firm foundation upon which to use neuropsychological tests to confirm or disconfirm the diagnosis of ADHD (Schmitz et al., 2002; Schoechlin & Engel, 2005), but the clinical question of greatest interest with the neuropsychological assessment of ADHD is not diagnosis but rather the ruling out or in of other organic or functional conditions.

Rates of ADHD among relatives of each subtype group of ADHD have been found to be greater than among relatives of controls (Faraone, Biederman, & Friedman, 2000). These authors, however, found that rates of ADHD were not significantly higher among relatives of Combined Type probands compared with relatives of other probands. There appears to be little evidence that the *DSM–IV* subtypes of ADHD correspond to familial distinct conditions. The data also do not appear to confirm the idea that subtypes fall along a gradient of familial severity. Instead, the data suggest that symptom differences among subtypes are likely due to nonfamilial, environmental causes.

Additionally, current *DSM* criteria provide equal importance to all symptoms. This phenomena combined with the fact that more symptoms are listed than required for diagnosis, cannot help but introduce error variance, as not everyone with a diagnosis experiences similar symptoms. In an effort to identify or define essential core symptoms, Owens and Hoza (2003) developed a definition of ADHD based on a set of diagnostic algorithms. These algorithms place differential importance on specific symptoms relative to situation and reporter. Thus, symptom reports critical to confirming a diagnosis from parents have been found to be somewhat different than those confirming the diagnosis in teachers. This is true also for ruling out ADHD in the absence of certain key symptoms. These authors note that key symptoms for the Inattentive Type of ADHD include forgetfulness, disorganization, and shifting attention. Running or climbing excessively was critical for the Hyperactive Type of ADHD. Running or climbing, difficulty playing quietly, problems waiting turn, and engaging in dangerous activities were most characteristic of children with the Combined Type of ADHD (Faraone, Biederman, Sprich-Buckminster, Chen, & Tsuang, 1993). According to these authors, in order to make a positive diagnosis of ADHD across setting, one symptom in each of three symptom clusters is required. Cluster one includes impulsive behaviors (e.g., speaks out in class), cluster two includes problems with concentration (e.g., has difficulty finishing work), and cluster three includes restless behaviors (e.g., often fidgets when seated). It has yet to be determined whether research for *DSM–V* will investigate the inclusion of alogrithmic formulas in making psychiatric diagnoses. Such a change would represent a significant shift in the diagnostic process. Neuropsychologists should also be aware that there are no acceptable substitutes for using the *DSM* criteria. Checklists based on *DSM* criteria may provide organized, norm referenced summaries and as such may be a good place to start but not necessarily a good place to finish.

In 1978, Rutter suggested that for a syndrome to be useful it must predict something other than what was used to define the group in the first place. Suggesting that as a syndrome ADHD predicts poor attention span, poor impulse control, and hyperactive behavior does not make a particularly useful diagnosis. These behaviors are obvious. The value lies in the relationship between these behaviors and predicting future outcome. There has been a clinical quest over the past 50 years to determine if a diagnosis of ADHD or a specific subtype of ADHD might speak to more or less risk of future problems or respond differently to treatment. Although subtype analysis has attempted to evaluate ADHD based on its occurrence, pervasively or in a specific situation, comorbidly with other disruptive and nondisruptive disorders or occurring with and without the hyperactive–impulsive component, the debate continues as to the value of subtypes within the broader diagnostic category of ADHD. A large body of research has yielded equivocal findings as to whether the current delineation of ADHD Combined Type, Hyperactive-Impulsive Type, and Inattentive Type represent distinct types with differential risks, impairments, response to treatment, and prognosis. Anastopoulos, Barkley, and Shelton (1994) noted that the continued focus on inattention perpetuates a number of major misconceptions, including that the Inattentive Type of ADHD represents a subtype of the Combined Type. Current research suggests that it may not (Todd, Rasmussen, Wood, Levy, & Hay, 2004). More likely, the Inattentive Type represents a distinct disorder primarily reflecting difficulty attending to repetitive, effortful tasks and distinct problems with disorganization. The problems that this ADHD group experience may very well be the result of faulty skills rather than inconsistent or inadequate use of skills. Until *DSM–V* appears sometime in or after 2012, the Inattentive Type of ADHD is still considered part of a cluster of ADHD diagnoses. Ironically, though children with this diagnosis are not disturbing or disruptive, their condition is defined along the disruptive continuum.

As additional field studies are undertaken in the ongoing process of the evolving diagnostic systems and in the preparation for *DSM–V*, a number of questions will be addressed. Among these are those distinguishing the meaning and relationship of the Combined, Hyperactive-Impulsive, and Inattentive subtypes. Further, as the condition is increasingly appreciated, defined, and treated as a problem related to executive functioning and self-regulation, the question whether cognitive measures should be included in what has traditionally been a descriptive or behavioral diagnosis has been raised (Goldstein & Naglieri, 2006). Among additional questions raised and yet to be answered concerning the evolution of the ADHD diagnosis are:

- Age-related symptom issues
- Diagnostic symptoms for children under the age of 5
- Diagnostic symptoms for adults
- Age of onset and its meaning
- Lower age boundary in which the diagnosis should not be made
- Adjustment of diagnostic criteria based on gender
- The need for demonstration of symptoms in at least two or three environments
- The importance of functional measures of impairment as an essential criteria in making the diagnosis

A NEUROPSYCHOLOGICAL DEFINITION OF ADHD

BASED ON THE work of Douglas and Peters (1979) and Goldstein and Goldstein (1990) first proposed a four part practical definition of ADHD, which was later expanded to five parts (1998). This definition, modified for this chapter, provides a neuropsychological perspective of the condition. It is offered as a way to facilitate understanding, measure impairment, and design effective treatment. As Douglas and Peter (1979) noted, those with ADHD experience a constitutional predisposition to struggle with attention, effort, inhibitory control, and fully modulated arousal, and have a need to seek stimulation. They struggle with the executive processes well defined by Barkley (2006). The five components of this definition include impulsivity and planning, inattention, hyperactivity, problems modulating gratification, and emotional regulation.

IMPULSIVITY AND PLANNING

THIS GROUP OF individuals experiences difficulty with inhibition leading to problems in planning. Planning is a mental process by which an individual determines, selects, supplies, and evaluates solutions to problems (Naglieri & Das, 1997). Planning requires the efficient choice of strategies: the ability to self-monitor, self-correct, flexibly shift, and adjust to feedback. They often know what to do but don't do what they know. They have difficulty weighing the consequences of their actions before acting. They do not reasonably consider the consequences of their past behavior. They struggle with rule-governed behavior (Barkley, 1981) likely due to an inability to separate experience from response, thought from emotion, and action from reaction. This results in impetuous, unthinking behavior in individuals who seemingly do not appear to learn from experience. These individuals are often repeat offenders, a pattern that frustrates parents, teachers, friends, and spouses.

Scholnick (1995) reviewed an extensive literature of nearly 11,000 references concerning the development and implementation of planning. Planning requires an internal process of problem solving that precedes the external strategic action; requires the capacity to inhibit action while thinking through the best ways to obtain goals; and involves multiple stages, each of which is critical in designing, choosing, and following through with the problem-solving approach regardless of the nature of the task. Planning, first described by Luria, is an active process. Clearly this process requires selective inhibition or impulse control. Planning relies on working memory to construct and anticipate a plan and monitor its execution. Such a process, as Barkley (1997) has noted, requires prolongation, self-directed speech, and reconstitution at the very least. For example, if an individual is unable to anticipate future consequences of his actions or reflect while acting, he is likely to be accident prone. Adept planners make fast computations and think ahead several steps through the use of working memory. This skillful allocation of resources requires that attention be divided simultaneously between active construction and utilization of a plan. Planning is also likely influenced by long-term memory, motivation, personal attributes, and belief about personal capacities. Planning deficits have been repeatedly found to significantly discriminate youth with ADHD from those with other conditions and controls (Naglieri, Goldstein, Iseman, & Schwebach, 2003; Naglieri, Salter, & Edwards, 2004; Paolitto, 1999).

INATTENTION

INDIVIDUALS WITH ADHD have difficulty sustaining effort and functioning efficiently relative to their peers and ability. In new or novel settings and those that are less repetitive and effortful they appear to function better, suggesting that the fault lies not in failure to know what to do but an inefficiency in action. Thus, reinforcing an important point, ADHD represents an exaggeration on a dimensional basis of normal problems such as too much restlessness or an inadequate investment in tasks that must be completed. On a dimensional basis the behavior of these individuals represents the extreme of what is expected.

HYPERACTIVITY

INDIVIDUALS WITH ADHD tend to be excessively restless, overactive, and struggle in particular to control body movements when staying still is at a premium. Interestingly, even youth diagnosed with the Inattentive Type of ADHD demonstrate more restless, fidgety behavior than controls (Lahey, Pelham, Loney, Lee, & Willcutt, 2005).

PROBLEMS MODULATING GRATIFICATION

INDIVIDUALS WITH ADHD often appear driven toward immediate, frequent, predictable, and meaningful consequences. They demonstrate less sensitivity to changing parameters of reinforcement rate, which may be secondary to problems sustaining attention or faulty inhibition (Kollins, Lane, & Shapiro, 1997). These individuals demonstrate an excess or exaggeration in comparison to normals in regards to these variables. They experience greater difficulty working toward a long-term goal. They often require brief repeated payoffs rather than a single long-term reward. Individuals with ADHD also do not appear to respond to rewards in a manner similar to others (Haenlein & Caul, 1987). Rewards do not appear to be effective in changing their behavior on a long-term basis. They are quick to regress once the reward paradigm is removed. Impulsivity drives their behavior to remain consequentially bound. However, it also appears that given a sufficient number of trials and opportunities for generalization, their behavior, that is the capacity to do consistently what they know, is shaped in a way similar to that of unaffected individuals (Shure, 2004). In regard to consequences and behavior development, for those with ADHD the issue is not so much behavior modification as behavior management. The provision of a sufficient number of supervised, structured, and reinforced trials for everything from daily habits to social, academic, and work skills is essential.

This group of individuals also receive significantly more negative reinforcement than others. Their interactions with others are often shaped by an effort to avoid aversive consequences. Negative reinforcement offers a plausible, experiential explanation for the diverse problems individuals with ADHD develop. Efforts of helpers tend to reinforce passivity and helplessness. Over time the avoidance of aversive consequences tends to exert greater influence over their behavior than the seeking of positive consequences. Individuals with ADHD, children and adults alike, learn to respond to demands placed on them by the environment when an aversive stimulus is removed contingent upon performance rather than for the promise of a positive future reward.

Emotional Regulation

INDIVIDUALS WITH ADHD appear quicker to become aroused. Whether happy or sad the speed and intensity of which they move to the extremes of emotion is much greater than that of peers. This problem appears to reflect an impulsive inability to separate thought from emotion. They often appear to be on a roller coaster ride of emotions. When happy they tend to be so happy that people are disrupted. When unhappy they tend to be so unhappy that people are equally disrupted. A combination of these qualities, feedback when received for emotionality, lack of ability to develop the skills necessary to control emotions, and the disruption in relationships across the life span exert a significant influence on a sense of psychological well-being, locus of control, and personality style.

Problems with ADHD typically cause significant and pervasive impairment in day-to-day interaction in the environment across the life span. Familial, social, academic, and vocational demands of a fast paced culture require consistent, predictable, independent, and efficient approach to life. Failure to develop, maintain, and use these abilities efficiently leads to uneven and unpredictable behavior, characteristically a function of knowing what to do but being unable to do it in a consistent, predictable manner.

NEUROPSYCHOLOGICAL FINDINGS ACROSS THE LIFE SPAN

DESPITE EXTENSIVE EFFORTS, no single measure nor battery of neuropsychological tests has been found to meet stringent positive and negative predictive criteria and conclusively determine whether or not a child, adolescent, or adult suffers from ADHD (Murphy, 1994). However, despite convincing data, neuropsychologists and other clinical evaluators continue to commonly practice profile analysis when assessing ADHD (Anastasi & Urbina, 1997; Fiorello, Hale, McGrath, Ryan, & Quinn, 2001). Many neuropsychologists continue to rely upon the use of intelligence test data in making the diagnosis of ADHD (Molter, 1995). However, although verbal comprehension and perceptual organization factors may distinguish between children with and without learning disability, these factors have not been found to distinguish between children with and without ADHD (Semrud-Clikeman et al., 1992). In 1990, the first author of this chapter in fact recommended neuropsychological measures as part of the ADHD diagnosis (Goldstein & Goldstein, 1990). However, by 1998 a sufficient body of data had been collected demonstrating that such measures could not and should not be used in ruling in or out the diagnosis of ADHD (Goldstein & Goldstein, 1998). However, neuropsychological measures may provide useful data once the diagnosis of ADHD is made. Such data can assist in defining neuropsychological strengths and weaknesses facilitating an appreciation of the role ADHD and other neuropsychological factors may play in contributing to impairment as well as in designing effective interventions. The greatest strength of neuropsychological assessment with ADHD is in ruling in or out other organic and functional conditions.

Children and adults with ADHD have been shown to have difficulty with working memory involving backward digit span, mental arithmetic, paced auditory serial addition, and paired associate learning, to mention but a few tasks (Barkley, 1997; Chang, et al., 1999, Grodzinsky & Diamond, 1992; Kuntsci, et al., 2001). Additionally, children and adults with ADHD have been found to have difficulty with tasks falling broadly under the umbrella of executive functioning, including anticipation (Grodzinsky & Diamond, 1992), self-monitoring (Clark,

Priori, & Kinsella, 2000), and organizational strategies (Zentall, 1988). Yet not all children or adults receiving a diagnosis of ADHD demonstrate similar patterns of cognitive processing deficits (Bekker et al., 2005; Goldstein & Naglieri, 2006).

Continuous performance tests (CPT) have been aggressively marketed as neuropsychological measures capable of making the diagnosis of ADHD. However, a large body of research with CPTs has yielded mixed results (Homack & Reynolds, 2005). CPTs demonstrated limited correlations with cognitive measures, and behavior ratings have not been found to distinguish one *DSM–IV–TR* type of ADHD from another (Naglieri, Goldstein, Delauder, & Schwebach, 2005).

CRITICAL VARIABLES

THE FOLLOWING SECTION will briefly review a number of key variables relative to neuropsychological findings across the life span.

Gender

It is irrefutable that many more males are diagnosed with ADHD than females. It is also irrefutable that because these behaviors are most visible in males, the development of diagnostic criteria and research primarily focused on males rather than females. The question as to whether gender specific norms and diagnostic criteria should be considered in identifying females with ADHD is still debated and will likely be an issue for *DSM–V*. A careful review of the literature, however, suggests that it is comorbid disruptive problems that likely bring males with ADHD to clinical attention in greater frequency than females (Biederman et al., 2005; Goldstein & Gordon, 2003). Meta-analytic studies have revealed little variability of gender issues and no significant gender differences in the areas of impulsivity, basic academic performance, social skills, peer status, fine motor ability, parent education, and diagnostic history. Further, little variability has been demonstrated across studies in IQ, hyperactivity, and externalizing diagnoses, with females displaying slightly greater levels of intellectual impairment and lower levels of externalizing behaviors and hyperactivity (Biederman et al., 2005; Gaub & Carlson, 1997). Among nonreferred individuals identified with ADHD, lower rates of inattention, internalizing behavior, peer aggression, and peer dislike occur more frequently for females than for males. However, in clinic referred and identified populations, males and females appear similarly impaired despite unsupported theories to the contrary (Quinn & Nadeau, 2002; Solden, 2005). Further, studies have suggested that males referred for treatment of ADHD are representative of the population of males overall with ADHD in the prevalence of externalizing behavioral problems, whereas females referred with

ADHD appear to demonstrate more severe externalizing symptoms than the unreferred population. Faraone, Biederman, and Monuteaux (2000), using a family study methodology in a sample of 6- to 18-year-old females suggested that relatives of ADHD probands were at significantly greater risk for ADHD. These findings suggest that ADHD with and without antisocial problems in females may represent etiologically distinct disorders.

Intelligence

Children and adults with ADHD display lower levels of intellectual performance than either nondisabled children or their own siblings (Frazier, Demaree, & Youngstrom, 2004). The effect size for adults is somewhat smaller than children, but both are significant (Hervey, Epstein, & Curry, 2004). Three questions are frequently asked regarding the relationship between intelligence and ADHD:

- Does an ADHD sample reflect a normal distribution in terms of intellectual skills?
- Are there characteristics unique to individuals with ADHD demonstrating superior or better intellectual abilities?
- Are there similar or different characteristics of ADHD in those demonstrating deficient intellectual abilities?

A weak though significant link has been found between IQ and ADHD (Hinshaw, Morrison, Carte, & Cornsweet, 1987; Kaplan, Crawford, Dewey, & Fisher, 2000; Schmitz et al., 2002) as well as a link between IQ and behavior problems (Sonuga-Barke, Lamparelli, Stevenson, Thompson, & Henry, 1994). Rates of hyperactive-impulsive behavior and measures of intelligence appear to have a negative association. In contrast, the association between ratings of conduct problems and intelligence are often much smaller, in some cases insignificant. When efforts are not made to control for IQ, children with ADHD differ significantly from controls, particularly in lower verbal intelligence (McGee, Williams, & Feehan, 1992; Barkley & Cunningham, 1979). Measures of sustained attention and inhibition are associated to a small but significant degree with measures of IQ (Schonfeld, Shaffer, & Barmack, 1989). Matching subjects with ADHD with controls and statistically controlling for IQ differences appears to reduce or eliminate the effects of ADHD on intelligence. However, group differences in Verbal IQ should not be viewed as an artifact of group selection nor as a source of error to be statistically removed. These differences may in fact reflect real differences in these two populations. The preponderance of the data, however, suggest that less than 10% of the variance in Verbal IQ is accounted for by ADHD. As Barkley (1995) points out, ADHD likely has a unidirectional effect on intelligence to a small degree in the acquisition of ability and to a larger degree in the application of skills.

Anecdotes abound that those with ADHD fall inordinately at the higher end of the intellectual distribution. However, well controlled research has not been generated to demonstrate that this is the case (for review see Barkley, 2006). Some authors have argued that there is an overlap between the behavioral characteristics of creativity and ADHD (Hallowell & Ratey, 1994). However, once again, such theories remain unproven in children and adults (Weyandt, Mitzlaff, & Thomas, 2002). Further, a number of intervening variables have been studied as possibly creating a link between ADHD and weak intellectual performance. For example, in a study of ADHD and language disability, children with ADHD Combined Type did not demonstrate a general working memory deficit unless they experienced a comorbid language disorder (Jonsdottir, Bouma, Sergeant, & Scherder, 2005).

An intellectual measure, the Cognitive Assessment System (Naglieri & Das, 1997), based on Luria's PASS theory of intelligence, has yielded promising results in identifying deficits in cognitive functioning commonly found in children with ADHD (Paolitto, 1999). The PASS theory of intelligence proposes human cognitive functioning as based on four essential activities: planning, attention, simultaneous processes, and successive processes. A number of studies have demonstrated consistent weaknesses in planning and attention processes in youth with ADHD (Naglieri et al., 2003, 2004).

Language

As Beitchman and Inglis (1991) note, language is the window to the mind. The bidirectional relationship of language development and impulsivity has been questioned but not thoroughly evaluated. Baker and Cantwell's (1992) extensive review of the literature on speech/language disorders in children with ADHD, as well as their longitudinal data, finds a consistent pattern of elevated rates of speech/language disorders in individuals with ADHD and elevated rates of ADHD in persons with speech/language disorders. These authors suggest that some types of speech/language disorder found in children with ADHD may be related to other factors such as age, gender, or comorbid psychiatric conditions.

Are the language skills of impulsive children delayed because they don't practice or attend to their environment effectively, or are these children impulsive because they lack the efficient linguistic capacity necessary to develop appropriate inhibitory control? The play, social, and behavioral skills of language-impaired children are deficient relative to their same age, unaffected peers and are likely to increase the vulnerability for this population to receive comorbid diagnoses of disruptive behavioral problems such as ADHD (Donahue, Cole, & Hartas, 1994). Further, parents of children with slow language growth view their offspring as more active, inattentive, and difficult to manage than normally speaking peers (Paul & James, 1990).

Learning Disability

In 1994, DuPaul and Stoner reviewed 17 studies in an effort to determine the percentage of children with ADHD also experiencing a learning disability. Averaging across studies, approximately 1 out of every 3 children with ADHD was found to have a specific learning disability. In contrast, the prevalence of learning disabilities among normal controls is much lower than the lowest estimate of approximately 20% for children with ADHD (Semrud-Clikeman et al., 1992). DuPaul and Stoner note that the overlap of ADHD with learning disabilities range from a low of 18% to a high of 36%. As with language impairment the direction of the relationship between learning disability and ADHD symptoms has been repeatedly questioned and examined. A beyond chance level relationship between the two may in part be related to a third phenomena such as language delay (Cantwell & Baker, 1992). Part of the dilemma in examining the relationship between these conditions lies in the lack of clearly defined subtypes within each (Riccio, Gonzalez, & Hynd, 1994). The consensus of the literature, however, suggests that ADHD and learning disability represent two distinct problems (Shaywitz, Fletcher, & Shaywitz, 1995). These authors wrote that learning disability "represents a disorder of cognitive functioning. In contrast, ADHD is defined by the child's behaviors perceived by the child's parents and teachers; ADHD thus refers to a disorder affecting primarily the behavioral domain" (pg. 55).

At least one study has been used as the basis for the development of a working memory training program to reduce symptoms and impairment in children with ADHD (Klingberg et al., 2005). However, when working memory is described as containing components related to a visual-spatial sketch pad or phonological loop and a central executive, children with ADHD have not been reported to have significant working memory deficits (Baddeley, 1992). In a review of the literature, Roberts and Pennington (1996) concluded that deficits in voluntary motor inhibition in ADHD, not deficits in verbal working memory, appear to be responsible for academic performance problems. However, more recent conceptualizations of working memory suggest that children with ADHD likely struggle academically because of their working memory deficits (Barkley, 1997). In fact, executive function tasks reflecting the right pre-frontal cortex, organs of the basal ganglia, and cerebellum may differentiate those with ADHD from controls or those with other developmental problems such as learning disability (Semrud-Clikeman et al., 2000).

Neuropsychologists should be sensitive to Denckla's (1996) argument that the use of terms such as attention and learning in cognitive neuroscience differs from clinical practice. When encoding processes are considered a function of working memory, children with learning and attention problems are identified as deficient (Sonuga-Barke, Dalen, & Remington, 2003; Toplak & Tannock, 2005). Reading disabled children demonstrate significantly lower working memory scores; arithmetic disabled children demonstrate lower scores on a working memory counting task with the inattentive group performing similar to normals, except at the youngest age. Denckla's (1996) review of the literature supports Barkley's perception that "what looks like an attention deficit is primarily an intention deficit with prominent developmental failures as the first component of intention, namely inhibition" (p. 117). In this model intention is defined as initiating a movement, sustaining a movement or posture, and inhibiting extraneous, off-task movements while engaged in a task or shifting from one movement to another.

When learning is considered a function of acquisition, consolidation, storage, and retrieval, children with ADHD appear to demonstrate deficits in the process of acquisition due to their deficient use of proactive strategies when engaged in learning tasks (Barkley, Grodzinsky, & DuPaul, 1992). Further, individuals with ADHD demonstrate poor recall, because their approach to recall is disorganized and their memory system appears to be overloaded with random bits of information in a disorderly framework (Grodzinsky & Diamond, 1992). Coupled with inhibition, working memory may well be the essential element of executive function. This combined deficit has in turn been linked to the diagnosis of ADHD (Roberts & Pennington, 1996). If there is no inhibition allowing delay between stimulus and response, there can be no working memory. However, what is held in working memory must possess some content. Under this construct of working memory, the child with ADHD may experience problems very similar to those of the child with learning disability.

Using a liberal definition of learning disability, significant differences are found between ADHD and LD groups. Although some authors report a comorbidity as high as 90% (Semrud-Clikeman et al., 1992), it is likely that inconsistencies in samples and methodological problems contribute to very high numbers. It is reasonable to conclude that approximately 1 of 3 youth with ADHD suffer from a specific learning disability and vice versa (for review see Barkley, 2006). The preponderance of the data regarding the etiological and symptomatic relationship of ADHD and learning disabilities suggests that it is reasonable for neuropsychologists to screen for academic achievement in all individuals referred for ADHD assessment. There is a high probability that a significant minority of individuals with ADHD experience deficits in achievement that may be contributed to by the combination of ADHD and other specific neuropsychological deficits. The preponderance of the available data suggests that the majority of individuals experiencing a learning disability do so as the result of deficits in language and to a lesser extent visual skills and are not due to symptoms of ADHD. Deficits in language also present themselves in the area of reading for individuals experiencing learning disabilities due to poor phonological processing skills, which is not demonstrated in individuals with ADHD. In childhood, reading problems are related to word reading, word decoding, and spelling. In adulthood, deficiencies are associated with reading comprehension (Samuelsson, Lundberg, & Herkner, 2004).

Depression and Anxiety

A beyond chance relationship between ADHD and the internalizing conditions of anxiety and depression makes these disorders more than just a passing interest to neuropsychologists. The overlap between ADHD and depression occurs at a beyond chance level, with nearly 30% in children (McClelland, Rubert, Reichler, & Sylvester, 1989; Willcutt, Pennington, Chhabildas, Friedman, & Alexander, 1999) and continues into the adult years (Levitan, Jain, & Katzman, 1999; Reimherr et al., 2005). ADHD has been reported as comorbid with severe mental health problems as well (Goldstein & Brzostek, 2000). Rey (1994) reports a strong co-occurrence between depression and ADHD. However, neuropsychological tests have not been able to consistently discriminate between ADHD and internalizing conditions (Catz, Wood, Goldstein, et al., 1998). A familial link between ADHD and depression has been suggested to reflect shared familial risk factors as well as those contributed to by the environment (Faraone & Biederman, 1997). ADHD has also been suggested when comorbid with bipolar disorder to represent a familially distinct condition from other forms of ADHD. The authors suggest that this may represent the unique variant of childhood onset bipolar disorder (Faraone, Biederman, Mennan, Wozniak, & Spencer, 1997). Anxiety is also much more commonly associated with depression than ADHD. Approximately one-third of referred and non-referred youth with ADHD have been found to have a life-time history of anxiety disorder (Biederman et al., 1993; Biederman, Newcorn, & Sprich, 1991).

Prevalence rates for ADHD are significantly greater in offspring of parents with depression and panic disorders based upon parent report and in children of depressed parents based on consensus report. Consistently higher rates of ADHD are reported by children, parents, and in a consensus diagnosis when anxiety or depression is present (McClelland et al., 1989). It has further been suggested that major depression is likely the outcome rather than the cause of co-occurring disorders in ADHD (Biederman, Faraone, Mick, & Lelon, 1995).

The familial association of ADHD and bipolar disorder among first degree relatives of children with comorbid ADHD and bipolar disorder has been extensively studied (Wozniak, Biederman, Kiely, et al., 1995; Wozniak, Biederman, Mundy, Mennin, & Faraone, 1995). There appear to be high rates of comorbidity between bipolar disorder and ADHD in children and high rates of both bipolar disorder and ADHD in first degree relatives. The authors suggest that there is strong genetic evidence of the validity of bipolar disorder and ADHD when they exist comorbidly. The comorbid condition may represent a distinct nosological entity. Yet on a case by case basis, other authors have suggested that there is a genetic relationship between depressive and anxiety disorders that likely does not exist for ADHD (Cohen & Biederman, 1988).

Some authors report rates of bipolar disorder in adolescents with ADHD as high as 57% (West, McElroy, Strakowski, Keck, & McConville, 1995) and 22% in a hospitalized sample of ADHD patients (Butler, Arredondo, & McCloskey, 1995). These findings, plus those demonstrating that ADHD and bipolar disorder cosegregate in families, suggest that ADHD in children with bipolar disorder is familiarly distinct from other ADHD cases and may reflect what has been termed childhood onset bipolar disorder (Strober, 1992). It would appear that individuals with manic depressive illness demonstrate an overlap of symptoms and impairments with ADHD and may be at greater risk to be identified with both conditions. It likely continues to be the case that the lack of specificity and diagnostic instruments utilized may be partially responsible for some of the overlap between ADHD and bipolar disorder (Butler et al., 1995).

In 1992, Pliszka evaluated 107 pre-adolescent children meeting the criteria for ADHD. Populations were divided into those with and without comorbid anxiety. The two groups were then compared to a control group. Children with comorbid diagnosis were less impulsive and more hyperactive than those with ADHD alone but more impaired than controls. There was also a trend for the comorbid ADHD/anxiety group to show fewer disruptive symptoms than the purer ADHD group. Further, it has also been suggested that females when manifesting full symptoms of ADHD may demonstrate even higher rates of comorbidity for internalizing problems such as depression and anxiety (Rucklidge & Tannock, 2001).

Medical Conditions

A number of medical conditions, including thyroid dysfunction, asthma, and those with defined genetic etiology such as Williams syndrome, celiac disease, fragile X syndrome, and neurofibromatosis have been associated with a higher prevalence of ADHD and ADHD symptoms. It is beyond the scope of this chapter to review these conditions. Interested readers are referred to Goldstein and Reynolds (1999, 2005).

THE DIAGNOSTIC CONUNDRUM

THE NEUROPSYCHOLOGIST'S FIRST concern is misdiagnosing another disorder as ADHD. The second is missing comorbid diagnoses in a population of individuals with ADHD. Internalizing and externalizing disorders because they occur at such a high rate in those with ADHD represent a diagnostic conundrum when efforts are made to specifically tie symptoms to diagnoses. Problems with anxiety appear to occur at a significant but certainly lower rate than problems related to depression and other disruptive disorders in the ADHD population. Problems of oppositional defiance, particularly those related to resistance, appear characteristic of impulsive behavior while those reflecting spiteful, vindictive patterns are much more likely a consequence of an interaction between biological vulnerability and experience. Neuropsychologists should be aware that the increasing popularity of ADHD has resulted in more children with a variety of problems presenting for ADHD assessment. Desgranges, Desgranges, and Karsky (1995) reviewed 375 patient records. Of 119 cases requesting ADHD assessment, only 45 were confirmed by diagnosis. In remaining cases, problems related to anxiety, substance abuse, other disruptive disorders, and tic problems were suggested as contributing to ADHD-like behaviors. Finally, in significantly impaired populations, the false positive diagnosis of ADHD is easy to make. Kennemer and Goldstein (2005) demonstrated that in populations of institutionalized adolescents, one out of two youth with a diagnosis of ADHD upon admission, subsequent observation, and treatment over a period of time were deemed to not experience the condition.

TREATMENT OF ADHD ACROSS THE LIFE SPAN

TREATMENT OF ADHD must be multidisciplinary, multimodal, and maintained over a long period (for review see Goldstein & Goldstein, 1998; Goldstein & Ellison, 2002; Teeter, 1998). By far, the most effective short term interventions for ADHD reflect the combined use of medical, behavioral, and environmental techniques.

An extensive literature attests to the benefits of medicine, specifically stimulants, in reducing key symptoms of ADHD, and thus improving daily functioning across the life span. Side effects appear slightly greater and benefits slightly less in young children (Greenhill et al., 2006; for review see Barkley, 2006; Goldstein & Goldstein, 1998). Stimulants and other drugs principally impacting dopamine and norepinephrine (Volkow et al., 2001) have consistently been reported to improve academic achievement and productivity as well as accuracy of class work (Douglas, Barr, O'Neil, & Britton, 1986), attention span, reading comprehension, and complex problem solving, and to enhance inhibitory processes (Balthazor, Wagner, & Pelham, 1991). Related problems, including peer interactions, peer status, and even relationships with family members have been reported improved with these drugs as well (Whalen & Henker, 1991).

Behavior management increases the salience of behaving in a way consistent with environmental expectations. The manipulation of the environment (e.g., making tasks more interesting and payoffs more valuable) reduces the risk of problems within the natural setting. Goldstein and Goldstein (1998) suggests that students with ADHD possess an active learning style with a demonstrated need to move, talk, respond, question, choose, debate, and even provoke. Thus, in classroom settings children with ADHD do not fare well in sedentary situations. Managing interventions have included positive and negative contingent teacher attention, token economies, peer mediated and group contingencies, time out, home school contingencies, reductive techniques based on reinforcement, and cognitive behavioral strategies (Abramowitz & O'Leary, 1991). Environmental and task modifications are also critical for classroom success for the students with ADHD. However, additional research is needed, especially in the area of school-based intervention for adolescents with ADHD.

Though popular, the use of cognitive strategies (e.g., teaching a child to stop, look, and listen) as well as other nontraditional treatments (e.g., dietary manipulation, EEG biofeedback, etc.) to permanently alter the symptoms of ADHD have not stood the test of scientific research and thus should not be advocated as first line treatments of choice for children with ADHD. However, these strategies are effective when targeted to specific problems and impairments in the classroom for all students, with or without diagnoses. Shure (1994) suggests that the patient application of cognitive training over a long period of time, applied in the real world setting, can even improve the self-regulatory skills of children with ADHD. Safren et al. (2005) and Rostain and Ramsay (2006) have demonstrated that cognitive behavioral therapy for ADHD is an effective intervention reducing symptom severity and impairment, particularly when paired with medication treatment.

Regardless of the treatment modality employed, the basic underlying premise in managing problems of poor self-discipline and self-regulation involves increasing the individual's capacity to inhibit before acting. This is consistent with the theoretical construct that the core problem for ADHD reflects an inability to permit sufficient time to think or respond consistently to consequences.

Psychosocial treatments based on cognitive and neuropsychological theory figure prominently in the guidelines for treatment of ADHD from the American Academy of Pediatrics (AAP, 2001). It continues to be the case that adults and children find such treatments more acceptable than medication (Krain, Kendall, & Power, 2005). Further, more than 100 studies demonstrate that behavior change programs can exert a significant positive impact on children with ADHD and broadly reduce disruptive behavior (Evans, Langberg, Raggi, Allen, & Buvinger, 2005; Pelham et al., 2005). Despite the significant reductions in immediate symptoms of ADHD reported with medication (for review see Barkley, 2006), due to the chronicity, severity, cross situational nature, and myriad symptoms of ADHD leading to a host of impairments, treatment logically must be long-term requiring creativity, multimodality, and perseverance (Rapport, 1992). ADHD is a disorder that is managed, not cured. Secondary by-products of living with ADHD across the life span (e.g., low self-esteem) must be addressed through cognitive and psychotherapeutic approaches (Brooks, 2002). Additionally, systematically applied cognitive behavioral therapy has been found to lead to symptom and impairment reduction in adults with ADHD (Rostain & Ramsay, 2006; Wilens, McDermott, Biederman, & Abrantes, 1999).

Single treatment approaches to ADHD have included medication, behavioral techniques, cognitive techniques, parent training, and modifications in the educational environment. These treatment approaches have attempted to combine various combinations of these variables, typically pairing medication with parent training for children and with counseling for adults. Further, over the last 20 years there has been a dramatic increase in an interest in other nontraditional treatments from reportedly natural substances (e.g., Omega 3 fish oil) to biofeedback and sensory integration training. Many of these treatments have also proposed assessment measures to facilitate diagnosis and design intervention (EEG biofeedback; for review see Loo & Barkley, 2005). It is beyond the scope of this chapter to review these in depth. Interested readers are referred to a comprehensive discussion of these issues in Arnold (2001).

At this time, neuropsychological tests have not been demonstrated to be either necessary or sufficient to guide decisions about candidacy in individuals with ADHD for psychotherapy, skill-building activities, or medication titration. However, an emerging body of literature suggests that neuropsychological measures of planning and executive functioning may provide valuable differential diagnostic data that can facilitate treatment choice and expectations (Goldstein & Naglieri, 2006). The greatest value of neuropsychological assessment in ADHD is in assessing the wide variety of comorbid conditions that can contribute to and mimic ADHD.

REFERENCES

Abramowitz, A. J., & O'Leary, S. G. (1991). Behavior interventions for the classroom: Implications for students with ADHD. *School Psychology Review, 20,* 220–234.

Amen, D. G. (2002). *Healing ADHD*. Berkeley, CA: Berkeley Publishers.

American Academy of Pediatrics. (2001). Clinical practice guideline: Treatment of the school-aged child with attention-deficit/hyperactivity disorder. *Pediatrics, 108,* 1033–1044.

American Psychiatric Association. (2000). *Diagnostic and statistical manual of mental disorders* (4th ed., text revision). Washington, DC: Author.

Anastasi, A., & Urbina, S. (1997). *Psychological testing* (7th Edition). Upper Saddle River, NJ: Prentice Hall.

Anastopoulos, A. D., Barkley, R. A., & Shelton, T. (1994). The history and diagnosis of attention deficit/hyperactivity disorder. *Therapeutic Care and Education, 3,* 96–110.

Arnold, L. (2001). Alternative treatments for adults with attention-deficit hyperactivity disorder (ADHD). *Annals New York Academy of Sciences, 931,* 310–341.

Baddeley, A. (1992). Working memory. *Science, 255,* 556–559.

Baker, L., & Cantwell, D. P. (1992). Attention deficit disorder and speech/language disorders. *Comprehensive Mental Health Care, 2,* 3–16.

Balthazor, M. J., Wagner, R. K., & Pelham, W. E. (1991). The specificity of the effects of stimulant medication on classroom learning-related measures of cognitive processing for attention deficit disorder children. *Journal of Abnormal Child Psychology, 19,* 35–52.

Barkley, R. A. (1981). *Hyperactive children: A handbook for diagnosis and treatment.* New York: Guilford.

Barkley, R. (1994). What to look for in a school for a child with ADHD. *The ADHD Report, 2,* 1–3.

Barkley, R. (1995). ADHD and I.Q. *The ADHD Report, 3,* 1–3.

Barkley, R. (1997). *ADHD and the nature of self-control.* New York: Guilford.

Barkley, R. A. (2006). *Attention deficit hyperactivity disorder.* New York: Guilford Press.

Barkley, R. A., & Cunningham, C. E. (1979). The effects of methylphenidate on the mother-child interactions of hyperactive children. *Archives of General Psychiatry, 36,* 201–208.

Barkley, R. A., Grodzinsky, G., & DuPaul, G. J. (1992). Frontal lobe functions and attention deficit disorder with and without hyperactivity. A review and research report. *Journal of Abnormal Child Psychology, 20,* 163–188.

Barkley, R. A., & Murphy, K. R. (2006). Identifying new symptoms for diagnosing ADHD in adulthood. *ADHD Report, 14,* 7–11.

Beitchman, J. H., & Inglis, A. (1991). The continuum of linguistic dysfunction from pervasive developmental disorders to dsylexia. *Pervasive Developmental Disorders, 14,* 95–111.

Bekker, B. M., Overton, C. C., Kooij, J. S., Buitelaar, J. K., Verbaten, M. N., & Kenemans, J. L. (2005). Distinguishing deficits in adults with ADHD. *Archives of General Psychiatry, 62,* 1129–1136.

Biederman, J., Faraone, S. V., Mick, E., & Lelon, E. (1995). Psychiatric comorbidity among referred juveniles with major depression: Fact or artifact? *Journal of the American Academy of Child and Adolescent Psychiatry, 34,* 579–590.

Biederman, J., Faraone, S. V., Milberger, S., Jetton, J. G., Chen, L., Mick, E., et al. (1996). Is childhood oppositional defiant disorder a precursor to adolescent conduct disorder? Findings from a four-year follow-up study of children with ADHD. *Journal of the American Academy of Child and Adolescent Psychiatry, 35,* 1193–1204.

Biederman, J., Faraone, S. V., Spencer, T., & Wilens, T. (1993). Patterns of psychiatric comorbidity, cognition, and psychological functioning in adults with attention deficit hyperactivity disorder. *American Journal of Psychiatry, 150,* 1792–1798.

Biederman, J., Kwan, A., Aleardi, M., Chouinard, V. A., Marino, T., Cole, H., et al. (2005). Absence of gender effects on ADHD: Findings in non-referred subjects. *American Journal of Psychiatry, 162,* 1083–1089.

Biederman, J., Monuteaux, M. C., Mick, E., Spencer, T., Wilens, T. E., Silva, J. M., et al. (2006). Young adult outcome of ADHD: A controlled ten-year follow-up study. *Psychological Medicine, 36,* 167–179.

Biederman, J., Newcorn, J., & Sprich, S. (1991). Comorbidity of attention deficit hyperactivity disorder with conduct, depressive, anxiety and other disorders. *American Journal of Psychiatry, 148,* 564–577.

Brooks, R. B. (2002). Changing the mindset of adults with ADHD: Strategies for fostering hope, optimism and resilience. In S. Goldstein and A. Teeter Ellison (Eds.), *Clinician's guide to adult ADHD: Assessment and interventions.* New York: Academic Press.

Butler, F. S., Arredondo, D. E., & McCloskey, V. (1995). Affective comorbidity in children and adolescents with attention deficit hyperactivity disorder. *Annals of Clinical Psychiatry, 7,* 51–55.

Cantwell, D. P., & Baker, L. (1992). Attention deficit disorder with and without hyperactivity: A review and comparison of matched groups. *Journal of the American Academy of Child and Adolescent Psychiatry, 31,* 432–438.

Clark, C., Priori, M., & Kinsella, G. J. (2000). Do executive function deficits differentiate between adolescents with ADHD and oppositional defiant/conduct disorder: A neuropsychological study using the Six Elements Test and the Hayling Sentence Completion Test. *Journal of Abnormal Child Psychology, 28,* 403–414.

Cohen, L. S., & Biederman, J. (1988). Further evidence for an association between affective disorders and anxiety disorders: Review and case reports. *Journal of Clinical Psychiatry, 49,* 313–316.

Denckla, M. B. (1996). Research on executive function in a neurodevelopmental context: Application of clinical measures. *Developmental Neuropsychology, 12,* 5–15.

Desgranges, K., Desgranges, L., & Karsky, K. (1995). Attention deficit disorder: Problems with preconceived diagnosis. *Child and Adolescent Social Work Journal, 12,* 3–17.

Dickstein, D. P., Garvey, M., Pradella, A. G., Greenstein, D. K., Sharp, W. S., Castellanos, F. X., et al. (2005). Neurologic examination of abnormalities in children with Bipolar Disorder or ADHD. *Biological Psychiatry, 58,* 517–524.

Diller, L. H. (2006). *The last normal child.* Greenwood Publishing Group, Inc.

Diller, L., & Goldstein, S. (2006). Science, politics and the psychosocial treatments of ADHD (Editorial). *Journal of Attention Disorders, 9,* 571–574.

Donahue, M., Cole, D., & Hartas, D. (1994). Links between language and emotional behavioral disorders. *Education and Treatment of Children, 17,* 244–254.

Douglas, V. I., Barr, R. G., O'Neil, M. E., & Britton, B. G. (1986). Short-term effects of methylphenidate on the cognitive, learning, and academic performance of children with attention deficit disorder in the laboratory and classroom. *Journal of Child Psychology and Psychiatry, 27,* 191–211.

Douglas, V. I., & Peters, K. G. (1979). Toward a clearer definition of the attention deficit of hyperactive children. In G. A. Hale & M. Lewis (Eds.), *Attention and the development of cognitive skills.* New York: Plenum Press.

DuPaul, G. J., & Stoner, G. (1994). *ADHD in the schools: Assessment and intervention strategies.* New York: Guilford.

El-Sayed, E., Larsson, J., Persson, H. E., & Rydelius, P. (2002). Altered cortical activity in children with ADHD during attentional load task. *Journal of the American Academy of Child and Adolescent Psychiatry, 41,* 811–819.

Evans, S. W., Langberg, J., Raggi, V., Allen, J., & Buvinger, E. C. (2005). Development of a school-based treatment program for middle school youth with ADHD. *Journal of Attention Disorders, 9*(1), 333–342.

Faraone, S. V., & Biederman, J. (1997). Do ADHD and major depression share familial risk factors? *Journal of Nervous and Mental Disease, 185,* 533–541.

Faraone, S. V., Biederman, J., & Friedman, D. (2000). Validity of DSM–IV subtypes of attention-deficit/hyperactivity disorder: A family study perspective. *Journal of the American Academy of Child and Adolescent Psychiatry, 59,* 300–307.

Faraone, S. V., Biederman, J., Mennan, D., Wozniak, J., & Spencer, T. (1997). Attention-deficit hyperactivity disorder with bipolar disorder: A familial subtype? *Journal of the American Academy of Child and Adolescent Psychiatry, 36,* 1378–1387.

Faraone, S. V., Biederman, J., & Monuteaux, M. C. (2000). ADHD and conduct disorder in girls: Evidence for a familial subtype. *Biological Psychiatry, 48,* 21–29.

Faraone, S. V., Biederman, J., Sprich-Buckminster, S., Chen, W., & Tsuang, M. T. (1993). Efficiency of diagnostic criteria for attention deficit disorder. Towards an empirical approach to designing and validating diagnostic algorithms. *Journal of the American Academy of Child and Adolescent Psychiatry, 32,* 166–174.

Fiorello, C. A., Hale, J. B., McGrath, M., Ryan, K., & Quinn, S. (2001). I.Q. Interpretation for children with flat and variable test profiles. *Learning and Individual Differences, 13,* 115–125.

Fisher, S. E., Francks, C., McCracken, J. T., McGough, J. J., Marlow, A. J., MacPhie, L., et al. (2005). A genomewide scan for loci involved in ADHD. *American Journal of Human Genetics, 70,* 1183–1196.

Frazier, T. W., Demaree, H. A., & Youngstrom, E. A. (2004). Meta-analysis of intellectual neuropsychological test performance in attention deficit hyperactivity disorder. *Neuropsychology, 18,* 543–555.

Fuster, J. M. (1989). A theory of prefrontal functions: The prefrontal cortex and the temporal organization of behavior. In J. M. Fuster (Ed.), *The prefrontal cortex: Anatomy, physiology, and neuropsychology of the frontal lobe.* New York: Raven Press.

Gaub, M., & Carlson, C. L. (1997). Gender differences in ADHD: A meta-analysis and critical review. *Journal of the American Academy of Child and Adolescent Psychiatry, 36,* 1036–1045.

Goldstein, S. (2006). Is ADHD a growth industry? *Journal of Attention Disorders, 9,* 461–464.

Goldstein, S., & Brzostek, J.S. (2000). Prevalence of ADHD among high risk adolescents: Preliminary findings. *The ADHD Report, 8*(5), 10.

Goldstein, S., & Ellison, A. T. (Eds.). (2002). *Clinician's guide to adult ADHD: Assessment and intervention.* New York: Academic Press.

Goldstein, S., & Goldstein, M. (1990). *Managing attention deficit disorder in children: A guide for practitioners.* New York: Wiley.

Goldstein, S., & Goldstein, M. (1998). *Managing attention deficit hyperactivity disorder in children: A guide for practitioners* (2nd Ed.). New York: Wiley.

Goldstein, S., & Gordon, M. (2003). Gender issues and ADHD: Sorting fact from fiction. *The ADHD Report, 11*(4), 7–16.

Goldstein, S., & Naglieri, J. A. (2006). The role of intellectual processes in the DSM–V diagnosis of ADHD (editorial). *Journal of Attention Disorders, 10,* 3–8.

Goldstein, S., & Reynolds, C. (1999). *Handbook of neurodevelopmental and genetic disorders in children.* New York: Guilford Press.

Goldstein, S., Reynolds, C. R. (Eds.). (2005). *Handbook of neurodevelopmental and genetic disorders in adults.* New York: Guilford.

Goodman, G., & Poillion, M. J. (1992). ADD: Acronym for any dysfunction or difficulty. *Journal of Special Education, 26,* 37–56.

Greenhill, L., Kollins, S., Abikoff, H., McCracken, J., Riddle, M., Swanson, J., et al. (2006). Efficacy and safety of immediate-release methylphenidate treatment for preschoolers with ADHD. *Journal of the American Academy of Child and Adolescent Psychiatry, 45*(11), 1284–1293.

Grodzinsky, G. M., & Diamond, R. (1992). Frontal lobe functioning in boys with attention deficit hyperactivity disorder. *Developmental Neuropsychology, 8,* 427–445.

Haenlein, M., & Caul, W. F. (1987). Attention deficit disorder with hyperactivity: A specific hypothesis of reward dysfunction. *Journal of the American Academy of Child and Adolescent Psychiatry, 26,* 356–362.

Hallowell, E. M., & Ratey, J. J. (1994). *Driven to distraction.* New York: Pantheon Books.

Harrier, L. K., & DeOrnellas, K. (2005). Performance of children diagnosed with ADHD on selected planning and reconstitution tests. *Applied Neuropsychology, 12,* 106–119.

Hervey, A. S., Epstein, J. N., & Curry, J. F. (2004). Neuropsychology of adults with attention deficit hyperactivity disorder: A meta-analytic review. *Neuropsychology, 18,* 495–503.

Hinshaw, S. P., Morrison, D. C., Carte, E. T., & Cornsweet, C. (1987). Factorial dimensions of the revised behavior problem checklist: Replication and validation within a kindergarten sample. *Journal of Abnormal Child Psychology, 15,* 309–327.

Homack, S. R., & Reynolds, C. R. (2005). Continuous performance testing in the differential diagnosis of ADHD. *The ADHD Report, 13,* 5–9.

Ingersoll, B., & Goldstein, S. (1993). *Attention deficit disorder and learning disabilities: Realities, myths and controversial treatments.* New York: Wiley.

Jiron, C., Sherrill, R., & Chiodo, A. (1995, November). *Is ADHD being overdiagnosed?* Paper presented at the National Academy of Neuropsychology, San Francisco, CA.

Jonsdottir, S., Bouma, A., Sergeant, J. A., & Scherder, P. J. (2005). The impact of specific language impairments on working memory in children with ADHD combined subtype. *Archives of Clinical Neuropsychology, 20,* 443–456.

Kaiser, D. A., & Othmer, S. (2000). Effect of neurofeedback on variables of attention in a large multi-center trial. *Journal of Neurotherapy, 4,* 5–15.

Kaplan, B. J., Crawford, S. G., Dewey, D. M., & Fisher, G. C. (2000). The I.Q.'s of children with ADHD are normally distributed. *Journal of Learning Disabilities, 33,* 425–432.

Kennemer, K., & Goldstein, S. (2005). Incidence of ADHD in adults with severe mental health problems. *Applied Neuropsychology, 12*(2), 77–82.

Kessler, R. C., Adler, L., Barkley, R., Biederman, J., Conners, C. K., Demler, O., et al. (2006). The prevalence and correlates of adult ADHD in the national comorbidity survey replication. *American Journal of Psychiatry, 163,* 716–723.

Kollins, S. H., Lane, S. D., & Shapiro, S. K. (1997). Experimental analysis of childhood psychopathology: A laboratory analysis of the behavior of children diagnosed with ADHD. *Psychological Record, 47,* 25–44.

Krain, A. L., Kendall, P. C., & Power, T. J. (2005). The role of treatment acceptability in the initiation of treatment for ADHD. *Journal of Attention Disorders, 9*(2), 425–434.

Lahey, B. B., Pelham, W. E., Loney, J., Lee, S., & Willcutt, E. (2005). Instability of the DSM–IV subtypes of ADHD from preschool through elementary school. *Archives of General Psychiatry, 62,* 896–902.

Levitan, R., Jain, U., & Katzman, M. (1999). Seasonal affective symptoms in adults with residual ADHD. *Comprehensive Psychiatry, 40,* 261–267.

Loo, S. K., & Barkley, R. A. (2005). Clinical utility of the EEG in Attention Deficit Hyperactivity Disorder. *Applied Neuropsychology, 12,* 64–76.

McClelland, J. M., Rubert, M. P., Reichler, R. J., & Sylvester, C. E. (1989). Attention deficit disorder in children at risk for anxiety and depression. *Journal of the American Academy of Child and Adolescent Psychiatry, 29,* 534–539.

McGee, R., Williams, S., & Feehan, M. (1992). Attention deficit disorder and age of onset of problem behaviors. *Journal of Abnormal Child Psychology, 20,* 487–503.

Medco Health Solutions. (2005). ADHD medication use growing faster among adults than children. New Research. Retrieved from http://www.medco.com

Molter, R. (1995, March). *Freedom from distractibility auditory processing problems: A critical look at the WISC-III factor.* Paper presented at the Learning Disabilities Association Annual Conference, Orlando, Florida.

Murphy, K. (1994). Guarding against overdiagnosis of ADHD in adults. *The ADHD Report, 2*(6), 3–4.

Naglieri, J. A., & Das, J. P. (1997). *Cognitive Assessment System interpretive handbook.* Chicago: Riverside Publishing Company.

Naglieri, J., Goldstein, S., Delauder, B., & Schwebach, A. (2005). Relationships between the WISC-III and the Cognitive Assessment System with Conners' rating scales and continuous performance tests. *Archives of Clinical Neuropsychology, 20,* 385–401.

Naglieri, J. A., Goldstein, S., Iseman, J. S., & Schwebach, A. (2003). Performance of children with attention deficit hyperactivity disorder and anxiety/

depression on the WISC-III and Cognitive Assessment System (CAS). *Journal of Psychoeducational Assessment, 21,* 32–42.

Naglieri, J. A., Salter, C. J., & Edwards, G. H. (2004). Assessment of ADHD and reading disabilities using the PASS Theory and Cognitive Assessment System. *Journal of Psychoeducational Assessment, 22,* 93–105.

Owens, J. S., & Hoza, B. (2003). The role of inattention and hyperactivity/impulsivity in the positive illusory bias. *Journal of Consulting Clinical Psychology, 71,* 680–691.

Paul, R., & James, D. F. (1990). Language delay and parental perceptions. *Journal of the American Academy of Child and Adolescent Psychiatry, 29,* 669–670.

Pelham, W. E., Massetti, G. M., Wilson, T., Kipp, H., Myers, D., Newman Standley, B. B., et al. (2005). Implementation of a comprehensive school-wide behavioral intervention. *Journal of Attention Disorders, 9*(1), 248–260.

Pliszka, S. (1992). Comorbidity of attention-deficit hyperactivity disorder and overanxious disorder. *Journal of the American Academy of Child and Adolescent Psychiatry, 31,* 197–203.

Pliszka, S. (2005). Recent developments in neuroimaging of ADHD. *The ADHD Report, 13,* 1–5.

Quinn, P., & Nadeau, K. (2002). *Gender issues in ADHD: Research, diagnosis and treatment.* New York: Advantage Books.

Rapport, M. D. (1992). Treating children with attention-deficit hyperactivity disorder. *Behavior Modification, 16,* 155–163.

Reimherr, F. W., Marchant, B. K., Strong, R. E., Hedges, D. W., Adler, L., Spencer, T. J., et al. (2005). Emotional dysregulation in adult ADHD and response to atomoxetine. *Biological Psychiatry, 58,* 125–131.

Riccio, C. A., Gonzalez, J. J., & Hynd, G. W. (1994). Attention deficit hyperactivity disorder and learning disabilities. *Learning Disability Quarterly, 17,* 311–322.

Roberts, R. J., & Pennington, B. (1996). An interactive framework for examining pre-frontal cognitive processes. *Developmental Neuropsychology, 12,* 105–126.

Ross, D. M., & Ross, S. A. (1982). *Hyperactivity: Research, theory and action.* New York: Wiley.

Rostain, A. L., & Ramsay, J. R. (2006). A combined treatment approach for adults with ADHD: Results of an open study of 43 patients. *Journal of Attention Disorders, 10,* 150–159.

Rucklidge, J. J., & Tannock, R. (2001). Psychiatric, psychosocial and cognitive functioning of female adolescents with ADHD. *Journal of the American Academy of Child and Adolescent Psychiatry, 40,* 530–540.

Rutter, M. (1978). Diagnostic validity in child psychiatry. *Advances in Biological Psychiatry, 2,* 2–22.

Safer, D. J., Zito, J. M., & Fine, E. M. (1996). Increased methylphenidate usage for attention deficit disorder in the 1990's. *Pediatrics, 98,* 1084–1088.

Safren, S. A., Otto, M. W., Sprich, S., Winett, C. L., Wilens, T. E., & Biederman, J. (2005). Cognitive behavior therapy for ADHD in medication treated adults with continued symptoms. *Behavior Research and Therapy, 43,* 831–842.

Samuelsson, S., Lundberg, I., & Herkner, B. (2004). ADHD and reading disability in male adults: Is there a connection? *Journal of Learning Disabilities, 37*(2), 155–168.

Schmitz, M., Cadore, L., Paczko, M., Kipper, L., Chaves, M., Rohde, L. A., et al. (2002). Neuropsychological performance in DSM–IV ADHD subtypes: An exploratory study with untreated adolescents. *Canadian Journal of Psychiatry, 47,* 863–869.

Schoechlin, C., & Engel, R. (2005). Neuropsychological performance in adult ADHD: Meta-analysis of empirical data. *Archives of Clinical Neuropsychology, 20,* 727–744.

Scholnick, E. K. (1995, Fall). Knowing and constructing plans. *SRCD Newsletter,* 1–3.

Schonfeld, I. S., Shaffer, D., & Barmack, J. E. (1989). Neurological soft signs and school achievement. The mediating effects of sustained attention. *Journal of Abnormal Child Psychology, 17,* 575–596.

Semrud-Clikeman, M., Biederman, J., Sprich-Buckminster, S., Lehman, B. K., Faraone, S. V., & Norman, D. (1992). Comorbidity between ADDH and learning disability: A review and report on a clinically referred sample. *Journal of the American Academy of Child and Adolescent Psychiatry, 31,* 439–448.

Semrud-Clikeman, M., Steingard, R. J., Filipek, P., Biederman, J., Bekken, K., & Renshaw, P. F. (2000). Using MRI to examine brain-behavior relationships in males with attention deficit disorder with hyperactivity. *Journal of the American Academy of Child and Adolescent Psychiatry, 39,* 477–484.

Shaywitz, B. A., Fletcher, J. M., & Shaywitz, S. E. (1995). Discrepancy compared to Iowa achievement definitions of reading disability: Results from the Connecticut longitudinal study. *Journal of Learning Disability, 25,* 639–648.

Shure, M. (1994). *Raising a thinking child.* New York: Henry Holt.

Solden, S. (2005). *Women with attention deficit disorder: Embrace your differences and transform your life.* Chicago: Underwood Books.

Sonuga-Barke, E. J., Dalen, L., & Remington, B. (2003). Do executive deficits and delay aversion make independent contributions to preschool ADHD symptoms? *Journal of the American Academy of Child and Adolescent Psychiatry, 42,* 1335–1342.

Sonuga-Barke, E. J., Lamparelli, M., Stevenson, J., Thompson, M., & Henry, A. (1994). Behaviour problems and preschool intellectual attainment: The associations of hyperactivity and conduct problems. *Journal of Child Psychology and Psychiatry, 35,* 949–960.

Strober, M. (1992). Relevance of early age-of-onset in genetic studies of bipolar affective disorder. *Journal of the American Academy of Child and Adolescent Psychiatry, 31,* 606–610.

Teeter, P. A. (1998). *Interventions for ADHD: Treatment in developmental context.* New York: Guilford.

Todd, R., Rasmussen, E. R., Wood, C., Levy, F., & Hay, D. A. (2004). Should sluggish cognitive tempo symptoms be included in the diagnosis of attention deficit/hyperactivity disorder? *Journal of the American Academy of Child and Adolescent Psychiatry, 43,* 588–597.

Toplak, M. E., & Tannock, R. (2005). Time perception: Modality and duration effects in ADHD. *Journal of Abnormal Child Psychology, 33,* 639–654.

Unnever, G. D., & Cornell, D. G. (2003). Bullying, self-control and ADHD. *Journal of Interpersonal Violence, 18,* 129–147.

Volkow, N. D., Wang, G., Fowler, J. S., Logan, J., Gerasimov, M., Maynard, L., et al. (2001). Therapeutic doses of oral methylphenidate significantly increase extra cellular dopamine in the human brain. *Journal of Neuroscience, 21,* 1–5.

Wellington, T. M., Semrud-Clikeman, M., Gregory, A. L., Murphy, J. M., & Lancaster, J. L. (2006). Magnetic resonance imaging volumetric analysis of the Putamen in children with ADHD: Combined type versus control. *Journal of Attention Disorders, 10,* 171–180.

West, S. A., McElroy, S., Strakowski, P. E., Keck, B. J., & McConville, B. (1995). Attention deficit hyperactivity disorder in adolescent mania. *American Journal of Psychiatry, 152,* 271–274.

Weyandt, L. L., Mitzlaff, L., & Thomas, L. (2002). The relationship between intelligence and performance on the Test of Variables of Attention. *Journal of Learning Disabilities, 35,* 114–120.

Whalen, C. K., & Henker, B. (1991). Therapies for hyperactive children: Comparisons, combinations and compromises. *Journal of Consulting and Clinical Psychology, 59,* 126–137.

Wilens, T. E., McDermott, S. P., Biederman, J., & Abrantes, A. (1999). Cognitive therapy in the treatment of adults with ADHD. A systematic chart review of twenty-six cases. *Journal of Cognitive Psychotherapy, 13,* 215–226.

Willcutt, E. G., Pennington, B. F., Chhabildas, N. A., Friedman, M. C., & Alexander, J. (1999). Psychiatric comorbidity associated with DSM–IV ADHD in a non-referred sample of twins. *Journal of the American Academy of Child and Adolescent Psychiatry, 38,* 1355–1362.

Wozniak, J., Biederman, J., Kiely, K., Ablon, J. S., Faraone, S. V., Mundy, E., et al. (1995). Mania-like symptoms suggestive of childhood-onset bipolar disorder in clinically referred children. *Journal of the American Academy of Child and Adolescent Psychiatry, 34,* 867–876.

Wozniak, J., Biederman, J., Mundy, E., Mennin, D., & Faraone, S.V. (1995). A pilot family study of childhood-onset mania. *Journal of the American Academy of Child and Adolescent Psychiatry, 34,* 1577–1583.

Zentall, S. S. (1988). Production deficiencies in elicited language but not in the spontaneous verbalizations of hyperactive children. *Exceptional Children, 60,* 143–153.

22

Neuropsychology of Autism Spectrum Disorders

HENRY V. SOPER, STEPHEN WOLFSON,
AND FRANCIS CANAVAN

NEUROPSYCHOLOGY OF AUTISM SPECTRUM DISORDERS

AUTISM IS A complex neurodevelopmental disorder affecting aspects of learning, communication, and socialization. First described by Kanner in 1943, autism affects areas of functioning usually considered within the neuropsychological arena. These areas include social skills, language, attention, perception, and motor activity. However, identifying the basic natures of these disorders has proven difficult. Many of those diagnosed with autism have significant comorbidities, including developmental delays in cognition and adaptive functioning, often with clear neurological manifestations (e.g., epilepsy). Using data from such lower functioning individuals is problematic.

Author Note: The authors would like to acknowledge the assistance of Hugo M. Doig and Teri McHale for their help in putting together this manuscript. We would also like to thank the many people with ASD as well as their families and those who work with them, all of whom have been major contributors to this chapter.

Generally these people can be expected to manifest a variety of conditions at best only tangentially related to the autistic condition itself. For this reason it would be better to study those diagnosed with higher order autism spectrum disorders (ASD), such as Asperger's disorder, because they tend to show fewer symptoms beyond the core interpersonal and motor ones mentioned in the *Diagnostic and Statistical Manual of Mental Disorders* (American Psychiatric Association [APA], 1994).

As mentioned by Wing (2005), both autism and Asperger's disorder manifest qualitative impairments in social interaction and restricted repetitive and stereotyped patterns of behavior, interests, and activities. However, those who fulfill the Asperger's criteria do not show clinically significant delay in language, and they do not show significant cognitive or related delays (e.g., imagination, self-help skills; DuCharme & McGrady, 2003). Wing further states that many of those who fulfilled the criteria for autism when younger later present with a behavior pattern more consistent with Asperger's disorder. It is possible that at a given age two individuals could present with effectively the same behavioral arrays, but one, due to his or her history of language delays, could be labeled autistic and the other as having Asperger's disorder. This could have a major impact on the services available.

A third group of individuals consists of those who show the social impairments but often few if any of the other symptoms of autism. Although often deemed socially awkward or odd, most carry no diagnosis, for they are able to function adequately enough to avoid serious problems at work or school and to live independently with little or no help from outside resources. When given a diagnosis, it is most often pervasive developmental disorder—not otherwise specified (PDD-NOS). Wing (1992, 2005) has provided us with a very good description of the subgroups (aloof, passive, and active-but-odd) of these higher-functioning members of the ASD.

It would be useful to group those showing the features of ASD into four diagnostic groups. Those with pure autism would meet the current diagnostic criteria. Those with autism of the Asperger's variety consist of those who currently show no cognitive or language delays regardless of whether they have before. Those who are currently diagnosed with PDD-NOS are a bit of a problem. There are individuals outside the ASD who meet these criteria but who, for example, might have a psychogenic basis for their disorder (e.g., a very regressed woman who could have been considered normal until multiple rapes at age 8). We used to term these people as psychogenic PDD-NOS, versus the more biogenic autism spectrum PDD-NOS diagnosis. However, there are problems with this distinction too. Perhaps the designation PDD-NOS with autism spectrum features would be best for now. The fourth group would be those who are able to live in society and who do not now meet the definition of having a mental disorder ("A mental disorder is conceptualized as a clinically significant behavioral or psychologic syndrome or pattern that occurs in an individual and that typically is associated with either a painful symptom (distress) or impairment in one or more important areas of functioning (disability)," APA, 1980, p. 363).

It is important for families to recognize people who fulfill the criteria for the last two groups, for these are the ones who are particularly vulnerable to the influences of others, often with serious consequences. Later we will mention the man who was involved in kidnap, rape, and murder due to the influence of another. Quite likely, one of the Columbine killers may well have met one of the ASD criteria. Wing (1992) describes a young man who had a job counting money. Someone else, "recognizing an innocent when he saw one," (p. 136) conned him into keeping back a small amount each day that later they would share. Such people can be quite gullible and vulnerable to the persuasions of others.

FRIENDSHIP AND LOVE

HIGH FUNCTIONING INDIVIDUALS within the ASD, on the surface, can express a desire for friends, but the lack of interpersonal experience can cause confusion as to just what that term means. A young woman who works at a soda shop and who treats one nicely can become a "girlfriend," meaning no more than a female who treats him well. Lacking the ability to form a true reciprocal relationship, most with ASD would not fully understand what a true friendship consists of, and might at best understand that someone is or is not a friend because that person had told them so. They also understand that having a friend is a good thing, but, again, only because they have been told so. However, these people within the spectrum seldom if ever spontaneously call this supposed friend or show evidence of missing them even if they have not seen them in some time.

Much like friendship, those with ASD do not have the ability to form a true love relationship. Many who work long with such individuals have the feeling that the "love" is there, but right beneath the surface, encapsulated somehow, ready to come out. The need to believe in this love is certainly understandable. However, it appears right now that it is most parsimonious to state that interpersonal love is not possible.

CORE FEATURES OF THE AUTISM SPECTRUM

WING (1996) CONSIDERS a triad of impairments to be needed for a diagnosis of autism: impairments in social interaction, communication, and the development of imagination. Although many of the communication difficulties, as mentioned previously, might be attributable to the interpersonal ones, many, such as late onset mutism, certainly seem to go beyond that. The impairment in spontaneous make-believe play or social imitative play, however, is fully appreciable in view of the severe social deficits secondary to the inability to view others as human, as in this way different from other aspects of their environment.

Those with ASD do tend to show the full spectrum of emotions in that they can become happy, even ecstatic, angry, irritated, and the like. Although often diagnosed as "flat," this refers more to the relative unresponsiveness under circumstances when an affective or interpersonal response would be expected. However, they are basically devoid of interpersonal emotions such as love and envy, and they are unable to feel for others through empathy. One could say they have no conscience, but this would be more a reflection of their lack of interpersonal appreciation, as opposed to running roughshod over the rights of others and a lack of concern for how others might feel, as one sees in the antisocial personality. Rather, in many ways those with ASD appear to be interpersonally in a world unto themselves, and in this sense "alone" (Kanner, 1943). At times they are accused of wanting to avoid others. There is a wide range of individual differences (and experiences with "others"). However, if the others in their environment are not bothering them or placing confusing demands on them, usually there is no trouble. On the other hand, these people do not miss individuals in the way a nonautistic child might miss their parents when they go to live with someone else. When someone is missing from the environment of someone with ASD, problems may be brought about by the altered routines, especially if they do not understand the reason for the change. Put simplistically, this missing person is another object now no longer in their environment.

Getting at this core interpersonal aspect of the ASD has proven very difficult. Even with the help of those high functioning individuals with the disorder the features have been hard to pin down. In a way it is like a sighted person trying to understand what it is like to be congenitally blind. One wants to "see" it as a totally black world, yet those who are congenitally blind have no idea what it is they are missing, and so they will have difficulty conveying the subjective information, too. In the case of autism, many of us have an idea of the autism experience, or think we do, but putting this idea into words is very difficult. It is much easier to name the symptoms.

Although a lot has been said about the signs and symptoms of ASD, the core processing deficits have not been described very well. Kanner (1943) is accurate when he states that those with autism have an "inability to relate themselves in the ordinary way to people and situations from the beginning of life" (p. 242). Later he says that a profound aloneness dominates all behavior, which, though technically true, sounds as if there is suffering because of it, which is not true. It is certainly true there is impairment in reciprocal social interaction. However, more than this, there is an inability to make a genuine emotional bond with another. A teacher may work closely with a student for hours a day for years, but when it is time to move on there is no evidence of interpersonal loss. (As indicated previously, there may be disruption because the replacement is not familiar with the routines of the student, but this is quite different from an interpersonal loss.) It is almost as if the teacher never existed. Family members notice this lack of sense of loss or bereavement when someone close dies. Those who were interacted with on a regular basis at an old location tend not to be thought of after a move to a new one. There is no attempt to seek out or even call close relatives and associates. It is as if out of sight is out of mind. This is true even at the higher end of the spectrum and is in sharp contrast to the major disruption that can occur when highly familiar, regimented procedures are disrupted (e.g., changing meal times or the sequence of events). It is quite possible that this latter disruption is often related to the former impairment in that the inabilities to "read," understand, and hence empathize with others renders the environmental change unexpected, which would understandably be disruptive.

This lack of appreciation for affective contact with others, the inability to read the mind (or even appreciate the mind) of others, the total inability for a true interpersonal bond with others, and the inability to even appreciate these aspects of humanity, appear to be at the core of the symptoms we see within this spectrum of disorders. The basic neurobiological aspect of the ASD relates to these functions, although the specific manifestations will depend on other factors such as level of intellectual functioning, individual differences, other neurological problems, and the like. The core deficits of those displaying ASD include not being able to read the minds of others, and related to this they are unable to form a genuine human bond as normally exists in love or friendship. (Although this is similar to the "mindblindness" of Baron-Cohen, 1999, there are some subtle and basic differences, too.) This is often very difficult for those who work with such people, including relatives, to really appreciate. It is so far beyond their own experience they cannot imagine the dearth of appreciation, intimacy, and love. Those who are very high functioning and do get married show an emotional coldness and lack of attachment, even though all the essential duties are performed. Kanner (1943) was pretty accurate when he concluded, "We must, then, assume that these children have come into the world with innate inability to form the usual, biologically provided affective contact with people, just as other children come into the world with innate physical or intellectual handicaps" (p. 250).

One could go further and say that these deficits are not in uniquely human abilities. Dogs, chimpanzees, and others have shown clearly the ability to relate to both humans and conspecifics. Such animals exhibit very good eye contact, far better than most with ASD. It gives one pause to wonder if ASD is a uniquely human condition.

There is some recent neurobiological work that supports this impairment in the ability to relate to others. Interesting work with monkeys (Fogassi et al., 2005) has shown that certain neurons, called mirror neurons, respond similarly to the intentions of the monkey itself and to the perceived intention of an observed monkey. A similar phenomenon exists in humans, but not among those with ASD (Oberman et al., in press). At rest, sensorimotor neurons fire in synchrony, resulting in mu (8–13 Hz) frequency EEG oscillations. A significant mu suppression is observed in control subjects either when they move their own hands or when they observe others moving their hands. Among those with ASD, significant mu suppression occurs to self-performed hand movements but not to observing the same movements in others. The authors feel that the deficits observed in imitation, pragmatic language, theory of mind, and empathy among those with ASD are reflected in this lack of mu suppression to the actions of others but not to those of the self. To carry it one step further, one could say that such results support the contention that those with this spectrum of disorders have a severe neurobiologically based impairment in reading, or appreciating, the minds of others.

This is also supported when they are asked to take the mental position of another. One young person with Asperger's disorder was asked to tell the story of Snow White and the Seven Dwarfs from Grumpy's perspective. He agreed, but after trying for a while he admitted that he simply could not do it from Grumpy's perspective. When asked if Dopey's perspective would be easier, he tried, but gave up, unable to even initiate either task. He had no difficulty just telling the story, although he made reference to "seven small miners." Another child with autism was not only unable to perform the Grumpy task but could not tell at all what Santa Claus might say about him come Christmas.

Another example will show the extreme isolation from the feelings of others. A high functioning person with ASD PDD-NOS was coming up for trial on kidnap, rape, and murder charges. As a part of the evaluation he was asked to name all the emotions he could within a minute. He responded with four items: depressed, anxious, arrogant, and numb. He had been diagnosed with depression and anxiety, and in a concrete manner one can see how "numb" can become a feeling or emotion. "Arrogant" seems to be a bit different though. Due to his social deficits especially in regard to seeing the world from the view of another, one can see how "arrogant" can become considered an emotion. To most of us, depressed is how a person feels, and arrogant is how others feel about that person. The kind of mental gymnastics necessary to see this distinction is impossible for someone with ASD, and so when an individual with ASD hears someone is called arrogant, they will look for the most concrete meaning available.

When asked to relate his crimes, he did so in a flat, emotionless manner. He talked about himself and his partner (the one who came up with the idea and who planned it), but he made almost no reference to the victim. Periodically he was asked how the victim was feeling. Each time he would stop, ponder for a few seconds, and then he would say that because of what she was saying or doing this must have been how she felt. It was quite clear that he had no sense of her as a human being, he was totally unable to relate to her, to read her mind. It was not as if he did not care. He simply could not perceive what she was going through, especially as it was not relevant to the task at hand. He was relating to her as if she were a large piece of wood. He also had no sense of the gravity of his crimes. When asked what he thought was going to happen when he was first arrested. He responded that he thought he would have to pay a fine, because that was what happened the last time. When asked about this last time, it turns out he had been arrested before for throwing rocks at cars. This man has no idea of the difference in moral severity between throwing rocks at cars and kidnap, rape, and murder.

NEUROPSYCHOLOGICAL ANALYSIS OF THOSE WITH AUTISM SPECTRUM DISORDERS

I N T H E N E X T sections the neuropsychology of autism will be discussed domain by domain somewhat as one would do for an individual neuropsychological evaluation. The results will be discussed with reference to the core deficits in this spectrum of disorders as well as factors independent of those core deficits.

Many years ago Kevin Walsh (1985) mentioned that most behaviors are complex, in that there are many causes for each and just as many reasons why someone might fail a task. Someone with ASD may do poorly on a given task or class of tasks because of the core interpersonal impairment and not because of some primary sensory or motor defect. Such an impairment can result in hyper-responsivity to some stimuli, such as the sound of a wheel spinning or a toilet flushing, and hypo-responsivity to others, such as a human voice. In the same manner abnormal behaviors may be related to this core deficit as well. For example, most of those with ASD have very poor eye contact. In addition, many (Shore, 2003) report that most people without ASD send social cues with their eyes. Those with ASD are unable to understand these cues, or body language in general. This is not due to a right hemisphere problem, nonverbal learning disorder, or any similar impairment, but rather it is related to the core interpersonal impairment. Most of us, when we get mad at our car, do not stare menacingly at it in the headlights, because to do so would provide us with so little information. It would seem that this is the same reason so many with ASD have such poor eye contact. (By the way, poor eye contact does not always occur with the autism spectrum. Many at all levels of functioning display what would be described as moderate to good eye contact.)

In the following sections we shall look domain by domain at the neuropsychology of autism and try to understand the manifestations as derived from the core disorder or from something else. First we will look at the neuroanatomical findings, and then discuss attention and concentration. These will be followed by the findings on intelligence, sensory, motor, handedness, language, higher cerebral functioning, memory, and executive functioning.

Neuroanatomical Findings

According to the review by Minshew, Sweeney, Bauman, and Webb (2005), it would appear that the only prosencephalic areas consistently showing abnormalities are the hippocampus, amygdala, mammillary body, anterior cingulated gyrus, and the medial nucleus of the septum, all areas of the limbic system and thought to be involved in emotional regulation. No thalamic or cortical areas so far have been found to be structurally abnormal, and the telencephalic subcortical portions of the motor systems appear to be unaltered. Altered brain stem structures appear to be the cerebellar hemispheres and their associate nuclei as well as the related inferior olive. Minshew et al. suggest the possibility that these brain stem findings might be involved in the mediation and modulation of some aspects of language, learning, attention, and affective behavior. Furthermore, they suggest that the nature of the alterations indicate developmental curtailment of these areas, rather than being alterations secondary to the autistic condition.

Attention and Concentration

Attention and concentration, especially sustained attention and concentration, are highly variable among those with ASD. The critical variable appears to be whether the ongoing task is their agenda of that of another. The focus can become singular as to be termed perseveration. This is seen at all levels of the spectrum as well as a difficulty in switching attention either from one thing to another or off whatever is currently the focus of attention. In addition to difficulties in shifting attention, Rumsey (1992) concludes that such people also have difficulty with the ability to scan stimulus material rapidly and make a verbal or skilled motor response quickly. One can readily see why those with ASD might "take their own sweet time" performing actions without regard to externally imposed guides such as to do the task quickly. This does not mean they are under-responsive to urgings to go quickly. However, the urgings must be continuous in most cases or the performance reduces to the baseline rate. On the other hand, high functioning people within the spectrum perform well on the Continuous Performance Tests (see Tsatsanis, 2005) and externally imposed test of sustained attention but with minimal interpersonal involvement. In summary, it would appear that there is no systemic difficulty with attention and concentration, and in the areas where difficulties do arise these difficulties are attributable to the interpersonal deficits of the individuals.

INTELLECTUAL FUNCTIONING

INTELLECTUAL DIFFICULTIES CERTAINLY do occur in the majority of people within the autism spectrum, but many others show functioning and scores on tests well within the average range. Rutter (1983) states that even higher functioning patients with autism show what could be called intellectual impairments, such as literalness, as well as poor social comprehension, lack of empathy, lack of reciprocity, and inappropriate social behavior. One would not be surprised to find that individual strengths and weaknesses on intellectual subtests would be in accord with such deficits. Rumsey's (1992) summary of the literature found this to be true. For those whose intellectual scores lie outside the range of significant impairment (i.e., mental retardation) she found that these individuals tend to have the strongest Wechsler scores on Block Design and Digit Span. Digit Span, in fact, can be remarkable, both forward and backward. These two subtests tap minimally on the interpersonal and related areas where those with the spectrum would have the most difficulty. On the other hand, the poorest performance tends to be on Comprehension and Picture Arrangement. These subtests would tap relatively heavily into abstract reasoning and the interpersonal areas.

The intelligence of those with ASD is often odd in that they can be exceedingly good in certain areas, poor in other areas, and be very odd or unusual in still other areas. A vocabulary may contain many rare words yet not some common ones. One individual had Wechsler scale scores predominantly between the second and ninth percentile, yet Information was at the 95th. The lower scores clearly gave a better estimate of his actual functioning, as he was unable to do much with this large fund of knowledge.

SENSORY

THOSE WITH ASD have been described as both hypersensitive and hyposensitive to noise. Kootz, Marinelli, and Cohen (1982) suggested that there might be difficulty filtering sensory input. Reports 20 years ago of abnormalities in auditory evoked potentials seemed to hold promise in answering some of our questions. However, further investigation has shown these results to be inconsistent at best. A more parsimonious conclusion at present is that such abnormalities in auditory evoked potentials do not exist across the board in this spectrum of disorders.

Similarly, although individuals appear to reflect specific sensory difficulties (e.g., hyper- or hypo-responsivity), there are no specific sensory impairments or abnormalities that are consistent within the spectrum or major portions of it. For example, many lower functioning individuals, especially those who display self-injurious behaviors, have high background levels of endogenous endorphins, suggesting that they do not feel pain as acutely as others (Kootz, Marinelli, & Cohen, 1982). However, there are also many who do not show this trait.

However, those with ASD do display abnormal responses to sounds and visual stimuli. A classic example is a child who does not even appear to hear the spoken word and may ignore loud sounds, yet respond clearly to a familiar but quiet bell or a song on the radio. There would be hypo-responsivity to the spoken voice, yet hyper-responsivity to the bell or the song. There may be no response to a box of plastic toys dropped behind the child, yet some apparently innocuous noises can cause such a response that an observer might conclude that the person is overly sensitive to the sound. However, given the core features of autism, it would appear that despite a normal primary sensory system the person is highly responsive. It is easy to see how something that is foreground to us may be background to someone and vice versa. This noise that is "background" to him or her may be someone talking, and not appear to be background to others without the core ASD. On the other hand, the clicking of a bicycle wheel may be of great interest to such a child, but be so unimportant to others as to be ignored. In other words, the abnormalities of sensory stimulation may reflect the different interests and concerns of those with ASD rather than a core neurological abnormality. These individuals have their own agendas and often cannot comprehend those of others. What appears to be an inappropriate motor response may make perfect sense to a person with one of this spectrum of disorders.

MOTOR

INDIVIDUALS WITH ASD display abnormal movements, which might be more accurately described as inappropriate movements. However, to date no basic motor impairments or abnormalities have been found that universally apply to either the entire spectrum or to entire portions of it. With regard to abnormalities in more complex motor behaviors, these are a part of the diagnostic criteria for autism and Asperger's disorders. However, again there are no problems that apply universally.

Those diagnosed with autism or Asperger's disorder do display abnormal motor movements. These behaviors have been nicely grouped into three kinds of movements by Wing (1996). The first group consists of stereotyped movements, or "stereotopies." These include the finger flicking and hand flapping, toe walking, body rocking, and jumping up and down. As Wing says, these movements occur most often when the person is excited, agitated, or angry, or when something is absorbing their whole attention. Many of these stereotopies feel good and help focus on the task at hand and are not restricted to those with ASD. Very young normal children, people with severe to profound mental retardation, and the blind are prone to act in this manner. It appears that the development of such stereotopies themselves is not abnormal, but the extinction of such behavior through social cues does not occur in those with ASD. Elderly people rocking in a chair while the grandchildren are swinging in swings, a youngster jumping up and down waving his arms in glee at being given a present, and a football team jumping up and down in place prior to a game or after a touchdown are all stereotopies, but acceptable ones under those conditions. However, one can see how someone with minimal comprehension of social cues would not be able to use such cues to alter their behavior. They would not even appreciate that they should stop doing what they are doing. As they grow older, those who are high functioning can learn "prosocial" behavior and eliminate most inappropriate stereotopies. On the other hand, we have seen many people who show no signs of autism squeal, jump up and down, and flap their arms at receiving some particularly good news. Body rocking at very bad news is also common. Perhaps the stereotopies observed among those with ASD are not by themselves so abnormal. The social conditions under which they occur are abnormal, for the core autism deficits render such individuals unable to use (social) cues needed to inhibit the behaviors.

The second group of movements discussed by Wing (1996) includes abnormalities of gait and posture. Not all show such behaviors. This type of movement seems to occur more frequently among the lower functioning individuals, though it certainly exists among higher functioning ones too. Wing states that such abnormal movements are most noticeable in adolescents and adults. These abnormalities of gait appear to be immature ways of moving. Examples include holding arms in unusual positions or swinging them inappropriately, ascending or descending stairs one at a time rather than alternating, and clumsily sweeping the feet with the arms extended. Wing says that many children have odd postures: "They may hold their arms, hands and fingers stretched out or bent at peculiar angles" (p. 49). Although one reason for these behaviors may be attributable to lack of feedback from others, there is more to it than this. Usually the gait is very inefficient; one would think that sensorimotor feedback would result in a gait of greater efficiency. On the other hand, many of these people do not run very much, and at other times the abnormal gait does not interfere. This leaves us again with the most parsimonious explanation being that the abnormalities of gait and posture are a result of the inability to fully appreciate and understand feedback from others, especially nonverbal feedback.

The third group of movements Wing discusses is imitative movements. These include facial expressions, looking people in the eye, and waving goodbye. These, for the most part, are not things that are specifically taught, but movements that children usually pick up and use to help interact with others. Children with ASD can be taught, for example, to look people in the eye when talking or to wave goodbye. However, the intensity, direction, and other aspects of these behaviors make it clear they are really prosocial behaviors and not true attempts to communicate. Some, according to Wing, do begin to imitate, but as a form of echopraxia, not with the intention to communicate. This is similar to immediate and delayed echolalia, speech sounds not intended to communicate but uttered because they give pleasure to the vocalizer. To most of us, words stated in this manner have intent and meaning in the here and now. Words in songs do not have to meet those criteria. Echolalia meets the criteria of a song except there are no notes. The echolalic person does not comprehend that most will assume such stimuli are intended to convey information, much like other "statements." One young lady would rock and say over and over again, "Where is my father? Where is my father?" The staff had become irritated, because she had been told they could not find her father. Once, while doing this, she was asked, "I don't know. Where is your father?" Her response was, "At work!" She started rocking immediately and saying, "When will he be home?" When asked when he would be home, she replied, "Purty soon!"

HANDEDNESS

IN THE NORMAL adult population about 90% are right-handed and 10% are left-handed. An abnormal distribution of manual dominance has been seen among those with a diagnosis of autism (Soper et al., 1986). An older (mean age of 21 years) and lower functioning group (severe to profound mental retardation) and a younger (mean age of 11 years) and relatively higher functioning group (borderline level intelligence) were assessed, and both were found to have about 40% right-handers, 20% left-handers, and about 40% who were inconsistent in manual preference either between or within items (e.g., pick up a spoon, throw a ball). However, this may be attributable, at least in part, to the level of cognitive functioning rather than the autism, as those with mental retardation but no evidence of autism also show a very high incidence of non–right-handedness (Soper, Satz, Orsini, van Gorp, & Greene, 1987) as do those who are quite young (Soper, Barnhart, & McHale, 2005).

LANGUAGE

THE LANGUAGE DEFICITS of autism are well noted, even a defining property of those diagnosed with autism. However, these linguistic difficulties reflect more the core features and processing deficits of ASD rather than specific linguistic ones. For example, children diagnosed with autism often present with pronominal reversal. However, if one reflects on the complexity of the meanings of deictic terms such as "you" and "me," one can see how those who cannot comprehend the world from another point of view would have difficulty with the ever-shifting meaning of the words "you" and "me." To those with ASD, the word "you" at times refers to "Tom" and at times to me, "Henry," so why not make things easy and just use the proper name, which is a solution many with ASD come to. The core difficulty is one of reference, not one of semantics. Over time most individuals overcome this difficulty.

The semantic aspect of language of those with ASD is curious, because here words tend to have concrete meanings. For example, a picture is next to a wall, not on a wall. One adolescent of average intelligence but who displayed autism was asked to tell a story about a picture on a card from the Thematic Apperception Test. This card had a half-clad woman lying down and a male standing facing away with his hand to his head. The story he told included information about the picture "next to" the wall and the materials on the table, which no one in my experience has mentioned before. At the conclusion of the story he was asked how the man felt. The (concrete) response was, "Warm." When asked to tell me more, he replied that the heater must have been on, and so the room was warm. Not being able to read my mind, he had taken the question as referring to the sensory aspect of "feeling," not the emotional aspect, which should not be surprising.

It would prove useful to look at the basic elements of language— morphology, syntax, semantics, phonetics, and pragmatics—to locate any basic disruption. *Morphology* is the study of the structure of words; the component of the grammar that includes the rules of word formation. A morpheme is the smallest unit of linguistic meaning. In general those higher functioning adults with ASD have no particular difficulty in this area, though younger and lower functioning people do. Some lower functioning people with autism will on occasion make unintelligible speech-like sounds. When asked to say it again so it can be understood, they say it clearly. This makes it obvious that initially there was little attempt to communicate. In addition, Bartolucci, Pierce, and Streiner (1980) found that children with autism were more likely to omit articles (a, the), auxiliary and copula verbs, past tense, third-person present tense, and present progressive. Bartolucci and Albers (1974) found that children with autism are significantly impaired on the past tense. *Syntax* concerns the rules of sentence formation; the component of the mental grammar that represents the speaker's knowledge of the structure of phrases and sentences. Although some lower functioning individuals do speak in a chunking manner, frequently using several words in the same sequence even when not strictly appropriate, most have limited expressive difficulty in this area. Receptively, even a person with a higher functioning ASD can have great difficulty comprehending alterations made in syntax for emphasis or for expressing abstract ideas. However, for most syntax is generally appropriate for their level of cognitive development, even though a few may have more noticeable problems (Tager-Flushberg, Paul, & Lord, 2005).

Semantics is the study of the linguistic meaning of words, phrases, and sentences; the component of the grammar that specifies these meanings. Semantics refers to the meanings of language. Certainly many with high functioning forms of the autism spectrum have good vocabularies. The specific content of the vocabulary, but not the size, might differ from that of others with that level of intelligence. However, in general, for those who have language, basic semantics does not appear to be a problem beyond that attributable to intelligence and the lack of imagination, abstract ability, and other factors already mentioned. However, flexibility with semantics is, as we have seen, a real problem. Different shadings of meaning and abstract meanings can cause difficulty for those with ASD. Similarly phonetics, very closely related to basic sensorimotor processes, is not generally affected. *Phonetics* is the study of linguistic sounds, how they are produced (articulatory phonetics), how they are perceived (auditory or perceptual phonetics), and the physical aspects of speech (acoustic phonetics). Although general developmental delay can result in phonemic difficulty, most often mispronunciations are a result of minimal effort to communicate. The child knows what they are saying and, given the centrism from the core deficits, they cannot understand why others do not perceive it equally well.

Pragmatics is the study of how context influences the interpretation of meaning, considered by some to be a part of linguistic performance and by others to be a component of the grammar. Usually we are acutely aware of the importance of the context of the utterance. The context can add substantially to the meaning of the sentence. Pragmatics is the downfall of those with ASD. Their very limited ability to view the world from the perspective of another and hence to understand the social and other contexts of the utterance render them with limited ability in the area of pragmatics. In some ways, everyone is treated the same, and so the tone of voice used is regulated more by what is being said and little by whom it is being said to.

The obvious language deficits imply left hemisphere involvement, but the lack of prosody leads many like Damasio (1984) to suggest predominantly right or, more likely, bilateral involvement. On the other hand, one of our adolescents would go to the nursing station and ask, "May I go to the bathroom?" The response was always, "Yes, you may," and he was given the key. Then one day he started saying, "May I go to the bathroom yes you may." In this "mostly parrot-like repetitions of heard word combinations" (Kanner, 1943, p. 243) and many other ways he reflected a predominantly right hemisphere form of language processing, even though his verbal expression was monotonic.

HIGHER CEREBRAL FUNCTIONING

A FEW DECADES ago we were convinced that those showing features of autism would also display deficits in association cortex function. Almost 100 people diagnosed with autism and a similar number of people with equivalent levels of mental retardation but no evidence of autism were evaluated. After several years of effort on a series of tasks ranging from match-to-sample to making cross-modal associations we had found not one shred of evidence that those showing autistic features displayed any consistent form of impairment under these controlled conditions. It became quite clear that such an approach was not getting at the essential nature of autism.

What do we know about the higher-order sensory processing? One way to look at it is to compare the analytic and gestaltic, or right hemisphere and left hemisphere, forms of processing. (Other terms, such as successive and simultaneous, have also been used.) Hemispheric specialization really does refer to how the information is being processed, not what is being processed. We are used to thinking in terms of what is being processed, such as verbal or visual-spatial material, and less in terms of the mechanisms involved in appreciating the information. In a general way, details are the purview of the left hemisphere and the big picture, the relationships, are that of the right. And this is regardless of the modality (vision, audition, etc.) or dimension (pitch/frequency, amplitude, timbre, etc.) of the input. Of course, the same information can be, and usually is, processed in different manners by the two hemispheres. The right side may retain the gestalt or gist of the story, and the left side may retain the analytic aspects or details. Under normal circumstances, both hemispheres work together, producing an accurate recall or response.

Most people with ASD have difficulty with expressive prosody and, it would appear, receptive prosody as well. Similarly they have a great deal of difficulty reading the body language of others (Koning & Magill-Evans, 2001), including information from the eyes and face. This can result in poor eye contact and difficulty appreciating when they have insulted or hurt someone else. These symptoms would appear to point to a difficulty with the right hemisphere. Although those with nonverbal learning disabilities (Rourke, 1985, 1989) but no features of autism also have difficulty reading others, this is for a different reason. It is a result of hypofunction of the posterior right areas of the brain. However, many people with autistic features perform exceedingly well on tasks usually purported to tap into posterior right functions, such as the Street Completion (Street, 1931) and the Hooper (Hooper, 1983). Similarly, there appears to be no particular problem in appreciating spatial relations. Spatial span, as assessed by replicating a random sequence of taps on blocks or squares placed at various places on a board or card, can be remarkably good. At times we have "hidden" a desired toy (e.g., piece of string) from children with both autism and mental retardation by leaving the toy where they did before being called away. We rearranged the furniture so they would have to take a new path to access the toy. Even though the new arrangement made it difficult to see the object until they got near it, they had no difficulty going to the right place to secure the object. In other words, they remembered the spatial location of the object even though the rest of the room had changed.

Many of those with autism are mute, suggesting perhaps a left hemisphere involvement. However, many did speak until about 30 to 36 months and then ceased to talk. (It may be that the normal shift from right to left hemisphere dominance for language did not occur, but the inhibition of right hemisphere, assumedly by the left, did. We need more work on this.) However, items and details really seem to be a strength of many showing autistic features. They can have large, albeit unusual, vocabularies or stores of knowledge. Many of the drawings of those with autism show great care in the details but little concern for the gestalt, how and where the details are put together. Several items may be drawn on top of each other in a corner of the paper. On the other hand, many who show autism or Asperger's show great care in the more holistic, gestaltic aspects of their drawings, and some show great precision (as in strong left) and appreciation for spatial relations (right). Ramachandran (2004) speaks of Nadya, an "autistic savant," who at age 5 created great drawings of horses and such, and he states that these drawing were on a par with, if not better than, those of Leonardo da Vinci. Her drawings at that age reflected a very strong posterior right hemisphere. However, as Nadya grew up and developed her linguistic skills she lost her "artistic sense."

In summary, although many with ASD have deficits on tasks of higher cerebral functioning, these are a reflection of the core deficits described earlier. There is no evidence of consistent hemisphere compromise among those with ASD.

MEMORY

MEMORY CAN BE remarkably good among those within the ASD. Luria writes about a savant with an incredible memory for lists and such (1972). Many of the higher functioning individuals have digit spans of eight numbers or more. It would appear that the rote manner of retention is preferred as chunking or other aids are seldom used. Curiously, the ability to use information from this rote memory is often compromised. We have known two people with ASD who have memorized the multiplication table to 100 times 100. Today both would likely be diagnosed with Asperger's disorder. They had difficulty, however, using this knowledge. One was turning 30 the next month and was asked how many months old he was. He had no idea how to figure this out. He was able to repeat the question but lost as to how to solve the problem. The other was asked if John is going to turn 40 the next month, how many months old is he? This person responded, "About 480," but was unable to take it beyond that.

Neither of these people were true savants. Most of us could, if we chose to, memorize the times tables to that extent. Similarly we have met some "calendar savants," but these were not true savants either. They had memorized tables and methods for determining their results. Savantism certainly does appear to exist, and some day it may tell us something about the etiology of this spectrum of disorders.

This preference for rote retention is likely related to the concrete processing mentioned earlier and is responsible for the difficulties higher functioning people with autism have on more complex recall tasks. For example, they have problems on the immediate recall of paragraphs (Rumsey & Hamburger, 1988), a task analogous to retention of conversational speech. Later, Minshew, Goldstein, and Siegel (1997) found further deficits in the delayed retention of such paragraphs. In fact, Minshew et al. found no weaknesses in attention, sensory perception, elementary motor, simple memory, formal language, rule learning, or visuospatial processing. It is as if there are no deficits when there are limited ways to perform the task. However, there were cognitive weaknesses on complex motor, complex memory, complex language, and concept formation where many approaches for resolution are possible. Retention and processing of simple or basic material resulted in no deficits, but more complex processing and retention did.

Executive Functioning

Rumsey and Hamburger (1988) summarize the neuropsychological findings at that time as being characterized by a preponderance of deficits in abstraction and conceptual reasoning. They found relative sparing in memory and language and only a few impairments in visuospatial, sensory, and motor abilities. Since then, most have found a variety of dysfunctions on executive tasks among those with ASD, but the resultant profile is uneven. Few difficulties have been found with some such tasks, such as verbal fluency (FAS), Token Test, and Category Test (Minshew et al, 1997). In two studies (Rumsey & Hamburger, 1988; Minshew et al., 1997), the additional time needed to complete Trail Making B over that for Trail Making A was almost identical for the two groups (although in both studies those in the autism group took longer on Trail Making A than those in the matched control group). This would suggest that the difficulty many find with the Wisconsin Card Sort Test is not due to shifting attention. The findings show that performance can be, but is not consistently, poorer on the Wisconsin Card Sort Test for number of categories completed (Rumsey & Hamburger, 1988), though not for perseverative errors (Minshew et al., 1997). However, the reinforcement in this task is usually verbal, and as such the differences noted may have to do with the perceived strength of the reinforcement. (Would computer administration be any better?)

The executive functions, also known as frontal functions, involve incorporating all the available information into a decision prior to acting. It includes aspects such as planning and organizing material, problem solving, and maintaining goal-directed behavior. People with deficits in this area tend to act before they take everything relevant into account. Those with ASD have difficulty with many tasks of executive functioning, but often not for the same reasons as those with disruption of the frontal lobes. These prefrontal areas as a whole integrate information from the rest of the brain—the forms of information include sensory, affective, and memory. With frontal disruption, available information is not processed, and the resultant behavior can be viewed as what might be expected without that information. This does not mean that the person does not have the information, only that he does not use it. For example, an adolescent with prefrontal trauma may charge after a snake he just spied without taking into account that it is a rattlesnake, even though he knows about the danger. As another example, he might get on the first train that gets to a station without considering the direction it is going.

The deficits on executive tasks found among those within the ASD reflect less a lack of input, but more a misapplication of that input. Tsatsanis (2005) concludes that higher functioning people with ASD have no particular difficulty in learning rules and procedures or identifying concepts. Rather, they have difficulty abstracting information in order to attain concepts or to develop flexible problem-solving strategies. These individuals have difficulty with cognitive flexibility and limited ability to comprehend novel or abstract concepts.

This difference has been noted when comparing attention-deficit/hyperactivity disorder (ADHD) groups to high functioning autism groups (Tsatsanis, 2005). Those with ADHD tend to have difficulty inhibiting a prepotent response, a response that might be correct except under certain circumstances. Those in the autism groups showed deficits in cognitive flexibility. An aspect of this may be related to imagining or thinking about possible outcomes, which entails viewing a situation from various angles. Such imagining is certainly related to the core aspect of being unable to take different perspectives. However, this is more than just difficulty taking the perspective of others, but difficulty in taking different perspectives in general. There would be no difficulty in forming straightforward strategies, as we see for some of the "executive" tests (e.g., verbal fluency). When flexibility in thought is needed, when different views or outcomes must be surveyed, when an abstract strategy must be derived, those within the autism spectrum have great difficulty. This would also explain why those with ASD often appear to follow their own agenda rather than effectively pursuing an externally imposed goal. For example, people with this spectrum of disorders have particular difficulty with the 20 Questions task, the Binet Picture Absurdities Test (Minshew et al., 1997), and the Tower of Hanoi (see Tsatsanis, 2005), all tasks that require cognitive flexibility.

Although some of the "executive" deficits can be explained through the core interpersonal deficits there seems to be more to it. Those with the autism spectrum disorders appear to develop, or have, a unique, but not necessarily effective, form of logic. The explanations may have no rhyme or reason. Often they are able to do very difficult logical analyses only to fall flat in their final conclusion (e.g., the person who could easily multiply the 40 times 12 to see how old John will be next month, but then he had no idea how to proceed from there).

CONCLUSION

A SD IS A complex neurodevelopmental array of disorders with a high comorbidity with other significant problems including developmental delays in cognition. Those with ASD show difficulties in learning, communication, and socialization. The spectrum ranges from those who have epilepsy and have profound mental retardation to those who, for the most part, are able to function independently in our society. However, it is important for relatives and others to identify and understand those who are high functioning, for these are the ones who are particularly vulnerable to the influences of others, often with serious consequences.

From the onset people with ASD are unable to relate to others in what would be considered a normal manner. They are unable to feel for others as through empathy. They have little idea of their impact on others. They are unable to view others as having a mind, as human and somehow different than other aspects of the environment. Their aloneness does not bother them, and often they prefer to be alone. More than just a defect in reciprocal social interaction, those with ASD have an inability to make a genuine emotional bond with another. Although most with ASD are able to show the full array of emotions, they are unable to experience interpersonal emotions, such as love. This lack of appreciation for affective contact with others, the inability to read the mind (or even appreciate the mind) of others, the total inability for a true interpersonal bond with others, and the inability to even appreciate these aspects of humanity appear to be at the core of the symptoms we see within this spectrum of disorders.

Someone with ASD may do poorly on a given task or class of tasks because of the core interpersonal impairment and not because of some primary sensory or motor defect or other reason found within the non-ASD population. Most of the attention and concentration problems observed have more to do with whether the ongoing task is their agenda or that of another. Intellectually ASD people tend to be literal with poor social comprehension. The intellectual strengths tend to be in areas where there is the least need for appreciating interpersonal information and where concrete thinking is required. Such individuals have difficulty when abstract reasoning or mental flexibility is needed.

Although on the surface there appear to be substantial sensory and motor abnormalities, the basic biological processes appear to be intact. The abnormalities arise from individuals having their own agenda and not appreciating a more universally accepted one. Hence we get hyper-responsivity to some sounds and hypo-responsivity to others. Stereotopies by themselves are not abnormal, but the core deficits in interpersonal appreciation render those with ASD unable to control or to eliminate the stereotopies through social cues.

Language deficits of autism are a defining property. However, these linguistic features reflect more the core features and processing deficits of ASD than specific linguistic ones. Much of language, especially pragmatics, assumes the ability to take different viewpoints, especially those of other people. Those with ASD cannot do this. Related to this is expressive and receptive prosody, particular weaknesses of those with ASD. Semantics are concrete and language shows little flexibility or abstract reasoning. The very strong rote abilities of many with ASD may well be related to the concrete reasoning. In line with this, they often display a unique form of logic. Deficits often occur not because they do not use available information, but because they apply it in what to the rest of us appears to be an illogical manner. Working to understand the core interpersonal symptoms and their relationships to the concrete thinking, inflexibility, and poor abstract reasoning may help us gain an understanding of the neuropsychology of ASD.

REFERENCES

American Psychiatric Association. (1980). *Diagnostic and statistical manual of mental disorders* (3rd ed.). Washington, DC: Author.

American Psychiatric Association. (1994). *Diagnostic and statistical manual of mental disorders* (4th ed.). Washington, DC: Author.

Baron-Cohen, S. (1999). *Mindblindness: An essay on autism and theory of mind.* Cambridge, MA: MIT Press.

Bartolucci, G., & Albers, R. J. (1974). Deictic categories in the language of autistic children. *Journal of Autism and Childhood Schizophrenia, 4,* 131–141.

Bartolucci, G., Pierce, S. J., & Streiner, D. (1980). Cross-sectional studies of grammatical morphemes in autistic and mentally retarded children. *Journal of Autism and Developmental Disorders, 10,* 39–50.

Damasio, A. R. (1984). Autism. *Archives of Neurology, 41,* 481.

Ducharme, R. W., & McGrady, K. A. (2003). What is Asperger's syndrome? In R. W. Ducharme & T. P. Gullotta (Eds.), *Asperger's syndrome: A guide for professionals and families.* New York: Kluwer Academic/Plenum.

Fogassi, L., Ferrari, P. F., Gesierich, B., Rozzi, S., Chersi, F., & Rizzolatti, G. (2005). Parietal lobe: action organization to intention understanding. *Science, 308,* 662–667.

Hooper, H. E. (1983). *Hooper organization test manual.* Los Angeles: Western Psychological Services.

Kanner, L. (1943). Autistic disturbances of affective contact. *Nervous Child, 2,* 217–250.

Koning, C., & Magill-Evans, J. (2001). Social and language skills in adolescent boys with Asperger syndrome. *Autism: Journal of Research and Practice, 5,* 23–36.

Kootz, J. P., Marinelli, B., & Cohen, D. J. (1982) Modulation of response to environmental stimulation in autistic children. *Journal of Autism and Developmental Disorders, 12,* 185–193.

Luria, A. R. (1972). *The man with a shattered world.* New York: Basic Books.

Minshew, N. J., Goldstein, G., & Siegel, D. J. (1997). Neuropsychologic functioning in autism: Profile of a complex information processing disorder. *Journal of the International Neuropsychological Society, 3,* 303–316.

Minshew, N. J., Sweeney, J. A., Bauman, M. L., & Webb, S. J. (2005). Neurologic aspects of autism. In F. R. Volkmar, R. Paul, A. A. Klin, & D. Cohen (Eds.), *Handbook of autism and pervasive developmental disorders: Vol. 1. Diagnosis, development, neurobiology, and behavior* (3rd ed., pp. 473–514). Hoboken, NJ: Wiley.

Oberman, L. M., Hubbard, E. M., McCleery, J. P., Altschuler, E. L., Ramachandran, V. S., & Pineda, J. A. (in press). EEG evidence for mirror neuron dysfunction in autism spectrum disorders. *Cognitive Brain Research.*

Ramachandran, V. S. (2004). *A brief tour of human consciousness.* New York: Pi.

Rourke, B. P. (1985). *Neuropsychology of learning disabilities.* New York: Guilford.

Rourke, B. P. (1989). *Non-verbal learning disabilities: The syndrome and the model.* New York: Guilford.

Rumsey, J. M. (1992). Neuropsychological studies of high-level autism. In E. Schopler & G. B. Mesibov (Eds.), *High-functioning individuals with autism* (pp. 41–64). New York: Plenum.

Rumsey, J. M., & Hamburger, S. D. (1988). Neuropsychological findings in high-functioning men with infantile autism, residual state. *Journal of Clinical and Experimental Neuropsychology, 10,* 201–221.

Rutter, M. (1983). Cognitive deficits in the pathogenesis of autism. *Journal of Child Psychology and Psychiatry, 24,* 513–531.

Soper, H. V., Barnhart, M., & McHale, T. (2005). *Development of lateralization of performance.* Paper presented at the meeting of the National Academy of Neuropsychology, Tampa, FL.

Soper, H. V., Satz, P., Orsini, D. L., Henry, R. R., Zvi, J. C., & Schulman, M. (1986). Handedness patterns in autism suggest subtypes. *Journal of Autism and Developmental Disorders, 16,* 155–167.

Soper, H. V., Satz, P., Orsini, D. L., van Gorp, W. G., & Green, M. F. (1987). Handedness distribution in a residential population with severe or profound mental retardation. *American Journal of Mental Deficiency, 92,* 94–102.

Street, R. F. (1931). *A Gestalt Completion Test. Contributions to education 481.* New York: Teachers College, Columbia University.

Tager-Flushberg, H., Paul, R., & Lord, C. (2005). Language and communication in autism. In F. R. Volkmar, R. Paul, A. A. Klin, & D. Cohen (Eds.), *Handbook of autism and pervasive developmental disorders: Vol. 1. Diagnosis, development, neurobiology, and behavior* (3rd ed., pp. 335–364). Hoboken, NJ: Wiley.

Tsatsanis, K. (2005). Neuropsychological characteristics in autism and related conditions. In F. R. Volkmar, R. Paul, A. A. Klin, & D. Cohen (Eds.), *Handbook of autism and pervasive developmental disorders: Vol. 1. Diagnosis, development, neurobiology, and behavior* (3rd ed., pp. 365–381). Hoboken, NJ: Wiley.

Walsh, K. W. (Speaker). (1985). *Clinical evaluation in neuropsychology* (Cassette Recording No. INS 636–85A-B). Inglewood, CA: Audio-Stats.

Wing, L. (1992). Manifestations of social problems in high-functioning autistic people. In E. Schopler & G. B. Mesibov (Eds.), *High-functioning individuals with autism* (pp. 129–142). New York: Plenum.

Wing, L. (1996). *The autistic spectrum: A guide for parents and professionals.* London: Constable.

Wing, L. (2005). Problems of categorical classification systems. In F. R. Volkmar, R. Paul, A. A. Klin, & D. Cohen (Eds.), *Handbook of autism and pervasive developmental disorders: Vol. 1. Diagnosis, development, neurobiology, and behavior* (3rd ed., pp. 583–605). Hoboken, NJ: Wiley.

23

Neuropsychological Assessment of Individuals With Substance Use Disorders

DANIEL N. ALLEN, GREGORY P. STRAUSS,
BRIAN D. LEANY, AND BRAD DONOHUE

OVERVIEW

SUBSTANCE USE DISORDERS are highly prevalent in the United States (Grant, 1997), with males affected two to three times more frequently than females. The American Psychiatric Association's (APA) *Diagnostic and Statistical Manual of Mental Disorders,* 4th ed. *(DSM–IV)* divides substance related disorders into two general categories, substance use disorders and substance induced disorders. These disorders often have debilitating effects, as they are associated with increased mortality rates, homelessness, child maltreatment, homicide, suicide,

Acknowledgment: This work was partially supported by funding from NIDA (grant number DA020548–01A1).

and other problem behaviors that extensively tax the health care system. Neuropsychologists are often employed to assess the severity of neurocognitive impairments associated with the use of substances, as well as to provide recommendations for treatment and rehabilitation. The current chapter details neurocognitive and neurological abnormalities specific to the major drug classifications identified in the *DSM–IV* (cannabis, cocaine, opioids, amphetamines, hallucinogens), including recommendations for comprehensive assessment and treatment/rehabilitation.

CLINICAL DIAGNOSIS AND ASSESSMENT OF SUBSTANCE USE DISORDERS

IN THE DIAGNOSTIC *and Statistical Manual of Mental Disorders,* 4th Edition-Text Revision *(DSM–IV–TR)* substance-related disorders include: (1) substance use disorders and (2) substance induced disorders (APA, 2000). Substance use disorders, which are the focus of the current discussion, include the subcategories of substance abuse and substance dependence. These two diagnoses are the most common substance related disorders. Substance abuse is diagnosed when during a 12-month period substance use leads to significant problems in at least one of the following four domains: (1) legal, (2) interpersonal, (3) work or school, or (4) hazardous behaviors. The diagnosis of substance dependence is made when persistent substance use results in three or more cognitive, behavioral, or physiological symptoms that occur within the same 12-month period. Symptoms may include unsuccessful attempts to cut down, tolerance, withdrawal, and curtailment of social, occupational or recreational activities in order to use or obtain the substance. It is important to note that increased tolerance or withdrawal symptoms are not required in order to diagnose substance dependence. A primary distinction between substance abuse and dependence is that for substance abuse, there is no withdrawal, tolerance, or compulsive use.

An accurate clinical history is essential to the diagnosis, assessment, and treatment of substance use disorders. However, an accurate history can be difficult to obtain for several reasons. A primary consideration is that individuals who have substance use disorders often deny or underreport the extent and consequences of their substance use. Indeed, substance abusers are often externally motivated to keep their use of substances private, as they are notoriously involved in the legal system and evidence significant problems in their relationships. These individuals are also sometimes too intoxicated or delirious to provide accurate histories. Additionally, the neurocognitive deficits resulting from substance use may impair their ability to accurately report details of previous use. Moreover, individuals who have been indicated to evidence cognitive impairments are more likely to deny substance use in contrast to their noncognitively impaired counterparts (Burgard, Donohue, Azrin, & Teichner, 2000).

In many cases substance use will only be suspected, and clinicians may doubt the validity of patient self-report. However, several methods can be used to improve the utility of patient self-report. For instance, it is helpful to obtain collateral reports from significant others and to perform drug screening immediately prior to testing to validate sobriety. Medical records may assist in determining if physical problems are consistent with substance use, or if the individual has access to medications with high potential for abuse. In addition to an accurate history and routine laboratory tests, sound psychometric assessment and screening is necessary to evaluate the existence and extent of neuropsychological and cognitive impairment. Structured procedures, such as the Time-Line Follow Back assessment procedure (Sobell & Sobell, 1976), which has been used to document both alcohol and substance use over the past 4 months, may be particularly beneficial for patients with cognitive impairment, by providing a visual and structured format for which to recall instances of substance use (Burgard et al., 2000). Self-report measures, such as the Substance Abuse Subtle Screening Inventory-3 (SASSI; Miller, Roberts, Brooks, & Lazowski, 1997), may also be useful in identifying individuals at risk for substance use disorders. Measures such as the SASSI are brief, and provide information about a range of alcohol and drug use behaviors using established cut-off scores to determine level of risk for substance use disorders. Although screening measures, such as the SASSI, are insufficient in providing a comprehensive understanding of etiological and maintaining factors, these instruments are useful in identifying those at risk for substance abuse and dependence. Also instruments such as the SASSI do not establish the diagnosis of substance abuse or dependence, which requires additional interview and evaluation.

NEUROPSYCHOLOGICAL ASSESSMENT
OF SUBSTANCE USE DISORDERS

WHEN THERE IS limited time or expertise to administer and interpret full neuropsychological batteries, neuropsychological screening instruments can be employed. Neuropsychological screening instruments, such as the Cognistat (Kiernan, Mueller, Langston, & Van Dyke, 1987), Repeatable Battery for the Assessment of Neuropsychological Status (RBANS; Randolph, Tierney, Mohr, & Chase, 1998), and Neuropsychological Screening Battery (NSB; Heaton,

Thompson, Nelson, Filley, & Franklin, 1990) may have particular utility. Each screening method has advantages and disadvantages. Advantages of Cognistat and RBANS include that they require minimal training and administration time (i.e., < 30 minutes), although neither has been extensively validated with individuals who have substance use disorders. On the other hand, the NSB requires greater administration time, but reliably discriminates individuals with substance use disorders from controls. Cognistat subtests assess orientation, attention, language comprehension, language repetition, confrontational naming, construction, memory, calculation, verbal abstraction, and judgment and incorporate screening items into each of the individual subtests. However, recent research suggests some items in this instrument may be culturally/ethnically biased, necessitating recommendations to administer the full Cognistat when assessing substance use disorders (Schrimsher, O'Bryant, Parker, & Burke, 2004). The 12 subtests of the RBANS may be utilized to evaluate immediate and delayed memory, visuospatial/constructional abilities, attention, and language. The NSB consists of six commonly used neuropsychological tests. It provides assessment of attention, visual and verbal learning and memory, psychomotor speed, language and reading comprehension, verbal fluency, and visuoconstructional ability.

The subsequent sections focus on describing the typical neuropsychological deficits of individuals who abuse specific drugs. It should be noted that of all substances, alcohol is the most widely abused substance, and the neurocognitive effects of alcohol, as compared with other substances, have received considerably more attention in the scientific community. As the effects of alcohol are discussed elsewhere in this volume, this chapter focuses on cannabis, cocaine, amphetamines, opiates, benzodiazepines, and polysubstance abuse.

ASSESSMENT OF SPECIFIC SUBSTANCE USE DISORDERS

BECAUSE INDIVIDUAL SUBSTANCES are often associated with unique neurocognitive impairments, careful consideration should be given to the selection of a battery of neuropsychological tests that are sensitive to the unique deficits associated with each substance. Therefore, the following section delineates neurocognitive deficits that are particular to specific substances.

CANNABIS

THE MOST FREQUENTLY abused category of illicit drugs is the cannabinoids, with the most common form of use being marijuana. The lifetime prevalence rate for marijuana use in the United States is approximately 30%. The psychoactive effects of cannabinoids are caused by delta-9-tetrahydrocannabinol, or THC. Cannabis has several corresponding symptoms of intoxication. Physiological symptoms include blood-shot eyes, increased appetite, and dry mouth. Psychological symptoms may include impaired cognitive abilities (e.g., sensory perception, memory, and judgment), fluctuations in mood state (anxiety or euphoria), and psychotic symptoms (paranoia, grandiosity, hallucinations). It is uncertain if there are withdrawal symptoms associated with the cessation of cannabis use, so the *DSM–IV* does not include a diagnostic category for cannabis withdrawal. Nevertheless, there is some limited empirical support to suggest withdrawal occurs with very heavy and prolonged use in some individuals. Withdrawal symptoms may be physiological (nausea, tremor, insomnia) or psychological (anxiety and irritability). Cannabis use disorders are also associated with a variety of negative outcomes including poor social relationships, higher incidence of legal problems, lower employment status, poor work record, poor motivation, apathy, affective blunting, and decreased libido.

Neuropsychological deficits associated with cannabis use have been examined in relation to intoxicated, short-term, and long-term effects. Cannabis intoxication produces significant and widespread cognitive deficits in the areas of problem solving, abstraction, attention, expressive and receptive language, and memory. Several short-term deficits have also been reported to occur during the 24 hours following cessation of cannabis use, including impairments in attention, executive functioning, mental arithmetic, immediate recall of verbal information, and complex reaction times (Iverson, 2003; Pope & Yurgelun-Todd, 1986). Subtle long-term deficits may also be present in the ability to learn and recall new information (Grant, Gonzalez, Carey, Natarajan, & Wolfson, 2003). It is not clear whether these deficits reflect neurological damage caused by cannabis or if they are premorbid in nature. However, it appears that cannabis use disorders do not lead to marked long-term neurocognitive deficits.

Although the effects of cannabis on structure and function of the cerebrum have not been extensively investigated using neuroimaging techniques, a small number of studies suggest that cannabis use may be associated with distinct functional, but not structural abnormalities. Positron emission topography (PET) studies following acute administration of cannabis demonstrate increased regional cerebral blood flow (rCBF) in the cerebellum, which may be consistent with a high concentration of cannabinoid C1 receptors. Increased rCBF has also been reported in the orbitofrontal cortex, insula, and cingulate gyrus following acute intoxication (Matthew, Wilson, Coleman, Turkington, & Degrado, 1997). Although CT studies indicate no consistent differences between users and nonusers after neurological and medical risk factors are controlled, functional magnetic resonance imaging (fMRI) investigations of chronic users examined after short-term and long-term abstinence demonstrate abnormal activation of dorsolateral prefrontal cortex and left superior parietal cortex during working memory tasks (Jager, Kahn, Van Den Brink, Van Ree, & Ramsey, 2006). It also appears that even after 25 days of abstinence, heavy cannabis users demonstrate poorer performance on decision-making tasks, which is accompanied by decreased activation in the left medial orbital frontal cortex and increased activation in the cerebellum (Bolla, Eldreth, Matochik, & Cadet, 2005).

COCAINE

COCAINE IS A stimulant drug that causes cerebral vasoconstriction and hypertension, which may lead to ischemic stroke, cerebral vasculitis, subarachnoid and parenchymal brain hemorrhage, and seizures. Use of cocaine can also result in death from respiratory or cardiac failure. Physiological effects of intoxication include tachycardia, increased blood pressure, pupil dilation, and perspiration. Behavioral symptoms include hyperactivity, restlessness, and stereotyped behavior, and psychological symptoms of euphoria, grandiosity, increased alertness, anxiety, and depression are also common. Heavy chronic cocaine use typically results in physiological dependence, and withdrawal can occur within hours after cessation of use, and almost always within 2 or 3 days. During withdrawal physiological symptoms including disrupted sleep, appetite, and psychomotor functioning are common. These physiological symptoms are often accompanied by feelings of depression, sadness, and anxiety. While many of the symptoms abate after physiological withdrawal is complete (1 to 5 days), some may last much longer. For example, some individuals continue to report anhedonic symptoms for up to 10 weeks following cessation of heavy use.

Although general intellectual ability remains intact in most cases, cocaine use is associated with several distinct neuropsychological and neurological abnormalities. However, these deficits differ in relation to time since use, whether withdrawal symptoms are current, and extent of use. Current use is associated with impairments in verbal and visual recall, working memory, and attention (Simon et al., 2002). In a recent quantitative review of the cocaine neuropsychology literature, Jovanovski, Erb, and Zakzanis (2005) found that measures of attention, executive function, working memory, and declarative memory were the most frequently deficient following cessation of cocaine use. Most of the participants in the studies examined by Jovanovski et al. were heavy users who were in various stages of remission, with many no longer demonstrating withdrawal effects. A number of studies have also attempted to document improvement in brain function following cessation of cocaine use via neurocognitive tests (Berry et al., 1993; Block, Erwin, & Ghoneim, 2002; Bolla, Funderberk, & Cadet, 2000; Di Sclafani, Tolou-Shams, Price, & Fein, 2002; Van Gorp et al., 1999). These studies suggest that memory abilities improve over the first 5 or 6 weeks of abstinence, with relatively little improvement very early in the recovery process (< 2 weeks) and more gradual improvement later in recovery (6 weeks to 6 months). The pattern of recovery for other neurocognitive domains during the first 5 weeks of sobriety is unclear, although it appears that little recovery occurs even after 6 months of sobriety, particularly for attention, executive function, spatial processing, or delayed memory. Correlations between length of sobriety and a number of neurocognitive domains also suggest that little improvement is observed (Selby & Azrin 1998).

Abnormal brain imaging results provide additional evidence for the deleterious effects of cocaine use (Fein, Di Sclafani, & Meyerhoff, 2002; Goldstein et al., 2004; Gottschalk, Beauvais, Hart, & Kosten, 2001; Holman et al., 1991). Much like the neuropsychological literature, neuroimaging studies suggest that abnormalities observed differ in relation to pattern and length of use. During cocaine intoxication, fMRI findings indicate activation of the lateral prefrontal cortex, anterior cingulate gyrus, nucleus accumbens, and the hippocampal gyri, as well as decreased signal intensity in the medial prefrontal cortex, amygdala, and temporal pole. PET studies also indicate that intoxication is associated with decreased glucose metabolism throughout the brain (Goldstein & Volkow, 2002). Some of the most consistent findings following cessation of use include abnormality in frontal and prefrontal cortices, either reduced frontal and prefrontal gray matter volume and cortical density, including the anterior cingulate, as demonstrated through MRI (Fein et al., 2002; Matochik, London, Eldreth, Cadet, & Bolla, 2003; O'Neill, Cardenas, & Meyerhoff, 2001), or reduced cerebral blood flow or glucose metabolism, using single photon emission topography (SPECT) or PET (e.g., Holman et al., 1991; Strickland et al., 1993; Weber et al., 1993). Abnormalities in temporal and parietal cortices have also been identified. Additionally, while some improvement occurs, consistent with the neuropsychological findings, decreased regional cerebral blood flow in the frontal lobes persists up to 4 months following cessation of cocaine use (Volkow et al., 1992). These abnormalities appear to be related to dose and length of cocaine use.

AMPHETAMINES AND
METHYLENDIOXYMETHAMPHETAMINE (MDMA)

AMPHETAMINES ARE STIMULANT drugs with properties similar to cocaine. However, the psychostimulant actions tend to be longer lasting and sympathomimetic effects are generally more potent than with cocaine. MDMA (3,4-methylendioxymethamphetamine), also known as "Ecstasy," is a member of the amphetamine family, but is described here independently due to its hallucinogenic properties. MDMA use is associated with significant long-term serotonergic abnormalities, which lead to changes in a variety of psychological functions, such as behavior, mood, and sleep (Landry, 2002). For chronic users, long-term changes have also been reported in relation to neuronal pruning, with the extent of damage proportional to the amount and duration of use.

The intoxication and withdrawal effects associated with amphetamine and MDMA use are similar. Common physiological symptoms of intoxication reflect sympathetic nervous system arousal and include tachycardia, cardiac arrhythmias, pupillary dilation, as well as increased blood pressure, heart rate, and body temperature. Psychological symptoms of euphoria or anxiety are also common, along with decreased concentration, impaired judgment, and perceptual alterations. For a minority of individuals (as many as 25%), MDMA causes strong negative reactions during intoxication, which may include severe anxiety. Cessation of amphetamine use causes withdrawal symptoms to occur within a few hours or few days. Dysphoria and anhedonia are common, as are fatigue, disrupted sleep, increased appetite, and psychomotor agitation or retardation.

Distinct neuropsychological findings have been reported for both amphetamine and MDMA users. Few studies have been conducted on the neuropsychological effects of amphetamines (McKetin & Mattick, 1997), but findings are similar to those with cocaine abuse, which reveal deficits primarily in attention, executive functions, and memory. During intoxication, amphetamines produce general cognitive arousal and increased vigilance without a corresponding improvement in cognition or memory. Immediately following cessation of use, short-term deficits are present for attention, psychomotor speed, verbal fluency, and verbal learning and memory (Kalechstien, Newton, & Green, 2003). Even after 1 month of abstinence, amphetamine dependent users exhibit impaired verbal memory and learning, as well as impaired information-processing speed (Johanson et al., 2006). Memory impairment may not be observed when using verbal memory tasks that rely on recognition, even when these recognition tasks are delayed, because it appears that the verbal memory impairment results from poor organizational strategies and limitations in generating semantic relationships (Woods et al., 2005). Long-term deficits are also present in attention and motor skills in heavy stimulant users 1 or more years following cessation of use (Toomey et al., 2003).

Neuroimaging studies of individuals who are methamphetamine dependent have also provided evidence for the neurotoxic effects of this drug (Paulus et al., 2002). Overall reductions in temporal lobe volume, hippocampal volumes, anterior cingulate grey matter, and prefrontal grey matter have been identified when methamphetamine users are compared to controls (Bartizokis et al., 2000; Kim et al., 2006; Thompson et al., 2004). Recently, seemingly contradictory results have indicated increased volume in a number of structures including the parietal cortex, basal ganglia, and nucleus accumbens (Jernigan et al., 2005; but also see Thompson et al., 2004). These volume increases were associated with increased neurocognitive impairment, and while their cause remains undetermined, a number of mechanisms might account for the findings, such as astrocytosis, microgliosis, or premorbid neurodevelopmental conditions including attention-deficit/hyperactivity disorder (ADHD). Finally, there is recent evidence from PET studies indicating potential nerve terminal degeneration in the striatum of methamphetamine users who had not used for at least 30 days (Johanson et al., 2006).

For MDMA, a number of neurocognitive deficits have been identified in the days immediately following cessation of MDMA use. Verbal memory and working memory impairments have been demonstrated in MDMA users who have been abstinent for relatively short periods of time (at least 3 weeks). Both occasional and chronic users exhibit impairments in verbal fluency and immediate and delayed prose recall (Bhattachery & Powell, 2001). Long-term neurocognitive deficits have also been reported. In both occasional and heavy MDMA users, neurocognitive deficits have been found to persist up to 1 year post-abstinence (Parrot, 2001; Reneman, Booij, Majoie, van den Brink, & den Heeten, 2001). These deficits are most consistently reported in the domains of learning and memory, particularly verbal memory. Additional deficits have been found in the areas of executive function and planning, attention and vigilance, verbal fluency, and visual scanning. Task switching ability has been shown to be proportionally impaired with the level of lifetime usage, with those having higher levels of lifetime usage showing greater impairment on the task-switching ability (Dafters, 2006).

Neuroimaging findings also suggest that MDMA use results in significant functional impairment (for a review see Reneman et al., 2001). PET studies indicate that a single dose of MDMA causes increased regional cerebral blood flow in the ventromedial and occipital cortex, inferior temporal lobe, and the cerebellum with corresponding decreases in the motor and somatosensory cortex, temporal lobe, cingulate cortex, insula, and thalamus. For heavy MDMA users, global decreases in serotonin (5-HT) transporter densities are present primarily in the parieto-occipital, occipital, and sensory cortex, indicating serotonin neuronal injury. SPECT studies also demonstrate decreases in 5-HT transporter densities, as well as changes in postsynaptic 5-HT receptors indicative of down-regulation in most cortical regions, except for up-regulation in the occipital cortex. There is also electrophysiological evidence suggesting that MDMA causes 5-HT impairment, with greater impairment occuring with more frequent use (Croft, Klugman, Baldeweg, & Gruzelier, 2001).

OPIOIDS

THE DSM–IV CATEGORY of opioids includes naturally occurring, semi-synthetic, and synthetic substances. Although there are a number of opioids abused, heroin is the most frequent. Several medical and psychological factors are associated with heroin use, such as head trauma, poor school or occupational performance, and hyperactivity or attention problems. Although opioid use disorders are less prevalent than common cannabis or alcohol disorders, some evidence suggests that the prevalence of heroin use is increasing.

Intoxication effects resulting from opioid use include feelings of euphoria, impaired judgment and attention, slurred speech, lethargy, and constriction of the pupils, and dysphoria often follows the initial feelings of euphoria. Less common intoxication effects include hallucinations and delirium. Opioid withdrawal typically occurs within 24 hours following cessation of use and is characterized by feelings of anxiety and depression. Physical symptoms such as nausea, malaise, sweating, pupil dilation, insomnia, and muscle aches also commonly occur. Most of these withdrawal symptoms will resolve within a week, but some symptoms such as dysphoria can continue for several months.

Relatively few studies have investigated the neurocognitive deficits resulting from opioid use, and the results of these studies are conflicting particularly with regard to long-term effects. Similar to other substance use disorders, it appears that neurocognitive deficits vary in relation to duration and quantity of use. Studies examining cognitive effects during acute opioid administration suggest that heroin use impairs long-term verbal and visual memory, as well as attention and concentration. Investigations of current users indicate impairment in fine motor speed, visuospatial and visuomotor abilities, attention, verbal fluency, memory, as well as more generalized cognitive impairment (Grant et al., 1978; Hill & Mikhael, 1979). Deficits in executive functioning, impulse control, and nonverbal reasoning have been found to persist for weeks to months in chronic users after heroin use has stopped (Lee & Pau, 2002; Lyvers & Yakimoff, 2003; Pau, Lee, & Chan, 2002). However, these results are not wholly consistent across studies, and deficits may be influenced by polydrug or alcohol use, as well as comorbid psychiatric and medical disorders. Additionally, some preliminary results suggest that these deficits may resolve with sustained abstinence of 4 or more months (Gerra et al., 1998).

Structural imaging studies have produced discrepant results; however, differences may be due to imaging method and sample selection. A study using CT found no significant differences between heroin users and controls. Structural MRI findings indicated bilateral reduction in prefrontal cortex volume, with specific reductions in grey, but not white matter (Liu, Matochik, Cadet, & London, 1998).

Associated Risks of IV-Drug Use

Because opioids, in particular heroin, tend to be administered via intravenous injection, there is an associated risk of infectious diseases, such as HIV and concommitant neuropsychological impairment. This impairment is not restricted to dementia, which is typically considered when conducting a neuropsychological assessment for individuals diagnosed as HIV positive, but can include more subtle presentations of neurocognitive slowing as well as neurocognitive related motor dysfunction. AIDS dementia is a rapidly progressive deterioration of cerebral functioning that, left untreated, will become debilitating within 3 days to 2 months of the onset of presenting symptoms. It can have a broad presentation ranging from general mental slowing to more obvious motor impairments such as an altered gait, weakness, or motor-discoordination, or it may present in emotional disturbances and psychosis (Lezak, Howieson, & Loring, 2004). However, in the United States, current pharmacological treatment for AIDS has dramatically reduced the number of affected individuals who go on to develop dementia.

Recent research has shown that individuals who are asymptomatic may also show a variable pattern of neuropsychological impairment, and this impairment can be attributed to two different patterns of progression that may occur. HIV infection may continue along a progression that shows a gradual increase in neurological dysfunction until an eventual presentation of AIDS dementia, or it may follow a more insidious course in which there are several acute episodes of neurological disturbances that seem to remit. While the type of asymptomatic presentation may vary, research suggests that those individuals who show impairment in any two domains of neurological functioning are more likely to have functional difficulty in their everyday life. Those asymptomatic individuals who demonstrate neuropsychological impairment have greater difficulty in keeping and maintaining employment and show a decrease in driving abilities. Most importantly they have a higher mortality rate with those who also demonstrate a minor cognitive motor disorder having the highest mortality rate (Grant, Marcotte, Heaton, & the HNRC Group, 1999).

Benzodiazepines

BENZODIAZEPINES ARE CLASSIFIED as sedative/hypnotics in the *DSM–IV*. These drugs are among the most widely prescribed medications in the world and have a high potential for abuse because of their calming and sometimes euphoric effects. Although abused by individuals of all ages, elderly individuals, who receive almost 40% of all benzodiazepine prescriptions, more often abuse benzodiazepines. Prescription of benzodiazepines is common in the elderly because they are often used to treat disorders that increase in prevalence with age (e.g., insomnia). Elderly individuals who abuse benzodiazepines are at increased risk for adverse reactions, such as delirium and confusion. Therefore, it is recommended that clinicians pay special attention to the assessment of benzodiazepine use disorders in the elderly (for reviews see Allen & Landis, 1998; Mort & Aparasu, 2002).

Benzodiazepine intoxication effects include incoordination, ataxia, dysarthria, diplopia, and dizziness. Benzodiazepines typically induce relaxation, calmness, and euphoria although in some cases, feelings of depression and hostility may occur. Chronic benzodiazepine use leads to development of tolerance, but physiological dependence may also occur after only a few days of use. Withdrawal symptoms may include irritability, anxiety, insomnia, sweating, muscle twitching or aching, concentration difficulties, depression, and derealization. Severe withdrawal symptoms such as delirium, confusion, and seizures have also been reported (Tune & Bylsma, 1991). It appears that the abrupt discontinuation of benzodiazepines with long half-lives (e.g., diazepam) increases the risk for seizures within 3 days of discontinuation, although discontinuance of shorter-acting benzodiazepines may cause more intense withdrawal symptoms.

Neuropsychological deficits observed with benzodiazepine use depend upon the age of the user. Studies suggest that benzodiazepines have several acute cognitive effects on elderly individuals, although these effects are negligible (at least at low doses) in younger individuals. Additionally, elderly individuals display cognitive impairment even at low doses, and these impairments increase as dose increases. However, it has been reported that deficits become less severe with chronic administration.

Drug half-life also influences the type of neuropsychological deficits observed with benzodiazepine use. Long-acting benzodiazepines are associated with multiple neurocognitive abnormalities, including impairments in immediate and delayed verbal recall, delayed visual recall, processing speed, and psychomotor functioning, as well as higher rates of intrusion errors on list learning tasks. Short-acting benzodiazepines impair attention, as well as several memory functions, including explicit, working, and semantic memory. Neuropsychological impairments typically subside rapidly once benzodiazepine use is discontinued. However, chronic long-term benzodiazepine users have been found to display impairment up to 6 months after discontinuation of use (Tata, Rollings, Collins, Pickering, & Jacobson, 1994).

Structural and functional neuroimaging studies have also been conducted with benzodiazepine users. Structural imaging (CT) studies provide no evidence of anatomical differences between benzodiazepine users and controls. However, PET studies suggest that regional cerebral glucose metabolism is reduced with benzodiazepine administration, and fMRI indicates similar decreases (Streeter et al., 1998).

POLYSUBSTANCE USE

THE DSM–IV ALSO includes a diagnosis of polysubstance dependence, which requires use of three substances (excluding caffeine and nicotine) over a 1-year period, with a pattern of symptomatology produced by this combined use that meets criteria for substance dependence. However, in order for a diagnosis of polysubstance dependence to be made, no single substance can meet criteria for substance dependence. The majority of studies examining neuropsychological deficits in polysubstance use apply a broader definition of polysubstance dependence, which simply requires the presence of abuse of or dependence on more than one substance. Using *DSM–IV* nomenclature, multiple diagnoses of abuse and dependence would be given, rather than a single diagnosis of polysubstance dependence.

The symptoms of intoxication and withdrawal in polysubstance users reflect the specific symptoms associated with the particular substances that are being used. However, specific withdrawal and intoxication effects can be difficult to predict when multiple substances are used, because there are often interaction or potentiation effects that occur. For example, using benzodiazepines and alcohol together will produce greater sedation and euphoria than when either is used alone. Thus, when assessing individuals who use multiple substances, consideration of these interaction effects is warranted.

Neuropsychological deficits have been found to occur in up to 50% of current polysubstance users (Grant et al., 1978; Grant & Judd, 1976). Although the prevalence of neurocognitive deficits is relatively high in polysubstance users, the pattern of deficits observed varies widely and falls in line with the specific substances used. Additionally, neuropsychological impairments observed in polysubstance users are also affected by the many unique comorbid medical and psychiatric factors that are associated with particular substances. In general, however, the amalgam of polysubstance use disorders is most consistently associated with impairments in motor ability, perceptual motor skills, visuospatial abilities, problem solving, and verbal and visual memory.

As with neuropsychological profiles, structural and functional abnormalities associated with polysubstance use are variable and dependent upon the individual substances used. As such, studies examining neurological effects of polysubstance use have reported findings ranging from severe to benign impairment, with a range of structures implicated. It is also important to recognize that the types of impairment produced by the combination of various substances may not represent simple addition effects. Take for example, the common combination of cocaine and alcohol. Based on laboratory studies with animals and humans, some have suggested that their combined effects may cause greater impairment than use of either substance alone, due to a metabolite of cocaine derived from ethanol, cocaethylene (e.g., McCance-Katz, Kosten, & Jatlow, 1994). This hypothesis has received mixed support, with some studies showing greater neurocognitive impairment associated with cocaine–alcohol comorbidity (Bolla et al., 2000), most finding no effect (e.g., Lawton-Craddock, Nixon, & Tivis, 2003), and still others finding better performance in comorbid groups compared to those with cocaine dependence alone (e.g., Robinson, Heaton, & O'Malley, 1999). Some have suggested that because ethanol reduces platelet aggregation, it may actually reduce the likelihood of cocaine-related cerebral vascular accidents (e.g., Robinson et al., 1999), and thus protect against this cause of neurocognitive dysfunction. However, given this consideration, readers are encouraged to review other sections of this chapter to estimate the types of abnormalities that may occur in substances of interest.

COMORBIDITY IN SUBSTANCE USE DISORDERS

AMONG THOSE DIAGNOSED with substance use disorders, the presence of comorbid mental and physical disorders is common, and they often cause more severe neurocognitive impairments. For example, it has long been reported that substance use disorders have high comorbidity with several psychiatric conditions (Hubbard & Martin, 2001) such as schizophrenia, where as many as 65% of patients have lifetime diagnoses of substance use disorders (Cuffel, 1992; Mueser et al., 1990; Regier et al., 1990). This comorbidity appears to have compounding and interactive effects on brain dysfunction, so that the deficits observed in those with comorbid disorders are greater than what might be expected from the simple additive neurocognitive effects of one disorder to the other (Allen, 2004; Allen & Remy, 2000; Thoma et al., 2006), as well as causing an acceleration in age-associated cognitive decline (Allen, Goldstein, & Aldarondo, 1998; Mohamed, Bondi, Kasckow, Golshan, & Jeste, 2006). A number of other psychiatric disorders also occur at increased rates in substance users. Major depression is highly comorbid with alcohol, cannabis, cocaine, and polysubstance use disorders. Attention-deficit/hyperactivity disorder has increased incidence in alcohol and heroin use disorders, and in early onset (adolescent) substance use disorders. Anxiety disorders occur with greater frequency in alcohol use disorders, while antisocial personality disorder has increased incidence in alcohol, cannabis, cocaine, and polysubstance use disorders.

Thorough physical examination is advised in all patients who have substance use disorders, to rule out medical conditions that could affect neurocognitive functioning including infectious diseases (e.g., human immunodeficiency virus and hepatitis), cerebrovascular accident, subdural hematoma secondary to head injury, epileptic seizures, disorders resulting from malnutrition such as Wernicke-Korsakoff disorder (Victor, Adams, & Collins, 1971), and cirrhosis of the liver leading to hepatic encephalopathy (Tarter & Butters, 2001), among others. These conditions may have direct additive effects or interactive effects on neurocognitive deficits. A recent example of the former was reported for individuals who were HIV seropositive and also diagnosed with methamphetamine dependence. Individuals affected by both conditions exhibit higher levels of neuropsychological impairment (Carey et al., 2006) and grey matter abnormalities on MRI (Jernigan et al., 2005) than comparable groups affected by either condition alone.

AGE EFFECTS AND SUBSTANCE USE DISORDERS

A GE ALSO SIGNIFICANTLY impacts the type and severity of substance use, as well as the patterns of neurocognitive deficits observed (for review see Allen & Landis, 1998). Because the percentage of elderly individuals in the United States is gradually increasing, clinicians should anticipate seeing a rise in the number of elderly clients with substance use disorders in the years to come (Morgan, Dallosso, Ebrahim, Arie, & Fentem, 1988). When working with elderly individuals, clinicians should keep in mind that they differ from younger individuals in several important ways. First, there are several unique factors that place elderly individuals at risk for developing substance use disorders. Of primary consideration is that elderly individuals are the largest consumers of prescription medications, with estimates suggesting that the elderly consume approximately 30% of all prescription drugs. As previously mentioned, elderly individuals are at a particularly high risk for becoming dependent on benzodiazepines, which have high potential for abuse or addiction. Despite these risk factors, substance use disorders are typically less prevalent in older individuals. For males 18–29 years old, 1 year prevalence rates for drug use disorders are 4.0%; however, risk rapidly reduces with age, as estimates drop to .7% for individuals 30 years or older, and to one-tenth of 1% in individuals over age 65. These decreasing prevalence rates have been explained by the "maturing out" theory (Winick, 1962), which suggests that substance use decreases as individuals pass from one developmental stage to the next, or by increased mortality rates that occur in substance use disorders.

However, three others factors associated with under-detection may also explain the drop in prevalence that comes with age. The first factor involves inadequate or inappropriate diagnostic criteria. As individuals move into the latter part of life, age-appropriate physical, social, and community related tasks significantly differ from that of younger individuals. Due to this shift, elderly individuals may be exposed to fewer potential outlets where distress, dysfunction, or deviant behavior could be observed (Miller, Belkin, & Gold, 1991). Clinicians should be careful to consider that diagnostics criteria may fit younger, but not older clients for this reason. Lower prevalence rates among the elderly may also be due to under-detection of prescription substance abusers. This under-detection may occur because many health care providers fail to consider potential for abuse and dependence when prescribing to elderly individuals. The third factor involves late life onset of substance abuse. Health care providers may be less likely to assess for, and subsequently detect, substance use in elderly individuals with no prior history of substance related problems. However, there is evidence for late-onset substance disorders, which may be caused by a "maturing in" process (Allen & Landis, 1998), whereby the unique challenges of late life coupled with greater access to and potential for dependence on prescription medication causes late-onset substance problems in an otherwise low-risk elderly population.

NEUROCOGNITIVE DEFICITS AND TREATMENT

THERE IS INCREASED interest in the means by which neuro-cognitive deficits interfere with treatment response in substance use disorders (Allen, Goldstein, & Seaton, 1997). Indeed, as reported by Burgard et al. (2000), there is anecdotal support resulting from a controlled treatment outcome study that standardized treatments are relatively ineffective with cognitively impaired individuals. In contrast to substance abusers who did not evidence cognitive impairments, about a dozen participants who were identified to be cognitively impaired or functioning in the borderline range of intellectual functioning rarely completed treatment, and none achieved abstinence. Along similar lines, treatment response may be mediated by the type of neurocognitive deficits observed, and thereby differ based upon the types of substances abused. For instance, memory deficits have been linked to difficulty learning and retaining rationales for treatment, psychoeducational information, logic and rule-governed behavior involved in cognitive therapies, and appreciation of consequences involved in contingency management strategies (see Burgard et al., 2000). Whereas deficits in executive function may hinder the application of problem-solving strategies that have been indicated to (1) assist substance abusers from acting upon their urges to use drugs, (2) curb derogatory comments when angry, and (3) resist temptations to be truant or absent from work or school (e.g., Azrin et al., 2001). Nevertheless, the relationship between treatment outcome and neurocognitive deficits is complex, and it is likely that neurocognitive impairment exerts both mediating and moderating effects, depending on the outcome domains, risk factors, and neurocognitive abilities under consideration (Bates, Bowden, & Barry, 2002). Therefore, neuropsychologists should consider type and severity of neurocognitive deficits when planning treatment for individuals with substance use disorders. When deficits are present, cognitive rehabilitation procedures may help to remediate deficits and thereby increase treatment efficacy. Bates et al. (2002) provide specific suggestions for remediating substance-induced deficits.

CONCLUDING REMARKS

THE OVERARCHING GOAL in examining substance use disorders in relationship to neuropsychological functioning is trying to classify patterns of deficits associated with the substance of abuse. The corpus of research literature available for neurocognitive and neuroimaging research is centered on this attempt to isolate specific brain structures associated with corresponding functional abnormalities and neurocognitive deficits. While these studies suggest that such patterns of activation and associated deficits in cognition and behaviors exist, one must be aware that the observed effects may not be due solely to the neurotoxic effects of a substance of abuse. However, the individual diagnosed with a substance use disorder rarely presents with a single causal factor. Clinicians should take care to conduct an evaluation that relies upon a multimethod approach. This evaluation should include a reasonable assessment of physical, psychiatric, and psychosocial domains of functioning. There is also the apparent need to examine the interaction of these neurocognitive deficits with treatment in populations that exhibit high rates of substance abuse and have very high potential for harm, such as in cases of child abuse and neglect, HIV risk behaviors, and suicidal/homicidal behaviors. This research is crucial in order to develop interventions capable of accommodating the unique neurocognitive abnormalities that accompany substance use disorders. Finally, there is a need for a greater expansion of the neurocognitive and neuroimaging studies into the long-term effects of substance abuse on the brain. Ideally these studies would incorporate a methodology that allows examination of the interaction of factors that occur in an individual diagnosed with a substance use disorder, including comorbid substance use, as well as medical and psychiatric disorders.

REFERENCES

Allen, D. N. (2004). Substance abuse and schizophrenia [Abstract]. *The Clinical Neuropsychologist, 18,* 162.

Allen, D. N., Goldstein, G., & Aldarondo, F. (1998). Neurocognitive dysfunction in patients diagnosed with schizophrenia and alcoholism. *Neuropsychology, 13,* 62–68.

Allen, D. N., Goldstein, G., & Seaton, B. E. (1997). Cognitive rehabilitation of chronic alcohol abusers. *Neuropsychology Review, 7,* 21–39.

Allen, D. N., & Landis, R. K. B. (1998). Substance abuse in elderly individuals. In P. D. Nussbaum (Ed.), *Handbook of neuropsychology and aging* (pp. 111–137). New York: Plenum.

Allen, D. N., & Remy, C. J. (2000). Neuropsychological deficits in patients with schizophrenia and alcohol dependence [Abstract]. *Archives of Clinical Neuropsychology, 15,* 762–763.

American Psychiatric Association. (2000). *Diagnostic and Statistical Manual of Mental Disorder* (4th ed., text revision). Washington, DC: Author.

Azrin, N. H., Donohue, B., Teichner, G., Crum, T., Howell, J., & DeCato, L. (2001). A controlled evaluation and description of individual-cognitive problem solving and family-behavioral therapies in conduct-disordered and substance dependent youth. *Journal of Child and Adolescent Substance Abuse, 11,* 1–43.

Bartzokis, G., Beckson, M., Lu, P. H., Edwards, N., Rapoport, R., Wiseman, E., et al. (2000). Age-related brain volume reductions in amphetamine and cocaine addicts and normal controls: Implications for addiction research. *Psychiatry Research: Neuroimaging, 98,* 93–102.

Bates, M. E., Bowden, S. C., & Barry, D. (2002). Neurocognitive impairment associated with alcohol use disorders: Implications for treatment. *Experimental and Clinical Psychopharmacology, 10,* 193–212.

Berry, J., van Gorp, W. G., Herzberg, D. S., Hinkin, C., Boone, K., Steinman, L., et al. (1993). Neuropsychological deficits in abstinent

cocaine abusers: Preliminary findings after two weeks of abstinence. *Drug & Alcohol Dependence, 32,* 231–237.

Bhattachary, S., & Powell, J. H. (2001). Recreational use of 3,4 methylenedi-
oxymethamphetamine (MDMA) or 'ecstasy': Evidence for cognitive
impairment. *Psychological Medicine, 31,* 647–658.

Block, R. I., Erwin, W. J., & Ghoneim, M. M. (2002). Chronic drug use and cognitive impairments. *Pharmacology Biochemistry and Behavior, 73,* 491–504.

Bolla, K. I., Eldreth, D. A., Matochik, J. A., & Cadet, J. L. (2005). Neural substrates
of faulty decision-making in abstinent marijuana users. *Neuroimage, 26,*
480–92.

Bolla, K. I., Funderberk, F. R., & Cadet, J. L. (2000). Differential effects of
cocaine and cocaine alcohol on neurocognitive performance. *Neurology,*
54, 2285–2299.

Burgard, J., Donohue, B., Azrin, N. H., & Teichner, G. (2000). Prevalence and
treatment of substance abuse in the mentally retarded population: An
empirical review. *Journal of Psychoactive Drugs, 32,* 293–298.

Carey, C. L., Woods, S. P., Rippeth, J. D., Gonzalez, R., Heaton, R. K., et al. (2006).
Additive deleterious effects of methamphetamine dependence and
immunosuppression on neuropsychological functioning in HIV infection. *AIDS and Behavior, 10,* 185–190.

Croft, R. J., Klugman, A., Baldeweg, T., & Gruzelier, J. H. (2001). Electrophysiological evidence of serotonergic impairment in long-term MDMA
("ecstasy") users. *American Journal of Psychiatry, 158,* 1687–1689.

Cuffel, B. J. (1992). Prevalence estimates of substance abuse in schizophrenia and their correlates. *Journal of Nervous and Mental Disease, 180,*
589–592.

Dafters, R. I. (2006). Chronic ecstasy (MDMA) use is associated with deficits in
task-switching but not inhibition of memory updating executive functions. *Drug and Alcohol Dependence, 83,* 181–184.

Di Sclafani, V., Tolou-Shams, M., Price, L. J., & Fein, G. (2002). Neuropsychological
performance of individuals dependent on crack-cocaine or crack-
cocaine and alcohol at six weeks and six months abstinence. *Drug and*
Alcohol Dependence, 66, 161–171.

Fein, G., Di Sclafani, V., & Meyerhoff, D. J. (2002). Prefrontal cortical volume
reduction associated with frontal cortex function deficit in 6-week
abstinent crack-cocaine dependent men. *Drug and Alcohol Dependence,*
68, 87–93.

Gerra, G., Calbiani, B., Zaimovic, A., Sartori, R., Ugolotti, G., Ippolito, L., et al.
(1998). Regional cerebral blood flow and comorbid diagnosis in abstinent opioid addicts. *Psychiatry Research: Neuroimaging, 83,* 117–126.

Goldstein, R. Z., Leskovjan, A. C., Hoff, A. L., Hitzemann, R., Bashan, F., Khalsa,
S. S., et al. (2004). Severity of neuropsychological impairment in cocaine
and alcohol addiction: Association with metabolism in the prefrontal
cortex. *Neuropsychologia, 42,* 1447–1458.

Goldstein, R. Z., & Volkow, N. D. (2002). Drug addiction and its underlying neurological basis: Neuroimaging evidence for the involvement of the frontal cortex. *American Journal of Psychiatry, 159,* 1642–1652.

Gottschalk, C., Beauvais, J., Hart, R., & Kosten, T. (2001). Cognitive function and cerebral perfusion during cocaine abstinence. *American Journal of Psychiatry, 158,* 540–545.

Grant, B. F. (1997). The influence of comorbid major depression and substance use disorders on alcohol and drug treatment: Results of a national survey. In L. S. Onkin, J. D. Blaine, S. Genser & A. M. Horton, Jr. (Eds.), *Treatment of drug-dependent individuals with comorbid mental disorders* (pp. 4–15). NIDA Research Monograph 172, Rockville, MD: U.S. Department of Health and Human Services.

Grant, I., Adams, K. M., Carlin, A. S., Rennick, P.M., Judd, L. L., & Schoof, K. (1978). The collaborative neuropsychological study of polydrug users. *Archives of General Psychiatry, 35,* 1063–1074.

Grant, I., & Judd, L. (1976). Neuropsychological and EEG disturbances in polydrug users. *American Journal of Psychiatry, 133,* 1039–1042.

Grant, I., Gonzalez, R., Carey, C. L., Natarajan, L., & Wolfson, T. (2003). Nonacute (residual) neurocognitive effects of cannabis use: A meta-analytic study. *Journal of the International Neuropsychological Society, 9,* 679–689.

Grant, I., Marcotte, T. D., Heaton, R. K., & the HIV Neurobehavioral Research Center Group. (1999). Neurocognitive complications of HIV disease. *Psychological Science, 10*(3), 191–195.

Heaton, R. K., Thompson, L. L., Nelson, L. M., Filley, C. M., & Franklin, G. M. (1990). Brief and intermediate length screening of neuropsychological impairment in multiple sclerosis. In S. M. Rao (Ed.), *Multiple sclerosis: A neuropsychological perspective* (pp. 149–160). New York: Oxford University Press.

Hill, S. Y., & Mikhael, M. A. (1979). Computerized transaxial tomographic and neuropsychological evaluations in chronic alcoholics and heroin abusers. *American Journal of Psychiatry, 36,* 598–602.

Holman, B. L., Carvalho, P. A., Mendelson, J., Teoh, S. K., Nardin, R., Hallgring, E., et al. (1991): Brain perfusion is abnormal in cocaine-dependent polydrug users: A study using technetium-99m-HMPAO and ASPECT. *Journal of Nuclear Medicine, 32,* 1206–1210.

Hubbard, J. R., & Martin, P. R. (Eds.). (2001). *Substance abuse in the mentally and physically disabled.* New York: Marcel Dekker.

Iverson, L. (2003). Cannabis and the brain. *Brain, 126,* 1252–1270.

Jager, G., Kahn, R. S., Van Den Brink, W., Van Ree, J. M., & Ramsey, N. F. (2006). Long-term effects of frequent cannabis use on working memory and attention: An fMRI study. *Psychopharmacology (Berl), 185,* 358–68.

Jernigan, T. L., Gamst, A. C., Archibald, S. L., Fennema-Notestine, C., Mindt, M. R., Marcotte, T. D., et al. (2005). Effects of methamphetamine dependence and HIV infection on cerebral morphology. *American Journal of Psychiatry, 162,* 1461–1472.

Johanson, C., Frey, K. A., Lundahl, L. H., Keenan, P., Lockhart, N., Roll, J., et al. (2006). Cognitive function and nigrostriatal markers in abstinent methamphetamine abusers. *Psychopharmacology, 185,* 327–338.

Jovanovski, D., Erb, S., & Zakzanis, K. K. (2005). Neurocognitive deficits in cocaine users: A quantitative review of the evidence. *Journal of Clinical and Experimental Neuropsychology, 27,* 189–204.

Kalechstein, A. D., Newton, T. F., & Green, M. (2003). Methamphetamine dependence is associated with neurocognitive impairment in the initial phases of abstinence. *Journal of Neuropsychiatry and Clinical Neuroscience, 15,* 215–220.

Kiernan, R. J., Mueller, J., Langston, J. W., & Van Dyke, C. (1987). The neurobehavioral cognitive status examination. *Annals of Internal Medicine, 107,* 481–485.

Kim, S. J., Lyoo, I. K., Hwang, J., Chung, A., Sung, Y. H., Kim, J., et al. (2006). Prefrontal grey-matter changes in short-term and long-term abstinent methamphetamine abusers. *International Journal of Neuropsychopharmacology, 9,* 221–228.

Landry, M. J. (2002). MDMA: A review of epidemiologic data. *Journal of Psychoactive Drugs, 34,* 163–169.

Lawton-Craddock, A., Nixon, S. J., & Tivis, R. (2003). Cognitive efficiency in stimulant abusers with and without alcohol dependence. *Alcoholism: Clinical and Experimental Research, 27,* 457–464.

Lee, T.M.C., & Pau, C.W.H. (2002). Impulse control differences between abstinent heroin users and matched controls. *Brain Injury, 16,* 885–889.

Lezak, M. D., Howieson, D. B., & Loring, D. W. (with Hanay, H. J., & Fischer, J. S.). (2004). *Neuropsychological assessment* (4th ed.). New York: Oxford Press.

Liu, X., Matochik, J. A., Cadet, J. L., & London, E. D. (1998). Smaller volumes of prefrontal lobe in polysubstance abusers: A magnetic resonance imaging study. *Neuropsychopharmacology, 18,* 243–252.

Lyvers, M., & Yakimoff, M. (2003). Neuropsychological correlates of opioid dependence and withdrawal. *Addictive Behaviors, 28,* 605–611.

Matochik, J. A., London, E. D., Eldreth, D. A., Cadet, J. L., & Bolla, K. I. (2003). Frontal cortical tissue composition in abstinent cocaine abusers: A magnetic resonance imaging study. *Neuroimage, 19,* 1095–1102.

Matthew, R. J., Wilson, W. H., Coleman, R. E., Turkington, T. G., & DeGrado, T. R. (1997). Marijuana intoxification and brain activation in marijuana smokers. *Life Science, 60,* 2075–2089.

McCance-Katz, E. F., Kosten, T. R., & Jatlow, P. (1994). Concurrent use of cocaine and alcohol is more potent and potentially more toxic than use of either alone—A multiple-dose study. *Biological Psychiatry, 44,* 250–259.

McKetin, R., & Mattick, R. P. (1997). Attention and memory in illicit amphetamine users. *Drug and Alcohol Dependence, 50,* 181–184.

Miller, F. G., Roberts, J., Brooks, M. K., & Lazowski, L. E. (1997). *SASSI-3: A quick reference guide for administration and scoring.* Bloomington, IN: Baugh Enterprises.

Miller, N. S., Belkin, B. M., & Gold, M. S. (1991). Alcohol and drug dependence among the elderly: Epidemiology, diagnosis, and treatment. *Comprehensive Psychiatry, 32,* 153–165.

Mohamed, S., Bondi, M. W., Kasckow, J. W., Golshan, S., & Jeste, D. V. (2006). Neurocognitive functioning in dually diagnosed middle aged and elderly patients with alcoholism and schizophrenia. *International Journal of Geriatric Psychiatry, 21,* 711–718.

Morgan, K., Dallosso, H., Ebrahim, S., Arie, T., & Fentem, P. H. (1988). Prevalence, frequency, and duration of hypnotic drug use among the elderly living at home. *British Medical Journal Clinical Research Ed., 296,* 601–602.

Mort, J. R., & Aparasu, R. R. (2002). Prescribing of psychotropics in the elderly: Why is it so often inappropriate? *CNS Drugs, 16,* 99–109.

Mueser, K. T., Yarnold, P. R., Levinson, D. F., Singh, H., Bellack, A. S., & Kee, K. (1990). Prevalence of substance abuse in schizophrenia: Demographic and clinical correlates. *Schizophrenia Bulletin, 16,* 31–56.

O'Neill, J., Cardenas, V., & Meyerhoff, D. (2001). Separate and interactive effects of cocaine and alcohol dependence on brain structures and metabolites: Quantitative MRI and proton MR spectroscopic imaging. *Addiction Biology, 6,* 347–361.

Parrot, A. C. (2001). Human psychopharmacology of Ecstasy (MDMA): A review of 15 years of empirical research. *Human Psychopharmacology, 16,* 557–577.

Pau, C.W.H., Lee, T.M.C., & Chan, S. F. (2002). The impact of heroin on frontal executive functions. *Archives of Clinical Neuropsychology, 17,* 663–670.

Paulus, M. P., Hozack, N. E., Zauscher, B. E., Frank, L., Brown, G. G. Braff, d. L., et al. (2002). Behavioral and functional neuroimaging evidence for prefrontal dysfunction in methamphetamine-dependent subjects. *Neuropsychopharmacology, 26,* 53–63.

Pope, H. G., & Yurgelun-Todd, D. (1996). The residual cognitive effects of heavy marijuana use in college students. *Journal of the American Medical Association, 275,* 521–527.

Randolph, C., Tierney, M. C., Mohr, E., & Chase, T. N. (1998). The Repeatable Battery for the Assessment of Neuropsychological Status (RBANS): Preliminary clinical validity. *Journal of Clinical and Experimental Neuropsychology, 20,* 310–319.

Regier, D. A., Farmer, M. E., Rae, D. S., Locke, B. Z., Keith, S. J., Judd, L. L., et al. (1990). Comorbidity of mental disorders with alcohol and other drug abuse. Results from the Epidemiologic Catchment Area (ECA) Study. *Journal of the American Medical Association, 264,* 2511–2518.

Reneman, L., Booij, J., Majoie, C., van den Brink, W., & den Heeten, G. J. (2001). Investigating the potential neurotoxicity of Ecstasy (MDMA): An imaging approach. *Human Psychopharmacology, 16,* 579–588.

Robinson, J. E., Heaton, R. K., & O'Malley, S. S. (1999). Neuropsychological functioning in cocaine abusers with and without alcohol dependence. *Journal of the International Neuropsychological Society, 5,* 10–19.

Schrimsher, G. W., O'Bryant, S. E., Parker, T. D., & Burke, R. S. (2004). The relation between ethnicity and Cognistat performance in males seeking substance use disorder treatment. *Journal of Clinical and Experimental Neuropsychology, 27,* 873–885.

Selby, M. J., & Azrin, R. L. (1998). Neuropsychological functioning in drug abusers. *Drug and Alcohol Dependence, 50,* 39–45.

Simon, S. L., Domier, C. P., Sim, T., Richardson, K., Rawson, R. A., & Ling, W. (2002). Cognitive performance of current methamphetamine and cocaine abusers. *Journal of Addictive Diseases, 21,* 61–71.

Sobell, M. B., & Sobell, L. C. (1976). Second-year treatment outcome of alcoholics treated by individualized behavior theory: Results. *Behavior Research and Therapy, 14,* 195–215.

Streeter, C. C., Ciraulo, D. A., Harris, G. J., Kaufman, M. J., Lewis, R. F. Knapp, C. M., et al. if possible (1998). Functional magnetic resonance imaging of alprazolam-induced changes in humans with familial alcoholism. *Psychiatry Research, 82,* 69–82.

Strickland, T. L., Mena, I., Villanueva-Meyer, J., Miller, B. L., Cummings, J., Mehringer, C. M., et al. (1993). Cerebral perfusion and neuropsychological consequences of chronic cocaine use. *Journal of Neuropsychiatry and Clinical Neurosciences, 5,* 419–427.

Tarter, R. E., & Butters, M. (2001). Neuropsychological dysfunction due to liver disease. In R. E. Tarter, M. Butters, & S. R. Beers (Eds.), *Medical neuropsychology* (2nd ed., pp. 85–105). Dordrecht, The Netherlands: Kluwer Academic Publishers.

Tata, P. R., Rollings, J., Collins, M., Pickering, A., & Jacobson, R. R. (1994). Lack of cognitive recovery following withdrawal from long-term benzodiazepine use. *Psychological Medicine, 24,* 203–213.

Thoma, R. J., Hanlon, F. M., Miller, G. A., Huang, M. X., Weisend, M. P., Sanchez, F. P., et al. (2006). Neuropsychological and sensory gating deficits related to remote alcohol abuse history in schizophrenia. *Journal of the International Neuropsychological Society, 12,* 34–44.

Thompson, P. M., Hayashi, K. M., Simon, S. L., Geaga, J. A., Hong, M. S., Sui, Y., et al. (2004). Structural abnormalities in the brains of human subjects who use methamphetamine. *Journal of Neuroscience, 24,* 6028–6036.

Toomey, R., Lyons, M. J., Eisen, S. A., Hong, X., Sunanta, C., Seidman, L. J., et al. (2003). A twin study of the neuropsychological consequences of stimulant abuse. *Archives of General Psychiatry, 60,* 303–310.

Tune, L. E., & Bylsma, F. W. (1991). Benzodiazepine-induced and anticholinergic-induced delirium in the elderly. *International Psychogeriatrics, 3,* 397–408.

Van Gorp, W. G., Wilkins, J. N., Hinkin, C. H., Moore, L. H., Hull, J., Horner, M. D., et al. (1999). Declarative and procedural memory functioning in abstinent cocaine abusers. *Archives of General Psychiatry, 56,* 85–89.

Victor, M., Adams, R. D., & Collins, G. H. (1971). *The Wernicke-Korsakoff Syndrome.* Philadelphia: F. A. Davis.

Volkow, N. D., Hitzemann, R., Wang, G. J., Fowler, J. S., Wolf, A. P., Dewey, S. L., et al. (1992). Long-term frontal metabolic changes in cocaine abusers. *Synapse, 11,* 184–190.

Weber, D., Franceschi, D., Ivanovic, M., Atkins, H., Cabahug, C., Wong, C., et al. (1993). SPECT planar brain imaging in crack abuse: Iodine-123-iodoamphetamine uptake and localization. *Journal of Nuclear Medicine, 34,* 899–907.

Winick, C. (1962). Maturing out of narcotic addiction. *Bulletin on Narcotics, 14,* 1–7.

Woods, S. P., Rippeth, J. D., Conover, E., Gonzalez, R., Cherner, M., Heaton, R. K., et al. (2005). Deficient strategic control of verbal encoding and retrieval in individuals with methamphetamine dependence. *Neuropsychology, 19,* 35–43.

24

Neuropsychology of Alcoholism

DOUG JOHNSON-GREENE AND JOHN DENNING

T IS WELL recognized by health care providers that alcohol abuse is a relatively common problem in our society, the effects of which can include a wide range of devastating psychosocial, medical, and psychological consequences. Research examining the relationship between alcohol abuse and alteration in normal brain structure and cognitive function has gained considerable momentum during the past several decades, which has yielded important implications for treatment interventions and our understanding of the deleterious effects of alcohol use disorders (AUD). Neuropsychologists have an important role to play in evaluating persons with alcohol abuse, because many persons with acquired brain injury have comorbid substance abuse problems, and conversely, persons with alcohol abuse frequently have significant cognitive impairments. The goal of this chapter is to examine the epidemiologic characteristics, assessment and diagnostic considerations, neuropathologic, neuroimaging, neuropsychological, and psychological manifestations of AUD and their implications for treatment. While not representing an exhaustive review of the literature, the chapter should nonetheless provide a basic understanding of issues pertinent to AUD for the practicing neuropsychologist and other health professionals interested in the impact of AUD on brain structure and function.

EPIDEMIOLOGICAL CHARACTERISTICS AND COMORBIDITIES

IT IS ESTIMATED that 1 in 10 Americans has significant problems with alcohol (Miller & Brown, 1997). Exact estimates of the prevalence of alcoholism have historically been difficult to determine because of changes in diagnostic criteria and conceptualization over time, differences in or lack of specificity in the criteria and nomenclature employed at a given point in time (Spitzer, Endicott, & Robins, 1975), and because of lack of consistency in the instruments and methods employed to measure alcohol use disorders (Alanko, 1984). Despite these observations many researchers and clinicians continue to focus exclusively on the amount of alcohol someone consumes to make determinations about the presence of pathological drinking, though a multitude of factors can detract from the reliability and validity of this approach, including the self-report and retrospective nature of the information gathered (Dawson, 1998; Rehm, 1998). There are also methodological limitations associated with point in time estimates of consumption (Clarke, Shipley, & Lewington, 1999), which has prompted researchers to recommend focus on both point and lifetime estimates of consumption. These factors may partially account for the relatively consistent finding that there does not appear to be a dose-response relationship between alcohol consumption and pathological conditions, including neuropsychological impairments (Horner, Waid, Johnson, Lathan, & Anton, 1999).

Identification of possible alcohol-related consequences is often the key to determining the presence of previously undetected occult alcohol abuse. The current nomenclature for alcohol abuse as described in the *Diagnostic and Statistical Manual for Mental Disorders,* 4th ed. (*DSM–IV;* American Psychological Association [APA], 1994) focuses on continued use of alcohol despite its adverse consequences. It is well recognized that alcohol can have wide-ranging and adverse psychosocial effects including employment retention and productivity (Blum, Roman, & Martin, 1993), family relationships (Leonard & Rothbard, 1999), legal difficulties associated with aggression and crime (Chermack, Walton, Fugger, & Blow, 2001; Greenfield, 1998), and financial well-being.

The relationship between alcohol and traumatic injuries resulting in disability has been well documented (Gentilello, Donovan, Dunn, & Rivera, 1995). The rate for alcohol problems in consecutive trauma admissions has been as high as 44%, and up to 28% of all trauma admissions meet criteria for alcohol dependence (Rivara et al., 1993; Soderstrom et al., 1997). Acquired conditions such as traumatic brain injury (TBI) have long been associated with a high rate of premorbid and post-injury alcohol-related problems (Corrigan, 1995; Corrigan,

Rust, and Lamb-Hart, 1995). Studies have found alcohol to be a significant contributing factor in more than 50% of all cases of motor vehicle-related TBI, and alcohol use has also been linked specifically to motor vehicle crashes in the elderly (Higgins, Wright, & Wrenn, 1996). Similar percentages have been found for alcohol and falls, which is a common cause of traumatic brain injury (Brennan, Kagay, Geppert, & Moos, 2000). Other conditions that have been associated with alcohol abuse include spinal cord injury (Bombardier & Rimmele, 1998; Heinemann, Keen, Donohue, & Schnoll, 1988; Kiwerski & Krasuski, 1992) and burn injury (Bassett, Chase, Folstein, & Reiger, 1998). The conclusion that can be drawn from the literature is that there is a strong association between AUD and trauma-related disability.

AUD have also been shown to have an adverse impact on outcome from trauma-related disabling conditions. Not surprisingly, many post-traumatic injury patients continue to abuse alcohol, complicating their recovery and long-term rehabilitation. Alcohol abuse increases complications from and mortality during the acute phase of recovery in patients with TBI (Dikmen, Donovan, Loberg, Machmer, & Temkin, 1993), severe burn injury (Grobmyer, Maniscalco, Purdue, & Hunt, 1996; Kelley & Lynch, 1992), and in general trauma populations (Jurkovich et al., 1992). Alcohol may also affect post-injury outcome in persons with disability across a broad range of functional measures, including resumption of employment (Fauerbach, Engrav, & Kowalske, 2001), neurological complications (Kaplan & Corrigan, 1992), decreased activity, and rehabilitation participation (Heinemann, Goranson, Ginsburg, & Schnoll, 1989), and may also contribute to higher rates of suicide (Charlifue & Gerhart, 1991).

While there is general agreement that the incidence of AUD (i.e., alcohol abuse and dependence) decreases with age, recent epidemiological studies suggest that the extent of AUD in the elderly is significantly greater than previously reported (Adams, Barry, & Fleming, 1996; Clay, 1997; Holroyd & Duryee, 1997; Oslin, Streim, Parmelee, Boyce, & Katz, 1997; Reid & Anderson, 1997). It has been estimated that up to 10% of the elderly population are "problem" drinkers. Within this population, alcohol misuse is much more common in men than in women (Adams & Cox, 1995; Bucholz, Sheline, & Helzer, 1995), and there is reason to believe that African Americans may be more vulnerable to problem drinking in later life (Gomberg, 1995).

There are several implications for these findings. Because the elderly are at increased risk for cognitive impairments, they represent a special population that may be particularly vulnerable to the effects of alcohol abuse. Secondly, the elderly receive services from neuropsychologists and other health care providers at a disproportionate rate from younger populations because of the association between chronic illness and age, heightening the need to be familiar with AUD in this population. Finally, research suggests that the prevalence of AUD in persons with chronic disabling conditions is higher than in the general population. This has led to concern that alcohol may not only contribute to the development of a number of chronic conditions, but may also slow rates of recovery and produce secondary complications in persons who already have chronic conditions. It is also well known that the risk of substance abuse increases with higher levels of stress, as is frequently seen in persons coping with chronic illness. In turn, many chronic illnesses can be worsened by behaviors associated with substance abuse such as limited compliance with health regimens, decreased access to health care, and increased self-neglect. Exploration of the relationships between chronic illness and substance abuse is still in its infancy, but the prevalence of chronic illness in the elderly population highlights the increased risk for substance abuse in this population, given the research findings to date.

AUD is associated with significantly more adverse events including emergency room visits and hospital admissions (Holroyd & Currie, 1997). Other medical ailments that have been linked to AUD include delirium (Elie, Cole, & Primeau, 1998), various forms of cancer (Smith, 1995), liver disease, pancreatitis, peripheral neuropathy, poor nutrition, and late-onset seizures (Fink, Hays, Moore, & Beck, 1996). These alcohol-related complications can exert an independent effect on brain integrity and cognitive function, particularly where there is significant cardiac, hepatic, or endocrine dysfunction, which sometimes improve following successful resolution of the primary medical condition (Arria, Tarter, Starzi, & Thiel, 1991). These "secondary" effects represent one of the methodological hurdles that have made it difficult to determine the direct effects of AUD on cognitive impairments. Conversely, when attempts are made to recruit research subjects with AUD who are free of medical complications, they may not be very representative of the population of persons with AUD.

DIAGNOSTIC CONSIDERATIONS AND ALCOHOLISM ASSESSMENT

FOR MANY PATIENTS evaluated by health care workers there exists the possibility that AUD goes undiagnosed and untreated. AUD is largely unrecognized, because factors complicate assessment and diagnosis. There may be a tendency to be overly focused on cognitive functioning to the exclusion of psychosocial factors and inexperience in evaluating and identifying AUD. Another factor contributing to under-recognition of AUD is that current classification schemes used for diagnosis of AUD may have limited applicability to persons with disability. For example, the *DSM–IV* (APA, 1994) requires impairment in major life domains related to alcohol use, which may be difficult to demonstrate in persons with disability who are no longer employed or receive caregiver support for most activities of daily living because of their cognitive impairments. Because persons with cognitive impairments may be more susceptible to the effects of alcohol use, the classification scheme that has been proposed by the Substance Abuse and Mental Health Services Administration (SAMSHA; 1998) for elderly alcohol abuse may also have applicability to those with cognitive impairments. Specifically, they describe "at risk" drinkers whose alcohol use, although not currently causing problems, may bring about adverse consequences to the drinker or others; and "problem drinkers," which includes those with hazardous levels of consumption and drinking-related consequences.

Another factor related to under-recognition of AUD in persons with cognitive and medical disabilities includes difficulties with recognition of the problem and attitudes about alcohol use. AUD can mimic other medical and behavioral disorders common in persons with brain injury and illness, and it is not uncommon in these populations for somatic complaints, apathy, and emotional dysphoria to be erroneously associated with cognitive and medical disabilities. However, for a portion of individuals these complaints are actually signs of AUD. Increased efforts to educate health practitioners about common signs of alcohol abuse have resulted in reasonable success in increasing identification of problem drinking, particularly in general medical settings and emergency departments, though such training is typically not part of the typical education offered to doctoral students in psychology.

There may be a general reluctance to report problems with alcohol abuse by our patients and their family members. Family members may be hesitant to raise or confirm issues of alcohol abuse for fear of retribution, or they may simply choose to rationalize alcohol abuse by their family members because it is consistent with their own lifestyle choices and method of coping. A health care worker who asks reasonable questions about alcohol that are met with nonresponsive or angry responses has ample reason to suspect that alcohol concerns are present.

Lastly, the novice who focuses on self-reported alcohol consumption and fails to obtain corroboration is unlikely to detect AUD when it is present. Rather than focusing exclusively on the amount of alcohol consumed the health care worker should be focused on subtle "nonspecific" signs suggestive of AUD, such as physical, psychosocial, health, and safety concerns. A list of nonspecific signs of AUD can be found in Table 24.1.

Data gleaned from interviews can be supplemented with responses to alcohol screening measures. The advantage in doing both clinical interviews and alcohol screening measures is that there is an opportunity to determine the reliability of responses to similar questions separated by a brief interval of time. Inevitably, some patients with AUD who were not detected with clinical interview may be detected with the addition of an alcohol screening measure. For this reason, universal screening of patients is recommended, particularly given the higher prevalence of alcohol concerns in patients with acquired brain injury and chronic

TABLE 24.1   Nonspecific Signs of Alcohol Use Disorders (AUD)

Physical and Cognitive Signs
- Sleep complaints and change in sleeping patterns
- Change in eating habits and gastrointestinal complaints
- Vague cognitive complaints including confusion, mental fatigue, and impaired concentration
- Tremor, unexplained restlessness, unsteady gait, or poor coordination

Psychosocial Issues
- Signs of self-neglect such as poor nutrition, hygiene, or cleanliness of home
- Estrangement from most or all of family members with vague explanations
- Irritability and a tendency to react quickly to minor nuisances (i.e., short fuse)
- Altered mood (depression or anxiety)

Health and Safety
- Liver function abnormalities, pancreatitis, seizures
- Unexplained poor response to treatment or uncontrolled high blood pressure
- Gastrointestinal problems such as esophagitis and bleeding ulcer
- History of unexplained falls or bruising
- Recent history of car accidents

TABLE 24.2   Common Alcohol Screening Measures

Measure	Items	Max score	Impaired range	Format
CAGE (Ewing, 1984)	4	4	2 or more	Yes/No
AUDIT (Babor et al., 1992) Description	10	40	8 or more	5-Point
MAST (Selzer, 1971)	25	25	12 or more	Yes/No
SMAST (Selzer, Vinokur, & Rooijen, 1975)	13	13	5 or more	Yes/No
MAST-G (Blow et al., 1992)	24	24	5 or more	Yes/No

illness. A list of brief measures frequently utilized to screen for problem drinking is provided in Table 24.2. Of these measures, the CAGE is the shortest, the MAST-G was validated specifically for elderly patients, and the AUDIT enjoys the highest sensitivities and has been the most extensively validated in medical settings (Allen, Litten, Fertig, & Babor, 1997).

MAJOR MORPHOLOGICAL AND NEUROPATHOLOGICAL FINDINGS

THERE IS A rather large body of literature indicating that even in the absence of distinctive syndromes, such as Wernicke-Korsakoff syndrome, severe chronic alcoholism damages the central nervous system (CNS). One of the first comprehensive descriptions of neuropathological changes in the brains of alcoholics was written by Courville (1955). Since this seminal work others have documented that excessive amounts of alcohol produce major morphological changes in the aging human cerebral cortex (Courville, 1955; Harper & Kril, 1989, 1991; Kril & Harper, 1989) and correlated disorders of higher cerebral function.

The neuropathological changes associated with chronic heavy alcohol use are widespread in the brain and include both cortical and subcortical structural damage. Alcohol itself has a cytotoxic effect on brain tissue (Lishman, 1990). Postmortem and CT findings typically highlight the extent of whole brain atrophy with the greatest reductions in volume in the frontal and subcortical white matter, which results in sulcal and ventricular enlargement (Cala & Mastaglia, 1981). Even in nondependent alcohol drinkers there is evidence of slight enlargement of the ventricles and sulci compared to those who are nondrinkers. Older individuals with a history of chronic heavy alcohol use tend to show greater cortical and subcortical pathological changes compared to those who are younger (Pfefferbaum et al., 1992). MRI of chronic alcoholics has shown decreased volumes of subcortical white matter and cortical gray areas of the prefrontal and parietal lobes (Oscar-Berman & Marinkovic, 2003a). The decreased overall weight of alcoholic brains compared to normal brains tends to be the result of reductions in cell number and cell size including decreases in synaptic complexity and neuronal arborization across a variety of brain regions. Specifically, the hippocampus and the anterior cerebellar vermis (primarily responsible for coordination of gait and movement of the trunk and lower extremities), show decreased volumes, though there is some evidence that after a period of abstinence the hippocampus volume damage may improve (White, Matthews, & Best, 2000).

Deficits in memory are common in those with a history of heavy alcohol use as a function of disruption of the hippocampus and its connections with other memory-related structures. However, it is also important to note that even short-term heavy alcohol use can impair hippocampal (memory) functioning, and human and animal models link this to neurogenesis abnormalities in the dentate gyrus (Herrera et al., 2003). There has been speculation that some of the behavioral deficits found in many chronic alcoholics are similar to the deficits found in patients with right hemisphere damage (e.g., flat affect, decreased awareness of emotional cues, etc.) and also that there is a greater vulnerability of the right hemisphere to the toxic effects of alcohol. Some have found evidence showing smaller right compared to left hippocampal volumes in chronic alcoholics, but there is no consistent evidence of lateralized damage as a result of alcohol use (Oscar-Berman & Marinkovic, 2003a). It has also been hypothesized that females are more vulnerable to the toxic effects of alcohol due in part to evidence of atrophy of the corpus callosum in chronic alcoholic women compared to men. However, Pfefferbaum, Sullivan, Mathalon, and Lim (1997) suggested that there are too many confounding factors to make the assertion that there are significant gender differences, and they cite factors such as differences in the amounts of alcohol consumed, brain size, smoking frequency, and metabolic differences, which are typically not taken into account.

A small proportion of chronic heavy alcohol users may develop a rare and debilitating condition if they survive Wernicke's encephalopathy known as Wernicke-Korsakoff syndrome (WKS), which is thought to be primarily caused by chronic thiamine deficiency from malnutrition and reduced absorption in the gut. The constellation of cognitive deficits associated with the disorder sometimes shows slight improvement with high dose thiamine supplementation (Ambrose, Bowden, & Whelen, 2001), and at least one researcher has highlighted the importance of administering thiamine to persons with acute head injury because of its strong association with AUD (Ferguson, Soryal, & Pentland, 1997). Neuropathological evidence of the syndrome has found widespread diffuse cortical and subcortical abnormalities including areas of the orbitofrontal, cerebellar, and dienchephalic structures. These individuals tend to show greater reductions in subcortical white matter and overall brain atrophy than heavy drinkers with less severe cognitive impairments. The severe anterograde memory impairments characteristic of WKS have been associated with the loss of neurons specifically in the anterior and dorsomedial thalamic nuclei (Harding, Halliday, Caine, & Kril, 2000), though lesions can be found in a variety of other diencephalic structures such as the mammilary bodies. The cerebellum abnormalities are due to a decrease in the purkinje cell density, which is not a characteristic found in alcoholics free of significant medical complications (Baker, Harding, Halliday, Kril, & Harper, 1999). This degeneration in the cerebellum has been linked to many coordination-related behavioral features of the disorder as well as a loss in eye blink conditioning (McGlinchey-Berroth et al., 1995). Other anatomical abnormalities found in WKS include a significant loss of neurons in the basal forebrain and locus ceruleus, which in turn disrupts the normal regulation of acetylcholine and norepinephrine across a variety of brain areas.

FUNCTIONAL IMAGING STUDIES

FUNCTIONAL BRAIN IMAGING studies, such as functional magnetic resonance imaging (fMRI), single photon emission computed topography (SPECT), and positron emission tomography (PET) have suggested much about the nature of the impairments based on structural imaging and neuropsychological measures. Early functional studies showed global cerebral hypometabolism in the brains of persons with chronic alcohol abuse (Volkow, Hitzeman, & Wang, 1992), which is why imaging studies examining regions of interest (ROI) normalize their data to measures of whole brain cortex so that regional variations represent true variations and not global hypometabolic states.

Early CT and MRI studies showed brain shrinkage, which was more prominent in the frontal lobes and in the elderly (Oscar-Berman & Marinkovic, 2003b; Pfefferbaum et al., 1997). More recently, functional imaging studies examining the frontal lobes have shown that they are particularly vulnerable to decreased metabolism (Gilman, Adams, & Koeppe, 1990) and lower levels of specific neurotransmitters such as GABA (Gilman, Koeppe, & Adams, 1996). These findings have since been replicated in a number of functional imaging studies (Sullivan, Rosenbloom, Lim, & Pfefferbaum, 2000). Researchers have now started to link functional imaging deficits and neuropsychological impairments to treatment outcomes. For example, Noel and his colleagues (2002) found that in 20 patients who underwent treatment for alcoholism, low levels of cerebral blood flow in the medial frontal gyrus measured with SPECT and correlated deficits in inhibition and working memory were associated with difficulty in maintaining short-term abstinence.

NEUROPSYCHOLOGICAL IMPAIRMENTS
AND CHRONIC ALCOHOL ABUSE

THERE IS A growing body of literature suggesting that low to moderate consumption of alcohol can have beneficial effects across a number of physiological and cognitive domains, though these preliminary findings have multiple methodological shortcomings and may indeed be spurious findings related to failure to control for premorbid intellectual functioning (Krahn, Freese, Hauser, Barry, & Goodman, 2003). In contrast, a variety of cognitive impairments have been reliably associated with AUD. In addition to wide-ranging impairments in learning and memory functioning there are prominent impairments in executive type skills, particularly in the areas of rule and concept formation, selective attention, and the capacity to shift strategies in problem solving (Adams et al., 1993, 1995; Johnson-Greene et al., 1997b). In a recent study by Sullivan, Rosenbloom, and Pfefferbaum (2000) examining neuropsychological and motor functioning in 71 recently detoxified men and 74 healthy controls, impairments were found in six areas: executive functions, short-term memory, upper limb motor ability, declarative memory, visuospatial skills, and gait. The author postulated that the pattern of deficits implicated two distinct neural systems, the cerebellar-frontal system and the cortico-cortico system between the prefrontal and parietal cortices (Sullivan, Rosenbloom, & Pfefferbaum, 2000).

The extent of the relationship among cognition, alcohol, and aging has not been fully explored because of methodological complexities. However, there has been some limited support to suggest that alcohol may accelerate site-specific neuronal loss in older individuals (Freund, 1982; Pfefferbaum et al., 1992; Wiggins et al., 1988), which has been shown to correlate with cognitive impairment (Freund, 1982; Wiggins et al., 1988). The frontal lobes appear to be the most susceptible to neuronal loss related to alcohol abuse (Harper et al., 1998; Leuchter et al., 1994; Pfefferbaum et al., 1992), which is consistent with histological changes observed in normal aging. Acceleration of neuronal loss similar to patterns seen in elderly persons in response to chronic repeated alcohol exposure has led to development of a paradigm termed premature aging. However, this paradigm is not well-validated, because a clear dose response relationship between alcohol intake, neuronal loss, and cognitive dysfunction has not been established (Christian et al., 1995). Thus, the interaction between alcohol and aging as it relates to neuropathology for now must be considered inconclusive.

Much has been made of genetics and family history as it relates to increased risk for development of AUD, but several studies now suggest that the offspring of persons with AUD exhibit cognitive impairments similar to probands prior to using alcohol themselves (Poon, Ellis, Fitzgerald, & Zucker, 2000; Tarter, Hegedus, Goldstein, Shelly, & Alterman, 1993). It is possible that if there is a genetic risk factor for AUD its phenotypic expression is a set of cognitive impairments that interfere with reasonable decision making as it relates to alcohol use. Once a person develops chronic AUD, family history appears to have no impact on impairments in cerebral metabolism or cognitive functioning (Adams et al., 1998). Other "premorbid" factors have been implicated in studies of the cognitive impairments associated with AUD, including past history of traumatic brain injury, learning disabilities such as attention-deficit disorder, and psychiatric illness. Unfortunately, few studies correct for comorbid conditions, which has greatly complicated interpretation of much of the literature in this area.

The role of alcohol abuse in the development of alcoholic cerebellar degeneration (ACD) has also been well documented (Jernigan et al., 1991; Jernigan, Schafer, Butters, & Cermak, 1991). ACD is thought to represent a more severe course of chronic AUD, so it has been of interest to researchers attempting to segregate differing levels of alcohol use severity. Studies of neuropathological changes in the brains of persons with chronic alcoholism have shown asymptomatic degeneration of the cerebellum in up to 27% of chronic alcoholics, particularly neurons in the anterior superior vermis (Coffey et al., 1992; Johnson-Greene et al., 1997a). While cerebellar findings are relatively common in chronic AUD, the clinical syndrome of ACD develops in only a small proportion of persons with chronic AUD. In one of the few recent studies of ACD, Johnson-Greene and his colleagues (1997a) found that persons with ACD compared to persons with AUD but no ACD showed signs of motor slowing and decreased coordination of the upper extremities, but differences in cognition or duration of alcohol use.

There are several implications for alcohol-related cerebellar degeneration. Impaired coordination associated with cerebellar pathology may complicate recovery of ambulation after disabling illness and may contribute to increased risk of falls, potentially leading to multiple head injuries. Secondly, there is a growing body of literature suggesting that the cerebellum has a broader role than simply coordination of motor functioning and plays a role in learning memory, emotional regulation, and other cognitive functions. Third, because ACD is thought to be more common in persons with severe alcohol-related malnutrition, the persons represent a distinct group for research activities examining the effects of chronic AUD.

In summary, chronic alcohol use has been associated with site specific neuropathological changes in the brain and correlated cognitive impairments, primarily in the frontal lobe regions and the cognitive domain of executive functioning. We will next explore the potential for reversibility of these impairments.

REVERSIBILITY OF NEUROPSYCHOLOGICAL IMPAIRMENTS ASSOCIATED WITH ALCOHOLISM

THE PERMANENCE OF cognitive and metabolic changes in chronic alcoholics has been the subject of much debate. With abstinence of 1 to 5 months, deficits in brain mass diminish, which has been attributed in animal models to increase in neuronal cell size, increases in glial cells, and dendritic arborization (Franke, Kittner, Berger, Wirkner, & Schramek, 1997). However, cognitive deficits may continue to improve over the course of as much as 4–5 years (Parsons, 1993). Johnson-Greene and his colleagues (1997b) found in a small sample of patients with severe chronic alcoholism that abstinence was associated with improved performance on neuropsychological tests of general and executive functioning as well as recovery of local cerebral metabolic rates for glucose measured using PET.

Others have found more permanent impairments (Eckardt et al., 1996; Sclafani et al., 1995), though the length of follow-up appears to be an integral variable in interpreting such findings. The implication of these findings is that problem drinking may worsen cognitive changes associated with normal aging and contribute to brain trauma and illness, though there are indications of at least partial recovery with abstinence (Bates, Bowden, & Barry, 2002).

PSYCHOLOGICAL MANIFESTATIONS OF ALCOHOL ABUSE

PROBLEM DRINKING APPEARS to have a relationship to negative emotional states, such as depression and anxiety. This relationship has important implications for interpretation of neuropsychological measures inasmuch as emotional state is known to adversely affect performance on neuropsychological measures, and it can be difficult to determine the proportion of impaired performance attributable to CNS impairment in persons with significant levels of depression or anxiety. In particular, there is a growing body of literature focusing on the detrimental impact of depression on neuropsychological performance (Basso & Bornstein, 1999; Rohling, Green, & Iverson, 2003). Deficits have been noted on more challenging tasks as well as on those involving executive functioning, problem solving, memory, and attention. There is also empirical support to suggest that depression and age have a synergistic relationship and that depression can produce differentially worse impairments in elderly patients (Boone et al., 1995; King, Cox, & Lyness, 1995; King, Caine, & Cox, 1993).

Research has revealed that patients with histories of alcohol abuse have a higher prevalence of comorbid psychological disorders than the general population (Helzer & Pryzbeck, 1988; Hesselbrock, Hesselbrock, Tenmen, Meyer, & Workman, 1983; Ross, Glaser, & Germanson, 1988; Weisman, Meyers, & Harding, 1980). Specifically, anxiety and depression are frequently associated with chronic alcoholism (Grant, Adams, & Reed, 1984; Loberg, 1981; Merikangas & Gelernter, 1990). In many patients who abuse alcohol, initially high levels of depressive symptoms have been found to decrease after several weeks (Brown et al., 1995; Brown & Schuckit, 1988; Dackis, Gold, Pottash, & Sweeney, 1986; Schuckit & Hesselbrock, 1994). However, despite improvement following abstinence, many patients with a history of alcohol abuse continue to experience elevated levels of emotional distress and may meet diagnostic criteria for a mood or other psychiatric disorder (Schuckit et al., 1995; Schuckit, Irwin, & Brown, 1990; Schuckit, Irwin, & Smith, 1994). Patients with comorbid alcohol and psychiatric disorders have heightened severity of alcohol problems (Helzer & Pryzbeck, 1988), increased utilization of treatment services (Ross et al., 1988), and increased relapse rates after treatment (Booth, Yates, & Petty, 1991; Brown, Irwin, & Schuckit, 1991; Overall, Reilly, Kelley, & Hollister, 1985). Psychological conditions have also been implicated in the initiation and maintenance of alcohol abuse, as alcohol has been implicated as a form of self-medication (Kuschner, Sher, & Beitman, 1990; Weiss & Rosenberg, 1985). These findings are particularly important considering the strong link between depression and recovery from disabilities (Parikh, Lipsey, Robinson, & Price, 1990; Turner & Noh, 1988; Turner & Wood, 1978; Westbrook & Viney, 1982) and the high prevalence of depression in elderly medical patients (Blazer, 1989; Kessler, Foster, Webster, & House, 1992; Koenig et al., 1991; Langer, 1994; Mulsant & Ganguli, 1999), particularly those with stroke (Sinyor, Amato, & Kaloupek, 1986).

There has been more modest research examining the relationship between emotional states and neuropsychological test performance in patients with alcohol abuse. Goldstein and his colleagues (Goldstein, Shelly, Mascia, & Tarter, 1985) demonstrated a significant correlation only for a subset of patients with alcoholism who had "psychotic" profiles on the MMPI and measures of neuropsychological functioning. Though this was the first study to show an association between neuropsychological functioning and emotional functioning in persons who abuse alcohol, the use of the MMPI to classify broad profile types was a shortcoming of this investigation. In another study, Johnson-Greene and his colleagues (2002) conducted a factor analytic study of the MMPI that showed a relationship between emotional distress and executive dysfunction measured with the Halstead Category Test. This study suggests that there is an association between different facets of frontal lobe dysfunction common to cognitive and affective domains in persons with chronic alcohol abuse.

TREATMENT CONSIDERATIONS

P ERSONS WITH DISABILITIES, including those with cognitive disabilities, have been shown to be at greater risk for AUD (Corrigan et al., 1995). Nonetheless, persons with disabilities are less likely to receive effective treatment for AUD compared to persons without disabilities (Helwig & Holicky, 1994; Moore & Li, 1994). Common barriers encountered by persons with disabilities may include: (1) attitudinal barriers; (2) discriminatory policies, practices, and procedures; (3) communication barriers; and (4) architectural barriers.

As we have previously described, persons with AUD may have alcohol-related cognitive impairments, and conversely, persons with brain injury and illness may have comorbid difficulties with AUD. The commonalities are that both groups have both cognitive impairments and AUD. However, the type and severity of these impairments varies, and this variation is partially responsible for the type of treatment setting that is most likely to provide optimal service to the patient. For example, patients with severe cognitive impairments but low severity substance AUD may be best served with a brief intervention approach in a rehabilitation setting, whereas the same person but with more severe AUD may need the services of a specialized program that works with persons with severe cognitive impairments and AUD. A model outlining these cognitive and alcohol use severity parameters was first proposed by Corrigan (Corrigan, 2006). A modified version of the model pertaining to cognition and AUD can be found in Figure 24.1.

The underlying premise for all intervention strategies is to avoid approaches that blame or punish the drinker and focus more on edu-

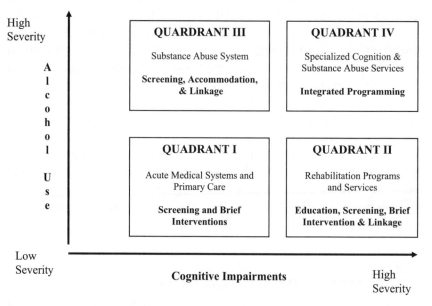

FIGURE 24.1 Cognition and alcohol use disorders.
Adapted from Corrigan (2006).

cation and mutual exploration of behavior change options. There remains an ongoing debate over the goal of alcohol interventions with some clinicians promoting abstinence and others focusing on harm reduction as a means of reducing alcohol-related consequences.

Once alcohol problems have been identified there are several treatment options that have been shown to be effective depending on the severity of the AUD and cognitive impairments. Those with low severity AUD and low to high severity cognitive impairments may benefit from brief interventions that focus on education, linkages with community support systems, behavioral contracting, goal setting, and other behavior modification techniques. In fact, brief interventions have been successful in reducing consumption in 10 to 30% of non-dependent AUD (Fleming, Barry, Manwell, Johnson, & London, 1997). Motivational interviewing techniques have also been shown to be effective with problem drinkers (Miller & Rollnick, 1991).

On the other hand, high severity AUD with low to high severity cognitive impairments may require more specialized intervention where substance abuse is provided in specialized neurorehabilitation programs using communication, behavioral, and learning techniques that have been shown to be helpful to persons with brain injury and illness. By necessity such approaches must account for a patient's self-awareness of their capacities and limitations and their relationship to their use of alcohol. For a comprehensive review of standards for providing substance abuse services to persons with cognitive impairments the reader is referred to the Treatment Improvement Protocol Series Book 29 by the Substance Abuse and Mental Health Services Administration (Miller & Rollnick, 1991; Moore, 1998).

REFERENCES

Adams, W. L., Barry, K. L., & Fleming, M. F. (1996). Screening for problem drinking in older primary care patients. *Journal of the American Medical Association, 276*, 1964–1967.

Adams, W. L., & Cox, N. S. (1995). Epidemiology of problem drinking among elderly people. *International Journal of Addictions, 30*, 1469–1492.

Adams, K. M., Gilman, S., Johnson-Greene, D., Koeppe, R. A., Junck, L., Kluin, K. J., et al. (1998). Significance of family history status in relation to neuropsychological test performance and cerebral glucose metabolism studied with positron emission tomography in older alcoholic patients. *Alcoholism: Clinical and Experimental Research, 22*(1), 105–110.

Adams, K. M., Gilman, S., Koeppe, R. A., Kluin, K. J., Junck, L., & Lohman, M. (1995). Correlation of neuropsychological function with cerebral metabolic rate in subdivisions of the frontal lobes of older alcoholic patients measured with [18f]fluorodeoxyglucose and positron emission tomography. *Neuropsychology, 9,* 275–280.

Adams, K. M., Oilman, S., Koeppe, R. A., Kluin, K. J., Brunberg, J. A., Dede, D., et al. (1993). Neuropsychological deficits are correlated with frontal hypometabolism in positron emission tomography studies of older alcoholic patients. *Alcoholism: Clinical and Experimental Research, 17,* 205–210.

Alanko, T. (1984). An overview of techniques and problems in the measurement of alcohol consumption. *Research Advances in Alcohol and Drug Problems, 8,* 209–226.

Allen, J., Litten, R., Fertig, J., & Babor, T. (1997). A review of research on the alcohol use identification test (audit). *Alcoholism: Clinical and Experimental Research, 21,* 613–619.

Ambrose, M. L., Bowden, S. C., & Whelan, G. (2001). Thiamin treatment and working memory function of alcohol-dependent people: Preliminary findings. *Alcoholism: Clinical and Experimental Research, 25*(1), 112–116.

American Psychiatric Association. (1994). *Diagnostic and statistical manual of mental disorders* (4th ed.). Washington, DC: Author.

Arria, A. M., Tarter, R. E., Starzi, T. E., & Thiel, D.H.V. (1991). Improvement in cognitive functioning of alcoholics following orthotopic liver transplantation. *Alcoholism: Clinical and Experimental Research, 15,* 956–962.

Baker, K., Harding, A., Halliday, G., Kril, J., & Harper, C. (1999). Neuronal loss in functional zones of the cerebellum of chronic alcoholics with and without Wernicke's encephalopathy. *Neuroscience, 91*(2), 429–438.

Babor, T. F., de la Fuente, J. R., Saunders, J., & Grant, M. (1992). AUDIT: *The alcohol use disorders identification test: Guidelines for use in primary health care.* Geneva, Switzerland: World Health Organization.

Bassett, S. S., Chase, G. A., Folstein, M. F., & Reiger, D. A. (1998). Disability and psychiatric disorders in an urban community: Measurement, prevalence, and outcomes. *Psychological Medicine, 28,* 509–517.

Basso, M. R., & Bornstein, R. A. (1999). Neuropsychological deficits in psychotic versus non-psychotic unipolar depression. *Neuropsychology, 13,* 69–75.

Bates, M. E., Bowden, S. C., & Barry, D. (2002). Neurocognitive impairment associated with alcohol use disorders: Implications for treatment. *Experimental and Clinical Psychopharmacology, 10*(3), 193–212.

Blazer, D. (1989). The epidemiology of depression in late life. *Geriatric Psychiatry, 22,* 35–52.

Blow, F. C., Brower, K. J., Schulenberg, J. E., Demo-Dananberg, L. M., Young, J. P., & Beresford, T. P. (1992). The Michigan alcohol screening test—geriatric version (mast-g): A newly elderly-specific screening instrument. *Alcoholism: Clinical and Experimental Research, 16,* 372.

Blum, T. C., Roman, P. M., & Martin, J. K. (1993). Alcohol consumption and work performance. *Journal of Studies on Alcohol, 54*(1), 61–70.

Bombardier, C., & Rimmele, C. (1998). Alcohol use and readiness to change after spinal cord injury. *Archives of Physical Medicine and Rehabilitation, 79,* 1110–1115.

Boone, K. B., Lesser, I. M., Miller, B. L., Wohl, M., Berman, N., Lee, A., et al. (1995). Cognitive functioning in older depressed outpatients: Relationship of presence and severity of depression to neuropsychological test scores. *Neuropsychology, 9,* 390–398.

Booth, B. M., Yates, W. R., & Petty, F. (1991). Patient factors predicting early alcohol-related readmissions for alcoholics: Role of alcoholism severity and psychiatric comorbidity. *Journal of Studies on Alcohol, 52,* 37–43.

Brennan, P. L., Kagay, C. R., Geppert, J. J., & Moos, R. H. (2000). Elderly medicare inpatients with substance use disorders: Characteristics and predictors of hospital readmissions over a four-year interval. *Journal of Studies on Alcohol, 61*(6), 891–895.

Brown, S. A., Inaba, R. K., Gillin, C. J., Schuckit, M. A., Stewart, M. A., & Irwin, M. R. (1995). Alcoholism and affective disorder; clinical course of depressive symptoms. *The American Journal of Psychiatry, 152*(1), 45–52.

Brown, S. A., Irwin, M., & Schuckit, M. A. (1991). Changes in anxiety among abstinent male alcoholics. *Journal of Studies on Alcohol, 52,* 55–61.

Brown, S. A., & Schuckit, M. A. (1988). Changes in depression among abstinent alcoholics. *Journal of Studies on Alcohol, 49,* 412–417.

Bucholz, K. K., Sheline, Y. I., & Helzer, J. E. (1995). *The epidemiology of alcohol use, problems, and dependence in elders: A review.* New York: Oxford University Press.

Cala, L. A., & Mastaglia, F. L. (1981). Computerized tomography in chronic alcoholics. *Alcoholism: Clinical and Experimental Research, 5*(2), 283–294.

Charlifue, S., & Gerhart, K. (1991). Behavioral and demographic predictors of suicide after spinal cord injury. *Archives of Physical Medicine Rehabilitation, 72,* 488–492.

Chermack, S. T., Walton, M. A., Fuller, B. E., & Blow, F. C. (2001). Correlates of expressed and received violence across relationship types among men and women substance abusers. *Psychology of Addictive Behaviors, 15*(2), 140–151.

Christian, J. C., Reed, T., Carmelli, D., Page, W. F., Norton, J. A., Breitner, J. C. S., et al. (1995). Self-reported alcohol intake and cognition in aging twins. *Journal of Studies on Alcohol, 56,* 414–416.

Clarke, R., Shipley, M., & Lewington, S. (1999). Underestimation of risk associations due to regression dilution in long-term follow-up of prospective studies. *American Journal of Epidemiology, 150,* 341–353.

Clay, S. W. (1997). Comparison of audit and cage questionnaires in screening for alcohol use disorders in elderly primary care outpatients. *Journal of the American Osteopathic Association, 10,* 588–592.

Coffey, C. E., Wildinson, W. E., Parashos, L. A., Soady, S. A. R., Sullivan, R. J., Patterson, L. J., et al. (1992). Quantitative cerebral anatomy of the aging human brain: A cross-sectional study using magnetic resonance imaging. *Neurology, 42,* 527–536.

Corrigan, J. (2006). *Personal communication. Four quadrant model of cognitive and AUD services.* Ohio State University.

Corrigan, J. D. (1995). Substance abuse as a mediating factor in outcome from traumatic brain injury. *Archives of Physical Medicine and Rehabilitation, 76,* 302–309.

Corrigan, J. D., Rust, E., & Lamb-Hart, G. (1995). The nature and extent of substance abuse problems in persons with traumatic brain injury. *Journal of Head Trauma Rehabilitation, 10,* 29–46.

Courville, C. B. (1955). *Effects of alcohol in the central nervous system of man.* Los Angeles: San Lucas Press.

Dackis, C. A., Gold, M. S., Pottash, A. L., & Sweeney, D. R. (1986). Evaluating depression in alcoholics. *Psychiatry Research, 17,* 105–109.

Dawson, D. A. (1998). Volume of ethanol consumption: Effects of different approaches to measurement. *Journal of Studies on Alcohol, 59,* 191–197.

Dikmen, S., Donovan, D., Loberg, T., Machmer, J., & Temkin, N. (1993). Alcohol use and its effects on neuropsychological outcome in head injury. *Neuropsychology, 7,* 296–305.

Eckardt, M. J., Rohrbaugh, J. W., Stapleton, J. M., Davis, E. Z., Martin, P. R., & Weingartner, H. J. (1996). Attention-related brain potential and cognition in alcoholism-associated organic brain disorders. *Biological Psychiatry, 39*(2), 143–146.

Elie, M., Cole, M. G., & Primeau, F. J. (1998). Delirium risk factors in elderly hospitalized patients. *Journal of General Internal Medicine, 13,* 204–212.

Ewing, J. A. (1984). Detecting alcoholism: The CAGE questionnaire. *Journal of the American Medical Association, 252,* 1905–1907.

Fauerbach, J. A., Engrav, L., & Kowalske, K. (2001). Barriers to employment among working-aged patients with major burn injury. *Journal of Burn Care Rehabilitation, 22,* 26–34.

Ferguson, R. K., Soryal, I. N., & Pentland, B. (1997). Thimine deficiency in head injury: A missed insult? *Alcohol and Alcoholism, 32*(4), 493–500.

Fink, A., Hays, R. D., Moore, A. A., & Beck, J. C. (1996). Alcohol-related problems on older persons: Determinents, consequences, and screening. *Archives of Internal Medicine, 156,* 1150–1156.

Fleming, M. F., Barry, K. L., Manwell, L. B., Johnson, K., & London, R. (1997). Brief physician advice for problem alcohol drinkers: A randomized controlled trial in community-based primary care practices. *Journal of the American Medical Association, 277,* 1039–1045.

Franke, H., Kittner, H., Berger, P., Wirkner, K., & Schramek, J. (1997). The reaction of astrocytes and neurons in the hippocampus of adult rats during chronic ethanol treatment and correlations to behavioral impairments. *Alcohol and Alcoholism, 14*(5), 445–454.

Freund, G. (1982). The interaction of chronic alcohol consumption and aging on brain structure and function. *Alcoholism Clinical and Experimental Research, 6,* 13–21.

Gentilello, L., Donovan, D., Dunn, C., & Rivera, F. (1995). Alcohol interventions in trauma centers. *Journal of the American Medical Association, 274,* 1043–1048.

Gilman, S., Adams, K., & Koeppe, R. A. (1990). Cerebellar and frontal hypometabolism in alcoholic cerebellar degeneration studies with positron emission tomography. *Annals of Neurology, 28,* 775–785.

Gilman, S., Koeppe, R. A., & Adams, K. M. (1996). Positron emission tomographic studies of cerebral benzodiazapine receptor binding in chronic alcoholics. *Annals of Neurology, 40,* 163–171.

Goldstein, G., Shelly, C., Mascia, G. V. & Tarter, R. E. (1985). Realtionships between neuropsychological and psychopathological dimensions in male alcoholics. *Addictive Behavior, 10,* 365–372.

Gomberg, E.S.L. (1995). *Older women and alcohol use and abuse.* New York: Plenum Press.

Grant, I., Adams, K. A., & Reed, R. (1984). Aging, abstinence, and medical risk factors in the prediction of neuropsychologic deficit among long-term alcoholics. *Archives of General Psychiatry, 41,* 710–718.

Greenfield, L. A. (1998). *Alcohol and crime: An analysis of national data on the prevalence of alcohol involvement in crime. Report prepared for the assistant attorney general's national symposium on alcohol abuse and crime.* Washington, DC: U.S. Department of Justice.

Grobmyer, S. R., Maniscalco, S. P., Purdue, G. F., & Hunt, J. L. (1996). Alcohol, drug intoxication, or both at the time of burn injury as a predictor of complications and mortality in hospitalized patients with burns. *Journal of Burn Care Rehabilitation, 17,* 532–539.

Harding, A., Halliday, G., Caine, D., & Kril, J. (2000). Degeneration of anterior thalamic nuclei differentiates alcoholics with amnesia. *Brain, 1,* 141–154.

Harper, C., & Kril, J. (1989). Patterns of neuronal loss in the cerebral cortex in chronic alcoholic patients. *Journal of Neurological Sciences, 92,* 81–89.

Harper, C., Sheedy, D., Halliday, G., Double, K., Dodd, P., Lewohl, J., et al. (1998). *Neuropathological studies: The relationship between alcohol and aging* (Vol. Monograph 33). Bethesda, MD: U.S. Department of Health and Human Services.

Harper, C. G., & Kril, J. (1991). If you drink your brain will shrink. Neuropathological considerations. *Alcohol and Alcoholism, Suppl 1,* 375–380.

Heinemann, A., Goranson, N., Ginsburg, K., & Schnoll, S. (1989). Alcohol use and activity patterns following spinal cord injury. *Rehabilitation Psychology, 34,* 191–206.

Heinemann, A., Keen, M., Donohue, R., & Schnoll, S. (1988). Alcohol use in persons with recent spinal cord injuries. *Archives of Physical Medicine and Rehabilitation, 69,* 619–624.

Helwig, A. A., & Holicky, R. (1994). Substance abuse in persons with disabilities: Treatment considerations. *Journal of Counseling and Development, 72*(2), 227–233.

Helzer, J. E., & Pryzbeck, T. R. (1988). The co-occurrence of alcoholism with other psychiatric disorders in the general population and its impact on treatment. *Journal of Studies on Alcohol, 49,* 219–224.

Herrera, D. G., Yague, A. G., Johnson-Soriano, S., Bosch-Morell, F., Collado-Morente, L., Muriach, M., et al. (2003). Selective impairment of hippocampal neurogenesis by chronic alcoholism: Protective effects of an antioxidant. *Proceedings of the National Academy of Sciences, 100*(13), 7919–7924.

Hesselbrock, M. M., Hesselbrock, V. M., Tenmen, H., Meyer, R. E., & Workman, K. L. (1983). Methodological considerations in the assessment of depression in alcoholics. *Journal of Consulting and Clinical Psychology, 51,* 399–405.

Higgins, J. P., Wright, S. W., & Wrenn, K. D. (1996). Alcohol, the elderly, and motor vehicle crashes. *American Journal of Emergency Medicine, 14,* 265–267.

Holroyd, S., & Currie, L. (1997). A descriptive study of elderly community-dwelling alcoholic patients in the rural south. *American Journal of Geriatric Psychiatry, 5,* 221–228.

Holroyd, S., & Duryee, J. J. (1997). Substance use disorders in a geriatric psychiatry outpatient clinic: Prevalence and epidemiologic characteristics. *American Journal of Geriatric Psychiatry, 5,* 221–228.

Horner, M. D., Waid, L. R., Johnson, D. E., Latham, P. K., & Anton, R. F. (1999). The relationship of cognitive functioning to amount of recent and lifetime alcohol consumption in outpatient alcoholics. *Addictive Behaviors, 24*(3), 449.

Jernigan, T. L., Butters, N., DiTriaglia, G., Schafer, K., Smith, T., Irwin, M., et al. (1991). Reduced cerebral grey matter observed in alcoholics using magnetic resonance imaging. *Alcoholism Clinical and Experimental Research, 15,* 418–427.

Jernigan, T. L., Schafer, K., Butters, N., & Cermak, L. S. (1991). Magnetic resonance imaging of alcoholic korsakoff's patients. *Neuropsychopharmacology, 4,* 175–186.

Johnson-Greene, D., Adams, K. M., Gilman, S., Kluin, K., Junck, L., Martorello, S., et al. (1997a). Impaired upper limb coordination in alcoholic cerebellar degeneration. *Archives of Neurology, 54,* 436–439.

Johnson-Greene, D., Adams, K. M., Gilman, S., Koeppe, R. A., Kluin, K., Junck, L., et al. (1997b). Effects of abstinence and relapse upon neuropsychological function and cerebral glucose metabolism in severe chronic alcoholism. *Journal of Clinical and Experimental Neuropsychology, 22,* 378–385.

Johnson-Greene, D., Adams, K. M., Gilman, S., &, Junck, L. (2002). Relationship between neuropsychological and emotional functioning in severe chronic alcoholism. *The Clinical Neuropsychologist, 16,* 300–309.

Jurkovich, G. J., Rivera, F. P., Gurney, J. G., Seguin, D., Fligner, C. L., & Copass, M. (1992). Effects of alcohol intoxication on the initial assessment of trauma patients. *Annals of Emergency Medicine, 21,* 704–708.

Kaplan, C., & Corrigan, J. (1992). Effect of blood alcohol level on recovery from severe closed head injury. *Brain Injury, 6,* 337–349.

Kelley, D., & Lynch, J. (1992). Burns in alcohol and drug users result in longer treatment times with more complications. *Journal of Burn Care Rehabilitation, 13,* 218–220.

Kessler, R. C., Foster, C., Webster, P. S., & House, J. S. (1992). The relationship between age and depressive symptoms in two national surveys. *Psychological Aging, 7,* 119–126.

King, D. A., Cox, C., & Lyness, J. M. (1995). Neuropsychological effects of depression and age in an elderly sample: A confirmatory study. *Neuropsychology, 9,* 399–408.

King, G. D., Caine, E. D., & Cox, C. (1993). Influence of depression and age on selected cognitive functions. *Clinical Neuropsychologist, 7,* 443–453.

Kiwerski, J., & Krasuski, M. (1992). Influence of alcohol intake on the course and consequences of spinal cord injury. *International Journal of Rehabilitation Research, 15,* 240–245.

Koenig, H. G., Meador, K. G., Shelp, F., Goli, V., Cohen, H. J., & Blazer, D. G. (1991). Major depressive disorder in hospitalized medically ill patients: An examination of young and elderly male veterans. *Journal of the American Geriatrics Society, 39,* 881–890.

Krahn, D., Freese, J., Hauser, R., Barry, K., & Goodman, B. (2003). Alcohol use and cognition at mid-life: The importance of adjusting for baseline cognitive ability and educational attainment. *Alcoholism: Clinical and Experimental Research, 27*(7), 1162–1166.

Kril, J. J., & Harper, C. G. (1989). Neuronal counts from four cortical regions of alcoholic brains. *Acta Neuropathologica, 79,* 200–204.

Kuschner, M. G., Sher, K. J., & Beitman, B. D. (1990). The relation between alcohol problems and the anxiety disorders. *American Journal of Psychology, 147,* 685–695.

Langer, K. G. (1994). Depression in disabling illness: Severity and patterns of self-reported symptoms in three groups. *Journal of Geriatric Psychiatry and Neurology, 7,* 121–128.

Leonard, K. E., & Rothbard, J. C. (1999). Alcohol and the marriage effect. *Journal of Studies on Alcohol, 13*(Suppl. 13), 139–146.

Leuchter, A. F., Dunkin, J. J., Lufkin, R. B., Anzai, Y., Cook, I. A., & Newton, T. F. (1994). Effect of white matter disease on functional connections in the aging brain. *Journal of Neurology Neurosurgery and Psychiatry, 57,* 1347–1354.

Lishman, W. A. (1990). Alcohol and the brain. *British Journal of Psychiatry, 156,* 635–644.

Loberg, T. (1981). Mmpi-based personality subtypes of alcoholics. *Journal of Studies on Alcohol, 42,* 766–782.

McGlinchey-Berroth, R., Cermak, L. S., Carrillo, M. C., Armfield, S., Gabrieli, J. D. E., & Disterhoft, J. F. (1995). Impaired delay eyeblink conditioning in amnesic korsakoff's patients and recovered alcoholics. *Alcoholism: Clinical and Experimental Research, 19,* 1127–1132.

Merikangas, K. R., & Gelernter, C. S. (1990). Comorbidity for alcoholism and depression. *Psychiatric Clinics of North America, 13*, 613–632.

Miller, W. R., & Brown, S. (1997). Why psychologists should treat alcohol and drug problems. *American Psychologist, 52*, 1269–1279.

Miller, W. R., & Rollnick, S. (1991). *Motivational interviewing*. New York: Guilford Press.

Moore, D. (1998). *Substance use disorder treatment for persons with physical and cognitive disabilities. Treatment improvement protocol series 29*. Rockville, MD: U.S. Department of Health and Human Services.

Moore, D., & Li, L. (1994). Substance abuse among consumers for vocational rehabilitation services. *Journal of Rehabilitation, 38*(2), 124–133.

Mulsant, B. H., & Ganguli, M. (1999). Epidemiology and diagnosis of depression in late life. *Journal of Clinical Psychiatry, 60*(suppl 20), 9–15.

Noel, X., Sferrazza, R., Linden, M. V. D., Paternot, J., Verhas, M., Hanak, C., et al. (2002). Contribution of frontal cerebral blood flow measured by 99mtc-bicisate spect and executive function deficits to predicting treatment outcome in alcohol-dependent patients. *Alcohol and Alcoholism, 37*(4), 347–354.

Oscar-Berman, M., & Marinkovic, K. (2003a). Alcoholism and the brain: An overview. *Alcohol Research and Health, 27*(2), 125–133.

Oscar-Berman, M., & Marinkovic, K. (2003b). Alcoholism and the brain: An overview. *Alcoholism: Clinical and Experimental Research, 27*(2), 125–133.

Oslin, D. W., Streim, J. E., Parmelee, P., Boyce, A. A., & Katz, I. R. (1997). Alcohol abuse: A source of reversible functional disability among residents of a VA nursing home. *International Journal of Geriatric Psychiatry, 12*, 825–832.

Overall, J. E., Reilly, E. L., Kelley, J. T., & Hollister, L. E. (1985). Persistence of depression in detoxified alcoholics. *Alcoholism: Clinical and Experimental Research, 9*, 331–333.

Parikh, R. M., Lipsey, J. R., Robinson, R. G., & Price, T. R. (1990). Post-stroke depression: Impact on daily living over two years. *Archives of Neurology, 47*, 785–790.

Parsons, O. A. (1993). Impaired neuropsychological cognitive functioning in sober alcoholics. In W. A. Hunt & S. J. Nixon (Eds.), *Alcohol-induced brain damage* (Vol. Research Monograph 22, pp. 173–194). Rockville, MD: National Institute on Alcohol Abuse and Alcoholism.

Pfefferbaum, A., Lim, K. O., Zipursky, R. B., Mathalon, D. H., Rosenbloom, M. J., Lane, B., et al. (1992). Brain grey and white matter volume loss accelerates with aging in chronic alcoholics: A quantitative MRI study. *Alcoholism Clinical and Experimental Research, 16*, 1078–1089.

Pfefferbaum, A., Sullivan, E. V., Mathalon, D. H., & Lim, K. O. (1997). Frontal lobe volume loss observed with magnetic ressonance imaging in older chronic alcoholics. *Alcoholism: Clinical and Experimental Research, 21*, 521–529.

Poon, E., Ellis, D. A., Fitzgerald, H. E., & Zucker, R. A. (2000). Intellectual, cognitive, and academic performance among sons of alcoholics during the early school years: Differences related to subtypes of familial alcoholism. *Alcoholism: Clinical and Experimental Research, 24*(7), 1020–1027.

Rehm, J. (1998). Measuring quantity, frequency, and volume of drinking. *Alcoholism: Clinical and Experimental research, 22,* 4–14S.

Reid, M. C., & Anderson, P. A. (1997). Geriatric substance abuse disorders. *Medical Clinics of North America, 81,* 999–1016.

Rivara, F., Jurkovich, G., Gurney, J., Seguin, D., Flinger, C., Ries, R., et al. (1993). The magnitude of acute and chronic alcohol abuse in trauma patients. *Archives of Surgery, 128,* 907–913.

Rohling, M. L., Green, P. A., & Iverson, G. L. (2003). Depressive symptoms and neurocognitive test scores in patients passing symptom validity tests. *Archives of Clinical Neuropsychology, 17,* 205–222.

Ross, H. E., Glaser, F. B., & Germanson, T. (1988). The prevalence of psychiatric disorders in patients with alcohol and other drug problems. *Archives of General Psychiatry, 45,* 1023–1031.

Substance Abuse and Mental Health Services Administration. (1998). Substance abuse among older adults: Treatment improvement protocol (tip) series 26. Department of Health and Human Services. Rockville, MD: U.S. Government Printing Office

Schuckit, M. A., & Hesselbrock, V. (1994). Alcohol dependence and anxiety disorders: What is the relationship? *American Journal of Psychiatry, 15,* 1723–1734.

Schuckit, M. A., Hesselbrock, V. M., Tipp, J., Nurnberger, J. I., Anthenelli, R. M., & Crowe, R. R. (1995). The prevalence of major anxiety disorders in relatives of alcohol dependent men and women. *Journal of Studies on Alcohol, 56,* 309–317.

Schuckit, M. A., Irwin, M., & Brown, S. A. (1990). The history of anxiety symptoms among 171 primary alcoholics. *Journal of Studies on Alcohol, 51*(1), 34–41.

Schuckit, M. A., Irwin, M., & Smith, T. L. (1994). One-year incidence rate of major depression and other psychiatric disorders in 239 alcoholic men. *Addiction (Abingdon, England), 89,* 441–445.

Sclafani, V. D., Ezekial, F., Myerhoff, D. J., MacKay, S., Dillon, W. P., & Weiner, M. W. (1995). Brain atrophy and cognitive function in older abstinent men. *Alcoholism: Clinical and Experimental Research, 19*(5), 1121–1126.

Selzer, M. (1971). The Michigan alcohol screening test. *American Journal of Psychiatry, 127,* 1653–1658.

Selzer, M., Vinokur, A., & Rooijen, L. V. (1975). A self-administered short Michigan alcoholism screening test (smast). *Journal of Studies on Alcohol, 36,* 127–132.

Sinyor, D., Amato, P., & Kaloupek, D. (1986). Post-stroke depression: Relationship to functional impairment, coping strategies, and rehabilitation outcome. *Stroke, 17,* 1102–1107.

Smith, J. W. (1995). Medical manifestations of alcoholism in the elderly. *International Journal of Addictions, 30,* 1749–1798.

Soderstrom, C., Smith, G., Dischinger, P., McDuff, D., Hebel, J., Golick, D., et al. (1997). Psychoactive substance abuse disorders among seriously injured trauma center patients. *Journal of the American Medical Association, 277,* 1769–1774.

Spitzer, L., Endicott, J., & Robins, E. (1975). Clinical criteria for psychiatric diagnosis, DSM-III. *American Journal of Psychiatry, 132,* 1187–1192.

Sullivan, E. V., Rosenbloom, M. J., Lim, K. O., & Pfefferbaum, A. (2000). Longitudinal changes in cognition, gait, and balance in abstinent and relapsed alcoholic men: Relationships to changes in brain structure. *Neuropsychology, 14,* 178–188.

Sullivan, E. V., Rosenbloom, M. J., & Pfefferbaum, A. (2000). Pattern of motor and cognitive deficits in detoxified alcoholic men. *Alcoholism: Clinical and Experimental Research, 24*(5), 611–621.

Tarter, R. E., Hegedus, A., Goldstein, G., Shelly, C., & Alterman, A. (1993). Learning and memory capacity in sons of alcoholic men. *American Journal of Addictions, 2,* 219–224.

Turner, R. J., & Noh, S. (1988). Physical disability and depression: Longitudinal analysis. *Journal of Health and Social Behavior, 29,* 23–37.

Turner, R. J., & Wood, D. W. (1978). Depression and disability: The stress process in a chronically strained population. *Research in Community Mental Health, 5,* 46–51.

Volkow, N. D., Hitzeman, R., & Wang, G.-J. (1992). Decreased brain metabolism in neurologically intact healthy alcoholics. *American Journal of Psychiatry, 149*(8), 1016–1022.

Weisman, M. M., Meyers, J. K., & Harding, P. S. (1980). Prevalence and psychiatric heterogeneity of alcoholism in united states urban community. *Journal of Studies on Alcohol, 41,* 672–681.

Weiss, K. J., & Rosenberg, D. J. (1985). Prevalence of anxiety disorder among alcoholics. *Journal of Clinical Psychiatry, 46,* 3–5.

Westbrook, M. T., & Viney, L. L. (1982). Psychological reactions to the onset of chronic illness. *Social Science and Medicine, 16,* 899–905.

White, A. M., Matthews, D. B., & Best, P. J. (2000). Ethanol, memory, and hippocampal function: A review of recent findings. *Hippocampus, 10,* 88–93.

Wiggins, R. C., Gorman, A., Rolsten, C., Samorajski, T., Ballinger, W. E. J., & Freund, G. (1988). Effects of aging and alcohol on the biochemical composition of histologically normal human brain. *Metabolism and Brain Disease, 3,* 67–80.

25

Neuropsychological Assessment of Toxic Exposures

RAYMOND SINGER

INTRODUCTION

NEUROTOXICITY DESCRIBES THE harmful effects of toxic substances on the nervous system. All parts and aspects of the nervous system are susceptible to neurotoxicity, including the central and peripheral nerves, the brain, sensory organs, autonomic function, motor function, neurochemical processes, cognition, emotion, conation, perception, personality, and so forth. Neuropsychologists are the best qualified professionals to assess functional effects of neurotoxic substances, due to their comprehensive background in function of the entire nervous system function and their specialized training and experience in assessment.

Exceedingly few commercial products have been adequately tested prior to marketing for their potential to cause neurotoxic injuries (Kilburn, 1998; Singer, 1990a). In 1976, it was estimated that more than 1,000 new compounds were being developed each year and added to the approximately 40,000 chemicals and 2,000,000 mixtures already in industrial use (Environmental Protection Agency [EPA], 1976). Most commercial substances have not even been examined for neurotoxicity (Williams et al., 1987).

More than 850 chemicals have been identified as producers of neu-robehavioral disorders (Anger & Johnson, 1985). Most of these chemicals fall into the categories of solvents, pesticides, and metals. Workplace regulations were set for 200 chemicals in part because of neurotoxic-ity. Regulations may underestimate the risk from neurotoxic chemi-cals, as the effects of chronic exposure to low levels of neurotoxicants are often unrecognized.

However, the scientific literature is replete with reports of the neu-rotoxicity of common substances, such as carbon monoxide and other asphyxiants, pesticides, some herbicides (Singer, Moses, Valciukas, Lilis, & Selikoff, 1982), fumigants, solvents, and some metals. Many sub-stances are known to be neurotoxic based on clinical experience, case reports, epidemiologic studies, and animal testing.

The number of people with significant neurotoxic chemical expo-sures and potential chemical brain injuries remains very high and uncharted. Factors affecting neurotoxic outcomes include exposure levels, duration of exposure over levels of exposure, and host factors such as gender; age; race; prior function of the immune, hepatic, and renal systems; prior neurotoxic chemical exposures; concomitant expo-sures; possible additive or synergistic effects of all of these factors, and so forth. In the final analysis, the clinical judgment of the neuropsy-chologist must be relied upon to reach an accurate diagnosis.

Every person touched by modern civilization is at risk of significant chemical exposure and neurotoxicity. Significant neurotoxic injury may result from occupational exposures in such diverse occupations as insurance office personnel (Singer, 1997a), automobile sales managers (Singer, 1997a), dentists (Singer, 1995), electrical products (transformer) salvage (Singer, 1994), herbicide workers (Singer et al., 1982), postal workers (Singer, 1985), and soldiers (Sloyan 1996a, 1996b).

Even if a person does not work, they may suffer neurotoxicity from use of consumer products (Singer, 1996a), prescription drugs (Singer, 1997b; 1997c), medical devices (Singer, 1996b), drinking water at home (Singer, 1990b), or drinking beverages at a restaurant (Singer, 2000).

Simply going to school can be hazardous for both students and teachers (Singer, 1999a) if your school district is repairing the roof of your school while school is in session. Or, when trying to get away from the pressures of modern life and building a life in a beautiful rural county, one can be exposed to a witch's brew of human and industrial waste called sewage sludge. Municipalities can pay your neighbor to accept sewage sludge, thus creating a hazardous dump for your neigh-borhood (Singer, 1999b).

Pesticides are especially promiscuous in their targets. Even if a per-son does not work or consume, they may live in or enter a structure with pesticide over-application, or be drizzled by pesticide drift when walking down a country lane, or sitting in their rocking chair on their front porch, or sleeping in their bed in an agricultural area (Singer, 1999c).

A product as seemingly innocuous as carbonless copy paper can cause relentless neurotoxicity when it is amassed in large quantities in an office, under poor ventilation conditions, and with lengthy exposure time periods (Singer, 1998).

Living very far from industrialization may not always provide protection from hazardous chemical products: the highest blood levels of the neurotoxic polychlorinated biphenyl (PCB) have been found among the Inuit (Eskimo) people of Baffin Island, near the Arctic circle, thousands of miles from where PCB is used. Due to various atmospheric processes, industrial effluent discharged into the air in the tropics can collect in the North and South Poles (Lean, 1996).

Once neurotoxic chemicals have been used in manufacture and production of consumer goods, and the product is stabilized, this does not mean that we are forever safe from its reach. For example, neurotoxic substances can be released by fire, as found in the wake of the World Trade Center attack, with high levels of neurotoxic substances such as benzene, dioxin, metals, and other substances being discharged at ground zero into the air and water (Gonzales, 2001). Currently, a number of people exposed to debris from this attack are complaining of nervous system symptoms.

When people are hurt by neurotoxic products, they have the judicial right to demand compensation for their injuries. These matters are often brought to court for adjudication. The forensic neurotoxicologist and neuropsychologist will be called upon to help the judge and jury understand the nature and extent of possible nervous system injury.

With that in mind, let us now examine the common symptoms of neurotoxicity.

SYMPTOMS OF NEUROTOXICITY

THE RESIDUAL NEUROBEHAVIORAL symptoms of neurotoxicity from various substances are similar (Singer, 1990a) and form what I term the *neurotoxicity syndrome*, as virtually all neurotoxic substances have the same core residual outcomes,[1] including:

1. Cognitive changes

    a. Attentional dysfunction, concentration difficulties: The affected person reports difficulty with keeping his mind in focus. His thoughts may drift and seem fuzzy, with increased susceptibility to distraction.

b. Learning dysfunction, due to disruption of memory processes, often sparing memory traces prior to exposure and onset of illness. This symptom affects short-term memory.

c. Cognitive and psychomotor slowing, which may be described by the subject as confusion or "brain fog."

2. Personality changes

a. Irritability: Reduction of cognitive and emotional capacities from neurotoxicity can be frustrating and perplexing, resulting in irritability and anger. The subject may report frequent strife with family members, friends, and coworkers, or difficulty conforming to norms.

b. Increased sadness, depression, crying. Helplessness and hopelessness can result from disabilities developing from neurotoxic injuries.

c. Social withdrawal often occurs as the person becomes increasingly frustrated with his disabilities. He may feel that people are staring at or scrutinizing him. Word dysfluency often is present. Personality testing often indicates avoidant personality disorder, as the person withdraws from an active social life. Withdrawal and avoidance may also result from multiple chemical sensitivity, a symptom that often accompanies neurotoxicity.

3. Disturbance of executive function: Difficulty with planning, multitasking, organizing, assessing outcomes, and changing plans accordingly. Coupled with anger, this disturbance can result in criminal behavior. Neuropsychologists are increasingly called upon by courts to help assess the impact of neurotoxicants on a criminal defendant's sanity and his ability to form a reasonable intention to commit a crime. The crime can include serious offenses such as felonious robbery, embezzlement, and murder.

4. Sleep disturbance: Choppy sleep patterns, frequent awakening. Disruption of endocrine and hormonal systems, as well as other autonomic functions, can occur with neurotoxicity. Sleep disturbance contributes to memory disruption, learning dysfunction, and chronic fatigue.

5. Chronic fatigue: Subjects may report that they are always tired, with reduced ability to lift, carry, climb stairs, walk distances, stay awake, and conduct activities of daily living.

6. Headache, which may be diagnosed as migraine, cluster, tension, or other types.

7. Sexual dysfunction: Males may have difficulty achieving or main-taining an erection. In both genders, there is usually reduced desire for sexual activities. This outcome is a combined effect of central, autonomic, and peripheral neurotoxicity, as well as fatigue, emotional dysfunction (i.e., irritability), or self-concept issues resulting from neurotoxically induced disabilities.

8. Numbness in the hands or feet (depends upon the substance). Some neurotoxic agents damage peripheral nerves. Nerves that have very long axons, such as nerves that serve the feet (and the hands to a lesser extent), are more susceptible to damage from neurotoxic agents. Disruption of the peripheral nervous system may be described by the patient as numbness, tingling, "pins and needles" sensation, or a feeling that the limb "falls asleep."

9. Multiple chemical sensitivity (MCS). A discussion of this topic is beyond the scope of this chapter. However, there is extensive literature on this topic, including original research on World War II German nerve gas workers (Spiegelberg, 1961) demonstrating symptoms of MCS, attributed by the author to neurotoxic symptoms, in workers exposed in the 1940s.

Other frequent symptoms include:

1. Motor dysfunction (tremor, reduced dexterity, etc.). This symptom may be expressed as difficulty in walking or handling tools and can progress to severe motor loss. Neurotoxicity may be misdiagnosed as multiple sclerosis (Singer, 1996a), "MS-like" disease (Singer, 1990b), amyotrophic lateral sclerosis, opsoclonos or myoclonos, seizures, and other diseases affecting the neuromotor system.

2. Sensory-perceptual disturbances: Blindness, hearing loss, pain, burning sensations, and kinesthetic dysfunction are examples of sensory disturbance that can occur with neurotoxicity. If the peripheral and central nervous system degenerate, the nerves have reduced ability to transmit accurate information to the central nervous system. Any sensory system can be affected to the point of system failure.

Less common outcomes of neurotoxicity include panic disorder (Singer, 2002) and suicide (Singer, 2006).

Virtually any neurological disease can be caused by neurotoxicity, as neurotoxic chemicals can damage any part of the brain and nervous system. For example, there have been a number of recent reports associating Parkinson's disease with neurotoxicity, including Ascherio et al. (2006).

SCOPE OF NEUROTOXICITY

THE MAIN CLASSES of neurotoxic substances include pesticides, solvents, some metals, and gases such as carbon monoxide. Pesticides are perhaps the most egregious neurotoxic offender, developed specifically to attack the nervous system (Ecobichon & Joy, 1982). A common pesticide type, organophosphates, were originally designed for use as chemical warfare agents, then later adapted or scaled down to kill insects—yet they have not lost their human toxicity.

EXPOSURE OF AGRICULTURAL WORKERS TO PESTICIDES

PESTICIDES ARE A very significant commercial product. Approximately 1 billion pounds of pesticides are used annually in agriculture in the United States, costing $5 billion, with potential exposure of agricultural workers such as farm field workers, pesticide applicators, food transporters, and food storage personnel (Office of Technology Assessment [OTA], 1990).

An estimated 5 million Americans farm as a primary source of income. Farms often employ children under the age of 16. Three million workers in the United States are migrant and seasonal agricultural workers, and there are an additional estimated 1 million certified pesticide handlers (OTA, 1990).

The estimated prevalence of pesticide poisoning in the United States is 300,000 cases, only 1–2% of which are reported (OTA, 1990). Estimated prevalence rates need to account for the low rate of identification of pesticide neurotoxicity, as few clinicians are trained to diagnose neurotoxicity. Cases of neurotoxicity (1) may not come to the attention of health care workers, (2) may be dismissed without a diagnosis, and (3) may be diagnosed as psychiatric or neurologic disorders, without awareness of the cause of the illness.

EXAMPLES OF NEUROTOXIC PESTICIDES

ORGANOPHOSPHATE AND CARBAMATE pesticides are widely used. Because of their rapid toxicity, they are the most common cause of acute pesticide poisoning. These pesticides affect insects and humans by interfering with the biochemistry of nerve transmission. Acute symptoms can include hyperactivity, breathing difficulties, sweating, tearing, urinary frequency, abnormal heartbeat, anxiety, gastrointestinal disturbance, weakness, dizziness, convulsions, coma, and death. Typical organophosphorus pesticides include Parathion, Thimet, EPN, chlorpyrifos, Dursban, DDVP, and Vapona. Carbamate pesticides include aldicarb, Temik, carbaryl, and Sevin (OTA, 1990).

Organochlorine pesticides are less acutely toxic than organophosphate and carbamate pesticides, but they have a greater potential for chronic toxicity due to their persistence in the environment and in the affected person's body. From 1940 through the 1970s, several organochlorine pesticides were widely used, including DDT, aldrin, mirex, lindane, chlordane, and heptachlor. Chlordane, introduced in 1947, was banned in 1978 for most uses except termite control (OTA, 1990). Chlordane is highly persistent and has an estimated half-life of 20 years.

Pyrethroids are a group of insecticides that are highly toxic to insects but less toxic to humans than the organophosphate and organochlorine pesticides. They are replacing the more toxic pesticides.

Fumigants are gases used to kill insects (including termites) and their eggs and are the most acutely toxic pesticides used in agriculture. Methyl bromide is a particularly problematic pesticide, as it is colorless, almost odorless, and relatively inexpensive. It has caused death and severe neurotoxic effects in fumigators, applicators, and structural pest control workers (exterminators) (OTA, 1990).

Neurotoxic herbicides include 2,4-D; 2,4,5-T; MCPA; and Silvex. Although EPA suspended some of their uses, they continue to be used widely in forest management and weed control in agricultural and urban settings, including children's soccer fields. These herbicides may be contaminated with dioxins (TCDD; OTA, 1990).

NONAGRICULTURAL EXPOSURE TO PESTICIDES

IN ADDITION TO the $5 billion spent annually on agricultural pesticides, $2 billion is spent annually on nonagricultural pesticide products (OTA, 1990). Pesticides used to control termites, cockroaches, and other household insects usually have human neurotoxic potential. The elderly, adults, and children are exposed to these substances in environments including the home, school, public and private offices, restaurants and other public stores, and public parks. The person being exposed is almost always unaware that an exposure is occurring, nor is there awareness of the potential for neurotoxicity. Additional exposures to pesticides and herbicides can occur during chemical treatment of lawns, golf courses, and playing fields. With overexposure, neither the person nor their doctor would have sufficient understanding of the cause of their illness. In addition, brain damage is cumulative, so effects can be subtle but ultimately debilitating.

PESTICIDE RESIDUE IN FOODS

AN ESTIMATED 17% of the preschool population in the United States is exposed to neurotoxic pesticides in food above levels the Federal government has declared as safe (National Resources Defense Council [NRDC], 1989; OTA, 1990). This analysis was based upon raw fruits and vegetables alone and does not consider other sources of pesticide exposure. Children are considered to be more at risk of neurotoxicity than adults, because they absorb more pesticides per pound of body weight; their immature development makes them less able to detoxify substances; and their nervous system is developing and may be more vulnerable to permanent disruption (OTA, 1990).

Pesticides banned for use in the United States can return to the food supply via produce from other countries with fewer regulations. For example, DDT, which was banned in the United States many years prior, could still be found in foods sold in the United States (NRDC, 1984; General Accounting Office [GAO], 1989a). This phenomena has been termed "banned pesticide rebound." Pesticides may be overapplied by applicators who have difficulty reading the manufacturer's instructions, which may only be available in English. The U.S. Food and Drug Administration is too short-staffed to adequately monitor the pesticide status of imported food (GAO, 1989b).

Pesticides can also contaminate water supplies. Highly persistent pesticides, such as aldicarb, have been found in groundwater supplies (Barrette, 1988).

EFFECTS OF BOTH ACUTE AND CHRONIC LOW-LEVEL EXPOSURE TO PESTICIDES AND OTHER NEUROTOXIC SUBSTANCES

THE EFFECTS OF chronic exposure to pesticides may be difficult to detect for a number of reasons.

1. *Unawareness of exposure.*
2. *Accumulation of neurotoxicity.* Dead brain cells are not replaced, so many of the functional deficits caused by damage to the brain and spinal cord are permanent (Aguayo, 1987).
3. *Potential for neurotoxicity to cause Alzheimer's disease (AD) and other degenerative nervous system conditions.* Determination of the possible relationship between neurotoxic chemical exposure and such neural diseases as senile dementia, AD, and similar diagnostic categories, are hampered by the delayed or cumulative effects of neurotoxicants. We are now aware that some diseases, such as cancer from asbestos exposure, may take 20

years to develop. Without careful study, the causal connection of asbestos and cancer could have been overlooked. Degenerative brain disease could have a long latency period after exposure has occurred.

The relationship between dementia and neurotoxicity has been discussed by Butler (1987), former head of the National Institute of Aging. Function of the central nervous system provides a primary marker of aging. Neurotoxic damage to the central nervous system tends to be irreversible and cumulative. Neurotoxic damage is not all-or-nothing; neurotoxic nervous system deterioration is produced on a continuum.

Some scientists have theorized that AD and other neurological and neuropsychological conditions may be due to exposure to environmental toxic substances occurring years before the onset of the disease. Spencer et al. (1987) have linked an environmental (food) chemical exposure, occurring many years earlier with no apparent effects, with neural disease occurring later, specifically amyotrophic lateral sclerosis, Parkinson's disease (PD), and dementia, and thought that other environmental chemicals may also act as triggers for neuronal death. Although damage may remain subclinical for several decades, it may make those affected especially prone to the consequences of age-related neuronal attrition (Lewin, 1987). Arezzo and Schaumburg (1989) also suggested that neurotoxic damage early in life can enhance central nervous system dysfunction that occurs late in life, such as PD.

Current thinking indicates that degenerative disease such as AD and PD actually are the same with different symptoms (Calne, McGeer, Eisen, & Spencer, 1986). Perl, Olanow, and Calne (1998) wrote that "a considerable amount of evidence demonstrates that these disorders share common clinical and neuropathologic features and that overlap between the two conditions is extensive. For example, a significant percentage of AD patients exhibit extrapyramidal features, and many PD patients develop dementia. Similarly, at autopsy many AD patients not only exhibit the neuropathologic features of that disorder but also exhibit nigral pathology, including Lewy bodies. The vast majority of demented PD patients show widespread neurofibrillary tangles and senile plaques as well as Lewy body formation and nigral degeneration. The extent of such overlap is far greater than one would anticipate by chance alone…[reflecting] a common pathogenic mechanism for the neurodegeneration encountered within specific vulnerable neuronal populations.

Furthermore, we suggest that the current nosologic approach, which attempts to separate AD from PD, fails to properly deal with the issue of overlap and that a new classification of the neurodegenerative disorders should be considered."

Chemically induced neurological disorders are often virtually indistinguishable from other causes of disease, suggesting the possibility that environmental chemicals mimic the action of metabolically generated chemical substances circulating in the blood. The decline of neurologic integrity associated with the aging process might be linked with the cumulative effects of endogenous or exogenous poisons (Williams et al., 1987).

4. *Difficulties for detection of neurotoxicity by the untrained observer.* Mental deterioration from exposure to low levels of neurotoxic chemicals may not be noticed by the person, because (1) the brain lacks the ability to detect pain resulting from brain cell death or injury, so therefore lacks sensitivity to destruction of brain tissue itself; and (2) mental deterioration often occurs in small increments, so that gradual and subtle change is difficult to notice. Over time, such gradual decrements can cause significant decline in mental function. As the person's mental processes deteriorate, he is less able to use logic, perception, memory, and other mental processes to determine the extent or cause of mental deterioration.

5. *Lack of knowledge.* Doctors are often unaware of the acute effects of pesticides and other neurotoxic substances and are usually unaware of chronic or residual effects of pesticides or neurotoxic substances in general. Acute exposure to neurotoxic agents also may have a delayed effect, which further confounds the ability of the physician to determine the cause of subsequent neurobehavioral deterioration.

ELEMENTS OF THE NEUROPSYCHOLOGICAL ASSESSMENT FOR NEUROTOXICITY

Symptoms

Perhaps the most important element of the neuropsychological evaluation for neurotoxicity is the detection and assessment of symptoms. The examiner should assess for the presence of a constellation of symptoms characteristic of neurotoxicity. An instrument that I have found helpful is the *Neurotoxicity Screening Survey* (Singer 1990a, 1990c), which quantifies the frequency and severity of neurotoxicity symptoms in 10 factors. This instrument also aids in determining the onset of symptoms relative to the person's chemical exposure, as it helps assesses the extent to which the subject may have had similar symptoms prior to exposure (confounding factors). It also has a measure of symptom distortion, so that the examiner can determine if the subject is over-reporting symptoms. (One reason why examinees may over-report symptoms is confusion.) Of course, neuropsychologists do not rely upon symptoms alone for diagnosing, as this method can be unreliable.

INTERVIEW

THE INTERVIEW PROVIDES an opportunity to take or clarify the examinee's history, as well as assess his overall neuropsychological condition. With careful observation, useful information can emerge regarding the degree of the subject's ability and willingness to accurately report symptoms. Although neuropsychologists are often eager to detect malingering, it is also important to assess under-reporting of symptoms, which frequently occurs. People with memory problems may forget to report some of their symptoms.

To help keep a record of the interview, behavioral observations can be recorded on an extended checklist, such as that provided by Zuckerman (2000). A head and shoulder photograph for the case records can help refresh the expert's memory if testimony is needed.

Collateral interviews can help an examiner review the consistency of the examinee's symptoms and history with other's observations of the examinee (Sbordone, 2000). Consistency or discrepancy are important factors in determining the reliability (and veracity) of self-reported symptoms, and so forth. Examiners can interview members of the family and the household to obtain their perspective on the examinee's neuropsychological function, including possible disabilities, and to help determine the impact of the illness on family members. In addition to close family and cohabitors, interviews or statements of employers, clergy, and long-time friends can be helpful.

HISTORICAL RECORDS

RECORDS HELPFUL FOR diagnoses include records of exposure, any records of exposure levels, past and present employment supervisor records, all medical records (prior to onset of illness to current time), military records, and any other records or documents of past level of achievement, including academic, artistic, and athletic documents.

In order to know if the person has suffered a decline in function on neuropsychological tests, it is important to develop numerical criteria for the expected, premorbid level of function. To develop this pre-exposure criterion of cognitive function, pre-exposure record examination may include records of all educational and scholastic activities; any standardized tests; military service; evidence of intellectual achievement, such as papers, patents, and so forth. These materials can be used to both quantify overall prior mental function and to determine specific levels of cognitive function in various cognitive, perceptual, and emotional domains. Supervisor and other work records are often helpful for this purpose.

In addition, demographic equations can be used to predict premorbid intellectual function (Vanderploeg & Schinka, 1995). Because crystallized cognitive function is more resistant to recent nervous system injury than the fluid cognitive functions, the differential between the two types of functions can be helpful in estimating overall premorbid intellectual function and determining possible declines. Collateral and family interviews as described previously may also be helpful.

PSYCHOMETRIC TESTS

INTERPRETATION OF TEST results must account for prior neuropsychological ability, as described previously. The person should not be compared with the hypothetical average, because the person may not have been average.

Cognitive Function

Cognitive function can be assessed using the numerous commercially available tests for intellectual, memory, and other cognitive functions, such as the Wechsler Intelligence Scales (WIS), which provides a well-recognized method to develop a comprehensive view of cognitive function. Of course, the overall intelligence quotient may be a misleading indicator of a person's actual ability in his activities of daily living, as specific deficits may be debilitating or disabling in the examinee's profession.

Generally in neurotoxicity cases, there will tend to be declines in the WIS composite indices Perceptual Organization, Processing Speed, and Working Memory. This is consistent with the observation that crystallized cognitive functions are more resistant to neurotoxic effects than fluid cognitive functions.

Executive Function

Executive function is usually disrupted in neurotoxicity cases. Tests to assess this function include the various trailmaking tests, the Color-Word tests (also affecting processing speed), and the fluency tests. The various fluency tests (verbal, visual, etc.) offer a window into the types of difficulties the neurotoxic patient may be experiencing. While these tests do not exclusively measure executive function, they do offer general insight into the patient's executive functioning.

Perceptual Function

Perception is often distorted with neurotoxicity. Tests of this function can include the Visual Search and Attention Test (VSAT), a test that measures an indicator of function (attention and factors of visual perception) often depressed with neurotoxicity.

Emotional Function

It is often helpful for diagnostic purposes to quantify emotional function. Tests such as the Beck Depression and Anxiety Scales can help assess the extent of emotional factors in the cases' pathology.

Depression and anxiety can be factors that exist independently of neurotoxicity, or they may be caused by neurotoxicity. Neurotoxicity can cause emotional disorders in at least two ways: by direct action of the neurotoxic substance on areas of the brain that control emotion, and as factors secondary to loss of cognitive and physical functions.

If depression is found, the responses should be checked to determine if the depression shows the classic stigmata of feelings of guilt and low self-worth, or whether responses are more weighted toward psychomotor slowing and hopelessness, which often accompanies neurotoxicity.

Because neurotoxicity can affect any part of the brain and neural systems, including the autonomic nervous system, the outcome could include any type of emotional illness (such as panic disorder, to name one).

Personality Function

Many neuropsychologists routinely use the MMPI-2 to identify personality pathology. However, the MMPI-2 has not been normed on patients with neurotoxicity or other neurological disorders, so it is not valid for differentiating between neurotoxicity and personality disorders. The MMPI-2 test results are often difficult to explain to lay consumers, such as juries, in part due to the antiquated names that have been applied to the scales. More modern tests, such as the NEO Personality Inventory, offer clearer evidence to help juries adjudicate cases.

General Well-Being

Instruments such as the Human Activity Profile or the General Well-Being Schedule help quantify the impact of the sickness on general functioning.

Malingering and Distortion

These issues are beyond the scope of this chapter but are carefully discussed in chapter 6 of this book. When assessing these functions, care must be taken to choose tests that are insensitive to neurotoxicity. Because all of the specific effects of neurotoxicity for a given individual cannot be entirely specified in advance, nor can the degree of impairment, it is possible that functions affecting test results, damaged by neurotoxicity, can cause a false diagnosis of malingering.

Neurophysiological Tests

Many neurotoxic substances also affect the peripheral nervous system. Nerve conduction velocity tests offer a reliable way to evaluate peripheral nerve function (Kimura, 1989; Singer, 1990a). Assess nerves that are most susceptible to neurotoxicity, such as the median sensory and sural nerves, and measure both sides of the body. However, decreases in nerve function may be nonspecific, and peripheral nerves are not always affected with neurotoxicity, so Nerve Conduction Velocity (NCV) assessment is not always a reliable indicator of neurotoxicity. These tests are best recommended when numbness and other perceptual irregularities are found in the feet, as the longer axons are more susceptible to metabolic disruption such as can occur with neurotoxicity.

Other techniques that may provide helpful information include the various brain potential tests (somatosensory, etc.) and evoked potential measures of attentional processes. Because sleep is so often disrupted, laboratory sleep studies might also provide helpful information to the examiner. Again, findings are not specific to neurotoxicity.

CNS Imaging

Routine CAT and MRI brain imaging are often only helpful to rule out other causes of pathology. However, nonspecific changes on the MRI, such as changes in brain size and white matter changes, can be found with neurotoxicity. PET and SPECT scans are more sensitive tests, but the attribution of changes on these tests to neurotoxicity is controversial and may require expert assistance.

Testing for Traces, Metabolites, or Other Indications of Exposure in Blood

While these measures might be valuable when assessing acute exposures, in general, these tests are of little value for assessing the effects of a substance months or years after exposure. As with any nonfunction test, the meaning and significance of any elevation of blood indicators in a person's life and medical condition needs to be carefully interpreted.

Anti-Myelin Antibody

Measures are often elevated in neurotoxic conditions, and can provide helpful corroborative evidence.

SUMMARY

NEUROPSYCHOLOGICAL EVALUATION IS the most important diagnostic tool for most neurotoxic cases as it is comprehensive and assesses function, which is often the most significant factor in a case assessment.

NOTE

1. Additional symptoms are often related to prior susceptibilities, as well as factors such as areas of the brain affected, systems of the brain affected, and the particular neurotoxic substance, as well as factors of the exposure.

REFERENCES

Anger, W. K., & Johnson, B. (1985). Chemicals affecting behavior. In J. O. Donoghue (Ed.), *Neurotoxicity of industrial and commercial chemicals* (Vol. 1, pp. 51–148). Boca Raton, FL: CRC Press.

Arezzo, J. C., & Schaumburg, H. H. (1989). Screening for neurotoxic disease in humans. *Journal of the American College of Toxicology., 8,* 147–155.

Ascherio, A., Chen, H., Weisskopf, M. G., O'Reilly, E., McCullough, M. L., Calle, E. E., et al. (2006, August). Pesticide exposure and risk of Parkinson's disease. *Annals of Neurology, 60*(2), 197–203.

Barrette, B. (1988). The Rhode Island Department of Health (DOH) Private Well Surveillance Program. *Northeast. Regional. Environmental. Public. Health. Center. Newsletter, 2,* 1–2.

Butler, R. (1987). Keynote address, Workshop on Environmental toxicity and the aging process. In S. R. Baker & M. Rogul (Eds.), *Environmental toxicity and the aging process* (1st ed., Vol. 1, pp. 11–18). New York: Alan R. Liss.

Calne, D. B., McGeer, E., Eisen, A., & Spencer, P. (1986). Alzheimer's disease, Parkinson's disease, and motoneurone disease: Abiotropic interaction between ageing and environment? *Lancet, 103,* 1067–1070.

Ecobichon, D., & Joy, R. (1982). *Pesticides and neurological disease* (1st ed.). Boca Raton: CRC Press.

Environmental Protection Agency. (1976). Core activities of the office of Toxic Substances (Draft Program Plan), EPA Publication 560/4-76-005, Washington, DC. Cited in Landrigan, P. J., Kreiss, K., Xintaras, C., Feldman,

R. G., and Clark, W. H. (1980). Clinical epidemiology of occupational neurotoxic disease. *Neurobeh. Toxicol. 2,* 43–48.

General Accounting Office. (1989a). *Pesticides: Export of unregistered pesticides is not adequately monitored by EPA* (GRD/HRD-89-128). Washington, DC: U.S. General Accounting Office.

General Accounting Office. (1989b). *Imported foods: Opportunities to improve FDA's inspection program* (GAO/HRD-89-128). Washington, DC: U.S. General Accounting Office.

Gonzales, J. (2001, October 26). A toxic nightmare at disaster site air, water, soil contaminated. *News and Views, City Beat.*

Kilburn, K. (1998). *Chemical brain injury.* Van Nostrand Reinhold: New York.

Kimura, J. (1989). *Electrodiagnosis in diseases of nerve and muscle: Principles and practice* (2nd ed.). Philadelphia: F.A. Davis.

Lean, G. (1996, December 15). World industry poisons Arctic purity. *Independent on Sunday,* page 15, London, England.

Lewin, R. (1987). Environmental hypothesis for brain diseases strengthened by new data. *Science,* 583–584.

National Resources Defense Council. (1984). *Pesticides in food: What the public needs to know.* San Francisco: Author.

National Resources Defense Council. (1989). *Intolerable risk: Pesticides in our children's food.* Washington, DC: Author.

Office of Technology Assessment. (1990). *Neurotoxicity. Identifying and controlling poisons of the nervous system* (OTA-BA-436). Washington, DC: Office of Technology Assessment, Congress of the United States.

Perl, D. P., Olanow, C. W., & Calne, D. (1998) Alzheimer's disease and Parkinson's disease: Distinct entities or extremes of a spectrum of neurodegeneration? *Ann Neurol. Sep., 44*(3 Suppl 1), S19–31.

Sbordone, R. J., Seyranian, G. D., & Ruff, R. M. (2000). The use of significant others to enhance the detection of malingerers from traumatically brain-injured patients. *Archives of Clinical Neuropsychology, 15*(6), 465–477.

Singer, R. (1985, August). Neuropsychological evaluation of neurotoxicity. In R. Singer (Ed.), *Neurobehavioural methods in occupational and environmental health: Document 3. Environmental health* (pp. 86–90). Copenhagen, Denmark: Second International Symposium, World Health Organization Regional Office for Europe.

Singer, R. (1990a). *Neurotoxicity guidebook.* New York: Van Nostrand Reinhold.

Singer, R. (1990b). Neurotoxicity can produce "MS-like" symptoms. *Journal of Clinical and Experimental Neuropsychology, 12*(1), 68.

Singer, R. (1990c). *The Neurotoxicity Screening Survey.* Doctoral dissertation, Santa Fe, New Mexico: Author.

Singer, R. (1994). Chronic polychlorinated biphenyl exposure and neurobehavioral effects. *The Toxicologist, 14,* 1.

Singer, R. (1995). Neuropsychological assessment of a practicing dentist with elevated urinary mercury. *The Toxicologist, 15.* 1.

Singer, R. (1996a). Neurotoxicity from outdoor, consumer exposure to a methylene chloride product. *The Toxicologist, 30* Part 2, 1.

Singer, R. (1996b). Neurobehavioral screening of breast implant women. *Archives of Clinical Neuropsychology, 11,* 5.

Singer, R. (1997a). Wood-preserving chemicals, multiple sclerosis, and neuropsychological function. *Archives of Clinical Neuropsychology, 12*(4), 404.

Singer, R. (1997b, March). Sick building syndrome: Neuropsychological study. Fundamental and Applied Toxicology, Supplement. *The Toxicologist, 36*(1), 59, Part 2.

Singer, R. (1997c). Neuropsychological evaluation of desipramine toxicity. *The Journal of Neuropsychiatry and Clinical Neurosciences, 9*(1), 167.

Singer, R. (1998, January). Evaluating a carbonless copy paper neurotoxicity case. *Archives of Clinical Neuropsychology, 13*(1), 127.

Singer, R. (1999a, Winter). Neuropsychological evaluation of bystander exposure to pesticides. *Journal of Neuropsychiatry and Clinical Neurosciences, 11*(1), 161–162.

Singer, R. (1999b, March). Neurobehavioral screening of child and adult bystander exposure to toluene diisocyanate application. Fundamental and Applied Toxicology, Supplement. *The Toxicologist, 48*(1-S), 359.

Singer, R. (1999c). Neurotoxicity from municipal sewage sludge. *Archives of Clinical Neuropsychology, 14,* 160.

Singer, R. (2000, March). Neurobehavioral evaluation of residual effects of acute chlorine ingestion. Fundamental and Applied Toxicology, Supplement. *The Toxicologist, 54*(1), 181.

Singer, R. (2002). Panic disorder can be caused by neurotoxicity. *Archives of Clinical Neuropsychology, 17*(8), 813–814.

Singer, R. (2006). Forensic neuropsychological autopsy of a suicide following occupational solvent exposure. *Archives of Clinical Neuropsychology, 21*(6), 606.

Singer, R., Moses, M., Valciukas, J., Lilis, R., & Selikoff, I. J. (1982). Nerve conduction velocity studies of workers employed in the manufacture of phenoxy herbicides. *Environmental Research, 29,* 297–311.

Sloyan, P. J. (1996a, October 11). Release of Gulf War study postponed. *Newsday.*

Sloyan, P. J. (1996b, September 27). CIA reports 120,000 exposed to nerve gas. *Newsday.*

Spencer, P. S., Nunn, P. B., Hugon, J., Ludolph, A. C., Ross, S. M., Roy, D. N., et al. (1987). Guam amyotrophic lateral sclerosis—Parkinsonism—dementia linked to a plant excitant neurotoxin. *Science, 213,* 517–522.

Spiegelberg, U. (1961). Psychopathologisch-neurologische Schaden nach Einwirkung synthetischer Gifte [Psychopathological-neurological injuries after exposure to synthetic toxins]. In U. Spiegelberg (Ed.)., *Wehrdienst und Gesundheit* (Vol. III). Darmstadt: Wehr und Wissen Verlagsgesellschaft mbH.

Vanderploeg, R., & Schinka, J. (1995). Predicting WAIS-R premorbid ability: Combining subtest performance and demographic variable predictors. *Archives of Clinical Neuropsychology 10*(3), 225–239.

Williams, J. R., Spencer, P. S., Stahl, S. M., Borzelleca, J. F., Nichols, W., & Pfitzer, E. (1987). Interactions of aging and environmental agents: The toxicological perspective. In S. R. Baker and M. Rogul (Eds.), *Environmental toxicity and the aging process* (pp. 81–135). New York: John Wiley & Sons.

Zuckerman, E. (2000). *The clinician's thesaurus*. New York: Guilford Press.

26

Sports Neuropsychology

FRANK M. WEBBE

Mike Webster (1952–2002)*

By Kimberly Powell

Wednesday, September 25, 2002

Hall of Fame center Mike Webster, a member of the Steelers' 1970s dynasty team, died September 24, 2002 at the age of 50 following complications from a heart attack.

Mike Webster played more seasons (15) and more games (220) than any other player in Pittsburgh Steelers' history. Considered one of the greatest centers in professional football, Mike Webster's superlative 17-year career in the National Football League included four Super Bowl rings and nine Pro Bowls, an NFL record for an offensive lineman. He was inducted into the Pro Football Hall of Fame in 1997, during his second year of eligibility, and was voted to the NFL's all-time team in 2000.

Unfortunately, retirement did not treat Mike Webster as well as his football career. In 1999, the lineman was diagnosed with brain damage caused by repeated head injuries sustained during his time in the NFL.

Multiple concussions had damaged his frontal lobe, and the effects of the injuries grew worse in recent years. The rest of his life, unfortunately, deteriorated along with his health, leaving him unemployed, debt-ridden, and occasionally homeless. He also suffered a brief brush with the law when he was charged with forging prescriptions for the drug Ritalin, and he accepted 5 years probation.

At his 1997 Hall of Fame induction, Hall of Fame quarterback and fellow Steelers teammate Terry Bradshaw summed up Mike Webster in a few moving words. "There never has been and never will be another man as committed and totally dedicated to making himself the very best he could possibly be."

Mike Webster is survived by two sons, Garrett, 17, who wears his father's No. 52 for the Moon High School football team, and Colin, 23, a corporal in the U.S. Marines, and two daughters, Brooke, 25, and Hillary Webster, 15, of Madison, Wisconsin.

W HY AND HOW did one of the greatest players in NFL history come to such an untimely and undignified end? How was it that "multiple concussions" rendered this most powerful of men a homeless, confused derelict who stymied the efforts of his family to care for him? The discipline of sports neuropsychology illuminates these issues and suggests answers to the questions. In this chapter we undertake an examination of the historical underpinnings of sports neuropsychology and the core of the resultant modern discipline.

HISTORICAL ORIGINS OF SPORTS NEUROPSYCHOLOGY

S PORTS NEUROPSYCHOLOGY DEFINES a discipline of recent origin that combined two extant fields: sport psychology and neuropsychology. Each of these fields, disciplines in their own right, can trace their proximal history back for a little more than a century. That may appear to be a short duration but, in reality, these fields began nearly contemporaneously with Wundt's publication of his *Grundzüge der physiologischen Psychologie* in the 19th century and the founding of his laboratory of experimental psychology at Leipzig 6 years later (Reisman, 1981). Those twin events are commonly used as the marker for the beginning of modern, scientific psychology.

The origin of neuropsychology often is linked to Paul Broca's study in 1861 of the brain origins of the speech difficulties exhibited by the aphasic patient Tan (Broca, 1861). Sport psychology traces its origin to a series of studies of social-facilitation effects in bicyclists conducted by Norman Triplett in the 1890s (Triplett, 1898).

Sport psychology can be defined as "the scientific study of people and their behaviors in sport and exercise activities and the practical application of that knowledge" (Weinberg & Gould, 2003, p. 1). Neuropsychology comprises "the study of the relationships between the brain and behavior, including the use of psychological tests and assessment techniques to diagnose specific cognitive and behavioral deficits" (University of California, 2005). Both parent fields exhibit several similarities. Each has its scientific and applied sides. Experimental neuropsychology uses methods from experimental psychology to uncover the relationship between the nervous system and cognitive function. This approach involves studying healthy humans in a laboratory setting, although animal experiments are not uncommon. Clinical neuropsychology applies neuropsychological knowledge to the assessment, management, and rehabilitation of people with neurocognitive problems due to illness or brain injury. It brings a psychological viewpoint to treatment, to understand how such illness and injury may affect and be affected by psychological factors. In sport psychology, the split is more complex. Exercise science is the predominant scientific side, but the psychology half also is divided into clinical versus scientific aspects. Table 26.1, adapted from Weinberg and Gould (2003), indicates the various subareas within the sport science–exercise versus psychology domains.

Obvious areas of overlapping interest exist between sport psychology and neuropsychology. For example, exercise science studies motor control and motor learning in sport. Brain injuries might obviously impact such learning and performance, and the rehabilitative effects of relearning motoric behavior might in turn affect recovery processes in the brain. A sport neuropsychological approach would map such relationships. Another study might examine the role of excessive metabolic demands in endurance sports in altering brain function and cognitive performance. Many other questions have already been studied. Most, however, are waiting to be asked. Because the potential topics are boundless, the discussion here will highlight already existing developments in sports neuropsychology.

TABLE 26.1   Categorization of Sport v. Exercise Psychology
Disciplines

Sport science—exercise	Sport psychology
Biomechanics	Abnormal Psychology
Exercise Physiology	Clinical Psychology
Motor Development	Counseling Psychology
Motor Learning and Control	Developmental Psychology
Sport Pedagogy	Personality Psychology
Sport Sociology	Physiological Psychology

TABLE 26.2   Areas of Research and Application in Sport-Related Concussion

Sport-related concussion topics

- Epidemiology
- Relationship between concussion occurrence and type of sport
- Role of previous concussions
- Recovery curve
- Role of subconcussive brain insults in neurocognitive performance
- Interaction of concussion with premorbid factors such as LD and ADHD
- Return to play

MODERN ORIGINS OF SPORTS NEUROPSYCHOLOGY

Two major research and practice areas define sports neuropsychology in the new millennium: sport-related concussion and neurocognitive/medical well-being. Sport-related concussion defines a phenomenon of mild traumatic brain injury (MTBI) that occurs within a sport context. For example, when a hockey player is smashed into the boards and comes off the ice wobbly, confused, and amnestic for the event, an instance of sport-related concussion has happened. Other focus areas in sport-related concussion are shown in Table 26.2. These will be described later in detail.

Neurocognitive/medical well-being defines the use of neurocognitive assessment of athletes to determine the role that normal sport activities might have in affecting quality and duration of cognitive capacity and in quality of life. These types of studies can identify costs or benefits of sport activities. For example, the role of aerobic activities in facilitating cerebral blood flow may point toward beneficial effects. The role of soccer heading may suggest a downside to normal play of a sport.

SPORT-RELATED CONCUSSION

Since the study of concussion and its after effects represents such a large chunk of research and practice in sports neuropsychology, it is worthwhile to define the term.

> Cerebral concussion is a closed head injury that represents a usually transient alteration in normal consciousness and brain processes as a result of traumatic insult to the brain. The alterations may include loss of consciousness, amnesia, impairment of reflex activity, and confusion regarding orientation. Although most symptoms resolve within

a few days in the majority of cases, some physical symptoms such as headache, and cognitive symptoms such as memory dysfunction may persist for an undetermined time. (Webbe, 2006, p. 48)

Just as Triplett's study of cyclists and Broca's study of Tan were seminal in the origins of the parent disciplines, Barth's study of sport-related concussion spurred the evolution of sports neuropsychology. In the early 1980s, Barth and colleagues, including Macciocchi, Alves, Rimel, and Jane began studying college football players who suffered a concussion (Barth, et al., 1989; Macciocchi, Barth, Alves, Rimel, & Jane, 1996). Table 26.3 summarizes the original athlete sample and the study results.

Realizing the improbability of multiple prospective participants for the study of brain injury in the general population, Barth identified college football players as individuals at a significantly high risk of brain injury. Neuropsychological tests were administered before the playing season began and were repeated for those players who suffered concussion as well as for a nonconcussed control group. From a medical, individual, and social perspective, the results were optimistic in that they portrayed the typical sport concussion in football as an event with transient neurocognitive impact. Much more importantly, however, the methodology of the study established for the future a standard that has shaped the discipline. Specifically, Barth's approach of using the sport setting as a laboratory to study mild traumatic brain injury (sport as a laboratory assessment model—SLAM) established prospective, longitudinal methodology as the gold standard in the field (Barth, Freeman, & Broshek, 2002). When athletes engage in rough, physical play there is an inevitability of injury, including head injury. The notion of establishing baselines of neurocognitive performance against

TABLE 26.3 University of Virginia Study of Mild Head Injury in Football (Barth et al., 1989).

Population	Findings
• 10 Center Study • Prospective, Longitudinal Data Collection • 195 athletes sustaining concussion compared to 2350 orthopedic and normal control subjects	• Single mild head injury causes cognitive & information processing deficits • Effects of concussion can be assessed by neuropsychological measures • Relatively rapid recovery occurs in 5 to 10 days

which post-head injury performance could be compared represented a monumental improvement over the group, normative comparisons that otherwise were the only choice. Moreover, along with preinjury neurocognitive testing, researchers also could collect information on premorbid physical and cognitive symptomatology. Thus, the baseline assessment model greatly diminished the variance inherent in making group normative comparisons. The remaining variance associated with repeated testing, history, and maturation could be understood better within the individual context. What has not been eliminated, indeed it has been enhanced, is the observation of considerable individual differences in such critical and basic areas as: (a) differences in the severity of outcome between individuals who receive apparently similar head insults, (b) differences between individuals in duration of recovery from concussions of apparently similar magnitude, (c) differences between individuals in ultimate recovery from concussion such that they can resume their previous activities, (d) effects of recurrent concussions on neurocognitive performance, and (e) effects of subconcussive blows on neurocognitive performance (Webbe & Barth, 2003).

Epidemiology

More than 10% of all adult participants in formal athletic events can be expected to suffer a concussion this year (Cantu, 2001). The Centers for Disease Control translate these statistics into the prediction that about 300,000 sport-related concussions will be reported each year (Kelly, 2000). Because many athletes participate in leagues where medical oversight is lacking, they likely will have no examination by a trainer or physician following MTBI. Thus, it is highly likely that many more than this number of concussions actually occur (Echemendia & Julian, 2001).

With children the picture remains fuzzy. We know that for children under 15 years of age, we can expect about 400,000 mild head injuries from all causes in a given year in the United States (McCrory, Collie, Anderson, & Davis, 2004). We don't know how many of these might be sport related, and we don't know how many will go undetected. The unknown incidence of sport-related concussion in children is not trivial. For example, Guskiewicz, Weaver, Padua, and Garrett (2000) reported that high-school athletes were at higher risk for concussion than were most collegiate players. Moser and Schatz (2002) reported that considerably more of their concussed high-school-level athlete participants (age 14–19) appeared to have longer lasting neurocognitive and somatic symptoms than would have been expected based upon previous studies of older athletes. In their studies of neurological indices in soccer players, Tysvaer and Storli (1989) reported a higher incidence of abnormal EEGs and poorer neurocognitive outcomes in younger versus older soccer players. In player samples that ranged from age 15 to 64 (retired players were included) EEG abnormalities occurred most frequently in the players younger than age 24 (Tysvaer, 1992). The authors presumed that the abnormalities related to concussions suffered during the course of play, although no documentation of concussions existed. If these injury patterns were to extend lower into the childhood range, then the risk of rough play in children's sports would represent an even greater concern. Fueling such concern and also guiding caution in return-to-play following concussion is the unknown risk of mortal injury as a result of second-impact syndrome (SIS).

SECOND-IMPACT SYNDROME AND CONCUSSION PATHOPHYSIOLOGY

SECOND-IMPACT SYNDROME DESCRIBES injury-induced vulnerability to further cerebral concussion. Over the past 20 years, there have been approximately 55 reports of sudden collapse and death following seemingly minor concussive incidents. In several of these incidents, it was discovered that the individual had recently suffered another concussion (Cantu & Voy, 1995; McCrory, 2001). Although the original observations of SIS occurred in human case history studies, the fundamental data that support the phenomenon have arisen in animal studies. In the animal experimental literature we now have clear documentation that two or more concussive blows in close succession may produce significantly greater neurologic impairment and resulting neurobehavioral deficits than a simple sum of these singular blows would have predicted (Fu, Smith, Thomas, & Hovda, 1992; Laurer et al., 2001).

Hovda and his colleagues have shown that the initial concussion creates a neurometabolic cascade of events whereby energy stores are depleted through excitotoxic mechanisms, with accompanying ionic fluxes of great magnitude, and neuronal/axonal impairment and injury (Giza & Hovda, 2001; Hovda et al., 1999). In rats, if a second concussive event occurs within a 3-day period of metabolic instability and vulnerability, then the brain may be incapable of dealing with the decreased cerebral blood flow accompanying the new event in combination with the hypermetabolic phenomena of the second concussion. In such an instance the probability of neuronal mortality increases greatly (Giza & Hovda, 2001). Of great importance, Hovda and colleagues also have extended these findings to humans. They have now documented that glucose hypometabolism characterizes the post-TBI patient. Subsequent events that create the need for increased energy utilization may prove disastrous to the temporarily fragile brain (Bergsneider et al., 2000).

Thus, these researchers (Giza & Hovda, 2001; Hovda et al., 1999) have provided a mechanism that can explain disastrous outcomes of further head injury following an initial concussion.

Although some controversy exists over how well documented and extensive the SIS phenomenon may be, there appears to be no argument that the more compelling cases have occurred with youthful individuals, typically mid-adolescents (McCrory, 2001). A rapid, generalized cerebral edema that has been reported in some children following MTBI is one possible mechanism that may underlie both SIS and differential concussion outcome based upon age (Bruce et al., 1981). The good news is that SIS continues to be a rare phenomenon.

Gender

MOST STUDIES OF gender differences in incidence of and recovery from sport-related concussion have employed intercollegiate athletes. In cross-comparisons of gender by sport, college females appear more often than college males to have a somewhat increased likelihood of concussion, a greater risk of more serious head injury, and also a more problematic recovery (Covassin, Swanik, & Sachs, 2003a, 2003b). Because college football has been the predominant sport from which to obtain concussion data, the bulk of sport-comparison studies have come from other sports that each gender plays, mostly soccer and basketball. In a prospective study of 2,340 high school and college athletes who were tested in preseason with the computerized Concussion Resolution Index (CRI), Broshek et al. (2005) found that female athletes exhibited significantly greater declines in simple and complex reaction times than did males. Moreover, females were found to have significantly more subjective and objective symptoms in the initial follow-up 1–2 days post-concussion. Although one must use caution in comparing sport-related mild head injuries to those arising in other contexts, this apparent higher risk for females is not an isolated phenomenon. For example, in studies of mild head injury due to all causes, it also has been noted that females more than males report more symptoms and exhibit longer recovery times (Bazarian et al., 1999; Rutherford, Merrett, & McDonald, 1979). Thus, gender may be a critical variable in determining recovery following sport-related concussion. This conclusion naturally stimulates the question, *why*. Women may be at greater risk for more severe injury and post-concussion effects due to lower body mass and smaller neck size and supporting musculature. Conversely, it could be argued that concussion-inducing collisions in women's sports may be less severe because of overall lower body mass entering into the force-mass relationship. Moreover, the general finding that women's brains are less lateralized than men's suggests that neurocognitive outcomes of concussion in women may be ameliorated due to more distributed functional capacity (Webbe & Barth, 2003).

From a physiological standpoint, gender differences in hormonal systems, cerebral organization, and musculature may partially explain the differential findings. Results of studies with animals have implicated the sex steroid hormone, estrogen, as important in gendered differences in outcome from experimentally induced brain injury. However, some studies support a protective effect of estrogen; some demonstrate an exacerbation of injury (Roof & Hall, 2000). These discrepant findings may be due to major differences in methodology including the mechanism for producing brain injury, pretreatment regimen, and even to inherent differences in effects of exogenous versus endogenous estrogen. Progesterone appears to reduce post-TBI neural impairment in humans, most likely by inhibiting destructive membrane changes and the resulting vasogenic edema (Roof, Duvdevani, & Stein, 1993; Roof & Hall, 2000). In summary, despite some conflicting studies regarding estrogen's role following TBI, the bulk of the hormonal data supports a neuroprotective role for both estrogen and progesterone.

The fact that gender may differentially determine TBI incidence, severity, and symptom resolution is a common thread of discussion in experimental neurology, but less well known in neuropsychology. There are considerable gender differences in the neural anatomy and physiology, cerebrovascular organization, and cellular response to concussive stimuli. For example, cortical neuronal densities are greater in males, while number of neuronal processes is greater in females (de Courten-Myers, 1999). Females also exhibit greater blood flow rates and higher basal rates of glucose metabolism (Andreason, Zametkin, Guo, Baldwin, & Cohen, 1994; Esposito, Van Horn, Weinberger, & Berman, 1996). To the extent that female brains may have higher cortical metabolic demands, the typical decrease in cerebral blood flow along with the increased glycemic demands caused by TBI may interact with the already high gendered demands and result in greater impairment in females than males.

ROLE OF SPECIFIC SPORT IN DETERMINING CONCUSSION

MOST PHYSICAL SPORTS have the potential for causing brain injuries to their participants. In some such as golf or bowling, the risk is low, but golfers do get hit with balls and clubs, and bowlers, curlers, and even shuffleboard participants do slip, fall, and crack their heads. Typically, though, we consider the roughness and speed of play as critical factors that determine risk of concussion. American football has been the "model" sport because of the roughness, speed, and player size factors in interaction with a large number of participants (Barth et al., 1989). Soccer, the most popular sport in the world, appears to have a somewhat lower risk of concussion than American football. Equestrian sports have high relative percentages of head injuries but many fewer participants overall. Wrestling, rodeo, skiing, snowboarding, Australian Rules football, rugby, lacrosse, and ice hockey are other sports where concussions are frequent enough to garner reports in the literature (Ruchinskas, Francis, & Barth, 1997). The player size, speed of action, and gear such as sticks, balls, and pucks all contribute to the possibility of abrupt changes in acceleration of the head and brain. More than physical blows, it is the differential acceleration of brain tissue (such as where white and gray matter interact or at areas of different tissue density) that determines concussion. Moreover, sports where acceleration exists in multiple planes may carry the highest risk of concussion. For example, in bull riding in rodeo, the rider experiences simultaneous accelerations in vertical, lateral, and horizontal planes.

ASSESSMENT

Sideline Assessment

Although not purely neuropsychological, the first assessment of sport-related concussion in organized leagues is likely to take place on the sideline or in a locker room during or immediately following a game. The most common instrument for this assessment is the Sideline Assessment of Concussion (SAC; McCrea et al., 1998), administered by an athletic trainer or a team physician. The SAC aims to determine the instant level of confusion, disorientation, and amnesia of the injured player. This standardized, quantifiable approach represents a considerable leap over the qualitative and inexact attempts to assess mental status previously common on the football sidelines (e.g., "where are you; what's the score; what's your name"). In addition to a brief series of orientation questions, the SAC also employs a short word-learning list, digits backwards, exertional exercises to observe motor coordination and ability to follow directions, and a brief neurological exam. The likelihood that players who suffer a "ding" and who are administered the SAC will re-enter a game generally is inversely related to the level of play (youth, amateur, professional). This represents a change in practice from several years ago. Players' careers and lives may be affected by a premature return to play, especially given fear of a repeat concussion (Kelly et al., 1991). The SAC provides subtest and total scores. Although group data indicated that the maximum score of 30 is above the average score, the SAC is susceptible to ceiling effects. Moreover, it may be difficult for a tester to determine the meaning of a player's score in the absence of a baseline on this test. Nonetheless, the SAC has proven to be a very useful tool for an initial screening, generally showing statistically significant decreases in score of about 4 points for concussed versus nonconcussed players. These differences tend to disappear after 48 hours (McCrea, 2001). Players who score positive on the SAC will commonly be referred for follow-up medical treatment. This typically implies a neurological evaluation. If a protocol has been established, neuropsychological testing may also be mandated, but that outcome is highly variable. In professional football and hockey leagues where concussions are a fact of life, follow-up neuropsychological evaluation is very likely to occur (Lovell & Barr, 2004).

NEUROPSYCHOLOGICAL ASSESSMENT

Baseline Testing

Best practice calls for preseason neurocognitive baseline testing to establish a player's premorbid level of functioning. Most professional leagues have implemented such testing. For example, in the National Football League (NFL) and National Hockey League (NHL), such testing is mandatory. Following several horror stories of the recent past, neuropsychologists such as Mark Lovell, Mickey Collins, and Ruben Echemendia have been successful in creating an entire network of qualified practitioners who are ready and accessible to test players who have suffered a head injury (Lovell, Echemendia, & Burke, 2004).

Common neuropsychological tests employed to assess baseline cognitive performance are shown in Table 26.4.

Because of the large number of athletes who may have to be tested and the limitations on hours of availability, neuropsychological batteries used in sports neuropsychology are generally briefer than might be used in normal clinical practice. Forty-five minutes to an hour is the typical time frame. The batteries consist of tests that measure critical domains of functioning known to be at risk for impairment following TBI. Thus, processing speed, memory, and executive functioning have priority for assessment (Gronwall, 1989).

Although baseline testing is commonly conducted in a standard office environment, the first post-concussion test may occur in locker rooms, hotel rooms, or other environments. Measures of effort may be necessary in nonsport settings to insure validity of outcome. Effort has generally not been considered a critical factor with athlete examinees (Lovell et al., 2004). Instead, faking good is the more likely outcome, because most athletes aim to return to play as soon as possible. Thus, even with nonstandard testing conditions, motivation is high. Nonetheless, with

TABLE 26.4 Common Neuropsychological Tests Used in Sports Neuropsychology

Test category	Test
Learning and memory: Verbal/Auditory	California Verbal Learning Test
	Hopkins Verbal Learning Test
	Rey Auditory Verbal Learning Test
Learning and memory: Visual	Brief Visuospatial Memory Test-Revised (BVMT-R)
Processing speed	Symbol Digit Modalities test
	Trail Making Test
	Controlled Oral Word Association test
	Paced Auditory Serial Addition Test
	WAIS-III Digit Symbol Test
Executive Function	Stroop Color Word Test
	Tower of London-Drexel
Attention	WAIS-III Digit Span
Word Fluency	Controlled Oral Word Association Test (COWAT)

the advent of high profile sport-concussion injuries and the undoubted potential for liability claims, good practice suggests that tests of effort should become commonplace in the sports neuropsychology setting. A greater historic problem in the post-concussion testing is that of repeated measurement. Following a suspected concussion, anywhere from one to five assessments may occur within a 2-week time frame. Thus, it is most important to understand the re-test validity of the measures selected and make provision for positive change as a function of testing. For this reason, the sports neuropsychology domain has contributed considerably to studies of reliable change in testing (Hinton-Bayre, Geffen, Geffen, McFarland, & Friis, 1999).

THE NFL NEUROPSYCHOLOGY PROGRAM AND THE NHL CONCUSSION PROGRAMS

BARTH AND COLLEAGUES' (1989) seminal study with college athletes from the University of Virginia and other schools paved the way for the modern prospective approach to the study of sport-related concussion. The application of that approach is best represented in the concussion management programs of the NFL and NHL. The business of sport has often translated into the treatment of athletes as interchangeable parts of the teams. If one is injured, bring in the back-up and continue play. Maybe the first one recovers, maybe not. If not, find a permanent replacement. The team and the game must go on. As long as injuries were not life threatening, the personal ramifications of this approach garnered only passing attention. For example, in 1905, aghast at the 19 deaths that had occurred that year in college football (there was no viable professional football alternative), President Theodore Roosevelt intervened. He called several college presidents to the White House and "strongly" suggested that unless the game could be made safer, football programs should be abandoned. That meeting spurred the development of the Intercollegiate Athletic Association of the United States (IAAUS), which morphed into the National Collegiate Athletic Association (NCAA) in 1910. Rules and equipment were introduced to reduce injuries and deaths, and the game continued (Crowley, 2006).

All athletes risk injury when they take the field, court, ice, and so forth. There is a presumption, however, that the ruling bodies of sport have taken steps to reduce the risk of injuries, particularly those that are debilitating or life-threatening. And although few would characterize most present-day professional sports organizations as humanistic in nature, the financial and public-relations ramifications of player injury have positively impacted the development and introduction of protective equipment and legislation of protective rules.

For the NFL, it was the interaction of this latter reality with the warnings given by the medical and neuropsychology community that spurred development of the NFL Neuropsychology Program in 1993. Mark Lovell, Joseph Maroon, and colleagues began this program with 23 of the players from the Pittsburgh Steelers football club. At the present time, all 32 teams participate (Lovell & Barr, 2004). The program tests each player prospectively in the preseason, often at conditioning camps. Because of the practical issues of access to players, the battery that has been developed is brief, taking approximately 30 minutes to administer. A similar program was developed in the NHL in 1997. The batteries employed in each program are listed in Table 26.5 (adapted from Lovell & Barr, 2004 and Lovell et al., 2004).

SEVERITY

CONCUSSION, OF COURSE, is considered to mark the mild end of a continuum of brain injury. The historic notion was that brain activity is disrupted temporarily and then returns quickly to normal with few or no residual symptoms and no morphological damage. As better measurement devices have been developed, that style of definition has lost credibility, because we now know that morphological change, including axonal and somatic necrosis, does occur in some cases of concussion (Hovda et al., 1999). What still remains problematic is differentiating and predicting whether a given individual who suffers concussion will exhibit a quick, unremarkable recovery, versus a lengthy

TABLE 26.5 NFL and NHL Neuropsychological Test Batteries

Ability evaluated	NFL battery	NHL battery
Retrograde and anterograde amnesia, orientation to place and time	Orientation Questions	Orientation Questions
Verbal memory	Hopkins Verbal Learning Test (HVLT)	Hopkins Verbal Learning Test (HVLT)
Visual memory	Brief Visuospatial Memory Test-Revised (BVMT-R)	Brief Visuospatial Memory Test-Revised (BVMT-R)
Visual scanning, mental flexibility	Trail Making Test	Color Trail Making Test
Word fluency, word retrieval	Controlled Oral Word Association Test (COWAT)	Controlled Oral Word Association Test (COWAT)
Visual scanning, visual search	WAIS-III Symbol Search	Penn State Cancellation Test
Visual scanning, information processing	WAIS-III Digit Symbol	Symbol Digit Modalities
Attention span	WAIS-III Digit Span	
MTBI symptoms	Post-Concussion Symptom Inventory	Concussion Symptom Inventory

period—possibly months or years—filled with physical and cognitive disturbances. A typical first step in documenting concussion severity occurs shortly after injury. Particularly, as health care professionals became more involved in evaluating athletes following head injury, it became clear that useful guidelines for estimating concussion severity and making decisions on return-to-play were both necessary and critical. The concussion classification system proposed by Ommaya and Gennarelli (1974) to describe experimentally produced concussion has formed the basic model from which the applied systems have been derived. According to that system, concussion could be graded in five steps. Only grades 4 and 5 incorporated loss of conciousness (LOC) and were considered to be very serious. A description of their grades is shown in Table 26.6.

Clearly, the development of the most widely used of the contemporary, clinical concussion grading systems followed the same basic pattern that Ommaya and Gennarelli established. In Table 26.7, the systems developed by Cantu (1986, 2001) and the American Academy of Neurology (AAN; Kelly & Rosenberg, 1997) are contrasted. Similar to Ommaya and Gennarelli's schema, LOC is seen as representing greater severity. Cantu's system weighs amnestic and other symptoms more

TABLE 26.6   Categories of Experimental Concussion

Grade	Defining characteristic	Symptoms
1	Confusion	Normal consciousness without amnesia
2	Confusion	Normal consciousness with PTA only
3	Confusion + amnesia	Normal consciousness with PTA plus RGA
4	LOC—Paralytic coma	Confusion plus PTA and RGA
5	LOC—Coma	Persistent vegetative state

Adapted from Ommaya & Gennarelli (1974).

TABLE 26.7   Concussion Severity Grading Guidelines

	AAN	Cantu (2001)
Grade I	Symptoms < 15 minutes *and* No LOC	All Symptoms < 30 minutes *and* No LOC
Grade II	Symptoms > 15 minutes	Symptoms > 30 minutes but < 7 days *and/or* PTA > 30 minutes but < 24 hours *and/or* LOC < 1 minute
Grade III	Any LOC	Symptoms > 7 days *and/or* PTA > 24 hours *and/or* LOC > 1 minute

Adapted from Erlanger et al. (2003).

heavily in assessment than do the AAN guidelines. These schemata make most sense when interpreted within Ommaya and Gennarelli's (1974) centripetal theory. That is, in showing that rotational as opposed to linear accelerations were most responsible for causing concussions, they suggested that concussion could best be understood as:

> a graded set of clinical syndromes following head injury wherein increasing severity of disturbance in level and content of consciousness is caused by mechanically induced strains affecting the brain in a centripetal sequence of disruptive effect on function and structure. The effects of this sequence always begin at the surfaces of the brain in the mild cases and extend inwards to affect the diencephalic-mesencephalic core at the most severe levels of trauma. (pp. 637–638)

Thus, the notion that LOC represented greater concussive severity follows clearly from this concept. Among others, McCrory has suggested that we uncouple LOC and post-traumatic amnesia (PTA) from notions of severity, because the cortical post-concussive effects may ultimately be the most serious.

Moreover, several recent studies have shown a disconnect between LOC duration and severity as measured by neurocognitive symptoms (Erlanger et al., 2003; Lovell, Iverson, Collins, McKeag, & Maroon, 1999). Thus, although the duration of PTA appears to be an important predictor of severity, there has been a tendency in recent years to use other or additional measures. Gronwall (1989) has categorized these, and two appear to have been particularly important: scores between 13–15 on the Glasgow Coma Scale (Teasdale & Jennett, 1974) and duration of hospital stay (Rimel, Giordani, Barth, Boll, & Jane, 1981). It is important to note that these measures were derived within the sport context and are best applied within that frame.

Severity of concussion can be considered in five ways: (1) the actual physical forces of impact/acceleration, (2) the documented disruption in brain function, (3) actual cytoarchitectural and morphological changes, (4) frequency and duration of peri- and post-concussion symptoms, and (5) role of cumulative or repetitive concussive and subconcussive blows.

Physical Forces

Barth and colleagues have suggested that severity of injury and subsequent neurocognitive impairment can be estimated by the acceleration–deceleration forces acting on the brain (Barth, Freeman, Broshek, & Varney, 2001; Barth, Varney, Ruchinskas, & Francis, 1999). Most such data on the forces necessary to cause concussion have been derived from animal experiments. However, because of the vast differences between animals and humans in the ability to withstand major blows with impunity—the specific values of force, mass, rotation, and duration that are sufficient to cause concussion or worse brain injuries in animals may have little bearing on humans. Two measures, derived from the potential for brain injury resulting from decelerative forces in auto crashes, shed some light on the forces necessary to cause concussion and more severe injuries in humans. The head injury criterion (HIC) and the Gadd severity index were calculated using human cadavers in crash testing settings. Unfortunately, in the sport context, there rarely is an opportunity for prospective methods that would measure such forces. We can speak in generalities; for example, it is clear that when peak decelerative forces occur over a very brief duration the risk of brain injury greatly increases. Naunheim, Standeven, Richter, and Lewis (2000) indicated after their review that a score in excess of 1,500 on the Gadd Severity Index, or above 1,000 on the Head Injury Criterion (HIC), or a peak accelerative force of 200 g should be considered thresholds for single impacts likely to "cause a significant brain injury" in humans. These values were estimated based upon the animal studies and observations of accident outcomes in humans. Naunheim et al. (2000) also measured peak accelerative forces in athletic competition by using an accelerometer embedded in helmets worn by soccer, football, and ice hockey players. They recorded no impacts that approached the 200 g level but also observed no events that were correlated with reports of concussion. That limits any possible conclusion other than the obvious observation that concussive level forces likely occur with relative (and fortunate) infrequency in these sport contexts. Schneider and Zernicke (1988) studied concussion risk in soccer heading via a computer simulation model, within which the characteristics of the human participant along with the ball factors (acceleration, vector, and mass) were varied. After first calculating typical accelerative forces in players and nonplayers who were participating in a moderate heading drill, they applied the obtained acceleration, mass ratio, and duration values to the model. They reported that unsafe values of the HIC (>1,000) occurred when children were modeled in both translational and rotational acceleration conditions and for adults in the rotational condition. Because the outcomes with children suggested an interaction between the mass of the individual with the mass of the ball as a critical variable in the equation, Schneider and Zernicke recommended the use of small soccer balls in contexts in which children might be heading.

THE NORMAL RECOVERY CURVE

THE TYPICAL MILD closed head injury of the sort most often seen in sport settings is notable for a period of confusion and disorientation immediately post-injury and may be accompanied by brief LOC or PTA (Barth et al., 1989). The musings on concussion by early observers, such as by Barth (Barth et al., 1989), emphasized the transient presentation in concussion and the full recovery of the senses. Because such writers were looking primarily at LOC, which required no sophisticated instruments for measurement, there was an obvious emphasis on that symptom and a common ignoring of others. Even in more modern times, the mistaken focus that concussion was primarily a vascular phenomenon continued to promote the complete reversibility or remission notion (e.g., Trotter, 1924). However, beginning in the mid-twentieth century, researchers and clinicians began expressing doubt about the sudden and full "recovery" side of the concussion curve. For example, 40 years ago, Symonds (1962) cautioned that the effects of even mild concussion were never fully reversible and buttressed his claims with clinical data from his patients. Similarly, Rimel et al. (1981) noted persisting concussion symptoms in many patients after seemingly mild

TBI. Symonds and Rimel et al., of course, dealt with concussions arising within the general population. In contrast, Barth and colleagues showed that for the vast majority of athletes who suffered concussion, most exhibited complete resolution within 5–10 days (Barth et al., 1989). Both Symonds and Barth et al., however, concluded that complete recovery following *multiple* concussive or even subconcussive blows might be less probable. It is not uncommon for post-concussive symptomatology to persist for weeks or months under these conditions in some athletes (Moser & Schatz, 2002) similar to findings reported in more general clinical populations (Arcia & Gualtieri, 1993). This confusing differential duration of symptoms poses significant difficulties for choosing methods of assessment generally (Jagoda & Riggio, 2000) and differentiation of guidelines for return-to-play in athlete populations (Guskiewicz, 2001). Moreover, the factors that predict which athlete will have a quick versus long symptom resolution have not been identified clearly and unambiguously. Two athletes who suffer similar head trauma may differ widely in their recovery and return to play despite no obvious differences in injury mechanics, diagnostic imaging, and sideline symptoms, including presence or absence of LOC and PTA. Other factors such as number and recency of previous concussions may critically determine symptom resolution (Erlanger, Kutner, Barth, & Barnes, 1999; Guskiewicz et al., 2003; Macciocchi, Barth, Littlefield, & Cantu, 2001). In the absence of clear physical data, the severity and duration of symptom involvement remains the clearest estimate of severity.

RETURN TO PLAY

AS HAS BEEN noted in several instances, severity of concussion is often a *post hoc* determination based upon the persistence of concussion-related symptoms. The earliest definitions and conceptualizations of concussion included that recovery was quite rapid. The vestige of that concept remains in sport when players attempt to re-enter games as quickly as possible or deny any recurring symptoms that might persuade others to keep them from returning to play. Similarly, coaches and team owners in professional sports want their players to resume training and playing as soon after concussion as possible. Studies of athletic head injuries most typically report on immediate, short-term, and long-term outcomes for recovery of normal cognitive function and resolution of physical symptoms such as headache and nausea. Assuming that an immediate, sideline judgment has been made that a player suffered a concussion, then subsequent neurocognitive assessments are typically initiated within 24 hours in this model. If symptoms still are present, then additional measurement is likely after 3–5 days, and again at 7–10 days. If symptoms or cognitive functions have not returned to normal within 10 days, it would be common to make further observations at regular intervals until symptoms have resolved and the player returns to their baseline neurocognitive function. With respect to physical and cognitive markers, in most instances, athletes who have suffered concussion are generally symptom-free within 5–10 days (Barth et al., 1989). This appears to capture the majority of cases as represented in the scientific and applied literature to date, employing many types of measuring instruments, across a variety of sports. The somatic symptoms that predominate during these times are headache and confusion or disorientation, which are reported by about 50–75% of the athletes (Barth et al., 1989; Macciocchi et al. 1996; McCrea et al., 2003). The significant minority of athletes and others whose concussion symptoms persist for weeks, months, or longer have yet to be studied in sufficient microscopic detail to determine underlying causes. Thus, what remains to be fine-tuned is to correlate the underlying functional and structural changes with recovery from concussion. Although it is tempting to speculate, for example, that hypometabolic alterations are responsible for symptoms in the short term, and that lasting cytoarchitectural alterations and cellular morbidity controls are more persisting symptoms, data from human studies still are insufficient to support such conclusions.

So, when should athletes return to play? The conservative approach is the most followed: (1) resolution of physical symptoms as determined by self-report; (2) clear neurological examination results; and (3) neurocognitive test data showing return to or maintenance of premorbid functioning.

CURRENT ISSUES IN SPORT NEUROPSYCHOLOGY

VALUE-ADDED ROLE OF NEUROPSYCHOLOGICAL TESTING

A PRESSING QUESTION that currently vexes sports neuropsychology and return-to-play decisions is whether neuropsychological testing offers sufficient data to occupy a role in managing sport-related concussion and in clearing athletes to return to competition. Randolph, McCrea, and Barr (2005) have recently challenged the profession to demonstrate that neuropsychological evaluation following concussion actually provides unequivocal conclusions regarding impaired versus recovered functioning. Coming on the heels of the summary report from the 2nd International Conference on Concussion in Sport that found no need for post-concussion neuropsychological testing in "simple concussion" (McCrory et al., 2005), this article has struck at the heart of the developing discipline of sports neuropsychology. The basic questions raised in the article are appropriate. Specifically, the authors are concerned to know (1) are the batteries used in concussion assessment valid, (2) is information provided by the neuropsychological assessment unique versus other categories of testing (e.g., neurological, scanning/imaging, balance testing), and (3) do the neuropsychological outcomes reveal information regarding recovery of function that would otherwise not be known and that is critical for the return-to-play decision. In asking the first question on validity, Randolph et al. (2005) considered the reliability, sensitivity, validity, change scores/classification rate, and clinical utility of sport neuropsychological assessment batteries used in many published studies. The authors found these test batteries to be lacking in several areas. The chances are good, however, that similar findings would have been obtained had the authors sampled neuropsychological batteries in more general settings. One of the key issues at play is that assessment in the sport domain often carries with it the requirement for briefer batteries than might be chosen for general practice. A practitioner might be comfortable with the sensitivity and clinical utility of the Halstead-Reitan Neuropsychological Test Battery (HRNTB), for example, and choose that as the gold standard. The likelihood of HRNTB actually being of use in the sport setting is near zero. Thus, clinicians and researchers have pieced together short batteries that assess major areas of functioning known to be impacted in many sport-related head trauma cases. A second issue of note in Randolph et al.'s (2005) criticism is that they tend to consider group differences as the key arena for evaluating such critical issues as the sensitivity of tests. In many research studies that is certainly critical. However, the outcomes of mild brain trauma clearly differ greatly across individuals. Two people of similar morphology may be exposed to similar concussive forces in similar settings. One may be notably affected and the other not, and neuropsychological and other tests may clearly discern this outcome. The variables that determined the differential outcome remain unknown. They may relate to subtle differences in the actual event, or they may relate to characteristics of the individual. Should we fault the test battery for not classifying both persons as symptomatic? Subtle differences in the actual concussive event may also result in somewhat different brain areas receiving differential injury. Individual tests within a battery should exhibit different outcomes, and this may appear to create unreliability. Thus, too great a focus on group data and on considering concussion more unitary in the expression of dysfunction may easily cloud good science and good practice.

In demanding that post-concussion neurological assessment contribute more knowledge of concussion severity, potential for recovery, and determination of return to play than can be garnered through neurological imaging, symptom inventories, or other present methods, Randolph et al. are on safe ground. However, their suggestion that such demonstrations are lacking appears to be incorrect. For example, Erlanger et al. (2001) clearly showed that of their participants who completed prospective and post-concussion testing with the computerized Concussion Resolution Index, individuals who otherwise were asymptomatic continued to test in impaired ranges. Lovell and colleagues have shown in several studies that their computerized ImPACT system uncovered continued neurocognitive weakness in concussed athletes who reported themselves as asymptomatic, and for whom neurological tests were clear (Van Kampen, Lovell, Pardini, Collins, & Fu, in press).

ETHICS

CLINICAL PSYCHOLOGISTS WOULD be aghast at the prospect of nonclinical personality specialists advertising their services for clinical assessment. Neuropsychologists would be aghast at the prospect of neuropsychologically naïve clinical psychologists advertising their services for neuropsychological evaluations. Sport psychologists would be aghast at either clinical or neuropsychologists advertising their services for sport-related assessment of athletes. Moreover, licensing and certification bodies would take a dim view of the first two of these examples. The third is less known, because the practice of sport psychology is protected neither by state laws or certification agencies. Nonetheless, the major sport psychology organizations (Association for the Advancement of Applied Sport Psychology and Division 47 of the American Psychological Association [APA]) have issued clear guidelines for educational and experiential qualifications of such practice (APA, Division 47). When it comes to sport neuropsychology, practice qualifications are even more obscure, because a combination of knowledge and skills from the twin domains of sport psychology and neuropsychology must be considered. Most commonly, a potential consultant will have the neuropsychology background but may lack the sport specific background or knowledge. As Parker, Echemendia, and Milhouse (2004) have indicated, that background may be crucial for understanding the context in which neurocognitive deficits occur and the issues that the athlete–patient faces in recovery and adaptation. For example, neuropsychological testing may reveal some slight psychomotor slowing that may be borderline on an impairment index. For an athlete, such a change may well be catastrophic, because exceptional capabilities in this area are likely the norm and separate a successful from an unsuccessful performer. The sport-naïve practitioner may totally miss such implications. Moreover, it may be necessary to counsel the athlete in life and career choices given lack of full recovery from a seeming mild brain injury.

WHO IS THE CLIENT?

UNLIKE TYPICAL CLINICAL consulting situations, the question of who the client is may be fuzzy in sports neuropsychology and more generally in sport psychology. For example, the practitioner may be employed by the team or organization to examine players prospectively and following head trauma. The identity of the patient is clear— it is the athlete. However, she or he may not be the client; that may be the organization/employer. The normal issues of client confidentiality become blurred in such a situation. The team wants to know unequivocally whether the player is disabled or ready to return to action. How will such a revelation affect the player and their future livelihood? Is this the concern of the psychologist? Sport psychology is not the only arena where such ticklish ethical issues arise. Industrial/ organizational and military psychologists often face similar dilemmas. The key in any of these settings is for the psychologists to clarify the issues ahead of time, and potentially, refuse a consultation if their ethical obligations are compromised. Sport neuropsychologists also face a potential adversary in the media. Particularly when high profile professional athletes suffer traumatic brain injury, a media circus can ensue. Again, the issue of ethics remains paramount, but the extensions become even more arcane. For example, betting on professional sports is legal in Nevada. Dr. X has evaluated a starting quarterback who suffered a concussion 2 weeks earlier. Although the team neurologist has cleared the quarterback, Dr. X is well aware that the athlete's reaction times and speed of processing remain impaired. Are there added ethical considerations here, or does patient and client confidentiality apply? What if the league office asks about the quarterback's mental state because they are concerned for the integrity of the game? These questions derive from actual cases. They are complex and can entangle the unwary sports neuropsychologist in a sticky web that is not easily escaped. As Parker, Echemendia, and Milhouse (2004) suggest, the savvy consultant will consider such issues before accepting a case and consult experts and ethicists along the way.

CULTURE AND DIVERSITY

THE DAYS HAVE long passed when sport participants at the college and professional levels represented cultural or ethnic homogeneity.

Increasingly at the collegiate level and commonly at the professional level, foreign-born athletes comprise a significant minority, if not a majority, of players in leagues. For example, in the National Hockey League it has been estimated that more than 80% of players are foreign born, representing more than 15 countries (Echemendia, 2004). EuroLeague basketball teams commonly have more than 50% foreign born players. For example, the 11-man roster of the German RheinEnergie team boasts only three Germans, with four players from the United States, two from Serbia, one from Poland, and one from Estonia (EuroLeague Basketball). Of the 24 members of the Real Madrid soccer club, 10 are foreign born, including players from Brazil, Italy, Mali, the Netherlands, and England (Real Madrid.com). The first critical issue that faces the sports neuropsychologist who works with such diverse groups is, of course, the language barrier. Your language and the player's language may be different. Understanding and communicating pose a significant validity threat beginning with the interview. The bulk of evaluation measures are in English, so selection of instruments must be done with care so as to avoid bias. Echemendia (2004) recommends the use of nonverbal tests when possible to reduce the language bias. Of course, at some point, language-based measures will be critical to fully assess abilities. Interesting questions arise when testing such diverse athletes. For example, given that many current athletes arise from Eastern European countries, how does a history of using Greek or Cyrillic characters manifest itself on tests using Roman-based alphanumeric systems? Echemendia reports that early data from the NHL suggests that these players may score low even on nonverbal instruments such as the Symbol Digit Modality Test. Clearly, the existence of baseline performance data with such individuals is critical to understanding later performance following TBI. In addition to the diversity arising from national and ethnic origins, there also is diversity related to the culture of sports. For example, many athletes have learned to live and work in the presence of chronic pain. For some, there may be recourse to prescription or nonprescription analgesics. The use of alcohol may be common. Others grin and bear it. Regardless of the attempt or nonattempt to mask the pain, the neuropsychologist must understand that results of assessment may be colored either by drugs or by the distracting presence of pain. Interpretation must occur within this context.

COUNSELING AND PSYCHOTHERAPY

THE THERAPEUTIC ASPECTS of sports neuropsychology have been long in coming. Not unlike the history of neuropsychology, where practitioners might only have interpreted test results and never actually laid eyes on the patient, so also in sports neuropsychology, the practitioner might formerly have assessed, interpreted, and recommended but never actually intervened in a psychotherapeutic manner. Broshek (2003) described the evolution of *therapeutic neuropsychology* within the context of comprehensive psychological and neuropsychological services delivered to student-athletes within the athletic department of a major state university. Although concussion management provided the initial entrée, the prospect of a continuum of care appealed to the athletic department. Such services came to include academic evaluations, preseason academic and neurocognitive screening, psychotherapeutic interventions, treatment of eating disorders, and learning disorder (LD) and attention-deficit/hyperactivity disorder (ADHD) assessments. Commonly, concussion management was a linchpin connecting several of the practice areas. For example, Broshek (2003) described a sequence where a varsity player suffered a third concussion that resulted in persistent post-concussive symptomatology in conjunction with lingering neurocognitive deficits. A psychotherapeutic intervention was initiated to prepare the student for the termination of her playing days. Psychoeducational approaches ensued to demonstrate to the student exactly how her brain had been damaged and why further play was dangerous. Such intervention recognizes the incredible motivation to compete that would drive such an individual to leave one program for another where her injury history was unknown and where she might play once again. Because this student's identity was intricately wrapped within her sport and performance, the transition from being an active player was arduous. Unfortunately, in professional sports, such concern for the individual is often mitigated by economic investment and liability concerns. Moreover, because the individual is often very willing to continue participation despite medical and psychological advice to the contrary, there will always be a potential employer for the skilled but progressively impaired athlete. As an example, consider the hockey career of Eric Lindros. A powerful man himself who has dished out much punishment to other players, Lindros became equally known for his susceptibility to concussions. With at least eight documented concussions in his 16-year NHL career, and many months of associated recovery time off the ice, Lindros has still never lacked employment. His tenure as a member of the Philadelphia Flyers club was notable for complaints in the media from the Flyers' management about his toughness. Specifically, he was called to task for missing games following concussions and other injuries. A man who valued toughness was chided for letting such trifling—and possibly phantom—injuries keep him off the ice. This brings us full circle to Mike Webster, a player who also prided himself on his toughness. The culture of toughness and "manliness" is common in contact sports as described previously.

Such a culture may have spurred Lindros and Webster to demonstrate their toughness by continuing to place themselves in harm's way. The danger of the situation is more apparent for Lindros than for Webster because of the different generations and the modern prevalence of neurocognitive testing. Clearly, the work of the sports neuropsychologist does not end with the delivery of the findings of the evaluation in cases such as these. The prominent extension relates to counseling for adaptation to post-concussive symptoms and associated decrements in neurocognitive abilities. Although there remains some controversy over the uniqueness of post-concussion symptoms vis-a-vis their ubiquity in other syndromes such as chronic pain (Iverson & McCracken, 1997), there is little doubt that headache, confusion, fatigue, and other symptoms are common correlates of the immediate post-concussion period and may extend out many months in time (Ruff, Camenzuli, & Mueller, 1996). Moreover, the concomitant occurrence of cognitive weakness may require both psychotherapeutic as well as cognitive rehabilitative interventions.

REFERENCES

American Psychological Association, Division 47. *Becoming a sport psychologist.* Retrieved January 10, 2006, from http://www.psyc.unt.edu/apadiv47/about_becomingsportpsych.html

Andreason, P. J., Zametkin, A. J., Guo, A. C., Baldwin, P., & Cohen, R. M. (1994). Gender-related differences in regional cerebral glucose metabolism and normal volunteers. *Psychiatry Research, 51,* 175–183.

Arcia, E., & Gualtieri, C. T. (1993). Association between patient report of symptoms after mild head injury and neurobehavioral performance. *Brain Injury, 7,* 481–489.

Barth, J. T., Alves, W. M., Ryan, T. V., Macciocchi, S. N., Rimel, R. W., Jane, J. A., et al. (1989). Mild head injuries in sports: Neuropsychological sequelae and recovery of function. In H. Levin, H. Eisenberg, & A. Benton (Eds.), *Mild head injury* (pp 257–277). New York: Oxford University Press.

Barth, J. T., Freeman, J. R., & Broshek, D. R. (2002). Mild head injury. In V. S. Ramachandran (Ed.), *Encyclopedia of the human brain: Vol. 3* (pp. 81–92). San Diego, CA: Academic Press.

Barth, J. T., Freeman, J. R., Broshek, D. K., & Varney, R. N. (2001). Acceleration-deceleration sport-related concussion: The gravity of it all. *Journal of Athletic Training, 36,* 253–256.

Barth, J. T., Varney, R. N., Ruchinskas, R. A., & Francis, J. P. (1999). Mild head injury: The new frontier in sports medicine. In R. N. Varney & R. J. Roberts (Eds.), *The evaluation and treatment of mild traumatic brain injury* (pp. 81–98). Mahwah, NJ: L. Erlbaum.

Bazarian, J. J., Wong, T., Harris, M., Leahey, N., Mookerjee, S., & Dombovy, M. (1999). Epidemiology and predictors of post-concussive syndrome after minor head injury in an emergency population. *Brain Injury, 13*, 173–189.

Bergsneider, M., Hovda, D. A., Lee, S. M., Kelly, D. F., McArthur, D. L., Vespa, P. M., et al. (2000). Dissociation of cerebral glucose metabolism and level of consciousness during the period of metabolic depression following human traumatic brain injury. *Journal of Neurotrauma, 17*, 389–401.

Broca, P. P. (1861). Loss of speech, chronic softening and partial destruction of the anterior left lobe of the brain. *Bulletin de la Société Anthropologique, 2*, 235–238.

Broshek, D. R. (2003, October). *Comprehensive neuropsychology in athletics: A new frontier in sports medicine*. Special Topics presentation to the 23rd Annual Conference of the National Academy of Neuropsychology, Dallas, TX.

Broshek, D. K., Kaushik, T., Freeman, J. R., Erlanger, D., Webbe, F. M., & Barth, J. T. (2005). Gender differences in outcome from sports-related concussion. *Journal of Neurosurgery, 102*(5), 856–863.

Bruce, D. A., Alavi, A., Bilaniuk, L., Dolinskas, C., Obrist, W., & Uzzell, B. (1981). Diffuse cerebral swelling following head injuries in children: The syndrome of "malignant brain edema." *Journal of Neurosurgery, 54*, 170–178.

Cantu, R. C. (1986). Guidelines for return to contact sports after a cerebral concussion. *The Physician and Sportsmedicine, 13*, 76–79.

Cantu, R. C. (2001). Post-traumatic retrograde and anterograde amnesia. Pathophysiology and implications in grading and safe return to play. *Journal of Athletic Training, 36*, 244–248.

Cantu, R. C., & Voy, R. (1995). Second-impact syndrome: A risk in any contact sport. *Physician and Sportsmedicine, 23*, 27–34.

Covassin, T., Swanik, C. B., & Sachs, M. L. (2003a). Epidemiological considerations of concussions among intercollegiate athletes. *Applied Neuropsychology, 10*, 12–22.

Covassin, T., Swanik, C. B., & Sachs, M. L. (2003b). Sex differences and the incidence of concussions among collegiate athletes. *Journal of Athletic Training, 38*, 238–244.

Crowley, J. N. (2006). *In the arena: The NCAA's first century*. Denver, CO: AB Hirschfeld Press.

de Courten-Myers, G. M. (1999). The human cerebral cortex: Gender differences in structure and function. *Journal of Neuropathology and Experimental Neurology, 58*, 217–226.

Echemendia, R. J. (2004). Cultural aspects of neuropsychological evaluations in sports. In M. R. Lovell, R. J. Echemendia, J. T. Barth, & M. W. Collins (Eds.), *Traumatic brain injury in sports* (pp. 435–442). Lisse, The Netherlands: Swets & Zeitlinger Publishers.

Echemendia, R. J., & Julian, L. J. (2001). Mild traumatic brain injury in sports: Neuropsychology's contributions to a developing field. *Neuropsychology Review, 11*(2), 69–88.

Erlanger. D., Kaushik, T., Cantu, R., Barth, J., Broshek, D., Freeman, J., et al. (2003). Symptom-based assessment of concussion severity. *Journal of Neurosurgery, 98,* 477–484.

Erlanger, D. M., Kutner, K. C., Barth, J. T., & Barnes, R. (1999). Neuropsychology of sports-related head injury: Dementia pugilistica to post concussion syndrome. *The Clinical Neuropsychologist, 13*(2), 193–209.

Erlanger, D. M., Saliba, E., Barth, J., Almquist, J., Webright, W., & Freeman, J. (2001). Monitoring resolution of post-concussion symptoms in athletes: Preliminary results of a web-based neuropsychological test protocol. *Journal of Athletic Training, 36*(3), 280–287.

Esposito, G., Van Horn, J. D., Weinberger, D. R., & Berman, K. F. (1996). Gender differences in cerebral blood flow as a function of cognitive state with PET. *The Journal of Nuclear Medicine, 37,* 559–564.

EuroLeague Basketball. Retrieved January 10, 2006, from http://www.euroleague.net/main/teams/showteam?clubcode=COL

Fu, K., Smith, M. L., Thomas, S., & Hovda, D. A. (1992). Cerebral concussion produces a state of vulnerability lasting as long as 5 hours [Abstract]. *Journal of Neurotrauma, 9,* 59.

Giza, C. C., & Hovda, D. A. (2001). The neurometabolic cascade of concussion. *Journal of Athletic Training, 36,* 228–235.

Gronwall, D. (1989). Cumulative and persisting effects of concussion on attention and cognition. In H. S. Levin, H. M. Eisenberg, & A. L. Benton (Eds.), *Mild head injury* (pp 153–162). New York: Oxford University Press.

Guskiewicz, K. M. (2001). The concussion puzzle: 5 compelling questions. *Journal of Athletic Training, 36,* 255.

Guskiewicz, K. M., McCrea, M., Marshall, S. W., Cantu, R. C., Randolph, C., Barr, W., et al. (2003). Cumulative effects associated with recurrent concussion in collegiate football players. *Journal of the American Medical Association, 290,* 2549–2555.

Guskiewicz, K. M., Weaver, N. L., Padua, D. A., & Garrett, W. E. (2000). Epidemiology of concussion in collegiate and high school football players. *American Journal of Sports Medicine, 28,* 643–650.

Hinton-Bayre, A. D., Geffen, G. M., Geffen, L. B., McFarland, K. A., & Friis, P. (1999). Concussion in contact sports: Reliable change indices of impairment and recovery. *Journal of Clinical and Experimental Neuropsychology, 21,* 70–86.

Hovda, D. A., Prins, M., Becker, D. P., Lee, S., Bergsneider, M., & Martin, N. A. (1999). Neurobiology of concussion. In J. E. Bailes, M. R. Lovell, & J. C. Maroon (Eds.), *Sports-related concussion* (pp. 12–51). St. Louis, MO: Quality Medical Publishing, Inc.

Iverson, G. L., & McCracken, L. M. (1997). Postconcussive symptoms in persons with chronic pain. *Brain Injury, 11.* 783–790.

Jagoda, A., &, Riggio, S. (2000). Mild traumatic brain injury and the postconcussive syndrome. *Emergency Medicine Clinics of North America 18,* 355–363.

Kelly, J. P. (2000). Concussion in sports and recreation. *Seminars in neurology, 20*(2), 165–171.

Kelly, J. P., Nichols, J. S., Filley, C. M., Lillihei, K. O., Rubinstein, D., & Kleinschmidt-DeMaasters, B. K. (1991). Concussion in sports: Guidelines for the prevention of catastrophic outcome. *Journal of the American Medical Association, 226,* 2867–2869.

Kelly, J. P., & Rosenberg, J. H. (1997). Diagnosis and management of concussion in sports. *Neurology, 48,* 575–580.

Laurer, H. L., Bareyre, F. M., Lee, V.M.Y.C., Trojanowski, J. Q., Longhi, L., Hoover, R, et al. (2001). Mild head injury increasing the brain's vulnerability to a second concussive impact. *Journal of Neurosurgery, 95,* 859–870.

Lovell, M. R., & Barr, W. (2004). American professional football. In M. R. Lovell, R. J. Echemendia, J. T. Barth, & M. W. Collins (Eds.), *Traumatic brain injury in sports* (pp 209–219). Lisse, The Netherlands: Swets & Zeitlinger Publishers.

Lovell, M. R., Echemendia, R. J., & Burke, C. J. (2004). Professional ice hockey. In M. R. Lovell, R. J. Echemendia, J. T. Barth, & M. W. Collins (Eds.), *Traumatic brain injury in sports* (pp. 221–229). Lisse, The Netherlands: Swets & Zeitlinger Publishers.

Lovell, M. R., Iverson, G. L., Collins, M. W., McKeag, D., & Maroon, J. C. (1999). Does loss of consciousness predict neuropsychological decrements after concussion? *Clinical Journal of Sport Medicine, 9,* 193–198.

Macciocchi, S. N., Barth, J. T., Alves, W., Rimel, R. W., & Jane, J. A. (1996). Neuropsychological functioning and recovery after mild head injury in college athletes. *Neurosurgery, 39,* 510–514.

Macciocchi, S. N., Barth, J. T., & Littlefield, L. M. (1998). Neurologic athletic head and neck injuries. *Clinics in Sports Medicine, 17*(1), 27–37.

Macciocchi, S. N., Barth, J. T., Littlefield, L., & Cantu, R. C. (2001). Multiple concussions and neuropsychological functioning in collegiate football players. *Journal of Athletic Training 36,* 303–306.

McCrea, M. (2001). Standardized mental status assessment of sports concussion. *Clinical Journal of Sports Medicine, 11,* 176–181.

McCrea, M., Guskiewicz, K. M., Marshall, S. W., Barr, W., Randolph, C., Cantu, R. C., et al. (2003). Acute effects and recovery time following concussion in collegiate football players: The NCAA concussion study. *Journal of the American Medical Association, 290,* 2556–2563.

McCrea, M., Kelly, J. P., Randolph, C., Kluge, J., Bartolic, E., Finn, G., et al. (1998). Standardized assessment of concussion (SAC): On-site mental status evaluation of the athlete. *The Journal of Head Trauma Rehabilitation, 13,* 27–35.

McCrory, P. (2001). Does second impact syndrome exist? *Clinical Journal of Sport Medicine, 11,* 144–149.

McCrory, P., Collie, A., Anderson, A. V., & Davis. G. (2004). Can we manage sport related concussion in children the same as in adults? *British Journal of Sports Medicine, 38,* 516–519.

McCrory, P., Johnston, K., Meeuwisse, W., Aubry, M., Cantu. R., Dvorak, J., et al. (2005). Summary and agreement of the 2nd International Conference on Concussion in Sport, Prague 2004. *British Journal of Sports Medicine, 39,* 196–204.

Moser, R. S., & Schatz, P. (2002). Enduring effects of concussion in youth athletes. *Archives of Clinical Neuropsychology, 17,* 91–100.

Naunheim, R. S., Standeven, J., Richter, C., & Lewis, L. M. (2000). Comparison of impact data in hockey, football, and soccer. *The Journal of Trauma, 48,* 938–941.

Ommaya, A. K., & Gennaretti, T. A. (1974). Cerebral concussion and traumatic unconsciousness. *Brain, 9*(7), 633–654.

Parker, E. S., Echemendia, R. J., & Milhouse, C. (2004). Ethical issues in the evaluation of athletes. In M. R. Lovell, R. J. Echemendia, J. T. Barth, & M. W. Collins (Eds.), *Traumatic brain injury in sports* (pp. 467–477). Lisse, The Netherlands: Swets & Zeitlinger Publishers.

Randolph, C., McCrea, M., & Barr, W. B. (2005). Is neuropsychological testing useful in the management of sport-related concussion? *Journal of Athletic Training, 40,* 139–154.

RealMadrid.com. Retrieved January 12, 2006, from http://www.realmadrid.com/plantilla/portada_eng.htm#

Reisman, J. M. (1981). History and current trends in clinical psychology. In C. E. Walker (Ed.), *Clinical practice of psychology: A guide for mental health professionals* (pp. 163–185). New York: Pergamon Press.

Rimel, R. W., Giordani, B., Barth, J. T., Boll, T. J., & Jane, J. A. (1981). Disability caused by minor head injury. *Neurosurgery, 9,* 221–228.

Roof, R. L., Duvdevani, R., & Stein, D. G. (1993). Gender influences outcome of brain injury: Progesterone plays a protective role. *Brain Research, 607,* 333–336.

Roof, R. L., & Hall, E. D. (2000). Gender differences in acute CNS trauma and stroke: Neuroprotective effects of estrogen and progesterone. *Journal of Neurotrauma, 17,* 367–388.

Ruchinskas, R. A., Francis, J. P., & Barth, J. T. (1997). Mild head injury in sports. *Applied Neuropsychology 4,* 43–49.

Ruff, R. M., Camenzuli, L. F., & Mueller, J. (1996). Miserable minority: Emotional risk factors that influence the outcome of mild traumatic brain injury. *Brain Injury, 10,* 551–556.

Rutherford, W. H., Merrett, J. D., & McDonald, J. R. (1979). Symptoms at one year following concussion from minor head injuries. *Injury, 10,* 225–230.

Schneider, K., & Zernicke, R. F. (1988). Computer simulation of head impact: Estimation of head-injury risk during soccer heading. *International Journal of Sport Biomechanics, 4,* 358–371.

Symonds, C. (1962). Concussion and its sequelae. *The Lancet, 1,* 1–5.

Teasdale, G., & Jennett, B. (1974). Assessment of coma and impaired consciousness. A practical scale. *Lancet, 2*(7872), 81–84.

Triplett, N. (1898). The dynamogenic factors in pacemaking and competition. *American Journal of Psychology, 9,* 507–553.

Trotter, W. (1924). Certain minor injuries of the brain. *The Lancet, 1,* 935–939.

Tysvaer, A. (1992). Head and neck injuries in soccer: Impact of minor trauma. *Sports Medicine, 14,* 200–213.

Tysvaer, A., & Storli, V. (1989). Soccer injuries to the brain: A neurologic and electroencephalographic study of active players. *American Journal of Sports Medicine, 17,* 573–578.

University of California, San Francisco. (2005). Glossary: Memory and aging center. Retrieved August 18, 2005, from http://memory.ucsf.edu/glossary.html

Van Kampen, D. A., Lovell, M. R., Pardini, J. E., Collins, M. W., & Fu, F. H. (in press). The "value added" of neurocognitive testing after sports-related concussion. *American Journal of Sports Medicine.*

Webbe, F. M.. (2006). Definition, physiology, and severity of cerebral concussion. In R. J. Echemendia (Ed.), *Sports neuropsychology: Assessment and management of traumatic brain injury* (pp. 45–70). New York: The Guilford Press.

Webbe, F. M., & Barth, J. T. (2003). Short-term and long-term outcome of athletic closed head injuries. *Clinics in Sports Medicine, 22,* 577–592.

Weinberg, R. S., & Gould, D. (2003). *Foundations of sport and exercise psychology* (3rd ed.). Champaign, IL; Human Kinetics.

Section V

Conclusion

27

The Future of Clinical Neuropsychology

Arthur MacNeill Horton, Jr.

I N THE PRECEDING chapters, efforts were made to describe the current status of clinical neuropsychology. Chapters dealt with foundations of clinical neuropsychology, ethical issues, issues unique to brain injury, practice issues, and special areas in clinical neuropsychology. In this chapter, however, the intent is to speculate regarding possible future directions in clinical neuropsychology. The focus will be upon what might be likely development in clinical neuropsychology. At the same time, it should be stated that these speculations are based on the judgments of the chapter author and no guarantees are provided, nor should any be expected.

In terms of organizing this chapter, the future developments are listed in terms of new concepts, new techniques, and new populations.

NEW CONCEPTS

I N THIS SECTION the new concepts of managed care, the Internet, and credentialing will be addressed.

Managed Care and Clinical Neuropsychology

IT IS FAIRLY clear that future clinical neuropsychology directions will involve activities that will be strongly influenced by changing the U.S. health care system (Sbordone & Saul, 2000). There is ample warrant to expect significant health care changes in the near future. The history of health care in the last two decades has been one of drastic change (Cummings, 1986).

While in the 1970s and perhaps in the early '80s, there was great attention to the quality of health care services, this has changed. In the late '80s and '90s, the watchword in health care has become cost containment. Essentially, national health care costs have been increasing over the years at a rate greater than the inflation rate and at a far greater rate than the production of other goods and services for the United States (Strosahi, 1994). Simply put, while the productivity of the American worker had been increasing up until perhaps the early '70s, year by year that productivity appeared to level off in the 1970s.

This has created a rather difficult situation as inflation has continued to rise, and there is continued pressure from employees to have annual wage increases. Unfortunately, new productivity to pay for wage increases has not been available in the American economic system. Therefore, one has greater demands for wages and health care with fewer resources to pay for wages and health care.

Health care has perhaps taken an even more disturbing trend in that as earlier noted the rate of increase has gone up exponentially over the past few decades. To a large extent, this is or should be due to greater use of expensive technological procedures and the use of heroic efforts to keep terminally ill patients alive through artificial means. In addition, however, there is increasing concern regarding runaway physician fees and inefficient health care systems. In health care, the public perception has been that there is basically no accountability with respect to cost of procedures (Armenti, 1993).

In recent years, the specter of managed care has arisen in such a way as to make everyday Halloween for U.S. health care providers. To put it in simplest perspective, managed care applies a cost metric to health care. That is to say, there is review of the allocation of the health care dollars and questioning as to whether money should have been spent. In recent years, this has led at times to a maddening array of paperwork and health care treatment plans in managed care organizations, which have bedeviled doctors, nurses, physicians, assistants, psychologists, and other health care professionals almost to the point of major mental disturbance (Strosahi, 1994). As managed care reduces the incomes of clinical psychologists, many will likely move into the forensic area in order to gain income (Otto & Heinbrum, 2002).

What is most unfortunate is the perception that managed care organizations, which review the utilization of care, may disavow services that have in many cases been delivered without a research base to make these decisions. As noted by Peterson and Harbeck (1988) regarding pediatric psychology, the development of a research base is critical to the maturing of any field, and their comments are relevant to managed care. Relatively little is known about the impact of managed care, and less research has gone on in terms evaluating the effects of managed care on clinical neuropsychology services (Armenti, 1993). As far as clinical neuropsychologists are concerned, however, the extant research findings regarding managed care influences on clinical neuropsychology are gloomy at best and disastrous at worse (Sweet, Westergaard, & Moberg, 1995).

Nonetheless, because of federal budget deficits and the need to reduce health care cost, there have been efforts to apply rigid cost containment strategies in the form of managed care. That is to say the plans imposed are based on the fact that health care costs need to be cut and there is little thoughtful planning as to how to do this best (Cummings, 1986).

How will clinical neuropsychologists' roles change in order to deal with managed care settings and the pressures of the evolving health care system? It would appear clear that there are going to be greater pressures on cost accountability and specification of problem and outcome. In addition, clinical neuropsychology will have to include explicit methods to promote generalization of effects to other settings, demonstrating ecological validity of findings (Purish & Sbordone, 1997) and to evaluate the degree to which the person treated approximates, after treatment, the untreated members of their peer groups who, at least initially, were without the identified problem.

It would be expected that clinical neuropsychologists would be encouraged to be very precise in terms of the problems they are addressing and to collect specific outcome data demonstrating that their interventions were effective. While that is all well and good, it would appear quite likely there would be pressures to treat even complex clinical cases in a limited number of hours.

As a result, it may be difficult to treat cases with appropriate amounts of resources unless proper attention is given to the issue of making determinations of the degree of complexity of specific cases. In medicine, there are descriptors to whether the services provided may be relatively uninvolved and brief or complex and difficult. There would need to be some sort of consideration producing a similar system for clinical neuropsychology.

In most cases clinical neuropsychology activity would require quite some time. Therefore, clinical neuropsychologists will have to take great care to document what they do and also demonstrate that they are efficient. The time component will be very important in terms of delivery of services as long as services are calculated on an hour for hour basis.

The focus of outcome care, at least in the foreseeable decade, will be on cost containment. Health care providers will be pressured and in some cases severely pressured to contain costs to provide adequate clinical services economically. In time the hope is that there would be some efforts to move toward the direction of a greater emphasis on quality of care. The great danger in managed care is that an excessive focus on cost containment will cause a diminution of quality service to the point that clinical care may be given, but the clinical care may be so watered down as to be relatively inefficient.

Therefore, while some treatment services are provided, the treatment provided could be inadequate to argue for the abolishment of the service. In some cases, the effect of managed care appears to have been to reduce the quality of health care. This could be a very serious development as the denial of adequate care can have horrible consequences to ill and impaired individuals.

Many health care providers have their horror stories of managed care errors. There is the case of one young woman who complained of severe headaches and went to her HMO; she was not even examined, because they had felt that she was somewhat hysterical. The woman was made to sit down on a bed in the clinic, was never examined by a physician, physician assistant, nurse, or nurse practitioner, and then was sent home. The woman unfortunately was having transient ischemic attacks and later had a stroke. The fact that she was relatively young, in this case about 29, was apparently no barrier to stroke, and a lawsuit ensued. The woman's clinical history was noteworthy for the fact that she had a clear family history of relatives having strokes in their thirties. This unfortunate situation is an example of or at least appears to be an example of where efforts to curtail the use of health care services may cause significant harm to patients and destroy the confidence of consumers in the U.S. health care system.

THE INTERNET AND CLINICAL NEUROPSYCHOLOGY

THE PRACTICE OF real estate can be summed up in the phrase: "location, location, location, and location." The issue of technological influences on clinical neuropsychology might be summed up as "computers, computers, computers, and computers." The explosive development of the Internet and the World Wide Web has definitely changed the way that human beings in the United States and indeed the whole world approach information processing, information transfer, and information storage and will continue to do so for centuries to come. The Information Superhighway is a reality for citizens of the world. The computer revolution is such that individuals can trade information with others halfway around the world in moments. Internet news groups regularly have international contributions from individuals in South American, Australia, England, and Canada, as well as the United States.

One of the most fascinating aspects of the news groups with respect to clinical neuropsychology is that very often a member of a news group will present a clinical neuropsychological case and ask for comments, and within 24 hours, the person posting the message in the news group can receive relatively specific advice and suggestions from individuals that they have never previously heard from, half a world away.

It is also remarkable how the comments on the news group can provide a wide range of suggestions to the point where it almost seems like a very good case conference in clinical neuropsychology. The value for clinical neuropsychology might be that in the future, there could be electronic chat rooms devoted to clinical neuropsychology problems where a master consultant moderates interactions among individuals seeking advice and those who can provide advice in such a way that suggestions can be given and participants can be helped in a positive manner.

The speed with which information can be transferred is truly amazing and potentially of fantastic value in terms of clinical neuropsychology on the treatment of patients. In addition to information transfer, the computer can facilitate the development of expert systems. That is to say that various problems in clinical neuropsychology could be reduced to a number of key considerations and essential factors. Computer programs in a computer network could be developed to provide clinical neuropsychology guidance in elementary cases. Software could be developed such that suggestions can be made to persons seeking clinical neuropsychology. There are already a number of computer programs, for instance, for making neuropsychological interpretation in terms of patients' neuropsychological test data. While these appear to be best for making a simple diagnosis of brain damage and are relatively less capable when one deals with the questions of etiology, localization, or process of cerebral injury, nonetheless, the potential for further development is available. Additional work could possibly develop systems of training individuals in clinical neuropsychology and specifically in terms of behavioral procedures that could be useful in behavioral neuropsychology.

It could be that a person could put in various parameters of a problem and then come back with possible suggestions based on research literature and expert judgment of what would be seen as state of the art methods of approaching various neurobehavioral problems. While such an undertaking would require a great deal of time and effort it nonetheless could yield particularly powerful and positive results.

One need only to consider the ubiquitous computer interpretations of psychological tests to realize the potential value. While MMPI-2, MCMI-III and PAI interpretations may or may not fit individual clients, in all cases, nonetheless, their use over a number of years has definitely established them as significant aids to clinicians. The production of computerized psychological test interpretations is now a very significant economic activity for psychologically oriented business persons.

It might be expected that clinical neuropsychology services could be operated in the same way over the Internet, whereby anyone in any setting could request some initial suggestions regarding clinical neuropsychology services. In addition, when various problems come up, the computer can provide additional suggestions as to what would be possible viable strategies for overcoming various difficulties. The potential to improve clinical neuropsychology practice is truly amazing.

On a more personal level, there is always a possibility of case conferences done through video services, where people at various locations can be visually linked through transmission of pictures of persons in other settings. Even movies are transmitted through the Internet. For example, this could include observations of a child in a free play situation going through a behavioral treatment session. Experts, hundreds and even thousands miles away, could consult on the case and make suggestions regarding the appropriate strategies to deal with the child.

Such technological avenues of information could allow world-famous experts to consult widely and significantly enhance the standardization of high quality clinical neuropsychology services on a national, even international basis.

CREDENTIALING AND CLINICAL NEUROPSYCHOLOGY

CLINICAL NEUROPSYCHOLOGY AS a specialty is at a crossroads, and efforts need to be made to respond to current challenges. Perhaps the most serious challenge lies in the area of credentialing. Indeed there is a long and controversial history of credentialing efforts in clinical neuropsychology. As this history has been treated elsewhere (Horton, 1997a) only very brief comments will be offered here.

In clinical neuropsychology, there are two major diplomate boards offering board certification credentials in clinical neuropsychology. These are the American Board of Clinical Psychology (ABCN), which is affiliated with the American Board of Professional Psychology (ABPP), and the American Board of Professional Neuropsychology (ABPN).

In the interests of appropriate disclosure, it might be mentioned that the chapter author is a past president of ABPN. Both ABCN and ABPN utilize an application process and work sample review and oral examination procedures. ABCN uses a multiple choice test, and ABPN uses an essay exam but is developing a multiple choice examination.

Recently, ABPN has begun to offer advance qualifications in a number of specialty areas. The expectation is that professional practice standards in clinical neuropsychology will show continual development.

In addition, the Coalition for Clinical Practitioners of Neuropsychology (CCPN) recently developed a draft set of guidelines for the professional practice of neuropsychology (Horton & Reitan, 2005). The draft guidelines identified empirically validated clinical neuropsychological test batteries, listed core neuropsychological abilities that should be assessed in a comprehensive clinical neuropsychological evaluation, and defined a clinical neuropsychologist. The definition of a clinical neuropsychologist included having earned a doctoral degree based on a dissertation on a psychological topic, with an internship or equivalent in a clinically relevant area of professional psychology and having the equivalent of 2 years of experience and specialized training in the science and practice of clinical neuropsychology and related neurosciences. The 2 years (one would be post-doctoral) of experience and specialized training would include supervision by a clinical neuropsychologist (except for senior citizens in neuropsychology who entered the field prior to the development of training programs). The clinical neuropsychologist would also have to be licensed in a state or province to practice psychology independently or would have to be employed as a neuropsychologist in an exempt agency.

NEW TECHNIQUES

IN THIS SECTION the new techniques of neuropsychological measures, neurodiagnostic measures, and malingering measures will be covered. At the same time, however, it must be noted that the Daubert decision (*Daubert vs. Merril Dow Pharmaceuticals,* 1993) has imposed new standards for technique assessment. While it is not possible to adequately deal with the complex issues posed by the Daubert decision in the very limited space available in this chapter, nonetheless some brief and oversimplified remarks will be offered. The Daubert decision has promulgated standards for helping trial judges to assess the value of scientific evidence offered in the context of litigation. The intent is to weed out "junk science" from the courtroom. The intent, of course, is praiseworthy, but many clinical neuropsychologists are very concerned about the actual application of scientific standards in the hands of individuals such as trial judges who, while highly intelligent and astute, are not usually formally trained in science. Future clarification of the Daubert decision in actual court decisions is expected, and the degree to which Daubert achieves its purpose will determine if a lasting contribution is made.

Neuropsychology Assessment Measures and Clinical Neuropsychology

The hallmark of neuropsychological assessment measures has been their careful validation relative to neurological criteria (Horton, 1997b; Reitan, 1974; Reitan & Davison, 1974; Reitan & Wolfson, 1993). There is clear agreement among scientists and researchers as to the impressive empirical validity of neuropsychological tests to determine the presence of brain damage and lateralization of the brain damage (Horton, 1997b). On the other hand, there has been a relative paucity of specific research with neuropsychological tests addressing questions related to ecological validity issues, and the argument has been made that empirical evidence for the ecological validity of neuropsychological tests needs to be much better developed (Sbordone & Saul, 2000). It is to be expected that a future trend will be to address this important area.

Neurodiagnostic Assessment Measures and Clinical Neuropsychology

Neurodiagnostic measures such as magnetic resonance imaging (MRI) and positron emission topography (PET) scanning have provided new windows through which to visualize the human brain (Bigler, Lowry, & Porter, 1997).

The expectation is that increased use of these exciting brain imaging techniques will be the norm in clinical neuropsychology. The interactive use of neuropsychological testing and neurodiagnostic measures such as MRI and PET scans might be expected to yield new dramatic insights into the workings of the human brain and further develop the empirical basis for clinical neuropsychology.

Malingering Measures and Clinical Neuropsychology

In the last decade the most dramatic development in clinical neuropsychology has been the explosive growth of test measures designed to detect biased responding on neuropsychological tests (Franzen & Iverson, 1997). The development of new measures, use of specific profiles, item response patterns, and cut-off scores on standard neuropsychological tests have been investigated. Future research in this area is expected.

NEW POPULATIONS

IN THIS SECTION, possible new populations that clinical neuropsychology may address will be mentioned. Such populations might include medical/health care patients and minority groups.

MEDICAL/HEALTH CARE PATIENTS AND CLINICAL NEUROPSYCHOLOGY

IN THE AREA of medical neuropsychology (Horton, 1997a) there are many opportunities for clinical neuropsychologists to make important contributions. Patients that have had systemic illnesses that have secondary brain effects (such as lung disease, cardiovascular disorders, liver disease, and selected ontological disorders, among many others), as well as cases where the effects of pharmaceuticals are at question, are clear candidates for clinical neuropsychological assessment to determine if brain damage has occurred. In addition, cases where medical complications or treatment may have a direct or indirect impact on neural integrity and where neurotoxic effects of chemicals/substances is suspected are considered within the possible scope of clinical neuropsychology (Hartman, 1995). In addition, in cases where patients have survived brain injury and now are being rehabilitated, neuropsychologists can be of assistance (Hall & Cope, 1995).

MINORITY GROUPS AND CLINICAL NEUROPSYCHOLOGY

AS THE POPULATION of the United States grows increasingly more diverse, greater attention to the neuropsychological assessment of minority groups is an inevitable development. The expectation is that appropriate neuropsychological assessment may have to be tailored to fit the cultural context of new immigrants to the United States and those who maintain a different cultural perspective than the majority culture. The extant research on neuropsychological assessment in a multicultural context, however, is actually quite rudimentary (Horton, Carrington, & Lewis-Jack, 2001). When minority group members are neuropsychologically assessed a firm empirical basis for decision making is needed. At present, much additional work is needed to address the area of clinical neuropsychological assessment within a multicultural context.

SUMMARY

THIS CHAPTER HAS discussed the possible impact of the future on clinical neuropsychology practices in the United States. It is postulated that the advent of managed care will require much more extensive documentation of services and justification of added clinical value. Health care practices will be as influential as legal developments in shaping the focus of clinical neuropsychology. In addition, the potential value of computers and the Internet for improving clinical neuropsychology practices and facilitating access to experts in clinical neuropsychology was briefly outlined. Issues related to credentialing were also very briefly mentioned in an oversimplified manner.

Also, there is need for greater ecological validity for neuropsychological tests and the future uses of MRI and PET scans and need for measures to assess biased responding were mentioned. The new populations of medical/health care patients and minority group members were proposed as areas in great need of future clinical neuropsychological assessments. The hope and expectation is that this chapter will serve to expedite the future progress of clinical neuropsychology.

REFERENCES

Armenti, N. (1993). Managed health care and the behaviorally trained professional. *The Behavior Therapist, 14*, 13–15.

Bigler, E. D., Lowry, C. M., & Porter, S. S. (1997). Neuroimaging in clinical neuropsychology. In A. M. Horton, Jr., D. Wedding, & J. S. Webster (Eds.), *The neuropsychology handbook, Vol. 1* (2nd ed., pp. 171–220). New York: Springer Publishing.

Cummings, N. (1986). The dismantling of our health care systems: Strategies for the survival of psychological practice. *American Psychologist, 41*, 426–431.

Daubert vs. Merril Dow Pharmaceuticals, 113 S. Ct. 2786 (1993).

Franzen, M. D., & Iverson, G. L. (1997). Detection of biased responding in neuropsychological assessment. In A. M. Horton, Jr., D. Wedding, & J. S. Webster (Eds.), *The neuropsychology handbook, Vol. 2* (2nd ed., pp. 393–423). New York: Springer Publishing.

Hall, K. M., & Cope, D. N. (1995). The benefits of rehabilitation in traumatic brain injury: A literature review. *Journal of Head Trauma Rehabilitation, 10*(1), 1–13.

Hartman, D. (1995). *Neuropsychological toxicology* (2nd Ed.). New York: Plenum Press.

Horton, A. M., Jr. (1997a). Human neuropsychology: Current status. In A. M. Horton, Jr., D. Wedding, & J. S. Webster (Eds.), *The neuropsychology handbook, Vol. 1* (2nd ed., pp. 3–29). New York: Springer Publishing.

Horton, A. M., Jr. (1997b). Halstead-Reitan neuropsychological test battery: Problems and prospects. In A. M. Horton, Jr., D. Wedding, & J. S. Webster (Eds.), *The neuropsychology handbook, Vol. 1* (2nd ed., pp. 221–254). New York: Springer Publishing.

Horton, A. M., Jr., Carrington, C. H., & Lewis-Jack, O. (2001). Neuropsychological assessment in a multicultural context. In L. A. Suzuki, J. G. Ponterotto, & P. J. Meller (Eds.), *Handbook of multicultural assessment* (2nd ed., pp. 233–260). San Francisco: Jossey-Bass.

Horton, A. M. Jr., & Reitan, R. M. (2005, January). *Professional standards in clinical neuropsychology: Draft suggested guidelines.* Paper presented at the Coalition of Clinical Practitioners of Neuropsychology (CCPN), Las Vegas, NV.

Otto, R. K., & Heinbrum, K. (2002). The practice of clinical psychology. *American Psychologist, 57*(1), 5–18.

Peterson, L., & Harbeck, C. (1988). *The pediatric psychologist.* Champaign, IL: Research Press.

Purish, A. D., & Sbordone, R. J. (1997). Clinical neuropsychology: Clinical issues and practice. In A. M. Horton, Jr., D. Wedding, & J. S. Webster (Eds.), *The neuropsychology handbook, Vol. 2* (2nd ed., pp. 309–373). New York: Springer.

Reitan, R. M. (1974). Psychological effects of cerebral lesions in children of early school age. In R. M. Reitan, & L. A. Davison (Eds.). *Clinical neuropsychology: Current status and applications* (pp. 53–90). New York: John Wiley.

Reitan, R. M., & Davison, L. A. (Eds.). (1974). *Clinical neuropsychology: Current status and applications.* New York: John Wiley.

Reitan, R. M., & Wolfson, D. (1993). *Halstead-Reitan Neuropsychological Test Battery.* Tucson, AZ: Neuropsychology Press.

Sbordone, R. J., & Saul, R. E. (2000). *Neuropsychology for health care professionals and attorneys* (2nd ed.). Boca Raton, FL: CRC Press LLC.

Strosahi, K. (1994). Entering the new frontier of managed mental health care: Gold mines and land mines. *Cognitive and Behavioral Practice, 1,* 5–23.

Sweet, J. J., Westergaard, C. K., & Moberg, P. J. (1995). Managed care experiences of clinical neuropsychologists. *The Clinical Neuropsychologist, 9*(3), 214–218.

Index